THE MOTHERS

THE MOTHERS

A STUDY OF THE ORIGINS OF SENTIMENTS AND INSTITUTIONS

BY

ROBERT BRIFFAULT

VOL. III

NEW YORK
THE MACMILLAN COMPANY
1927

PRINTED IN THE UNITED STATES OF AMERICA
By J. J. Little & Ives Company, New York

CONTENTS

Chapter XXIII

THE MAGICAL ORIGIN OF QUEENS

CHAPTER XXIV

THE GREAT MOTHERS

CHAPTER XXV

HOLY MATRIMONY

CHAPTER XXVI

MODESTY

CHAPTER XXVII

PURITY

CHAPTER XXVIII

ROMANCE

THE MOTHERS

CHAPTER XXIII

THE MAGICAL ORIGIN OF QUEENS

THE reinterpretations of cosmic religious conceptions and the transformation of primitive lunar deities into solar or heavenly gods are often associated with the transfer of magical and priestly functions to the men and the development of male priesthoods. Thus, in Egypt, while priestesses were prominent in the early period, their sacerdotal functions were abolished in later times.[1] Or again, in Peru, the official cult of the lunar deity at Cuzco was served by colleges of priestesses, while the service of the Sun-god was performed by male priests. But the Peruvian priestesses were not an institution founded by the Incas or specially connected with the official lunar deity of Cuzco; those priestesses were an immemorial native institution and constituted the original priesthood of the deities of the land before the establishment of the Inca monarchy.[2] The transformation of primitive lunar deities into solar gods is commonly associated with the establishment of powerful rulers, conquering military monarchs or priest-kings, who are disposed to claim the special protection of a deity distinct from the ordinary gods of the common people, and superior to them in power and splendour. "The effects of the moon," observes Plutarch, "are similar to the effects of reason and wisdom," that is to say, of magic knowledge and art, "whereas those of the sun appear to be brought about by the power of physical force and violence."[3] The ordinary epithet of the sun was, among the ancients, the 'unconquered,' as that of the moon was the 'eternal.' Hence monarchical rulers who have extended and consolidated their power by force of arms tend almost invariably to regard the sun as their special deity; regular solar cults are nowhere found in societies that have retained their primitive democratic character. The development of agriculture, which is

[1] See above, vol. i, p. 387.
[2] A. F. Bandelier, *The Islands of Titicaca and Koati*, p. 278.
[3] Plutarch, *De Iside et Osiride*, xli.

the foundation of higher civilisation, also tends, of course, to impart a solar character to primitive cosmic conceptions, for the yearly cycle of the seasons and the helpful heat of the sun which brings seeds to maturity acquire a direct importance, and the cycle of changes which had originally reference to the lunar period becomes translated in terms of the yearly cycle which governs the fertility of the fields. Agricultural pursuits, when they have so far developed in importance as to render superfluous those of the primitive hunter, are taken up by the men. Male priests and male rulers become accordingly concerned in the cultural and magical practices connected with the control of the seasons and with promoting the growth of vegetation and the fertility of the earth.

Agricultural Magic.

Yet those functions originally appertain to the prescriptive sphere of the women and not of the men. In the primitive division of labour the gathering and the cultivation of vegetable food are the special occupation of the women as hunting is that of the men. The yam-digging stick is among the Australian aborigines as inseparable and personal a part of the woman as weapons are appurtenances of the man.[1] The art of cultivation has developed exclusively in the hands of women. The invention of agriculture by woman is commemorated in savage myth. Thus among the Cherokee, corn is supposed to have been discovered in the forest by the first woman. When she died, she gave directions that her body should be dragged over the earth; wherever it touched the soil there sprang an abundant crop.[2] The traditions of the Cheyennes likewise ascribe the discovery of agriculture and of corn to a woman.[3] The Tupis of Brazil have a legend to the effect that a virgin conceived, and from the body of the babe to which she gave birth, and which died in infancy, grew the first plant of manioc.[4] The Basutos of South Africa and the natives of West Africa likewise assign the invention of agriculture to the first woman.[5]

The art of cultivation is regarded by all uncivilised peoples

[1] W. B. Spencer and F. J. Gillen, *The Native Tribes of Central Australia*, p. 220.

[2] J. B. Davis, "Some Cherokee Stories," *Annals of Archaeology and Anthropology, Liverpool University*, iii, p. 47.

[3] G. A. Dorsey, "The Cheyennes," *Field Columbian Museum Publications: Anthropological Series*, vol. ix, No. 1, p. 40.

[4] J. V. Couto de Magalhães, *O Selvagem*, pp. 134 sq.

[5] E. Casalis, *Les Bassoutos*, p. 255; A. Bastian, *Geographische und ethnologische Bilder*, pp. 193 sq.

as depending, in an even higher degree than other operations, upon magical power and procedures rather than on skill and manual labour.   Nothing so astonished the Pueblo Indians when Europeans first settled amongst them, as to see them plant corn without performing any religious ceremonies; and it was the profoundest shock to all their ideas to see that the corn grew nevertheless, and that abundant crops were produced.   The fact did more to shatter their faith than all the missionary crusades of the Padres.[1]   In ancient Mexico every operation of agriculture, however trifling, was accompanied with elaborate ceremonies, incantations, and prayers addressed to the Goddess of Fertility.[2]   In South Africa "the Shumba women will not hoe their lands if their dance has not been held, as they say that if they do not respect their spirits there will be no crops."[3]   In northern Borneo "the whole labour of farming," says Mrs. Bryan Scott, "is for the Dyaks no mere prosaic routine, but a supernaturally protected process with constant festal interruptions."[4]

The magical or religious rites intended to secure the fertility of the fields were naturally within the special competence of the women who cultivated them, and whose fertility was likened to the earth's. Many of the women's religious associations were doubtless concerned originally with discharging that important function.   Thus the Raruba women's society in Sierra Leone "has for its chief function to prepare 'medicine' or magical charm, which is sprinkled over the rice-fields, thus insuring their fertility."[5] Among the Cheyennes "the Corn Dance was, they say, practised by young girls and middle-aged women, who danced in a circle.   Men sang for the dance, and shook a gourd rattle, which they called and which represented a squash.   The woman who led the dance carried the sacred ear of corn on a stick which was fitted into a hole in the butt of the ear."[6] Among the Sioux the women performed each spring with considerable ceremonial the magical rites which ensured the fertility of the fields. Rows of poles were erected in front of every village, and on them were hung meat-offerings to the 'Old Woman

[1] D. G. Brinton, *Religions of Primitive Peoples*, p. 39.

[2] H. Ruiz Alarcon, "Tratado de las supersticiones y costumbres gentilicos que oy vivan entre los Indios naturales desta Nueva España," *Annales del Museo Nacional de Messico*, vi, pp. 178 sq.; Pedro Ponce, "Breve relacion de los dioses y ritos de la gentilidad," *ibid.*, p. 8.

[3] H. W. Garbutt, "Native Witchcraft and Superstitions in South Africa," *Journal of the Royal Anthropological Institute*, xxxix, p. 550.

[4] Mrs. S. B. Scott, "Harvest Festivals of the Land Dyaks," *Journal of the American Oriental Society*, xxix, p. 240.

[5] N. W. Thomas, *Anthropological Report on Sierra Leone*, vol. i, p. 151.

[6] G. B. Grinnell, *The Cheyenne Indians*, vol. i, p. 252.

who never dies.' That divine patroness was impersonated by the elder women, who, acting as priestesses, consumed, as priests usually do, the offerings presented to the deity. The women danced round the sacred poles to music provided by the men. After the dance the young women fed the elder priestesses with meat, and received in exchange grains of consecrated corn from cobs which the old women carried at the end of long sticks. One of these grains they ate, the others were carefully mixed with the seed-corn used in sowing, thus imparting to the seed the fertility bestowed by the 'Old Woman who never dies.'[1] Among the Hidatsas, the women, at the corn festival, carried at the end of sticks samples of all the vegetables which they cultivated, maize, pumpkin, melons, etc. They proceeded with them to the lodge. Here they stripped naked, and the elder men sprinkled both the fruits and the women with consecrated water.[2] The men, in this instance, performed the fertilising function; but the festival was, we are told, "instituted by the women."[3] Among the Seminols, Chicassee, Natchez, and the tribes of the southern plains, when the last frosts were over, "women provided themselves with a hoe of walnut wood; they placed on their heads baskets divided into various compartments filled with seeds of maize, water melons, beans, sun-flowers, and so forth. They then proceeded to the communal field, which was usually situated at a place easy to defend, such as a tongue of land between two rivers, or amid a circle of hills. At one end of the field the women disposed themselves in a row, and began breaking the ground with their hoes, walking backwards. While they thus performed their primitive ploughing without forming a seam, other women followed, sowing the ground prepared by their companions. The beans and the grains of maize were sown together, so that the climbing vegetable might train on the maize stalks. Young girls meanwhile busied themselves spreading layers of a black washed earth, and over it were sown the melons and sunflowers. All round the fields and beds, fires of green wood were lit in order to hasten germination."[4]

Vestal Fires.

The practice of lighting fires or of carrying lighted torches round the newly-sown fields is one form of the rites in which

---

[1] Maximilian, Prinz zu Wied-Neuwied, *Reise in das Innere Nord-America*, vol. ii, pp. 182 sqq.

[2] E. James, *Account of an Expedition from Pittsburgh to the Rocky Mountains*, vol. ii, pp. 58 sq.

[3] J. O. Dorsey, "A Study of Siouan Cult," *Eleventh Annual Report of the Bureau of Ethnology*, p. 505.

[4] F. R. de Chateaubriand, *Voyages en Amérique*, vol. i, p. 137.

fire is associated with the success of agriculture, and which have assumed so many significances and associations that their original intention is often forgotten and undiscoverable. Among the Basutos a fire is lit in the middle of every cornfield; and on the wide plains columns of smoke may be seen rising everywhere, each marking the site of a patch of cultivation. Special magic herbs are burnt, but the most potent 'medicine' is the skin of a boa serpent which, when consumed in the field fire, is an infallible means of causing the crops to grow.[1] Fires are lit in Korea in the same manner as by the North American squaws, and avowedly with the same purpose.[2] The practice is observed in most parts of Europe.[3] In ancient Umbria it was the custom to light fires round the fields, and young boys ran round with torches, "in order to render the land more fertile." The custom was general in France and was repeatedly condemned by ecclesiastical councils as a relic of paganism. In gardens it was customary to place, on the first Sunday in Lent, a lighted log, because "that did good to the garden and made onions grow."[4] The farmers in Lancashire observed until quite lately the same practice as the American squaws. With a whisp of straw at the point of a fork, on the eve of All Hallows, the farmer in some districts of the Fylde encircles his field to protect the coming crop from noxious weeds, the tare and darnel.[5]

Among the Zuñis the object of lighting fires in the fields is said to be to produce rain.[6] Similarly, among the Bechuanas the lighting of sacred fires by the women, from herbs specially gathered by them for the purpose, is to produce rain.[7] Among the more primitive Bushmen also, the fires are lit for the express purpose of controlling the rainfall, but in this instance the fire was thought

[1] E. Casalis, *Les Bassoutos*, pp. 273 sq., 288. Cf. H. Callaway, *The Religious System of the Amazulu*, p. 447. The faith of the women in the beneficial effects of such fires is in part justified. "The natives," remarks Livingstone, "show their skill in agriculture by collecting all the weeds and grass into heaps, covering them with soil and then setting fire to them. They burn slowly, and all the ashes and much of the smoke is retained in the overlying soil. The mounds thus formed, when sown upon, yield abundantly" (D. and C. Livingstone, *Narrative of an Expedition to the Zambesi*, pp. 498 sq.).

[2] I. L. Bishop, *Korea and her Neighbours*, vol. ii, pp. 56 sq.

[3] J. G. Frazer, *The Golden Bough*, vol. x, pp. 113, 142, 170, 233.

[4] J. B. Thiers, *Traité des superstitions qui regardent les sacrements*, vol. i, p. 263.

[5] W. Thornber, *An historical and descriptive Account of Blackpool*, p. 99.

[6] M. C. Stevenson, "The Zuñi Indians," *Twenty-third Annual Report of the Bureau of American Ethnology*, pp. 2 sq., 158.

[7] See below, p. 15.

to check excessive rain.[1]   In the Vosges district the fires lit on
St. John's night were also thought to be particularly useful in
checking too plentiful a supply of rain.[2]   As in many other parts
of France the ceremony has a religious character, though this is
derived from surviving pagan ideas rather than from Christian
doctrine.   The midsummer bonfire was, however, lit, after pronouncing a suitable benediction, by the parish priest.[3]

Fire is everywhere accounted sacred. That sacred character is
sometimes described as constituting a 'fire-cult.'   Fire must be
protected against polluting or inauspicious influences.   Thus
the household fire amongst the Persians and Parsis, and in many
other parts of the world, must be carefully protected against
the evil influence of a menstruating woman.   The Ojibwa, for
example, when a woman menstruates, "are very careful to remove
the fire and the ashes from the wigwam in which the family reside,
and to strike fresh fires, believing that if this be not done sickness
would immediately follow."[4]   The occurrence of a death, or the
presence of a corpse, is in the same manner considered to have a
polluting influence upon the fire.   In Uganda, on the death of
the king, all fires are immediately put out, and they may not be
relit until his successor has been appointed.[5]   Similarly, at
Mechoacan, in the West Indies, when a ruler dies, and during the
whole period of his obsequies, "no fire was permitted to be kindled
in the city."[6]   The same usage is observed among the Mishmis of
northern Bengal.[7]   It is still the custom in some parts of the Highlands of Scotland to put out every fire in the house as soon as a
person dies.[8]   Fires must in like manner be extinguished on inauspicious, or Sabbath days.   During the observance of the Hawaiian
Sabbaths all fires were extinguished, and only cold food could be
eaten.[9]   The same rule, we saw, was observed in Babylon;[10] and
it was laid down in Jewish law that "Ye shall kindle no fire
throughout your habitations upon the Sabbath day."[11] So strictly
was the rule observed in the Middle Ages that Rabbi Solomon
Ben Andret took the precaution to have a lock affixed to his

---

[1] D. O. Dapper, *Description de l'Afrique*, p. 389.
[2] A. Bertrand, *La religion des Gaulois*, p. 407.
[3] *Ibid.*, pp. 116 sq.
[4] P. Jones, *History of the Ojebway Indians*, p. 62.
[5] J. Roscoe, *The Baganda*, p. 304.
[6] T. Cage, *A New Survey of the West-Indies*, p. 160.
[7] R. P. Krick, in *Annals de la propagation de la Foi*, xxvi, p. 817.
[8] J. Logan, *The Scottish Gael*, vol. ii, p. 374.
[9] W. Ellis, *Narrative of a Tour through Hawaii*, p. 367; H. T. Cheever, *The Is'and World of the Pacific*, p. 63.
[10] See above, vol. ii, p. 435.
[11] *Exodus*, xxxv. 3; cf. xvi. 3.

kitchen oven, and kept the key in his pocket during the Sabbath day, lest his cook, through misguided kindness, should be tempted to light a fire and warm up his dinner.[1]   The rekindling of the fire after the Sabbath was performed with the solemnity of a ritual ceremony.[2]

The Andamanese Islanders extinguish or cover up all fires whenever the moon rises after sundown.   "This," says Mr. Man, "is owing to the belief that he is jealous of attention being distracted to other objects than himself at such time, or of any other light being employed than that which he had been graciously pleased to afford so abundantly."[3]   On much the same principle it is considered necessary to extinguish all fires when a sacred fire is being rekindled.   Among the Zuñi, for several days before the lighting of the new fire no other fire must be lit, and it is even regarded as grossly sacrilegious to light a cigarette.[4]   The Eskimo also are careful to extinguish all fires before the new fire is lit, with appropriate ceremonies, for the year.[5]   In China, on the 105th day after the winter solstice a solemn religious feast is held which is known as the 'Feast of Cold Eating'; for at that time, during three days, the Chinese may not eat any warm food.   All fires are extinguished, and are solemnly relit after three days.   It is believed that if those observances were neglected the fields would suffer and not bear a good harvest.   The 'Feast of Cold Eating' was formerly, and is still in some parts of China, observed four times a year, but it is now generally accounted sufficient to hold it once a year.[6]   Among the ancient Irish, sacred fires were, as we have seen, tended by holy priestesses in the same manner as by similar vestals in other parts of the world.   One of those perpetual fires was kept in the hall of the royal palace at Tara, and at the great festival of Belthane, was relit with elaborate ceremony.[7]   Fires had then to be extinguished in every home.   When St. Patrick first came among the heathen Irish, and, on the day of Belthane, lit candles in a little chapel which he had built, such was the horror caused by the sacrilegious act that he was

[1] I. Abrahams, *Jewish Life in the Middle Ages*, p. 83.

[2] M. Friedmann, "The Sabbath Light," *Jewish Quarterly Review*, iii. p. 709.

[3] E. H. Man, "On the Aboriginal Inhabitants of the Andaman Islands," *Journal of the Anthropological Institute*, xii, p. 152.

[4] M. C. Stevenson, "The Zuñi Indians," *Twenty-third Annual Report of the Bureau of American Ethnology*, pp. 108 sq., 114 sqq.

[5] C. F. Hall, *Arctic Researches and Life among the Esquimaux*, p. 576

[6] J. J. M. de Groot, *Les fêtes annuellement célébrées à Émoui*, vol. i, pp. 210 sq.

[7] R. A. S. Macalister, "Tremair Breg: A Study of the Remains and Traditions of Tara," *Proceedings of the Irish Academy*, xxxiv, Section C, pp. 370 sq.

obliged to extinguish them.[1] Similarly, in Rome, at the same
time as the three bonfires, which were connected with the cult
of primitive agricultural deities, were lit, the sacred fire in the
temple of Vesta was extinguished, and was subsequently cere-
moniously rekindled.[2]   In the island of Lemnos all fires were put
out for nine days at the time of the summer solstice, and they
could not be rekindled until a fire had been brought by a ship from
Delos.[3] The universal rite is observed in most countries by the
Christian Church on the Saturday before Easter. All lights are
extinguished in the churches and they are then relit with the
spark from a flint. The ceremony constitutes one of the great
festivals observed at the Church of the Holy Sepulchre at Jerusalem, and enormous crowds gather to witness the relighting of the
sacred fire. Indeed, with many Eastern Christians this is regarded
as the chief ceremony of their religion, and to witness it and
obtain a taper lighted at the sacred fire is the sole object of their
pilgrimage to the Holy City. The new fire is believed to be
supplied by the Holy Ghost, who comes down from heaven and
sets the consecrated candles alight.[4]

It is very commonly supposed that rituals connected with
fire, and the tending of perpetual fires, are a sure index of
a cult of the sun. But there is no ground for the assumption.
Those rites are much older than any solar cult. The Sabbath
observances of the Babylonians and of the Jews were monthly,
and not yearly ceremonies. The renewal of fire is interpreted
in the 'Satapatha-Brâhmana' as assisting the renewal of life:
"along with the renewal of his fires does the sacrificer renew
himself; and beneficial to life, indeed, is that redemption of his
own self." The renewal of life is not associated in primitive
religion with the sun, but with the moon.[5] Sacred fires, in ancient
Greece, were kept burning in the shrines of countless deities, who
had no connection with solar cults, such as Demeter and Kore,[6]
Aphrodite at Argyros,[7] Pan at Akakesia.[8] Nor can the sacred fires
of the Eskimo be set down to worship of the sun. The vestals of
Timor maintained a perpetual sacred fire in the temple, not of the
sun, but of the moon.[9] In Rome a fire was maintained in the

---

[1] A. Bertrand, *La religion des Gaulois*, p. 106.
[2] Ovid, *Fasti*, iii. 143 sq.; Macrobius, *Saturnalia*, i. 12. 6.
[3] Philostratus, *Heroica*, i.
[4] M. C. d'Arvieux, *Mémoires*, vol. ii, pp. 139 sqq.
[5] *Satapatha-Brâhmana*, xi. 7. 1. 1., *The Sacred Books of the East*, vol. xliv,
pp. 118 sq.
[6] Pausanias, viii. 9. 1.
[7] Apeleius, *Liber memorialis*, viii. 16.
[8] Pausanias, viii. 37. 8.
[9] See above, vol. ii, p. 710.

temple of 'Luna noctiluca.'[1] In New Britain human life is thought
to depend on tending the moon's, not the sun's fire.[2] It is an
obvious idea, which obtains in all stages of culture, that fire is
latent in the wood of trees out of which it is kindled.[3] Agni is
regarded in the Vedic hymns as being hidden in the sacred wood.[4]
But trees and the sacred spirit which they contain are, it has been
seen, associated everywhere with the moon and not with the sun.
According to the myths of the Huitoto, fire was first obtained
from the moon by a woman.[5] Among the tribes of the Orinoco,
when there is an eclipse of the moon, lighted brands are carefully
put away underground, for it is believed that if the moon were to
be extinguished, all fires on the surface of the earth would go out
also.[6] The rites of the sacred fire at equinoxial festivals and in
connection with solar religions are rituals derived from more
primitive cults, and the vestal priestesses who tend perpetual
fires are the descendants of the most ancient wielders of agricultural magic.

Rain-making.

Among the Pueblo tribes the rites of fertility have reached the
highest degree of ceremonial elaboration. In the famous Snake-
Dance of the Hopis the men, headed by an elder swinging a
bull-roarer, dance round a sacred rock, holding serpents in their
mouths. The women, both young and old, uttering solemn prayers,
sprinkle maize-flour over the animals and the men until the air is
thick with flour-dust and the ground white as snow. The snakes
are then cast on the ground and the women again scatter meal over
them.[7] The traditions of the Hopis ascribe the institution of the
Snake-Dance to their tribal ancestress.[8] Similar dances are held in

[1] A. Preuner, *Hestia-Vesta*, p. 197 n.
[2] O. Meyer, "Mythen und Erzählungen von dem Insel Vuatom (Bismarck-
Archipel)," *Anthropos*, v, p. 724. Cf. above, vol. ii, p. 645.
[3] E.g. S. Powers, *Tribes of California*, pp. 171, 287; M. Girschner, "Die
Karolinen und Namöluk und ihre Bewohner," *Baessler-Archiv*, 1912, p. 141.
Cf. J. G. Frazer, *The Golden Bough*, vol. xi, pp. 295 sq.
[4] *Rig-Veda*, x. 79 (E. Ludwig's transl., vol. i, p. 460); cf. vi. 33 (*ibid.*, vol. ii,
p. 138). Compare also the language of a modern French writer cited above,
vol. i, p. 51.
[5] K. T. Preuss, *Religion und Mythologie der Uitoto*, vol. i, p. 119.
[6] J. Gumilla, *El Orinoco ilustrado*, p. 499.
[7] J. G. Bourke, *The Snake-Dance of the Moquis of Arizona*, pp. 180 sqq.
[8] J. W. Fewkes, "Tusayan Migration Traditions," *Nineteenth Annual
Report of the Bureau of American Ethnology*, Part i, p. 622; Id., "Tusayan
Snake Ceremonies," *Sixteenth Annual Report of the Bureau of Ethnology*,
p. 304.

most Pueblo villages.[1] The Zuñi Indians have numerous rain-making ceremonies. In one of these a sacred spring is cleaned out by the men of the Frog clan, who then hand the bowls full of water to the women; these pour the water from the bowls, deck them with feathers and place them on the ledge of the spring.[2] In another rite, flour and powdered roots are mixed with the water in bowls and the priestess whips the mixture into a froth, while the male priests utter appropriate prayers.[3]

The object of the rites performed by the women in these instances is the production of rain. No rites connected with the success of agricultural operations are of such paramount importance as those designed to control the rainfall. Those rites are commonly regarded as appertaining to the women's special sphere. Not only is rain the primary condition for the successful cultivation of the soil, which, as well as the care of springs and wells and the supplying of water in pitchers, is women's work, but all waters are associated with the moon, the patron of women. Among the native tribes of Peru and the Araucanians of Chili, the care of regulating the supply of rain devolved entirely upon sacred women or priestesses.[4] Among the Abipones of the Gran Chaco no one but the eldest woman of the tribe was regarded as qualified to provide the water required in the village.[5] Among the Guanches of the Canary Islands the production of rain was the business of priestesses; they proceeded for that purpose to the sea-shore and beat the water with rods.[6] Throughout India the magical operations intended to secure a supply of rain are performed almost exclusively by the women. Thus among the Kholarian tribes of Bengal, intercession for rain is the concern of the women. They ascend the hills, and pray to Mrang Buru to send rain.[7] In the Koch tribes of eastern Bengal, the ceremonies intended to secure a good harvest and to procure rain are carried out by the women, and men are excluded during the performance of the rites.[8] The

[1] M. C. Stevenson, "The Zuñi Indians," Twenty-third Annual Report of the Bureau of American Ethnology, pp. 86 sq.; J. W. Fewkes, "Tusayan Migration Traditions," Nineteenth Annual Report of the Bureau of American Ethnology, pp. 963 sqq.; Id., "A Comparison of Sia and Tusayan Snake Ceremonials," The American Anthropologist, viii, pp. 137 sqq.

[2] M. C. Stevenson, op. cit., pp. 58 sqq.

[3] Ibid., pp. 21, 163 sqq.

[4] See below, p. 17.

[5] M. Dobrizhoffer, An Account of the Abipones, vol. ii, p. 152.

[6] J. B. Bérenger-Féraud, Superstitions et survivances, vol. i, p. 473.

[7] E. T. Dalton, "The Kols of Chota-Nagpore," Transactions of the Ethnological Society, N.S., vi, p. 34.

[8] W. Crooke, "Nudity in India, in Custom and Ritual," Journal of the Royal Anthropological Institute, xlix, p. 247.

rain-making ceremonies are likewise carried out by the women among the tribes of Muzaffarpur, on the Ganges.[1] In most of those rites the women dance naked at night in the fields round a clay image which they have fashioned, and sing lewd songs to stimulate the god of fertility. Often the nude sorceresses draw a plough across the field.[2] So also in southern India, rain-making is generally performed by the women. When rain is wanted, the women make a small clay figure of a man, which they set on a palanquin. They carry it from house to house singing obscene songs, and then place it in a field. The ceremony is regarded as a powerful rain-charm and fertiliser. Elsewhere, instead of a clay man, a frog is carried.[3]

Abundant traces of the rain-making functions of the priestesses of primitive Europe survive in the attributes and activities of their successors the witches of mediaeval and modern times. The raising of storms has always been regarded as one of their favourite deeds of malice; it is the power of rain-making turned to evil account. "No one indued with meane sense," says Reginald Scott, "but will denie that the elements are obedient to witches and at their commandement, or that they may at their pleasure send rain, hail, tempests, thunder, lightning, when she, being but an old doting woman, casteth a flint over her left shoulder towards the west, or hurleth a little sea-sand up into the element, or wetteth a broom sprig in water, and sprinkleth the same in the air; or diggeth a pit in the earth and putting water therein, stirreth it about with her finger; or boileth hogs' bristles; or layeth sticks across upon a banke where never was a drop of water; or burieth sage till it be rotten; all which things are confessed by witches, and affirmed by writers to be the means that witches used to move extraordinary tempests and raine."[4] According to a German chronicle of the sixteenth or seventeenth century the witches were in the habit of assembling on the banks of ponds and streams, and of beating the water with wands until out of them rose fogs and rain-clouds, which

[1] C. J. Stevenson-Moore, "Harvest Festivals in Muzaffarpur," *Journal of the Asiatic Society of Bengal*, lxxii, part 3, p. 39.

[2] H. H. Risley, *The Tribes and Castes of Bengal*, vol. i, p. 498; Sarat Chandra Mitra, "On the Har Parauri, or the Behari Women's Ceremony for producing Rain," *Journal of the Royal Asiatic Society*, N.S., xxix, pp. 471 sqq.; Id., "On some Ceremonies for producing Rain," *Journal of the Anthropological Society of Bombay*, iii, p. 25; *North Indian Notes and Queries*, i, p. 210; *Panjab Notes and Queries*, iii, pp. 41, 115; W. Crooke, *Popular Religion and Folklore of Northern India*, vol. i, pp. 68 sqq.

[3] W. Francis, "Agricultural Superstitions in Bellany," *Folk-lore*, xviii, pp. 332 sq. Cf. E. Thurston, *Castes and Tribes of Southern India*, vol. iii, pp. 244 sq.

[4] R. Scott, *The Discoverie of Witchcraft*, p. 47.

they directed whither they pleased.   A Swiss chronicle informs us that in the year 1382 a certain count of Kyburg, being besieged by his enemies, secretly sent for an old woman, who, standing on the battlements of his castle, raised clouds and a rain so violent that it scattered the forces of his opponents.[1]   A common story, of which many variants are found, is that of a hunter who, being annoyed at a prolonged spell of rainy weather, fired a shot at the blackest rain-cloud.   A naked woman fell from it, mortally wounded, and the rain-clouds at once dispersed.[2]   The notion is embodied in the current expression that "it is raining cats and dogs, and old women."   The cats and the dogs are, of course, but disguises of the 'old women.'   The Germans have a similar expression, and say, when it snows, that "the old women are shaking their cloaks."[3]   The Walkyries rode in the clouds, and from them poured dews and water over the earth.[4]

Rain-making ceremonies take place at the present day in some parts of Germany.   When rain is badly needed a little girl is stripped and led to some out-of-the-way spot, where she has to dig up some henbane with her foot and perform other ritual acts. After this water is poured over her.[5]   In Worms, when a severe drought was experienced, the young women stripped one of the younger girls and led her to the nearest stream to bathe, while they flogged the water vigorously with wands.   The girl was then led back to the village, walking backwards.[6]   In Silesia the young women are, in case of drought, roused in the middle of the night and led to the wells and springs.[7]   It is customary in many parts of Germany, the Tyrol, and Hungary, if the country needs rain, to throw buckets of water over the women and girls.[8]   Similar customs are widespread in south-eastern Europe.   Thus in Wallachia, when rain is badly needed, the women and girls, having stripped themselves naked, go round the boundaries of the commune watering the ground.[9]   In Rumania the girls, clothed in a scanty attire of greenery, go from house to house singing songs, while the

---

[1] J. Grimm, *Teutonic Mythology*, p. 1087.

[2] *Ibid.*   It will be remembered that King James I narrowly escaped being drowned in consequence of the doings of some witches, who "had baptized and drowned a black cat, thereby raising a dreadful storm." The women were, of course, tortured, the King taking a personal interest in the proceedings, and they were eventually duly burned alive at the stake.   His son Charles I also nearly fell a victim to storm-raising witches (C. Hardwick, *Traditions, Superstitions and Folk-Lore*, p. 108).

[3] Cf. J. Grimm, *op. cit.*, p. 268.

[4] *Ibid.*, pp. 421, 641, 1088.   [5] *Ibid.*, p. 593.

[6] W. Mannhardt, *Wald- und Feldkulte*, vol. i, pp. 330 sq.

[7] *Ibid.*, p. 332.   [8] *Ibid.*, pp. 259 n., 328 sqq.

[9] R. F. von Kaindl, "Zauberglaube bei den Huzulen," *Globus*, lxxvi, p. 253.

people throw water over them.[1]   In Serbia the young women of
the village dance in a circle and sing round one of their number,
who stands in the midst of them wearing only a skirt of leaves.[2]
In Russia likewise, it is the women who, in case of drought, provide for the needs of the community by bathing a manikin in
the river, or by seizing a passing stranger and giving him a
thorough ducking.[3]

In Africa, where rain-making is so prominent a function of
the sacred king, the association of that function with the
special powers and activities of women is nevertheless apparent.
Thus among the Baronga, one of the few southern Bantu
tribes whose customs have been systematically investigated, the
magical production of rain when a drought threatens the country
is done entirely by the women. "The ceremony," says the Rev.H.
Junod, "is accompanied by very savage customs."   The women
remove their clothing and array themselves in head-dresses and
girdles made from a particular creeping plant. They set out in procession uttering special cries, and singing songs "of a revolting
obscenity, in which all must join." They first proceed to the house
of a woman who has borne twins and sprinkle her with water. The
procession, still singing obscene songs and performing lascivious
dances, then proceeds to the wells, which are ceremonially cleaned
out.   They then go to the grove where the tribal ancestors are
buried and pour water over their graves. During the proceedings
no man must be found in the path of the women; should any
male intruder be met, he is soundly thrashed and otherwise
maltreated, and thrust out of the way.   The ceremony, remarks
the Rev. H. Junod, "strongly recalls those of the Bacchantes
among the ancient Greeks, who performed their mysterious rites
far from the eyes of any male."[4] Similar ceremonies have been
observed in Nyasaland.   When there is a drought, the women
go in procession, early in the morning, to the wells, and clean
them out, pouring water over their leader and throwing it in the
air.[5] Among the tribes which formerly inhabited the Transvaal,
it was the special office of girls, known as 'itsugwana,' to call for
rain. Painted with stripes like zebras, they ran naked from
kraal to kraal, singing songs while they ran around the corn-

[1] W. Schmidt, Das Jahr und seine Tage in Meinung und Brauch der Romänen
Siebenbürgens, p. 17; E. Fischer, "Paparuda und Scaloian," Globus, xciii,
pp. 14 sq.
[2] W. Mannhardt, op. cit., p. 330; E. Gerard, The Land beyond the Forest,
vol. ii, p. 13. Cf. W. R. S. Ralston, Songs of the Russian People, pp. 227 sqq.
[3] J. Polek, "Regenzauber in Osteuropa," Zeitschrift des Vereins für Volkskunde, iii, p. 85; W. Mannhardt, op. cit., p. 331.
[4] H. A. Junod, Les Ba-Ronga, pp. 417 sq.
[5] A. Werner, The Natives of Central Africa, p. 56.

fields. On reaching the chief kraal of the neighbourhood they were given some corn by the headman and brewed beer from it.[1] Among the Zulus, the girls attend to the supply of rain by carrying pots of water to a certain sacred tree and watering it.[2] One of the most famous rain-makers in Natal was a certain witch whose power over the weather was regarded as unbounded.[3] In Loango at the present day, should the local rain-maker fail to obtain rain, recourse is had to an aged woman who lives at Abako and holds a position of unique influence in all the neighbouring tribes. "She is not a rain-maker and professes to have no power over the elements, but is the priestess of Atida, called by all, except the very few initiated, Min Jok, or Mother of God. As the priestess she has the power of divination and prophecy, and her advice is sought, with gifts, on a diversity of matters, including rain."[4] Among the southern Bantu "one of the most famous rain doctors was Modjaji, a chieftainess who resided in the Northern Transvaal."[5] In Angoniland the weather is considered to be under the control of the women.[6] Among the Makololo likewise it is upon the witches that the supply of rain is thought to depend.[7] At Chigunda, in Central Africa, the rain-making ceremonies are carried out exclusively by the women; the whole assembled tribe is present, but the women are the only officiating members. The chief priestess is the chief's sister, who, after performing some magical rites consisting of dropping 'ufa' on the ground, invokes Heaven in an intoned prayer of which the burden is: "Hear Thou, O God, and send rain!" The people answer in solemn responses. The women then pour water over one another.[8] Among the Damaras it is the daughter of the chief who prays for the success of agricultural operations. "This woman is called Ondangere, and is to the Damaras what the Vestal was among the ancient Romans." Like them she tends a perpetual sacred fire.[9] Among the Herero the eldest daughter of the chief discharges the same functions, and has charge of a sacred fire which is kept burning in the hut of the chief's principal wife.[10]

[1] H. W. Garbutt, "Native Witchcraft and Superstition in South Africa," *Journal of the Royal Anthropological Institute*, xxxix, p. 550.

[2] D. Kidd, *The Essential Kafir*, p. 115; cf. pp. 117 sq.

[3] J. Shooter, *The Kafirs of Natal and the Zulu Country*, pp. 212 sqq.

[4] J. H. Dribers, "Rain-making among the Loango," *Journal of the Royal Anthropological Institute*, xlix, pp. 70 sq.

[5] H. W. Garbutt, *loc. cit.*

[6] *The British Central Africa Gazette*, vol. v, No. 6, p. 3.

[7] D. and C. Livingstone, *Expedition to the Zambesi*, p. 46.

[8] H. Rowley, *Story of the Universities' Mission to Central Africa*, pp. 226 sq.

[9] C. J. Andersson, *Lake Ngami*, p. 223.

[10] A. Werner, "The Evolution of Agriculture," *Journal of the African Society*, ix, p. 408.

Among the Bechuana the rain-making ceremonies are performed by, or under the direction of, a professional rain-making magician; but it is the women who gather the appropriate herbs for the ceremony, and who light the sacred fires.[1] The male rain-maker is often 'assisted' by his wife or by other women. Some light is thrown upon the nature of that assistance by an incident related of a Bechuana rain-maker. After a long period of drought, during which the official rain-maker and his female assistants had exerted themselves with little apparent success, the welcome shower fell at last. The delighted elders of the tribe betook themselves to the rain-maker's hut to congratulate him and to thank him for the success of his labours. But, to their embarrassment, they found that the magician was sound asleep and when roused he appeared to be quite unaware of the arrival of the rain. He, however, pointed to his wife, who was sitting on the floor vigorously shaking a milk-sack, and said to the chiefs: "Do you not see my wife churning rain as fast as she can?"[2] Mr. Andersson, who relates the anecdote, represents the answer of the rain-maker as a subterfuge to save his face, and he is doubtless right. Nevertheless, the subterfuge presupposes that the part of the female assistants of rain-makers is recognised as being more than subsidiary.

The magical powers of a wizard are often thought to be to a great extent dependent upon the character of his wife. Thus, among the Cheyenne Indians, "a man cannot become a doctor by himself; when he receives the power, his wife, who afterwards is his assistant, must also be taught and receive certain secrets. If the wife of the man who is receiving the power does not wish to become a doctor, the man must find another woman to act for him. A man may become a doctor through a dream, thus receiving spiritual power directly from above, but even in this case he must have a woman to help him."[3] Among the Zulus a rain-maker loses his power altogether if his wife becomes pregnant, for pregnancy is believed to impair the magical powers of women.[4] Similar ideas obtain among the Seri Indians. The functions of chief, among those primitive people, are like those of archaic monarchs in much more advanced cultural stages, essentially magical; it is mainly in view of those magical functions that the chief is elected. But, as with the medicine-men of the Cheyenne and the Zulu rain-maker, it is not so much his own personal qualifications which are of moment, but those of his wife. The Seri chief is selected, not with

[1] C. J. Andersson, *op. cit.*, p. 460.
[2] *Ibid.*, p. 461.
[3] G. B. Grinnell, *The Cheyenne Indians*, vol. ii, pp. 128 sq.
[4] H. Callaway, *The Religious System of the Amazulu*, p. 443.

reference to his own magic powers, but with reference to those of his wife.[1]   The notion appears Gilbertian, but it is by no means a whimsical peculiarity of those savages.   Very much the same principle is, in fact, implied in many archaic forms of the institution of royalty.

Magical Functions of Queens.

The Bechuana magician is not the only instance of a rain-making wizard leaving the actual work to his wives, while he remains content with the honour and credit accruing from the results of the operation.   In Dahomey, as in all African kingdoms, the monarch is the great rain-maker.   His title to that office is particularly definite, for he is regarded as the direct descendant of the rain-god, and the temple where his divine ancestor dwells in spirit, and where the rites necessary for the maintenance of the water-supply are performed is part of the royal palace.   That god of whom the sacred monarch is the living representative, is moreover, in this instance, not a sky-god or sun-god, but the moon-god.[2]   The qualifications of the king of Dahomey to act as rain-maker thus appear to be exceptionally high.   Yet, strangely enough, it is not he who takes the most important part in the rites upon which the water-supply depends, but his wives.   It is the special office of those ladies, with the assistance of the virgin Amazons who are officially the King's wives, to serve the temple of the rain-god, and their daily task consists in going to sacred wells whence, in holy vessels manufactured by the Amazons themselves, they draw the water required for the secret rites of the temple.   The wives of the King of Dahomey are in fact the priestesses of the rain-making god. They are spoken of as 'the Mothers.'[3]

The vestal priestesses of Peru were also called 'the Mothers,' 'Mama-cuna.'   They were, under the Inca domination, regarded as the wives of the Great Inca, who had the right to take any of

[1] W. J. McGee, "The Seri Indians," *Seventeenth Annual Report of the Bureau of Ethnology*, Part ii, p. 276.

[2] The tutelary god of the king of Dahomey is known as Nesu. He is a special water-god, and water-pots are sacred to him.   Mau, on the other hand, "controls the rain supply, and keeps a vast store of water in the firmament, which he lets out at will.   This seems to be his only function with regard to man."   Skertchly says that the priestesses of Mau are distinguished by necklaces of alternate cowries and dark seeds; and Sir A. B. Ellis says the same thing of the priestesses of Nesu.   It is thus fairly evident that Nesu, the king's special god, is only another name for Mau, the moon-god (A. B. Ellis, *The Ewe-speaking Peoples*, pp. 34, 67; J. A. Skertchly, *Dahomey as it is*, p. 472; cf. above, vol. ii, p. 761).

[3] A. B. Ellis, *op. cit.*, p. 67; J. A. Skertchly, *op. cit.*, pp. 206 sqq.

them as his actual wives, and they were also bestowed upon the Inca princes and upon provincial governors and chieftains.[1] The institution of the Peruvian 'Mothers,' which was adopted by the Incas, was far older than their rule. It belonged to the most ancient religious usages of the people, and the priestesses were, in all probability, regarded 'ex officio' as the wives of the local chieftains. The vestals of Cuzco, although employed in all branches of the official cult of the dynasty, were specially addicted to the cult of the official Moon-deity, Mama-Quilla, whose image they carried on their shoulders on ceremonial occasions.[2] They tended night and day a perpetual fire, baked the bread and prepared the beer of the gods, and spun and wove the sacred garments of white wool for the use of the Incas and the idols.[3] The native priestesses of Peru and of Chili, commonly known as 'machi,' who were the prototyes of the sacred wives of the Incas, were, of course, consecrated to the cult of the native deities; they served in particular the 'Mother of Maize' who presided over agricultural rites, and the rain-giving gods, whose cult occupied a prominent place in native rites. The rain-making ceremonies were performed by the 'machi' priestesses, and consisted in the lighting of sacred fires, and in the performance of ritual dances to the accompaniment of music which was supplied by the men.[4] The Inca monarchy developed in all probability out of the temporary chieftainship of war-leaders, known as 'sinchi.' "Although the tribes all lived in simple liberty without recognising any lord, there were always some ambitious men among them, aspiring for mastery; they committed violence among their countrymen and among strangers to subject them and bring them to obedience under their command." In the mythical history of the Incas the first four traditional founders of the

---

[1] J. de Torquemada, *Viente i un libros rituales i Monarchia Indiana*, vol. ii, p. 195; Bartolome de las Casas, *De las antiguas gentes del Peru*, p. 84; J. Roman y Zamora, *Republicas de Indias, idolatria y gobierno en Mexico y Peru*, vol. i, p. 117; Gregorio Garcia, *Origen de los Indios*, pp. 180 sq.; Polo de Ondogardo, in C. R. Markham, *Narrative of the Rites and Laws of the Yncas*, p. 166. Although the severest punishments were inflicted in case of unchastity, a vestal who became pregnant had only to declare that she had conceived through the Sun, and her statement was never questioned (P. de Andagoya, *Relación de los sucesos de Pedrarias Davila*, in M. Fernandez de Navarrete, *Coleccion de los viages y descubrimentos*, vol. iii, p. 166).

[2] Christobal de Molina, *An Account of the Fables and Rites of the Yncas*, p. 37.

[3] Garcilasso de la Vega, *Royal Commentaries of the Yncas*, vol. i, pp. 292 sqq.; vol. ii, pp. 155 sq.; P. Cieza de Leon, *Second Part of the Chronicle of Peru*, pp. 85 sq.; B. de las Casas, *op. cit.*, p. 82; J. de Torquemada, *loc. cit.*

[4] T. Guevara, "Folklore Araucano," *Anales de la Universidad de Chile*, cxxvii, pp. 559, 566 sqq., 576 sq., 578; P. J. de Arriaga, *Extirpacion de la idolatria nel Piru*, pp. 25, 35.

dynasty are associated with four women.[1]   These may have been priestesses, or 'machis,' who as wives of the tyrants would impart a sacred character to the usurpers.

The similarity between the priestesses of the most advanced states of America and of Africa and the Vestals of Rome is manifest.   The current conception of the cult of the Vestals is that which has been transmitted to us by the tradition of later Roman times, in which the aspect of the cult that was deliberately emphasised represented it as the emblem of the service of the hearth and the home.   The Vestal virgins were expressly held up as symbols and models of domestic virtue to Roman women.[2]   But that was a late conception of the cult; its original significance and functions were very different.   As Dr. Fowler remarks: "There must have been many stages of growth from the beginning to the fully developed Vesta of the Republic and Empire."[3] The goddess Vesta was not the sole deity served in the temple of the Forum. With her was associated a male god, Pales, who, according to Servius, was together with Vesta, the deity of 'pabulum,' that is, of food.[4] Pales was a deity of supreme importance among the old Italic populations, not only in Rome, but throughout Italy as far south as Brindisi.   The Palatine mount, as well as other sacred places, was named after him, and the home of the sacred king came to be known as the 'palace,' or 'house of Pales.'   The mythical ancestor-king Evander was said to be the grandson, or in other traditions, the father, of Pales, or Pallas.[5]   Pales appears to have been identical with Priapus, and was represented in the temple of the Vestals by a phallic image.[6]   He was also impersonated by a sacred serpent which in olden times was kept in the grove of Vesta, and tended by the priestesses.[7]   The goddess who came later to be generally known as Vesta and was indistinguishable from the Good Mother, or Mater Matuta, and the Good Goddess, was in all probability a female counterpart of Pales, who appears sometimes in female form as Diva Palatua.[8]   One of the chief festivals of the cult was the Feast of Bakers, held on the 9th of June, when all mills and millstones were decorated with

---

[1] P. Sarmiento de Gamboa, *History of the Incas*, pp. 38 sqq., 43.

[2] See below, p. 350.

[3] W. Warde Fowler, *The Roman Festivals of the Period of the Republic*, p. 148.

[4] Servius, *ad Georgic.*, iii. 1.

[5] L. Preller, *Römische Mythologie*, pp. 365 sq.   The name 'Latium' itself is probably connected with the god Pales.

[6] Pliny, *Nat. Hist.*, xxviii. 39.

[7] A. Preuner, *Hestia-Vesta*, p. 337.

[8] L. Preller, *loc. cit.*   Servius actually speaks of Pales as a goddess (on *Georgics*, iii. i.   Cf. Arnobius, *Contra Gentes*, iii. 40; Martianus Capella, i. 50, v. 425).

garlands of flowers, and the Roman matrons brought offerings of bread to the temple.[1] The Vestals themselves prepared loaves of bread, observing a most elaborate ritual in the process.[2] One of the most prominent functions of the Vestals, however, was the care of the water-supply; and, like the priestesses of Dahomey, they proceeded daily to a sacred spring outside the Porta Camena and brought water to the temple in special earthenware vessels, for no water that had been conveyed through pipes might be used in the ceremonies of the cult.[3] They were also called upon to regulate the flow of the Tiber. At the Ides of May the Vestals proceeded with much pomp to the Pons Sublicius, and after certain ceremonies had been performed, they threw into the river twenty-four dummy figures fashioned out of reeds, which had their hands and feet firmly bound.[4] The reed figures represented, as Dionysius of Halicarnassus tells us, "men whom they used to cast into the stream of the Tiber, bound hand and foot."[5]

Sir James Frazer has brought together much evidence to show that the Roman Vestals were originally, like their American and African sisters, the wives of the Roman kings.[6] Several Vestals were, we know, the mothers of kings of Rome; and every Vestal, on her consecration, received the name of Amata, 'beloved,' which, it will be remembered, was the name, or title, of the wife of the Latin king. It is therefore probable that when the emperor Heliogabalus, like the Inca and Dahomian monarchs, married one of the Vestals, he was unconsciously following a venerable precedent. In republican and imperial times, the representative of the sacred king was the Flamen Dialis, who dwelt in the Regia by the temple of Vesta, and occupied the position of head of the college of the sacred priestesses. That holy personage was subject to innumerable tabus and rules which had to be very strictly observed, and which, in republican and imperial Rome, preserved the memory of a primitive stage of Italian culture. Among those rules were some which appear very peculiar in a society so professedly patriarchal as that of Rome. Although the chief object of the tabus to which the Flamen was subject was to maintain him in a condition of ritual purity, he

---

[1] Ovid, *Fasti*, vi. 304 sq., 389 sq.; Propertius, iv. i. 21 sqq.

[2] Servius, *ad Bucolic.*, viii. 82; Festus, in *Jurisprudentiae antejustinianae quae supersunt*, ed. Huschke, p. 40.

[3] Plutarch, *Numa*, 13; Livy, i. 11; Valerius Maximus, ix. 6. 1; Cedrenus, p. 122 (ed. Oporin); Festus, *ut supra*, p. 160; Servius, *ad Aeneid.*, xi. 339.

[4] Plutarch, *Quaest. Rom.*, xxxii. lxxxvi; Macrobius, i. 11. 47; Ovid, *Fasti*, v. 621 sqq.

[5] Dionysius Halicarnassensis, i. 38.

[6] J. G. Frazer, *The Magical Origin of Kings*, 219 sqq.

was not vowed to chastity; on the contrary, it was compulsory that he should be a married man. His wife, the Flaminica Dialis, was a scarcely less sacred and important personage than her husband. Plutarch speaks of her as the priestess of Juno,[1] but it does not appear that the Flaminica was specially attached to the cult of the goddess.[2] Every nine days, that is, at every phase of the old lunar month, she had to sacrifice with her own hands a ram to Jupiter in the Regia.[3] If there was a thunder-storm, it was her duty to take immediate steps to appease the gods.[4] She was subject to at least as many peculiar tabus as the Flamen, as, for instance, that she should not comb her hair or trim her nails while the temple of Vesta was being purified, or when the Salic priests, or 'Jumpers,' performed their dances, or when, at the head of the Vestal priestesses, she took part in the ceremony of casting the figures representing human victims into the Tiber.[5] Although the wife of the Flamen Dialis was always a Flaminica, it appears that in the provinces the husband of the priestess need not necessarily have been a priest, and that she might indeed have been unmarried.[6] The Flaminica had to belong to one of the most ancient and noble Roman families. Her marriage with the Flamen Dialis had to be celebrated according to the old ritual of 'confarreatio.'[7] It was indissoluble, the laws of divorce being inapplicable to the sacred couple.[8] But the most remarkable of those rules was that, if the Flaminica should happen to die before her husband, the latter automatically ceased to hold office and at once lost his sacred character; he became an ordinary private citizen and was moreover strictly debarred from marrying again.[9]

It thus appears that the title of the Flamen Dialis, the repre-sentative of the Roman sacred kings, did not essentially differ from that of the headman of the Seri Indians, and that the magic power of the sacred personage depended, like that of American and Zulu wizards, upon the magical faculties of his wife. It would be quite impossible to account for those strange rules if we were content to accept the old conception that Roman society had from the first been

---

[1] Plutarch, *Quaest. Rom.*, 86.
[2] Cf. C. Jullian, art. "Flamen," in C. Daremberg and E. Saglio, *Dictionnaire des antiquités grecques et romaines*, vol. ii, part ii, p. 1163.
[3] Macrobius, *Saturnalia*, i. 16. 30.
[4] *Ibid.*, i. 16. 7.
[5] Ovid, *Fasti*, iii. 97, vi. 229 sq.
[6] C. Jullian, *loc. cit.*, p. 1185.
[7] Servius, *ad Aeneid.*, iv. 103. 374; Gaius, *Institut.*, i. 112; Tacitus, *Annales*, iv. 16.
[8] Aulus Gellius, x. 15. 23; Plutarch, *Quaest. Rom.*, 50.
[9] Aulus Gellius, x. 15. 22; Plutarch, *loc. cit.;* Priscian, v. 12.

strenuously patriarchal, and that priestly functions had accordingly been chiefly exercised by male priests.   Had that been the case it would be inconceivable that priestesses, such as the Vestals and the Flaminicae, should have come into existence at all and should have come to occupy the sacrosanct and exalted position which they held in the most essential rites of Roman cult.   The truth is probably very different from the traditional patriarchal picture. There was a legend that Hercules, when he visited the site of Rome for the first time, approached a spring near the Aventine Hill to quench his thirst; but he was met by a priestess and a number of women who informed him that no man was allowed near the spot while the sacred rites were being performed.[1]   The rites in question were those of the Good Goddess, who was the same as the great Italic goddess Fauna, or Fatua.   Her male counterpart was a serpent-god Faunus, that is, the Good God, who is apparently identical with Pales, the serpent-god worshipped by the Vestals.[2]   The cult of the Good Goddess, from which even in later times men were entirely excluded, was said to be one of the oldest and most sacred in Roman religion, and was served by the Vestal priestesses.   In primitive times priestesses were of even more importance than priests in Roman religion; and the magical powers of priests and of sacred kings were, in Rome as elsewhere, derived in the first instance from an older priesthood of magical women.

Archaic Queenship.

In the primitive monarchies of America, Africa and archaic Italy it was, then, considered appropriate that the wives of the god, or of his representative the sacred king, should take an important part in the performance of the rites designed to promote the success of agriculture, and more especially in those ceremonies connected with the cult of water, which originally belonged to woman's sphere, but which were also the special magic function of the king as rain-maker.   It is difficult to suppose that women were introduced into religious rituals which were originally in the hands of male officiants; and it may even appear surprising that they should have been allowed to retain those functions under monarchies so despotic as that of Dahomey or so definitely patriarchal as that of Rome.

The office of royalty and the sacred and semi-divine character attaching to it had their origin, as has been abundantly shown by Sir James Frazer, not in administrative and political organisation,

---

[1] Propertius, iv. 9. 23 sqq.; Macrobius, i. 12. 28.
[2] L. Preller, *Römische Mythologie*, pp. 351 sq.

but in the magical functions which archaic monarchs were expected to discharge on behalf of the community, and sacred kings have evolved from primitive magicians and medicine-men.   Despotic power, is, however, far from being a characteristic feature of the most ancient forms of kingship; the burdens and disabilities of primitive royalty are indeed much more conspicuous than its privileges and authority. Like primitive magicians, and primitive gods themselves, magical chiefs are frequently treated with scanty reverence; they are very generally regarded as being employed by the community, like any other servant, for the purpose of carrying out certain necessary work, and the sacred personage is sometimes scarcely distinguished from the rest of the community except by his miserable poverty.   It is the majesty and power of the fully developed king, the 'god on earth,' which have to a large extent helped to impart an august and majestic nature to the deity whom he impersonated, rather than the deity who has transmitted his character to the king.   But the development of the monarchical office has almost invariably taken place through the acquisition of power by war-leaders and mighty military conquerors.   The war-leader and the chief magician, or headman of a particularly sacred clan, are often one and the same person.   The two may, however, be distinct; the sacred king, or spiritual monarch, and the temporal remaining quite separate to the last.   In general the powerful and successful war-leader, being anxious to combine the two characters and to legitimise, so to speak, his claims to supreme power, becomes assimilated to the magical and sacred personage, whether he was originally identical with him or not.

War-leaders are, of course, usually from the first men, and the royal office is, in the relatively advanced phases where it has developed, habitually vested in a king.   The magical and religious functions of kingship, which constitute its peculiar sacredness, are not, however, in the primary division of labour between the sexes exclusively masculine functions. The primitive magic worker was on the contrary, there is every reason to think, a woman. Accordingly, not only may the royal office, even in the most advanced stages of civilisation, be filled by a woman, but the queen is in every phase of the development of that office considerably more than merely the wife of the king.   Full-blown royalty, being mainly the product of military power and conquest, belongs to a stage of social development which is a long way from primitive; it is unknown in the most uncultured societies.   Where such royal institutiones have developed, social organisation has, as a rule, long lost its primitive matriarchal character.

Matriarchal society may, however, persist until advanced stages of culture. The transference of magic functions from the women to the men may in such cases not become completely effected, or may not take place at all. The war-leader, remaining what he is originally, the appointed delegate of the community, may never have the opportunity of combining with his temporal duties the exercise of magical functions which still belong to the sphere of women. The office of sacred ruler, in those conditions, will develop exclusively in the hands of priestesses, and such a matriarchal society may become an actual gynaecocracy, in which supreme power is vested, not in a king, but in a queen. An example of such a development of administrative, as well as magical, functions in the hands of women is supplied by the matriarchal communities of Assam. In the matriarchal clans of the Khasis and Syntegs the religious and sacerdotal functions have remained in the hands of the women. "Priestesses assist at all sacrifices, and the male officiants are only deputies." In one important State, Khyrim, the High Priestess and actual head of the State is a woman who "combines in her person sacerdotal and regal functions."[1] In southern China, in the Su-Mu, a tribe of the Man-Tseu, which numbers some three and a half million people, the ruler is likewise a queen, and the office is said to be hereditary within the sacred clan, but can never be held except by a woman.[2] In another tribe of southern China, the Nue'Kun, the supreme authority is exercised by a female ruler, and its transmission is confined to the female descendants of the royal family.[3] A large province of Tibet, the principality of Po-mo, in the north-eastern portion of the country, is, or was until lately, ruled by a queen; but we have no definite information as to whether female rule was permanently established.[4] In any case, it appears that a regular gynaecocratic government was the established constitution a thousand years ago throughout the northern part of Tibet. The Chinese annals of the Sui and of the T'ang dynasties (A.D. 581–905) contain accounts of the Kingdom of Su-pi, or as it was called by the Chinese, Nu-kuo, that is, the 'Kingdom of Women,' which comprised the whole of northern Tibet. The accounts in the Sui-shu and T'ang-shu run as follows:[5] "The Kingdom of Women is south of the Tsung-ling mountains, and is a division of the Ch'iang. From east to west it is nine days' journey, from north to south twenty days' journey. It has eighty towns,

---

[1] Sir C. J. Lyall, in P. R. T. Gurdon, *The Khasis*, p. xxiv.
[2] W. Gill, *The River of Golden Sand*, vol. i, p. 365.
[3] J. Gray, *China*, vol. ii, p. 307.
[4] W. W. Rockhill, *The Land of the Lamas*, p. 219; cf. p. 213.
[5] For the sake of clearness and in order to avoid repetition I have combined the two accounts, that of the T'ang-shu and that of the Sui-shu, as given by Mr. Rockhill. They differ verbally only in minor details.

and there are over 40,000 families and 10,000 soldiers. In this country the sovereign is a woman, who resides in the K'ang yen valley, a narrow, precipitous gorge around which flows the Jo River in a southerly direction. The queen's husband is called Chin-tsu, but he has nothing to do with the government of the State. There is also a 'little queen,' the two together ruling the kingdom. As to their customs, the women hold in light esteem their husbands, nor are they jealous. Both men and women paint their faces with different coloured clays. They wear raw-hide boots. The climate is very cold and they live by the chase. Their domestic animals comprise sheep and horses. The country produces copper, cinnabar, musk, yak, and salt in great abundance, which they carry to India and make great profit by the trade. The sons take the family name of their mother. Rich women have always men-servants who arrange their hair and paint their faces with clay. The men do also the fighting and till the soil. They have often waged war with Hindustan and the T'anghsiang. The sovereign has near her person several hundred women, and once every five days there is a council of state. They depute men to perform all outside duties, and these are thence known as 'women's deputies.' From the interior of the palace the men receive and transmit the order. When the sovereign dies the people pay several myriad of gold coins, and select from the royal clan two clever women, one to reign, the other as assistant sovereign to succeed her in case of death. If the one who dies is a maiden, the other, a married woman, succeeds her, so that there is no possibility of the dynasty becoming extinct, or of a revolution. The sovereign wears a black (or blue) plaited skirt of a rough texture, with a black robe with sleeves trailing on the ground, and in winter a lambskin gown ornamented with embroideries. She wears her hair done up in little plaits, also earrings, and on her feet a kind of leather boot, known as 'so-i.' In the sixth year of Sui-k'ai-huang (A.D. 586) this country sent tribute to court; since then it has discontinued doing so."[1] There is no ground to doubt the substantial accuracy of those accounts. The gynaecocratic organisation of the kingdom of Su-pi merely represents on a somewhat larger scale the matriarchal tribal organisation which is found in Assam. It does not essentially differ in constitution from that which appears to have obtained in many kingdoms of Arabia and Western Asia, in which the consort of the queen had no official functions. It is not improbable that many such gynaecocratic monarchies have existed. But since monarchical institutions belong to advanced and matriarchal institutions in general to primitive social phases, the complete combination of the two into a gynaecocratic government must be regarded as exceptional.

[1] W. W. Rockhill, *The Land of the Lamas*, pp. 339 sqq.

The matriarchal constitution of royalty, however, far from being exceptional, is, on the contrary, the general rule in barbaric kingdoms. The first qualification of a king, as all kings are careful to inform us, is not his personal merit, but his legitimacy, that is to say, his right by birth and descent. In primitive monarchies the sacred king is not merely a magician possessing special individual magical powers; he is the headman of a magical clan, or royal family, and it is upon his membership in that family that his magical qualifications, in other words, his divine right, rest. That right is thought of as a magical power, or rather an actual substance, on the transmission of which the qualification of a monarch depends. Speaking of a powerful African king, Livingstone observes that "he was a firm believer in the divine right of kings. He was an ordinary man, he said, when his father died, and left him the chieftainship; but directly he succeeded to the high office, he was conscious of power passing into his head and down his back; he felt it enter and knew he was a Chief, clothed with authority, and possessed of wisdom; and people began to fear and reverence him. He mentioned this as one would a fact of natural history, any doubt being out of the question."[1] In societies where the primitive matriarchal rules of succession still obtain, those rules apply, of course, to the transmission of the kingly office, which is handed down in the female line, the heir to the throne being, not the king's son, but his brother or his sister's child. That rule is sometimes observed in royal families after it has fallen into disuse among the common people, as is the case, for instance, in Uganda. There is nothing surprising in the circumstance that royalty, being an archaic and conservative institution, should tend to preserve the usages of a more primitive order of society. But the constitution and the rules of succession of primitive royal families go much farther than the matriarchal rule of transmission in the female line. The royal office, in those earlier forms of the institution, is not even transmitted by the king, according to the matriarchal law, to his sister's children; the succession does not take place in the king's family at all, but remains within the direct line of the queen's family, the king being a stranger.

In North America, where the democratic and equalitarian character of primitive society has in general been so fully maintained, a system of royal institutions developed, nevertheless, among the agricultural tribes of the lower Mississippi valley, in particular among the Natchez. The royal power was with them not so much the attribute of an autocrat as of an aristocratic clan, which enjoyed the faculty of influencing the seasons by virtue of their descent from the sun. In the Sun-clan the female genealogy alone counted.

[1] D. and C. Livingstone, *Narrative of an Expedition to the Zambesi*, p. 79.

Indeed, the husbands were not members of the royal clan. The women might take as their sexual partners whomsoever they pleased from the common people, and they were in fact debarred from mating with men of the clan. Their husbands or lovers had no status, but were treated as servants. They waited on their royal mistresses in the humble attitude of slaves, and might not even sit down in their presence. The Sun-women could have as many lovers as they chose, and could dismiss them as their fancy dictated; they could order them to be tomahawked if they so pleased, or if the 'curs'—for so they spoke of them—were suspected of infidelity. When a royal woman died, her slave-husband was strangled on her grave. If a child of his died, the father was obliged to die also. The royal status of the men of the Sun-clan was thus derived solely from their mothers, not from their fathers, who were commoners and slaves. The headman of the clan, the 'sacred king,' or Great Sun, was the representative of his mother, the clan-mother, who occupied a position equal, if not superior, to that of the executive monarch.[1]

The surmise to which we were led that the Incas of Peru may in the first instance have founded their claim to be regarded as sacred personages upon their connection with the ancient sacred priestesses of the country, is confirmed by the circumstances governing the rules of succession amongst them. The office of Inca did not pass automatically either to the king's son or to his sister's children, but to one of the sons of the queen, the Mama-Ccoya, or Mother of the royal clan. A device was, however, adopted by the later Incas which has been resorted to again and again by royal families in other parts of the world, and which, while preserving the original rule that the throne should pass to a son of the Royal Mother, provided that the king's own son should not be excluded from the succession. The only way to effect this is for the king to marry one of his sisters or half-sisters; and the Incas of Peru accordingly adopted that practice of dynastic incest which is the only means of combining a male succession with the original female succession.[2] The device for transmitting the throne to their sons was also employed by the kings of Bogota.[3]

The same method was adopted in Hawaii. At the beginning of the last century three of the king's sisters were queens; the other

[1] F. X. de Charlevoix, *Histoire de la Nouvelle France*, vol. vi, pp. 177 sqq.

[2] P. Sarmiento de Gamboa, *History of the Incas*, pp. 127 sq., 123, 129; Garcilasso de la Vega, *Royal Commentaries of the Yncas*, vol. i, p. 93; Cieza de Leon, *La cronica del Peru*, p. 402.

[3] L. Fernandez de Piedrahita, *Historia general de las conquistas del nuevo Reyno de Granada*, p. 16.

princesses did not marry, but enjoyed the same freedom of taking any man they pleased as their lover or temporary husband which no doubt originally belonged to all the women of the royal clan. The Queen-Mother occupied, as in America, an exalted position; her authority was at least equal to that of the king. The king negotiated all business relating to foreign relations, while the Queen-Mother was the sole head of internal affairs. In the absence of the king the whole government devolved upon her. "The singular feature of a double executive, mutually checking or strengthening, without the sanction of both no act being valid, has been retained to this day. It is an anomaly," Mr. Jarves thought, "but the principle is so well understood and recognised by the Hawaiians that the harmony of the kingdom has never been endangered."[1]

In Tahiti royalty was hereditary through the women, and as many queens as kings appear in the dynastic records of the islands. Oberea was queen at the time that Tahiti was visited by Wallis; and Aimata exercised supreme authority, which her consort, the king of Tahaa, who married her in order to unite the two crowns, did not share with her. The daughter of the king of Raiatea was also sovereign of the island of Huahine.[2] In Tonga the eldest sister of the sacred king, or Tui-Tonga, the Tamaha, as she was called, or failing her his aunt, was regarded as more sacred than himself. He had to pay homage to her, and to prostrate himself in her presence in the same manner as the people prostrated themselves before him. She was the "first person in the Tonga Islands." His own daughters also were regarded as nobler than the Tui-Tonga, and received homage from him. They were not permitted to marry, but might have as many lovers as they pleased.[3]

Polynesian society was not by any means in a matriarchal phase, but it appears that the magical or sacred character of royalty was regarded as being transmitted through the women and not through the men. In Samoa the family religious rites, when not performed by the paterfamilias, were celebrated by his sister and not by his brother or any other male relative, and it was usually the eldest sister of a chief who exercised the functions of priestess.[4] Remarking upon that usage and on the extraordinary ceremonial veneration which was shown by chiefs

[1] J. J. Jarves, *History of the Hawaii, or Sandwich Islands*, pp. 213 sqq.

[2] W. Ellis, *Polynesian Researches*, vol. iii, pp. 99, 287 sq.

[3] O. W. Brierly, "Brief Geographical Sketch of the Friendly Islands," *Journal of the Royal Geographical Society*, xxii, p. 98; J. S. C. Dumont d'Urville, *Voyages de la corvette l'Astrolabe*, vol. iv, p. 274; J. E. Erskine, *Journal of a Cruise among the Islands of the Western Pacific*, pp. 127 sq.; T. B. Wilson, *Narrative of a Voyage round the World*, p. 355.

[4] J. B. Stair, *Old Samoa*, p. 222.

towards their sisters, Mr. Williamson observes that the deity of the group was apparently thought of as observing the older matriarchal rules of descent; "it was into descendants of the sister, and not into those of the brother, that the family-god would enter more especially."[1]

It is in Africa that the development and significance of primitive royalty may be most easily followed. With all African rulers the magical functions attaching to the royal office are very definitely emphasised, every African monarch being the controller of the fertility of the soil and a rain-maker. Royal power has, however, in Africa as elsewhere, become greatly developed as a result of military conquests, which have brought large territories and numerous populations under the domination of a victorious war-leader. The character of the primitive king, originally the head-man of a sacred or priestly clan, and possessing little or no temporal and political power, has thus undergone a profound transformation, the priest becoming a military and political ruler. The realms of African potentates have, during the last two or three centuries, been steadily decaying, owing chiefly to the slave-trade, which has brought about their mutual extermination and depopulation. They were at one time much more powerful and prosperous than since they have been open to the observation of European travellers. Over the whole region of the Congo, for instance, extended a vast empire under the rule of Mani-Congo, or Emperor of Congo, by whose representatives were governed the various provinces or sub-kingdoms into which the territory was divided. Women were not infrequently appointed provincial governors. The empire of Congo has since broken up into the kingdoms of Dongo, Loango, Cacondo, Engoi, Matamba, Benguela, and others, whose rulers proclaimed their independence. Cambolo, the governor of Matamba, for instance, made himself king, and the Mani-Congo had to relinquish the province. But a woman, probably a princess of the Royal House of Congo, gathered an army, gained several victories over Cambolo, and finally defeated him; and after branding his wives and daughters with hot irons, proclaimed herself Queen of Matamba.[2]

Queens have frequently held the reins of government in African kingdoms. The kingdom of Agonna was at the beginning of the last century, and had been for some time, governed by a queen "with as much courage and conduct as other countries are ruled by men. This governess is so wise," says our informer, "that to keep

---

[1] R. W. Williamson, *The Social and Political System of Central Polynesia*, vol. ii, p. 105.

[2] J. B. Labat, *Relation historique de l'Éthiopie occidentale*, vol. i, pp. 57 sqq., vol. ii, p. 314.

the government in her own hands she lives unmarried." But "she is so perfectly mistress of her favours that she may confer them on whom she pleases without fear of scandal."[1] Such an arrangement is not, as Bosman thought, a matter of personal choice and taste, but was customary in all Bantu kingdoms; in such cases there is not even a prince consort, the spouses or lovers of the reigning queen being commoners or slaves.[2] The kingdom of Angola was frequently ruled by women; the names of seven female rulers who occupied the throne within recent times survive in the memory of the peoples. The last queen of Angola, Singa N'Gola,[3] waged a heroic struggle to maintain the independence of her country against the Portuguese. She entered into an alliance with the Dutch, and during many years conducted an incessant war against the European invader. When at last her resources were exhausted, her feudatory chiefs having fallen away one by one, she received from the Portuguese authorities an offer that she should keep her title and crown on condition of recognising the Portuguese suzerainty. But she proudly refused to be a queen in name only, and preferred to abdicate, leaving the throne to the puppet-king nominated by the conqueror, who took the name of Alfonso.[4]

A queen was in recent years holding royal power among the Fanti of the Gold Coast.[5] In Latuka, in the extreme northern part of the Uganda Protectorate, the throne has for many years been occupied by an aged queen. "There is no doubt," says Mr. Cunningham, "that the queen is universally respected by her people, and there is not a whisper of rivalry for her throne." She, however, like other African queens, has no husband, and expresses the view that there is not a man in her kingdom worthy of being her spouse.[6] In East Central Africa, at Mpororo, two powerful queens have ruled for many years. They are, properly speaking, high-priestesses of the god Niawingi, and they hold the allegiance of the people rather by virtue of their sacred and religious, than of

[1] W. Bosman, "A New Description of the Coast of Guinea," in Pinkerton, *Voyages and Travels*, vol. xvi, p. 365.

[2] Cf. D. Livingstone, *Missionary Travels and Researches*, p. 179.

[3] Her name appears variously as Zingha, Ginga, Linga, and, like the names of most African royalty, is an honorific title, and not a personal name. The word would appear to belong to the same root as Kinkayi, which means "the house of the mother's family," and 'kinkenti,' 'female nature,' 'womanhood,' or 'motherhood' (see G. Bentley, *Dictionary and Grammar of the Kongo Language*, s.v.).

[4] J. B. Labat, *op. cit.*, vol. ii, p. 454; vol. iv, pp. 28 sqq. A long and detailed account of the career of this remarkable woman is given in Father Labat's work. The events happened in the middle of the eighteenth century.

[5] R. M. Connolly, "Social Life in Fanti-Land," *Journal of the Anthropological Institute*, xxvi, p. 146.

[6] J. F. Cunningham, *Uganda and its People*, pp. 366 sqq.

their political, title.   They are so sacred that it would be a breach of tabu for them to touch the ground, and they are accordingly carried about in baskets by their ministers of state.[1]   A consideration of other existing or recently existing African monarchies will dispose us to believe that such supreme female rule was formerly by no means uncommon on that continent.

One of the best known kingdoms of the Gold Coast is that of Ashanti.   The organisation of royal power there was almost identical with that which we have noted among the Natchez of America.   So unimportant is the paternal descent of the king that the princesses of the royal house are free to marry whomsoever they please, be he the meanest slave.   All that is expected of them is that he shall be handsome in appearance.   The prince-consort, if we may so call him, that is, the father of the heir to the throne, is of no importance whatever.   If the princess dies before him, he is obliged to commit suicide on her grave.[2]   When a male child is born to the princess "the father does it homage and acknowledges his vassalage in the most abject manner; and if the child dies, the father must die with him."   The chief position among the princesses is occupied by the one who is called Queen-Mother. She draws her own tribute and administers the State when the king is absent from the capital.   The election of a son of one of the princesses to the royal stool is conducted by four officers, but requires to be confirmed by the Queen-Mother; she also has the power to depose the king, and has been known to exercise it.[3] That gynaecocratic character of the great African kingdom persisted to the very last day of its existence, and was found unmodified when, in 1895–96, the British Protectorate was established.   Major Barter, the commander of the expedition which put an end to Ashanti royalty at the point of the bayonet, found that "the real rule of Ashanti was the Queen-Mother."   The king, Prempeh, was indeed a mere puppet; he was not even permitted to speak in the course of negotiations with the British officials, but had to nod his approval to whatever was said by one of the ministers who received his directions from the Queen-Mother.   "A very disagreeable-looking object was the old woman," says Major Barter, "with a thin bony body and a cruel face.   She is credited on good authority with having possessed several dozen husbands, all of whom she had executed, with the sole exception of Prempeh's father.   We were informed from a local source that when displeased

---

[1] M. Weiss, "Land und Leute von Mpororo (Nord-west von Deutschen Ostakrika)," *Globus*, xci, pp. 168 sq.

[2] A. B. Ellis, *The Tshi-speaking People*, pp. 287, 297 sqq.

[3] T. E. Bodwich, *Mission from Cape Coast Castle to Ashantee*, pp. 239 sqq., 245, 291.

she would wipe out her whole suite, and start with a completely fresh retinue, and it is said the changes were frequent."[1]

As in Ashanti, so also in Loango the princesses are free to marry whom they please, and generally choose sturdy plebeians who are, however, treated more as slaves and prisoners than as husbands. They may be dismissed at the will of the princess, and another temporary husband taken; they are kept under an armed guard, are not allowed to leave the royal palace without an escort, and they run the risk of being instantly beheaded by order of their royal wives on the slightest pretext. The chief princess is called Mani-Lombo, that is, King. She chooses her husband, and treats him as the other princesses do theirs. The king is elected from among the children of the princesses; none of the king's children ever becomes king, for, indeed, he does not marry a princess, and the queen is not his wife, but the Mani-Lombo, whom he addresses as 'Mother.' He is expected to consult her on all matters of State.[2] In the kingdom of Daura, the royal princesses were in like manner married to slaves, and the king was chosen from their children, not from the children of the late king. The Queen-Mother occupied the same position as in Ashanti and Loango.[3] The like constitution of the reigning family is found among the Abrons of the interior of the Ivory Coast. The royal princesses occasionally marry, but as a rule remain single and take as many lovers as they please. They do the same even if they have a husband. The lover of a princess is executed if she dies. The king is not the husband of a queen, but her son by a plebeian father.[4] In northern Rhodesia, near Lake Bangeulu, the little kingdom of Ubemba was until lately ruled exclusively by queens. The reigning queen bore the title of Manfumer, that is, Mother of Kings, but it does not appear that the kings to whom she gave birth took any part in the government of the country. "The privileges attaching to the position of the queen," says Father Guillemé, "are many. The most singular is that the queens may choose for themselves husbands from among the common people. The selected who thus becomes the royal consort does not, how-

[1] C. Barter, "Notes on Ashanti," *The Scottish Geographical Magazine*, xii, pp. 451 sq.

[2] L. B. Proyart, *Histoire de Loango, Kakongo et autres royaumes d'Afrique*, pp. 134 sqq.; "Adventures of Andrew Battel," in Pinkerton, *Voyages and Travels*, vol. xvi, p. 331; A. Bastian, *Die deutsche Expedition an der Loango-Küste*, vol. i, pp. 197 sqq.; L. Degrandpré, *Voyage à la côte occidentale d'Afrique*, pp. 110 sqq.; R. E. Dennett, *At the Back of the Black Man's Mind*, pp. 36 sq., 134.

[3] J. G. Frazer, *Totemism and Exogamy*, vol. ii, pp. 607 sq., from material supplied by Mr. H. R. Palmer.

[4] F.-J. Closel and R. Villamur, *Les coutumes indigènes de la Côte d'Ivoire*, p. 203.

ever, take any share in the administration of the realm. When
selected, he is obliged to leave everything and to follow his royal
spouse, who is often anything but considerate."[1]

In those primitive types of African monarchy, then, the royal
family, or sacred clan, consisted of women only. The head-woman
of the clan might herself exercise all the functions of royalty, or
mighty depute one of her sons to act for her under her authority
and control. That conception of the constitution of a royal house
appears to have been deeply rooted among African peoples.
Livingstone relates how the Bechuana chief Sebituane associated
his daughter with him in the government, and advised her to retain
the chieftainship in her own hands after his death, and not to
marry any man, but to take as many lovers as she pleased.[2] "In
the oldest times," says Dr. Rehse, "there were no reigning princes
in Africa, but the negroes had large kingdoms which were ruled by
goddesses. The goddesses had priests and priestesses, who trans-
acted the affairs of government in the name of their divine
mistresses."[3] Those divine rulers appear, however, to have
generally been impersonated by the sacred women who acted as
their representatives.

In the kingdom of Dahomey the same usages obtained
until quite recent times, the princesses being free to choose
whom they pleased as their husbands.[4] That state of things,
however, was violently amended by some ambitious monarch, and
the royal court presented after that reformation a very different
appearance. Instead of the plebeian husbands being guarded
under lock and key by their tyrannous wives, the tables were
turned, and it is the wives of the kings who are now immured
and guarded, and who, when they issue forth on their priestly
duties, are preceded by a bell warning men out of their path, in
the same manner as is done with regard to the husbands of
the princesses of Ashanti. The Dahomian queens now perform
their rites in the temple as 'vestal virgins.' But that inversion
of the former state of things, and the establishment of a male
line of succession by the male despots, could be brought about
only by adopting the same device as that employed by the Incas
of Peru and the kings of Hawaii, namely, by the king marrying one
of his sisters. Even the Dahomian despot could not claim to hand
over the throne to his son unless the latter was, by virtue of that
arrangement, also the son of one of the dispossessed royal princesses.
When the king dies one of the king's sons is elected as his successor,

[1] R. P. Guillemé, "Au Bengouéolo," Les Missions Catholiques, xxxiv, p. 16.
[2] D. Livingstone, Missionary Travels and Researches in South Africa, p. 179.
[3] H. Rehse, Kiziba, Land und Leute, p. 126.
[4] A. B. Ellis, The Ewe-speaking Peoples, p. 204.

but during the lifetime of the king the princes enjoy no privileges and have no rank[1]; and during the interregnum which takes place before the new king is elected, and which sometimes lasts a considerable time, the Queen-Mother occupies the throne.[2]

The vast kingdom of Lunda was one of the most powerful monarchies of Central Africa. Its ruler is known as the Muata Jamwo. One of the royal princesses, called the Lukokesha, shares, however, the government with him. She is officially regarded as his mother; she is unmarried, does as she pleases, and keeps slave-lovers. Her children are killed at birth. This practice, which is common in such cases, is necessary in order to secure the succession to a son of the king; for the Muata Jamwo has adopted the same method of achieving this as the king of Dahomey, two of the royal princesses being his wives, and his successor being elected from among their children. The Central African potentate has not, however, succeeded so completely as the king of Dahomey in establishing a purely male dynasty. The power of the Queen-Mother, or Lukokesha, is still supreme; she is inviolable, has her own court and draws her own revenues, and the king can do nothing without previously obtaining her approval. She accompanies him at every function and administers all affairs when he is absent from the court.[3] In the year 1873 the Lukokesha deposed the Muata Jamwo, and appointed a new king.[4] The usages in the kingdom of Urua, a territory to the west of Lake Tanganyika, as large as Great Britain and France put together, are identical with those of Lunda. The king marries his sisters or first cousins, and the queen has to be consulted in all matters, and exercises absolute power in his absence. When one of the princesses dies, the king must remain with the corpse night and day for a week.[5]

In the rich barbaric kingdom of Benin the Queen-Mother had her separate court "at a little distance outside the town, beautifully built, where she resides with many women and daughters. She is consulted in all state affairs. She did everything which the king did." But the curious usage was observed that "from the day that the king had fulfilled the last rite which made him king, she never saw his face." As in other African kingdoms, the royal princesses did not marry, but took any man they pleased as their lover.[6]

The power of the Queen-Mother and of the Queen-Sister was

[1] A. B. Ellis, *op. cit.*, pp. 161 sqq., 182 sqq., 210.
[2] A. Giraud-Teulon, *Les origines du mariage et de la famille*, p. 216.
[3] P. Pogge, *Im Reiche des Muata Jamwo*, pp. 153 sq., 227 sq., 231 sq.
[4] V. L. Cameron, *Across Africa*, p. 396; O. Schmidt, *Reise in Südwestlichen Becken des Congo*, p. 136.
[5] V. L. Cameron, *op. cit.*, pp. 334, 337 sq., 362.
[6] H. Ling Roth, *Great Benin*, pp. 119, 180, 37.

not by any means always formal and nominal. Much of it, no doubt, became so in later stages of the evolution of those monarchies, in the same way as the high-sounding formulas applied in regard to constitutional monarchs in Europe have now become empty phrases. But those phrases which are now meaningless are the relics of powers which were once absolute, and could not have come into existence if they had not stood at one time for realities. In the kingdom of Dwabin, for instance, the Queen-Mother ruled energetically, the king being a mere weakling.[1] The king of Ashanti once tried to levy tribute from the king of Buntooko, taking advantage of the absence of the queen, "a woman of masculine spirit and talent, and the soul of the government." When she returned, however, she severely reprimanded the king for his weakness in yielding to the demands of the Ashanti monarch, and declared war on the latter, saying that "she would fight to the last rather than be so constantly despoiled."[2]

The kings of Uganda, whose subjects have advanced to a higher degree of civilisation than any other of the African races of the interior, are nevertheless fierce and warlike potentates, and very jealous of their power. But by their side reign two women, the Queen-Mother ('Namasole') and the Queen ('Lubuga'); the latter is the king's sister. Each of those women bears the title of 'Kabaka,' that is, King; each has her court and extensive estates in various parts of the kingdom which she administers, appointing her own officials. The Queen-Mother lives in a separate enclosure at some distance from that of the king, and separated from it by a stream of running water, "because it was said that she also was a king, and that two kings could not live on the same hill." After the various elaborate ceremonies of investiture were ended it was a rule that the king of Uganda, like the king of Benin, should never set eyes again on his mother. She had to send him some food every day, and the king manifested great annoyance if that were omitted. If the Queen-Mother died, "fear seized the people," and the king was so disturbed that it was dangerous to approach him. Another 'Queen-Mother' was at once provided from the same clan as the deceased queen. While the Baganda took their totem from their father—though they were formerly matrilineal—the royal family took theirs from their mothers. The sacred fetich of the king was provided by his grandmother, or by one of her relatives in the same clan, and was in the keeping of one of the king's wives. The Queen-Sister was chosen by the Queen-Mother. She sat on the same throne as the king at the coronation ceremonies, and took the same oath. When the king died the queen at once took charge of

[1] T. E. Bodwich, *Mission from Cape Coast Castle to Ashantee*, p. 246.
[2] *Ibid.*, p. 245.

her brother's body, and did not leave it until it was handed over to the embalmers.[1]

In the instance of the kings of Uganda the rather ludicrous feature of the whole business is that, notwithstanding the elaborate show of respecting the principle of inheritance in the female line in regard to the royal title, the kings were after all the sons of common Baganda women belonging indiscriminately to a diversity of clans. The formal tradition has here outlasted its significance and the discharge of its function.

Among the Banyoro of East Africa the same principles obtained as in other African monarchies. The king was the high-priest of the people, and such was his sacred character that his existence was burdened with innumerable tabus and regulations. Every month, as soon as the new moon had been perceived from a mound whence official observers watched for her first appearance, a messenger was despatched to the king. He informed him of the event by saying: "You have outlived the moon." The king was obliged to marry one of his half-sisters. Even if, as was usually the case, he was already married at the time of his election, his wife could acquire no official status. The Queen-Sister could have no children, and when she became pregnant by the king, she procured abortion. The reason given for this practice was that, if she had a child, she would necessarily be separated from the king during the period of her pregnancy and nursing. Such a cessation of intercourse with the royal princess might, it was apparently supposed, imperil the magic power of the king. The Queen-Mother held the same position as in other African kingdoms, and, as in Uganda and Dahomey, was not supposed to meet the king after his coronation.[2] The Banyoro kingdom has now been converted to Christianity, and it is, of course, inconsistent with the new faith to carry out the ancient usages. "Since the present king became a Christian he has had only one wife, who, however, as she is neither his half-sister nor a princess, cannot take the position nor the title of queen; and the rank is held by a princess who is only nominally the wife of the king."[3] A similar compromise is adopted by the Banyankole. One of the king's sisters, and not his wife, is the most important woman in the kingdom, and is held responsible for the health and general efficiency of the monarch.[4] The devolution of the original scheme of African royalty has thus reached the last stage of decay.

The rules regulating the office of royalty in the barbaric kingdoms of Africa thus present various phases which, though differing

[1] J. Roscoe, *The Baganda*, pp. 104, 114, 205, 210, 325.
[2] Id., *The Bakitara, or Banyoro*, pp. 90, 107, 136 sqq., 140 sq., 147.
[3] Id., *The Soul of Central Africa*, pp. 172 sq.
[4] Id., *The Banyankole*, pp. 59 sq.

materially in their practical outcome, rest upon the same principles. In some the royal power is exclusively in the hands of sacred women, who remain unmarried so as not to share that power with a recognised husband; in others the prince consort is excluded from the business of government; in others again a variously limited executive power, subject to the jurisdiction of the queen, is conferred upon a son of the royal women. Those gynaecocratic monarchies pass by imperceptible gradations into systems of government in which power is wholly in the hands of male autocrats, and the status of the royal women, as Queen-Sister or as Queen-Mother, has come to consist of little more than empty ceremonial and hollow titles. But the same principles upon which the exercise and transmission of the right divine depend are observed in the latter as in the more archaic forms of the institution.

Those principles and usages are not peculiar to the Bantu races; they are observed in those kingdoms of East Africa where the ruling classes are predominantly Hamitic. We come upon similar principles among the Shilluk of Fashoda, on the White Nile. The sacred kingship of the Shilluk, which has been investigated by Dr. Seligman, offers an interesting illustration of Sir James Frazer's well-known theory that the royal office was in some of its primitive forms temporary, the sacred king being ritually put to death before his powers suffered decay from senility. Such treatment of the king's majesty is readily intelligible if the monarch was originally little more than the slave-husband of imperious royal women who might deal with him according to their pleasure. Unlike the Banyoro king,[1] the divine personage impersonating the deity might not be permitted to outlive the moon, his assimilation to the god being carried to the extent of requiring him to renew himself in another generation every month; or, as with the Egyptian Pharaohs, the assimilation might be more liberally interpreted by translating the lunar period into terms of years, the monarch renewing his life after a period of twenty-eight or thirty years. Among the Shilluk the term of the king's office and of his life was, it appears, determined by the queens, who decreed his demise as soon as his generative powers began to fail; and Dr. Seligman was told that it was formerly the custom for the royal women to strangle the king with their own hands. The princesses do not marry, but, as elsewhere in Africa, are free to have as many lovers as they please; they are not, however, permitted to bear children, and terminate their pregnancies by abortion. We have little definite information as to the rules of succession and marriage; the king is chosen from among the children of the royal wives, and it may be presumed that he inherits the right, or rather the duty,

---

[1] See above, p. 35.

of access to the numerous queens. But the whole institution is at the present day in an advanced state of decay, and evidently differs in many particulars from its original form.[1] The sacred kings of the Shilluk trace their descent and royal right from a divine ancestress.[2]

The same principles which we find in force in the institutions of barbaric kingdoms throughout Africa obtained in the ancient and opulent monarchy of the Pharaohs. The legitimacy of the Egyptian kings depended upon the female line of descent. "It is very doubtful," says Sir Flinders Petrie, "if a king could reign except as the husband of the heiress of the kingdom, the right to which descended in the female line."[3] The queen was not so much the wife of the king as the wife of the god; and it was as a temporary incarnation of the deity that the king was spouse to the queen. Her conception by the god who comes down from heaven, and her delivery of the son of god, are minutely represented in the reliefs of Luxor, Deir Al-Bahri, and Erment. The queen was accordingly high-priestess, that is, wife of Amen-Rā, and all princesses were by birthright, and from the moment of their birth, 'Royal Wives.' A daughter of king Makeri, who lived only a few days, is styled on her sarcophagus, "Beloved wife of the god, Lady of both Lands."[4] Princesses were allowed to marry commoners, in which case their children were potential heirs to the throne.[5] On the other hand, the son of the king was but a commoner, and had no right to the throne unless he was also the son of a royal princess. "When a legitimate princess bore a son, that son was nearer to the throne than the son of the Pharaoh himself."[6] Tahutmes III, son of Tahutmes II, had no claim to the throne, being the son of a woman, Aset, not of royal blood. Accordingly, his aunt, Queen Hapteshu, who wished to hand the succession over to him, had to marry him to her daughter, his half-sister.[7] Any commoner might reign as king provided he married a royal princess.[8] But although a king might reign as husband and delegate of a queen, he could have a personal right to the throne only by being the son of a

[1] C. G. Seligman, "The Cult of Nyakang and the Divine Kings of the Shilluk," *Fourth Report of the Wellcome Tropical Research Laboratory at the Gordon Memorial College, Khartoum*, pp. 217 sq., 221 sq.

[2] Count Gleichen, *The Anglo-Egyptian Sudan*, p. 197.

[3] W. M. Flinders Petrie, *History of Egypt*, vol. ii, p. 183.

[4] G. Maspéro, *Les momies royales de Deir el Bahari*, p. 377.

[5] F. L. Griffith, "Notes on some Royal Names and Families," *Proceedings of the Society of Biblical Archaeology*, xiv, p. 41; P. E. Newberry, *Beni Hasan*, 82, No. 14.

[6] A. Wiedemann, "Le roi dans l'ancienne Égypte," *Le Muséon*, xiii, p. 373.

[7] W. M. Flinders Petrie, *op. cit.*, vol. ii, p. 96.

[8] *Ibid.*, p. 240; E. A. Wallis Budge, *History of Egypt*, vol. iv, p. 145.

queen, and therefore of the god.   Accordingly, the Queen-Mother occupied in Egypt a position exactly similar to that which she held in other African kingdoms.   Kings are generally represented on their monuments accompanied by the Queen-Mother.[1] The title of 'Royal Mother,' which belonged by right of birth to every princess of the royal house, was the most exalted of honorific titles, and marriage to a reigning monarch added nothing, either in title or in status, to the position of a princess.   The chief title of the king, on the other hand, was 'Suten net,' which means high-priest of Herakleopolis and of Koptos, and only later was given the signification of 'King of Upper and Lower Egypt.'[2] The queen and the princesses had accordingly as their crown the royal totem, the Hawk, to which they were entitled from birth; while the king wore only the crown of high-priest, and did not receive his Horus-name until his coronation.   In fact, according to the conceptions which governed the functions of royalty in ancient Egypt, queens were born and not made, while kings were made, not born.   The statement of Diodorus that "it had been appointed that the queen should receive more power and more honour than the king," thus appears to be amply borne out.[3]   Egyptian history, from its first dim page to its closing scene in the death-chamber of Cleopatra, reflects the exalted significance attached to the office of the queens.

The oldest inscription in Egyptian writing which we possess is the name of a queen, "Ha, wife of Horus Ka," on a pre-dynastic vase dating from about 4900 B.C.[4]   The first historical dynasty, beginning with king Mena (Aha-Men), was founded by his marriage to Neit-hotep, who bears the 'Ka' name, that is to say, is styled, like other African queens, 'King'; and it was therefore she who transmitted the crown of Egypt from pre-dynastic times to the first dynasty.   In the second dynasty, queen Ne-Maat-Hap reigned alone during the minority of her children.   Manetho says that the right of women to the throne was decreed by a king,

---

[1] W. M. Flinders Petrie, op. cit., vol. i, p. 138.

[2] A. Wiedemann, "Le roi dans l'ancienne Égypte," Le Muséon, xiii, p. 367.

[3] Diodorus Siculus, i. 27.

[4] W. M. Flinders Petrie, op. cit., vol. i, p. 14. She is surmised by Sir Flinders Petrie to have been the daughter of the last pre-dynastic king, Sma; but it would appear to be more probable that she was his widow, for her name is mentioned in conjunction with that of Sma (W. M. Flinders Petrie, The Royal Tombs of the First Dynasty, Part ii, p. 7), which would be unlikely had she been his daughter and not his queen. The first Egyptian dynasty under whom the North and the South were first united was naturally founded by the queen; and the break between the pre-dynastic lines and the first dynasty was bridged over by the reign of the queen who handed over her executive power to her consort, the first king of Egypt.

Binothris (Ba-En-Neter), of the IInd Dynasty.[1] But this is manifestly an aetiological explanation of the same kind as that which accounted for the matrilinear reckoning of descent in Lykia by a 'decree.'[2] Among the early Egyptian queens who figure prominently in tradition is Net-Akerti, called by Greek authors Nitokris. According to Herodotus, her brother was murdered, and the queen relentlessly tracked the murderers and at last succeeded in wreaking awful vengeance upon them.[3] She is, according to Manetho, the last queen of the IVth Dynasty, and reigned twelve years.[4] She completed the building of the third pyramid, which Herodotus ascribed to the fair Rhodopis,[5] and which the Arabs still regard as being haunted by a beautiful witch.[6] A recently discovered plaque represents her in the character of Isis with her husband, Mankaura.[7] She was worshipped long after her death, and a sacred fire and incense were kept burning night and day in her temple.[8]

The restoration of the Egyptian dynasties after the expulsion of the Hyksos, and the dawn of the golden age of the Second Empire, are marked by the reign of a woman who eclipsed her brother-spouse, even though he was the liberator of his country from the foreigner. Queen Nefertari wielded sole authority after his death. She was, says Sir G. Maspéro, "the first of those queens by divine right who, scorning the inaction of the harem, took upon themselves the right to fulfil the active duties of a sovereign and claimed recognition of the equality or superiority of their titles to those of their

[1] *Fragm. Hist. Graec.*, vol. ii, p. 543.

[2] Plutarch, *De virt. mulier.*, ix.

[3] Herodotus, ii. 100.

[4] Ἐβασίλευσε Νίτωκρις γυνὴ ἀντὶ τοῦ ἄνδρὸς, says of her Erastothenes, in Syncellus, *Chronographia*, 104C, vol. i, p. 195.

[5] Herodotus, ii. 134. The third pyramid was, according to Sir Flinders Petrie, built by Menkaura of the IVth Dynasty. But, as the pyramid has been enlarged, and additional chambers built (Baedecker, *Egypt*, p. 123), there appears no reason for not regarding the traditional history which refers it to Net-Akerti, the queen of Menkara of the VIth Dynasty, as accurate.

[6] "It is said that the spirit of the southern pyramid appears without in the form of a nude young woman, most beautiful, and whose manners are such that when she wishes to bestow her love upon someone and rob him of his reason, she smiles at him, and forthwith he approaches her, and she draws him towards her, and makes him mad with love, so that he loses his mind, and thereafter runs as a vagabond through the country" (*L'Égypte, de Murtadi, fils de Graphiphe*, trad. par M. P. Wattier, p. 65). Nitocris has furnished the theme for a poem by a recent French writer: J. F. L. Merlet, *Nitokris, légende de l'ancienne Égypte*, Paris, 1912.

[7] Discovered by G. A. Reisner, and now in the Boston Museum of Fine Arts.

[8] Herodotus, ii. 130; G. F. C. Parthey, "Das Orakel und die Oase Ammon," *Abhandlungen der königlichen Akademie der Wissenschaften*, 1862, p. 144.

husbands or sons."[1]　After her death she was worshipped as the national heroine, the 'Ancestress and Foundress,' of restored Egypt; and her cult, which lasted over six hundred years, eclipsed that of any hero of Egyptian history.　"Her image was placed as an equal among the inhabitants of the Egyptian heaven.　In the united assembly of the sainted kings of the New Empire she sits enthroned at the head of all the Pharaonic pairs, and before all the royal children of their race, as the specially venerated ancestress and founder of the XVIIIth Dynasty."[2]　Her glory has, for us, been eclipsed by the splendour of her grand-daughter, the famous Hapteshu, "King of the North and South, Ka-Ma-Ra, the Golden Horus, Bestower of years, Goddess of risings, Conqueror of all Lands, Life-giver of all Hearts, Chief spouse of Amen, The Mighty One."[3]　The great queen, who was associated with her father, Tahutmes I, reigned supreme for thirty-three years, and it is significant that, although her nephew, Tahutmes III, proved after her death one of the most brilliant and aggressive kings of Egypt, he was, during the period of his official association with her, entirely eclipsed by Queen Hapteshu.　Tyi, the queen of Amenhotep III, also exercised the regency during her son's minority, and her influence during her husband's reign appears to have been scarcely less pronounced.　"She appears closely associated with the king on his monuments, her figure is seen side by side with his on scarabs, her name appears along with the king's on innumerable objects, a temple was built in her honour at Sedeinga."[4]　Since her son, Amenhotep IV, was but a youth when he initiated the peculiar religious reformation which is associated with his name, it appears more than probable that the Queen-Mother had a considerable share in that adventure.　Her daughter Nefertiti, and the latter's daughter Ankhsenamen, appear in turn as the dominating figures during the reign of Tutankhamen, who, like many other Egyptian monarchs, derived his title to the crown from his wife and assumed her name.　Writing long before the discovery of his famous tomb, Sir Flanders Petrie remarks: "The queen, Ankhsenamen, was very important, and her name is almost as often found as that of her husband."[5]

By the eighth century B.C. the ancient glories of Egypt had departed for ever, and the Nilotic realm was breaking up.　It was saved for a while from dissolution by the Sudanese rulers of Napata

---

[1] G. Maspéro, *The Struggle of the Nations*, p. 95.

[2] H. Brugsch, *Egypt under the Pharaohs*, vol. i, p. 279.

[3] J. R. Butter, *The Queens of Egypt*, p. 96.

[4] W. M. Flinders Petrie, *op. cit.*, vol. ii, p. 183.　The temple at Sedeinga bears the inscription: "Made for the great and mighty heiress, the mistress of all lands, Tyi" (*ibid.*, p. 193).

[5] W. M. Flinders Petrie, *op. cit.*, vol. ii, p. 238.

and Meroe, who took charge of the government of Egypt, founding
their claim on some old connection with the priest-kings of Thebes
and on descent from an Egyptian princess. That reversion of
Pharaonic royalty into the hands of a semi-barbaric African dynasty
was, as might be expected, marked by a notable accentuation of its
archaic matriarchial features. The sacred and official head of the
Nubian kingdom was and always had been the Queen-Mother,
or 'Kandake.'[1] On the walls of the pylons and chapels of Meroe
and Naga are depicted imitations of the conventional apotheoses
of the Egyptian Pharaohs; but the glorified divine monarchs are
in this instance not kings, but queens. Their prince-consorts are
represented in smaller proportions standing behind them;[2] and
the amazonic queens are pictured in the traditional attitude,
spearing their defeated enemies or slaughtering them with their
swords.[3] Piankhi, who established the Nubian dynasty in Egypt,
describes himself on the stele of Aspaleta as the son of the "Queen
of Kush," and traces his descent through eight generations of
queens, no kings and no fathers being mentioned.[4] Queen Amen-
ardes, the most prominent figure in the records of the Nubian
dynasties of Egypt, "always appears as the main personage where
she is named. . . . As a mere appendage to her power appears that
of her husband, Pankhy II."[5] Queen Nesikhonsu (XXIst
Dynasty) acted as viceroy of Middle Egypt and Ethiopia; she is
styled on a stele at University College Museum, "Viceroy of Kush,
Administrator of the Middle Country."[6] Under the Ethiopian
dynasties each king had two Great Queens, the one ruling at
Napata, the other at Thebes, both exercising royal authority with
the assistance of a prime minister. Indeed, during the last
dynasties, the Theban queens, ruling personally as 'Divine Spouses
of Amen,' were independent of the Saite rulers of Lower Egypt.[7]

[1] Strabo, xvii. 54; Bion Solensis, in *Fragmenta Historicorum Graecorum*,
vol. iv, p. 351. Cf. Hesychius, s.v. κάνδη.
[2] C. R. Lepsius, *Denkmäler aus Ägypten und Ëthiopen*, Abth. v, ppl. 30,
32, 59; 19, 41, 52, 53, 54.
[3] *Ibid.*, ppl. 40, 56.
[4] *Records of the Past*, vol. vi, p. 76; W. M. Flinders Petrie, *op. cit.*, vol. iii,
p. 309. Matriarchal rules of succession obtained in Nubia till mediaeval times.
"Among the Nubians," says the Arab historian Abu-Selah, "when a king
dies leaving a son and a nephew, the son of his sister, it is the latter who
succeeds to the throne to the exclusion of the natural heir" (E. M. Quatremère,
*Mémoires géographiques et historiques sur l'Égypte et sur quelques contrées
voisines, recueillis des manuscrits coptes, arabes*, etc., de la Bibliothèque Impériale,
vol. i, p. 32).
[5] W. M. Flinders Petrie, *op. cit.*, vol. iii, p. 289.
[6] A. B. Edwards, "Relics from the Tomb of the Priest-Kings at Dayr-el-
Baharee," *Recueil de Travaux relatifs à la philologie et à l'archélogie Égyptiennes
et Assyriennes*, iv, pp. 81 sqq.
[7] W. M. Flinders Petrie, *op. cit.*, vol. iii, pp. 303 sq., 308.

Psamtek got one of his daughters adopted by Queen Shepenapt of Thebes, who was only officially his wife.[1]

The kings of Egypt adopted, in order to transmit the office to their own heirs, the device of dynastic incest which we have already several times noted.[2]   It is significant that the most powerful and vainglorious despot among Egyptian kings, Rameses II, appears to have been the most anxious to clinch the legitimacy of his dynastic title by emphasising the fusion of the male and female lines.   He married two of his sisters.[3] He is everywhere represented in association with the Queen-Mother or with one of the queens, and the association is emphasised in the most sumptuous of his monuments.   At Abu-Simbel, Queen Nefertari stands beside him, both on the colossal façade and in the scenes of adoration on the walls of the temple;[4] and the Hathor temple close by is dedicated exclusively to the queen. In the Ramesseum the Queen-Mother is styled "the mighty mistress of the world."[5]

Failing the artificial combination of the male and female lines

---

[1] W. M. Flinders Petrie, *op. cit.*, vol. iii, p. 357; Karnak Stele, Cairo, T. 673.

[2] The practice, with which we are familiar during the Ptolemaic period, which is known to us from less formal histories than those available in the monuments, was a very ancient usage which the Lagides could not afford to disregard, repugnant as it was to Hellenic ideas, without jeopardising their authority and prestige with a people jealous of its traditions.   In the golden age of the Theban Empire, the only other period of Egyptian history for which documentary material is sufficiently detailed to enable us to reconstruct genealogical tables, we find that, in the XVIIIth Dynasty, seven kings married their sisters; in the XIXth Dynasty all but three are known to have done so; in the XXth Dynasty every king married his sister.   Kings married their sisters in the XVIIth, XIIIth, XIIth, and as early as the IVth Dynasty.   Dynastic incest, besides being practised by the African, Peruvian, and Hawaiian royal families, as we have already seen, was the rule among the Gallas (N. Pearce, *Life and Adventure in Abyssinia*, vol. i, p. 96), and also in Persia and among the Phoenicians (F. Justi, in W. Geiger and F. Kuhn, *Grundriss der Iranischen Philologie*, vol. ii, p. 435).   Tacitus notes it among the Iberians (*Annales*, xii. 46), and it was adopted in Karia (Arrianus, *Exped. Alex.*, i. 25; Dionysius Sic., xvii. 24).   It was also the rule in Siam (J. Bowring, *The Kingdom and People of Siam*, vol. i, p. 436; M. Turpin, *Histoire civile et naturelle du Royaume de Siam*, vol. i, p. 56).

[3] E. A. Wallis Budge, *A History of Egypt*, vol. v, p. 69.   It has been thought that Rameses also married three of his own daughters (E. A. Wallis Budge, *loc. cit.*; G. Maspéro, *The Struggle of the Nations*, p. 424; W. M. Flinders Petrie, *op. cit.*, vol. iii, p. 88; A. Wiedemann, *Aegyptische Geschichte*, p. 466).   But as that conclusion rests only upon the title of 'Royal Wife,' which is known to have been borne by a royal princess even in infancy, the grounds for the view appear to be insufficient.

[4] C. R. Lepsius, *op. cit.*, Abth. iii, plates 185, 189B.

[5] J. E. Quibell, *The Ramesseum*, plate xxix; cf. M. Duncker, *The History of Antiquity*, vol. i, p. 172.

of descent, the succession reverted to the female line; and the royal office could not be transmitted by a king to his descendants, but could only be delegated by a princess of the royal clan to her husband. Hence the essential condition for legitimising a new dynasty is that the king shall marry the deceased monarch's wife, for if she were to have a child by another husband, that child would be the legitimate heir. In African kingdoms the new king, when elected, has a right to the wives of his predecessor.[1] In Ashanti the heir apparent "no sooner hears of the king's death than he immediately makes his interest with this friends to take possession of the late king's court and wives, and, succeeding happily in these particulars, he need not doubt the remainder."[2] It is needless, however, to go to savage Africa for examples of the practice of elected kings and usurpers legalising their title by marrying the widows of their predecessors. Almost every conqueror and usurper shows the same anxiety. Absalom obtains possession of the wives of King David; Alexander marries Roxana; Musa, after the conquest of Spain by his general Al-Tarif, marries the widow of the Visigothic King Roderick; Alboin, the Lombard king, marries Rosamund, the daughter of the slain Cunimund; Hamlet's uncle, Feng, marries Hamlet's mother, and the latter's successor, Wiglet, does the same; Canute marries the aged widow of Ethelbert; and so forth throughout barbaric history.

In Egypt the connecting link between the male dynasties is established by the marriage of the founder of the new dynasty to the widow of the last king, or to a princess of the royal blood. After the long dark centuries of the Hyksos domination, when the Egyptian princes of the old dynasty had probably all perished in the severe struggle, the succession was established by the surviving princesses. "As soon as the veil over this period of history begins to be lifted we distinguish among the personages emerging from the obscurity as many queens as kings presiding over the destinies of Egypt."[3] "Every time that a dynasty becomes extinguished the founder of the new dynasty, whose greatest anxiety is to become connected with the royal family, married princesses of the blood royal, or gave them in marriage to his son. Such a marriage reunited the temporarily severed chain of the divine dynasty and legalised the usurpation."[4] According to the story of Manetho, when the king whom he calls Sethosis, on setting out on a journey, appointed his brother as regent over the kingdom, he handed over to him the full royal authority with the proviso "that he should

[1] A. B. Ellis, *The Ewe-speaking Peoples*, p. 205; V. L. Cameron, *Across Africa*, p. 337.

[2] W. Bosman, *A New Description of the Coast of Guinea*, p. 345.

[3] G. Maspéro, *The Struggle of the Nations*, p. 77.

[4] Id., *Histoire ancienne des peuples de l'orient*, p. 53.

forbear from touching the queen, the mother of the royal children, or the royal wives." The faithless brother, however, did not consider that he had become master of the kingdom until he had married his brother's wife.[1] The Persian Kambyses, before conquering Egypt, sought out an Egyptian princess in order to have a title to the throne.[2] The famous intrigue of Mark Antony with Cleopatra was, no doubt, much more political than romantic, and the Roman adventurer endeavoured to follow the immemorial precedent of all aspirants to the double crown of Egypt.[3]

It is apparent that there is an unbroken continuity between the principles which traditionally governed the institution of monarchy in the kingdom of the Pharaohs and those which obtained in primitive African monarchies, where the spouses of the princesses of the royal house were but maltreated slaves at the mercy of the royal women. The mysterious power, which was thus originally an attribute of the women of the royal family and not of the men, was not in its origin political or administrative, but was, as Sir James Frazer has shown, of a magical or magic-wielding nature; and it was that magical power which was transmitted by the women, or rather was primitively possessed exclusively by the women of the royal family. It was in view of the transmission of that magic power that so much importance was attached to legitimacy in the royal succession. Among the Kuku of the Upper Congo, although the rain-maker has not developed into a sacred king or risen above the status of an ordinary practitioner of magic, the magic power is regarded, as by African kings, as being transmissible through the women only. If a rain-maker has no son by his wives, it is incumbent upon one of his sister's sons to beget an heir to his magic from one of the rain-maker's wives. No man can become a rainmaker except he is born of a rain-making woman.[4]

The character of primitive and archaic sacred monarchies affords a strong confirmation of the conclusion to which we were previously led, that magic and priestly functions were originally exercised by women. The power of sacred monarchs and of priesthoods, which is so important an element of established agricultural civilisations, is founded upon magical attributes which originally belonged prescriptively to women and are regarded as being transmitted through women. Agricultural religions have developed out of rites and beliefs that were as much the particular domain of the women as the plying of their wooden hoe and the watering of the seeds which they planted. The cults which those primitive priestesses served were addressed to powers that derived their

---

[1] Josephus, *De bello Judaico*, i. 15.
[2] Herodotus, ii. 1.
[3] Cf. G. Ferrero, *Grandezza e decadenza di Roma*, vol. iii, pp. 414 sqq.
[4] J. van den Plas, *Les Kuku*, pp. 393 sqq.

significance from their association with the functions of women. Those conclusions take us a long way from the assumption that women have had little or nothing to do with the development of religious ideas.   In its advanced phases and intellectualised forms religious development has, indeed, been the work of men.   By powerful and leisured priesthoods, under the aegis of established monarchies, the crude conceptions of primitive cult have become systematised and have undergone the transformations which have ultimately converted them into interpretations of nature, of the universe, and of life.   In the same manner as primitive emotions and sentiments have become transmuted into the products of creative art by the intellectual operation of the masculine mind, so primitive magic and superstition have been transformed by the male intellect into theological religions.

CHAPTER XXIV

THE GREAT MOTHERS

IN accordance with their primary function as 'the real husband of all women' and source of all fertility, primitive lunar deities are predominantly masculine; the moon is a man and the sun is commonly his wife. With the transference of the attribute of fertilising agent to solar gods or to more generalised heavenly deities, the fundamental ground for the masculine sex of the lunar deity ceases to exist. The sexes of the heavenly bodies commonly become reversed, the moon becoming the wife of the sun. That change of sex is facilitated by the intimate association of the moon with women and with all their functions and activities. The primitive moon-god presents, indeed, the incongruity of a male who is nevertheless the patron of all the pursuits and attributes which appertain to the sphere of women. As a result of those feminine associations and functions the primitive moon-deity, although predominantly male, may, if occasion requires, be regarded as a female. Among those pre-agricultural peoples with whom the moon is almost invariably regarded as a male, occasional contradictions are found. Thus among the Eskimo, the Ainu of Japan, the Nagas of Manipur, although the moon is usually looked upon as a male, odd examples are met with in folk-lore stories where the moon plays the part of a female.[1] Among the Akamba the moon, we are informed, is treated indifferently as a male or as a female according to the occasion.[2] Some of those contradictions may be due to contact with more advanced peoples, who regard the moon as a female. But apart from such influences there is nothing surprising in that occasional change of sex of the primitive lunar deity. Primitive theology is not a fixed and dogmatic system, and the nature of the gods is not an article of orthodox faith. The moon-deity is the particular deity of women, and exercises,

---

[1] F. Boas, "The Central Eskimo," *Sixth Annual Report of the Bureau of Ethnology*, p. 597; J. Batchelor, *The Ainu and their Folklore*, pp. 273 sq.; J. H. Hutton, *The Angami Nagas*, p. 410.
[2] G. Lindblom, *The Akamba*, p. 337.

apart from sex, all feminine functions. The incongruity of a male deity traditionally engaged in spinning, weaving, making pots, drawing water, carrying firewood, cooking and acting as a midwife cannot but prove at times perplexing. The difficulty is sometimes met by placing two persons of opposite sex in the moon. The male moon-god, the lover of women, is everywhere in the habit of kidnapping women; the ravished woman naturally undertakes those feminine occupations which are unsuited to a male deity.[1] In later cultural phases the myth is commonly reversed: the female moon kidnaps a male lover, as Artemis Endymion. The feminine attributes of the moon are thus reconciled with its primary masculine functions. There is no occasion to have recourse to theories of 'bisexual deities.' Such a conception is foreign to primitive thought. The sexual character of primitive deities is, on the contrary, emphatic; the primitive moon-god is the very principle of masculine generative power. The 'bisexual' character of primitive deities is not the expression of a transcendental conception of metaphysical hermaphroditism, but a natural result of the combination of male attributes and feminine interests in the primitive lunar deity and of the facile inconsistency of primitive thought and tradition. The change of sex of the moon from male to female does not, then, entail any violent subversion of established ideas. When the primary notions which gave rise to the sexual functions of the deity have lost their original force, when the change has become necessitated by definite causes, the way to it has been prepared by the confusion resulting from the combination of masculine and feminine attributes in the lunar deity. As soon as it has lost its functionally male character, the lunar power readily assumes the form of a female divinity and becomes the heavenly prototype of womanhood, the Woman or the Mother.

The Primitive Goddess as Mother of God and as Primal Ancestress.

In primitive cosmic myths, moreover, the moon, though a male, is, as has been seen, generally associated with a female deity.

---

[1] E.g., A. Krause, *Die Tlinkit Indianer*, pp. 270 sq.; F. A. Golder, "The Songs and Stories of the Aleuts," *Journal of American Folk-Lore*, xx, p. 28; J. Teit, "The Lilloet Indians," *Publications of the Jesup North Pacific Expedition*, vol. i, p. 275; W. E. Stanbridge, "Some Particulars of the General Characteristics, etc., of the Tribes in the Central Part of Victoria, Southern Australia," *Transactions of the Ethnological Society*, N.S., i, p. 301; J. Bonwick, *Daily Life and Origin of the Tasmanians*, p. 192; W. W. Gill, Myths and Songs of the Southern Pacific, p. 45; H. G. Wissendorff, "Légendes mythologiques lataviennes," *Revue des Traditions Populaires*, vii, p. 553.

In matriarchal societies it would be an inconceivable incongruity that a masculine personage should have no mother. The metaphysical notion of a self-begotten god does not enter into the conceptions of primitive theology. A male god may very well have no father, but it would be opposed to the most fundamental notions of a primitive society that he should be without a mother. Generation begins with females, not with males; women procreate by immaculate conception, men do not; a mother is indispensable, a father is not. Primitive moon-gods, accordingly, have usually a mother. That mother is not in primitive lunar myths, such, for example, as those of Melanesia, so intimately associated with the functions and cosmic attributes of the moon as are the moon-gods themselves. With the latter, and not with their mother, the primary and fundamental attributes of the moon are connected; the connection of the mother-goddess with those attributes is therefore more remote. She indeed often dies in giving birth to her son, or sons; she becomes the wife of her own son; but the vicissitudes which are characteristic of lunar gods are, in general, not so marked in the conception of their mother. She is not a dying goddess. Her function and the reason of her existence is primarily that of bringing forth the moon-god; she is essentially the Mother of God. And accordingly it is her enduring, her eternal character, persisting through all vicissitudes, which is most prominent. She is the 'Power over the Manitu,' the fatal goddess, the goddess of Fate, and often therefore the inexorable one, the goddess of death, whom even the efforts and entreaties of her son cannot mollify.

Those characteristics of the Mother of God render her, from the first, a more generalised deity than the moon-god. Although personified abstractions are foreign to primitive thought, the primal Mother partakes from her very nature of an abstract character as the prototype of motherhood in general. She is not only the Mother of God, or as the Algonkin called her, emphasising her primal and timeless character, the 'Grandmother,' she is also generally the Mother of mankind, the primal Mother. The Mother of American or of Melanesian myth is indistinguishable from the First Woman, the Eve of Semitic myth. Often each tribe or clan has its eponymous primal Mother. The Pelew Islanders, for example, have an ancestral goddess for each family, and each tribe amongst them has its eponymous mother. They are the active and important deities of the people, and their cult constitutes the bulk of the religious practices and sentiment in those islands. All good and bad luck comes from the Mothers; it is they who, when angry, send diseases and death.[1]

[1] J. Kubary, "Die Religion der Pelauer," in A. Bastian, *Allerlei aus Volk und Menschenkunde*, vol. i, pp. 12, 22, 27.

Similarly, among the aboriginal populations of India, more especially in the southern provinces, where Aryan influence has never
been so strong as in the north, the native cults are represented by
local deities, whose numerous little shrines may be seen in the
neighbourhood of every village. In the larger towns imposing
temples of Siva or of Vishnu may be found, but these are alien
importations. The real cult of the aboriginal population is addressed
to the deities of the shrines, who represent the worship of the land
before the Aryan came. Those village deities, or ' grama-davata,'
are with few exceptions female.[1] The goddesses bear a multitude
of names, and are associated with an equal diversity of attributes ; but the people acknowledge that those numerous
goddesses " are only different names for the same goddess." [2]
Frequently she is simply spoken of as Mata—that is, ' the Mother,' [3]
or Pedama, ' the World Mother.' [4] Like the Pelew goddesses, the
Indian village Mothers have often become conspicuously associated
with the diseases with which they are supposed to afflict mankind.
There is Gangamma, the goddess of small-pox; Maramma, the
goddess of cholera; Kokkalamma, the goddess of cough; Sukha-
lamma, the goddess of measles; Udalamma, the goddess of swollen
necks.[5] There is even, in the Canara district, a goddess Chamundi,
or the ' Mistress of Death'; [6] and, like the Greek Demeter, the
goddess is often spoken of as ' the Black One.' [7] The power of
death is, however, as usual the correlative of the power of life.
In the Chamba State the goddesses have the power to cure all
diseases of man and beast,[8] and they are, of course, goddesses of
childbirth and fertility. They have also a special relation to the
food supply and the products of the earth, and the Mother may
be spoken of as ' she who fills with grain,' Annapurna.[9]

The goddesses are worshipped by men and women alike, though
the women are often the more devout worshippers, especially in
connection with their functions and when asking for help in
childbed or desiring children. The little shrines are usually served
by men of the menial class; but it is worthy of note that the

[1] H. Whitehead, *The Village Gods of South India*, p. 17.
[2] *Ibid.*, p. 26.
[3] W. Crooke, " The Cult of the Mother Goddesses in India," *Folk-lore*,
xxx, p. 300.
[4] H. Whitehead, *op. cit.*, p. 24.
[5] *Ibid.*, p. 23.
[6] M. J. Walhouse, " Devil and Ghost Worship in Western India," *Journal
of the Anthropological Institute*, v, p. 418.
[7] W. Crooke, *op. cit.*, p. 300.
[8] H. A. Rose, *Glossary of the Tribes and Castes of the Punjab and the
North-West Frontier Province*, vol. i, p. 331.
[9] H. Whitehead, *op. cit.*, p. 17. Cf. H. A. Rose, *op. cit.*, vol. i,
p. 479.

incumbent generally belongs to a profession which was formerly
exercised by women, such as that of washerman or potter. At
Coconada the office is exercised by a woman of the fisherman class,
and it is hereditary in her family, but she generally appoints one of
her male relatives as her deputy.[1] At Guichivada, in the Telugu
country, the priest assumes the dress of a woman when officiating.[2]
Elsewhere in Malabar the goddess is impersonated at her festival
by an unmarried woman, who is called by the name of the goddess
and takes the chief part in the ceremonies ; she touches all persons
with a wand, and spits on them, thereby cleansing them of all
defilements, physical and spiritual.[3] Near Bangalore, at the festival
of the seven goddesses, a fire-walking ceremony takes place, the
performers being women.[4] In Mysore, " on the first day of the
festival a woman comes from every household to the place of
worship with a lighted lamp made of rice flour, called ' arati,' and
then all together wave their lamps in a circle from left to right above
their heads, and from right to left below. When the festival is
over, the washerman of the village, who acts as ' pujari,' accompanied by all the villagers, takes the image to the tank, and leaves
it there." [5]

The general opinion is that the Indian aboriginal Mothers are
primarily tribal ancestresses, and they are in several instances
overtly recognised as such.[6] But the tribal ancestress or ancestor
may be anything, from a totem to a moon-deity, and usually about
the last thing which he is in reality is an actual historical progenitor. Most deities are regarded as the first parent, male or
female. The character of the Indian goddesses as controllers of
life and disease, as arbiters of destiny, suggests that they may
have originally been derived from the fateful and magic-wielding
lunar deities who exercise those functions in primitive thought.
On the other hand, it is plain that they contain at least the
germ of agricultural goddesses, mothers of corn, Earth-mothers,
and that but for the proximity of the Brahmanical Sivas and
Vishnus, and the influence of Hindu religion, which is essentially
non-agricultural, they might easily have developed into Great
Mothers similar in type to those of Western Asia and Europe.

The goddesses of the Pueblo tribes of New Mexico and Arizona

---

[1] H. Whitehead, op. cit., pp. 63 sq.
[2] Ibid., p. 57.
[3] E. Thurston, Omens and Superstitions of Southern India, p. 27.
[4] H. Whitehead, op. cit., p. 83.
[5] Ibid., p. 40.
[6] M. Monier Williams, Brahmanism and Hinduism, pp. 225 sq. ; Gazetteer
of the Bombay Presidency, vol. v, p. 76 ; vol. vii, pp. 609 sqq. ; vol. ix, part i,
p. xxxvi ; A. K. Forbes, Ras Mala, pp. 426 sqq.

are likewise the central figures of cults which prefigure the rituals of Eleusis, and the Great Mother and her daughters present barbaric counterparts of Demeter and Kore in the agricultural rites of ancient Greece. As has been shown in detail by Mr. Fewkes, those deities, which are invoked as Corn Mother, Corn Maidens, Mother of Germs, are regarded by their votaries as actual ancestresses of the clans. The fundamental object of the ' Katcina ' ceremonies, as of all savage ' secret societies,' is to establish a communion between the living and the deceased members of the clan. Every deceased tribesman becomes a deity capable of controlling the conditions of agricultural prosperity, and is addressed with the prayer : " You have become a ' katcina '; bring us rain." [1] The Great Mother, as her name clearly indicates, is at the same time the Moon, the Mother of God.[2] The Arapahos have very similar ceremonies, which also bear a striking likeness to the mysteries of the agricultural religions of Greece and Western Asia. Much after the manner of the hierophant at Eleusis, the Arapaho high priest bears forth, after a rite of symbolic fecundation performed by the light of the moon, in which the high priestess personifies the Great Mother, a pod of maize, the emblem of the fruits of the earth. When questioned on the nature of the Great Goddess, the priest has no other explanation to offer than that " the woman represents the mother of the tribe." [3]

The Primitive Goddess as Mother of Animals.

Since cosmic gods are commonly assimilated to the animal ancestor of the clan, the totem, the Mother deity is often the mother of the totem, or tribal hero. In her character of generating goddess she is the mother of animals as well as of men, which, as we have seen, are scarcely differentiated from one another in the thought of totemic societies. As mother of the tribe she is, above all, the dispenser of food. One of the most common attributes of the Great Mother is accordingly the control of animals and of the food supply. Artemis, the hunting goddess of the Greeks, was specially thought of as the protectress of wild creatures, and curiously, not of land animals only, but also of fish.[4] In India

[1] J. W. Fewkes, " An Interpretation of Katcina Worship," *Journal of American Folk-Lore*, xiv, p. 82 ; Id., " The Group of Tusayan Ceremonials called Katcinas," *Fifteenth Annual Report of the Bureau of Ethnology*, pp. 251 sqq. ; Id., in *Handbook of American Indians*, vol. i, pp. 566 sq.

[2] See above, vol. ii, p. 738.

[3] G. A. Dorsey, " The Arapaho Sun Dance," *Field Columbian Museum Publications, Anthropological Series*, vol. iv, p. 173.

[4] Plutarch, *De rat. anim.*, viii.

there are likewise goddesses of the jungle whose chief attribute is to protect or control the denizens of the woods, and
who must be conciliated by the hunter.[1] The Finns have
a similar goddess, Mimmerkki, and to gain her favour was the
chief anxiety of hunters.[2] The Yoruba and the Fjort have a
goddess, called Zambici, who is " the mother of all animals." [3]
The Germanic goddess Harke bore a strong likeness in this respect
to the Greek Artemis and the Latin Diana ; she also was the
protectress of wild creatures.[4]

Among the Eskimo the Great Goddess, called Sedna, or Arna-
kuagsak—that is, ' the Woman '—holds so important a place in
their conceptions and rites that she is described as their chief
deity. Her principal attribute and function is the control of the
animals which provide the Eskimo with food, and which in this
instance are chiefly sea animals. " She sends out all animals that
serve for food ; but in certain cases withholds the supply, causing
want and famine " [5] The Great Goddess of the Eskimo is identified
with the cosmic power which they regard as controlling their
destinies, namely, the moon. She occupies in Eskimo myths the
place which in a version already noted [6] is taken by one of the
two conflicting moon-beings. She is said to dwell on the one
side, while " her father "—who seems to be also at times her
brother and her lover—dwells on the opposite side. As with
the Egyptian Horus and the South American moon-god, Eskimo
mythology has a good deal to say about what happens to Sedna's
eye. She is said to have only one eye, and her father likewise has but one eye. He pierces the eye of the Great Goddess.
She periodically dies and comes to life again.[7] On first seeing a
European look at the moon through a telescope the Eskimo were
convinced that he must have been performing an incantation to call
forth from the moon an abundant supply of seals.[8] The Great
Goddess is also represented as dwelling in a house at the bottom
of the sea. She has the attributes which are everywhere characteristic of lunar deities ; she is the controller of atmospheric conditions, of rain and storms, of the sea ; she has the character of
an inexorable fate-deity ; she " has boundless command over the

---

[1] W. Crooke, " The Cult of the Mother Goddesses in India," *Folk-lore*,
xxx, pp. 297 sq.
[2] M. A. Castrén, *Vorlesungen über die Finnische Mythologie*, p. 93.
[3] R. E. Dennett, *At the Back of the Black Man's Mind*, p. 152 ; Id.,
Folklore of the Fjort, p. 127.   [4] See above, vol. ii, p. 618.
[5] H. J. Rink, *Tales and Traditions of the Eskimos*, pp. 39 sq.
[6] See above, vol. ii, p. 721.
[7] F. Boas, " The Central Eskimo," *Sixth Annual Report of the Bureau of
Ethnology*, pp. 583 sq. ; H. N. Wardle, " The Sedna Cycle : A Study in Myth
Evolution," *The American Anthropologist*, N.S., ii, pp. 573, 575.
[8] E. Petitot, *Les Grands Esquimaux*, p. 82.

destinies of mankind"; she rules the land of the dead, and, like Hekate, is attended by a dog.[1]

The Chukchi have a goddess which appears to be identical with the Great Goddess of the Eskimo; she is called 'The Mother of Walruses,' lives at the bottom of the sea, and is represented in the form of a walrus.[2] The chief cult of the Samoyeds is also addressed to Grandmother Yanman, who controls the supply of fish and dwells at the mouth of the Ob River.[3] Similar goddesses wielding power over the food-supplying sea animals are worshipped by the Buryat[4] and the Koryak.[5] We have thus among peoples with whom the Earth-Mother, bearer of golden harvests, would clearly be out of the question, her counterpart, an unagricultural Demeter, the giver of all food, who, without being in any way associated with the earth, partakes nevertheless of the characters which are everywhere typical of the Great Mother. If we imagine the Eskimo transported from their frozen abode to fertile plains, and transformed into an agricultural people, their Great Goddess of fertility and of food would inevitably assume the character of a corn-goddess and deity of harvests, and become assimilated to Mother Earth.

The Primitive Goddess as Mother of Corn.

The Great Goddess of the Siouan tribes of North America, the ancestress of mankind, or First Woman, the 'Old Woman who never dies,' has actually assumed the character of Corn-mother so completely, in all but her name, that her attributes and the rites by means of which she is encouraged to bring forth the fruits of the earth, present the most manifest primitive parallel to those of the Asiatic corn-goddesses and the Hellenic Demeter. But the 'Old Woman who never dies' is expressly said to be the moon, and is never regarded as anything else.[6] She is identical with the Aataentsic of the Algonkin tribes, and it is but a step from her to the Mother of Germs, whose name is also Moon, of the more advanced agricultural Pueblo tribes.

The Great Mother, the mother of the Manitu, or Great Hare, is also, like the Eskimo goddess, the mother of the food animals, or the mother of the totem, the cosmic god, or moon-god, being conceived in animal form, and being assimilated to a totem-animal.

---

[1] F. Boas, *loc. cit.*   [2] W. Bogoras, *The Chukchee*, p. 317.
[3] M. A. Czaplicka, in Hastings's *Encyclopaedia of Religion and Ethics*, vol. xi, pp. 175 sq.
[4] Id., *Aboriginal Siberia*, p. 284.
[5] W. Jochelson, *The Koryak*, pp. 30 sq.
[6] See above, vol. ii, pp. 728 sq.

As source of all food, she is, when food comes to be mainly cereal, equally the mother of vegetable as of animal food, the mother of corn. The precious corn which she produces is her offspring, and is therefore the same as her son, the Manitu, or moon-god. Like him, it dies and is born again. The corn is regarded as a sacred food-totem, as is the animal-totem by the primitive hunter. " The corn," said an American Indian to a missionary, " is the same to us as Jesus Christ is to you." [1] Among the Tupis of Brazil Mother Moon is chiefly regarded as the mother of all vegetables. They have the following myth concerning the origin of the manioc plant. A young woman became pregnant without intercourse, after a young man, white and shining, had appeared to her. She presently gave birth to a child as white as snow, which, however, died after a year. It was buried, and from its grave there presently arose a plant which bore fruit. On tasting some of the fruit men felt as if the spirit of a god had entered into them. That was the first manioc plant.[2] The mother of the manioc plant is clearly the ' Mother of Vegetables,' that is, Mother Moon. Her child, in the form of the manioc plant, dies after a year instead of dying, like her heavenly child, after a month. Mother Moon is here, as with the North American tribes, a Corn-mother, and her offspring, or divine son, is a dying ' vegetation-god.'

Mother Earth.

The Great Goddesses who occupied so important a place in the religions of Western Asia and of Europe owe their prominence chiefly to their association with agricultural rites, and are thought of as mothers of the harvests, or as the Earth-Mother who brings forth the golden corn. The successful carrying out of the agricultural labours of women is regarded in primitive thought as due to the magical powers with which they are credited, and is thought to be, like their power of child-bearing, inherent in their sex and to appertain to the very nature of womanhood. Primitive man thinks of the cultivation of the soil as being " magically dependent for success on woman, and connected with child-bearing." [3] " When women plant maize," said an Orinoco chief to Father Gumilla, " the stalk produces two or three ears ; when they set manioc, the plant produces two or three baskets of roots. Why ? Because women know how to produce children ; and in like manner they cause fruits to multiply. They alone know what

[1] G. B. Grinnell, " Pawnee Mythology," Journal of American Folk-Lore, vi, p. 112.

[2] J. V. Couto de Magelhães, O Selvagem, pp. 134 sqq.

[3] E. J. Payne, History of the New World called America, vol. ii, p. 8.

to do to cause the corn which they sow to germinate. There-fore let them plant it ; they know more about the matter than we do."[1] In Uganda "a sterile wife is said to be injurious to a garden ; it won't yield fruit ; while that of a pro-lific woman bears plentifully." A man has, accordingly, a recognised right to divorce a sterile wife on grounds of agricultural economics.[2] In New Zealand the same ritual precautions and tabus apply to a woman who is with child and to one who has a patch of sweet potatoes under cultivation.[3] The Nicobar Islanders consider that seed will germinate and prosper best if it is planted by a pregnant woman.[4] Similar ideas are current in Europe. The peasants of southern Italy believe that whatsoever is sown and planted by a pregnant woman will grow and increase as the foetus in her womb.[5]

The fecundity of the earth and the fecundity of women are viewed as being one and the same quality. The peasants of Greece at the present day reproduce unconsciously in their songs the ideas out of which arose the myths of the Corn Goddess among their ancestors. "A Jewish maiden," they sing, "reaps the corn ; Ah ! the maiden is with child. At times she reaps, at times she stoops and leans upon a wheat-sheaf, and she bears a golden child."[6] In many parts of Europe it is the custom for a bride to be crowned, like Ceres, with ears of corn.[7] In wedding rites of world-wide dis-tribution, which survive amongst ourselves, the bride is strewn with corn or rice. Among the Jews it was customary to adorn the wed-ding tent, or 'huppah,' with ears of corn, and to throw roasted grains of corn on the bride, "to signify," as an old Rabbi explains, "Be fruitful and multiply."[8] The rite was similarly observed in Vedic India ; the bride threw green roasted corn on the fire.[9] In the Eifel district if a baby does not thrive and put on weight, his parents take to church an offering of corn exactly equal in weight to that of the child, hoping, doubtless, that if the corn is blessed and made to increase, the child will increase also.[10] In Russia it

---

[1] J. Gumilla, *El Orinoco ilustrado*, vol. i, pp. 274 sq.
[2] J. Roscoe, " Notes on the Manners and Customs of the Baganda," *Journal of the Anthropological Institute*, xxxi, p. 56.
[3] E. Tregear, " The Maoris of New Zealand," *Journal of the Anthropological Institute*, xix, p. 107.
[4] R. C. Temple, in Hastings's *Encyclopaedia of Religion and Ethics*, vol. ix, p. 362.
[5] G. Finamore, *Tradizioni popolari abruzzesi*, p. 59.
[6] J. M. Firmenich Richartz, Τραγουδια 'Ρωμαικα, *Neugriechische Volk-gesange*, p. 63.
[7] See W. Mannhardt, *Mythologische Forschungen*, p. 369.
[8] *Ibid.*, p. 355.
[9] A. Hillebrandt, *Ritualliteratur ; Vedische Offer und Zauber*, p. 64.
[10] J. H. Schmitz, *Sitten und Sagen . . . des Eifler Volkes*, vol. i, p. 65.

was the custom to make the wedding-bed of a newly married couple on a heap of rye-sheaves.[1] The Greeks spoke of a corn-field as λοχαῖος, lochial.[2] In New Caledonia the fertility of the earth and of women was stimulated by burying a girl at puberty in the earth.[3]

The same means which fertilise the earth are also thought to fertilise women, and vice versa. Thus the fertilising rains and all the flowing waters which fecundate the earth can also fecundate women. In Australia and in South Africa women lie in a shower of rain when they desire to conceive.[4] Vergil echoes in mouth-filling lines the conceptions of the Australian aborigines :—

> Uere tument terrae et genitalia semina poscunt ;
> tum pater omnipotens fecundis imbribus Aether
> conjugis in gremium laetae descendit, et omnes
> magnus alit magno commixtus corpore fetus.[5]

What may have been poetical metaphor with the Roman poet is literal truth in primitive thought. In early Rome itself " the Earth presided over all nuptials ; and virgins, as they proceeded to their husband's home, sacrificed to the earth under various names." [6] Similar usages are universal in India at the present day. Thus in Byapur, when a Rajput marries, one of his relatives goes to some sacred spot and makes offerings to Mother Earth, pouring water on her surface, and strewing the ground with rice and with flowers.[7] In all parts of the country the women proceed, before a wedding, to the village clay-pit, and bring thence some ' lucky earth ' with which generally is built the fireplace where the wedding meal is cooked.[8] In the Telugu country five women proceed with great pomp, under a canopy and accompanied by a band of music, to the clay-pit and bring the earth which they build up into a seat in the marriage booth ; and on this the bride and bridegroom sit.[9]

The identification of the earth with women pervades the thought of all stages of culture, and pages could be filled with illustrations of the universal equation. " The mother and the soil are

---

[1] W. Mannhardt, op. cit., p. 355.

[2] Photius, s.v. λοχαῖος.

[3] W. Mannhardt, op. cit., p. 303.

[4] See above, vol. ii, p. 452.

[5] Vergil, Georgics, ii. 324 sqq.

[6] Servius, ad Aeneid., iv. 166.

[7] Gazetteer of the Bombay Presidency, vol. xxii, p. 159.

[8] W. Crooke, Introduction to the Popular Religion and Folklore of Northern India, vol. i, p. 27 ; E. Thurston, Tribes and Castes of Southern India, vol. vi, p. 355.

[9] J. A. Padfield, The Hindu at Home, p. 144.

alike," was a principle of Roman jurisprudence;[1] and the poets
express themselves in the same terms as the lawyers.[2] In ancient
India, at the wedding ceremony, the woman was called 'a seed-
field,' and the priest exhorted the bridegroom, saying, "Sow her
with thy seed."[3] "Your women are your field," says the Kuran.[4]
The mother's womb and the womb of the earth are forms of the
same thing; "naked came I out of my mother's womb, and naked
shall I return thither."[5] The earth is the All-Mother, παμμῆτόρ γή;[6]
from her all things are issued, "for all are of the earth, and all
turn to earth again."[7] "Hail mother of harvests, Saturn's Earth,"
sings Vergil; "hail mighty mother of men."[8] In words almost
identical the rude Germans sang: "Hail Earth, mother of men;
may you grow in the embrace of God, filled with nourishment for
the welfare of men."[9] In the Vedic hymns the Earth is the mother
of man, and he the son of earth;[10] and in Persian religion man
was created out of the earth.[11] In many savage cosmologies the first
men arose out of the earth.[12] The word 'homo' is itself a derivative
of 'humus.'[13] Although Adam was fashioned out of the earth,

---

[1] J. Cuiacus, *Opera*, vol. vi, p. 219.

[2] E.g., Euripides, *Herakles*, 839; Sophokles, *Antigone*, 569. For numerous
citations from Greek literature see L. Preller, *Demeter und Persephone*,
pp. 254 sqq.

[3] *Atharvaveda*, xiv. 2. 14. Cf. A. Weber, "Vedische Hochzeitssprüche,"
Indische Studien, vol. v, p. 205.

[4] *The Kuran*, Sura, ii. [5] *Job*, i. 21.

[6] Aeschylus, *Prometheus*, 90.

[7] *Ecclesiastes*, iii. 20. Cf. *Genesis*, iii. 19; *Job*, x. 9, xxxiv. 15; *Psalms*,
ciii. 14; Cicero, *De natur. De.*, ii. 26: "Et recidunt omnia in terras et
oriuntur e terris"; Aeschylus, *Fragm.*, 195: ἄπαντα τίκῖει χθών πάλιν τε
λαμβάνει.

[8] Vergil, *Georgics*, ii. 173 sq. Cf. Livy, i. 56; iv. 54.

[9] E. H. Meyer, *Germanische Mythologie*, p. 287.

[10] *Rig-Veda*, xii. 1. 12.

[11] *The Sacred Books of the East*, vol. viii, p. 401.

[12] E. Casalis, *Les Bassoutos*, p. 255; T. Hahn, *Tsuni-Goam*, p. 91;
H. Callaway, *The Religious System of the Amazulu*, p. 34; C. J. Andersson,
Lake Ngami, p. 221; H. A. Junod, *Les Ba-Ronga*, p. 402; L. Frobenius,
Volksmärchen der Kabylen, vol. i, p. 55; A. C. Kruijt, *Het Animisme in den
Indischen Archipels*, p. 469; Schoolcraft, *Indian Tribes*, vol. ii, p. 132;
J. Tanner, *Narrative of a Captivity among the Indians*, p. 203; J. G. E.
Heckewelder, *History, Manners, and Customs of the Indian Nations*, p. 429;
L. Hennepin, *Voyage*, pp. 90 sq.; J. R. Swanton, *Early History of the Creek
Indians*, p. 192; F. H. Cushing, "Outlines of Zuñi Creation Myths,"
Thirteenth Annual Report of the Bureau of Ethnology, p. 13; J. G. Müller,
Geschichte der amerikanischen Urreligionen, pp. 56, 110, 221, 369, 494;
Garcia, *Origen de los Indios*, vol. iv, p. 26; Torquemada, *Monarquia Indiana*,
vi. 41; H. Egede, *A Description of Greenland*, p. 195; T. Falkner, *A
Description of Patagonia*, pp. 114 sq.; J. 'Arnason, *Islenzkar þjoðsögur og
aefintyri*, vol. ii, p. 409.

[13] H. Oslhoff, *Etymologische Parerga*, vol. i, p. 221.

Lactantius blames Demokritos for believing that men came out of the earth like worms.[1] Lucretius, however, declares that "animals cannot have fallen from the sky, nor the inhabitants of earth have issued out of lagoons of salt water ; rightly is the earth called 'mother,' for out of the earth all things have been created."[2]

The belief in the intimate connection of children with the earth is manifested in the widespread custom of depositing a child directly after its birth on the ground. It was honoured by the Romans, and is similarly observed by very rude savages. The Veddahs of Ceylon, for instance, place the child on the ground and put an arrow in its hand ; "this ceremony is never omitted, and they attach the greatest importance to it."[3] The same thing is done by the Tupis of Brazil,[4] and by the African natives on the Gold Coast and in Central Africa.[5] At Nierstein, in Hessia, as among the Australian and North American aborigines, the women believe that they get their children from a cave in the earth ; and they assert that if you place your ear to the ground in the neighbourhood you can hear quite clearly the cries and voices of the unborn.[6] The apostles of Christianity in northern Europe had great trouble in combating such beliefs. In an old English homily it is lamented that "men believe in the earth because she feeds all things" ;[7] and Abbot Aelfric complains that "also many foolish women go to the crossways and drag their children over the earth, and thereby give both themselves and their children to the Devil."[8] In Sicily it is believed that if a child is not laid on the earth immediately after it is born it will certainly die in hospital.[9] An African chief, on being offered a chair, replied that the lap of his mother was good enough for him, and squatted on the ground. With the Bari of the Upper Nile, the same notion leads to an opposite course of conduct, for they will on no account desecrate the earth by sitting on the ground, and accordingly always carry about with them a little stool.[10]

The conception of Mother Earth is a far more obvious one

---

[1] Lactantius, *Inst. Div.*, vii. 7, 9, cited by Diels, *Fragmenten der Vorsokratiker*, p. 397.

[2] Lucretius, 790 sqq.

[3] P. and F. Sarasin, *Ergebnisse naturwissenschaftlicher Forschungen auf Ceylon*, vol. iii, pp. 580 sq.

[4] *Globus*, lxxxix, pp. 60, 63.

[5] B. Struck, "Die Erdmutter in Afrika," *Archiv für Religionswissenschaft*, x, p. 158.

[6] J. W. Wolf, *Hessische Sagen*, p. 13.

[7] F. Kluge, *Mittelenglisches Lesebuch*, p. 89.

[8] *Aelfric's Lives of Saints*, ed. W. W. Skeat, p. 374.

[9] G. Pitré, *Usi e costumi, credenze e pregiudizzi del popolo Siciliano*, vol. ii, p. 145.

[10] A. Bastian, *Allerlei aus Volks- und Menschenkunde*, vol. ii, p. cviii.

than that of Mother Moon, and the assimilation of the fruit-bearing soil to the child-bearing woman is universal. Nevertheless, Mother Earth has scarcely any place in the cosmological or religious conceptions and rites of peoples in pre-agricultural stages. Even far above the level of primitive culture, where advanced material and intellectual civilisation has been attained by peoples who have never truly become cultivators of the soil, Mother Earth plays no part. The Hindu Aryans, for example, developed the highest type of Oriental civilisation and culture without ever becoming agriculturists. It was as a society of pastoral warriors that they established themselves in the fertile plains of northern India ; they never took up the cultivation of the soil, leaving it to the native inhabitants ; and, indeed, they, like all pastoral warriors, profoundly despised agriculture as the occupation of conquered races. ' The Laws of Manu ' forbid agricultural work to members of the Brahmanical and warrior castes. " Some declare that agriculture is something excellent," states the official code of Brahmanical laws, " but that means of subsistence is blamed by the virtuous." [1] A Brahman at the present day will not so much as touch a plough. In Vedic literature, accordingly, and in Hindu religion we find no great Earth Mother. The earth is indeed personified as Prithivi, ' the Broad One,' but there is no worship and scarcely any significance attached to her. " The earth herself makes no remarkable figure ; she is indeed deified, at least partially, is addressed as mother and substance of all things, is generally in company with the sky invoked to grant blessings. Yet this never advanced farther than a lively personification might go." [2] Goddesses occupy a subordinate position in Vedic religion. Only two, Ushas, a personification of the dawn, and Sarasvati, an impersonation of a sacred river, acquired any importance. [3]

In the earlier and more archaic stages of agriculture, the bringing forth of the fruits of the earth, the bearing and production of vegetable food, is ascribed not to the earth, but to the moon. With the native tribes of Brazil the moon and not the earth is the ' mother of all vegetation ' ; the ' Old Woman,' the agricultural Great Mother of the Siouan tribes, who bears so close a likeness to the Asiatic agricultural goddesses, is not the earth but the moon. The apparent incongruity of setting aside and passing over the obvious and recognised analogies which mark the earth as the mother of the life-giving fruits which she brings forth, and of

---

[1] *The Laws of Manu*, x. 84 sq.
[2] W. D. Whitney, *Oriental and Linguistic Studies*, p. 32.
[3] W. Crooke, " The Cult of Mother Goddesses in India," *Folk-lore*, xxx, pp. 284 sq. ; A. A. Macdonell, *Vedic Mythology*, pp. 124 sq. ; R. G. Bhandarkar, " Vaisnavism, Saivism, and Minor Religious Systems," in G. Bühler, *Grundriss der indo-arischen Philologie*, vol. iii, pp. 142 sqq.

assigning the function to the moon, arises from the circumstance
that religious conceptions have nowhere originally developed as a
symbolism, as a ' symbolic interpretation of nature.' They have
arisen out of functional magic. The universal mother, the mother
of men, the bestower of food, the source of all fertility, the eternal
prototype of women, the source of their magic power, of their
own fertility and of that which they imparted to the earth, existed
long before their labours and their magic became the chief factors
in the sustenance of life and in the development of new forms of
society. In spite of the recognised motherhood of the earth, Mother
Earth is not a primitive deity. No clear instance is to be found in
any culture, either primitive or advanced, of a worshipped female
divinity who originally arose solely or chiefly as a personification
of the earth. The symbolism which has become familiar to us
is for the most part the elaborated product of advanced phases
of agricultural civilisation. Primitive humanity might recognise
the motherly functions of the earth, but those functions were only
one aspect of all motherhood which had its prototype in the primitive
goddess. The attributes of the earth goddess were extended to
her by an older and more primitive divine mother. She is the
heiress of antecedent deities.

The moon and the earth are curiously identified in all primitive
thought as aspects of the same thing. Thus the Caribbean savages
have a myth representing both moon and earth as created out of
one amorphous substance.[1] The ancient Mexicans regarded the
earth and the moon as the same power.[2] The Maori identify the
moon, Hine, ' The Woman,' with the earth, and say that the moon
was formed out of the earth.[3] Among Nordic nations the moon
was said to be the progeny of the earth, born out of her womb.[4] A
Chaldean myth transmitted by Berosus relates that the moon-god
split into two, one portion becoming the earth.[5] It is, no doubt,
the same myth which is referred to on a coin of Syracuse showing
the ' world-egg ' split in two.[6] The division of the world-egg,
which is originally no other than the moon, plays a prominent part
in the cosmogony of the Orphics.[7] In the 'Satapatha-Brâhmana,'

[1] J. G. Müller, *Geschichte der amerikanischen Urreligionen*, p. 229.

[2] K. T. Preuss, "Die Astralreligion in Mexiko, in vorspanischer Zeit und
der Gegenwart," *Transactions of the Third International Congress for the
History of Religion* (Oxford, 1908), vol. i, p. 29.

[3] E. Best, " Ceremonial Performances pertaining to Birth as performed
by the Maoris of New Zealand," *Journal of the Royal Anthropological Institute*,
xliv, p. 131.

[4] O. Rudbeck, *Atlantis*, Part ii, p. 607.

[5] *Fragmenta Historicorum Graecorum*, vol. ii, p. 497.

[6] H. Goltzius, *Sicilia et Magna Graecia*, tab. v, fig. 3.

[7] Cf. *Orphica*, ed. E. Abel, p. 173 ; G. F. Schömann, *Opuscula academica*,

we are told that " the full moon is the earth." [1] The Chinese, in
whose metaphysical speculations primitive notions are reduced to
systematised definition, represent both the moon and the earth as
belonging to one and the same cosmic principle, the Feminine
Principle.[2] The Greeks expressly called the moon " a heavenly
earth," and " a part of the earth." [3] That persistent identification
of the moon with the earth would be unintelligible in peoples
ignorant of modern astronomical conceptions, let alone in uncultured races such as the Caribs and the Polynesians. When the
earth is conceived as a huge, solid, immovable surface contrasted in every respect with the wandering sphere or disc of
the moon in the heavens, there appears to be no imaginable
ground for assimilating the one to the other. The identification cannot arise from any analogy in appearance or function ;
it becomes intelligible only when the ideas intimately connecting
both the moon and the earth with women and their functions,
and the transference of the attributes of the latter to the former,
are apprehended.

There is not, in fact, an earth-goddess who is not at the
same time a moon-goddess. All Earth Mothers, as Bachofen
remarked, " lead a double life, as Earth and as Moon." [4] The
converse is often, but not universally, true ; a moon-deity need
not necessarily be an earth-deity. Primitive agricultural goddesses
retain consciously the character of the primitive universal mother,
the Mother of God.

The Great Mother in Mexico.

Among the ancient Mexicans, for example, with whom agriculture had advanced to a higher stage of development than among
the North American tribes, and who, moreover, had a definite
solar cult established by monarchical rulers, the assimilation of
the Great Mother to the Earth and the Corn-mother had proceeded
much farther than among Siouan or Pueblo tribes.

The Mexicans commonly referred to their Great Goddess as
' Our Ancestress ' (Tonantzin), or as ' Our Mother ' (Toci). She

vol. ii, p. 60 ; J. E. Harrison, *Prolegomena to the Study of Greek Religion*,
pp. 625 sqq. ; P. N. Rolle, *Recherches sur le culte de Bacchus*, vol. i,
pp. 204 sq.

[1] *Satapatha-Brâhmana*, xi. 2. 4. 3 (*The Sacred Books of the East*, vol. xliv,
p. 30).

[2] J. Legge, Introduction to the *Yî King* (*The Sacred Books of the East*,
vol. xvi, p. 32).

[3] Plutarch, *De defect. orac.*, xiii ; Proclus, *Commentarius in Platonis
Timoeum*, i. 23E ; iii. 32B, 36D ; iv. 40B.

[4] J. J. Bachofen, *Das Mutterrecht*, p. 37.

was called, 'The Mother of God' (Tetevinan).[1] Father Clavigero
tells us that in his day, those heathenish cults and ignorant
superstitions having happily disappeared, there rose on the site
of her chief temple a church dedicated to the Mother of the True
God, which contained an image of her famed throughout the country
for its miraculous powers.[2] The church and the miraculous image
of Our Lady of Guadalupe are still in existence in the northern
quarter of Mexico city.[3] The statue of the Mexican Great Mother
which the Christian image displaced presented a remarkable
appearance ; for the upper part of the face of the goddess was
white, while the lower part, from the mouth down, was black,[4]
thus resembling the black and white Greek Erinyes. The Christian
Indians of the present day have, however, been but imperfectly
weaned from their ancient conceptions. " All they know of
Christianity," observes one traveller, " are the words ' Señor San
José,' and ' Maria santissima ; ' the Virgin Mary becomes a
substitute for Mother Moon." [5] The Mexican women recite a
Paternoster at the first appearance of the new moon.[6] Formerly
they held up their children to Mother Moon, beseeching her to
grant them an ever-renewed life like her own ; [7] and they regarded
an eclipse of the moon as fatal to the progress of gestation.[8]

The Mexican Great Mother fulfils, under a variety of names, the
many functions commonly assigned to lunar deities. She was the
goddess of all waters, of rain, of the ocean ; [9] and a statue of
her stood by the side of every stream and fountain.[10] She was
represented in that character as a green frog, of which a
figure carved out of a huge emerald was to be seen in one of her
temples.[11] She was also a Serpent goddess.[12] She was the source of
all maleficent influences and diseases ; [13] but was also the goddess

---

[1] F. S. Clavigero, *Storia antica del Messico*, vol. ii, pp. 16, 22 ; B. De
Sahagun, *Historia general de las cosas de Nueva España*, vol. i, pp. 6 sq.

[2] F. S. Clavigero, *op. cit.*, vol. ii, p. 22.

[3] C. A. Robelo, *Diccionario de mitologia Nahoa*, p. 620.

[4] *Ibid.*

[5] C. Lumholtz, *Unknown Mexico*, vol. i, p. 295.

[6] J. G. Bourke, " Superstitions of Rio Grande," *Journal of American
Folk-Lore*, vii, p. 136.

[7] F. S. Clavigero, *op. cit.*, vol. ii, p. 17.

[8] B. de Sahagun, *op. cit.* vol. ii, p. 250.

[9] *Ibid.*, p. 9 ; J. de Torquemada, *Veinte i un libros rituales i Monarchia
Indiana*, vol. ii, p. 46 ; P. Ponce, " Breve relación de los dioses y ritos de
la gentilidad," *Anales del Museo Nacional*, vi, p. 5.

[10] Jesús Sanchez, " Estatua colosal de la diosa del Agua," *Anales del
Museo Nacional*, iii, p. 29.

[11] B. de Sahagun, *op. cit.*, vol. i, p. 9 ; C. A. Robelo, *Diccionario de mitologia Nahoa*, p. 444.

[12] B. de Sahagun, *op. cit.*, vol. i, p. 5.

[13] *Ibid.*, vol. i, pp. 5 sq.

of healing and the patroness and instructress of the feminine medical profession in Mexico.[1] She was the special protectress of all women, and the goddess of childbearing.[2]

But although the Mexican Great Mother is Mother Moon, it is in a different character that she commonly appears in the accounts of Mexican religion at the time of the Spanish conquest. Her most familiar name is Centeotl, that is to say, ' She of the Maize-plant.' [3] She presided over, and was invoked in connection with, every operation of agriculture,[4] and is constantly compared to Ceres or Demeter.[5] It is a common feature of moon-deities, who preside over all vegetation, to be identified with a particular plant ; the moon-god in India, for instance, was identified with the soma-plant in the same manner as the moon-goddess in Mexico was identified with the maize-plant,[6] The Maize-goddess was, in fact, conceived as a heavenly deity, who came down to earth in the spring, was born as the maize-plant, was killed at harvest time, and re-ascended to heaven.[7] The Mexican Great Goddess is even, under the name of Toze, or Tatech, definitely identified with the earth, and is sometimes called Tlalli Iyolta, ' The Heart of the Earth,' and regarded as the cause of earthquakes.[8] That the various forms and aspects and the numberless and formidable consonantal names of ' Our Mother,' are but cult-forms of one and the same Great Goddess is generally admitted. The ease with which such a multiplication of names took place is illustrated by the fact that in her character of goddess of the maize-plant she bore a variety of different appellations, such as Xilonen, Isloccenteotl, Tlallanhqui, etc., referring to the various stages in the growth of the plant. As water-goddess she had as many names as there were streams, rivers, and ponds.[9] "All these goddesses, without any doubt," says Dr. Seler, one of the highest authorities on the subject, "were originally moon-goddesses ; but developed into goddesses of fertility and generation, into earth-goddesses and patronesses of women's arts." [10] Towards the sixth century of

---

[1] B. de Sahagun, op. cit., vol. i, p. 6.

[2] Ibid., p. 5.

[3] C. A. Robelo, op. cit., p. 71.

[4] Pedro Ponce, " Breve relación de los dioses y ritos de la gentilidad," Anales del Museo Nacional, vi, p. 8 ; H. Ruiz Alarcon, " Tratado de las supersticiones y costumbres gentilicas," ibid., pp. 176 sq.

[5] C. A. Robelo, op. cit., p. 77 ; P. Ponce, op. cit., p. 5.

[6] See below, pp. 131 sqq.

[7] K. T. Preuss, " Die Astralreligion in Mexiko," Transactions of the Third International Congress for the History of Religions (Oxford, 1908), vol. i, p. 39.

[8] C. A. Robelo, op. cit., p. 620.   [9] Ibid., pp. 72, 138.

[10] E. Seler, in Hastings's Encyclopaedia of Religion and Ethics, vol. viii, p. 614.

our era a religious 'reformation' took place in Mexico with the introduction of monarchical institutions and the establishment of the cult of the sun as the official deity of the royal clans.[1] The lunar aspect of the primal goddess was probably officially relegated into the background, the agricultural and earth attributes of the national Great Mother being emphasised at the expense of her lunar character.   But there is no real opposition or inconsistency between the two aspects.   As everywhere else, moon and earth were conceived in Mexico as similar and related powers. According to Dr. Preuss, 'Our Mother' was at the same time the earth and the moon ; and the moon is the heavenly counterpart of the earth.[2] In Maya manuscripts and on monuments the god Xmhtletl is represented bearing the symbols of both the moon and the earth.[3]

Nordic Goddesses.

The Great Mothers, who have played so prominent a part in the religious development of Europe and of the Near East, have often been regarded as being primarily personifications of the earth, Mother Earth.

Goddesses were conspicuous in the cults and mythological conceptions of the barbarians of northern Europe.   Those goddesses are known by a variety of names, but their attributes and characters are in general so similar that writers on the subject have trouble in disentangling their several personalities.   The current impression concerning them is that they are essentially 'personifications of Mother Earth.'   The view emanates in the first instance from the classical reference to them by Tacitus.   Nearly all the Germans, he tells us, "unite in worshipping Nerthus, that is to say, Mother Earth." [4]   Jacob Grimm in his prodigious work on Teutonic mythology accepts the classical tradition, and it is also repeated in one of the most exhaustive and authoritative of more recent treatises on the subject, that of Mogk.[5]   The Great Goddesses of the ancient Germans were, according to those authorities, nothing else but personifications of the Earth Mother. But when the attributes of those goddesses come to be examined, it must be admitted that they present a picture which suggests almost anything rather than an allegorical presentment of the broad-based earth.   Tacitus was led to identify the goddess

---

[1] See above, vol. ii, pp. 740 sq.
[2] K. T. Preuss, *op. cit.*, p. 39.
[3] Id., in D. V. Riva Palacio, *Mexico a través de los siglos*, vol. i, p. 284.
[4] Tacitus, *Germania*, xl.
[5] E. Mogk, " Mythologie," in H. Paul, *Grundriss der germanischen Philologie*, vol. iii, pp. 366 sqq.

whom he calls Nerthus with Mother Earth chiefly by the fact that, at her great festival, she was drawn about in a chariot, like Cybele and other goddesses whom the Romans were accustomed to regard as Earth-goddesses. But nothing surely would seem more inappropriate as an allegorical presentment of Mother Earth than such peregrinations in a carriage. Those peripatetic habits are characteristic of all German goddesses. "They are thought of chiefly," says Grimm, "as divine mothers who travel round and visit houses, from whom the human race learns the occupations and arts of housekeeping and husbandry, spinning, weaving, tending the hearth, sowing, reaping."[1] It would no more occur to think of a 'personification of the earth' as spinning, weaving, and tending the hearth, than to picture her as careering about the country in a wagon.

In some of her most popular forms the goddess does not use a wagon as a means of transport, but a ship mounted on wheels and drawn on dry land, an even more startling mode of locomotion for Mother Earth. Even Tacitus felt the inappropriateness of the identification, and called accordingly the ship-faring goddess not Mother Earth but Isis.[2] The Egyptian Moon-goddess Isis is a very different personage, cosmologically considered, from Mother Earth. The ship-faring goddess of the Germans was honoured until late in the Middle Ages in Flanders, where she was the patroness of the famous Flemish weavers, who had taken over the ancient feminine industry. She was drawn at night in her ship by teams of weavers, and was accompanied by noisy crowds of women whose behaviour and costume, or lack of decent costume, were, according to an indignant cleric's account of those heathen rites, somewhat bacchanalian.[3]

Not only does our supposed Earth-goddess rumble about on carts and on boats provided with wheels and drawn by weavers; she also rushes through the air. She is part of the 'Furious Host' that may be seen rushing past at night. Freija, who, like other Teutonic goddesses, usually rides in a cart, drawn in this instance by cats, assumes as an alternative means of locomotion the wings of a falcon, and flies through the air.[4]

The Egyptian Isis was provided with a boat for a definite purpose, namely, to navigate the upper and the nether waters in her pilgrimage through the heavens and beneath the earth.

[1] J. Grimm, *Teutonic Mythology*, p. 250.
[2] Tacitus, *Germania*, ix.
[3] Rodulfus, *Gesta Abbatium Trudoniensium*, in Pertz, *Monumenta Germaniae Historica, Scriptores*, vol. x, pp. 309 sqq.
[4] P. D. Chantepie de la Saussaye, *The Religion of the Teutons*, p. 277; J. Grimm, *op. cit.*, p. 305.

Celestial bodies are in like manner habitually provided with chariots for the purpose of conveying them on their wanderings through the heavens. The moon and the sun are everywhere thought of, like the planets, as ' wanderers '; and are furnished with special means of transport, generally some car or carriage. If Teutonic goddesses must needs have chariots or ships, it is because they are by nature wanderers. The most definite of those goddesses is Freija, who appears to have gathered together in her personality, among the more northern Germanic tribes at any rate, all local goddesses. We retain her memory in the name of Friday. Freija was expressly a wanderer. Like Isis in search of Osiris, like Io and innumerable other goddesses, she wanders disconsolate in search of Odhr, or Odin.[1] It is not surprising that such wanderers should require carts and ships to convey them, but the picture scarcely fits with the conception of broad-based stability of Mother Earth as she was viewed in pre-Copernican times.

The other particular which Tacitus gives us concerning the Great Goddess of the Germans is that, after her journeys in a cart, she was given a bath.[2] Mother Earth certainly requires watering, but why she should be immersed in a pond is not obvious. It is usually with the heavenly bodies that such periodical immersions and ablutions are associated.

There is, as a matter of fact, a true personification of the earth in Nordic mythology. She is called Jordh, and is one of the wives of the Sky-god and the mother of the earth-born Thor. But that is all about her; she has no myth, no cult, no personality. She is, as all mere personifications of the earth are, a vague, inactive, otiose and unworshipped deity.[3]

The fundamental incongruities in the conception of the German goddesses as pure and simple personifications of the earth have not failed to attract at times the attention of investigators. Meyer gives up the classical identification and advances the theory that the German goddesses are clouds.[4] Jacob Grimm, although in his great work he does not venture to depart from the established tradition canonised by the authority of Tacitus, expresses in a later writing a very different view. He arrives at the conclusion that Freija resembles most closely the Thracian Moon-goddess whom Herodotus calls Artemis.[5] Freija was probably

---

[1] P. D. Chantepie de la Saussaye, op. cit., pp. 277 sq.; E. H. Meyer, Germanische Mythologie, pp. 197, 357.

[2] Tacitus, Germania, xl.

[3] P. D. Chantepie de la Saussaye, op. cit., pp. 239, 305.

[4] E. H. Meyer, Germanische Mythologie, pp. 267 sqq., 294 sqq., 349 sqq.

[5] J. Grimm, Kleinere Schriften, vol. v, pp. 416 sqq. On the Thracian Artemis, see below, p. 138.

the 'Isis' of Tacitus.[1] In mediaeval legend she figures as the 'Venus' famous from her association with Tannhäuser;[2] in Nordic mythology one of her favourite surnames is Mardoll, or Menglodh, that is, " She who shines over the sea." [3]

Teutonic mythology, barbaric though it be, is a complex growth which has undergone many transformations. The form in which it has reached us consists of very late and corrupted versions of old epics, the productions of Nordic ' scalds,' who used myths and legends as poetical themes with little regard for their religious or cosmogonic significances. In the euhemerised sagas we catch only dim glimpses of the myths whence they originated. There are indications that Freija, who is the possessor of a golden necklace—which is probably the Ring of the Nibelung—was originally the Sun-goddess. She appears to have been the heroine of a myth similar to those which we come upon in Melanesia, where the moon-god and his brother contend for the favours of the beautiful sun-woman.[4] As Freija-Venus, she conjoins beneath the earth with the moon-god, impersonated in the familiar version by Tannhäuser, in the same manner as in most savage mythologies.

Freija, the radicle of whose name is the same as in ' fru,' ' frau,' ' froon,' and means ' the woman,' was but vaguely differentiated from Frigga,[5] the horned goddess, who is avowedly the moon.[6] The Nordic peoples, says Olaus Magnus, " worship the moon." [7] " Many," says Olf Rudbeck, " are of opinion that the moon was honoured by them more than either the sun or the earth, and that the attributes and titles of the latter were assigned to the moon." [8] Caesar, who was perhaps in a better position than Tacitus to know something of the German barbarians, says that " the only gods of the Germans are the Sun, Vulcan, and the Moon." [9]

The most prominent male figure of the Nordic pantheon was Wotan, who is identical with Odin. Like the Egyptian Horus throughout most of his career, Wotan is one-eyed; and the story of how he lost his other eye is of interest. Wotan, like most male gods of the Nordic pantheon, was, in spite of the exalted

---

[1] P. D. Chantepie de la Saussaye, *op. cit.*, p. 104.

[2] J. Grimm, *Teutonic Mythology*, p. 306 n.

[3] P. D. Chantepie de la Saussaye, *op. cit.*, p. 279.

[4] O. L. Jiriczek, *Northern Hero Legends*, pp. 131 sq. Cf. p. 51.

[5] O. Rudbeck, *Atlantis*, Part ii, p. 493.

[6] *Ibid.*, pp. 215, 240, 319, 607.

[7] Olaus Magnus, *Historia de gentibus septentrionalibus*, iii. 2.

[8] O. Rudbeck, *op. cit.*, p. 609.

[9] Caesar, *De bello Gallico*, vi. 21.

position he occupied, deficient in prophetic powers. When he wanted to know the future he was compelled to have recourse to goddesses, in the same manner as his earthly counterparts had to resort to prophetic women.[1] He had, however, access to another oracle, a male god, who served him as adviser, and assisted him in the difficult task of fulfilling adequately his duties as Supreme God under the serious handicap of lacking information as to the course which events might take. That helpful god was an old primitive watery deity of springs, wells, and vegetation, who became somewhat forgotten in the luxuriant growth of heroic sagas, although he still plays an alleged comic part in Wagner's operas. His name was Mime, or Mimir. Wotan consulted Mime by looking down a well; but as a fee to the oracular god for his vaticinations Wotan had to leave him one of his eyes, which remained in the well.[2] The watery god thus appears to have been in the habit of swallowing one of Wotan's eyes. And in fact the dwelling-place of Wotan's lost eye was the world-tree Yggdrasil, which was no other than Mime's tree, growing out of his well.[3] Wotan, who is usually called ' The Wanderer,' had, like the Sun-maiden, a ring, Draupnir, from which every ninth night there dropped eight equal parts.[4] The nature of the supreme Teutonic god, Wotan, who is generally described as a ' wind-god,' would thus seem to be fairly transparent.[5]

The Great Goddesses of the Celts.

The Great Goddess was as primeval among the Celts as among the Teutonic races.[6] The Irish Gaels called themselves Fir Dea,

[1] Knut Gjerset, *History of the Norwegian Peoples*, vol. i, p. 96.

[2] E. Morgk, " Mythologie," in H. Paul, *Grundriss der Germanischen Philologie*, vol. iii, p. 305. Mime was in later mythology a decayed god, but there is evidence that he had seen better days. We know him as a dwarf, but in older sagas he appears, on the contrary, as a giant. Towns were named after him, and the waves of the sea were his sons (E. Morgk, *op. cit.*, p. 306 ; P. D. Chantepie de la Saussaye, *op. cit.*, p. 232).

[3] P. D. Chantepie de la Saussaye, *op. cit.*, pp. 348 sq. Cf. above, vol. ii, p. 630.

[4] K. Müllenhoff, *Deutsche Alterthumskunde*, vol. iv, pp. 642 sqq.

[5] So-called wind gods are generally moon-gods, the winds being, like all atmospheric disturbances, regarded as manifestations of the moon. The Mexican Quetzalcoatl, for example, is commonly described as a wind-god. The identification of Wotan with the wind in particular is of comparatively recent origin (see W. Golther, *Handbuch der germanischen Mythologie*, pp. 283 sqq.). He is sometimes a triune god : Wotan-Donar-Ziu, the Mercury, Mars, Hercules of Tacitus (see H. Usener, " Dreiheit," *Rheinisches Museum*, lviii, p. 31).

[6] " The goddesses are, comparatively speaking, more conspicuous than

'The men of the Goddess.'[1] The mythical race of gods and heroes from which they were descended were the Tuatha De Danann, 'the tribes of the goddess Danu.'[2] 'Danu' is probably a contraction of Dea Anu, for she was also called Anu, or Aine, 'The Mother,' and Bu Anu, 'The Good Mother.'[3] She was "the mother of the Irish gods."[4] One of her most usual names was Brigit, or Brigantia.[5] The great goddess Anu, or Brigit, was by no means a special Irish goddess; she was the great goddess of all the Celts, both in Britain and in Gaul. Although some thirty-five appellatives or epithets of Celtic goddesses are known,[6] it would appear that they were not only identical in type, but recognised as such, and were for the most part referred to by the same names, Brigantia in Britain,[7] Briginto in Gaul.[8] The popularity of the great goddess Brigit in Ireland survived till recent times. The Irish, says a writer quoted by Camden, "make a practice of swearing at every third word, by the Trinity, God, St. Patrick, and Brigit."[9] "The piety of the Irish," says a recent author, "went so far as to some extent to confound Brigit with the Mother of God. Her votaries called her 'The Mary of the Gaels,' and even 'the Mother of Jesus.'"[10]

Celtic heathenism was, as regards the female form of the deity, like most religions, monotheistic and at the same time trinitarian. There were 'three Brigits,' represented either as sisters, or as the three daughters of the goddess.[11] The three Brigits are also 'The

the gods in Irish legend" (J. Rhys, *Transactions of the Third International Congress for the History of Religions*, Section VII, President's Address, vol. ii, p. 212).

[1] J. Rhys, *Lectures on the Origin and Growth of Religion as Illustrated by Celtic Heathendom*, p. 579; J. A. MacCulloch, *The Religion of the Ancient Celts*, p. 63.

[2] J. Rhys, *loc. cit.*

[3] J. A. MacCulloch, *op. cit.*, p. 73. From Bu-Anu are probably derived 'Bononia,' and the names of the many towns in France and Panonia which bear that name. Boulogne-sur-mer was known to the Anglo-Saxons as Bunne (J. Rhys, in *Transactions of the Third International Congress for the History of Religions*, vol. ii, p. 213).

[4] *Sanas Chormaic*, p. 4.

[5] J. A. MacCulloch, *op. cit.*, p. 68; H. D'Arbois de Jubainville, *Le cycle mythologique irlandais et la mythologie celtique*, p. 155.

[6] E. Anwyl, "Ancient Celtic Deities," *Transactions of the Gaelic Society of Inverness*, xxvi, pp. 413 sq.

[7] J. Rhys, *Lectures on . . . Celtic Heathendom*, p. 89.

[8] H. D'Arbois de Jubainville, *op. cit.*, p. 146. All Celtic goddesses are referred to by Caesar as Minerva (Caesar, *De bello Gallico*, vi. 17).

[9] W. Camden, *Britannia*, vol. iii, p. 659.

[10] L. Gougard, "Les saints irlandais dans la tradition populaire des pays continentaux," *Revue Celtique*, xxxix, p. 202.

[11] J. A. MacCulloch, *op. cit.*, p. 68.

Three Blessed Ladies of Britain.'[1] The innumerable altars and inscriptions found in France and Britain and western Germany dedicated to the Three Mothers, or Ladies, refer, there can be no doubt, to the triune Celtic goddess.[2] Brigit had three sons, Bryan, Iuchar, and Uar, who are usually represented by Bryan alone ; [3] they had three wives, Erin, Bamba, and Fotla, of whom the first generally stands for all three.[4] They had also three concubines, but had only one son between them.[5]

'The Mothers' are usually represented bearing babes on their laps, or carrying baskets containing the fruits of the earth, and are thus regarded as goddesses of fertility. The Celtic Mother, Anu, comes close to being identified with Mother Earth ; two hills in county Kerry are called her paps.[6] Dionysius Periegetes identifies the deities served by the priestesses of Nantes with Demeter and Persephone.[7] Like the Germanic goddesses, the Celtic goddess was, at Autun, under the name of Berecynthia—obviously a Latinised form of Brigindo—perambulated round the cornfields and the vineyards ; [8] and an inscription at Vaucluse refers to the chariot of Anu.[9] In his life of Saint Martin, Saint Sulpicius tells us that " it was the custom of the Gaulish peasants to carry round their fields the wretched emblems of their false gods, the productions of insanity, covered with a white veil." [10]

The rites of the Celtic goddess were not, however, purely bucolic. The Nantes priestesses offered her human victims.[11] The warriors of the queen-priestess Boudicca impaled men on trees in honour of her goddess, Andaste, whose name looks like a compound of Anu.[12] At Dane's Hill, in Leicestershire, there is a cave which is known at the present day as 'Black Annis's Bower,' that is, 'Black Anu's Bower' ; and she is represented as a

[1] J. Rhys, op. cit., p. 527.
[2] E. Anwyl, " Ancient Celtic Goddesses," The Celtic Review, iii, pp. 29 sqq. Cf. below, p. 160.
[3] H. D'Arbois de Jubainville, op. cit., p. 68.
[4] J. A. MacCulloch, op. cit., p. 73.
[5] H. D'Arbois de Jubainville, op. cit., pp. 373 sq.
[6] Sanas Chormaic, p. 4.
[7] Dionysius Periegetes, Orbis descriptio, v. 570.
[8] Gregory of Tours, Liber de gloria confessorum, in J. P. Migne, Patrologiae Cursus, vol. lxxi, col. 884.
[9] J. Rhys, in Transactions of the Third International Congress for the History of Religions, vol. ii, p. 213.
[10] S. Sulpicius Severus, Vita S. Martini, in Corpus Scriptorum Ecclesiasticorum Latinorum, vol. i, p. 122.
[11] Strabo, iv. 4. 6.
[12] Xiphilinus, lxii. The name is variously spelt Andraste, Andaste ; the latter appears to be the reading of the oldest MSS. An inscription found near Southampton mentions the Dea Ancasta (E. Anwyl, " Ancient Celtic Goddesses," The Celtic Review, iii, p. 46).

savage woman who eats men.[1] Anu was supposed to make men mad. There is a stone near Dunany known as " the chair of Aine, or the chair of lunatics " ; anyone sitting on it went raving mad.[2]

Anu ruled the sea.[3] The Three Brigits had, like the goddess of the Eskimo, a palace at the bottom of the sea.[4] The goddess presided over all rivers, springs and wells, and many, such as Bridewell, are named after her.[5] The stepping-stones over streams in Ireland are believed to have been placed there by Anu, and floods, it is said, can never rise above them.[6] In Wales the Three Brigits are the three sisters Arianrhod, that is ' Silver Wheel,' who descend into the sea.[7] The sorceresses who play the part of heroines in the Arthurian cycle are undoubtedly the ancient Celtic goddesses, or ' fées,' or fates.[8] One of them is called in the Norman-French version, Luned, or Lunéte.[9] In the south of France the goddess was called ' The Shining One.' [10] In her temples, not in Ireland alone, but also at Bath and in Hesse, perpetual fires were maintained.[11] She was in some of her forms identified by the Romans with Diana, and temples of the goddess are known to have existed in Monmouth-shire, in Westmorland, and in London.[12] Nehelauia, who is said to be the same as Anu, was the new moon.[13] By the Sequani she was worshipped as Mona, or Mena, that is, the moon, and the Gauls prayed to her for the welfare of their women.[14] The goddess is reputed to have been a wonderful reaper ; she " carries, that is, the moon's sickle." [15] A popular name for her in Ireland was Cailleach Bhiarach, that is, ' the old woman with the horns.' [16] In county Clare she is declared to have been a cow.[17] Irish antiquaries

[1] *Leicestershire County Folklore*, p. 4.

[2] N. O'Kearney, " Folk-Lore," *Transactions of the Kilkenny Archaeological Society*, ii, p. 35.

[3] *Ibid.*, p. 36.

[4] J. Rhys, *Lectures on . . . Celtic Heathendom*, p. 161.

[5] J. A. MacCulloch, *op. cit.*, pp. 42 sq.

[6] D. Fitzgerald, " Popular Tales of Ireland," *Revue Celtique*, iv, p. 189.

[7] J. Rhys, *op. cit.*, p. 161 ; J. A. MacCulloch, *op. cit.*, p. 109.

[8] See A. Nutt, *Studies on the Legend of the Holy Grail*, pp. 232 sqq.

[9] *The Mabinogion*, transl. by Lady Charlotte Guest, pp. 3 sqq.

[10] J. A. MacCulloch, *op. cit.*, p. 41.

[11] *Ibid.*

[12] W. Camden, *Britannia*, vol. ii, pp. 5, 480 ; vol. iii, p. 153.

[13] James Logan, *The Scottish Gaël*, vol. ii, p. 332.

[14] *Ibid.* For the prevalence of the worship of Diana among the Britons, see also Jehan de Waurin, " Recueil des croniques et anchiennes istories de la Grant Bretaigne, à présent nommé Engleterre," *Chronicles and Memorials of England and Scotland* (1864), vol. i, p. 65.

[15] D. Fitzgerald, *op. cit.*, p. 189.

[16] *Ibid.*, p. 188.

[17] *Ibid.*, p. 189.

would appear to be justified in the conclusion that "Cailleach Bhiarach seems, like Anu, to be the moon." [1]

The great midsummer festival was called in the Limousin ' La Lunade.' [2] At Vallon de la Suille the wood where the festival was held is called ' Bois de la Lune.' [3] Solstice festivals are not, as is sometimes assumed, necessarily solar festivals. Many primitive peoples who have no inkling of the solar year are yet familiar with the periodical changes in the seasons, which they recognise by the concomitant changes in vegetation, or, as in some parts of Indonesia and New Guinea, by the changes in the prevailing winds. The yearly winter and summer festivals have quite commonly reference to the moon and not to the sun. Where the solar year is unknown the midsummer and midwinter ceremonies correspond only roughly to the solstices, and their yearly date is not fixed, but variable within considerable limits. This was the case with the great Irish festivals of Samhain and Belthane held at midwinter and midsummer respectively. [4] The French midsummer ' Lunade ' began not at sunrise, but at the rising of the moon ; [5] and so did the Irish festivals. One of the chief sites of the Belthane festivals in Ireland was Cnoc Aine, that is, the ' Hill of Anu,' and the ceremony could not be performed unless the moon stood in a certain position with regard to the hill. [6] Even in later times " Aine was much dreaded by the old people on the Friday, Saturday and Sunday following La Lughnasa (Lammas Day), for these three days were supposed to have been sacred to her in conjunction with Crom Dubh, or Crom Cruaich." All work was abstained from during those days, and the Irish were particularly careful to avoid bathing or fishing. [7] The winter festival, or Samhain, was said to have been instituted by a legendary king, who " erected a magnificent temple, called Fluchta, sacred to the fire of Samhain and to the Samnothei, or priests of the Moon." [8]

---

[1] D. Fitzgerald, op. cit. ; N. O'Kearney, " Folk-Lore," Transactions of the Kilkenny Archaeological Society, ii, p. 36.

[2] M. Deloche, " La procession dite ' de la Lunade ' et les feux de la Saint-Jean à Tulle (Bas Limousin). La Fête du solstice d'été," Revue Celtique, ix, p. 439.

[3] D. Monnier, Traditions populaires comparées, pp. 174, 222.

[4] J. A. MacCulloch, op. cit., pp. 175 sq.; Id., in Hastings's Encyclopaedia of Religion and Ethics, vol. iii, pp. 78 sq.

[5] M. Deloche, " La procession dite de la Lunade," Revue Celtique, ix, p. 439.

[6] D. Fitzgerald, " Popular Tales of Ireand," Revue Celtique, iv, pp. 186 sqq.

[7] N. O'Kearney, " Folk-Lore," Transactions of the Kilkenny Archaeological Society, ii, pp. 35 sq.

[8] S. O'Halloran, A General History of Ireland from the Earliest Accounts, vol. i, p. 221.

Such temples were doubtless originally circles of megalithic stones such as abound in Celtic and Nordic countries. In his account of the priestesses of Nantes, Strabo mentions that their temple was roofed with thatch, but that the curious rule was observed of unroofing it once a year at the time of the chief festival.[1] " This," as Sir John Rhys observes, " clearly implies that originally it had no roof but the sky, as is the case with Stonehenge and other stone circles." [2] Those stone circles are known in Norway as ' horgs ' ; and in the Edda the goddess Freija refers, in speaking of the hero Ottar, to the

> horg he built me
> made of stone ;
> now the stones have turned to glass.
> With fresh blood
> of oxen he sprinkled them.
> Ottar always believed in the Goddesses.[3]

In the Orkneys such a stone circle is known at the present day to the native inhabitants as " the temple of the moon." [4]

Crom Cruaich, the god who was associated with Anu in the festival of Dalhain, was a huge idol, the largest in Ireland, to whom human sacrifices were offered ; he represented the god Dagda, and his name means " The Bloody Crescent." [5] Dagda was the supreme god of the Irish, the chief of the Tuatha De Danann, and therefore the racial ancestor of the Irish people. The Crescent god was, like the goddess, triune, bearing three names and being three persons while yet remaining one.[4] Like the great goddess, he was not a special Irish deity, but common to all the Celts. " The Gauls affirm," says Caesar, " that they are all descended from Pluto (Dis pater)." [7] The Celtic deities equated by the Romans with Pluto or Dis have generally been described as " gods of the dead," or " deities of the underworld." But such expressions are misleading. All ancestral gods are ' deities of the dead ' in the sense that the privileged and initiated dead join their ancestors, and all primitive religions are ' ghost

---

[1] Strabo, iv. 4. 6.
[2] J. Rhys, Lectures on . . . Celtic Heathendom, p. 197.
[3] Knut Gjerset, History of the Norwegian Peoples, vol. i, p. 108.
[4] James Logan, The Scottish Gaël, vol. ii, p. 360.
[5] H. D'Arbois de Jubainville, op. cit., p. 106 ; J. A. MacCulloch, The Religion of the Ancient Celts, p. 79 ; Whitley Stokes, " Rennes Dindsenchas," Revue Celtique, xvi, pp. 35 sqq. ; " The versified Dinnshenchas of Mag Slecht," in The Voyage of Bran, ed. by K. Meyer, vol. ii, pp. 301 sqq. ; cf. A. Nutt, ibid., pp. 149 sq.
[6] Sanas Chormaic, pp. 47, 444 ; H. D'Arbois de Jubainville, op. cit., p. 375.
[7] Caesar, De bello Gallico, vi. 28.

religions.' In primitive eschatology the main aim as regards the after-life is not reward or paradise, but the privilege of being united with one's own people, the tribal ancestors. The ancestral god— and all gods are originally ancestral gods—is thus invariably a 'god of the dead,' in the same sense as Abraham, in whose bosom Jews hoped to rest, might be called therefore a 'god of the dead.' But there is no 'underworld' character necessarily attaching to such a function; the charge of ghosts belonging 'ex officio' to the ancestral god nowise debars him from exercising other functions.

Dagda gave harvests and kine, and was a god of fertility, as was Pluto. The Gaulish form of the Crescent god of Samhain is readily recognisable in Cernunnos, the horned god pictured and named on a considerable number of monuments in France.[1] He is probably equivalent to the three-headed god, who also commonly occurs.[2] In his enumeration of the gods of the Gauls, Caesar does not mention Pluto, but places Mercury first.[3] The two are in all probability the same, Mercury being, like Pluto, the giver of wealth, and his purse being equivalent to Pluto's horn of abundance. The Gaulish 'Mercury' was the largest idol of the Gauls, as the Crom Cruaich statue of Dagda of the Irish; it stood on the top of Puy de Dôme, the highest mountain in Gaul.[4]

As in other mythologies, the 'father' was duplicated in 'the son.' The divine son of Dagda was Lug, who frequently changes places with him, and is also equated with Nuada Argetlan, " of the silver hand," king of the Tuath De Dannan.[5] He is the British Ludd, and the Gaulish Lugd, or Lugus, patron and founder of many cities in Gaul and Britain, such as Lyons (Lugdunum) and London (Caer Ludd).[6] He was worshipped at Ludgate Hill, in association with the moon-goddess called by the Romans Diana.[7]

---

[1] A. Bertrand, *Religion des Gaulois*, pp. 314 sqq. Particularly interesting is the Beaune altar (*op. cit.*, p. 317) in which a triad of gods is represented, one of whom is three-headed, and another horned. Above the triad is a figure crowned with the lunar crescent.

[2] *Ibid.*, pp. 341 sqq.; J. A. MacCulloch, *op. cit.*, p. 33.

[3] Caesar, *De bello Gallico*, vi.

[4] Pliny, *Nat. Hist.*, xxxiv. 18.

[5] H. D'Arbois de Jubainville, *op. cit.*, pp. 175, 293; J. Rhys, *op. cit.*, p. 124.

[6] J. A. MacCulloch, *op. cit.*, p. 114; J. Rhys, *op. cit.*, pp. 125, 129; H. D'Arbois de Jubainville *op. cit.*, pp. 304 sq. Professor de Jubainville counts four cities of the name of Lugdunum in France. Carlisle was anciently called Lug Ballum (W. Camden, *Britannia*, vol. iii, p. 174). The original name of the city of the Parisii was Lug-tetia (*ibid.*), so that both Paris and London were named after the same god.

[7] J. Rhys, *op. cit.*, pp. 125, 129; J. A. MacCulloch, *op. cit.*, p. 114;

This prominent double of the chief Celtic god is still honoured in various parts of Ireland as a Christian saint, under the names of St. Luan, Eluan, Lugidus, Lugad. " The foundations with which the saint under some of his aliases is connected," writes an Irish antiquary, " extend over eight counties in the provinces of Ulster, Leinster, and Munster. Luan is to this day the common Irish word for the moon. We read that there were fifteen saints of the name of Lugadius ; and as Lugidus was one of Luan's aliases, I have set them all down as representing the moon in the several places where the planet was worshipped as the symbol of female nature." [1]

Celtic, like Hebrew mythology, has reached us in the euhemerised form of professed mythical annals, which were edited in Christian times and in which all gods are reduced to the proportions of heroes and wizards, and their doings are represented as ' invasions of Ireland,' and pseudo-history. Sir John Rhys's Hibbert Lectures on Celtic Heathendom are still perhaps the most charming general account of those myths ; but it was composed in the eighties, when Professor Max Müller pontificated over the nascent science of comparative religion. The myths of the Celts, liberally seasoned with references to the Vedas and to Sanskrit etymologies, are accordingly presented by Sir John Rhys exclusively in the guise of solar myths. Some of the resulting incongruities have been pointed out by Canon MacCulloch and others ; but the most startling one is exhibited to his readers by Sir John Rhys himself. After close on six hundred pages of warlike sun-gods, including Lug, sun-heroes, and solar battles, we are suddenly brought up with a shock against the fact that in all Celtic languages and dialects the sun is without exception feminine.[2] Sir John Rhys points out the fact with perfect candour, though with some distress, and is at a loss to account for that extraordinary disregard on the part of his ancestors for the views of Professor Max Müller. But there could not be allegories of the sun's course where that course was not known or

W. Camden, *Britannia*, vol. ii, p. 5. The annexes of old St. Paul's were referred to in the Church Records seen by Camden as ' Camera Dianae.'

[1] M. Keane, *The Towers and Temples of Ancient Ireland*, p. 59. It appears beyond doubt that St. Leger, the Saint under whose special patronage the midsummer festival was held in the Limousin, in France, was likewise a successor of Lugidus, or Lugd (M. Deloche, " La procession dite de la Lunade," *Revue Celtique*, ix, pp. 429 sqq.).

[2] J. Rhys, *Lectures on . . . Celtic Heathendom*, pp. 572 sqq. Cf. A. B. Cook, " The European Sky God," *Folk-lore*, xviii, p. 49. Mr. Cook suggests that, the sun being feminine and the moon masculine in Celtic languages, the Celtic goddesses must have been sun-goddesses and the gods moon-gods. But the attributes and characters of Celtic goddesses which have been noted above render Mr. Cook's hypothesis inadmissible.

observed. The Celtic year was lunar. Pliny tells us that
the Celts counted the beginnings of years and of months by the
moon;[1] and Caesar says, " they reckon all time, not by days,
but by nights, and when they calculate the dates of births, or the
beginnings of months or years, they are always careful to put the
night before the day," [2] a mode of reckoning which is common to
all early cultures, and of which traces survive in such terms as
' fortnight ' and ' sennight.' [3]

It is more than doubtful whether there ever were any native sun-
gods among the Celts. " Perhaps the most important object in
nature to the early Celts as to most primitive folks," remarks Canon
MacCulloch, " was the moon." [4] The orisons which peasant women
in the north of England address to the moon are older than Christianity.[5] The observance is carried out in every part of Scotland.[6]
In Ireland, according to a writer quoted by Camden, the common
people, when they first see the moon, " fall down on their knees and
repeat the Lord's prayer ; and near the wane address themselves to
the moon with a loud voice, ' Leave us as well as thou hast found
us.' " [7] In Brittany likewise " it was the established custom to
kneel before the moon and recite the Sunday prayer in her
honour." [8] In other parts of France the Church had, as late as
the seventeenth century, not succeeded in weaning the people
from their habit of speaking of the moon as ' Our Lord,' or, as
they did at Noyon, as ' The Lord of Lords.' [9]

The moon was the supreme deity of the Basques, and the word
which is used at the present day in the Basque language for ' God '
is the same as for ' moon.' [10] How far the Celtiberians, that is, the
Celtic populations which crossed the Pyrenees and established
themselves in Spain, adopted the cults of the country or imported
their own, is not known. However that may be, they worshipped
the moon after the orthodox manner of primitive savages ; men,
women and children turned out of doors at the full moon, and
danced unremittingly the whole night regardless of fatigue.[11]

[1] Pliny, Nat. Hist., xvi. 45.

[2] Caesar, De bello gallico, vi. 18.

[3] In some parts of France the word ' ennuit ' is still used instead of
' aujourd'hui ' ; M. Deloche, " La procession dite de la Lunade," Revue
Celtique, ix, p. 444.

[4] J. A. MacCulloch, op. cit., p. 175.   [5] See above, vol. ii, p. 433.

[6] R. C. Maclagan, Our Ancestors, Scots, Picts, and Cymri, p. 4.

[7] W. Camden, Britannia, vol. iii, p. 659.

[8] H. Gaidoz, " Superstitions de la Basse-Bretagne au XVIIᵉ siècle,"
Revue Celtique, xi, p. 435.

[9] J.-B. Thiers, Traité des superstitions qui regardent les sacremens, etc.,
vol. i, p. 14 ; S. Owen (Audaenus), Vita S. Eligii, p. 216.

[10] A. H. Hovelacque, E. Picot et J. Vinson, Mélanges de linguistique et
d'anthropologie, p. 209.

[11] Strabo, iii. 4. 16.

The worship of the Celtiberians did not differ from that which was general among the inhabitants of the peninsula. At Ebura, near Cordova, there was in the time of Strabo a famous temple of the native Moon-god; [1] the Sacred Promontory of Cape St. Vincent was probably dedicated to the same deity, which was represented by standing stones and was believed to haunt the spot at night; [2] and the goddess ' Noctiluca ' was worshipped at Malaga.[3] The usual symbol on native Spanish coins is the lunar crescent.[4]

Primitive Semitic Religion.

With the whole Semitic race the cult of the moon as representing the supreme cosmic power was from earliest known times, and remained, the foundation of all theological development, even after the migrants from Arabia settled in the fertile lands of Mesopotamia and Syria and became agriculturists. " With all Semitic peoples, who at one time were all nomads," remarks Weber, " the moon was originally the supreme deity." [5] A curious Talmudic tradition represents the moon as complaining to Yahweh on account of the latter having caused the pristine importance of the luminary to become diminished. " The moon," says Rabbi Simeon Ben Asai, " spake to God, and said, ' O Lord of the world, it is not possible for two kings to wear the same crown.' Then said the Lord God, ' Begone, and become thou smaller.' And the moon answered, ' Because I have spoken a reasonable thing, why should I on that account become smaller ? ' Then said God, ' Go and rule thou by day as well as by night.' But the moon replied, ' O Lord of the world, of what use is a light at midday ? ' And God said, ' Go, Israel shall reckon his days and his years by thee.' Whereupon the moon said, ' That is not enough.' And God said, ' The righteous shall be named after thee.' But as the moon was not even then satisfied, the Lord God said, ' Make ye a sin-offering on my behalf, for I have caused the moon to become smaller.' " [6] That strange dialogue appears to be inspired by the tradition that the religion of Yahweh, among the Jews, displaced an older cult in which the moon occupied a position of greater importance.

[1] Strabo, iii. 1. 9.

[2] Avienus, *Ora maritima*, 215 sq., 309 sqq.; Diodorus Siculus, iii. 59. 1; Strabo, iii. 1. 4. Cf. C. Philipon, *Les Ibères*, p. 203.

[3] Avienus, *Ora maritima*, 429 sq.; cf. 367.

[4] P. A. Boudard, *Études sur l'alphabet ibérien et sur quelques monnaies autonomes d'Espagne*, pp. 74 sq.; J. Zobel de Zangronitz, " Spanische Münzen und bisher unerklärte Aufschriften," *Zeitschrift der deutschen morgenländische Gesellschaft*, xvii, pp. 337 sqq.

[5] O. Weber, *Arabien vor dem Islam*, p. 19.

[6] Rabbi Simeon Ben Asai, *Jalkut Shimoni*, fol. 4 (*Monumenta Hebraica*, vol. i, p. 206); J. A. Eisenmenger, *Entdecktes Judenthum*, vol. i, pp. 39 sq.

Moses Maimonides expressed the consciousness of the same fact in the traditions of the race by saying that moon-worship was the religion of Adam.[1] The crescent is still the badge of Islam,[2] as it was the emblem of Israel,[3] and when Muhammad overthrew the old religion of Arabia he was not strong enough to defy and offend the immemorial sentiment of the Arab people. The divine mission of the prophet was reconciled with the old religion by representing the Islamic reform as receiving the sanction of the immemorial deity. The moon, according to Arab tradition, had descended from heaven and had bowed down, doing homage to the Prophet. According to another version, he was transfigured in the rays of the moon, which penetrated his garments and filled his body with light.[4] Arab women at the present day insist that the moon is the parent of mankind.[5]

Herodotus says that the Arabs " have no other divinities than Dionysos and Urania."[6] As both Dionysos and Urania, that is, Ishtar or Aphrodite, are definitely lunar deities, the statement implies that the sole divinities of the Arabs were the male and the female form of the Moon deity. In some parts of Abyssinia, which was originally peopled from Arabia, the character of the ancient Arabian religion appears to have been preserved until the present day. The Shangalla are said to " worship various trees, serpents, and the moon."[7] The deciphering of the numerous inscriptions of ancient Arabia has of late years elucidated much that was obscure in the history of the country before Islamic times. They show everywhere the moon deity as the most prominent object of cult, whether in Hadramaut, Kataban, or the Minaean kingdom.[8] In

[1] T. Harley, *Moon Lore*, p. 90.
[2] Some think that the crescent moon, which was the badge of Ephesus, the sacred city of the Asiatic Artemis, and thus became the badge of the Ephesian colony of Byzantium, was adopted by the Turks together with many usages and traditions of the Byanztine empire (see A. Zernitz, *La Luna*, p. 6). But the national emblem of Byzantium was not the crescent, but the double-headed eagle, which originated with the Hittites. The crescent as symbol of Islam is far older than the conquest of Constantinople, and figures in the same capacity in the time of Omar. It is the most conspicuous symbol in the oldest Arabian inscriptions of the Yemen and of every other part of Arabia.
[3] M. Seligsohn, in *The Jewish Encyclopaedia*, vol. viii, p. 678.
[4] F. von Schlegel, *The Philosophy of History*, p. 325; A. Zernitz, *La Luna*, p. 6.
[5] S. I. Curtiss, *Primitive Semitic Religion To-day*, p. 106.
[6] Herodotus, i. 8.
[7] J. Bruce, *Travels to Discover the Sources of the Nile*, vol. ii, p. 554.
[8] D. Nielsen, *Die altarabische Mondreligion und die mosaische Ueberlieferung*, pp. 13, 19, 37; F. Hommel, *Der Gestirndienst der alten Araber und die altisraelitische Ueberlieferung*, pp. 9 sq.; Id., *The Ancient Hebrew Tradition and the Monuments*, p. 80; E. Glaser, *Die Abessinier in Arabien*

early Babylonia the cult of the lunar deity constituted the national religion. The name Chaldeans means 'moon worshippers.' " With respect to the name Chaldean," says Sir G. Rawlinson, " perhaps the most probable account of the origin of the word is that it designates properly the inhabitants of the ancient capital, Ur or Hur, Khaldi being in the Burbur dialect the exact equivalent of Hur, which was the proper name of the Moon-god, and 'Chaldeans' being thus either 'moon-worshippers,' or simply the inhabitants of the town dedicated to, and called after the moon." [1]

The most general name of the moon-god, in ancient Babylonia, was Sinn, which is still the ordinary Syrian name for the moon ; the Kurds at the present day speak of the moon as Sheikh Sinn.[2] The name is equally prominent in Arabian inscriptions down to the farthest southern extremity of the peninsula.[3] He bore, however, innumerable local names and cult-epithets ; the most common Minaean name, for example, was Wadd, which means 'Love.' [4] In Sumerian religion he appears under the names of Uru-ki, Nannar, and allied forms of those words.[5]

As with the moon-gods of all primitive peoples, we find from earliest times a tendency in the moon-god of the Semites, who, like all others, was " the special deity and protector of women," [6] to give rise to, or be associated with, a female counterpart. In fact, almost every name of the god has its corresponding feminine form.

The Great Goddess of Arabia was most generally known as Al-Uzza. We are told by Al-Kindy that Al-Uzza was the moon.[7] Her chief shrine, and the most famous and sacred spot of Arabia, was the Ka'aba at Mecca. The Khuraish, the tribe that had charge of the holy place, were in pre-Islamic times her priestly

---

und in Afrika, p. 72 ; F. Tuch, "Sinaitischen Inschriften,' *Zeitschrift der deutschen morgenländische Gesellschaft*, iii, p. 202.

[1] G. Rawlinson, *The Five Great Monarchies*, vol. i, p. 56.

[2] E. Combe, *Histoire du culte de Sin en Babylonie et en Assyrie*, p. 90.

[3] F. Hommel, *The Ancient Hebrew Tradition and the Monuments*, p. 80 ; Id., *Aufsätze und Abhandlungen*, pp. 149 sq., 156, 158 sq. ; E. Osiander, "Studien über die vorislamische Religion der Araber," *Zeitschrift der deutschen morgenländische Gesellschaft*, xix, p. 288.

[4] D. Nielsen, *Die altarabische Mondreligion*, p. 37. "The Father is Wadd" is a stereotyped expression in Minaean inscriptions. The Nazarenes in their spiritualisation of the old Semitic deity, may possibly have had in their mind some allusion to the ancient Minaean name of the god when they declared that "God is love." The pre-Islamic god Vadd mentioned in the Kuran (see J. Wellhausen, *Reste des arabischen Heidentums*, pp. 14 sqq.) is clearly the old Minaean god.

[5] M. Jastrow, *The Religion of Babylon and Assyria*, p. 68 ; L. W. King, *Babylonian Religion and Mythology*, p. 17 ; F. Hommel *op. cit.*, p. 64.

[6] D. Nielsen, *op. cit.*, p. 35.

[7] Al-Kindy, *The Apology*, p. 17.

caste and bore the title of ' Abd al-Ussah,' that is, ' the servants of Al-Uzza ' ; but her immediate service in the temple of Mecca was performed by aged priestesses.[1] At the present day the guardians of the Ka'aba are known as the Beni Shaybah, that is, ' the Sons of the Old Woman.' Popular tradition relates how Abraham, when he founded the Ka'aba, bought the ground from an old woman to which it belonged. She, however, consented to part with it only on the condition that she and her descendants for all time should have the key of the place in their keeping.[2] The tradition manifestly refers to the priestesses of Al-Uzza, and represents the male god, Abraham, as a later intruder in the sanctuary. The Great Goddess was worshipped in the Ka'aba in the form of a sacred stone,[3] which, there can be no doubt, was none other than the famous black stone which is still the most sacred object in Islam.[4] When he abolished the ' idols ' of the old religion, Muhammad, whose dominating ideal was to unite all Arabian tribes into a single political body bound by a common cult, felt it to be undesirable or impracticable to do away with the most sacrosanct object or symbol of the old religion. Thus Muslim pilgrims from all quarters of the globe proceed to Mecca to this day chiefly with the purpose of kissing the ancient image of the Great Goddess of Arabia.[5] As in most other shrines in Semitic and also in Greek lands, the aniconic stone of the deity stood by a sacred spring, or well, the Zemzem, whose sacred waters are drunk by all good Muslims. She was also represented in the form of three samura palms, which stood, and still stand, by her stone ; for, like so many other moon-deities, the Great Goddess was threefold, being at the same time one and three, "the three Holy Virgins," Al-Ilat, Al-Uzza, and Manat.[6] ' Al-Uzza,' is merely a cult epithet, meaning ' the Powerful One ' ; Al-Ilat is the feminine form of Ilu, or Allah, and may be rendered ' the Goddess.' [7]   Manat, which is the feminine form

---

[1] L. Krehl, *Ueber die Religion der vorislamischen Araber*, pp. 76 sq. ; E. Osiander, *op. cit.*, pp. 482 sq. ; J. Wellhausen, *Reste des arabischen Heidentums*, pp. 34 sqq.

[2] R. F. Burton, *Personal Narrative of a Pilgrimage to Al-Madinah and Meccah*, vol ii, p. 161, n.

[3] L. Krehl, *loc. cit.* Cf. J. Hamilton, *Sinai, the Hedjaz and Soudan*, p. 151.

[4] The identity of the Black Stone with the Great Goddess and with the moon is recognised by the Hulama, or rationalist school of Islam (R. F. Burton, *op. cit.*, vol. ii, p. 162).

[5] Muslims are charged with inconsistency by the Hindus, who taunt the denouncers of idols with being idol-worshippers themselves (R. F. Burton, *loc. cit.*, pp. 162 sq.).

[6] L. Krehl, *op. cit.*, p. 76 ; J. Wellhausen, *op. cit.*, pp. 24 sqq.

[7] L. Krehl, *op. cit.*, p. 80. For the wide diffusion of the cult of Al-Uzza

of Meni, stood particularly for the conception of fate or destiny. The word 'mana' is still commonly used by the Arabs in the sense of 'luck.' The threefold Arabian Goddess thus corresponds in character to the Greek Moirai, the Fates, and the Nordic Nornes.[1]

The great Arabian goddess was regarded by the Babylonians as identical with their goddess Ishtar.[2] Ishtar, however, appears to have had a somewhat different origin. Although she is very definitely a moon-goddess, her name is not that of the moon, but of the planet we still call Venus, using the Latin name of the Greek homologue of Ishtar, Aphrodite. Al-Uzza, on the other hand, is never identified with the planet Venus.[3] The identification of Ishtar with the morning and evening stars, throws an interesting light on her origin and on that of other goddesses.

The pre-Islamic Arabs are said to have worshipped the stars. Each tribe had its protecting star. Thus the Kais tribe were under the protection of Sirius, the Gudam tribe of the planet Jupiter, the Asad of Mercury, the Tajj under that of Canopus, and so forth.[4] The adoption of 'lucky stars' by the Arabian tribes, their so-called 'worship of the stars,' was, it is generally held by scholars, of comparatively late origin, and due to the influence of Babylonian astrology. Not only was Ishtar associated with the planet Venus, but all other Babylonian deities were similarly associated with some particular planet ; Bel-Marduk, for instance, with Jupiter, Nirgal with Saturn, Nabu with Mercury.[5] Of those astrological associations there is no indication before the time of Hammurabi.[6] The zodiacal stars were known to the ancient Arabs as "the houses of the moon." [7] Ishtar was associated not only with Venus, but also with Sirius, with the star

throughout Arabia see E. Osiander, *op. cit.*, p. 487 ; H. Dérembourg, "Le culte de la déesse Al'Ouzza dans l'ancienne Arabie vers l'an 300 de notre ère," *Verhandlungen der zweiten Kongress für allgemeine Religionsgeschichte* (1904), pp. 234 sq.; C. M. Doughty, *Travels in Arabia Deserta*, vol. ii, pp. 515 sq.

[1] Th. Nöldeke, "Vorstellung der Araber vom Schicksal," *Zeitschrift für Volkspsychologie und Sprachwissenschaft*, iii, pp. 132 sq.

[2] Herodotus, i. 131. Herodotus says that 'Mylitta' was identical with Al-Ilat. Mylitta is probably a corruption of Belitta, i.e. 'Our Lady,' and is a cult-epithet of Ishtar.

[3] J. Wellhausen, *op. cit.*, p. 44.

[4] E. Osiander, *op. cit.*, p. 498 ; L. Krehl, *op. cit.*, pp. 8 sq.

[5] F. Hommel, *The Ancient Hebrew Tradition as illustrated by the Monuments*, pp. 64 sq.; A. Jeremias, *Handbuch der altorientalischen Geisteskultur*, pp. 82 sqq.

[6] T. G. Pinches, "The Goddess Ištar in Assyro-Babylonian Literature," *Proceedings of the Society of Biblical Archaeology*, xxxi, p. 22 ; J. Wellhausen, *Reste des arabischen Heidentums*, p. 211.

[7] Abu'l Fadah, *Historia Ante-Islamica*, p. 181.

Virgo; in fact, with a different star for every month of the year.[1] She is the "Queen of the Stars."[2] The identification of Ishtar with the planet Venus has, however, nothing to do with those late astrological ideas, but is made clear by reference to the notions obtaining in other cosmologies. Among the Baluba of the Congo the morning and the evening stars are the two wives of the moon.[3] The natives of Sierra Leone likewise regard the planet Venus in her two aspects as the wife of the moon,[4] as do also the Ochi of West Africa.[5] The Australian natives of the Pennefather river have the same conception; the morning and evening stars are with them the two wives of the moon.[6] In Egypt, according to our information, Isis was identified with the star Sirius.[7] But it appears probable that Isis and Nephthys, the two wives of Osiris, were originally the evening and the morning star. The Hebrew god Yahweh was worshipped in the Jewish synagogue at Elephantine with two wives,[8] and the arrangement is found again in regard to the god Abraham and his two wives, Sarah and Hagar. The morning and evening star was, there can be little doubt, the 'wife,' that is to say the female counterpart, of the Moon-god.[9] When that female aspect of the lunar deity came to displace the male, the 'wife' of the Moon-god became identified with the moon itself, while the goddess Ishtar retained her association with the planet Venus. That identification is commonly represented in a symbolic manner by the astronomically incongruous emblem of the lunar crescent enclosing the star within its horns, which is still the crest of Islam.[10]

[1] T. G. Pinches, "Assyro-Babylonian Astrologers and their Lore," *The Expository Times*, xxx, p. 166; H. C. Rawlinson, *The Cuneiform Inscriptions of Western Asia*, vol. iii, pl. 30, 58, 316.

[2] Herodian, v. 6.

[3] R. P. Colle, *Les Baluba*, vol. ii, p. 715.

[4] N. W. Thomas, *Anthropological Report on Sierra Leone*, Part i, p. 179.

[5] R. A. Freman, *Travels in Ashanti and Jaman*, p. 289.

[6] W. E. Roth, *North Queensland Ethnography*, Bulletin No. 5, p. 7.

[7] R. V. Lanzone, *Dizionario di mitologia egizia*, pp. 825 sq.; Diodorus Siculus, i. 27. 4; Plutarch, *De Iside et Osiride*, xxi sq., xxxviii; Porphyry, *De antro nympharum*, xxiv.

[8] E. Meyer, *Der Papyrusfund von Elephantine*, pp. 59 sqq.; S. A. Cook, in *The Cambridge Ancieni History*, vol. i, p. 204.

[9] The 'wife' of the male Moon-god was known in Harran as Nigal, "The Lady," or "The Queen" (M. Jastrow, *The Religion of Babylonia and Assyria*, p. 411; D. Nielsen, *op. cit.*, p. 21; E. Osiander, *op. cit.*, p. 483).

[10] It has been supposed by some that in the clear sky of Babylonia the acute Chaldean observers succeeded in making out the phases of Venus. In support of that conjecture it is adduced that the "horns of Ishtar" are mentioned in the texts (A. Jeremias, *Handbuch der altorientalischen Geistes-kultur*, p. 79; T. G. Pinches, "The Goddess Ištar in Assyro-Babylonian

There was, however, nothing definite or constant about the relationship between the male and the female counterparts of the moon deity.   Ishtar is most commonly described in Babylonian religion as the daughter of Sinn;[1] in Hadramaut, Sinn is, on the contrary, the son of her male form Ashtar;[2] and in later Syrian cult that relationship is once more reverted to, the god being the son of the goddess.

The same variability and confusion obtain in all the genealogical relationships of Semitic mythology.   Various name-forms of deities are indifferently related to one another as father and son, or as son and father, as husband and wife or with sexes reversed, as wife and husband.   Nothing more is indicated by those relationships than the greater or lesser prominence of a given aspect or form at a given place or time.   " In Hebrew mythology," remarks Goldziher, " the figures represented as children are frequently only repetitions of one of their parents."[3]   The remark holds good of all Semitic mythology.   In the same manner as the male and female forms do not represent two different principles, such as heaven and earth, but duplications of one principle or deity, so the relationship of father or mother and offspring represents the latter as an emanation or aspect of the parent.   Each Arab tribe had its patron star ; nay, every individual had also his particular patron deity who was represented in his name.   But the tribal or individual patron was regarded as the hypostasis of the higher deity from which it emanated.   The principle, which was familiar as regards individual names, was no less clearly recognised in the tribal and local names of the gods ; they were consciously viewed as local forms of one another.   Hence the prevalence among the Semites of general names for those deities, such as ' The King,' ' The Lord,' ' Our Lady,' and thence, as also in accordance with the principle of

---

Literature," *Proceedings of the Society of Biblical Archaeology*, xxxi, pp. 23 sq.; J. Offord, "Ashteroth Karnaim," *ibid.*, xxi, pp. 173 sq.).   There is no need of such texts to inform us that Ishtar was horned.   Like Hathor and all Moon-goddesses of Western Asia, she was assimilated to a cow, but in her lunar, not in her planetary aspect.   It appears exceedingly improbable that the phases of Venus were observed by the Babylonians ; for considering that all the astronomical views of the ancients were directly derived from the discoveries of the Babylonian astronomers, so remarkable a fact could not have failed to be recorded and to have become generally known.   The phases of Venus were, on the contrary, unsuspected until discovered by Galilei, and nowhere is there any representation of the planet Venus as crescent-shaped. The supposition is quite unnecessary to account for the association of the moon-deity with the planet.

[1] M. Jastrow, *op. cit.*, p. 84.

[2] F. Hommel, *op. cit.*, p. 80.

[3] I. Goldziher, *Mythology among the Hebrews*, p. 126.

keeping the 'real name' of a deity secret, the practice of referring to that deity simply by a pronoun. The terms El, Ilu, Allah, and their feminine forms are merely the definite article, and have the force of pronouns ; they essentially signify He or She. The patron deity is frequently represented in proper names by such expressions as 'Ili,' 'My God,' or 'Ilu,' God.[1] The bearing of those views and usages on the development of monotheism is obvious.

Many of the more familiar deities in the Babylonian and Assyrian pantheons are of comparatively late growth. Bel-Marduk, the chief city-god of Babylon, is first heard of on the establishment of Hammurabi's empire, when Babylon displaced the ancient Ur and became the capital of an extended Mesopotamian dominion. He is the local god of Babylon and, whatever he may originally have been, his character is essentially that of a national and nationalistic god, and his cosmic features are subordinate to his political functions and character. The same is true of the majority of later Babylonian deities, and of Asshur, the national god of Assyria. They are political, not cosmic, gods. The two characters are necessarily conflicting and incompatible. A cosmic god representing a universal force of nature stands in the same relation to all countries and to all men ; a nationalistic and local god cannot assume cosmic functions without weakening his nationalism and patriotism. What cosmic significances and associations were retained by the political gods of Babylon were taken over from the older deities.

The oldest and most fundamental Babylonian deities recorded are a triad of male gods, Anu, En-Lil, and Ea, who are intimately associated with one another, are worshipped together, and are in fact three aspects of a triune god.[2] Anu is characterised as the heavenly deity, or rather, the deity of the waters above the earth, and pours those fertilising waters down from heaven, bringing forth vegetation. En-Lil, the original Bel, whose attributes as well as name were taken over by the national god Marduk,[3] has often been described as a deity of the earth, but is so only incidentally. He is said to be " the Lord of the Heavenly Earth," [4] and is represented in a clay shrine from Nippur as standing in the vault of heaven, surrounded by the stars.[5] He is the father of the moon, which is called " the calf of Lil." [6] He is likewise

[1] F. Hommel, op. cit., p. 81 ; O. Weber, Arabien vor dem Islam, p. 20.

[2] R. W. Rogers, The Religion of Babylonia and Assyria, pp. 82 sq.

[3] A. T. Clay, " Ellil, the God of Nippur," The American Journal of Semitic Languages and Literatures, vol. xxiii, pp. 275 sq.

[4] A. Jeremias, op. cit., p. 237.

[5] A. T. Clay, Light on the Old Testament from Babel, p. 103.

[6] A. Jeremias, op. cit., p. 237 ; Id., art. 'Marduk' in W. H. Roscher, Ausführliches Lexikon, vol. ii, Part ii, p. 2354.

the ' master of the wind,' ' the king of storms,' and a god of waters.[1]
Ea is definitely associated with the waters, and is the primal ocean,
Tiamat, the Deep out of which all things arose. He is the Ancient
Serpent, Oannes, the fish-god or Leviathan mentioned by Berosus.
But he is at the same time " The Lord of the Earth," and his path
is filled with fruitfulness.[2] The attributes of the Babylonian triad
thus overlap, and its three persons have reference to the
three spheres of Heaven, Earth, and Water, like the threefold
Zeus, Olympian, Plutonic, and Poseidonic, of Greek mythology,
without, however, being fully separated and departmentalised.
The great goddess Ishtar is mentioned as the daughter or
female counterpart of each of the three members of the triad.[3]
She is also usually the daughter of the moon-god Sinn. The
names of the members of the Babylonian triad, which, unlike those of
other Semitic gods, are not used as components of proper names,
are, for that purpose, replaced by the name of Sinn.[4] Ea is
stated to be the same as Sinn.[5] If any doubt remains as to the
original character of the three persons of the Babylonian trinity,
it should be dispelled by the explicit statement of an early text :
" The moon is during the period of his visibility, in the first five
days, the god Anu ; from the sixth to the tenth day, the god Ea ;
from the eleventh to the fifteenth day, the god En-Lil." [6]

There were sun-gods in Semitic religion. The sun is mentioned
as being worshipped by several Arabian tribes.[7] It appears
in several city-cults on the eastern bank of the Euphrates, and
was the special god of the city of Hammurabi. When the latter
established his empire the sun was raised to a position of greater

---

[1] L. B. Paton, art. ' Baal, Beel, Bel,' in Hastings's *Encyclopaedia of
Religion and Ethics*, vol. ii, p. 295 ; A. Jeremias, in Roscher's *Lexikon*, *loc.
cit.*, pp. 2354 sq. ; H. Radau, *Sumerian Hymns and Prayers to God Nin-Ib*,
pp. 19 sqq.

[2] R. W. Rogers, *The Religion of Babylonia and Assyria*, p. 81 ; F. Hommel,
The Ancient Hebrew Tradition as illustrated by the Monuments, p. 63 ;
T. G. Pinches, " The Babylonian Paradise and its Rivers," *The Expository
Times*, xxix, pp. 182 sqq.

[3] R. W. Rogers, *op. cit.*, p. 85 ; M. Jastrow, *The Religion of Babylonia
and Assyria*, p. 84 (Daughter of Anu) ; T. G. Pinches, " The Goddess Ištar
in Assyro-Babylonian Literature," *Proceedings of the Society of Biblical
Archaeology*, xxxi, p. 21 (Spouse of Anu) ; R. W. Rogers, *op. cit.*, p. 81
(Female counterpart of En-Lil) ; *Ibid.*, p. 85 ; F. Hommel, *op. cit.*, pp. 65 sq.
(Daughter of Ea).

[4] F. Hommel, *op. cit.*, pp. 63 sq.

[5] *Ibid.*, pp. 65 sq.

[6] H. C. Rawlinson, *The Cuneiform Inscriptions of Western Asia*, vol. iii,
55. 3 ; A. Jeremias, *op. cit.*, p. 162.

[7] E. Osiander, " Studien über die vorislamische Religion der Araber,"
Zeitschrift der deutschen morgenländische Gesellschaft, xix, p. 498 ; L. Krehl,
Ueber die Religion der vorislamischen Araber, pp. 8 sq.

importance than it occupied before. That character became more pronounced in later periods ; the triumphant war-gods, the city-gods of Babylon and Assyria, assumed a solar character. But the sun, which was regarded as one of the planets, never, even in later periods, acquired anything like a supreme cosmological significance. The sun-god is always the agent, the champion, the interpreter of the gods. The sun, Shamash, was originally regarded as a female, the daughter or wife of the moon,[1] and had no cult until relatively late.[2] Shamash occupies to the last in Babylonian religion a position which is avowedly and consistently subordinate to that of the Moon-deity. Indeed, that position of the Sun-god in Babylonian cult and cosmology is, to our notions, positively humiliating and degraded. The sun " bears a name which signifies ' attendant,' or ' servitor,' and which sufficiently shows the subsidiary position that he occupied in the Babylonian pantheon. One of the rulers belonging to the IInd Dynasty of Ur calls the sun-god the offspring of Nannar, one of the names of the moon-god, and the last king of Babylon, Nabbonedos, does the same. In combination with the moon-god, the latter takes the precedence of Shamash, and in the enumeration of the complete pantheon in the inscriptions of both Assyrian and Babylonian kings the same order is preserved." [3] In no instance is the sun regarded as the promoter of growth, life, or vegetation ; on the contrary, the heat and rays of the sun are invariably represented as injurious things which blast, consume, and cause death.[4] Curiously enough, while the moon is viewed as the giver of life, the promoter of growth, and the power of light, the sun is associated with death, darkness, and the underworld. The paradox becomes intelligible when the astronomical system of the Babylonians is taken into account ; for when the moon is at its highest and brightest, the sun, in opposition, occupies the lowest place, and is therefore, in a system which takes its starting-point from the moon and remains purely lunar, opposed to the moon as darkness to light.[5] The curious notion of the Caribbean

---

[1] D. Nielsen, *Die altarabische Mondreligion*, pp. 20, 29 ; F. Hommel, *op. cit.*, p. 81.

[2] L. W. King, *The Religion of Babylon and Assyria*, p. 18.

[3] M. Jastrow, *The Religion of the Babylonians and Assyrians*, p. 68. Cf. L. W. King, *op. cit.*, p. 17 ; F. Thureau-Dangin, *Les inscriptions de Sumer et d'Akkade*, pp. 246 sq., 298 sq., 302 sq. ; F. Delitzsch, *Assyrisches Handwörterbuch*, p. 234a ; E. Combe, *Le Culte du dieu Sin*, p. 18 ; F. Hommel, *op. cit.*, p. 65 ; E. Schrader, *Die Höllenfahrt der Istar*, p. 45.

[4] A. Jeremias, *op. cit.*, p. 248. The natives of Brazil have the same conception of the sun as a withering power particularly injurious to vegetation (F. J. de Santa-Anna Nery, *Folk-Lore Brésilien*, p. 250).

[5] *Ibid.*, pp. 74 sq.

savages who " esteem the moon more than the sun," which Tylor
thought singular, was thus shared by a people who are regarded
as being particularly advanced and enlightened in both their
astronomical and their religious views.

While the sun-god is regarded as an attendant deity, the
moon-god is called " the father of the great gods " and
the " father of all gods " ; " the lord of heaven, whose sickle
shines among the gods " ; " the king of the universe " ; " the
lord and giver of life " ; " he who fashioned men and all things
with his hands." [1] " He is supreme ; there is none like him ;
and all the gods are subservient to him." [2] " In the Heavens, who
is great ? " sings one psalmist to the god Sinn ; " Thou alone art
great. On earth who is great ? Thou alone art great." [3] " In
heaven and on earth," states another text, " thou hast, among
the gods, no rival." [4] In another cuneiform hymn he is addressed,
" Sinn, thou alone givest light from above ; thou art the light of
the world ; thy light shines bright as the light of thy first-begotten
son Shamash. Before thee all the gods lie in the dust, O Lord of
Fate." [5] The cult of Sinn is found in every Semitic land, and
" was undoubtedly more popular than that of any other deity." [6]

That supreme character of the primal moon-god of the Semites
and Sumerians passed, however, in later times, to his female
counterpart, who came to replace him almost entirely. That
transfer of supremacy from the male to the female form of
the moon-deity in Western Asia probably determined the
conceptions of classical Greece in regard to the moon, and
the moon has hence come to be regarded in European culture
as a female. Although Ishtar is called " the daughter of
Sinn," nothing more is expressed by that relation than her
derivation from the Moon-god and her identity with him. In
one inscription she describes herself as being both " the master "
(en-lit) and " the mistress " (ni-lit). [7] As female avatar of the male

[1] E. Combe, *Histoire du culte du dieu Sin en Babylonie et en Assyrie*,
pp. 24–27.

[2] M. Jastrow, *op. cit.*, p. 79. Cf. R. W. Rogers, *op. cit.*, p. 84.

[3] A. Jeremias, *op. cit.*, p. 229.

[4] H. C. Rawlinson, *The Cuneiform Inscriptions of Western Asia*, vol. iv,
9. 11. 12.

[5] L. Bergström, " Semitisk mändyrka," *Nordisk Tidskrift*, 1909, p. 301.

[6] F. Hommel, *op. cit.*, p. 73.

[7] J. Dyneley Prince, " The Hymn to Bêlit," *Journal of the American
Oriental Society*, xxiv, p. 106. No importance can be attached to the
reference to her as ' bearded ' (J. A. Craig, *Assyrian and Babylonian Religious
Texts*, pl. 7 ; T. G. Pinches, " Assyro-Babylonian Astrologers and their
Lore," *The Expository Times*, xxx, p. 167), which probably means merely
' radiant ' (cf. M. Jastrow, in *Revue Assyriologique*, xvii, pp. 271 sqq.), nor
can she be in any way regarded as bi-sexual (see J. D. Prince, *loc. cit.*).

moon-god she possesses all his attributes. But the Great Goddess Ishtar, or, as she was called in older synonymic names, Nana, Innini, is not in Babylonian religion a departmental deity presiding over particular domains of nature or of human life, for she is equally related to all, and is best described as the Deity in a monotheistic sense. She does not even represent a ' female principle,' for, although she has purely feminine functions, such as presiding over childbirth, she is equally capable of assuming the most masculine offices, such as that of legislator, of huntress, and even of Lady of Hosts, and goddess of battles. She appears, in fact, as a universal deity, the creatrix and governess of the universe. She is " the creatrix of all things." [1] She is " the Mother of men," [2] and " the mother of the gods." [3] She fashioned men out of clay, and one of her appellatives is " the Potter." [4]

The character of the goddess and the manner in which she was regarded may be illustrated by the following extracts from a prayer addressed to her :—

I beseech thee, Lady of ladies, Goddess of goddesses, Ishtar, Queen of all cities, leadress of all men.
Thou art the light of the world, thou art the light of heaven, mighty daughter of Sinn.
Thou leadest the hosts in battle and ordainest the combat ;
Thou givest forth all commands and deckest thyself with the crown of kings.
Supreme is thy might, O Lady, exalted art thou above all gods.
Thou renderest judgment and thy decision is righteous ;
Unto thee are subject the laws of the earth and the laws of heaven, the laws of the temple and of the shrine, and the laws of the private apartment and of the secret chamber.
Where is the place where thy name is not, and where is the spot where thy commandments are not known ?
At thy name the earth and the heavens shake, and the gods they tremble ; the spirits of heaven tremble at thy name and the men hold it in awe.
Thou art great, thou art exalted ; all the men of Sumer, and all creatures, and all mankind glorify thy name.
With righteousness dost thou judge the deeds of men, even thou ;
Thou lookest upon the oppressed and to the down-trodden thou bringest justice every day.
How long, Queen of Heaven and of Earth, how long,
How long, Shepherdess of pale-faced men, wilt thou tarry ?
How long, O Queen whose feet are not weary and whose knees make haste ?

[1] S. Langdon, *Sumerian and Babylonian Psalms*, p. 256.
[2] J. A. Craig, *Assyrian and Babylonian Religious Texts*, p. 256.
[3] *Ibid.* ; A. Jeremias, *Handbuch der altorientalischen Geisteskultur*, p. 253.
[4] A. Jeremias, *loc. cit.*

How long, Lady of Hosts, Lady of battles ?
Glorious one whom all the spirits of heaven fear, who subduest all angry
  gods ; mighty above all rulers, who holdest the reins of kings.
Opener of the womb of all women, great is thy light.
Shining light of heaven, light of the world, enlightener of all the places
  where men dwell, who gatherest together the hosts of the nations.
Goddess of men, Divinity of women, thy counsel passeth understanding.
Where thou glancest the dead come to life, and the sick rise and
  walk ; and the mind that is diseased is healed when it looks upon
  thy face.
How long, O Lady, shall mine enemy triumph over me ?
Command, and at thy command the angry god will turn back.
Ishtar is great ! Ishtar is Queen ! My Lady is exalted, My Lady is
  Queen ; Irnini, the mighty daughter of Sinn.
There is none like unto her.[1]

Notwithstanding her character of universal deity, creatrix and
governess of the world, the original nature of Ishtar was never forgotten, though her association with the moon may in course of time
have become looser and more symbolic. The title of Queen of Heaven,
as she expanded into a supreme and universal deity, acquired a
theological rather than an astronomical significance. But she was,
nevertheless, still the Queen of Heaven in the literal sense, that
is, " the Queen of the stars." [2] She was horned,[3] and was, indeed,
a cow,[4] all lunar goddesses being commonly represented as the
heavenly cow in the same manner as the male moon-god is the
heavenly bull. A myth of late source, but which may nevertheless
represent a very ancient tradition, describes Ishtar as having fallen
from heaven into the Euphrates or the sea, whence she was brought
ashore by a troop of attendant fishes or water-gods, and tended
by doves.[5] Hence the birth of the Moon-goddess, who, like all
lunar deities, was also a goddess of the waters, from the sea-foam,
in some of her derivative forms. The great Semitic goddess was
threefold or triune. In her Arabian form she was, as has been
seen, three persons, the threefold goddess Al-Ilat, Al-Uzza,
Al-Manat. She is commonly represented in aniconic form on the

[1] British Museum, 26. 187 ; L. W. King, *The Seven Tablets of Creation*,
Appendix v ; R. W. Rogers, *Cuneiform Parallels to the Old Testament*,
pp. 153 sqq. ; F. Delitzsch, *Babel und Bibel*, pp. 65 sqq. ; A. Jeremias,
Handbuch der altorientalischen Geisteskultur, pp. 261 sq.

[2] Herodian, v. 6.

[3] T. G. Pinches, " The Goddess Ištar in Assyro-Babylonian Literature,"
Proceedings of the Society of Biblical Archaeology, xxxi, p. 23. Cf. ' Asheroth
Karnaim,' *Genesis*, xiv. 5.

[4] A. Jeremias, *Handbuch der altorientalischen Geisteskultur*, p. 242 n. ;
J. Offord, " Ashteroth-Karnaim," *Proceedings of the Society of Biblical
Archaeology*, xxi, p. 173.

[5] Hyginus, 197.

steles and monuments of Phoenicia and Carthage as three pillars, three trees, or a pillar and two trees.[1] The Syrian goddess is represented in triple form on a monument from Ascalon.[2] Vergil was well aware of the threefold character of the Semitic goddess, and makes Dido invoke her as three-faced.[3] St. Augustine with scathing irony taunts his pagan countrymen with the absurdity of the notion that a goddess could be at the same time one person and yet three persons.[4]

But although no goddess could be more distinctly celestial and lunar than Ishtar, she is yet capable of assuming the characters and functions of an Earth-goddess. Sinn himself, the pure and simple Moon-god, possessed those chthonic attributes before her. He is " the creator of the land," " the lord of territories " ; he is " the lord of vegetables," he is " the creator of plants." One of his names means " the Fruit." [5] His crescent is represented on a cylinder as lying in a field.[6] His oldest appellation in Chaldean cult is " Urikittu," that is, " the Green One." [7] Ishtar bears the same title.[8] It required no great feat of metamorphosis or evolution on the part of the Moon-goddess Ishtar to become an Earth-goddess ; she was so from the first, in the sense of being the producer of all vegetation and of all earthly life, the Great Mother. She is styled not only " the first in Heaven," but " the first on Earth." [9] She is a special deity of mountains, and is called " Lady of Mountains." [10] She is described in another text as " Queen of the earth and mistress of the fields." [11] She it is who " causes verdure to spring forth." [12] She is " the mother of the vine-stalk." [13] " I have heaped up grain for man-

[1] *Corpus Inscriptionum Semiticarum*, vol. i, tab. xliv ; vol. ii, tab. liii, vi, etc.

[2] A. Héron de Villefosse, *Notice des monuments provenant de la Palestine et conservés au Musée du Louvre*, p. 45.

[3] Vergil, *Aeneid*, iv. 510.

[4] Augustine, *De civit. Dei*, iv. 10.

[5] E. Combe, *Histoire du culte de Sin en Babylonie et en Assyrie*, pp. 24, 25, 26.

[6] J. Menant, *Catalogue des cylindres orientaux du Cabinet Royal des Médailles de La Haye*, pl. III, 14.

[7] F. Hommel, *The Ancient Hebrew Tradition as illustrated by the Monuments*, pp. 64, 68.

[8] J. A. Craig, *Assyrian and Babylonian Religious Texts*, vol. i, pp. 15 sq.

[9] E. Schrader, *Die Keilinschriften und das Alte Testament*, pp. 178 sq.

[10] J. Dyreley Prince, " The Hymn to Bêlit," *Journal of the American Oriental Society*, xxiv, p. 107.

[11] L. B. Paton, in Hastings's *Encyclopaedia of Religion and Ethics*, vol. vii, p. 430.

[12] P. Haupt, *Akkadische und Sumerische Keilschrifttexte*, pp. 116 sq.

[13] S. Langdon, *Tammuz and Ishtar*, pp. 7, 14, 43.

kind and I have produced fodder for the cattle," she says in one inscription.[1]   On Babylonian cylinders she is commonly represented with sheaves of grain.[2]

It is manifest that such a goddess is not far removed, if at all, from a Ceres or a Demeter.   In Syria the earth-attributes of the Great Goddess became even more conspicuous.   The Syrian goddess, Atargatis, who is identical with Ishtar, the Queen of Heaven,[3] is almost more prominent as a goddess of vegetation than as a heavenly deity.   Lucian, himself a Syrian, though reluctant to equate her with any Greek goddess, chooses Rhea as an appropriate equivalent.[4]   Macrobius identifies her with the Earth.[5]   Her picture on the coins of Syria, with a castellated crown, in a chariot drawn by lions, is indistinguishable from the presentment of the typical Earth-goddess Cybele.[6]   But on some of the coins of Sidon the occupant of her chariot is the lunar crescent.[7]

The character of earth-deity is rendered more pronounced in the Syrian form of the Babylonian goddess by the intimate association of her cult with that of the god Tammuz, or, as he was usually called by the Greeks, Adonis.   For that divine personage presents perhaps the most complete type of that class of gods whom Sir James Frazer has made familiar to us under the name of ' vegetation gods ' ; and her relation to a god representing the fruits of the earth naturally assimilates the goddess to Mother Earth. Although Tammuz appears as the lover or spouse of the goddess, he is more especially her son.   His name indeed, in its Babylonian and Sumerian forms Dumuzi, Damu, means ' the true Son,' or ' the only Son.'   His yearly death, corresponding to the decay of vegetation after the harvest, and his resurrection in spring ; his descent into the nether-world, where the sorrowing Mother-goddess goes down to seek him ; the cult in which that cycle is reflected, the ritual wailings and lamentations of the women over the dead god ; the rites designed to assist his resurrection, in which the women carried basin-shaped vases containing representative seedlings, and called ' gardens of Adonis,' are generally known from the references of Greek authors as well as from the pages of ' The Golden Bough.'   But we were until quite recently under a profound misapprehension in regard to Tammuz ; for the

[1] L. B. Paton, loc. cit.

[2] W. H. Ward, The Seal Cylinders of Western Asia, pp. 133 sqq.

[3] Herodotus, v. 6, 4 ; Plutarch, De Isid. et Osir., xv ; Cicero, De natur. deor., iii. 5. 6.

[4] Lucian, De dea Syria, xv.

[5] Macrobius, Satur., i. 23. 18.

[6] B. V. Head, Historia numorum, pp. 777, 778, 797.

[7] E. Meyer, art. ' Astarte,' in W. Roscher, Ausführliches Lexikon, vol. i, col. 652.

impression was derived from the prominence of his cult at Byblos that this was a comparatively late and local development, and that the cult had become grafted, as a more or less adventitious growth, on the religion of the Semitic goddess.

Nothing could be more remote from the truth. The dying and resurrecting god Tammuz, the Divine Son, is one of the oldest elements in Babylonian religion, and figures in it as far back as our records reach; his cult was established from time immemorial in the cities of Sumer before the Babylonian empire existed, as early as 3000, or, according to other authorities, 4000 B.C. As Professor Langdon observes, we do not know among historical peoples possessing written records of a more ancient god. He was in Mesopotamia, as in Syria, closely connected with vegetable life, and was called " the father of plants and vegetation." [1] His cult was intimately associated with the magic of agriculture; and the baskets, or vases, containing representative seedlings figured in the ceremonies of his cult in pre-Babylonian Sumer, as at Byblos.[2] We have already come upon them among the North American Indians. Tammuz was represented as having been born out of a tree; his material image was a rough wooden figure, or an aniconic log of wood. At the festival which symbolised his death the log was anointed and mourned over by the women, and was thereafter cast upon the waters, and the god sacrificed by drowning.[3] Similar rites, in which the temporary deity is drowned, have been noted in other parts of the world. Thus among the Chicora and Duhare tribes of the Creeks, the early Spanish adventurers witnessed the following ceremony: " Another feast is celebrated every year, when a roughly carved wooden statue is carried into the country and fixed upon a high pole planted in the ground. From sunrise till evening the people dance round this statue, clapping their hands; and when nightfall has barely set in, the image and the pole on which it was fixed are carried away and thrown into the sea, if the country is on the coast, or into the river, if it is along a river's bank. Nothing more is seen of it, and each year a new statue is made." [4] Among the Oraons of Bengal, before the harvest, the young men go into the forest and fetch a branch or sapling of a karam tree. This is stuck in the ground in the middle of the village and adorned with bright flowers and with lights, much after the manner of our Christmas trees. After holding a banquet and making merry, the people spend the night dancing round the tree. At dawn it

[1] S. Langdon, *Tammuz and Ishtar*, p. 8.
[2] *Ibid.*, p. 13.
[3] *Ibid.*, pp. 10 sq.
[4] Peter Martir, *De orbi novo*, pp. 263 sq.

is carried to the nearest river and is thrown into it.[1] God-desses are also frequently sacrificed in India by drowning them. "One of the most remarkable ceremonies in the festivals of the Indian Goddess," remarked Warren Hastings, "is that of casting her image into the river. The Pundit of whom I have inquired concerning its origin and import answered that it was prescribed by the Veda, they know not why."[2] The image of Parvati is made from rice-flour and red grain by the women and adorned with rich garments and flowers. It is carried about for nine days in a palanquin; thereafter it is borne, accompanied by crowds of women, to a sacred pool and thrown into the water.[3] In Egypt likewise Osiris was in some of the earliest forms of his ritual sacrificed, like Tammuz, by drowning him. His image, which often consisted of a bundle of branches or corn, was thrown into the Nile, whence he was supposed to rise again.[4]

Most prominent in the oldest records of the cult of Dumuzi which have come down to us are the liturgies of 'lamentations.' The date at which those 'lamentations' were held is marked in the Babylonian calendar as far back as our information extends.[5] We possess an extensive literature of such dirges over the dead god, some of them very beautiful, which depict the sorrow of the bereaved mother, the Mater Dolorosa, or Lady of Sorrows, as in the following passage :—

> His mother wailing begins the lamentations for him;
> Wailing and sobbing she begins to lament for him.
> She wanders, bringing a burden of tears;
> She sits and puts her hand to her heart;
> She wails; her sorrow is bitter;
> She laments; her lament is bitter.[6]

The immemorial Son and his cult in Sumer and in ancient Babylonia were in all respects identical with the Syrian cult of later ages, and Dumuzi is a typical dying god of vegetation. Nevertheless, contrary to what we should expect had he originated as a personification or allegory of the dying and resurrecting vegetation, the earlier and more primitive form of

---

[1] F. Hahn, " Some Notes on the Religion and Superstition of the Oraos," *Journal of the Asiatic Society of Bengal*, lxxii, Part 3, p. 13.

[2] Warren Hastings, " On the Gods of Greece, Italy, and India," *Asiatick Researches*, i, p. 255.

[3] J.-F. Bernard and B. Picart, *Cérémonies et coutumes religieuses de tous les peuples du Monde*, vol. i, p. 2.

[4] A. Erman, ' Ein Denkmal memphitischer Theologie," *Sitzungsberichte der königlich preussiche Akademie der Wissenschaften*, xliii, pp. 929, 934.

[5] A. Jeremias, *Handbuch der altorientalischen Geisteskultur*, p. 264.

[6] S. Langdon, *Sumerian and Babylonian Psalms*, p. 313. Cf. the description of the later cult given by Macrobius (i. 2. 1).

the dying god is far less exclusively characterised by that aspect than is his descendant in a later age ; and the supposition that he arose as an emblem of vegetation and of the cycle of its yearly vicissitudes is excluded. In the earliest records Dumuzi is intimately associated with water, whether as brooks, rivers, canals or sea, and he is one of the principal gods of Eridu, the city of Ea, a shrine specially devoted to water and aquatic or marine deities.[1] He is spoken of as ' Dumuzi of the deep sea ' ; [2] he was worshipped at Lagash as the ' Lord of the freshets,' and the ' Lord of the Flood,' [3] and it is said that without him all water-courses and canals would cease to flow.[4] He is associated with springs and brooks, and the river Adonis which flowed by Byblos was but one of the many streams over which he presided. Those functions might be in accordance with the character of a god of vegetation whose life depended upon moisture and irrigation, although we should expect him to be irrigated rather than to act as an irrigator. But his association with the life of plants is but an aspect of his attributes as " Giver of the breath of life " ; not vegetables only cease to grow and reproduce when he is absent, but also cattle, sheep, human beings, and particularly kings. He is the " Healer," the " Saviour." [5] A common title of

---

[1] T. G. Pinches, " The Babylonian Paradise and its Rivers," *Expository Times*, xxix, pp. 182 sq.

[2] S. Langdon, *Tammuz and Ishtar*, p. 6.

[3] *Ibid.*, pp. 6, 45.

[4] J. A. Craig, *Assyrian and Babylonian Religious Texts*, vol. ii, p. 13.

[5] S. Langdon, *op. cit.*, pp. 33 sq. Some of the epithets of the ancient Tammuz are of particular interest. From the practice of anointing his image—a universally prevalent method, among savages, of conveying the spirit of a god or totem by inunction with the fat of the animal—Dumuzi was called " The Anointed, " a term which would be translated in Hebrew by ' Messiah,' and in Greek by ' Christ.' One of the liturgies of ' lamentation ' runs as follows :—

> For him who has been taken away there is wailing,
> Ah me, my child has been taken away,
> My Damu that has been taken away,
> My Christ that has been taken away,
> From the sacred cedar where the Mother bore him.
> The wailing is for the plants, they grow not ;
> For the houses and for the flocks ; they produce not ;
> For the perishing wedded couples, for perishing children, the people of
>   Sumer, they reproduce not.
> The wailing is for the great river, it brings the flood no more.
> The wailing is for the fish-ponds ; the fish spawn not.
> The wailing is for the forests ; the tamarisks grow not.
> The wailing is for the store-house ; the honey and wine are not produced.
> The wailing is for the palace ; life unto old age is not.

(S. Langdon, *Sumerian and Babylonian Psalms*, p. 332 ; Id., *Tammuz and Ishtar*, pp. 10 sq.)

Tammuz is 'The Shepherd,'[1] He is usually described as a shepherd bearing a crook. It might be suggested that the character has reference to the dependence of flocks upon the pasture-grass, and that when Tammuz is absent " the hungry sheep look up and are not fed." But the constancy of the character of Tammuz as the Shepherd is out of all proportion to such an incidental connection ; he is represented not as an earthly, but as a heavenly shepherd ; he is styled " The Lord Tammuz, the Shepherd of Heaven."[2] The flocks which the Heavenly Shepherd originally tended were not earthly sheep, but the flocks of the stars.

Next to the title of Shepherd the most common appellative of Tammuz is ' The Wanderer.' He is addressed in a liturgy :—

> O Wanderer, Wanderer, my brother Wanderer,
> In the fields of Arallu, Wanderer, my brother Wanderer.[3]

The epithet is, as has been noted, a common one applied to the moon ; and, taken in conjunction with the title of Heavenly Shepherd and the other attributes of Tammuz as lord of moisture and of generation, suggests that he was originally a lunar god. He is, in fact, expressly addressed in one liturgy as the Moon-god.[4] It is true that he is also in the same liturgy called the sun ; but his career is in any case assimilated not to the birth and death of vegetation, but to the birth and death of a heavenly body. And the heavenly body originally associated with the cycle of death and rebirth is the moon.

Even the Sumerian cult of some 5,000 or 6,000 years ago, such as it is known from cuneiform documents, was far from being a primitive type of religion. It was, on the contrary, a very advanced and even sophisticated phase of religious evolution, for

---

[1] The Sumerian psalmist sings :—

> Why have they slain him, him of the plains ?
> The Shepherd, The Man of Wisdom,
> The Man of Sorrow why have they slain ?
> The Lady of the Vine languishes,
> The lambs and the claves languish.
> The Lord, the Shepherd of the folds lives no more,
> The spouse of the Queen of Heaven lives no more,
> The lord of the cattle stalls lives no more.
> When he slumbers, the sheep and the lambs slumber also.

(S. Langdon, *Sumerian and Babylonian Psalms*, pp. 319, 323 ; Id., *Tammuz and Ishtar*, pp. 14 sq.)

[2] H. Zimmern, " Zur Vollständigung von K. 2001," *Zeitschrift für Assyriologie*, xxv, p. 195.

[3] S. Langdon, *Sumerian and Babylonian Psalms*, p. 330. Arallu is the dark aspect of the Queen of Heaven, as ruler of the dead, and the " fields of Arallu " are therefore the dark sky.

[4] S. Langdon, *op. cit.*, p. 330.

it had an organised theology in which earlier beliefs were systematically standardised and remodelled; and there are not wanting
traces of conflicts between the official doctrines upheld by priestly
classes and less orthodox and more popular views and 'superstitions.'[1] The Sumerians were in a very advanced state of
civilisation; they had an extensive written literature to which
they constantly added. They had not only discovered the solar
year, but had laid the foundations of all subsequent astronomy,
and traced the apparent course of the heavenly bodies through
those constellations of the zodiacal belt, the girdle of Ishtar, which
still go by the names which they gave to them. It can scarcely
be supposed that in those circumstances the immemorially established conception of the dying and resurrecting god represents the
most primitive form of the notion. Although the familiar cycle of
death, descent into the nether-world, and rebirth, and the rites of
lamentation and rejoicing are as definitely expressed in the most
ancient as in the most highly developed forms of the cult of the
dying god, the personality of Tammuz and his place in the myth-
cycle are, in the earlier forms of the cult, more vaguely and indefi-
nitely conceived. The Divine Son is not so much a separate god
as a complex of attributes which may be ascribed in turn to any
Son of God. "There is not a single Babylonian trinity in which
the 'Son' does not appear as the 'Saviour.'"[2] He has many
alternative local names and forms, such as Ninib at Nippur,[3]
Ningirsu, Abu at Lagash,[4] Nergal at Kutha,[5] Esmun at Sidon,
Melqart at Tyre. Gilgamesh, the hero of the Babylonian epic,
was a Tammuz god;[6] Bel-Marduk was a Divine Son, and is called
"the Lord of Lamentations."[7] The Hebrew god Yahweh was
identified with Tammuz.[8] Any god conceived as waxing and
waning, or as dying and returning to life, was a Divine Son, or
Tammuz. The relation of the Dying-god to the Mother-goddess,
always somewhat complex, was in primitive stages more indefinite.
In some texts Dumuzi appears to be confounded with the Goddess.
He is sometimes spoken of as feminine.[9] In some lamentation

[1] Cf. H. Radau, "Miscellaneous Sumerian Texts," in *Hilprecht Anniversary Volume*, p. 389; Id., *Sumerian Hymns and Prayers to God Nin-ib*,
p. 14.

[2] *Ibid.*, p. 65.

[3] *Ibid.*

[4] S. Langdon, *Tammuz and Ishtar*, p. 9 n.

[5] *Ibid.*, p. 54.

[6] E. Schrader, *Die Keilinschriften und das Alte Testament*, p. 374.

[7] *Ibid.*

[8] See below, p. 114.

[9] H. C. Rawlinson, *The Cuneiform Inscriptions of Western Asia*, vol. ii,
pp. 54, 349; T. G. Pinches, "Assyro-Babylonian Astrologers and their
Lore," *Expository Times*, xxx, p. 167.

rituals the Goddess appears to mourn not so much with reference to a specific dead god as for men and all creatures. She descends into the nether-world without any specific purpose of seeking the dead god. It would seem that the conception of the Divine Son, who dies and rises again, and the rite of ' lamentations ' are older than any formal myth.[1]

The cult of Tammuz was general throughout Mesopotamia and Syria.[2] A mediaeval traveller reports that grottos or caves where the rites of Adonis were celebrated abounded in Cyprus.[3] One of the chief shrines of Tammuz in Palestine was at Bethlehem. " Bethlehem," says St. Jerome, " which now belongs to our faith and is one of the most sacred places in the whole world, lay formerly under the shadow of a grove dedicated to Tammuz, that is to say, Adonis, and the very grotto where the infant Christ uttered his first cries resounded formerly with the lamentations over the lover of Aphrodite." [4]

The cult continued in many parts of Asia long after the Christian era, and was more particularly observed by the Sabaeans, the most persistent worshippers of the original male lunar deity among the Semites. An Arab writer of the tenth century tells us that " all the Sabaeans of our time, those of Babylonia as well as those of Harran, lament and weep to this day over Tammuz at a festival which they, more particularly the women, hold in the month of the same name. They fable concerning it much absurd nonsense ; but it is clear to me that none of the sects has any definite knowledge concerning Tammuz, and that none of them knows the reason why they mourn over him." [5] Another writer mentions that in the year A.D. 1063 a hunting party near Baghdad came upon a black tent in the desert, wherein were a multitude of people of both sexes beating their faces and uttering loud cries, as is customary in the East when someone dies. The burden of those lamentations was " The great King of the Djinns is dead ; woe unto the land ! " " And there issued afterwards from the tent," continues the writer, " a great troop of women followed by other rabble, who went to the cemetery still beating and wailing in sign of grief." [6] Again, in the thirteenth century, when an epidemic

[1] Cf. S. Langdon, *op. cit.*, pp. 16, 89.
[2] Firmicus Maternus, *De errore profanarum religionum*, p. 14. (ed. Wover).
[3] Felix Faber, *Evagatorium in Terrae Sanctae, Arabiae et Egypti Peregrinationem*, vol. iv, pp. 220 sq.
[4] Jerome, *Epist.* lviij, *ad Paulinum*, in Migne, *Patrologiae Cursus Completus*, vol. xxii, col. 581.
[5] D. Chwolson, *Ueber Tammuz, und die Menschenverehrung bei den alten Babyloniern*, pp. 56 sq., after Abu-Bakr A'hmed Ibn Wa'hschijah.
[6] B. d'Herbelot, *Bibliothèque orientale*, p. 375.

raged in Mosul, it was said by the people that a great female Djinn, named Omm Ankud, having lost her son, all those who did not comfort her would be attacked by the disease. The women assembled and beat their cheeks, crying out with all their might, " O Mother Ankud, forgive us ! Ankud is dead, and we did not think of it." A similar incident in reported from Egypt. During an epidemic the people prepared a broth of meal and threw it into the Nile, crying, " O Mother Halkum, forgive us our trespasses ! Halkum is dead, and we forgot." [1]

The immemorial rites and ideas characteristic of the cult of Tammuz thus become readily transferred not only to other gods, but to an occasion for devotional exercises apparently as irrelevant to the traditional objects and associations of the cult as the outbreak of an epidemic. The same rites have been adapted to the cults of heroes, prophets, and martyrs. For example, the feast of the martyr Hussain, the son of Ali and Fatima, who died in the massacre of Kerbela, is celebrated by the Muhammadans of Persia and of India in the following manner : " From the first appearance of the new moon on the horizon the devout Muslim utters sighs and groans, and prepares the mourning feast, or ' Bazm matam ka.' Each worshipper, after having donned black clothes, planted banners and arranged the representation of the Tomb of Hussain, weeps, striking his head, to express his grief. A chamber hung with black cloth and containing a pulpit is made ready ; and every evening, during the ten days of the festival, is read the sad narrative of the events which it commemorates. The reader accompanies his words with loud wailing, passing all conception ; and the congregation give external marks of their grief by cries and lamentations. An elegiac poem in honour of the saint is then chanted, full of harrowing details of his martyrdom, which cause the assembly to break out into renewed weeping. The representations of the Tomb of Hussain, or rather of the chapel which contains his sepulchre, are more or less richly ornamented. They are given the metaphoric name of ' ta'ziya,' that is, ' mourning,' or ' lamentations.' They are carried in procession through the streets, and are afterwards deposited in special cemeteries, or, if there is a river or pond available, they are cast into the water." [2] It is not unlikely that the

---

[1] *Ibid.* ' Ankud,' or ' Halkum,' means simply ' throat,' and has reference to the disease, probably diphtheria—which is particularly prevalent in Egypt and was first known as ' the Egyptian ulcer '—which was the occasion of those observances. The goddess was, as in India, named after the disease which she was supposed to have produced.

[2] J. H. G. de Tassy, *L'Islamisme*, pp. 299, 324. The Persian theologian, Hussain Vaez, in order to justify the enormous importance attached to the cult of Hussain, goes to much pains to argue that Hussain should be regarded

name 'ta'ziya' which is given to the festival is, as the writer suggests, a corrupt reminiscence of 'ta'uz,' or Tammuz. The rite is celebrated with as much fervour by Muslims in India as in Persia. Their manifestations of grief and mourning, their wails and piercing cries, are so heartrending that even Christian spectators have been known to be so affected by them as to burst into tears. This is one of the few ceremonies of Indian Muslims in which most Hindus feel bound to join, out of respect for its solemn character. During its celebration they put on mourning and go barefooted, excusing themselves by saying that all religions address themselves, after all, to the same God and have the same foundations. In the districts on the banks of the Ganges and Jumna the wooden 'ta'ziya' are solemnly thrown into the river.[1] The assimilation of Hussain to Tammuz is rendered all the more intelligible by the fact that Ali, the husband of Fatima and son-in-law of the Prophet, who also was cruelly murdered, is declared by the peasants of Syria at the present day to be the same as the moon.[2]

Like Muslim hero-martyrs in modern times, the kings and princes of the city-states of Mesopotamia were, in the early days of Sumerian and Babylonian civilisation, regarded as representatives or impersonations of the Divine Son. A list of the traditional kings of Eridu mentions Damuzi as having reigned over the city a hundred years; one of his immediate successors was Gilgamesh, the hero of the Babylonian epic and a double of Damuzi.[3] There is evidence that in primitive Semitic states the king, or a prince chosen from among his sons, was sometimes actually sacrificed for the good of the people, as was done until lately by the Shilluks of the Upper Nile and other uncultured peoples in various parts of the world, and thus impersonated the Dying God in a realistic manner. "It was the custom of the ancients," says Philo of Alexandria, "in great crises of danger for the rulers of a city or nation to give up the most beloved of their children for sacrifice as a ransom to avenging daemons in order to avert the common ruin; and those who were thus given up were sacrificed with mystic rites." He tells us further that a

as the son of the Prophet. "According to Holy Scripture," he says, "descent may well be traced from the side of the mother, since Jesus Christ is said to be the son of Abraham, although he only descended from him through the Blessed Virgin, his mother." An attempt was thus made to assimilate the cult of Hussain to that of Jesus Christ (B. D. d'Herbelot, *Bibliothèque orientale*, p. 463).

[1] E. Roberts, *Scenes and Characteristics of Hindostan*, vol. ii, pp. 186 sqq.
[2] S. I. Curtiss, *Primitive Semitic Religion To-day*, pp. 104, 106.
[3] T. G. Pinches, "Early Babylonian Chronology and the Book of Genesis," *The Expository Times*, xxvii (1916), p. 519.

certain king, El, " who was king over the country and subsequently after his death was deified as the star Saturn, had by a nymph named Anobret, an only begotten son, whom they on this account called Jehud, that is to say, the Only Begotten, being so called among the Phoenicians. And when very great dangers from war had beset the country, he arrayed his son in royal apparel, and prepared an altar, and sacrificed him." [1] The sacrificed prince or king thus enacted the part of the Divine Saviour whose death and resurrection was the token of life to the people.

Ideas and cults similar to those connected with Tammuz appear to have been widespread in Asia far beyond the limits of Meso-potamia. A Chinese writer of the second century B.C. gives the following account of the beliefs of the inhabitants of Samarkand at that time. " They adore," he says, " a divine being and show themselves very zealous in the cult which they address to him. They relate how the Son of God died with the seventh moon, and that his remains disappeared. Every month the persons conse-crated to his cult, and on the seventh month all the inhabitants, without distinction, appear dressed in robes of black wool. They go barefooted, striking their breasts, uttering loud wails and weeping copious tears. Three hundred persons, both men and women, go about the fields scattering grass, and looking for the remains of the Son of God." [2] With the people of Samarkand, it will be noticed, the lamentations over the death of the Son of God were observed by his priests once every month, whereas the mass of the people celebrated the same rites, with the intention apparently of imparting fertility to the fields, once a year only. The cult seems, therefore, in this instance to have been in a state of transition from a monthly lunar observance to a yearly agricultural rite, the more conservative clergy adhering to the monthly ritual, while the agricultural population observed it in relation to the yearly cycle.

There can be little doubt that among the Semites also the ideas and observances which originally applied to the lunar cycle became transferred to the cycle of the seasons, and that the rites with which in later times the birth and death of the solar year were celebrated were the same which, in more primitive stages, had marked the significance attached to the lunar changes in the course of the month. Indeed, both the mourning rites of death and the rejoicings over the resurrection continued to be observed by the women at their monthly Sabbath, and persisted even in Christian times. St. Augustine complained that the heathen rites were observed in his day by the women of Carthaginian Africa. The

[1] Philo of Alexandria, in Eusebius, *Praeparatio Evangelica*, p. 156 E 40.
[2] A. Wahlen. *Moeurs, usages et costumes de tous les peuples du monde Asie*, p. 96.

old Roundhead, Northbrooke, reports the passage as follows:
" It is better that women should picke wool or spinne upon the
Sabbaoth day, than they should dance impudently and filthily all
day long upon the daye of the New Moone." [1] Concerning the
observance of the ritual in Harran, the immemorial site of the cult
of the Moon-god, a Christian writer of the tenth century, Abu-Sa'id
Wahb Ibn Ibrahim, gives us the following particulars: " In the
middle of this month is the feast of Al-Baqât, that is, of the
Mourning Women ; and this is the Ta'uz feast which is celebrated
in honour of the god Ta'uz.   The women bewail over him, lamenting that their Lord has been so cruelly slain.   They grind his bones
in the mill, and scatter them to the winds.   The women, during the
feast, abstain from eating any grain food, or from grinding flour." [2]
That abstinence from work and from food during the period of
seven days of the ' lamentations ' for Tammuz, which is not
mentioned in our accounts of the cult in more ancient times, had
probably a wider application than the aetiological interpretation
mentioned by the Syrian writer would indicate.   The period,
which in the older Babylonian documents is expressly referred to
as " unpropitious," [3] and is analogous to our Lent, was in
the observances it called for identical with the " unpropitious
day," or Sabbath of the women.   That, as we have seen, was
originally a monthly observance. [4]   Similarly, all rites, observances,
and ideas which in the more advanced stages of society are connected with the cycle of the solar year were, previous to the
development of that cult, part of the ritual practices connected with
the cycle of the lunar month.

The nations of Europe also practised rites, and entertained
conceptions in every essential respect identical with those which
we find at the dawn of historic times in Babylonia.   The Christian
Church repeatedly denounced and vainly tried to put down those
heathen beliefs and observances which have survived to our own
day.   In the south of France the Yule-log, or as it is often called,
the Christ-log, was solemnly anointed with olive oil, and thus,
like the log which constituted the image of the god Tammuz,
became a ' Christ ' in fact as well as in name. [5]   On Christmas Eve

---

[1] John Northbrooke, *A Treatise against Dicing, Dancing, Plays and
Interludes, with other Idle Pastimes*, p. 165.

[2] D. A. Chwolson, *Ueber Tammuz und die Menschenverehrung bei der
alten Babyloniern*, pp. 38 sq. ; Id., *Die Ssabier und der Ssabismus*, vol. ii,
pp. 604 sq.

[3] T. G. Pinches, in Hastings's *Encyclopaedia of Religion and Ethics*,
vol. xii, p. 190.

[4] See above, vol. ii, p. 435.

[5] A. Millin de Grandmaison, *Voyage dans les départements du Midi de la
France*, vol. iii, p. 336.

the anointed log was brought with much ceremony into the common-room or kitchen, or into the bedroom of the master and mistress of the house. It was then solemnly addressed in an invocation in Provençal verse sung as a chorus, which ran as follows :—

> Rejoice, O Noël Log,
> For to-morrow is the Day of Bread,
> Let all good things enter hither,
> Let women bear children,
> Let goats kid,
> Let the ewes lamb,
> Let there be much corn and much bread,
> And of wine a vat full.

The log was then placed on the fire, and such was the respect paid to it that all stood by in solemn silence until it was consumed.[1] In southern Italy it was the custom to place on the Christ-log a portion of all the food that was eaten and to pour wine over it, and this was said to be the share of Jesus Christ.[2] The ashes, which were carefully preserved and regarded as sacred, were in some districts of Germany scattered over the fields to ensure their fertility.[3] In Montenegro they are placed round the fruit-trees with the same object.[4] In France they were mixed with the fodder of cattle in order to make them calve.[5] In Italy they were scattered over the fields and were believed to be a sure protection against storms and disease.[6]

When the Yule-log was lit, it was the custom in Belgium to extinguish every other fire or light in the house.[7] The French country people believed that the fire from the sacred log was no ordinary material fire, and that if a brand from it were placed on the table, it would not consume the finest linen tablecloth. The observances did not terminate with the burning of the log. On the next day the Christmas bread was baked ; and such was its marvellous nature that it was believed that it might be kept for ten years without growing mouldy. Small pieces were treasured by each participant, and were regarded as a talisman against every disease and misfortune. Like their sisters in Harran, the French women baked no bread thereafter until Twelfth

---

[1] J.-B. Thiers, *Traité des superstitions qui regardent les sacremens*, etc., vol. i, pp. 263 sq.
[2] G. Finamore, *Credenze, usi e costumi abruzzesi*, p. 65.
[3] Montanus, *Die deutschen Volksfeste*, p. 12.
[4] K. S. Vuk, *Montenegro und die Montenegriner*, pp. 103 sq.
[5] J.-B. Thiers, *op. cit.*, vol. i, pp. 238, 231.
[6] G. Finamore, *loc. cit.*
[7] W. Mannhardt, *Wald und Feldkulte*, vol. i, p. 227.

Night ; nor was it permissible to spin or to weave, or to wash clothes during that period. It was even considered impious to wash one's feet. At such a cold time of the year it would have been inconvenient to extinguish all the fires ; but the next best thing was done, for it was a rule that no fire should be taken out of the house, and if a neighbour whose fire had gone out came to borrow a light, she was to be sternly refused. Further, during the period between Christmas and Twelfth Night a table was laid, and on it a loaf of bread ; the table was set day and night for the whole period in order that the Holy Virgin might come and partake of the food. The tablecloth was thereafter carefully preserved, to be used as a sack for the seeds at sowing-time, thereby securing their fertility.[1]

Those observances and beliefs found among the country-side populations of Europe, and now degraded to the level of ignorant superstitions condemned by the Church, were substantially equivalent to the cult of Tammuz in ancient Babylonia 6000 years ago. For Tammuz was simply an anointed log of wood. The Provençal chorus is perhaps not of such high literary merit as the beautiful psalms which have been transmitted to us, but the import of the requests which it expressed was essentially similar. What was expected of Tammuz was that he should impart fertility to the fields and orchards, to the vineyards, to the sheep and cattle, and to the women ; and no less was expected of the Yule-log. In ancient Babylon Tammuz was sacrificed by drowning him in the river, as was done by the Egyptians with Osiris, by the Indians of Florida with their log-god, and by the Oraons with their sacred tree or branch, which bears a strong resemblance to the Yule-log and Christmas tree. But it was also a common practice among the Semites to sacrifice Tammuz, like the Yule-log, by burning him. This was the custom at Tyre, where the god Melqart, that is, "the Lord of the City," was the local form of Tammuz. His great festival was known as the ' Feast of the Resurrection ' ; a large fire was lit in the precincts of the temple in which the god was consumed, and was thought to renew his life.[2] The story of Phoenix, the father of Europa, who was represented as being periodically burned, and as rising again out of his ashes, is a version of the myth and ritual

---

[1] J.-B. Thiers, *op. cit.*, pp. 263 sq., 260, 265, 268. The ' Twelve Nights ' are an unpropitious period, a period of mourning (see P. D. Chantepie de la Saussaye, *The Religion of the Teutons*, pp. 289, 225). With us at the present day they constitute the ' festive season ' par excellence ; but that is only because the Nativity feast has been shifted from the end of the period (Epiphany) to the beginning.

[2] Clement of Rome, *Recogn.*, x. 24 ; Nonnus, *Dionysiaca*, xl. 388.

of the Tyrian Tammuz. Among the Jews Talmudic tradition
ascribes the same fate to Abraham. It is related that Nimrod
caused Abraham to be cast into a burning furnace, and that he
rose again out of the fire.[1] The Jewish tradition evidently has
reference to a ritual identical with that of the Tyrians, which was
observed either in regard to the god Abraham or to some homo-
logous deity in Harran.

Similar rituals are found in other religions. The Algonkin
Indians of North America used to perform a ceremony exactly
similar to the burning and resurrection of Melqart. The occasion
for its observance in the instance to which our report refers
was an epidemic sickness, and the procedure was intended to
promote the restoration of the people to health. " They
looked out the handsomest and most sprightly young man in
the assembly, and put him into an entire new wigwam, built of
everything new for the purpose. They then formed into two files
at a small distance from each other. One standing in the space
at each end put fire to the bottom of the wigwam on all parts, and
they fell to singing and dancing. Presently the youth would leap
out of the flames, and fall down to appearances dead. Him they
committed to the care of five virgins, prepared for the purpose,
to restore to life again. The time required for this would be uncertain, from six to forty-eight hours—during which time the
dance must be kept up. When he was restored he would tell that
he had been carried in a large thing high up in the air where he
came to a great company of white people, with whom he inter-
ceded hard to have the distemper layed ; and generally after much
persuasion would obtain a promise, or answer of peace which never
failed of laying the distemper." [2] The resurrection of the sacrificial victim would, however, according to the rules of sympathetic magic, be of itself effectual without his intercession.
Although in this instance the effect of the procedure was to promote
the health of the people, it would be equally beneficial in
bringing about the recovery of the moon, or in promoting
the growth of crops, and the Algonkin ceremony might thus
become the central rite of the cult of a ' vegetation-god.'
In Thrace, Dionysos suffered yearly sacrifice by fire in the
same manner as Melqart at Tyre. A great flame appeared in his
temple, which was regarded as the symbol of his death and resurrection, and presaged, according to whether the fire burned well
or badly, a good or a poor harvest.[3] A ceremony almost identical

[1] J. A. Eisenmenger, *Endecktes Judenthum*, vol. i, pp. 490 sqq.

[2] T. Cooper, " Fabulous Traditions and Customs of the Indians of Martha's
Vineyard," *Collections of the Massachusetts Historical Society*, vol. i,
p. 140.

[3] Aristotle, *De mirabilibus auscultationibus*, cxxii.

with those observed in ancient Tyre and in Thrace may be witnessed at the present day at Florence. On the Saturday before
Easter an ancient wooden structure shaped like a catafalque
is placed in front of the main entrance of the Cathedral
and is covered with fireworks. At midday a wooden dove,
which moves along a wire connecting the Sepulchre, or ' Carro,'
with the high altar of the Cathedral, carries a taper lit at the altar
and sets fire to the pyrotechnic apparatus. Crowds of peasants
from all parts of Tuscany gather to witness the ceremony, for if the
fireworks go off successfully the harvest, they are convinced, will
be good, if not it will be poor.

It has been suggested by some Assyriologists that the cult of
Tammuz in early times was of the nature of a ' mystery,' and that
the essential rites of the cult were probably accessible to
initiates only.[1] The preponderant part played by women in
those rites in historical times—they were essentially a women's
religion—suggests that the cult was carried out in earlier
times by a kind of women's ' Secret society,' which possessed
the secrets of agricultural magic. Ancient Sumerian and Semitic
queens were regarded as impersonations of Ishtar, as is indicated
by the traditions of Semiramis and Dido, and Babylonian kings
were supposed to be the husbands of the Queen of Heaven.[2] The
Queen would thus, as the earthly Ishtar, and as high-priestess
of the rites of fertility, be the chief ministrant of the Dying God,
and would preside over the women's ' mysteries ' upon which
depended the magic of fertility. Such agricultural women's rites
would, no doubt, be an important factor in the rise to supremacy
of the Queen of Heaven and in the eventual displacement of the
primitive Moon-god by the goddess.

Be that as it may, the Great Goddess did not, in Semitic
or Sumerian lands, either originate as, or develop into, a

---

[1] S. Langdon, *Tammuz and Ishtar*, p. 24. In spite of the abundance
of literary remains referring to the cult, and of its evident widespread
popularity, there exist, with the exception of figures representing the mother
and child, no pictorial representations of the Dying God on Babylonian
monuments. It should, however, be noted that representations of the
death of a god would probably be regarded as extremely inauspicious by
the superstitious Babylonians. In Egypt, it is true, we have innumerable
pictorial representations of the dead god ; but in Egyptian religion the
Dying God stood emphatically for the earnest of the immortality of the soul.
The Sumerians and the Semites had no such doctrine. Tammuz is invoked
in prayer and asked to prolong life to a ripe old age, but there is no
expression in the rituals that can be interpreted as having reference to human
survival after death.

[2] F. Thureau-Dangin, *Les inscriptions de Sumer et d'Akkade*, p. 204 ;
H. Radau, " Miscellaneous Sumerian Texts," in *Hilprecht Anniversary
Volume*, pp. 393 sqq ; S. Langdon, *Sumerian Grammar*, pp. 196 sq. ; Id.,
Tammuz and Ishtar, p. 64.

personification of the earth, although she acquired every function of an earth-goddess and controlled agricultural rites. But even while fulfilling those functions it was as the Queen of Heaven that in all her forms she was consistently regarded. If the Semitic goddess never became overtly and officially the Earth-Mother, it was chiefly owing to the fact that the prominence of her character as a moon deity was too strongly established in the traditions of the race to allow of such a transformation. Ishtar was not a departmental moon-goddess in the midst of a pantheon of deities representing natural elements and forces. She stood as the chief representative of the cosmic divine powers of Semitic gods, and was the heiress of the supreme Moon-god, the only cosmic deity of Semitic religions.

That primitive simplicity and unity, that reference of all the powers of life and nature to a single source, and the absence of departmental deities, facilitated among the Semites the development of monotheistic conceptions. " In the faith of ancient Arabia," remarks Prince Teano, " in the cult of the moon, regarded as supreme male deity, conceived as a cause to which all worship refers, there lies manifestly the germ of monotheism, although only the Jews first, in Judaism and in Christianity, and Muhammad afterwards in Islam, attained to a clear enunciation of the monotheistic formula." [1] The great Yahwistic movement which resulted in Jewish monotheism was conditioned by many political circumstances, and owed its triumph in great measure to its nationalistic character. But from the religious point of view it was essentially much what it claimed to be, a return to " the faith of our fathers," a purging of Jewish cult from accretions which, if not exactly ' foreign,' were at any rate extraneous in many of their aspects to the primitive conceptions and cult of the Hebrew people. " There are abundant indications," observes again Prince Teano, " which seem to demonstrate that the Jehovah of the Hebrews and the Allah of Islam are merely transformations of the primitive lunar deity of Arabia." [2]

The Hebrews—the term is not an ethnical, but a political one, and refers not to a separate Semitic race, but to a confederation of Bedawi tribes—were the latest wave of migrants from the home of the race. Their last abode had been the region of the Minaean dependency, to which they referred as Sinim, ' The Land of the Moon,' [3] and one of the great centres of lunar worship in

---

[1] L. Caetani, *Studi di Storia Orientale*, vol. i, p. 225.

[2] *Loc. cit.*

[3] *Isaiah*, xlix. 12. Jewish traditional history is profoundly distorted by the disproportionate place assigned in the Yahwistic editing to the legend of the ' Exodus from Egypt.' Nothing is more probable than

Arabia in its purest, and at the same time most elaborate, Minaean form. The cult of the god was there, as in most other parts of Arabia, associated with a sacred mountain, the mount of Sinai, that is, the Mountain of the Moon.[1] The service of the god of Sinai was, as we learn from the very ancient inscription of Al-Ola, in the care of a special tribe of priests and priestesses called 'law'iu,' or by assimilation with the god, 'lawî-atan.'[2] To that sacred clan of 'law'iu,' or Levites, belonged the traditional leaders, Moses, or in more primitive Semitic speech Musa, the Musrian, Jethro, Aaron,

---

that bands of northern Arabian Semites settled at various times on the Egyptian side of the isthmus and that some obtained employment in the building of the storehouses of Ramesses and Pithom, an occupation which they found intensely distasteful. Nothing is more improbable than that the Hebrew tribes as a whole were at any time in Egypt. Generations of scholars have since the birth of archaeological history sought to fit the legend into the frame of known historical outlines ; they are no nearer to imparting to it a semblance of historicity than they were a century ago. The legend is a tissue of inconsistencies ; the Egyptian scenario is a clumsy fabrication ; the scene shifts without regard for dramatic verisimilitude from the Egyptian court at Memphis—under Theban dynasties !—to Arabia ; the actors are Midianites. Northern Arabian inscriptions prove that the 'Midianite' country, the home of all the 'dramatis personae' in the Exodus legend, was a Minaean colony in northern Arabia (*Corpus Inscriptionum Semiticarum*, Glaser, 1083, 1155 ; O. Weber, " Studien zur südarabischen Alterthumskunde," *Mittheilungen der vorderasiatische Gesellschaft*, vi, i, p. 27 ; F. Hommel, *Aufsätze und Abhandlungen*, vol. ii, pp. 235 sqq.) ; and a mass of circumstantial evidence confirms the intrinsic probability that this and not Egypt, of whose culture not a trace is to be found in theirs, was the home of the Hebrew tribes before they entered Canaan (see in particular H. Winckler, *Altorientalische Forchungen*, vol. i, pp. 24 sqq. ; Id., *Musri, Meluhla, Ma'in* ; Id., " North Arabia and the Bible," *The Hibbert Journal*, 1904, pp. 571 sqq. ; O. Weber, *op. cit.*, pp. 34 sqq.). Sir E. A. Wallis Budge, Dr. H. R. Hall, and a few other scholars regard the view as having been 'discredited' ; but no adequate consideration has been adduced to do so. Considerable trouble has been taken to show that by 'Musri' the Hebrew writers mean Egypt, a fact which nobody has disputed. But geography was never a strong point with the Semites, and the diplomatic inaccuracy of Hebrew scribes is notorious. The Masoteric text of *Judges* x. 12 has מעון where the Septuagint reads Μαδιαμ. A similar confusion is found in *Job* ii. 11 (ציפר הבעמתי ; *Sept.* : Μιναίων βασιλεύς). Such geographical confusions are common (cf. O. Weber, *op. cit.*, pp. 30 sq. ; L. Caetani, *Studi di storia orientale*, vol. i, pp. 121, 125, 131, 243). It would require much more solid evidence than that afforded by the contradictory and inconsistent Hebrew legend to prove that the Hebrews were naturalised Egyptians and not north Arabian Bedawi.

[1] H. Zimmern, in E. Schrader, *Die Keilinschriften und das Alte Testament*, p. 365 ; M. Jastrow, *The Religion of Babylonia and Assyria*, p. 77 ; D. Nielsen, *Die altrabische Mondreligion*, p. 154 ; W. Rendell Harriss, in Hastings's *Dictionary of the Bible*, s.v. ' Sinai.'

[2] J. H. Mordtmann, *Beiträge zur minaischen Epigraphik*, p. 43 ; F. Hommel, *Aufsätze und Abhandlungen*, pp. 30 sq. ; O. Weber, *op. cit.*, pp. 2, 29.

Joshua, Miriam, the high-priestess Mary, who organised the Hebrew
confederation and led the tribes out of the land of Musri into Canaan,
or Phoenicia. The name Levi means " serpent " ; and the deity
was commonly worshipped under the common form of the Semitic
moon-god as a serpent.[1] The sacred serpent remained the symbol
of the God of Israel in the Temple for many centuries and " the
children of Israel did burn incense to it." [2] The Levite priests wore
as their headdress a lunar crescent, a form of headgear which occurs
in many other cults and has given rise to the episcopal mitre. The
high-priest sometimes wore a large globular white turban representing the full moon. The moon is regarded as the emblem of
Israel in Talmudic literature and Hebrew tradition.[3] The mythical
ancestor of the Hebrews was Abraham of Ur, who is no other than
the god of Ur, the Moon-city. As if to emphasise his connection
with the racial god, he is made to migrate to Harran, the other
great centre of Semitic moon-cult.[4] The Levite god Yahweh was

---

[1] The serpent is even more constant as a lunar symbol among the Semites
than in other parts of the world. In southern Arabian inscriptions the
serpent and the crescent are in association with one another a constantly
recurring symbol (D. Nielsen, *Die altarabische Mondreligion*, p. 108). Sinn
is represented in Ur as a serpent with human head ; the Sumerian moon-
god was a serpent-god, or Leviathan. Throughout Babylonian pictography
the moon is represented as a snake (*Ibid.*, p. 107. Cf. W. W. Baudissin,
Studien zur semitischen Religionsgeschichte, vol. i, pp. 255–292 ; O. Weber,
Altorientalische Siegelbilder, pp. 103 sq.).

[2] *II Kings*, xviii. 4.

[3] M. Seligsohn, in *The Jewish Encyclopaedia*, vol. viii, p. 678.

[4] Abraham, or Ab-Ram, means ' the high father,' or ' the father on
high,' ' the heavenly father.' By a strange violence to Semitic speech the
name is twisted in apologetic literature into ' My father is the Most
High.' In accordance with such dog-Semitic we should have to translate
Abu-Kamil, for instance, by ' My father is the Most Excellent,' a process
of inversion which would surprise Arab genealogists. The name Ab-ram
occurs in personal names, like all divine names, in very ancient documents,
and curiously is employed as a synonym of ' Ab-Sinn ' (B. Meissner, *Beiträge
zum altbabylonischen Privatrecht*, No. 111). A tradition reported by
Eutychius runs as follows : " At the time of Abraham there reigned Shabib,
the wife of Sinn, priestess of the mountain, who built Nisib and Edessa
and surrounded them with walls. She founded also the sanctuary of
Harran, and made an idol of gold, called Sinn " (Eutychius, *Annales*, i. 72,
in Migne, *Patrologiae Cursus, Ser. Graec.*, vol. iii, cols. 923 sq.). For the
identification of Abraham with Sinn, see further A. Jeremias, *Das Alte
Testament im Lichte des alten Orients*, pp. 182, 211. Al-Kindi reports in the
tenth century the tradition that " Abraham lived with his people four-score
years and ten in the land of Harran, worshipping none other than Al-Uzza,
an idol famous in the land and adored by the men of Harran under the
name of the moon, which same custom prevails among them to the present
day " (*The Apology of Al-Kindy*, ed. by Sir W. Muir, p. 17). The Millat
Ibrahim, or religion of Abraham, was widespread among Semitic peoples
(see T. Hyde, *Historia religionis veterum Persarum*, pp. 28, 36). He was

not only " the god of Abraham, the god of Isaac, the god of Jacob " ;
he was also " the god of Shem," that is to say, the god of all the
Semites.[1]

worshipped in the Ka'aba (E. Pocock, *Specimen Historiae Arabum*, p. 100 ;
A. P. Caussin de Perceval, *Essai sur l'histoire des Arabes avant l'Islamisme*,
vol. i, p. 270). Abraham and Israel were also numbered among the mythical
kings of Damascus (F. C. Movers, *Die Phönizier*, vol. i, p. 87). Abraham
was identified with Bel of Babylon (Josephus, *Antiquit.*, i. 7. 2 ; Eusebius,
Praep. Evang., ix p. 449 ; Clement Alexandr., *Rom. recog.*, i. 33).
    [1] *Genesis*, ix. 26. Theories which sought to assign a foreign origin to
Yahweh are now untenable. He was purely Semitic, and the god of the Jews
from earliest times. There is nothing peculiar or extraneous about the name.
Its more usual form, as with many other Semitic names, appears to have been
the syncopated Yaho or Yah. This was the form in which it was known, when
known at all, among the ancients (Diodorus Siculus, i. 94 : " To the Jews
Moses gave the laws of the god called Yaho (*'Ιάω*) " ; and St. Jerome expressly
says : " The name of the Lord among the Jews consists of four letters,
Jod, He, Vau, He, which is the proper name of God, and may be read
Yaho " (Jerome, *Epist.* xxv, *ad Marcellam*, in Migne, *Patrologiae Cursus
Completus*, vol. xxii, col. 429. Cf. Origen, *In Joh.*, ii. i, *op. cit.*, *Series Graeca*,
vol. xiv, col. 105 ; Clement of Alexandria, *Stromates*, v. 6, *ibid.*, vol. ix,
col. 60 ; Theodoret, ed. Sirmond, vol. i, p. 364 ; W. W. Baudissin, *Studien
zur semitischen Religionsgeschichte*, vol. i, pp. 183 sqq.). The Ophites and
the Valentinians always wrote the name Yaho (Irenaeus, *Adv. haeres.* i. iv. 1,
in Migne, *op. cit.*, *Series Graeca*, vol. vii, col. 481), and it is in that form that
it appears on cabalistic gems. The name is not uncommon in proper
names in Babylonia from earliest times (A. T. Clay, *Light on the Old Testament
from Babel*, pp. 236, 239 ; G. A. Barton, " Yaweh before Moses," *Studies in
the History of Religions presented to Crawford Howell Toy*, pp. 188 sq.).
On a beautiful stele from Byblos, for instance, the king Yaveh-Melek,
that is, Yahweh the King, is represented as worshipping the Queen of
Heaven (*Corpus Inscriptionum Semiticarum*, vol. i, p. 8, pl. 1). There
are indications that Yaho may have been one of the ' secret names,' the
' real name,' of the Semitic god in Babylonia. Johannes Lydus expressly
asserts that " the Chaldeans called their god Yaho " (J. Lydus, *De
Mensibus*, p. 74. Cf. Macrobius, *Sat. Conv.*, i. 18). A Babylonian
private text reads : " The god Ib is my god Yau " (*Essays on some Biblical
Questions*, p. 49). It must be borne in mind that the ' true name ' of
deities, which if divulged among the profane would give them power
over the gods, is everywhere kept secret, and the names that are current
are mere cult-epithets. That particularly applies to Semitic deities.
In Islam Allah has ' a hundred names,' but no one knows the true name
of Allah. In Egypt the true names of the gods were never uttered (Cicero,
De nat. deor., iii. 16). He who spoke the true name of Isis was " a child
of death " (Joannes Malala, *Chronographia*, p. 61). The Samaritans declared
that the god they worshipped " had no name " (Josephus, *Antiq.*, xii. 5. 5).
The same was said of the Jews (*ibid.*, ii. 12. 4 ; Philo, *Vita Mosis*,
iii. 4). Indeed, it was a crime among the Jews to utter the name of
Yahweh ; in *Leviticus*, xxv. 16—" And he that blasphemeth the name
of the Lord, he shall surely be put to death, and all the congregation
shall certainly stone him "—the word ' noqedh,' which is translated ' blas-
pheme,' means properly ' articulate,' or ' utter.' It may well be that, as
Lydus states, the name of the god of the Levites as it appeared in their

When the Hebrew tribes under the leadership of the votaries
of the god of Sinai came out of the " land of great drought " into
a land flowing with the milk and honey of the Queen of Heaven,
they found their own race there and their own religion, but
modified by the effects of agricultural civilisation. The Baal
of Sinai had, like all other Semitic gods, his female form or
counterpart. The Queen of Heaven, under whatever name
she may have been worshipped—possibly Miriam, who figures
as the high-priestess among the Levites, bore the name of the
goddess—belonged from time immemorial to Jewish cult.[1] The
Elohim of ancient Jewish religion were in all probability the male
and female moon deities. The temple of Jerusalem was simultane-
ously dedicated to Yahweh and to the Queen of Heaven. Before
it stood the ' asherah,' the symbolic trees that are throughout
Semitic lands associated with the female aspect of the deity.[2] In
all probability the two figures in the temple's sanctuary, which were
later interpreted as cherubim, were the images of the male and
female deities, as the two so-called ' tables of the law ' in the Ark
were their sacred stones. Among the Jews of Elephantine in the
fifth century B.C. Yahweh was associated with his goddess, and the
names of the Elohim were blended, as Anath-Yahu.[3] In the
excavations of Gezer, in Palestine, a number of figures of bulls have
been found, the usual representation of Yahweh ; with them are
the corresponding figures of cows, the animal form of the great
goddess.[4] Abraham, a close double of Yahweh, was worshipped
with his female counterpart, Sarah, " The Queen." [5]

immemorial cult cry, Hallelu Yah, was the true name of the Semitic god in
all his local forms. The first part of the cry is still the usual form of salutation to the new moon among the Bedawi and in Abyssinia (F. Hommel,
Der Gestirndienst der alten Araber, p. 28 ; E. Liltmann, " Sternsagen und
Astrologisches aus Nordabessinien," *Archiv für Religionswissenschaft*, xii,
p. 313). Yahuq was a divine name among the pre-Islamic Arabs ; there
was an idol of Yahuq among the Hamdan, and a hill near Ghaymar is called
the mountain of Yahuq (J. Wellhausen, *Reste des arabischen Heidentums*,
pp. 13, 22).

[1] Besides *Jeremiah*, xiv. 22, see *Amos*, v. 25 ; *Genesis*, xiv. 5.

[2] W. W. Baudissin, *Studien zur semitischen Religionsgeschichte*, vol. ii,
pp. 22 sq. The asherah were special objects of denunciation with the
prophets (*Judges*, iii. 7 ; *Kings*, xxiii. 4). The derivation of the asherah
from the trees which represented in Mecca the goddess Al-Uzza is clearly
shown on a stele from Carthage on which, instead of the three pillars
as asherah which commonly represent the threefold goddess, two trees
and one pillar are pictured (*Corpus Inscriptionum Semiticarum*, vol. ii,
part i, tab. vi, fig. 619). The goddess herself is sometimes called Asherah.

[3] E. Meyer, *Der Papyrusfund von Elephantine*, p. 63.

[4] R. A. S. Macalister, *Bible Side-lights from the Mound of Gezer*,
p. 115.

[5] Cf. above, pp. 82 n[9], 108 n[4].

But the relation and respective status of the male and female Semitic deities were, in agricultural Canaan, profoundly modified. The Queen of Heaven eclipsed the male god. Adon, the Lord, instead of being the spouse or the father, was the son of the Queen of Heaven, and a subordinate deity by her side. The bulk of the Jewish people, especially the women, readily adapted themselves to the more advanced view, the richer form of the racial religion, and their devotion became to an increasing extent transferred from the Baal to the Holy Mother. But to the more conservative elements among the Hebrew tribes those agricultural forms of the Semitic cult were an abomination. The profound antipathy of the true pastoralist to agriculture and agricultural rites and conceptions has already been noted with reference to the Aryan Hindu.[1] The nomads of Central Asia have the same unbounded dislike of agricultural populations.[2] The Bahima of Central Africa, a purely pastoral people, look with contempt upon the neighbouring agricultural tribes, and will not intermarry with them.[3] Nothing could induce the Germans, says Tacitus, to set their hand to a plough.[4] That characteristic of all true pastoral peoples is in the highest degree pronounced among the Semites. The Jew has never adopted farming as an occupation. In contrast to the sentiments of the Greeks and Italians, with whom the life of the farmer represented the ideal of beatitude and stood for the golden age of humanity, "to eat bread in the sweat of his brow" is to the pastoral nomad the symbol of a curse, of a fall from a state of happiness. Muhammad looked with contempt upon the Kuryshites and Ansari "for they employ themselves with sowing seed, but we Arabs of the desert are not engaged in sowing"; [5] and pointing to a ploughshare and other agricultural implements, he said, "those implements do not enter into the house of a nation unless Allah causes lowmindedness to enter there also." [6] "The divine glory," the Prophet is again reported to have said, "is among the shepherds; vanity and impudence among agricultural peoples." [7] Even the Hellenised Jew Philo glorifies the shepherd in contrast with the agriculturist.[8]

---

[1] See above, p. 59.
[2] P. S. Pallas, *Voyages en différentes provinces de l'Empire de Russie,* vol. i, p. 539.
[3] J. Roscoe, *The Soul of Central Africa,* p. 66.
[4] Tacitus, *Germania,* xiv. xv.
[5] Al-Bokhari, *Recueil des traditions mahométanes,* ed. L. Krehl, vol. ii, p. 385; I. Goldziher's translation, *Mythology among the Hebrews,* p. 79.
[6] Al-Bokhari, *Les traditions islamiques,* ed. O. Houdas and W. Marçais, vol. ii, p. 91.
[7] *Ibid.,* p. 537.
[8] Philo Judaeus, *De sacrificio Kajin,* p. 169.

In the fierce nationalistic struggles of the Hebrews the local homologues of Yahweh were repudiated as false Baalim, instead of being, as by other Semites, recognised as identical with the national god. It was declared by the Yahwists that Yahweh's leadership of the Hebrew tribes into Canaan had been undertaken under a covenant or oath of fidelity to him ; and it was also claimed that he was a better rain-maker than the Baal of the Phoenicians.[1] As happened with the Babylonian gods, he became dissociated from his darker aspect, or double, discharging upon him his darker, maleficent, lunar attributes, as cause of death and of disease. El or Bel came to be in Babylonian myth the opponent and conqueror of his own double, Ea, or Tiamat, the serpent-god, or, as in the Phoenician version, Melqarto was opposed to the fish-god Dagon.[2] The god of Sinai dissociated himself from his serpent-form Levia-

FIG. 20.—THE CONTEST BETWEEN SINN AND THE DARK MOON.
From a tablet in the Berlin Museum (*Vat.* 7851).

than, who became ' the enemy,' and whose sacred image in the temple was destroyed by Hezekiah.[3] The contest between the two aspects of the lunar divinity refers, of course, originally to the conflict between the bright and dark moon, which is represented on a Babylonian tablet (Fig. 20) ; and the process of translation of that contest into terms of moral values was analogous to that which has been noted in ancient Egypt.[4] The most familair example of that translation is presented by Persian Mazdaism, from which post-exilic Yahwism drew much inspiration. In the prose Avesta the dualism between good and evil, which is unknown to primitive religion, becomes a veritable obsession. All things fall strictly

---

[1] *Jeremiah*, xiv. 22. According to the version of the Phoenician priests Yahweh was, of course, completely defeated in his contest as a rain-maker with the Phoenician Baal, and the priests of the latter brought the drought to an end by their prayers (Josephus, *Antiq.*, viii. 13. 2, after Menander of Ephesus).

[2] C. B. Stark, *Gaza und die philistäische Küste*, p. 249.

[3] *II Kings*, xviii. 4. Leviathan, the god of the Levites, is in the Talmud expressly identified with ' the ancient serpent,' or Satan (J. A. Eisenmenger, *Endecktes Judenthum*, vol. i, p. 823).

[4] See above, vol. ii, pp. 784 sq.

into the two categories; even words belong to either one or the other of the two sharply contrasted classes. The good spirit, Ahura Mazda, is the creator of all things good; the evil spirit, Ahriman, the creator of all things evil; and existence consists in the eternal contest between the two principles. The prose Avesta is the latest of the Zoroastrian sacred texts; it bears every mark of having been composed in a language that was no longer a living language. If we turn to the earlier sacred books of Persian religion, the Gathas and the Yashts, we come upon a remarkable fact: there is not a word of this elaborate dualism, there is no trace of the polarity between good and evil values. Instead of Ahura Mazda being the creator of good things, and Ahriman of evil ones, he is expressly stated to have created darkness as well as light, the night as well as the day.[1] Ahriman is not mentioned in the Gathas; and so little was he differentiated from Ahura Mazda that the Magi, the primitive Persian priesthood, continued, under the reformed religion, to offer sacrifices to Ahriman in the old shamanistic spirit, " to avert things ill and things of gloom." [2] In the Vedas, Aryaman is an alternative form of Agni; he is " the Lord of all Beings "; [3] " Mitra and Aryaman, the givers of good rain, are glorious." [4] The only hint of his potential dark nature in the great god Aryaman is the fact that he is the Lord of the dead and of the underworld, in his capacity, doubtless, of dark moon-god.[5]

It was not, however, on political and nationalistic grounds alone that the differentiation of Yahweh from other forms of the Semitic god was, from the point of view of the Hebrew conservatives, desirable and necessary. His local homologue, the Phoenician

---

[1] *Yasts*, xliv. 5; E. H. Moulton, *Early Zoroastrianism*, p. 95.

[2] See E. H. Moulton, *op. cit.*, pp. 425 sq. In Persian religion, as in most other religions, the dissociated good principle became identified with the sun, " the conqueror," and the dark, fatal, inexorable aspects were left in their old association with the lunar powers. Yet, as elsewhere, it was not possible to obliterate altogether, even in the most emphatically solar religion, the immemorial lunar cult. Herodotus tells us that the Persians worshipped both the sun and the moon (Herodotus, i. 131). As Gibbon remarks, " the Persians of every age have denied the charge, and explained the equivocal conduct which might appear to give colour to it " (E. Gibbon, *The Decline and Fall of the Roman Empire*, vol. i, p. 200). But, as Harley observes, " it will certainly require considerable explanation to free from lunar idolatry the following passage : ' We sacrifice to the moon, the holy master of holiness we sacrifice to the full moon, the holy master of holiness ' " (*Zend Avesta* Yast, vii. 4; *The Sacred Books of the East*, vol. xxiii, p. 90).

[3] *Rig-Veda*, ii. i (*The Sacred Books of the East*, vol. xlvi, p. 186. C v. 3, *ibid.*, p. 371).

[4] *Rig-Veda*, i. 41, *ibid.*, p. 148.

[5] *Bhagavadgîtâ*, x. 30 (*The Sacred Books of the East*, vol. viii, p. 89).

Baal, was no other than Tammuz, or Adon, the Lord. So completely had Yahweh become assimilated to him that not only were the two cults confounded, the Jewish women celebrating the ' lamentations ' of Tammuz in the national temple, but the very names had become inextricably blended ; Yahweh was as often as not spoken of as ' The Lord,' Adon. The tetragrammaton was sometimes vocalised with the vowels of the name of Adonai, a confusion which gave occasion at the time of the Lutheran reformation to the production by persons unconversant with the Hebrew language of the barbarism ' Jehovah.' That identification, natural enough and in itself unobjectionable, meant, however, that Yahweh must stand in the same relation to the Queen of Heaven as Adonai. It meant the ultimate supremacy of the goddess over the god, the eclipse of the primitive moon-god by his agriculturalised feminine counterpart.

The Jewish god had, in fact, but one real and formidable rival. It was not his homologues, whom all Semitic peoples recognised as equivalent, who endangered his position, but the Goddess, the Queen of Heaven, who, from being a subsidiary aspect of the primitive male moon-deity, had, among the agricultural populations, come to displace him well-nigh entirely. And it was no easy task for the Yahwistic reformers to press on the people the claims of Yahweh to their fidelity in his solitary male form. They were met with the answer : " We will certainly do whatever thing goeth out of our mouths, to burn incense unto the Queen of Heaven, and to pour drink offerings unto her, as we have done, we and our fathers, our kings, and our princes in the cities of Judah and in the streets of Jerusalem. For then had we plenty of victual and were well, and saw no evil. But since we left off to burn incense to the Queen of Heaven and to pour drink offerings to her, we have wanted all things, and we have been consumed by the sword and by famine." [1]

One aspect of the contest was neither purely religious nor political. The religious Hebrew opposition to the Great Goddess was also a struggle of patriarchal principles against the survivals of matriarchal society. The chief opponents of the Yahwistic priests and prophets throughout the old prophetic reformation, the opponents whom the reformers recognised as their true enemies, and against whom they never wearied of hurling their invectives, were the women. It was the women who answered

---

[1] *Jeremiah*, xliv. 17–18. The popularity of the Queen of Heaven is reflected in the poem of Esther and Mordecai—but slightly modified dialectical variants of Ishtar and Marduk (cf. H. Winckler, *Altorientalische Forschungen*, vol. iii, pp. 1 sqq. ; C. Fries, *Die Griechischen Götter und Heroen,* p. 113).

them by refusing to give up their allegiance to the Queen of Heaven and their motherly lamentations over the Dying God ; it was the women who delighted in keeping up their Sabbaths and their feasts ; it was the women of the harems of the Jewish kings, not by any means all ' foreign ' women as the prophets chose to represent, who defied them in defence of the Great Mother, and urged their lords against the enthusiasts. It was a Queen who wrought fierce vengeance upon the enemies of the Queen of Heaven. As the Jewish reformers experienced to their cost, it was no mere idle fancy of the votaries of the Semitic Moon-god in Harran, when they remarked that if they were to honour the moon as a female they would become subject to their women.[1]

Although the ideal of his votaries was the restoration of the conception of Yahweh and of his cult to their primitive purity and supremacy, that restoration, as always happens, could not take place without involving profound changes in those conceptions. The past, in human evolution, cannot be recalled without being transformed. In order to sever completely the connection with his rival, the Queen of Heaven, it was necessary to abolish the old conception of a female aspect or counterpart ; Yahweh could no longer remain Elohim. The doctrine of his unity and oneness, the conception of him as the only god, had reference primarily not so much to the repudiation of his homologues, as to the repudiation of his female counterpart. The repudiation of other Baalim became extravagantly exaggerated by nationalistic sentiment and priestly interests. In the campaigns of Hezekiah and of Josiah not only were the local Baalim attacked and denounced, but all other Yahwehs, except the Yahweh of Jerusalem, were likewise abolished.[2] The ancient Yahweh had been willing to be worshipped wherever a stone was erected in his honour. " In all places where I record my name," he said, " I will come unto thee, and I will bless thee." [3] But now all his shrines, his chief shrine in Gideon, the great shrines of Bethel and of Dan, those of Nob, Gilgal, Gerizim, Tabor, Carmel, Shiloh, all the sacred places of his cult, were put down ; and it was decreed : " Take heed to thyself that thou offer not thy burnt-offerings in every place thou seest." [4] Not only was there to be no other Baal but Yahweh, but there should be no other Yahweh but the Yahweh of Jerusalem, the Yahweh of Zion, and his temple was the only place where he could be worshipped at all. The religious ground of that nationalistic doctrine was that

[1] See above, vol ii, p. 639.
[2] *II Kings*, xviii. 4, 22 ; xxiii. 5, 8, 9, 14, 15.
[3] *Exodus*, xx. 24.
[4] *Deuteronomy*, xii. 13. The Book of ' Deuteronomy ' was composed the priest Hilkiah to give divine sanction to these reforms (*II Kin* xxiii. 2, 24).

Yahweh was not like other Baalim, that they were impure, that they acknowledged relations to other deities, to a female consort or Mother, which meant an agricultural religion, and the virtual eclipse of the male god.

Hence the chief task of the reformers was to edit and adapt the traditional myths so as to obliterate all mythology. The character of the new Yahweh which is most persistently insisted on is that he is unchanging, he changes not.[1] It might appear puzzling—and it has puzzled more than one theologian—why insistence should be laid on the unchanging character of the god. Abidingness is, to be sure, a divine character, though even progressive revelation is not inconsistent with divine attributes ; but it is not obvious why that unchanging nature should be so dwelt upon as the chief characteristic of the Hebrew god. To declare that he was unchanging was but a way of affirming that he was not as other Semitic gods, that he was not a moon-god. He did not wax or wane ; he did not successively take the aspect of three different gods ; above all he did not die and rise again after the third day : in other words, he was not Tammuz, he was not the male double of the Queen of Heaven. He was unchanging. All astral myths and allusions had to be expunged. The Old Testament carried farther than any book the principles for which Euhemerus of Agrigentum was accused of atheism. The fragments of the supposed ' Sacred History' of the Phoenicians or Canaanites by Sanchoniathon have been described as " after the manner of Euhemerus." [2] In the introduction to those fragments we are told that " the most ancient peoples, especially the Phoenicians and the Egyptians, from whom other peoples derived the custom, accounted those the greatest gods who had found out things most necessary and useful in life, and had been benefactors of mankind." The Hebrew scriptures edited and composed by Ezra went farther than either Euhemerus or Sanchoniathon ; all gods are there reduced to the status of men, and cosmological myths translated into history. The primitive moon-god of the Semites has obliterated as far as possible l traces of his original nature. Nevertheless, even at the present day, in Palestine, Jewish women are not forgetful of the immemorial

[1] *Psalms*, cii. 25–28 ; *Isaiah*, xl. 28 xli. 4 ; *Lamentations*, v. 19 ; *Malachi*, iii. 6.

[2] F. C. Movers, *Die Phönizier*, vol. i, p. xiv. It is exceedingly unlikely at Sanchoniathon was, as has sometimes been supposed, " evolved from e inner consciousness of Philo " (G. Rawlinson, *History of Phoenicia*, p. 385). o doubt he had before him some of the numerous compendia of the Sacred riptures of the Phoenicians, though there can be little doubt that he freely ited them in accordance with his own ideas, a procedure which was iversal in his day, and has not yet entirely fallen into disuse.

object of Semitic cult, and when the new moon appears they recite reverently a prayer, saying : " May God cause thee to increase ; and mayest thou be enabled to bestow upon us a blessed month." [1]

It was the great development of agriculture that laid the foundations of Western civilisation, which gave rise to the pre-eminent position which the Great Goddesses occupied at the dawn of our culture.   The fertility of the soil retained its immemorial association with the women who had been the tillers of the earth and were regarded as the depositaries of agricultural magic ; and, the masculine functions of the primitive moon-gods having to a large extent lost their original direct significance, the mother-goddess, whose motherhood was assimilated to the fruit-bearing earth's, overshadowed for a time the masculine deities.   Men, how-ever, not only took up the labours which primitively appertained to the exclusive sphere of women, but, as has happened in far ruder phases of culture, in Australia, in South America, were as anxious to obtain control of those magic powers which, in the conditions of early civilisation, were thought to be essential to the successful cultivation of the soil.   The male gods, rein-terpreted and transformed into solar or more generalised deities, ultimately ousted the Great Mothers, not only among the pastoral Semites, but throughout the Western world.   The religious evolu-tion thus constituted an aspect of the social evolution that led to the final obliteration of the matriarchal character which Western society had retained until a very late phase of its development, and the substitution of a patriarchal social organisation.   Not only the cultivation, but the ownership of the soil passed from the women to the men ; the rites which were associated with the food-supply passed also from the hands of the women into those of powerful male priesthoods.   That process took place in the cradle of European civilisation, in Europe proper, as it had taken place among the pastoral Semites, but in a somewhat different manner ; for the Mediterranean peoples were not pastoralists and had none of the pastoralists' prejudices against agriculture and its rites. The Bedawi last-comers, who would make no compromise with the rites of agricultural populations, alone succeeded in entirely abolishing the Great Goddess and her ' abominations.'   The circumstance that it was their religion which ultimately imposed itself upon the Western world, is perhaps not unconnected with the natural tendency to obliterate the last traces of matriarchal society.

[1] T. Canaan, *Aberglaube und Volksmedizin in Lande der Bibel*, pp. 96 sq

The Divine Mother and
Child in Greek Religion.

In the earliest Aegean civilisation, of which the great centre
was Krete, the most striking religious phenomenon is the pre-
ponderance of female deities, surpassing perhaps anything of the
kind to be found elsewhere. While from the earliest neolithic
tombs to the last Minoan epoch innumerable figures and representations of goddesses are met with, no male idol has been found,
and there are not above two representations of a male god on seals
of a late date, picturing the youthful deity in complete subordination to goddesses.[1] Some six types of representations of goddesses
may be distinguished, but their attributes are interchangeable, the
serpent-goddess being sometimes found with doves, the mountain-
goddess with serpents, and so forth ;[2] and those various forms,
all are agreed, refer to a female divinity who, under varying attributes, " seems from first to last to have been the main object of
worship in the island."[3] The attributes of the goddess are virtually
identical with those of the Asiatic goddess whose type is Ishtar.
The Kretan goddess appears more often with serpents than does
the Babylonian ; but the latter was also a serpent-goddess, and is
represented in the same attitude with serpents in her hands.[4] The
doves, the lions and other beasts, the conventionalised representation of a mountain, are symbols common, both in substance and
treatment, to the Great Mother in Western Asia and in Krete. It
is, in fact, difficult to escape the conclusion that Kretan religion
was in great part derived from, or profoundly influenced by, the
religion of Syria and of Babylon. The Kretan Great Mother was,
like the Semitic goddess, triune, and was, like her, commonly
represented under the attributes of the tree, the pillar, and the
cross.[5] That identity of symbols and attributes between the Kretan
Great Mother and the Semitic Ishtar would naturally lead us to
regard the former as being, like the latter, a moon-goddess. That
conclusion is confirmed by other data. In a representation, on a

---

[1] A. J. Evans, "Mycenaean Tree and Pillar Cult," *The Journal of Hellenic
Studies*, xxi, p. 168.

[2] H. Prinz, " Bemerkungen zur altkretische Religion," *Mitteilungen der
Kaiserlich deutsche archäologischer Institut, Athenische Abteilung*, xxxv,
pp. 174 sq., 156 sqq.

[3] D. G. Hogarth, " Aegean Religions," in Hastings's *Encyclopaedia of
Religion and Ethics*, vol. i, p. 143. Cf. A. J. Evans, *op. cit.*, p. 175 ; Id.,
" The Palace of Knossos," *Annual of the British School at Athens*, ix, p. 87 ;
H. Prinz, *op. cit.*, p. 173 ; B. E. Williams, in H. B. Hawes, *Gournia*, p. 51 ;
R. M. Burrows, *The Discoveries in Crete*, p. 137 ; R. Dussaud, " Questions
Mycénéennes," *Revue de l'Histoire des Religions*, li, p. 26.

[4] A. Jeremias, *Handbuch der altorientalischen Geisteskultur*, pp. 254.

[5] See below, p. 161 ; above, vol. ii, p. 753.

lentoid from Ligortino, of the temple of the goddess, which is marked
by a sacred tree growing before it, the deity is indicated by a large
crescent moon within the shrine.[1]   The lunar crescent is a ubiqui-
tous symbol in Krete under the form of the so-called ' horns of
consecration.' [2]

The paramount prominence of goddesses, or rather of the Great
Goddess, in Kretan religion, which is revealed by archaeological
exploration, is reflected in the traditional mythology of the island
as it appears in Greek literature.   Every Kretan goddess or divine
queen is identified with the moon.   Britomartis-Diktynna is stated
to be Artemis, Hekate, and the moon.[3]   The cow-goddess Pasiphae,
that is, ' the all-shining one,' is the moon.[4]   Europa, another cow-
goddess, is recognised as being a moon-goddess,[5] and so is Ariadne,
' the clear shining.' [6]

The Kretan goddess has attributes which are commonly
regarded as ' chthonic,' or earthly, such as lions, trees, and the
truncated cone which represents a mountain.   But those attributes
are identical with those of the Asiatic Ishtar, and they did not
make her a personification of the earth.   There is therefore no
justification for the opinion of some scholars that the ancient
Kretans worshipped the personified earth.[7]   Demetrios of Skepsis
expressly stated that Rhea, the term usually employed to denote
an earth-goddess, was never worshipped in Krete.[8]

The youthful god who appears on gems as a figure drawn

[1] A. J. Evans, *op. cit.*, p. 185 ; R. Dussaud, *Les civilisations préhelléniques*,
p. 273 ; J. E. Harrison, *Themis*, p. 190.
[2] A. J. Evans, *op. cit.*, p. 137.   Cf. below, p. 195.
[3] Pausanias, ii. 30. 3 ; Callimachus, *Hymn in Dian.*, 189 ; Euripides,
Hypol., 141, and Scholiast, *ad loc.* ; Hesychius, *s.v.* Βριτόμαρτις ; Scholiast
to Apollonius Rhodius, 1353.   On the coins of Kydonia she is represented
as the moon (K. Hoeck, *Kreta*, vol. ii, p. 169).
[4] Pausanias, iii. 26. 1 ; A. J. Evans, *op. cit.*, p. 181.   The epithet
' Pasiphae' is applied to Artemis and to Selene (*Orphic Hymn*, xxxvi. 3 ;
H. Usener, *Götternamen*, p. 57).
[5] Helbig, in W. H. Roscher, *Ausführliches Lexikon der griechischen und*
römischen Mythologie, vol. i, p. 1418 ; A. J. Evans, *op. cit.*, p. 181 ; K. Hoeck,
Kreta, vol. i, pp. 90 sqq.
[6] K. Hoeck, *op. cit.*, vol. ii, pp. 144 sqq.   Cf. Hesychius, s.v. Ἀριδήλαν ;
K. Welkker, *Griechische Mythologie*, vol. ii, pp. 559 sqq. ; O. Ribbeck,
Anfänge und Entwickelung des Dionysoscultus in Attika, p. 6.   " Whatever
name may have originally belonged to the goddess of the Mycenean cult
scenes, whether in Cyprus or Greece proper, a part of her mythic being
survived in that of the goddess who in Crete is best known by her epithet,
Ariadne " (A. J. Evans, *op. cit.*, p. 175).
[7] R. Dussaud, " Questions Mycénéennes," *Revue de l'Histoire des Reli-*
gions, li, p. 26 ; B. E. Williams, " Religion of the Minoans," in H. Boyd
Hawes, *Gournia*, p. 53.
[8] Strabo, 472.

much smaller than the goddesses [1] is, there can be no doubt, the same as the god whom the Greeks called Zeus, and who bore some twenty-five different appellatives and epithets.[2] His indigenous name appears to have been Zan ; [3] and under the name of Zagreos he was identified with Dionysos. He bore no resemblance to the Olympian Zeus. He was, like Tammuz, a dying-god, who is never met with full grown, but, having been nursed by The Mothers, died and was born again. His shrines were Holy Sepulchres where his passion was represented and his death ritually lamented.[4]

In Anatolia and the northern portion of the Aegean region the son of the Great Mother bears the name which in all languages of the Aryan family is the name of the moon, Men. That, in fact, and not Selene, is the proper Greek term for the moon, and, as in all other languages, it is masculine. " The masculine form was the original one, and was formerly common to both Greeks and Italians." [5] The term Men, or Mene, never Selene, is used by Homer and by writers who pride themselves on precision.[6] In spite of the general feminisation of the moon in Hellenic mythology, " the mystics," that is, those who liked to hark back to primitive conceptions, " regarded the moon as masculine." [7] It is remarkable that, notwithstanding the classical Greek representation of the moon as a female, which is the source of our European view of the sex of the luminary, the Greek peasants persist to this day in representing the moon as a man.[8]

The cult of the god Moon was prominent and general throughout Anatolia, in Phrygia and Lydia, in Ionia, Karia, and Cilicia.[9] His most noted shrine was at Kabeira in the Pontus, where,

---

[1] A. J. Evans, *op. cit.*, pp. 107 sq., 170, 175.

[2] W. Aly, " Ursprung und Entwiklung der kretischen Zeus-Religion," *Philologus*, lxxi, p. 459.

[3] Chrysostom on *Epist. Paul. ad Titum*, iii (Migne, *Patrologiae Cursus, Series Graeca*, vol. lxii, col. 676) : " The Kretans have a sepulchre of Zeus, with the inscription : ' Here lies Zan, whom they call Zeus.' "

[4] Pomponius Mela, ii. 7 ; Lucian, *Jupit. tragaed.*, 45 ; Id., *De sacrificiis*, xiii ; Porphyry, *Vit. Pythag.*, xvii ; Lactantius, *De falsa religione*, i. 11 ; Scholiast to Callimachus, *Hymn.*, i ; J. Firmicus Maternus, *De errore profanarum religionum*, vii. 6 ; K. Hoeck, *Kreta*, vol. iii, p. 36 ; J. Meursius, *Creta, Cyprus et Rhodus*, p. 80 ; A. J. Evans, *op. cit.*, pp. 119 sqq.

[5] H. Usener, *Götternamen*, p. 36.

[6] Pindar, *Olympic.*, iii. 36 ; Aeschylus, *Promet.*, 797 ; Euripides, *Rhes.*, 534 ; *Fragm.*, 997.

[7] Spartianus, *Caracalla*, vi. 6.

[8] N. G. Politis, in W. H. Roscher, *Über Selene und Verwandtes*, p. 173.

[9] P. Le Bas and W. H. Waddington, *Voyage archéologique en Grèce et en Asie Mineure ; Inscriptions*, pp. 667 sq. ; P. Perdrizet, " Mên," *Bulletin de Correspondance Hellénique*, xx, pp. 60 sqq.

in a rich temple, hierodules pontificated and he delivered oracles.[1] Men is associated with a goddess who is sometimes known as Anaitis, sometimes as Hekate, and was identified with Artemis, the ' Diana of the Ephesians,' the great Mother Moon " whom all Asia and all the world worshippeth." [2] He was connected in Phrygia with rain and water.[3] One of his common epithets is ' the Saviour,' and, like all youthful moon-gods, he is regarded as identical with his father, Paean.[4] He is also called Ascanios, the name familiar as that of the son of the Trojan hero-god Aeneas, the son of Aphrodite, who thus appears to have been a form of the Father moon-god.[5] He is also freely identified with Attis,[6] Sabasios,[7] and Dionysos.[8] Men was, of course, a dying god, and, like the Egyptian gods, appeared in infant and in adult form.[9]

Men does not seem to have been worshipped under that name in Greece proper in classical times ; inscriptions dedicated to him have been found in Attica,[10] but they doubtless represent late and adventitious importations. The cult of the male lunar deity occupied, nevertheless, from earliest times a foremost position in Greek religion. The name by which he is best known in classical theology is Dionysos.

Dionysos has always presented a problem of peculiar interest to students of Greek religious ideas. He stands obviously apart from the circle of the Olympian gods ; he is not one of them. That isolation has commonly been accounted for by regarding him as a comparatively late importation into Greek religion ; but that

[1] Strabo, xii. 3. 31 ; A. Bouché-Leclercq, *Histoire de la divination dans l'antiquité*, vol. iii, p. 409.

[2] J. A. R. Munro, " Inscriptions from Mysia," *The Journal of Hellenic, Studies*, xvii, pp. 284 sq. ; P. Perdrizet, *op. cit.*, pp. 55 sqq.

[3] H. B. Walters, in *The Classical Review*, 1894, p. 229.

[4] W. M. Ramsay, *The Cities and Bishoprics of Phrygia*, vol. ii, pp. 625 sq. ; J. A. R. Munro, *loc. cit.*

[5] E. Thrämer, *Pergamos*, p. 413 ; P. Perdrizet, *op. cit.*, pp. 90 sq. Cf, Strabo, p. 577. The relations of mother and son, wife and husband, are conspicuously interchangeable among the deities of Anatolia, and of the Men group in particular (see J. A. R. Munro, *loc. cit.*) ; and it is therefore more than probable that Aeneas was in reality the husband of Aphrodite, as he was of her homologue Dido.

[6] F. Wieseler, *Der Hildesheimer Silberfund*, p. 17 n. ; W. H. Ramsay, *op. cit.*, p. 169.

[7] Proclus, *Commentarius in Platonis Timaeum*, iv. 251 ; W. H. Ramsay, *op. cit.*, vol. i, pp. 263 sq.

[8] Drexler, in W. H. Roscher, *Ausführliches Lexikon der griechischen und römischen Mythologie*, vol. ii, p. 2755.

[9] P. Perdrizet, *op. cit.*, pp. 59 sq.

[10] *Corpus Inscriptionum Atticarum*, ii, 1587 ; iii, 73, 74. He was also worshipped at Delos (Am. Hauvette-Besnault, " Fouilles de Délos," *Bulletin de Correspondance Hellénique*, vi, p. 345).

view is the more misleading because of the element of truth which it contains. As a fundamental statement it is incompatible with the facts and with the primitive significance of the cult of Dionysos. It was from that cult that Greek drama professedly derived ; and the evolution from rude religious dances, such as are prevalent among savage peoples, to classical Greek drama as we know it, must have been a long one, and have had its roots in the most primitive religious usages and conceptions of the race. The cult of Dionysos was immemorial among the Spartans, the most archaic and conservative representatives of that race ; and it is intimately associated with the most hoary and venerated institutions of Greek cult, such, for instance, as the oracle of Delphi. The deity, admittedly protean and many-named, appears in every region of Greece, no less than in Attica and in Laconia, in the most primitive strata of religious ideas and customs. Rather than say that Dionysos was a late importation into Olympian religion, it would probably be nearer the truth to say that Olympian religion was a comparatively late importation into Dionysian cults.

Greek legend, in glaring contradiction with those facts, does, it is true, constantly represent Dionysos as a new god coming from abroad, in particular from the wilder northern country of Thrace, and even from Asia and India, to take possession of the Greek cities ; and it depicts the opposition offered to the god by the rulers of those cities. Such, for example, is the theme of the great mystery-play of Euripides, the ' Bakchai.' Pentheos, the Theban king, complains that

our own
Wives, our own sisters, from their hearths are flown
To wild and secret rites ; and cluster there
High on the shadowy hills, with dance and prayer
To adore this new-made God, this Dionyse.[1]

The drama might be a poetical version, transfigured by the glory of Hellenic art, of the tradition which we have met with among the

---

[1] Euripides, *Bakchai*, 217 sqq., G. Murray's translation. The opposition of the rulers to Dionysos, as pictured in the myths of Lykourgos and of Pentheos, belongs to a universal theme, that of the ' enemies of the god,' who is persecuted and rejected. The theme, which is part of the Osiris-myth also, is found in every quarter of the world. Thus among the Indians of California the moon-god Wiyot, who has come down to earth and been incarnated in human form to instruct mankind, is the victim of the hostility and machinations of his enemies, prompted by his ' dark-god ' antagonist, the serpent or lizard. The human god patiently submits to his fate, which he knows to be inevitable, and predicts his own death, the triumph of his enemies, and his second coming (A. L. Kroeber, " The Mythology of the Mission Indians of California,"

savages of Tierra del Fuego, and which they commemorate in masked festivals which might be regarded as crude primitive germs of the ' Bakchai.'

Dionysos was a culture-god who was not only represented as teaching a religion, but also as 'inventing and introducing agriculture,'[1] and such culture-gods always come down as strangers to dwell amongst men. Dionysos, as in Boeotia, came to Egypt under the name of Osiris, and taught men agriculture and a 'new religion.'[2] Few would be prepared to regard Osiris as an 'imported' god in Egypt—though even that theory has been put forward—or Ea, who came to Babylonia and taught men all things, as an exotic deity.

The rites which the Boeotian women celebrated were very far from being new-fangled; they were the immemorial rites indispensable to the successful cultivation of the soil. The Boeotian 'trieterica' took place every third year; the period,

---

Journal of American Folk-Lore, xix, pp. 310 sqq.). Variants are to be found in almost every mythology. The persecuted god who appears incognito as his own prophet is done to death by his enemies, who are thus the instruments of the sacrifice of which he is the foredoomed and unresisting victim. In the ' Bakchai,' when the guards come to arrest him, he

> never flinched, nor thought to flee,
> But held both hands out unresistingly.
> No change, no blanching of the wine-red cheek;
> He waited while we came, and bade us wreak
> All the decree; yea laughed, and made my hest
> Easy, till I, for very shame confessed
> And said : " O stranger, not of mine own will
> I bind thee, but his bidding to fulfil
> Who sent me."—(*Bakchai*, 436 sqq.)

The divine prisoner maintains before his judges a dignified silence as to the truth he has come to announce, for they have eyes and cannot see, and they know not what they do (*ibid.*, 472, 504, 506). The first coming and predication of Dionysos was contrasted in Orphic theology with his second coming, when he would return finally and establish his Kingdom (Proclus, *Commentarius in Timaeum*, v. 291 ; Fréret, " Recherches sur le culte de Bacchus parmi les Grecs," *Mémoires de Littérature de l'Académie des Inscriptions*, xxiii, p. 265 ; P. N. Rolle, *Recherches sur le culte de Bacchus*, vol. iii, p. 28).

It is clearly unsafe to draw conclusions from such stereotyped myth themes, and to regard them as referring to historical events. That there was an opposition to the popular agrarian religion of the women on the part of the aristocratic military classes is probable ; but no conclusion as to the importation of a foreign cult can be derived from the myths of the persecuted god. In Argos the opponent to the 'introduction' of Dionysian religion is the Sun-hero, Perseus (Pausanias, ii. 20. 4 ; 22. 1 ; Nonnus, *Dionysiaca*, xlvii, 475 sqq.).

[1] L. Preller, *Griechische Mythologie*, p. 709.
[2] Diodorus Siculus, iii. 74. 1.

as Dr. Farnell convincingly suggests, corresponding to " the original shifting of land-cultivation which is frequent in every society owing to the backward nature of agricultural processes." New fields had to be laid out from time to time, and the duty of selecting the ground and of imparting to it the required fertility fell to the women, " who held the vegetation magic in their hands."[1] The ' Mainads ' were the priestesses of the Dionysiac agricultural cult, and were assimilated to the mythical ' Nurses,' or ' Mothers,' variously identified with the Charites, the Horai, the Hesperides, the Muses, the Dodonean nymphs, the Hyades, who tended the god, in the same manner as Teutonic priestesses were assimilated to the Norns. Like them, the Mainads were three in number,[2] each having charge of a troupe, or ' thiasos,' of women, both maids and matrons. They performed on ' tympana,' which were no other than the magic drums used by shamanesses throughout Asia and Indonesia, and which survive among the populations of southern Europe as the tambourine. They carried spears or javelins, which were probably used, like the spears of the priestesses in the Philippines,[3] to kill the sacrificial victims. When not in use the points of the spears were protected by a fir cone, and the weapon constituted the magic thyrsos. They were also armed with swords, and with the double-axe used in sacrifices,[4] and also with pitch-forks. Before taking part in the ceremonies the women partook of a purificatory bath, praying to Dionysos to assist them.[5]

Rites in every respect identical with the Theban magic ceremonies of the agricultural Mainads took place from immemorial

---

[1] L. R. Farnell, *The Cults of the Greek States*, vol. v, pp. 180 sq. As an example of those usages the practice of the Kioga women in Central Africa may be mentioned. " It is the women in this country," says the Rev. J. Roscoe, " who own the fields and do all the ordinary work of digging and attending to the crops. . . . They work on the same land year after year without any attempt to fertilise it ; but when, after four or five years, the crops show signs of deterioration, the field will be left fallow for two or three years, and new ground will be broken up " (J. Roscoe, *The Soul of Central Africa*, p. 227). The period of three years, it may be added, corresponded to the symbolic triplicity which runs through every emblem of the cult of Dionysos. The classical picture of the ' orgiastic ' nature of the ritual celebrated at night on ' high places ' by the women is doubtless coloured by the mystery attaching to rites to which men were not admitted. As Euripides himself surmised, that ' orgiastic ' character was greatly exaggerated (cf. *Bakchai*, 683 sqq.).

[2] Euripides, *Bakchai*, 680 sqq. ; Theocritus, xxvi ; Propertius, iv. 17. 24. The traditional Mainads were called Ino, Autonoe, and Agave, or, according to other traditions, Kosko, Baubo, Thettale (E. Rohde, *Psyche*, vol. ii, p. 55).

[3] See above, vol. ii, p. 528.

[4] J. E. Harrison, *Prolegomena to the Study of Greek Religion*, p. 462.

[5] Pausanias, ix. 20. 4.

time in every part of Greece and in all Greek lands.   At Delphi
the priestesses were known as Thyades, or ' frantic women,' after
Thya, the ancestress of the race, or First Woman, the mother of
Delphos, who " established the cult of Dionysos." [1]   In Attica, so
ancient was the mainadic ritual, that, in its primitive form, it had
already passed away " before the time at which our records begin."
The officiating priestesses were called Lenai, ' the raging ones,' an
old equivalent of ' mainad.' [2]   It was also at the festival known
later as Dionysiac that the ' manhood ceremonies ' of the Attic tribes,
the initiation of young men and their inscription on the roll of the
phratries, took place under the auspices of the Moon-deity.[3]

Greek cult illustrates the common rule that religious ceremonies have not arisen as the worship of preconceived deities,
but that the presiding deities are, on the contrary, outcomes
of the utilitarian magic rites.   Frequently the festivals of
Greece are not named after any god or goddess ; they are the
three-yearly festival, the harvest-feast, the feast of seedlings, the
feast of greenery, the bread-feast, the threshing feast, the straw
feast, the feast of the grove, the mountain, the village, or field.
The Greeks did not speak of the festival of a given god so much
as of the gods of a given festival.   It is not the rite, but the name
of the deity under whose patronage it may be placed, that changes.
The same is, of course, true of all religions ; totemic ritual survives
in the religions of advanced civilisations ; venerable pagan festivals
continue under the auspices of Christianity ; the Paschal feast of
the Jews was naturalised in the cult of Yahweh.   Gods are mortal
and pass away ; cult endures.

The agricultural rites of primitive Greece, unlike those of many
ruder savage tribes among whom men have at an early stage of
culture snatched the monopoly of magical arts, remained even in
historic times conspicuously a special, and often an exclusive,
women's cult.   Men were in later times admitted to the trieterica,
but, as the story of Pentheos itself shows, they were originally
in danger of being torn to pieces should they so much as spy upon
the women's mysteries.[4]   No man was permitted, even as late as

---

[1] Pausanias, x. 6. 2 ; cf. 4. 2 ; Herodotus, vii. 178.

[2] L. R. Farnell, *The Cults of the Greek States*, vol. v, pp. 208 sq.   The
name λήναια was later, by an impossible etymology, derived from ληνός,
a wine-press.   Cf. O. Ribbeck, *Anfänge und Entwickelung des Dionysoscultus
in Attika*, p. 13.

[3] Hesychius, s.v. χουρεῶτις.

[4] The fate of Pentheos' grandson, Actaeon, who also spied on the purificatory rites of the female attendants of the Moon-deity, was probably of
like significance.   In one version of the myth it is not Artemis, but Semele,
the mother of Dionysos, whom Actaeon offended (Apollodorus, *Bibliotheka*,
iii. 4).   The tearing to pieces, besides being the threatened punishment of
any male intruder on the sacred rites, was also a part of the rites them-

the time of Pausanias, to enter the chapel which represented the birth-chamber of Dionysos at Thebes.[1]

Men were likewise excluded, and in the most rigorous manner, down to latest times, from other agricultural rites accounted of supreme importance, and known in Attica as the 'thesmophoria,' which took place in October at the time of seed-sowing. The ritual, enriched by the accretions of centuries, was complex and lasted over five days. The women prepared themselves, as for the trieterica, by purificatory baths and by rigorous chastity. They proceeded, in Attica, to the shrine of Eleusis for the purpose of bringing back the 'kalathos,' or sacred 'kernos.' This was a large wide-mouthed earthenware vessel, in which were placed a number of small pots, or 'kotyloi,' forming compartments, and containing seeds and seedlings of rye, barley, peas, lentils, and other vegetables.[2] The 'kernos' was thus similar to the so-called 'gardens of Adonis,' and was the counterpart of the baskets divided into compartments used by North American squaws in their sowing-festival, and which contained the selected consecrated seeds to which the virtue of the fertilising 'medicine' had been imparted.[3] The 'kernos' bore a lighted taper in the centre,[4] and also contained phallic fetiches made of paste,[5] to impart fertility to the seeds. The sacred seed-pots have been found in the oldest strata of Mykenean culture and in Krete;[6] and, with tapers substituted for the seeds, they are used at the present day in the ritual of the Greek Church.[7] The great 'kernos,' or 'kalathos' was brought on a chariot, and the women accompanied it bearing the kernoi. The procession wended its way to the temple of Thesmophoros, where, after the sacrifices, the priestess uttered some such prayer as the following : " Preserve the City in peace and plenty ; cause all the fruits in our fields to ripen ; fatten our kine ; render fruitful our orchards ; make the ears of corn to grow large, and the harvest to be plentiful. Give peace in our time,

selves, for there is no doubt that originally the Greek priestesses, like the Celtic ones, offered human sacrifices, for which animal victims were later substituted (see L. R. Farnell, op. cit., vol. v, pp. 167 sqq.).

[1] Pausanias, ix. 12.

[2] Athenaeus, xi. 8 ; Scholiast to Callimachus. Hymn. in Cer., i. Cf. O. Jahn, "Die Cista mystica," Hermes, iii, pp. 326 sqq.

[3] See above, p. 4.

[4] R. C. Bosanquet, "Notes from the Cyclades," Annual of the British School at Athens, iii, p. 59.

[5] Scholiast to Nicander of Kolophon, Alexipharmaca, 217 ; L. Couve, art. "Kernos," in C. V. Daremberg and E. Saglio, Dictionnaire des antiquités grecques et romaines, vol. iii, p. 823.

[6] S. Xanthoudides, "Cretan Kernoi," Annual of the British School at Athens, xii. pp. 1 sqq.

[7] Ibid., pp. 20 sqq.

that the hand which soweth may also reap." [1] The sacrifices were pigs, which the women buried in an underground vault; the remains of the last year's sacrifice were collected and mixed with the seed-corn, as a 'medicine' to impart fertility to it. [2] Among other rites performed during the ceremonies was a solemn march round the arable land, during which the women waved pine torches over the fields. [3] "The whole ministration was in the hands of the women : the women elected their own representatives and officials, and from at least the essential part of the mystery, the solemnity in the Thesmophorion, the men were rigidly excluded. The men seem to have played no part at all." [4] The cult was in charge of a college of fourteen aged matrons, 'gerarai,' presided over by the Queen Archon. [5]

The rites, in essentially the same form, were common to the whole Hellenic world, from Ionia and the Islands to Syracuse, Cumae and Naples. [6] The term 'thesmophoria' appears to have been used loosely for all the agricultural rites of Greece. [7] They were associated in Attica with the god Iakchos, and everywhere with Dionysos. Herodotus states that the 'thesmophoria,' which were celebrated primitively throughout Greece, were discontinued at the time of the Doric invasion, and that only in the secluded rural

[1] Callimachus, *Hymn to Demeter*, 135 sqq., 138 sqq.

[2] Scholiast to Lucian, in *Rheinisches Museum*, xxv, p. 548.

[3] L. Preller, *Griechische Mythologie*, p. 797.

[4] L. R. Farnell, *The Cults of the Greek States*, vol. iii, p. 83.

[5] Demosthenes, *Contra Neaeram*, 78 ; Hesychius, s.v. Γεραραί.

[6] L. R. Farnell, *op. cit.*, vol. iii, pp. 99, 100 sq. ; N. P. Nillson, *Griechische Feste*, pp. 313 sqq. An inscription to the priestess of Demeter Thesmophoros has been found in Pompeii (*Corpus Inscriptionum Graecorum*, 5865).

[7] The only use of θεσμός that we know is as an archaic term corresponding to νόμος, and meaning 'law,' 'order' (Hesychius, s.v.). The laws of Drakon are spoken of as θεσμοί. The bearing of 'law and order' on agricultural fertility has given rise to some astonishing interpretations. Some speak of the women "carrying the books of the law"; others of the sanctification of the civil order ; others even of the commemoration of the institution of monogamic marriage. Although the votaries in festivals are commonly called "carriers," so are deities, and it was in this instance the presiding deity, and not the celebrant, who was θεσμοφόρος, for not only is the deity distinctly so called, while the votaries are called θεσμοφοριάζουσαι, but variants of the same word, such as θεσμια (Pausanias, viii. 25. 4), θεσμοδότειρα (*Orphic Hymn*, i. 25) are also applied to him or to her. The term θεσμός is allied in meaning as well as in form to θέμις. No more natural and common epithet could be given to the regulator of the seasons, the establisher of order, the legislator of the agricultural cycle. The deity who performs those functions is everywhere known as 'the Measurer,' Mas, Harmonia. The 'Measurer,' or 'orderer,' is identified with Themis (Ovid, *Fasti*, iii. 657). In Babylon Ishtar was the establisher of the Laws of Heaven and Earth (see above, p. 88 ; cf. H. Zimmern, *Babylonische Hymnen und Gebete*, p. 66).

districts of Arcadia was their observance uninterrupted. The ancient mysteries were afterwards restored.[1] All other Attic festivals of agriculture and fertility, such as the 'aretophoria,' 'sthenia,' 'skira,' 'haloa,' were likewise celebrated by the women ;[2] and during the sacrifice of Kourotropos, in the Dionysiac feast of the 'apathuria,' at Athens and also at Samos, no man might approach.[3] At Pyreai, in the temple of Dionysos, Demeter, and Kore, women alone were allowed to enter.[4] At Briseai, in Laconia, men were not admitted to the cult of Dionysos, "women alone performed in secrecy the rites."[5] At Pellene men were admitted during the first three days only of the nine-day festival of Demeter.[6] At Tegea, in the rites of the so-called Ares, "the Entertainer of Women"—probably a form of Dionysos—no man might enter the temple.[7] At Kos the cult of Dionysos was in the hands of a high-priestess.[8] Mainads sacrificed at Orchomenos, in Arcadia.[9] At Mantinea the cult was in charge of a college of priestesses ;[10] and at Elis the rites were in the care of a priesthood of sixteen women.[11] At Karnea, in Laconia, the eleven priestesses who performed the sacrifices were called Dionysiades; other Dionysiades ran a ritual race traditionally associated with Penelope.[12] The famous gymnopaedic dance of the Spartan maidens was a Dionysian rite. There were two forms of it, the 'oschophories,' or 'vine-bearing dance,' and the Dionysiad.[13] It would, in fact, appear that the whole cult associated with Dionysos was originally a women's religion, from the rites of which men were excluded. When Dionysian religion was introduced into Italy no men were, under the severest penalties, allowed to be present at the celebrations.[14]

It is probable that men were originally excluded from the mysteries of Eleusis.[15] The cult, one of the most ancient in

---

[1] Herodotus, ii. 171.

[2] L. R. Farnell, *op. cit.*, vol. iii, p. 83 ; J. E. Harrison, *Prolegomena to the Study of Greek Religion*, pp. 131, 134, 146 ; Suidas, s.v. σθενια. The 'haloa' were specially associated with the vintage, and though they were conducted mainly by women, men were admitted.

[3] Pollux, *Onamastikon*, i. 3.

[4] Pausanias, ix. 20. 4.

[5] *Ibid.*, iii. 20. 4.   [6] *Ibid.*, vii. 27.

[7] *Ibid.*, viii. 48. 5.

[8] L. R. Farnell, *op. cit.*, vol. v. p. 160.

[9] Plutarch, *Quaest. Graec.*, xxxviii.

[10] C. Michel, *Recueil d'inscriptions grecques*, No. 993.

[11] Plutarch, *De mulierum virtute*, xv.

[12] Pausanias, iii. 13. 5. Penelope, 'the Weaver,' whose web is continually unravelled, is undoubtedly a moon-goddess.

[13] Athenaeus, xiv. 30.

[14] Livy, xxxix. 8. 13.

[15] J. E. Harrison, *op. cit.*, p. 151, n.

Attica, was closely connected with, if not an essential part of, the
'thesmophoria'; this is clearly shown by a remark of Plutarch,
who says that "the ancients used to begin the sowing earlier than
is now done, and this is evident from the Eleusynian Mysteries." [1]
The high-priestess of Demeter initiated catechumens; [2] and in
certain of the ceremonies she presented the offerings to the exclusion
of the male hierophant. [3] An interesting series of paintings in
a house at Pompeii almost certainly represents the ritual of the
'lesser mysteries.' All the votaries and officiants are women;
"the liturgy is exclusively feminine." [4] The term 'Mystery' in
Greek cult would appear, indeed, to have been used primarily with
reference to the secrecy attaching to cults exercised by women's
religious societies, from which men were excluded. [5] According to
an old scholiast the name Iakchos, which was the Attic appellation
of Dionysos, and the ritual cry in his rites, means "the cry of
women." [6]

As elsewhere, when men took part in the cult of the women's
god, they frequently donned feminine attire. Pentheos, like the
male members of the women's society in Sierra Leone, had to
become a woman, and assume a woman's dress to approach
the Dionysiac celebrations. [7] In Attica Dionysian priests were

[1] Plutarch, *Fragm.*, xxiii.
[2] Suidas, s.v. φιλλειδαι.
[3] Demosthenes, *Contra Neaeram*, 116.
[4] V. Macchioro, *Zagreus*, pp. 68 sqq. *et passim*.
[5] Cf. L. R. Farnell, *op. cit.*, vol. iii, p. 129. Dr. Farnell is in this matter
a hostile witness. In spite of the wealth of evidence which his own collections afford, and of brilliant suggestions which further enhance the significance
of that evidence, he is bent on minimising the part played by women in Greek
religion; and he has written an article specially to discourage any interpretation that might be put upon the facts by the partisans of the hypothesis
of matriarchy (L. R. Farnell, " Sociological Hypotheses concerning the Position of Women in Ancient Religion," *Archiv für Religionswissenschaft*, vii,
pp. 70 sq.). It is difficult to perceive on what grounds he commends his attitude. The consideration on which he appears chiefly to rely is that officiants
in primitive cults were not, as far as we know, 'officially' appointed, and
therefore were not legally qualified priestesses. But no one supposes that
primitive priestesses, shamanesses, witches, owed their influences and power
to diplomas bearing an official stamp. The argument, so far as it goes—for
there is no lack of 'officially appointed' priestesses—brings out precisely
the character of the changes which took place in Greek cult, as in those of most
other peoples. The male priests belong chiefly to the phase of official religions,
of civically organised cults; their position is as much political as religious.
As Dr. Farnell himself says, the women "held the vegetation-magic in their
hands," and I cannot recall an instance mentioned by him or anyone else
of male priests in early or later times performing unaided the rites of that
agricultural magic.
[6] Scholiast to Aeschylus, *Septem contra Thebas*, 141.
[7] Euripides, *Bakchai*, 822; Nonnus, *Dionysiaca*, xlvi. 82.

arrayed in women's attire.[1] Dionysos himself, like the primitive
moon-gods whose sex is rendered unstable by their feminine
associations, has a feminine character. He also wears women's
clothes, and the Charites weave a peplos for him.[2] According to
one myth he was brought up as a girl.[3] He is referred to as ' girl-
faced,' and ' womanish,' [4] as a ' half-man.' [5] In Macedonia he was
called ' pseudanor,' or ' sham-man.' [6] He was called χοιροψάλαν,
and at Sikyon was worshipped as the " lord of vulvae." [7]

It is clear from the facts already noted that the rites which constituted the cult of Dionysos, under whatever divine name they may
have been originally celebrated, belonged to the most primitive and
archaic elements in Greek religion. That many ideas which formed
no part of those primitive cults were, in the course of cultural and
religious growth, grafted on to them, and that some of those ideas
may have been in a sense imported, is to be expected. Among those
superadded conceptions the most conspicuous was the intimate
association of the god with the vine. We do not know at what
date the vine was imported into Greece. It is probable that the
primitive inhabitants of the Aegean region drank beer. In Italy
the vine was unknown until comparatively late times ; Pliny
tells us that in sacrifices milk only was used, and that Romulus
drank nothing but milk.[8] " The terms ' oinos,' ' vinum,' " says
M. Halévy, " are not found in Asiatic Aryan languages, while
' wai'n ' is the Arabic word for grape." [9] The vine appears to
have been first brought to Greece by the Phoenicians, who carried
on a large trade in wine in the eastern Mediterranean. The people
of Tyre asserted that all the vines in Greece came from a
stock brought from their country.[10] One of the first miracles
ascribed to Dionysos was the turning of water into wine ; [11] and
similar miracles of transubstantiation took place in his chapels

---

[1] Lucian, *Calumniae non temere credendum*, xvi ; Photius, *Bibliotheka*,
p. 322 (ed. Bekker) ; Hesychius and Suidas, s.v. *Ἰθύφαλλοι* ; Plutarch,
Theseus, 23.

[2] Apollonius Rhodius, iv. 424 ; Nonnus, *Dionysiaca*, xvi. 270.

[3] Apollodorus, iii. 4. 3.

[4] Euripides, *Bakchai*, 353 ; Scholiast to Aristophanes, *Thesm.*, 135 ;
Orphic Hymn, xliv. 4.

[5] Lucian, *Dial. deor.*, xxiii. Cf. Aristides, *Dionysos*, vol. i, p. 49 (ed.
Dindorf). Some statues represent him with two heads, a man's and a
woman's (B. de Montfaucon, *L'Antiquité expliquée*, vol. i, pp. 248 sq.).

[6] Polyaenus, *Strategemata*, iv. 1 ; Suidas, s.v. *Ψευδάνωρ*.

[7] Clement of Alexandria, *Exhortatio*, ii. 39.

[8] Pliny, *Nat. Hist.*, xviii. 24.

[9] J. Halévy, *Mélanges de critique et d'histoire relatifs aux peuples Sémitiques*, p. 423.

[10] Achilles Tatius, ii. 2. Cf. F. C. Movers, *Die Phönizier*, vol. i, p. 330.

[11] Diodorus Siculus, iii. 66 ; Pliny, *Nat. Hist.*, ii. 231.

during the celebration of his festivals, at Elis and at Andros.[1] He is commonly thought of as the god of the vine.

In that character he presents a remarkable likeness to the Indian Moon-god Soma. Soma, or Homa, was with the ancient Aryan populations the name of a climbing-plant (*Sarcostema viminalis*, or *Asclepias acida*), an evergreen which does not decay, bears no fruit, and resembles the ivy in appearance.[2] From it was prepared a fermented beverage possessing intoxicating properties. In ancient Persian and in Vedic ritual it was used as an ingredient in sacrificial offerings to which the greatest significance and importance were attached. " Homa is the first of the trees planted by Ahura Mazda in the fountains of life. He who drinks of its juice never dies. According to the Bundehesh, the Gogard or Gaokerena tree bears Homa, which gives health and generative power, and bestows the gifts of life and resurrection." [3] The cult and ritual of Soma occupy the foremost place in ancient Vedic religion ; a whole book of the Rig-Veda, the ninth, is devoted to Soma, and a special compilation, the Sama-Veda, was made in which the regulations referring to the ritual of Soma were collected. The terms ' Soma-drinkers,' ' Soma-pressers,' were those by which the Aryans, in India and Persia, distinguished their own coreligionists from barbarians and infidels ; their religion was regarded by them primarily as the religion of Soma. The plant was called ' The King of Plants,' and was regarded as the special vehicle of that power which controls vegetable life and the generative and renewing forces of nature, and has, according to primitive conceptions, its source in the moon. Soma and the moon, or Moon-god, were completely identified, so that the word ' Soma ' in Vedic literature and at the present day means the Moon-god.[4] It has been shown by Hillebrandt, whose studies of Vedic religious literature have superseded in exhaustiveness previous work in that field, that " the moon occupied the central place in Vedic belief and cult. The sun lies in the background, and in its stead the moon rules in the world of ancient Indian thought. In a much higher degree than the sun, the moon is,

---

[1] Pausanias, vi. 26. 1 ; Athenaeus, I. 34A.

[2] M. Monier-Williams, *Sanskrit Dictionary*, s.v. ' soma '; F. H. Windisham, " Ueber den Somacultus der Arier," *Abhandlungen der Münchener Akademie*, 1846, p. 131.

[3] F. H. Windisham, *loc. cit.* Cf. Shams-ul-Ulma Jivangi Jamshady Modi, " Haoma in the Avesta," *Journal of the Anthropological Society of Bombay*, v, pp. 202 sqq.

[4] A. Hillebrandt, *Vedische Mythologie*, p. 309. It was contended, in accordance with the preconceived views of Vedic religion which were until lately current, that Soma was identified with the moon in later times only. That statement has been conclusively shown by Hillebrandt to be entirely erroneous ; throughout the Vedas Soma is the moon.

in the Vedas, the Creator and Governor of the universe." [1]   Soma was the sustainer of all life, not only that of men and animals, but of the gods also; [2] for the privilege of immortality which is connected with the ever-renewed moon was communicated by partaking of the fluid sap which was the essence and emanation of the lunar power.   Thus in the Atharva-Veda mortal man is exhorted by Soma with these words : " Breathe with the breath of those that breathe ; do not die ! I free thee from all evil and disease and unite thee with life. Do thou rise up with life ; unite thyself with life, with the sap of plants." [3]   Again Soma is addressed by the worshipper, saying, " All the gods approach thee, thou deathless one ; by thy offerings they are wont to attain immortality." [4]   The life, or soul of man is regarded in Vedic philosophy as returning after death to the moon whence it originally derived, and thus, being consumed by the gods, it is united with them.   The souls of the dead proceed to " the moon, that is, Soma the King.   Here they are loved by the Devas, yea the Devas eat them." [5]   In the Upanishads the faithful is exhorted to " worship on the day of the full moon, as it is seen in the east, saying, ' Thou art Soma, the king, the wise, the five-mouthed, the lord of creatures. . . . Do not decrease by our life, by our offspring, by our cattle ; he who hates us and

[1] A. Hillebrandt, *op. cit.*, vol. i, pp. 277, 313. In the same manner as the ritual of Soma has long since disappeared, so Hinduism has, like other religious systems, lost its original character with the obsolescence of primitive beliefs and the growth of theological priesthoods. Vedic religion, which centred round the moon-god Soma, who was regarded as the universal principle of life and of generation, presents one of the clearest examples, among religious systems having a developed literature, of the purely lunar character of cosmic religions. Agni, the brilliant god, and Siva, the dark god, were no doubt forms of the moon-deity. Owing to its having supplied the text for the first attempts at interpretation of an ancient and unfamiliar religion and mythology, at a time when the comparative study of religions and scientific anthropology scarcely existed, Vedic religion has currently become regarded as a type of solar religions and of so-called ' nature worship ' ; and the older writings on primitive religions are filled with appeals to supposed Vedic parallels. Many Sanskrit scholars still speak of Hillebrandt's thorough and scientific analysis of the Vedic material in terms of scorn as " lunar fancies." So deep a hold has that attitude obtained in the sphere of these studies, that it is probable that it will continue yet awhile. I venture to entertain some hope that the present work may perhaps hasten in some small measure the dismissal of those preconceptions to the limbo of pre-scientific assumptions.

[2] A. A. Macdonell, " Vedic Mythology," in G. Bühler, *Grundriss der Indo-Arischen Philologie und Altertumskunde*, vol. iii, p. 109.

[3] *Atharva-Veda*, iii. 31 (*The Sacred Books of the East*, vol. xliii, p. 52).

[4] *Sâma-Veda*, ii. 4. 2. 3 (T. Benfey, *Die Hymnen des Sama-Veda*, vol. ii, p. 262).

[5] *Khandogya-Upanishad*, ii. 9 (*The Sacred Books of the East*, vol. i, p. 80).

whom we hate, decrease by his life, by his offspring, by his cattle." [1] Soma is the source of all prophetic and poetical gifts, the two being originally identical; he is " he who with the mind of a prophet makes prophets, the bestower of heaven, praised in a thousand hymns, the pathway of poets." [2] Some of the epithets of Soma are ' Seer,' ' Healer,' and ' The raging one.' [3] He is, as we saw, the ' owner ' of all women. [4]

The notion of an intimate association between heady vegetable beverages and the moon is widely diffused, and derives from the most universal conceptions of the nature and attributes of the lunar power. As the source of moisture and of vegetation the moon is specially connected with the sap of plants and with all fluids that exude from them; hence the sacred character of gums, resins, and incense. [5] They were regarded as the special vehicles of the magic and prophetic powers derived from the moon. Terebinth was, among the Semites, spoken of as " prophetic terebinth." [6] " Erebinthios " was one of the epithets of Dionysos. [7] The mistletoe of the Celts derived its significance from being regarded as " the sap of the oak." [8] In Greece prophetic women prepared themselves for their functions by chewing leaves of ivy or laurel. [9] When the juice of a plant is observed to give rise to symptoms of intoxication, symptoms which are identified with the state of inspiration, enthusiasm, ecstasy or divine madness due to the moon, that vegetable fluid is naturally regarded as rich in the divine essence. Among the peoples of northern Europe and the Celts, beer was regarded in much the same manner as Soma among the Iranians and Aryans. It was the ambrosia that gave the gods their immortality; there was a God of Beer, Braciaca. [10] Dionysos himself, or his Thracian form Sabasios, appears to have been connected with a fermented beverage, or beer made from rye, before he became a vine-god. [11] The plant which produces those magic beverages

[1] *Kanshitaki-Upanishad*, ii. 9 (*ibid.*, vol. i, p. 287).
[2] *Sâma-Veda*, ii. 5. 1. 1 (T. Benfey, *op. cit.*, vol. ii, p. 264).
[3] G. M. N. Davis, *The Asiatic Dionysos*, pp. 141, 195, 139. Numerous other illustrations of the parallelism between Soma and Dionysos are given in Miss Davis's book.
[4] See above, vol. ii, p. 585.
[5] See above, vol. ii, p. 631.
[6] W. W. von Baudissin, *Studien zur semitischen Religionsgeschichte*, vol. ii, p. 224.
[7] P. N. Rolle, *Recherches sur le culte de Bacchus*, vol. iii, p. 416.
[8] J. A. MacCulloch, *The Religion of the Ancient Celts*, p. 206.
[9] See below, pp. 136, 150.
[10] J. A. MacCulloch, *op. cit.*, pp. 76, 28 sq.
[11] J. E. Harrison, *Prolegomena to the Study of Greek Religion*, pp. 415 sq.

and is the source of those divine feelings is looked upon as an embodiment, or avatar, of the lunar divinity itself. Thus the Indian tribes of Mexico pay an elaborate cult, and offer sacrifices to the cactus plant, from which a drink is prepared which produces a state of ecstasy ; it is " therefore considered a demi-god." [1] In Peru the cocoa-plant was regarded with equal veneration, and was looked upon as a god, in consequence of the effects of mild cocaine poisoning.[2] Throughout Central and South America, ' chicha,' the fermented beverage brewed from Indian corn, is not only the favourite article of consumption of the people, who are perhaps the only uncultered races among whom drunkenness was prevalent before contact with Europeans, but the beverage plays an essential part in all their religious rites and ceremonies, and is regarded as communicating the divine spirit to the worshippers.[3] The Huitoto consider that the moon waxes by drinking ' chicha,' and regard the liquor as the blood of the moon.[4]

Osiris was in Egypt regarded as the discoverer of the vine and as having taught men how to make wine.[5] He is pictured on papyri as old as 1550 B.C. surrounded by vines and grapes.[6] A Hittite god, who appears to have been a Divine Son of the Great Goddess, is represented at Ivriz bearing bunches of grapes ; [7] and a similar image existed, according to local tradition, at Damascus.[8] On Punic steles the grape is, indeed, a common attribute of the Baal.[9] The Babylonian Tammuz, in his most ancient form among the early Sumerians, was identified with the vine. In the great shrine of Eridu, where he was worshipped in connection with the ancient Sumerian triad, Anu-El-Ea, he was represented by a Sacred Vine which occupied a conspicuous place in the sanctuary, and one of his favourite titles was " the Heavenly

---

[1] C. Lumholtz, *Unknown Mexico*, vol. i, pp. 357 sqq.

[2] J. de Acosta, *The Natural and Moral History of the Indies*, pp. 244 sqq.; C. F. Ph. von Martius, *Beiträge zur Ethnographie und Sprachenkunde Amerika's*, vol. i, p. 521.

[3] J. V. Couto de Magalhães, *O Selvagem*, pp. 133 sqq.; F. X. de Charlevoix, *Histoire du Paraguay*, vol. ii, p. 234 ; H. Coudreau, *La France équinoxiale*, vol. ii, pp. 185, 189.

[4] Th. Preuss, *Religion und Mythologie der Uitoto*, vol. i, p. 79. Cf. above, vol. ii, p. 631.

[5] Diodorus Siculus, i. 15 ; Martianus Capella, *De nuptiis Philologiae et Mercurii*, ii. 40.

[6] E. A. Wallis Budge, *Osiris and the Egyptian Resurrection*, vol. i, pp. 39, 45.

[7] J. Garstang, *The Land of the Hittites*, pl. lvii.

[8] J. E. Hanauer, in *Palestine Exploration Fund, Quarterly Statement*, April 1910, pp. 85 sq.

[9] F. Lenormant, " Quelques observations sur les symboles religieux des stèles puniques," *Gazette Archéologique*, ii, p. 146.

Vine." [1] The Great Goddess, his mother, was habitually called
" The Mother of the Vine-stalk," and had a temple under that
name at Lagash.[2] Delilah, a form of the Semitic goddess, dwelt
in Nachal Sorek, ' the Valley of the Vine,' [3] and her name may be
interpreted ' Branch,' or ' Vine-shoot.' [4] The vine was called by
the Babylonians the ' Tree of Life,' and wine the ' drink of life.' [5]
The Heavenly Vine, wrought in gold, was represented in the temple
of Jerusalem.[6]

It is thus unnecessary to go to India for homologues of
the identification of Dionysos with the vine. The association
of Dionysos with India in myth merely expresses the recognition by the Greeks of the similarity between the cult of
Soma and the theology of Dionysos. The other ' travels
of Dionysos ' which form part of the classical myth of the god,
and represent him as having journeyed to Arabia, Egypt, Syria,
as well as India, express in all probability the fact that the gods
of those countries were recognised as essentially identical with the
primitive Greek god. The only male god whom the Arabs worshipped was, according to Greek ideas, Dionysos ; [7] Osiris was
Dionysos ; [8] Bel, Tammuz, Adonis were Dionysos ; [9] Yahweh, the
Hebrew god, was Dionysos ; [10] the Phrygian Attis was Dionysos ; [11]
the Persian Mithra was Dionysos.[12] In fact, as Euripides stated,
" All the barbarians dance his rites." [13] The ' new god ' was justified
by pointing out that the lunar gods of other countries were manifestly identical with Dionysos.

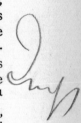

In those assimilations of the gods of other peoples to their
own, the ancients seized as a rule the essential grounds of identity,
often more surely than the modern critic. Dionysos is not regarded
in those equations as the god of the vine. There could be no
greater error than to suppose that Dionysos was a manifestation of
the vine ; the vine was, on the contrary, a manifestation of Dionysos.

[1] T. G. Pinches, " The Babylonian Paradise and its Rivers," *The
Expository Times*, xxix, pp. 182 sq. Cf. A. Jeremias, *Handbuch der Altorientalischen Geisteskultur*, p. 339, n. 1.
[2] S. Langdon, *Tammuz and Ishtar*, p. 43.
[3] *Judges*, xvi. 4.
[4] H. Steinthal, " The Legend of Samson," in I. Goldziher, *Mythology
among the Hebrews*, p. 405.
[5] T. G. Pinches, *The Old Testament in the light of Historical Records*, p. 75.
[6] Josephus, *Antiq. Judaeor.*, xv. 11. 3.
[7] Herodotus, iii. 8.
[8] Diodorus Siculus, i. 11 ; iii. 73 ; Plutarch, *De Iside et Osiride*, xxxiv ;
Quaest. Conv., iv. 5. 3.
[9] F. C. Movers, *Die Phönizier*, vol. i, pp. 337 sqq., 234.
[10] Plutarch, *Quaest. Conv.*, iv. 6. 2.
[11] Pindar, *Isthm.* vii. 3 sqq. ; Euripides, *Bakchai*, 75 sqq.
[12] Martianus Capella, *De nuptiis Philologiae et Mercurii*, ii. 43.
[13] Euripides, *Bakchai*, 482.

But the vine was by no means the only plant with which Dionysos was intimately connected. With the ivy his association was even closer and more ancient : it was " one of the most primitive emblems of the god." [1] He and his votaries are crowned with ivy ; he is called " ivy-haired." [2] The Dionysiac women chewed ivy-leaves.[3] Men were dedicated to him by marking them with an ivy-leaf.[4] His thyrsus is encircled with ivy. His cup is called the " ivy-cup " ; [5] it was so large that it stood him in lieu of a shield.[6] Archaic figures of the god represent him as a wooden post shooting forth ivy leaves, or covered with ivy.[7] He was worshipped at Acharnae as Kissos, ' The Ivy.' [8] The significance of the association between Dionysos and the ivy had been forgotten in classical times ; futile reasons for it were adduced.[9] Yet it was doubtless direct enough ; the ever-green ivy, which survives while other plants die, is, like the soma-plant, the vegetable emblem of immortality. The mother of Dionysos, ' the eternal moon,' crowned herself with ivy before giving birth to him.[10] In Egypt the ivy was called " the plant of Osiris." [11]

The ever-green and resinous pine is almost as closely associated with Dionysos.[12] The dendrophori carried pine-branches in his honour at his festivals,[13] and it was from the pine that the torches used in his rites were made.[14] The pine-cone was one of

[1] J. E. Sandys, edit. of the *Bakchai*, p. 105. Cf. Plutarch, *De Iside et Osiride*, xxxvii.

[2] *Homeric Hymn*, xxvi. 1.   [3] Plutarch, *Quaest. Rom.*, cxii.

[4] *Etymologicum Magnum*, s.v. γάλλος ;   C. A. Lobeck, *Aglaophamus*, p. 657 ; *III Maccabees*, ii. 29 ; P. Perdrizet, " Le fragment de Satyros sur les dèmes d'Alexandrie," *Revue des études anciennes*, xii, pp. 235 sqq. ; Id., " La miraculeuse histoire de Pandare et d'Echédore," *Archiv für Religionswissenschaft*, xiv, p. 104.

[5] Macrobius, *Sat.*, v. 21.

[6] Vergil, *Eclog.*, vi. 17 ; Aristides, *Dionysos*, vol. i, p. 50 (ed. Dindorf).

[7] C. V. Daremberg and E. Saglio, *Dictionnaire des antiquités grecques et romaines*, vol. i, pp. 361, 626 sq. ; C. Bötticher, *Baumkultus der Hellenen*, pp. 42-44 ; W. H. Roscher, *Ausführliches Lexikon*, vol. i, part i, p. 1091.

[8] Pausanias, i. 31. 3. The ivy was regarded as sacred in Thrace. Pliny, *Nat. Hist.*, xvi. 144.

[9] Plutarch, *Quaest. Conviv.*, iii. 2 ; Tertullian, *De Coron. milt.*, vii ; Athenaeus, v. 7 : Because ivy cools the brow and cures drunkenness ; Plutarch, *Queast. Rom.*, cxiii : because ivy when chewed produces madness. Dr. Farnell's explanation is little better ; he sees in the ivy a symbol of " wanton movement and luxuriant life." The correct interpretation is given by Miss Harrison (*Themis*, p. 133), and by Perdrizet (*op. cit.*, p. 238).

[10] Nonnus, *Dionysiaca*, viii. 8 sqq.

[11] Plutarch, *De Iside et Osiride*, xxxvii.

[12] " Maxime aeternam putant hebenum, et cypressum, cedrumque " (Pliny, *Nat. Hist.*, xvi. 79). L. Preller, *Griechische Mythologie*, p. 713 ; O. F. Gruppe, *Griechische Mythologie und Religionsgeschichte*, p. 1418.

[13] Nonnus, *op. cit.*, xlvii, p. 1204.

[14] L. Preller, *Griechische Mythologie*, p. 797.

the favourite emblems of the god, and crowned the point of his thyrsus. The pine-tree from which Pentheos was fabled to have watched the rites of the women was, by order of the Delphic Pythia, made into statues of Dionysos.[1] He was frequently represented, like Tammuz, by a mere rough log, or tree stump ; even at his shrine at Thebes he had no other image than a log " supposed to have fallen from heaven, which later piety decorated with bronze, but never changed into human semblance." [2]

At Sparta Dionysos was called Sykites, and was the ' inventor ' of the fig-tree.[3] At Philippi the maple and the oak were sacred to him ; [4] and at Magnesia the plane-tree.[5] He was also called ' Protyges,' as being the giver of barley ; [6] and he had a temple near Athens as ' Kyametes,' the God of Beans.[7] He was the god of apples also, and, in fact, of all fruits.[8]

Dionysos was, thus, a ' vegetation god.' He is ' Endendros,' " the god who dwells in trees," [9] ' Dendrites,' [10] ' Antheos.' [11] He is " the producer of the fruits of the earth." [12] He is " the inventor of ploughing and sowing " ; [13] and is called in an ancient hymn " the beloved son of the plough." [14] The Romans identified him with their old phallic gods of fertility, and his image was drawn round the fields in a chariot and crowned by the matrons.[15] At Krastonia, in Thrace, during the festival of Dionysos, a great flame appeared in the temple " when the deity intended to give a good harvest, but this was never seen when he intended a dearth." [16]

In the character of deity of vegetation it is obvious how Dionysos was recognised as identical with Osiris, Attis, Adonis, with all other ' vegetation gods.' Yet it was probably not as

[1] Pausanias, ii. 2. 6.

[2] L. R. Farnell, *The Cults of the Greek States*, vol. v, p. 240. Cf. C. G. W. Bötticher, *Baumkultus*, pp. 226 sqq.

[3] Athenaeus, iii. 14 ; Hesychius, s.v. συκίτης. Cf. C. G. W. Bötticher, *op. cit.*, p. 437.

[4] *Bulletin de Correspondance Hellénique*, 1900, pp. 322 sq.

[5] Ch. Michel, *Recueil d'inscriptions grecques*, No. 856 ; P. Wendland and O. Kern, *Beiträge zur Geschichte der griechischen Philosophie und Religion*, pp. 79 sqq.

[6] Pollux, i. 24.

[7] Hesychius, s.v. κυαμῆτης.

[8] Athenaeus, i. 21.

[9] Hesychius, s.v.

[10] Plutarch, *Quaest. Conv.*, v. 3. 1.

[11] Pausanias, vii. 21. 6.

[12] Suidas, s.v. Βρόμιος. Cf. Plutarch, *Quaest. Conv.*, ix. iv. 3 : Dionysos " increases all seeds, for his chaste light produces all fruits."

[13] Diodorus Siculus, iii. 73. 5.

[14] Martianus Capella, *op. cit.*, ii. 43 ; P. N. Rolle, *Recherches sur le culte de Bacchus*, vol. i, p. 100.

[15] Augustine, *Civit. Dei*, vii. 21.

[16] Aristotle, *De mirabilibus auscultationibus*, cxxii.

'vegetation gods' that those divine personages were assimilated
by the Greeks to one another ; the Greeks had not read Sir James
Frazer, and knew of no 'vegetation gods,' and not one of those
deities was, in fact, a pure and simple vegetation god. Their
association with vegetable life, its growth, death, and rebirth,
constitutes but one aspect of attributes and characters which
extend much farther. Not one is a mere impersonation of
the growing fruit of the earth ; the fruit is, on the contrary,
a manifestation of their generative force. " Dionysos," says Plutarch,
" is the generative principle which gives life to all."[1] In him,
Plutarch tells us again, "is seated the humour which gives generating
power."[2] That ' generative power,' dependent upon moisture or
' humour ' is, in turn, not an abstract principle represented by the
gods, but an attribute of the primitive cosmic deity of peoples in
stages of culture where there is little place for abstract principles.

It was commonly reported amongst the Greeks that Dionysos
came from Thrace. The Thracian god who became known as
Dionysos was, like his Asiatic and Egyptian homologues, the Divine
Son of the Great Mother. " He was united," says Dr. Farnell, " with
a goddess, with whom his relation was mainly regarded as filial."[3]
Herodotus tells us that " the Thracians worshipped no other gods
but Dionysos, Ares, and Artemis."[4] The ' Ares ' appears to have
been but a form of the Dionysos, in his tribal, national aspect ;
he was a dying-god and had his Holy Sepulchre.[5] The Mother-
goddess whom Herodotus calls Artemis, was generally known
as Bendis,[6] and was, as his identification indicates, a lunar
goddess. " The moon," says Hesychius, " is called Bendis and
Artemis."[7] One of her favourite appellations was, as elsewhere, " The Queen of Heaven."[8] Thus the Thracian Dionysos
was, like his foreign homologues, related to the Great Mother in
her heavenly or lunar aspect and not in her terrestrial form. The
god, while prominently a vegetation god, was also conspicuous in
his oracular character. He was fond of dwelling in caves ; at
Satrai there was a great oracle of his at which he vaticinated through
a prophetess.[9]

---

[1] Plutarch, *De Iside et Osiride*, xxxiv.

[2] Id., *Quaest. de arati signis.* Cf. C. A. Lobeck, *Aglaophamus*, vol. i,
p. 661 n[b.]

[3] L. R. Farnell, *The Cults of the Greek States*, vol. v, p. 101.

[4] Herodotus, v. 7.

[5] L. R. Farnell, *loc. cit.* ; Clement Alexandrinus, *Recogn.*, x. 24.

[6] Strabo, p. 470 ; Lucan, *Icaromen.*, 24 ; Livy, xxxviii. 41 ; Hesychius,
s.v. δίλογχον.

[7] Hesychius, *loc. cit.*   [8] Herodotus, iv. 32.

[9] *Ibid.*, vii. 111. There were numerous other Dionysian oracles in
Thrace : e.g. Pausanias, ix. 30. 9 ; Macrobius, *Satur.*, i. 18. 1 ; Plutarch,
Vit. Crassi, viii ; Suetonius, *Octavian*, xciv ; Dio Cassius, liv. 34. 5 ; li. 25. 5.

In the same manner as Dionysos " of the many names " [1] was identified with the vegetation gods of the barbarians, and also with many other gods, such as the Sinn of the Arabs, who were not typically vegetation gods, so the Thracian god, assuming him to be originally Thracian, had been assimilated to, and had absorbed, a multitude of very primitive local gods in Greece itself. " Dionysos," as Professor Wernicke remarks, " took in many localities the place of male nature-deities allied to Artemis," [2] that is to say, of primitive moon-gods. It is in that sense that Dionysos had been 'imported,' or was a 'new god.' But for the same reason he represented, at the same time, the oldest deities of Greece, older essentially than the Olympians. They became unified under the name of Dionysos. [3]

Those primitive deities belonged to lunar not to solar cults. The moon, according to Aristophanes, complained of the neglect into which her cult had fallen in Greece. [4] Yet despite that comparative decay, her cult played, even in classical times, a part out of all proportion to the importance of a subordinate luminary, and quite incompatible with the development of a lunar cult by the side of, and supplementary to, the cult of a solar deity. That disproportion is emphasised in the more primitive and rural districts. In Arcadia, where primitive cults survived when, at the time of the Dorian invasion, they disappeared in all the rest of Greece, moon-worship was supreme. The Arcadians were indeed commonly referred to as " the moon-worshippers," προσέληνοι, σεληνῖται. [5] And, on the other hand, it is noted by Immerwahr that there is a striking absence of any cult of Helios. [6] Nowhere are so many temples of the moon-deity to be found, K. O. Müller remarks, as in Arcadia. [7] The

[1] Sophokles, *Antigone*, 1115.

[2] K. Wernicke, in Pauly-Wissowa, *Real-Encyclopaedie der classischen Alterthumswissenschaft*, vol. v, p. 1365.

[3] No great profit is to be derived from discussing the name Dionysos. The interpretations are countless, and none is conclusive. It appears certain that the name is a compound, Dio-Nysos. (It appears in the divided form in Aristophanes, *Ranae*, 214, and in Apollodorus, *Argonautica*, iv. 1132.) 'Nysos' has, on insufficient evidence, been interpreted as 'son,' deducing it from a Thracian feminine, meaning 'girl'; thus making out the name to mean " The Son of God " (P. W. Kretschmer, in *Aus der Anomia*, p. 22). Dionysos does not, however, appear to have been the ordinary Thracian name of the god, who seems to have been known there as Bromios and Sabos. There are numerous mountains and groves called Nysa with which the god is identified. 'Nysa' is said to be an old term for 'grove' or 'wood'; and Dionysos might thus mean 'the god of the grove.'

[4] Aristophanes, *Nubes*, 610.

[5] W. Immerwahr, *Die Kulte und Mythen Arkadiens*, p. 209 ; V. Bérard, *De l'origine des cultes arcadiens*, p. 62.

[6] W. Immerwahr, *op. cit.*, p. 205.

[7] C. O. Müller, *The History and Antiquities of the Doric Race*, vol. i, p. 376.

moon-goddess, though referred to in classical terminology by the
name of Artemis, bore a number of local names, such as Kallisto,
Linatis, Heleia, and had no connection with Artemis or Apollo,
whose cult is never, as it invariably is in Olympian religion,
conjoined with hers, and who is not mentioned in relation
to her.[1] Utterly different in her attributes from the classical
moon-goddess, the Arcadian Artemis was represented at Mega-
lopolis, in company with Demeter, with a torch in one hand
and two serpents in the other,[2] and she is described as " raging
and foaming like a Bacchanalian." [3] The moon-goddess of Arcadia
was the primal ancestress, the First Woman ; she was the mother
of Arcas, that is, of the Arcadians.[4] But she was even more
ancient, for we are told that she was older than the earth.[5]

The Spartans themselves were, like all primitive peoples, super-
stitiously observant of lunar influences ; in all their undertakings
they took account of the phase of the moon, and they missed taking
part in the battle of Marathon because the moon was not in the
proper quarter for a journey.[6] The eponymous mother of the
Hellenes, Helen, was a special object of worship at Sparta, where
the women wore lotus-flowers at her festival.[7] The daughter of
the Swan-woman, sister of the Heavenly Twins, and wife of the
Moon-man, Menelaos, was born from an egg which had fallen from
the moon.[8] Her name was regarded by the Gnostics as identical
with that of the moon, Selene.[9]

Although, as elsewhere in Greece, the moon was in Arcadia
and in Elis worshipped as a female divinity, there is evidence
of the more primitive usage in place-names, for the name
of the river Menios could not have been given to it by a people
who regarded the moon as Selene or Artemis.[10] Yet the district

---

[1] W. Immerwahr, op. cit., pp. 153 sqq.   [2] Pausanias, viii. 37. 2.
[3] Plutarch, De superstitione, 9.   [4] Pausanias, viii. 35. 7.
[5] Stephanus Byzantinum, s.v. 'Αρκαδία : Scholiast on Apollonius Rhodius,
iv. 264 ; Aristophanes, Nubae., 397 ; Lucian, De astrologia, xxvi.
[6] Herodotus, vi. 106 ; Lucian, De astrologia, xxv.
[7] Theocritus, xviii. 43 sqq. ; Pausanias, iii. 15. 3 ; iii. 19. 9 ; Herodotus,
vi. 61 ; Hesychius, s.v. 'Ελένεια.
[8] Athenaeus, ii. 16 ; cf. ix. 4. Helen was also identified with Nemesis
(Cypria, vi., in Epicorum Fragmenta, ed. G. Kinkel, p. 24). She was also a
deity of trees and waters ; she was worshipped at Rhodes as ' dendritis '
(cf. Pausanias, iii. 19. 10 ; Stephanus Byzantinus, s.v. 'Ελενη). Menelaos,
who was worshipped in conjunction with Helen, was likewise a tree-god
(S. Wide, Lakonische Kulte, pp. 345 sq.). Her introduction into the saga of
Troy, partly in the character of Nemesis, is an adaptation of a myth of
which an earlier form appears in her abduction by Theseus.
[9] Irenaeus, Contra haereses, i. 20 ; Tertullian, De anima, 34 ; Epiphanius,
Adversus octoginta haereses, xxi. 2.
[10] Pausanias, vi. 24. 6.

is the scene of the myth of Endymion, the tribal ancestor of the
Epeioi, who had fifty daughters by the moon,[1] and possessed the
gift of eternal youth.[2] The great local god of Elis and Arcadia
was a very primitive god called Pan.[3] The story was told, not
many miles from the scene of the Endymion myth, of his having
ravished the moon.[4] Parallels from all parts of the savage world
would suggest that the sexes of the personages had become trans-
posed ; and that, as is the habit of moon-gods, Pan was given to
carrying away women whom he caught fetching water at wells
and streams. Pan was worshipped in caves in association with
Selene.[5] According to one tradition he was the son of the moon-
goddess Penelope.[6] He was a dying god,[7] who " slept by day." [8]
Like the Eleusinian Dionysos, he bears a torch, and is worshipped
by the light of torches.[9] At his great sanctuary at Lykosura an
undying fire was maintained, and he there delivered oracles through
his prophetess, who bore the name of Erato.[10] Apollo was represented as the pupil of Pan in the arts of prophecy.[11]

There is considerable evidence that in Attica itself the moon's
complaint that her cult had fallen into neglect in latter days was
not unjustified. The Athenians of the classic age did not, like
the Arcadians, regard the moon as the creator of the world and

[1] *Pausanias*, v. 1. 4.

[2] Apollodorus, *Bibliotheca*, i. 7.

[3] Pan, who was transmuted by the Orphics into " the great god Pan,"
that is, ' All,' is named from a root which appears in πάομαι, επἁσάμην,
etc., and is the same as that of the Latin ' pabulum.' He was simply ' food,'
or ' the nourisher.' Arcadian hunters depended on him for success in the
chase, and if they found no game they whipped his image (Theocritus,
vii. 106 sqq., and Scholiast, M. P. Nilsson, *Griechische Feste*, pp. 443 sq.).
Zeus Lykaios, the wolf-god, has, like every other god, been interpreted as a
sun-god. But Immerwahr has shown that the assumption for which there
exists no evidence is positively inadmissible (W. Immerwahr, *op. cit.*,
p. 17).

[4] Macrobius, *Satur.*, v. 22. 9 sq. ; Vergil, *Georg.*, iii. 392 ; Porphyrius,
De antro nymph., xx. The myth is figured in numerous pictorial representations in which Pan is depicted carrying the moon. He appears thus
on the coins of Patrai.

[5] Porphyrius, *De antro nymph.*, xx.

[6] Herodotus, ii. 145 ; Scholiast ad Theocritus, i. 123 ; Pindar, *Fragm.*,
100 ; cf. " Apollodori Bibliothecae Fragmenta Sabbaitica," *Rheinisches
Museum*, xlvi, p. 181.

[7] Plutarch, *De defectu oraculorum*, xvii.

[8] Theocritus, *Id.*, i. 15 sqq. ; Ovid, *Fasti*, iv. 762. Pan was specially
associated with dreams (Servius, on *Aeneid*, vi. 776 ; Scholiast, on Aristophanes, *Vespae*, 1038 ; Augustin, *De Civit. Dei*, xv. 23).

[9] L. Preller, *Griechische Mythologie*, p. 741.

[10] Pausanias, viii. 37. 8–9. Welcker regards Pan as a god of light—surely
not of sunlight (F. G. Welcker, *Griechische Götterlehre*, vol. i, pp. 454
sqq.).

[11] Apollodorus, i. 4. 13 ; Argum. to Pindar, *Pyth*, p. 297.

the ancestor of mankind; but that very similar views once obtained among their forefathers is suggested by the fact that the manhood ceremonies of the Athenians and their registration as citizens in the rolls of the phratries, continued to be carried out under the auspices of the Moon-deity, Artemis, and that they dedicated the hair which they cut off on that occasion— the only surviving relic of old initiation rites—to the Moon-goddess.[1] The most ancient and sacred shrine of Athenian religion was not the Parthenon, but the Erechtheion; and a large portion of that sacred building was occupied by a temple, the Pandroseia, dedicated to the "All dewyone," or deity of all the dews. The "All-dewy one" was the name of one of the Horai; but Pandrosos was originally worshipped in intimate conjunction with Athene, and was in fact indistinguishable from her.[2] Close by the Pandroseia was the sacred olive-tree which was likewise worshipped in the shrines of old Mykenean cults as the emblem, or rather the dwelling-place of the moon. Athene herself bore the moon on her shield and the lunar serpents all over her; and her priestesses wore moon-haloes. Athenian coins bear the symbols of the tribal goddess, the owl, the twig of olive, and the crescent moon.[3]

Like all the gods with whom he was identified, Dionysos was certainly in nature and origin a moon-god. Whatever attributes of his may at one time or another have become prominent, they constitute the complex of characters which belong to the primitive lunar deity; and he has no others. He is, like all primitive moon-gods, the lord of vegetation because he is the lord of generation and of moisture. 'Hyes,' or 'Hyeus,' 'the raining one,' was one of his oldest appellatives; his priestesses, the Mainads, were called 'Hyades,' and 'Hye' was a name of the moon.[4] Dionysos controlled rivers and the ocean,[5] was assimilated to Poseidon, and at Argos was actually a sea-god, 'Pelagios.'[6] At Elis he was supposed to rise, when invoked, from the water.[7] The connection between moisture, vegetation, and generation is thus referred to by Plutarch:

---

[1] Hesychius, s.v. κουρεῶτις; Diodorus Siculus, v. 73.

[2] *Corpus Inscriptionum Atticarum*, ii. 3 n. 1383, 1390; iii. n. 887; H. Usener, *Götternamen*, p. 138.

[3] J. E. Harrison, *Themis*, pp. 190 sq.

[4] Hesychius, s.v. Ὑη, εναςτος ὥςτεμαιγας. Cf. *Etymologicum Magnum*, p. 775 I. Bekker, *Anecdota Graeca*, p. 207; H. Usener, *Götternamen* pp. 45; qq.

[5] Horace, *Od.*, ii. 19. 17: "Tu flectis amnes, tu mare barbarum."

[6] Pausanias, xi. 23. Cf. S. Wide, *De Sacris Traezeniorum*, p. 44. Conversely, Poseidon was a god of vegetation, and was called the "Producer of Plants" (Plutarch, *Quaestiones conviviales*, iii. 1, viii. 4; Cornutus, *De Natura Deorum*, xx.).

[7] Plutarch, *De Iside et Osiride*, **xxxv**.

"The Greeks," he says, "call a son 'hyon,' from water and rain, which are called 'hydor' and 'hyein'; and they call Dionysos Hyes, who presides over all moisture."[1] It is interesting to set by the side of that passage one from the Vedanta: "Water," says the Indian philosopher, "becomes in succession moon (which attracts water), rain, food, seed, embryo; and thus water becomes man."[2]

"The Nocturnal" is one of the most common epithets of Dionysos, and he had a temple under that name.[3] All his festivals were celebrated at night; Aristophanes calls him "the lighter of nocturnal feasts."[4] Sophokles terms him "the Leader of the fiery stars";[5] Nonnus, "night-shining Dionysos."[6] His ritual vestment is a dark star-spangled robe and a crescent-shaped mitre.[7] In Phrygia he was identified with the moon-god, Men.[8] "Bull-faced Mene" is made to say: "I love the grape and tend the Bacchic rites, for the earth can ripen no fruit save after receiving the bright germinating dew of the moon. . . . I lead the raging choruses; Bacchic Mene am I, not merely because I accomplish in the Aether the cycle of the months, but because I excite mania and rule the raging spirits."[9]

The Thracian Dionysos was the son of the Moon-goddess whom Herodotus calls Artemis. The Theban Dionysos is, in the classical legend the son of Semele, also called Thyone, "the raging one," who is generally regarded as an Earth-goddess,[10] which, however, by no means prevents her from being a moon-goddess. The race of Kadmos, the father of Semele, out of which the Theban Dionysos sprang, had for its mythical tribal ancestress Io, a Moon-goddess assimilated to Isis, who was also represented as one of the mothers

---

[1] Plutarch, *De Iside et Osiride*, 34.

[2] *Vedanta-Sutra*, iii. 1. 5 (*The Sacred Books of the East*, vol. xlviii, p. 587).

[3] Aristophanes, *Ranae*, 218; Pausanias, i. 40. 6.

[4] Aristophanes, *Ranae*, 746.

[5] Sophokles, *Antigone*, 148 sq.

[6] Nonnus, *Dionysiaca*, xliv. 218.　　　　　[7] *Ibid.*

[8] Proclus, *Comment. in Timaeum*, iv. 251; L. Preller, *Griechische Mythologie*, pp. 577, 701.

[9] Nonnus, *Dionysiaca*, xliv. 217 sqq. Nonnus makes here what a commentator calls a pun with the words 'Men,' moon or month, and 'mania,' 'mainad.' But in the light of the universal attributes of the moon in primitive culture it appears far from improbable that the supposed 'pun' rests upon philological identity. The Mainads would thus be the 'moon-women.'

[10] Diodorus Siculus, iii. 62. Kretschmer has identified Semele with a Phrygian appellation of the earth (P. W. Kretschmer, *Aus der Anomia*, pp. 17 sqq.; cf. L. R. Farnell, *The Cult of the Greek States*, vol. v, p. 94; J. E. Harrison, *Prolegomena to the Study of Greek Religion*, p. 404). One of her names is 'Υή, 'the rainy one' (Hesychius, s.v. 'Υή). It is difficult to imagine a 'rainy earth.'

of Dionysos.[1] Ulpian says that "some call Dionysos the son of Selene."[2] Eusebius says that the mother of Dionysos was either Persephone or Selene.[3] Cicero states that he was the son of the Moon.[4]

Dionysos, though alien to the Olympian deities, is everywhere associated in Greek cult with the moon-goddess Artemis. They were worshipped in the same temples.[5] On the day following the Dionysiac festival, the Athenians celebrated the feast of the Moon, or Pandia.[6] The relation of Dionysos to Artemis is usually represented as a brotherly one, a relation which, in this instance, denoted interchangeable identity. The temple of Artemis 'the Saviour,' at Delos, was professedly erected on the spot where, not Artemis, but Dionysos had saved Demeter from the nether-world.[7] On the coins of Delos are pictured three crescent moons enclosing asterisks representing Artemis, Dionysos, and Apollo.[8] Dionysos was likewise intimately associated with the moon-goddess Ariadne ; she was his wife. They were worshipped together at Naxos,[9] and at Kos,[10] and their sacred marriage constituted a holy mystery. The tomb of Ariadne was shown in the sanctury of the Kretan Dionysos.[11]

Although Dionysos was everywhere regarded as dying and coming to life again, the myth of his vicissitudes had evidently been, like most cosmological myths, half-forgotten by the Greeks of classical times, except for those features which survived in his dramatic rituals. The essential points of the story were told in Krete as follows. Dionysos was born as a horned infant, and soon after mounted the throne of his father, who is called Zeus, and who according to one version surrendered his throne to him and made him "the king of all gods." While thus enthroned in glory

[1] Nonnus, *Dionysiaca*, iii. 360 ; Hesychius, s.v. 'Ιώ.

[2] C. A. Lobeck, *Aglaophamus*, vol. ii, p. 1133.

[3] Eusebius, *Praeparatio Evangelica*, iii. 13. 120. The reading is arbitrarily emended by Cuperus into ' Semele.' Cf. C. A. Lobeck, *loc. cit.*

[4] Cicero, *De natura deorum.*, iii. 23. 58. The suggestion of Foucart, approved by Farnell, that the precisian Cicero, in writing concerning the gods, was guilty of an illiterate confusion between Semele and Selene is, to put it mildly, inadmissible. Cicero does not say ' Selene,' but ' Luna.'

[5] Pausanias, i. 31. 4 ; ii. 31. 4 sq. ; iii. 26. 11 ; iv. 34. 6 ; vii. 26. 11 ; viii. 23. 1 ; viii. 27. 3 ; Strabo, viii. 363.

[6] Demosthenes, *In Midian*, 517.

[7] Pausanias, ii. 1.

[8] P. N. Rolle, *Recherches sur le culte de Bacchus*, vol. i, p. 75.

[9] Hesiod, *Theogony*, 948 ; Euripides, *Hyppolitus*, 339 ; K. Hoeck, *Kreta*, vol. ii, pp. 148 sq.

[10] *Archäologische Zeitung*, 1846, Tab. xlii.

[11] Pausanias, ii. 23. 7.

Dionysos employed himself contemplating his image in a mirror. His reign was, however, a brief one, for he fell a victim to the assaults of the Titans, who cut him up into a number of pieces—some say fourteen—and devoured him. Only his heart remained, which was eaten by his mother, from whom consequently he was presently born again.[1] The type of story should by now be familiar to the reader. The outline of the myth has come to us through late sources; but a theme which is identical with those of the savages of Melanesia and of America is manifestly not a late invention. Such primitive myths had melted away in the exuberance of Greek poetical imagination, which had long outgrown primitive cosmic conceptions. It is only by snatches that we can catch through the rich veil of Hellenic poetry and drama glimpses of the rude savage folklore which formed the germ of that growth, as, for instance, in the myth of Oedipus, who kills his father and becomes his mother's husband. The ritual representations of those primitive myths suffered less change than the stories, whose meaning had faded. The growth of the infant Dionysos was promoted by the dances and saltations of the Kouretes, as the growth of the young moon is assisted by the dances of its savage votaries. The 'Titans,' or 'clay-men,' derived their name from being bedaubed with white clay in the same manner as the Australian aborigines at their lunar festivals.[2]

As most readers are aware, Greek cult contained two disparate elements, one might almost say two distinct and different religions. On the one hand were the Olympian gods grouped about the central figure of the sky-god Zeus, and typically represented by the sun-god Apollo. Other deities of the Olympian pantheon, such as Poseidon, Ares, Hephaistos, Hera, Aphrodite, Athene, Artemis,

---

[1] Nonnus, Dionysiaca, vi. 155–205; Orphica, fragm. 200, ed. Abel; Firmicus Maternus, De errore profanarum religionum, 6; Clement of Alexandria, Protrept., ii. 17; Proclus, on Plato, Cratylus, p. 59; C. A. Lobeck, Aglaophamus, vol. i, pp. 547 sqq. Dionysos, alone amongst Greek gods, is represented under three distinct aspects: as infant, as mature man, and as an old man. Cf. Macrobius, Saturn., i. 28. The triplicity of his aspects pervades his cult symbolism. At Patrai he was represented by three statues (Pausanias, vii. 21. 6; cf. 18 sq.). He appears also to have been worshipped as threefold at Athens (Nonnus, Dionysiaca, xlvii. 962 sqq. Cf. R. Köhler, Über die Dionysiaka des Nonnus von Panoplis, p. 92). At Sekyon the god was represented by a single statue in gold and ivory; but on the night of his festival two other statues were brought out. So that for the duration of the feast he was threefold (Pausanias, ii. 7. 5 sq.). On an inscription from the island of Nisyros his priest is referred to as the priest of the Dionysoi, ιερέως των Διονύσων (Inscriptiones Graecae Insularum, iii. n. 164).

[2] Harpocration, s.v., 'απομάττων.

whatever might have been their original character, assumed in the Olympian atmosphere frankly, almost coarsely anthropomorphic natures, taking sides as tribal deities, in the disputes of mankind, and presiding as well-defined departmental divinities over the several provinces of nature. Apart from their tribal partisanships they were in general good-natured and helpful to their votaries. Their attributes and characters lay on the surface ; there were no mystic depths in their constitution. They were, in fact, as the Greeks themselves more than once felt, and as every adverse critic has represented, somewhat superficial and trivial gods. They had, but for their tribal attributes, no intimate relation to the individual, to his life, his destiny, his soul.

There was, on the other hand, a totally different set of divinities whom systematic mythologists never succeeded in quite naturalising in the Olympian pantheon. To that order of non-Olympian deities belonged Demeter, the Great Mother, and her various forms, Kore, Persephone, and numerous, by comparison with the Olympian somewhat shadowy, beings, such as Moira, Nemesis, Erynis, Charis, Hades, in some aspects of his functions Hermes, and Dionysos. These were related not so much to departments of nature and natural forces, as to the very forces of life and death. Their realm, unlike that of the Olympians, extended beyond the affairs of this life ; they determined the fate of the dead. But they controlled the forces which bring to life as well as those which destroy, the forces which generate and nourish, and which blight and cause to perish ; they were the ultimate arbiters of the destinies of existence for good and for evil. They were the source of punishment and death, but with that dark character went also the control of the sources of life ; with judgment and retribution the promise of redemption, with fateful death the hope of life everlasting.

That composite, dual character of Greek religion, which has been made familiar to English readers by the delightful studies of Miss Jane Harrison, was, among modern scholars, first clearly perceived by Friederich Nietzsche who, with the intuition of genius, distinguished and contrasted, in his brilliant essay on the Origin of Greek Tragedy, the two opposite elements in Greek religious ideas. To those he gave the names, not as has now become customary, of ' chthonic,' or terrestrial, and ' uranian,' ' Olympian ' or celestial, but of Dionysian and Apollonian.[1] Those names indicate more fundamentally and accurately than do the current ones the nature of the contrast. For those deities which are called ' chthonic ' or earthly are, as a matter of fact, not in any sense deities of the earth. They are, in one of their aspects associated with the ' underworld,' but that underworld is but a

---

[1] F. Nietzsche, *Die Geburt der Tragödie*, p. 51 *et passim.*

segment of their cycle; they are deities of the underworld not because they appertain to the earth or are in any sense a personification of it, but because they are, on the contrary, heavenly bodies which, in the course of their cycle, pass under the earth. They are therefore just as much ' uranian ' as are the Olympians. Those ' chthonic ' deities appertain to the cycle of the primitive lunar religion of which the male moon-god represented in Greek cult by Dionysos, is the prototype; and that older cosmological religion was not displaced so much by the Olympian Sky-god Zeus, as by the Sun-god who appropriated the functions of the older heavenly deity.

When, as in all primitive cosmological ideas and in pre-agricultural religion, the moon is the heavenly ruler, the controller of time, of life and death, of magic and prophetic powers, the source of the heavenly influences that produce fertility and growth, the sun is without any functions. When he becomes in turn the measurer and controller of the agricultural year and of the seasons, and rises to a position of new importance, the sun can acquire his attributes of heavenly power only by taking them over from his predecessor in the government of heaven, the lunar deity. Hence, whenever those attributes are found ascribed, even in part, to a lunar deity, the fact alone is proof that the deity was once supreme in the heavens and the sun subordinate; for no lunar deity could acquire heavenly powers as regards the fertility of the earth while a solar deity existed by its side to exercise those functions. In Greek religion the position of the sun deity never became supreme; the function of fertilising the earth and of controlling the rain belonged to the Sky-god, Zeus. The Sun-god, being raised to importance by agricultural religion, had therefore no functions or attributes to mark that importance except such as could be transferred to him from the lunar god. Apollo, the Sun-god, is in Greek religion in the incongruous position of possessing none of the specific attributes of a heavenly fertiliser and producer of vegetation; he is associated instead with functions and attributes which appertain prescriptively to the lunar god, with prophecy and divination, with the control of diseases and with the healing art. " Apollo," says Servius, " has not the power to give, but only the power to speak." [1]

Apollo is, in classical Olympian mythology, the god of Parnassus, where, on the Helikonian height, he leads the chorus of the Muses. He is, however, but an intruder there. Parnassus was the sacred mountain of Dionysos, the great centre of his trieteric festivals.[2] Sophokles calls the mountain ' Nysa,' the

[1] Servius, *ad Aeneid.*, iii. 85.
[2] Pausanias, x. 32. 7; Hyginus, *Fab.*, iv; Euripides, *Iphig. in Taur.*,

mount of Dionysos, " whose summit is crowned with ivy, and its flanks clad with vine ; whose echoes reverberate with the Bakchai's plaintive hymns."[1] The Helikonian height in particular was sacred to Dionysos.[2] The Muses, divinities of ' poetry ' in the primitive sense, that is, of spells and vaticinations, originally three, and a form of the threefold goddess of fate, were the nurses of Dionysos,[3] who bears the title of " Leader of the Muses," Musagetes.[4] In a temple in the Keramikon he was worshipped as ' Melpomenos.'[5] He was the special protector of poets ; and was celebrated by them at a festival in which they were crowned not with laurel but ivy.[6]

The position of Apollo was consecrated by establishing him at Delphi, the holiest spot in Greek cult, the " navel of the earth." But " it was not forgotten by the ancients themselves that at Delphi, the central site of his cult, Apollo was an intruder."[7] " The oracle was not founded by the god, but inherited by him from a still older cult."[8] The Delphic oracle was, in fact, like all other Greek oracles, a mantic shrine of the Mother Goddesses, in their threefold fatidic aspect, and of the Divine Son. Aeschylus tells us that Apollo inherited the oracle from Gaia, Themis, and Phoibe.[9] Those are but names for the triune Great Goddess in her three aspects, earthly, fatidic, and heavenly. The Moirai had a chapel in the Delphic shrine.[10] The Delphic deities were more usually referred to simply as ' The Three.'[11] " What strikes us as most alien to Apollo in the Delphic ritual," remarks Dr. Farnell, " is the idea that the source of the inspiration is in the subterranean world, for he of all Greek deities has no part or lot in this."[12]

1243 sq. ; Id., Phoenic., 234 sq. ; Sophokles, Antigon., 1126 sqq. ; Aristophanes, Nubes, 603 sqq. ; Stephanus Byzantinus, s.v. Νῦσαι ; Macrobius, Saturn., i. 18. 3.

[1] Sophokles, Antigon., 11 ; Plutarch, Quaest. Conviv., viii. 1 ; Diodorus Siculus, iv. 4.

[2] Sophokles, Oedip. Tyr., 1098.

[3] Plutarch, Quaest. Conviv., viii. praef.

[4] Inscription from Naxos, in Bulletin de Correspondance Hellénique, 1878, p. 587 ; Inscriptiones Graecae Insularum, v. 46.

[5] Pausanias, i. 2. 5 ; Athenaeus, v. 215 ; Corpus Inscriptionum Atticarum, iii. 20. 274. 278.

[6] Ovid, Eleg., v. 3 ; P. N. Rolle, Recherches sur le culte de Bacchus, vol. iii, pp. 212 sq.

[7] E. Rohde, Psyche, vol. ii, p. 54.

[8] L. R. Farnell, The Cults of the Greek States, vol. iii, p. 193.

[9] Aeschylus, Eumenides, 2 sqq.

[10] Plutarch, De EI ap. Delph., 2 ; Pausanias, x. 24. 4.

[11] Homeric Hymn to Mercury, 552 ; Apollodorus, iii. 19. 2 ; Pherekydes, Fragm., 2a (Fragm. Hist. Graec., vol. iv, p. 637) ; Zenobius, v. 75 ; Hesychius, s.v. Θριά ; Scholiast to Callimachus, in Apoll., 45 ; Lobeck, Aglaophamus, pp. 814 sq.

[12] L. R. Farnell, op. cit., vol. iii, p. 193. Euripides calls Delphi an ' oracle

Euripides represents Apollo as protesting to Zeus against the Earth-goddess being allowed to continue her oracular functions at Delphi.[1] Ge had in fact to the last her shrine at Delphi.[2] But The Three were not here any more than elsewhere, purely earth-deities. Aeschylus mentions amongst them Phoibe, that is to say, the moon.[3] According to local tradition one of the first Delphic Sibyls, Herophile, was the same as the moon-goddess Artemis.[4] Plutarch, whose authority in the matter is enhanced by the circumstance that he was himself a Delphic priest, says that the oracle was inspired by Night and the Moon;[5] and Lucian tells us that "the Delphic virgin has the gift of divination as the representative of the Heavenly Virgin."[6] The Delphian priestesses bore the name of Melissai, "a term," remarks Dr. Farnell, "specially reserved to priestesses of Demeter";[7] but it was also borne by the priestesses of the moon-goddess,[8] and was indeed a favourite epithet of the moon, from which all honey was supposed to derive, and which is assimilated to a hive whose bees are the stars.[9] The original mantic shrine of Delphi was, in fact, a hut frequented by bees, and was likened to a hive.[10] It would appear, according to Plutarch, that the oracle could be consulted

---

of the earth,' ᾿μαντεῖον χθόνιον (*Iphig. in Taur.*, 1249). The story of the mephitic vapours rising out of the ground is, however, pure fiction. The French excavations have shown that there was neither chasm, nor cave, or opening of any kind, in the floor of the temple to give vent to vapours, which, in that situation, would be a geological absurdity (A. P. Oppé, "The Chasm at Delphi," *Journal of Hellenic Studies*, xxiv, p. 214).

[1] Euripides, *Iphigenia in Taur.*, 1259 sqq.

[2] *Bulletin de Correspondance Hellénique*, 1902, p. 65; H. Pontow, "Die Kultstätte der 'anderen Götter' von Delphi," *Philologus*, lxxi, p. 30.

[3] Porphyry in Eusebius, *Praeparatio Evangelica*, iv. 23. 175 :—

> "Lo! here the Virgin, who changing forms
> Runs forth o'er highest heaven, with bovine face,
> Three-headed, ruthless, arm'd with shafts of gold,
> Chaste Phoebe, Illythia, light of men."

Cf. Vergil, *Aeneid*, x. 215; Ovid, *Amores*, iii. 2. 51.

[4] Pausanias, x. 12.

[5] Plutarch, *De ser. num. vindic.*, xxii.

[6] Lucian, *De astrologia*, xxiii.

[7] L. R. Farnell, *op. cit.*, vol. iii, p. 193.

[8] Porphyry, *De antro nympharum*, xviii; Scholiast to Pindar, *Pythic*, iv. 106. The priest of Artemis at Ephesos was called ἐσσήν, that is, 'the king-bee' (Pausanias, viii. 13. 1; cf. Hesychius, Suidas, s.v. ᾿Εσσην).

[9] F. L. W. Schwartz, *Sonne, Mond und Sterne*, p. 87; W. H. Roscher, *Selene und Verwandtes*, pp. 49, 65; Id., *Nektar und Ambrosia*, pp. 13 sqq.; A. B. Cook, "The Bee in Greek Mythology," *Journal of Hellenic Studies*, xv, pp. 3 sqq. Dionysos himself was the discoverer of honey (Ovid, *Fasti*, iii. 735 sq.). He is said to have been fed on honey (Apollonius Rhodius, iv. 1129 sqq.).

[10] Pausanias, x.

once a month only;[1] there were, at any rate, "unlucky days," on which it could not be made use of.[2] The Three were represented by the prophetic tripod, which had no connection with Apollo.

As elsewhere the Three were associated at Delphi with a male god. Among the deities whom Apollo displaced there, Dionysos is expressly named.[3] According to tradition, Delphos, the eponymous founder of the shrine, was the son of Thyia, "who was the first priestess of Dionysos and introduced his orgies." [4] The sungod, in truth, never completely succeeded in ousting the older deities from the official centre of Apollonian cult. "Dionysos," says Plutarch, "had as much to do with Delphi as Apollo." [5] He had his own priests there, and sacrifices were solemnly offered to him in the shrine; [6] he was represented with his 'Nurses,' the Thyades, the first priestesses of the Delphian sanctuary, on the pediment of the temple.[7] The oracle was actually delivered from "the grave of Dionysos," [8] which was no other than the sacred 'omphalos,' the centre of the world, an old aniconic sacred stone fetich of the Delphic bethel. He represented the serpent-god of waters and trees, Pytho, who was the original prophet and spokesman of the Three.[9] The Pythia prepared herself for her office by drinking from the sacred spring of the god,[10] and by chewing leaves of laurel.[11] "Apollo," remarks Dr. Verrall interpreting

---

[1] Plutarch, *Quaest. Graec.*, ix.

[2] Id., *Vita Alexandris*, xiv.

[3] Scholiast to Pindar, *Pyth.*, *Argum.* (ed. Bokh, p. 297).

[4] Pausanias, x. 6.

[5] Plutarch, *De EI apud Delphos*, ix.

[6] H. Pontow, "Die Kultstätte der 'anderen Götter' von Delphi," *Philologus*, lxxi, pp. 62, 64.

[7] Pausanias, x. 19. 3.

[8] Plutarch, *De Iside et Osiride*, xxxv; Callimachus, *Fragm.*, 374; Kephalion, *Fragm.*, 5 (*Fragm. Hist. Graec.*, vol. iii, p. 628); J. Malala, *Chronographia*, ii. 52; Tatian, *Adv. Graec.*, viii. 25; Philochoros, *Fragm.*, 22. Cf. C. A. Lobeck, *Aglaophamus*, p. 572.

[9] Hyginus, *Fab.*, 140; Hesychius and Suidas, s.v. Πυθώ.

[10] Lucian, *Hermotimus*, 60.

[11] Id., *Bis accus.*, 2. Like all trees the laurel was sacred to Dionysos (Euripides, *Fragm.*, 480, ed. Nauck.) and also to the moon and Hekate (Porphyry, in Eusebius, *Praep. Evang.*, v. 12. 200; Diogenes Tragicus, in Athenaeus, xiv. 38; Pausanias, iii. 24. 6). "The legend of Apollo and Daphne," says Rohde, "symbolises the conquest of chthonic divination by Apollo " (E. Rohde, *Psyche*, vol. ii, p. 58, n.). The gratuitous suggestion put forward by Bouché-Leclercq (*Histoire de la divination dans l'antiquité*, vol. iii, p. 88), by Rohde (*op. cit.*, vol. ii, pp. 56 sqq.), and by Farnell (*op. cit.*, vol. ii, pp. 190 sq.) that Pythian prophesying was a late introduction, or "assumed a Maenadic character," having been preceded by "more sober forms," is opposed to local evidence, and assumes an ethnological paradox. On the contrary, as Preller remarks, "the characteristic of

Euripides, "is not, properly speaking, a prophet at all. The inspiration belongs to the place, to the oracular cave, and, if we trace it deeper, it would seem to come either from Earth or (much rather) from Dionysos, by whom the whole sacred mountain is 'possessed' or 'inspired,' like one of his bacchants into whom the god has entered."[1]

Dionysos stood at Delphi for the primitive god Pytho, and in the same relation to the goddesses. Similarly, he was regarded as the son of the mantic goddesses of the other great oracle of Greece, that of Dodona ; the female deities being there identified with Thyone,[2] or represented as the 'Nurses' of the god, the Hyades.[3] Dodona, the oldest oracle in Greece, was not appropriated by Apollo, but by Zeus, who was linked with it through the sacred tree of the shrine, represented as the oak of Zeus. As it happens the sacred trees of Dodona were not oaks but beeches.[4] Besides their tree-symbols the prophetic goddesses were represented there in orthodox Mykenean fashion by pillars surmounted by doves.[5] They were known as the Mother Erinyes.[6]

Besides setting up as a prophet Apollo professed to be a doctor, and pretended to be the same as the serpent-god Asklepios. But here again he found Dionysos in the field before him. Dionysos was "The Physician."[7] He was "an expert in cures."[8] He had a special sanatorium at Ophitea, 'Snake-town,' where he cured people by dreams.[9] In Phrygia Apollo had to be satisfied with a third share of the medical practice, and is represented on the

Apollonian divination was its operation by direct prophecy, which lay the future, or that which was concealed, before the mind, so that revelation took sudden and violent possession of the chosen vessel, which, in the oldest traditions, was generally a woman or a maid " (L. Preller, *Griechische Mythologie*, pp. 281 sq.). Dr. Farnell speaks of "a woman being chosen as the medium," and generally endeavours to minimise the part of the prophetess. Doubtless the Pythic prophetess was in later times but a tool in the hands of the priestly corporation, but to suppose that the primitive prophetess was so likewise would be opposed to all evidence. In primitive as well as in later times, as regards oracles which had not acquired political importance, there were no male priests. Pausanias expressly states that at Delphi " tradition makes women the first utterers of the oracle " (x. 5).

[1] A. W. Verrall, *Euripides the Rationalist*, p. 228.
[2] Johannes Lydus, *De mensibus*, iv. 3. 5 ; Cicero, *De natura deorum*, iii. 23.
[3] Scholiast, Germanic. ad Taurum, *Fragm. Hist. Graec.*, vol. i, p. 84.
[4] Stephanus Byzantinus, *De Urbibus*, s.v. Δωδώνη.
[5] *Ibid.*
[6] *Ibid.*
[7] Athenaeus, i. 22 ; Plutarch, *Quaestiones conviviales*, iii. 1. 3. Cf. Hesychius, s.v. παιώγιος.
[8] Lucian, *Deor. Dialog.*, xxiv. 2.
[9] Pausanias, x. 23.

coins of Dionysopolis with his senior partners Asklepios and Dionysos.[1]

The sun-god Apollo has in fact no functions or attributes except such as belong primarily and in a far higher degree to Dionysos, while, on the other hand, Dionysos possesses in addition those generative powers, and vegetation-producing functions, which, if any, might be thought to appertain prescriptively to an agricultural sun-god. Apollo was, in truth, never the sun-god of an agricultural cult.[2] In his purely solar aspect he is generally referred to not by the name of Apollo, but as Phoibos, or simply as Helios, the sun.[3] So manifest was the fact that the attributes of Apollo were merely repetitions of some of the attributes of Dionysos that the ancients constantly declared Dionysos and Apollo to be the same. "What we have said of Apollo," writes Macrobius, "may also be considered to apply to Dionysos, for, as the Aristotle who wrote the Theologumena says, Apollo and Dionysos are one and the same god, which he proves by many arguments." [4] From that equation they deduced that Dionysos was a sun-god ; [5] assuredly a strange sun-god who was 'Nocturnal,' and whose cult was celebrated almost exclusively at night.[6] Apollo was not, of course, originally a sun-god at all ; his solar character is merely the expression of his claim to supremacy in an age when tribal gods displaced as 'conquerors' the primitive cosmic deity.[7] The presumption that Apollo himself derived from some local moon-god is strengthened by the fact that his name Paean was that of the father of the god Moon, Men. In

---

[1] F. Imhof-Blumer, *Kleinasiatische Münzen*, vol. i, p. 220.

[2] The power of the sun-god was regarded by the primitive Greeks in much the same way as by the Babylonians, as destructive and dangerous. Apollo was the sender of plagues, the archer of the laetal shafts. His name has by some been interpreted as 'the destroyer' (see H. Usener, *Götternamen*, p. 333).

[3] It is noteworthy that the memory of Apollo, unlike that of most Greek gods, does not seem to survive in modern Greek folklore, though he appears as the daemon Apollion in mediaeval story. Greek peasants, on the other hand, remember quite well Helios, who has become St. Helias, or the prophet Elias, and to whom nearly every highest hill in the Aegean islands is dedicated. He is invoked when rain is desired.

[4] Macrobius, *Saturn.*, i. 18.

[5] In Orphic and mystic theology Dionysos, under the name of Phanes, is uniformly assimilated to the sun, which is but a way of marking his supreme character. The association with either sun or moon loses, of course, all importance in the more advanced stages of religious development.

[6] It has been the custom to endeavour to meet such incongruities by speaking of the "Night-Sun." If I should have an opportunity, I intend to ask an Australian black, or any other primitive man, to explain what he understands by the "Night-Sun."

[7] Cf. L. R. Farnell, *op. cit.*, vol. iv, pp. 136 sqq.

Phrygia " Men is not to be distinguished from Apollo." [1] The
chief character of Apollo was that of a political god. His very
name was commonly derived, whether rightly or wrongly, from
ἄπελλα, ' an assembly ' ; [2] and his statue occupied the chief position,
like the portrait of the king in a government office, at political
meetings and State functions. His favourite epithet is Patroos ;
he is the founder of States ; [3] he presides over emigrations and
colonies to mark the bond between them and the mother-country ; [4]
he presides over law and order, and is the special protector of the
rights of private property.[5] At Corinth he was called " the Guardian
of the Streets," [6] and was thus a sort of deified policeman. He is a
conquering god, that is, the god of conquerors. At what
corresponded to the primitive manhood ceremonies in Athens,
at the feast of Dionysos, every youth had his hair cut ; the
' eupatrids,' that is, the aristocratic families, dedicated their hair
to Apollo, and it was considered respectable to send it to the god's
own official home at Delphi.[7] The mass of the people, on
the other hand, dedicated their hair to the moon-goddess
Artemis.[8]

Apollo appears chiefly, almost solely, in the character of a
deliverer of oracles. That is his special function, and his cult
is consequently centred in the great seat of mantic authority at
Delphi He is the leader of the Muses, the god of poetry, that is,
of vaticination. But we have just seen that those prophetic
functions, which everywhere belonged originally to the threefold
goddess, were admittedly usurped by Apollo. There exists no
oracular shrine associated from the first with Apollo, the alleged
special god of prophecy. There is no evidence that he was originally a god of prophecy ; why did he become one ? The same
phenomenon is met with in Babylonia. The sun-god Shamash,
who originally had no cult, and whose position remained to the
last definitely subordinate, assumed importance in relation to
political conquests, and became the symbol of political power and
government. His chief religious office was that of deliverer of
oracles, albeit primitive oracles appertained to older fatidic
deities.[9] The reason why a deity associated with political conquest

[1] J. A. R. Munro, " Inscriptions from Mysia," *The Journal of Hellenic
Studies*, xvii, p. 294.

[2] Plutarch, *De defectu oraculorum*, 413A ; L. R. Farnell, *op. cit.*, vol. iv,
pp. 98 sq.

[3] Theognis, 773 ; Pausanias, i. 42. 5.

[4] L. R. Farnell, *op. cit.*, vol. iv, pp. 161 sq.

[5] *Ibid.*, p. 176.　　　　　[6] Pausanias, ii. 19.

[7] Plutarch, *Vita Thesaei*, iv.

[8] Hesychius, s.v. κουρεῶτις ; Diodorus Siculus, v. 73.

[9] A. Jeremias, *Handbuch der altorientalischen Geisteskultur*, p. 281 ;
M. Jastrow, *The Religion of Babylon and Assyria*, pp. 334 sq., 344.

and order should take possession of oracular shrines is obvious ; oracles were the chief means of controlling public opinion and public action, and to control the oracles was as necessary to a political god as it is to later politicians to control the press or education.

The triumph of Apollo was symbolised by his victory over Pytho and his conquest of the shrine of Delphi. The contest of the sun-god with the serpent-god naturally recalls a universal myth-theme, represented, for example, by the conflict between Bel and Tiamat, Ahura Mazda and Ahriman. But in this instance the parallel is misleading. The Apollonian myth has reference to Delphi only ; Pytho represents nothing but his own oracle taken possession of by Apollo. In one curious variant of the myth it is Pytho who comes off victorious in the contest and kills Apollo ; and the corpse of the invading sun-god is buried at Delphi.[1] In other circumstances the contest of the sun-god with the more primitive lunar serpent-god would no doubt have developed as elsewhere into a symbolism of the conflict between light and darkness, between the forces of good and evil, into a Manichaean opposition between the radiant conqueror and the evil primitive god. But Greek gods remained to the last amoral; they never became differentiated into 'good' and 'evil.' The contests between them remained political, racial, social; but opponents were never stigmatised as evil and wicked. The attributes of the primitive gods of the land, of Dionysos, for instance, never became represented, as they easily might have been, as those of Satan. But although no moral interpretation was attached to the contests of the gods, there were ample records of

[1] Porphyry, *Vita Pithagori*, xvi. The central theme of Apollonian myth was an adaptation of an ancient ritual of Delphi, known as the 'stepterion,' in which apparently the serpent-god was ceremonially sacrificed. The immolation of the sacred serpent took place, as with the Tyrian Melqart, by burning him. The ceremony was accompanied by rites of mourning and by a mimetic resurrection of the god impersonated by a young boy crowned with laurel (Plutarch, *De defect. orac.*, xiv ; cf. M. P. Nilsson, *Griechische Feste*, p. 151 ; J. E. Harrison, *Prolegomena to the Study of Greek Religion*, pp. 113 sq.). Plutarch, whose account of a primitive ritual which he did not understand is somewhat confused, does not expressly state that the sacred serpent was sacrificed, but he mentions that the richly decorated hut which was set on fire looked like anything rather than a serpent's lair ; from which it may be inferred that it contained, or was understood to contain, the sacred serpent. The Pythic games, which were held in connection with the ritual, are referred to by Clement of Alexandria, who calls them " a solemn assembly of the Greeks, held in honour of a dead serpent," and the odes which were sung at the festival were, he adds, not in honour of Apollo, but " in praise of the serpent and in lamentation over it " (Clement Alexandrinus, *Exhortatio*, i. 2).

the feud between the Olympians and the 'Chthonian' deities. In Athens the priests of Hera, the typical Olympian goddess, were not permitted to hold any communication with the priests of Dionysos, and it was regarded as a gross insult and sacrilege to introduce so much as a leaf of ivy into the temple of Hera.[1] Apollo treats the Moirai themselves, the venerable Fates of the Oracle of Delphi, in the most insulting manner. On one occasion he actually makes the old ladies drunk—a form of horseplay which, one might have thought, would have been more in the line of Dionysos.[2]

In that strange play of Aeschylos, the 'Eumenides,' the contest between the Olympian deities and the old religions is significantly identified, as somewhat differently in the 'Bakchai,' with the change in the social position of women, and takes in fact the form of a set disputation on the respective merits of matriarchal and patriarchal right, of female and male kinship. Orestes has killed his mother to avenge the murder of his father at her hands ; he is charged by the old Mother-deity, the Erinys, with the most heinous of all deeds, matricide. In defence he alleges that he did no more than his duty in avenging his father's death, and that if such vengeance can be called murder, so was the deed of his mother, and a much more heinous one.

Or.   She killed her husband and my father to boot.

Er.   Thou, however, still livest, while she has paid the penalty of her deed.

Or.   Why then didst thou not pursue *her* while she lived ?

Er.   She was not related by blood to the man she slew.

Or.   And dost thou call *me* a blood-relation of my mother ?

At this astounding expression of patriarchal theory—one cannot but suspect some irony on the part of the dramatist—the Mother Goddess bursts out into indignation : " Thou bloody murderer, did she not bear thee in her womb ? Dost thou disown the dear blood of thine own mother ? " Here Apollo, at whose instigation the deed of Orestes has been committed, intervenes in the dispute, and gives a little lecture on a new physiological theory of his own. " The so-called offspring is not produced by the mother," he says ; " she is no more than the nurse, as it were, of the newly conceived foetus. It is the male who is the author of its being ; while she, as a stranger and for a stranger, takes charge of the young plant on behalf of those for whom the gods have decided to spare it and not blight it in the bud. And I will show you a proof of this assertion ; it is quite possible to become a father without the assistance of a woman : there stands the daughter of Olympian

[1] Plutarch, *Fragm.*, ix.

[2] Aeschylus, *Eumenides*, 173. 734 ; Euripides, *Alk.*, 32.

Zeus, who was not even nursed in the darkness of a woman's womb. And yet no god could show a more worthy child than our colleague the fair Athene." The jury of the gods is entirely convinced by this masterly piece of reasoning and by the force of the evidence produced, and Athene, gratified by the advocate's flattering reference to herself, gives the casting vote for the patriarchal theory, on the very spot where once, according to the legend, the Athenian women had decided the contest between her and Poseidon in her favour. Erinys then gives way to her despair and utters her, " Thou hast conquered, O Galilean ! " " The powers of the grey old time," she exclaims, " are over-thrown. . . . Thou art hounding us down, O new God, us, the old ones. . . . It is the old law, the immemorial right, which ye are tearing down, ye New Gods . . . tearing out of my hands." [1]

It is not here Dionysos who is the new god, but Olympian Apollo. The old agricultural cults of primitive, rural Greece, which the Olympian religion of a race of pastoral warriors had attempted to absorb and ignore, was, however, restored in a new form by a religious revival ; and it is this revival which imparts to Dionysian religion the outward appearance of a new cult. The phenomenon bears more than a superficial resemblance to the prophetic and Yahwistic movement in Palestine. As in the latter, the Greek reformers aimed essentially at the restoration of an old cult and at purging religion from extraneous elements. In the one movement as in the other what was restored was not a primitive religion, but one transformed, heightened, and enriched by abstract conceptions foreign to primitive thought. A new significance was imparted to the immemorial agricultural rites and cycle of ideas by those enthusiasts who in Greece, as in Phoenicia and Judaea, formed a fringe of emotional sentiment and prophetic exaltation around the somewhat cold and official State religion, and, from their haunting the neighbourhood of the fanes, were known as ' fanatics.'

The old rural deities of the women's religion, syncretically gathered together under the name of Dionysos, contained, it was perceived, those very elements out of which the wealth of mystic and emotional significances had grown, that made so strong an appeal in the elaborate theologies of Egypt and of the Orient, and which the Olympians of the warriors conspicuously lacked. Dionysos was, like Osiris, Attis, Adonis, a dying god, and his death was the emblem and token of immortality. He had been persecuted and done to death by his enemies.[2] His sufferings and his

---

[1] Aeschylos, *Eumenides*, 573 sqq., 627 sqq.

[2] Justin, *Apolog.*, i. 54, in Migne, *Patrologiae Cursus, Series Graeca*, vol. vi, col. 408 ; Id., *Dialog. cum Tryphone Judaeo*, 69 (*op. cit.*, col. 636) ; Origen, *Contra Celsum*, iv. 17.

passion were celebrated during the Holy Week of his festival. In Krete, for instance, his votaries "represented in order all those things which the young god had done and had suffered at the time of his death."[1] At his shrines his Holy Sepulchre was shown. He had descended into the nether world. He had been brought to life again by his father, and had risen into heaven, where he had been placed upon the throne of Zeus and been appointed to rule over the Kingdom of Heaven.[2] Those features of his mythical cycle, as his ancient votaries, no less than his modern interpreters had forgotten, belonged to him by virtue of his primitive lunar nature ; they were reproduced in his character of spirit of vegetation—the direct corollary of his original attributes —and offspring of the Great Mother.

It was that parentage which imparted to him the rich and varied significance for which he was valued. Hence it is that Dionysos, although historically and genetically he has no connection with the goddess who came to be the representative of the Great Mother, Demeter, is yet inseparably and in the closest manner associated with her. According to the generally accepted view Dionysos came from Thrace and Demeter from Krete, one from the north, the other from the south ; there is no connection between the two as regards their origin. In myth, with the exception of some late stories, such as that which makes Dionysos act as guide or rescuer to Demeter in her journey to Hades, the two do not meet, and it would be difficult to find in Greek mythology two personages who are more complete strangers to one another. Yet in cult they are inseparable ; it may be said that the cult of Dionysos is at the same time the cult of Demeter, and with almost every form of the cult of Demeter Dionysos is associated. " The ancients," says Plutarch, " worshipped Dionysos and Demeter together."[3] The sanctuary of Eleusis, a venerable primitive centre of the cult of the agricultural goddess, is, we are told, " a temple of Dionysos."[4] The temple of Demeter Thesmophoros at Holimos is referred to as a place where they celebrate the mysteries of Dionysos.[5] Dionysos and Demeter everywhere share the same shrines and the same cults.[6] Dionysos was represented

---

[1] Firmicus Maternus, *De err. prof. rel.*, 5 (ed. Ziegler).
[2] Origen, *Contr. Celsum*, iv. 17.
[3] Plutarch, *Quaest. de aratr. sign.*, vii.
[4] Scholiast to Apollonius Rhodius, 746.
[5] Arnobius, *Adversus Gentes*, v. 25.
[6] Pausanias, viii. 54. 5 ; Scholiast to Aristophanes, *Ranae*, 338 ; Hippolitus, *Ref. omn. Haeres.*, v. 20 ; *Corpus Inscriptionum Latinarum*, vi. 1870 ; P. Foucart, *Recherches sur l'origine et la nature des mystères d'Eleusis*, pp. 448 sq.

seated on the same throne as Demeter,[1] nay, on the lap of the goddess.[2] When the Romans adopted the cult, they straightway made Dionysos the son of Demeter ; they called him Liber and Demeter's daughter, Persephone, Libera.[3] At Rome there was a temple of Demeter (Ceres), Liber, and Libera.[4]

The reason of that intimate association of two deities who were historically strangers lies in the essence of the significance of both. Demeter, in organised Greek mythology, was the name of the Great Mother, as Dionysos was the name of the Dying God and Divine Son ; and, however disparate and heterogeneous the origins of those two representatives of primitive deities, they were of necessity indissolubly associated by virtue of their nature and character. Demeter who was without a Divine Son, was bound to adopt Dionysos, whose Divine Mother had also faded away. For the classical Demeter of later cult was anomalous among Divine Mothers in that her child was a daughter and not a son. But the myth of Persephone, in spite of its classical prominence, forms, all are agreed, no part of the original mythology of the goddess. Although the classical myth is of late date, the association of Demeter with another goddess, or other goddesses, is not. Demeter is never worshipped alone. The relation and the names of her associates matter little ; as often as not they are simply referred to as " The Goddesses." In the same way as the deities of the European peasantry are simply " Our Lady," " The Child," " The White Lady," " The Good People," so in primitive Greece the deities of the cult of Demeter were primarily known as " The Goddesses," " The Three," or as at Dodona, " The Nymphs," or as in countless cults, " The Mothers." The same group will receive as many different names as there are interpreters, and a god will accordingly have as many " Nurses," or " Mothers," to the distraction of the systematic mythologist who desires to set down genealogies of ' personifications ' ; for the original conception is not represented by the proper names, but by the generic appellations. " The Goddesses " were not necessarily related as mother and daughter, though that relation might without impropriety be introduced. " The Three," at Delphi were, according to Aeschylos, Ge, who in later theology is interchangeable with Demeter, her daughter Themis, and Phoibe.[5] The reference occurs in the prologue of the ' Eumenides,' who themselves, though commonly forming a triad, are represented in the play by a single goddess, Erinys. Demeter was worshipped at Lykaion as

[1] Scholiast to Aristophanes, *Ranae*, 324.
[2] Sophokles, *Antigone*, 1119. Cf. Scholiast to Pindar, *Isthm.*, vii. 3.
[3] Cicero, *De natur. deor.*, ii. 24.
[4] Tacitus, *Annales*, ii. 49 ; Dionysius Halicarnassensis, vi. 17.
[5] Aeschylus, *Eumenides*, 7.

threefold ; her three altars were dedicated to Demeter, Despoina, and the Great Mother.[1] In Arcadia she is no other than Erinys. The story related by Pausanias tells that she had a child, Persephone, by Poseidon, the god of waters and moisture.[2] In another version of the story Poseidon begat Persephone from " one of the Erinyes." [3] On the coins of Thelpusa and of Tegea, Demeter is represented with serpent-hair in the character of an Erinys.[4] In Krete the triad sometimes consisted of Demeter, Persephone, and Erinys.[5] In the same manner Demeter is connected with almost every other similar triad. At Corinth she was worshipped with the Moirai, [6] presumably, as at primitive Delphi, as one of the Moirai. At Pellene, in Achaia, she was worshipped as a Muse, and her temple was called the Museum.[7] Again, we are told that she is always in the company of the " Nymphs," she is worshipped with " the Nymphs." [8] When there was a famine Medea ordered the Corinthians to offer sacrifice to Demeter and the Lemnean Nymphs.[9] ' The Nymphs ' is the generic name for the local ' Three,' as at Dodona, for instance, where they are the same as the Hyades,[10] and for ' the Nurses,' or ' the Charites.' [11]

The threefold goddess is as conspicuous in Greek, as in Semitic, in Teutonic, and in Celtic, religion ; there is not, in fact, a Greek goddess who does not form part of a triad of goddesses.[12] In the more primitive cults the goddess is triune ; no distinction being drawn between the unitarian and the trinitarian view of her, between the Great Mother and The Mothers. Erinys was one or three, the Charites appear in Homer as a single Charis. In their transplanted cult in Sicily the temple of The Mothers at

---

[1] Pausanias, viii. 37. 2.

[2] Ibid., viii. 25. 364.

[3] Hesychius, s.v. 'Αρίων. Cf. Tzetzes on Lycophron, 153.

[4] J. A. Overbeck, Griechische Kunstmythologie, vol. ii, Münztafeln, vi No. 26, vii, Nos. 15, 34. Cg. Photius, p. 148 (ed. Bekker). Persephone was the daughter of Styx (Apollodorus, i. 3. 1).

[5] Παρνασσος, xv, p. 615 ; Mitteilungen des Kaiserlich deutschen Archäologischen Institut. Athenische Abteilung, xviii, p. 211.

[6] Pausanias, ii. 11. 6 ; cf. viii. 36. 5. 7, ii. 14. 1. 2.

[7] Pausanias, vii. 27.

[8] Scholiast to Pindar, Pyth., iv. 104. Cf. L. Preller, Demeter und Persephone, p. 324.

[9] Scholiast to Pindar, Olymp., xiii. 74.

[10] See above, p. 151. The Hyades were represented as pigs, the sacred animal of Demeter (Servius ad Georg., i. 138).

[11] The connection of the Charites with Demeter in cult is referred to by Aristophanes (Thesmoph., 300). The threefold Mothers of the Celts and Germans are sometimes referred to in inscriptions as the ' Nymphs ' (J. W. C. Steiner, Codex Inscriptionum Romanarum Rheni, No. 994).

[12] See, e.g., J. E. Harrison, Prolegomena to the Study of Greek Religion, pp. 286 sqq. ; V. Bérard, De l'origine des cultes Arcadiens, pp. 166 sqq.

Engyon was spoken of by Cicero as the temple of The Great Mother.[1]
The threefold aspect of the goddess continues most marked in
later cult in relation to her fatidic and mantic functions; when
delivering oracles she is projected into the past and the future.
She also retains her threefold character when acting as the Nurse,
or Nurses of a god; for she then represents the threefold Fate-
deity who determines the destiny of the child.   Throughout Europe
The Three visit the new-born and determine the course of his
existence; and in ancient Germany they were impersonated by
three priestesses who were called in to bestow their blessing on
the nursling.   In Bohemia it is still the custom, soon after the
birth of a child, to set simple refreshments on a table, and a
lighted lamp, so that when the divine visitors come at night
they should be favourably impressed with the preparations made
for their reception.[2]   The same thing is done at the present
day by the peasants throughout Greece.   " Provision for their
arrival is scrupulously made.   The dog is chained up.   Any
obstacle over which the visitors might trip in the darkness is
removed.   The house-door is left open, or at any rate unlatched.
Inside a light is kept burning, and in the middle of the room is
set a low table with three cushions or low stools placed round it—
religious conservatism apparently forbidding the use of so modern
an invention as chairs.   On the table are set such dainties as the
Fates love, including always honey.   In Athens formerly the
essentials were a dish of honey, three white almonds, a loaf of
bread, and a glass of water; and ready to hand, as presents from
which the goddesses may choose what they will, may be laid all
the most costly treasures of the family, such as jewellery and even
money, in token that nothing has been spared to give them welcome.
These preparations made, their visit is awaited in solemn silence;
for none must speak when the Fates draw near.   Most often they
are neither seen nor heard; but sometimes, it is said, a wakeful
mother has seen their forms as they bent over her child." [3]   The
belief of the Greek peasantry in the three Moirai " is one of the
most deeply rooted and most widely spread superstitions that have
survived from ancient times." [4]   The Moirai, or Charites, who act
as foster-mothers to every Greek child at the present day are no
other than The Three who tended the Divine Child in Krete, who

[1] Cicero, *Cont. Verr.*, iv. 44.   Cf. Diodorus Siculus, iv. 80; Plutarch,
Vit. Marcell., 20.

[2] O. Henne-Am Rhyn, *Deutsche Volksage*, pp. 441 sq.

[3] J. C. Lawson, *Modern Greek Folklore and Ancient Greek Religion*,
pp. 125 sq.   Cf. G. F. Abbott, *Macedonian Folklore*, p. 125; J. G. v. Hahn,
Griechische und albanesische Märchen, p. 137;   F. C. H. L. Pouqueville,
Voyage en Morée, vol. i, p. 262; G. Georgeakis and L. Pineau, *Le folk-lore
de Lesbos*, p. 330.

[4] G. F. Abbott, *op. cit.*, p. 126.

were the Nurses and The Mothers, and, in their unitarian aspect, the universal Mother and the Mother of the Gods. They are represented in a group found at Haghia Triadha, one large, two small ; [1] and again at Palaikastro.[2] More commonly they are represented, as on Semitic monuments,[3] in the aniconic form of three pillars, usually surmounted by doves ; [4] or as three trees.[5] At Orchomenos the Charites were worshipped as three rough stones said to have fallen from heaven.[6] On a stele from Hadrumetum the pillars are fashioned in the upper part as females, and the threefold goddess holds the crescent moon and orb.[7] The antiquity of the cult of the three Charites, or Mothers, in Krete was well known to the ancients, for, according to Apollodorus, the festival of the Charites in the island of Paros was instituted by King Minos.[8]

Sometimes, though more rarely, the multiple deity instead of being threefold is merely double. The Charites are said to have been sometimes regarded in Athens as two in number.[9] Thales only mentions two Hyades.[10] At Dodona the prophetic goddesses were represented by two dove-crowned pillars ; [11] similarly, at Delphi the Moirai were represented by two statues ; [12] and the goddess Tyche is represented as double on the coins of Cilicia.[13] In most of those instances, as also with the Semitic ashera, or double pillars, the threefold goddess becomes twofold when associated with a male god, the triad being thus preserved. But as has been abundantly seen, lunar phases are often simplified into two. The old Latin god Janus, the male counterpart of Jana, or Diana, the moon-deity, was, like many savage and Egyptian deities, represented with two faces. The conception which gave rise to the ancient Italic moon-god is still current among the Italian peasantry. They regard the changes of the moon as being due to her turning her face round ; she presents her full face only at the instant of turning it from one

[1] *Monumenti Antichi, Accademia dei Lincei,* xiii.
[2] R. M. Dawkins, "Excavations at Palaikastro," *Annual of the British School at Athens,* x, p. 217.
[3] See above, pp. 89 sq.
[4] A. J. Evans, *Annual of the British School in Athens,* viii, p. 29, fig. 14.
[5] Id., "Mycenean Tree and Pillar Cult," *Journal of Hellenic Studies,* xxi, pp. 101, 141 sq.
[6] Pindar, *Olymp.,* xiv. 1 ; Pausanias, ix. 35. 1 ; 38. 1 ; Strabo, ix. 414.
[7] *Gazette Archéologique,* 1884, pl. vii.
[8] Apollodorus, iii. 15. 7.
[9] Pausanias, ix. 35. 1.
[10] Stoll, in Roscher, *Ausführliches Lexikon,* p. 2758.
[11] Stephanus Byzantinus, s.v. Δόδονα.
[12] Plutarch, *De EI apud Delphos.,* 2.
[13] *Revue Numismatique,* 1898, p. 159.

side to the other, and thus, in the course of her monthly cycle, faces both ways like the god Janus.[1]

The Kretan goddess, or The Mothers, had a son. The Divine Son in Krete was the youthful dying god whom the Greeks called Zeus. He was called the Diktean Zeus from his shrine in the Diktean cave on Mount Ida. The name was supposed to derive from " the nymph Dikte." The latter is the Kretan goddess, Britomartis-Diktynna.[2] One of the names given to the mother of the Kretan god was Amalthea, the goat-goddess with the horn of plenty ; another was Melissa, who is represented as the first priestess of Demeter.[3] Amalthea is also mentioned as the mother of Dionysos,[4] the Kretan Zeus being recognised as identical with the Kretan Dionysos, Zagreos.[5] In a more classical version the son of Demeter was Pluto, that is ' Plenty.' Hesiod says :—

> Demeter brought forth Pluto; and kindly was the birth
> Of him whose way is on the sea and over all the earth.
> Happy, happy is the mortal who doth meet him as he goes
> For his hands are full of blessings and his treasure overflows.[6]

The father of Pluto was Iason, the hero of the Minyan race, who marries the double of the moon-goddess Hekate, Medea,[7] identified by the Romans with Bona Dea, the Good Goddess.[8] The Good Tyche, as she was called, that is to say, ' Good Luck,' was one of the Moirai, and, so some optimists said, the mightiest of the Three.[9] An Attic poet goes so far as to call her the ruler of all the gods.[10] Her images represented her holding the horn of Amalthea, that is, the horn of Pluto ; and she appeared as the Divine Mother bearing the Holy Infant, Pluto, in her arms.[11] The Divine Child is sometimes simply known as ' the Saviour.' [12] In

---

[1] G. Finamore, *Credenze, usi e costumi abruzzesi*, p. 45.

[2] Servius, on *Aeneid*, iii. 171. Cf. H. Usener, *Götternamen*, p. 41.

[3] Hyginus, *Fabulae*, 182 ; Lactantius, i. 22. 19.

[4] Diodorus Siculus, iii. 74. 1.

[5] L. Preller, *Griechische Mythologie*, p. 701, note 2.

[6] Hesiod, *Theogon.*, 909 sqq., Miss J. E. Harrison's version, *Themis*, p. 286.

[7] H. Usener, *op. cit.*, p. 156.

[8] Macrobius, *Saturn.*, i. 12 ; Servius, on *Aeneid*, vii. 750.

[9] Plutarch, *De fortun. Roman.*, iv ; Pausanias, vii. 26. 6. Cf. L. Preller, *Griechische Mythologie*, p. 540. On a Roman sarcophagus Tyche is represented as Lachesis with the other two Fates (F. Allègre, *Étude sur la déesse Tyché*, p. 233). She is still well known in the folklore of Macedonia as one of the Moirai (G. F. Abbott, *Macedonian Folklore*, p. 128).

[10] H. Usener, *Götternamen*, p. 340.

[11] Pausanias, ix. 16. 1.

[12] Pausanias, vi. 20. 2 ; C. Robert, " Sosipolis in Olympia," *Mittheilungen des kaiserlich deutschen archaeologischen Institut, Athenische Abtheilung*, xviii, pp. 37 sqq. ; F. M. Cornford, in J. E. Harrison, *Themis*, pp. 239 sqq.

one representation Tyche, instead of bearing Pluto in her arms, carries Dionysos.[1] The Moira, Tyche, is thus evidently much the same as the Moira, Demeter, the other mother of Pluto. At Sparta, Tyche, Demeter and Persephone were worshipped together as a triad of Moirai ; [2] and at Lebadia, Moira replaced Demeter as the companion goddess of Persephone-Kore.[3]

Demeter, again, is the same as Iason's other wife, Hekate ; Porphyry tells us that Demeter is the same as Hekate,[4] who, in turn, is commonly regarded as identical with Demeter's double, Persephone.[5] Two aspects of Demeter-Persephone were distinguished, the bright and the dark aspect,[6] in the same manner as the white Charites and the black Erinyes constituted the two aspects of The Three.[7]

Among other components or aliases of the classical Demeter is the cow-goddess Io.[8] She is identified with Pasiphae and is scarcely distinguishable from another cow-goddess, Europa, the mother of the race of Minos. Demeter herself is called Europa, and was worshipped under that name at Lebadaia in Boeotia.[9] Another goddess, Ino, the ancestress of the Danaoi, was constantly confounded with Io. She is called Leukothea, the White Lady. The Romans identified her with Mater Matuta, the Good Mother.[10] The Italian ' Good Mother ' "causes the new moon to shine in the sky, and, as the moon, acts upon the constitution of women in view of maternity." [11] Io is also called Themisto,[12] and is assimilated to the Arcadian Moon-goddess.[13] She had an oracle at Thalamai, and in her temple was an image which Pausanias identified with the cow-goddess Pasiphae, and one of a god whom

---

[1] H. G. Schültz, in *Annali del Instituto di corrispondenza archeologica*, 1839, pp. 101 sqq. Pluto, or Hades, and Dionysos are, in fact, commonly equated (Plutarch, *De Iside et Osiride*, 28. 79 ; Herakleitos, *Fragment*, xv [Diels]).

[2] *Corpus Inscriptionum Graecarum*, 1464. Cf. F. Allègre, *op. cit.*, p. 143.

[3] Pausanias, ix. 30. 5.

[4] Porphyry, in Eusebius, *Praeparatio Evangelica*, v. 13. 201.

[5] Plutarch, *De facie in orbe lunae*, **xxix** ; Porphyry, *De antr. Nymph.*, 29. Cf. E. Gerhard, *Griechische Mythologie*, par. 429.

[6] Aelian, *Hist. anima.*, xii. 10 ; Artemidorus, *Oneirocr.*, ii. 34 ; L. Preller, *Demeter und Persephone*, p. 23.

[7] V. Bérard, *De l'origine des cultes arcadiens*, pp. 165 sq. ; A. Bouché-Leclerq, *L'astrologie grecque*, pp. 735 sq. Cf. C. Fries, *Greichische Götter und Heroen*, p. 24.

[8] Apollodorus, ii. 1.

[9] Pausanias, ix. 39. 4. 5.

[10] Plutarch, *Quaest. Rom.*, xvi ; *Vit. Camill.*, v ; Cicero, *Tuscul.*, i. 28 ; *De nat. deor.*, iii. 4. 8 ; Ovid, *Fasti*, vi. 545 sqq. ; Servius, on *Georgic.*, i. 437.

[11] Strabo, v. 266.

[12] Scholiast to Apollonius Rhodius, ii. 1185.

[13] Stephanus Byzantinus, s.v. Ἀρκάς.

he took to be the sun.[1] Both Io and Ino are ancestresses of the
house of Kadmos and mothers of Dionysos; and both, like all
mother-goddesses of primitive Greek religion, are persecuted by
Olympian Hera. Demeter was linked up with them and with
their offspring Dionysos by saying that she had established her
first temple in the very house of Kadmos.[2]

In the great Attic centre of the cult of Demeter the deities of
the fane were usually referred to, especially in earlier times, as
" the Goddesses and the God." [3] The goddesses were Demeter
and Kore, or Persephone; the god was Pluto.[4] The relations
and the myth of the goddesses, which, as will be seen, were already
somewhat confused and complicated, were rendered still more
perplexing by the growth of a local myth which made the position
of Pluto as the Divine Son of the Great Goddess untenable.
As everyone knows, Pluto became the wicked underworld
god who carried away the Mother's beloved daughter Persephone. She became his wife instead of his sister, the Greeks
being averse to recognising the dynastic incest by which such
multiple relations are explained in the East. Another son had to
be found for Demeter and another god for the Eleusinian shrine,
and she was made the mother of Iakchos, the local god who was
identified with Dionysos.[5]

The myth, which all are agreed is a very late one, of Demeter's
loss of her daughter Persephone, of the Sorrowing Mother, the
Demeter Achaia, or Mater Dolorosa, of her wanderings in search
of her child, constitutes the whole of the classical mythology of
Demeter and of its reflection in cult; and it would seem that if
we deprive her of it there is nothing left but a figure without a story.
But it has already been noted that such a mythical cycle is
quite independent of the dramatis personae who may be made
to take a part in it. There can be little doubt that in earlier times
it was not Persephone, but Pluto whom the goddess sought and
mourned for. Ishtar lamented in the same manner over Tammuz
and sought him in the netherworld; she lamented, wandered,
and descended into the lower world even apart from any clearly
definite Tammuz. The theme of the mythologies of Io and of
Ino is likewise their sorrows and their wanderings. The cow-
goddess Io wanders all over the country pursued by her enemy

---

[1] Pausanias, iii. 26. 1.

[2] *Ibid.*, ix. 16. 5. Cf. H. D. Müller, *Mythologie der Griechischen
Stämme*, vol. i, p. 289.

[3] P. Foucart, " Le culte de Pluton dans la religion Eleusinienne," *Bulletin
de Correspondance Hellénique*, vii, p. 400.

[4] *Ibid.*, pp. 396 sqq. Cf. *Corpus Inscriptionum Atticarum*, ii. 2. 8346. 112.

[5] Diodorus Siculus, iii. 641; Suidas and Photius, s.v. Ἴακχος; C. A.
Lobeck, *Aglaophamus*, pp. 919 sq.

Hera in the form of a gad-fly ; and the Bosporus owes its name to
the Cow-goddess being driven by that troublesome fly to swim
across from one continent to another. Ino, the White Lady, the
mother of Dionysos, is no less of a wanderer ; she is in fact a
protecting goddess of travellers. The wanderings of Io are, however, not wholly caused by her being worried by a fly ; she wanders
in search of her son, Epaphos, whom, according to the Egyptian-
ising Herodotus, who recognised in him Apis-Osiris, she calved in
Egypt.[1] But according to the more scientific Strabo she bore
him in a cave in Euboea.[2] Ino's son is sometimes called Palaimon,
sometimes Melikertes,[3] which is, there can be little doubt, a Greek
corruption of Melqart, the cult-epithet of the Tyrian Tammuz.
She is also the ' nurse ' of Dionysos.[4] The lamentations of the
Mater Dolorosa are an immemorial attitude of all Mother goddesses.
Isis laments in like manner over Osiris and wanders in search of
him. The Celtic Brigit laments over her son Ruadan, and her
wail is said to have been the first wail heard in Ireland.[5] All the
' Nurses,' ' Mothers,' and ' Nymphs,' lament in like manner. Eos
laments over her son Memnon, and is pictured in the attitude of
the Mater Dolorosa over his lifeless body. Aeschylos describes the
inconsolable sorrow of the Pleiades,[6] and Pindar speaks of the
lamenting Naiads.[7] Elsewhere, after mentioning " the lays, which
amid the crowns of flourishing ivy, long for the dithyramb of
Dionysos," he sings : " But in another kind of song did The Three
lull to rest the bodies of their sons. The first sang a dirge over
clear-voiced Linos ; the second lamented with her latest song
Hymenaios, whom fate seized as he lay with another ; and the
third grieved over Ialemos, when his strength was arrested by a
raging sickness." [8] The lamentations of The Three were reproduced in their ritual by the Argive women. Once a year clad in
mourning they wailed over the grave of Linos ; the ceremony was
called " the day of lamentations." [9] Commenting upon the absence
of such ceremonies among the Romans in his time, Dionysius of
Halicarnassus says that " there is not held any black-robed or
mournful festival with women's wailings and lamentations over a

---

[1] Herodotus, ii. 153.

[2] Strabo, x. 445.

[3] Apollodorus, iii. 4.

[4] *Ibid.* The Isthmic games were celebrated in honour of the dying son
of Ino, no doubt to promote his resurrection.

[5] Whitley Stokes, " The Second Battle of Moytura," *Revue Celtique*, xii,
pp. 95, 97.

[6] Aeschylus, *Fragm.*, 312 ; ap. Athenaeum, xi. 491.

[7] Pindar, *Fragm.*, 208.

[8] *Ibid.*, 139.

[9] Aelian, *Nat. Anim.*, xiii. 34.

god vanished from sight, such as are celebrated among the Greeks in reference to the rape of Persephone and the passion of Dionysos, and all other things of the kind." [1]

To the general reader, and to many a professed student, the tangle of Greek divine names and attributes, and the equation of their bearers with one another, cannot but appear hopelessly confusing; every goddess is almost everything in turn, and is identified with every other goddess. That confusion and perplexity arise from the traditional assumption that the deities of polytheistic cults are primarily 'departmental' deities, gods and goddesses 'of' this or that special sphere of natural objects and forces. So long as such an assumption is made the starting-point and fundamental postulate of attempts at interpretation, all is indeed perplexity and confusion; and we must expect to be hopelessly puzzled when we find a wine-god assuming the character of a sea-god, or a corn-goddess masquerading as a Fury, a Fate, or a cow.[2] That confusion and perplexity disappear, however, when we view the departmental attributes of those deities not as primary characters to which they owe their origin, but as adventitiously specialised aspects of divinities who did not preside over any particular department of nature or form of power, but in whom all nature and all supernatural power were conceived to have their source, and who were, under a variety of local names and cult-epithets, in their essential nature identical. Demeter is as much an Erinys, a Moira, and a ruler of the dead as she is a 'corn-goddess.'

In current impressions of Greek mythology Demeter has long stood for the typical personification of the Earth Mother. Her name was once very commonly translated by the change of its first consonant, into Ge-Meter, the Earth-Mother; but such philological legerdemain is now happily recognised as inadmissible.[3] Demeter, it appears probable, is merely a contraction

[1] Dionysius Halicarnassensis, ii. 18.

[2] Dr. Farnell, for example, is sorely troubled about Demeter-Erinys, that being about the last travesty under which we might expect to find a corn-goddess or a personification of the earth; and he falls back, to get over the incongruity, upon the theory of a 'contaminatio' from quite different cults (L. R. Farnell, *op. cit.*, vol. iii, pp. 53 sq.).

[3] G and D are among the least interchangeable of consonants. Appeal to dialects does not help the case; there is no more tendency for a *g* to become a *d* in Doric or other Greek dialects than in any other language. Preller, the most learned advocate of the $\Delta\acute{\eta}=\Gamma\acute{\eta}$ theory, whose book starts from the 'petitio principii' that Demeter is the earth, adduces examples where a hard *g* sound by gradual attrition into a soft *dg* might conceivably become eventually a dental. But such doubtful arguments, which might pass in reference to some trivial current word which has undergone transformations in the course of centuries, are irrelevant as regards so

of Dea, or Deo-Meter, the Goddess Mother.[1] A pure and simple personification of the earth, it is evident enough that she was not, any more than any other goddess. Many modern scholars have recognised the incongruity of such an equation, and have regarded her as having celestial significances. Thus Kuhn, writing in the days of Max Müllerian mythology, when every deity was under the obligation of being either the dawn or the sunset, or a white cloud, or a grey cloud, or a pink cloud, asserted that "Demeter is no other than the storm-cloud."[2] Schwartz takes a similar view and states that "Demeter has hitherto been erroneously regarded, from her habitual abode, as a pure earth divinity."[3] H. D. Müller affirms that she is almost as much related to the moon as to the earth.[4] Fries states that she is a moon-goddess.[5] Among the ancients Demeter was freely identified with Ino, with Isis, with Hekate, deities purely and conspicuously lunar. Porphyry says "also the power productive of corn-crops, which is Demeter, they associate with the moon, as her productive power. The moon is also a supporter of Kore ; they set Dionysos also beside her."[6] Servius states that "the Stoics say that the moon, Diana, Ceres, Juno, Proserpine are all one."[7] Arnobius, writing against the Gentiles, remarks that "men of learning amongst you, and who are not given to idle and capricious chatter, maintain that Diana, Ceres, and the Moon are but one deity, and that there are not three distinct persons as there are three different names, and that in each instance it is the moon which is invoked, the others being merely surnames added to her name."[8] As Fries observes, all Greek goddesses whatsoever have lunar attributes.[9]

definite a word as *Γή*, which is never anything else than *γή*, and remains *γή* in all compounds and derivatives without exception. No amount of references to doubtful examples of slurred pronunciation will account for the transformation, without any parallel or transition, of *Γή* into *Δή* in just this one divine name alone, and nowhere else.

[1] *Δηώ* appears to have been the proper appellation of the goddess in Arcadia, though she was invariably referred to as *Δημήτηρ* (see V. Bérard, *De l'origine des cultes Arcadiens*, p. 200).

[2] A. Kuhn, "Sanranyû-'*Ερινύς*," *Zeitschrift für Sprachenforschung*, i, p. 455. Clouds, according to Hillebrandt, play scarcely any part in Vedic mythology (A. Hillebrandt, *Vedische Mythol.*, vol. i, p. 313).

[3] F. L. W. Schwartz, *Der Ursprung der Mythologie*, p. 67.

[4] H. D. Müller, *Mythologie der griechischen Stämme*, vol. ii, p. 290. Other scholars, such as B. Delbruck (*Zeitschrift für Völkerpsychologie*, iii, pp. 292, 295) and B. E. Petersen (*Kritische Bemerkungen zur alteste Geschichte der griechische Kunst*, p. 38), adopt similar views.

[5] C. Fries, *Die griechischen Götter und Heroen*, p. 253.

[6] Porphyry, in Eusebius, *Praeparat. Evangel.*, 114.

[7] Servius, *ad Georg.*, i. 7.

[8] Arnobius, *Adversus gentes*, iii. 34.   [9] C. Fries, *loc. cit.*

However closely Demeter and analogous goddesses may have become assimilated to the Earth-Mother, whatever earthly and agricultural symbolism may have clustered round them, they could never become entirely of the earth earthy, nor lose their heavenly character, because the cults of advanced agriculture did not create their divinities. Gods are uncreated; they are evolved. And no agricultural earth-goddess had any pre-agricultual divine antecedent from whom she could draw her being.[1] Nor had they need of one; the Great Goddesses owed their existence not to the earth, but to their motherhood, and the Great Mother, whom we find in the frozen ice-fields of the arctic no less than among the corn-fields of Krete or Boeotia, existed before an ear of corn had ever been ground in the mill. Her origin was heavenly, not earthly; she was the Queen of Heaven and had fertilised the dark earth and been the mother of all her fruits long before she was crowned with corn.

Her primitive character, which was never forgotten, was preserved above all by her relation to the male god with whom she was associated. The gods who accompany the Great Mothers are not merely male counterparts of her; they are not her 'husbands.' With divine pairs that are purely male and female aspects of the same divinity, the relation is usually that of husband and wife. Such divine pairs, scarcely differentiated except in sex, were the general rule in primitive Semitic religion. In native Italian cults also we find the same duplication applied to every deity— Saturnus and Juturna, Janus and Diana, Lupercus and Luperca, Faunus and Fauna, etc.[2] At other times the male and the female deity stand sharply contrasted as masculine and feminine principles, as heaven and earth, which are for the most part simply called by their own names, Aether and Ge, Imber and Tellus, or, as in Indonesia, Mr. Heaven and Mrs. Earth, without

[1] Dr. Farnell, following the classical tradition, regards Demeter as an emanation of Ge. But when it comes to discovering that supposed divine ancestress, nothing but the vaguest metaphors and figures of speech are to be found, and we are thrown back upon the purely imaginary conjecture that " there may have been in Greece, as elsewhere, some period of fluid animism that had not yet deposited those concrete personalities of divinities, to whom the world of nature with its phenomena serves merely as a residence." We hear, indeed, a great deal about ' Mother Earth ' from the poets and from ancient and modern mythologists ; but of any primitive cult of her no more trace is discoverable in Greece than elsewhere. Homer regarded her " from the same point of view as the later cultivated Greek or the modern civilised man, as a great physical entity, living in some sense, but not personal nor fraught with such a life as man's." Dr. Farnell's profession of classical faith is prefaced with the words, " We must believe " (L. R. Farnell, *The Cults of the Greek States*, vol. iii, p. 4).

[2] See L. Preller, *Römische Mythologie*, p. 56.

any traditional names or mythological circumlocutions. The relation of the Great Mothers to the gods associated with them is entirely different. The supremacy of the Great Mothers in agricultural religions is generally marked by their complete dissociation from the male supreme god. The circumstance, we may note, is fundamentally significant of their evolution ; had they been essentially personifications of the earth, it would have been well-nigh inevitable that their position as wives of the supreme god, who generally tends to assume the generalised character of a Sky-god, should have been emphasised in the clearest manner. Of such a relation to a corresponding Sky-god or Sun-god there is almost no trace. Demeter, who as Mother-Earth should be the legal wife of the Sky-god Zeus, is a total stranger to him, and scarcely ever so much as meets him in the course of mythological story.

It is by that dissociation from a divine consort that the rise to matriarchal predominance of the agricultural goddesses is above all characterised. They have no husband ; they are ' Virgins.' Ishtar, the morning star, was doubtless originally the wife of the moon-god ; but with her rise to supremacy she is divorced from him, the abolition of the relation being marked by making her his daughter, a relationship destitute of significance. She is, " in accordance with her whole nature, not the exclusive wife of any male god." [1] She is habitually referred to as ' The Virgin,' ' The Holy Virgin,' ' The Virgin Mother.' [2] The term ' virgin ' is, if course, used in those titles in its primitive sense as denoting ' unwed,' and connoting the very reverse of what the term has come to imply. The virgin Ishtar is also frequently addressed as ' The Prostitute ' ; and she herself says, " A prostitute compassionate am I." [3] She wears the ' posin,' or veil, which, as among the Jews, was the mark of both ' virgins ' and prostitutes.[4] The hierodules, or sacred prostitutes of her temples, were also called " the holy virgins." [5] Such an application of the epithet, however startling it may be to us, was in accordance with the only meaning of the term in primitive and ancient societies. The Greek word ' parthenos ' had the same meaning as the Semitic term ' bathur,' ' batim,' for ' unwed.' Children born out of wedlock were called ' parthenioi,'

---

[1] H. Zimmern, in E. Schrader, *Die Keilinschriften und das Alte Testament*, vol. ii, pp. 432 ; cf. p. 424.

[2] S. Langdon, *Tammuz and Ishtar*, pp. 75, 83.

[3] *Ibid.*, pp. 18, 76 ; G. Reisner, *Sumerische-babylonische Hymnen*, p. 106 ; M. I. Hussey, " Some Sumerian-Babylonian Hymns of the Berlin Collection," *American Journal of Semitic Languages*, xxiii, pp. 145, 149.

[4] H. Zimmern, *loc. cit.*

[5] S. Langdon, *op. cit.*, p. 75.

'virgin-born.'[1]   The word 'virgin' itself has not, strictly speaking,
the meaning which we attach to it ; the correct Latin expression for
an untouched virgin is not ' virgo,' but ' virgo intacta.' Aphrodite
herself was a Virgin.[2]   The term was applied to all the goddesses
of early Aegean cults, and the wide diffusion of the worship of the
Virgin is evidenced by the many place-names, such as Parthenia,
the ancient Samos, Mount Parthenon in Arcadia, Parthenion in
Euboea, the river Parthenios in Paphagonia, and many others.
Hera herself, although in later mythology the type of the matronly
spouse, retained a reminiscence of her earlier character in the title
of ' Virgin.' [3]   In later patriarchal society, when the term had come
to acquire a new meaning, it was sought to justify its application
to unattached goddesses, and they were transformed into types
of maidenly purity. Artemis, though she was the mother of
Telephos and of the fifty daughters of Endymion, was regarded as
a virgin-goddess in the later acceptation of the term, and indeed
as the patroness of fierce virginity and chastity.   The motherhood
of Athene, the ancestral mother of the Athenians and the mother
of Erechthonios by the Fire-god, was explained away by a somewhat coarse story, and Erechthonios was made the son of Earth,
Athene acting merely as his foster-mother.[4]   In the same
manner the Roman Vesta was deliberately set up as the patroness
and example of chaste virginity, though she retained her title of
Mother and was even the Mother of the Gods, and phallic emblems
continued to figure in her cult.[5] Her relation to Priapus was
obliterated by an expedient similar to that employed in the
Athenian story ; the virginity of the goddess was saved from the
assaults of the rustic god by the timely interference of an ass—
incongruously enough, the representative of the god himself, and
the emblem of lubricity.[6]   The association of the goddess with the
ass-god was not, however, entirely effaced ; on a fresco in Pompeii
the Italian Virgin Mother is represented riding an ass and bearing
the Divine Child in her arms.[7]   The ancient British Moon-goddess,
Arianrhod, was called ' the Virgin,' although she had several
children, and her unbridled amours were in later times regarded

---

[1] Homer, *Iliad*, xvi. 180; Pindar, *Olymp*. vi. 51; Suidas, s.v. παρ θένιοι.
Cf. above, vol. i, p. 400.

[2] Firmicus Maternus, *De errore profanarum religionum*, in Migne, *Patrologiae Cursus Completus*, vol. iv, col. 989.

[3] Pausanias, ii. 36. Cf. S. Casson, " Hera of Kanathos and the Ludovisi
Throne," *Journal of Hellenic Studies*, xl, p. 139 ; E. Fehrle, *Die kultische
Keuscheit im Altertum*, pp. 162 sqq., 223.

[4] Pausanias, v. 33 ; Apollodorus, iii. 14. Cf. Clement of Alexandria,
Exhortatio, ii. 24.

[5] A. Preuner, *Hestia-Vesta*, pp. 333 sqq.

[6] Ovid, *Fasti*, vi. 319 sqq.

[7] *Annali del Instituto di Corrispondenza archeologica*, 1872, Tab. D.

as somewhat scandalous.[1] The Chinese Holy Virgin, like those of Western patriarchal societies, has become the pattern of purity and her conception is immaculate, but a trace of her former character survives in the circumstance that she is the special patroness of prostitutes.[2] The character of Virgin, in its primitive sense of free and unwed, is everywhere the denotation of the independence of the goddess in the phase of her supremacy. The Great Goddess of the Eskimo is spoken of as ' uinigumsuitung,' which means. " She who will not have a husband." [3] The Great Goddess of the Chams has ninety-seven lovers, but no husband.[4] Demeter " execrated marriage," and she presided, Servius tells us, not over marriage, but over divorce.[5] The same character appertains to all the Great Goddesses of the Eastern Mediterranean world. Isis alone presents an apparent exception. In the conservative world of Egypt she retained her primitive character of wedded wife and faithful spouse of the Moon-god. But her relation to him is strangely complex. She is his sister and wife, but conceives from him after his death ; she is at the same time his mother, and becomes the wife of her perpetually ageing and dying son. Such, in fact, is inevitably the composite relation of the Mother of God in the primitive lunar myths of uncultured peoples, from the American continent to the Pacific and the South African veldt. Such it remains essentially with the Great Mothers in the cradles of Western civilisation on the Mediterranean shores. The relation of the youthful god to the goddess is seemingly ' confused,' and differs altogether from the simple relation which obtains between divine pairs that are merely male and female aspects of the same divinity. Tammuz is at the same time the son and the lover of the goddess ; Attis is the son and the husband of Kybele ; the god Moon is the son and lover of the Phrygian goddess.

The attributes of the original moon-god who has become eclipsed, in agricultural religion, by the goddess and generalised, are reproduced in his duplicated form, the younger god whose outstanding relation to the goddess is the original ground of the association, and who is thought of mainly as her son. The Divine Son, from the first of the same nature as the Father, became the more conspicuous form of the god. While the original

[1] J. A. McCulloch, *The Religion of the Ancient Celts*, pp. 109 sq. The Walkyries, who solaced the heroes in Walhalla, were ' virgins,' and, what is the same thing, it was a strict rule that they should not marry (J. Grimm, *Teutonic Mythology*, p. 425).

[2] J. J. M. de Groot, *Les fêtes annuellement célébrées à Émoui*, vol. i, p. 200.

[3] F. Boas, " The Central Eskimo," *Sixth Annual Report of the Bureau of Ethnology*, p. 586.

[4] H. Baudesson, *Indo-China and its Primitive People*, p. 277.

[5] Servius, on *Aeneid*, iv. 58 ; cf. iii. 139.

moon-god became immutable and eternal instead of subject to vicissitudes and periodic death, the Son retained those primitive attributes, and was preeminently a dying god and a culture-god who assumed human form and as a Man-god instructed men. The supreme moon-god, the Father, transformed by the side of the Great Goddess, loses his primitive attributes, assumes the character of a solar god, or of a sky-god, becomes an 'Olympian.' Not so the Son. Whether definitely and consciously identified with the moon or not, he of necessity retains those attributes which constitute the original nature and functions of the primitive moon-god. He is a generative force ; he is associated with waters and moisture ; he is the lord of vegetation ; he is the animating force of the fruits of the earth, of generation, in animals, in mankind ; he is oracular and prophetic, the cause of divine madness and enthusiasm ; he is the master of magic, the lord of spells and charms ; he causes death and he heals ; he is the lord of time, the judge of the dead ; he is a 'chthonic' god who periodically descends into the dark underworld, rises again, and ascends to heaven ; he is the lord of the resurrection and the life everlasting. Those are the attributes of the primitive moon-god ; they are also the attributes of the son of the Great Mother. The Divine Son is at once the youngest and the oldest of the gods.

He is identified in agricultural religion with the fruits which the Divine Mother bears forth ; the bread is his body, the juice of the grape his blood. In the yearly seasonal cycle the son of the Great Mother is born and dies, is buried in the dark womb of the earth and rises again. His birth is celebrated with rejoicings, his growth with dances and music, his passion, his persecution at the hands of the enemies by whom he is done to death are set forth in sacred mystery-plays, his death is lamented and honoured with the rites that will ensure his resurrection. But that cycle and those rites are not new, have not developed on the seed and harvest field. They are the immemorial myth of an older cycle, the observances of the most primitive pre-agricultural times. The rejoicings of the votaries of the agricultural god, their wails and fasts at his death, the rites by which his resurrection is assisted, are the rejoicings of the savage at the appearance of the new moon, his wails and terrors when it is dead. They are the rites which the primitive cultivators of the soil employed to secure success in the rudimentary agricultural arts which gradually developed in their hands. But not for that purpose alone. They are the rites of all magical societies, of the religious associations, the institution of which tradition in every part of the savage world ascribes to primitive witches. Those rites are not solely or chiefly intended to secure the fertility of the earth and the resurrection of vegetation, but the resurrection of all life, of the tribe through the fertility of its women, of the individual through his new birth and his admittance to the company of the immortal dead.

The rites of mourning, of ' lamentation,' the earliest cult, as distinguished from purely magical operations, had themselves a magical effect upon the fate of the departed and their consequent attitude towards survivors, by placating their anger and honouring them. Those rites and ' lamentations ' are throughout primitive society performed by the women. Thus among the Sioux the winding of the dead in the mortuary garments, the building of the scaffold upon which the corpse is placed, is done by the women, and it is they who maintain the mortuary fire and sit by it.[1] The same vestal offices are performed by the women in Australia.[2] All wailing, however ritualistic, devolves everywhere upon the women, and it is they who ' cut themselves for the dead.' In the Banks Islands they perform the horrible duty of drinking the liquids from the putrefying corpse.[3] In Ashanti " it is chiefly the women who fill the chamber of the dead. The men generally seat themselves outside, and until the funeral customs commence, take no very active part in the proceedings." [4] The Patagonians, like most other races, pay great attention to the honouring and propitiating of their dead, and that ancestor-worship constitutes an important portion of their religion. The bones of the dead are periodically taken up, cleaned, and adorned ; they are then buried anew in large graves which are curiously surrounded by the remains of dead horses propped up on sticks in a standing position. At those graves they make periodical offerings of food and libations. The care and service of those ancestral graves is in charge of a woman. "An old matron is chosen out of each tribe to take care of these graves, and on account of her employment is held in great veneration." [5] In pre-Islamic Arabia the honouring of the dead was regarded as the particular function of the women. Some of the most beautiful specimens of ancient Arabian poetry are the elegies, ' rithas,' composed by women in honour of the dead. The talents of Arabian poetesses were " bestowed chiefly on the dead ; it is a proof of the high character and position of women in pre-Islamic Arabia," says Professor Nicholson, " that the hero's mother and sister were deemed the

---

[1] T. L. McKenney, *Sketches of a Tour to the Lakes*, p. 292 ; H. C. Yarrow, " A Further Contribution to the Study of the Mortuary Customs of the North American Indians," *First Annual Report of the Bureau of Ethnology*, pp. 198, 184 sq., 186.

[2] J. Fraser, *The Aborigines of Australia*, p. 85.

[3] R. H. Codrington, *The Melanesians*, p. 268.

[4] B. Cruikshank, *Eighteen Years on the Gold Coast*, vol. ii, p. 216.

[5] T. Falkner, *A Description of Patagonia*, p. 120.

most worthy to mourn and praise him."[1] But the circumstance, far from being peculiar to Arabia, is a universal rule.
Among the Romans the mother and sister of the deceased were
regarded as the mourners; they were referred to as 'personae
funereae,' that is, "ad quas funus pertinet."[2] As in all primitive
communities, women alone took part in the mourning rites among
the ancient Karians and Lokrians;[3] and among the Lykians,
when a man mourned for a beloved dead, it was the custom for him
to dress in female clothes.[4] The Houris and the Walkyries, whose
function it was to collect the souls of fallen warriors on the battle-
field, were the immortal counterparts of the women who, in a more
literal sense, sought out and gathered their dead, and, mourning
over them, sent them on their way to their eternal abode. The
fate of the dead is not in primitive society an enviable one; the
ghost is thought to wander cold, hungry, and in pain, and it is
chiefly his envy of the living that renders him dangerous
and calls for placatory rites. But that fate has gradually
become ameliorated. In the Banks Islands, for example, there
is a portion of the underworld "where youths go who die in the
flower of their age, a place more pleasant than the rest, where all
kinds of flowers abound and scented plants. This fancy was mostly
that of the women, who thought much of all who died young, and
above all of those who had been shot for them, who had died on
their account—'me matewalira,' and paid for them the price of
their death."[5]

The lamentations of the women of Syria, Babylon, Egypt, and
Greece over the Divine Son were also for the Saviour who had
"paid for them the price of death," and were the counterpart of
the rites and of the emotions of those whose office was to
offer the last comforts of their love to the departed. For
the Divine Son was ever the 'Saviour' whose death is the
pledge of the moon's gift of eternal life, a gift which he is
willing to impart to those who will follow him.[6] Initiation into
the mysteries of Dionysos, like initiation into the mysteries of
savage 'ghost societies,' was believed to secure for the chosen
votary the benefits of eternal salvation. In the Homeric hymn
to Demeter we are assured that "he is indeed blessed who has
beheld these things; but he who has been deprived of the holy

---

[1] R. A. Nicholson, *Literary History of the Arabs*, p. 89. Cf. Th. Nöldeke,
Beiträge zur Kenntniss der Poesie der alten Araber, p. 175.

[2] Servius, *ad Aeneid.*, ix. 486.

[3] Heraclides Ponticus, *Fragm.*, ix.

[4] Plutarch, *Consolatio ad Apollonium*, xxii.

[5] R. H. Codrington, *The Melanesians*, p. 273.

[6] Cf. above, p. 96. 'The Saviour' was one of the cult-epithets of
Dionysos (C. H. Tzchucke, note to Pomponius Mela, iii. 2; K. Hoeck, *Kreta*,
vol. ii. p. 236).

sacraments does not enjoy the same fate when he dies." [1]   The profane were destined to wallow in slime,[2] whereas the initiated would ascend to heaven,[3] and dwell with the gods ; [4] they will occupy the foremost place in the other world.[5] He who had received the sacraments of initiation lived in joy and hope ; [6] for him death was robbed of her sting and the grave of her victory ; [7] he lived in the sweet prospect and hope of a better world.[8]

That hope was the gift of the god. But not of him alone ; it is the Great Mother that possesses the secret of eternal life, who gives her son to the world, that men may live. The moon is not only thought of as imparting renewed life by its resurrection, and causing its votaries to be born again, but also as removing evil by acting as a substitute or scapegoat. It is a current belief among the peasants of southern Italy that if a person is suffering from boils, warts, swollen glands, varicose veins, goitre, or in fact any evil or uncleanness, and the affected part be touched at the very instant when the change, or turn, of the moon takes place, the affliction will certainly be cured, and the body of the patient rendered whole, the moon carrying away the disease.[9] The Southern Slavs similarly request the moon to take away their children's ailments.[10]

The Divine Son of the Great Mother, the youngest of the gods, though the lineal descendant of the primitive moon-god and possessing his attributes, differs in many respects from all previous divine beings ; and that difference depends chiefly upon the fact that he is, first and foremost, the divine child, the nursling of The Mothers, who rejoice in him and mourn over him. It is in that relation that the powers and attributes of the primitive moon-god have passed over to the younger god. He is not the primitive moon-god in his aspects of Father, of fighter, of dark destroyer, but in his youthful aspect of son of the Divine Mother. Pictorial art in both Christian and pre-Christian times

[1] Homeric *Hymn to Demeter*, 466 sq.

[2] Plato, *Phaedo*, 69.

[3] Diogenes Laertius, viii. 1. 31 ; Proclus, Commentary on Plato's *Republic*, ii. 129. 1 ; *Ibid.*, ii. 132. 19 ; Pindar, *Fragm.*, cxxxii ; *Corpus Inscriptionum Atticarum*, i. 442.

[4] Plato, *Phaed.*, 69 c.

[5] Pseudo-Plato, *Axiochos*, p. 196 (ed. Bekker) ; Diogenes Laertius, vi. 12. 39.

[6] Cicero, *De legibus*, ii. 14.

[7] Plutarch, *De an.*, vi. 2 ; Sophokles, *Fragm.*, 753 ; *Revue Archéologique*, iii (1883), p. 81, n.

[8] Aristides, *Orat.*, xix. 1, xiii. 1 ; Isocrates, *Panegyr.*, 59.

[9] G. Finamore, *Credenze, usi e costumi abruzzesi*, p. 45. For similar ideas in Germany, see L. Strackerjan, *Aberglaube und Sagen aus dem Herzogthum Oldenburg*, vol. i, p. 74.

[10] F. S. Krauss, *Sitte und Brauch der Südslaven*, p. 547.

seldom depicts the Son in the company of his Father, but always in that of his mother, and as the young god, who at most is never more than thirty. That form alone of the primitive moon-god has been bequeathed to him by his relation to the Great Mother. He is the inseparable symbol of her motherhood, deriving his significance and character from his association with her. When the Jesuit missionary, Le Jeune, asked the Iroquois how they could imagine that the moon is a woman, since she had no arms, they replied that he was miserably ignorant about such matters; for everyone knew that if her arms did not project it was because they were folded against her breast as she held her child.[1] The Mexican goddess is represented nursing an infant;[2] and people sometimes caught glimpses of her by lonely pools as a woman with a kindly face bearing the Divine Child in her arms.[3] Of the religious beliefs of the natives of Darien what the first Spanish conquerors gathered was that " in heaven there is a woman, very beautiful, with a baby." [4] In South Africa the Kaffirs regarded the moon as a man; but an alternative view represents it as a woman carrying her infant on her back.[5] The favourite representations of Isis and of Ishtar are the familiar presentment of the Divine Mother and Child.[6] In China " the most common of female deities is the Shing-Moo, or Holy Mother. This lady is the exact counterpart of the Indian Ganga, or goddess of the river, the Isis of the Egyptians, and the Ceres of the Greeks. Nothing shocked the missionaries so much on their first arrival in China as the image of this lady, in whom they discovered, or thought they discovered, the most striking resemblance to the Virgin Mary. They found her generally shut up with great care in a recess at the back of the altar, and veiled with a silken screen to hide her from common observation, sometimes with a child in her hands, at other times on her knees, and a glory round her head. On hearing the story of Shing-Moo they were confirmed in their opinion. They were told that she conceived and bore her son while yet a virgin." [7] Dr. Medhurst referring to the same difficulties, says: " The very

[1] *Relations des Jésuites*, 1634, p. 26.

[2] A. Chavero, " Los dioses astronomicos de los antiguos Mexicanos," *Anales del Museo Nacional de Mexico*, v, plate facing p. 457.

[3] J. de Torquemada, *Veinte i un libros rituales i Monarchia Indiana*, vol. ii, p. 61.

[4] P. de Andagoya, " Relación de los sucesos de Pedrarias Davila," in M. Fernandez de Navarrete, *Coleccion de los viages*, vol. iii, p. 401.

[5] D. Kidd, *Savage Childhood*, p. 149.

[6] For the nursing Ishtar see W. H. Ward, *Seal Cylinders of Western Asia*, p. 154; A. Jeremias, *Das Alte Testament im Lichte des alten Orient*, p. 107. Ishtar is called " the mother of the faithful breast " (S. Langdon, *Sumerian and Babylonian Psalms*, p. 288).

[7] J. Barrow, *Travels in China*, pp. 472 sq.

titles of their intercessors, such as 'goddess of mercy,' 'holy mother,' 'queen of heaven,' with the image of a virgin having a child in her arms, holding a cross, are all such striking coincidences that the Catholic missionaries were greatly stumbled at the resemblance between the Chinese worship and their own when they came over to convert the natives to Christianity." [1]

As regards the origin and nature of the Queen of Heaven in China, as good an idea of it may be gathered from the old account of Mendez Pinto as from more learned disquisitions. Describing the chief temples outside the city of Peking, he says : " A third building we saw without the walls, sumptuous and rich, named Nacaperau, which signifieth 'The Queen of Heaven,' which they mean not of the Virgin Marie, but thinke that as temporal kings are married so also is the heavenly, and the children which hee getteth of Nicaperau are the starres ; and when the starres seem to shoute or fall in the ayre, that then one of these children dye, all his brethren weeping so many teares that the clouds are therewith filled, and water the earth, and make it fruitful." He goes on to relate that he was informed by the priests of the temple how, after the flood, the moon sent her representative to the earth to re-people the world. She stood upon the reappearing dry land, and " a great quantitie of creatures issued from down her arms ; down the right-hand males, and females down the left ; having no other place in her bodie whence to bring them forth as other women of the world, whom for sinne God hath subjected to filthinesse of corruption, to show how filthy sinne is. After she had finished this travell or child-birth of 33,333 creatures, as they number, one-third part males and two parts females, she remayned so weake having no bodie to provide her any thing, that with dizziness she fell to the ground dead without recoverie. Whereat the Moone in condoling her death covered herself with sorrow, which are the shadows we see from the earth ; which they say shall remaine so many years as the produced creatures (33,333) and then the Moone shall put off her maske of sorrow, and the night shall bee as cleare as the day. Such and other like mad stuffe they tell, which make one wonder, or more weepe, that the Devil should gull them with such manifest lyes, being otherwise so understanding a people." [2]

It is chiefly by his relation to the Divine Mother, by that tie of intimate sentiment and by his recurring birth, passion, and death, that the Divine Son is made to partake of a human as well as of a divine nature ; he is God and Man in one. The Divine Son came down among men, was his own prophet, established his

[1] W. H. Medhurst, *China : Its State and Prospects*, p. 217.

[2] F. Mendez Pinto, " Observations of China, Tartaria and other Easterne parts of the World," in *Hakluytus Posthumus, or Purchas His Pilgrimes*, vol. xii, pp. 124, 133 sq.

own religion. Men doubt whether he is god or man; so marked is the human aspect that even the modern critic is sometimes taken in by it. Egyptologists still seriously entertain the possibility of Osiris-Horus having been an actual king.[1] Tammuz reigned in Babylonia, and every Semitic martyr-hero or prophet has been identified with the Anointed One. The Dionysos of Euripides has been regarded as a human prophet impersonating the god.[2] Miss Harrison is persuaded that his double, Orpheus, the lover of 'The Broad One,' is a historical personage; and many still regard Musaios, the Muse-man, son of the Moon, and Eumolphos, the husband of the Moon,[3] as historical realities. It would require strong evidence to establish the historicity of such Divine Sons. Their human character is part and parcel of their attributes.

The old tribal moon-gods, culture heroes, were likewise indeterminate as regards their human and their divine character; no distinction, indeed, was drawn between the two. But that primitive confusion differs wholly from the human nature deliberately acquired by the Divine Infant. By the time that he appears primitive society has long since passed away; the heavenly gods, the Olympians, the transformed and generalised Supreme Beings have become exalted to such aethereal spheres that they have in the process of abstraction lost their humanity, or become cold and passionless, remote and unapproachable. The Divine Son, the Holy Child of the Great Mother, brings the god down to earth again and into contact with humanity.

And it is with women's sentiments that the human contact takes place. In the divine group of Mother and Child, which comes to dominate religion, and before which the entire pantheon of male divinities fades into insignificance, is presented not only the culmination of the religion of women, but the one definite development by which religion has been transformed. Hitherto all spirits, manitus, tribal gods, rain-gods, sky-gods, had been 'feared,' controlled, placated, propitiated, exorcised. For the first time in the history of religious evolution was a divine object, a deity regarded with other sentiments. The Great Mother, the Divine Child, were the first divinities to whom women at any rate turned with feelings other than mere dread and secret hostility. Tenderness, love, springing from its fountain-head, the maternal instinct, entered for the first time the sphere of religion. At the outset of the foregoing rough attempt to outline in some of its aspects the relation of women to the evolution of religious cult

[1] T. E. Peet, in *The Cambridge Ancient History*, vol. i, p. 333.

[2] A. W. Verrall, *The Bacchants and Other Essays*, pp. 30 sqq.; G. Norwood, *The Riddle of the ' Bacchae.'*

[3] *Orphica* (ed. Abel), *Fragm.*, iv; Plato, *Respub.*, 364 E; Scholiast to Aristophanes, *Ranae*, 1033; Athenaeus, 597; Suidas, s.v. Μουσαῖος.

and ideas, I declined to commit myself to definitions. When we are considering the utilitarian magical practices of the totemic medicine-man and the witch we may seriously doubt whether the term religion is rightly applicable ; when we come upon the maleficent daemons before whom the savage quails in terror, we are compelled to recognise that the description of early missionaries who stigmatised those cults as devil-worship was not merely ignorant and inaccurate ; when we are confronted with the otiose, inactive, unworshipped Sky-gods of whom their votaries take little note except to curse them when they do not send rain, we may, in spite of theological definitions, hesitate whether to call the conception a religious one. Religious persons will be the first to agree that, whatever definition we may choose to adopt, it is in the character of the sentiments which move the votary that the essence of religion lies. And if a distinction is anywhere to be drawn between that which we like to think of as religion in a legitimate sense, and that from which it sprang, it is here or nowhere that the line of demar-cation is definitely crossed. Religious sentiment became, with the development of the Divine Mother, assimilated from the very nature of its central object, with the love of the mother for the child. The whole ritual of that religion consisted in mourning with the mother over her beloved son, in rejoicing with her at his birth. Over the dead Osiris, the dead Tammuz, the dead Dionysos, the women wailed by the side of the bereaved and disconsolate mother ; and there was, we may be sure, more than mere ritual and ceremonial in their sobs. That veiled and bowed figure of the Divine Mourner, The Lady of Sorrow, was indeed a new deity to whom they could securely appeal for sympathy with human suffering.

The women who were by nature possessed of the powers of magic and witchcraft, who held the secrets of agricultural magic, who were the chief ministrants in the cult of the dead, would appear to have had no unimportant share in the evolution of religious ideas, if indeed, religion, of which they are regarded as the last bulwarks and ultimate support, has not been from first to last mainly their creation. For it is improbable that they have ever been the mere recipients of the ideas and conceptions associated with their mysteries and their cults. It is assuredly improbable that the Mother and Child were fashioned by the hands of man. And it was in the religion of the Mother and her Divine Son that the rites and conceptions of the primitive savage became trans-muted. The fierce, tribal, nationalistic gods of hunters and herding tribesmen became transformed under the influence of the women's religion ; they grew gentler, their attributes changed in harmony with the character of the Universal Mother. The transition from the fierce and dreaded tribal god into the moral Creator and Governor of the universe has often been traced. But it was not with the male god, but with the Great Goddess that the transition first took place. The All-Mother is older than the All-Father. Ishtar and Isis were the universal mother long before any sky-god or tribal male deity had evolved into universal fatherhood. The conception of universal rule and of universal parenthood originated with the cosmic deity of women, not with the tribal deity of the men. It was chiefly in relation to the Great Mother that those more highly developed theological notions were held in the ancient world. The Great Mother differed fundamentally from the tribal deities, the political gods, the triumphant Sun-gods; she was not tribal, not national, not the jealous deity of a chosen people. She was the Mother of all without respect of persons; and the brotherhood of her children was not tribal brotherhood, but the brotherhood of all men. " I am Nature, the mother of all things," Apuleius made her say, " the ruler of the elements, the original principle of the ages, the supreme divinity, the queen of souls, the first in heaven, the one presentment of all gods and of all goddesses. The luminous spheres of heaven, and the health-giving breath of the sea, and the dark silences of Hades obey my laws. There is no other power but I; I am worshipped under as many aspects, under as many forms, with as many rites as there are peoples on the earth. To the primitive race of the Phrygians I am Pessinunte, the Mother of the Gods; in Athens I am Kekropean Athene; in Cyprus, Paphian Aphrodite; in Krete, Artemis Diktynna; in Sicily, Stygian Proserpine; at Eleusis, Demeter, the ancient goddess; unto others I am Hera or Bellona; unto others again Hekate or Rhamnusia." [1]

As the conditions which gave rise to the religion of the Great Mothers passed away, as agriculture ceased to be associated with women's sphere and they no longer wielded the monopoly of the magic of fertility, as woman herself fell more and more under patri-archal supremacy, the Great Gods, the Sky-gods, the Heavenly Fathers, who had almost faded out of existence in the glow of the religion of the Mothers, reasserted themselves. But they were no longer the same. They might cast aside the idolatries of agricultural religion as " the abominations of the Gentiles," and " the whoredoms of Eleusis," but it was nevertheless from those ' abominations ' that the influences has been derived that softened the harsh and narrow features of the old tribal divinities.

The Queen of Heaven was put away by the solitary god. Gnostic and Christian theology restored, however, his original threefold nature. The Son, the Logos, was the offspring of the Father and of Divine Sophia—for the Queen of Heaven had ever been the Goddess of Wisdom; [2] the Holy Ghost, which is identical

---

[1] Apuleius, *Metamorphoses*, xi. 5.   [2] *Wisdom of Solomon*, vii. sq.

with her, and, in Hebrew, feminine, was regarded by the Nazarenes and early Christians as the mother of Christ.[1] It was by a grammatical accident, πνεῦμα in Greek being neuter, that the third Person of the Holy Trinity came to be dissociated from the Mother of God.   Nevertheless, it was represented by the dove, the immemorial bird of the Great Goddess, the 'Patroness of Israel.'[2] Philo regarded the sacred bird as identical with Sophia.[3]   Jesuit theologians have asserted that the Holy Virgin was omniscient, and describe her in that aspect as the 'noetic dove.'[4] The early Christians adopted Roman sarcophagi upon which were depicted the doves of Venus Libitina drinking from a cup, and the symbol was universally reproduced in Christian Churches.[5] In the popular mind the dove was completely identified with the third Person of the Trinity. "Mary," says Alphonso de Liguori, "was prefigured by the Dove of the ark," and she is addressed as "the beautiful Dove."[6] In eastern Europe the dove is still associated with the Holy Virgin rather than with the Holy Ghost. In Bosnia a holy monk was said to have notes brought to him daily from the Holy Virgin by her bird, the dove;[7] and Russian peasants to this day will not eat pigeons, thinking they would thereby commit a sacrilege.[8]

The Great Mother continued to share popular devotion with the Divine Son whom she had borne. Epiphanius complained that the women of eastern Europe offered, like the Jewish women of old, cakes to the Queen of Heaven.[9] In truth they have never ceased to do so; they continue to this day to observe the immemorial rite as they did when they celebrated the

---

[1] Origen, *In Jeremiah Homilia*, xv. 4 (Migne, *Patrologia Graeca*, vol. xiii, col. 453); *Commentarium in Evangelium Johannis*, xi. 6 (*ibid.*, vol. xiv, coll. 132 sq.); Jerome, *Comm. in Michaeam*, vii. 6 (*Patrologia Latina*, vol. xxv, coll. 1221 sq.); *In Ezechielem*, xvi. 13 (*ibid.*, col., 137); Epiphanius, *Adversus octoginta haereses*, xxi. 2, liii. 1 (*Patrologia Graeca*, vol. xli, coll. 288, 960). Justin speaks of the Holy Ghost as feminine, and assimilates it to Persephone-Kore (*Apologia I pro Christianis*, lxiv., in Migne, *op. cit.*, *Series Graeca*, vol. vi, col. 426).

[2] See above, p. 78.   [3] Philo, *Quis rerum divinarum heres sit*, c. 44.

[4] Christophorus de Vega, *Theologia Mariana*, fol. 254.

[5] M. A. Boldetti, *Osservazioni sopra i cimiteri de santi martiri*, pp. 339 sq.; R. Rochette, "Sur l'archéologie chrétienne," *Mémoires de l'Académie des Inscriptions*, xiii, p. 297.

[6] St. Alphonso de Liguori, *The Glories of Mary*, p. 176. Cf. C. de Vega, *op. cit.*, fol. 55; H. Marraccius, *Polyanthea Mariana*, pp. 124 sqq.

[7] A. Chaumette-des-Fossés, *Voyage en Bosnie*, p. 71.

[8] J.-B. May, *Saint Pétersbourg et la Russie en 1829*, vol. i, p. 95. There is at Boulogne a church dedicated to Our Lady of the Dove (A. Maury, *Croyances et légendes du moyen-âge*, p. 270).

[9] Epiphanius, *Adversus octoginta haereses*, lxxviii. 23. St. Augustine's mother was in the habit of bringing cakes and wine to Church until it was pointed out to her that such a practice savoured of heathenism (Augustine, *Confess.*, vi. 2).

thesmophoria, and as they have done from prehistoric times. In Athens itself it was quite recently the custom for girls to offer cakes with honey and salt at a small cave called the " hollow hill." " The same practice, I was informed in Sparta," says Mr. Lawson, " is known at the present day to the peasant women of the surrounding plain, who will undertake even a long and wearisome journey to lay a honey-cake in a certain cave on one of the eastern spurs of Taygetus." Mr. Lawson mentions several other places where the custom is observed ; " and from the testimony of many other observers," he adds, " I conclude that it is, or was till recently, universal in Greek lands." [1] The practice of offering cakes to the Queen of Heaven has survived not only in Greece, but also in modern France.[2]

Demeter was worshipped at Eleusis until the year 1801, not in a vicarious form, but in her own name and in the shape of her ancient statue, which was crowned with flowers, " in the avowed hope of obtaining good harvests." The cult was put to an end only by the vandalism of two Englishmen, named Clarke and Cripps, who armed with a Turkish warrant removed the venerable goddess, causing a riot among the exasperated peasants.[3] Throughout Greece the peasant knows 'Despoina,' the Mistress, as she is called by her ancient title. " He has learnt from his ancestors of a woman beautiful, revered, deathless, who dwells within a mountain of his land. . . . She is a real person, not a personification of any natural force. . . . The blessing which rests on field and fold is the work of a living goddess' hands.   Flesh and blood she is, even as they themselves, but immortal and very mighty, nobler than many of whom the priests preach, stronger to help the good and punish the wicked." [4] In Sicily, as at Eleusis, the Great Goddess Ceres did duty for the Madonna in Christian

[1] J. Cuthbert Lawson, *Modern Greek Folklore and Ancient Greek Religion*, pp. 120 sq.   The ' Ishtar cakes,' as they were called in Sumerian ritual, are a constant feature of her ritual in the oldest records (see F. Delitsch *Assyrisches Handwörtebuch*, p. 448).   The Christians of Syria are said to " pay even higher adoration to the Virgin Mary than either Greeks or Catholics " (S. Buckingham, *Travels in Mesopotamia*, vol. i, p. 341).

[2] See above, p. 103.   The Ishtar cakes survive in some form or other in most countries.   In Nottingham the bakers used to send to their customers at Christmas large buns with the image of the Virgin stamped upon them.   T. Inman, *Ancient Faiths embodied in Ancient Names*, vol. i, p. 379.

[3] J. Cuthbert Lawson, *op. cit.*, pp. 79 sq.   The goddess is now in the Fitzwilliam Museum in Cambridge, catalogued as " No. XIV (much mutilated)."

[4] *Ibid.*, p. 89.   Despoina is, in Greece, distinct from the Holy Virgin, the name of the latter being Panagia, the All-Holy One, the same name which was borne by the priestess of Demeter at Eleusis, who impersonated the younger of the two goddesses (Hesychius, s.v. Παναεις ; cf, ᾽Αρχαιολογικη ᾽Εφημερις, 1894, p. 176 ; *ibid.*, 1900, p. 79).

churches, and at Castrogiovanni, on the site of the ancient Enna, the great shrine of her worship, there is still a statue of the Virgin whose Divine Child is not a boy, but a girl, the figure having served as Ceres and Proserpine in a previous sanctuary of the goddess.[1]

The substitution of Mary for Sophia or the Holy Ghost as the Divine Mother did not acquire importance until after the doctrine of the Incarnation had become, in consequence of the Nestorian controversy, the central dogma of the Catholic Church.[2]   The deity immemorially enthroned in the religious consciousness of the people was soon incorporated in the new religion.   The Marianites were condemned in the fifth century for regarding the Holy Virgin as a goddess ; [3] but the ascription to her of divine attributes and titles was an accepted commonplace a few centuries later, and she came to be pronounced identical in nature with the First Person of the Trinity,[4] coeval with the world, and one with the first light and primal matter.[5]   It was even asserted that she created the world and that its existence depended upon her.   " At the command of Mary," says Alphonso de Liguori, " all obey, even God." [6]

Of the assimilation of the Divine Mother to the earth, the mother of corn, few traces have remained in later conceptions. The Virgin Mary is compared by Epiphanius to the earth fecundated by the heavenly rain.[7]   St. Ambrose, commenting on the Song of Songs, remarks : " In the most pure womb of Mary there was sown one sole grain of wheat, yet it is called a garden of wheat because all the elect were included in the chosen grain." [8]   Like Persephone, she is the Queen of the Underworld : " The most blessed Virgin rules over the Infernal regions.   She is sovereign mistress of the devils, she is therefore called the ruling Mistress of the devils." [9]   But those chthonic aspects of the Queen of Heaven, which mythologists have

---

[1] Douglas Sladen, *In Sicily*, vol. i, p. 335.

[2] A. Harnack, *History of Dogma*, vol. iv, p. 315.   The first invocation to her occurs in Gregory of Nazianzus, and is from a woman, St. Justina, (Gregorius Nazanzenus, *Oratio*, xxiv, in Migne, *Patrologiae Cursus Completus, Series Graeca*, vol. xxxv, col. 1151).   For the growth of the official worship of the Virgin in the Christian Church, see J. C. W. Augusti, *Denkwürdigkeiten aus der Christliche Archaeologie*, vol. ii, pp. 1 sqq. ; G. F. H. Rheinwald, *Die Kirchliche Archäologie*, p. 233 ;   C. Benrath, " Zur Geschichte der Marienverehrung," *Theologische Studien und Kritiken*, 1886, pp. 1 sqq.

[3] J. A. Fabricius, *Codex epigraphicus*, vol. ii, p. 317, from the Council of Ephesus, A.D. 431.

[4] H. Marraccius, *Polyanthea Mariana*, p. 156.   The Holy Virgin is called " Dea dearum," " Dea ecclesiae universalis," " Dea deorum," " Dea amoris."

[5] C. de Vega, *Theologia Mariana*, fols. 38, 255.

[6] Alphonso de Liguori, *The Glories of Mary*, pp. 334, 155.

[7] Epiphanius, *Adversus octoginta haereses*, lxxiv. 3 (in Migne, *Patrologia Graeca*, vol. xlii, coll. 477, 480).

[8] Alphonso de Liguori, *op. cit.*, p. 23.

[9] *Ibid.*, p. 119.

mistaken for primary characters, faded almost completely, and her primal nature alone survived. The Divine Mother retained her ancient association with the planet Venus, the star of Ishtar.[1] She is " the Star of the Sea," and " the ruler of the Ocean." [2] Her more fundamental cosmic aspect is, however, by far the most prominent one. The Holy Virgin is universally identified with the moon.[3] She is called " the Moon of the Church," " Our Moon," " the Spiritual Moon," the " Perfect and Eternal Moon." [4] She is said to control the moon, and through the moon the stars and all the planets.[5] The peasantry in most parts of Europe fail to distinguish clearly between the Virgin Mary and the moon. Thus in France the peasants of the Perche district call the moon " Notre Dame." [6] In Portugal no distinction is drawn between the two ; the country people call the moon " the Mother of God." [7] The Virgin is habitually represented with her ancient symbols, the moon and the serpent. " As the moon is between the heavens and the earth," says St. Bonaventure, " so does Mary continuously place herself between God and sinners in order to appease our Lord in their regard, and to enlighten their return to Him." [8] " God, having created the heavens and the earth," says the blessed Alphonso, " made two great luminaries, the Sun to rule the day, the Moon to preside over the night. ' The former,' says Hugo, ' is a figure of Jesus Christ, whose splendid rays illumine the just who live in the day of grace ; the latter is typical of Mary, whose mild lustre illumines sinners mid the dreary night of sin.' ' Towards the Moon it is,' says Innocent III, ' he should look, who is buried in the shades of sin and iniquity. Having lost divine grace, the day disappears, there is no more sun for him ; but the Moon is still in the horizon. Let him address himself to Mary ; under her influence thousands every day find their way to God.' " [9]

---

[1] Alphonso de Liguori, *The Glories of Mary*, p. 96.
[2] C. de Vega, *op. cit.*, p. 94.
[3] Alphonso de Liguori, *op. cit.*, p. 177 ; C. de Vega, *op. cit.*, fol. 379 ; H. Marraccius, *op. cit.*, s.v. ' Luna,' pp. 846 sqq. Cf. ' Index Marianus,' in Migne, *Patrologiae Cursus Completus*, vol. ccxix, col. 511, s.v. ' Luna.'
[4] H. Marraccius, *op. cit.*, pp. 348, 350.
[5] C. de Vega, *op. cit.*, p. 379.
[6] F. Petigny, in *Revue des Traditions Populaires*, xvii, p. 453.
[7] T. Braga, *O Povo Portuguez, nos sens costumes, crenças e tradiciones*, vol. ii, p. 49.
[8] Alphonso de Liguori, *op. cit.*, pp. 177 sq.
[9] *Ibid.* (carefully revised by a Catholic Priest), p. 84.

CHAPTER XXV

HOLY MATRIMONY

Marriage of Women to Beasts.

WOMEN probably played an essential part in the rites intended by primitive hunters to promote an increase in the supply of food-animals. The spring ceremonies performed by the Sioux to bring about the multiplication of buffaloes, which are their staple food, take several forms, all of which are imitative of the intended effect. In one form of the rite the younger men offered their wives to the old men, and these had sexual intercourse with them in the sacred lodge.[1] In another the men danced dressed in the skins of buffaloes. The ceremony was under the management of the women. One man impersonated the buffalo-bull, while others took the part of the cows. At the end of the dance, the man who impersonated the bull retired at some distance, and was pursued by the women, who surrounded him, mocking and bespattering him. The wooden phallic appendage with which he was provided was wrested from him by one of the women, who then wrapped it in sage leaves and returned to the village accompanied by the other matrons. She was hoisted on to the roof of the lodge, and proceeded thence to harangue the people, saying, " she held the power of creation and also the power of life and death over them, that she was the father of the buffaloes, and that she could make them come or stay away as she pleased." [2] The Hidastas, another tribe of Sioux, had a similar festival for the multiplication of buffaloes. Promiscuous intercourse took place during the magical ceremony. They state that the festival was instituted by the women.[3]

---

[1] M. Lewis and W. Clarke, *Travels to the Source of the Missouri River*, vol. i, p. 209.

[2] G. Catlin, *O-Kee-pa, a Religious Ceremony, and other Customs of the Mandans*, pp. 23 sq., 33.

[3] J. Owen Dorsey, " A Study of Siouan Cult," *Eleventh Annual Report of the Bureau of Ethnology*, p. 505.

In Australia ritual sexual intercourse, general promiscuity and suspension of individual marital rites accompany almost every religious ceremony ; the men place their wives at the disposal of the chief ministrants, who have intercourse with them on the sacred ground.[1] " The idea," says Mr. Brough Smyth, " is that sexual intercourse assists in some way in the proper performance of the ceremony." [2] Such rites of promiscuity are believed by the Dieri to cause an increase in the supply of wild dogs and of snakes.[3]

Those rites of primitive hunting tribes to promote the fertility of animals have, there can be no doubt, been far more widespread than is shown by our present records ; for little attention has been paid to them, and they are kept from the knowledge of travellers, besides having now long since disappeared in almost every part of the world. Similar rites were, however, prevalent among our own ancestors. A neolithic picture in the rock-shelter of Cogul, near Lerida, in northern Spain, which is probably some twenty thousand years old, might serve as an illustration of the scene in the Buffalo Dance of the Mandans described by Catlin.[4] It was a universal usage with the peoples of Western Europe, from southern Gaul to Britain and Germany, to dress at their great yearly festival of the winter solstice, in the skins of animals, such as deer, oxen, goats. The animals represented males and females, bulls and cows, bucks and hinds, the female principle being, however, sometimes impersonated by an old woman. None of the customs or rites of their pagan religions was more persistently adhered to by the barbarians, even long after their conversion to Christianity, and none called forth more denunciations from the Church.[5] We are not expressly told that, as in the similar festivals of the Mandans,

---

[1] A. W. Howitt, The Native Tribes of South-East Australia, pp. 175 sqq. ; W. B. Spencer and F. G. Gillen, The Native Tribes of Central Australia, pp. 96 sq. ; Id., The Northern Tribes of Central Australia, pp. 136 sq. ; S. Gason, in J. D. Woods, The Native Tribes of South Australia, p. 280 ; R. H. Mathews, " Ethnological Notes on the Aboriginal Tribes of New South Wales and Victoria," Journal and Proceedings of the Royal Society of New South Wales, xxxviii, p. 18 ; E. Eylmann, Die Eingeborenen der Kolonie Südaustralien, pp. 152 sq. ; A. Oldfield, " The Aborigines of Australia," Transactions of the Ethnological Society, iii, pp. 230 sq.

[2] R. Brough Smyth, The Aborigines of Victoria, vol. ii, p. 319.

[3] A. L. P. Cameron, " Notes on some Tribes of New South Wales," Journal of the Anthropological Institute, xiv, p. 353. Cf. S. Gason, in J. D. Woods, loc. cit.

[4] S. Reinach, Répertoire de l'Art Quaternaire, p. 56 ; Id., in L'Anthropologie, 1909, p. 17.

[5] Augustine, Sermo, cclxv, " De Christiano nomine cum operibus non Christianis," in Migne, Patrologiae Cursus, vol. xxxix, col. 2239 ; Priminius, De singulis libris scarapsus, in C. P. Caspari, Kirchenhistorische Anecdota, p. 175 ; S. Audoenus, Vita S. Eligii, ii. 15 ; S. Theodorus, Paenitentiale, in H. Spelman, Concilia, Decreta, Leges, Constitutiones in re Ecclesiarum Orbis

sexual congress formed a part of those European animal rites. We have, however, conclusive evidence that it constituted an essential part of the magic ritual of European witches, who were united to the devil in the form of a he-goat ; and Miss Murray has brought together much evidence showing that the ritual, in which an artificial phallus played a conspicuous part, was in all probability the survival of the essential rites of religious festivals in pre-Christian times.[1] Among the tribes of the northern terri- tories of the Gold Coast, at the present day, women offer themselves to animals in the belief that their own fertility will be benefited.[2]

The clan or tribe is commonly regarded as having sprung from the union of the totem, or some other animal, with a woman. Thus, for example, the Iroquois tribes of New Netherlands regarded themselves as derived from the intercourse of women with bears, deers, or wolves.[3] The same idea is reflected in countless myths. The Eskimo of Smith Sound trace some of their clans to the union of a woman with a bear ; [4] other Eskimo tribes believe themselves to be descended from a woman and a dog.[5] The Tlinkit of Alaska say that some clans sprang from the union of women with sharks.[6] The Déné regard themselves as issued from the union of the first woman with a dog.[7] The Ainu of Japan also believe that they are the progeny of women who had intercourse with dogs.[8] Such a traditional genealogy is very widespread. Steller says that Kamchadal women formerly had intercourse with dogs,[9] a state- ment which probably refers to a similar tradition. The Kirghis Tartars reckon their descent from forty girls (= kirg kiss) who had intercourse with a red-haired dog.[10] The inhabitants of Babi

Britannici, vol. i, tit. 33 ; C. du Fresne Du Cange, *Glossarium Mediae et Infimae Latinitatis*, s.vv. ' cervula ' and ' vetula,' where many other references are cited.

[1] M. A. Murray, " Witches and Fertility," *Man*, xix, pp. 35 sq. ; Id., *The Witch-Cult in Western Europe*, pp. 175 sqq.

[2] A. W. Cardinall, *The Natives of the Northern Territories of the Gold Coast*, p. 66.

[3] J. G. Müller, *Geschichte der amerikanischen Urreligionen*, pp. 108 sq.

[4] A. L. Kroeber, " Tales of the Smith Sound Eskimo," *Journal of American Folk-Lore*, xii, p. 176.

[5] H. J. Rink, *Tales and Traditions of the Eskimo*, p. 186.

[6] A. Krause, *Die Tlinkit-Indianer*, p. 269.

[7] E. Petitot, *Autour du Grand Lac des Esclaves*, pp. 296 sqq. ; H. H. Bancroft, *The Native Races of the Pacific States*, vol. iii, p. 507.

[8] I. L. Bird, *Unbeaten Tracts in Japan*, pp. 250, 255, 315 ; W. H. Wood, " The Hairy Men of Yesso," *Transactions of the Ethnological Society*, N.S., iv, p. 37 ; H. C. St. John, *Notes and Sketches from the Wild Country of Nipon*, pp. 29 sq.

[9] G. W. Steller, *Beschreibung von dem Lande Kamtschatka*, p. 289.

[10] Radloff, " Observations sur les Kirghis," *Journal Asiatique*, VIᵉ Série, ii, pp. 311 sq.

likewise regard themselves as descended from a woman and a dog.[1]
The kings of Kandy traced their origin to the union of a woman
with a lion.[2] The rajahs of Chuta Nagpur claimed to be sprung
from the union of a woman with a serpent,[3] a genealogy which is
found the world over. The house of Cleves traced its descent
from a woman and a swan.[4] Saxo Grammaticus tells us that a
line of Swedish princes was descended from a woman and a bear.[5]

Many rituals contain direct allusions to the union of a woman
with a divine animal. Thus in the Asvamedha, or Sacrifice of
the Horse, the most important ceremony in the religious cult
of the ancient Hindus, upon which the welfare of the people was
thought to depend, the queen was ritually united to the sacred
animal. The horse represented, we are told, the god Agni ;[6]
but as the worship of the sacred horse is common among the nomad
populations of Central Asia, the god Agni possibly represented the
horse. Every year a horse was chosen and treated with extravagant deference, a troop of four hundred young men of the noblest
families being specially appointed to the honour of waiting on the
animal. At the end of the year the sacred horse was solemnly
sacrificed with great pomp. As soon as it had been killed, the
queen lay alongside the slaughtered animal, a rich cloth was spread
over them, ponebatque in gremium regina genitale victimae mem-
brum. As she did so she uttered the words : " May the vigorous
male, the layer of the seed, lay seed," in order to secure the union.[7]
It will be remembered that Semiramis was fabled to have contracted a union with a horse.[8] The myth may have had reference
to a ritual practice similar to that of the ancient Aryans. Incredible
as it may appear, it is not unlikely that at one time the union of
the woman with the sacred horse was even more realistically effected.
At any rate, such a union is said to have been inflicted as a punishment upon the wives of the king of Siam when they proved

---

[1] T. Waitz, *Anthropologie*, vol. v, p. 33.

[2] *The Rájávaliya : or a Historical Narrative of the Sinhalese Kings*, ed. by
B. Gunasékara, pp. 14 sqq.

[3] E. T. Dalton, *Descriptive Ethnology of Bengal*, pp. 165 sq.

[4] F. de Reiffenberg, *Le Chevalier du Cygne et Godefroy de Bouillon*, vol. i,
p. iii ; J. F. D. Blöte, " Das aufkommen des clevischen Schwanritters,"
Zeitschrift für deutsches Alterthum, xlii, pp. 1 sqq. ; P. S. Barto, *Tannhäuser
and the Mountain of Venus*, pp. 58 sqq.

[5] Saxo Grammaticus, *Gesta Danorum*, 1. x, p. 345. Our own reigning
Royal House was in all probability originally descended from a wolf, for
the name Guelf, or Welf, is no other than the word ' wolf ' or ' welp '
(J. Grimm, *Geschichte der deutschen Sprache*, p. 468).

[6] *Satapatha-Brâhmana*, x. 6. 4. 1 (*The Sacred Books of the East*, vol. xliii,
p. 401).

[7] *Ibid.*, xiii. 2. 8. 5 (*The Sacred Books of the East*, vol. xliv, p. 324) ;
A. Hillebrandt, *Rituallitteratur : Vedische Opfer und Zauber*, p. 152.

[8] Pliny, *Nat. Hist.*, viii. 155 ; Hyginus, 243.

unfaithful. " Le supplice qu'on fait souffrir à ces dernières c'est de les abandonner à un cheval dressé tout exprès." [1]

In Egypt, where the gods of a highly developed religion preserved to the last much of their primitive totemic animal character, unions of women with the animal-god were a prominent feature. The bull Apis, who represented Osiris, was treated with honours similar to those bestowed upon the sacred horse in Vedic India. During the first forty days after his installation in his temple at Memphis, the women stood before him and, raising their clothes, exposed their persons.[2] Egyptian princesses were assimilated to cows. Herodotus tells us that when the beloved daughter of King Mykerinos (Menkaura) died, her body was placed in a wooden cow.[3] Such cow-shaped coffins have been found in the cliff-tombs of Ghizeh.[4] Theban princesses in the earlier period of the Middle Kingdom acted as priestesses of Hathor, the cow-form of Isis ; they were buried in the company of sacred bulls,[5] which were presumably their divine husbands. In one tomb a large mummified phallus, apparently that of a bull, was found with the body of the princess.[5] The god Anubis was represented by a priest clothed in the skin of a jackal, who in that animal form had ritual connection with a woman. A notorious scandal was caused in Rome, under the reign of Tiberius, when a priest was bribed to allow a gentleman to take his place while a Roman matron was participating in the primitive ritual.[5] The union of the woman with the sacred animal continued to take place in Egypt even more realistically. The women at Mendes had ritual

---

[1] J.-F. Bernard and B. Picart, *Cérémonies et coutumes religieuses de tous les peoples du monde*, vol. ii, part i, p. 81.

[2] Diodorus Siculus, i. 85.

[3] Herodotus, ii. 29. Cf. Stephanus Byzantinus, s.v. Βουσιρις.

[4] C. R. Lepsius, *Die Chronologie der Aegypter*, p. 309 n3.

[5] V. Lortet and C. Gaillard, " La faune momifiée de l'ancienne Égypte," *Archives du Muséum d'Histoire Naturelle de Lyon*, vol ix, pp. 67 sqq. The two mummified bulls described were found in the tomb of Princess Amenit at Deir el-Bahri by M. Grébaut in 1891 (Cairo Museum, No. 115). Remains of cattle were found by Mr. E. Naville and Dr. H. R. Hall in the tombs of the eleventh-dynasty temple at the same place (E. R. Ayrton and H. R. Hall, in E. Naville, *The XIth Dynasty Temple at Deir El-Bahari* (*Memoirs of the Egypt Exploration Fund*, xxviii), pp. 46, 50). The remains were assumed to be those of cows ; but, as Dr. Hall kindly informs me, this is merely an assumption, and seeing that those skeletons which have been minutely examined by competent zoologists have been found to be beyond doubt those of bulls, it may be presumed that those in the other tombs of Hathor priestesses were likewise bulls and not cows.

[6] M. and M. Vaerting, *The Dominant Sex*, p. 109. The only objects found in the famous Hathor-cow shrine at Deir el-Bahri were wooden phalli (E. Naville, *The XIth Dynasty Temple at Deir El-Bahari*, Part i, p. 65).

[7] Josephus, *Antiq.*, xviii. 72 sq. ; Zonara, vi. 5 ; Hegisippus, ii. 4.

connection with the divine he-goat ; the rite, which was celebrated at the time of Herodotus, was still practised as late as the time of Plutarch, who mentions that the most beautiful women were offered to the divine animal.[1] A similar rite was perhaps observed by the early Semites, for Jewish women were forbidden " to stand before a beast to lie down thereto," and to offer sacrifices to goats with which they had fornicated.[2] The myth of Pasiphae, in her character of queen of Krete, shows that similar ideas were current among the early populations of the Aegean. The queen of Krete was, like the Egyptian royal women, married to a divine bull, as was also the queen of Athens.[3] In Rome the women had in primitive times ritual connection with the sacred ass, the representative of the god Pales ; the ritual, no doubt in some modified form, continued to be observed by Roman matrons under the auspices of the Bona Dea.[4]

A vivid reminiscence of sacred zoogamy survived in England down to Tudor times. In the meadows of the manor of Habyrdon, now known as Haberden meadows, near Bury St. Edmunds, a white bull was kept, which was never yoked to a plough and enjoyed ease and plenty. Whenever a married woman was desirous of offspring, the bull " was led in procession through the principal streets of the town to the principal gate of the monastery, attended by all the monks singing, and a shouting crowd, the woman walking by him and stroking his milk-white sides and pendulous dew-laps. The bull being dismissed, the woman entered the church and paid her vows at the altar of St. Edmund, kissing the stone, and entreating with tears the blessing of a child." [5]

In the crude rites of primitive religion or magic from which those notions and usages originally derived, women were thought of as united to the totem animal, the food-supplier of the tribe, and thus as multiplying the animal food and also the children of the tribe which depended on that food. But the primitive totem

---

[1] Herodotus, ii. 46 ; Strabo, xvii. 18 ; Plutarch, *Bruta animalia ratione uti*, v. Cf. the remarks of D'Hancarville, *Recherches sur l'origine, l'esprit et les progrès des arts de la Grèce*, vol. i, p. 320.

[2] *Leviticus*, xviii. 23 ; xvii. 7.

[3] See below, p. 193. The Athenian and the Kretan ritual were in all probability originally identical (cf. K. Hoeck, *Kreta*, vol. ii, pp. 115 sq.).

[4] Ovid, *Fasti*, ii. 410 sqq. ; Juvenal, vi. 333 sq.

[5] *County Folk-lore*, vol. i, pp. 124 sq., from a contemporary account. Several entries referring to the sacred bull appear in the registers of the monastery. One reads : " This indenture certifies that Master John Swassham, sacrist, with the consent of the prior and convent . . . shall find, or cause to be found, one white bull every year of his term, so often as it shall happen that any gentlewoman, or any other woman, from devotion or vows by them made shall visit the tomb of the glorious martyr St. Edmund to make oblation of the same white bull," etc.

merges by imperceptible degrees into the mythical tribal ancestor, the god, and gods tend to preserve, even in advanced stages of culture, primitive theriomorphic attributes.

The Divine Bull.

By far the most common of those animal forms of the god are the serpent and the bull. The serpent is, as we have seen, well-nigh invariably the emblem of the lunar deity in its aspect of eternally renewed source of life and of fertilising waters ; and the notion that gods in the form of serpents have intercourse with women is, we also saw, equally universal. The bull is perhaps an even more prevalent embodiment of the god. In ancient Persian religion the ' Primal Bull ' was regarded as representing the soul of the world, and more especially its generative power, which was thought to reside in the moon. The conception was evidently much older than Zoroastrian religion, and the Lunar Bull, the first of all beings, was no doubt the form of the supreme deity. The Great Bull is said to have dwindled little by little, and ultimately perished, leaving its seed in the moon.[1] From the Primal Bull came all the good of the world.[2] " I invoke and glorify the Supreme Bull who causes the grass to grow in abundance," runs an ancient Persian hymn, " the pure bull who has given being to the pure man." [3] " Address your prayers to the excellent bull," we read in another hymn, " address your prayers to the principle of all good, address your prayers to the source of all abundance, address your prayers to the pure, heavenly bull, holy and un-created." [4] The divine bull of Mithraic religion was, there can be little doubt, the same as the divine bull of primitive Persian religion. In India the bull was the form of Agni, to whom, in conjunction with Soma, bulls were sacrificed in the ' agni-shomiya ' ceremonies, in which Agni and the moon-god Soma were treated as one god, Agni-Soma.[5] The bull was also an impersonation of Indra [6] and of Siva.[7]

[1] A. Hovelacque, L'Aveste, Zoroastre et le Mazdéisme, pp. 334 sq.

[2] A. H. Anquetil du Perron, Zend-Avesta, vol. i, Part ii, p. 201.

[3] Ibid., pp. 86 sq.

[4] Ibid. (Vendidad, Fargad xxi. 1), p. 424. Cf. The Sacred Books of the East, vol. iv, p. 231.

[5] Rig-Veda, i. 140., viii. 49., x. 155 ; Satapatha-Brâhmana (The Sacred Books of the East, vol. xxvi, p. 162) ; Apastamba's Yagna-Paribibhasha-Sutras, cxv (ibid., vol. xxx, p. 346).

[6] Satapatha-Brâhmana, ii. 5. 3. 18 (The Sacred Books of the East, vol. xii, p. 416).

[7] J. A. Dubois, Hindu Manners, Customs and Ceremonies, vol. i, p. 21, vol. ii, p. 634 ; W. Crooke, The Popular Religion and Folk-lore of Northern India, vol. ii, pp. 156, 230, 234.

Among the Semites the bull form of the god is particularly prominent ; there is not a god in Semitic religions who is not assimilated to, and represented as, a bull. The god Moon, Sinn, is specially termed " the bearer of the mighty horns." [1] The word ' mighty,' ' abbîr,' signifies ' bull,' and the passages in which it occurs in the Hebrew scriptures " should be rendered ' bull ' rather than ' Mighty one.' " Yahweh, who was throughout earlier times worshipped in the form of a bull, was ' the Bull of Israel.' [2] In Egypt bull-worship, that is, the representation of the gods as bulls, was one of the oldest features of religious cult. The Moon-god, Khons, was, as we saw, more especially conceived as ' the Fiery Bull,' and was thought to be in that form the source of all fertility and the cause of women's pregnancy. [3] Osiris was no less a bull-god than Khons ; he is repeatedly addressed and referred to as " the Bull of Heaven," [4] a title which is likewise applied to the moon. [5] His oldest and most intimate incarnation was the moon-bull Apis, who was the very soul, Ka, of Osiris, and the bearer of his mighty horns. Most other Egyptian gods, being identical in nature with one another, were also represented by sacred bulls. Mnevis was the bull-form of Ptah ; early texts mention four sacred bulls of Temu ; [6] and, as Strabo tells us, sacred bulls impersonating the gods abounded in Lower Egypt. [7] The divine kings, as impersonations of the god, constantly compared themselves to bulls. [8] In much the same manner the sacred kings of the Shilluks trace their descent from a divine cow. [9]

As the myths of the Minotaur and Pasiphae, of Europa and the bull-god, clearly show, the divine generative power corresponding to the cow moon-goddesses was conceived in Kretan religion in the form of a bull. To the rationalistic and idealising mind of the Greeks of the classical age such primitive theriomorphic conceptions were as repugnant as to ourselves. The typical representative of the archaic gods of Greece, Dionysos, remained, however, a bull-god. " Many of the Greeks," says Plutarch, " represent Dionysos in the form of a bull." [10] He was called ' bull-shaped,'

---

[1] A. Jeremias, *Handbuch der altorientalischen Geisteskultur*, p. 242.

[2] A. H. Sayce, *Hibbert Lectures on the Origin and Growth of Religion as illustrated by the Religion of the Babylonians*, p. 289 ; Id., in Hastings's *Encyclopaedia of Religion and Ethics*, vol. ii, p. 888.

[3] See above, vol. ii, p. 772.

[4] E. A. Wallis Budge, *Osiris and the Egyptian Resurrection*, vol. i, p. 399.

[5] A. Erman, *A Handbook of Egyptian Religion*, p. 11.

[6] E. A. Wallis Budge, *loc. cit.*

[7] Strabo, xvii. 1. 22.

[8] E. A. Wallis Budge, *op. cit.*, pp. 397 sq.

[9] Count Gleichen, *The Anglo-Egyptian Sudan*, p. 197.

[10] Plutarch, *De Iside et Osiride*, xxxvi. Cf. Athenaeus, xi. 51.

'bull-headed,' 'bull-horned,' and so forth;[1] and like 'bull-faced Men,' the god Moon,[2] Dionysos, who was born a horned child,[3] is often represented with horns,[4] or even as a bull pure and simple crowned with ivy.[5] It was in the form of a bull that the god led Pentheos to his mysteries;[6] he was invoked by the Theban Mainads as 'The Bull,'[7] and it appears from the whole Theban myth that this was his usual form at Thebes in archaic times.[8] At Kyzikos the festivals of Dionysos were called "the cattle-herding feasts," and the hierophant bore the title of " chief cowherd," 'Αρχιβουκόλος.[9] The women of Elis called upon Dionysos to come to them as a " bull-footed " god;[10] and the priestesses of Dionysos Laphystios, wore horns,[11] thus assimilating themselves to cows while invoking the god.   In Athens itself, opposed as such barbaric notions were to Attic taste, there persisted a survival of their crudest form. The Queen Archon, the representative of the primitive queen, was every year married to Dionysos, the marriage being supposed to be consummated; and from the fact that it took place in a cattle-stall, there can be little doubt that the god was, originally at least, represented by a bull.[12]

Celtic gods are commonly horned, and Celtic myth refers to bull-gods.[13] The sacred bull of Cooley, called Donn, forms the

[1] P. N. Rolle, *Recherches sur le culte de Bacchus*, vol. i, pp. 138 sq. ; J. G. Frazer, *The Golden Bough*, vol. vii, p. 16 ; Plutarch, *Quaest. Graec.*, xxxvi ; Euripides, *Bakchai*, 99 ; Scholiast on Aristophanes, *Ranae*, 357 ; Nicander, *Alexipharmaca*, xxxi ; *Orphica*, Hymn xxx. 3. 4, xlv. 20, 1, lii. 2, liii. 8 ; Lucian, *Bacchus*, ii ; Clement of Alexandria, *Exhortatio*, ii. 16.

[2] Nonnus, *Dionysiaca*, xliv. 217.

[3] See above, p. 145. Cf. Euripides, *Bakchai*, 99.

[4] C. Daremberg and E. Saglio, *Dictionnaire des antiquités grecques et romaines*, vol. i, pp. 619 sq., 631 ; W. H. Roscher, *Ausführliches Lexikon*. vol. i, pp. 1149 sq. ; K. O. Müller, *Denkmäler der alten Kunst*, vol. ii, pl. xxxiii,

[5] He appears in that form on a Sicilian coin (H. Goltzius, *Sicilia et Magna Graecia*, tab. v, fig. 3).   On a red-figured vase he is depicted as a child with a calf's head on the lap of his mother (*Gazette archéologique*, 1879, pl. iii).

[6] Euripides, *Bakchai*, 918 sqq.

[7] *Ibid.*, 1017.

[8] See Pausanias, ix. 12.

[9] Hesychius, s.v. Ταυρόκολια ; J. Gruterus, *Inscriptiones Antiquae totius orbis Romani*, No. xvii.

[10] Plutarch, *De Iside et Osiride*, xxxvi.

[11] Scholiast on Lycophron, *Alexandra*, 1237.

[12] Demosthenes, *Contra Neaeram*, 1369 sqq. ; Hesychius, s.v. Διονύσου γάμος ; Id. and *Etymologicum Magnum*, s.v. γεραραί ; Aristotle, *Constitutio Athenien.*, iii. 5 ; U. von Wilamowitz-Moellendorff, *Aristoteles und Athen*, vol. ii, p. 42 ; J. E. Harrison, *Prolegomena to the Study of Greek Religion*, p. 537.

[13] J. A. MacCulloch, *The Religion of the Ancient Celts*, pp. 32 sqq. ; H. d'Arbois de Jubainville, *Les Druides et les dieux celtiques à forme d'animaux*, pp. 153 sqq.

theme of the most important Irish epic that has come down to us,
the 'Táin bó Cúalnge.' The divine bull was apparently venerated
among all the Celts, for Caesar mentions a Gallic chieftain called
Donno-taurus,[1] whose name would seem to be identical with that
of the bull of the Irish epic. The Cimbri, according to Plutarch,
swore their most solemn oaths in the name of a certain brazen
bull.[2] The Nordic god Freijr was spoken of as a bull.[3]

The bull is an obvious emblem of generative power. Not only
is it representative of masculine procreative force, but as the usual
drawer of the plough among agricultural peoples, the bull is also
apt to be regarded as fertilising the earth. Diodorus says that
the sacred bulls Apis and Mnevis " were dedicated to Osiris, and
it was ordained that they should be worshipped as gods in common
by all the Egyptians, since these animals above all others had
helped the discoverers of corn in sowing seed and procuring the
benefits of agriculture." [4] Bulls are, in fact, specially connected
with the transfer of agricultural work from the women to the men ;
for as cattle are generally regarded in pastoral societies as appertaining prescriptively to the men, the yoking of oxen to the plough
marked the turning-point in the transfer of agriculture to the
men who drove them. Among the natives of South Africa, "the
women do all the work with the exception of ploughing which in-
volves the use of oxen, and the men only do this on account of
their superstition which does not allow women to have anything
to do with cattle." [5] In the Canton de Vaud in Switzerland, women
are believed to have an injurious influence on cattle, and old wiseacres say that when cattle are taken up to the summer pastures the
women should be left at home.[6] The ancient Romans, when they
performed religious or magical ceremonies for the health of their
cattle, were particular that no woman should be present, or
should learn the formulas used.[7] That supposed injurious effect
of women on cattle is probably a special instance of the emas-
culating influence which women are thought to exercise on men's
weapons and appliances, a superstition which has thus reinforced
the special proprietary claim of the men to domesticated animals.

But although the bull is a natural emblem of fertilising power,
it appears, I think, conclusively that the primary ground for the
equation and for the widespread identification of gods with bulls
was the assimilation of the horned animal to the moon. In the

[1] Caesar, *De bello Gallico*, vii. 65.   [2] Plutarch, *Vita Marii*, xxiii.

[3] K. von Müllenhoff, *Deutsche Alterthumskunde*, vol. iv, pp. 472, 528.

[4] Diodorus Siculus, i. 21.

[5] H. E. Rouquette, " A few Notes on the Farming, etc., of the Kafirs
and Basutos," *Journal of the Anthropological Institute*, xvi, p. 134.

[6] A. Céresole, *Légendes des Alpes Vaudoises*, p. 188.

[7] Cato, *De re rustica*, lxxxiii, p. 53.

great religions in which bull-gods are most prominent, the divine bull is either expressly identified with the moon, or it is specially associated with those gods who are most unequivocally regarded as moon-gods.   The horns of cattle and the lunar crescent are inter-changeable, and the lunar disc is placed between the horns of the Apis bull or the Hathor cow as between those of the moon-crescent. The horned god, the horned moon, and the horned bull are similarly interchangeable in all Semitic pictography.   The horns of the bull-formed Kretan Zeus were likened to those of the moon.[1]   The assimilation is almost equally prevalent among peoples who keep no cattle, have no agriculture, or only rudimentary cultivation, and who do not use cattle for ploughing.   When Captain Cook first visited the Sandwich Islands, the natives described the European visitors, who wore cocked hats, as being " horned like the moon." [2] The North American Indians assimilated the horns of buffaloes to the crescent of the moon in the same way as did the Semites and the Egyptians.   They represent the disc of the full-moon between the horns of buffalo-skulls ; [3]   and they describe the moon-serpent as ' horned.' [4]   The Akamba of East Africa, when the new moon is not clearly visible, say, according to Dr. Lindblom, that it is only visible "to the horns of cattle." [5]   The expression is somewhat obscure, and may not have been quite correctly understood, but it is clear that they associate the horns of cattle with the lunar crescent.   The Neo-Caledonians represent the lunar disc within a crescent with everted points, assimilated to animal horns, in the same manner as did the ancient Egyptians.[6]   The same assimilation is found in every part of the globe.   Throughout the Lake-dwellings of the bronze and early iron ages, lunar crescents are found, modelled in clay, which vary in form from regular crescents to bull's horns, and angular horns similar in all points to the Kretan ' horns of consecration.' [7]

[1] Moschus, ii, 87 sq.

[2] " Die Sandwich Inseln, einst und jets," *Evangelisches Missions-Magazine*, N.F., 1865, p. 267.

[3] F. W. Putnam, " Symbolism in Ancient American Art," *Proceedings of the American Association for the Advancement of Science, 44th Meeting*, p. 322.

[4] See above, vol. ii, pp. 704, 733.

[5] G. Lindblom, *The Akamba*, p. 337.

[6] Père Lambert, *Moeurs et superstitions des Néo-Calédoniens*, p. 121.

[7] J. Déchelette, " Croissants lacustres et cornes sacrées," *La Revue pré-historique et de paléontologie*, iii (1908), pp. 300 sqq. ; F. Keller, *The Lake Dwellings of Switzerland and other Parts of Europe*, vol. i, pp. 177 sqq., 501 sqq., 567 sq. ; vol. ii, tab. lxxx, lxxxi ; R. Munro, *The Lake Dwellings in Europe*, pp. 17, 45 ; E. Desor, *Die Pfahlbauten des Neuenburger Sees*, p. 82 ; F. Troyon, *Habitations lacustres*, pp. 184, 384 ; R. Paribeni, " Corni di conse-crazione nella prima età del ferro europea," *Bollettino di Paletnologia Italiana*,

Rites of Sexual Licence.

The rites immemorially associated with the multiplication of the tribe's food were, when that food came to be derived chiefly from the cultivation of the soil instead of from hunting, naturally extended to the promotion of the earth's fertility by ritual magic. The belief that the sexual act assists the production of an abundant harvest of the earth's fruits, and is indeed indispensable to secure it, is universal in the lower phases of culture. It might perhaps be supposed that in barbarous communities sexual licence, as a manifestation of exuberance, would tend to accompany agricultural feasts in which men and women joined as in an occasion of rejoicing. But, however that traditional licence may have come to be viewed in later times, it is clear that it was originally regarded with a very different sentiment. Thus among the Pipeles of Central America, on the night of the planting of the seed, certain persons were specially appointed to perform the sexual act at the exact moment when the seed was deposited in the ground.[1] Among the Musquaki Indians it is an old custom that, at the sowing festival, one of the young women is given a husband ; the latter goes out to seek his wife in the fields. Children that are born nine months after the sowing festival are regarded as possessing divine gifts and are accounted great prophets.[2] The magic sexual union of the woman is in this instance regarded as having taken place with a more than mortal husband. The husband is in fact but the representative or medium of a divine spouse who fertilises both the fields and the woman. Among the Peruvians the festival held at the ripening of the ' palta,' or alligator pear, was preceded by a period of severe fasts and abstinence. Men and women then assembled naked, and at a given signal ran a race, and every man had intercourse with the woman he caught.[3] Similar yearly festivals at which sexual licence was unchecked took place in Chili,[4] in Nicaragua,[5] among the tribes of New Mexico,[6] and are

xxx, pp. 304 sqq. ; A. Mosso, *Le origini della civiltà mediterranea*, pp. 268 sq. ; G. A. F. de La Marmora, *Voyage en Sardaigne*, p. 330 ; H. and L. Siret, *Les premiers âges du métal dans le sud-est de l'Espagne*, pp. 8, 58.

[1] H. H. Bancroft, *The Native Races of the Pacific States*, vol. ii, pp. 719 sq. ; cf. vol. iii, p. 507.

[2] M. A. Owen, *Folk-lore of the Musquakie Indians of North America*, p. 51.

[3] J. J. von Tschudi, " Culturhistorische und sprachliche Beiträge zur Kentniss des alten Peru," *Denkschriften der Kaiserliche Akademie der Wissenschaften, Wien. Philosophische-historische Classe*, xxxix, p. 26 ; P. J. de Arriaga, *Extirpacion de la idolatria del Piru*, pp. 36 sq.

[4] R. E. Latcham, " Ethnology of the Araucanos," *Journal of the Royal Anthropological Institute*, xxxix, p. 354.

[5] J. G. Müller, *Die amerikanischen Urreligionen*, p. 663.

[6] H. H. Bancroft, *The Native Races of the Pacific States*, vol. i, pp. 551 sq.

observed by the native tribes of Mexico at the present day.[1] The sacred festivals of Jurupari among the Uaupes and other tribes of the Amazon region are scenes of unrestricted sexual licence in which old and young join without restraint.[2] Among the Choroti every ritual dance is followed by public promiscuity,[3] and similar rites are observed among the Bororo.[4] Among the Patagonians the chief religious festival, or Kamaruko, concludes with a general sexual orgy.[5] Among the tribes of the plains of North America and of the lower Mississippi valley the harvest festivals were attended with general licence, and the old men and women exhorted the younger ones to indulge without restraint.[6]

In Java the husbandmen and their wives secure the fertility of the rice-fields by having sexual intercourse in the midst of them.[7] Throughout the Northern Moluccas and adjacent islands the great religious festival called Poreka takes place at the time of the eastern monsoon to celebrate the union of Grandfather Sun and Grandmother Earth, and the union by which the earth is fertilised is imitated by the people, who have sexual intercourse under the sacred nunu-tree.[8] Among the Dayaks of British North Borneo, at the festival called Bunut by which the fertility of the soil and a plentiful harvest of paddy are secured, general licence takes place lasting exactly a quarter of an hour, after which perfect order and beseemingness are restored. During that time a naked man wanders in and out among the men and women, and each woman touches him as he passes.[9] In the Malay Peninsula, during the rice-harvest the men of the Jakun tribes exchange wives.[10]

---

[1] C. Lumholtz, *Unknown Mexico*, vol. i, p. 352.

[2] H. A. Coudreau, *La France équinoxiale*, vol. ii, p. 190.

[3] E. Nordenskiöld, *Indianerleben*, pp. 86 sqq.

[4] V. Frič and P. Radin, " Contribution to the Study of the Bororo Indians," *Journal of the Anthropological Institute*, xxxvi, p. 390.

[5] Comte H. de La Vaulx, *Voyage en Patagonie*, pp. 143 sq.

[6] A. L. Kroeber, " The Arapaho," *Bulletin of the American Museum of Natural History*, xviii, p. 15 ; Id., " Ethnology of the Gros Ventres," *Anthropological Papers of the American Museum of Natural History*, i, p. 244 ; M. Lewis and W. Clarke, *Travels to the Source of the Missouri River*, vol. i, p. 211 ; J. R. Swanton, *The Tribes of the Lower Mississippi Valley* (*Bureau of American Ethnology, Bulletin No. 43*), p. 121 ; D. Brinton, *Myths of the New World*, p. 159.

[7] G. A. Wilken, *De verspreide geschriften*, vol. iii, p. 41.

[8] J. G. F. Riedel, *De sluik- en kruisharige rassen tusschen Selebes en Papua*, pp. 337, 372 sqq., 410 sq. ; G. W. W. C. Baron von Hoëvell, " Einige weitere Notizen über die Forme der Götterverehrung auf den süd-wester und süd-öster Inseln," *Internationales Archiv für Ethnographie*, viii, p. 134.

[9] H. Ling Roth, *The Natives of Sarawak and British North Borneo*, vol. i, p. 117.

[10] W. W. Skeat and C. O. Blagden, *Pagan Races of the Malay Peninsula*, vol. ii, p. 70 ; cf. pp. 76, 145.

Throughout India the sexual licence which marks the agricultural festivals is a well-known feature, not perhaps because it is more prevalent there than elsewhere, but because our information is fuller. The Holi festival, which is celebrated in every part of Hindustan in honour of the goddess Vasanti is an occasion on which " the most licentious debauchery and disorder reign throughout every class of society. It is the regular Saturnalia of India. Persons of the greatest respectability, without regard to rank or age, are not ashamed to take part in the orgies which mark this season of the year." [1] Phallic emblems operated mechanically are carried, and the loves of the gods are represented in ' tableaux vivants ' on stages and chariots. In ancient times the festival was called Basantotsava, and the noblest princesses danced in public in honour of the god of love.[2] The original intention of the carnival, says Mr. Crooke, is to promote the fertility of man, animals, and crops.[3] In Chota Nagpur, among the Hos, the harvest is the signal for general licence, and such licence is looked upon as a matter of absolute necessity. Men set aside all conventions and women all modesty, and complete liberty is given to the girls.[4] In Orissa, among the Bhuiyas, during the spring festival called Magh Porai, "all respect for blood relations and husbands is set at nought."[5] The Parganait, a caste of husbandmen in the Rājmahāl Hills, have a great yearly agricultural festival, called Sohrai, at which the unmarried of both sexes indulge in promiscuous sexual intercourse.[6] In Jeypore promiscuity and changes of partners last for a month at the new year festival of the Punjas.[7] The Kotas of the Nilgiri Hills have a similar festival of continuous licentiousness.[8] In Assam spring festivals are observed by all the tribes, and women are allowed complete freedom without "any stain, blemish, or loss of reputation."[9] Similar

[1] L. Rousselet, *India and its Native Princes*, p. 173.

[2] J. Campbell Oman, *The Brahmans, Theists, and Muslims of India*, pp. 241 sqq.

[3] W. W. Crooke, "The Holi : a Vernal Festival of the Hindus," *Folk-lore*, xxv, p. 83 ; Id., *Introduction to the Popular Religion and Folklore of Northern India*, vol. ii, pp. 314 sqq. Cf. S. M. Natesa Sastri, *Hindu Feasts, Fasts and Ceremonies*, pp. 44 sq. ; J. E. Padfield, *The Hindu at Home*, p. 152.

[4] E. T. Dalton, *Descriptive Ethnology of Bengal*, pp. 196 sq.

[5] D. A. Macmillan, " The Bhuiyas," *Calcutta Review*, ciii, p. 188.

[6] *Imperial Gazetteer of India*, vol. xxii, p. 68.

[7] J. Shortt, *The Hill Ranges of Southern India*, vol. iii, pp. 11 sq. ; Id., " Contributions to the Ethnology of Jeypore," *Transactions of the Ethnological Society*, N.S., vi, p. 269.

[8] Id. " Account of the Hill Tribes of the Neilgherries," *Transactions of the Ethnological Society*, N.S., vii, p. 282.

[9] J. Butler, *Travels and Adventures in the Provinces of Assam*, pp. 226 sq. Cf. F. Hahn, " Some Notes on the Religion and Superstition of the Oraos,"

festivals are observed in Khondistan,[1] among the wild tribes of Manipur[2] and of northern Burma.[3] Unseasonable showers are usually set down by wiseacres in India to the circumstance that too many marriages have taken place.[4]

In Ashanti the yam festival is the chief religious function of the year, and is celebrated with great pomp and many sacrifices. It takes place just after the maturity of the vegetable, which may not be eaten until after the conclusion of the feast. Another similar festival is held at the time when it is planted. The yam-custom, says Bowdich, " is like a Saturnalia ; the grossest liberty prevails, and each sex abandons itself to its passions."[5] It was formerly a custom with the Yoruba, who guard their daughters with the utmost strictness and at ordinary times .do not allow them to speak to a man save in the presence of their mother, to give the girls full freedom to attend the harvest in the company of a boy and his friends.[6] The harvest is celebrated with similar festivals of sexual licence in the Cameroons,[7] in the Congo,[8] in British Central Africa,[9] among the Kaffirs and the Hottentots,[10] and in fact among Bantu peoples in every part of Africa. " Their harvest festivals." says the Rev. H. Rowley, " are akin in character to the feasts of Bacchus. It is impossible to witness them without being ashamed. Men and women, who in ordinary circumstances are modest in behaviour and speech, then abandon themselves to licentiousness."[11] The festivals attending the circumcision of young men are so timed as to coincide with the harvest.[12] Not only is

Journal of the Asiatic Society of Bengal, lxxii, 3, p. 12 ; H. Kausch and Ferd. Hahn, *Fünfzig Bilder aus der gossnerscher Kols-Mission*, pp. 92, 99 ; T. C. Hodson, " The ' Genna ' amongst the Tribes of Assam," *Journal of the Anthropological Institute*, xxxvi, p. 94.

[1] J. Campbell, *A Personal Narrative of Thirteen Years' Service amongst the Wild Tribes of Khondistan*, pp. 52 sq.

[2] T. C. Hodson, *The Naga Tribes of Manipur*, p. 168.

[3] J. A. Anderson, *Report of an Expedition to Northern Yaman*, p. 123.

[1] W. Crooke, *The Popular Religion and Folk-lore of Northern India*, vol. i, p. 109.

[5] T. E. Bowdich, *Narrative of a Mission from Cape Coast Castle to Ashantee*, p. 226 ; A. B. Ellis, *The Ewe-speaking Peoples of the Gold Coast*, pp. 229 sq.

[6] S. and O. Johnson, *The History of the Yoruba*, p. 102. The Rev. S. Johnson says that misconduct was rare on those occasions. That may, of course, have been the case in later times, but it is unlikely that it was the original intention.

[7] P. A. Talbot, *In the Shadow of the Bush*, pp. 74, 78.

[8] G. Bentley, *Pioneering in the Congo*, vol. i, p. 283.

[9] H. H. Johnston, *British Central Africa*, p. 408 ; Duff Macdonald, *Africana*, vol. i, pp. 119, 126, 173.

[10] G. Fritsch, *Die Eingeborenen Süd-Afrika's*, p. 328.

[11] H. Rowley, *Africa Unveiled*, p. 165.

[12] D. Kidd, *The Essential Kafir*, p. 207.

full sexual licence permitted to the neophytes, and indeed in most
cases enjoined, but any visitor attending the festivals is encouraged to indulge in licentiousness. " Prostitution is freely
indulged in, and adultery is not viewed with any sense of heinousness on account of the surroundings. No man attending the
festival is allowed to have intercourse with his wife." [1]

In Morocco and North Africa the most solemn religious feasts
are made occasions for sexual licence and prostitution.[2] In the
region inhabited by the Walad 'Abdi tribe the women lead the
most dissolute life ; they are constantly divorcing their husbands,
and in the interval between one marriage and another, are common
prostitutes, though continuing to dwell in the midst of their
families. The French authorities have repeatedly attempted to
put a stop to these scandalous disorders, but they have met with
fanatical opposition on the part of the agricultural population, who
allege that such a state of things is necessary in order to obtain
an abundance of crops.[3]

The same practices were observed by the ancient Germans,
and the peasants in the southern districts of Holland regard them
at the present day as necessary to fertilise their fields. They
employ the same means which are adopted by the husbandmen
in Java.[4] The method of imparting fertility to the fields was
probably usual among the ancient populations of the Aegean, for
there can be little doubt that the myth of Demeter and Iason, who
are described as securing the fruitfulness of the ploughed fields of
Krete in the same manner as the Dutch peasants,[5] represents a similar
practice or ritual.

Festivals of promiscuity, or of general relaxation of sexual moral
codes, reminiscent of such promiscuity, have survived in most
countries in relation to what originally were agricultural festivals
to evoke the magic powers of fertility. The Roman Saturnalia
were the feasts of sowing, and there is every reason to believe
that in earlier times the general relaxation of ordinary decorum

[1] C. A. Wheelright, " Native Circumcision Lodges in the Zoutpansberg
District," *Journal of the Anthropological Institute*, xxxv, pp. 254 sq. ; C. T.
Nauhaus, "Familienleben, Heirathsgebraüche und Erbrecht der Kaffern,"
Verhandlungen der Berliner Gessellschaft für Anthropologie, 1882, p. 205.

[2] A. Mouliéras, *Le Maroc inconnu*, vol. ii, pp. 14 sq., 18 sq., 20, 30 ; Id.,
Une tribu Zénète Anti-Musulmane au Maroc, pp. 100, 102 ; G. Salmon,
" Les Bd'âd'ona," *Archives Marocaines*, ii, p. 362 ; Leo Africanus, in Ramusio,
Navigationi et Viaggi, vol. i, fol. 61.

[3] E. Doutté, *La société musulmane du Maghreb. Magie et religion dans
l'Afrique du Nord*, pp. 560 sq.

[4] G. W. W. C. van Hoëvell, " Einige weitere Notizen über die Forme
der Götterverehrung auf den süd-wester und süd-öster Inseln," *Internationales
Archiv für Ethnographie*, viii, p. 134 n.

[5] Hesiod, *Theogonia*, 969.

and the freedom granted even to slaves included, as in other similar festivals, the suspension of sexual codes and general promiscuity.[1] The Carnival is the old licence festival. May-Day celebrations were denounced by the English Puritans as being occasions for general licence. "I have heard it credibly reported," one of them writes, "by men of great gravity and reputation, that of fortie, threescore, or a hundred maides going to the wood over night, there have scarcely the third part of them returned home undefiled."[2] In Russia promiscuity took place as late as the sixteenth century at the festivals of Midsummer Day and Christmas.[3] Church festivals involving scenes of riot and indecency abounded in Europe up to late times. The 'Fête des Fous,' during which general licence took place among both priests and laymen, persisted in France until the seventeenth century.[4] The licentious character which marked the cults of the Great Mothers throughout Mediterranean countries appears to have survived in some parts of Italy down to the present day. Alphonso de Liguori declares that the great festivals of the Holy Virgin in some country districts, such as Montevergine, are utterly profaned "with dances, excesses, and immodest conduct." He warns all good Christians to abstain from attending those festivals of the Church. "I entreat the clients of Mary," he says, "to keep away as much as possible from such sanctuaries during festivals, and also, as far as possible, to prevent others from going there; for on such occasions the Devil gains more profit than the Blessed Virgin derives honour from it."[5]

Rites of sexual licence among savages are not by any means confined to promoting the fertility of nature by imitative magic. In many instances it is clear that such is not the object in view. Among the North American Indians almost every religious occasion was attended with ritual promiscuity. If a chief was ill, some young girls were chosen to perform the sacred rites of promiscuity. Young women vied for the honour of being chosen and were filled with pride in consequence.[6] The Patagonians, when they are in distress and dogged by misfortune, send their wives into the forest, and require them to give themselves to the first man who happens

---

[1] See J. G. Frazer, *The Golden Bough*, vol. ii, pp. 311 sqq.; J. J. Bachofen, *Die Sage von Tanaquil*, pp. 133 sqq.

[2] P. Stubbes, *The Anatomie of Abuses*, p. 149.

[3] M. Kovalewski, *Modern Customs and Ancient Laws of Russia*, pp. 6 sqq.

[4] A. Dulaure, *Les divinités génératrices*, pp. 315 sqq.; J. Brand, *Observations on Popular Antiquities*, vol. i, pp. 36, 66.

[5] Alphonso de Liguori, *The Glories of Mary*, p. 516. Cf. below, p. 219.

[6] *Jesuit Relations and Allied Documents*, vol. vii, pp. 147 sq.; vol. xxxiv, p. 106; vol. xlviii, p. 269; vol. liv, p. 36; cf. vol. xv, p. 170; vol. xxxix, p. 122.

to pass by.[1] Similarly, the Australian natives, when terrified by the appearance of an aurora australis, which they take to be a host of angry spirits advancing to destroy them, or when threatened with an epidemic, give themselves up to general promiscuity, hoping thereby to pacify and conciliate the gods.[2]

Similar ideas were familiar to the Greeks of the luxurious colony of Lokria in Magna Grecia. When they were hard pressed by the Rhegians they vowed that, if they should be saved from defeat, they would expose their women for sacred prostitution in the temple of Aphrodite. Having secured the victory they, however, neglected to fulfil their vow. On a subsequent occasion, when again the fortune of war seemed to go against them in their contest with the Lucanians, it was decided in council, at the suggestion of Dionysios, that they should send their wives and daughters, arrayed in their richest apparel, to the temple of Aphrodite, and that one hundred of the women should be selected by lot. These were to spend one month in the public brothels of the city ; but, at the same time, all Lokrian men were to bind themselves solemnly not to enter those places during that time. As it turned out this was merely a fraudulent artifice of the tyrant Dionysios who with his men-at-arms, when the women assembled at the temple of Aphrodite, took occasion to rob them of their jewels.[3] The account is of all the more interest because such a proceeding was evidently obsolete, and so opposed to existing sentiments that the Lokrians could not bring themselves to carry it out ; after on one occasion neglecting to fulfil their vow, they evaded, on the other occasion, by a subterfuge, the actual prostitution of their women. The principle that the anger of the gods might be averted by promiscuous sexual intercourse was, however, as clearly recognised by them as by the savages of Patagonia and of Australia ; and the practice which was then opposed to Greek sentiment must clearly have been, in more ancient times, an actual custom with the Lokrians, and, since we can hardly suppose them to have been singular in this respect, with the Greeks in general.

Why should the removal of all tabus on sexual relations, and indulgence in unrestricted promiscuity be regarded as pleasant to the gods, who are generally credited with having imposed those very restrictions ?   The reason is, I think, plain when those usages

---

[1] T. Falkner, *A Description of Patagonia*, p. 126.
[2] A. W. Howitt, *The Native Tribes of South-East Australia*, p. 277 ; L. Fison and A. W. Howitt, *Kamilaroi and Kurnai*, p. 290 ; Id., " The Jereail, or Initiation Ceremonies of the Kurnai Tribe," *Journal of the Anthropological Institute*, xiv, p. 353.
[3] Justin, *Historiae Philippicae,* xxi. 3.

are considered in correlation with other facts. By the removal of personal claims to individual women, the latter are, as it were, offered to whomsoever it may please to take them, and therefore to the god or gods, who are given the same opportunity as any other person. The Patagonians, no doubt, argue that the first stranger who comes upon the woman in the forest is no other than the angry god himself, for the woman being once offered in that manner, the god is then at liberty to come and claim her if he wishes. In an Indian tale a king whose wife was barren sent her into the street in much the same way as is done by the Patagonians ; the first person she met was no other than the god Vishnu, disguised as a Brahman priest. Her fertility was, of course, at once restored by the divine stranger.[1] In many of the rites of sacred prostitution among uncultured peoples and in the ancient world, the man who is invited to take advantage of them is expressly described as a 'stranger.' To the primitive mind there is always a possibility that a stranger may be a god in disguise, and that when the stranger is honoured, a god has been entertained unawares. When a woman, instead of reserving her favours for a man of her own choice or for her husband, gives herself indiscriminately to the first man she may happen to meet, that surrender to the decision of chance is tantamount to an invitation to the god to avail himself of the offer and to present himself in the form of the unknown stranger. If he does not do so, that is his fault ; he has been given the opportunity. We are indeed expressly told in some instances that every man taking part in rites of promiscuity is the avatar of the god. The rites known as Sakti-puja are practised by most Brahmans and by about three-fourths of the Hindu population of Bengal. A number of couples meet in the middle of the night. The goddess Sakti is represented by a nude woman adorned with jewels, and is worshipped with strange ceremonies. A banquet takes place, and is followed by promiscuous intercourse, " all distinctions of caste, rank, and kindred being temporarily suspended. During their orgiastic religious rites, every man present is, according to their pantheistic notions, Siva himself, and every woman there none other than Siva's consort."[2]

It was thought by earlier anthropologists that rites of promiscuity were an atonement for the breach of primitive communal rights by the appropriation of women in individual

[1] *The Jātaka, or Stories of the Buddha's former Births*, translated from the Pâli, under the editorship of E. B. Cowell, vol. v, p. 141.

[2] J. C. Oman, *The Brahmans, Theists, and Muslims of India*, pp. 26 sqq. Cf. W. Ward, *A View of the History, Literature, and Religions of the Hindus*, pp. 152 sq., 232 sqq. ; J. A. Dubois, *Hindu Manners, Customs and Ceremonies*, vol. i, p. 288.

marriage. That view is now generally discredited. Those practices, nevertheless, essentially consist in a surrender of individual
rights ; but that surrender is made not so much in view of the
rights of other men as in view of the rights of the gods. Sacred
prostitution is, in fact, the equivalent of a propitiatory and piatory
sacrifice. To primitive man the necessaries and good things of
life are food and women. He naturally regards the gods as having
the same needs as himself ; he offers food to them in the form
of sacrifice and women in the form of sacred prostitution. A portion
of his food must be surrendered to the gods in order that they
may not be jealous and envious ; a portion of his claims over
women must in like manner be surrendered to the gods.

The sacrifice is, however, not only due to the gods and offered
to them in order to propitiate them ; it is essentially a necessity
because the generative powers of women and their special powers
and functions proceed from the gods. The deity is the real giver
of children as well as of food. Women not only belong to the god
by right, he being, as we have seen, their real husband, but the
functions of women cannot be properly exercised without that
sacred union, however mystically effected.

The operation of the divine generative power which brings
about the fertility of nature, of animals, of women, is believed to
be stimulated not only by sexual intercourse, but also by any act
or speech of a lascivious and sensual character. In the primitive rites
of fertility we do not come upon free love and sexual promiscuity
only ; even where that is absent, even where the rites are carried
out by women alone, and men are, as is so often the case,
excluded, those rites are invariably characterised by what to us
is indecency and obscenity. All the primitive magic ceremonies
of women are indelicate. The rain-making ceremonies of the
Baronga women, which no man is permitted to witness, are, says
the Rev. H. Junod, marked throughout by a sensual character ; their
dances are lascivious and the obscenity of their songs is revolting.[1]
Against the rites of the various women's societies in the Congo
the same charge is repeatedly brought. Nothing can exceed
their obscenity ; the rites are performed by the women naked,
and it is even said that masturbation regularly takes place.[2]
In the Loyalty Islands the women have their separate dances to
which men are not admitted ; and they are marked by " a licence
equalling anything of the kind ever manifested in the mysteries
of the Bona Dea." [3] Dayak shamanesses in the course of their

---

[1] See above, p. 13.
[2] R. P. Colle, Les Baluba, vol. ii, p. 619.
[3] V. de Rochas, " Îles Loyalty," Bulletin de la Société de Géographie,
4ᵉ Série, xx, p. 25.

incantations and hypnotic trances make ribald jests.[1] The rites
of the women of barbarian Europe were marked by the same indelicate character. The Flemish women, in rites which were
probably those of the great goddess Freija, were semi-naked, and
the whole proceedings were denounced by Christian priests as
scandalous.[2] In Russia, in Bohemia, the women, even in Christian
times, performed their heathen ceremonies in their shifts.[3] The
rites of the Gaulish women were equally immodest.[4] British
priestesses danced naked painted with woad.[5] The Godiva procession in Coventry refers, no doubt, to an ancient ritual which
has many parallels.[6] In India the great Pongol festival, which
is probably in its origin agricultural, is characterised by the
indecency of the officiating women.[7] At the Vedic sacrifice of
the horse, not only did the queen go through the ritual of
symbolic union with the animal, but obscene jests were exchanged between the priests and the attendant women.[8] The
same usages obtained among the ancient populations of Italy.
The term ' Fescennine jests ' which is frequently used in reference
to that ritual ribaldry comes from the name of the Etruscan city
Fescennium, and we are told by Horace that those religious
obscenities of speech were used in the course of ceremonies connected with the harvest festival.[9] In ancient Egypt the women
carried phallic images operated by strings,[10] as is still done in West
Africa and the Congo.[11] When they proceeded to Bubastis for the
great corn festival, they exchanged obscene jests with all the
women they met, and repeated the gesture of Baubo which made
Demeter laugh.[12] The practice appears to have survived in Egypt
until the present day, or at least a very few years since, for I
myself witnessed it. It was the invariable custom at the more
respectable Egyptian weddings for a man on horseback to head the

[1] I. H. N. Evans, " Notes on Some Beliefs and Customs of the Orang
Dusu of British North Borneo," *Journal of the Royal Anthropological Institute*,
xlvii, p. 158.

[2] See above, p. 65.

[3] See above, vol. ii, 562.

[4] A. de Nore, *Coutumes, mythes et traditions des provinces de France*, p. 131.

[5] Pliny, *Nat. Hist.*, xxii. 1.

[6] See E. S. Hartland, *The Science of Fairy Tales*, pp. 71 sqq.

[7] J. A. Dubois, *Hindu Manners, Customs and Ceremonies*, vol. ii, p. 581.

[8] *Satapatha-Brâhmana*, xiii. 2. 9. 6-9 (*The Sacred Books of the East*, vol.
xliv, pp. 325 sq.).

[9] Horace, *Epistolae*, ii. i. 148. Cf. Servius, on *Aeneid*, vii.

[10] Herodotus, ii. 48.

[11] L. De Grandpré, *Voyage à la côte occidentale de l'Afrique*, vol. i, p. 118;
A. B. Ellis, *The Ewe-speaking Peoples of the Slave Coast*, p. 44 ; Id., *The
Yoruba-speaking Peoples of the Slave Coast*, p. 65.

[12] Herodotus, ii. 60.

procession adorned with a phallus about two feet long, which he waved about to the delight of all beholders.[1]

Those are not the depravities of savages, of barbarians, or of sensual Orientals. Athenian women of the most noble families were under the religious obligation to exchange Fescennine jests at the Thesmophoria; they carried phallic images, and that obscenity was an essential part of the ritual.[2] Roman matrons in their special women's rites at the feast of the Bona Dea did the same;[3] and those obscene utterances and phallic emblems formed part of the cult of Vesta, the patroness of matronly virtue.[4] With the Roman matrons the immodest character of the rituals was reduced to a minimum; the obscenities which are loudly chanted by African women were whispered by the Roman women in one another's ears. The ritual importance of the act is thereby emphasised. The obscenity is no more a gratuitous manifestation of depravity in Africa than it was in Rome. We are expressly told by Dr. Nassau, who gives an unsparing account of the indecency of the proceedings in the women's sacred rites in West Africa, that as soon as they are over the behaviour of the women leaves nothing to be desired in point of perfect modesty of bearing and conduct.[5] Traces of the belief in the efficacy of obscene words in religious functions survive to this day in Christian countries. Thus among the Portuguese population of Brazil at the feast of the Holy Virgin, the women have a dance in which they sing: "Eu cago fogo! Donna Maria quer lamber."[6]

The lasciviousness which characterises women's rites in every part of the world is regarded as necessary for the success of those rites and has a definite object. Like ritual sexual intercourse it is thought to stimulate the generative powers of nature. "Some gods," says Porphyry, "are subject to passions, and for this reason, they say, phalli set up to these latter, and obscene phrases are used."[7] So among the Kochs of Bengal, the god "is pleased to see nude women dancing before him, and to hear obscene songs, in consideration of which he sends rain and a good harvest."[8] "I have seen," says the Rev. F. Metz, "the most indelicate

[1] Cf. J. L. Burckhardt, Arabic Proverbs, p. 138.

[2] Apollodorus, i. 5. 1; Homeric Hymn to Demeter, 203 sqq.; Diodorus Siculus, v. 4. Cf. Euripides, Bakchai, 225, Ion, 533 sq.

[3] Plutarch, Caesar, ix; Cicero, Ad Att., xv. 25. Cf. Juvenal, ii. 83; vi. 314 sqq.

[4] See above, p. 18.

[5] R. H. Nassau, Fetichism in West Africa, pp. 260 sq.

[6] K. von den Steiner, Unter den Naturvölkern Zentral-Brasiliens, p. 561.

[7] Porphyry, in Eusebius, Praeparatio Evangelica, v. 10. 199.

[8] W. Crooke, "Nudity in India, in Custom and Ritual," Journal of the Royal Anthropological Institute, xlix, p. 247.

performances in the shape of dances or theatrical pieces in front of the Badago temples, and on bearing witness to their wickedness have been told that the god delighted in them " [1] Marco Polo was told that misfortunes were due to the god being angry owing to his having quarrelled with his wives, but that when lascivious dances were performed before him, he had connection with his wives and became well disposed.[2] According to St. Cyril of Jerusalem, the Manichaens regarded rain as the effect of amatory excitement on the part of the Deity.[3]

All religion, not only in its crude and primitive phases, but in its highly developed forms in the great civilisations of India, of Babylon, of Egypt, of Greece, is pervaded with conceptions, symbols and practices which, in our modern European view, appear the very reverse of religious and holy. It is permeated with indecency and sensuality. The charge constantly reiterated by the Christian Fathers that all heathen religions were impure is, it must be admitted, not unjustified ; the whole subject is indelicate. That fact is commonly expressed by saying that the generative powers of nature have everywhere been the object of worship. But the statement is rendered unsatisfactory by the obscurity attaching to the latter term. The word ' worship ' does not express the rationale or motive of any primitive religious phenomenon ; the objects of primitive cults are not such by virtue of their being worshipful, but by virtue of the practical utilities or dangers that are supposed to derive from them. To say that primitive man ' worshipped the generative powers of nature,' is little more than a phrase destitute of applicable meaning ; for the notion of worship is as unknown to the primitive mind as is the abstract conception of ' the generative powers of nature.' To acquire a meaning the phrase must be translated into terms of concrete and functional purposes. And the explanation of the sensual and sexual character of religious rites lies in the notion that every function of woman, whether as mother, as wife, as supplier of food, as cultivator of the soil, as sorceress, witch, prophetess, or priestess, postulates her union with the god who is the bestower of those powers. The indecency so conspicuous as a feature of all heathen religions has everywhere reference to that union, in some form or other, of women with divine beings. The union of men with goddesses plays virtually no part in those conceptions and practices.[4] It is to women that the sacred marriage with the

---

[1] F. Metz, *The Tribes inhabiting the Neilgherry Hills, their Social Culture and Religious Rites*, p. 61.

[2] *The Book of Ser Marco Polo*, vol. ii, pp. 345 sq.

[3] St. Cyril of Jerusalem, *Cateclesis* VI, xxxiv, in Migne, *Patrologiae Cursus Completus, Series Graeca*, vol. xxxiii, col. 600.

[4] In the cults of Western Asia, as in those of many uncultured peoples,

Divine Bridegroom is a functional necessity ; men do not require
to be united with a divine bride in order to fulfil their functions
But every religion, from the most primitive to the highest, is pervaded with the idea that union with a god, a ' hieros gamos,' or
' Holy Matrimony,' is a necessity to every woman.

The character which marks the religious rituals of women in
early society appertains equally to all magical operations carried
out by women. It is a universal rule that a witch, in order to perform her incantations effectually, must divest herself of all clothing.
In ancient Greece and Italy witches stripped when performing
their magical operations.[1] We have seen that one of the most
constant features of rain-making ceremonies, even in the forms
which have survived in modern Europe, is the nudity of the performers.[2] In Italy, when girls consult the cards in order to gain
information concerning the success of their love-affairs, they are
in the habit of stripping naked.[3] In mediaeval Europe a witch
proceeding to the Sabbath gathering stripped herself naked. A
picture, now in the Vienna Museum, represents witches, both
young and old, in the act of preparing themselves for the Sabbath, and divesting themselves of their clothes.[4] Nudity is
regarded as a requirement for the successful performance of an

male prostitutes are found as well as hierodules (E. Schrader, *Die Keilinschriften und das Alte Testament*, pp. 422 sq. ; Lucian, *Lucius*, xxxviii ;
Jerome, *In Osee*, i. 4. 14 ; *Deuteronomy*, xxiii. 17 ; *I Kings*, xiv. 24., xv. 12.,
xxii. 46 ; *II Kings*, xxiii. 7 ; *Job*, xxxvi. 14 ; *The Laws of Hammurabi*, 187).
The men are assimilated to women, and that sacred sodomy is but part
of the elaborate mimicry of femininity, which goes so far as to counterfeit
parturition and to give rise to emasculation, which characterises the male
priest of goddesses. Among the Chukchi, a male shaman not only dresses
as a woman, but is married to a husband (W. Bogoras, *The Chukchee*, p. 452).
Similar practices are found in every part of the world. It appears to me
extremely probable that the prevalence of homosexual vice in Western Asia
and in Greece owes its origin chiefly to the immemorial mimicry of the female
sex by male priests and male hierodules. The adoption of women's priestly
functions by men may have thus been one of the chief factors in developing
unnatural vices.

   [1] Pliny, *Nat. Hist.*, xxviii. 7. 23 ; Vergil, *Aeneid*, iv. 518 ; E. Riess, art.
" Aberglaube," in Pauly-Wissowa, *Real-Encyclopädie der classischen Altertumswissenschaft*, vol. i, p. 35 ; R. Heim, *Incantamenta magica graeca latina*,
p. 507 ; E. Gerhard, *Gesammelte akademische Abhandlungen*, vol. iii, p. 8 ;
L. Deubner, *De incubatione*, p. 26 ; O. Jahn, " Über den Aberglauben des
bösen Blicks bei den Alten," *Berichte über Verhandlungen der Königlich
Sächsischen Gesellschaft der Wissenschaften. Phil.-hist. Classe*, vii, p. 80 sqq.,
93 sqq. ; C. Daremberg and E. Saglio, *Dictionnaire des antiquités grecques et
romaines*, vol. iii, p. 1515.

   [2] See above, pp. 12 sq.

   [3] C. G. Leland, *Etruscan and Roman Remains in Popular Tradition*,
pp. 148, 301.

   [4] The picture is by F. Francken, and is reproduced in Ploss-Bartels, *Das
Weib*, vol. ii, p. 690.

incantation in India,[1] in Africa.[2] By an extension of the rule even men are supposed to strip in order to perform successfully an act of powerful witchcraft. A Kikuyu man, on being required to strip for the performance of a particular task, objected on the ground that he would be suspected of being engaged in the practice of witchcraft. If he retained his clothing, he argued, people would say, " No, he cannot be a witch because he is dressed." [3] The nudity which is thus universally regarded as indispensable in the practice of the magic arts of witchcraft has the same object as the nudity and lasciviousness of women's religious rituals and mysteries. All powers of magic, as well as of prophecy and religious inter-cession, possessed by women postulate the union of the woman exercising those powers with a supernatural being or god ; and the union is primitively thought of as actual sexual intercourse with the god. Where that inspiring spirit is located in some sacred fetich object, that fetich is the husband of the fetich-woman. A Chukchi shamaness whose spirit was located in a fetich-stone called the stone her real husband, although she had also a human husband. Nor did she use the expression in a purely figurative sense ; she asserted that her children had been conceived by her from the stone.[4] In mediaeval Europe, witches were universally regarded as having given themselves body and soul to Satan, and as being his paramours. " It pleaseth their new maister often times," says an old writer, " to offer himself familiarly unto them, to dally and lye with them, in token of their more neere conjunction, and, as it were, marriage unto him." [5] And, in fact, all witches actually believed that they had intercourse with the superhuman power whence they derived their faculties. At the Sabbath they had carnal intercourse with him, sometimes in human form, sometimes in the form of a goat, and witch-children were pointed out as the offspring of such unions. Satan is, of course, the homologue of gods in older religions, and the union of the witch with him was in its original form the mystic union of the priestess with a god. " In studying the cult of the witches," says Miss Murray, " plain and irrefragable proof is found that the person-age called by Christian writers ' the Devil ' was considered by the witches themselves to be God incarnate as a man." [6]

[1] W. Crooke, The Popular Religion and Folk-lore of Northern India, vol. i, p. 69.

[2] R. H. Nassau, Fetichism in West Africa, p. 279.

[3] R. E. Dennett, At the Back of the Black Man's Mind, p. 149. Cf. W. Bogoras, The Chukchee, p. 448.

[4] W. Bogoras, The Chukchee, p. 344.

[5] T. Cooper, Mystery of Witchcraft, p. 22. Cf. P. De Lancre, Tableau de l'inconstance des mauvais anges et des démons, p. 233.

[6] M. A. Murray, " Child-sacrifice among European Witches," Man, xviii, p. 60. Cf. Id., The Witch-cult of Western Europe, pp. 31 sqq.

Holy Matrimony of Priestesses and Queens.

That union with the Divine Bridegroom, sacramentally celebrated, forms the central ritual in many religious ceremonies. The
high-priestess, or the queen, celebrates, as representative of all
womankind, the sacred union with the god. That holy matrimony
was, we have seen, celebrated by the queen in ancient India by her
union with the god in theriomorphic form ; this was followed by
her union with the sacrificing king.[1] In modern India, during the
feast of the Juggernaut, a young woman is conducted in triumph
to the temple of the god ; she is solemnly married to him, and the
marriage is consummated during the night, an abundant harvest
being thereby insured.[2] In ancient Scandinavia the same ritual
was performed as on the banks of the Ganges. The priestess of
the god Freijr, after following him while he was drawn in a wagon
through the land, lay with him or his representative in the temple
of Upsala.[3] The Arapahos of Colorado celebrated the most
solemn ceremony of their religion in a great lodge built for the
purpose. After long and intense ascetic preparations, purifications and fastings, the hierophant and the high-priestess retired
at midnight amid the solemn and tense silence of the worshippers.
When they returned the hierophant announced : " I have returned,
having performed the holy act which was commanded." In later
times the union of the priest, who was regarded as representing
' the Man above,' with the priestess was not actually consummated ; but the woman, with a quick movement, threw her
blanket on the ground, and fell, exposing her body to the moon.[4]
Perhaps the latter form of the rite, attenuated in deference to
European ideas, is an even closer approximation to the original
conception which gave rise to it than the ritual union with the
priest. In Babylon the holy matrimony was consummated in the
Holy of Holies of the temple of Baal, the woman being a princess
of the royal blood, and possibly the queen herself.[5] At the present
day, in Irak, when there has been a long drought, the Christian
peasants dress up a figure in woman's clothes. She is placed in
the middle of the field, and is called ' the Bride of God.' [6] The

---

[1] *Satapatha-Brâhmana,* xiii. 4. 1. 9.

[2] Delaflotte, *Essais historiques sur l'Inde,* p. 218.

[3] J. Grimm, *Deutsche Mythologie,* p. 176 ; E. H. Meyer, *Mythologie der
Germanen,* pp. 366 sq.

[4] G. A. Dorsey, " The Arapaho Sun-Dance," *Field Columbian Museum
Publication* 75, Anthropological Series, vol. iv, pp. 173 sqq.

[5] Herodotus, i. 181 sq.

[6] S. I. Curtiss, *Primitive Semitic Religion To-day,* p. 114. The same ritual
is observed by the Muslim peasants (A. Jausser, *Coutumes des Arabes au
Pays de Moab,* p. 328).

queen of Egypt observed the same ritual, and her chief title was 'Divine Spouse of Rā,' originally, in all probability, of Osiris or Horus. Herodotus says that at Thebes a woman slept in the temple of the god as his wife, and was said to have intercourse with him in human form.[1] As the marriage of the queen to the god is mentioned in numerous Egyptian texts, it is probable that the holy matrimony to which Herodotus refers was that of the queen herself. " In the same manner also the priestess who utters the oracles at Patarai in Lykia, when the god is there, for there is not an oracle there at all times, is shut up during the night in the temple with the god." [2] The holy matrimony was celebrated at Athens also, the queen, represented by the Queen Archon, being solemnly wedded to Dionysos.[3] The holy sacrament of matrimony constituted the central feature of the ritual in the Mysteries of Eleusis. We are told of " the underground chamber and the solemn meeting of the hierophant and the priestess, each with the other alone, when the torches are extinguished, and the vast crowd believes that its salvation depends on what goes on there." [4]

The priestess of a god is the wife of the god. Her special consecration to his service consists in her marriage to him, and the magical and oracular powers which she wields are derived from her union with the god. It is improbable that the marriage of priestesses to the god originally implied chastity ; commonly they are free from such an obligation. Among the Tshi-speaking peoples of the Gold Coast, for instance, priestesses are never married, for " a priestess belongs to the god she serves, and therefore cannot become the property of a man." But " this prohibition extends to marriage only, and a priestess is not debarred from sexual commerce." Priestesses are, on the contrary, " most licentious, and custom allows them to gratify their passions with any man who may chance to take their fancy. A priestess who is favourably impressed by a man sends for him to her house, and this command he is sure to obey, through fear of the consequences of her anger. She then tells him that the god she serves

---

[1] Herodotus, i. 182.

[2] *Ibid.*

[3] See above, p. 193.

[4] Asterius Amasenus, *Encomium in sanctos martyres*, in Migne, *Patrologiae Cursus Completus, Series Graeca*, vol. xl, col. 324. Cf. Tertullian, *Ad nationes*, ii. 7 ; Hippolytus, *Refutatio omnium haeresium*, v. 8 ; Psellus, *Queanam sunt Graecorum opiniones de daemonibus*, p. 39 ; Scholiast on Plato, *Gorgias*, 497c ; P.Foucart, *Recherches sur l'origine et la nature des mystères d'Éleusis*, pp. 48 sq. ; J. E. Harrison, *Prolegomena to the Study of Greek Religion*, pp. 549 sq. ; J. G. Frazer, *The Golden Bough*, vol. ii, pp. 138 sqq. ; L. R. Farnell, *The Cults of the Greek States*, vol. iii, p. 176.

has directed her to love him. . . . Some priestesses have as many as half a dozen men in their train at one time, and may, on great occasions, be seen walking in state followed by them." Priests, on the other hand, marry like other men. They are said to be licentious, " but social considerations oblige them to be so less openly than the priestesses." [1] The priestesses of Bel-Marduk in Babylon, who were called " the brides of the god," [2] commonly had numerous children.[3] In India the priestesses of Siva and of Vishnu are called the " wives of the gods." [4] Nautch girls, or Bayaderes, are also regarded as being married to the god, and their consecration is celebrated with the same ceremonies as a marriage. They are of two classes, the ' thassis ' and the ' vashis '; the former, like the priestesses in ancient Babylon and Egypt, belong to the highest castes; they are sometimes spoken of as Begum, or ' noble dames,' and Indian drama shows that in former times they occupied a foremost place in Indian society. It is not long since the hierodules constituted the only class of educated women in India. A hymn intoned in the temples proclaims that " to have intercourse with a prostitute is a virtue which takes away sin." In some places, as among the Kaikolans, a caste of Tamil weavers, it is regarded as proper that in every family at least one daughter should be dedicated to the service of the god as a hierodule.[5] In Greece and in Rome, in classical times, the priestess of a god had usually an earthly husband, who was generally a priest.

We know of virgin priestesses only where the power of the sacred king is already highly developed, and the rigorous tabu on his wives is reflected in the corresponding requirements of the god. The priestesses of the god are usually the wives or brides of the king, the office of queen being, of course, equivalent to that of high-priestess. The claims of the god are often met by appointing to his service very young girls, who terminate their

---

[1] A. B. Ellis, *The Tshi-Speaking Peoples*, pp. 121 sq.

[2] *The Code of Hammurabi*, 110, 127, 178 sq.

[3] *Babylonian Expedition of the University of Pennsylvania*, vol. vi, 6, 31, 45.

[4] J. A. Dubois, *Hindu Manners, Customs and Ceremonies*, vol i, pp. 133 sq.

[5] J. Shortt, " The Bayadere, or Dancing Girls of Southern India," *Memoirs read before the Anthropological Society*, iii, pp. 182 sqq. ; J. A. Dubois, *Hindu Manners, Customs and Ceremonies*, vol. i, p. 313, vol. ii, pp. 592 sq.; R. V. Russell, *The Tribes and Castes of the Central Provinces of India*, vol. iii, pp. 376, 379 ; E. Thurston, *Ethnographic Notes in Southern India*, p. 121; Id., *Castes and Tribes of Southern India*, vol. iii, pp. 37 sqq.; Thyagaraja Ayar, *Census of India*, 1911, vol. xxi, p. 99 ; H. Risley, *Census of India*, 1901, vol. xv, p. 151 ; G. Le Bon, *Les Civilisations de l'Inde*, p. 399 ; A. K. Forbes, *Râs Mâlâ : Hindoo Annals of Goozerat*, vol. i, p. 247 ; W. Crooke, *Tribes and Castes of the North-Western Provinces of India*, vol. iv, p. 368.

period of duty when they reach nubile age. Such was the rule with the virgin priestesses of Uganda,[1] with those of Mexico,[2] of Peru ;[3] and it was probably the original rule with the Roman Vestals.[4] The marriage of consecrated virgins to the god is thus in earlier instances a preliminary to human marriage.

Goddesses—that is, true Great Goddesses—on the other hand, have no priest-husbands as gods have priestess-wives ; for theirs is the primitive matriarchal law of the free woman, and it is inconsistent with their character to recognise the rule of any patriarchal husband. When men serve them it is, accordingly, not as husbands or lovers, but by renouncing their sex and assimilating themselves to women. They dress as women ; they emasculate themselves, as did the priests of Ishtar,[5] of the Syrian goddess,[6] the Galli and Kouretes,[7] the priests of Pessinos,[8] the Hittite priests,[9] and those of the Ephesian Artemis.[10] In Central Africa the priests of a lunar deity are eunuchs.[11] In Mexico men were admitted as priests of the Great Goddess after the age of sixty only.[12] Those emasculate priests are doubtless secondary introductions in the cult of goddesses who originally were served exclusively by women.

With the priestesses of goddesses the considerations which tend to lay upon the wife-priestesses of a god the tabu of chastity have no application, and their hierodulic character is retained. They are sacred prostitutes ; it is upon them that the rites of fruitfulness by which the fertilising powers of the world are invited to fecundate the female principle of Nature specially devolve. In Borneo, among the Dayaks of Sarawak, " in spite of their sublime vocation as mediatresses between gods and men, the Bilin also constitute a class of public women." [13] Among the Tahus, a primitive tribe of western Mexico, girls dedicated to the service of the deity were held in high

[1] J. Roscoe, *The Baganda*, pp. 9, 275.
[2] B. de Sahagun, *Historia de las cosas de la Nueva España*, vol. i, pp. 227 sq.
[3] J. de Torquemada, *Veinte i un libros rituales i Monarchia Indiana*, vol. ii, p. 205 ; B. de las Casas, *De las antiguas gentes del Peru*, p. 83.
[4] The Vestals were bound by their vows for a period of thirty years, after which they were at liberty to retire from their office and marry, although they are not known to have ever availed themselves of the liberty (Dionysius Halicarnassensis, ii. 67 ; Plutarch, *Numa*, x; Seneca, *De otio*, ii. 2).
[5] E. Schrader, *Keilinschriftliche Bibliothek*, vol. vi, pp. 62 sq.
[6] Lucian, *De dea Syria*, 50–53.
[7] Martial, ix. 16.
[8] Strabo, xii. 5. 3.
[9] J. Garstang, *The Land of the Hittites*, p. 361.
[10] J. C. Farnell, *The Cults of the Greek States*, vol. ii, p. 481.
[11] H. H. Johnston, *The River Congo*, p. 409.
[12] F. S. Clavigero, *Storia antica del Messico*, vol. ii, p. 44.
[13] H. Ling Roth, *The Natives of Sarawak and British North Borneo*, vol. ii, p. clxxv.

honour, and were consecrated with much ceremony at the great annual festivals, which were attended by all the chiefs of neighbouring districts. The candidate for the sacred office of priestess appeared splendidly dressed and decorated with bracelets of turquoise. After the dances and songs had ceased, she retired to a neighbouring hut, " and the chiefs went one by one to lie with her, and all the others who wish to do so follow them. From that time those women cannot refuse anyone who pays a certain amount agreed upon." The sacred hierodules may later marry, but the obligation which they have undertaken at their consecration does not cease after their marriage.[1] The institution of consecrated hierodules, apart from the sacred prostitution incumbent upon all women, which was universal in Western Asia, probably dated back to the earliest forms of the cult of the Great Goddess in Arabia, and traces of it existed at Mecca in the last century.[2] The cloister-like buildings attached to the temples in Babylonia, where the sacred hierodules lived, were known as 'kaluttu,' 'the house of the bride'; and the name 'kadishtu' (among the Hebrews 'kadesha'), by which the consecrated prostitutes were known, means 'the pure,' or 'holy ones.'[3] Identical institutions were found throughout Syria,[4] in Armenia [5] and the Pontus,[6] in Lydia,[7] among the Canaanites and the Jews,[8] in Cyprus,[9] at Eryx,[10] in Carthage.[11] Herodotus says that "nearly all people, except the Egyptians and the Greeks, have intercourse with women in sacred places."[12] But the exceptions which he mentions are certainly not borne out, even by his own testimony. In Egypt sacred

[1] P. de Castañeda de Naçera, *Relación de la Jornada de Cibola*, p. 448. Father Domenech, anticipating the methods of some modern anthropological historians, thus reports the above information which he derived from Castañeda : " Although the men were very immoral, yet such was their respect for all women who led a life of celibacy that they celebrated great festivals in their honour " (E. Domenech, *Seven Years in the Deserts of North America*, vol. i, p. 120).

[2] C. M. Doughty, *Travels in Arabia Deserta*, vol. i, p. 340 ; C. Snouck Hurgronje, *Mekka*, vol. ii, pp. 59 sq.

[3] A. Jeremias, *Handbuch der altorientalischen Geisteskultur*, pp. 340 sq.

[4] Eusebius, *Vita Constantini*, iii. 58 ; Sozomenus, *Historia Ecclesiastica*, ii. 4, v. 10. 7 ; Socrates, *Historia Ecclesiastica*, i. xviii. 7–9 ; Athenaeus, xii. 11.

[5] Strabo, xii. 559., xi. 532 ; Diodorus Siculus, v. 77.

[6] Strabo, xii. 3. 36 ; 31. 3.

[7] Herodotus, i. 92 ; Aelian, *Var. Hist.*, iv. 1.

[8] *Judges*, ii. 39 sq ; *I Kings*, iv. 23, 27 ; *II Kings*, xxiii. 7 ; *Deuteronomy*, xxiii. 17–18 ; *Hosea*, iv. 14.

[9] Herodotus, i. 99 ; *Corpus Inscriptionum Semiticarum*, vol. i, p. 86.

[10] Strabo, vi. 2. 6 ; *Corpus Inscriptionum Semiticarum*, vol. i, pp. 135, 140.

[11] Justin, xviii ; *Corpus Inscriptionum Semiticarum*, vol. i, p. 340.

[12] Herodotus, i. 93.

hierodules were attached to temples.[1] Sacred prostitution among Hellenic peoples has been represented as " due to Asiatic influence." The apologetic interpretation might pass as regards the colleges of hierodules attached to the temple of Artemis at Ephesus,[2] and perhaps in reference to those of Corinth ;[3] but to suppose that the ideas found in all early stages of culture were strange, at those stages, to the Greeks, and had to be imported from abroad, would be to ignore the perspective presented by the facts of comparative anthropology. The same conceptions in their most primitive form were, as we have seen, represented in Greek myth, and were so deeply rooted, even though they had become opposed to later Greek sentiment, that the Lokrians in time of need had doubts as to the impiety of neglecting them.[4] Those are not the manifestations of adventitiously imported customs. The famous hetairai of Corinth were in later times regarded in the light of ' filles de joie,' but their function was originally religious. " It is an ancient custom," says Chamaelon of Heraklea, " whenever the city addresses supplications to Aphrodite about any important matter, to employ as many courtesans as possible to join in the supplications ; and they pray to the goddess, and afterwards they are present at the sacrifice."[5] During the Persian invasion, the Corinthian courtesans offered prayers in the temple for the safety of the city, and a picture was painted with their portraits in commemoration of their devotion and services.[6] A sacred brothel of ancient date was attached to the temple of Dionysos at Sparta.[7] Sparta is not the place where we should look for imported Asiatic customs.

The Greek courtesans were the direct successors of sacred hierodules, and the transition from the institution as it existed immemorially in ancient cults to the traffic in much the same form as it exists amongst ourselves at the present day took place among the Greeks within historical times. Organised prostitution derives directly from the religious institutions which prevailed in ancient Mediterranean civilisations. Brothels are still commonly spoken of on the continent as ' abbeys.' The term is, no doubt, used in a jocular way, but those who use it in jest are unaware

---

[1] Strabo, xvii. 8. 46 ; Diodorus Siculus, i. 47 ; J. H. Breastead, *Ancient Records of Egypt*, vol. v, p. 132, vol. iv, p. 128 ; B. Peyron, " Papiri Greci del Museo Britannico di Londra e della Biblioteca Vaticana," *Memorie della Reale Accademia delle Scienze di Torino*, Ser. ii, iii, pp. 15 sqq.

[2] J. R. Farnell, *The Cults of the Greek States*, vol. ii, p. 481.

[3] *Ibid.*, vol. ii, p. 746 ; Strabo, viii. 6. 20.

[4] See above, pp. 200, 202.

[5] Athenaeus, xiii. 32.

[6] *Ibid.*

[7] *Ibid.*, 34.

that it derives from an actual historical tradition. Brothels were frequently attached to churches and religious houses. A brothel called ' The Abbey ' was instituted in the papal city of Avignon under the patronage of Queen Joanna of Naples. It was regulated by strict rules after the model of religious houses. None but good Christians were admitted, Jews and infidels being excluded; it was closed on Good Friday and Easter Day and, what is more notable, a system of medical inspection and of quarantine was enforced.[1] Pope Julius II, by a papal Bull, instituted a similar brothel in Rome, and the foundation prospered under the patronage of Leo X and Clement VII, part of the proceeds being devoted to providing for the comfort of the Holy Sisters of the Order of St. Mary Magdalene.[2] In Antwerp at the present day it is, I am informed, a practice with the prostitutes of regular brothels to proceed in a body on certain feast days to the churches, carrying candles which they dedicate to the Holy Virgin, fervently praying to her for the success of their affairs. In that practice we may perhaps see a reminiscent association of their calling with the cult of the goddess. The Holy Virgin is, in China, the special patroness of prostitutes.[3]

Consecrated hierodules and consecrated virgins were regarded as equally sacred, and the honour in which the former were held in America, in India, in Western Asia, was the equivalent of the honour with which in later phases of culture virgins vowed to chastity were regarded. Europeanised Orientals residing in England never regard prostitutes in the same light as do Europeans; the stigma which attaches to them is still unintelligible to the Oriental mind. As sacred prostitution fell into disuse and was supplanted by secular prostitution, and as the conception of virginity acquired a new significance, the principle of ritual chastity became greatly extended. Even the priestesses of a goddess came sometimes to be vowed to chastity, as were those of Athene at Tegea, and, strangely enough, at Sikyon the priestesses of Aphrodite.[4] Originally, however, it was an essential part of the functions of priestesses, whether serving a god or a goddess, to promote the fertility of Nature and the prosperity of mankind by union with generative powers represented by the god under any human disguise which he might assume in the freedom of sacred promiscuity. It is a fundamental rule of the latter that the hierodule is not free to choose her temporary partner, but is under the obligation not to refuse any man who proffers the appointed price.

Like priests, priestesses and sacred hierodules were often

---

[1] J. P. Papon, *Histoire générale de Provence*, vol. iii, pp. 180 sq.
[2] J. A. Dulaure, *Les Divinités génératrices*, p. 285.
[3] See above, p. 171.
[4] Pausanias, viii. 47. 3 ; ii. 10. 4.

members of a sacred clan or religious association. In India the women of particular castes or clans are vowed from birth to the service of the gods as sacred prostitutes.[1] In Algeria the women of the sacred clan of the Walad 'Abdi, which claims descent from a saint, exercise the profession of sacred prostitutes and are regarded as holy women, the prosperity of the country depending upon their ministrations.[2] In Egypt there was until recently a special class of prostitutes, known as 'ghowazy' (sing. 'ghazye'), who belonged to a particular clan of pure Arab blood called the Barmaky. They were regarded with special honour and reverence, and were never confounded with common prostitutes; they would not only strongly resent the comparison, but regarded themselves as more noble than the general Egyptian population. They frequently, after retiring from their profession, marry sheikhs or dignitaries, " who consider it an honour to carry off so fair a prize, nor would the ghazye bestow herself in matrimony on any common peasant. When such an event is to take place, the ghazye, before she marries the sheikh, makes a solemn vow upon the tomb of some saint never to be unfaithful to her husband, and I have been assured," says Burckhardt, " that no ghazye married under these circumstances was ever known to violate her vow." They have their own female sheikh, and many attain great wealth and perform the pilgrimage to Mecca, assuming thereafter the title of ' hadjy.' In the time of the Mameluks their influence was very great, and their protection was courted by the most respectable persons. All the females of the tribe perform the office of prostitutes, though it is also a rule with them that they must marry one of the men of the tribe, who perform the functions of ' souteneurs,' and " are as much despised as their females are distinguished." Before marrying, however, it is obligatory for a ghazye to have intercourse with a stranger. " They have made it a law among them, never to refuse the embraces of any person, whatever may be his condition, so that he pays." [3]

Obligatory Sacred Marriage.

Although intercession with the divine power may be effected, and the religious and magic needs of the community served by priestesses and sacred clans, the religious requirements of every woman cannot be wholly supplied by appointed delegates. The

[1] See above, p. 212.
[2] E. Doutté, *La société musulmane du Maghreb. Magie et Religion dans l'Afrique du Nord*, pp. 560 sq. Cf. above, p. 200.
[3] J. L. Burckhardt, *Arabic Proverbs*, pp. 173 sqq. Cf. E. W. Lane, *Manners and Customs of the Northern Egyptians*, pp. 347 sqq.

fulfilment of a woman's functions, her capacity to bear children, is believed, in the highest no less than in the most primitive culture, to depend upon her fertilisation, not by an earthly husband, but by the god. As in New Guinea, in New Zealand, in India, the signs of a woman's puberty are the effects of her intercourse with the moon-god, so among the Déné Indians, it is necessary that she should have intercourse with some stranger before her 'moon' can appear.[1]

The union of a woman with the divine power, which is regarded as a necessary preliminary or accessory to her human marriage, is sometimes effected directly by her marriage to the image of the god himself, as in the defloration of brides by the sacred 'lingam' in India.[2] It appears probable that in the usage which is general in India of marrying a girl to a tree before she is handed over to her human husband,[3] the tree is regarded as the representative of the god, Such trees, more especially the Pipal, or fig-tree, are believed to impregnate women,[4] and those women who are desirous of obtaining offspring embrace the sacred tree.[5] The union of the bride with the statue of the god took place among the Romans as it did in India.[6] In China, ladies desiring offspring undertake pilgrimages to reputed pagodas, and "rub their bellies against certain little copper gods."[8] In India, as everywhere else, women who are afflicted with barrenness go from shrine to shrine to obtain from the gods the capacity to fulfil the functions of womanhood. They spend the night in the temple of the god, who, impersonated by one of his priests, visits them in the darkness. "Fully convinced that the god has deigned to have intercourse with them, the poor creatures return home enchanted, flattering themselves that they will soon procure for their husbands the honour of paternity."[8] Elsewhere the god, instead of being incarnated in a priest is sought under the avatar of a stranger. "Children are promised to women who, laying aside

[1] See above, vol. ii, pp. 31, 447.

[2] J. H. van Linschoten, *Voyage to the East Indies*, vol. i, p. 224 ; J. Fryer, *A New Account of East India and Persia*, p. 179 ; Du Quesne, *Journal d'un voyage fait aux Indes Orientales*, vol. ii, pp. 204 sq.

[3] W. Crooke, *The Popular Religion and Folk-lore of Northern India*, vol. ii, pp. 115 sqq. ; H. H. Risley, *Tribes and Castes of Bengal*, vol. i, p. 531 ; J. G. Frazer, *The Golden Bough*, vol. ii, pp. 57 sq. ; Id., *Totemism and Exogamy*, vol. i, pp. 32 sq., vol. iv, pp. 210 sqq.

[4] R. V. Russell, *Tribes and Castes of the Central Provinces of India*, vol. iv, p. 33.

[5] See J. G. Frazer, *The Golden Bough*, vol. ii, pp. 56 sqq. ; W. Mannhardt, *Wald und Feldkulte*, vol. i, pp. 51 sq.

[6] See below, pp. 246 sq.

[7] J. Barrow, *Travels in China*, p. 480.

[8] J. A. Dubois, *Hindu Manners, Customs and Ceremonies*, vol. ii, p. 601.

all shame, grant their favours to all persons indiscriminately. At such places a feast is celebrated every year in the month of January, at which both sexes, the scum of the country-side, meet. Barren women, in the hope that they will cease to be so, visit them after binding themselves by a vow to grant their favours to a fixed number of libertines. Others, who have entirely lost all sense of decency, go there in order to testify their reverence for the deity of the place by prostituting themselves, openly and without shame, even at the very gates of the temple." [1] Similar practices obtained as late as the end of the eighteenth century in southern Italy. At Isernia in the Abruzzi, some fifty miles from Naples, the great yearly feast of Saints Cosmo and Damianus was celebrated on the 27th of September, lasting three days, and was largely attended by women from the surrounding country. The Saints had a special reputation for assisting women afflicted with sterility During the time of the celebrations a holy relic, the ' big toe ' of Saint Cosmo, was exhibited in the church. A large trade took place in votive offerings, which consisted of wax phalli of all sizes, and which were purchased by the women and deposited with their contributions on salvers in which the priests collected them. The women lodged during the nights of the festival in the church and adjoining monastery, in charge of the Chapter assisted by the good friars. Miracles frequently took place, says the Italian reporter irreverently, " with little assistance from the Saints." [2]

Resort to the unfailing fertilising power of the gods was not, however, originally confined to women afflicted with sterility ; every woman's power to bear children was dependent upon her union with the divine bridegroom. At Telkûpi Ghât, Santal girls were under the obligation of acting once in their lives as public prostitutes.[3] The obligation was similar to that which obtained in Babylonia. The institution of sacred hierodules in the cults of Western Asia was not the only form in which women offered themselves to the gods. It did not dispense any woman from the necessity of becoming united with the Divine Bridegroom. In Babylonia every woman was under the obligation of proceeding once in her lifetime, most probably before her marriage, to the temple of the Great Goddess, arrayed in her most splendid apparel, and of waiting there until a stranger threw a piece of money in her lap with the words, " I beseech Our Lady to favour thee." She

[1] J. A. Dubois, *Hindu Manners, Customs and Ceremonies*, p. 603. Father Dubois mentions Jungingatta, Kara-madai, in the Coimbatore district, Mudu-dorai in eastern Mysore, as places where, to his knowledge, the rites were celebrated.

[2] R. Payne Knight, *Le culte de Priape*, pp. 5 sqq.

[3] Beglar, in *Archaeological Survey of India*, Xth Report, p. 177.

then retired with the stranger to an adjoining house, and surrendered to his embraces.[1] The same rule appears to have been observed at one time throughout Semitic lands. The practice was abolished at Hierapolis in the time of Constantine.[2] In Phoenician temples women prostituted themselves for hire in the belief that they thereby won the favour of the divinity.[3] Among the Amorites it was a law "that she who was about to marry should sit in fornication seven days by the gate." [4] In Cyprus every woman, whether princess or peasant, offered herself at the temple of the Goddess before marriage.[5] In Lydia all girls were under the obligation to act as prostitutes before marriage,[6] and the pious deed is found recorded with devout pride on monuments erected by noble matrons.[7] Those customs have survived until quite recently in the islands of the Anatolian coast. At Chios it was in the eighteenth century the custom for girls to earn their dowry by prostitution.[8] In Armenia it was considered the duty of girls of noble family to serve for a considerable time as sacred prostitutes in the temples before they married.[9] The same rule obtained in Egypt. Every girl of a noble family was, before marriage, and indeed, before the age of puberty, appointed to serve for a period in the temple of the god, and gave herself to any stranger who paid the required amount into the temple treasury. That promiscuous intercourse ceased when the first menstruation appeared, and the young woman was then married as befitted her station.[10] In later times, at Byblos, the surrender of a woman's virginity to a stranger could be commuted by her cutting off her hair, as is done at the present day by Catholic nuns when becoming mystically married to the Divine Bridegroom.[11]

Survivals of those rites and of the ideas which they represented

---

[1] Herodotus, i. 199 ; Strabo, xvi. i. 20.

[2] Eusebius, *Vita Constantini*, iii. 58 ; Socrates, *Historia Ecclesiatica*, i. 18. 7 sqq. ; Sozomenus, *Historia Ecclesiatica*, v. 10. 7.

[3] Athanasius, *Contra Gentes*, xxvi, in Migne, *Patrologiae Cursus Completus*, Series Graeca, vol. xxv, col. 52 ; Augustine, *De civitate Dei*, iv. 10.

[4] "Testament of Judah," in *The Testaments of the Twelve Patriarchs*, translated and edited by R. H. Charles, p. 81.

[5] Herodotus, i. 199 ; Clement of Alexandria, *Exhortatio*, ii ; Justin, xviii. 5. 4 ; Athenaeus, xii. 11 ; Lactantius, *Divin. Instit.*, i. 17.

[6] Herodotus, i. 93 sq ; Athenaeus xii. 11.

[7] W. M. Ramsay, *Cities and Bishoprics of Phrygia*, vol. i, pp. 94 sq., 115 ; *Bulletin de Correspondance Hellénique*, vii, p. 276.

[8] J. A. Guer, *Moeurs et usages des Turcs*, vol. i, pp. 430 sq.

[9] Strabo, xi. 14. 16.

[10] *Ibid.*, xvii. 1. 46.

[11] Lucian, *De dea Syria*, vi. The cutting off of a woman's hair was a marriage rite among the Spartans (Plutarch, *Lykurgus*, xv. 4), and was habitual until quite lately amongst the peasants of Southern Italy (F. G. Finamore, *Tradizioni popolari abruzzesi*, p. 54).

have persisted down to our day. In Egypt, in the populous city of Tanta, the great annual ' mulid,' or Saint's feast, of Ahmed al-Bedawi, is one of the most popular festivals of the Muslim world. Enormous crowds from all parts of Lower Egypt gather during the celebrations. Special tents used, until recent years, to be pitched by the Egyptian Government, for the use of ' ghowazy,' of whom no fewer than six hundred established themselves there during the festival, acting as sacred hierodules. It is the custom at the present day for women of the most respectable families who desire any special grace to make a vow to attend the holy festival, and to yield themselves to the first man who happens to approach them.[1] The usage, there can be little doubt, dates from the times of the Pharaohs. Throughout Syria and Armenia aberrant sects survive among the hill populations, which have but imperfectly adopted the new religions, and continue to observe, as an essential part of their cults, the ancient rites of promiscuity. The Kissilbasis, a sect resembling the Druses, in the mountains of Armenia, celebrate a yearly festival during which all sexual restrictions are suspended.[2] In the Dersin mountains, the Dusik Kurds have a similar yearly feast at which promiscuous intercourse is obligatory.[3] At Kerrund a sect who call themselves the Ali-Ullaheeahs, that is, worshippers of Ali, but are regarded by Muhammadans as pagans, have the same annual feasts. The women remove their nether garments and suspend them to the wall ; each man, as he enters takes one, the owner becoming his partner for the night. The Nessereah, near Aleppo, observe the same ritual promiscuity.[4] At the immemorial shrine of Al-Uzza, at Mecca, it is a practice for women to offer themselves to the holy pilgrims.[5] With the Persian Shi'ites it is the custom to form temporary unions during the period of the holy pilgrimage. It is stipulated that at a fixed date all relations must cease, and the parties to such unions do not give signs of recognition if they subsequently meet. Any children resulting from such unions are regarded as a blessing in the family, and are looked upon as divine children or saints.[6]

The ' stranger ' is in those sacred rites the procreator of a more than human offspring. The eagerness of savages to offer their women to white men proceeds, no doubt, in part from such a notion. In Australia, among the northern tribes, the mothers,

---

[1] S. I. Curtiss, *Primitive Semitic Religion To-day*, pp. 154 sq. Cf. J. L. Burckhardt, *Arabic Proverbs*, p. 177.

[2] J. Creagh, *Armenians, Koords, and Turks*, vol. i, pp. 145 sqq.

[3] C. Blau, " Nachrichten über kurdische Stämme," *Zeitschrift der deutschen morgenländischen Gesellschaft*, xvi, pp. 623 sq. Cf. below, p. 247.

[4] J. S. Buckingham, *Travels in Assyria, Media, and Persia*, vol. i, pp. 110 sq.

[5] C. Snouck Hurgronje, *Mekka*, vol. i, pp. 60 sq.

[6] F. Eugénieu, " Les Chiites d'aujourd'hui," *Anthropos*, ii, p. 418.

we are told, were particularly anxious to get white men to deflower their daughters.[1] When Amerigo Vespucci landed on the
coast of Honduras the first act of the natives was to place some
girls in the boats of the Europeans.[2] The Guaranis of Brazil
created a very favourable impression in the minds of the first
missionaries who visited them ; but, says one of them, " il y a
une chose qui gaste tout : que avant que marier leurs filles les
pères et mères les prosternent au premier venu pour quelque petite
chose, principalement aux Chrétiens allans par lá, s'ils veulent en
user." [3] The Comanches, when they captured a white man in
battle, compelled him to have intercourse with their women.[4]
When the Indians of Colombia saw for the first time a negro they
offered him their women, in order to propitiate the black god.[5]

In Tibet mothers took their daughters to passing strangers and
requested the latter to deflower them.[6] In Malabar a man's
services were similarly sought by mothers in order that he might
have intercourse with their daughters before their marriage ; and
the Portuguese were besought by native merchants to do them
the favour to deflower their brides. The strangers performing
that office were lavishly entertained ; but if they attempted to
repeat the act, " it would have meant death to the man and to the
woman." The girls themselves begged strangers to take their
virginity, " for while they were virgins they could not find a husband." [7] Similar usages were observed throughout the East, as,
for instance, in Burma,[8] Pegu,[9] Tonkin ; [10] among the Alfurs of
Celebes,[11] and the Savunese.[12] Among the Todas a man from another
village is invited to have intercourse with every girl before she is
married ; " it might be a subject of reproach and abuse for the

---

[1] R. Brough Smyth, *The Aborigines of Australia*, vol. ii, p. 319.
[2] Amerigo Vespucci, *Quatuor navigationes*, in M. Fernandez de Navarrete,
Colección de los viages y descubrimientos, vol. iii, pp. 219 sq.
[3] A. Thevet, *Les singularitez de la France antarctique*, p. 214.
[4] M. de Foney, *Le Mexique*, p. 462.
[5] P. Castañeda de Naçera, *Relación de la jornada de Cibola*, p. 418 ; A. F.
Bandelier, " Contributions to the History of the South-western Portion of
the United States," *Papers of the Archaeological Institute of America*, American
Series, v, pp. 154 sq.
[6] *The Book of Ser Marco Polo*, vol. ii, p. 44.
[7] L. Barthema, in G. B. Ramusio, *Navigationi et Viaggi*, vol. i, fol. 180 ;
P. Alvares, *ibid.*, fol. 137 ; P. W. Verhoeven, *Kurtze Beschreibung einer Reyse
in die Öst-Indien*, p. 56.
[8] J. W. Jones, in *Travels of L. di Vathema*, p. lxxix.
[9] J. H. van Linschoten, *Voyage to the East Indies*, vol. i, pp. 98 sq.
[10] J. Richard, " History of Tonquin," in Pinkerton, *Voyages and Travels*,
vol. ix, pp. 760 sq.
[11] J. G. F. Riedel, " De Minahassa in 1825," *Tijdschrift voor Indische taal-,
land- en volkenkunde*, xviii, p. 486.
[12] G. A. Wilken, *De verspreide geschriften*, vol. i, p. 588.

remainder of the woman's life, and it was said that men might even refuse to marry her, if this ceremony had not been performed at the proper time." [1]   In the Philippines special officials were appointed to deflower girls before marriage, and were highly paid for their trouble.[2]   In Central Africa the father of the bride hires a man to have intercourse with his daughter before she is married.[3] Elsewhere the bridegroom himself provides a man to perform the office.[4]   In New Caledonia also men are hired by the husbands to deflower their brides.[5]

The religious prostitution incumbent upon the women of Lydia has sometimes been described as " earning their dowry by prostitution," and the same description has been given of similar usages in various parts of the world.[6]   In Japan it was until quite lately the general rule for unmarried girls to spend some time in the ' green houses ' before settling down to married life.   " Except with the daughters of some of the highest functionaries," says a Japanese gentleman, " all girls may from the tenderest age give themselves without any loss of reputation to public prostitution." [7] We are told, indeed, that unless they did so no man would have consented to marry them.[8]   In view of the manner in which sacred prostitution is regarded, it is probable that in those instances the usage of earning their dowry by prostitution is not solely or chiefly founded on economic considerations.

The Nasamonian Custom.

The practice generally known as the Nasamonian custom, namely, that the bride, before her husband exercises his rights, should yield herself to all the wedding guests, is in some respects

[1] W. H. Rivers, *The Todas*, p. 503.

[2] J. Mallat, *Les Philippines*, vol. i, p. 61 ; A. de Morga, *The Philippine Islands*, pp. 304 sq. ; G. F. Gemelli Careri, *Giro del Mondo*, vol. v, p. 87.

[3] H. Crawfurd Angus, in *Verhandlungen der berliner Gesellschaft für Anthropologie*, 1898, pp. 479 sq. ; Gaud, *Les Mandja*, p. 275.

[4] H. H. Johnston, *British Central Africa*, p. 410.

[5] L. Moncelon, " Réponse au questionnaire de la Société," *Bulletin de la Société d'Anthropologie*, Série iii, ix, p. 368.

[6] E. Doutté, *La société musulmane du Maghreb. Magie et Religion dans l'Afrique du Nord*, p. 560 ; P. Soleillet, *L'Afrique occidentale*, p. 118 ; Le Page du Pratz, *History of Louisiana*, p. 343 ; P. de Andagoya, *Narrative of the Proceedings of Pedrarias Davila in the Province of Tierra Firme*, p. 33 ; A. de Herrera, *The General History of the West Indies*, vol. iii, p. 340 ; A. Bastian, *Die deutsche Expedition an der Loango-Küste*, vol. i, pp. 151, 727 ; H. Soyaux, *Aus West-Afrika*, p. 161 ; J. Kubary, *Die socialen Einrichtungen der Pelauer*, p. 51.

[7] Kouri-Moto Tei-ziro, "Sur la condition de la femme au Japon," *Revue orientale et américaine*, xi, p. 239.

[8] F. Cartelli, *Viaggi da lui racontati in dodici raggionamenti*, pp. 228 sqq.

analogous to the obligation that every woman should prostitute herself to a stranger before her marriage. The name given to the usage is derived from the oldest account, by Herodotus, of the practice observed by the Nasamonians of Cyrenaica. " When a Nasamonian marries," he says, " it is the custom for the bride on the first night to lie with all the guests in turn, and each, when he has intercourse with her, gives her some present which he has brought with him." [1] The same thing is reported by Pomponius Mela concerning the Augilae of the same region. The custom, he says, is regarded in the light of a solemn obligation, and the bride is bound to give herself to any man who comes and claims her, bringing a reward ; it is regarded as a great honour to have had relations with many men on that occasion, although the women are not dissolute and are exceedingly chaste after marriage.[2] Speaking of the inhabitants of the Balearic Isles, Diodorus says : " They have a strange custom at their weddings ; for on the wedding-night the oldest friends and guests lie first with the bride ; then the others in the order of their ages. The bridegroom is the last man who is admitted to that honour." [3] Similar usages are observed at the present day among the Barea of Abyssinia,[4] and among the Waitata [5] and the Wataveta [6] of East Africa. The Nasamonian custom is general among the Australian aborigines. Thus among the Queensland tribes, after certain ritual operations to which I shall have to refer later, a young woman who is about to be married is taken into the bush and has connection with all the men present. " Men come forward from all directions, and the struggling victim has to submit in rotation to promiscuous coition with all the ' bucks ' present. She has now attained the degree in which she is allowed to marry." [7] The usage has been reported from several parts of Australia, and the bridegroom himself does not usually have access to the bride for two or three nights, or more, after marriage.[8] In

[1] Herodotus, iv. 172.

[2] Pomponius Mela, De situ orbis, i. 8. Cf. C. J. Solinus, Collectanea rerum memorabilia, xxxi. 4.

[3] Diodorus Siculus, xiv. 4. 25.

[4] W. Munzinger, Ostafrikanische Studien, p. 273.

[5] H. H. Johnston, " The People of Eastern Equatorial Africa," Journal of the Anthropological Institute, xv, p. 8 ; J. Thomson, Through Masai Land, p. 51.

[6] H. H. Johnston, The Kilima-njaro Expedition, p. 431 ; Mrs. French-Sheldon, " Customs of the Natives of East Africa from Tieta to Kilimegalia," Journal of the Anthropological Institute, xxi, p. 366.

[7] W. E. Roth, Ethnological Studies among the North-West Central Queensland Aborigines, pp. 174 sq.

[8] W. E. Roth, " North Queensland Ethnography, Bulletin No. 10," Records of the Australian Museum, vii, p. 11 ; W. B. Spencer and F. J. Gillen, The Native Tribes of Central Australia, pp. 92 sqq. ; Id., The Northern Tribes

the Marquesas Islands the bride lay with her head on the bride-groom's lap, and all the men present filed past dancing and singing ; each in turn had connection with the bride, and it was a point of honour among the women that as many men as possible should avail themselves of the right.[1] Similar usages obtain among some Massim tribes of New Guinea.[2] The Nasamonian rite appears to have been a prevalent institution among the natives of Central America ; it has been reported of the Caribs of Cuba,[3] and of Porto Rico,[4] of the Manta and other tribes of Peru.[5]

In nearly every country usages are observed at weddings which suggest that they may be attenuated reminiscences of similar customs. Thus in Baluchistan it is usual for a mock-bride and bridegroom, represented by a man and a boy attired in the same manner as the real bride and bridegroom, to make their appearance at the wedding-feast. They are received with much clapping of hands and bawling of wedding-songs. When they are seated, up comes a man who calls upon the mock-bride to choose between the paltry bridegroom at her side and one who is famed throughout the country for his virility. Scuffles take place in which the mock-bride is seized by the challenger and the other male guests, the duplicate bridegroom being invariably thrust aside ignominiously. The scenes that follow, says Mr. Bray, are too obscene for descrip-tion.[6] Among the Southern Slavs it is the custom for the two best men at a wedding to spend the night in the bride's chamber, the bridegroom being excluded. At the present day they occupy a separate bed in a corner of the room, while two old women sleep

---

of Central Australia, pp. 133 sqq. ; F. J. Gillen, in Report on the Work of the Horn Expedition, vol. iv, p. 165 ; A. W. Howitt, The Native Tribes of South-East Australia, p. 664 ; Id., " Diery and other kindred Tribes of Central Australia," Journal of the Anthropological Institute, xx, p. 87 ; J. F. Small, " Customs and Traditions of the Clarence River Aboriginals," Science of Man, 1898, p. 17 ; B. H. Purcell, " Rites and Customs of the Australian Aborigines," Verhandlungen der Berliner Gesellschaft für Anthropologie, 1893, p. 288 ; R. Schomburgk, " Über einige Sitten und Gebräuche der tief im Innern Süd-australiens, am Peake-Flusse und dessen Umgebung hausenden Stämme," ibid., 1879, pp. 235 sq.

[1] L. Tautain, " Étude sur le mariage chez les Polynésiens (Mao'i) des îles Marquises," L'Anthropologie, vi, p. 642. Cf. G. H. von Langsdorf, Voyages and Travels in various Parts of the World, vol. i, p. 153.

[2] W. Seligman, The Melanesians of British New Guinea, p. 473.

[3] F. Lopez de Gomara, Historia general de las Indias, p. 185 ; F. Coréal, Voyage aux Indes occidentales, vol. i. p. 49.

[4] J. W. Fewkes, " The Aborigines of Porto Rico and the Neighbouring Islands," Twenty-fifth Annual Report of the Bureau of American Ethnology, p. 48.

[5] Garcilasso de la Vega, First Part of the Royal Commentaries of the Incas, vol. i, p. 59 ; vol. ii, p. 442 ; P. Cieza de Leon, La Crónica del Peru, p. 402.

[6] D. Bray, Census of India, 1911, vol. iv, p. 108.

with the bride ; but not long since the respective places were reversed.[1] I am told that it was the custom in the West of Ireland fifty years ago, for the male guests to follow the bride into the nuptial chamber and undress her. Even at Chinese weddings a custom is observed which, when one remembers the extravagant notions of propriety and decency which obtain in that country, is somewhat startling. It is called ' the inspection of the bride.' After the ceremonies and festivities are over, the bride retires to her apartments, and sits in state arrayed in all the splendour of her finery. Presently the guests are invited to follow her. A female attendant stands by her side with a candle, and draws attention to the bride's ' points ' amid admiring exclamations. She asks the guests which particular feature of the young lady they would like to inspect ; and the survey goes so far that her arms are exposed and her skirts drawn above her knees.[2] The custom can have survived amid the excessive prudishness of existing standards only by reason of long-established recognition, and in its present form is doubtless a residuary survival of the original usage. The widespread custom giving to all male guests at a wedding the right to kiss the bride, or to dance with her, may be merely a symbolic farewell to her days of freedom, but the attenuated usage may date back from times when that farewell took a more primitive form. In France, in the Marche district, the bride embraced without distinction every man she met on the way to Church.[3] The more ancient usages from which such customs may have originally derived are strongly suggested in those instances where the male guests are obliged to pay the bride a small fee for her kisses and dances.[4]

The Divine Bridegroom Impersonated by a Priest, or Sacred Personage.

Several confluent motives are included in those customs, as also in those of pre-nuptial defloration. The Nasamonian usages are undoubtedly in some instances regarded as a recognition of communal rights and tribal brotherhood before the husband asserts his individual proprietary claims. Such a recognition sometimes takes the form of a perquisite appertaining to those tribal brothers who have assisted the bridegroom in the

[1] F. S. Krauss, *Sitte und Brauch der Südslaven*, pp. 382, 456, 608.

[2] W. G. Walshe, *Ways that are Dark*, p. 118.

[3] Laisnel de la Salle, *Croyances et légendes du centre de la France*, vol. ii, p. 66.

[4] C. Rogers, *Scotland, Social and Domestic*, p. 112 ; J. Piprek, *Slawische Brautwerbungs- und Hochzeitgebräuche*, p. 108.

real or simulated capture of the bride. But those conceptions merge into, and are associated with, others. In Australia, where the Nasamonian custom appears to have chiefly the character of an acknowledgment of tribal communism, all such practices of promiscuity are, as has been seen, regarded as having a conciliatory effect upon the higher powers, and as being beneficial in bringing luck and averting the wrath of spirits. Where the bride acts for a time as a prostitute for payment, and is bound to yield herself to any man who comes forward with the prescribed fee, the usage is scarcely distinguishable from the sacred prostitution which was regarded in Western Asia as incumbent upon every woman before her marriage. The requirement that a bride should be deflowered before her marriage proceeds, as we shall see, from the dread which attaches to the haemorrhage resulting from rupture of the hymen, which is regarded as analogous to menstrual blood.[1] But that is not the sole motive why the services of a stranger are sought by the husband. The place of the stranger is often taken by a priest, or by the sacred king, or a prince of noble race. The two forms of the practice are frequently combined. Thus the Brahman priests officiating in the temples constantly have intercourse with the hierodules, although these are also public prostitutes.[2] In Nicaragua " the parents had the custom that when they had a girl of age to marry, they sent her away to earn money in view of her marriage, and the girls went through all the land earning money publicly, and when they had enough for their house or to set up in some trade, they returned home to their parents and married. They had another custom that when anyone got married, on the night before the wedding a man whom they regarded as a pope and who lived in the temple, had to sleep with the bride." [3] The notion that for a woman to have intercourse with a person of holy or divine character is desirable and meritorious is very general. Thus among the Eskimo, " the women think themselves happy if an ' angikok,' or prophet, will honour them with his caresses ; there are even men so generous that they will pay the ' angikok ' for it." [4] Among the Kushkuwak of Alaska, unless a girl had previously been relieved of her virginity by a shaman, she was deemed unworthy to take part in any religious ceremony.[5] Among the Algonkin and Huron tribes of North

[1] See below, pp. 316 sqq.

[2] W. Ward, *A View of the History, Literature, and Religion of the Hindoos,* vol. ii, p. 134.

[3] P. de Andagoya, *Relación de los sucesos de Pedrarias Davila en las provinvias de Tierra firme,* p. 414.

[4] H. Egede, *A Description of Greenland,* p. 140.

[5] F. von Wrangell, *Statistische und ethnographische Nachrichten über die russischen Besitzungen an der Nordwestkuste von Amerika,* p. 133.

America, medicine-men are constantly sought out by girls and women, and when the magic man retires to solitude in order to commune with the higher powers, he is followed by eager female votaries anxious to partake of the divine afflatus.[1]

Among the Yezidis, a semi-Christian sect of Armenia, the priests, or bishops, are regarded with the deepest veneration ; they lead an itinerant life, visiting in turn the various districts of their diocese. " These Yezidi prelates no sooner arrive in a village where they intend passing a day or two, than they at once get married ; and the young lady selected for the honour becomes, in consequence, so holy that she is looked upon as a kind of saint." [2] In Egypt, saints, or ' maslub,' go about stark naked, and women who are desirous of having children kneel before such a holy man, when they meet one. Should the saint come upon a troop of women, he will frequently seize one, and have connection with her there and then in the public street ; and this, instead of being resented, is regarded as a great blessing and honour. Her companions, far from defending her against the assault of the holy personage, close round singing joyfully, and congratulating the fortunate woman selected by the representative of God.[3] The outrages of one of these saints in Damascus were so scandalous that the pasha had him locked up. Shortly after the pasha died, and the people were persuaded that his death was a just punishment from heaven for having laid hands on the holy man. The latter had to be released and sent back to the city, " where he was permitted to indulge his depraved propensities without limit or restriction as to time, place, or condition ; violating, it is even said, the sanctity of the Great Mosque, when women passed through it as a thoroughfare." [4] The assaults of a saintly personage are regarded in the same manner by the women in Morocco.[5] Among the Tachtadshys of Lykia, the priest, or ' dede,' has the right of intercourse with any woman he pleases, and the husband " feels considerably honoured by this distinction." [6]

The desirable and meritorious character of union with a holy personage is universally recognised in India. " All India," remarks Reclus, " is imbued with the belief that sacerdotal blood is gifted

---

[1] Le Jeune, in *Jesuit Relations and Allied Documents*, vol. vi, p. 208.

[2] J. Creagh, *Armenians, Koords, and Turks*, vol. i, p. 154.

[3] M. C. d'Arvieux, *Mémoires*, vol. i, pp. 210 sq. ; E. W. Lane, *Manners and Customs of the Modern Egyptians*, vol. i, pp. 345 sq. ; I. Pallme, *Beschreibung von Kordofan*, p. 50, 52 sq. It is in fact considered wrong for a woman to refuse her favour to a ' Whyman ' (S. I. Curtis, *Primitive Semitic Religions To-day*, p. 150). Cf. above, vol. ii, p. 609.

[4] J. S. Buckingham, *Travels among the Arab Tribes inhabiting the Countries East of Syria and Palestine*, pp. 376 sqq.

[5] L. de Chenier, *The Present State of the Empire of Morocco*, vol. i, p. 187.

[6] E. Petersen and F. von Luschan, *Reisen in Lykien, Milyas und Kibyratis*, p. 199 n. 1.

with regenerating virtues." [1] The holy rishis, the paradigms and
predecessors of the Brahmans, are constantly represented in the
Mahâbhârata as being requested by kings and nobles to honour
them by having sexual connection with their wives and daughters.
Holy men, or ' yogis,' instead of performing wonders of ascetic
penance, sometimes " make a vow to deflower two or three
thousand girls, and go about performing this charity, wherefore
they are held in great veneration, and are preceded by a brigade
who hold the people at a distance with the equivalent of a ' procul,
o procul.' " [2] Fakirs and saintly personages of every kind are
regarded as having free access to all women.[3] A Gond song describes the pleasure of the village women at the arrival of a saint,
owing to the sexual gratification which they expect to receive
from him.[4] The priests of Siva and ' gurus,' or spiritual advisers,
called in the western provinces ' jangamas,' are throughout India
regarded as the means of effecting the spiritual communion of
women with the divine powers. " When a guru travels about
his district he lodges with some member of the sect, and the
members contend amongst themselves for the honour of receiving
him. When he has selected the house he wishes to stay in, the
master and all the other male inmates are obliged, out of respect
for him, to leave it and go elsewhere. The holy man remains
there day and night with only the women of the house." [5] Brahmans play in some districts the part of " thoroughbred stallions,
upon whom it is incumbent to ennoble the race and to cohabit
with virgins of inferior caste. The venerable personage scours town
and country ; the people give him presents in money and stuff ;
they wash his feet, drink some of the dirty water, and preserve
the rest. After a repast of dainty meats, he is conducted to the
nuptial couch, where, crowned with flowers, the virgin awaits
him." [6]

Such a union is frequently considered not only desirable, but
an imperative condition of marriage. Among some Eskimo tribes
it is regarded as indispensable that a girl before her marriage
should have intercourse with an ' angakut.' [7] Throughout Central

[1] E. Reclus, *Primitive Folk*, p. 172.

[2] F. Sassetti, " Lettere," in A. de Gubernatis, *Storia dei viaggiatori italiani
nelle Indie Orientali*, p. 193.

[3] J. C. Oman, *The Mystics, Ascetics, and Saints of India*, p. 91 ; R. V.
Russell, *The Tribes and Castes of the Central Provinces of India*, vol. iii, p. 138 ;
E. Maclagan, in *Census of India*, 1891, " Punjab," p. 112.

[4] R. V. Russell, *loc. cit.*

[5] J. A. Dubois, *Hindu Manners, Customs and Ceremonies*, vol. i, p. 118.

[6] E. Reclus, *Primitive Folk*, pp. 171 sq., after E. Roberts, *Notes of an
Overland Journey to Bombay*.

[7] H. W. Klutschak, *Als Eskimo unter Eskimos*, p. 234.

America, in Guiana, in Brazil, it was an established usage that the
'paje' should have intercourse with the bride before her marriage.[1]
The same necessity was recognised in Patagonia.[2] Among the
Zhara of Morocco the services of a spiritual leader, or 'rusma,' are
required to deflower every bride before she can marry.[3] It is
necessary in Cambodia for every girl to be deflowered by a Buddhist
or Taoist priest, and the ceremony is performed annually on girls
after the manner of a first communion.[4]

The practice constitutes the 'jus primae noctis' assigned to
priests and chiefs ; but although it may, under systems of established
despotism, have sometimes assumed the form of a tyrannous claim,
the facts show that this was not its original character. The
people are, in archaic societies, as eager that their daughters and
their brides should be united to the priestly or kingly representative
of the god as they are to induce strangers to act in that capacity.
Kings themselves are no less anxious than their subjects to seek out
a representative of the god to deflower their brides.[5] In ancient
Ireland it was not only a right, but a duty of the king to deflower
brides before they were handed over to their husbands ; and King
Conchobar is praised in an ancient record for his punctilious devotion
to his duties in having taken the virginity of every maid in Ulster.[6]
Among the Guanches of the Canaries it was a matter of considerable
anxiety to the bridegroom that the services of a prince of the
blood royal should be obtained to deflower his bride, for unless

---

[1] Castañeda de Naçera, "Relación de la Jornada de Cibola," in *Fourteenth
Report of the Bureau of Ethnology*, Part i, pp. 513 sq. ; A. de Herrera, *The
General History of the West Indies*, vol. iii, p. 341 ; G. F. de Oviedo y
Valdes, *Historia general y natural de las Indias*, vol. i, p. 222 ; F. Lopez
de Gomara, *Historia general de las Indias*, pp. 206, 283 ; F. Coréal,
Voyages aux Indes Occidentales, vol. i, pp. 139 sq. ; P. de Andagoya,
*Narrative of the Proceedings of Pedrarias Davila in the Province of Tierra
Firme*, pp. 33 sq. ; C. Lumholtz, *Unknown Mexico*, vol. i, p. 270 ; J. B.
von Spix and C. F. Ph. von Martius, *Reise in Brasilien*, vol. iii, pp. 1182,
1189 ; C. F. Ph. von Martius, *Beiträge zur Ethnographie Amerika's*, vol. i,
p. 113.

[2] B. F. Bourne, *The Captive in Patagonia*, pp. 56 sq.

[3] A. Mouliéras, *Une tribu Zénète anti-musulmane au Maroc (les Zhara)*,
pp. 85 sqq.

[4] Tcheou Ta-Kouan, "Mémoire sur les coutumes du Cambodge," traduit
et annoté par M. P. Pelliot, *Bulletin de l'École Française d'Extrême Orient*,
ii, p. 153 ; J. P. Rémusat, *Nouveaux mélanges asiatiques*, vol. i, pp. 116 sq.

[5] J. H. von Linschoten, *Voyage to the East Indies*, vol. i, p. 99 ;
A. Hamilton, "A New Account of the East Indies," in Pinkerton, *Voyages and
Travels*, vol. viii, p. 374 ; P. Sonnerat, *Voyage aux Indes Orientales*, vol. i,
p. 68 ; T. Herbert, *Some Years' Travels into Divers Parts of Africa and Asia
the Great*, p. 337.

[6] H. d'Arbois de Jubainville, "Le droit du roi dans l'épopée irlandaise,"
Revue archéologique, xliii, pp. 332 sqq. ; K. Schmidt, "Das Streit über das
jus primae noctis," *Zeitschrift für Ethnologie*, xvi, p. 50.

such a prince could be persuaded to bestow this favour upon him, a man's children would be regarded as bastards, and the marriage as good as null. "When they had a marriageable damsel in the house, after the marriage had been arranged, they shut her up for several days to fatten ; and when she came out she was married. And cavaliers and noblemen came before her, and one of them, whichever she might choose, had to lie with her before the bridegroom, and if she became pregnant from that knight the son she bore would be noble, otherwise the children of the husband were commoners." [1] Other accounts tell us that the first child of a woman was alone regarded as 'legitimate,' while subsequent children were regarded as 'bastards.' [2] But according to our ideas it would be the other way about ; the children whom they called 'legitimate' we should call bastards, and those whom they called 'bastards' we should call legitimate. The view taken by the Guanches was virtually identical with that which was held in India, where the first-born, being begotten by a Brahman or sacred personage, is nearly always spurious, but is spoken of as "born by the grace of God." [3]

The same view is taken by some tribes of the interior of Papua ; and the grounds for their opinion are set forth in a particularly explicit and lucid manner in their customs. Among the Banaro, marriage takes place between members of inter-marrying groups or septs, and is arranged by the parents while the parties concerned are still minors. The puberty rites, or mysteries of initiation of both sexes, and the marriage ceremony are all one ; the initiation of the children, male and female, is regarded as equivalent to their marriage, the partners having been selected previous to the ceremony. Those ceremonies are similar in character to those which we have noted as characteristic of New Guinea tribes. The sacred hut, or 'goblin hall,' in which the candidates are isolated, the magic flutes which are supposed to represent the voice of the god, the men disguised as goblins, play the same part as in other Papuan initiation rites. After the preliminary instruction and proper sacrifices have been offered, the bride is taken by her future father-in-law to the goblin hall, and is handed over by him to a 'goblin,' that is, to one of the

---

[1] A. Bernaldez, *Historia de los reyes catolicos D. Fernando y Dona Isabel*, vol. i, pp. 186 sq. Cf. J. de Abreu de Galindo, *Historia de la conquista de las siete Islas de Gran Canaria*, p. 97 ; A. Ca da Mosto, "Navigationi," in G. B. Ramusio, *Navigationi et Viaggi*, vol. i, fol. 106 ; A. Galvano, in *Hakluytus Posthumus, or Purchas His Pilgrimes*, vol. x, p. 6.

[2] Sir Edmund Scory, in *Purchas His Pilgrimage*, p. 787 ; A. de Espinosa, *Del origen y milagros de N.S. de Candelaria*, p. 12.

[3] A. de Gubernatis, *Storia dei viaggiatori italiani nelle Indie orientali*, pp. 352 sq.

hierophants who impersonate the spirit, or deity, who presides over
the rites.   The 'goblin' takes the girl to the Holy of Holies of the
sanctuary, to the very spot, in fact, where the sacred pipes are
kept.   "Before these hidden gods the couple unite."   The rite is
repeated on several occasions, but always in the goblin hall.   The
bridegroom or husband himself is not permitted to have any
relations with his bride.   It is not until she has borne a child that
he is allowed to cohabit with her and start married life.   The child
is called "the goblin-child."[1]   The first-born child is thus regarded
as the offspring of a god, and is in fact the offspring of the
impersonation of the god.

Nuptial Continence.

It is a usage prevalent in most parts of the world for
newly married people to observe continence during one or
more nights, or even for much longer periods.[2]   A simple
enumeration of those instances, taken by themselves, makes
edifying reading, but any rash supposition that the custom points
to exalted ideas of the merits of continence and chastity is soon
dispelled ; for the practice is observed by people who are conspicuous for the freedom and licentiousness of their sexual customs.
Thus in Greenland, among the Eskimo, of whom it is said that
"it would be difficult to find a people more cynical and more
devoid of shame,"[3] it is considered highly indecent for a young
woman to have a child until well after a year of marriage.[4]   In
Europe among the peasants of Esthonia, the bride's girdle must
not be undone on the wedding night, and the bridegroom must on
no account touch even her breast.   As Dr. Kreutzwald remarks,
his marital rights appear to be terribly limited, but he was
amply compensated for such continence by the freedom which he
enjoyed before marriage ; for nowhere probably, in Europe, did
the licence which was accorded to young women, and even regarded
as obligatory, approximate more closely to the condition of things

[1] R. Thurnwald, *Bánaro Society ; Social Organisation and Kinship System
of a Tribe in the Interior of New Guinea* (*Memoirs of the American Anthropological Association*, vol. iii, No. 4), pp. 260 sqq.

[2] A. E. Crawley, *The Mystic Rose*, pp. 344 sqq. ; H. Ploss, *Das Weib
in der Natur- und Völkerkunde*, vol. i, pp. 548 sqq. ; F. von Reitzenstein,
" Der Kasualzusammenhang zwischen Geschlechtsverkehr und Empfängniss,"
Zeitschrift für Ethnologie, xli, pp. 677 sq. ; J. G. Frazer, *Folk-Lore in the
Old Testament*, vol. i, pp. 497 sqq. ; E. Westermarck, *The History of Human
Marriage*, vol. ii, pp. 547 sqq.

[3] E. Petitot, in *Annales de la Propagation de la Foi*, xliii (1871), p. 470.

[4] H. Egede, *A Description of Greenland*, p. 143 n.

found in the more primitive savage societies.[1]   Among the Pathans
of Baluchistan the newly married bride is protected by a kinswoman who shares her bed, "and when her husband eventually
joins her, he is expected in some tribes to defer consummation for
a considerable period."   Yet the Pathans are noted for conceptions
of sexual morality which are the reverse of Puritanical, and " the
custom prevails more particularly in those tribes that still
go in wholesale for · pre-nuptial amours." [2]   Again, among the
Khyoung of the Chittagong Hills, husband and wife sleep apart
for the first seven nights after marriage, " although, according to
European ideas, the standard of morality among the Khyoung is
low." [3]   The Naga tribes of Manipur are not people to whom any
prudish notions can be imputed ; although, at the present day,
customs vary in different tribes and clans, the common house to
which unmarried girls resort is an immemorial institution amongst
them all, and in some tribes, such as the Ao, it is, even at the
present time, obligatory for them to receive lovers.   Among the
Angami virginity is regarded as disgraceful.[4]   Yet it is part of
the elaborate observances which accompany marriage in all
tribes that marital intercourse is prohibited to the newly married
for periods sometimes as long as a month.[5]   Among the Lhota
Nagas small boys sleep with the bridal pair to prevent them from
having intercourse ; [6] among the Ao a bodyguard of six men and
six women perform the same office ; [7] among the Angami a girl-
friend sleeps with the bride at her husband's house, while he goes
to the club-house ; he calls, on the wedding night, and ordering
everyone out of the house, consummates the marriage, but directly
after returns to the bachelors' quarters, and does not cohabit with
his wife again for three nights, or, according to another account,
for nine or ten nights.[8]   Similar delays are observed by the wild
tribes of Assam,[9] and the Kachin of Upper Burma,[10] who are

[1] J. W. Boecler, *Der Ehsten abergläubische Gebräuche, Weisen und Gewohnheiten*, pp. 25 sq.

[2] D. Bray, *Census of India*, 1911, vol. iv, " Baluchistan," p. 113.

[3] T. H. Lewin, *The Hill Tracts of Chittagong*, p. 51 ; Id., *Wild Races of
South-Eastern India*, p. 130.

[4] T. C. Hodson, *The Naga Tribes of Manipur*, pp. 78, 87 ; G. Watt,
" The Aboriginal Tribes of Manipur," *Journal of the Anthropological Institute*,
xvi, p. 358 ; D. Prain, " The Angami Nagas," *Revue Coloniale Internationale*,
v, pp. 47 sq. ; J. H. Hunter, *The Angami Nagas*, p. 169.

[5] T. C. Hodson, *op. cit.*, p. 87.

[6] J. P. Mills, *The Lhota Nagas*, pp. 150, 152 sq.

[7] E. Gait, *Census of India*, 1891, "Assam," vol. i, p. 245.

[8] J. H. Hunter, *The Angami Nagas*, p. 223 ; E. Gait, *op. cit.*, p. 239.

[9] T. C. Hodson, " The ' Genna ' amongst the Tribes of Assam," *Journal
of the Anthropological Institute*, xxxvi, p. 97.

[10] J. G. Scott and J. P. Hardiman, *Gazetteer of Upper Burmah*, Part i,
vol. i, p. 407.

conspicuous for the freedom of their sexual relations. Similarly, in the Malay Archipelago, in the island of Flores, the bride and bridegroom are guarded on their wedding night and for the three following nights by eight matrons, who watch in pairs to make sure that the marriage is not consummated.[1] Yet the morals of those islanders are disgraceful, and promiscuous inter- course is the rule before marriage.[2] The moral code is no better in the Kei Islands, sexual relations being entirely unrestricted before marriage ; yet the chastity of the newly married is main- tained by an old woman or a boy who sleeps between them.[3] In the Babar Archipelago the bride and bridegroom are surrounded by a guard of female and male relatives respectively, who prevent them from approaching one another for several nights after marriage ; but before marriage the relations between them take the form of sanctioned nocturnal visits.[4] Among the Dayaks of Dutch Borneo it is a rule that the bride and bridegroom must not sleep together on the wedding night, but their conduct before marriage is unrestricted.[5] In the Solomon Islands marriage is said, in many instances, not to be consummated for a long time ; [6] but before marriage the bride leads the life of a prostitute.[7] In Fiji when a man and woman are married " they remain in strict seclusion for three days ; on the fourth day the women of the same town assemble and escort the newly married female to a stream to bathe ; and her husband is now supposed to abstain for a lengthened period from sexual indulgence. This custom, however, belongs to a time when the Fijians were polygamists. Missionary influence established monogamy amongst them, and nowadays the golden maxims which in former times regulated marital relations are ignored and forgotten." [8] But in those days the depravity of the Fijians in sexual matters, the Rev. Lorimer Fison thought, was " probably unparalleled in any other part of the world." [9] Among the For tribe of Central Africa the

---

[1] S. Roos, " Iets over Endeh," *Tijdschrift voor indische taal- land- en volkenkunde*, xxiv, p. 525.

[2] J. G. F. Riedel, "The Island of Flores," *Revue Coloniale Internationale*, 1886, pp. 67 sq.

[3] Id., *De sluik- en kroesharige rassen tusschen Selebes en Papua*, pp. 219, 236.

[4] *Ibid.*, pp. 350 sq.

[5] M. T. H. Perelaer, *Ethnographische beschrijving der Dajaks*, pp. 53, 59.

[6] R. H. Codrington, *The Melanesians*, p. 239.

[7] H. B. Guppy, *The Solomon Islands*, p. 43 ; C. Ribbe, *Zwei Jahre unter den Kannibalen der Solomo-Inseln*, p. 270.

[8] D. Blyth, " Notes on the Traditions and Customs of the Natives of Fiji relative to Conception, Pregnancy, and Parturition," *Glasgow Medical Journal*, xxviii, pp. 179 sq.

[9] C. Wilkes, *Narrative of the United States Exploring Expedition*, vol. iii,

bride and bridegroom do not so much as meet for seven days after marriage, and consummation is even then deferred. Yet prenuptial relations are wholly free, and virginity is neither found nor expected.[1] Among the Pangwe consummation of the marriage is not permitted on the first night, and it is alleged that the bride would be ashamed of such indecent haste; but sexual relations are free before marriage.[2] Among the Bohindu of the Congo it is a rule that no relations are permitted between husband and wife immediately after marriage; in the interval between that event and her betrothal, the bride " prostitutes herself until she is with child," when she informs the bridegroom that she is ready to receive his embraces.[3] Among the Bawenda the husband is not even permitted to enter his wife's hut until the first night of the third month after marriage; but the behaviour of the young people after initiation and immediately before marriage " does not bear description." [4] Marriage among the Nandi is not consummated for two or three nights, but the prenuptial state is one of free love.[5] Among the Banyoro it is considered proper to abstain from consummating the marriage for two or three nights; as is the custom with the neighbouring Baganda and many other peoples, the bride is protected by a female relative, generally her aunt, who sleeps with the newly-wedded pair. In order, however, to instruct the bride, her chaperon has intercourse with the bridegroom.[6] Among the Swahili it is the rule that marriage must not be completely consummated on the wedding night; the bridegroom has only partial connection with his wife, and completes the act with a slave-girl who is at hand for the purpose.[7]

Several of the peoples who observe the custom of remaining chaste during the first few nights after marriage are polyandrous in their matrimonial arrangements, and a woman, after marriage, enjoys the greatest freedom. Thus among the Bahima a bridegroom is held bound to observe continence for three nights, and

p. 363. Cf. L. Fison, " The Nanga, or Sacred Stone Enclosure of Wainimala, Fiji," *Journal of the Anthropological Institute*, xiv, p. 28.

[1] R. W. Felkin, " Notes on the For Tribe of Central Africa," *Proceedings of the Royal Society of Edinburgh*, xiii, pp. 228 sq., 233.

[2] G. Tessmann, *Die Pangwe*, vol. ii, pp. 255 sq., 233.

[3] E. Torday et T. A. Joyce, *Notes ethnographiques sur les peuples communément appelés Bakuba, ainsi que sur les peuplades apparentées. Les Bushongo* (*Annales du Musée du Congo Belge*), p. 271.

[4] E. Gottschling, " The Bawenda, a Sketch of their History and Customs," *Journal of the Anthropological Institute*, xxxv, p. 373.

[5] H. H. Johnston, *The Uganda Protectorate*, p. 878; A. C. Hollis, *The Nandi*, p. 63.

[6] J. Roscoe, *The Bakitara, or Banyoro*, p. 272.

[7] H. Zache, " Sitten und Gebräuche der Suaheli," *Zeitschrift für Ethnologie*, xxxi, p. 75.

his wife is equally under the obligation not to deny herself to any of his clan brothers, or to any visitor that may call upon her husband.[1] So likewise among the Banyoro, whose practice of nuptial continence has already been noted, " any man's wife was common to him and the other members of his clan." [2]   Again, among the Tlinkit of Alaska the family, as we have seen, is a polyandrous one, a couple of brothers or other relatives of the husband being associated with him in his marital rights.[3]   But the chief bridegroom is very scrupulous to fast and to defer the consummation of the marriage for as long as four weeks.[4]

It is manifest from such examples that the practice of observing continence for a certain period after marriage is unrelated in its origin to any notion concerning the meritorious character of chastity.   In some of its forms the practice is part and parcel of the Nasamonian usage or of other similar customs of pre-nuptial defloration by a person or persons other than the husband. The bridegroom is, of course, ' ipso facto ' obliged to observe continence as regards the bride.   Thus in the Arunta tribe of Central Australia the bridegroom is not allowed access to the bride for two or three nights ; the other men who have the right of previous access to her using meanwhile their privilege.[5]   In the Narrinyeri tribe of South Australia also, the companions of the bridegroom claim the right of access to the bride ; [6] and the bridegroom is not supposed to have any relations with her until the third or fourth night, and after all guests have departed.   This, the Rev. George Taplin informs us, " is a point of decency. . . . This arrangement is for the sake of decency." [7]   The reader may form his own conclusions as to Narrinyeri conceptions of decency. The custom of excluding the bridegroom from access to the bride would naturally be kept up even where the Nasamonian usage was no longer practised, as is said to be the case in the above-mentioned tribes, and among other Australian aborigines.   Thus among the Euahlayi the bride is kept from her husband for a whole month, or until her mother gives her permission to join him ; [8] and among the tribes of Western Victoria one of the

---

[1] J. Roscoe, *The Northern Bantu*, pp. 120 sq.

[2] Id., *The Bakitara, or Banyoro*, pp. 279, 265, 239.

[3] See above, vol. i, p. 642.

[4] A. Krause, *Die Tlinkit Indianer*, p. 220 ; H. H. Bancroft, *The Native Races of the Pacific States*, vol. i, p. 111.

[5] See above, p. 224.   Cf. C. Strehlow, *Die Aranda- und Loritja-Stämme in Zentral-Australien*, vol. iv, part i, pp. 90 sq.

[6] For the Nasamonian usage, A. W. Howitt, *The Native Tribes of South-East Australia*, p. 261 ; for the nuptial continence, G. Taplin, *The Folklore, Manners, Customs, and Languages of the South Australian Aborigines*, p. 35.

[7] G. Taplin, *loc. cit.*

[8] L. Parker, *The Euahlayi Tribe*, p. 58.

bridegroom's friends sleeps with him for two months after his marriage to see that he does not take possession of his wife.[1] Similarly, among the Wataveta of East Africa, among whom it is customary for the bridesmen to lie with the bride in turn before the bridegroom has access to her, it is a rule that he shall not approach her for four or five nights.[2] Among the Ankwe of Northern Nigeria the bride is very modestly secluded after her marriage and her food is brought to her ; consummation is not permitted for a period varying from three to six months. The groom is, however, sometimes anticipated by his father ; and among the Lala of the same province this is claimed as a right.[3] Similarly, among the Mekeo of New Guinea the bride takes up her abode for two or three weeks with the bridegroom's father, and during that time her future husband is not permitted to approach her.[4] The custom would appear to be allied to that of the Banaro, among whom the man who impersonates the spirit or goblin is sometimes the bridegroom's own father.

It is not improbable that in many instances where the custom of deferring consummation of the marriage is observed, it was formerly accompanied by some form of union of the bride with a representative of the god, either in the form of indiscriminate prostitution, or by intercourse with some priest, prince, or holy man. Indeed, learned ecclesiastical writers, in refuting " the vile and abominable calumny " that such practices ever existed in mediaeval Europe, lay the greatest stress upon the observance of the custom forbidding the bridegroom to approach the bride for some nights after marriage, inferring that the latter custom was confounded with a ' jus primae noctis ' of the priest or prince.[5] The distribution of those usages among some heathen peoples outside Europe lends countenance to the argument. Among the ancient Mexicans consummation was deferred for three, or according to another account five, nights, which were spent in devotion and mortification. When the general prevalence among the ruder populations of Central America of the custom of requesting a priest or medicine-man to spend the first few nights with the bride is borne in mind, it is difficult to dismiss the surmise that the usage of the more civilised Mexicans was originally connected

[1] J. Dawson, *Australian Aborigines*, pp. 31 sq.

[2] See above, p. 224. Cf. A. C. Hollis, " Notes on the History and Customs of the People of Taveta," *Journal of the African Society*, i, pp. 115 sqq.

[3] O. Temple, *Notes on the Tribes, Provinces*, etc. . . . *of the Northern Provinces of Nigeria*, pp. 21, 257.

[4] R. W. Williamson, " Some unrecorded Customs of the Mekeo People of British New Guinea," *Journal of the Royal Anthropological Institute*, xliii, p. 276.

[5] L. Veuillot, *Le droit du seigneur au moyen-âge*, pp. 183 sqq. ; Abbé Hanauer, *Les paysans de l'Alsace au moyen-âge*, pp. 136 sq.

with similar functions exercised by the priests. That surmise is strengthened by the fact that, if the priest did not attend the bride on the wedding night, it was at least his duty to make her bed, and to place upon it the sacred emerald which was the emblem of the deity, together with other symbols of the gods. Unless chastity was observed by the bridegroom, the anger of the gods was, they believed, sure to fall upon him and his bride.[1] Again, the custom of nuptial abstinence is observed by the Persians,[2] and it is likewise observed by those curious representatives of primitive Persian religion, the Yezidis, who make it a rule to defer consummation of a marriage for three nights.[3] We have seen how eager the latter people still are that their daughters should become united to a holy sheikh, and how highly their desirability as wives is thought to be enhanced by such a sanctifying connection.[4] The rule of continence for a period of at least three nights is prescribed by ancient Hindu law,[5] and is equally observed by many representatives of the aboriginal non-Aryan populations of India ;[6] and nowhere is the notion of the desirability, or obligation, of intercourse with a representative of a god before the consummation of human marriage more deeply and immemorially established than among those races.

It is not by any means invariably necessary that the divine spouse, spirit, god, or demon, should be incarnated in a human representative. As we know, the fecundation of a woman by a supernatural agent is commonly believed even among the most primitive peoples, to take place without her actual knowledge. In the Vedic ritual the god was represented by a staff annointed with perfumed oils, and wrapped round with a garment or with thread, which was laid on the bridal bed while the spouses spent the night in continence.[7] This was obviously equivalent to the

[1] D. F. Clavigero, *Storia antica dell Messico*, vol. ii, pp. 91 sq. ; G. de Mendieta, *Historia ecclesiatica Indiana*, p. 128 ; F. L. de Gomara, *Conquista del Méjico*, p. 439.

[2] J. Chardin, *Voyages en Perse et autres lieux de l'Orient*, vol. ii, p. 235.

[3] H. O. Parry, *Six Months in a Syrian Monastery*, p. 365.

[4] See above, p. 228.

[5] *The Grihya-Sutras*, trans. by H. Oldenberg, *The Sacred Books of the East*, vol. xxiv, pp. 286, 384 ; vol. xxx, pp. 48, 267 ; M. Winternitz, *Das altindische Hochzeitsrituell nach dem Apastambiya-Grihyasutra und einigen anderen verwandten Werken* (*Denkschriften der kaiserlischen Akademie der Wissenschaften, Wien, Philosophische-historische Classe*, vol. xl), p. 86 ; A. Weber, " Vedische Hochzeitssprüche," *Indische Studien*, v, p. 325.

[6] Thyagaraja Aiyar, in *Census of India*, 1911, vol. xxi, p. 100; R. V. Russell, *The Tribes and Castes of the Central Provinces of India*, vol. iv, p. 407 ; Anantha Krishna Iyer, *Cochin Tribes and Castes*, vol. i, p. 61 ; vol. ii, pp. 139, 143, 192 ; E. Thurston, *Castes and Tribes of Southern India*, vol. iii, pp. 103 sq.

[7] *The Grihya-Sutras of Apastamba*, iii. 8. 8 sqq. (*The Sacred Books of the East*, vol. xxx, p. 267).

sacred emerald placed on the bed of the Mexican bridal pair, and
to the sword which in many European customs was placed between
the newly-wedded couple, professedly to keep them separated and
help them to remain continent, but doubtless fulfilling originally
the same office as the anointed manikin employed in ancient
India. The Moon-god, Soma, was, we saw, expressly declared in
the Vedic marriage service to have the first claim to the bride
before she came into the possession of her husband. In some
formulas he is associated with other gods : " Soma has her first,
next she is received by Gandhara, the third to have her is Agni,
fourthly she belongs to the man born of mortals." [1] The gods
appear to play a similar Nasamonian function in the notions which
are current at the present day among the peasants of Brittany.
The usage of observing chastity during the first three nights of
marriage is an old-established one among them also ; the first
night is generally regarded as belonging to the Good God, the
second night is in some districts considered to belong to St. Joseph,
while the third night belongs to the patron saint of the husband,
the fourth night only being ' the husband's night.' [2] The result
of such continence is, according to the Grihya-Sutras, offspring
of a divine character ; indeed, if the husband exercises so much
self-control as not to approach his wife for a whole year after
marriage, she will give birth to a god. A period of abstinence
lasting six months will result in the birth of a Rishi, four months'
abstention will produce a holy Brahman, while shorter periods,
down to the minimum of three nights, will be rewarded by the
birth of a distinguished Vedic scholar.[3]

When the confusion to which the character of primitive deities
has given rise is borne in mind, it is not surprising that the
supernatural power to which the primitiae of marriage are devoted,
instead of being regarded as a god, should very commonly be
said to be a devil. The Esthonians, for instance, say that it
is the devil who prevents the bride and bridegroom from coming
together.[4] Similarly, in Java, where the custom of observing
nuptial abstinence is prevalent,[5] the devil is said to hover round

[1] *Rig-Veda*, x. 85. 40, ed. Lüdwig, vol. ii, p. 537.

[2] P. Sébillot, *Coutumes populaires de la Haute-Bretagne*, pp. 132 sq.
Cf. A. de Nore, *Coutumes, mythes et traditions des provinces de France*, p. 195.
The allocations vary in different districts and in different accounts ; the
Virgin Mary is also mentioned as claiming one of the wedding-nights, and in
some districts the first—possibly in her character of moon-deity.

[3] M. Winternitz, *Das altindische Hochzeitsrituell*, p. 86.

[4] J. W. Boecler, *Der Ehsten abergläubische Gebräuche, Weisen und Gewohnheiten*, p. 29.

[5] P. J. Veth, *Java, geographisch, ethnologisch, historisch*, vol. iv, p. 396 ;
T. S. Raffles, *The History of Java*, vol. i, p. 369 ; E. Hardouin and W. L.
Ritter, *Java*, p. 29.

the nuptial bed, ready to carry off one of the pair.[1] The Dayaks,
who also are forbidden to have sexual relations, or even to go
to sleep on the night of their marriage, say that they act thus
from fear of the devil.[2] In China devils were said to be on the
look-out to seize the bride when she was being carried to her
husband's house.[3] Countless precautions are taken by various
peoples to protect the bride from the devils who are lusting after
her. In Bulgaria the custom of nuptial abstinence was observed
as among other Southern Slavs ; but the bridegroom nevertheless
seized an early opportunity of enjoying the embraces of his
bride. This had, however, to be done before midnight ; after
that fateful hour, in which spirits are wont to be abroad, all
relations between him and the bride had to cease until the following
Tuesday.[4] As an additional precaution, during the hurried consummation of the marriage, a friend stood by fully armed and
with drawn sword, lest the devil should come to claim his prey
before the appointed hour.[5] Among the Canelos Indians of
Ecuador abstinence is demanded of the bridegroom on the wedding-
night, and his life would be endangered if he did not observe
chastity. He does not even spend the night with his bride. The
reason which is given by the natives for this practice is that a
dangerous demon, called ' supai,' claims the right to spend that
night with the bride, and that the husband voluntarily cedes him
the right. The danger is not over after the first night, for the
demon is jealous of the husband and wants to continue to possess
the bride ; the rivalry lasts sometimes until two or three children
are born of the marriage.[6]

In the last instance, as in many others, fear of the supernatural
generative power rather than desire to secure the benefit of its
divine fecundity, as in India, is given as the motive for yielding
the bride ; and instead of the Good God to whom the first night
is dedicated in Brittany, we have an awful demon. But such
differences of point of view are commonplaces in religious evolution.
Dr. Oldenberg is of opinion that even in India the heavenly bridegroom, who is now invited to confer the benefits of divine generation
on the newly wedded bride, was formerly viewed as a dreaded
demon who slipped into the woman, and whom it was important
to conciliate or deceive.[7] The two aspects or points of view still

---

[1] W. B. d'Almeida, *Life in Java*, pp. 160 sq.
[2] M. T. H. Perelaer, *Ethnographische beschrijving der Dajaks*, p. 53.
[3] J. Doolittle, *Social Life of the Chinese*, vol. i, p. 95.
[4] F. S. Krauss, *Sitte und Brauch der Südslaven*, p. 451.
[5] J. Piprek, *Slavische Brautwerbungs- und Hochzeitsgebräuche*, p. 149.
[6] R. Karsten, *Contributions to the Sociology of the Indian Tribes of Ecuador*
(*Acta Academiae Aboensis, Humaniora*, i, No. 3), pp. 72 sqq.
[7] H. Oldenberg, *Die Religion des Veda*, p. 271.

exist side by side throughout the Muhammadan world; for, on the one hand, it is believed that the devil desires to have intercourse with the bride;[1] and, on the other, it cannot be doubted that the elaborate religious rituals with which the act of procreation is attended are designed to call down upon the bride powers of fecundity from a divine source. In Egypt, according to Lane, when the bridegroom is first admitted to the presence of his wife, he " takes off every article of the bride's clothing, except her shirt; seats her upon a mattress or bed, the head of which is turned towards the direction of Mekkeh, placing her so that her back is also turned in that direction; and draws forward and spreads upon the bed the lower part of the front of her shirt. Having done this, he stands at the distance of rather less than three feet before her, and performs the prayers of two rekkehs; laying his head and hands, in prostration, upon the part of her shirt that is extended before her lap." These devotional observances are followed by the digital defloration of the bride, after which the bridegroom retires and strictly abstains from approaching his bride for several days.[2]

The practice of deferring the consummation of marriage was upheld and recommended by the Christian Church, which, as in regard to many other heathen rites and customs, claimed to have introduced it.[3] In the Eastern Church it was a punishable offence

---

[1] El-Bukhari, *Traditions musulmanes*, trans. by Houdas and Marçais, vol. iii, p. 578.

[2] E. W. Lane, *An Account of the Manners and Customs of the Modern Egyptians*, vol. i, p. 218. Cf. J. L. Burckhardt, *Arabic Proverbs*, p. 140.

[3] It is enacted by the Council of Trent that " if any provinces have herein in use any praiseworthy customs or ceremonies, the holy Synod earnestly desires that they shall be by all means retained " (*The Canons and Decrees of the Sacred and Oecumenical Council of Trent*, Session xxiv, chap. i, p. 198). It would appear that the practice of nuptial continence in Europe belongs more particularly to the barbaric races. It is found among the Slavs, in Germany, Switzerland, and Alsace (A. Wuttke, *Der deutsche Volksaberglaube der Gegenwart*, p. 375; K. Simrock, *Handbuch der Deutschen Mythologie*, pp. 600 sq.; E. H. Meyer, *Badisches Volksleben, in neunzehnten Jahrhundert*, pp. 272, 319; A. Birlinger, *Volksthümliches aus Schwaben*, vol. i, p. 479, vol. ii, pp. 334, 354; E. Hanauer, *Les Paysans de l'Alsace au moyen-âge*, p. 137 n.), in Brittany, in Scotland (Lord Hailes, *Annals of Scotland*, vol. iii, p. 15 n.). On the other hand it does not appear to obtain in Southern Europe. It was sometimes observed in Italy (L. A. Muratori, *Antiquitates Italicae medii aevi*, disc. xx, vol. ii, p. 110), but only in obedience to the prescriptions of the clergy. An instance reported from Romagna (M. Placucci, *Usi e pregiudizi dei contadini della Romagna*, pp. 59 sq.) appears to refer rather to a matter of convenience, the departure of the guests from a crowded house being awaited, than to a ritual custom. In Greece, Italy, and Spain, the opposite usage of exhibiting the ' proofs of virginity ' is more prominent, and that usage is not conspicuous, if found at all, among the northern peoples. The latter were still, at the time of the introduction of

to consummate a marriage on the first night.[1]   The observance was recommended by St. Augustine at the fourth Council of Carthage ; [2] it is laid down in the Carolingian capitularies,[3] and reference to it occurs pretty frequently in early mediaeval ecclesiastical literature.[4]   In the Life of St. Emmeramus by the monk Arnoldus, for instance, a holy man thus addresses his bride : " We should be careful, my beloved sister, seeing that we have been joined by a Christian marriage, not to fall into the rites of the Gentiles, but rather exercise continence for three nights, praying God that he may procreate children for us." [5]   The idea that by dedicating the first nights of marriage to God, who is the true procreator of children, that divine function will be promoted, is, it will be noted, by no means absent in the Christian interpretation of the custom.   Not only is the fertility of the bride thought to be promoted by the observance, but it is sometimes thought the number of children she will bear will be proportional to the number of nights during which continence has been observed by the husband.[6]

Yet there is here the same confusion that we have noted elsewhere as regards the character of the supernatural being to whom the first nights of marriage are yielded.   A scriptural sanction for the adoption of the immemorial usage by the Christian Church was found in the now apocryphal ' Book of Tobit,' where the custom is described as having been observed in regard to his wife Sarah by Tobit, or Tobias, " a name," observes an ecclesiastical writer, " which in relation to the sanctity of Christian

---

Christianity, in a more matriarchal social phase than the lands of Latin culture, and their societies were as yet more accustomed to pre-nuptial freedom, and ignorant of the traditional value of virginity.   The notion that the god, rather than the human husband was the true generator of a woman's offspring was, accordingly, more familiar to them than to the patriarchalised lands of Mediterranean civilisation.   In the religious East, on the other hand, the conception of divine generation survived amid a patriarchal order of society ; and it was re-introduced thence with Oriental religious ideas.

[1] L. Veuillot, *Le droit du seigneur*, p. 194.

[2] *Concilium Carthaginense Quartum,* in Migne, *op. cit.*, vol. lxxxiv, col. 201.

[3] *Caroli Magni Capitularia, Benedicti Diaconi Collectio*, Migne, *op. cit.*, vol. xcvii, col. 859.

[4] J. Michelet, *Origines du droit français*, p. 37 ; L. Veuillot, *Le droit du seigneur*, pp. 184 sqq. ; *Decretum Magistri Gratian*, Pars sec., Caus. xxx, quaest. v, c. 7 (*Corpus Juris Canonicus*, vol. i, p. 1106) ; Regino Pruniensis, *Chronicon*, in Migne, *op. cit.*, vol. cxxxii, col. 139, 251 ; L. Thomassin, *Dictionnaire de discipline ecclésiastique*, vol. i, p. 1053 ; E. Martène, *De antiquis Ecclesiae ritibus*, vol. ii, i. ix. 5 ; J.-B.-E. Pascal, *Origines et raison de la liturgie Catholique*, in Migne, *Encyclopédie théologique*, vol. viii, col. 753.

[5] Arnoldus Emmeramensis, " De miraculis et memoria Beati Emmerammi libri duo," in Migne, *Patrologiae Cursus*, vol. cxli, col. 1000.

[6] Rajacsich, *Das Leben, die Sitten und Gebräuche, der im Kaiserthume Oesterreich lebenden Südslaven*, p. 147.

marriage stands second only to the most holy name of God." [1]
The traditional three nights of abstinence were commonly known
as 'Tobias nights.' The narrative relates that Sarah had already
had seven husbands, but that each had been slain on his wedding-
night by the jealous devil Asmodaeus. Tobias, aware of the
circumstance, took the precaution to avoid any clash with his
supernatural rival by leaving the field clear, and not visiting his
wife for three nights. The story is evidently very old, and as we have
it, in various versions, is a composite one which has passed through
several editings. In the Septuagint and the English translation
made from it, the three nights of continence are not mentioned;
while in the Vulgate and the Aramaic version from which it was
taken Tobias not only refrains from challenging the claims of
the demon, but, on the advice of his guardian angel, performs
elaborate magic incantations by burning the heart and liver of
a fish, a well-known fertility charm, thus driving the demon
away as far as Ecbatana. [2] Such inconsistencies are commonplaces in folklore tales, which are repeated from age to age, the
point of the original narrative being as often as not entirely lost.
The daemon Asmodeus is clearly no other than the Persian Aëshma
daëva, who is frequently mentioned in the Zend-Avesta as the
chief angel of Ahriman, [3] apparently a double of the dark god;
and, as has been seen, [4] there is every reason for thinking that the
evil character of Ahriman was no part of the original nature of
that divinity.

The Divine Bridegroom impersonated by the Husband.

Whether marriage be entered upon with the observance of strict
chastity, or with rites of promiscuity, or the defloration of the
bride by a sacred personage, the intention is in each case the same,
namely, to secure the union, or Holy Matrimony, of the woman with
the god. In the Christian view, as in that of the Papuans or the
Polynesians, as well as among most other peoples, savage or civilised,
it is, in fact, from the deity that the generative power which causes
women to bear children truly comes; it is the god who is 'the

---

[1] L. Veuillot, *Le droit du seigneur*, p. 183.

[2] *The Book of Tobit*, iii. vi, *The Apocrypha and Pseudepigrapha of the
Old Testament*, vol. i, pp. 218 sqq. For a full discussion of the origin of the
texts of the *Book of Tobit* see pp. 174 sqq., and E. Schürer, *History of the
Jewish People in the Time of Jesus Christ*, div. ii, vol. iii, pp. 40 sqq.

[3] E.g. *Samyad Yast*, viii. 46 (*The Sacred Books of the East*, vol. xxiii, p. 297);
Bandahis, xxviii. 14 (*ibid.*, vol. v, pp. 107 sq.).

[4] See above, p. 113.

real husband of all women.' The human husband is but accessory,
or is at best the vehicle of the divine source of fertility and
generation. The union with the Divine Bridegroom, which is
regarded as essential to secure not only the fecundity of a woman
but also the fulfilment of all her functions, is by the majority of
peoples considered to be quite separate from human marriage ;
it commonly takes place in magical or religious rituals and ceremonies which have no direct relation to human marriage.

Marriage, as we have had ample opportunity of noting, is not
regarded by peoples in lower stages of culture as in any way
partaking of the character of a religious institution or ceremony.
It is, on the contrary, almost universally viewed in a very practical
and matter-of-fact light as a business transaction. Among most
primitive peoples a marriage is merely a mutual understanding
between marriage-groups, the members of which are 'born married,'
or between smaller groups or families, or between individuals.
With the vast majority of uncultured races marriages are not
celebrated with any special ceremony. Among the Bushongo of
the Congo, " the couple meet in the bush, and the man makes his
declaration, if it is accepted the marriage is consummated there
and then." [1] Such an unceremonious procedure is typical of the
simpler phases of culture. There is no marriage ceremony in
Australia. With the exception of one or two peoples of more
advanced culture in Central America, there was a conspicuous
absence of all solemnity in relation to marriage throughout the
American continent. The simpler peoples in Africa, in Asia, in
Indonesia do not celebrate a marriage by any ceremony. Marriage
ceremonies, where they exist as observances of a religious character
among peoples of relatively advanced culture, have generally other
purposes than that of establishing a fast union between the bride
and bridegroom. A large proportion of marriage rites are intended
to promote the fertility of the union. Numerous rites in the
elaborate ceremonies of Eastern peoples are magical measures to
secure good luck and to avert supposed dangers ; purifications,
baths, protection by means of amulets and talismans, the scaring
away of evil influences by drumming, wedding bells, the waving
of swords and the firing of muskets, the observance of silence,
fasting, magic robes, bridal veils, complete seclusion, are some of
the means adopted to avert the evils which are supposed to threaten
the bridal couple. That the ' happy pair ' should be thought to
be specially exposed to envy is very natural. Among Greek
peasants it is remarked that " the fear of the evil eye poisons the

---

[1] E. Torday and T. A. Joyce, *Notes ethnographiques sur les peuples communément appelés Bakuba, ainsi que sur les peuplades apparentées. Les Bushongo*, p. 115.

very joys of love. It is generally believed that its influence, or the power of witchcraft, can bind the fires of the spouse. Therefore appropriate precautions are taken on marriages or even before. Gifts are offered to any witch whom one may have reason to suspect ; and the people endeavour to become reconciled with any enemies they may have." [1] But the envy of mortals is not the only danger that threatens married bliss. The bridegroom is avowedly an usurper. That such an usurpation should be attended with particular dangers, more especially as regards the fulfilment of the reproductive functions of marriage, is not therefore surprising. Ceremonial rites are compacted of precautionary measures, not merely on account of the malice of envious eyes, but because the bridal pair are in fact objects of just resentment and displeasure, inasmuch as by the act of entering the married state they more or less set aside the claims of the Divine Bridegroom. Other marriage rites, such as those of the wedding meal or other forms of communion, have reference to establishing an alliance of friendship between the two families or groups concerned. In the more patriarchal types of society, rites are performed, such as placing a mark on the bride, or a ring on her finger, or tying the bride and bridegroom together, which constitute a symbolic taking possession of the woman, or mark her transference from her own family to that of her husband. But it may be said that nowhere, except in a few advanced phases of patriarchal society, is the solemnisation of a marriage regarded as in itself a religious act ; and, indeed, it is only in Christian times that such a view of marriage has become definitely developed and emphasised.

Where such a view has come to be adopted, the sacred character imparted to the transaction arises from combining the human marriage with, or assimilating it to, a Holy Matrimony. In India, as has been seen, the necessity for the divine union, and the prior claim of the god to the woman, are explicitly and even emphatically recognised. The bridegroom is careful to declare repeatedly that not he, but the moon-god Soma, is the rightful husband of the bride, and formally surrenders her to the god before advancing any claim to her himself. [2] Nevertheless, that formal acknowledgment being made, he proceeds on the supposition that, no action being taken by the god, he may himself impersonate the deity and act as his representative. It is, in fact, as to the god that the woman is married, and she is instructed that whatever the character of his earthly representative, she must regard him as the god himself. " Though

[1] F. C. H. L. Pouqueville, *Voyage en Morée, à Constantinople, en Albanie,* etc., vol. i, pp. 257 sq.

[2] See above, p. 239, vol. ii, p. 585.

of bad conduct or debauched, or even devoid of good qualities, a husband must always be worshipped like a god." [1] In China the theory that the husband is the representative of the god, and that the marriage union is in fact a Holy Matrimony, or union of the woman with a god, is even more explicitly conceived. The husband is the representative of Heaven, and the wife the representative of the Earth.[2] In the two pronounced patriarchal societies of India and China human marriage is, thus, definitely assimilated to Holy Matrimony, and the human husband to the divine spouse.

Among the Jews, marriage never assumed a pronounced religious character. Nevertheless, there is no doubt that some notion of identifying it with a Holy Matrimony existed, though only vaguely. Rabbi Jehudah expressly refers to the bridegroom as ' Sanajim,' that is to say, ' Heaven.' [3] It was also the custom among the Jews until quite recent times that, when the greater part of the marriage ceremony had been celebrated in the synagogue or in the house, the wedding party should proceed out of doors, and the essential act by which the bride and bridegroom were joined took place " under the tent of heaven." [4] It is possible that the intention was that the bride should be regarded not as entering the tent of an earthly bridegroom, but as being joined to God Himself under His heavenly tent. The custom of erecting the bridal tent, where the newly married spend the wedding night, on the roof of the house may also have been associated with the same notion.

Among the Romans, marriage was, as we have seen, regarded as a civil contract, and in the later days of the republic and during the empire, religious celebrations were habitually dispensed with altogether. But in the religious ceremonies which originally accompanied patrician marriages there lingered distinct traces of older views. The previous marriage of the bride to the god was vividly represented by the custom that the bride should sit on the lap of the god's statue.[5] The custom was associated with the notion that such a ' hieros gamos ' was necessary

---

[1] The Laws of Manu, v. 154 (The Sacred Books of the East, vol. xxv, p. 196).

[2] Yî King, Appendices, ii. xxxvii. liv (The Sacred Books of the East, vol. xvi. pp. 242, 257).

[3] R. Eisler, Weltenmantel und Himmelszelt, vol. i, p. 603.

[4] Kaufmann Kohler in The Jewish Encyclopaedia, vol. vi, p. 506. It was likewise a common custom in the Middle Ages to conclude the marriage service at the door of the church (J.-B.-E. Pascal, Origines et raison de la liturgie Catholique, in Migne, Encyclopédie Théologique, vol. viii, col. 754).

[5] Augustine, De civitati Dei, iv. 11, vi. 9, vii. 24 ; Arnobius, Contra Gentes, iv. 7 ; Lactantius, Divinae Institutiones, i. 20. 36 ; Tertullian, ad Nat., ii. 11 ; Id., Apolog., 25.

to ensure the woman's fertility, and married women who desired offspring repeated the iconic union with the phallic god in an even more realistic fashion.[1]

That the husband himself had been, in earlier patriarchal times, regarded as the representative of the god is shown by a formula the meaning of which had come to be entirely forgotten. At the wedding ceremony the bride pronounced the words " Ubi tu Caius ego Caia," or, according to the older pronunciation, " Ubi tu Gaius ego Gaia." [2] The name Caius, which was so common among the Romans, means ' bull,' and its feminine form means ' cow.' The Sanskrit root from which the words are derived is ' gau,' which means ' cow,' and the English word, as also the word ' calf,' are derivatives of the same linguistic root. In the Aeolian dialect γαῖος and γαῖα retain their original meaning of 'bull' and ' cow.'[3] The formula " Ubi tu Gaius ego Gaia " therefore means literally "Where thou art the bull, I am the cow."[4] The bull is, as we know, the common form under which the god in his fertilising aspect is represented, and the goddess is correspondingly pictured as a cow; the name Gaia, by which the Great Goddess in her character of earth-deity fertilised by the heavenly male power was known to the Greeks, is, in fact, the unaltered original term, and means ' The Cow.' In the Dersin mountains of Kurdistan, among the Dusik Kurds, the rites of fertility and the Holy Matrimony of the women with the god are still cele-brated in the crude primitive manner. During the great yearly festival, when the men and women assemble in a large room which serves as a temple, the lights are suddenly turned out, and promiscuous sexual intercourse takes place. Earlier in the course of the ceremony the priest calls in a loud voice: " I am the Great Bull! " Whereupon a woman who has been recently married, perferably the same day, steps forward and gives the response: " I am the young Cow." The lights are then turned out, and the Holy Matrimony between the priest of the bull-god and the young cow is consummated.[5] Among the ancient Celts, a woman would signify her choice to a man by saying: " You are the bull, and I am the young cow." [6] The Roman formula was thus the exact equivalent of that with which the Holy

---

[1] Arnobius, *loc. cit.*

[2] Plutarch, *Quaest. Rom.* xxx; Valerius Maximus, x ; Cicero, *Pro Murena*, xii. 27.

[3] Hesychius, s.v. γαῖος.

[4] See F. Liebnecht, *Zur Volkskunde*, p. 423 ; F. G. Bergmann, *Les Gètes*, p. 171.

[5] O. Blau, "Nachrichten über kurdische Stämme," *Zeitschrift der deutschen morgenländischen Gesellschaft*, xvi, pp. 623 sq.

[6] A. H. Leahy, *The Heroic Romances of Ireland*, vol. i, p. 95.

Matrimony is celebrated in more primitive forms; the crude
union of the woman with the god in the form of the stranger who
possesses her in promiscuous intercourse, or of the priest, being,
in accordance with more advanced sentiments, eliminated by the
assimilation of the husband to the Divine Bridegroom. Plutarch
tells us that the senator Manilius never had intercourse with his
wife except during a thunderstorm, for he thus felt himself to be
more thoroughly assimilated to Jupiter.[1]

The religious or sacred character which the contract of marriage
has assumed in the more pronounced patriarchal societies, contrasting as it does with the secular and business nature of the
institution in primitive social phases, is imparted to it by the
identification of the human husband with the god who is united
to the woman in earlier fertility rites; the human marriage thus
becomes itself a Holy Matrimony. The conception of marriage as
a sacred and religious bond did not, however, attain its clear
expression until Christian times, and did not indeed become an
established dogma until the sixteenth century of our era. To
Christian authorities in the Patristic age, and for long after, it
was, as we shall see, more than doubtful whether the state of
matrimony were not a state of sin.[2] Married men commonly
regarded themselves as unworthy of partaking of the sacraments,
and deferred doing so, even as regards baptism, until their
wife's death or their own approaching end had placed them
in a state of grace. The very suggestion that marriage should
be regarded as a sacrament would, to the Christian Fathers, have
been gross blasphemy. " Nothing is further from the truth,"
remarks Dr. Conybeare, " than the contention of modern divines
that the Church from the first patronised and sanctified an
institution which was in reality only imposed upon her "; and
" nothing is more remarkable than the tardiness with which
liturgical forms for the marriage ceremony were evolved in the
Church." [3] Among the early Christians, as in the Graeco-Roman
world generally, marriage was usually viewed in the light of a civil
contract, and the function of any religious ceremony connected
with it was to seal the contract and bring prosperity and blessing
upon the union. Although it was recommended by some that
marriages should be solemnised with a priestly benediction, and
that due publicity should be given to them by obtaining the
approval of the congregation,[4] most Christians continued to follow

---

[1] Plutarch, *Vita Catonis*, xvii.

[2] See below, pp. 372 sqq.

[3] F. C. Conybeare, *Myth, Magic, and Morals*, pp. 216, 371.

[4] Tertullian, *Ad uxorem*, ii. 9; *De pudicitia*, iv (Migne, *Patrologiae
Cursus*, vol. i, cols. 1415 sqq.; vol. ii, cols. 1038 sq.).

the Roman usage and dispensed with a religious ceremony at their marriages. In the fifth century the constitution of Theodosius and Valentinian recognised the consent of both parties as sufficient to constitute a valid marriage.[1] In A.D. 537 it was laid down that marriages among the noble classes should be celebrated in a church ; but "the common people may continue to contract valid marriages without any external solemnity."[2] The solemnity was, it is clear, regarded, as in early Rome, as merely lending greater weight to the contract. That was also the view of its function which was generally taken by the Fathers. St. Basil speaks of "the yoke imposed by the blessing."[3] The 'blessing' was the general term by which the matrimonial ceremony was referred to, thus clearly indicating the purport of its function. The Christian Church continued to recognise the validity of marriages, whether contracted with or without blessing. In the middle of the eighth century the Eclogue of Leo the Isaurian and Constantine lays it down that marriage is recognised whether it be contracted by written instruments, or by verbal consent of the parties or of their parents, or whether solemnised in a church or not.[4] The religious ceremony was for the first time pronounced to be an indispensable condition of the validity of a marriage by the Council of Trent in the year 1563. The pronouncement does not hold in those countries where the decrees of the Council have not been published, and a religious ceremony was not made a condition of the legality of a marriage in England until the passing of Lord Harwicke's Act in 1753. "Before this Act, the canon law was in force in England, and according to its provisions the mere consent of the parties, followed by cohabitation, constituted, for many purposes, a valid marriage."[5]

It was out of the expression used by St. Paul that the complete doctrine of religious marriage developed in Europe. St. Paul referred to marriage as a 'mysterion,'[6] thus assimilating it to the

---

[1] J. Zhishman, *Das Eherecht der orientalischen Kirche*, p. 140.

[2] *Ibid.*, p. 141.

[3] St. Basil, *Homelia vii in Hexaemeron*, in Migne, *op. cit.*, *Series Graeca*, vol. xxix. col. 160.

[4] J. Zhishman, *op. cit.*, p. 158.

[5] W. E. H. Lecky, *A History of England in the Eighteenth Century*, vol. ii, p. 115. The beautiful words of the Marriage Service are not, in this instance, the product of the Church's literary genius, but are the terms of the Anglo-Saxon plighting in heathen days, which was couched in the same language as was used in deeds of transfer of land, and was adopted by the Anglican Church : "I take thee, John, to be my wedded husband, to have and to hold, from this day forward, for better for worse, for richer for poorer, in sickness and health, to be bonny and buxom, in bed and at board, till death do us part, and thereto plight I my troth " (M. B. Synge, *A Short History of Social Life in England*, p. 38).

[6] *Ephesians*, v. 32.

'hieros gamos,' or Holy Matrimony, which constitutes so general a feature in the mysteries of uncultured races and ancient religions; and he deliberately identified the marriage of bride and bridegroom with the union of a woman to the Divine Bridegroom, which in primitive and archaic societies is regarded as a necessary antecedent to human marriage. The expression used by St. Paul, which was the usual one by which those ceremonies were denominated, was translated in the Vulgate by the word 'sacramentum,' a use of the term for which no precedent is known, and which was applied elsewhere by the translators to the " sacrament of the Woman and the Beast." [1] The Holy Matrimony came thereby to be regarded as a sacrament of the Christian Church. Thus was reached the culmination of the regulations imposed from the dawn of primitive society upon sexual relations. Not only was the economic aspect of the relation conjoined with the sexual aspect from which it was originally distinct, but those two aspects of the institution were themselves blended with the magic and religious conceptions which formerly had reference to a divine marriage separate from, and even directly opposed to, the human economic union; and the full force of the primitive tabus came to extend to all sexual relations save those of the Holy Matrimony of a woman with one man acting as the representative of her God.

[1] *Revelation*, xvii. 7.

CHAPTER XXVI

MODESTY

WE have seen that a strange paradox is presented by ethical ideas in primitive society. While those rules and principles which bear directly upon the welfare and harmony of the social order, and appear indispensable to its existence, are not insisted on or invested with any solemnity, and are often not formulated at all, the greatest importance and awe attach to rules of conduct which have no apparent utilitarian function, to those prohibitions, namely, which come under the denomination of tabus. Murder, theft, fraud may or may not be explicitly condemned ; they are, in any case, viewed as civil offences, and in the vast majority of primitive societies as personal offences which are the private concern of the injured individuals or families, but to which no awful and supernatural prohibition attaches. The breach of traditional tabus, on the other hand, such as holding converse with one's mother-in-law, eating forbidden foods, neglecting to observe tabu days, coming in contact with menstrual blood, or, in many tribes, exposing one's open mouth while in the act of eating, is regarded in a totally different light. They are offences fraught with consequences, vague but dreadful, not only to the guilty party, but to the whole community, which is defiled and laid under a curse by the infringement of those awful rules. The sentiments they evoke differ from any which offences against the social order may call forth ; these may be perpetrated callously and brazenly, but the breach, even accidental, of a tabu fills a man with a sense of utter shame, and he shrinks from meeting the gaze of his fellow-men. To avoid the breach of tabus is with most primitive peoples an anxiety which dominates conduct, private and public, and the most essential part of religion. Among the Eskimo " it is the chief duty of the Shaman or angokok to discover who has infringed tribal tabus, and thus brought down the wrath of the spiritual beings." [1]

[1] P. Rodin and L. H. Gray, art. " Eskimo," in Hastings's *Encyclopaedia of Religion and Ethics*, vol. ii, p. 394.

Nothing, perhaps, strikes us as so incongruous in the notions of primitive peoples as that paradoxical disproportion between their attitude towards manifest offences against utilitarian social ethics, and offences as regards what to us are meaningless and absurd superstitions. No feature in their 'manners and customs' is more apt to be regarded in a humorous light and to afford occasion for amusement at the expense of the poor savages than the awful character which they ascribe to their tabus.

But we have, in truth, little right to laugh at the savage in this respect. The paradox is not peculiar to uncultured society; it is no less marked in our own, and it is only the very sanctity with which our tabus are invested which prevents us from perceiving amongst ourselves the same incongruity which strikes us so forcibly in primitive societies. The European missionary among savages is filled with horror and distress at many of their customs and ideas, and the pages of his accounts are filled with lamentations over their evil ways. That horror and reprobation on the part of the European often appear to the savage in much the same light as his own superstitious fears and traditional tabus do in the eyes of the European. When the savage refers in awe-struck tones to his confusion at meeting his mother-in-law, the European cannot refrain from laughing; when the missionary expresses indignation at the pre-nuptial promiscuity of the savage the latter turns aside to have a hearty laugh. Savage tabus may differ to some extent in their form from those of the European, but the paradoxical estimate of their relative importance and of that of social ethical rules is as pronounced in European as in any primitive or ' savage ' society.

When we speak of morality we are understood, nine hundred and ninety-nine times out of a thousand, to refer not to abstention from fraud, violence, or injustice, or any principle of social utilitarian ethics, but to sexual morality. Sexual morality belongs to a different order of moral principles from utilitarian ethics. The latter, however their sanction and obligation may be conceived, refer to acts which are the cause of injury and suffering to others, and, by extension, assign a positive value to acts calculated to promote their welfare and well-being. Sexual morality rests on entirely different ideas. It is not on the injury or suffering that may be caused to others that the notion of sexual morality depends. Sexual immorality may, it is true, and frequently does, involve the infliction of suffering. But the suffering so inflicted is to a large extent the effect of the very condemnation which attaches to the offence; it is the punishment meted out by social dis-approval or by social conditions which repudiate such conduct. It may, of course, be easily maintained that, apart from that automatically injurious effect, sexual immorality is, all things

considered, injurious, and sexual morality beneficial. But whatever latitude and force may be allowed to those considerations,
the fact remains that it is not upon them that sexual morality
rests. It lies outside the sphere of utilitarian and rationalistic
sanctions ; its moral values refer to absolute and categorical
imperatives, or, what is the same thing, to what are termed
'natural sentiments.' And it is precisely to that sphere of moral
prohibitions that the term 'morality' attaches to a degree altogether incommensurate with the moral values appertaining to
utilitarian social ethics. Grave people will unhesitatingly speak
of the public exhibition of a woman's limbs as 'immoral,' while
they will dispute as to whether paying a woman 10½d. a dozen
for the manufacture of shirts is, or is not, an immoral act.
Sexual morality is morality 'par excellence' ; it is not dependent
for its sanction upon mere rationalistic and utilitarian considerations,
but is a true categorical imperative irreducible to terms of irrelevant
rational principles.

Feminine Power and Sexual Restrictions.

It is manifest from such facts as we have had abundant occasion
to review that standards of sexual morality are products of social
evolution ; they differ widely in primitive and in civilised humanity.
It will be found on examination that existing notions of sexual
morality are composed of at least two distinct elements which
have by no means developed concomitantly in the course of social
evolution. They have originated from certain primitive tabus,
but those tabus have been greatly reinforced and extended by
the development of masculine proprietary claims. If my view is
correct, the first tabu prohibition imposed, and the prototype of
all subsequent prohibitions, was the curse pronounced by women
in repulsing sexual intercourse at such times as they were
physiologically unfitted for it. The tabu against incest was
probably also imposed by women, actuated by maternal jealousy.
Tabu prohibitions were thus from the outset directed against
sexual functions ; the disproportionate importance attached to
sexual tabus is thus part of the original nature of tabu prohibitions
in general. Those tabus were imposed by women, not by men ;
the dread and awful character with which they are regarded is the
character attaching to the curse of a witch. No stronger foundation
for a moral prohibition could exist in the primitive mind.

But women, who laid the foundation of sexual tabus, would
seem to have had very little part in their subsequent development
and extension. There is no original disposition in women to
chastity. The sexual instinct in woman differs from that of the
male chiefly in its periodicity. Sexual indifference, or frigidity,

is perhaps more common in women than in men, and sensuality
more rare ; but even frigidity is a very different thing from a bias
towards principles of chastity.   Generalisations as to the respective
physiological dispositions of the sexes are very unreliable, owing
chiefly, I believe, to the fact that the character of the sexual
instincts tends more than any other to be equally transmitted to
both sexes, and thus equilibrated, any excessive development of
those instincts in the male being communicated to the female
also, and vice versa.   Considerable differences in temperament are
found as regards those instincts in different races and societies,
but those differences usually include both sexes ; and there is,
I think, no authentic instance showing that in the same race and
in the same society one sex is temperamentally frigid and the
other lascivious.   Whatever physiological differences may exist,
they are to a large extent neutralised by the racial equilibration
between the sexes ; and there is little evidence of any influence
upon the development of ideas and standards of sexual morality
arising from the temperament of one sex alone.

    We are on much more solid ground when we turn from physio-
logical speculations to social and ethnological facts.   These afford
no evidence that the influence of women has ever been exercised in
the direction of extending sexual restrictions and tabus, and of
imposing chastity on men.   Where such principles are already
recognised and established women are often found to be staunch
upholders of them ; but that upholding of established principles is
a universal character of the profound conformity of the feminine
mind and of its disposition to acquiesce in current views and
standards.   Feminine morality consists in unquestioning assent
to established estimates and usages.   Woman is constitutionally
orthodox ; all heresy is alien to her character.   The established
sentiment has for her a hundredfold greater force than it has for
man ; its authority is for her absolute, her devotion to it passionate.
That conformity is naturally greater where her own value and
position are concerned.   It is equally tenacious of any established
sexual value which may happen to have the status of a generally
approved and established view ; feminine conservatism defends
polygamy and sexual freedom as staunchly as it does monogamy
and morality.   The only influence which the relative sexual
indifference of woman may have had on the course of development
of standards of sexual morality is manifested in the ease with
which she accepts a change in those standards when once that
change is duly recognised.   Women, as compared with men, are
easily corrupted and easily reformed.

    In those uncultured races among which the task of imposing the
Christian religion has been comparatively easy, as in many parts
of America, and particularly in Polynesia and Melanesia, where no

strong religious beliefs or ideas opposed the change, the missionaries have succeeded in effecting a complete transformation in the sexual standards of the people within a few years, one might almost say instantaneously. Since the sexual customs of the savage do not proceed, as some are prone to suppose, from corruption or temperamental lasciviousness, but from amorality in that respect, he is quite ready to adopt the most puritanical ideas when they are imposed upon him with religious authority. Reformed Papuans speak of the sexual customs which were immemorially established amongst themselves until within a few years in the same terms of horror and reprobation as do their religious instructors. In Polynesia the girls and women whose mothers offered themselves to strangers and knew of no restrictions in sexual life, now generally excel in prudish beseemingness their European sisters. Andagoya mentions that a Paraguayan woman who had been but a few months converted to Christianity received the advances of a Spaniard with an indignant rebuff: " How, sir, could you ask me to do such a thing ? I am a married woman, and the Holy Virgin would be angry with me." Before her conversion it would have been a point of honour with her not to refuse the request.[1] Those facts must be borne in mind in estimating the value of reports on the subject. An illustration of transformation in the standards of chastity is afforded by the following instance. The women of Kumul, on the outskirts of Chinese Turkestan, were notorious for the freedom of their sexual habits. A recent traveller, however, notes that " the excessive shyness of the ladies of Kumul appeared strange to us after the easy manners of the Mongols and the Kirghiz. In Kumul it was almost impossible to catch a glimpse of a woman in the streets. They were as shy as rabbits, and dived into their houses when they saw us approaching, and even locked the doors until we were well passed ! It was obvious that the reputation which Kumul possessed in the days of Marco Polo has been entirely changed. This change cannot have been the result of their conversion to Islam, and can only have taken place in recent years, for Prejevalsky, who visited the oasis in 1879, said that ' the women were free and easy in their manners, just as they were in Marco Polo's time.' Now, however, morality is a feature—a profound contrast to olden days, in order to produce which some very strong cause must have been at work." The cause is the rapid increase of Chinese influence in the place, where in recent years Chinese manners, dress, and ideas have been adopted—as likewise Chinese notions in regard to the seclusion and virtue of women.[2]

[1] P. de Andagoya, *Narrative of the Proceedings of Pedrarias Davila in the Province of Tierra Firme*, p. 68.
[2] D. Carruthers, *Unknown Mongolia*, pp. 483 sq.

But while strict standards of sexual morality are in general readily adopted by women, no facts exist to show that women have been at any time instrumental in establishing such standards. Those societies where the influence and power wielded by women have been greatest are, on the contrary, uniformly characterised by greater sexual freedom as compared with patriarchal societies. Bachofen, who supposed that matriarchal society had become established as a result of a revolt of women against conditions of promiscuity, recognised, with a strange inconsistency, that 'hetaerism' is a characteristic of all matriarchal societies. In none of the most pronounced surviving examples of such societies do we find any development of stringent codes of sexual morality. Among the Pueblos before the advent of Europeans, pre-nuptial freedom obtained, and marriage relations, if not actually communal, were of the loosest.[1] Even at the present day the sexual code is characterised by the utmost freedom. "Though the Sia are monogamous," writes Mrs. Stevenson, "it is common for the married as well as the unmarried to live promiscuously with one another, the husband being as fond of his wife's children as if he were sure of their paternal parentage." Married women boast of the numbers of their lovers, and girls cohabit with married men.[2] Among the Hopis, pre-nuptial motherhood is common and does not affect marriage prospects; the dissolution of the tie, as with all other Pueblo Indians, presents no difficulty to either party.[3] We have seen that there existed no trace of any rigid sexual code among the matriarchal Iroquois.[4] The extreme sexual immorality of Targi society, where women wield paramount power, is notorious.[5] In the matriarchal societies of the Malays and of the Nayars, the adoption of more stringent sexual standards has gone hand in hand with the decay of matriarchal institutions. In the age-old society of Tibet, which was originally matriarchal, and where women still wield great influence and power, sexual freedom prevails. Tonga is distinguished among patriarchal Polynesian islands for the high status of the women and the great influence they wield; women occupied "an easy and honoured position which they have held from time immemorial; they were idolised." Yet "great licence existed between the sexes," and in fact their sexual morality was such, we are told by the same missionary, as "to show how low humanity could fall when without the restraints and sanction of a

---

[1] See above, vol. ii, p. 86.

[2] M. C. Stevenson, "The Sia," *Eleventh Report of the Bureau of Ethnology*, p. 20.

[3] O. Solberg, "Gebräuche der Mittelmesa-Hopi bei Namengebung, Heirat and Tod," *Zeitschrift für Ethnologie*, xxxvii, p. 269.

[4] See above, vol. ii, pp. 33 sq.

[5] See above, vol. ii, pp. 113, 288.

Divine faith."[1] An ancient account gives us a high idea of the exalted position of the women of Central Asia : " They receive more attendance than the men from handmaidens and young pages ; they promenade on horseback with great show, and adorn their houses with gold and precious stones."   But, adds the same writer, " they are not chaste, and consort promiscuously with their slaves and with strangers, having immunity in this respect, and are not blamed by their husbands, over whom they, in a manner, domineer."[2] The women of Java, owing to their industry and to favourable economic conditions, are generally quite independent economically of their husbands.   " Does this state of things," asks Crawfurd, " give rise to the singular libertinism of Javanese women ? "[3] Among the Mumbake, a Nigerian tribe, who are in a state of transition from matriarchal to patriarchal customs, the women remain in their parental home for some years after marriage.   In case of adultery the aggrieved husband has a right to kill the offender or to exact compensation.   But if the offence be committed in the woman's own home, the husband is not entitled to any compensation, and no blame attaches to the act.   Thus adultery is an offence under patriarchal, but not under matriarchal conditions.[4]

In countries where marriage customs are still, or were until recently, polyandrous, the system is, we have seen, emphatically favoured by the women and regarded by them as superior to those of other countries ; nothing, as regards those matrimonial arrangements, is done without their express sanction and approval.   Far from the number of husbands being imposed upon them, that number is frequently increased at their express wish and desire. In Ladakh, women who have two, three, four, or even five husbands, have, and generally use, the right of selecting additional husbands or lovers, who are known as ' magpa.'   The supplementary husband is regarded as the property of the wife ; she can dismiss him whenever she chooses, and take another.   The women, as a very general rule, avail themselves of those privileges.[5] Among the Todas also, the women exercise the right to have recognised lovers, in addition to their regular husbands.[6]   In Ceylon it was, according to Tennent, the women of noblest birth and greatest wealth who had the most husbands.[7]   So likewise in the Marquesas it was with the princesses that polyandry on the most extensive scale

---

[1] T. West, *Ten Years in South-Central Polynesia,* pp. 260 sq., 270.
[2] Bardesanes, in Eusebius, *Praeparatio evangelica,* p. 276.
[3] J. Crawfurd, *History of the Indian Archipelago,* vol. i, p. 79.
[4] O. Temple, *Notes on the Tribes of Northern Nigeria,* pp. 284 sq.
[5] See above, vol. i, p. 664.
[6] See above, vol. i, p. 698.
[7] J. E. Tennent, *Ceylon,* vol. i, p. 428.

was practised.[1]   Among the Aleuts, according to Bancroft, it was the
wealthiest women and those whose position was therefore of greatest
influence, who were the most polyandrous in their relations.[2]

Wherever individual women enjoy, in uncultured society, a
position of dominant power, far from imposing or observing
chastity and purity, they avail themselves of their independence
to exercise greater liberty in their sexual relations.   Queens and
princesses in the old matriarchal kingdoms of Africa used their
privileges to the utmost.   The princesses and Queen-Mother of
Uganda used their position in such a manner that " all Uganda
was said to be their husbands "[3]; and the Queen-Mother of
Ashanti is similarly described as a Messalina.[4]   Among the Basonge
of the Congo, the daughters of chiefs refuse even their parents'
entreaties that they should marry, and prefer to set up their
own house and to have as many lovers as they please.[5]   The
same freedom was claimed by queens and princesses in Hawaii,[6]
in Tahiti.[7]   In Paraguay ' noblesse oblige ' was the motto: a
lady of the highest rank is reported to have said that, although
common and vulgar women, who had no breeding, might behave
rudely, no lady of good birth and natural refinement would be so
mannerless as to refuse her favours to an admirer.[8]   So likewise in
Sierra Leone " it is reckoned extremely impolite and ill-bred for a
married woman to reject the offers of a lover." [9]   In Akra and in
Loango, although amongst commoners girls and women are strictly
guarded, women of wealth and noble birth entertain as many
lovers as they please without any loss of respectability.[10]   Noble
women and heiresses in Madagascar have as many lovers as they
choose.[11]   In the Marshall Islands every woman who is of noble
birth and independent has a recognised right to have sexual
intercourse with her underlings.[12]   In Arabia high-born women
refused to bind themselves to one man by marriage, and claimed
complete freedom in the disposal of their favours.[13]

[1] M. Radiguet, " Les derniers sauvages," *Revue des Deux Mondes*, 1859,
vol. ii, p. 613.

[2] H. H. Bancroft, *The Native Races of the Pacific States*, vol. i, p. 92.

[3] J. Roscoe, " Notes on the Manners and Customs of the Baganda,"
Journal of the Anthropological Institute, xxxi, p. 122.

[4] W. Hutton, *A Voyage to Africa*, p. 354.

[5] C. van Overbergh, *Les Basonge*, p. 254.

[6] J. J. Jarves, *History of the Hawaiian Islands*, p. 90.

[7] M. Radiguet, *loc. cit.*

[8] G. Hernandez de Oviedo y Valdés, *Sumario de la natural historia de
las Indias*, p. 182.

[9] J. Matthews, *A Voyage to the River Sierra-Leone*, p. 119.

[10] H. C. Monrad, *Gemälde von der Küste von Guinea*, p. 51.

[11] J. Sibree, *The Great African Island*, p. 217.

[12] P. A. Erdland, *Die Marshall Insularen*, p. 121.

[13] W. Robertson Smith, *Kinship and Marriage in Early Arabia*, p. 69.

It may be supposed that feminine jealousy might have tended to foster the development of monogamous marriage institutions. But we have, I think, seen conclusive evidence that there is in polygamous societies no more disposition on the part of the women to favour the adoption of monogamous institutions than there is a disposition among the women of our own society to bring about the reverse change. Matrilocal marriage, where it has persisted until advanced stages of culture, as in Egypt or in early Greece, has certainly been a factor in the development of monogamous marriage, for it is generally impracticable in those stages of culture for a man to contribute adequately to the maintenance of several households, as appears to have been sometimes done in Egypt. But the operation of that factor is economic, not psychological. In the northern Ṭargi tribes, where marriage is matrilocal and monogamous, the presence of concubines in the household is not in the least resented by the wife,[1] and the same appears to have been the case in early Greece. Feminine jealousy may in some instances have assisted in the transition from polygamous to monogamous institutions by hastening the elimination of 'secondary' wives and concubines. Women of another race or nation are liable to be objected to by wives who have no objection to women of the same race, especially if, as primitively is the case, they are relatives. Thus among the Chiriguanos of the Gran Chaco a man is at liberty to keep as many concubines as he pleases, who assist the chief wife and lighten her labours; but it was as much as his life was worth to bring home a Spanish woman whom he might have captured in warfare.[2] Whatever influence feminine jealousy may have exercised in the direction of monogamy, it has not counted as a fundamental factor; the whole development of the institution has been, as has been seen, conditioned by economic causes in which considerations of sentiment or of abstract morality have had but little part. While we everywhere find chastity imposed by men upon women, it would be difficult to find instances of any corresponding imposition of chastity by women upon men, apart from the observance of the primitive tabus which have reference to menstruation, pregnancy and suckling.

*Concealment during Sexual Intercourse
not the primary object of Modesty.*

It has been very generally supposed that an innate or 'natural' tendency towards sexual purity is evidenced in woman by the sentiment of modesty or pudicity. No order of sentiments has

[1] Ibn-Batuta, *Travels*, transl. by S. Lee, pp. 234 sq.
[2] P. Lozano, *Descripción Chorographica del terreno*, etc., *del Gran Chaco*, p. 82.

been more commonly regarded as being an inborn and spontaneous character. The stereotyped phrases used by old writers referred to those manifestations as due to sentiments "which nature has implanted in the human mind," and they usually alluded modestly to the sexual organs as "those parts which nature has taught human beings to conceal." Those expressions are destitute of meaning; either the sentiment of modesty has been inherited from animal ancestors or it has developed in some manner as a result of conditions and ideas arising in social humanity. As to the existence of any germ of the sentiment in animals, so entirely absent is any trace of such a reaction that grossly indecent behaviour has always been described as identical with that of animals.

In support of a biological origin of the sentiment it has, however, been adduced that some animals retire to secluded places, such as the depth of the forest, for sexual intercourse. There is no very definite evidence of this, but it would, of course, be natural that animals should seek seclusion while pairing, in the same way as carnivorous animals often drag their prey to some sheltered and hidden place in order that they may to some extent be relieved from the necessity for watchfulness while engaged in feeding. It has been argued by some authors that a similar necessity would render it desirable for primitive man to seek concealment during the sexual act, and it has been suggested with some confidence that such a necessity or desirability has been the chief factor leading to concealment and secrecy in regard to sexual functions.[1]

Such a view is not in accordance with either sociological or psychological facts. It is not round the sexual act but the exposure of the sexual organs that the sentiment of modesty centres. It is, of course, true that privacy is almost universally sought for the performance of the sexual act. But our ethnological information appears to show that, so long as the act is regarded as licit, the desire for concealment and privacy is far from being a general sentiment in the lower cultures, and that no sense of embarrassment attends the satisfaction of sexual desire before witnesses. This is the case with regard to the Australian aborigines. The habitual communal defloration of girls previous to marriage takes place in the presence of all concerned. Any native man will, on request, call a woman from the camp and copulate with her before the visitors and any other witnesses without the slightest manifestation of embarrassment or self-consciousness on the part of

---

[1] L. Tillier, *L'instinct sexuel chez l'homme et chez les animaux*, p. 254; G. Mortimer, *Chapters on Human Love*, p. 40; A. E. Crawley, *The Mystic Rose*, pp. 150, 180; F. Lester Ward, *Dynamic Sociology, or Applied Social Science*, vol. i, pp. 634 sq.

either the man or the woman.[1] In Tahiti, as Cook testifies in
detail, copulation commonly took place in public, and the highest
ladies of the Court looked on without any indication that they
found anything unusual in such an exhibition.[2] Even at the present
day complete indifference in this respect is observable among the
Maori. Among the Eskimo races also the evidence is definite that
no privacy is thought necessary for the performance of the sexual
act.[3] Among the Creeks, Schoolcraft notes that sexual intercourse
was indulged in without secrecy or shame.[4] Among the tribes of
New Mexico, Castañeda tells us, the sexes united in public wherever
and whenever they chose—"como animales."[5] The Botocudos are
in this respect completely indifferent to the presence of other members of the family or neighbours, including children and young
girls.[6] The same is said of the Indians of Paraguay.[7] Among the
Chorotis of the Pilcomayo, after their dances, the young women
place themselves in front of their huts, and there receive male
visitors in succession. " The so-called sense of shame does not
appear to be greatly developed ; several pairs lie together, and
the presence of spectators is not unusual."[8] Among the Negritos
of the Andaman Islands, privacy is not regarded as necessary for
sexual intercourse ; copulation takes place anywhere, in the
presence of men, women, and children.[9] The Fuegians have no
notion that the sexual act should not be, like all other natural
acts, performed in public.[10] Such indifference is, in the promiscuity
of savage life, quite usual. For juridical or ritual reasons marriage
is not infrequently consummated in public.[11]

[1] N. von Miklucho-Maclay, " Über der Mika-Operation in Central-
Australien," *Verhandlungen der Berliner Gesellschaft für Anthropologie*, 1880,
p. 89.
[2] J. Cook, *An Account of a Voyage round the World*, in Hawkesworth,
An Account of Voyages, etc., vol. ii, p. 128.
[3] H. Egede, *A Description of Greenland*, pp. 126 sq. ; E. Petitot, *Les
Grands Esquimaux*, p. 37.
[4] H. R. Schoolcraft, *Indian Tribes*, vol. v, pp. 195 sq.
[5] P. de Castañeda de Naçera, *Relación de la jornada de Cibola*, p. 448.
[6] P. Ehrenreich, " Ueber die Botocudos der brasilianischen Provinzen
Espiritu Santo und Minas Geraes," *Zeitschrift für Ethnologie*, xix, p. 31.
[7] F. X. de Charlevoix, *History of Paraguay*, vol. i, p. 92.
[8] E. Nordenskiöld, *Indianerleben*, p. 88.
[9] E. Owen, " On the Osteology and Dentition of the Inhabitants of the
Andaman Islands," *Transactions of the Ethnological Society*, N.S., ii, p. 35.
[10] C. Spegazzini, " Costumbres de los habitantes de la Tierra de Fuego,"
Anales de la Sociedad Científica Argentina, xiv, pp. 176 sq. The Continental
visitor to Hyde Park derives the impression that spontaneous sentiments
in this respect among the lower classes in England do not differ greatly from
those reported concerning peoples of lower cultures. It would seem that
the only bar to the consummation of the sexual act in public is the police.
[11] E.g. L. Tautain, " Ethnographie des Îles Marquises," *L'Anthropologie*,

Although it appears that no sense of indecency attaches among many, probably most, uncultured races to the sexual act, and primitive man in general has no such sentiment, it is nevertheless the rule that privacy is sought for its performance, and even legitimate marital relations are, among many primitive peoples, clandestine. This, we saw, is probably the effect of actual danger attending such relations in their primitive form. The privacy demanded remains, in fact, desirable chiefly for its own sake, and the main consideration in seeking it is the desire to be sheltered from all disturbing influences. Such secrecy is quite commonly, even at the present day in civilised society, motived above all by the fear of detection ; so that no transformation of the desire for privacy into a quite different sentiment has taken place, as would be the case if that desire for privacy were the primitive root of the transformed sentiment. Feminine modesty commonly operates concomitantly with the complete and willing yielding of herself by the woman, and manifests itself in a desire for darkness and avoidance of exposure even in the act of giving herself to her lover ; and it continues to operate quite irrespectively of the sexual act itself. It is not the sexual act which is the main object of the sentiment, but the sexual organs. Exposure of the latter wounds the sentiment of modesty, while nothing could be added to that pain by the sexual act itself—on the contrary, the latter, as a natural fulfilment of the most important functions of womanhood, is commonly associated by women in a far less degree with sentiments of modesty than exposure of the body. In fact, where relations are legitimate and recognised, there is no indelicacy, even for the most modest woman, in being seen lying in bed with her legitimate partner, as, for instance, by servants, while the slightest exposure of the body may cause her agonies of wounded modesty. Those facts are significant ; they show that the sentiment of sexual modesty has not arisen primarily in reference to the sexual act and become subsequently extended to the sexual organs, but that, on the contrary, it has primarily reference to the latter, and only secondarily and by extension to the sexual functions themselves.

The contrary view that the sentiment of modesty has primarily reference to the sexual act, and only by extension to the organs concerned in that act, has been maintained by several writers, notably by Dr. Westermarck. Countless manifestations of shyness and sentiments of modesty in reference to the sexual act itself are even more pronounced in primitive than in civilised

vii, p. 546 ; Tutuila, " The Line Islanders," *Journal of the Polynesian Society,* i, pp. 270 sq.; H. H. Johnston, *The Uganda Protectorate,* p. 747 ; J. H. Weeks, " Notes on some Customs of the Lower Congo People " *Folk-lore,* xix, p. 413.

societies, in spite of the fact that among many who cover their sexual organs, sexual relations may take place in public. There are numerous reasons, apart from the grounds for secrecy which we have already noted, for that shyness. In the view which I have put forward of primitive sexual restrictions they originally applied virtually to all sexual relations, and these were of necessity clandestine. Those restrictions abound in even the most primitive human society. Tabus on sexual relations do not, however, explain the special notions and sentiments attaching to the exposure of the sexual organs, as Dr. Westermarck appears to acknowledge, since he puts forward a separate theory to account for their concealment. There is, in the most primitive social phases, no correlation between the importance attached to sexual restrictions and that connected with bodily modesty ; and, on the other hand, the most rudimentary forms of protection and concealment of the sexual organs have reference not to their attraction or suggestiveness in regard to the sexual impulse, but, on the contrary, to supposed injuries that might impair their functions in the satisfaction of that impulse. In later stages the two orders of tabus and sentiments, those attaching to sexual relations in general and those which have reference to bodily exposure, or pudicity proper, have to some extent coalesced, and, the primitive motives which led to the covering of the sexual organs having disappeared, the secrecy or impurity attaching to all sexual matters has become substituted for it as the rationale of concealment by clothing. The two sentiments have thus become fused and mutually reinforced. But in their primitive forms we find their manifestations entirely distinct.

*Clothing used for purposes
other than Modesty.*

The practice of covering the sexual organs is far from being primitive in humanity. To effect that object is by no means the first purpose which has given rise to the use of clothing. Personal apparel, often of a very elaborate character, is used by many peoples without serving any purpose of modesty. Among the Bororo, for example, as among the majority of South American tribes, the women are usually completely naked ; the men are elaborately decorated with crowns, armlets, garters of bright parrots' feathers, and they wear an abundant array of collars and girdles ; but the sexual organs are left exposed.[1] The natives of Peru wore a kind of shirt, but it only reached down to the navel.[2] In New Britain,

---

[1] K. von den Steinen, *Unter den Naturvölkern Zentral-Brasiliens,* pl. i.
[2] F. L. Gomara, *Historia general de las Indias,* p. 273.

clothing for the purposes of covering and decency was "absolutely non-existent" with both men and women; yet they were loaded with articles of apparel of the most elaborate character.[1] Some Melanesians who, as regards all purposes of modesty go naked, are yet so sophisticated in the arts of the toilet that they actually wear wigs.[2] Similarly, in many parts of western New Guinea the toilet of the men is certainly more elaborate than that of any European, and more trouble is bestowed upon it than we should care to bestow upon ours; but the penis is left exposed.[3] The Australian natives of New South Wales, when seen by Captain Cook, were naked, both men and women, but the elaborate character of the ornaments they wore was a matter for remark.[4] Among the Fuegians men and women are entirely naked; they, however, sometimes use a skin cloak, but they wear it on their back as a protection against the wind.[5] Among the Suk and the Nandi the men are loaded with apparel, and, in addition to the elaborate articles with which almost every part of their body is covered, they wear a substantial mantle over their shoulders; but the sexual organs are left exposed.[6] Among the Munshi of Nigeria, men and women habitually wear quite decent cloth robes; but on gala occasions, and on a market day, they take them off and go stark naked, their bodies being merely painted.[7]

The ample and skilfully constructed garments with which arctic peoples are covered are intended solely for warmth and protection. The total lack of bodily modesty amongst them is conspicuous. "What in civilised countries is called 'shame,'" says Father Weniaminof, "is entirely unknown among the Aleuts."[8] Dr. Middendorff relates how, when he was very hospitably entertained in the large yurta of a well-to-do Samoyed, half the

[1] H. Strauch, "Allgemeine Bemerkungen ethnologischen Inhalts über Neu-Guinea," etc., Zeitschrift für Ethnologie, ix, p. 9.

[2] G. Brown, Melanesians and Polynesians, p. 311.

[3] A. J. Gooszen, "De Bewoners van Nederlandsch Nieuw-Guinea," in J. C. van Eerde, De volken van Nederlandsch-Indië, vol. ii, pp. 107, 112; H. N. Moseley, "On the Inhabitants of the Admiralty Island," etc., Journal of the Anthropological Institute, vi, p. 399.

[4] J. Cook, An Account of a Voyage round the World, in Hawkesworth, An Account of Voyages, etc., vol. iii, p. 633.

[5] C. Darwin, Journal of Researches, p. 228; P. P. King and R. Fitzroy, Narrative of the Surveying Voyages of the "Adventure" and "Beagle," vol. i, p. 23.

[6] H. H. Johnston, The Uganda Protectorate, pp. 843, 863. The Beirs of the Sudan are similarly arrayed (M. H. Logan, "The Beirs," Sudan Notes and Records, i, p. 242).

[7] O. Temple, Notes on the Tribes . . . of Northern Nigeria, p. 300.

[8] I. Weniaminof, "Charakter-Züge der Aleuten von den Fuchs-Inseln," in F. Wrangell, Statistische und ethnographische Nachrichten über die russischen Besitzungen an der Nordwestküste von Amerika, p. 203.

village being present, he mistook his host's daughter for a young man, and referred to her as the gentleman's son. The Samoyed, in the most natural manner, called his daughter, removed her pantaloons, and gave the traveller an ocular demonstration of his error.[1] Eskimo men and women, when inside their huts, take off their clothing, which they place outside in order to get rid of vermin, and they remain completely naked no matter what strangers may be present, manifesting no self-consciousness in so doing.[2] At festive entertainments which are held in a sort of public hall, the women likewise remove their clothing and sit naked while viewing the performance.[3] The Eskimo, says Father Petitot, " is completely ignorant of morality, and cannot imagine that what is natural and necessary should not be done openly," The women " are so accustomed from birth to see themselves in the costume of Eve that they manifest no shame. They learn from their parents the most cynical indifference. Where, then, should they learn sentiments of modesty or decency ? Are these innate in the human mind ? Are they not received from the family and from education ? "[4] Those arctic peoples who have been compelled to adopt elaborate clothing from climatic necessity, and not as sexual coverings, are of all races the most devoid of any notion of modesty. The necessary development of clothing apart from motives of modesty has, with them, prevented the development of that sentiment.

The North American peoples, who possessed more elaborate clothes than the majority of uncultured races, and who probably reached their habitat from the north, also removed all their clothes when indoors, and when the weather was warm. In some tribes, at the time of European settlement, the men retained a pair of drawers and the women a petticoat ;[5] while in other tribes both men and women had no scruple in undressing completely. Thus among the tribes of Canada the men, when the weather was warm,

[1] A. Th. v. Middendorff, *Reise in den äussersten Norden und Osten Sibiriens*, vol. iv, Part ii, p. 1429.

[2] H. Egede, *A Description of Greenland*, p. 126 ; E. Petitot, *Les Grands Esquimaux*, pp. 55 sqq.

[3] A. L. Kroeber, " The Eskimo of Smith Sound," *Bulletin of the American Museum of Natural History*, No. X, pp. 302 sq.

[4] E. Petitot, *op. cit.*, pp. 198 sq. " They do not blush to sit down and ease themselves in the presence of others. Every family has a urine tub placed before the entry, in which they make water " (H. Egede, *op. cit.*, pp. 127 sq.).

[5] L. Carr, " Dress and Ornaments of Certain American Indians," *Proceedings of the American Antiquarian Society*, N.S., xi, pp. 382, 406 sq. ; Charlevoix, *Histoire de la Nouvelle France*, vol. vi, p. 39 ; Le Page du Pratz, *Histoire de la Louisiane*, vol. ii, pp. 190 sq. ; John Megapolensis, " A Short Account of the Maquaas Indians in New Netherland," in E. Hazard, *Historical Collections*, vol. i, p. 154.

"went stark naked without reserve," [1] and the women, if they had to cross a stream, had no hesitation in stripping completely, no matter who might be present. [2] At dances whether purely religious, or given in order to honour visitors or victories in war, both men and women stripped naked. [3] Clothing was probably adopted by them chiefly for the sake of warmth, [4] and, as with the Eskimo, sentiments of modesty were very feebly, if at all, developed. Like other uncultured peoples, they rapidly adopted the habit of avoiding exposure on learning that the European strangers entertained strong sentiments on the subject. "The old people still remember and praise," said a traveller in the second part of the eighteenth century, "the ancient days before they were acquainted with the whites, when they had little dress, except a bit of skin about their middle, moccasins, and a mantle of buffalo for the winter, a light one of feathers for the summer." [5] In the southern tribes complete nudity was more habitual. Thus among the natives of the Mississippi valley, all girls and even women of twenty-five or thirty went about completely naked. [6]

The use of clothing for purposes of warmth and protection is limited to a very few peoples in primitive stages of culture. By far the bulk of primitive clothing consists of what is commonly described as 'ornaments.' The term is naturally employed in accounts of strange peoples to describe any object worn on the person which does not serve the purposes of protection or of decency, and the use of which is not known. As our acquaintance with the ideas and usages of a people becomes extended, the number of articles in their attire serving no other purpose than that of decoration becomes greatly reduced; for it is found that most savage 'ornaments' possess, apart from their decorative value, quite other uses and significances which are of the greatest importance to the wearer. When Captain Cook first visited Botany Bay he found the native

---

[1] *Relations des Jésuites*, 1641, p. 50; F. G. Sagard Théodat, *Le Grand Voyage du Pays des Hurons*, p. 53; S. de Champlain, *Les Voyages de la Nouvelle France*, vol. i, p. 357; H. Timberlake, *Memoirs*, p. 56.

[2] S. de Champlain, *op. cit.*, vol. i, p. 206.

[3] L. Carr, *op. cit.*, p. 384; *Le Jeune's Relation, Jesuit Relations and Allied Documents*, vol. xi, p. 214; M. Lescarbot, *Histoire de la Nouvelle France*, vol. iii, pp. 281 sq.: "Toutes les femmes et filles commencèrent à quitter leur robes et peaux et se mirent toutes nues montrant leur nature"; *ibid.*, p. 738; A. Henry, *Travels and Adventures in the Years* 1760–1776, p. 279. H. Timberlake, *Memoirs*, p. 37; F. Parkman, *The Jesuits in North America in the Seventeenth Century*, p. xxxix.

[4] *Relations des Jésuites*, 1634, p. 46; F. G. Sagard, Théodat, *Le Grand voyage du pays des Hurons*, vol. i, p. 51.

[5] H. Timberlake, *Memoirs*, p. 51.

[6] J. Gilmary Shea, *Early Voyages up and down the Mississippi*, pp. 77, 80, 83.

Australians elaborately ornamented with various gewgaws, the beautiful workmanship of some of which excited his admiration. They wore through the cartilages of their noses skewers as thick as a man's finger ; they had necklaces and bracelets made from threaded discs of shell material, and over their breasts hung gorgets and discs of mother-of-pearl. " Upon such ornaments," he says, " they set so great a value that they would never part with the least article for anything we could offer, which was the more extraordinary as our beads and ribbons were ornaments of the same kind, but of a more regular form and more showy materials." [1] When given bright ornaments much more conspicuous than their own, the North Australian natives, says Major Campbell, accepted them through politeness, but took the first opportunity, when they thought they were out of sight, of quietly dropping them or throwing them away.[2] The articles which they wore were not regarded by the primitive Australians in the light of merely decorative ornaments. However great the personal vanity and love of self-decoration of primitive man may be, a careful survey of the most primitive forms of such decoration forces upon us the conclusion that he has never in any instance been led to take the first step in attaching foreign materials to his body by a pure instinct of self-embellishment, but that his pleasure in apparel as mere finery has only developed subsequently to its adoption from quite other motives.

Primitive peoples have even been extremely slow in bethinking themselves of employing easily available materials, such as the skins of animals, to protect themselves from cold. Professor Stirling observes that it is very remarkable that the natives of the MacDonell ranges in central Australia, where the nights are extremely cold and the temperature is often uncomfortably chilly even in the daytime, have not thought of using the fur of the bandicoots, which abound throughout the neighbourhood, as a protection.[3] Father Parkinson makes a similar remark in reference to the natives of the interior of the Solomon Islands, who are completely naked, notwithstanding that the temperature is commonly very low.[4] The climate of Tierra de Fuego is one of the most inclement in the world, yet the natives have for ages been content to shiver in the cold, crowding with chattering teeth round their fires till they sustain serious burns, and only occasionally providing themselves with

---

[1] J. Cook, An Account of a Voyage round the World, in J. Hawkesworth, An Account of the Voyages undertaken by order of His present Majesty for Making Discoveries in the Southern Hemisphere, vol. ii, p. 634.

[2] Campbell, " Geographical Memoir of Melville Island, or the Cobourg Peninsula, North Australia," The Geographical Journal, iv, p. 153.

[3] E. C. Stirling, Report on the Work of the Horn Scientific Expedition to Central Australia, part iv, p. 18.

[4] R. Parkinson, Dreissig Jahre in der Südsee, pp. 490 sq.

minute mantles against the direct blast of the wind.[1]   Except under
the stress of absolutely arctic conditions, primitive man has remained
naked ; he has no more bethought himself of covering his body
than have his animal ancestors.

Magical purposes of Primitive Attire.

There is undoubtedly an innate personal vanity in humanity
which is identical with the instincts of self-display among animals,
and is a sexual manifestation.   But that instinct, though it causes
pleasure in decoration, does not appear to have led to self-
decoration in man any more than in animals.   Primitive
women are, we saw, remarkably devoid of those instincts of self-
decoration, and even of that appreciation of gewgaws and bright
colours, which are generally regarded as strong innate characteristics
of feminine nature.   Only where personal ornaments have already
been adopted from other motives and are in general use is the
taste for further decoration found to be developed.   That does not
prevent those decorations which have been adopted for other
purposes being valued for their ornamental function.   Any object
worn on the person may, and generally does, acquire an aesthetic
value and becomes a ground of sexual vanity.   That is substantially true of the apparel of civilised man no less than of the
savage's.   Military uniforms are ornamental and are forms of self-
decoration, although their overt purpose is different.   Ordinary
clothes, those of men no less than those of women, although their
primary object would be generally described as being related to the
needs of comfort, warmth, and decency, are nevertheless required
to be becoming and attractive, however much the standards of such
becomingness may vary.   But because dainty shoes show off an
ankle to advantage, it does not follow that footwear was invented
in the first place as a means of sexual attraction.   The features
and forms of the body itself are objects of vanity no less than
clothing ; but although a savage may be vain about his features
or his limbs, the primary function of eyes or of arms is not that
of sexual display.   " I believe," says Mr. Dall, " that the idea
of ornament in connection with the object worn as a symbol
would always follow, though closely, its adoption on other grounds.
The idea that it was a symbol of vigour, fortitude, and mature
development would connect with the symbol the admiration
which is excited by the qualities symbolised, which are in the
highest esteem in uncivilised peoples, and therefore it would be
considered as an ornament without any reference to any inherent
elegance of forms, material, or colour.   These would afterwards
develop as a matter of course with the development of aesthetics in

[1] C. Darwin, *A Naturalist's Voyage round the World*, p. 8.

other directions, and if the development in another direction did not take place, the original rudeness of the symbol (as in the wooden plug of the Botocudos) would be likely to remain unchanged." [1] When uncultured peoples are asked the purpose of a particular decoration they will commonly reply that it is thought becoming and is appreciated by the opposite sex ; but such answers are no more authoritative as regards the origin of those decorations than are savage aetiological theories as regards their customs. In Polynesia, Melanesia, the Indian Archipelago, where both religious ideas and tribal organisations are in a state of disintegration, the natives will say that the object of the women's tatuings is " to please the men," [2] or that the men tatu themselves " to please the women." [3] But we have, in undisorganised primitive societies, overwhelming evidence that the motives which primarily led to the practice were different. Even objects and decorations which are employed for the express purpose of exercising sexual attraction are, among primitive peoples, believed to act not by virtue of their aesthetic value, but by their power as magic charms. Among the Chans only the men wear tatuings ; but if a girl is crossed in love she will have a small tatu design imprinted on one of her arms, believing that it will act as a magic charm.[4] The Samoyeds do not as a rule use tatuings ; but some of the young women have three small lines scratched on the inside of the right elbow and permanently marked with charcoal. This, they say, is to protect them from diseases.[5] As M. van Gennep remarks, " it seems superfluous at the present day to insist on the fact that the origin of tatuing lies not in any ' aesthetic instinct ' or in ' desire for means of sexual attraction,' but in medico-magical mutilations." [6]

Some savage ornaments and articles of apparel appear to have originated from the desire to accentuate the wearer's resemblance to his totemic animal, or to a supernatural being or ghost, especially during the performance of religious ceremonies. The naked Fuegians who perish with cold from want of protective clothing, and who have not developed any other form of bodily amulets or ornaments, dress themselves up in the

---

[1] W. H. Dall, " On Masks, Labrets, and Certain Aboriginal Customs," *Third Annual Report of the Bureau of Ethnology*, p. 81.

[2] J. Chalmers, *Pioneering in New Guinea*, p. 166.

[3] J. G. F. Riedel, *De sluik- en kroesharige rassen tusschen Selebes en Papua*, p. 288. Cf. E. Westermarck, *The History of Human Marriage*, vol. i, pp. 520 sqq.

[4] Mrs. Leslie Milne, *Shans at Home*, p. 68.

[5] A. Th. v. Middendorff, *Reise in den äussersten Norden und Osten Sibiriens*, vol. iv, Part ii, p. 1461.

[6] A. van Gennep, *Études d'ethnographie algérienne*, p. 87.

most elaborate manner during their religious ceremonies and wear hideous masks. One of their motives, in this instance, is not to attract, but to repel and terrify the opposite sex.[1] Among organised totemic peoples the ornaments used in their religious ceremonies constitute tribal distinguishing marks. They have also a derivative personal value ; for many savages suppose that their welfare in the life hereafter depends upon their being admitted to the company of their deceased ancestors, and a definite mark is therefore indispensable to secure their being recognised as relatives. In several parts of New Guinea, for instance, the admission of a person's ghost to the company of his ancestors will depend upon the septum of his nose having been perforated, and a quill, or skewer, inserted in it. Should a child die before having undergone the operation, it is per-formed ' post-mortem,' so that he may not be excluded on that account from the abode of his fathers.[2] Similarly, among the Eskimo the women, who alone are tatued, do not regard those marks as mere ornaments. " This tatuing is done from principle, the theory being that the lines they make will be regarded in the next world as a sign of goodness." [3] In Fiji " the women believe that to be tatued is a passport to the other world . . . So strong is this superstition that when girls died before being tatued their friends have painted the resemblance of it upon them in order to deceive the priest and to escape the anger of the gods." [4] Among the Bechuana of the hare totem, it is the practice for children to have their ears bored when they are about twelve years old. But if a woman has lost a child or two in infancy, she will insist that her next baby's ears shall be pierced shortly after birth.[5] Tupi children in Brazil were firmly held down and had their nose, ears, and lips perforated by the medicine-man " for the honour of the family." [6] The enormous importance attached to those decorations or mutilations, such as nose-skewers, ear-orna-ments, labrets, the knocking out or filing of teeth, etc., rests largely upon the far-reaching consequences which they entail. Without them a man or a woman is not a member of the tribal

---

[1] See above, vol. ii, p. 545. Australian savages paint themselves during their dances so as to represent skeletons.

[2] J. Chalmers, *Pioneering in New Guinea*, p. 168 ; C. G. Seligman, *The Melanesians of British New Guinea*, p. 192.

[3] C. F. Hall, *Arctic Researches and Life among the Esquimaux*, p. 570.

[4] C. Wilkes, *Narrative of the United States Exploring Expedition*, vol. iii, p. 355.

[5] W. C. Willoughby, " Notes on the Totemism of the Becwana," *Journal of the Anthropological Institute*, xxxv, pp. 299 sq.

[6] S. de Vasconcellos, *Noticias curiosas e necessarias das cousas do Brasil*, p. 149.

community ; they are not fitted for reproduction, they are not recognised members of the company of their ancestors in the next world.

Those ornaments play at the same time the part of charms or amulets, which are believed to act magically, imparting to the wearer peculiar virtues and warding off evil influences. The Eskimo is not only protected by clothes from the weather, he is loaded with magic objects. " This bric-à-brac hangs on him in front, behind, at the side ; there is some for the head, some for the spine, etc." [1] Women, in addition to their tatuings, have innumerable amulets. One, accounted very effectual in promoting fertility, is a piece of a European's old shoe, which they hang round their body ; " for, as they take our nation to be more fertile and of a stronger disposition of body than theirs, they fancy the virtue of our body communicates itself to our clothing." [2] A woman is careful to place her trinkets and amulets for three days and three nights in the bladder of a female bear, so that the magic virtues emanating from the spirit of the animal may be communicated to her articles of jewellery. [3] With arctic peoples those amulets and charms are distinct from, and subsidiary to, clothing worn for protective purposes ; but with the majority of uncultured peoples dwelling in warmer climates the physical protective function of clothing does not exist, and the articles which are worn on the person belong entirely to the same class as the amulets of the Eskimo. Speaking of the amulets worn by the Baila, Messrs Smith and Dale say : " It is impossible to exaggerate the part which these . . . play in the life of the Ba-Ila. It is not too much to say that apart from these it is impossible to understand any side of their life. Their use constitutes a system of insurance against the ills and calamities of life." [4] According to an old writer the articles of apparel worn by the natives of the coast of Guinea were all treated as sacred. "They weare," he says, "many strange wreathes which they call fetissos, which name they derive from their idolatry, for when they eate or drinke, then they power meat or drink upon them, or first give them to eate and drinke . . . and if they have fetissos on their arms or feet, they spit out of their mouthes upon them, as if they gave them drink also." [5] In the Congo, fetiches or amulets

[1] E. Petitot, *Les Grands Esquimaux*, p. 187.

[2] H. Egede, *A Description of Greenland*, p. 194.

[3] C. F. Hall, *Arctic Researches, and Life among the Esquimaux*, p. 582.

[4] E. W. Smith and A. M. Dale, *The Ila-speaking Peoples of Northern Rhodesia*, vol. i, p. 252.

[5] " A Description and Historical Declaration of the Gold Kingdom of Guinea," *Hakluytus Posthumus, or Purchas His Pilgrimes*, vol. vi, pp. 267, 275. Cf. T. Winterbottom, *An Account of the Native Africans in the Neighbourhood of Sierra Leone*, vol. i, p. 123.

consist of the simplest articles, the most common being " blades of
grass, a banana leaf, a palm branch, a hen's feather, a wild-cat's
skin, earth from a grave wrapped in a piece of cloth, a leopard's
claw." [1]   Among the Gallas, according to Father Soleillet, " everything which with us is called an ' ornament ' or a ' jewel ' is, in
truth, with them an amulet or a medicine.   Thus a copper ring
suspended from the neck cures skin diseases ; a ring or piece of
tortoise shell worn on the second phalanx of the left forefinger is
an infallible remedy against affections of the urinary organs, and so
forth." [2]   A native of Sierra Leone would not have hesitated to
jump into the sea, although he saw a shark near, provided he had
on him his loin-cloth of goat-skin ; but he would not so much
as put his foot in the water for fear of those animals, if his only
' article of apparel ' or ' ornament ' were removed.[3]

Of all the various forms of ' ornaments ' worn by either cultured
or uncultured peoples there is none to which magic properties
and talismanic virtues are not ascribed.   Necklaces are but strings
of charms and amulets, and, as Dr. Winterbottom remarked,
" it is not improbable that the necklace which at present forms
so ornamental a part of female dress, owed its origin to these
superstitious practices." [4]   A necklace is sometimes regarded as
containing the very soul of the wearer, so that, if it is lost or
worn by another person, the original owner will die.[5]   When
a Déné girl loses her girdle of beads, her relatives are in serious
doubt whether she will be able to survive the loss.[6]   When the
Jesuits first settled in Canada, the Indians ascribed the ability
and accomplishments of the good Fathers to the rosaries which
they constantly carried with them, and many natives were greatly
influenced in their conversion to the Christian religion by their
desire to possess one of those magic talismans.   They believed that
these " have the power and property not only of succouring the
Indians in sickness and all most pressing necessities, but also of
preserving them from surprises, from persecution and from the
fury of enemies."   Old women who had succeeded in obtaining
possession of rosaries at once set up in business on their own account
as sorceresses.[7]   In Louisiana an Indian accused a woman who had

---

[1] A.-J. Wauters, L'état indépendant du Congo, p. 301.

[2] P. Soleillet, Voyages en Ethiopie, p. 260.

[3] T. Winterbottom, An Account of the Native Africans in the Neighbourhood of Sierra Leone, vol. i, p. 256.

[4] Ibid., vol. i, p. 258.

[5] E. Thurston, Omens and Superstitions of Southern India, p. 189.

[6] J. Jetté, " On the Superstitions of the Ten'a Indians (Middle Yukon
Valley, Alaska)," Anthropos, vi, p. 257.

[7] P. C. le Clercq, Nouvelle Relation de la Gaspesie, pp. 367 sq.   Cf. Jesuit
Relations and Allied Documents, vol. xxvi, p. 286.

become converted to the Catholic faith, and possessed a rosary, of having killed his father by means of it.[1] The feather garters worn by many savages appear to be purely ornamental articles ; but the Lenguas of the Gran Chaco regard them as a protection against snake-bite ; [2] and the Negritos of the Philippines, who wear garters of wild boar's bristles, say that they " give the wearer greater powers of endurance and are efficacious in making long journeys less tiresome, for is not the wild boar the most hardy of animals ? " [3] The Wambuti pygmies of the Congo put on their bracelets of antelope skin only when they go hunting, believing that their success in the chase will thereby be facilitated.[4] Bracelets are also sometimes fertility charms.[5] Even the colours and patterns of cloths and silks worn by richly garbed Orientals are regarded by them as having each its occult virtue and significance. A young Shan woman, having obtained some European dress material, was chiefly anxious to know the special virtues of the charms which were imprinted upon it. The magic formula consisted of the words : " Made in Germany." [6]

By wearing the skin of an animal, primitive man not only assimilates himself physically to that animal, but also acquires its psychical qualities. It seems probable that animal skins were used in the first instance by primitive humanity for that purpose long before any utilitarian notion of their advantage as a physical protection was thought of. The skins, claws, horns, and other parts of animals are universally thought to impart to the wearer the qualities, real or imaginary, of those animals, in the same manner as does the eating of their flesh.[7] Attacks from animals of the same species are also warded off by such means. Nandi hunters take care to provide themselves with a piece of lion's skin in order not to be attacked by lions. The Nandi also wear rings made from the hide of bulls and goats as aphrodisiac charms.[8] Among the Thonga, wearing the skin of a goat is regarded as an effective remedy for sterility.[9] In India a piece of antelope's

[1] Relation of Father Marquette, in J. G. Shea, *Discovery and Exploration of the Mississippi Valley. Historical Collections of Louisiana*, Part iv, p. 27.

[2] W. B. Grubb, *An Unknown People in an Unknown Land*, p. 72.

[3] W. A. Reed, *Negritos of Zambales*, p. 38.

[4] J. Maes, " Notes sur quelques objets des Pygmées-Wambuti," *Anthropos*, vi, p. 133.

[5] *Atharva-Veda*, vi. 81, *The Sacred Books of the East*, vol. xlvii, pp. 96 sq.

[6] L. Milne, *Shans at Home*, p. 62.

[7] Cf. E. B. Tylor, *Researches into the Early History of Mankind*, p. 131 ; A. C. Haddon, *Magic and Fetichism*, p. 32 ; A. L. Kroeber, " Ethnology of the Gros Ventres," *Anthropological Papers of the American Museum of Natural History*, i, pp. 192 sqq.

[8] A. B. Hollis, *The Nandi*, p. 87.

[9] H. A. Junod, *The Life of a South African Tribe*, vol. i, pp. 187 sq.

skin was accounted an infallible cure for all inherited diseases.[1]
The claws and teeth of animals, the tusks of boars, which are inserted
by savages in their nostrils, hung to their ears, and worn round
their necks, are all powerful amulets and talismans. " Their use,"
remark Messrs Skeat and Blagden, speaking of the tribes of the Malay
Peninsula, " is probably due, as in other parts of the world, rather
to magical ideas than to pride of capture. The bristles, teeth,
claws of tigers are all certainly used much more for magical than
for merely ornamental or decorative purposes." [2]

The feathers of birds are among the most decorative ornaments
worn by uncultured peoples. The hawk's wings which adorned
the helmets of our barbaric forefathers were most picturesque.
But the barbarians did not only wear the wings of hawks on
their heads, they also carried the bones of the birds secreted about
their person.[3] The Déné Indians carry the feet of hawks about
them to impart swiftness to their movements.[4] The Shoshone
Indians believe that the wings and feathers of buzzards are a
sure protection against missiles.[5] The elaborate feather helmets
of the Lengua Indians are regarded by them as charms especially
efficacious against the evil spirits that dwell in swamps.[6] " The
habit of wearing feathers, common among the forest tribes, is
probably due more to a desire for protection than for ornament,"
remarks Mr. Crooke.[7] Among the Bororo, " to be befeathered
was a ' medicine ' in daily use. Intermittent fever was very
prevalent in the colony, and the children were ' befeathered ' at
every moment, so that it was absolutely impossible to perceive
where the boundary line lay between ' medicine ' and ' ornament.' " [8]

[1] *Atharva-Veda*, iii. 7 (*The Sacred Books of the East*, vol. xlvii, pp. 15,383 sq.).

[2] W. W. Skeat and C. O. Blagden, *Pagan Races of the Malay Peninsula*, vol. ii, p. 202. Cf. *Jesuit Relations and Allied Documents*, vol. x, p. 200 ; E. Thurston, *Omens and Superstitions of Southern India*, pp. 189, 191 ; H. S. Stannus, "Note on some Tribes of British Central Africa," *Journal of the Royal Anthropological Institute*, xl, p. 320 ; O. Temple, *Notes on the Tribes, Provinces, Emirates and States of the Northern Provinces of Nigeria*, p. 261.

[3] G. Bellucci, *Il feticismo primitivo in Italia*, pp. 31 sq. Cf. G. Rasmussen, *The People of the Polar North*, pp. 138 sq.

[4] J. Jetté, "On the Superstitions of the Ten'a Indians," *Anthropos*, vi, p. 256.

[5] R. H. Lowie, "The Northern Shoshone," *Anthropological Papers of the American Museum of Natural History*, ii, part 2, pp. 229 sq.

[6] W. B. Grubb, *An Unknown People in an Unknown Land*, p. 71.

[7] W. Crooke, art. "Charms and Amulets (Indian)," Hastings's *Encyclopaedia of Religion and Ethics*, vol. iii, p. 442. Cf. T. H. Lewin, *Wild Races of South-Eastern India*, pp. 284, 309.

[8] K. von den Steinen, *Unter den Naturvölkern Zentral-Brasiliens*, p. 476. It is notable that in primitive societies feather ornaments are very rarely worn by women. Their peculiar virtues are associated with the pursuits of

Shells play an even more important part in the most primitive forms of clothing than the skins of mammals and birds. Their origin from the fertilising waters causes them to be regarded as life-giving and as promoting fertility. The ancients believed that shells wax and wane with the moon, the controller of waters.[1] As Aphrodite was represented rising out of a shell, so also in India the moon-god was described as having been born out of a shell. " At the mouth of this shell," it is said in an Indian hymn, " is the God of the Moon. Glory to thee, sacred shell, blessed of all the gods, born of the waters." [2] In Melanesia, on the island of Aurora, the First Woman is reported to have issued from a cowry shell.[3] The cowry is probably the most common and widespread material of savage clothing. Its use as a means of exchange, or ' shell-money,' extends over five continents.[4] In the commercial relations between ancient Egypt and India, payment was made in cowry shells.[5] But the value of the cowry as a standard of exchange is subsequent to, and derivative from, the enormous value and significance which attached to it for its own sake.[6] In the Shortland Islands cowry shells are regarded with the utmost veneration. " There is some sacredness attached to them, but what it is, is not at all clear," says the Rev. George Brown ; " the natives will not talk about them at all, and will not give any information about them." [7] There is, however, no obscurity as to the primary significance of the cowry, which is expressly acknowledged by many peoples. It is universally identified, from its appearance, with the female genital organs.[8]

warriors and hunters, and have little or no bearing on female functions. Among the Aleuts, feather garments are worn by the men only, the women wearing nothing but furs.

[1] Pliny, *Nat. Hist.*, ii. 41.

[2] J. Hornell, " The Indian Conch (*Turbinella pyrum*, Linn.) and its Relation to Hindu Life and Religion," *Report to the Government of Baroda on the Marine Zoology of Okhamandal in Kattiawar*, part ii, p. 22. Chank shells are much used as amulets by girls and women in Tibet (W. L. Hildburgh, " Notes on some Tibetans and Bhutia Amulets and Folk Medicines," *Journal of the Royal Anthropological Institute*, xxxix, p. 393).

[3] R. H. Codrington, *The Melanesians*, p. 26. Cf. G. Turner, *Samoa*, pp. 8, 12, 17. The systematic names of the most common kinds of shells still retain the indication of their immemorial association with the Great Mother : *Venus, Cypraea, Pecten. Haliotis* is commonly known as ' Ear of Venus.'

[4] See, O. Schneider, *Muschelgeld-Studien* ; J. Wilfrid Jackson, *Shells as Evidence of the Migrations of Early Culture*, pp. 126 sqq.

[5] A. del Mar, *History of Money in Ancient Countries*, p. 149.

[6] This is proved by the use of the cowry for its magical properties where no shell-money and no commerce exist, as in Australia (see below, p. 278).

[7] G. Brown, *Melanesians and Polynesians*, p. 207.

[8] G. E. Rumphius, *D'Amboinsche rareteikamer, behelzende eene beschrijvinge van . . . schaalvisschen . . . die men in d'Amboinsche zee vierdt*

Its associations with the sea and with the moon have marked it as the most direct emblem of female fertility.[1]

Cowry shells are found employed as articles of primitive clothing, as they are still throughout the savage world, in prehistoric tombs of the Stone Age and of the early Bronze and Iron Ages in all parts of Europe.[2] In the tomb of Laugerie Basse, in Dordogne, the skeleton had cowries placed in pairs on the forehead, each arm, each thigh, and each foot.[3] They are found in equal abundance in graves of pre-dynastic Egypt,[4] and of Krete.[5] The women of Pompeii wore cowry shells as a charm against sterility ; [6] and, like them and their prehistoric mothers, the women of Italy still provide themselves with cowry shells.[7] They are worn in Greece, in Corfu, in Montenegro.[8] In Egypt cowries are among the most

(Amsterdam, 1741), p. 113 ; M. Adanson, *Histoire naturelle du Sénégal ; Coquillages*, p. 65 ; J. Wilfrid Jackson, *op. cit.*, pp. 171, 205 ; G. Elliot Smith, *ibid.*,. Introduction, p. xiii ; Id., *The Evolution of the Dragon*, pp. 150 sq. ; O. Jahn, " Über den Aberglauben des bösen Blicks bei den Alten," *Berichte über die Verhandlungen der königlich Sächsischen Gesellschaft der Wissenschaften*, vii, p. 80 ; S. Seligmann, *Der Böse Blick und Verwandtes*, vol. ii, pp. 126 sq., 204 sq. ; A. Abt, *Die Apologie des Apuleius von Madaura und die Antike Zauberei*, pp. 15, 211 ; G. Bellucci, *Il feticismo primitivo in Italia*, p. 38 ; J. Herber, "Tatouage du pubis au Maroc," *Revue d'Ethnographie et des Traditions Populaires*, iii, p. 42 ; W. Hildburgh, " Some Japanese Charms connected with the Making of Clothes," *Man*, xvii, p. 28 n. ; Suidas and Hesychius, s.v. χοιρῖναι. Ennius calls the cowry shell ' matriculus ' (G. E. Rumphius, *loc. cit.*). The Greek name χοιρίνη was rendered by the equivalent Latin term ' porculum,' a name applied to the vulva, whence our term ' porcelain.' The Warega sometimes wear in their girdle an ivory amulet representing the vulva (C. Delhaise, *Les Warega*, p. 93). The natives of Easter Island have a vulva tatued on their chest (Geiseler, *Die Oster-Insel*, p. 29).

[1] Dr. Elliot Smith appears to go so far as to regard the Mediterranean Great Mother as a personification of the cowry.

[2] E. Lartet and H. Christy, *Reliquiae Aquitanicae*, pp. 48, 288 ; O. Schneider, *Muschelgeld-Studien*, p. 115 (Germany) ; G. Bellucci, *Il Feticismo primitivo in Italia*, pp. 38 sq. ; H. et L. Siret, *Les premiers âges du métal dans le sud-est de l'Espagne*, pp. 16, 29, 30, 57, etc. ; W. L. H. Duckworth, " Cave Exploration at Gibraltar," *Journal of the Royal Anthropological Institute*, xli, p. 362.

[3] E. Massenat, Ph. Lalande, and Cartailhac, "Description d'un squelette humain de l'âge du renne à Lugerie Basse (Dordogne)," *Comptes Rendus de l'Académie des Sciences*, lxxiv (1872), pp. 1060 sqq.

[4] W. M. Flinders Petrie, *Amulets*, p. 27 ; V. Lortet and C. Gaillard, " La Faune momifiée de l'ancienne Égypte : Mollusques," *Archives du Muséum d'Histoire Naturelle de Lyon*, x, pp. 108 sqq. ; G. A. Reisner, *Early Dynastic Cemeteries of Naga-ed-Dêr*, pl. vi and vii.

[5] R. M. Dawkins, " Excavations at Palaikastro, " *Annual of the British School in Athens*, ix, pp. 291, 335.

[6] Tiberi, *Le conchiglie Pompeiane* (Naples, 1879), cited by J. W. Jackson, *op. cit.*, pp. 133, 139.

[7] G. Bellucci, *op. cit.*, pp. 38 sq.

[8] W. Ridgway, " The Origin of the Turkish Crescent," *Journal of the Royal Anthropological Institute*, xxxviii, p. 248.

common amulets, and " are especially considered preservatives against the evil eye." [1] They are equally valued for their magic virtues in Morocco.[2] Women's and girls' girdles throughout the Sudan and Somaliland consist mainly of cowries.[3] In Abyssinia the women wear them sown to their skirts.[4] In Nigeria a girdle adorned with cowry shells is a " sign of virginity," and is removed on marriage.[5] Hottentot women wear them fastened, with the aperture outwards, to the border of their aprons.[6] The prudishly dressed Baganda women carry some cowry shells in a small bag suspended over their abdomen to secure fertility.[7] The women of Hadramaut wear cowry shells in their girdles, as did their predecessors in the time of Strabo.[8] Muhammadan women in the Panjab wear a cowry on their abdomen under their clothes during pregnancy, in order that their child should not be still-born.[9] Cowries are worn by the women in Central Asia, among the Tartars and Kirghis,[10] and Tibetan women make a point of wearing some in their girdle.[11]

Like all fertility charms the cowry and other shells have come to acquire general magic protective virtues against all evils, in much the same manner as the greenstone tiki, which formerly was worn exclusively by Maori women as a fertility charm, has come to be worn by men also as a protective amulet.[12] Among the Didinga of the Upper Sudan a string of cowries is placed round the neck of a woman when she is believed to be possessed by a spirit.[13] In the Raymahak hills sorcerers commence their incantations by attaching five cowry shells round their brows.[14] The cowry is a magic

[1] E. W. Lane, *An Account of the Manners and Customs of the Modern Egyptians*, p. 230.

[2] J. Herber, " Tatouage du pubis au Maroc," *Revue d'Ethnographie et des Traditions Populaires*, iii, p. 42.

[3] J. W. Crowfoot, "Wedding Customs in the Northern Sudan," *Sudan Notes and Records*, v, p. 6 ; O. Schneider, *Muschelgeld-Studien*, p. 173.

[4] P. Soleillet, *Voyages en Éthiopie*, p. 265.

[5] A. J. Tremearne, " Notes on the Kagoro and other Nigerian Headhunters," *Journal of the Royal Anthropological Institute*, xlii, p. 153.

[6] J. Barrow, *An Account of Travels into the Interior of Southern Africa*, vol. i, p. 155.

[7] J. Roscoe, *The Baganda*, p. 331 ; H. H. Johnston, *The Uganda Protectorate*, p. 771.

[8] A. von Wrede, *Reise in Hadramaut*, p. 90 ; Strabo, xvi. 14.

[9] H. A. Rose, " Muhammedan Pregnancy Observances in the Panjab," *Journal of the Anthropological Institute*, xxxv, p. 279.

[10] J. W. Jackson, *op. cit.*, p. 139.

[11] O. Schneider, *op. cit.*, p. 117.

[12] See above, vol. ii, p. 584.

[13] J. H. Driberg, " A Preliminary Account of the Didinga," *Sudan Notes and Records*, v, p. 221.

[14] C. F. Gordon Cumming, *From the Hebrides to the Himalayas*, vol. i, pp. 201 sq.

talisman in Australia. A Western Australian medicine-man, in a desperate case, will rub his patient all over with a cowry shell.[1] The Gallas, " in order to secure protection against Djair, or evil spirits, or from persons who are possessed by them and have the evil eye, wear shells or beads, especially over any affected part of the body." [2] The richly attired Japanese are far above the sartorial phase in which a girdle of cowry shells serves as a complete costume, but they make a point of placing cowry shells with their clothes, when they put them away, ' for luck.' If a cowry shell happens to be unobtainable, a pornographic picture exhibiting the female genital organs serves as a substitute.[3] Fishermen and hunters affix cowry shells to their nets and their weapons.[4]

Coral, where it is obtainable, ranks almost as high as the cowry as a talisman. In some parts of Africa it constituted the sole material of clothing. Its use as an amulet against the evil eye and sorcery is still universal in Europe ; it was regarded as particularly effective in all affections of children, a notion which still survives in its use for babies' rattles and gewgaws at teething time. This is equally prevalent in Syria.[5] Its virtue as a charm, it is interesting to note, is in inverse ratio to its aesthetic and decorative worth, for it is a principle recognised no less in the Congo than in Southern Europe that polish and artistic treatment deprives it of its magical virtue.[6] The original conception of that virtue still appears in the beliefs of the peasant women of Italy. It is regarded by them as possessing the specific power of regulating the menstrual flow. Fragments of coral are worn by women for that purpose segregated under their clothes. It is believed that coral becomes pale during the menstrual period of the wearer, and regains its bright-red colour when the catamenia has ceased.[7] The blood-red, water-born coral is thus regarded as an emanation of the power that governs the fertilising waters and the monthly cycle. In India it is associated with the waxing moon,[8] and is looked upon as protective

---

[1] E. Clements, " Ethnological Notes on the Western Australian Aborigines," *Internationales Archiv für Ethnographie*, xvi, p. 8.

[2] P. Soleillet, *Voyages en Éthiopie*, p. 260.

[3] W. L. Hildburgh, " Some Japanese Charms connected with the Making of Clothes," *Man*, xvii, p. 28.

[4] J. W. Jackson, *op. cit.*, p. 127.

[5] Béchara Chimali, "Naissance et premier âge au Liban," *Anthropos*, v, p. 746.

[6] G. Bellucci, *Il Feticismo primitivo in Italia*, pp. 22 sq. ; Id., *Un capitolo di psicologia popolare : Gli amuleti*, p. 29.

[7] Id., *Il Feticismo primitivo in Italia*, pp. 23 sq. White coral, on the other hand, is regarded as regulating the flow of milk (G. Bellucci, *Gli amuleti italiani contemporanei*, p. 50).

[8] J. E. Padfield, *The Hindu at Home*, p. 319.

against the influences of the sun.[1] By Roman women it was worn as a charm against sterility.[2] In Algeria, as in most parts of Asia and Africa, coral is regarded as an indispensable part of a woman's attire.[3]

Mother-of-pearl and the pearl itself possess in a high degree the virtues of shells and of the products of the sea. In Arabia the same term is applied to both pearls and coral.[4] A hymn of the Atharva-Veda is devoted to the praise of the pearl : " With the shell that was born of the sea, foremost among bright substances, we slay the Rakshas and conjure the Atrins ; with the shell we conquer disease and poverty ; the shell is our universal remedy. Thou art the daughter of the Moon ; the bones of the gods turned into the sea-dwelling pearl. I fasten it upon thee that thy life may be long, lustrous and mighty, that it may last a hundred autumns protected by the pearl." [5]

We have already noted the profound importance that attaches to crystals and all kinds of gems, which are regarded as containing the very quintessence of magic powers derived from the moon.[6] Amethysts play the same part among the shamans of Alaska as quartz crystals among Australian medicine-men.[7] Emeralds were called in ancient Peru ' daughters of the moon,' and assisted women in child-birth,[8] and they represented, as we have seen, the god on the bridal couch in Mexico.[9] They are likewise called ' the sons of the moon ' in India.[10] Every precious stone is regarded as having special virtues. Thus beryls increase married love ; sapphires protect chastity ; lapis lazuli brings success in love ; turquoises draw upon themselves any evil that threatens the wearer ; carbuncles protect from wounds in battle ; cornelians protect from witchcraft ; chrysoprase defends the wearer against the assaults of demons ; [11] topazes bring wealth.[12] Glass beads, on which savages set so high a value, are believed by them to possess virtues scarcely less potent than the most precious gems. In the interior

[1] W. Crooke, *Popular Religion and Folklore of Northern India*, vol. ii, pp. 15 sq. ; J. M. Campbell, *Notes on the Spirit Basis of Belief and Custom*, p. 69.

[2] W. T. and K. Pavitt, *The Book of Talismans*, p. 221.

[3] P. Gaffarel, *L'Algérie conquise*, p. 281.

[4] G. Elliot Smith, *The Evolution of the Dragon*, p. 203.

[5] *Atharva-Veda*, iv. 10 (*The Sacred Books of the East*, vol. xlvii, pp. 62, 383 sq.).

[6] See above, vol. ii, pp. 702 sqq.

[7] J. Jetté, " On the Superstitions of the Ten'a Indians," *Anthropos*, vi, p. 255.

[8] W. T. and K. Pavitt, *The Book of Talismans*, p. 180.

[9] See above, p. 238.

[10] J. E. Padfield, *The Hindu at Home*, p. 319.

[11] W. T. and K. Pavitt, *op. cit.*, pp. 155, 158 sq., 172, 180 sq., 208, 233.

[12] J. E. Padfield, *op. cit.*, p. 321.

parts of Africa, before the days of European penetration, if a native
were given the choice between a gold sovereign and a glass bead,
he would generally prefer the latter.[1]   One of the reasons given for
the preference is that beads are perforated, which is sufficient to
associate the object in the mind of the savage, like the cowry, with
the female principle of generation.[2]   The Zulus call glass beads
' eggs.'[3]   The girdles of glass beads which are in general use among
Bantu women, are at the present day often worn beneath their
undergarments.[4]   In British Central Africa girdles of glass beads
are worn by women only, and their use is discontinued during
menstruation.[5]   In India the Jatni place pieces of glass on their
sleeping-rugs and sheets, in order to ward off evil influences.[6]

The discovery of metals which marked an era in the history
of mankind was accounted a miraculous revelation of magic power ;
and all metals are regarded as possessing talismanic properties of
the highest order.   Iron and copper are no less endowed with magic
qualities than the so-called ' precious metals,' but gold, probably
from its permanent brightness and incorruptibility is generally
accounted particularly potent as an amulet.[7]   The magic power of
these metals depends upon the substances themselves and not on
their decorative value.   In Burma pieces of gold and silver wire
or little discs of the metals are inserted through a cut under the skin,
thus being more thoroughly assimilated than if used as collars or
bracelets, and the metals thus worn subcutaneously are accounted
a most powerful charm to ward off evil spirits.[8]   Such is the
reverence with which gold is regarded in India that it is not
considered proper to wear any below the waist, as this would be
an indignity to the holy material.   There can be little doubt that
the adoption of a gold standard of currency was, as with cowry-
shell money, due in the first instance to magical and superstitious
notions.   When nickel annas were introduced into India, the
natives entertained great doubts as to their worth, and did not

[1] D. Livingstone, *Missionary Travels and Researches in South Africa*,
p. 189.

[2] *Loc. cit.*;   C. F. Gordon Cumming, *From the Hebrides to the Himalayas*,
vol. i, pp. 313 sqq.;   F. T. Elworthy, " On Perforated Stone Amulets,"
Man, iii, pp. 17 sqq.

[3] A. Delegorgue, *Voyages dans l'Afrique Australe*, vol. ii, p. 226.

[4] E. Torday and T. A. Joyce, " Notes on the Ethnography of the Ba-
Mbala," *Journal of the Anthropological Institute*, xxxv, p. 401.

[5] H. S. Stannus, " Notes on Some Tribes of British Central Africa,"
Journal of the Royal Anthropological Institute, xl, pp. 319, 321.

[6] W. Crooke, *Popular Religion and Folklore of Northern India*, vol. ii,
p. 36.

[7] *Ibid.*, vol. ii, pp. 15 sq.

[8] L. Milne, *Shans at Home*, p. 67

consider that they could be used for any solemn purpose, such as offerings in the temples.[1]

Amulets or ornaments are worn more particularly in the neighbourhood of the various openings of the body, through which, according to universal belief, evil spirits and influences may enter, or the soul may escape or be drawn out. The nostrils are guarded by skewers and nose-rings, the ears by ear-rings or huge discs or cylinders passed through the transfixed and elongated lobes; the mouth is protected by tooth-filings, the knocking out of teeth, labrets, skewers, rings, and even strings of beads passed through the lips. A warrior of the Juri tribe on the Amazon, for example, presented an extraordinary appearance: a huge disc was inserted in his lower lip, one in the lobe of each ear, one in each wing of his nostrils.[2] The women of Darien likewise wore rings in their ears, their nose, and their lips.[3] On the coast of Guinea it was the custom for women to wear rings and charms over every opening of their body; a gold ring was inserted in the labia.[4] Among the Pelew Islanders, when a child is in a critical condition, protective pellets are inserted in every opening of the body.[5] Little figures are found in museums representing a man, woman, or child covering the upper opening of the body with one hand and the lower with the other. They were worn by the ancients as amulets.[6]

When a portion or opening of the body is thus protected by an amulet it is thought foolhardy or grossly indelicate to remove it, or to be seen without it, and the person who meets with such an accident is filled with confusion and shame. The Australian aborigines, in early days, would on no account be seen by a stranger for whom they had any respect without their nose-skewer.[7] American Indians, when the overstretched lobes of their ears became torn, so that they were unable to wear the huge ear-ornaments which they were in the habit of inserting

[1] R. V. Russell, *The Tribes and Castes of the Central Provinces of India*, vol. iv, pp. 523 sq.

[2] J. Debret, *Voyage pittoresque et historique au Brésil*, pl. xxviii.

[3] *Purchas His Pilgrimes* (1626), p. 872. For numerous other examples see W. H. Dall, " On Masks, Labrets, and Certain Aboriginal Customs," *Third Annual Report of the Bureau of Ethnology*, pp. 81 sqq.

[4] A. Ca da Mosto, " Navigationi," in G. B. Ramusio, *Navigationi et Viaggi*, vol. i, fol. 110e.

[5] J. Kubary, " Die Religion der Pelauer," in A. Bastian, *Allerlei aus Volks- und Menschenkunde*, vol. i, p. 9.

[6] O. Jahn, " Über den Aberglauben des bösen Blicks bei den Alten," *Berichte über die Verhandlungen der Königlich Sächsischen Gesellschaft der Wissenschaften*, vii, pp. 48 sq. ; S. Seligmann, *Der böse Blick*, vol. i, p. 326.

[7] B. McKiernan, " Some Notes on the Aborigines of the Lower Hunter River, New South Wales," *Anthropos*, vi, p. 886.

in the distended lobe, were so overcome with shame that they were with difficulty prevented from committing suicide.[1] The women of Alaska, who wore large discs inserted in their lower lip, could hardly be induced to remove them ; when at last they yielded to persistent requests and bribes, they hid their mouth with their hands, and manifested the same confusion as a European woman who should be discovered semi-naked.[2] The nose-ring, or 'nathni,' worn by Hindu women is regarded in the same manner. A woman who should remove it would be looked upon as having quite lost her virtue and sense of modesty, and would be for ever dishonoured.[3] It is even considered indelicate to draw attention or to allude to the amulet, and the mention of it constitutes a gross breach of decency.[4]

Magical Protection of the Sexual Organs.

The sexual openings are naturally the most important that call for protection against magical influences. Apart from the intrinsic importance of their functions, the need of protecting them is apparent when it is remembered to what constant dangers they are, in primitive conceptions, exposed. Impregnation at a distance may take place through the agency of countless supernatural and magical agencies. The soul of the unborn and those of the dying, the rays of the moon and those of the sun, wind, sandstorms, and rain, the innumerable spirits that people the air, may cause a woman to fall pregnant unawares. That ascription of impregnation to unseen agencies sometimes constitutes a ground for the purposive neglect of means of protection. Among the tribes of Kavirondo, the women believe that if they were to put a cloth round their loins they could not have children.[5] Similarly, the native women of the Cross Rivers, who wear only the most minute apron, believe that "more clothing would be detrimental to child-bearing."[6] The dreaded nature of the many spiritual beings who are on the look-out to take possession of women renders, however, protection against their assaults far more generally desirable. Throughout India, women

[1] J. G. E. Heckewelder, *History, Manners, and Customs of the Indian Nations*, p. 207 ; J. Adair, *The History of the American Indians*, p. 171.
[2] La Pérouse, *Voyage*, vol. ii, pp. 226 sq. ; U. Lisiansky, *A Voyage round the World*, p. 195.
[3] R. V. Russell, *The Tribes and Castes of the Central Provinces of India*, vol. iv, pp. 524 sq.
[4] W. Crooke, *Popular Religion and Folklore of Northern India*, vol. ii, p. 43.
[5] A. Bland Sutton, *Man and Beast in Eastern Aethiopia*, p. 143.
[6] C. Partridge, *Cross River Natives*, p. 153.

are believed to be in constant danger of being outraged by spirits ; and such is the violence and persistence of their embraces that their victims are reputed to die from lassitude.[1] Singhalese women believe that if the sexual organs were left carelessly exposed " a devil, imagined as a white and hairy being, might have intercourse with them." [2] In ancient Greece and Italy women stood in the same danger from Fauns and Satyrs.[3] In Tonga and in Samoa women are often rendered pregnant by invisible assailants.[4] Throughout South America girls and women are constantly liable to assaults from snakes and evil spirits.[5] Eskimo women are careful to rub saliva on their abdomen in order to protect themselves from the embraces of the moon-god.[6]

Women are not menaced by supernatural beings alone : pregnancy, sterility, and abortion may result from incantations, witchcraft, spells, or from the mere look of a person who is moved by envy or desire. In Sierra Leone, if two women are walking along the road, and a man passes between them, the women, it is firmly believed, are liable to fall pregnant in consequence ; if two men should pass between the women, the latter will have twins.[7] In North-Western Australia it is believed that a man may become the father of a woman's child by merely willing it, or by means of secret incantations ; [8] and I am further informed that such impregnation at a distance is thought to take place through the power of the evil eye. The injurious power of the evil eye is essentially the effect of a look charged with envy, malice, or cupidity. In primitive thought the principle that " he that looketh upon a woman to lust after her has already committed adultery with her in his heart," has a literal signification. Pregnancy, it is believed by primitive people, may quite well result from such a look.[9]

Men are scarcely less exposed than women to such perilous influences. Any organ of the body is constantly exposed to magic

---

[1] J. A. Dubois, *Hindu Manners, Customs, and Ceremonies*, vol. ii, pp. 389 sq.

[2] E. Westermarck, *The History of Human Marriage*, vol. i, p. 537, giving an incorrect reference to H. H. Ellis.

[3] L. Preller, *Römische Mythologie*, p. 337.

[4] T. Waitz and G. Gerland, *Anthropologie der Naturvölker*, vol. vi, p. 315.

[5] R. Southey, *History of Brazil*, vol. i, p. 240 ; R. Karsten, *Studies in South American Anthropology*, vol. i, p. 164.

[6] H. Egede, *A Description of Greenland*, p. 209.

[7] G. A. L. Banbury, *Sierra Leone ; or the White Man's Grave*, p. 185.

[8] A. R. Brown, " Beliefs concerning Childbirth in some Australian Tribes," *Man*, xii, p. 182.

[9] D. S. Oyler, " The Shilluk's Belief in the Evil Eye," *Sudan Notes and Records*, ii, p. 124.

dangers   The Shilluk believe that the evil eye may affect the
eyes, the hands, the liver, the feet, or indeed any portion of
the body upon which the influence may happen to fall.   It is the
universal belief that impotence is due in every instance to some
act of witchcraft.[1]   " There are some," writes a Turkish author,
" who deny the influence of sortilege and of the evil eye on the
male sexual powers.   It is easy enough to deny what one does not
understand, I reply to all such sceptics.   But the testimony of
the Holy Prophet proves that impotence may be caused by the
evil eye, by evil incantations, by envy and ill-will, and the ' knotting
of the aiguillette.' "[2]   In Spain the fear of a woman's evil eye is
extremely prevalent.   In order to counteract it, the men, when
they suspect that they have incurred the danger, are in the habit
of drinking horn shavings, presumably on principles of sympathetic
magic, as an antidote against impotence.[3]   The men in the
Cameroons are so much afraid of the evil eye causing them to become
impotent that they are most careful not to expose the penis even
during a medical examination.[4]   In the New Hebrides " the
closest secrecy is adopted with regard to the penis, not at all from
a sense of decency, but to avoid ' narak,' " that is, witchcraft.[5]
The protection of the sexual organs of both women and men from
such dangers is therefore as essential as any form of self-protection
from physical violence.

The purposes for which articles are employed in relation to the
protection of the sexual organs and their functions are quite
commonly achieved without covering those organs.   In India
children were wont to go entirely naked, but wore amulets in the
neighbourhood of the genital organs.   " The private parts of
children," says Abbé Dubois, " have their own particular decoration.   Little girls wear a gold or silver shield, or cod-piece, on
which is graven an indecent picture ; while a boy's ornament, also
of gold or silver, is an exact copy of the member it is meant to

[1] S. Seligmann, *Der böse Blick und Verwandtes*, vol. i, pp. 199 sqq. ;
E. Doutté, *La société musulmane du Maghreb. Magic et religion de l'Afrique
du Nord*, pp. 288 sq. ;   F. C. H. L. de Pouqueville, *Voyage en Morée, à Constantinople en Albanie*, vol. i, pp. 257 sq. ;   D. Bray, in *Census of India*, 1911,
vol. iv, "Baluchistan," p. 105 ; W. B. Heard, "Notes on the Yezidis," *Journal
of the Royal Anthropological Institute*, xl, p. 213 ;   G. Sandys, *A Relation of a
Journey begun An. Dom. 1610*, p. 7.

[2] B. Stern, *Medizin, Aberglaube und Geschlechtsleben in Turkei*, vol. i,
p. 291.

[3] R. Ford, in *Murray's Handbook to Spain* (1885), p. 632.

[4] A. Plehn, " Beobachtungen in Kamerun," *Zeitschrift für Ethnologie*,
xxxvi, p. 720.

[5] B. T. Somerville, " Ethnological Notes on the New Hebrides," *Journal
of the Anthropological Institute*, xxiii, p. 368.   Cf. W. H. Rivers, *The History
of Melanesian Society*, vol. ii, p. 432.

decorate." [1]   Similar amulets are worn by little girls in Siam over the vulva.[2]   In Central Australia the men fastened a shell or some beads to their pubic hair.[3]   Similarly, among the Buruns, a secluded tribe of the Upper Nile, the men sometimes wear a small cowry shell fastened on one side of the pubis.[4]   The primary object of such sexual ' clothing ' is frequently effected by a belt or girdle worn round the abdomen.   The women among the Buruns wear nothing but a string of cowry shells round their waist.[5]   In Nubia, according to an old traveller, " the young girls and those who are not married wear rosaries of paternosters, which married women wear round their necks, tied round them above their natural parts." [6]   In Sennar and in some parts of Senegal the entire costume of unmarried girls likewise consists of a string of cowry shells tied round the waist.[7]   The same form of attire is employed by the Washuma unmarried females.[8]   Among the Didinga and the Turkana unmarried women wear nothing but a few chips of ostrich egg-shells tied to a string.[9]   Among some tribes of the Congo the only costume of the women consists of a girdle of beads.[10]   In the upper Ubangi district unmarried girls wear nothing but a string plaited from the hairs of elephants.[11]   Among the Ababua " very frequently the younger women wear absolutely no clothing, and have for all ornament two or three strings threaded with iron rings as a girdle." [12]   Among the Tiapys of the Senegal unmarried girls wear nothing but a shell suspended by a string.[13]   In Benin young girls wore " nothing but some strings of coral twisted round their

---

[1] A. Dubois, *Hindu Manners, Customs and Ceremonies*, vol. i, p. 336.

[2] Pallegroix, *Description du royaume de Thaï, ou Siam*, vol. i, p. 203.

[3] E. C. Stirling, in *Report of the Work of the Horn Scientific Expedition to Central Australia*, Part iv, p. 18.

[4] D. Waterson, " Report upon the Physical Characters of some Nilotic Negroid Tribes," *Third Report of the Wellcome Research Laboratories*, p. 343.

[5] *Ibid.*, p. 333.

[6] F. Alvarez, " Viaggio nella Ethiopia," in G. B. Ramusio, *Navigationi et Viaggi*, vol. i, fol. 203.

[7] O. Schreiner, *Muschelgeld-Studien*, p. 173 ; A. da Ca da Mosto, " Navigationi," in G. B. Ramusio, *op. cit.*, vol. i, fol. 100 sq.

[8] O. Schreiner, *op. cit.*, p. 172.

[9] J. H. Driberg, " A Preliminary Account of the Didinga," *Sudan Notes and Records*, v, p. 221.   Cf. H. H. Johnston, *The Uganda Protectorate*, p. 846. Egg-shells are, of course, regarded as a fertility-charm.   In the district about Stanley Pool the women use egg-shells strung together and hung over the fowl-run, to make the hens lay (Lieutenant Costermans, " Le district de Stanley-Pool," *Bulletin de la Société d'Études Coloniales*, ii, p. 45).

[10] E. D. Morgan, in *Journal of the Anthropological Institute*, xvii, p. 235.

[11] A.-J. Wauters, *L'État indépendent du Congo*, pp. 314 sq.

[12] J. Halkin, *Les Ababua*, p. 174.

[13] H. Hecquard, *Voyage sur la côte et dans l'intérieur de l'Afrique occidentale*, p. 232.

middle, which is not sufficient to hide their nudities." [1]   In New
Caledonia the women simply wore " a string round the middle and
another round the neck." [2]   These strings were made of swans'
feathers mixed with human hair, and they were tied round them,
they said, " to secure a long life." [3]   The same costume is common
for both men and women among the tribes of Brazil ; a necklace
of pieces of shell is sometimes deemed sufficient. [4]   Among the
Tupi tribes marriageable girls wear for all costume a string of
cotton fastened round their waist, and two similar strings round
the arms.   These " were magical things which were put on the
girl at the critical epoch of her life, when she became a woman,
in order to protect her against the Anhanga," or evil spirits. [5]
Such belts are often discarded on marriage, or after the birth of
the first child.

The belt or girdle tied round the waist, the primal rudiment
of all apparel, is universally regarded not as a utilitarian
contrivance, but as a magic instrument to which transcendent
virtue and importance are attached.   Japanese women, who are
noted for their ingenuous lack of prudery, and were in the habit
of bathing publicly in the company of the men, never lay aside
their girdle except at the bath, and not always then ; for it contains
the charm upon which depends " their capacity to bear children
and feed them." [6]   Among the Ainu, the most effective remedy
for barrenness is to drink some water in which the leather girdle
of a woman who has borne children has been boiled. [7]   The girdle
of Déné girls, with which their very existence is supposed to be
bound up, is made of the guts of porcupines, because the animal
gives birth to its young with great rapidity, and it is accordingly
supposed that such a girdle will " enable her to bring forth children
without difficulty." [8]   In Central Australia a girl is provided by
her friends with a girdle for the purpose of promoting her fertility. [9]

[1] W. Bosman, " A New Description of the Coast of Guinea," in Pinkerton's
Voyages and Travels, vol. xvi, p. 524.

[2] J. G. A. Foster, *A Voyage round the World*, vol. ii, p. 383.

[3] G. Hamilton, " Customs of the New Caledonian women belonging to
the Nancaushy Tribe," etc., *Journal of the Anthropological Institute*, vii,
p. 206.

[4] K. von den Steinen, *Unter den Naturvölkern Zentral-Brasiliens*, p. 182.

[5] R. Karsten, *Studies in South American Anthropology*, vol. i, p. 164.

[6] E. Jung, " Japanisches Aberglaube," *Zeitschrift für Ethnologie*, ix, p. 333.

[7] B. Pilsudski, " Schwangerschaft, Entbindung und Fehlgeburt bei den
Bewohnern der Insel Sachalen," *Anthropos*, v, pp. 772 sq.

[8] J. Jetté, " On the Superstitions of the Ten'a Indians," *Anthropos*, vi,
p. 701.

[9] N. von Milklucho-Maclay, " Ueber die Mika-Operationen in Central
Australien," *Verhandlungen der Berliner Gesellschaft für Anthropologie*, 1880,
p. 89.

Among the Acholi of the Upper Nile, the unmarried girls go naked but for bracelets and anklets of beads ; women after marriage wear a small apron covered with bead chains, called a ' cip.' If a married woman runs away with a lover, all that the husband has to do is to obtain possession of her ' cip ' and conceal it. If this is done the woman will be unable to bear a child, and may possibly die.[1] Similarly, among the Lotuko, "if a woman's apron be stolen, she will be barren till it is restored." [2] Among the more civilised Arab tribes of the Sudan, as in many other instances, the primitive sexual talisman is worn in conjunction with the elaborate robes of a more advanced culture. The leather belt adorned with tassels and fringes of cowry shells, which is the most prevalent form of garment among the women of Africa, is worn by Sudanese women outside their robes ; it is known as the ' rahab.' It is regarded as the most important portion of their attire, and when offering prayers for the fulfilment of some wish at the tomb of a saint, girls break off a tassel of cowries from their ' rahab ' and suspend it on the tomb as a votive offering. The essential part of the marriage ceremony is also known as the day of the ' rahab,' and consists in tearing off one by one the tassels of the bride's girdle.[3] The bridegroom is himself elaborately dressed and covered with ornaments, the most important consisting of four necklaces of white and black beads. These are specially prepared by his female relatives, who soak them in an infusion of dura which has begun to germinate. This, they say, is done " to make the marriage fruitful." [4] In Persia, a woman who has been bewitched, is sedulously rubbed with a girdle.[5] Among the Arabs, the girdle, or ' berim,' has the same significance with both men and women. The circles of camel's or goat's hair worn by Bedawi on their heads are miniature ' herim,' sometimes spoken of as ' berim ' and they are professedly worn for the purpose of warding off the evil eye.[6] Among the Gallas the men call their girdle ' gourda,' that is, ' the guardian of the body ' ; it is worn in

[1] E. T. N. Grove, " Customs of the Acholi," Sudan Notes and Records, ii, pp. 158 sq., 162.

[2] Hon. Fitz R. R. Somerset, " The Lotuko," Sudan Notes and Records, i, p. 157.

[3] J. W. Crowfoot, " Wedding Customs in the Northern Sudan," Sudan Notes and Records, v, p. 6 ; Id., " Customs of the Rubatab," ibid., i, pp. 123, 127.

[4] Id., Sudan Notes and Records, v, pp. 4 sq.

[5] S. Seligmann, Der böse Blick und Verwandtes, vol. i, p. 306.

[6] S. Hillelson, " Arabic Proverbs, Sayings, Riddles, and Popular Beliefs," Sudan Notes and Records, iv, p. 78 ; R. Dozy, Dictionnaire détaillé des noms de vêtements chez les Arabes, pp. 71 sqq.

honour of Ayana, the good spirit.[1] The men's belts are commonly manufactured by the women.   Thus Veddah girls, on their
marriage, place round their husband's loins a girdle which he
must wear all his life.[2]   In some Australian clans a man's belt must
be made by his mother-in-law from her own hair.   It is obligatory
for her to present such a belt to the man who marries her eldest
daughter, and he may not accept one from any other woman.[3]   In
those instances the effects of the girdle are doubtless similar to
those of the girdle given to her royal lover, Peter of Castille, by
Maria de Padilla, which caused the king to become madly infatuated
with her.[4]   The magic importance ascribed by primitive peoples
to the girdle or belt has passed into the myths of higher
cultures as the mystic virtues with which the sacred girdles of
Isis, Ishtar, Aphrodite, Brynhild, were endowed.   To remove his
girdle is as degrading for a man as for a woman. ' Belted
knights ' were publicly degraded, when guilty of a serious offence,
by removing their belt.   The act was in the Middle Ages a token
of submission and homage ; and the refusal of the Duke of
Brittany to remove his belt before King Charles VII nearly led to
civil war.[5]

In the province of Magalhan in Brazil, the costume of the women,
in pre-European times, consisted of a minute triangle of earthenware
which fitted closely over the mons veneris.   These articles, which
are known as ' tangas, or ' babals,' are found in large quantities
in the mounds of that region, and are unique as articles of clothing,
and of singular interest.   They are made with special care from fine
clay of better quality than the native pottery ; they closely
resemble in form the pubic portion of the palm-leaf ' uluri ' worn
in some tribes of the Amazon, and these have in all probability
been derived from the clay ' tangas ' of the more advanced ancient
inhabitants.   At each angle is a small hole, little larger than the
eye of a darning-needle, for the insertion of the fine strings by
which it was attached.   The appliance does not reach down to the
vulva, and the string which passed between the thighs served
no purpose of covering.   The surface bears elaborate geometrical
designs, which are different in each specimen.   There can be little
doubt that Senhor Netto is right in his view that they had a

[1] P. Soleillet, *Voyages en Éthiopie*, p. 260.

[2] J. Bailey, " An Account of the Wild Tribes of the Veddahs of Ceylon,"
Transactions of the Ethnological Society, N.S., ii, pp. 293 sq. ; C. G. and B. Z.
Seligman, *The Veddas*, p. 97.

[3] F. G. Gillen, " Notes on some Manners and Customs of the Aborigines
of the McDonell Ranges belonging to the Arunta Tribe," *Report on the Work
of the Horn Expedition*, vol. iv, p. 165.

[4] J. de Mariana, *Historia general de España*, vol. ix, p. 260.

[5] Madame de Barbera, *Gems and Jewels*, pp. 298 sq.

magical or ritual significance. Phallic emblems and ' yonis' are conspicuous among the clay objects found in the Brazilian mounds.[1] The ' mound-builders' of Brazil belonged in all probability to the same race as the ' mound-builders' of the southern United States. In North America, " when savages went naked they made the same use of shells as our first parents did of fig leaves." [2] The shells, or round discs of nacreous shell-substance used, were not unlike the ' tangas' of the Brazilian women; they were engraved with designs, and perforated with holes for suspension. Mr. Carr remarks that it is extremely unlikely that they were used from motives of self-decoration, for the nacreous and most orna- mental surface of the shell was worn next to the body instead of being exposed.[3] Shells, cocoons, and carved gourds and tubes of bamboo are widely used by the men in Melanesia and New Guinea, the penis being inserted in the receptacle, or merely clipped to it.[4]

In the last instances the articles worn serve the purpose of occluding the openings in the genital organs rather than of covering them. This is also the case with many forms of primitive sexual clothing. Thus the tape, or ' ururi,' worn by the women in the Bakairi tribe of Brazil is less than an inch in width and does not conceal the labia, but occludes the opening of the vagina.[5] The same mode of protection is adopted in New Guinea. Among the Mafulu " one is tempted to think as regards both men and women, that from a point of view of covering, the bands might be dispensed with altogether." Those worn by full-grown women " can hardly be regarded as more than nominal." [6] It cannot, however, be sup- posed that peoples at such a stage of culture have adopted measures whose function is merely nominal; the bands completely fulfil the purpose for which they are intended, namely, the closing of the sexual openings. Similarly, the men in many Brazilian tribes and also in some parts of Polynesia and Melanesia, tie a piece of tape or string round the prepuce, thus occluding the urethra.[7] Disarrange-

[1] L. Netto, " Investigaçoes sobre a archeologia Braziliera," *Archivos do Museu Nacional de Rio de Janeiro*, vi, pp. 423 sqq.; C. F. Hartt, " Contri- buiçoes para a ethnologia do valle do Amazonas," *ibid.*, pp. 52 sq.

[2] F. X. de Charlevoix, *Histoire de la Nouvelle France*, vol. v, p. 308.

[3] L. Carr, " Dress and Ornaments of certain American Indians," *Pro- ceedings of the American Antiquarian Society*, N.S., xi, p. 452.

[4] H. N. Moseley, " On the Inhabitants of the Admiralty Islands," *Journal of the Anthropological Institute*, vi, pp. 397 sq.; R. Parkinson, *Dreissig Jahre in der Südsee*, p. 368; A. F. R. Wollaston, *Pygmies and Papuans*, pp. 113 sq.

[5] K. ven den Steinen, *Unter den Naturvölkern Zentral-Brasiliens*, p. 194.

[6] R. W. Williamson, *The Mafulu People of British New Guinea*, pp. 26 sq.

[7] J. B. Debret, *Voyage pittoresque et historique au Brésil*, vol. i, pp. iii, ix; K. von den Steinen, *op. cit.*, pp. 192 sq.; R. Karsten, *Studies in South American Anthropology*, vol. i, p. 180; P. Ehrenreich, *Beiträge zur Volker- kunde Brasiliens*, pp. 11, 52 sq.; F. Krause, *In den Wildnissen Brasiliens*,

ment of this piece of string causes the greatest distress and embarrassment.[1] The Zulus wear a minute cap fitted over the prepuce.[2] In some parts of Melanesia and Australia, though nothing is worn, great care is taken by the natives that the prepuce shall not be retracted.[3]

The idea in those instances is very similar to the reluctance shown by many primitive peoples to being seen with their mouth open. Thus among the Ewe-speaking peoples of the Gold Coast, " it behoves a man to be careful about opening his mouth, lest a homeless spirit should take advantage of the opportunity, and enter his body." [4] In some parts of Central Africa a man, on being invited to eat with a European, will request the loan of a napkin so that he may hold it in front of his mouth. He thus avoids the possibility of evil influences entering through the unguarded aperture, at the same time sparing, according to his notions, the shock to the feelings of those present and the confusion and embarrassment to himself that would naturally result from such a gross breach of the sentiments of modesty and decorum ' which nature has implanted in the human mind.' [5] In Madagascar, among the Zafimanelo, a man when he wants to eat, retires to his room and locks the door.[6] In Ashanti a man of consequence never drinks before his inferiors without hiding his face, for it is believed that an enemy " can thus impose a spell on his faculties." [7] Most Hindus intensely dislike to be seen eating, and if too persistently stared at by a stranger while at their meal, will desist and throw away the food.[8] In Samoa, when a man cooked a mess of turtle, he was careful to apply a bandage over his mouth lest the fumes from the soup should convey into his inside an embryo turtle, which would grow there and ultimately kill him.[9] In Tonga it is extremely rude to eat before anyone, and should a person be caught in the act of

p. 204 ; A. de Saint-Hilaire, *Voyages dans l'intérieur du Brésil*, Part i, vol. iii, p. 44 ; A. J. von Krusenstern, *Voyage round the World*, vol. i, p. 156 ; U. Lisinasky, *A Voyage round the World*, pp. 85 sq. ; J. J. H. de Labillardière, *An Account of a Voyage in search of La Pérouse*, vol. ii, p. 193 ; G. von Koenigswald, " Die Caraja-Indianern," *Globus*, xciv, p. 223.

[1] U. Lisiansky, *loc. cit.* ; A. de Saint-Hilaire, *loc. cit.*

[2] A. Delegorgue, *Voyage dans l'Afrique australe*, vol. ii, p. 221.

[3] W. H. R. Rivers, *The History of Melanesian Society*, vol. ii, p. 433 ; W. E. Roth, *North Queensland Ethnography, Bulletin No. 8*, p. 7.

[4] A. B. Ellis, *The Ewe-speaking Peoples of the Slave Coast*, p. 107.

[5] V. L. Cameron, *Across Africa*, p. 337.

[6] J. Richardson, " Tanala Customs, Superstitions, and Beliefs," *Antananarivo Annual and Madagascar Magazine*, ii, p. 92.

[7] T. E. Bowdich, *Mission from Cape Coast Castle to Ashantee*, p. 438.

[8] W. Crooke, *Popular Religion and Folk-lore of Northern India*, vol. i, p. 293.

[9] G. Turner, *Samoa*, pp. 66 sq.

eating, it is common decency to turn one's head away.[1] In New Zealand only common people eat in public.[2] In Tahiti, when men and boys wished to eat a snack of lunch, they would sit down on the ground at a distance of two or three yards from one another, and turn their faces against the wall or away from the company. It was thought particularly obscene for a woman to be seen eating. The ladies with whom the officers of Captain Cook's ships had such a good time, sometimes forgot themselves so far as to take some light refreshments in their cabins ; but they begged their lovers not to let it be known that they had been guilty of such a gross breach of modesty, for their countrymen would have regarded them with utter disgust.[3] In Polynesia and Melanesia, when a man is surprised or moved with admiration, he claps his hand over his mouth, to prevent himself from gaping.[4] In south-eastern Australia, a newly initiated youth must cover his mouth in the presence of a woman.[5] In the island of Timor a man always holds his right hand in front of his mouth when speaking to anyone, lest a demon should enter his body, or the person to whom he is speaking should injure his soul by magic.[6] Among the Orang Laut a woman leaves the hut and seeks some private spot in order to eat, if men are present, and she brings up her children to observe the same modesty.[7] In Brazil, the traveller, von den Steinen, who was on terms of the most friendly intimacy with the Bakairi, once shocked his companions' feelings horribly by eating in their presence a fish which one of them had given him. The group of Indians, who had not a stitch of clothing on their persons, were filled with utter confusion at the immodest act, and although it was too delicate a matter, and they were too shy, to offer any open protest, the poor people were made so uncomfortable that they did not know which way to look.[8]

---

[1] W. Mariner, *An Account of the Natives of the Tonga Islands*, vol. ii, p. 235.

[2] W. Yate, *An Account of New Zealand*, p. 20.

[3] J. Cook, *An Account of a Voyage round the World*, in J. Hawkesworth, *An Account of Voyages undertaken by the order of His present Majesty*, vol. ii, pp. 203 sq.

[4] G. Brown, *Melanesians and Polynesians*, pp. 53, 58.

[5] A. W. Howitt, " On some Australian Ceremonies of Initiation," *Journal of the Anthropological Institute*, xiii, p. 456.

[6] J. G. Frazer. *The Golden Bough*, vol. iii, p. 122, after J. G. F. Riedel, " Die Landschaft Dawacode, West-Timor," *Deutsche Geographische Blätter*, x. p. 230.

[7] H. V. Stevens, " Mittheilungen aus dem Frauenbeben der Orang Belendas, der Orang Djâkun und der Orang Laut," *Zeitschrift für Ethnologie*, xxviii, p. 167.

[8] K. von den Steinen, *Unter den Naturvölkern Zentral-Brasiliens*, pp. 66 sq.

We may regard such notions with amusement, but it is on similar grounds that we have acquired the habit of covering our mouths when yawning. Among the peasants of Germany and Tyrol it is a rule that if one yawns " he should cross himself in the name of the Holy Trinity in order that no evil thing may enter his mouth." [1] In Norway, when a child yawns, his mother makes the sign of the cross over its mouth, saying " In Jesu's name." [2] The same precautions are observed in Italy and in Spain.[3] The Hindus, when a man yawns, snap their finger and thumb and repeat the name of some god, such as Rama. To neglect this is a sin as great as the murder of a Brahman.[4] Fear of untoward consequences from yawning is universal among the Arabs. " If anyone happen to yawn," says an Arab writer, " let him cover his mouth with his left hand." All Arabs believe "that the devil would jump into their mouths if they were to yawn without covering it." [5]

The sexual organs may be protected by paintings or tatuings. In Morocco the women of the lower classes have small tatu marks over the pubis. These are quite small and inconspicuous, and in no way ornamental, consisting of two or three crosses only ; their avowed purpose is to protect the organs from evil influences.[6] Among the Mangbetu of the Congo the women, in most clans, wear a small flap-covering over the sexual organs ; but in some clans none is worn, the women, it is said, being forbidden to do so. In their stead little designs, such as crosses and stars, are painted in the sexual region.[7]   " Tatuing," we are told, " is regarded by the natives as a protection against their fetich, or evil spirits." [8] Among the Baholoholo and the Basonge, girls, when they reach the age of puberty, are marked by their mothers with incisions over the nates, in the absence of which sexual

---

[1] A. Wuttke, *Der deutsche Volksaberglaube der Gegenwart*, p. 284.

[2] G. O. Hylten-Cavallius, *Warend och Wirdarne*, vol. i, p. v.

[3] F. Liebrecht, *Volkskunde*, pp. 320 sq. ; Id., ed. of G. Basile, *Der Pentameron*, vol. i, p. 405 ; G. Tassoni, *La Secchia rapita*, iv. 48. Cf. J. Aubrey, *Remaines of Gentilisme and Judaisme*, pp. 177, 194.

[4] W. Ward, *View of the Literature, History, and Mythology of the Hindoos*, vol. i, p. 142 ; W. Crooke, *Popular Religion and Folk-lore of Northern India*, vol. i, p. 240.

[5] C. Defremery, review of Macrizi's *De valle Hadramaut libellus* (ed. P. B. Noskowyi, Bonn, 1866), in *Journal Asiatique*, vi^e Ser., ix, pp. 411 sq. n., referring to Lane's Dictionary.

[6] J. Herber, " Tatouage du pubis au Maroc," *Revue d'Ethnographie et des Traditions Populaires*, iii, pp. 37 sqq.

[7] C. van Overbergh, *Les Mangbetu*, p. 197, after Levy.

[8] E. D. Morgan in discussion on R. C. Phillips, " The Lower Congo, a Sociological Study," *Journal of the Anthropological Institute*, xvii, p. 235.

relations would be thought to be ineffectual.[1] The same practice
is observed by the Tupis of Brazil; lamp-black is rubbed in
the incisions so as to colour them permanently.[2] In Polynesia
likewise a series of arched tatuings on the nates was indispensable
for females after puberty had been reached, and any man had the
right to request to see those tatu marks.[3] Forster relates how
at O-Raiedra, in the Tahiti group, a chief, on seeing his two
sisters approaching, told him to say to the younger, ' Veheina
puwa.' " I did so," says Forster, " not knowing what would
be the consequences, and her elder sister immediately lifted up
the garments of the younger, showing that she had the marks of
puberty." On further inquiry he learnt that " in these isles it is
a kind of reproach or want of dignity not to be of age and to be
destitute of the marks of puberty. These curious marks are
reputed honourable, and it is thought a mark of pre-eminence
to be capable of bearing children." [4] During Cook's first voyage a
young woman, when presenting some plants as a gift to Mr. Banks,
" with as much decency as one could possibly conceive, exposed
herself entirely naked from the waist downwards; in this manner
she turned herself once or twice round and dropped down her
clothes." [5] Similar tatuings were worn in Fiji under the loin-
cloth; doubtless their use preceded that of the latter.[6] Dr.
Finsch comments upon the entire absence of any manifestations
of modesty on the part of the girls in Ponape, in the Caroline
Islands. They are elaborately tatued, the most complex designs
being placed round the vulva. Dr. Finsch, wishing to copy some
of those designs, requested from some of the girls' parents permission
to do so. This was readily granted, and the girls lay on the deck
of the ship, in what would be termed medically the ' lithotomy
position,' without manifesting the least sign of embarrassment,
or, what is more, any simper of lubricity or self-consciousness,
but went on smoking in absolute unconcern while the tatuings
were being copied in the presence of the crew.[7] It should be

[1] C. van Overbergh, Les Basonge, p. 251; R. Schmitz, Les Baholoholo,
p. 160.

[2] " Noticia sopre os Indios Tupinambas," Revista Trimensal do Historia
e Geographia, i, pp. 197 sq.

[3] J. Cook, " An Account of a Voyage round the World," in J. Hawkesworth,
An Account of the Voyages undertaken by the order of His present Majesty,
vol. ii, p. 190; S. Wallis, " An Account of a Voyage round the World," ibid.,
vol. i, p. 482; J. R. Forster, Observations made during a Voyage round the
World, pp. 433 sq.

[4] J. R. Forster, loc. cit.

[5] J. Cook, Journal of Last Voyage, p. 73.

[6] B. H. Thomson, The Fijians, pp. 217 sqq.

[7] O. Finsch, " Ueber die Bewohner von Ponapé," Zeitschrift für Ethnologie,
xii, pp. 317 sq.

noted, however, that the organs, although exposed, were amply protected from evil influences by those very tatuings.

Ornaments and bright objects are effective against the evil eye, not only through their special virtue as amulets, but also in a physiological manner by diverting the glance of the onlooker to themselves. In southern Italy the harness of horses and mules is made up of innumerable protective charms against the evil eye ; but, in addition to the talismanic designs which they embody, they are made of copper, and kept highly polished, so that they cannot be ' overlooked.' [1] In India " all beads which shine and reflect the light are considered efficacious in averting the evil eye." [2] The Romans wore the lunar crescents upon which they relied chiefly for protection against the evil eye by preference on their sandals, so as to divert looks as far as possible from their face.[3] Hindu brides wear on their foreheads an ornament called ' bassinam,' made of gold-leaf or glittering tinsel. " The object of the bassinam is to avert the effects of the evil eye. Placed thus on the most conspicuous part of the body it is supposed to attract the eyes of the malevolent, and thus prevent them from exercising their malign influence." [4] Women and girls in Tibet and Bhutia wear large discs of polished metal on their heads.[5] Similarly, in Kordofan large metal discs two inches in diameter are worn, and their purpose, we are told, is to act as a protection against the evil eye.[6] " Everything which shines (gems, glass, metal)," remarks Professor Doutté, " may play the same part. There is no doubt that primitive adornment was partly a manifestation of the same belief." [7] The natives of Australia wore large discs, three to four inches wide, of nacreous shell-substances either on their chest or in the neighbourhood of the sexual organs.[8] " When

[1] F. T. Elworthy, *The Evil Eye*, p. 204.

[2] R. V. Russell, *The Tribes and Castes of the Central Provinces of India*, vol. iv, p. 525.

[3] Plutarch, *Quaest. Rom.*, lxxvi.

[4] J. A. Dubois, *Hindu Manners, Customs and Ceremonies*, vol. i, p. 230. The ' potta ' or spot of paint worn by Hindu women on the middle of the forehead has, of course, a similar effect.

[5] W. L. Hildburgh, " Notes on some Tibetan and Bhutia Amulets and Folk Medicines and a few Nepalese Amulets," *Journal of the Anthropological Institute*, xxxix, pp. 389 sq.

[6] R. G. Anderson, " Medical Practices and Superstitions amongst the People of Kordofan," *Third Report of the Wellcome Research Laboratories*, p. 282.

[7] E. Doutté, *La Société musulmane du Maghreb. Magie et Religion de l'Afrique du Nord*, pp. 323 sq.

[8] E. C. Stirling, *Report on the Work of the Horn Scientific Expedition to Central Australia*, part iv, p. 18; J. Cook, " Account of a Voyage round the World," in Hawkesworth, *An Account of the Voyages*, etc., vol. ii, p. 633;

a man wishes to charm a particular woman he takes off his ornament, and attaching it to a stake fixed in the ground, he sings
chants, the burden of which is an invitation to the lightning to
come and reside in the shell. At night he wears the shell at the
corroboree." [1] Hottentot women wore large discs of some brilliant
material, such as mother-of-pearl or polished metal, when this
was procurable, well above the pubis, so as to divert attention
from the vulva.[2] Similar discs of polished metal were a common
feature in the women's belts among ancient northern European
nations.[3]

When amulets or veils are placed over the sexual organs
themselves, they are frequently as ineffective for the purpose of
concealing them as when worn round the waist or over the pubis.
Thus among Australian tribes, when they were not entirely naked,
the men and women wore "a small fan-shaped tassel made out
of fine string, and not much larger than a postage-stamp. This
is attached to the pubic hair, and is much less efficient as a covering
than the vine-leaf of the sculptor." [4] In the Anchorete Islands
the men wore a perineal tape of bast-fibre, but were quite careless
as to whether the penis was under or outside it.[5] The fringe of
springbok leather worn by Hottentot women was cut into threads
" so small and thin that they served no sort of use as a covering." [6]
Of the little fringe, consisting of a dozen leather threads, worn by
the Zulus, Delegorgue remarks "that they are designed more for
ornament than with the object of concealing." [7] The same is
true of the majority of fringes, miniature aprons, tassels, bandages,
shells, cocoons, worn as sexual coverings by primitive peoples.

The Hebrew tradition which represents clothing as having
originated in the most easily available material, the leaves of

W. E. Roth, *Ethnological Studies among the North-West-Central Queensland
Aborigines*, p. 113.

[1] F. J. Gillen, "The Natives of Central Australia," *Proceedings of the
Royal Geographical Society of Australasia, South Australian Branch*, iv, p. 26.

[2] J. Barrow, *An Account of Travels into the Interior of South Africa*,
vol. i, p. 276.

[3] O. Montelius, *Les temps préhistoriques en Suède*, pp. 81 sq.

[4] E. C. Stirling, in *Report of the Horn Scientific Expedition to Central Australia*, Part iv, p. 18. Cf. B. W. Spencer and F. J. Gillen, *The Northern
Tribes of Central Australia*, pp. 683 sq.

[5] H. Strauch, "Allgemeine Bemerkungen ethnologischen Inhalts,"
Zeitschrift für Ethnologie, ix, p. 35.

[6] J. Barrow, *loc. cit.* The sentiment which inspired its adoption appears
to have become obsolete at the beginning of the seventeenth century. Sir
Thomas Herbert says : " I cannot commend their modesty ; the woman,
upon receipt of anything, returning her gratitude by discovering her shame "
(T. Herbert, *Some Yeares Travels into Africa and Asia the Great*, p. 16).

[7] A. Delegorgue, *Voyage dans l'Afrique Australe*, vol. ii, pp. 220 sq.

trees, for the purpose of covering the sexual organs is scarcely borne out by ethnological facts.[1] The use of leaves and branches as sexual coverings, although common in some parts of Africa and Melanesia, is by no means the most general form of primitive clothing. Leaves and boughs are regarded as partaking of the magic properties associated with trees, and are widely used as protective charms. Thus in some parts of Manipur " each house has over its door a branch of dried leaves to keep away the evil spirits." The same mode of protection is employed for a variety of purposes, for it is believed that " evil spirits are frightened off by grass and herbs." [2] Among the Kammas a bunch of dhal leaves is tied to the wedding booth and to the front door of the house when a woman is in labour.[3] Among the Thompson Indians of British Columbia a widow sometimes wears a bunch of grass for the purpose of preventing her husband's ghost from having connection with her.[4] Among the Kagoro of Nigeria the wearing of leaves in front is a sign of marriage, that is to say, of fertility.[5] Among the tribes of the Northern Territory of the Gold Coast, who are great treeworshippers, the women, who before marriage go naked but for a string round the waist, wear after marriage a bunch of leaves, which they renew every day. If a man wishes to cause a woman to become barren, all he has to do is to procure her leaf-apron and to hide it under the hut with appropriate incantations. " As it dies, so will the womb of the woman one wishes to harm." Hence the precaution of renewing the leaf-apron each day. It is also believed that spirits may take shelter in the leaves which a woman uses for her apron, and that she may thus become impregnated by her

[1] The Hebrew myth is doubtless a comparatively late one. It has been suggested with much plausibility by Mr. W. R. Paton (" The φαρμακοί and the Story of the Fall," *Revue Archéologique*, 4ᵉ Sér., vol. ix, pp. 51 sqq.) that it owed its origin to an agricultural ritual which was practised at Thargelion, and may have had a wide distribution. Its object was to promote the fertility of fig-trees, which, according to common primitive ideas, were regarded as male and female, by a sacred marriage, in which the trees were represented by a man and woman, or a man impersonating a woman, clad in fig-leaves. The fig-tree was one of the most common emblems of fertility and reproduction, the wood being the usual material for phallic emblems, such as the statues of Priapus, and the fruit being regarded as a surrogate of the female genital organs.

The hideous use of leaves on statues is a quite recent practice introduced by the Jesuits in the seventeenth century.

[2] C. Hodson, *The Naga Tribes of Manipur*, pp. 134 sq.

[3] E. Thurston, *Castes and Tribes of Southern India*, vol. iii, pp. 100, 104.

[4] J. A. Teit, " The Thompson Indians of British Columbia," *Publications of the Jesup North Pacific Expedition*, vol. i, p. 333.

[5] A. J. N. Tremearne, " Notes on the Kagoro and other Nigerian Headhunters," *Journal of the Royal Anthropological Institute*, xlii, p. 154.

own clothes.[1] Women and girls, among the Kikuyu, change their attire for one of leaves or grass during religious ceremonies ;[2] and branches of trees are worn as fertility charms.[3] The women of the Marghi tribe in Nigeria, although their attire is quite elaborate and they wear handsome gowns, complete their costume by wearing a bunch of leaves in their girdle.[4] Similarly, the women of the Koragars caste in south Canara were until lately clad in the classical costume of Eve, and wore the traditional leaves. At the present day they are fully clothed in Manchester goods, but they still wear their leaf-apron over their clothes. They maintain that "leaving it off would be extremely unlucky."[5] In Ross-shire, girls are in the habit of sewing ivy-leaves to their petticoats " to bring luck throughout the year."[6]

Thus the traditional primitive sexual covering of leaves is not a veil fashioned out of the most readily available material to serve the requirements of instinctive modesty, but is, like all other primitive forms of sexual clothing, an amulet or charm employed for its magical properties and as a protection against occult influences. Had the object of primitive clothing been merely to cover the organs of generation, abundant means of doing so effectively are easily within the reach of the most uncultured peoples. That their clothing, when they have any, does not fulfil that purpose is not due to their inability or want of opportunity, but to absence of the notion that such clothing is desirable.

Where the custom of covering the sexual organs has not become established, the use of such covering, when suggested, is not understood. In Brazil, according to the description of an old author, " all of them goe naked, as well men as women, and have no kind of apparell, and are nothing ashamed ; rather it seemeth that they are in a state of inocencies touching this behalf. . . . Now alreadie some doe weare apparell, but esteem it so little that they wear it rather for fashion than for honesties sake, and because they are commanded to weare it ; as it is well seene by some that sometimes come abroad with certaine garments no further than the navell, without any other thing, or others onely a cap on their heads and leave the other garments at home."[7] The Jesuit fathers in

---

[1] A. W. Cardinall, *The Natives of the Northern Territories of the Gold Coast*, pp. 27 sq., 48.

[2] Cayzac, " La religion des Kikuyu," *Anthropos*, v, p. 317.

[3] C. W. Hobley, *Bantu Beliefs and Magic*, p. 197.

[4] O. Temple, *Notes on the Tribes of Northern Nigeria*, p. 273.

[5] M. J. Walhouse, " Some Account of a Leaf-wearing Tribe on the Western Coast of India," *Journal of the Anthropological Institute*, iv, p. 370.

[6] C. F. Gordon Cumming, *From the Hebrides to the Himalaya*, vol. i, p. 201.

[7] " A Treatise of Brazil, written by a Portugall which had long lived there," *Hakluytus Posthumus, or Purchas His Pilgrimes*, vol. xvi, pp 422 sq.

the Orinoco were grievously distressed that the women would insist on tearing up the materials with which they supplied them and putting it on their heads or round their necks. They positively refused to wear clothes, saying in so many words that " they would be ashamed to do so." [1] The women of New Ireland had similar notions ; they much preferred to wear the petticoats with which they were supplied on their heads than round their bodies.[2] Father Salvado had the same trouble in Australia. The natives " did not cover themselves at all, their complete nudity not producing any effect on them in the state of degradation in which they found themselves ; wherefore both men and women presented themselves before us naked without even suspecting that they were doing any improper thing and were an occasion of scandal. In order to initiate the work of civilising them and of rescuing them from this miserable state, we proceeded to make a law that whoso- ever came to the monastery to fetch soup or any other thing, or to work in our fields, should be covered with the mantel of kangaru skin. . . . Two women perfectly naked came nevertheless to receive their portion of soup ; as we refused it because they were not covered they immediately ran to the place where they had slept, took their rug, and having slung it over their left shoulder presented themselves again asking for soup ; for although they were quite as naked as before, they believed that they had complied with the order." [3] In the Congo some of the natives are now being supplied with trousers ; but, for the sake of convenience, they leave them completely unbuttoned, thus defeating the purpose of the garments.[4]

Those peoples who are altogether nude have, nevertheless, the notions and sentiments which have led to the protection of the sexual organs ; and the fact has served to confirm the idea of a natural ' sentiment of modesty.' Among the Brazilian tribes, where women are wholly unclothed, if strangers are suddenly introduced there will be a certain amount of commotion among the women, and they will alter their position so as to conceal the vulva by means of their foot, or in some other way. This is a regular practice with them, and this " little pantomime " is done with a certain amount of deliberate and fussy ostentation, as the observance of a routine rule. After the strangers have been among them for some time, the precaution is dropped without

[1] J. Gumilla, *El Orinoco ilustrado*, vol. i, p. 137 ; F. S. Gilii, *Saggio di storia americana*, vol. ii, pp. 46 sq., 49. Cf. A. Wallace, *Travels on the Amazon and Rio Negro*, p. 357.

[2] A. J. Duffield, " On the Natives of New Ireland," *Journal of the Anthro- pological Institute*, xv, p. 116.

[3] P. Salvado, *Memorie storiche dell' Australia*, p. 220.

[4] J. Vanden Plas, *Les Kuku*, p. 113.

any immodesty.[1] The same conduct has been observed among the Fuegians. " Men and women," says an old traveller, " leave their nudity uncovered. But when they see strangers, such as ourselves when they first perceived us, they cover themselves with their little mantles so as to hide themselves. But amongst themselves they have no objection to being naked, and even as soon as they knew us a little, they made no more fuss ; they took off their mantles, and men and women warmed themselves and stood in front of us quite naked." [2] The conduct does not point to any sentiment or motive other than those which have led us to the use of amulets and coverings. Those motives are, in fact, equally valid among savages who have not yet adopted the use of these objects, and the behaviour of naked tribes is, therefore, particularly instructive as regards the original character of the notions. A stranger may have the evil eye, and until reasonable assurance is acquired that he has no intention of bewitching the sexual organs of the women or of the men, it is common wisdom to take some precaution against such a contingency. It has been noted among the Fuegians that if a person, though he be a close relative, or even a husband or wife, is observed to be looking directly at the sexual organs of another person, man or woman, the act arouses suspicion and causes the latter person to turn away.[3] But it is not to the sexual organs only that such fears and precautions apply. All savages have a strong objection to being stared at. It is the experience of anyone who has been among a primitive people that the visitor who idly gazes at the unfamiliar figures of men and women who may be quietly pursuing their occupation, causes them to manifest their uneasiness or their resentment by frowns or looks of suspicion. The dignified Iroquois never looked a person straight in the face. " They seldom turn their eyes on the person they are speaking to," remarks one traveller, " and are always suspicious when people's eyes are fixed upon them." [4] In India " all natives dread being stared at, particularly by Europeans." [5] The fear and suspicion aroused by staring are naturally more pronounced when so vulnerable and important a part of the

[1] J. B. Debret, *Voyage pittoresque et historique au Brésil*, vol. i, p. 22 ; A. M. G. Tocantins, " Estudos sobre a tribu ' Mundurucu,' " *Revista trimensal do Instituto Historico Geographicoe Ethnographico do Brazil*, xi, part ii, p. 113.

[2] M. G. Marcel, " Les Fuégiens à la fin du XVII siècle d'après des documents français inédits," *Congrès international des Américanistes*, VIIIe Session, pp. 489 sq.

[3] P. Hyades and J. Deniker, *Mission scientifique de Cap Horn*, vol. vii, p. 239.

[4] H. Timberlake, *Memoirs*, p. 55.

[5] W. Crooke, *The Popular Religion and Folk-lore of Northern India*, vol. ii, p. 9.

body as the reproductive organs are the object of attention, but that uneasiness is only a particular case, albeit perhaps the most important, of the dread which attaches to any fixed and impertinent gaze. The effect of such direct staring is, however, also dreaded in reference to other portions of the body. The feet, as organs of movement, are very liable to be injured or paralysed by being stared at. Von den Steinen notes that the naked Brazilian savages are extremely shy about their feet being the object of too much attention, and are careful to adopt attitudes in squatting that will prevent those parts of the body from being too prominently exposed.[1] The same thing may, I think, be observed in most savages; they will draw back their feet if these are stared at directly. In Africa it is considered extremely rude and indecent to sit with legs outstretched and the sole of one's feet exposed. As von den Steinen remarks, some savage philosopher might plausibly maintain that nature has implanted a special sense of modesty in the mind of man in regard to the exposure of his organs of locomotion.

Drs. Ploss and Bartels, who were, one would have thought, in a position to take a scientific view of the facts, fall back, in their discussion of modesty, on a reference to " a natural sentiment "; and they found their conclusion upon the fact that in photographs published by MM. Hyades and Deniker, some Fuegian girls are seen in attitudes reminiscent of the Venus de Medici. The learned authors were apparently unaware that similar attitudes are adopted by them on the first appearance of strange persons. But they should have known something of the universal terror with which the camera is looked upon by savages. Making a picture of them is, according to the ideas of all primitive peoples, regarded as placing them at the mercy of whatever magic powers the possessor of such a picture may please to wield. The fear is particularly manifested by women. Seri women absolutely refused to have their heads photographed by Dr. McGee, and it was only at the command of their chieftainess that they were induced or compelled to sit, twitching with terror, before the camera.[2] In the island of Engano, when Dr. Modigliani approached with a camera, men, women, and children took to the woods, so that in a moment the village was deserted.[3] The men in Nias were after some trouble persuaded by means of liberal bribes to surmount their prejudices, but nothing could induce a woman to submit

[1] K. von den Steinen, *Unter den Naturvölkern Zentral-Brasiliens*, p. 199.

[2] W. J. McGee, " The Seri Indians," *Seventeenth Annual Report of the Bureau of Ethnology*, p. 271.

[3] E. Modigliani, *L'isola delle Donne*, p. 126.

to being photographed.[1] In Borneo, Dr. Lumholtz found that
" women as usual were timid about being photographed, for it is
a universal belief that such an operation prevents women bearing
children. If a woman is pregnant, or has care of a small child, no
inducements are of any avail, as any exposure to the camera would
give the child bad luck, or a disease that might kill it." [2] The
attitude of the Fuegian women before the camera, far from being
indicative of any natural instinct, illustrates significantly the
notions which have given rise to the appearance of such an instinct.
" The Fuegians," says Dr. Spegazzini, " are, like all savages,
ignorant of the conventions which we term moral. All natural
acts of any kind whatever are performed publicly, and what we
term modesty does not exist, except in the most rudimentary
form, in the women." [3]

A woman's breasts are not by the great majority of peoples,
up to very advanced stages of civilisation, such as those of
India and ancient Egypt, associated with sentiments of modesty ;
they are left exposed with as complete an absence of any sense
of indecency as the face. Yet there are circumstances when,
even among the most uncultured peoples, exposure of the breasts
is regarded as highly undesirable. In Loango, where it is the
universal custom to leave the upper part of the body exposed,
women are extremely averse to suckling their children in the
presence of strangers. As Dr. Pechuël-Loesche remarks, " they
appear to be influenced by the fear of the evil eye, rather than
by a feeling of modesty." [4] Among the Hausa and the Filani,
the women will not allow their own husbands to see them suckling
a child, especially if it be the first-born. In their phraseology,
they say that they do this " on account of a sense of shame." [5]
In the Sudan, women will on no account suckle a child before men,
although exposure of the breasts is habitual.[6] Zulu women, whose
ordinary clothing is of the scantiest, cover their breasts when
they are pregnant.[7] In Kikuyu it is believed that if a man

---

[1] E. Modigliani, *Un Viaggio a Nias*, pp. 208 sq., 438. Cf. V. Frič and
P. Radin, " Contribution to the Study of the Bororo Indians," *Journal of
the Anthropological Institute*, xxxvi, p. 388.

[2] C. Lumholtz, *Through Central Borneo*, p. 75 ; cf. p. 217.

[3] C. Spegazzini, " Costumbres de los habitantes de la Tierra de Fuego,"
Anales de la Sociedad Cientifica Argentina, xiv, pp. 176 sq.

[4] E. Pechuël-Loesche, " Indiscretes aus Loango," *Zeitschrift für Ethnologie*, x, p. 31.

[5] A. J. N. Tremearne, " Notes on Some Nigerian Head-hunters," *Journal
of the Royal Anthropological Institute*, xlii, p. 164.

[6] J. W. Crowfoot, " Customs of the Rubatab," *Sudan Notes and Records*,
vol. i, p. 130.

[7] A. Delegorgue, *Voyage dans l'Afrique australe*, vol. ii, p. 227.

expresses his admiration for a woman who happens to be pregnant, this will cause her to abort, or will cause her breasts to become inflamed. In order to remedy the mischief which he has caused, the unwitting offender is requested to rub some of his saliva on the woman's breasts.[1] Among the tribes of the Upper Congo, where complete nakedness is the rule, women who are pregnant are sensitive about their breasts. In photographs of a pregnant girl published by Messrs. Torday and Joyce, the Venus de Medici attitude is adopted as regards the breasts, while other girls and women are indifferent as to exposing themselves.[2] The ancient Germans had the same notions, and thought that milk could be dried up in a feeding mother's breast by an envious look.[3] Witches have been burned at a quite late epoch in Burgundy for that very crime.[4] Special precautions against magic evils are very commonly taken by primitive women while they are nursing, and, vicariously, for the protection of their children, it being their belief that injurious influences affecting them may by proxy injure their children. Thus in the Shortland Islands the women, whose ordinary attire is infinitesimal, wrap themselves up when they are nursing in a bulky mantle of dried grass which would satisfy the most prudish European notions of decency. Nor are such precautions, indeed, sufficient to set their minds at rest ; " the mother is very much afraid of witchcraft, and if strangers come she hurries away with the child." [5] In Scotland it used to be the common practice of nursing mothers to tie a thread or a piece of coloured wool round their necks until the child was weaned.[6]

Care is everywhere taken to provide children with charms and amulets. In India children of the better classes are so loaded with

[1] C. W. Hobley, *Bantu Beliefs and Magic*, p. 178. The saliva of the offender is the universal antidote against the injuries resulting from the ' evil eye.' Cf. below, p. 359.

[2] E. Torday and T. A. Joyce, *Notes ethnographiques sur les peuplades communément appelées Bakuba, ainsi que les peuplades apparentées. Les Bushongo* (*Annales du Musée du Congo Belge*), p. 281, figs. 395, 397. Savage modesty as regards the breasts is the exact reverse of the civilised sentiment, and shows clearly the difference in the motives. With European women the function of motherhood is regarded as sanctifying the nursing mother and as excluding sexual associations. I have seen refined young mothers in Italy bare their bosom in public to nurse their baby, without any gesture of prudery. With the primitive woman, on the contrary, no self-consciousness attends the exposure of the breasts at ordinary times, but fear of evil influences leads to concealment and shyness while nursing.

[3] J. Grimm, *Deutsche Mythologie*, p. 920.

[4] S. Seligmann, *Der böse Blick*, vol. i, p. 201.

[5] G. Brown, *Melanesians and Polynesians*, p. 36.

[6] W. Henderson, *Notes of the Folk-lore of the Northern Counties of England and the Borders*, p. 20.

gold jewellery that they totter under the burden.[1] Among the
Cross River natives of West Africa " as a rule children wear more
ornaments than adults. Probably most of them are charms, to
preserve the wearer from natural and magic evils. Infants and
toddling mites are often loaded with ornaments all over their
bodies and limbs, and little bells and charms hang therefrom." [2]
The same thing is noticeable among the wild tribes of the Congo ;
Arande children are so loaded with amulets that they can hardly
walk.[3] North American Indians used to put a string of beads on
a baby as soon as it was born.[4]

The sexual organs are not only particularly liable to be
affected by magic influences, but are themselves apt to be the
source of similar influences. The primary menstrual and lochial
tabus establish the sentiment of such dangers.[5] That dreaded
influence is, as we have already had occasion to note, frequently
turned to account in magic practices. On the coast of Guinea
it used to be the custom, when a negress of noble family was

---

[1] W. Crooke, *Popular Religion and Folklore of Northern India*, vol. ii, p. 15.

[2] C. Partridge, *Cross River Natives*, p. 168.

[3] *Annales du Musée du Congo Belge*, Sér. iii, vol. i, " Les Arts, Religion,"
p. 156.

[4] S. de Champlain, *Voyage et découverte de la Nouvelle France, Oeuvres*,
vol. iv, p. 85.

[5] Professor Durkheim and M. S. Reinach regard the menstrual tabu
as the primary ground for the use of sexual coverings, and hence
as the source of sentiments of bodily modesty (E. Durkheim, " La
prohibition de l'inceste et ses origines," *L'Année Sociologique*, i. p. 50.
S. Reinach, *Cultes, Mythes et Religions*, vol. i, pp. 166 sqq.). There can be
no doubt that the primary menstrual tabu has been a most important
factor in the development of those usages and sentiments ; it may even have
first suggested the appropriateness of permanently covering the female
sexual organs. But I do not think that it is possible to regard it as the sole
and direct ground of the development of bodily modesty. Menstruation
among the most primitive peoples necessitates much more than mere covering, for it is thought to require complete seclusion or segregation, thus
rendering covering superfluous. The risk of an unexpected or irregular
appearance of the periods might, of course, call for the precaution. But
there is no correlation between the extreme importance attached to the menstrual tabu and the much rarer, slighter, and later employment of sexual
covering. A survey of the usages referring to the latter shows definitely
that the protection of the sexual organs from injuries coming from without,
and the magical promotion of their functions are much more prominent
than the protection of others from evil influences emanating from the
organs. The vast majority of devices are clearly designed for the benefit of
the wearer and not for the protection of beholders. Scarcely any of the
common forms of sexual covering in use among savages would be regarded
by them as an adequate protection against the dreaded influence of
menstruation. The mentrual tabu must therefore be regarded as a component, but not as the prime origin, of sexual protection and covering.

pregnant and approaching the time of her confinement, for her
to walk in state through the streets of the town completely naked,
all her coral ornaments and amulets being laid aside.[1] Belief in
the efficacy of similar procedures is world-wide. In the Madras
province women expose their persons in order to quell a storm,
and the same measure was adopted to drive away evil spirits at
the dedication of a temple.[2] The women in ancient Egypt used,
as we saw, the same means to drive evil spirits from the harvest
field,[3] and it would seem from some Theban wall-pictures that
the method was adopted by hired mourners at funerals.[4] The
idea was familiar to the ancients. In the myth of Bellerophon,
when the irate hero with Poseidon in his train invades the land of
the Lykians, he is unmoved by the entreaties of the men ; but
both hero and god are driven back in horror when the women
come forward ἀνασυράμεναι τοὺς χιτωνίσχους.[5] Pliny vouches for
the fact that ghosts can be laid by a woman exposing herself.[6]
A sixteenth-century traveller in Northern Africa tells us that he
was assured that if a woman were to meet a lion in some lonely
spot, she had only to expose her private parts and the lion would
at once lower its eyes in confusion and depart.[7]

In the developed form of the sentiment, bodily modesty having
reference to sexual purity, offensive breaches against it consist in
exposure of a woman's body before men, as constituting an un-
reserved invitation, and in exposure of a man's sexual organs before
women as constituting an insulting assumption of their lack of
modesty and virtue. But in the primitive form of the notion, the
reference being not to sexual purity, but to magic dangers, the
relations are necessarily somewhat different. As regards women,
the principle is in general similar in primitive and in advanced
cultures, the female organs being particularly vulnerable from
the effects of evil influences, and more especially from those resulting
from the desire of men. With regard to men, however, the dangers
from magic influences are scarcely less great than with women,
and may come equally from women or from men. Hence male
' modesty ' is in primitive societies more conspicuous than in higher
cultures, and has reference to exposure before other men as much

[1] F. Römer, Nachrichten von der Küste Guinea, p. 72.

[2] W. W. Crooke, The Popular Religion and Folk-lore of Northern India,
vol. i, pp. 71, 76.

[3] Herodotus, ii. 60.

[4] J. G. Wilkinson, Manners and Customs of the Ancient Egyptians, vol. iii,
p. 334.

[5] Plutarch, De virt. mulier. ix.

[6] Pliny, Nat. Hist., xxviii. 23.

[7] G. Leo Africanus, Descrittione del l'Africa, in Ramusio, Navigationi et
Viaggi, vol. i, fol. 100.

as to exposure before women. Among a considerable number of peoples the men alone wear protective charms or coverings.[1] In the Admiralty Islands a man is filled with utter confusion when the shell which he wears over his sexual organs is removed,[2] and in the New Hebrides the sight of another man's penis is regarded as fraught with the gravest magic dangers; the organ is accordingly wrapped in yards of cloth, forming a preposterous bundle sometimes two feet in length.[3] The pygmies of Dutch New Guinea wear as their sole article of clothing a prodigious case made of a gourd, in which they enclose the penis; its length commonly equals one-fourth the total height of the man. They are most unwilling to expose themselves; " when with some difficulty we had persuaded a man to part with his case," says Mr. Wollaston, " he would not remove it then and there, but always disappeared into the jungle and returned after an interval decently covered with leaves." [4] The Siamese were shocked at the shamelessness of the French soldiers, when they saw them bathe naked in one another's presence.[5] And the Fijians were so scandalised at seeing sailors naked, while engaged in fetching water, that they sent a deputation to the commanding officer requesting him to put an end to the disorder and the offence to their feelings.[6] On the other hand, not only do the men among a large number of peoples wear no covering, but many utterly scorn the idea that any such covering is called for. The Masai, for example, glory in their nakedness and consider it wicked to cover their sexual organs; [7] while the natives of some parts of British New Guinea also " glory in their nudeness, and consider clothing to be fit only for women." [8] The Kikuyu likewise say that modesty and clothes are only for women; yet if a boy, or even an animal, happens accidentally to touch a man's penis, they are much distressed and the offender is driven out of the camp.[9] It is thus clear that the extreme modesty of Papuan men is the outcome of special notions and traditions.

[1] E.g., H. Barth, *Reisen und Entdeckungen in Nord- und Central Afrika*, vol. ii, p. 473; A. von Humboldt, *Personal Narrative of Travels to the Equinoctial Regions of the New Continent*, vol. vi, p. 10; E. Nordenskiöld, *Indianerleben*, pp. 78 sq.

[2] H. N. Moseley, " On the Inhabitants of the Admiralty Islands," *Journal of the Anthropological Institute*, vi, p. 398.

[3] B. T. Sommerville, " Ethnological Notes on the New Hebrides," *Journal of the Anthropological Institute*, xxiii, p. 368.

[4] A. F. R. Wollaston, *Pygmies and Papuans*, pp. 161, 198 sq.

[5] Turpin, *Histoire civile et naturelle du royaume de Siam*, vol. i, p. 72.

[6] C. Wilkes, *Report of United States Expedition*, vol. v, p. 356.

[7] H. H. Johnston, *The Kilima-njaro Expedition*, p. 413 n.

[8] W. W. Gill, *Life in the Southern Isles*, p. 230.

[9] Cayzac, " La religion des Kikuyu," *Anthropos*, v, p 317.

Such a traditional sentiment, which in the cultured societies where it is established is instilled into every individual from childhood, is likewise very rapidly acquired by any people provided they are sufficiently impressed with the solemn and awful character of the tabu. The same savage women who, in their natural state, are devoid of self-consciousness and repel the exhortations of missionaries with shame and indignation, become, when they have been thoroughly indoctrinated, more extravagantly prudish than old maids in the missionary's native home. Father Gilii had the joy of bringing the nude Orinoco women, who had repulsed his first efforts, to such a sense of modesty that they would on no account remove any part of their clothing even when going to bed. "This," exclaims the good Father, "is a matter of great consolation." [1]

Extension of Sentiments of Modesty through Marital Proprietorship.

Like the vast majority of human sentiments and usages, the protection of the sexual organs originally intended to ward off magical influences from them and from those beholding them, and to promote the functions of those organs, has become reinforced and modified in its significance by confluent ideas and motives, and has ultimately become transformed into sentiments differing so completely in their rationale from the original notions which gave rise to the practice as to be quite inapplicable to its primitive forms. The covering of the sexual organs of women has become associated with the proprietary rights acquired over a woman by her husband through individual marriage. Among some tribes of the Congo the women, who wear but the scantiest pubic flap, have a notion that they should not expose themselves except to their husbands.[2] Among numerous peoples girls, who are completely naked before marriage, or wear only amulets that do not conceal the vulva, assume an effective covering after marriage; [3] and it

[1] J. F. Gilii, *Saggio di storia americana*, vol. ii, p. 47.
[2] J. Vanden Plas, *Les Kukus*, p. 112.
[3] E.g., J. H. Driberg, " A Preliminary Account of the Didinga," *Sudan Notes and Records*, v, p. 221 ; E. T. N. Grove, " Customs of the Acholi," *ibid.*, ii, p. 162 ; S. W. Baker, *The Albert N'yanza*, vol. i, pp. 62, 316 ; L. von Höhnel, *Discovery of Lakes Rudolf and Stefanie*, vol. i, p. 103 ; H. Hecquard, *Voyage sur la côte et dans l'intérieur de l'Afrique occidentale*, p. 232 ; H. H. Johnston, *The Uganda Protectorate*, p. 770 ; Id., *The River Congo*, p. 212 ; J. G. Shea, *Early Voyages up and down the Mississippi*, pp. 80 sqq. ; R. Parkinson, *Dreissig Jahre in der Südsee*, p. 491 ; L. Tauxier, *Le Noir du Soudan*, p. 250 ; O. Temple, *Notes on the Tribes . . . of Northern Nigeria*, pp. 15, 32, 366 ; G. Brown, *Melanesians and Polynesians*, p. 378.

is a very general rule in primitive societies that the clothing of women is lengthened and extended after marriage.[1] Among the Tiapy, women, who before marriage go completely naked, assume when they marry an ample wrap which they wind round their waist. If, however, the weather is cold, they take it off and put it round their shoulders, without any concern about their remaining exposed.[2] Among the Bagesu, when a woman's husband dies, she removes all her clothing, and either goes naked or resumes the small apron worn by unmarried girls.[3] Throughout West Africa, as well as other parts of the continent, one of the essential procedures in a marriage is for the bridegroom to give his intended wife a piece of cloth. Thus in Sierra Leone unmarried girls wear nothing but a loin-cloth, while married women wear a cloth skirt. The expression " he has given her a cloth " is thus equivalent to " he married her." If, however, the husband dies, the widow removes her skirt and returns to her pre-nuptial state of nudity.[4] Among the Kukuruku of northern Nigeria unmarried girls are naked. The ceremony of marriage consists in the groom adjusting a piece of locally woven cloth round the bride's loins. " Should a woman remove her marriage-cloth and, leaving it on her husband's sleeping-mat, appear naked in the town, or should she remove the cloth in the presence of others and turn her buttocks to her husband, he is forced to divorce her, and cannot demand either dower or a child." [5]

[1] F. Elton, " Notes on the Natives of the Solomon Islands," *Journal of the Anthropological Institute*, xvii, p. 96 ; G. Turner, *Samoa*, p. 6 ; J. G. A. Forster, *A Voyage round the World*, vol. ii, p. 280 ; H. Strauch, " Allgemeine Bemerkungen ethnologischen Inhalts über Neu-Guinea," etc., *Zeitschrift für Ethnologie*, ix, pp. 40 sq. ; C. Wilkes, *Narrative of the United States Expedition*, vol. iii, p. 355 ; J. Shooter, *The Kafirs of Natal*, p. 6 ; A. Delegorgue, *Voyage dans l'Afrique Australe*, vol. ii, p. 227 ; W. Bosman, " A Description of Guinea," in Pinkerton, *Voyages and Travels*, vol. xvi, p. 524 ; C. Partridge, *Cross River Natives*, p. 28 ; J. Matthews, *A Voyage to the River Sierra Leone*, p. 108 ; J. Halkin, *Les Ababua*, p. 174 ; H. H. Johnston, *The Uganda Protectorate*, p. 846 ; A. M. Champion, " The Ataraka," *Journal of the Royal Anthropological Institute*, xlii, p. 75 ; A. C. Hollis, *The Nandi*, pp. 27 sq. ; G. Lindblom, *The Akamba*, pp. 373 sqq. ; O. Temple, *Notes on the Tribes* . . . *of Northern Nigeria*, pp. 229, 250, 307, 315, 344 ; L. Tauxier, *Études Soudanaises. Le Noir de Boudoukou*, p. 254 ; G. von Koenigswald, " Die Caranja-Indianer," *Globus*, xciv, p. 223 ; J. Menant, *Les Yézidis*, p. 69.
[2] H. Hecquard, *Voyage sur la côte et dans l'intérieur de l'Afrique occidentale*, p. 232.
[3] J. Roscoe, *The Bagesu and other Tribes of the Uganda Protectorate*, pp. 40 sq.
[4] T. Winterbottom, *An Account of the Native Africans in the Neighbourhood of Sierra Leone*, vol. i, p. 101.
[5] O. Temple, *Notes on the Tribes* . . . *of Northern Nigeria*, pp. 250 sq.

Queens in their own right, however, often show their independence by dispensing with those imposed proprieties. An African queen, who was loaded with ornaments which were " supposed to act as charms," but was " otherwise in a state of frightful nudity," when repeatedly urged by Livingstone to clothe herself, replied that " it is not considered proper for a chief to appear effeminate." [1]

Marital concealment of women has gone to every extreme, such as the seclusion and elaborate veiling of Oriental women, which, however, was in the first instance intended, like the primitive sexual amulet, as a protection against the evil eye.[2] In some parts of Sumatra it is regarded as indecent for a woman to expose her knee ; [3] among the Baganda it is accounted highly improper for her to reveal her calf.[4] In China the costume of the women is specially designed with a view to effacing the lines of the figure, and the breasts are artificially flattened ; exposure of the neck, of the bare hand, and of the foot, even in pictures, constitute obscenities. When the Jesuit Fathers displayed some beautifully coloured pictures of male and female saints attired in classical drapery, they were horrified to discover that their attempts at pictorial edification were regarded in the light of pornographic exhibitions.[5]

The motives and ideas which have led to the adoption of measures to protect or conceal the sexual organs are, then, entirely different from those which have subsequently become assumed as the purpose of that practice. Primitive ' modesty ' has no reference to any notion of ' impurity ' attaching to the organs or their functions,

---

[1] D. Livingstone, *Missionary Travels and Researches*, pp. 276, 282.

[2] Even at the present day " the fear of the evil eye is a powerful motive for many Muslim women to cover themselves with care " (A. Jaussen, *Coutumes des Arabes au Pays de Moab*, p. 377). Young men of particularly handsome appearance have not infrequently been led to adopt veils as a means of protection against the envious looks which their beauty might excite (J. Wellhausen, *Reste des arabischen Heidentums*, p. 196).

[3] J. Crawfurd, *History of the Indian Archipelago*, vol. i, p. 209.

[4] H. H. Johnston, *The Uganda Protectorate*, p. 771.

[5] " A Description of China," in Astley's *New Collection of Voyages and Travels*, vol. iv, p. 74, after Magalhaens ; W. Gilbert Walshe, *Ways that are Dark*, p. 73 ; W. Stricker, " Der Fuss der Chinesinen," *Archiv für Anthropologie*, iv, p. 243. The earliest accounts of China from fifteenth-century travellers, though giving considerable details of costume, etc., make no mention of the deformation of Chinese women's feet. At the time of Genghis Khan the Emperor was attended at public functions by semi-nude girls, and Chinese women habitually bathed in public in the Yellow River (J. Barrow, *Travels in China*, p. 75). It would thus seem that Chinese prudery is of comparatively late growth.

but to the magical influences which may affect them or emanate from them.   There is, in fact, in primitive societies no correlation between the importance attached to covering the sexual regions of the body and sexual morality or restrictions.   Confusion at exposure of the sexual organs may exist where sexual relations are free from any pretence of restraint ; while, on the other hand, where nudity is the rule, sexual relations are no looser than where clothing is customary.   The most licentious woman in the Marquesas Islands, where licentiousness is notorious, would on no consideration have parted with the minute flap worn over the pubis.[1]   Mr. Cross remarks that in Africa, as a rule, " modesty is in inverse proportion to clothing." [2]

The painful sentiment of wounded pudicity is but a particular instance of the mental state which primitively attends the breach of a tabu.   The confusion of an American Indian or of a negro when brought face to face with his mother-in-law, that of a Brazilian Bakairi on seeing a person eat, are in all points identical with the confusion of a European maiden whose pudicity is subjected to a shock.   The sentiment of the savage at the breach of a tabu is invariably described as ' shame ' ; it is the sentiment of wounded modesty.   That ' shame ' and that ' pudicity ' have passed away in reference to many primitive tabus, which, having lost their force, have become merely ridiculous ; it has remained and has become reinforced as regards sexual tabus, which have assumed new developments and received new interpretations.   But even as it exists at the present day amongst ourselves the sentiment of wounded modesty refers to a tabu ; it is not evoked by the fact of exposure, but by the fact that such exposure constitutes the breach of a social tabu.   The exposure of the body, which in given circumstances is sanctioned by usage, does not call forth feelings of pudicity ; a fraction of that exposure which is customary on the sea-beach would give rise to sentiments of utter confusion in the street or in the drawing-room.   The sentiment is called forth almost, if not quite, as strongly by any gross breach of usage in regard to dress, even though no exposure is involved.   The nightmare of the lady in ' Punch,' who dreamed that she appeared at a ball in her nightgown and was pronounced to be shockingly overdressed, inflicted upon her the pains of wounded modesty.   We would as

[1] U. Lisiansky, *A Voyage round the World*, pp. 85 sq.   How entirely unrelated the sentiment was to one of corporal modesty may be judged from the fact that Marquesan women cultivated a ' Hottentot apron ' for purposes of exhibitionism at their dances (Berchon, in *Bulletin de la Société d'Anthropologie*, Série i, i, p. 523).

[2] D. K. Cross, " Notes on the Country lying between Lakes Nyassa and Tanganyika," *Proceedings of the Royal Geographical Society*, N.S., xiii, p. 88. Cf. H. H. Johnston, *The Uganda Protectorate*, p. 730.

soon appear in the street naked as in shirt and drawers. Elderly gentlemen may be seen filled with confusion and suffused with blushes on being surprised collarless and in their shirt-sleeves.

The strength of the traditional preconceptions which militate against our seeing the facts as to the nature of modesty in their true light is illustrated by the evidences that are some-times adduced in support of those preconceptions. Sikovsky mentions as a convincing proof of the innate and spontaneous nature of the sentiment the fact that a child three-and-a-half years old was filled with confusion when his father entered the room where he was washing himself, with the upper part of his body uncovered, and cried : " Please don't come in ; I have got no shirt on ! " [1]   Dr. A. Moll also cites the commonplace incident as a clinching demonstration of the innate nature of a sentiment of modesty.[2] To me it appears to testify as clearly as possible to the opposite. Such a sentiment is manifestly one of somewhat priggish assimilation of instilled principles, for no one can seriously suppose that children, who throughout most ages have gone naked, have inherited as a natural instinct notions concerning the exposure of their chest. The spontaneous manifestation of such a sentiment at that age illustrates the enormous power of traditional heredity and the facility with which it can mimic instinct and create a ' second nature.' That ' second nature ' has reference to breaches of custom and not to sexual purity. Those sentiments which, according to the consecrated phrase, " Nature has implanted in the human mind," do not, in fact, even at the present day and in the most developed civilisation, exist at all ; what exist are established tabus, and the sentiments in question have reference to breaches of those tabus and to those only. There can be no doubt that if complete nudity were once more to become general, it would, in spite of the traditional sentiments of millenniums, cease after a brief while to produce either sentiments of offended pudicity or of stimulated lubricity. No feminine attire that has been devised is sexually less stimulating than complete, unaffected nudity, provided that no contrast is suggested with the clothed figure ; the imagination is disarmed, and the artificial stimulation of the sexual instincts which is the effect of the tabus that constitute bodily modesty is abolished. It is not the unclothed body, but the unclothing of the body, which is an offence against those tabus, and which at the same time is the sole foundation of pruriency.

The latter result of the development of the modesties of clothing has had far more momentous consequences than the former. It

---

[1] I. A. Sikovsky, *Die seelische Entwicklung des Kindes*, p. 90.
[2] A. Moll, *The Sexual Life of the Child*, p. 253.

may be doubted whether the tabus of modesty have at any stage of culture had a restraining or regulative effect upon sexual relations. Ethnological and social history afford no indication that the development of clothing and modesty has at any time promoted sexual morality ; and if any correlation is exhibited between the two, it is, as has been remarked of African peoples, an inverse one. On the other hand, what distinguishes the sexual instincts of civilised man from those of primitive humanity is above all their reinforcements by the powers of the imagination which, in civilised humanity, constitutes by far the most important element in the operation of those instincts. The youthful Goethe described the feeling produced by his first contemplation of the female body " divested of extraneous coverings " as one akin to fear, such as might be called forth by the sight of some strange and unknown monster.[1] Flaubert, in his autobiographical fragments, says : " The first time that I saw the two breasts of a woman entirely unclothed I nearly fainted." [2] Such an avowal constitutes the severest indictment against the ' modesty ' which the evolution of the tabus of sexual clothing has developed, and affords a measure of the abyss which they have created between the natural sexual instincts of humanity and the artificially stimulated instincts of the civilised male. Pruriency and obscenity depend, like modesty, upon the breach of tabus and not upon natural sexual values. It is in the violation of the tabu that they find satisfaction. Where no tabu exists lubricity is devoid of scope and has no existence.

[1] Goethe, *Briefe aus der Schweiz, Werke,* vol. iv, p. 469.
[2] G. Flaubert, *Mémoires d'un fou (Oeuvres de jeunesse inédites)*, p. 521.

CHAPTER XXVII

PURITY

IF the primitive sexual tabus have been established by women, the extension and transmutation which have resulted in the moral character of sexual modesty and of chastity, have been brought about through the agency of men, and have been imposed by them upon women. While the primary tabus and the sentiments connected with them are universal among existing races, the sexual morality which owes its origin to male claims is comparatively rare in its distribution, and makes its appearance in relatively advanced stages of culture only. The fact affords an indirect but significant indication of the original matriarchal character of human society and of the relatively late growth of patriarchal influence. Throughout the earlier stages of culture the value which is attached in our own society to virginity in a bride, and therefore to female chastity apart from the immediate proprietary rights of the husband, is unknown. Among some peoples—more particularly in those parts of Hamitic East Africa and of West Africa and in northern Asia, where the theory of marriage by purchase is, by assimilation to slave purchase, most fully developed—virginity is claimed and the chastity of unmarried girls is guarded. But the peoples who have those usages are far removed from a primitive state, and the view they take of the matter differs, as we shall presently see, profoundly from European conceptions of the merit and worth of virginity. Those conceptions are relatively late products of culture and of strongly patriarchal conditions.

In European society itself the sentiment with which virginity is regarded, which is part of our cultural ideals, is by no means universal amongst the social classes where those cultural influences are weaker. In the lower orders and among the peasant populations of many parts of Europe retrospective jealousy is but feebly developed, and little importance, from a sentimental point of view, is attached to the virginity of a bride. In some districts of Holland girls, it is said, are seldom virgins at their marriage, and are often in an advanced state of pregnancy at the ceremony ;

pre-nuptial unchastity, multiplicity of lovers, and illegitimate children are not looked upon as a bar to marriage.[1] Similar views are said to obtain in the rural parts of Austria, Bavaria, Switzerland, Norway.[2] Indeed, in some country districts of Europe the same sentiments in this respect appear to obtain as we find in many savage societies. Thus of a village near Lisbon, Señor Pedroso says that " young girls who reach the age of about sixteen and are still virgins are the object of so much ridicule that in order to avoid the shame they yield themselves with the greatest readiness to the first man who courts their favours, and those ephemeral and unmoral unions continue until the girl is pregnant. Then a new life begins for her. He who thinks he is the father marries the girl, quite forgetting the past." [3] In many parts of Italy, says a sixteenth-century writer, the men would not think of marrying a woman who had not given proof of her popularity by the multitude of her amours.[4] The full force of the sentiment with which the bridegroom regards the chastity of his bride is, in reality, confined to some of the most highly developed phases of social evolution.

Preference for Women who are not Virgins.

Antecedently to the development of those sentiments, it is directly opposed to the objects of marriage that it should be contracted with a girl who is a virgin. If it be borne in mind that in primitive society marriage is not regarded as an avenue to sexual life, but as an economic measure, and that one of its chief objects is to obtain children, it will be apparent that to enter into anything of the nature of a binding contract with a virgin bride would be, in the Scotch phrase, " to buy a pig in a poke." It would be equivalent to accepting the risk of the woman being sterile, and such a transaction is inadmissible in primitive phases of society. Marriage is, indeed, not regarded in those phases as being fully contracted and consummated until a child is born. In stages slightly above the primitive, where a regular transaction takes place with payment of a bride-price, sterility either annuls the contract and the bride-price is returned, or another woman is supplied by the bride's parents.

---

[1] H. Havard, *La Hollande pittoresque. Le coeur du pays*, p. 219.

[2] F. von Hellwald, *Die menschliche Familie*, p. 223; H. A. Berlepsch, *Die Alpen in Natur- und Lebensbildern*, p. 468; G. Hartung and A. F. B. Dulk, *Fahrten durch Norwegen und die Lappmark*, pp. 244 sq.

[3] Consiglieri Pedroso, " Sur quelques formes du mariage populaire en Portugal," *Congrès international d'Anthropologie et d'Archéologie préhistorique*, IXe Session (Lisbon, 1884), pp. 636 sq.

[4] G. B. Modio, *Il Convito*, p. 159.

It is manifest that the development of a sentimental value attached to virginity could scarcely take place in those conditions ; it is fertility, not virginity, which is the dominant consideration in the qualifications of a bride. In many parts of Africa a girl who has already borne a child is preferred as a wife, her fertility having been proved.[1] The Akamba, says Sir Charles Eliot, " regard a pregnant girl as the most eligible spouse, exactly as if she were a cow with calf." [2] Among the Nandi, not only is a girl who has borne an illegitimate child specially sought after and a source of pride to her family, but in one clan it is an indispensable condition of marriage for a girl to have previously conceived. A young man marrying for the first time " must select a girl who has previously conceived ; if he has difficulty in finding one, he must capture one." [3] Among the Kaje of Nigeria the price of a virgin is a goat, together with some additional trifles ; that of a girl who has already borne a child is a horse.[4] Among the Mongwandi of the Congo a woman who has borne a child is entitled to a bride-price six times greater than a virgin.[5] Among the Tuareg of the southern Sahara, widows and divorced women are in greater demand than virgins, and command double the bride-price paid for the latter.[6] Similarly, among the Indians of Canada " it is not a crime for a girl to have children ; she is married all the sooner, because one is then assured that she is not barren." [7] " The men," says Champlain, " were so eager to marry a girl who was with child that such a girl could take her pick of all the bachelors." [8] Among the Pueblo Indians the wife's pre-nuptial children are cherished by the husband, who is as proud

[1] J. B. Labat, *Voyage du Chevalier des Marchais en Guinée*, vol. i, p. 103, vol. ii, p. 70 ; G. Tessmann, *Die Pangwe*, vol. ii, pp. 258 sq. ; A. L. Cureau, *Savage Man in Central Africa*, pp. 195 sq. ; G. Bruel, *L'Afrique équatoriale française*, p. 187 ; M. Delafosse, " Le peuple Siéna, ou Sénoufou," *Revue des études ethnographiques et sociologiques*, i, p. 483 ; R. Arnaud, " Notes sur les montagnards Habe des cercles de Bandiagoro et de Homlosi," *Revue d'Ethnographie et des Traditions Populaires*, iii, p. 245 ; J. B. Douville, *Voyage au Congo et dans l'Afrique équinoxiale*, vol. i, p. 158 ; R. Schmitz, *Les Baholoholo*, p. 161 ; P. Panceri, " Lettera a Mantegazza," *Archivio per 'anthropologia e l'etnologia*, iii, p. 361 (Maagh of Kordofan) ; P. Camboué, " Notes sur quelques moeurs et coutumes malgaches," *Anthropos*, ii, p. 983 ; J. Roscoe, *The Northern Bantu*, p. 171.

[2] C. Eliot, *The East African Protectorate*, p. 125.

[3] A. B. Hollis, *The Nandi*, p. 8. Cf. below, pp. 339 sq.

[4] O. Temple, *Notes on the Tribes of Northern Nigeria*, p. 196.

[5] H. H. Johnston, *George Grenfell and the Congo*, p. 677.

[6] C. Jean, *Les Touaregs du Sud-Est : l'Aïr*, p. 203.

[7] N. Denys, *Description géographique et historique des côtes de l'Amérique septentrionale*, vol. ii, p. 475.

[8] S. Champlain, " Voyages et découvertes," *Oeuvres*, vol. iv, p. 83.

of them as if they were his own.[1]   Among the Buryat a girl with a
child is much preferred as a bride ; nearly every young woman has a
child before marriage.[2]   The same thing is stated with reference
to the Mordvin.[3]   Among the Votyak also a girl with an illegitimate child commands a higher bride-price and is sure of
marrying a wealthy man.[4]   Among the Mekeo of British
Papua, when a young man courts a girl who already has
a child he proudly advertises the fact by wearing a yellow
cockatoo's feather on his head.[5]   In Nukahiva, where sterility is
common, when a girl became pregnant the men vied with one
another in their eagerness to marry her.[6]   The same thing was also
a strong recommendation in New Zealand.[7]   Among the Poggi
islanders " a young woman is rather liked the better and more
desired in marriage for having borne a child ; sometimes they
have two or three when marriage takes place." [8]

Apart from the consideration of fertility, the desirability of a
woman is often thought to be enhanced by her being sought
after by many lovers.   Thus among the Indians of Carolina a girl
who had many lovers was much in request as a wife ; " the more
whoreish, the more honourable." [9]   The same estimate obtained
among the Natchez.[10]   Among the Peruvians " it was lawful and
even praiseworthy," says Garcilasso de la Vega, " for the girls to be
as immodest and abandoned as they pleased ; and the most dissolute
were more certain of marriage than those who were faithful.   At
all events the abandoned sort of girls were held to be more lusty,
while of the modest it was said that they had no desire for anyone
because they were torpid." [11]   The Kamchadal bridegroom who

---

[1] M. C. Stevenson, " The Sia," *Eleventh Annual Report of the Bureau of
Ethnology*, p. 20.

[2] P. Labbé, *Chez les Lamas de Sibérie*, p. 56.

[3] J. Abercromby, " Marriage Customs of the Mordvins," *Folk-lore*, i, p. 419.

[4] N. Melnikow, " Die Burjäten des Irkutskischen Governments," *Verhandlungen der Berliner Gesellschaft für Anthropologie*, 1899, p. 442.

[5] R. W. Williamson, " Some unrecorded Customs of the Mekeo People
of British New Guinea," *Journal of the Royal Anthropological Institute*, xlii,
p. 273.

[6] M. Radiguet, " La Reine blanche aux Îles Marquises," *Revue des Deux
Mondes*, xxiii, p. 613 ; G. H. von Langsdorf, *Bemerkungen auf einer Reise
um die Welt*, vol. i, p. 128.

[7] J. Batty Tuke, " Medical Notes on New Zealand," *Edinburgh Medical
and Surgical Journal*, ix, p. 224.

[8] J. Crisp, " An Account of the Inhabitants of the Poggy or Nassau
Islands," *Asiatick Researches*, vi, p. 88.

[9] J. Lawson, *The History of Carolina*, pp. 62 sq.

[10] F. X. de Charlevoix, *Histoire de la Nouvelle France*, vol. vi, p. 4.

[11] Garcilasso de la Vega, *First Part of the Royal Commentaries of the Incas*,
vol. i, p. 59 ; G. J. and A. de Ulloa, " A Voyage to South America," in
Pinkerton, *Voyages and Travels*, vol. xiv, p. 521.

finds his bride to be a virgin is greatly put about, and roundly abuses her mother for the negligent way in which she has brought up her daughter.[1] In the Philippine Islands, among the Bisayos, " if a man finds his wife a virgin, he regards her as no good, because she has not been desired and deflowered." [2] In the Sunda Islands the men prefer a woman who is not a maiden.[3] Marco Polo says that in Tibet the more tokens from her lovers a girl carried round her neck, the sooner she got married and the more her husband thought of her.[4] The Afikbo of the Cross River district in West Africa have the same usage at the present day : a large number of ornaments worn round the neck mean so many lovers.[5] Plautus mentions the same thing of the ancient Etruscans,[6] and Herodotus of the Gindani of Lybia.[7] Even a husband's vanity is flattered by the attentions paid to his wife. Thus among the Brames a husband reckons it a special merit in his wife to have many lovers.[8]

Those views are clearly not exceptional. The conception of female chastity, apart from the husband's right to dispose of his wife, does not exist in primitive society, and virginity in a bride can have no meaning where no restrictions exist previously to marriage. Those claims have gradually come to be established, but in very advanced social stages only.

Fundamental primitive ideas have operated powerfully in preventing the retrospective extension of proprietary claims and the development of the value attached to virginity ; but for those ideas, such claims would probably have tended to become established much earlier. To say that no importance is attached to virginity in primitive society is scarcely accurate : virginity is, on the contrary, the object of superstitious dread and the utmost care is taken to guard against it. And it is obvious enough why that should be so ; the haemorrhage from hymeneal rupture is regarded as similar to the menstrual flow, the most dreaded and fundamental of all tabu objects of fear, no distinction being, in fact, drawn between the two phenomena. Menstruation is thought to be the effect of sexual intercourse, and the latter is therefore accounted necessary for the establishment of the physiological function.[9] Hence precocious sexual intercourse is

[1] G. W. Steller, *Beschreibung von dem Lande Kamtschatka*, p. 346.
[2] F. Gemelli Carreri, *Giro del Mondo*, vol. v, p. 87.
[3] J. G. F. Riedel, " The Sawu Group," *Revue Coloniale Internationale*, i, p. 305.
[4] *The Book of Ser Marco Polo* (ed. by Yule), vol. ii, p. 44.
[5] C. Partridge, *Cross River Natives*, p. 166.
[6] Plautus, *Cistell.*, ii. 3. 20.
[7] Herodotus, iv. 176.
[8] A. H. Post, *Afrikanische Jurisprudenz*, vol. i, p. 468.
[9] See above, vol. ii, p. 447.

not merely looked upon as 'permissible,' but as indispensable, and is encouraged and enjoined.[1] In some instances sexual relations cease at the appearance of puberty.[2] Those fundamental primitive conceptions persist in relatively advanced societies. Hindu law enjoins as a rule of the highest importance that a girl shall be married before the age of puberty.[3] Among the Nayar defloration had to take place before puberty " in order that the girl may not be deflowered by the regular operation of nature." [4] The same rule is observed by the Todas.[5] In ancient Egypt a girl had to be deflowered by promiscuous intercourse before the age of puberty ; on the appearance of menstruation such relations ceased.[6] In Nubia defloration, digitally performed, takes place shortly before puberty.[7]

Other considerations render, as we have seen, pre-nuptial intercourse imperative. Human marriage cannot achieve its object and be fruitful unless it is preceded by a divine marriage of the woman with the powers whence her fertility truly derives. That union is, we saw, effected by various means, by unrestricted promiscuity, prostitution with strangers, ritual defloration by priest or prince, hierodulic prostitution in temples, mechanical defloration by the image of the god. Those measures achieve more than one purpose ; the Holy Matrimony not only secures the fertility of the woman, and that of the fields and cattle, but also protects the husband against the perils of defloration. Those perils are minimised or abolished by the ritual character of the Holy Matrimony ; the participants in rites of promiscuity, the stranger, the priest do not incur the dangers attaching to defloration, for they are representatives of the god.

In the ' Nasamonian ' promiscuity which precedes the consummation of marriage among many peoples,[8] a remarkable feature is sometimes noted. Sir W. B. Spencer and Mr. Gillen state that among the Arunta tribes of Australia the girl's nearest relatives,

[1] E. W. Smith and A. M. Dale, The Ila-speaking Peoples of Northern Rhodesia, vol. ii, p. 36 ; J. Sibree, " Relationships and the Names used for them among the Peoples of Madagascar," Journal of the Anthropological Institute, ix, p. 39 ; J. H. Weeks, " Notes on some Customs of the Lower Congo," Folk-lore, xx, p. 309 ; F. X. de Charlevoix, Histoire de la Nouvelle France, vol. vi, p 38 ; M. Lescarbot, Histoire de la Nouvelle France, vol. iii, p. 714 ; J. H. Hutton, The Angami Nagas, p. 169 n.

[2] E. Torday and T. A. Joyce, Les Bushongo, p. 272.

[3] H. H. Risley and E. Gait, Census of India, 1901, vol. i, pp. 431 sqq.

[4] F. Buchanan, " A Journey from Madras," in Pinkerton's Voyages and Travels, vol. viii, p. 737.

[5] W. H. R. Rivers, The Todas, p. 503.

[6] Strabo, xvii. 1. 46.

[7] See below, p. 342.

[8] See above, pp. 223 sqq.

men belonging to the same division of the tribe as herself, are selected to have first intercourse with her.[1] The account given by Diodorus of the usage among the ancient inhabitants of the Balearic Islands would seem to indicate that the same rule was observed by them.[2] Cieza de Leon also mentions in his account of the custom in New Granada that the bride's " parents and friends took the girl's maidenhead and gave her away under that condition." [3] Among the tribes of Assam and Manipur, where pre-nuptial freedom is unrestricted and encouraged, a girl's pre-nuptial lover is often one of her own clan, " a man whom she may not marry." [4] Again in Fiji, where general promiscuity took place after the puberty cere-monies of boys and girls, not only does it appear that tribal brothers and sisters were not excluded from this temporary communism, but Mr. Fison expressly mentions that they were intentionally coupled. " We cannot for a moment believe," he justly remarks, " that it is a mere licentious outbreak." [5] At ordinary times " it would be indecent " for a Fijian to have any communication whatever with a tribal sister, " to be alone with her, to touch her, or even to speak to her." [6] In a considerable number of instances the deflora-tion of the bride is performed by her father, and this among peoples who are by no means in the lowest phases of culture.[7]

When the dread of incest is borne in mind it cannot be supposed that anything but a very definite purpose can be the motive of such deliberate breaches of the tabu. A person of the same blood, a near relative is in fact among the few persons who are immune from the perils attaching to menstrual or hymeneal blood. The exogamic tabu is distinct from the menstrual tabu, and those to whom the first applies are the only ones to whom the latter does not. They are ' of the same blood,'

---

[1] W. B. Spencer and F. J. Gillen, *The Native Tribes of Central Australia*, pp. 92 sqq.

[2] Diodorus Siculus, xiv. 4. 25. Cf. above, p. 224.

[3] P. Cieza de Leon, *Cronica del Peru*, p. 402.

[4] A. W. Davis, *Census of India*, 1891, " Assam," vol. i, p. 250. The accu-racy of this statement is, however, disputed by Captain Hutton (see J. H. Hutton, *The Angami Nagas*, p. 170).

[5] L. Fison, " The Nanga, or Sacred Stone Enclosure of Wainimala, Fiji," *Journal of the Anthropological Institute*, xiv, pp. 28, 30.

[6] Id., " The Classificatory System of Relationship," *Journal of the Anthropological Institute*, xxi, p. 363.

[7] R. Schmidt, *Liebe und Ehe im alten und modernen Indien*, p. 227 ; A. Herport, *Eine kurze Ost-indianische Reiss-Beschreibung*, pp. 178 sq. (Singhalese) ; N. von Miklucho-Maclay, " Ethnological Excursions in the Malay Peninsula," *Journal of the Straits Branch of the Asiatic Society*, No. 2, p. 216 ; E. Ketjen, " De Kalangers," *Tijdschrift voor Indische taal-, land-en volkenkunde*, xxiv, pp. 86, 427 ; A. G. Wilken, *De verspreide geschriften*, vol. i, p. 217 (Bataks).

and therefore can incur no peril from that blood. There is no breach of a tabu when an act is performed ritually with a religious purpose in view ; the latter overrules the tabu, which is itself a religious obligation, and cannot therefore be in opposition to another religious obligation. Tabu food is eaten ritually ; the sacred object which ' defiles the hands ' is handled in all rites ; parricide and adultery are sacred acts when performed as religious rituals. The breach of the incest tabu by those who are immune from the blood tabu is, like all rites of defloration, a religious act which secures against the unconsecrated breach of the blood tabu.

Mechanical Defloration and Circumcision of Girls.

The fear attaching to intercourse with a virgin has very generally led to the use of artificial means of defloration. The material instrument sometimes represents the god, as in India and in primitive Rome. In Morea in the last century, the bride " avant de se mettre au lit est admise à l'épreuve de sa virginité, qu'elle doit prouver en enfonçant un crible en peau sur lequel elle monte." [1] In Baluchistan, among the Jats, defloration is performed with a razor a few hours before marriage. [2] In China and most parts of the Far East it is customary to carry out processes of ablution so thoroughly on female children that the manipulations do not leave any trace of the hymeneal membrane. Chinese ' ammas ' in the service of Europeans think it their duty to treat their charges in the same manner, and parents who are not acquainted with the customs of the country are sometimes horrified to discover that their daughters have lost all physical signs of virginity. [3] In Kamchatka it was a mother's duty to assure herself that her daughter was deflowered. [4] In many parts of Africa artificial defloration by means of a wooden instrument is carried out by old women in the course of the girls' puberty ceremonies. [5] In Madagascar " the young girls deflower themselves if this has not already been done by their mother while they were in infancy ; and a father never gives his daughter in marriage

[1] F. C. H. L. Pouqueville, Voyage en Morée, à Constantinople, en Albanie et dans plusieurs autres parties de l'Empire Ottoman, vol. i, p. 314.

[2] D. Bray, in Census of India, 1911, vol. iv, " Baluchistan," p. 106.

[3] H. de Villeneuve, De l'accouchement dans la race jaune, p. 20. Cf. J. G. F. Riedel, De sluik- en kroesharige rassen tusschen Selebes en Papua, p. 151.

[4] G. W. Steller, Beschreibung von dem Lande Kamtschatka, p. 346.

[5] H. H. Johnston, British Central Africa, p. 410 ; F. Gaud, Les Mandja, p. 275 ; J. Roscoe, " Notes on the Manners and Customs of the Baganda," Journal of the Anthropological Institute, xxxi, p. 121 ; E. W. Smith and A. M. Dale, The Ila-speaking Peoples of Northern Rhodesia, vol. ii, p. 20.

unless that operation has been satisfactorily carried out." [1] Among the ancient Mexicans artificial defloration was performed by the high-priest and an assistant. The child was taken when only a few months old to the temple. If a boy, he was circumcised. "With regard to girls," says Father Mendieta, "the two above-mentioned priests corrupted her with their fingers, and they ordered that when she should have reached the age of six years, the mother should with her fingers renew the same corruption which the priests had begun. An abominable thing, truly, and disgraceful to hear, this custom of a people more than bestial." [2] In some parts of Peru the girl was deflowered publicly by her mother before her marriage.[3] In Ecuador, Jivaro girls are deflowered by means of a bone [4]; and similar methods are adopted at the present day in Paraguay,[5] and among some Brazilian tribes.[6] Girls are instrumentally deflowered and dilated in the Pelew Islands,[7] and in the Philippines.[8] In Samoa defloration is usually performed digitally, but sometimes a shark's tooth is used.[9] Among Australian tribes the operation is sometimes performed with a stick.[10] More commonly, however, defloration is carried out in the most thorough manner with a flint knife. It is called by the Arunta ' atna-aritha-kuma,' that is, cutting the vulva; the incision is carried down through most of the perineum, and, in the absence of very exact anatomical knowledge, portions of the labia minora and clitoris are often cut off as well. The procedure constitutes in fact a very thorough form of female circumcision.[11]

The operation performed on girls at puberty among the wild tribes of the Conivos dwelling on the banks of the Urubamba and

---

[1] V. Noël, " Île de Madagascar. Recherches sur les Sakkalava," *Bulletin de la Société de Géographie*, Sér. ii, xx, p. 294.

[2] G. de Mendieta, *Historia ecclesiastica Indiana*, p. 107.

[3] Garcilasso de la Vega, *First Part of the Royal Commentaries of the Incas*, vol. i, p. 59 ; P. de Cieza de Leon, *La Cronica del Peru*, p. 402.

[4] P. Rivet, " Les Indiens Jivaros," *L'Anthropologie*, xvii, p. 607.

[5] H. Ploss and B. Renz, *Das Kind im Brauch und Sitte der Völker*, vol. ii, p. 219, after Mantegazza.

[6] W. Ch. G. von Feldner, *Reisen durch mehrere Provinzen Brasiliens*, vol. ii, p. 148.

[7] J. Kubary, *Die socialen Einrichtungen der Pelauer*, p. 51.

[8] J. Mallat, *Les Philippines*, vol. i, p. 61.

[9] G. Brown, *Melanesians and Polynesians*, pp. 424, 97.

[10] F. J. Gillen, in *Report on the Work of the Horn Scientific Expedition to Central Australia*, pt. iv, p. 165.

[11] W. B. Spencer and F. J. Gillen, *The Native Tribes of Central Australia*, p. 93 ; Idd., *Northern Tribes of Central Australia*, pp. 133 sqq. ; N. von Miklucho-Maclay, " Über die Mika-Operation in Central-Australien," *Verhandlungen der Berliner Gesellschaft für Anthropologie*, 1880, p. 89 ; W. E. Roth, *Ethnological Studies among the North-West-Central Queensland Aborigines*, p. 174.

Ucayali rivers in northern Peru, may likewise be described either as an artificial defloration or as a circumcision. A feast is held with much pomp, and people indulge in a free consumption of ' chicha.' The girl, after she has reached a state of semi-unconsciousness from the liberal potations, is stretched on a stage before the assembled company. The operation is performed by " an old and experienced woman with a knife made from the bamboo used for the manufacture of arrows ; she cuts all round the ' introitus vaginae,' separating the hymen from the ' labia minora ' and freeing the clitoris." After the parts have been swabbed with styptic leaves, a phallus fashioned from clay and made to correspond in dimensions with the organ of her intended husband, is moistened and introduced into the vagina. The girl is now ready to be handed over to her husband.[1] Circumcision is performed in a similar manner among the Ticunas,[2] and other tribes of the Amazon.[3]

The practice of female circumcision by trimming the lesser labia and clitoris is very widespread in every part of Africa.[4] It

[1] A. Reich, " Die Kampa und die Kunibo des Urubamba," *Globus*, lxxxiii, p. 134. Cf. E. Grandidier, *Voyage dans l'Amérique du Sud, Pérou et Bolivie*, p. 129 ; F. Xavier Veigl, *Gründliche Nachrichten über die Verfassung der Landschaft von Maynas in Süd-America*, p. 63 ; P. Marcoy, *Voyage à travers l'Amérique du Sud*, vol. i, pp. 669 sq. ; F. de Castelnau, *Expédition dans les parties centrales de l'Amérique du sud*, vol. iv, p. 379. As there appears to be a good deal of confusion in references to these tribes, I may take the occasion to mention on the authority of Grandidier that they are collectively known as Chunchos, that is, ' heathens ' ; the chief tribes are the Campas or Antis, Chuntaquiros or Piros, Mascos, Amoacas, Conivos, Sepivos, Remos, Cacivos, Sensis or Mayorunos (E. Grandidier, *op. cit.*, p. 127).

[2] J. B. von Spix und C. F. Ph. Martius, *Reise in Brasil*, vol. iii, p. 1188 ; C. F. Ph. von Martius, *Beiträge zur Ethnographie und Sprachenkunde Amerika's*, vol. i, p. 445.

[3] A. F. de Souza, " Noticias geographicas da Capitania do Rio Negro no grande Rio Amazonas," *Revista Trimensal de Historia e Geographia*, Ser. ii, iii, p. 497. P. Mantegazza, *Gli Amori degli uomini*, vol. i, p. 203.

[4] T. Winterbottom, *An Account of the Native Africans in the Neighbourhood of Sierra Leone*, vol. ii, p. 235 ; J. Matthews, *A Voyage to the River Sierra Leone*, pp. 70 sqq. ; G. A. L. Banbury, *Sierra Leone, the White Man's Grave*, pp. 186 sq. ; J. M. Harris, " Some Remarks on the Origin, Manners, Customs, and Superstitions of the Gallinas People of Sierra Leone," *Memoirs of the Anthropological Society*, ii, p. 33 ; Mungo Park, " Travels in Africa," in Pinkerton, *Voyages and Travels*, vol. xvi, p. 84 ; H. Hecquard, *Voyage sur la côte et dans l'intérieur de l'Afrique occidentale*, p. 323 ; A. Hovelacque, *Les nègres de l'Afrique sus-équatoriale*, pp. 151, 272 ; L. Tauxier, *Le Noir Yatenga*, p. 251 ; R. Arnaud, " Notes sur les montagnards Habe des cercles de Bandiagoro et de Homlori," *Revue d'Ethnographie et des Traditions Populaires*, iii, p. 244 ; J. S. Gallieni, *Voyage au Soudan français*, pp. 432 sq. ; L. Tautain, " Études critique sur l'ethnologie et l'ethnographie des peuples du bassin de Sénégal," *Revue d'Ethnographie*, 1885, p. 140 ; Bellamy, " Notes ethnographiques sur le Haut-Sénégal," *ibid.*, 1886, p. 84 ; A. W. Cardinall,

was observed until recently by all classes throughout Egypt, both in
Cairo and in the Upper Nile valley.[1]   With the Copts female circumcision is regarded as of more importance than male circumcision ;

The Natives of the Northern Territories of the Gold Coast, p. 76 ; O. Temple,
Notes on the Tribes of the Northern Provinces of Nigeria, pp. 381, 105, 109, 262 ;
A. Raffenel, *Nouveau voyage au pays des nègres*, vol. i, p. 233 ; C. Partridge,
Cross River Natives, p. 216 ; A. Hewan, " On some Customs of the People
of Old Calabar," *The Edinburgh Medical Journal*, x, p. 221 ; H. Ling Roth,
Great Benin, p. 35 ; F. Müller, " Fetischistiches aus Atapame (Deutsch-
Togo)," *Globus*, lxxxi, p. 280 ; J. H. Weeks, " Notes on some Customs of
the Lower Congo People," *Folk-lore*, xx, p. 307 ; Id., *The Primitive Bakongo*,
pp. 175 sq. ; F. Gaud, *Les Mandja*, p. 269 ; R. P. Colle, *Les Baluba*, vol. ii,
p. 619 ; J. B. Douville, *Voyage au Congo et dans l'intérieur de l'Afrique
équatoriale*, vol. i, p. 57 ; A. Delegorgue, *Voyage dans l'Afrique australe*,
vol. ii, p. 561 ; J. Chapman, *Travels in the Interior of South Africa*, pp. 44 sqq. ;
M. Zoborowski, " La circoncision, ses origines et sa repartition en Afrique
et à Madagascar," *L'Anthropologie*, vii, p. 663 ; T. Herbert, *Some Years'
Travels into Africa and Asia the Great*, p. 17 (Hottentots) ; J. Irle, *Die
Herero*, p. 101 ; C. W. Hobley, " British East Africa," *Journal of the Royal
Anthropological Institute*, xxxv, p. 351 ; Id., *Ethnology of the A-Kamba and
other East African Tribes*, pp. 68 sqq. ; Id., *Bantu Beliefs and Magic*, p. 85 ;
H. Cole, " Notes on the Wagogo of German East Africa," *Journal of the
Royal Anthropological Institute*, xxxii, p. 309 ; J. M. Hildebrandt, " Ethnolo-
gischen Notizen über Wakamba und ihre Nachbaren," *Zeitschrift für
Ethnologie*, x, p. 398 sq. ; J. Thomson, *Through Masai Land*, p. 580 ;
A. C. Hollis, *The Masai*, p. 299 ; Id., *The Nandi*, p. 299 ; L. von Höhnel,
Discovery of Lakes Rudolf and Stefanie, vol. i, p. 103 ; H. H. Johnston,
The Uganda Protectorate, p. 864 ; W. S. and K. Routledge, *With a Prehistoric
People, the Akikuyu*, p. 164 ; A. M. Champion, " The Ataraka," *Journal of
the Royal Anthropological Institute*, xliii, p. 84 ; G. St. J. Orde Brown,
" Circumcision Ceremonies among the Awimbe," *Man*, xiii, pp. 139 sq. ;
Id., " Circumcision Ceremonies of the Chuka," *ibid.*, xv, pp. 66 sqq. ;
J. Roscoe, *The Bagesu and other Tribes of the Uganda Protectorate*, p. 79 ;
J. Bruce, *Travels in Africa*, vol. iii, p. 348 ; J. A. W. Munzinger, *Ueber
die Sitten und das Recht des Bogos*, pp. 38 sq. ; E. Rüppell, *Reisen in Abyssinien*, vol. i, p. 201 ; H. Ludolfus, *Ad suam historiam Aethiopicam Commentarius*, p. 272 ; Courbon, " Observations topographiques et médicales
recueillies dans un voyage en Abyssinie," *Bulletin de la Société d'Anthropologie*, iii, p. 15 ; J. Burckhardt, *Travels in Nubia*, p. 297 ; L. Pallme,
Beschreibung von Kordofan, pp. 52 sq. ; Al-Tunisi, *Voyage au Darfour*,
p. 217 ; P. Ascherson, " Die Bewohner der kleinen Oase in der Libischen
Wuste," *Zeitschrift für Ethnologie*, viii, p. 76 ; A. Ecker, " Ueber die Excision
der Clitoris bei afrikanische Völkerschaften," *Archiv für Anthropologie*, 1872,
p. 225 ; A. Bilharz, " Beschreibung der Genitalorganen einiger schwarzen
Eunuchen nebst Bemerkungen über Beschneidung der Clitoris und
klein Schamlippen," *Zeitschrift für wissenschaftlichen Zoologie*, x, p. 281 ;
H. Sarrazin, *Races du Soudan Français*, p. 188 (Tuareg).

[1] E. Godard, *Égypte et Palestine, observations médicales et scientifique*,
pp. 49 sqq., 58 sqq. ; R. F. Burton, *Personal Narrative of a Pilgrimage to
Al-Madinah and Meccah*, vol. ii, p. 20, note ; C. Niebuhr, " Travels in
Arabia," in Pinkerton, *Voyages and Travels*, vol. x, p. 162 ; P. Ascherson,
loc. cit. ; R. Hartmann, *Naturgeschichtlich-medicinische Skisse der Nillander*,
vol. i, p. 278.

the operation on the female " is observed among the Copts without exception." [1] It was regularly observed by the ancient Egyptians.[2]

Female circumcision was an immemorial practice among the Arabs. Indeed, according to Arab tradition, it preceded male circumcision ; it was said to have been first practised by Sarah on Hagar ; afterwards both Sarah and Abraham, by order of Allah, circumcised themselves.[3] Its prevalence in Arabia was known to Strabo,[4] and it is frequently referred to by Arab authors.[5] " A mother circumcised is a happy mother," is a common saying among the Arabs.[6] It is still universally practised in the Hedjaz and by many Arab tribes, and the Bedawi will not marry an uncircumcised woman.[7] As everywhere else, it has gradually tended to become neglected and is carried out secretly, while male circumcision has acquired greater emphasis. According to Ibn-al-Athir, Muhammad pronounced circumcision to be " an ordinance for men and honourable for women." [8] There can be no doubt that it was originally equally obligatory on both men and women. In southern Persia female circumcision is observed as regularly as male circumcision ; but it has fallen into disuse in the interior.[9] We have no direct and conclusive evidence that circumcision of girls was practised among the Jews, though Strabo states that it was,[10] and

---

[1] E. W. Lane, *Manners and Customs of the Modern Egyptians*, vol. ii, p. 275.

[2] Strabo, xvii. 11. 5 ; St. Ambrose, *De Abraham*, ii. 11, in Migne, *Patrologiae Cursus Completus*, vol. xiv, col. 494 ; B. Peyron, " Papiri Greci del Museo Britannico di Londra e della Biblioteca Vaticana," *Memorie della Reale Accademia delle Scienze di Torino*, Ser. ii, iii, Part ii, pp. 86 sqq.

[3] R. F. Burton, *Personal Narrative of a Pilgrimage to Al-Madinah and Meccah*, vol. ii, p. 19.

[4] Strabo, xvii. 2. 5.

[5] J. Wellhausen, *Reste des arabischen Heidenthum*, p. 175 ; I. Broyde, *ut infra*.

[6] A. Jaussen, *Coutumes des Arabes au pays de Moab*, p. 35.

[7] *Ibid.* ; R. F. Burton, *loc. cit.* ; C. Niebuhr, " Travel in Arabia," in Pinkerton, *Voyages and Travels*, vol. x, p. 161 ; C. Snouck, Hurgronje, *Mekka*, vol. ii, p. 142.

[8] I. Broyde, art. " Circumcision among the Arabs," in *The Jewish Encyclopaedia*, vol. iv, p. 102.

[9] J. Chardin, *Voyages en Perse et autres lieux de l'Orient*, vol. x, p. 76.

[10] Strabo, xvii. 11. 5. Strabo says that " the Egyptians circumcised their boys and girls, as do the Jews." It is just possible that the grammar of the statement may be careless, although that would be unlike Strabo. It should be borne in mind that by the Arabs, as well as by most peoples who practice female circumcision, the utmost secrecy is observed in regard to it, and nothing is ever said about it. So that our information is very far from representing the full extent of the distribution of the practice.

the Virgin Mary was said to have been circumcised.[1] The Jews of Abyssinia, who represent a very primitive form of pre-Talmudic Judaism, regard female circumcision as obligatory.[2]

The defloration of the bride by means of a razor, practised by the Baluchi, is, of course, a form of circumcision. In fact, it is often carried out in childhood instead of immediately before marriage, and the two forms of operation " are usually lumped together in Baluchistan as mere varieties of one and the same practice, female circumcision." Although it is apt to be represented as a demonstration of virginity, it is regularly observed by the Jats, who allow complete sexual freedom to their women, both before and after marriage. The Brahuin, who do not regularly perform female circumcision, believe that snipping the tip of the clitoris is a sure means of overcoming either complete barrenness or a stubborn perversity in bearing nothing but girls.[3] Among the Kehal, a caste of boatmen on the Indus, " a newly married wife waits six months, and if not pregnant by then she gets herself circumcised, whereon pregnancy usually ensues."[4] Female circumcision is also commonly performed among the natives of the North-West Frontier Province.[5] Among the Sheikhs and Mogals of Rajputana the circumcision of girls is regarded as being as important as that of boys.[6] In Baroda and Bombay proper it is performed by the Dandi Bohoras and other Shiahs. "It is said to be dying out, and is now performed secretly only in a few ' orthodox ' families."[7]

It is therefore quite possible that female circumcision may have been practised, even in late times, by the Jews without any statement on the subject being available.

[1] A. Maury, Croyances et légendes du moyen-âge, p. 125. This was probably done on the principle that every incident in the biography of Christ had to have its exact counterpart in that of the Virgin ; but it nevertheless shows that it was thought quite natural that the Jews should circumcise their girls, a belief for which it would be difficult to account, in the absence of information on the subject, where anthropological knowledge did not exist.

[2] S. Weissemberg, " Die Falascha," Globus, xlvi, p. 257 ; R. Andree, Zur Volkskunde der Juden, p. 84 ; M. Flad, Kurze Schilderung der abissinischen Juden, p. 31. The practice might have been adopted from the Abyssinians by the Jews, but they themselves affirm that they observed it before they left Palestine (J. Bruce, Travels in Africa, vol. iii, p. 348).

[3] D. Bray, Census of India, 1911, vol. iv, " Baluchistan," Part i, Report, pp. 106 sq.

[4] H. A. Rose, A Glossary of the Tribes and Castes of the Panjab and North-West Frontier Province, vol. ii, p. 487.

[5] E. A. Gait, Census of India, 1911, vol. i, " India," Report, p. 177.

[6] Munshi Din Dayal, in Census of India, 1911, vol. xxii, " Rajputana and Amjer-Merwara," Report, p. 154.

[7] E. A. Gait, loc. cit.

Circumcision of females is practised by the Menangkabau Malays and several of the more primitive peoples of the Malay Archipelago.[1] It is in use in Java,[2] and in Celebes.[3]

Circumcision of Males.

Circumcision of girls, as is manifest from some of the examples above mentioned, is originally identical with mechanical defloration, and is often undistinguishable from it. There are grounds for regarding the practice of circumcision in the male as having arisen in the first instance as an imitation of those mutilations of the female genital organs which were themselves originally forms of instrumental defloration. Like all puberty rites, those mutilations are an essential part of the ceremonies of initiation into the tribal organisation or religious association, and are therefore tribal marks and passports to the ancestral paradise, or means of salvation. If, as we have seen reason to conclude, those religious or magic rites and ceremonies of re-birth and resurrection originated with the women and were taken over by the men, it would naturally follow that the operations or mutilations which constituted an essential part of those rites would also be adopted, in an analogous form, by the men.

Amputation of the prepuce is not by any means the most primitive or the most widespread form of the male mutilation. With the most primitive Australian tribes the essential operation, to which preputial excision is sometimes a preliminary, consists in slitting the penis along the whole length of the urethra.[4] The tribes among

[1] G. A. Wilken, " De Besnijdenis bij de volken van den Indischen Archipels," *De verspreide geschriften*, vol. iv, p. 238 ; A. L. van Hasselt, *Volksbeschrijving van Midden-Sumatra*, p. 66.

[2] J. Kögel, " Notizen über Sitten und Gebräuche der Javanen und Maduresen," *Das Ausland*, 1863, p. 280 ; F. Epp, reviewed in *Allgemeine Medicinische Central-Zeitung*, 1853, p. 37.

[3] J. G. F. Riedel, " Die Landschaft Holontalo, Limveto, Bone, Boaleom, und Kattingola," etc., *Zeitschrift für Ethnologie*, iii, p. 402.

[4] E. J. Eyre, *Journals of Expeditions of Discovery into Central Australia*, vol. i, pp. 212 sq. ; G. Tobin, in Woods, *The Native Tribes of South Australia*, p. xiv ; S. Gason, *ibid.*, p. 273 ; C. W. Schuemann, *ibid.*, p. 231 ; A. W. Howitt, " The Diery and other kindred Tribes of South-East Australia," *Journal of the Anthropological Institute*, xx, pp. 86 sq. ; W. B. Spencer and F. J. Gillen, *The Native Tribes of Central Australia*, pp. 251 sqq. ; N. von Miklucho-Maclay, " Über die Mika-Operation in Central-Australien," *Verhandlungen der Berliner Gesellschaft für Anthropologie*, 1880, pp. 85 sqq. ; W. E. Roth, *Ethnological Studies among the North-West-Central Queensland Aborigines*, pp. 170 sq., 178 ; T. P. A. Stuart, " The ' Mika ' or ' Kulpi ' Operation of the Australian Aborigines," *Journal and Proceedings of the Royal Society of New South Wales*, xxx, pp. 115 sqq. ; T. L. Bancroft, " Notes on Mutilations practised by Australian Aborigines," *ibid.*, xxxi, p. xxvi ;

which this ghastly operation is customary are those who practise also a complete subincision of the perineum in the female ; those which do not practise the latter operation do not incise the male urethra. The name by which the slit penis is known in the Boulia district is derived from the word for ' vulva.' The conclusion of Dr. Roth is a fairly obvious one : the puberty operation of the males is an imitation of the puberty operation of the females. " On the principle of a form of mimicry, the analogous sign was inflicted on the male to denote a corresponding degree of fitness on his part." [1] That conclusion has not only been amply confirmed by later information, but its literal accuracy goes beyond anything that one would imagine. It appears that subincised men, who are known as ' the possessors of a vulva,' are used by the youths who have not yet been initiated and have not undergone the operation for homosexual practices, the subincised penis being treated as a vulva—nay, there are recognised marriages between men who have undergone the operation and youths who have not yet done so.[2] Another observer reports that " in the Tomkinson Range members of the Ullparidga tribe were observed to dance about a man who had killed a kangaroo . . . all the while they held their subincised urethras to view, widening the slit to its utmost extent." [3]

Throughout Polynesia and the greater part of Melanesia the operation of circumcision does not consist in excision of the prepuce, but in making a longitudinal slit over the foreskin or the dorsum of the penis.[4] In New Guinea, as far as we know,

J. Mathew, *Eaglehawk and Crow*, p. 121 ; E. Eylmann, *Die Eingeborenen der Kolonie Südaustralien*, pp. 118 sqq. ; W. D. Campbell, " An Account of the Aboriginals of Sunday Island, King Sound, Kimberley, Western Australia," *Journal and Proceedings of the Royal Society of Western Australia*, i, p. 59 ; J. C. Cox, " Notes on some of the Habits and Customs of Australian Natives of Queensland," *Proceedings of the Linnean Society of New South Wales*, v, p. 633 ; J. G. Edge, " The Mika Ceremony," *Science of Man*, 1899, pp. 102 sq.

[1] W. E. Roth, *op. cit.*, pp. 179 sq.

[2] H. Klaatsch, " Some Notes in Scientific Travels amongst the Black Population of Tropical Australia in 1904, 1905, 1906," *Proceedings of the Australasian Association for the Advancement of Science, Adelaide*, 1907, pp. 581 sq.

[3] H. Basedow, " Anthropological Notes made on the South Australian Government North-West Prospecting Expedition, 1903," *Transactions of the Royal Society of South Australia*, xxviii (1903), p. 3.

[4] J. Remy, *Ka Moolelo Hawai*, p. xliii ; G. Turner, *Nineteen Years in Polynesia*, p. 177 ; G. Brown, *Melanesians and Polynesians*, p. 382 (Samoa) ; W. Mariner, *An Account of the Natives of the Tonga Islands*, vol. ii, p. 252 ; W. T. Pritchard, " Notes on Certain Anthropological Matters respecting the South Sea Islanders," *Memoirs read before the Anthropological Society of London*, i, p. 326 ; C. Clavel, *Les Marquisiens*, p. 35 ; J. A. Moerenhout, *Voyages aux isles du Grand Océan*, vol. i, p. 338 ; F. W. Beechey, *Narrative*

the same method obtained everywhere.　Thus in the south-western districts " circumcision was general, and appeared to be performed by a straight incision through the dorsum of the prepuce, there being no ablation of supernumerary skin or mucous membrane ; the cicatrices left were very unsightly, and did not speak at all highly for the surgical skill of the operator." [1]　Probably, however, those ' unsightly ' cicatrices were intentional, for the natives of New Guinea are particularly noted among savages for their surgical skill. The same mode of operation obtains in the northern districts.[2] In the Island of Rook the operation consists in a longitudinal incision.[3]　The people of the Malay Archipelago are for the most part Muhammadans, and the Semitic form of circumcision is accordingly practised.　But that method has only partially supplanted the older indigenous form of operation, which is identical with that employed in Polynesia.[4]　Even in Java, the stronghold of Islam in Indonesia, slitting is, it is stated, more extensively practised than excision.[5]　With all the more primitive populations of Indonesia circumcision takes the form of a longitudinal incision and not of an amputation.　Thus, for example, in the Moluccas the people perform circumcision " not after the manner of the Jews and Muhammadans, but in a way which is peculiar to themselves, inasmuch as it is not

---

of a Voyage to the Pacific and Behring's Strait, vol. i, p. 149 ;　G. Heinrich Langsdorf, *Voyages and Travels in Various Parts of the World*, vol. i, p. 158 ; F. Speiser, *Two Years with the Natives of the Western Pacific*, p. 113 ; H. N. Moseley, " On the Inhabitants of the Admiralty Islands," *Journal of the Anthropological Institute*, vi, p. 326 ;　R. Parkinson, *Dreissig Jahre in der Südsee*, pp. 181 sq., 336 sq., 342, 399 ;　W. H. R. Rivers, *The History of Melanesia Society*, vol. i, p. 292 n. :　" The prepuce is slit longitudinally without the removal of any part.　This is the usual mode of performing the rite which is usually known as circumcision in Melanesia and Polynesia." The exceptions occur in Fiji (L. Fison, " The Nanga or Sacred Stone Enclosure of Wainimala, Fiji," *Journal of the Anthropological Institute*, xiv, p. 28) and the Bismark Archipelago (Rascher, " Die Sulka, ein Beitrag zur Ethnographie Neu-Pommern," *Archiv für Anthropologie*, xxix, p. 209) ; but there is some doubt as to whether those accounts may not be inaccurate. Mr. Brewster says that " usually the foreskin was only split," and he mentions men being circumcised several times—that is, having blood drawn (A. B. Brewster, " Circumcision in Noikoro, Noemolu and Mboumbudho, *Journal of the Royal Anthropological Institute*, xlix, pp. 314 sq., 310).　The late Dr. Rivers' hypothesis that the Polynesian incision was a modification of circumcision by amputation is put out of court by the history of the practice in Indonesia.

[1] P. Comrie, " Anthropological Notes in New Guinea," *Journal of the Anthropological Institute*, vi, p. 109.

[2] R. Neuhauss, *Deutsch Neu-Guinea*, vol. i, pp. 155 sqq.

[3] P. Reina, "Ueber die Bewohner der Insel Rook östlich von Neu-Guinea," *Zeitschrift für allgemeine Erdkunde*, N.F., iv, p. 357.

[4] See G. A. Wilken, " De Besnijdenis bij de volken van den Indischen Archipel," *Verspreide geschriften*, vol. iv, pp. 206 sqq.

[5] J. F. G. Brumund, *Indiana*, vol. ii, p. 255.

so much what might properly be termed a circumcision as an incision."[1] Far from this form of the operation being peculiar to the Moluccas, however, it is the rule among all the more primitive peoples of the Archipelago ; it is found in Ceram, Celebes, among all the Alfur peoples,[2] and among the Dayaks of Borneo.[3] In Nias the operation consists in slitting the foreskin. It is not regarded as a religious rite, but the natives believe that unless it is done and the glans exposed a man is not capable of generation. A youth who has not undergone the operation is therefore the object of endless ridicule. Among the peoples of the Philippines " circumcision is performed by cutting from above downwards."[4]

Among the Papuans of a small island off the northern coast of New Guinea a different form of operation has been noted ; the penis is bored through.[5] The same mutilation is found in Celebes,[6] among the Bataks, the Dayaks of Borneo,[7] and the Bisaya of the Philippine Islands.[8] The mutilation was described by old travellers as a voluptuary device, and the interpretation has been accepted by some modern writers. Foreign bodies are inserted in the transfixed organ, which would otherwise cicatrise, and the women are said to appreciate the additional stimulation, although the vagina is frightfully lacerated and excoriated by the use of those articles. It seems quite untenable to anyone familiar with the psychology of savages, who, however licentious, are entirely ignorant of the refinements of vice, to suppose that the perforation originated among secluded Papuans as a form of vicious ingenuity. The distribution of the practice, which, as far as we know, is confined to a line running from New Guinea to the Philippines,

---

[1] F. Valentijn, *Oud en Nieuw Oost Indie*, vol. iii, p. 13.

[2] E. Modigliani, *Un Viaggio a Nias*, p. 702 ; G. A. Wilken, *op. cit.*, pp. 214 sqq., 218 ; Paul F. Sarasin, *Reisen in Celebes*, vol. ii, p. 53.

[3] J. R. Logan, " The Orang Binua of Johore," *Journal of the Indian Archipelago*, i, p. 271 ; F. A. Hervey, " The Endau and its Tributaries," *Journal of the Straits Branch of the Royal Asiatic Society*, 1881, p. 119.

[4] F. Blumentritt, *Versuch einer Ethnographie der Philippinen*, p. 14.

[5] H. Ploss and B. Renz, *Das Kind im Brauch und Sitte der Völker*, vol. ii, p. 197.

[6] A. B. Mayer, " Ueber die Perforation des Penis bei den Malayen," *Mittheilungen der anthropologischen Gesellschaft in Wien*, vii, pp. 242 sqq.

[7] S. St. John, *Life in the Forests of the Far East*, vol. i, p. 113 ; N. von Miklucho-Maclay, " Ueber die künstliche Perforatio Penis bei den Dajaks auf Borneo," *Verhandlungen der Berliner Gesellschaft für Anthropologie*, 1876, p. 24 ; H. van Deevall, " Aanteekeningen omtrent de Nordoostkust van Borneo," *Tijdschrift voor Indische taal-, land- en volkenkunde*, iv, p. 457.

[8] F. Carletti, *Viaggi da lui racontati in dodici ragionamenti*, pp. 143 sq. ; A. de Morga, *Sucesos de las islas Filipinas*, in E. H. Blair and J. A. Robertson, *The Philippine Islands*, 1493–1803, vol. xvi, p. 130 ; T. Candish, " Eerste Scheepstogt," in P. van den Aa, *Naaukeurige versameling der gedenk-waardigste zee- en land-reysen na Oost- en West-Indien*, vol. xx, p. 28.

and is there found among the most primitive and unsophisticated, and not among the more advanced and corrupt races,
shows that it is traditional and ritualistic, and not a corrupt invention.   Perforation would naturally be an alternative to slitting
as an imitation of female defloration. Theories of voluptuary
ingenuity would appear to be more felicitously illustrated by the
practice reported by old travellers from Pegu, i.e. Burma.
" Peguans," says the old Dutch traveller Linschoten, " weare a
bell upon their yard, and sometimes as big as an acorne, which is
made fast between the flesh and the skin." [1] But even in this
instance it turns out that the practice of inserting objects under
the skin is a well-known general usage among all Burmese populations ; and those objects are in every instance amulets intended
to ward off evil spirits.[2] A notorious thief was not long since
found to have small foreign objects inserted under the skin all over
his body, and it was suspected by the police in Burma that he
had thus secreted stolen gems, but it turned out that the objects
were magic amulets of no intrinsic worth.[3]

On the American continent, where cultural influence as regards
the diffusion of the practice is out of the question, artificial
defloration and complete circumcision of the female, in the most
literal sense, are far more prevalent than circumcision of the male.
Where the latter was practised it consisted in a cut or scarification.[4]
In Africa circumcision was practised by making a slit in the prepuce.

[1] J. H. von Linschoten, *Voyage to the East Indies*, vol. i, p 99.   Cf. Nicolò
Conti, " The Travels of," in R. H. Major, *India in the Fifteenth Century*,
p. 11 ; F. Carletti, *op. cit.*, pp. 347 sqq.

[2] See above, p. 280.

[3] D. A. C. Burnell in note to the above-cited passage of Linschoten.

[4] Father Mendieta, who had a shrewd notion that the Aztecs were the
lost tribes of Israel, and Torquemada, who copied his account, state
that among the ancient Mexicans the prepuce was cut off (G. de Mendieta,
Historia eclesiatica Indiana, p. 107 ; J. de Torquemada, *Veinte i un libros
rituales i Monarchia Indiana*, vol. ii, p. 83) ; but this, like the statement
of Zuazo that the Aztecs " practised circumcision like the Moors and the
Jews " (A. Zuazo, " Carta del licenciato A.Z. . . . al Padre Fray Luis de
Figueroa," in J. G. Icazbalceta, *Coleccion de Documentos para la Historia de
Mexico*, vol. i, p. 564), is but an assumption that all circumcision must
consist in the same form of operation.   Acosta, on the contrary, expressly
states that " they scarified the male organ " (J. de Acosta, *Historia natural
y moros de los Indios*, p. 374), and other witnesses testify to the same effect
(E. C. Brasseur de Bourbourg, *Histoire des Nations civilisées de l'Amérique
centrale*, vol. iii, p. 526 ; cf. H. H. Bancroft, *The Native Races of the Pacific
States*, vol. ii, p. 279, n.).   Among Brazilian tribes ' circumcision ' consisted
in " a small and imperceptible incision in the prepuce " (A. F. de Souza,
" Noticias geographicas da Capitania do Rio Negro," *Revista Trimensal*,
Ser. ii, iii, p. 497 ; cf. J. B. von Spix and C. F. Ph. von Martius, *Reise in
Brasiliens*, vol. iii, p. 1188 ; C. F. Ph. von Martius, *Beiträge zur Ethnographie
und Sprachenkunde Amerika's*, pp. 445, 583).

The form of the operation was originally that employed by the
Basuto, but in later times they adopted the amputation of the
prepuce.[1] Among the tribes of East Central Africa—the Yao,
Amangada, Machinga—circumcision likewise consisted formerly in
slitting the foreskin in the median line, but the Muhammadan
method is now being adopted.[2] The Masai, Wadgaga, and Kikuyu
likewise perform the operation by slitting and not by amputation,[3]
and among the Atharaka also there is no excision.[4] Among the
Amwimbe, the Meru, and the Chuka a small portion of the prepuce is
first sliced off and thrown aside, as a preliminary to perforating
the prepuce with a button-hole incision, through which the glans
is thrust.[5] The assimilation of the mutilation of the male organs
to the process of defloration in the female is here represented as
vividly as in Australia. Among the Bissagos and the Feluppus of
Senegambia simple incision without any excision takes place.[6]
The facts further show that the practice of circumcision in Africa
is not due, as has been sometimes supposed, to Arab influence ;
nor is that of female circumcision, for it is practised by those
tribes which preserve the original Bantu mode of male mutilation
and have not adopted the Muhammadan form of the rite. In the
Northern Territories of the Gold Coast female circumcision is
observed, while male circumcision is unknown.[7]

Circumcision by amputation of the prepuce appears, indeed,
with comparatively few exceptions, to be confined to the Semitic
races and to those peoples who have come under their influence.
The operation may possibly, among the Semites themselves, have
originally taken another form, such as the gruesome evulsion, or

[1] North, " Puberty Rites of the Basuto," *Report of the Seventh Annual
Meeting of the South African Association for the Advancement of Science,
Bloemfontein*, 1909, p. 199.
[2] H. S. Stannus, "Notes on Some Tribes of British Central Africa,"
Journal of the Royal Anthropological Institute, xl, p. 296 ; J. Thomson,
Through Masai Land, p. 580 ; H. H. Johnston, *Uganda*, p. 804 ; Widenmann, " Beschneidung bei den Massai," *Verhandlungen der Berliner Gesell
schaft für Anthropologie*, 1895, pp. 302 sq.
[3] J. M. Hildebrandt, " Ethnographische Notizen über Wakamba und
ihre Nachbaren," *Zeitschrift für Ethnologie*, x, p. 398.
[4] A. M. Champion, " The Atharaka," *Journal of the Royal Anthropological
Institute*, xlii, p. 84.
[5] G. St. J. Orde Browne, " Circumcision Ceremonies among the Amwimbe,"
Man, xiii, p. 138 ; Id., " Circumcision Ceremonies of the Chuka," *Man*,
xv, p. 65.
[6] M. Zaborowski, " De la circoncision des garçons et de l'excision des
filles comme pratiques d'initiation," *Bulletins de la Société d'Anthropologie*,
4e Série, v, p. 97.
[7] Cf. A. Hovelacque, *Les nègres de l'Afrique sus-équatoriale*, p. 271 ;
M. Zaborowski, " La circoncision, ses origines, et sa repartition en Afrique
et à Madagascar," *L'Anthropologie*, vii, pp. 653 sqq.

' salkh,' still in use in some Arab tribes—an operation which has its analogue in some forms of female circumcision among Semitic peoples.[1] More probably it was, as elsewhere, an incision. Be that as it may, we know that the Jewish rite did not assume its present form until so late a period as that of the Maccabees. At that date it was still performed in such a manner that the jibes of Gentile women could be evaded, little trace of the operation being perceptible. The nationalistic priesthood therefore enacted that the prepuce should be completely removed.[2]

The origin and primitive intention of the rite were long since forgotten by the Semites, as they are among the majority of primitive races who practise it. It was, however, generally understood among the Jews that it was in some way necessary or beneficial for procreation.[3] Among the Arabs it continued to be regarded as a civic and not a religious rite, and it is not prescribed by the Kuran. The general view among jurists and theologians is that it is intended to prepare for procreation.[4] Among the Jews it assumed, like all their customs, a religious significance, and aetiological interpretations drawn from the conceptions of later theologies, such as the notion of a sacrificial offering or of the casting off an impurity, represented the amputation as the essential

[1] See above, vol. ii, p. 193.

[2] A. Glassberg, *Die Beschneidung*, p. 223 ; *I Maccabees*, i. 16 ; *IV Maccabees*, v. 1.

[3] G. A. Barton, *A Sketch of Semitic Origins, Social and Religious*, pp. 100, 280 sqq.

[4] I. Ludolfus, *Ad suam Historiam Aethiopicam Commentarius*, p. 269. The sanitary theory of circumcision illustrates the interpretation of primitive customs in the light of the prejudices which those customs have created. There is nothing of which uncultured peoples are more careless and innocent than sanitary precautions. The supposed sanitary advantages of circumcision are doubtful, hypothetical, and unproved. Yet circumcision continues to be highly preconised on medical grounds and extensively inflicted, and the primitive rite, whatever view be taken of its origin, is very generally regarded as a wise and beneficial provision. Female circumcision, or artificial defloration, on the other hand, is referred to with horror as ' infamous,' ' disgusting,' ' worse than bestial.' Yet of the two operations, that upon the female has infinitely more to recommend it from a sanitary point of view ; and there is a good deal more to be said for the Chinese nurses' notions of cleanliness than in justification of the mutilation of the male organs. Had the practice of artificial defloration or female circumcision survived among the Jews or the Romans, we should no doubt have a large medical literature setting forth the sanitary advantages of the measure. The Greek physician, Paul of Aegina, recommended, indeed, the performance of female circumcision after the Egyptian manner to the ladies of Greece, on medical grounds (Paulus Aegineta, vii. 70). Male circumcision, on the other hand, apart from the status which the mutilation owes to Biblical sanction, can only be regarded, as Dr. Mantegazza justly opines, as a savage, senseless, and disgusting procedure.

feature of the operation. As an initiatory rite and a part of the ceremonies associated with new-birth, as in Australia and in the religious societies of women in West Africa and the Congo, circumcision, male and female, partook from the first of the latter character. In the male it imitated not only the defloration of the female, but also the tabu, or sacred state resulting from the hymeneal blood. In the Biblical account of the origin of circumcision, which is evidently an old one and somewhat obscurely and imperfectly reproduced, Zibborah rescues her husband Moses, whom Yahweh is attempting to kill, by pretending to circumcise him. He thus becomes " a bloody husband," and Yahweh dare not touch him.[1]

The blood from the operation of circumcision is, in Kikuyu, regarded as tabu, and anyone coming in contact with it must undergo a process of purification.[2] Boys after circumcision are strictly tabu until the wound is healed. They are secluded, like girls at their first menstruation; no one may approach them, and they are sometimes provided with sticks to scratch their own bodies. Their clothes and mats are destroyed after the function is completed.[3] Sometimes they are " dressed as girls." [4] Even among Egyptian Muslims, boys undergoing circumcision are attired in a woman's skirt and cap.[5] It is a primitive rule that newly circumcised boys are not only allowed complete sexual freedom, but that intercourse as soon as possible after circumcision is imperative. The reason for the rule, taken by itself, appears obscure. With regard to girls, there is a very definite reason for the necessity of early intercourse after artificial surgical defloration, Unless appropriate steps are taken, adhesions will be formed, and the very purpose of the operation will be more than defeated, a condition of infibulation resulting.[6] In Peru an artificial penis is inserted after the operation to prevent the formation of adhesions.[7] In Baluchistan, when a girl has been circumcised, " the one and only permanent cure is consummation of the marriage." [8] In Australia wholesale copulation must take place immediately after the performance of the operation. In Africa as soon as circum-

---

[1] *Exodus*, iv. 24 sq.

[2] C. W. Hobley, *Bantu Beliefs and Magic*, p. 82.

[3] A. W. Howitt, *Native Tribes of South-East Australia*, p. 596; A. S. Gatschett, *Migration Legend of the Creek Indians*, vol. i, pp. 185 sq.; D. Kidd, *The Essential Kafir*, p. 208; L. Alberti, *De Kaffers aan de Zuidkust van Afrika*, pp. 76 sq.; H. Lichtenstein, *Reisen im südlichen Afrika*, vol. i, p. 427; S. Kay, *Travels and Researches in Caffraria*, pp. 273 sq.

[4] A. C. Hollis, *The Masai*, p. 298; Id., *The Nandi*, pp. 53 sqq.

[5] C. B. Klunzinger, *Upper Egypt*, p. 195.

[6] See below, pp. 344 sq.

[7] See above, p. 321.

[8] D. Bray, *Census of India*, 1911, vol. iv, " Baluchistan," Part i, Report, p. 106.

cision has been performed promiscuous intercourse is ordered.[1] In British Central Africa a girl must have intercourse directly after the operation, and the services of a man are called in, who " is asked to oblige " ; he must, however, be careful not to ejaculate.[2] The surgical necessity of preventing adhesions following the rough primitive methods of artificial defloration by intercourse immediately after the operation would thus, if the corresponding mutilation of the male organs was originally intended as an imitation of that carried out in the female, imply a like necessity as regards the newly circumcised males ; that obligation confirms the view here taken of the origin of the widespread rite. As among the Arabs and other Muslim peoples, the practice of circumcision, which was at one time as incumbent on the females as on the males, has generally tended to fall into disuse and become discountenanced as regards the former, and even to be looked upon as objectionable, while the rite, as regards males, has acquired special nationalistic and semi-religious significances. Hence at the present day, although the two corresponding rites are found to be equally obligatory among some peoples, and among others the female rite alone is observed, yet the male rite is more prevalent than the corresponding female rite. Artificial defloration of the females, which is practised by all Mongol peoples and by most Muslims, is still nevertheless the rule with an actual majority of the human race.

Claim to Virginity of Bride.

The importance attached in primitive societies to the circumstance that a bride shall not be a virgin at the time of marriage stands in sharp contrast with the conceptions current in our own and in many of the higher cultures as to the intrinsic merit and value of the state of virginity. In primitive societies the conception is almost unknown ; no words exist to represent it, and when asked for some term to describe the condition the Congolese savage can think of none more appropriate than one meaning ' fool ' or ' mental defective.' Among the Basoga-Batamba of Uganda " virginity in a woman of a marriageable age is considered almost a crime." [3] There is, however, no obscurity as to the origin and cause of the transformation in the sentiments with which female virginity has come to be regarded.

[1] F. Müller, " Fetischistiches aus Atakpane," *Globus*, lxxxi, p. 280.

[2] H. S. Stannus, " Notes on Some Tribes of British Central Africa," *Journal of the Royal Anthropological Institute*, xl, p. 298.

[3] M. A. Condon, " Contribution to the Ethnography of the Basoga-Batamba, Uganda Protectorate," *Anthropos*, vi, p. 372.

The value set upon virginity in a bride owes its origin to the practice of infant betrothal. The bespeaking of a female infant shortly after birth, or even before, prevails among all uncivilised peoples. I have cited some examples of the practice ;[1] to give an exhaustive account of its distribution would be to enumerate all races and tribes known to ethnological science. The practice is particularly common where capacity to pay a high bride-price is the chief consideration in such a contract. On the West Coast of Africa and in Nigeria it is in many districts the universal rule ; among some Nigerian tribes a female baby is regarded as betrothed to the first man, outside her family, who happens to see her after she is born.[2] A medical resident in Old Calabar says : " I have seen a strapping man, in the prime and vigour of life, dandling on his knees and kissing a baby two or three weeks old that he expects to become his wife and the mother of his children some fifteen or twenty years after. Pointing to her he says, ' You see my new wife ? ' "[3] The child usually remains in the charge of her mother until near the age of puberty, though often she may join the household of her future husband when very young and be brought up as one of the family. The mother of a betrothed child is thus regarded as acting for the future husband, and the latter accordingly often pays her for her services and expenses while the immature child is in her care. He may thus naturally consider that he has the same claim on his child-wife as he would were she mature and living with him That is, in fact, the view taken in West Africa, and " no man except the husband dares touch or come near a betrothed or married woman, not even to shake hands."[4]

Nevertheless, throughout the more primitive stages of social culture no such claims are put forward. The contract is interpreted in its literal sense—namely, that the child shall be handed over to the husband when she is considered old enough, or that he shall at least have the first claim to her, for no violence is done, as a rule, to the girl's inclination should she object to the union. The claim to pre-nuptial fidelity on the part of the betrothed child is not practicable or regarded as of importance in the most primitive societies. Thus the bespeaking and promising of a female child at birth is more prevalent among the Australian aborigines than anywhere else, but no claim to her virginity is contemplated.[5]

[1] See above, vol. i, pp. 522 sqq.

[2] O. Temple, *Notes on the Tribes . . . of Northern Nigeria*, pp. 163, 181.

[3] A. Hewan, " On some Customs of the People of Old Calabar relative to Pregnancy and Parturition," *The Edinburgh Medical and Surgical Journal*, x, p. 220.

[4] *Ibid.*, p. 221.

[5] See above. vol. ii, pp. 60 sqq.

So likewise among the Todas betrothal of girls in infancy is the universal rule; but not the slightest importance is attached to virginity, and intercourse is unrestricted from childhood.[1] Among the Kugamma of Nigeria, where every girl is betrothed at birth, it is expressly recognised by tribal law that adultery previous to final marriage does not constitute an offence.[2] Among the Bambara " a betrothed girl does not entirely dispose of herself, neither does she, however, belong definitely to her future husband; she retains the right of disposing of her person." [3] Among the Bushongo the first thing which a girl does when she becomes betrothed is to have intercourse with as many men as possible, in order to become pregnant and to satisfy her intended that she is not sterile.[4]

In somewhat higher cultural stages a clear distinction is sometimes drawn between a girl who is betrothed and one who is not. Thus in New Zealand a girl or a widow is ' noa,' that is to say, free from all tabu. She is under no obligation to any man to observe chastity; sexual relations are, in fact, wholly unrestrained, and she is valued all the more for having proved her fertility. " I don't think that the young woman knows when she was a virgin," says Mr. Tregoar, " for she had love-affairs with the boys from the cradle." [5] Such recognised liberty in an unbetrothed young woman was taken so much as a matter of course that even in the latter part of the last century, among the Christianised Maori round mission stations, different notions had not succeeded in establishing themselves.[6] This is true at the present day in many Maori tribes. On the other hand, when a girl had once been given away by her relatives and betrothed to some future master, she became strictly ' tapu,' and was even liable to be put to death should she be guilty of unchastity.[7] " We were often requested by elderly chiefs and their wives," relates Polack, " to allow their daughters—children perhaps five years of age—to be affianced to a son or younger brother, enquiring of us if we could accommodate their paternal wishes with either, and promising that the most rigid ' tapu ' should be placed over the young lady when she should arrive at years of discretion, and that nothing short of a refusal

[1] W. H. R. Rivers, The Todas, p. 523.
[2] O. Temple, Notes on the Tribes of the Northern Provinces of Nigeria, p. 245.
[3] J. Henry, L'âme d'un peuple Africain : les Bambara, pp. 162 sq.
[4] E. Torday, Les Bushongo, p. 271.
[5] E. Tregoar, " The Maoris of New Zealand," Journal of the Anthropological Institute, xix, p. 101.
[6] J. Batty Tuke, " Medical Notes on New Zealand," Edinburgh Medical and Surgical Journal, ix, p. 224.
[7] R. Taylor, Te Ika a Maui ; or New Zealand and its Inhabitants, p. 167.

should militate against the 'tapu' with which she would become invested." [1]

It is probable that in some societies, such as those of Polynesia, such a tabu and the claim to the virginity of the bride which consequently followed, was first put forward in regard to chiefs, who, apart from any despotic privileges, are in their sacred character more or less immune from the dangers attaching to virginity. In Samoa, though the strictest precautions were taken to secure the chastity of the betrothed bride of a chief, among the common people there was no such claim and no attempt at maintaining pre-nuptial chastity. [2] Among the Sakalavas of Madagascar, where sexual relations were notoriously of the loosest, and where pre-nuptial loss of virginity was, as we saw, regarded as so imperative that, if necessary, girls adopted artificial measures to secure it, princesses, who married only in noble families, dispensed with the operation. [3] On the same principle the Tui-tonga, or sacred king of Tonga, was the only person in the community who dispensed with circumcision. [4] It is part of the tabu attaching to all that belongs to a sacred chief that his women shall be untouched by any other man, and accordingly much more importance is everywhere attached to the chastity of a girl betrothed to a noble or a king than with reference to the bride of a commoner.

The claim to the virginity of the bride and the importance attached to it is, among uncultured races, found more especially developed in those regions where the theory of marriage by purchase has attained its crudest mercenary form—namely, in some parts of Africa, Siberia, and Indonesia. In Africa, side by side with the general prevalence of pre-nuptial licence and the marked looseness of sexual relations, inistence upon virginity as a requirement in a bride and the strict guarding of the chastity of unmarried girls are found among some peoples, more especially where the influence of slave-traffic has been greatest. Among the Bobos of the French Sudan, for example, complete sexual liberty is recognised and freely taken advantage of by unmarried girls, but where betrothal takes place in infancy, the girl is regarded as in duty bound to remain a virgin until marriage takes place. [5] Among the Tiapy

---

[1] J. S. Polack, *Manners and Customs of the New Zealanders*, vol. i, p. 136. Cf. E. Dieffenbach, *Travels in New Zealand*, vol. ii, p. 36 ; E. J. Wakefield, *Adventures in New Zealand*, vol. i, p. 257.

[2] G. Brown, *Melanesians and Polynesians*, pp. 119 sqq. Cf. above, vol. ii, p. 57.

[3] V. Noël, " Île de Madagascar. Recherches sur les Sakkalava," *Bulletin de la Société de Géographie*, Sér. ii, xx, p. 294.

[4] W. Mariner, *An Account of the Natives of the Tonga Islands*, vol. ii, p. 86.

[5] L. Tauxier, *Le Noir de Soudan*, p. 55.

young girls wear a shell suspended to their belt, and this is a token of virginity. When a girl marries, " if she is still wearing her shell and proves not to be a virgin, the husband has the right to send her back to her parents and to demand the cattle which he paid for her. Those cases are extremely rare, because among that people the loss of virginity does not carry with it any dishonour, and if the newly married bride has removed her shell no reproach is ever made to her. Thus it is not the loss of virginity which is punished, but the deception, for in this country women who have borne children are sought after with as much eagerness as young girls." [1] We have seen that in West Africa, where infant-betrothal is prevalent, the strictest care is observed as to the seclusion of unmarried girls from male society. Father Proyart long ago took the custom as a text for enlarging on " the common misconception " that female chastity is not regarded as of any account in savage societies. On the contrary, he points out, in West Africa girls are so strictly guarded that " a youth durst not speak to a girl except in her mother's presence "; and " the crime of a maid who has not resisted seduction would be sufficient to draw down a total ruin on the whole country, were it not expiated by a public avowal before the king." [2] That edifying puritanism is, however, entirely conditional on the girl being betrothed from babyhood. " Girls of the better classes are almost always betrothed when mere children, frequently when infants, the husband ' in futuro ' being sometimes a grown man, sometimes a boy. Non-virginity in a bride is a valid ground for repudiation only when the girl has been betrothed at a tender age ; for unbetrothed girls can bestow their favours upon whom they please. Thus no man who marries a girl without early betrothal feels aggrieved if she should prove not to be a virgin, for unless she is married or betrothed she is perfectly mistress of her own actions. Girls of the lower classes who are seldom betrothed can lead any life they choose without incurring reproach, and without affecting their future prospects of marriage ; but girls of the upper classes who are almost always betrothed must be chaste." [3] In Ashanti, according to Bowdich's account, " infants are frequently married to infants for the connexion of families, and infants are as frequently wedded by adults and elderly men. The ceremony is to send the smaller piece of cloth worn round the middle to the infant, and a handsome dash of gold to the mother, as her care then ceases to be a duty and becomes a service performed to the husband, who also sends frequent presents for the support of the child.

[1] H. Hecquard, *Voyage sur la côte et dans l'intérieur de l'Afrique occidentale*, p. 232.

[2] L. B. Proyart, " History of Loango, Kakongo, and other Kingdoms of Africa," in *Pinkerton, Voyages and Travels*, vol. xvi, p. 568.

[3] A. B. Ellis, *The Yoruba-speaking Peoples*, pp. 183 sqq.

Apokoo told me it was a good plan for a man to adopt who wished to get gold, for as the circumstance was seldom generally known, the most innocent freedom when the girl became ten or eleven years old grounded a palaver against the individual, though he might consider he was but fondling a child, and be wholly ignorant of her marriage. I afterwards understood from several others that this view was the leading motive." [1]

The guarding of virginity is, in Africa, undertaken by parents in view of its value on the marriage market. Thus among the Ibo of Nigeria, if a daughter is required to remain at home in order to help in the housework, she is not in any way guarded, but, on the contrary, the father assists in arranging liaisons for her entertainment.[2] In a number of African tribes the seducer of a girl, if he does not marry her, is required to pay the bride-price which would have been demanded for her. Thus on the Gold Coast, " if a man betrays a virgin he is compelled to marry her or to pay the price of her dowry." [3] But when the bride-price has thus been paid, " her marketable value having been received, any excesses she may commit are regarded as of no importance." [4] It has been acknowledged by missionaries themselves that in many parts of Africa the standard of pre-nuptial chastity has fallen considerably in the mission stations among the Christianised natives. The missionaries have abolished the bride-price. " The consequence is that the native girls have no longer a market value, and the control exerted over them by their parents, and especially the mothers, is relaxed." [5] Among the Pardhi of the Central Provinces of India, if a girl had been seduced, the offence was compensated for by providing the injured family with another girl.[6]

Of many uncultured peoples it is stated that the seducer of a girl is obliged to marry her, and that it is a disgrace sometimes severely punished for an unmarried girl to have a child. Such statements, taken by themselves, may easily give the impression that the standards of pre-nuptial chastity are identical with those obtaining amongst ourselves, if not, indeed, more strict. But that impression is often misleading. Unacknowledged children are objectionable for several reasons which have little to do with any ideal of chastity. Their maintenance falls on the parents of the girl. In many instances an intending husband is unwilling to undertake

[1] T. E. Bowdich, *Mission from Cape Coast Castle to Ashantee*, pp. 251 sq.

[2] G. T. Basden, *Among the Ibos of Nigeria*, p. 76.

[3] B. Cruikshank, *Eighteen Years on the Gold Coast*, vol. ii, pp. 195 sq.

[4] A. B. Ellis, *The Tshi-speaking Peoples of the Gold Coast*, p. 286.

[5] C. R. Conder, " The Natives of Bechuanaland," *Journal of the Anthropological Institute*, xvi, p. 81.

[6] R. V. Russell, *Tribes and Castes of the Central Provinces of India*, vol. iv, p. 361.

the maintenance of the girl's pre-nuptial offspring. The value of the girl and her chances of marrying are thus in many cases lessened, and the parents of the girl are doubly penalised. A large proportion of those instances which are set down as examples of the value attached to pre-nuptial chastity have no reference to such chastity, but to the bearing of pre-nuptial children. We have seen that the strictest rules and the most severe penalties are enforced among several of the Hamitic-Bantu peoples of East-Central Africa as regards pre-nuptial motherhood, while organised pre-nuptial free love is, at the same time, among their most conspicuous institutions.[1] The same distinction is drawn by several peoples who do not carry the interdiction of pre-nuptial motherhood to such extremes. Among the Bambala no reproach whatever attaches to an unbetrothed girl who bears a child, " for she has not yet been given." But if she is betrothed, although she enjoys complete and recognised freedom, the ' seducer,' should she bear a child, is punishable with a fine amounting to the value of two francs.[2] Among the Baila, pre-nuptial licence is not only permitted but recommended and looked upon as a necessity ; but when a girl has been betrothed from infancy to a man, a compensation is demanded if she is pregnant when handed over to him.[3] Among the Basutos " so long as a girl is not pregnant, she is ' in order.' " [4] Among the Bawenda, as among many other African peoples, the moral commandment as regards female chastity is understood to mean : " Thou shalt be careful not to bring a child into the world by extra-connubial intercourse." [5]

Usages as regards the pre-nuptial chastity of a bride are commonly found to vary within wide limits among tribes of the same race living in close proximity to one another ; in other words, the matter depends upon local custom. Entirely different usages may even obtain in various clans of one and the same people. Thus, for example, among the Nandi the same regular institution of pre-nuptial promiscuity obtains as among the related Masai, and virginity is, of course, not considered. But rules as to pre-nuptial conception vary considerably in the different clans. In several clans the fact that a girl has already borne a child adds greatly to her value, and in one clan that condition is an absolute necessity in order that she should be eligible for marriage. In

[1] See above, vol. ii, pp. 25 sq.

[2] J. Henry, L'âme d'un peuple africain : les Bambala, pp. 163, 164 sq.

[3] E. W. Smith and A. M. Dale, The Ila-speaking Peoples of Northern Rhodesia, vol. ii, pp. 39, 36.

[4] H. Grübner, " Ueber die Gebräuche der Basutos," Verhandlungen der Berliner Gesellschaft für Anthropologie, 1877, pp. 82 sq.

[5] R. Wessman, ibid., 1896, pp. 363 sq.

other clans the matter is optional. On the other hand, in the Elephant, Chameleon, and Buzzard clans, a man is debarred from marrying a girl who has previously conceived. In the Jackal and Cockroach clans a man may not take as his wife a girl who has previously conceived, but if he himself is the father of the child, he may take her as a junior wife. In the Baboon, Rat, and Lion clans, a man may marry a girl who has previously conceived, provided she is pregnant by him or by one of his brothers.[1]

With the Masai the object of guarding the bride for some time before her marriage would appear to be to secure that her husband shall be the father of her first child, since it can have no reference to her virginity; the rules observed by some clans of the Nandi with reference to the previous pregnancy of the bride have evidently the same object. The anxiety to secure assured fatherhood of the first child may thus become extended into a claim to the virginity of the bride. Among some Nigerian tribes which attach considerable importance to the virginity of a bride, no notice whatever is taken by the husband of her conduct after marriage, her amours being entirely ignored.[2] The Bahima of Ankole are perhaps the strictest puritans in regard to the preservation of pre-nuptial chastity in girls. These are guarded with unceasing watchfulness, and are practically kept under lock and key. A transgression is usually punished with death by drowning. But after marriage the utmost looseness prevails. For a man to place his wife at the disposal of his guest is a recognised rule of hospitality, and polyandrous marriages are recognised.[3]

The claim to the virginity of the bride thus represents sentiments entirely different from those which we attach to it. It is quite commonly thought to be nowise inconsistent with the defloration of the bride by a priest or by another man. It would have been a gross insult to a king of Uganda or of Calicut to offer him as a bride a girl that was not a virgin; yet she was, at her royal husband's desire, deflowered by proxy. Similarly among the Tahus of Mexico virginity was claimed, and if it was found wanting, the repayment of a portion of the bride-price was demanded from the bride's parents. But the first act of the bridegroom after marriage was to take his bride to a priest, requesting him to keep her for the night, and it was upon his report that the decision in the matter rested.[4] Analogous views obtained until recently in Southern Russia. If

[1] A. C. Hollis, *The Nandi*, p. 8.

[2] O. Temple, *Notes on the Tribes, Provinces, Emirates and States of the Northern Provinces of Nigeria*, p. 196.

[3] J. Roscoe, *The Soul of Central Africa*, pp. 62 sq.

[4] P. de Castañeda de Nacera, *Relacion de la jornada de Cibola*, p. 448. The Tahus, however, as we have seen, also married sacred prostitutes, who continued to exercise their office after marriage (see above, pp. 213 sqq.).

the bridegroom was unable to consummate the marriage on the wedding night, while the guests were still assembled to be apprised of the all-important proofs of virginity, the most vigorous-looking among them was requested to take the bridegroom's place, so that those proofs might be forthcoming.[1] It is manifest that in all such instances the value attached to the virginity of the bride does not, as Dr. Westermarck suggests, "spring from a feeling akin to jealousy towards women who have had previous intercourse with other men."[2] Such a feeling, which in its fully developed form embodies the appreciation of more than merely physical union, is a very advanced product of psychological development, which has been built upon the scaffolding of much grosser and quite different conceptions.

The demand for virginity in the bride is in the first instance a claim established by the contract of child-marriage ; the lack of virginity is not an offence against sexual sentiments of possession, but a breach of faith and an act of commercial dishonesty, the ' seducer ' being legally liable for the bride-price which has been disbursed by the intending husband. In those countries where marriage by purchase has attained its most fully developed form, as among the slave-holding populations of Africa and Asia, infant betrothal is the general rule. The claim thus becomes an established rule, and the ' honour ' of the man who does not obtain the same standard of exclusive possession as others is thereby injured.

The satisfaction of that claim consists, accordingly, not in the consciousness of obtaining the primitiae of the woman's sexual life, as it would were it founded upon sentiments of retrospective jealousy, but in the public demonstration and broadcast publication of its satisfaction. Not only may those primitiae be handed over to, and the satisfaction of the claim attested by, a credible deputy, but it is the common rule in early societies that the demonstration should be made public. In some provinces of Peru the mother, as we saw, deflowered the bride digitally in a public assembly and before the witnesses to the marriage contract.[3] In Samoa, in the case of the bride of a chief, the defloration was performed digitally by the bridegroom or by an uncle or other relative, at a public function held with much pomp before the assembled multitude.[4] Among the Mandigo the Mosaic ' proofs of vir-

---

[1] O. Asboth, " Ein Hochzeitsbrauch in Südrussland," *Archiv für Anthropologie*, xiii, pp. 318 sq.

[2] E. Westermarck, *The History of Human Marriage*, vol. i, p. 163.

[3] See above, p. 320.

[4] G. Brown, *Melanesians and Polynesians*, pp. 121 sq. ; A. Kramer, *Die Samoa-Inseln*, vol. i, pp. 36 sqq. ; O. Stubel, *Samoanische Texte* (*Königliches Museum für Volkerkunde*, iv), pp. 116 sq.

ginity' were carried through the streets of the village.[1] They are similarly exhibited in public among the Kulngo negroes of the French Sudan.[2] In southern Celebes the proofs of virginity are exhibited to the guests on a silver salver.[3] They are similarly presented for the inspection of the wedding-guests by the Tchurwash.[4] In Baluchistan, among the Brahui, the proofs of virginity are examined by a jury of matrons.[5]

Great importance is attached to the demonstration among Semitic peoples. Among the Bedawi it used to be the rule to hang the blood-stained cloth bearing the proofs of the bride's virginity on a lance in the middle of the camp or village, and to leave it there for several days.[6] Throughout Egypt and the Sudan those ' proofs ' are obtained by digital defloration. In Nubia, early betrothal being customary, it is usual for the bride-groom to ascertain the intended bride's virginity by a prelim-inary digital examination when she is about eight or nine years old. When she reaches the age of ten, but in any case before the appearance of menstruation, dilatation is effected, first with one, then with two fingers, the process being repeated on several successive days.[7] In Egypt digital defloration, the finger being covered with a cloth, is the rule among all classes ; it was habitually carried out in the presence of the mothers of the bride and bridegroom and of an experienced midwife, and the proofs were in every case exhibited to the guests, hung out of the window, or carried in triumph to neighbours' houses.[8] The custom was scrupulously observed by the Copts.[9] Among Catholic Christians defloration took place in the natural way, in the presence of the respective mothers of the bride and bridegroom.[10] The Turks do not attach so much importance to the virginity of the bride as do the Arabs ; it was customary, however, for the marriage to be consummated in the presence of the mothers of the parties concerned. They were careful not to allow the bridegroom to complete the connection,

    [1] J. Matthews, *A Voyage to the River Sierra-Leone on the Coast of Africa*, p. 118.
    [2] L. Tauxier, *Études Soudanaises. Le Noir de Bondoukou*, p. 235.
    [3] B. F. Matthes, *Bijdragen tot de ethnologie van Zuid-Celebes*, p. 42.
    [4] A. Vámbéry, *Das Türkenvolk*, p. 461.
    [5] D. Bray, in *Census of India*, 1911, vol. iv, " Baluchistan," pp. 105 sq.
    [6] A. M. St. Elie, " La femme du désert autrefois et aujourd'hui," *Anthropos*, iii, p. 185.
    [7] E. Godard, *Égypte et Palestine*, pp. 85 sq.
    [8] *Ibid.*, p. 87 ; A.-B. Clot, *Aperçu général sur l'Égypte*, vol. ii, p. 44 ; J. L. Burckhardt, *Arabic Proverbs*, p. 140 ; M. C. d'Arvieux, *Mémoires*, vol. iii, p. 306 ; Al-Tunisi, *Voyage au Darfour*, p. 441.
    [9] E. Godard, *op. cit.*, p. 86.
    [10] *Ibid.*, p. 87.

for they believed that mixture of the semen with blood would be injurious to the bride's fertility.[1]

Measures are, of course, readily adopted to insure that the required ' proofs ' shall be forthcoming in every case, as by the judicious use of pigeon's or chicken's blood, or by timing the procedure so that menstruation shall not have entirely ceased. In Egypt, if a young bridegroom should raise a complaint that the proofs of virginity are not available, an experienced midwife is called in who, with a well-cultivated finger-nail, excoriates the vagina and produces the required blood-stained napkin, to the confusion of the inexperienced bridegroom, who is roundly abused by the bride's mother and relatives and compelled to tender an apology. More commonly, however, the bridegroom himself takes care to connive at any fraud that may be required ; for the sentiment which is chiefly involved has no reference to his feelings towards the bride, but to the public upholding of the established standards as regards his ' honour,' and he is the first to desire any breach of those standards to remain secret.[2] In Nigeria, where the custom of exhibiting publicly the ' proofs of virginity ' is perhaps more general than elsewhere among uncultured peoples, the husband spares no pains to secure that they shall be forthcoming. Among the Fulah he invariably provides himself with some fowl's blood, and makes it a point of honour to affirm that he has found his wife a virgin.[3] Among the Mandingo it is usual for the husband to protest and swear by all that is holy that his bride was a virgin, even though it is well known to everyone that she has had several children.[4] The public exhibition of the ' proofs of virginity ' was until lately customary among the peasantry in most countries of southern Europe. In Greece the bride's nightgown was left hanging for some days at the window,[5] and the same custom obtained in Sicily.[6] At the present day it is generally considered sufficient that the bridal couch should be examined by the mothers. The custom was one of the ceremonials observed at royal weddings in Spain, and when the Emperor Charles V married Isabel of Braganza the ' proofs ' were solemnly exhibited for the inspection of the assembled grandees.[7] In Little

[1] E. Godard, Égypte et Palestine, p. 85.

[2] Ibid., p. 88 ; R. F. Burton, Personal Narrative of a Pilgrimage to Al-Madinah and Meccah, vol. iii, pp. 82 sq. n.

[3] F. de Coutouly, " Le mariage et ses coutumes chez les Foula du Kolu," Revue d'ethnographie et de sociologie, i, p. 285.

[4] H. Hecquard, Voyage sur la côte et dans l'intérieur de l'Afrique occidentale, p. 174.

[5] A. de Gubernatis, Storia comparata degli usi nuziali, p. 209.

[6] G. Pitré, Usi natalizi, nuziali e funebri del popolo siciliano, p. 115.

[7] F. von Hellwald, Die menschliche Familie, p. 345, after A. Navigiero.

Russia they were paraded at the end of a pole through the streets of the village. A red flag is now substituted.[1]

The chastity of a bride is, throughout barbaric cultures, not regarded as a virtue in the disposition of the young woman herself; its merit is ascribed entirely to her parents and in particular to her mother. This is usually recognised by praise and presents bestowed upon the mother as an acknowledgment of the watchfulness which she has exercised. The marketable value of virginity is not embodied in moral principles, but is secured by 'guarding' the girls. In Samoa, for instance, the bride of a chief " was always guarded and accompanied wherever she went by some woman of the family, as well as by a number of girl companions of her own age." [2] Among the Yakut virginity was protected by an intricate arrangement of leather trousers secured with straps, which a girl was not allowed to remove even at night.[3] The most thorough method of securing the virginity of the bride is by the operation of infibulation.[4] This is a variety of female circumcision. As with innumerable other primitive practices, it has become adapted to a purpose the very opposite of that which originally led to its adoption. Unless special means are employed, as is done in all primitive societies by the introduction of a foreign body or by immediate sexual intercourse, female circumcision, when completely carried out in its original form, results in an occlusion by cicatricial tissue more complete than that presented by the hymeneal membrane. In Egypt, where, in the lower classes, the operation is usually carried out by a barber, who, seizing all the soft parts in one hand, cuts them at one stroke with a razor, adhesions invariably result which necessitate considerable cutting at the time of the first delivery.[5] The original intention of the operation having long since become obsolete, the cicatricial closure has been utilised as a means of securing virginity; the formation of adhesions is encouraged by immobilising the parts or by stitches, only a small opening being contrived by inserting a quill during the healing process. The practice is universal in Nubia, south of Gebel Silsilleh and in the Sudan, and is also in use in Abyssinia, Somaliland and West Africa.[6] In some parts of Darfur and Kordofan no girl can find

[1] A. de Gubernatis, loc. cit.

[2] G. Brown, Melanesians and Polynesians, p. 120.

[3] M. A. Czaplicka, Aboriginal Siberia, p. 108.

[4] The name is derived from the practice which was occasionally employed by the Romans of fastening a brooch, or 'fibula,' to the prepuce of singers, whose voice it was desired to preserve at its best by enforced chastity (Juvenal, vi. 73, 378; Martial, vii. 821, xi. 758; Tertullian, De Pudicitia, xvi.).

[5] E. Godard, op. cit., pp. 60 sqq.

[6] Id., loc. cit.; Peney, " Études sur l'ethnologie, la physiologie,

a husband unless she has undergone the operation. The assistance of a midwife has generally to be invoked in order to render possible the consummation of the marriage, and the operation is frequently repeated after each confinement. The introduction of the practice is generally set down by writers to the Arabs ; but this is denied both by the Arabs and by the natives. Infibulation is condemned by Muslims.[1] It is practised in Siam at the present day; and in Burma they " sowe up the privie member of the female children as soon as they are born, leaving but a little hole to avoid the water." [2] Infibulation has also been reported in Java.[3] In Sind the procedure has been modified by the use of a detachable metal ring passed through the labia,[4] a contrivance which approximates to the chastity girdles in use in Europe during the Middle Ages.[5]

The honour of the man which is thus guarded by watchful custodians, by seclusion, by veils and draperies, by surgical procedures, has led to the conception of the honour and virtue of woman. There are considerable diversities in the

l'anatomie et les maladies des races du Soudan," *Bulletin de la Société de Géographie*, Sér. IV, xvii, pp. 338 sqq. ; J. W. Crowfoot, " Wedding Customs in North Sudan," *Sudan Notes and Records*, v, p. 9 ; C. C. Seligman, " Some Aspects of the Hamitic Problem in the Anglo-Egyptian Sudan," *Journal of the Royal Anthropological Institute*, xliii, p. 13 ; H. Sarrazin, *Races humaines du Soudan Français*, p. 189; Panceri, " Lettera al Prof. Mantegazza," *Archivio per l'antropologia e l'etnologia*, iii (1873), p. 353.

[1] Peney, *loc. cit.*

[2] J. W. L. v. Linschoten, *The Voyage of . . . to the East Indies*, vol. i, p. 110, and D. O. Burnet, note to the passage.

[3] F. Epp, reported in *Allgemeine Medicinischer Central-Zeitung*, 1853, p. 37.

[4] E. Gait, *Census of India*, 1911, vol. i, p. 260.

[5] " Du temps du roy Henry il y eut un certain quinquailleur qui apporta une douzaine de certains engins à la foire de St. Germain pour brider le cas des femmes, qui estaoient faicts de fer et ceinturoient comme une ceinture, et venoient à prendre par le bas et se fermer à clef, si subtilement faicts qu'il n'estoit pas possible que la femme, en estant bridée une fois, s'en peust jamais prévaloir pour ce doulx plaisir, n'ayant que quelques petits trous menus pour servir à pisser" (Brantôme, *Oeuvres*, vol. ix, p. 133). The contrivance was said to have been derived from Italy, and was sometimes known as a ' Bergamesque.' It is heard of in France as late as the eighteenth century, when a lady brought an action against her husband for desiring her to wear one of those appliances (P. Mantegazza, *Gli Amori degli uomini*, vol. i, p. 201. Cf. A. Bonneau, *Les cadenas et ceintures de chastété* (Paris, 1883); Caufeynon, *La ceinture de chastété* (Paris, 1905); E. Rodocanachi, *La femme italienne à l'époque de la Renaissance*, p. 323 ; P. d'Estrée, " La ceinture de chastété," *Journal de Médecine de Paris*, 3e Série, xiv, pp. 45 sqq.; P. Noury, "Les entraves mécaniques à la fonction de reproduction," *Chronique médicale*, xiii (1906), p. 610).

nature of those conceptions, and those variations bear in general a direct relation to the marriage customs of the people concerned. Thus among the Hindus, since by immemorial usage which has acquired the force of a moral obligation every girl must be married before she reaches the age of puberty, no occasion has arisen for guarding unmarried girls. A girl who has passed the age of nine years without becoming betrothed is practically excluded from any chance of marrying at all, and the only alternative is for her to become a hierodule or a concubine. A widow, again, if she does not commit suttee on the funeral pyre of her husband, is debarred by Hindu law from re-marrying, and although she is supposed to remain as chaste as though her husband were living, any amours she may indulge in, provided she avoids too glaring a publicity, are not judged severely by the moral code of the country. The requirements of feminine virtue thus reduce themselves, as in societies of a quite primitive type, to fidelity during the married state, and no preparation for such virtue by guarding and by the inculcation of moral principles is necessary outside that state. Consequently, not only has there been no development of the notions centring round the importance and merits of virginity, but no ideals or principles of feminine virtue and of the moral worth of female chastity can be said to have been formed. Adultery itself on the part of the woman, though, of course, condemned and resented, is not invested with an exaggerated heinousness or punished with a fierceness proportionate to the absolute domination claimed by the patriarchal husband. Modesty and mental purity are not a part of the established ideal of the wife. She owes fidelity to her husband ; but no special character or disposition, no uncontaminated sexual ignorance or conventional frigidity, is looked upon as a condition of that fidelity. Such a virtuous amputation of amorousness would, according to Hindu ideas, be accounted a defect and not a virtue in a wife.

Feminine Purity in China.

In China, on the other hand, where marriage does not take place until maturity,[1] and is therefore preceded by the strictest guarding and seclusion, a lofty standard of female virtue has been created which cannot be matched in any other country, and even surpasses the highest ideals of primitive Christianity. " In this species of factitious virtue," observes Sir G. Staunton, " the Chinese have

---

[1] Betrothal of an unborn infant, which is so common a practice among Oriental peoples, is in China a legal offence, although it was practised in the sixth century (P. Hoang, *Le mariage Chinois au point de vue légal*, p. 21).

preceded as well as surpassed most other nations." [1] The first
Jesuit missionaries were put to shame by the ingenious prudery
of the Chinese, and were compelled to acknowledge that in this
respect the latter were their superiors. " The modesty of the
Chinese," writes one missionary, " is not to be paralleled in all
the world, and no less the reservedness and precaution of the
women." [2] Chinese girls have been known to commit suicide
because they felt themselves dishonoured by having been in
the company of a man, albeit for the inadequate reason, as it
seemed to them, of saving him from imminent death. [3] In desperate
cases of illness the advice of a physician of high repute is sometimes resorted to by Chinese ladies ; in order that he may feel
their pulse a silk thread is tied to their wrist and is passed through
a hole in a partition. The physician, being enlightened by studying the tremors of the thread by means of his learned touch,
proceeds to prescribe for the patient. [4] The Jesuit Fathers were
sorely perplexed what they should do if called upon to administer
the sacrament of baptism or extreme unction to a female convert.
" The occasion of making this doubt is the incredible modesty
of the Chinese women, their reservedness, and their commend-
able avoiding not only of the conversation of men, but even the
sight of them ; in which particular, unless the missionaries be
extraordinarily cautious, a mighty scandal will be given to the
Chinese, and the whole body of Christians there may be exposed
to imminent danger." [5] In war-time or during a rebellion, when
a town has been in danger of being taken, the girls and women have
thrown themselves into the river to save their honour ; [6] and a
well is shown at Hang Chou into which hundreds of girls cast themselves rather than run the risk of falling into the hands of the T'ai
Ping rebels. [7] A vast literature is devoted to the recital of edifying
examples of female virtue and to singing the praises of noble women.
There was a special Imperial Order the decorations of which were
awarded to women signalised for their chastity and fidelity, such
as young widows who led a life of chastity and devotion to the
service of their deceased husbands' parents, and betrothed virgins
who remained single after the demise of the fiancé they had never

[1] G. Staunton, *An authentic Account of an Embassy from the King of Great
Britain to the Emperor of China*, vol. ii, p. 348.

[2] D. Fernandes Navarrete, " An Account of the Empire of China," in
Churchill, *A Collection of Voyages*, vol. i, p. 17.

[3] W. G. Walshe, art. " Chastity (Chinese)," in Hastings's *Encyclopaedia of
Religion and Ethics*, vol. iii, p. 491.

[4] J. Barrow, *Travels in China*, pp. 348 sq.

[5] D. F. Navarrete, *op. cit.*, p. 379.

[6] *Ibid.*, p. 11.

[7] W. G. Walshe, *loc. cit.*

seen.[1] Innumerable monuments, tablets and 'triumphal arches,' or 'P'Ai-fang,' of elaborate architecture commemorate similar exalted examples of feminine virtue.[2]

There is, on the other hand, in the vast and minute Chinese literature of moral precepts not a single reference to chastity or purity as virtues applicable to the male sex. No form of sexual indulgence is regarded as detracting from the character of the most dignified and honoured mandarin, and if he receives male friends, he is expected to supply prostitutes for their entertainment. The sexual habits of the men are of more than average licentiousness, and they are adepts at ingenious vice ; the state apartments of the most exalted officials are adorned with obscene pictures and statues depicting unnatural vices.[3] The ideals of female chastity and purity have reference to the character and functions of the Great Wife only ; and men in the highest families commonly marry as Little Wives women with whom they have first become acquainted in brothels. Men commonly keep female slaves, and resort to the company of accomplished courtesans as a relief from the perfection of purity to which they have so successfully trained their wives.

Greek Sexual Morality.

In Greece, where the position of women, whether as wives or as hetairai, was in the classical age closely similar to their position in China, conceptions of sexual morality were modified by the clear naturalism of the Greek mind, the extreme opposite of the inveterate conventionalism and formalism of the Chinese. Chastity and fidelity were claimed and regarded as essential virtues in wives and prospective wives. It can scarcely be said that the claim constituted an ideal. Women were consistently regarded in Greek thought as inferior beings ; the Greek social system, in fact, made them so. Their virtue as wives and daughters was viewed as a family obligation towards their husbands or relatives rather than as an ethical quality, and we find no heroic view of the seriousness of transgression and of the dishonour attaching to it. Chastity was neither elaborately held up as a moral ideal to the women, nor exalted by them to the status of a faith claiming their devotional enthusiasm, as in China. Adultery appears to have been common ; it was the concern of husbands

---

[1] P. Hoang, *op. cit.*, p. 244.

[2] *Ibid.*, pp. 244 sq. The inscriptions on commemorative tablets, or Pei, are in some such style as " This woman in her misery has preserved pure and unsullied a widow's chastity."

[3] J. Barrow, *Travels in China*, p. 150.

or guardians not to afford women the chance.[1] Euripides sets down the continual intrigues and adulteries of Greek wives to their seclusion, but the only remedy that suggested itself to him was a yet stricter seclusion.[2] Socrates, who gave his gratified approval to all that Isomachos said touching the proper sphere of a wife as housekeeper,[3] resorted, like all cultured Greeks, for congenial female companionship to the society of hetairai. Unlike him, some of the great minds of Greece felt, as did Euripides, a profound dissatisfaction with woman such as the Greek social system had shaped her. Plato, in disgust at the product of male proprietary morality, turned back as to an ideal to the primitive Greek social order such as it survived in Sparta, and advocated sexual communism.[4] So did the Cynics;[5] the Epicureans are said to have practised it.[6] In a somewhat later age the Stoics,[7] in spite of their ascetic tendencies, attached no special merit to chastity, and "did not regard loose sexual indulgence as 'per se' immoral." The conception of such a virtue as chastity, regarded as a moral merit and applicable to both sexes, was unthought of by the Greeks. "There does not appear to have been any respect for moral purity in the modern sense," says Mr. W. H. S. Jones. "The virtue of chastity was confined within narrow limits, such as loyalty to husband on the part of a wife, or to master and mistress on the part of a maid-servant. . . . Men were under no obligation except that of avoiding adultery or dishonour to a neighbour's family. Chastity, in fact, was a family and not a personal matter. . . . It is hard to find passages in pre-Christian literature where loose intercourse is looked upon as itself an offence. Indulgence might bring with it ceremonial defilement, but in itself was no sin. This attitude is in perfect accordance with the Greek spirit, which considered no natural impulse as evil. Sexual indulgence stood upon exactly the same level as eating and drinking."[8]

Thus at the phase of human social evolution when the foundations of Western civilisation were being laid, the conception of sexual virtue and purity remained essentially what it is in the most primitive phases of human society. Continence was no more accounted a virtue than abstinence in regard to food and to drink. The idea of morality 'par excellence'—that is, of sexual morality

---

[1] W. H. S. Jones, *Greek Morality*, p. 87.
[2] Euripides, *Hyppolit.*, 645 sqq.
[3] Xenophon, *Memorabilia*, iii. 11.
[4] Plato, *Republic*, v. 7.
[5] Diogenes Laertius, vi. 72.
[6] *Ibid.*, vii. 188; W. H. S. Jones, *op. cit.*, p. 119.
[7] Athenaeus, xiii. 588.
[8] W. H. S. Jones, *op. cit.*, pp. 118 sq.

as it has come to be regarded in modern Europe, as a virtue transcending in importance all other moral obligations, while disregard of it constitutes corruption and sin—was, when the basis of Western culture, thought, and civilisation were laid in Greece, as yet unborn. The germs of those ideas had, indeed, already appeared in lower cultural phases and had developed in certain aspects of Oriental culture; but they were absent from that culture which was the cradle of European civilisation. It was not until a later stage of Western culture that the current values which have been regarded in European sentiment as of absolute validity, as grounded in the constitution of human nature, and in the light of which it has been sought to interpret primitive society, have been developed.

Roman Sexual Morality.

As in all else, Roman views and usages came nearer to those of our society in regard to sexual morality than those of any other people. We have noted the peculiar combination in Roman patriarchy of many features arising from a highly developed matriarchal influence. The manner in which the principles of patriarchal morality were imposed upon Roman women differed fundamentally from that which was adopted in Greece. Those principles were not enforced by precautionary and coercive measures, but inculcated as precepts; the Roman woman was placed upon her honour. She was not immured in Oriental fashion in a gynaikonitis, but enjoyed wellnigh complete freedom. Her ' virtue ' was assimilated to the civic ' virtus,' which was the moral ideal of the Roman citizen. Instead of man's honour being guarded by precautionary restrictions, the woman herself was made a partner in that honour; it became, by a sort of legal fiction, her honour. That ideal of female virtue—the very name remains somewhat incongruous, ' female manliness '—was embodied in Rome, and kept before the eyes of women in their ancient cult of Vesta. The old agrarian goddess, with her Priapic male associate, her phallic emblems, her symbolic ass, her ritual obscenities, and all the usual attributes of goddesses of fertility, had been strangely and deliberately transformed into a symbol and protectress of virginity and female virtue. The virgin goddess and her virgin priestesses were constantly kept before Roman women, as Cicero quaintly tells us, " in order that womankind might feel that it is woman's nature to suffer all forms of chastity "—" ut sentiant mulieres naturam feminarum omnem castitatem pati." [1] In addition, a special cult, that of the goddess Pudicitia, was instituted,

---

[1] Cicero, De legibus, ii. 29.

which, significantly enough, was at first an exclusive patrician cult.
no plebeian woman being allowed to take part in the rites of the
goddess of modesty.   Later a Pudicitia Plebeia was also instituted.[1]

To a large extent the traditional type of the virtuous Roman
matron of the old days was, like the Greek noble wedded
wife of the heroic age, a retrospective convention.   In all probability the type of the Italic woman of primitive matriarchal
times was, so far as regards sexual morality, represented by such
'noble courtesans' as we hear of as foundresses of the Roman
nation and by the proverbially free Etruscan women.   The fact
that in the year 285 B.C. a temple was erected to Venus out of
the proceeds of fines imposed on Roman matrons for adultery [2]
is in itself sufficiently significant.   Livy, who is always anxious
to uphold the tradition of primitive Roman austerity, is manifestly
embarrassed in recording such facts ; as also when he refers in
obscure terms to an event which happened in 328 B.C., when,
after a disastrous epidemic, one hundred and seventy patrician
matrons were put to death on a charge of disseminating poison.[3]
The latter occurrence was probably an outburst of witch persecution.   The ideal presentment of the Roman woman of the early
days is only slightly less exaggerated than the ideal picture of
'corruption' under the Empire.   Our earliest contemporary records
of Roman life show quite as much laxity and licentiousness as
those of times of so-called 'corruption.'   "There is hardly a fault
or vice attributed by Juvenal to the women of Domitian's time,"
says Professor Dill, who is disposed to take the most generous
view in such matters, "which may not find parallel in the nine or
ten generations before Juvenal penned his great indictment against
the womanhood of his age." [4]   In the days of the Republic, as in
the most luxurious days of the Empire, very much the same variety
of conduct in this respect was to be found in Roman society as in
our own.   In both epochs there existed an austere idea of loyalty
to the Roman conception of the family, which identified a woman's
honour with that of the 'familia.'

The principle had no application to men, and there is nothing
in Roman ideas that corresponds to a moral value attaching to
sexual restraint as an intrinsic virtue.   Nevertheless, owing to the
method resulting from the peculiar influence of the old matriarchal
power on Roman patriarchy, of relying for the enforcement of
female fidelity on moral influence rather than on compulsory
measures, the ideal of female purity had in Rome a restraining effect,
such as it had not in Greece, upon masculine conduct.   For it was
a logical consequence of that principle that no offence should be

[1] Livy, x. 23.   [2] *Ibid.*, x. 31.   [3] *Ibid.*, viii. 18.
[4] S. Dill, *Roman Society from Nero to Marcus Aurelius*, p. 79.

shown by the men, when in the presence of women, to the ideal which they imposed upon them. Grossness in such circumstances would be an insult to the woman's husband. Hence the Romans felt bound to observe a decent restraint in language and behaviour in the presence of women,[1] and that discipline was imposed upon their habitual conduct by the Roman woman's freedom to join in social intercourse. Proprietary purity, among the Romans, thus came as near as possible to the notion of meritorious purity as a moral principle, but it never actually gave rise to it. The provisions of the famous ' Lex Julia ' against adultery were almost barbaric in their severity, though they remained to a great extent a dead letter ; but the legal definition of the crime had reference to married women only, and had no application to men.[2] Several philosophical writers, indeed, expressed the view that equity demanded from the husband the same continence as he expected from his wife,[3] and Ulpian set down that " it would be inequitable to the last degree if a man demanded chastity from his wife when he himself in no way set her an example." [4] But many of Ulpian's abstract principles remain to this day in the realm of Utopias and counsels of perfection. Those words were, moreover, written in the third century, and Seneca, Plutarch, and Musonius belong to a late age when quite other ideas than those of Roman patriarchy had made their way into the metropolis of Europe.

The Roman conception of good ' mores,' of propriety in sexual relations and of decency was thus, on the whole, much the same as our own. But there was, nevertheless, an essential and fundamental difference between it and the sentiments represented in European tradition. The Roman ideal of sexual virtue remained a civic and secular ideal ; the only ground upon which chastity was demanded of a woman was fidelity to her husband, and the only ground upon which continence was preconised in a man was that of equitable reciprocity. The religious, mystic, paramount character which makes sexual morality ' morality ' par excellence, the conceptions of ' impurity ' and of ' sin,' were as unknown in Rome as in any other society,

---

[1] Plutarch, *Vita Romuli*, xx.

[2] Justinian, *Digesta*, i. 16. 1 ; Paulus, *Sententiae*, ii. 26 ; W. Rein, *Das Criminalrecht der Römer von Romulus bis auf Justinianus*, pp. 835 sqq. ; W. A. Hunter, *A Systematical and Historical Exposition of Roman Law*, p. 1071. Cf. the emphatic dictum of Cato (Aulus Gellius, x. 23 ; above, vol. ii, pp. 348 sq.).

[3] Plutarch, *Consolatio ad uxorem*, x ; *Conjugis praeces*, iv. xliv ; Seneca, *Epist.*, xciv. xcv ; J. Denis, *Histoire des théories et des idées morales dans l'antiquité*, vol. ii, p. 134 ; E. Zeller, *Die Philosophie der Griechen*, vol. iii, Part i, p. 660.

[4] Justinian, *Digesta*, xlviii. 5. 13.

primitive or civilised. Those conceptions are the products of the Christian religion. It was Christianity which effected the final synthesis in the long and somewhat complex evolution of those principles and sentiments. We have seen that several distinct elements and orders of motives have become fused in that evolution. On the one hand, it derives from the primitive tabus of sex, the menstrual tabu, from fears of magic influences, of the evil eye, of dangers which are thought to threaten the sexual organs and their functions. On the other hand, sexual morality derives from the establishment and extension of proprietary claims, from the development of individualistic marriage, from the combination of its economic with its sexual aspects, and from the combination and assimilation of those claims with the social products arising from primitive sexual tabus. But there is yet a third element in the synthesis which has resulted in the existing European form of the sentiments. It is from the accession of that third traditional element that the fully developed conception, such as it has become established by Christianity and such as we know it, has arisen.

Ritual Purity.

Continence is regarded as one of the conditions required for the successful carrying out of magical operations and for securing the satisfactory issue of important enterprises. It is often practised in combination with the ritual licentiousness which, in another aspect, and sometimes at a different stage of those operations, is likewise thought to promote magical efficiency. Festivals of licentiousness and promiscuity are not infrequently preceded by a period of preparatory abstinence and chastity. The inconsistency between the two principles is more apparent than real, and is in any case no greater than is found in many primitive conceptions and procedures. It is for the sake of their magical effect and not for any intrinsic moral character that ritual measures are adopted. The powers which they are intended to control often require to be regulated, and their indiscriminate exercise would be the reverse of beneficial. Thus, for example, in Motu, in New Guinea, when there has been abundant rain and a good crop is looked for, a tabu is imposed upon the chief, who must remain chaste.[1] If he did not, more rain would presumably come down and spoil the good effects of previous showers. Similarly in Assam, among the Sobyas, when the corn is nearly ready to be garnered, continence is exercised by the whole community, for any licentiousness would obviously

---

[1] J. Chalmers, *Pioneering in New Guinea*, p. 181.

tend to stimulate the rain-god inopportunely and ruin the crops.[1]
In Mekeo, in British New Guinea, a company of fourteen or
fifteen watchmen is appointed to guard the growing crops of coco
and areca nuts ; they stand about the fields disguised in masks
and fantastic costumes. Their morals must be of the most rigid
kind : not only must they observe chastity, but they must not
even look upon a woman. If they happen to pass one, it behoves
them to cast down their eyes modestly.[2] Among the Romans,
who celebrated the feast of sowing with Saturnalia, harvesters
were careful to remain chaste until the corn was safely gathered.[3]
In the Greek agricultural festivals, which were represented
by the Thesmophoriae, the women who participated had to
prepare themselves by strict chastity, not only abstaining
from the company of men, but by the use of anti-aphrodisiac
herbs and hard beds cultivating a mood of mental purity.[4]
Yet the rites which followed were orgiastic, and even in
their late form in civilised Athens obscene emblems and
Fescennine jests were an indispensable part of them. Similarly in
Rome, chastity had to be observed for a considerable period before
the celebration of the Bacchanalian feasts.[5] Sometimes the two
conflicting practices of continence calculated to avert the envy
of the gods, and of licentiousness designed to stimulate their
procreative powers, are, in cases of doubt, judiciously combined.
Thus among the wild tribes of Manipur agricultural operations
were accompanied in the usual manner by the wildest licence, but
the sacred headman was obliged to conciliate the gods by the
exercise of the severest self-denial and mortification. He was to
fast and remain chaste.[6]

Continence is very generally observed by hunters, fishermen,
warriors in the course of preparation for an expedition.[7] That
continence might naturally be thought to arise from a consideration
of its physiological advantages and to be part of a rational course
of training. It is, of course, possible that an appreciation of such
advantages may exist here and there among some of the more
advanced races ; but it is clear that such considerations have
had nothing to do with the origin of the observance, which
applies equally to every kind of magical operation and to both

---

[1] T. C. Hodson, " The ' Genna ' amongst the Tribes of Assam," *Journal
of the Anthropological Institute*, xxxvi, p. 94.

[2] A. C. Haddon, *Head-Hunters*, pp. 270 sqq., 75 sq.

[3] Plutarch, *Quaest. conviv.*, iii. 6.

[4] Hesychius, s.v. κνέωρον ; Pliny, *Nat. Hist.*, xxiv. 59 ; Ovid, *Meta-
morph.*, x. 431.

[5] Livy, xxxix. 9. 4.

[6] T. C. Hodson, *The Naga Tribes of Manipur*, pp. 168 sqq.

[7] See J. G. Frazer, *The Golden Bough*, vol. iii, pp. 157 sqq., 190 sqq.

men and women. The dictum commonly adduced in this connection, "omne animale post coitum triste," is of very doubtful
truth ; the normal condition of the healthy animal in this respect
is one of satisfaction, and has as little relation to a state of
depression as the repletion which follows a meal. The proposition
is even more doubtfully applicable to the usually moderate
sexuality of primitive man. The suggestion is, however, directly
negatived by facts. Ritual preparatory asceticism is often very
far from being calculated to promote efficiency on physiological
and rational principles. Dakota warriors prepared themselves
for any important expedition by the most elaborate measures,
including, of course, rigorous chastity. They starved themselves ;
they kept themselves awake all night ; they scrubbed their bodies
with briars until they streamed with blood ; they lacerated
themselves and gashed their limbs ; they even completed the
process by cutting off a finger or two. As a result of such effective
preparation they worked themselves up to such a pitch of delirium
that they saw visions, and entered the fray as raving lunatics.[1]
As Sir James Frazer remarks : "It is hard to conceive any course of
training which could more effectually incapacitate men from the
business of war than that which those foolish Indian athletes
adopted." [2]

The continence of warriors and of hunters may be thought to
arise from conceptions similar to those which lead them to consider
that the properties of their weapons and instruments would be
injuriously affected by the touch of a woman, which might rob
them of their masculine virtue and impart to them feminine qualities.
No doubt some such notion is entertained by the men when they
are anxious to retain their full efficiency as warriors or hunters,
but it can be at most but a particular aspect of the principle
governing the observance of ritual chastity, and a derivative
interpretation placed upon it. That principle does not by any
means apply solely to preparation for strenuous enterprises, but
is equally applicable to all operations in which magical power
is thought to be required, and is observed both by men and by
women. Thus among the Masai chastity is a necessary condition
for the successful brewing of poison.[3] Among the Kwakiutl of
British Columbia it is regarded as needful in order to derive the
full benefit from the digestion of a cannibalistic meal.[4] Women

[1] J. O. Dorsey, "Omaha Sociology," *Second Annual Report of the Bureau
of Ethnology*, pp. 436, 444.
[2] J. G. Frazer, *The Golden Bough*, vol. iii, p. 160.
[3] A. C. Hollis, "Notes on the Masai System of Relationship and Other
Matters connected therewith," *Journal of the Royal Anthropological Institute*,
xlv, p. 274.
[4] F. Boas, "The Social Organisation and the Secret Societies of the

in Nukahiva considered that it was essential to observe chastity while engaged in the preparation of hair-oil.[1] Purity is also required of cooks. The cook of the king of Angoi was expected to keep himself pure, and might not live with his wife during his period of duty.[2] The same purity was regarded as being desirable in cooks, bakers, and waiters in ancient Rome.[3]

Chastity is a requirement of 'ritual purity.' The notion of 'purity' is, we have seen, by no means a primitive one; it is, on the contrary, a derivative conception resulting from an advanced reinterpretation of primitive notions. Ritual purity, or godliness, is thought of as akin to cleanliness. But such is very far from being the case as regards the primitive requirements of magical efficiency. Saints and ascetics are as a rule very dirty. St. Jerome declares that for an adult person to wash is a practice to be wholly condemned, and he expresses his admiration for women who abstain altogether from ablutions.[4] With many pious country people on the continent of Europe, the early Christian notion still survives that cleanliness is akin to the works of Satan, and that it is sinful to wash too much. The monk of St. Gall refers, in his Life of the emperor Charlemagne, to a certain deacon, who "resisted the course of nature; for he took baths and had himself closely shaved, polished his skin, cleaned his nails, and had his hair cut." [5] Such cleanliness in the very reverse of ritual purity. In ancient Rome the Flaminica had to be ritually pure. Although she was a married woman, she was under the obligation of observing chastity for a considerable time when some of the more important ceremonies of the year had to be performed. In addition, she had to abstain from washing herself, combing her hair, or trimming her nails.[6] The conception of ceremonial cleanliness is not derived from the notion of purity, but it is, on the contrary, from the notion of the immemorial requirements of magic efficiency that the notion of ceremonial purity has been formed.

Sexual continence is a necessary part of that ritual efficiency in the same way, and on the same principles, as all abstinence, self-denial and self-mortification. The primary rationale of such

---

Kwakiutl Indians," *Report of the United States National Museum for* 1875, pp. 440, 537 sqq.

[1] G. H. von Langsdorff, *Reise um die Welt*, vol. i, pp. 118 sq.

[2] A. Bastian, *Die deutsche Expedition an der Loango-Kuste*, vol. i, p. 216.

[3] Columella, *De re rustica*, xii. 4. 2 sqq.

[4] Jerome, *Epistola*, cvii, 11, in Migne, *Patrologiae Cursus Completus*, vol. xxii, col. 376.

[5] The Monk of St. Gall, *De gestis Karoli imperatoris*, i. 32, in Pertz, *Monumenta Germaniae Historica, Scriptores*, vol. ii, p. 746.

[6] Aulus Gellius, x. 15; Plutarch, *Quaestionae Romanae*, 86; Ovid, *Fasti*, iii. 197.

ascetic practices is that the envy of maleficent powers must be disarmed and warded off by self-abasement and voluntary suffering. It is identical in theory with rites of mourning : in order to ward off the envy of the ghost, who is jealous of all who enjoy the pleasures of life from which he is debarred, those pleasures must be abstained from. The mourner neglects his person, goes ragged and dishevelled, does not wash, nor comb his hair, covers himself with dust and filth, rends his clothes, fasts, secludes himself, scarifies himself till he streams with blood, humbles himself to the dust, and remains chaste. The Greeks expressly identified ritual purity with rites of mourning, and used the same word, ἀγνεία, to denote the mourning ceremonies in honour of dying gods.[1] Similarly, it is a widespread principle that persons or objects that are particularly valued, or are regarded as being specially exposed to dangers from envious powers or persons, shall be deliberately defaced or rendered unattractive. Women are, in most primitive societies, greatly perturbed if their children are too enthusiastically admired, and it is customary for strangers to make disparaging remarks in order not to arouse the fears and susceptibilities of the mothers. Thus, for instance, Mr. Dodwell, when travelling in Corfu, caused the greatest alarm and confusion in the household of his hostess by expressing his admiration for her children, whom he thought particularly handsome. The endangered infants were at once bidden to run away ; but the mother's anxiety was not completely set at rest until, at her request, the incautious visitor had consented to allay her suspicions by spitting in their faces.[2] In Egypt it is not an uncommon sight to see a wealthy lady, attired in the richest silks and delicately hennaed and perfumed, leading by the hand her beloved child clad in filthy cotton rags that have not been washed for months, with hair uncombed and hands and face innocent of ablution. This is not the result of gross neglect and carelessness, but is a deliberate artifice in order that the precious offspring should be thoroughly protected against those ever-present dangers which arise from the envy of human and supernatural powers.[3] The same principles are, in fact, applied to modern Egyptian children as were carried out in the early centuries of Christianity by the famous saints of the same country. In Muslim lands no praise is ever bestowed upon a person or object without qualifying it by some formula, such as ' mashallah,' implying submission to the superior judgment of the Deity.[4] In India it is a

---

[1] E. Fehrle, *Die kultische Keuscheit im Altertum*, p. 46.
[2] E. Dodwell, *Classical and topographical tour through Greece*, vol. ii, p. 36.
[3] E. W. Lane, *Manners and Customs of the Modern Egyptians*, vol. i, p. 70.
[4] *Ibid.*, vol. i, p. 315.

rule with craftsmen never to produce a ware of particular beauty and perfect workmanship without some intentional flaw, so as not to 'tempt providence' by the perfection of the products of their skill. The most beautiful Oriental manuscripts are in like manner generally defaced in some part by an intentional blot.[1] By an apparently paradoxical, but consistent, application of the same principles even curses are sometimes sought and bestowed 'for luck.'[2] It is manifestly essential that any risk of arousing the envy of the powers invoked should be scrupulously avoided in the act of conciliating them. Chastity is regarded as tending to avert the dangers arising from such envy. In the kingdom of Congo, when the sacred pontiff undertook a journey through his diocese, all the people, single and married, had to observe strict continence lest any indulgence on their part should, by causing annoyance to the gods, endanger the safety of the sacred personage.[3]

It is significant that, unlike many other primordial ideas and sentiments, the conception of ritual purity has remained unaltered in profoundly theological Oriental cultures, such as that of India, where it has reached in many respects its highest degree of development. Ritual chastity is there observed, as in the most primitive phases, by priests and holy men solely as a magical qualification, and without any reference to its intrinsic meritoriousness as a virtue. Indian sorcerers and wizards, when about to perform powerful incantations, had to observe chastity for several days.[4] "According to Hindu theory," says Sir M. Monier-Williams, "the performance of penances was like making deposits in the bank of heaven. By degrees an enormous credit was accumulated, which enabled the depositor to draw to the amount of his savings without fear of his draft being refused payment. The power gained in this manner by weak mortals was so enormous that gods as well as men were equally at the mercy of these all but omnipotent ascetics; and it is remarkable that even the gods are described as engaging in penance and austerities in order, it may be presumed, not to be outdone by human beings. Siva was so engaged when the god of love shot an arrow at him." In the 'Râmâyana' the demon Râvana, who is the villain of the poem, derives his power from his indulgence in ascetic practices. "The secret of his power lay in a long course of penance which, according to the Hindu conception, gained for

[1] W. Crooke, *The Popular Religion and Folk-lore of Northern India*, vol. ii, p. 10.
[2] J. G. Frazer, *The Golden Bough*, vol. i, pp. 279 sqq.
[3] J. B. Labat, *Relation historique de l'Éthiopie occidentale*, vol. i, pp. 259 sq.
[4] W. Caland, *Altindisches Zauberritual: Probe eine Übersetzung der wichtigste Theile des Kauśka Sutra*, p. 79.

him who practised it, however evil his designs, superiority to the gods themselves, and enabled Râvana to extort from the god Brahma this remarkable boon, that neither gods, genii, demons, nor giants should be able to vanquish him." [1] Ritual purity and chastity are in India as intimately associated and intermingled with ritual licentiousness and obscenity as anywhere in the savage world. Thus the priests of Siva, while ministering to the god in the form of a gigantic phallus, and surrounded by the most obscene representations, are under the strictest obligation to be chaste and pure, not only in deed, but in thought, and their complete nakedness renders any breach of that necessary purity apparent. [2] With those experts in asceticism, the Fakirs and Yogis of India, sexual continence belongs to the same order of observances as self-tortures and mutilations similar to those practised by the Dakota warriors, and it is also an alternative to ritual licentiousness. An aspirant to sanctity may tie a heavy stone to his penis, and thus effectually mortify the flesh ; or he may make a vow to deflower a thousand virgins. There is not in the most exalted and mystic religious literature of India any conception of chastity as a virtue and a good in itself ; it is always regarded as a means. " The life of chastity, O Monks," it is said in a religious manual, " is lived for the purpose of Insight and Thorough Knowledge." [3] Indeed to attach too much importance to ascetic chastity is sometimes expressly discouraged : " Undue craving for chastity is, like all other forms of clinging to conditions of earthly existence, essentially evil." [4]

The fact that ritual chastity did not, even in India, change its primitive character is profoundly significant For had the value attached to chastity arisen as the effect of a deep-rooted primordial sentiment, and had the chastity required of those engaged in important enterprises and in priests been a manifestation of such a sentiment, we should expect ritual chastity to assume readily the character of a merit and moral virtue. We should certainly expect that where the importance of ritual chastity had come to occupy a foremost place in a highly developed religious culture, and where many other sentiments, such as the conceptions of a patriarchal society, operated strongly in the same direction, the moral merit of chastity as a generally applicable virtue should have become fully recognised. Yet nothing of the sort has happened. Even though the magical effect of chastity was constantly dwelt

---

[1] M. Monier-Williams, *Indian Epic Poetry*, p. 4.

[2] P. Sonnerat, *Voyage aux Indes orientales et à la Chine*, vol. i, p. 322.

[3] *Iti-vuttaka, or Sayings of Buddha*, translated by J. H. More, p. 49.

[4] *Ibid.*, pp. 67 sq.

on, there is not a trace in Indian thought of its being regarded as a substantial virtue.

The same is true of all the other cultures and civilisations out of which our own has, directly or indirectly, developed. In Western Asia, in Egypt, in Greece, chastity was recognised as a ritual condition of magical power, but not as in itself a moral virtue. The Greeks had the same conceptions of the magical action of ritual chastity as the Hindus. They regarded it as effective in the practice of witchcraft.[1] Priestesses, more especially those engaged in prophecy, had to observe chastity in the pursuit of their avocations. But that ritual chastity was never regarded by the Greeks as having any bearing on morality and did not affect the naturalism of their view of sexual functions. So far were they from drawing inferences from magic or religious ritual to morality, that to require young women appointed to the service of the gods to remain chaste was generally thought unreasonable and barbarous, and care was taken to choose old women for those offices.[2] The Delphic prophetess was usually an old married woman, and complied with ritual requirements by dressing in the costume of a virgin.[3] In Rome chastity was esteemed as a civic trait, but had no intrinsic ethical or religious significance. The conceptions and sentiments to which supreme ethical importance is attached in European tradition are, in the form in which they are familiar to us, products of the Christian religion.

Christian Morality.

It is usual to trace the ascetic tendencies of Christianity, together with many of its other elements, to Eastern influence and to Eastern monachism.[4] But, as just noted, Eastern asceticism had an entirely different character. The saints, the rishis of India, practised asceticism, but they were also regarded, owing to their very holiness, as above the common law in regard to sexual privileges. In no form of Eastern monachism is chastity stringently regarded. In the lands of Western Asia, where Christianity had its rise, ritual continence was, as elsewhere, a part of the requirements of ceremonial purity. The Jews were distinguished above all other peoples for the importance they attached to the state of ritual undefilement. Ritual purity was not with them a special condition of the

---

[1] E. Fehrle, *Die kultische Keuscheit im Altertum,* pp. 157 sq.

[2] Pausanias, viii. 5. 12; E. Fehrle, *op. cit,,* pp. 95, 224; J. A. Hild, in C. Daremberg and E. Saglio, *Dictionnaire des antiquités grecques et romaines,* vol. v, p. 753.

[3] Diodorus Siculus, xvi. 26.

[4] The view was mooted by Clement of Alexandria (*Stromata,* i. 15, in Migne, *Patrologiae Cursus Completus, Series Graeca,* vol. viii, col. 780).

priestly office, but a condition of citizenship, of Jewishdom. Jewish religion centred round strict and minute conformity with the ritual observances, the Torah—in other words, the traditional tabus laid down in the Law. The word 'Law' had a significance in Hebraic religion which is foreign to most other religious systems. In mediaeval language it came to be the usual term for 'religion'— the 'Jewish Law,' 'the Mahometan Law,' 'the Christian Law' are the current designations for those religions. Religion, that is to say, was regarded by the Jews as consisting in the observance of the rules laid down ; and moral excellence was synonymous in the Jewish conceptions with accurate observance of the prescriptions whereby the state of ritual purity, and therefore magic power over evil, might be attained. Undoubtedly the moral ideals and the moral character of the Jews were high, and their adherence to their moral principles was more strict than that of neighbouring peoples. But this was not so much because they had raised morality to the level of a religious observance as because they had raised religious observances to such paramount importance that they constituted the whole of morality. It is often said that the moral conceptions of the Jews were higher than those of other peoples. The judgment is ambiguous. No ethical principle was formulated by the Jews that was not recognised equally by the Egyptians, the Greeks, or the Romans. The difference lay not in the superiority of their ethical principles, but in the fact that, with the Jews, every moral principle rested upon a religious sanction and was an article of Jewish Divine Law. Infringement of any of those principles was not merely evil or immoral, but sacrilegious, a treason, an abomination, a sin. The rites and customs of the Gentiles, the whoredoms of Babylon, were not fiercely denounced on the ground that they were intrinsically immoral, but on the ground that they were opposed to Jewish Law—or, rather, no distinction was drawn by the Jews between the one point of view and the other, between the ethical law and the Torah. The consumption of pork was regarded with as much horror as the rites of Mylitta. We never find Jewish doctors discussing, as did Roman jurists or Greek philosophers, whether an act is just or unjust, beneficial or harmful ; their sole concern and criterion was whether it was prescribed by the Torah, whether it was conducive to defilement or to religious purity.

Chastity was not invested with any specially exalted merit in Jewish Law. The conceptions of sexual morality in their most stringent form, as developed under the influence of patriarchal ideals, as well as elaborate ceremonial requirements and tabus, were embodied in it ; adultery, fornication, breaches of the primitive tabus were regarded with utter horror. Indecency was so strongly tabued that a man was defiled by seeing himself naked or by being insufficiently clothed while in bed.[1] But the primitive passion for fatherhood, the importance of increasing the race, of multiplying, were far too strongly established in Jewish ideals to permit of any exaltation of celibacy or virginity. On the contrary, celibacy was looked upon as a religious crime, equivalent to murder and to diminishing the image of God, and men over twenty were compelled to marry.[2] Celibacy was not even tolerable in priests ; celibate saints and virgins were utterly abhorrent to Jewish ideas.

At the time when Christianity began to differentiate itself among Jewish communities, they were divided into three types of Judaism : the Pharisees, the Sadducees, and the Essaeans.[3] The Pharisees, who constituted the bulk of the people, were the most rigorous observers of the Torah according to traditional Jewish views ; they, in addition, attached an equal importance to all national tradition, whether written or oral, as in their scrupulousness in the manner of washing their hands or of cleaning plates and dishes, thus neglecting no means of achieving purity or holiness. Ths Sadducees who were disposed to adopt Hellenic ideas and to bring what they regarded as the more barbarous and obsolete ancestral customs into line with more modern sentiment, repudiated the ritualistic practices of uncanonical traditions, and confined themselves to the observance of the Torah interpreted in a liberal spirit.

The third great sect, that of the Essaeans,[4] denounced the

---

[1] J. A. Eisenmenger, *Entdecktes Judenthum*, vol. i, p. 427.

[2] M. L. Margolis, art. " Celibacy," in *The Jewish Encyclopaedia*, vol. iii, p. 636.

[3] Josephus, *De bello Judaico*, ix. 13 ; Hippolytus, *Refutatio omnium Haeresium*, ix. 13.

[4] Josephus writes Essaeans (*Antiquitates Judaeorum*, xv. 10. 4) and Essenes. The latter is probably an Hellenised form for Greek readers (cf. C. D. Ginsburg, art. " Essenes," in W. Smith and H. Wace, *Dictionary of Christian Biography, Literature, Sects, and Doctrines*, vol. i, p. 208). Philo writes Essaeans, Epiphanius Issaeans—also Essenes and Ossenes—St. Nilus Issaeans (in Migne, *Patrologiae Cursus Completus, Series Graeca*, vol. lxxix, col. 722). Numerous names are mentioned with reference to the less orthodox Jewish sects, such as the Poor (Ebionim), Dositheans, Gorthenans, Daily Baptists (Hemerobaptisti ; in Hebrew, Toble Shachrith, A. Edersheim, *Sketches of Jewish Social Life in the Days of Christ*, p. 245), Therapeuts, Nazarenes, Iessaeans. Those appellations appear to refer in most instances to particular aspects of doctrine rather than to distinct sects ; it was the fashion to give names to the holders of a given opinion or the observers of a given rite, irrespectively of what religious denomination they might belong to. John the Baptist, for example, is spoken of as a Daily Baptist, a Nazarene, and an Ebionite. The Essaeans, or Issaeans, were indistinguishable from the Nazarenes, or Iessaeans (see below, p. 367 n.[1]) ; both were identical with the Poor, or Ebionites (Epiphanius, *Adversus octoginta Haereses*, xx. 3, in Migne, *op. cit.*, vol. xli, col. 273) There were several Essaean sects which differed " on trifling points " (διά σμικρόν τι) ;

Pharisees and the Sadducees for their superficial ritualism and their worldly modernism respectively. They sought holiness not only by meticulous ritual observances, but by spiritual exercises that might place their whole soul in a state of grace. Most of them eschewed cities " in order to escape from the immorality that is rife therein," [1] and lived in coenobitic and communistic brother-hoods, contributing to the common funds, which were entrusted to the management of a purse-bearer or treasurer, by the exercise of some craft or of agriculture.[2] Others, however, lived in the cities, and representatives of the sect were to be found in every town in Palestine. Some even permitted themselves to take part in worldly affairs, and occupied positions of influence under the Government; for they were highly trusted because of their honesty, and it was one of their principles to be loyal to all authority, " for no one can hold authority without God's help." [3] All were under the rule of a strict organisation, and owed obedience to their elected presidents, or bishops (ἐπιμεληταί).[4] They were much given to travelling from one community to another, carrying, however, neither wallet nor money, but dwelling in each town with their brethren. None could receive their baptism or partake of their communion until he had undergone a period of probation and been thoroughly instructed in the tenets of the sect. After their day's work they donned white linen garments and partook of their meals in common and sacramentally, the food having been prepared by priests and been duly blessed and consecrated. They regarded that communion as of more value than sacrifices in the temple at Jerusalem.[5] " Their love of virtue revealed itself in their indiffer-ence to money, worldly position and pleasure, their love of man in their kindliness, their equality, their fellowship passing all words." [6] They succoured the afflicted, pitied all men, and fed the poor, and " were anxious to assist all those who are heavy laden." [7] They bound themselves " in no way to injure anyone, and not

and which, notwithstanding their elevated principles of universal charity, detested one another mortally (Hippolytus, *Refutatio omnium Haeresium*, ix. 21 ; Epiphanius, *op. cit.*, x. col. 232). " The aforesaid sects—namely, Essaeans, Dosithaeans, Daily Baptists, Nazarenes—arose before the coming of Our Lord. They flourished until the coming of Christ, and afterwards from that time until the destruction of Jerusalem by Titus " (Epiphanius, *op. cit.*, iv. v. coll. 280. 268 ; cf. Philaster, *De Haeresibus*, iv, viii, ix).

[1] Philo Judaeus, " Quod omnis probus liber," *Opera*, vol. ii, p. 457.

[2] Id., in Eusebius, *Praepartio evangelica*, viii. xi. 4. 10 sqq. ; Josephus, *De bell. Jud.*, ii. 8. 4 sqq.

[3] Hippolytus, *Refutatio omnium Haeresium*, ix. 18.

[4] Josephus, *De Bell. Jud.*, ii. 8. 6.

[5] Id., *ibid.*, 8. 5 ; Id., *Antiq.*, xviii. 1. 5 ; Hippolytus, *op. cit.*, ix. 16.

[6] Philo, *op cit.*, vol. ii, p. 458.

[7] Hippolytus, *op. cit.*, ix. 17.

to hate those who injured them, or be hostile to them, but to pray for them."[1] They scrupled to swear, and were on that account specially exempted by the Government from taking oaths.[2] Nor would they call anyone ' Lord,' but God only.[3]

All Essaean sects accepted the Jewish Scriptures, which they read and expounded, using, however, great freedom of criticism, adducing corruptions and interpolations, and even in some instances rejecting the authority of whole portions of the Pentateuch. They interpreted the Old Testament in a mantic and mystic manner, using allegories and parables, and holding the principle that the letter killeth, but the spirit giveth life.[4] They had, in addition, their own collection of sacred writings, which they held secret, and it was the duty of appointed members to preserve them carefully.[5] The Essaeans and Nazarenes regarded themselves as orthodox Jews, and were so regarded until, after the fall of Jerusalem, which they were said to have predicted, differences between them and the orthodox parties became more accentuated.

---

[1] Hippolytus, *op. cit.*, ix. 18.

[2] Josephus, *Antiq.*, xv. 10. 4.

[3] Id., *ibid.*, xviii. 1. 5 ; Hippolytus, *op. cit.*, ix. 17. 21 ; Philo, vol. ii, p. 457.

[4] Epiphanius, *op. cit.*, x, col. 231 ; xxix, col. 401 ; xxx. 18, col. 436 ; Philo, *Opera*, vol. ii, p. 458.

[5] Josephus, *De Bello Judaico*, ii. 8. 7. One of their sacred books was that known as the ' Book of Elxai ' (the fragments have been collected by A. Hilgenfeld, *Hermae Pastor ; Elxai libri Fragmenta*, Berlin, 1881), which was equally esteemed by Essaeans, Nazarenes, and Ebionim (Epiphanius, *op. cit.*, liii). It presents a striking similarity to the so-called Clementine Homilies, which, indeed, we are told were used by the Ebionim (Epiphanius, *op. cit.*, xxx. 15, coll. 429, 432). The author of the latter work, which was ascribed to the first pope of the Catholic Church, was obviously familiar with, and recognised the authority of, the Nazarene tractate, which, however, is much older. (For the question of date, see J. G. W. Uhlhorn, *Die Homilien und Recognitionen des Clemens Romanus*, p. 392.) The Essaeans and Nazarenes were very learned, and composed books, all their writings being in Hebrew (Aramaic). Epiphanius states that the Nazarenes used the New Testament (*op. cit.*, xxxix. 7) ; as it was not in existence, this can only be understood to refer to books similar to the Gospels. And in fact we are told that they possessed the Gospel according to St. Matthew, and their version of the work was generally held to be the original. St. Jerome translated it into Greek and Latin ; but as it differed substantially from the Catholic tradition, it was deemed unwise to publish it (Jerome, *Dialogus adversus Pelagius*, iii. 2, in Migne, *op. cit.*, *Series Latina*, vol. xxiii, col. 570 ; *Commentarium in Evangelium Matthiae*, xii. 13, *ibid.*, vol. xxvi, col. 78). This Gospel is thought by some to be the same as the ' Gospel according to the Hebrews ' (R. A. Lipsius, art. " Gospels, Apocryphal," in W. Smith and H. Wace, *Dictionary of Christian Biography*, vol. ii, p. 710) ; but others, apparently with better reason, regard the Nazarene ' Matthew ' as having been an entirely different work (A. Hilgenfeld, *Evangeliorum secundum Hebraeos*, etc., *quae supersunt*, pp. 15 sqq., 33 sq.).

They observed circumcision, but they refused to offer burnt sacrifices in the Temple.[1] The ritual observance to which they attached chief importance was baptism, which they used daily, being thence called Daily Baptists (Hemero-Baptisti). They regarded water as the medium of divine life, and as bestowing spiritual immortality and the remission of sins.[2] The doctrines of the Essaeans and Nazarenes contained no elements extraneous to Judaism. Their interpretation of Jewish religion evaded, however, to a large extent what had been the Yahwistic reformers' chief aim, the exclusion of conceptions associated with the agricultural Tammuz cults. " Must we then do whatever things we did when we were idolaters ? " the disciple is represented as asking. To which the teacher replies : " Verily I say unto you, not all things, but whatsoever you did well you must do now, and more." [3] Yahweh retained his unchangeable character and unity, but he was duplicated in a Logos, who was " not God, but the Son of God," [4] and to whom the religious themes which the prophetic reformers had been at such pains to put down were freely applied. Deeply tinged as their doctrines were with ' Gnostic ' conceptions, there was no need to go outside Palestine and Babylonia for these. The Messianic visions and prophecies

[1] Josephus, *Antiq.*, xviii. 1. 5 ; Hippolytus, *op. cit.*, ix. 17. 21 ; Philo, *Opera*, vol. ii, p. 457 ; Epiphanius, *op. cit.*, xix. 3, coll. 265. Cf. *Clementine Homilies*, iii. 45.

[2] Josephus, *De Bello Judaico*, ii. 8. 5 ; Id., *Antiq.*, xviii. 1. 5 ; Hippolytus, *op. cit.*, ix. 16 ; Epiphanius, *op. cit.*, xvii, col. 256 ; xxx, coll. 408. 432 ; xliii, col. 960. The ' Book of Elxai ' taught that whatever sins a man might have committed, " if only he be a believer, he should by baptism receive remission of sins " (Hippolytus, *op. cit.*, ix. 8. Cf. *Clementine Homilies*, vii. 8 : " To be baptised for the remission of sins, and thus by this pure baptism to be born again unto God by the saving water ; to wash after sexual intercourse "). The Waters of Life were opposed to the Fire of Sacrifice ; thus, again, ' Elxai ' taught : " My sons go not to the image of fire, for thereby would ye err ; go rather to the voice of Water " (Epiphanius, *op. cit.*, xix. 3, col. 265. Cf. *Clementine Homilies*, xi. 26 : " Flee to the Water, for this alone can quench the violence of Fire ; unless ye be regenerated by Living Water, you shall not enter the Kingdom of Heaven "). The ' Clementine Homilies ' refer to John the Baptist as " John, a Hemerobaptist " (ii. 23). The Baptists continued to honour the memory of " Al-'Hasaih " in the tenth century (D. A. Chwolsohn, *Die Ssabier und der Ssabismus*, vol. ii, pp. 543 sqq., quoting Muhammad ibn Ish'aq en Nedim ; A. Hilgenfeld, *Ketzergeschichte des Urchristenthums*, p. 232) ; and the same rites and conceptions are current at the present day among the Mandaya, or Mandaeans, of Mesopotamia and Persian Khusistan. They are called by the Arabs ' Zubba,' that is, Baptists, and claim to be disciples of John the Baptist, but know nothing of Jesus Christ (A. J. W. Brandt, *Die mandäische Religion*, pp. 9, 83, 141, 177 sq.).

[3] *Clementine Homilies*, xi. 31.

[4] *Ibid.*, xvi. 15. Cf. Epiphanius, *op. cit.*, liii, col. 960.

of the Jewish seers themselves supplied the material of Essaean apocalyptic Christology. They likened the Son of God, after the manner of the times, to the sun, and pronounced each morning the formula, " He is risen." [1] They are said by Josephus to have " honoured their legislator most of all after God himself." [2] They

---

[1] Josephus, *De Bello Judaico*, ii. 8. 5. The sects which used the ' Book of Elxai '—namely, the Essaeans, Ebionim, Nazarenes—ascribed a particular symbolic significance to the sun, and they are called by Epiphanius ' Heliaci,' sun-worshippers, or Samsaeans, after Samson, that is, Shamash, the sun (Epiphanius, *op. cit.*, liii. 2 ; cf. xxix. 5). There is no ground for regarding their so-called sun-worship as other than mystically symbolic. The Therapeuts of Alexandria are also described by Philo as offering prayers at dawn and even " that their minds might be filled with the heavenly light, the real sunshine " (Philo, *De Vita Contemplativa*, p. 893). The Messiah, as early as the second century B.C., was regularly likened to the sun (*The Testaments of the Twelve Patriarchs, Testament of Levi*, xviii, ed. R. H. Charles, pp. 62 sq.). The early Christians, who, like the Essaeans, turned to the East when praying, held their feasts on Sun-days, associated the death of Christ with an eclipse of the sun, and later celebrated His birthday on the Mithraic ' Natalis dies solis,' were likewise held by the pagans to be sun-worshippers (Tertullian, *Apologia*, xvi). Indeed, Christ was always assimilated to the sun. The Clementine Homilies state that the disciples of John, the Hemerobaptist, looked upon Jesus as the sun, and that he had therefore twelve apostles, whereas they regarded John the Baptist as the moon, and he accordingly had thirty disciples, or, more precisely, twenty-nine and a half, one being a woman, " for a woman, being half a man, made up the number of the triacontad, as with the moon whose revolution does not make the complete course of the month " (*Clementine Homilies*, ii. 23).

[2] Josephus, *De Bello Judaico*, ii. 8. 9. It was usual to ascribe to every sect a ' legislator,' or ' founder,' in the same manner as the social constitution of the Spartans was set down to the legislation of Lykurgus, Greek Orphism to Orpheus, Judaism to Moses. The ' Book of Elxai,' that is, ' of the Hidden Mind, or Meaning,' was regarded as having been written by a certain Elxai, or Elketai, and a birthplace was even invented for this supposed ' founder,' a village of ' Elkesei ' in Galilee (Jerome, *Commentarium in Nahum*, i. 1). The ' Poor ' were provided with an eponymous ' founder,' and circumstantial biographies of this ' Poor Man ' were reproduced until not very long ago by quite serious writers, with disparaging remarks on the ' historical sense ' of those who doubted his existence. The Essaeans and Nazarenes honoured a number of traditional personages, whom they regarded as successive incarnations of the Son of God, beginning with Adam, the first Christ, down to " Jesus, the son of Nun," that is to say, Joshua, the son of the Fish (Epiphanius, *op. cit.*, xviii. 1, col. 257 ; xxx. 3, col. 409). Joshua, who was, like the Messiah, associated with the Great Fish, or Leviathan (see above, vol. ii, p. 167), was regarded by the Jews as the second promulgator of the Law ; " Moses received the Torah on Sinai, and handed it down to Joshua, Joshua to the Elders " (*Authorised Daily Prayer Book of the United Hebrew Congregations*, edited and translated by the Rev. S. Singer, p. 184). " Only one Son of Man hath brought Israel into the Promised Land, Joshua, the son of the Fish, the son of Joseph " (*Beresit Rabba*, 97, cited by I. Scheftlowitz, " Das Fischsymbol im Judentum und Christentum," *Archiv für Religionswissenschaft*, xiv, p. 4). The Messiah Joshua, or, in Greek,

held that at his next coming he would appear as the recognised ruler of the Kingdom of Heaven. They believed in a day of judgment, when their bodies should put on incorruptibility and the wicked receive eternal punishment, and they prophesied that the world was about to be destroyed in a universal conflagration.[1]

Some of the Essaeans practised celibacy. Speaking of an Essaean coenobitic community on the shores of the Dead Sea,

Jesus Christ (cf. *Acts*, vii. 45; *Hebrews*, iv. 8), the son of Joseph, was thus regarded by the Essaean sects as the successor of Moses and the Son of God. In other mentions of the Essaean or Ebionite doctrine, the last incarnation of the Christ, instead of being given as " Joshua, the son of the Fish," is identified with Jesus Christ (Epiphanius, *op. cit.*, xxx. 3, col. 409; cf. Hyppolytus, *Refutatio omnium haeresium*, x. 35).

[1] Josephus, *De Bello Judaico*, ii. 8. 11; Hippolytus, *op. cit.*, ix. 22. The relation suggested by the views and principles of the Essaean sects to Nazarenism, or, as it was called later, Christianity, which no one has ever supposed to have originated among the Pharisees or Sadducees, is more definitely exhibited by historical documents such as the following. The Nazarenes " scarcely differed in anything from the Essaean sects " (Philaster, *De haeresibus*, ix.; cf. xvii.). " The sect of the Essaeans was intimately interwoven (παραπεπλεγμένη) with that just mentioned "—the Nazarenes (Epiphanius, *op. cit.*, xix. i, coll. 260 sq.). " The sect of the Nazarenes preceded Christ and did not know Christ. But all Christians were regarded as Nazarenes " (*ibid.*, xxix. 6, col. 400). " They did not call themselves Nazarenes after Christ, or after Jesus. All Christians were at that time called Nazarenes, although for a while they bore the name of Iessaeans . . . either after Jesse who was the father of David, or after Jesus Christ, Our Lord. Or they may have been so called after the etymology of Our Lord's name, for Jesus means in the Hebrew tongue Therapeut, that is, Healer or Saviour " (*ibid.*, xxix. 1, 4, 5, coll. 389, 397). According to Eusebius, the Therapeuts of Egypt formed the first Christian Church in that country (Eusebius, *Historia Ecclesiastica*, ii. 17, in Migne, *Patrologia Graeca*, vol. xx, col. 181). Epiphanius endeavours to draw a distinction between ' Nasarene ' and ' Nazarene,' as later writers have between ' Nazarene ' and ' Nazarite,' but as Father Petavius observes, " he scarcely succeeds in persuading us that the ones were different from the others " (note to Epiphanius, *ed. cit.*, col. 387). The denomination ' Nazarene,' or ' Nazarite,' which means ' dedicated ' or ' consecrated,' was a very ancient one among the Jews (see *Numbers*, vi. 2 sqq.; H. Ewald, *The Antiquities of Israel*, pp. 84 sqq.). The sun-hero of the Essaeans, Samson, was a Nazarene (*Judges*, xvi. 17). John the Baptist was a Nazarene (*Luke*, i. 15). Paul was " a ringleader of the Nazarenes " (*Acts*, xiv. 5). No place of the name of Nazareth is known to Palestinian geography before the fourth century A.D., although over sixty-three names of towns and villages in Galilee are recorded. By a play on words, such as the Jews delighted in, the term ' Nazar ' may have been assimilated to ' najjar,' the current Semitic word for ' carpenter,' thus giving rise to the late tradition representing Christ as a carpenter (cf. S. Krauss, *Das Leben Jesu nach jüdischen Quellen*, pp. 253 sqq.; T. K. Cheyne, art. " Joseph," in *Encyclopaedia Biblica*, vol. ii, p. 2598). The term ' Christian ' is Gentile, and was not used until after the foundation of the Church at Antioch (Epiphanius, *op. cit.*, xxix. 1; Tertullian, *Adversus Marcionem*, xlviii.).

Pliny says : "They live without women, renouncing sexual love
. . . yet their numbers are kept up, and day by day renewed;
for many who are weary of battling with the rough seas of life
flock to them from afar. Thus, strange as it may sound, their
race has been perpetuated, though no man is ever born in it, for
thousands of years." [1] "No Essene marries," says Philo, "but
all practise continence; for women are selfish and jealous, and
apt to pervert men's moral dispositions, and to bring them into
subjection by their coaxings and their wiles." [2] A Jewish community of Iessaeans, or Therapeuts, near Alexandria, which Philo
joined for a time, about the year A.D. 10, admitted both men and
women, who participated together in their communal meals, hymns
and religious dances, but lived in separate "monasteries."
"Women also share in their feasts," he says, "most of whom
have grown old in virginity, preserving their purity not from
necessity, like some priestesses among the Greeks, but rather of
their own free-will, through their zealous love of wisdom, to which
they are so eager to devote their lives that they pay no attention
to the pleasures of the body. Their longing is not for mortal
children, but for a deathless progeny which the soul that is in
love with God can alone bring forth." [3] The Dositheans, who are
described as disciples of John the Baptist,[4] but who were in
existence in 150 B.C.,[5] were noted among Essaean sects for their
asceticism. "They lived in continence after the death of their
wives; some of them preserved their virginity." [6]

That abstinence was not, however, general among the Essaeans.
Many of them married and lived with their families. "They do
not absolutely deny the fitness of marriage and the propagation of
mankind by its means," says Josephus, "but they guard against
the lascivious behaviour of women, and are persuaded that none
preserves her fidelity to one man. . . . They condemn sensual
desires as sinful." [7] In order to justify the purpose of marriage
for the propagation of the species, some Essaean sects practised
trial-marriage, marrying a woman only if after three years she
had proved her fertility.[8]

---

[1] Pliny, *Nat. Hist.*, v. 17.

[2] Philo, in Eusebius, *Praeparatio evangelica*, viii. ii. 14 sqq. Cf. Josephus,
Antiq., xviii. 8. 5 ; Hippolytus, *op. cit.*, ix. 13.

[3] Philo, *De Vita Contemplativa*, viii.

[4] *Clementine Homilies*, ii. 24.

[5] T. G. J. Juynboll, *Chronicon Samaritanum*, pp. 112, 114 ; Philaster,
De Haeresibus, iv.

[6] Epiphanius, *op. cit.*, xiii, col. 237.

[7] Josephus, *De Bell. Jud.*, ii. 8. 2.

[8] *Ibid.*, ii. 8. 13. There are indications that the Essaeans, as well as
the early Palestinian Christians themselves, continued to observe the traditional rites of ceremonial licence. They attached great importance to

The explanations given of the celibacy practised by Essaean sects show that their motives were not generally understood. They differed in a fundamental manner from the grounds upon which other Eastern ascetics practised continence. With the latter, chastity was but a form of self-mortification which entitled the ascetic to compensation by magical powers. With the Jews the conceptions of ritual purity and of defilement had supplanted that of self-mortification. Ritual purity not being regarded by them, as by most peoples, as a special qualification of priestly or tabu persons in the exercise of their functions, but as necessary for all men at all times, that condition of ritual purity came hence to be accounted a quality of personal character and equivalent to morality. Jewish Law enumerated with minute detail the sources of infection by which a man might be defiled, and which necessitated his purification by means of Holy Water containing the ashes of a red heifer without blemish.[1] The preparation of that purifying water impregnated with the divine essence of the Bull of Israel entailed precautions more elaborate than any procedure of modern aseptic surgery ; and doubt was always entertained as to whether every source of contamination had been successfully excluded. The priest who carried out the final stages of the operation was, in Jerusalem, insulated in mid-air on a specially constructed bridge.[2] The Essaeans regarded the methods of the Pharisees as superficial, and aimed at outdoing them in compassing ritual purity ; not only should purity extend to the soul as well as to outward actions, but defilement should, as regards the latter, be more thoroughly avoided. On joining the communion, the Essaeans were supplied with a spade, which they always carried with them. " When they wish to relieve nature they dig a small pit a foot deep with the spade that is given them at their first admittance. They cover themselves round with their garment that they may not offend the divine rays of the sun, and ease themselves in the pit, after which they put back the earth which they dug out of it. And this they do in a remote spot only, chosen for the purpose ; and although easement of the body be natural, yet it is a rule with them to undergo ablution immediately after, as if they had been defiled." [3] Sexual intercourse constituted defilement according

attending the yearly festival at Mambre, where there was a sacred tree which was assimilated to the Heavenly Vine. The festival, at which hierodules officiated in sacred brothels, was put down by Constantine on account of the scandalous disorders (Sozomenus, *Historia Ecclesiastica*, ii. 4 ; Epiphanius, *op. cit.*, xviii. 2).

[1] *Numbers*, xix. 2 sqq.

[2] *Mishnah Tohoroth, Parah*, iii. 6.

[3] Josephus, *De Bello Judaico*, ii. 8. 9 ; cf. Hippolytus, *op. cit.*, ix. 20. The

to Levitical Law,[1] in the same manner as any other form of pollution. The consumption of animal food was also regarded by the Essaeans as defiling, and vegetarianism was long looked upon by the early Christians as a moral virtue of the same nature as chastity. " Among ourselves, vegetarianism is regarded as a harmless eccentricity," remarks Dr. Salmon, " but in early times of Christianity, even those who used animal food themselves came to think of the vegetarian as one who lived a higher life, and approached more nearly to Christian perfection."[2]

The conceptions of ritual purity and of defilement, or sin, thus differed entirely from the Oriental notion of asceticism, and led to a view of the moral merit of chastity unlike any which had previously been held. But chastity did not at first occupy the paramount place which subsequently came to be assigned to it as a moral quality. The difficulty of avoiding all defilement, and the incompatibility between natural functions and perfect purity perplexed the Essaeans ; hence the importance which they attached to baptism, by which purity could be restored. Many Essaeans held that to abstain from procreating the image of God was as sinful as the pollution of sexual intercourse.[3] According to Epiphanius, the author of the ' Book of Elxai ' " detested virginity, condemned continence, and prescribed marriage."[4] The language of Epiphanius is coloured by denunciatory zeal ; what he appears to refer to is the statement that whatever impurity might have been contracted through incontinence, " a believer would by baptism obtain the remission of sin."[5] There is, however, no special horror of unchastity and no trace of the exaltation of virginity in anything that we know of early Nazarene thought. In the Clementine Homilies, chastity is spoken of in the sense of connubial fidelity on the part of married women ; the joys of married life and of family affection are dwelt upon in the most charming human tone, early marriage and the marriage of all

procedure described is merely the observance of the regulations laid down in *Deuteronomy*, xxiv. 12–13. The directions for the use of Pharisees are far more elaborate and circumstantial ; a whole chapter of the tractate Berakot is devoted to a minute discussion of the rules to be observed by an orthodox Jew in a privy (*Berakot*, iii., transl. A. Cohen, pp. 150 sqq. ; cf. pp. 408 sqq.).

[1] *Leviticus*, xv. 18.

[2] G. Salmon, *A Historical Introduction to the Study of the Books of the New Testament*, p. 185.

[3] Hippolytus, *op. cit.*, ix. 23.

[4] Epiphanius, *op. cit.*, xix. 1, col. 261.

[5] Hippolytus, *op. cit.*, ix. 8. The contrast between those views and the later Christian doctrine is shown by the indignation with which they are reported by the Christian Fathers.

priests are strongly insisted on.[1] In the Gospels no special stress is laid on chastity and there is no denunciation of unchastity.[2]

Not until Christianity had extended beyond the Palestinian country-side to populous Roman cities did the conception of sexual purity assume a significance unknown in any previous stage of the world's history. The senses, the flesh, the world had not been clearly perceived to be incompatible with holiness until the pursuit of it as a necessary means of salvation had spread beyond the seclusion of rural communities and the peaceful retreats of the Orient into the heart of a complex civilisation, where sexuality was stimulated by the opulence, the contrasts, and the luxury of advanced culture. Saturninus, who drew large crowds to the Church of Antioch towards the beginning of the second century, declaring that " marriage and procreation are of Satan," and persuading his followers to adopt vegetarianism and celibacy,[3] is thought to have been the first to introduce such doctrines " among those who called themselves Christians." [4] As Christianity spread among the highly strung populations of the Eastern cities of the Roman Empire, the conflict between the ideal of ritual purity and the sensuous stimulation of a luxurious civilisation became enormously accentuated. In proportion to the difficulty of the task, sexual purity became emphasised above all other requirements of holiness, and chastity came to be regarded as the supreme virtue upon which every other moral quality depended. That stress laid on chastity was the direct outcome of an overstimulated sensuality ; it was a protest against the difficulties which the latter placed in the way of holiness. The fierceness with which the sexual instincts were denounced bears witness to the power which they wielded. " How often," says St. Jerome, " when I was living in the desert and the solitude that affords hermits a savage dwelling-place, parched by a burning sun, how often did I fancy myself amid the pleasures of Rome ! I sought

[1] *Clementine Homilies*, iii. 48 ; xiii. 13 sqq., 18.

[2] *Matthew*, xix. 12, is manifestly figurative. *Matthew*, v. 28, has reference to adultery, not to ritual purity, and implies no more than was contained in current Jewish ideas. *Berakot*, iii. 5, has : " He who gazes at the little finger of a woman is as though he had gazed at her nakedness (or had connection with her) " (ed. A. Cohen, p. 157 ; cf. E. Screiber, *Die Principen des Judenthums verglichen mit denen des Christenthums*, pp. 192 sqq.).

[3] Hippolytus, *op. cit.*, vii. 16. Cf. Irenaeus, *Contra Haereses*, i. 28, in Migne, *op. cit., Series Graeca*, vol. vii, col. 690 ; *I Timothy*, iv. 3.

[4] G. Salmon, art. " Saturninus," in W. Smith and H. Wace, *Dictionary of Christian Biography*, vol. iv, p. 587. As Mr. Mead remarks, " Protestant theologians especially regard encratism as a heretical practice ; but there seems no sufficient reason for assuming that so common a feature of religious life can be traced to any particular teacher " (G. R. S. Mead, *Fragments of a Faith Forgotten*, p. 178).

solitude because I was filled with bitterness. Sackcloth disfigured my misshapen limbs and my skin had become by neglect as black as an Ethiopian's. Tears and groans were every day my portion. I, who from fear of hell had consigned myself to that prison where I had no other companions but scorpions and wild beasts, fancied myself amongst bevies of young girls. My face was pale and my frame chilled with fasting; yet my mind was burning with the cravings of desire, and the fires of lust flared up from my flesh that was as that of a corpse. I do not blush to avow my abject misery. . . . So long as we are borne down by this frail body, so long as we have treason within this earthly vessel, so long as the flesh lusteth against the spirit and the spirit against the flesh, there can be no sure victory." [1]

The sexual aspect of holiness came to eclipse all other issues, and morality came to mean, what it has ever since connoted in European tradition, sexual purity. Athanasius declared that the appreciation of virginity and of chastity, which had never before been regarded as meritorious, was the one supreme revelation and blessing brought into the world by Jesus Christ.[2] Sexual continence was not only regarded as of the same importance as the most essential doctrines of the Christian faith and the principles of Christian ethics, but it was proclaimed to be the chief of all virtues, and the first and indispensable condition of righteousness and of faith itself.[3] "A stain upon our chastity," said Tertullian, " is accounted by us as more dreadful than any punishment or any death." [4] " The Kingdom of Heaven," he proclaimed, " is thrown open to eunuchs." [5] Origen castrated himself.[6] Numerous Christians adopted the same course; surgeons were besieged with requests to perform the operation.[7] In the literature of apocryphal Acts of the Apostles which issued from the Churches of Asia Minor in the second century, " the married life is treated as absolutely unlawful. The Apostolic preachers are represented as having done

---

[1] Jerome, *Epistola*, xxii. 7. 4, in Migne, *Patrologiae Cursus completus, Series prima*, vol. xxii, cols. 398, 396.

[2] Athanasius, *In passionem et crucem Domini*, xxx., in Migne, *Patrologiae Cursus completus, Series Graeca*, vol. xxviii, col. 236. Cf. Id., *De virginitate, ibid.*, col. 279; Ambrose, *De virginibus, ibid., Series prima*, vol. xiv, coll. 192 sqq.

[3] Ambrose, *Commentaria in epistola ad Corinthiis prima*, in Migne, *op. cit.*, vol. xvii, coll. 221 sq.

[4] Tertullian, *Apologeticus*, in Migne, *op. cit., Series prima*, vol. i, col. 535.

[5] Id., *De monogamia*, iii., in Migne, *op. cit.*, vol. iii, col. 932.

[6] Eusebius, *Historia ecclesiastica*, vi. 8.

[7] Justin, *Apologia I pro Christianos*, xxix., in Migne, *op. cit., Series Graeca*, vol. vi, col. 373; Origen, *in Matt.*, xv. 1. This was a penal offence under Roman law (Suetonius, *Domitian*, vii.), and the Roman Government refused to sanction the practice.

a good work when a couple about to unite in wedlock have been prevailed on to abandon the design, or when a wife has been persuaded to refuse further intercourse with her husband. The persecution which the Christian preachers met with is frequently represented as arising from the natural resentment of husbands at such teaching." [1] No act of a married woman calls forth more admiration from the writers than her deserting her husband. It is denied that married persons, or any persons who have been guilty of sexual intercourse, can share in the resurrection.[2] Woman was regarded not as ' impure ' only, but as the obstacle to purity, the temptress, the enemy ; she was " the gate of Hell." [3] " Every woman," says Clement of Alexandria, " ought to be filled with shame at the thought that she is a woman." [4] St. Jerome pours scorn upon motherhood, " the tumefaction of the uterus, the care of yelling infants, all those fond feelings which death at last cuts short." [5]

The importance, the necessity of chastity was inconsistent with compromise. Tertullian insisted in lengthy arguments that marriage was nothing but fornication, and that captious distinctions drawn between it and adultery were mere legal fictions.[6] St. Ambrose said that " married people ought to blush at the state in which they are living." He argued that men and women were born in a state of virginity, and that to change that state was to deface the work of the Creator.[7] Jerome said that to do so was equivalent to prostituting the members of Christ.[8] The superficial sophism that men and women would not have been created with organs of generation had these been intended to remain functionless, was readily disposed of. Bishop Gregory of Nyssa held that Adam and Eve had, at first, been created sexless, and that the phrase " Male and female created He them " referred to a subsequent act necessitated by Adam's disobedience ; had this not taken place the human race would have been propagated by some harmless

---

[1] G. Salmon, *A Historical Introduction to the Study of the Books of the New Testament*, p. 327.

[2] *Ibid.*, pp. 333, 340. The Apostle John is represented in Christian tradition as having been on three occasions prevented from marrying by the direct interposition of Christ (*Acta Joannis*, ed. T. Zahn, p. 247).

[3] Tertullian, *De cultu faeminarum*, in Migne, *op. cit., Series prima*, vol. i, col. 1305.

[4] Clement of Alexandria, *Paedagogus*, ii. 2, in Migne, *op. cit., Series Graeca*, vol. viii, col. 429.

[5] Jerome, *Epistola*, xxii. 2, in Migne, *op. cit., Series prima*, vol. xxii, col. 395.

[6] Tertullian, *Liber de exhortatione castitatis*, ix., in Migne, *op. cit.*, vol. ii, coll. 924 sq.

[7] Ambrose, *Exhortatio virginitatis*, in Migne, *op. cit.*, vol. xvi, col. 346.

[8] Jerome, *Epistola*, xxii., in Migne, *op. cit.*, vol. xxii, col. 397.

mode of vegetation.[1] The view was endorsed by John of Damascus.[2] The logical consequences of the advocacy of virginity were faced without hesitation ; both Ambrose and Tertullian declared that the extinction of the human race was preferable to its propagation by sexual intercourse.[3] " What is better," said Tertullian, " than the good which we learn from the apostle who, indeed, permitteth to marry, but preferreth abstinence, the one because of the snares of temptation, the other because of the distress of the times ; which reasons being considered, it is easily discerned that the power to marry hath been granted to us through necessity. But what is yielded through necessity is lowered in value. Lastly, whereas it is written ' It is better to marry than to burn,' what sort of a good is this, pr'ythee, that is recommended by comparing it with an evil ? So that it is better to marry only because it is worse to burn ; but how much better, then, neither to marry nor to burn ! Men make themselves new pretexts for marriage in their anxiety for descendants, in the pleasure, so bitter, of children. With us this is idle. Whether marriage be for the sake of the flesh, or of the world, or of having descendants, not one of those reasons applies to the servants of God." [4]

These views were not, as has sometimes been represented, exceptional and extreme opinions. It would be hard to find many Christian writers in the first four centuries who have not composed a tractate in laudation of virginity ; and none speaks of marriage and family affection in the human tone of the Ebionite Clementine Homilies. There was division of opinion and much controversy on the question whether marriage was permissible or not, and several of the Fathers protested against the view that it is incompatible with the profession of the Christian religion ; but they were one and all agreed in regarding it as an evil, albeit a necessary evil. Clement of Alexandria devotes a whole book, the third, of his ' Stromata,' to combating the view that marriage is incompatible with salvation, but he has no doubt as to celibacy being infinitely superior and as to woman being the

[1] Gregorius Nyssenus, *De hominis opificio*, in Migne, *op. cit.*, *Series Graeca*, vol. xliv, col. 185.

[2] John of Damascus, *De fide orthodoxa*, iv. 24, in Migne, *op. cit.*, *Series Graeca*, vol. xciv, col. 1208. This was proved by pointing out that before the Fall Adam and Eve were not ashamed, which could not have been possible had they possessed reproductive organs, whereas after the Fall " they saw that they were naked." Jerome demonstrates that the organs of generation are the abode, if not the creation, of the devil (Jerome, *Epistola*, xxii. 11, in Migne, *op. cit.*, *Series prima*, vol. xxii, coll. 400 sq.).

[3] Ambrose, *Exhortatio virginitatis*, in Migne, *op. cit.*, vol. xvi, cols. 343 sqq. ; Tertullian, *Ad uxorem*, ix. 3. 5, in Migne, *op. cit.*, vol. i, col. 1278.

[4] Tertullian, *loc. cit.*

tool of Satan.[1] Cyril of Jerusalem was the most determined
opponent of those who disputed the permissibility of marriage ;
yet he pleaded that " one must not condemn marriage, but virginity
is better," and declared that through it men were made the equals
of angels.   His position was identical with that of Tertullian, save
that he regarded human nature as unequal to the task.[2] John
Chrysostom was among the most moderate of the Christian
Fathers.   He concludes his discussion of the question by saying :
" Marriage is good, but virginity is better than marriage. If
you would have my candid opinion on the matter, it is that I
consider virginity to be as high above marriage as the heavens
are above the earth." [3] In a subsequent age Thomas Aquinas
reiterated that virginity alone can make men equal to angels,
and declared that it was as much above chastity as magnificence
is above liberality.[4] The principles of the Fathers were confirmed
by the decrees of Synods,[5] and are embodied in the canon of the
Council of Trent, in which it is laid down that, " Whosoever saith
that the marriage state is to be placed above the state of virginity,
or of celibacy, and that it is not better and more blessed to remain
in virginity, or in celibacy, than to enter matrimony, let him be
anathema." [6]

---

[1] Clement of Alexandria, *Stromata*, vii. 12, in Migne, *Patrologia Graeca*,
vol. ix, coll. 497, 499 ; cf. N. Le Nourry, *Dissertationes de omnibus Clementis
Alexandrini Operibus*, *ibid.*, pp. 1181 sq.

[2] Cyril of Jerusalem, *Catechesis vi de Uno Deo*, in Migne, *op. cit.*, *Series
Graeca*, vol. xxxiii, col. 601.   Cf. *Catechesis xii de Christo Incarnato*, xxxiv,
ibid., col. 766 ; L. Ellies-Du Pin, *Nouvelle bibliothèque des auteurs ecclésiastiques*, vol. ii, p. 137.

[3] John Chrysostom, *De virginitate*, ix, in Migne, *op. cit.*, *Series Graeca*,
vol. xlviii, col. 540.   Cf. *De non iterando conjugio*, i, *ibid.*, coll. 611, 614 ;
L. Ellies-Du Pin, *op. cit.*, vol. iii, p. 35.   See also, Augustine, *De sanctis
virginibus*, xiv ; Migne, *op. cit.*, vol. xl, coll. 402 sq. ; Id., *De bono viduitatis*,
xi sq., *ibid.*, vol. xix, coll. 431 sq., 445 ; Cyprian, *De habitu virginarum*, xxiii,
op. cit., vol. iv, col. 463.

[4] Thomas Aquinas, *Summa Theologica*, II. ii, quaest. clii, art. iii, *Opera*,
vol. iii, col. 1063.

[5] *Concilium Gangrense*, can. i ; *Consilium Mediolanense*, A.D. 390, in
Ph. Labbe, *Sacrorum Conciliorum Collectio*, vol. ii, p. 1106, vol. iii, pp. 689 sq.

[6] *Canones et decreta Concilii Tridentini*, Sess. xxiv, can. x.

CHAPTER XXVIII

ROMANCE

*Sex Morality among the
European Barbarians.*

IT is not without interest to follow the effects of the Christian conceptions of sexual morality upon the barbarian peoples who were destined to become the heirs of Western civilisation. No more incongruous contact of radically opposite cultural elements, as of burning lava with water, could be imagined than that of the products of Eastern ritualism and asceticism imported into Mediterranean culture with the social, ethical, and traditional ideas and usages of the northern Teutonic and Celtic populations of Europe. Something of the conceptions which, among the latter, governed the relation of the sexes has already been noted. Those societies were as yet little removed from matriarchal traditions. Their sagas, the scraps of information out of which a picture of their social life may be constructed, show the presentment of free, masterful women, often holding the position of queens or chieftainesses, commonly exercising the functions of priestesses, almost invariably conceived as endowed with magic attributes and powers. Their lovers, or husbands, come to them at their invitation, and are dismissed at their pleasure. Marriage, in the case of chieftains, was almost invariably an economic transaction into which no other motives entered, and it mattered not at all whether the lady whose possessions were desired was a maid, a widow, or was already actually married. The latter was commonly the case. When, for instance, Kilydd, a British king, bethought himself of getting married, he " took counsel where he should find a wife. Said one of his counsellors, ' I know a wife that will suit thee well, and she is the wife of King Doged.' And they resolved to go and seek her ; and they slew the king, and brought away his wife and one daughter that she had along with her. And they conquered the king's lands." [1] The procedure is representative of the marriage

[1] *The Mabinogion*, translated by Lady Charlotte Guest (ed. A. Nutt), p. 102.

transactions met with in Celtic records. When a marriage was not founded upon economic considerations, but on love, it was frankly regarded as a temporary and provisional arrangement. In an Irish saga, Fionn, being the guest of the chieftain Eanna, is dazzled by the beauty of his daughter, the fair Sgâthach, and in fact falls passionately in love with her at first sight. He there and then asks her hand in marriage, offering two hundred head of cattle and a hundred ounces of gold if the chieftain will bestow her upon him as his wife—" for one year." Her father is honoured by the request and, after consulting the wishes of his daughter, who replies that she would not think of dishonouring her father by opposing his desire, the temporary nuptials are solemnised with much dignity.[1] The marriage bonds are in every instance of the loosest ; each party has complete freedom to leave and contract another marriage whenever he or she pleases. The famous queen Medb has at least three living husbands, who are constantly quarrelling about her.[2] Frequent changes of partners are common till late in mediaeval history.

Although polygamous households were rare, there was no recognised principle of monogamy, and among chieftains polygamy was not unusual. The supreme king of Ireland, Diarmaid mac Cerbaill, has two legitimate wives, apart from concubines ;[3] Conchobar is represented as marrying Derdri, or seeking her in marriage, although he is already married to Mugain Aitencaithrech.[4] When Cuchulainn woos Emer, after she has asked him a number of questions, carefully enquiring into his antecedents, she adds, as an afterthought : " Yet one more question, hast thou a wife already ? "[5] Folk-tales represent a hero with two wives living in perfect harmony as nothing unusual.[6]

---

[1] The Book of the Lays of Fionn, ed. E. MacNeill (Irish Text Society), Part i, p. 145. Similarly Princess Findabair is married to Faech " for one year " (R. Thurneysen, Die irische Helden- und Königsage, p. 291 ; cf. p. 286).

[2] E. Hull, The Cuchullin Saga in Irish Literature, p. liii.

[3] H. d'Arbois de Jubainville, Études sur le droit celtique, vol. i, p. 218 ; Id., La civilisation des Celtes, pp. 292 sq.

[4] Id., L'épopée celtique en Irlande, pp. 89, 101, 176.

[5] E. Hull, The Cuchullin Saga in Irish Literature, p. 67.

[6] A. Nutt, " The Lai of Eriduc and the Märchen of Little Snow-White," Folk-lore, iii, p. 32. Cf. C. De Smedt and J. De Backer, Acta sanctorum. Hiberniae, pp. 343 sq. ; Whitley Stokes, " Annals of Tigernach," Revue Celtique, xvii, pp. 139, 142 sqq., 146, 163, 165. " Genuine popular tradition implies a society in which a multiplicity of such rewards (a damsel as wife) causes no difficulty ; the prejudice against accepting more than one is a later racial and literary development " (G. Schoepperle, Tristan and Isolt, a Study of the Sources of Romance, vol. i, p. 527). Caesar speaks of the marriages of the Gauls as polygamous (De Bello Gallico, vi. 19. 3). In myths and records marriage is as a rule represented as monogamous. But

The fraternal polyandry which obtained among the Britons in the time of Caesar is mentioned in Irish literature about the first century; Clothru, Queen of Connaught, had three brothers for her husbands.[1] Brothers share the same mistress.[2] The traditions of clan-brotherhood, and the derivative notions of the duties of hospitality, make it a point of honour to supply the guest with a temporary partner. Cuchulainn and his companions, when entertained by the King of Ulster, are given their choice of fifty women each, including the king's daughter and the queen herself.[3] When King Conchobar travelled, his host placed his wife at his disposal.[4] We are told incidentally that the son of King Aed Mac Ainmerech, when travelling through Ireland, was provided each night with the wife of a different chieftain.[5] When the King and Queen of Connaught send ambassadors to Dare Mac Fiachna, to negotiate for the acquisition of a certain sacred bull, they mention, among other terms of payment, that the queen " will receive him in her bed." [6] Ordinary travellers enjoyed the same hospitality. A chieftain receiving a party of pilgrims for the night bids them " each take a woman." [7] Those customs survived in Ireland as

it must be borne in mind that those documents have undergone Christian editorship, and, however lenient and perfunctory that editorship might be, any recognition of polygamy would be strictly suppressed. Polygamous households, though by no means unknown, were infrequent ; in a matriarchal society, polygamy is usually polyaecious, and of such polyaecious marriage there is ample evidence. Gildas definitely states that the Britons "had a large number of wives," " quamplurimas conjuges habentes " (Gildas, *Epistola*, ed. J. Stevenson, p. 36) ; there is no ambiguity about the words, the authority is one of the best, and there is no question of misrepresentation, for the statement occurs in an exhortative epistle addressed to the Britons themselves. One of the tasks of early Christian legislation was to put down polygamy among the barbarians (see below, p. 422). There is, therefore, no solid ground for the assertion that marriage among the Celts was monogamous. It is certain that no legal principle of monogamy was recognised.

[1] R. Thurneysen, *Die irische Helden- und Königsage*, p. 584 ; K. Meyer, "The Edinburgh Gaelic Manuscript XL," *The Celtic Magazine*, xii, p. 211. Cf. above, vol. i, pp. 695 sqq.

[2] L.-C. Stern, " Le Manuscrit irlandais de Leide," *Revue Celtique*, xiii, p. 20.

[3] *Fled Bricrend. The Feast of Bricriu*, ed. and trans. by G. Henderson, pp. 69, 81 ; H. Zimmer, " Der kulturgeschichtliche Hintergrund in den Erzählungen der alter irische Heldensagen," *Sitzungsberichte der Königliche Preussische Akademie*, 1911, p. 197.

[4] H. d'Arbois de Jubainville, *L'épopée celtique en Irlande*, pp. 8, 29.

[5] H. Zimmer, " Keltische Beiträge," *Zeitschaift für deutsches Alterthum und deutsche Litteratur*, xxx, p. 284.

[6] *Táin bó Cúalnge*, translated by H. d'Arbois de Jubainville, p. 36. The same offer is also made to Fer Diad for his assistance, in addition to Princess Findabair, who meanwhile showers kisses upon him to induce him to accept the offer (R. Thurneysen, *Die irische Helden- und Königsage*, pp. 221 sq.).

[7] H. Zimmer, " Keltische Beiträge," *Zeitschrift für deutsches Alterthum und deutsche Litteratur*, xxxiii, p. 167.

late as the seventeenth century. Fynes Moryson tells us that a nobleman, on coming to the house of an Ulster chief, "was met at the door with sixteen women all naked except their loose mantles; whereof eight or ten were very faire and two seemed very nymphs." [1]

Irish heroes are unsurpassed in any literature for the multiplicity of their amatory adventures. While he is wooing Emer, and engaged in acquiring certain accomplishments which she requires of him, Cuchulainn becomes " the husband " (sic) of Uatach; [2] and, while he is the husband of the latter, he has a son by Queen Aife.[3] While still engaged in " wooing " Emer, he has an amatory interlude of some months with the goddess Fand, the wife of Manannan Mac Lir.[4]

There is no notion of pre-nuptial chastity; princesses of the noblest families, besides being freely offered to guests, bestow their favours on whomsoever they please. Medb, Queen of Connaught, boasted to her husband: " Before I was married, I was never without a secret lover in addition to my official lover." [5] Princess Findabair mentions to her mother that she rather fancies the messenger who has been sent from the opposing camp. The queen replies: " If you love him, then sleep with him at night." [6] The same customs obtained in Britain; of a troop of warriors we are told that they were " freely beloved by the daughters of kings of the island of Britain." The narrator adds his approval of the custom: " This they merit, for they were ever in the front and the rear in every peril." [7] " Unmarried girls and married women were taken as concubines without any difficulty." [8] It does not appear that the conception of virginity being desirable even in the bride of a king had become established. In Celtic sagas, when a girl betrothed from birth to a king is abducted by a lover, the royal claimant is no less eager to regain possession of her than if her ' honour ' had remained unsullied.[9]

---

[1] Fynes Moryson, *Itinerary*, fol. 181.

[2] E. Hull, *The Cuchullin Saga in Irish Literature*, p. 76.

[3] *Ibid.*, p. 79.

[4] H. d'Arbois de Jubainville, *L'épopée celtique en Irlande*, pp. 174 sqq.

[5] *Táin bó Cúalnge*, translated by H. d'Arbois de Jubainville, p. 35.

[6] H. Zimmer, " Der kulturgeschichtliche Hintergrund in den Erzählungen der alter irische Heldensagen," *Sitzungsberichte der Königliche Preussische Akademie*, 1911, p. 188.

[7] *The Mabinogion*, ed. A. Nutt, p. 152.

[8] J. von Pflugk-Harttung, " Les cycles épiques d'Irlande, leur date et leur charactère," *Revue Celtique*, xiii, p. 177.

[9] A. H. Leahy, *Heroic Romances of Ireland*, vol. i, pp. 23 sq. The same indifference is shown by British chieftains (*The Mabinogion*, ed. A. Nutt, p. 64).

Sualdam marries Dechtin, the sister of King Conchobar, knowing her to be pregnant.[1] A king of Ireland, when sending messengers through the provinces to seek the fairest bride for him, mentions as a special stipulation, and as if it were an unusual claim, " that no woman should be to him as a wife, unless she had never before been as a wife to any one of the men of the land." [2]

Sentiments of bodily modesty were undeveloped. Celtic warriors in full fighting costume were, but for their weapons and ornaments, entirely naked.[3] It was an invariable usage for young unmarried girls to attend on them and assist them with their ablutions, to massage them, and wait on them at their toilet.[4] Men and women bathed in public.[5] It is mentioned incidentally that, while a troop of warriors and women is on the march, a young woman strips herself naked, merely to attract the attention of a hero.[6] The absence of pudicity exceeds, indeed, anything reported of the manners of the Eskimo or North American Indians.[7] " It is certain that the bonds of modesty and

[1] L. Duvau, " Légende de la conception de Cuchulainn," Revue Celtique, ix, p. 12.

[2] Ibid., vol. ii, pp. 94 sqq. A similar claim is made by Cuchulainn when wooing Emer : " I have never accepted a woman who has known a man before me," he informs her (E. Hull, The Cuchullin Saga, p. 68). That, however, is plainly untrue. Besides innumerable connections with married women, he is eager to claim Blathnad after she has become the mistress of Caroi (K. Meyer, " Irish Miscellanies," Revue Celtique, vi, pp. 187 sq.). The claim in the ' Wooing of Emer ' looks as if it were a Christian interpolation, Cuchulainn having become an almost Christian hero.

[3] H. d'Arbois de Jubainville, La civilisation des Celtes et celle de l'épopée homérique, pp. 8, 371 sq. ; Livy, xxii. 46. 6 ; Polybius, ii. 28. 7 sq. The ' braca ' or breeches, which appears to have been imported from the East, is not part of the original Celtic apparel, and was not in general use among the Celts. Polybius, in the passage above referred to, mentions that the Gaesetes, before entering into battle, took off their breeches.

[4] See below, p. 413.

[5] K. Meyer, " The Death Tales of the Ulster Heroes," Royal Irish Academy, Todd Lectures Series, xiv, pp. 32 sq. ; K. Meyer, " The Edinburgh Gaelic Manuscript XL," The Celtic Magazine, xii, p. 212. The usage persisted till late in the Middle Ages in all northern lands. See A. Schultz, Das höfische Leben zur Zeit der Minnesinger, vol. i, p. 171.

[6] H. Zimmer, '' Der Kulturgeschichtliche Hintergrund in den Erzählungen der alter irische Heldensagen," Sitzungsberichte der Königliche Preussische Akademie der Wissenschaften, 1911, p. 208.

[7] The Queen of Ulster, and all the ladies of the court, to the number of six score and ten, come to meet Cuchulainn, naked to the waist, and raising their skirts "so as to expose their private parts" (H. Zimmer, ibid., pp. 194, 207). Similar incidents are repeatedly mentioned, and are treated as customary. Cf. Fled Bricrend. The Feast of Bricriu, ed. by G. Henderson (Irish Texts Society), p. 67 ; Caesar, De Bello Gallico, vii. 47. Rabelaisian details are given in the ' Táin bó Cúalgne ' as to the effects of fear on Queen Medb (Táin bó Cúalnge, translated by H. d'Arbois de Jubainville, pp. 242 sq.).

of morality have never been more lax than in Ireland during the first centuries." [1]

Owing to the earlier development of literary activity in Ireland as compared with other barbarian countries, our information concerning Irish pagan society is older and more detailed. But, as will presently be seen, there is ample evidence that the principles and social customs of other barbaric nations did not differ in any essential particular from those represented in the literary records of Ireland. Celtic-speaking peoples, in Britain and in Gaul, had identical usages. German writers draw a contrast between the looseness of sexual morality among Celtic nations and the supposed relative austerity of ancient German manners, appealing to the testimony of Tacitus, who, like the eighteenth-century doctrinaires, held up the picture of the ' noble savage ' as an indictment of the vices of civilisation. [2] But as soon as the Teutonic barbarians emerge into the light of recorded history, their vices and the brutaility of their licentiousness exceed anything in the records of other races. [3] Of the Nordic people, their latest English historian admits that they " were guilty of two besetting vices : immoderate love of wine and of women." The chronicles, he says, make constant reference to their ceaseless desire " to overcome the chastity of matrons and make concubines even of the daughters of the nobility." [4]

It appears that privacy was not accounted necessary by the women for the fulfilment of natural functions. The licentious entertainment of guests by queens and princesses at royal banquets is described with the remark, " as was the custom " (H. Zimmer, loc. cit., p. 198).

[1] J. von Pflugk-Harttung, " Les cycles épiques d'Irlande, leur date et leur charactère," Revue Celtique, xiii, p. 177.

[2] St. Boniface, in appealing to the English Saxons to mend their licentiousness, mentions that the Saxons " in olden times "—not, be it noted, in his own time and experience—punished adultery severely (Boniface, Epistola, lxii, in Migne, Patrologiae Cursus Completus, vol. lxxxix, cols. 759 sq.). The impression of greater austerity in German manners appears to arise chiefly from this fiercer proprietary jealousy and more brutal punishment of ' adultery ' in the barbaric sense of the term. The Germans were more cruel.

[3] This is set down by some to ' corruption.' The explanation, which is called into service whenever and wherever sexual manners which do not conform to modern European standards are found, has been so much abused that, in the absence of definite evidence, it has lost all force as an unsupported argument. Even the manners described in the oldest Irish literature have been, incredible as it may seem, apologised for by using the blessed word ' corruption ' (R. Thurneysen, Die irischen Helden- und Königsage, p. 81). It is perplexing to know when ' corruption ' began ; and it appears safest to accept the orthodox view of the Church, that it began in the Garden of Eden.

[4] A. Mawer, The Vikings, pp. 95, 84.

How were those customs and those conceptions affected when Christianity, with its obsessing horror of sex relations, even in marriage, became established among those populations ? Their immemorial customs and ideas could not become suddenly transformed by their wholesale conversion to the new religion. Such a transformation does, as we have noted, often take place rapidly and completely in savage societies under the influence of missionaries. But the conditions attending the conversion of the European barbarians were different. The chief motive of conversion with the present-day savage is his recognition of the superior power of European magic. That motive scarcely existed with the northern barbarians ; what magical power Roman missionaries could manifest by virtue of their connection with the decaying ruins of the first European civilisation was scarcely of a nature to impress the barbarians by any conspicuous superiority. To some extent the glamour and prestige attaching to the name of Rome compensated for that deficiency, and barbarian chieftains were flattered by assimilation to Roman patricians and the adoption of Roman religion. Above all, the superior knowledge and education of ' clercs ' was indispensable to them in the organisation and administration of their new kingdoms. But there was nothing of the prestige exercised by a European missionary among savages in the influence of the apostles over the mass of the people. The latter became converted ' en masse,' often being literally driven like flocks of sheep through the baptismal waters at the behest of their rulers. It would be difficult to imagine how, in those circumstances, their immemorial standards and customs could become instantly transformed. And they were not. In the barbarian society of the early Middle Ages, in the life of the warrior chieftains of the ' age of chivalry,' and in their conceptions as regards the relations of the sexes, the old customs and ideas are but slightly modified by Christian influence.

The ' Age of Chivalry.'

The tradition of an ' age of chivalry ' has contributed to draw a veil of vague misconceptions over the obscure origins of European societies. It was firmly believed in the later Middle Ages that the romances of chivalry composed in the twelfth and thirteenth centuries, which referred to the times of Charlemagne and his predecessors, and more especially to those of a British chieftain called Arthur and his warriors, represented accurately, if not actual historical events, at least the manners, customs, and ideas of European societies during those periods. That belief has been dealt with tenderly by modern historical criticism, and the mediaeval notion survives in vague current conceptions of barbarian society during the centuries which immediately followed the introduction of Christianity.[1] In the romantic literature which furnishes the elements of the picture of the 'age of chivalry,' we are in the midst of a fantastic world ; knight-errants roaming in search of 'adventure,' rescuing distressed damsels, joining in the pageantry of jousts and tourneys, holding exalted ideals and observing codes of knightly honour, appear scarcely more real than the giants and dragons which they overcome, the enchanters and enchantresses that cast their spells upon them, the magic castles which rise and vanish. If from the dream-pictures of romance we turn to anything in the nature of historical documents and records, we come upon a society which presents the reverse of those pictures, and surpasses in grossness any savage or barbaric community described in ethnological accounts.

The British monk Gildas spent his life in the midst of that society of barbarian chieftains and warriors who, in the romantic tradition of chivalry, came to be thought of as the knights of Arthur's

---

[1] It was in the Middle Ages a matter of Christian faith to accept implicitly as historical truth the romances of chivalry and, in particular, those which had reference to Charlemagne and his age. Charlemagne, the great ally, for his own political ends, of the Church, who had established her authority where her position had been doubtful and precarious, and had won new realms for the faith, was canonised by clerical gratitude, which showered honour and adulation upon the armed missionary. The first German emperor was the central figure round which the heroic sagas, 'chansons de geste,' and romances had gathered. Never, even in the remotest mythopoietic ages of the past, in Babylon or in India, had an unchecked imagination dealt more freely with contemporary or recent historical events. Not only did the ignominious raid of Charles into northern Spain, in which he never crossed swords with a Moor, furnish the theme of countless recitals of epic glory, but his imaginary expeditions to Constantinople and to Jerusalem were set forth with equal detail (cf. G. Paris, *Histoire poétique de Charlemagne*, pp. 337 sqq.). The decree of Pope Callixtus II (1122) pronouncing the authenticity of the chronicle of the supposed Archbishop Turpin, and the letter of the same pope recommending its perusal to the faithful, are apocryphal ; but they expressed the view which was universal by the end of the twelfth century (G. Paris, *op. cit.*, p. 58 ; cf. Id. *De Pseudo-Turpino*, p. 56). Any doubt concerning the veracity of those legends was looked upon as a manifestation of impiety and atheism. The French translations of the work are among the oldest monuments of French prose. The authors explain that they employed prose, instead of verse, which was at the time the usual medium for such works, " because the use of rhyme would lead to employing words which are not found in the Latin text " (P. Meyer, in *Notices et Extraits des manuscrits de la Bibliothèque Nationale*, vol. xxxiii, p. 31). The text of the chronicle was treated with the same reverence as Holy Scripture. Much of that attitude has survived to our day. A literature of historical apologetics is devoted to the glorification of Charlemagne as a ' civiliser ' and to the ' whitewashing ' of the Dark Ages.

Court and of the " great order of the Table Round." He describes
them in the following terms: "They are sanguinary, boastful,
murderous, addicted to vice, adulterous, and enemies of God, and
their names ought to be forgotten. They are generally engaged in
plunder and rapine, and they prey by preference upon the innocent ;
if they fight in order to avenge or protect anyone, it is sure to be
in favour of robbers and criminals. They wage wars, but mostly
against their own people and unjustly. They lose no opportunity
of exalting and celebrating the most bloody-minded amongst themselves. They are ever ready to take an oath, and as often perjure
themselves ; they make vows, and immediately act perfidiously
and treacherously. Although they keep a large number of wives,
they are fornicators and adulterers." [1] The good monk, indeed,
cannot find terms strong enough to express his disgust for the
manners and behaviour of the future ' knights of the Round
Table.' Allowance should be made for his grief and disappoint-
ment at their obstinate attachment to their pagan notions and
gods and their disregard for the Christian religion ; for, he
complains, " they are actuated by hatred of truth, they love
darkness rather than the light of the sun, and regard Satan as
an angel of light." [2] His charges cannot, however, be regarded
as imaginary, for, apart from their agreement with information
from other sources concerning the manners of British warriors,
he takes to task one by one all the chieftains, or ' kings,'
of his time, and calls them personally to account for their
individual misdeeds. The one he calls " a tyrannical whelp";
another he describes as " wallowing in the filth of the most horrible
murders, fornications, and adulteries"; while a third " exceeds all
others in power, malice, and licentiousness, and is utterly sunk in
the dark pool of his iniquities." [3] Gildas, for a very good reason,
as will presently be seen, makes no mention of Arthur, " the
flower of kings," in enumerating British chieftains ; but the earliest
references to that hero portray him as similar in character and
manners to the chieftains who excite the indignation of Gildas.
An old gloss in some of the manuscripts of Nennius informs us
that Arthur was " from his boyhood renowned for his cruelty." [4]
Layamon, who lived on the Welsh border and inserted many
ancient native traditions in his poem, confirms that reputation. Setting aside the customary atrocities and barbarities which

[1] Gildas, *Epistola*, ed. J. Stevenson (*English Historical Society's Publications*), p. 36.
[2] *Ibid.*, p. 27 ; cf. pp. 28 sq.
[3] *Ibid.*, pp. 37 sqq.
[4] Nennius, *Historia Britonum*, in Pertz, *Monumenta Germaniae Historica,
Auctores antiquissimi*, vol. xiii, *Chronica Minora*, vol. iii, p. 729.

he perpetrates on his enemies,[1] his dealings with his own people are represented as hardly less appalling. His warriors hold him in such dread that they are afraid to utter a word in his presence. Their fears appear to be justified, for he informs them that anyone disobeying him or incurring his displeasure will be " drawn by wild horses," or will have a limb lopped off. At one of his banquets, which are described as wild, drunken orgies,[2] Arthur's ' knights ' fell to quarrelling, and presently attacked one another with the carving-knives. After several of them have been killed, Arthur, who was absent when the brawl started, enters the hall, and orders the warrior who began the disturbance to be buried alive in a bog : he further orders his knights to strike off the heads of all the male relatives of the culprit and to cut off the noses of all the females.[3]

Such barbarity was not, of course, peculiar to the countrymen and contemporaries of ' King Arthur.' Gregory of Tours' history of the Franks—their ' chansons de geste ' furnished the basis for Carolingian romance, and were largely incorporated in those presentments of the ' age of chivalry ' [4]—although written in a spirit of astounding condonation and flattery,[5] presents a

---

[1] Layamon, *Le roman de Brut*, ed. Le Roux de Lincy, vv. 22267 sqq., 22615 sqq. Geoffrey of Monmouth says that Arthur tore the Irish " without pity," and that in the wars with the Scots and Picts " he indulged in unparalleled ferocity "—" incomparabili saevitae indulgens " (Geoffrey of Monmouth, *Historia Britonum*, ed. Giles (Caxton Society), ix, 6, 20–22 ; cf. ix, 11, 27).

[2] Hector Boece, *The Buik of the Chroniclis of Scotland*, ed. W. B. Turnbull (*Chronicles and Memorials of Great Britain and Ireland*), vol. ii, p. 228.

[3] Layamon, *op. cit.*, vol. ii, pp. 552 sqq. For the elements of Celtic tradition in Layamon, see A. C. L. Brown, " Welsh Tradition in Layamon's ' Brut,' " *Modern Philology*, i, pp. 98 sqq. ; R. H. Fletcher, *The Arthurian Matter in the Chronicles* (*Harvard Studies and Notes in Philology and Literature*, x), pp. 163 sqq.

[4] That derivation has been demonstrated by Professor Rajna, although his exaggerated view of the purely Germanic character of the poetical tradition cannot be accepted (see P. Rajna, *Le origini dell' epopea francese*, pp. 47 sqq. and *passim* ; also G. Kurth, *Histoire poétique des Mérovingiens*). A poet of the end of the ninth century, who celebrates Charlemagne, states :—

> Est quoque jam notus, vulgaria carmina magnis
>   Laudibus ejus avos et proavos celebrant ;
> Pippinos, Carolos, Hludowicos et Theodricos,
>   Et Carlomannos Hloteriosque canunt.

(Poeta Saxo, *Annales de gestis Caroli Magni*, in Pertz, *Monumenta Germaniae Historica, Poetae Latini*, vol. iv, Part i, p. 58).

[5] Clothwig induced the son of Sigbert, the king of the Ripuarian Franks, to murder his father in his sleep ; as soon as the deed is accomplished Cloth-

picture a thousand times more lurid than the declamatory invectives of Gildas. There is, indeed, no parallel in human annals to the interminable recital of murders, massacres, perfidies, and cruelties which fill the record. The pious annalist distributes praise or blame according as the princes he names are favourably or unfavourably disposed towards the Christian bishops; but they are all alike in their cruelty, treachery, crimes, and parricides.[1] The mass of the people do not differ from them; " the entire population is sunk in vice; each man loves evil, and indulges his criminal inclinations without restraint." [2] The sexual morals of Chilperic, which differ nowise from those of other Merovingians, are thus described : " It is not possible to picture in thought any form of licentiousness or vice which he did not perpetrate in deed." [3] The race became exhausted through the excesses of debauchery.[4] " Those abominable princes," observes Dunham, " generally, such were their premature vices, died of old age before thirty." [5]

Amid the flood of glorification, ancient and modern, which attends the transient semblance of political order established with ruthless vigour by Charlemagne, there is a great lack of direct historical information concerning the manners and characters of his warriors. The most famous hero in the cycle of

wig murders the son. He bribes with false gold the servants of his relatives to capture them and bring them to him bound in chains; he then knocks out their brains. Having dealt thus with all his relations, he complains that he is alone in the world ; " but," remarks the historian, " this was said through cunning, to find out whether any were left whom he might kill." Gregory concludes the recital of these murders with the following remark : " Thus did the Lord fell down each day by his hand some of his enemies and extend his dominions, for he walked before the Lord with an upright heart, and did what was pleasant in His eyes " (Gregory of Tours, *Historia Ecclesiastica Francorum*, in M. Bouquet, *Recueil des historiens des Gaules et de la France*, vol. ii, pp. 183 sqq.).

[1] One of the favourites of Gregory is " the good king Gontrar." Sismondi thus sums up his good qualities : " He is only known to have had two wives and one mistress. His temper was, moreover, reputed to be a kindly one, for, with the exception of his wife's physician, who was hewn to pieces because he was unable to cure her ; of his two brothers-in-law, whom he caused to be assassinated ; and of his bastard brother, Gondebald, who was slain by treachery, no other act of cruelty is recorded of him than that he razed the town of Cominges to the ground, and massacred all the inhabitants, men, women, and children " (J. C. L. de Sismondi, *History of the Fall of the Roman Empire*, vol. i, p. 246).

[2] Gregory of Tours, *op. cit.*, p. 326.

[3] Id., *ibid.*, p. 291.

[4] C. Bayet, C. Pfister, and A. Kleinhausz, in E. Lavisse, *Histoire de France*, vol. ii, Part i, p. 146.

[5] S. A. Dunham, *History of the Germanic Empire*, vol. i, p. 10. Cf. J. C. L. de Sismondi, *Histoire des Français*, vol. i, pp. 403 sq. ; Id., *History of the Fall of the Roman Empire*, vol. i, p. 263.

Carolingian romances, Roland, is probably mythical.[1]   There are, however, sufficient indications to confirm the presumption that they did not differ from their immediate predecessors and successors.   Charles himself, in his capacity of warrior, behaved like his Merovingian forerunners. Having accepted the submission of the Saxons, who delivered to him their arms and the leaders who had resisted his aggressions, he summoned their chief men to Verden, and after a conference in which they gave him what information they could, he had them beheaded on the same day, to the number of 4,500.   After this massacre, continues the annalist, " the king having satisfied his desire for vengeance, proceeded to his winter quarters at Thionville to celebrate the Nativity of our Blessed Lord." [2] " As soon as the grass began to sprout again . . . he spread massacre, arson, and pillage in every direction." [3]   The revolting

[1] The only historical mention of the name occurs in Einhard's life (*Vita Karoli Magni*, c. ix, ed. L. Halphen, p. 30 : " Hruodlandus Brittannici limitis praefectus ").   But that work, long regarded as the standard document on Carolingian history, is now known to be an unreliable farrago of cullings from Suetonius' *Lives of the Caesars*, eked out with information from the *Annales maiores*, which the author was not even able to transcribe correctly (see Professor Halphen's edition above mentioned and his *Études critiques sur l'histoire de Charlemagne*, pp. 88 sqq.).   The occurrence of the name in some diplomas (P. Graevell, *Die Charakteristik der Personen im Rolandsliede*, p. 109) throws no light on the subject.   It appears beyond doubt that there was a myth of Roland before Charlemagne and Roncesvalles.   The chief trait which is repeated in every traditional and popular version of that myth refers to Roland's phenomenal thirst, and represents him as having died in consequence of having drunk a whole stream to quench it (Le Roux de Lincy, *Le Livre des proverbes français*, vol. ii, p. 63 ; Rabelais, *Pantagruel*, ii. 7 ; J. B. Bruyerin, *De re cibaria*, xvi. 5.   Cf. C. Nyrop, *Storia dell' epopea francese nel medio evo*, p. 103).   A similar story is told of the Celtic mythological heroes Uther and Bran, who also died in consequence of drinking up a well to quench their thirst (J. Rhys, *Hibbert Lectures on . . . Celtic Heathendom*, pp. 161 sq.).   We have come upon the same trait in Papuan moon-gods (see above, vol. ii, p. 681), and, indeed, a Breton folk-tale ascribes it to the moon itself (see above, vol. ii, p. 636).   Roland is represented in Etienne's mythical chronicle as the leader or king of the Armorican Britons, and as requesting the help of Arthur, who is in the Otherworld, against the Franks (Etienne de Rouen, *Draco Normannicus* [*Chronicles and Memorials of Great Britain and Ireland, Chronicles of Stephen*, etc.], vol. ii, pp. 945 sqq.).   Everything, therefore, seems to point to Roland being a mythical hero of the Bretons ; and the mention in Einhard would be naturally accounted for by his having heard of him as a Breton hero, and inserting the name in his account of the disaster suffered by Charlemagne's host at Roncesvalles.   Professor Halphen is of opinion that the mention in Einhard's ' Life,' which was extremely popular in the Middle Ages, is the source of the whole connection of Roland with Roncesvalles, and of the famous ' Chanson ' (*op. cit.*, p. 31 n.).

[2] *Annales Regni Francorum*, ed. F. Kurze (*Scriptores Rerum Germanicarum ad Usum Scholarum*), ad. an. 782, pp. 63–65.

[3] *Ibid.*, p. 69.

'Capitularies concerning the country of the Saxons' have preserved the official record of the reign of terror by which Germanic Europe was won to the Christian religion. The administration of the Carolingian empire, in which what survived of commerce and industry was effectively ruined by the provisions of the Frankish king and his priestly advisers,[1] was entrusted to his courts and barons; but Alcuin laments that they were "rapacious wolves" rather than judges.[2] The chieftains of the Carolingian period are depicted in the older 'chansons de geste' in traits which do not differ from those of the savages of Gregory of Tours. Thus, for example, Charles's son, 'Charlot,' vexed at losing a game of chess, takes up the chessboard and brains his opponent with it.[3] The king himself, in the character of Charles Martel, is represented as informing an ambassador that he will hang every knight he takes prisoner, cut off his nose or put out his eyes, and that all common soldiers and also merchants will have their feet or hands lopped off.[4] One of the most distinguished

[1] *Capitularia Karoli Magni*, A.D. 805, art. v. "Charlemagne ruined the internal trade of his dominions by fixing a maximum of prices, and destroyed foreign commerce under the persuasion that, by discouraging luxury, he could enable his subjects to accumulate treasures which he might afterwards extort or filch into his own treasury" (G. Finlay, *History of the Byzantine Empire*, p. 194). Not many years ago a book was published devoted to exhibiting the revival of industry and commerce during the 'Carolingian Renaissance' (A. Dopsch, *Die Wirtshaftsentwicklung des Karolingerzeit*, Weimer, 1912–13). Professor Halphen has exposed its misrepresentations and shown the effects which the reign of this 'civiliser' had on European economic conditions (L. Halphen, *Études Critiques sur l'histoire de Charlemagne*, pp. 239 sqq., 277 sqq.).

[2] Alcuin, *Epistolae*, in Migne, *Patrologiae Cursus Completus*, vol. c. col. 159; cf. vol. ci, col. 628 sq.

[3] Raimbert de Paris, *La chevalerie Ogier de Danemarche*, vv. 3177 sq. :—

> Baudinet en feri el frontier,
> Le test le fent, s'en salt le cerveler.

When Ogier, the father of the victim, appeals to Charlemagne for redress, the emperor drives him out of his dominions. Subsequently, however, having need of Ogier's services, Charlemagne promises to kill his own son. The same incident appears to be referred to under different names in *Renaus de Montauban*. Here it is Charles's nephew who, losing his game of chess, strikes Renaud de Bayard. The latter complains to Charlemagne, but the emperor only replies by striking him with his fist. Renaud thereupon seeks out the emperor's nephew and breaks his skull (*Renaus de Montauban*, ed. H. Michelant, p. 51, vv. 35 sqq.).

[4] *Gerard de Rossillon*, ed. Fr. Michel, p. 45 :—

> Per mon cap, ditz lo reis, d'aquo n'ai soih.
> Non pretz vostra menassa, Folques, un codoig.
> No penrai chavalier tot no'l vergong,
> O del nas o dels oils no'l fassa mong,
> Sirven ni mercadier, o pe o poig.

' paladins ' of Charlemagne, Vivian, cuts off the noses, ears, hands, and feet of the ambassadors who are sent to treat with him.[1] Another Carolingian hero tears out the eyes, and cuts off the noses and lower lips, of his prisoners.[2] The ' serjeant ' of Duke Beringarius is treated in the same manner, and his right hand is also lopped off. The duke's young daughter is stripped, her hair is cut off, and she is handed over to "four vagabonds"; after which she is "thrown out of the town." [3] The ' chivalry ' of the heroes towards women is notable. When a lady contradicted a Carolingian knight " he raised his fist, which was large and square, and hit her full on the nose, so that the bright blood streamed down." [4] In one of the earliest ' chansons de geste ' that have reached us, the hero, Raoul de Cambrai, while engaged in dispossessing some neighbours of their domains, roasts one hundred nuns alive.[5] An ecclesiastical apologist

---

[1] *Covenant Vivien*, summarised in L. Gautier, *Les épopées françaises*, vol. iv, p. 444.

[2] *Siège de Narbonne, ibid.*, p. 330.

[3] *Li romans de Parise la Duchesse*, ed. G.-F. de Martonne, vv. 2074 sqq. :

> " Tot apres la ceinture li ont dras copez,
> Les tresces par desore li ont vilment ote ;
> A IIII pautoniers ont la dame livre,
> Puis l'ont fait de la ville vilainement giter.
> Et lo maistre serjant qui dou duc fu privez
> Se li ont baulevre et le nez raonie
> Devers la destre part li ont le poing oste."

In another ' chanson de geste,' Princess Mirabel having been taken prisoner by Rainer, he orders his soldiers :—

> " Ceste putain me faites en ma cartre lancier
> Le matin la ferai livrer as escuiers."

(*Ajol, chanson de geste*, ed. J. Normand and G. Raynaud, vv. 7699 sq.). Cf. *La Mort de Garin le Loherain*, ed. M. Edelestand Du Meril, pp. 102 sq. ; *Histoire littéraire de la France*, vol. xxii, p. 329.

[4] *Gaydon, chanson de geste*, ed. F. Guessnard and S. Luce, p. 129. Such gallantry is not unusual in chivalric times. We are told of a valiant knight, Chauvigny by name, who, having been wounded in Syria, limped badly. The queen of England, Berengaria, wife of Richard Coeur de Lion, had the bad taste to make fun of him on account of his honourable infirmity ; whereupon the angry knight " struck her in the face with such violence that the blood gushed " (G. Thaumas de la Thaumassière, *Histoire de Berry*, vol. ii, p. 399). In the romance of Perceval, ' the knight of the Glade,' while a page was serving queen Guineveve with a goblet, " dashed the liquor that was therein upon her face, and upon her stomacher, and gave her a violent blow on the face " (*The Mabinogion*, ed. A. Nutt, p. 248). When the mother of Raoul de Cambrai reproaches him on account of his barbarities, he strikes her in the face (Guillaume de Tudèle, *La chanson de la Croisade contre les Albigeois*, ed. P. Meyer, vol. i, p. 24).

[5] *Raoul de Cambrai*, ed. P. Meyer and A. Lognon (*Société des Anciens Textes Français*), pp. 49 sqq. The poem is a relation of actual events, probably by an eye-witness, and the personages and chief events, such as the one

of the Middle Ages admits that the worthy is representative
of all others. " The man is a Siou," he says, " a Redskin, who
lacks only some tatuings on his cheeks and some feathers on his
head." [1]

In the midst of such a society the ' age of chivalry ' was
retrospectively located. There is nothing unusual about the
anachronism ; throughout the Middle Ages, and much later, all
past periods were conceived as being identical in manners, ideas,
and social constitution with contemporary society. The romance-
writers of the twelfth and thirteenth centuries pictured the heroes
and heroines of traditional sagas as contemporary barons and
chatelaines ; Roland and King Arthur were represented as clad in
complete suits of armour and riding caparisoned horses, as dwelling
in feudal moated castles, and as actuated by the ideas and sentiments of the period. The ' age of chivalry ' was that of the
readers, not of the heroes of the romances ; it was not the age
of Charlemagne or of the Saxon invasions, but of the Crusades,
when those religious expeditions gave rise to the conception of
consecrated warriors and armed defenders of the faith.[2] The

mentioned, are referred to in chronicles (P. Meyer, *op. cit.*, Introduction,
pp. xvi sqq.). The above citations are from early specimens of romances
of the Carolingian cycle, none of which, in the original redaction, is later
than the eleventh century. In apologising for those features of the ' chansons
de geste,' Professor Nyrop remarks : " It must be admitted that, judged
from the point of view of our own age, they are cruel, abominable, bestial
. . . their brutality, their savage bloodthirstiness must cause horror to
every reader, unless he is very familiar with the Middle Ages. But the Middle
Ages were not otherwise ; the ancient French poets are certainly not guilty
of any exaggeration whatsoever. . . . It would be extremely unjust to
blame them for the condition of the times in which they lived " (C. Nyrop,
Storia dell' epopea francese, pp. 323 sqq.).

[1] L. Gautier, *Le chevalerie*, p. 26. Although the practice of scalping
an enemy, and of wearing the trophy on one's helmet, which was habitual
with the Huns (Ammianus Marcellinus, xxxi), was in use in Europe as late
as the twelfth century (A. Schultz, *Das höfische Leben zur Zeit der Minnesinger*,
vol. ii, pp. 389 sq.), the comparison is a gross libel on the American Indians.
No American Indian has ever been known to torture or to do violence to
women and children. The European savages " hung young children to the
branches of trees by the sciatic nerve (nervum femoris) ; they killed more
than two hundred young girls by tying them by the arms to the tails of horses
which they drove in opposite directions, so as to tear the victims to pieces ;
other girls they pinned down with stakes to the ruts of the roads, and drove
heavily loaded wagons over them " (Gregory of Tours, *op. cit.*, p. 190).
" Such were those savage ancestors," comments Gibbon, " whose imaginary
virtues have sometimes excited the praise and envy of civilised ages "
(E. Gibbon, *History of the Decline and Fall of the Roman Empire*, chap. xxxv,
ed. Bury, vol. iii, p. 467). It is out of recent savagedom that modern Europe
has developed ; it is to its cultural, not to its racial heredity, that the Western
world owes its civilisation.

[2] The fashion which made its appearance with the Crusades fell at once

enormous popularity of the romances of chivalry at that period reacted upon the ideas and usages of the feudal chieftains whose minds were saturated with those narratives ; they regarded themselves as the successors, although somewhat degenerate owing to the 'corruption of the times,' of the goodly and mighty knights of old.

The claim was not wholly unfounded, for, as we shall presently see, the usages and ideas connected with twelfth-century chivalry derived directly from those which had from time immemorial obtained among warlike European barbarians. But the manners of the knights of feudal Europe at the period of the Crusades were scarcely less rude and barbarous than those of their predecessors. "History tells us," admits a fervid panegyrist of feudal chivalry, "that from the end of the eleventh to the commencement of the fifteenth century, which is termed the age of chivalry in connection with feudalism, crime of all sorts was never so rife, honour was never so disregarded, nor war conducted so brutally." [1] Richard Coeur de Lion, who is described by one of his chroniclers as "endowed with the valour of Hector, the magnanimity of Achilles, nowise inferior to Alexander or to Roland, transcending by far the most praiseworthy men of our times . . . actuated by an inborn gentleness," etc.,[2] differs but slightly from the 'Sioux' of an earlier period. To revenge the defeat and loss of his wild Welsh auxiliaries, he had some prisoners thrown from a cliff into the Seine ; he put out the eyes of fifteen French knights, and sent them to the French camp led by one of them whose right eye had been spared. Philip Augustus, the pattern of French chivalry, retaliated by treating fifteen English knights in the same manner, "in order, he said, that it should not be thought that he was inferior to Richard in prowess and valour." [3] In enumerating

into decay when they ceased (cf. V. de Vaublanc, *La France au temps des croisades*, vol. ii, p. 229).

[1] J. Batty, *The Spirit and Influence of Chivalry*, pp. 135 sq. Abstract panegyrics concerning some unspecified 'spirit of chivalry' continue to figure in our historical literature ; but those sentimental generalities vanish as soon as the historian comes in contact with facts. Green speaks of chivalry as the "picturesque mimicry of high sentiment, of heroism, love, courtesy, before which all depth and reality of nobleness disappeared to make room for the coarsest profligacy, the narrowest caste-spirit, and a brutal indifference to human suffering" (J. R. Green, *A Short History of the English People*, pp. 182 sq.). Froude recognises that the chivalry of the time of the Wars of the Roses was "mere savage ferocity" (J. A. Froude, *A History of England from the Fall of Wolsey to the Death of Elizabeth*, vol. i, p. 64).

[2] *Itinerarium Peregrinorum et Gesta regis Ricardi*, ed. W. Stubbs (*Chronicles and Memorials of Great Britain and Ireland*), p. 143.

[3] Guillelmus Brito-Armoricus, *Phillipides, sive gesta Philippi Augusti, Francorum regis*, in M. Bouquet, *Recueil des Historiens des Gaules et de la France*,

the valour of English knights, Richard mentions Guy de la Marque, instancing as proof of his prowess that he killed his father's butler with a blow of his fist.[1] The brother of Henry III, being dissatisfied with his dinner, had his cook tortured to death with ingenious refinements of cruelty. When complaint was made to the king, the latter laughed.[2] The pages of Ordericus Vitalis, of Giraldus Cambrensis, of Guibert of Nogent are scarcely less full of atrocities than those of Gregory of Tours. Of a certain couple among his acquaintances, Abbott Guibert says that, "although chiefly devoted to the service of Venus, they were none the less cruel on that account when occasion offered." The husband "vented his rage, without satisfying it, upon innocent people, and on one occasion tore out the eyes of ten wretches, who died on the spot."[3] Such incidents are commonplaces. Of a certain baron, Bernard de Cahuzac, a chronicler says that "the cruelties, robberies, enormities of that monster were such and so many as to pass all belief or conception. And the devil gave him a wife worthy of himself, namely, the sister of the Count of Turenne. Both spent their lives robbing and destroying churches, stripping travellers, making widows and paupers, mutilating innocent persons. In one monastery alone, that of the black friars at Sarlat, we found a hundred and fifty men and women with their hands and feet amputated, their eyes torn out, or otherwise injured. The wife of this tyrant, oblivious of all pity, used to cut off the breasts of poor women or lop off their thumbs."[4] As usual the women excel the men in cruelty. Adelaide of Soissons, "through cupidity to possess the county," poisons her brother ; a deacon who incurred her displeasure had his tongue and his eyes torn out of his head.[5] Mabel, Countess of Belesne, who is described as "politic, shrewd, fluent, and

vol. xvii, pp. 177 sq. At Acre, Richard, in violation of his pledge and under circumstances of aggravated treachery and barbarity, had his hostages slaughtered ; their bodies were flayed, and the skins dried and preserved. His conduct stands in strong contrast with the dignity and forbearance of Saladin, before whose eyes the outrage was committed, and who would not stoop to retaliate on his dastardly opponent (W. Besant and E. H. Palmer, *Jerusalem*, p. 454 ; Benedict of Peterborough, *De gestis Henrici secundi et Riccardi* [*Chronicles and Memorials of England and Scotland*], vol. ii, p. 189).

[1] J.-B. Capefigue, *Histoire de Philippe-Auguste*, vol. i, p. 143.

[2] John of Oxenede, *Chronica*, ed. by Sir H. Ellis (*Chronicles and Memorials of Great Britain and Ireland*), p. 194.

[3] Guibert of Nogent, *Monodiae*, iii. 14, in Migne, *Patrologiae Cursus Completus, Series Latina*, vol. clvi, col. 943.

[4] Peirre de Vaux-de-Cernay, *Historia Albigensum et sacri belli in eos suscepti*, in Bouquet, *Recueil des historiens des Gaules et de la France*, vol. xix, p. 98.

[5] Guibert of Nogent, *op. cit.*, iii. 16. col. 949.

extremely cruel," rides about the country at the head of a large troop of men-at-arms, quartering herself and her men upon terror-stricken monks, upon whose larder and cellar the invasion descends like a flight of locusts. By guile, craft, and treachery she dispossesses one after another all her neighbours, who are reduced to beggary. One of them, with his two brothers, at last succeeds in gaining access to her bedroom and cuts off her head, an event which " caused much joy." [1]   Henry I of England, while besieging his illegitimate daughter, Juliana, in her castle, is invited by her to a parley, at which she attempts to murder him by stealth ; when at last he reduces her by famine, he compels her to descend from the battlements naked, and sends her thus in the middle of winter over the snow to her husband.[2]

Rapine and robbery were as much attributes of a knight in the age of professed as in that of mythical chivalry. In an enquiry into the origin of certain tolls, or ' customs,' claimed from travellers by a baron, the latter explains with amazing candour that those dues were originally collected by force of arms, the travellers and merchants being simply stripped of their belongings.[3] " Robbery and piracy were honourable, so far were they from reflecting any discredit on the ancient or modern ' redressers of wrongs.' " [4]   " Knights," says a troubadour of the thirteenth century, " distinguish themselves by stealing cattle, and robbing travellers and villeins." [5]   " The castles which should afford protection to the weak," says Humbert de Romans, " are the refuge of thieves and brigands." Their lords are " highway robbers who gather together troops to despoil wealthy passers-by, legates and their escorts, caravans of merchants, or to plunder the monasteries." [6]   Hugh, Duke of Burgundy, is described as a ' moult bon chevalier ' ; he was one of the most renowned knights of his day, and a leading crusader. When his men descried from their towers a party of travellers, they informed their lord, and the duke, lance in hand, and accompanied by his knights, sallied forth to meet them, and relieved them of every valuable. When Joanna, the daughter of Henry II, went to Naples to get married, she had the misfortune to pass near the noble knight's domain ; she and her escort were stripped of everything, and the

---

[1] Ordericus Vitalis, *Historia ecclesiastica*, iii. 3, v. 13.

[2] *Ibid.*, xii. 10.

[3] A. Luchaire, in E. Lavisse, *Histoire de France*, vol. ii, part ii, pp. 27 sq.

[4] R. Hurd, *Letters on Chivalry and Romance*, p. 100.

[5] Bernard Arnaut de Montcuc, in C. Raynouard, *Choix de poésies originales des troubadours*, vol. iv, pp. 254 sq.

[6] Humbert de Romans, in A. Lecoy de la Marche, *La chaire française au moyen-âge*, p. 388.

duke's knights, to amuse themselves, "caressoient les damoiselles." [1]
The feudal knights do not disdain to stoop to the pettiest thefts.
Monks complain that their servants have been stopped by Count
Pons du Vernet, and robbed of three sous and six deniers; that he
has stolen the cheese from a farm; that he has abstracted from
another house a tunic and breeches and a pair of boots. [2] Sheep,
horses, cows are habitually seized; when reclamations are made,
the noble lord replies: "Let the rustics be thankful that I left
them their lives." [3] Burglary operations do not detract from the
character of a knight. In a 'chanson de geste' one of the highest
nobles of Roussillon, having blackened his face and wrapped
himself in skins, gains access one night by means of a ladder to
the loft of the castle where the king is staying, and steals the
silver. [4] The exploits described in romances do not differ essentially
from those proceedings. If people dare so much as to grumble
when knights take their wine, their cattle, their wagons, they "are
hanged by the throat." [5] When a boatman has the impudence to
ask for a fee for ferrying a knight across a river, he is disembowelled. [6]
Such manners are even explicitly laid down as rules of chivalry.
When Perceval (Peredur) is instructed by his mother in the principles
of knighthood, she directs him: "If thou seest meat and drink,
and have need of them, and none have the kindness or the courtesy

---

[1] A. Capefigue, *Histoire de Philippe-Auguste*, vol. i, pp. 117 sq.
Spenser gives a realistic description of a similar gentleman, though he is,
of course, represented as a 'wicked knight':—

> "He is, said he, a man of great defence,
>   Expert in battle, and in deeds of arms;
>   And more embolden'd by the wicked charms
> With which his daughter doth him still support;
>   Having great Lordships got and goodly farms
>   Thro' strong oppression of his pow'r extort;
> By which he still them holds and keeps with strong effort.

> "And daily he his wrong encreaseth more:
>   For never wight he lets to pass that way
> Over his bridge, albee he rich or poor,
>   But he him makes his passage-money pay;
>   Else he doth hold him back or beat away"
>   (Spenser, *The Faerie Queene*, v. 2).

[2] A. Luchaire, *La société française au temps de Philippe-Auguste*, p. 265.
Many more instances are mentioned by Professor Luchaire in his chapter
on "La féodalité pillarde et sanguinaire." The material, as he remarks, "is
inexhaustible."

[3] A. Lecoy de la Marche, *La chaire française au moyen-âge*, p. 389.

[4] *Gerard de Rossillon*, p. 90.

[5] *Charroi de Nismes*, cited in *Histoire littéraire de la France*, vol. xxii,
p. 493.

[6] *Doon de Mayence*, ed. A. Pey, vv. 791 sqq.

to give them to thee, take them thyself. . . . If thou see a fair jewel, possess thyself of it." [1]

St. Bernard, while expressing his approbation of organised orders of crusaders, such as the Knights Templar, every blow of whose sword is a victory for Christ, speaks with disgust of the new-fangled style of secular militia—or ' malicia,' as he calls it by a horrible pun—which had lately been coming into fashion. " Their warfare and contests," he says, " never have any other cause but an insensate ferocity, an inane appetite for glory, or greed and cupidity for all manner of earthly possessions." [2] Peter of Blois, Archdeacon of Bath, is even more severe. " The order of chivalry," he says, " consists in living in the midst of every disorder. It is the art of indulging in every excess and of leading a life of folly. Our knights receive their swords from the hands of priests, and avow themselves sons of the Church, in order that they may defend religion, succour the afflicted, and punish evildoers. What they do is, as a matter of fact, the exact contrary. They despoil and ransom the subjects of the Church ; they crush down the poor with a cruelty which is without parallel ; they seek in the sufferings of others the satisfaction of their illicit lusts and boundless licentiousness. Our knights at the present day, instead of employing themselves against the enemies of Christ, vie with one another in debauchery and drunkenness ; their degenerate and foul lives, spent in crapulous idleness, are a dishonour to the name of knighthood." [3]

In one respect the knights of the twelfth and thirteenth centuries differed fundamentally from the heroes of primitive sagas whom they regarded as their models. The latter belonged to an equalitarian society in which warlike prowess was the sole criterion of distinction and merit, and any fighting man took his rank according to the measure of his valour and his exploits. The feudal system which grew out of the conquests and invasions, resulted in a state of things the reverse of that primitive tribal constitution of pagan society. Rank and power depended upon territorial possession, with which went absolute rule over the inhabitants. While the allegiance of feudal lords to their suzerain was, as among the Germans of Tacitus and in all primitive societies, of the loosest,[4] the subjects of a feudal lord, being originally con-

---

[1] *The Mabinogion*, ed. A. Nutt, pp. 246 sq.

[2] St. Bernard, *De laude novae militiae*, in Migne, *Patrologiae Cursus Completus, Series Latina*, vol. clxxxii, col. 923.

[3] Peter of Blois, *Epistola*, xciv, in Migne, *Patrologiae Cursus Completus*, vol. ccvii, coll. 293 sqq.

[4] Cf. Tacitus, *Germania*, xi : The chief ruled " auctoritate suadendi magis quam jubendi potestate." In no savage society, with the exception of the advanced despotism of some African empires, is the authority of chiefs

quered people, were his chattels and held their lives at his pleasure and discretion.[1] The gap between the territorial aristocracy and the rest of the population was an unbridgeable abyss. The former constituted a close corporation, the latter were regarded as scarcely human beings. " To the warrior knight, the labouring man was but an instrument of service to whom no courtesy was due." [2] Chivalry thus meant not only warlike valour, but nobility of birth, membership of the privileged class. A knight was not only a warrior, like those of the sagas, but a mounted warrior, that is, one entitled to fight on horseback, a ' chevalier,' ' ritter.' The English ' knight ' has reference to the position of a legitimate feudal retainer of the sovereign. The rite of investiture by which a knight was armed was a variation of the rite by which he was invested by the suzerain with a territorial domain.[3] The

of much account. Charlemagne himself, before the feudal system became established, is treated by his nobles in the most cavalier manner. One is represented as threatening to brain him and tear him to pieces if he does not grant his demands (*Doon de Mayence*, vv. 6442 sqq.) :—

> " Et se ne le m'octroies, par Dieu de majeste !
> Vous seres orendroit trestout escherveles
> De mon branc esmoulu, et tout vif desmembres.

[1] A charter of the Abbey of St.-Victor classes villein vassals with "bêtes en park, poissons en viviers, et oiseaux en cage " (cited by V. de Capefigue, *Histoire de Philippe Auguste*, vol. i, p. 35). The relation between villein and feudal lord has been misrepresented by juristic historians, and assimilated to that between feudal lord and sovereign, whereas it was utterly different. It was also one of the conventions of older historians that the invasions of Gaul by the Franks, of Britain by Saxons and Normans, were of the nature of ' peaceful penetrations.' The countless texts showing them to have been, on the contrary, savage conquests in which whole populations were slaughtered and driven from their homes, vast regions being reduced to deserts, were set aside and ignored. Only of late has historical criticism begun to sap the long-established fables of mediaeval history (see, e.g., E. Lavisse, *Histoire de France*, vol. ii, part i, pp. 79 sq.; P. Rajna, *Le origini dell' epopea francese*, pp. 336 sqq.). " Six centuries after its victory," remarks Capefigue, " the conquering nation retained its superiority over the conquered Gauls attached to the soil " (*op. cit.*, vol. i, p. 14). Social classes in Europe have thus, as in savage Africa, their original root in military conquest, in the distinction between conqueror and conquered.

[2] S. R. Gardiner and J. B. Mullinger, *Introduction to the Study of English History*, p. 91.

[3] Investiture, or ' dubbing,' by striking with a weapon, in later times a sword, but originally any weapon or even a stick, was an ancient mode of conferring authority. Ambassadors were " consecrated with sticks, according to the rites of the Franks " (Gregory of Tours, *Historia ecclesiastica Francorum*, vii. 32). Charlemagne invests a warrior with a vacant domain by striking him " with an arrow " (Girart de Vienne, in *Histoire littéraire de la France*, vol. xxii, p. 454). The same custom obtained among the Lombards (Paulus Diaconus, *Historia Langobardorum*, i. 13).

conception of aristocratic privilege and power, which was wholly foreign to primitive barbarian society, was thus as essential an element of the notion of chivalry as that of warlike prowess. A knight had not only to be valiant, but also 'gentle,' that is, well born.

Hence showy display, emphasising the aristocratic condition of the knight, was essential in feudal chivalry. St. Bernard taunts the impersonators of the heroes of romance with their extravagance and ostentation : " You deck your horses with silk and gewgaws, and cover yourselves with I know not what tawdry draperies ; you have your lances, shields, and saddles painted, your horses' bits and your spurs of silver and gold adorned with gems. And it is in this pompous guise that with shameful brutality and shameless stupidity you court death. Are those the trappings of soldiers, or are they not rather the fripperies of women ? "[1] " Our knights," it was said, "fight in wedding-garments."[2] "The apocryphal deeds of the imperial Paladins," says a military historian, " created a romantic desire of emulation which caused revenues to be squandered and chargers covered with iron. This was the beginning of the age of chivalry."[3]

Competition in luxurious display at tournaments was a source of ruin to many knights, none of whom possessed much cash ; they consequently became mortgaged to the neck to Jews and Lombards, whom they beat and maltreated, spitting in their faces, but with whom they could not dispense.[4] Contributions towards the expenses incurred in tournaments were among the legal dues which vassals owed their barons, "car il fesait alors force dépenses de tournois."[5] Knights hoped to recoup themselves by the prizes won in jousts. Of the father of Perceval, we are told that he " maintained himself not so much by his own possessions as by tournaments, and wars and combats."[6] Knights commonly spoke

---

To invest " par rain et par baston " was a current phrase in feudal times (P. Rajna, *op. cit.*, p. 389).   Pieces of stick which had been used in the investiture are sometimes found attached to mediaeval charters (V. de Capefigue, *op. cit.*, vol. i, p. 28).

[1] St. Bernard, *op. cit.*, col. 923.

[2] Vincent de Beauvais, *Speculum historiale*, vol. iv, col. 1230.   Cf. A. Lecoy de La Marche, *La chaire française au moyen-âge*, pp. 392 sqq.

[3] H. B. Stuart, *A History of Infantry from the Earliest Times to the Present*, p. 23.

[4] A. Méray, *La vie au temps des trouvères*, p. 55 ;   V. de Capefigue, *Histoire de Philippe de Auguste*, vol. i, pp. 145 sq.

[5] C. du F. Du Cange, *Glossarium mediae et infimae Latinitatis*, s.v. " Auxilium."

[6] *The Mabinogion*, p. 244.   Perceval himself is compelled to fight in a tournament in order to pay back the money which he has borrowed from a miller (*ibid.*, pp. 279 sq.).

of their sword as their ' bread-winner.' [1]   Often, however, the plight of the poor knights was piteous.   Mediaeval charters refer to " mendicant noblemen." [2]   " They are frequently without weapons, having been compelled to pawn them, and charitable chatelaines in whose manors they spend the night not infrequently provide them with cast-off clothes." [3]   We read of a lady assisting her chosen knight with the sum of five shillings.[4]   One scarcely ever hears of a knight presenting his lady-love with any gift of value ; " in most instances the gifts which the ladies bestowed upon them were more valuable than those which they received." [5]   When knights " did not obtain sufficient ransom from prisoners, or were not set on their feet by the prizes received in tournaments, or acquired through the adventures of the road, or from the largesse of their suzerains, they did not scruple to accept from their mistresses more substantial tokens of love than a golden vizor, a ring, or a silken girdle or embroidered scarf.   The gift of a heavy purse filled with golden bezants nowise caused them any confusion or embarrassment." [6]   " Many a knight lived exclusively on the bounties supplied by his lady-love." [7]

The great worth of chivalry lay in the conception of ' honour.' It has been remarked that the conception, which dominated the ideas of the French nobility in particular down to the sixteenth century, was an entirely new one.[8]   It was to a great extent new with reference to Graeco-Roman ideas, but it was immemorially established among the northern barbarians, as among all barbaric peoples who retain tribal organisation.   The sentiment was developed in a far higher degree among the Arabs, for, owing to the conditions of their tribal society, which remained markedly

---

[1] P. J. B. Legrand d'Aussy, *Fabliaux ou contes du XIIᵉ et XIIIᵉ siècles,* vol. i, pp. 250 sq.

[2] L. J.-B. Bérenger-Féraud, *Les Provençaux à travers les siècles,* p. 265.

[3] A. Méray, *loc. cit.*   Troubadours were likewise commonly rewarded with gifts of old clothes.   The noble troubadour Ademar is said to have received " mauh vielh vestimen " (F. Diez, *Die Poesie der Troubadours,* p. 43).

[4] " Parthénope, comte de Blois," in P. J. B. Legrand d'Aussy, *op. cit.,* vol. v, p. 287.

[5] A. Schultz, *Das höfische Leben zur Zeit der Minnesinger,* vol. i, p. 469.

[6] A. Méray, *La vie au temps des trouvères,* pp. 55 sq.

[7] A. Schultz, *loc. cit.*   Cf. *Poésies de Marie de France,* vol. i, p. 508.   A lady, in promising her love to a knight, tells him that she will give him plenty of cloth for clothes, and of money :—

> " Jeo vus dunrai mult richement
> Deniers et dras, or et argent."

Later she sends a man to pay his debts and settle his rent, and to supply him with clothes, a bed-cover, and much money (*ibid.,* pp. 512 sqq.).

[8] E. Lavisse and A. Rainbaut, *Histoire Générale,* vol. ii, p. 61.

equalitarian, it included conceptions of generosity and extravagant magnanimity which were unknown to European chivalry. When European knights came into contact with Islamic warriors, they freely acknowledged that the pagans surpassed them in knightly honour ; the ideal became accordingly extended and raised to a higher level. The chivalric honour of the northern barbarians was a very limited conception which corresponded only partially to the connotation the term bears. It contained nothing that was inconsistent with treachery, perfidy, deceit, lying, cruelty, and what we should account a degrading lack of self-respect.

'Honour' primarily means 'renown,' 'fame' ; the word 'praise' is commonly used in mediaeval literature as a synonym.[1] The first requirement of chivalric honour was a reputation for warlike courage ; in the 'chansons de geste' and earlier romances the terms 'chivalry,' 'chivalrous,' are used exclusively in reference to warlike prowess.[2] The stain of cowardice constituted the deepest 'dishonour.' A man's whole kith and kin were, among the pagan barbarians, held to be infected by an act of cowardice on his part, and lost their tribal rights.[3] A man was equally 'defamed,' or 'dishonoured,' by a slanderous imputation of cowardice as by his actual conduct ; he was under the obligation of disproving the charge, and was thus bound to accept any challenge that might be offered. Warfare among the barbarians, as with all uncivilised peoples, consisted mostly of single

---

[1] 'Pretz' is the usual Provençal term for 'honour.' In the 'Chanson de Roland' 'praise' is used as an equivalent of 'honour' and of 'goodness':

> " Tant n'el vus sais ne preiser ne loer
> Que plus n'i al d'onur e de bonter "

(*La chanson de Roland*, ed. L. Gautier, v. 532). Caesar, in referring to the motives which actuated the Gallic warriors, uses the very same term—" belli laudis " (Caesar, *De Bello Gallico*, vii. 76).

[2] 'To win honour' meant, of course, to gain distinction in combats.

> " En plusieurs gestes de lui sunt groz hunurs "

(*La chanson de Roland*, v. 3181. Cf. F. Settegast, " Der Ehrbegriff in alt-franzoesische Rolandsliede," *Zeitschrift für romanische Philologie*, xiv, pp. 206 sq.). Hence any other avocation than that of arms, such as trade or industry, is profoundly 'dishonourable.' In chivalric romances we frequently come upon boys of noble birth who, through some accident, have been brought up by tradesmen ; their innate nobility shows itself at once, however, by their using the money entrusted to them to buy a horse and weapons, and by their absconding to join in wars and tournaments (*Histoire littéraire de la France*, vol. xxii, pp. 588 sqq. ; vol. xxvi, p. 307 ; C. Nyrop, *Storia dell' epopea francese nel medio evo*, pp. 137 sq.).

[3] *Beowulf*, vv. 2884 sqq., pp. 181 sq. (ed. T. Arnold). Cf. Tacitus, *Germania*, vi : " A man thus disgraced may not be present at the sacred rites or enter the council."

combats between champions, in contrast with the ordered attacks of disciplined troops. When mediaeval writers translated scraps of classical history they represented the battles as a succession of duels. Gaulish warriors frequently came out of the ranks and challenged an astonished Roman to single combat.[1] Such single combats had to be fought under equal conditions, neither party having the advantage of weapons over the other. In Irish sagas, duels are sometimes fought ' blow for blow,' the challenger first submitting to the assault of the challenged, and the latter subsequently receiving an equal number of blows from the challenger.[2] Similar rules, we saw, are observed among the Australian aborigines, the Indians of Brazil, and other savages.[3] These rules of ' fair play ' were known amongst the ancient Irish as ' fir fer.' [4] In an Irish lay, a warrior coming upon his enemy asleep, first wakes him, and tells him to take up his weapons and defend himself.[5]

Those contests and tests of valour usually took place in connection with festal gatherings or banquets, called by the Irish ' fled.' [6] Such banquets and combats were an immemorial institution among Celtic nations. The Greek historian Posidonius of Apamea, who travelled in southern Gaul about the beginning of the first century B.C., tells us that " the Celts, in their banquets, seat themselves upon green rushes,[7] and set the dishes upon wooden tables but slightly raised above the ground. . . . And when a

---

[1] When the Gauls attacked Rome, a gigantic, naked Celtic warrior advanced, and, making a sign with his hand to stop the fighting, challenged any Roman to single combat (Livy, vi. 43. 3 ; Aulus Gellius, ix. 8). On another occasion the Gaulish king Britomartes, noticing the Roman consul, challenged him to single combat (Plutarch, *Vita Marcelli*, 6 sqq. ; Cicero, *Tusculanes*, iv. 22. 49). Other similar instances are related (Livy, vii. 26 ; Appian, *De rebus Hispanensibus*, 53). The same usuage obtained among the Germans (Tacitus, *Germania*, x. Cf. P. Rajna, *Le origini dell' epopea francese*, pp. 402 sqq.).

[2] This would appear to be the essential meaning of the usage referred to by Posidonius (Athenaeus, iv. 40), and which plays a conspicuous part in Celtic sagas and in the romances derived from them (*Fled Bricrend. The Feast of Bricriu*, ed. G. Henderson, pp. 99 sqq. ; cf. Dr. Henderson's note on " The Champion's Covenant," *ibid.*, pp. 199 sqq. ; F. Madden, *Sir Gawayne*, vv. 287 sqq. ; Heinrich von dem Türlin, *Diu Crône*, vv. 12869 sqq. ; " La mule sans frein," in D. M. Méon, *Nouveau recueil de fabliaux et de contes*, vol. i, pp. 1 sqq. ; *Histoire littéraire de la France*, vol. xxx, pp. 73 sqq.).

[3] See above, vol. ii, p. 119.

[4] E. Thurneysen, *Die irische Helden- und Königsage*, p. 81.

[5] *The Book of the Lays of Fionn*, ed. E. McNeill, Part i, p. 104.

[6] E. Windisch, *Irische texte mit Wörterbuch*, s.v., p. 552.

[7] Cf. *The Mabinogion*, ed. A. Nutt, p. 167 : " King Arthur sat upon a seat of green rushes, over which was spread a covering of flame-coloured satin," etc.

company is gathered, they sit round in a circle, the most distinguished by reason of warlike bravery, or birth, or wealth, acting, as it were, as leader of the chorus, and the provider of the feast sitting next to him, and all the other according to their rank and distinction . . . and the serving-boys go round the circle of guests helping them from right to left. . . . The armour-bearers of the warriors stand behind them holding large oblong shields, and at the opposite end of the hall the spear-bearers also feast, sitting in a circle in the same manner as their masters. . . . The Celts are wont, in connection with their banquets, to hold single combats, in which they appear fully armed and strive amongst themselves in mock-fights as an exercise ; but not infrequently they go so far as to inflict wounds on one another, and sometimes the combatants even lose their lives. In olden times they had a custom of putting a hind-quarter on the table, and this was the portion of the foremost man. And if anyone else laid claim to that portion, the two rose, and they fought till one was slain." [1] The latter custom is repeatedly referred to in Irish sagas,[2] and was a recognised practice of chivalry. " In solemn feasts a roasted peacock was presented to a knight when it was desired to honour him particularly, and to distinguish him as the most valiant." [3] From those circular banquets the name ' Round Table ' was also applied to the armed contests, or tournaments, held in connection with them, a term which was used throughout the Middle Ages in speaking of such military sports.[4] The word

---

[1] Posidonius, in Athenaeus, iv. 36. 40. Cf. Diodorus Siculus, v. 28. 5. 6. Celtic houses and banqueting-halls were circular. Strabo describes them as "large round houses constructed of boards and wicker-work, and covered with a heavy, thatched roof " (iv. 3). Cf. E. O'Curry, *On the Manners and Customs of the Ancient Irish*, vol. iii, p. 31. Mr. Petrie has collected a number of passages from Irish literature referring to the circular houses of the Celts (G. Petrie, " On the History and Antiquities of Tara Hill," *Transactions of the Royal Irish Academy, Department of Antiquities*, xviii, pp. 197 sqq.) ; he also shows the famous feasting-hall of the Irish kings at Tara to have been circular (*ibid.*, p. 84).

[2] See H. d'Arbois de Jubainville, *L'épopée celtique en Irlande*, pp. 66 sqq. ; *Fled Bricrend. The Feast of Bricriu*, ed. G. Henderson (*Irish Texts Society*), p. 15 ; *The Book of the Lays of Fionn*, ed. E. MacNeill, p. 169 ; K. Meyer, in E. Hull, *The Cuchullin Saga in Irish Literature*, p. 289 ; A. C. L. Brown, The Round Table before Wace," *Harvard Studies and Notes in Philology and Literature*, vii, p. 196.

[3] C. Nyrop, *Storia dell' epopea francese nel medio evo*, p. 191. Cf. below, p. 402 n[5].

[4] Matthew Paris, *Chronica Majora*, vol. v, p. 318 ; C. Du Cange, *Glossarium mediae et infimae Latinitatis*, vol. viii, pp. 7 sq. ; P. J. B. Legrand d'Aussy, *Fabliaux ou contes du xiie et xiiie siècles*, vol. i, p. 327 : " célébré par des tables-rondes, des fêtes, des tournois " ; *Le livre du chevalier de la Tour Landry*, ed. A. de Montaiglon, p. 55 : " une grant feste d'une table ronde de joustes."

'tournament' had probably reference to the same usage of the ancient Celts whereby the merit and honour of a warrior was marked by his place from right to left in the company as they sat at their round tables.

To the conception of chivalric honour, after the indispensable requisite of a good reputation for valour, was attached that of fidelity in the observance of promises. That meaning of the primitive conception of honour survives in such phrases as 'to honour a promise, a cheque.' The principle was deeply established in barbaric society. A large proportion of Celtic stories turns upon the obligation to fulfil a promise, however unreasonable or rashly yielded. A common form, in those tales, is a promise to grant whatever boon may be asked. Thus, when a stranger delivered the King of Lochlann from certain venomous sheep which spread disease in his army, the king offered him whatever reward he might ask and it was in his power to give. In this instance the stranger merely asked to spend the night with the queen.[1] The obligation imposed by a pledged word was in reality a conditional curse. Such a pledge was called by the Irish a 'geis.' The connotation of the term extended, however, much farther. It had also the meaning of 'tabu.' Thus Cuchulainn, whose name means 'the Hound of Culan,' was under a 'geis' not to eat dog's flesh; a breach of that totemic tabu caused loss of strength in his limbs.[2] Similarly, Conaire, who was descended from a bird, might not kill birds.[3] The hero Diarmaid was under a 'geis,' whenever the cry of hounds was heard, to follow the hunt, whatever he might have been engaged in doing at the time.[4] In the latter instance the 'geis' was equivalent to a 'vow' similar to those which play an important part in the conceptions of chivalry.[5] So again, the hero Aedh, wishing to retain the services

[1] K. Meyer and A. Nutt, *The Voyage of Bran, the son of Febal, to the Land of the Living*, vol. i, p. 72.

[2] W. Stokes, " Cuchulainn's Death, abridged from the Book of Leinster," *Revue Celtique*, iii, pp. 176 sq.

[3] R. Thurneysen, *Die irische Helden- und Königsage*, p. 629.

[4] "The Death of Diarmaid," translated by J. H. Lloyd, O. J. Bergin, and G. Schoepperle, *Revue Celtique*, xxxiii, pp. 162 sqq.

[5] A common form of vow was that the warrior should bind himself not to rest two nights in the same place before a certain exploit or quest had been accomplished (R. Thurneysen, *Die irische Helden- und Königsage*, p. 254). This form of vow is common in Arthurian romances, as, for instance, in the quest of the Holy Grail. Vows were often undertaken while solemnly partaking of a particular food, as in the so-called 'voeux du paon,' and ' voeux du héron,' in which each participant made a vow while eating his portion (cf. A. Tobler, "Plus a paroles an plain pot De vin qu'an un mui de cervoise," *Zeitschrift für romanische Philologie*, iv, pp. 81 sq.; C. Nyrop, *Storia dell' epopea francese nel medio evo*, p. 119). Edward I, at his famous ' Round Table of Kenil-

of his daughter, vowed a 'geis' that he would kill any man who asked her in marriage. She was carried off, one day while he was absent, by Conon. Aedh expressed himself satisfied, for she had not been asked in marriage, and his 'vow' was therefore unbroken.[1] A 'geis' might be laid upon one person by another, and the violation of the 'geis' entailed all the dangers of a curse. No Irish hero ever was so rash as to break a 'geis.' Such a disregard would at the same time render the offender an object of ridicule. When the wife of Conchobar endeavours to persuade the unwilling Naisi to abduct her she lays a 'geis' upon him; "shame and ridicule will fasten on your two ears," she says, "unless you take me away." He consequently felt in honour bound to elope with the queen.[2] The honouring of a pledged word was thus much more of the nature of a superstitious fear than of an ethical principle; it was in no way inconsistent with perfidy and lying. Celtic heroes, when they have redeemed their 'geis' by granting the promised gift, commonly pursue and attack, or endeavour to outwit, the person on whom they have conferred it, in order to recover what they have been deprived of by the fulfilment of their pledge.[3] Clever deceit and lying, far from being

worth,' "renewed the faded glories of Arthur's Court . . . in his 'Vow of the Swan,' when rising at the royal board he swore on the dish before him to avenge on Scotland the murder of Comyn" (J. R. Green, *A Short History of the English People*, p. 183). The usage was observed as late as 1454, when Philip the Good of Burgundy gave a banquet at which a magnificently dressed pheasant was served; while consuming his portion each knight had to vow to join a crusade to liberate Constantinople, which had just fallen, from the Turks. The origin of the usage, which is closely connected with that of the 'hero's portion,' goes back to the cult of Freijr, in which German warriors undertook vows while eating a portion of a sacrificial animal (K. Simrock, translation of *Beowulf*, Stuttgart, 1859, p. 199; P. Rajna, *Le origini dell' epopea francese*, p. 405; J. Grimm, *Deutsche Rechtsalterthüme*, p. 900; C. Nyrop, *loc. cit.*). The ancient Russians had a similar usage (A. Rambaud, *La Russie épique*, pp. 83, 135, 258). The vow sometimes took the form of a boast to perform some impossible feat, and was then called a 'gab.' Thus, for instance, the hero Oliver, one of Charlemagne's chief paladins, vowed to have sexual connection a hundred times in one night with the daughter of his host (*Charlemagne, An Anglo-Norman poem of the twelfth century*, ed. Francisque Michel, p. 20).

[1] *The Book of the Lays of Fionn* (ed. E. MacNiell, *Irish Text Society*), Part i, pp. 95 sqq.

[2] H. d'Arbois de Jubainville, *L'épopée celtique en Irlande*, p. 226.

[3] E.g., A. H. Leahy, *Heroic Romances of Ireland*, vol. i, pp. 95 sqq.; *The Mabinogion* (Lady Charlotte Guest's translation, ed. A. Nutt), pp. 14 sq. The knights of King Arthur act in the same way. On the conception of the 'geis,' see E. Windisch, *Irische Texte mit Wörterbuch*, vol. i, p. 590, s.v.; R. Thurneysen, *Die irische Helden- und Königsage*, p. 80; H. Zimmer, "Der Kulturgeschichtliche Hintergrund in den Erzählungen der alten irische Heldensage," *Sitzungsberichte der Königliche Preussische Akademie der Wissen-*

inconsistent with ' honour,' were talents which enhanced a knight's reputation.

As regards respect for women, the rules of chivalry are thus explained by Chrestien de Troyes : " The usage and rule at that time," he tells us, " were that if a knight found a damsel or wench alone, he would, if he wished to preserve his good name, sooner think of cutting his own throat than of offering her dishonour ; if he forced her against her will, he would have been scorned in every court. But, on the other hand, if the damsel were accompanied by another knight, and if it pleased him to give combat to that knight and win the lady by arms, then he might do his will with her just as he pleased, and no shame or blame whatsoever would be held to attach to him." [1] The first part of the rule does not seem, however, to have been so strictly regarded as the courtly poet here represents. " To judge from contemporary poems and romances, the first thought of every knight on finding a lady unprotected and alone was to do her violence." [2] Gawain, the pattern of knighthood and courtesy, when Gran de Lis refuses to grant him her favours, ravishes her in spite of her tears and screams.[3] In Marie de France's ' lai de Graelent,' when the hero, who is represented as a model of knighthood, meets a lady in a forest, and she rejects his advances, he knocks her down and ravishes her.[4] The lady, however, forgives him his too violent ardour, for she recognises that " he is courteous and well-behaved, a good, generous, and honourable knight." [5] When a

---

schaften, 1911, p. 220 n. ; G. Schoepperle, Tristan and Isolt, a Study of the Sources of the Romance, vol. ii, pp. 307 sq., 402 ; J. O'Donovan, Book of Rights p. xlv ; A. Nutt, Studies on the Legend of the Holy Grail, pp. 212 sqq. ; R. A. S. Macalister, " Tremair Breg : A Study of the Remains and Traditions of Tara," Proceedings of the Irish Academy, xxxiv, section C, pp. 362 sq.

[1] Chrestien de Troyes and Godefroy de Laigny, Le roman du Chevalier de la Charette, ed. P. Tarbé, v. 1302 sqq. ; G. Paris, " Lancelot du Lac," Romania, xii, pp. 670 sqq.

[2] H. D. Traill and J. S. Mann, Social England, vol. ii, p. 782.

[3] Perceval le Gallois, ed. C. Potevin, vol. v, pp. 57 sq. Cf. vol. iii, p. 101 ; J. L. Weston, The Legend of Sir Perceval, vol. i, pp. 303 sq.

[4] Marie de France, Poésies, vol. i, p. 506 :—

" Graelent la truve si fière
E bien entent que par proiière
Ne fera point de sun plaisir,
N'il ne s'en veut ensi partir ;
En l'espese de la forest
A fet de li ce que le plest."

[5] Ibid., p. 508 :—

" Voit qu'il est curteis e sage,
Buns chevaliers e prox e large."

knight enters the hall of King Arthur and carries away by
force a weeping and screaming lady, "the king was glad, for she
made such a noise." [1] To neglect to acquire a woman when the
occasion offered was accounted unchivalrous and dishonourable.
Among the instructions in chivalrous conduct given to Perceval
by his mother is the rule that "if thou see a fair woman,
pay thy court to her, whether she will or no ; for thus thou wilt
render thyself a better and more esteemed man than thou wast
before." [2]

If a knight performed any service, either as a warrior or sometimes as a hunter, on behalf of a lady, the latter was thereby
bound in honour to reward him with her favours, a pledge which
she had in general little reluctance in fulfilling. "The marked
feature of the sex-relations in the days of chivalry was the institution of love-service. The knight bound himself to serve a particular
lady, matron, or maid. To approve himself brave, hardy, daring,
patient, and discreet was his part of the bargain, and when fulfilled the lady must fulfil hers and pay her servant. The relation
must not for one moment be looked upon as platonic ; the last
favours were in every case exacted, or rather were freely granted,
as the lady, whether maid or wedded wife, thought it no wrong
thus to reward her knight. It would have been ' bad form ' to
deny payment when the service had been rendered, and the offender
guilty of such conduct would have been scouted by her fellow
women as well as by all men. . . . Not only was it the lady's duty
to yield after proper delay, but at times she might even make the
first advances, and be none the worse thought of." [3]

The ' love-service,' which constituted so distinctive a feature
of the conventions of chivalry, was in fact the ' service '
which is in all primitive societies an indispensable qualification for obtaining the favours of a woman. The tenderness
of the women for the knights in mediaeval times had more than
romantic motives, or rather, the attraction which a man possessed
in their eyes depended chiefly, as in primitive societies, upon
the primary utilitarian qualities which are the foundation of
feminine love. When Iseult first beholds Tristan naked in his
bath, she is impressed with his handsome body ; but the beauty
of his limbs is thought of by her only as an indication of his fighting
capacities. "If he is as valiant as he is handsome," she says to
herself, "he must be sufficiently strong to sustain a hard fight,
for he is of noble proportions." [4] Those were perilous times in

---

[1] Sir Thomas Malory, *Le Morte d'Arthur*, iii. 5.
[2] *The Mabinogion*, ed. cit., p. 247.
[3] A. Nutt, *Studies on the Legend of the Holy Grail*, pp. 240 sqq.
[4] *Le roman de Tristan*, par Thomas, ed. J. Bédier, vol. i, p. 133. Cf.

which force and violence ruled ; and although the women were astonishingly hard and hardened viragoes, able on occasion to look after themselves in the most vigorous fashion, a male protector was almost indispensable. Young girls, when left through the death of a father or brother without a male guardian, habitually applied to the sovereign or suzerain lord, and asked him to provide them with a husband.[1] They might leave it to the sovereign to make a suitable selection, but in general desired to satisfy themselves of the proposed husband's qualifications. In order to do so they sometimes insisted on his fighting a tourney before their eyes.[2] A nubile girl was thus commonly the willing prize of victory in a passage at arms. [3] We read, for example, how William Peverel of Whittington proclaimed a tournament in which the prize was his niece Melette, who refused to be disposed of in any other fashion.[4] No girl or woman would have anything to do with a man who had not the reputation of being a good warrior, and whose 'praise' was not in people's mouths. A man who was under the least suspicion of cowardice had no chance of obtaining a wife, of retaining one if he was already married, or of winning the favour of any woman. "Shame be on me if he lies by me ! " she would exclaim.[5]

In an age when men commonly died a violent death, women were frequently the owners and heiresses of lands and manors. "The women and the fief are inseparable." " ' Take that woman and her fief,' was a common expression by which kings

---

Amis et Amile und Jourdains de Blaivis, ed. C. Hofmann, vv. 659 sqq. ; *Histoire littéraire de la France,* vol. xxvi, p. 243 ; T. Krabbes, *Die Frau im altfranzoesischen Karls-Epos,* p. 21, note 81 ; C. Nyrop, *Storie del epopea francese nel medio evo,* p. 35. "The women succumb to the influence of bodily beauty," observes Professor Nyrop. "The inward worth of a man has for them no importance ; it is only his external appearance that matters. But it must be added that, according to the ideas of the time, a robust body was necessarily the abode of a valiant heart."

[1] L. Gautier, *La chevalerie,* pp. 343 sq. ; T. Krabbes, *Die Frau in altfranzoesischen Karls-Epos,* pp. 20 sq.

[2] Herbert de Damartin, *Le roman de Foulque de Candie,* ed. P. Tarbe, p. 103.

[3] A. Schultz, *Das höflische Leben zur Zeit der Minnesinger,* vol. i, pp. 122 sq.

[4] *The History of Fulk Fitz Warine,* ed. by T. Wright, pp. 17 sqq.

[5] Adenés li Rois, *Bueves de Commarchis,* ed. A. Scheler, v. 2967 : " Honnie soie je s'il gist à mon costé." The expressions by which the women voice their scorn in such cases are invariably vigorous : " Molt est vile celle qui de vos ateint fruit " (Herbert de Damartin, *Le roman de Foulque de Candie,* p. 28) ; "Pute soit la pucelle qui ja vous aura chier " (Adenés li Rois, *Le siège de Barbastre,* v. 2907, cited in T. Krabbes, *Die Frau im altfranzoesischen Karls-Epos,* p. 21, from British Museum MS. 20. B. xi).

endowed their barons." [1]   An heiress "is a prey which pretenders dispute to one another, tearing her away from her father, guardian, and even husband." [2]   A thirteenth-century petition in the Rolls of Parliament declares that heiresses in every part of the kingdom were, by guile or force, brought in the power of designing men.[3] In 'Raoul de Cambrai,' the king having been induced by rich gifts to bestow an heiress and her lands on one of his barons, although the lady is already married, threatens her unless she complies to give her to his grooms to ravish.   Her husband having been reported killed, she is ultimately seized with the connivance of her father and compelled to marry the baron ; some years later, however, she is recaptured by her first husband.[4]   An acquaintance of Guibert of Nogent, the Countess of Namur, was seized, together with her lands, by a neighbour, the Lord of Couci, during her husband's absence in Burgundy.   A bitter war ensued when the aggrieved husband attempted to regain his wife and lands, and all prisoners that fell into his hands had their eyes gouged out, their feet lopped off, or were hanged.   He was, however, unsuccessful, and the Bishop of Laon consecrated the victory of the usurper.[5]   It mattered little, where a rich dowry was concerned, whether the woman was maid, widow, or unmarried mother. Hugh, Duke of Tabarie, for instance, eagerly married Sinamonde, who had an illegitimate son by Baldwin of Bouillon.[6]

In the oldest sagas and romances of European peoples the marriage of the hero, when not 'by capture,' is 'marriage by service.'   The lady is bestowed upon him by her father as a payment for the assistance he has rendered.[7]   The adventure which a young and penurious knight sought above all others was of the same kind as his barbaric forefathers had sought before him, and as young Greek princes in the heroic age sought when they left the paternal home, namely, the chance of a rich heiress. Prowess in combats and competitive trials of valour were the time-honoured qualifications for success in such an adventure.   As in all 'marriage by service' in barbaric societies, the bride is not by any means a passive victim mercenarily sacrificed to pay a debt ;

---

[1] L. Gautier, *La chevalerie*, p. 345.

[2] A. Luchaire, in E. Lavisse, *Histoire de France*, vol. ii, part ii, p. 22. Cf. Id., *La société française au temps de Philippe-Auguste*, pp. 381 sqq.

[3] A. Abrams, *English Life and Manners in the Later Middle Ages*, p. 34.

[4] *Raoul de Cambrai*, ed. P. Meyer and A. Longnon, pp. 211 sqq., 232 sqq., 256 sqq.

[5] Guibert, abbot of Nogent, *Monodiae*, iii. 3, in Migne, *Patrologiae Cursus Completus, Series Latina*, vol. clvi, col. 909 sqq.

[6] *Li Bastard de Bouillon*, ed. A. Scheler, v. 6290.

[7] Cf. G. Schoepperle, *Tristan and Isolt*, vol. ii, pp. 163 sq. ; A. Schultz, *Das höfische Leben zur Zeit der Minnesinger*, vol. i, p. 462.

the ' services ' which win her as a prize are identical with the qualities which can gain her affection.   She herself refuses a man who has
not won her by service.   Thus when the Irish hero Cuchulainn woos
Emer, the daughter of Forgall, he recites the deeds of valour which
he has performed.   She, however, belittles them as " the fights of
a mere boy," and lays down the enterprises and exploits which
he must accomplish in order that she may be convinced of his
worth as a warrior, and yield herself to him.[1]

It does not appear that the girl or woman who is bestowed
upon a warrior as a reward for his services or in recognition of
his deeds of valour is invariably expected to become his wife ; the
prize consisted in the enjoyment of the lady's favours, and the
distinguished warrior might please himself with regard to retaining
her.   For example, in the ' Chevalier à deux épées,' the lord of the
Châteaux du Port promises his daughter to Gawain if he should
rid him of his enemy.   When the deed is accomplished, the girl is
without further ado brought to the hero undressed, after supper ;
there is no word of marriage, and she, indeed, makes it clear
that she is sufficiently honoured by the knight's attentions,
and does not expect him to marry her.[2]   The proceeding is
usual in the romances ; " having accomplished an exploit and
won the lady attached to it as a prize, the knight promptly
rides off and leaves her." [3]   When Charlemagne and his peers
pay a visit to the Emperor of Constantinople, the latter's
daughter, Jacqueline, is given to Oliver by the emperor, merely
to prove a boast made by the hero as to his phenomenal

---

[1] " The Wooing of Emer," translated by K. Meyer, in E. Hull, *The
Cuchullin Saga in Irish Literature*, p. 65.   " It was of mighty consequence
who should obtain the grace of a rich heiress. . . . When interest had begun
the habit, the language of love and flattery would soon do the rest.   And
to what that language tended you may see by the constant strain of the
Romances themselves.   Some distressed damsel was the spring and mover
of every knight's adventure.   She was to be rescued by his arms, or won
by the fame and admiration of his prowess.   The plain meaning of all which
was this : that, as in those turbulent feudal times, a protector was necessary
to the weakness of the sex, so the courteous and valorous knight was to
approve himself fully qualified for that office " (R. Hurd, *Letters on Chivalry
and Romance*, p. 105).

[2] *Li chevaliers as deus espées*, ed. W. Foerster, vv. 4804 sqq., 4912 sqq.,
5086 :—

> " La pucele vestu avoit sans plus une blance cemise
> E il l'ot prise entre ses bras
> E li fait oster sa cemise,
> Puis a toute la reube prise.
> Si l'a ruée aval ses pies."

[3] G. Schoepperle, *Tristan and Isolt, a Study of the Sources of Romance*,
vol. i, p. 162.

virility; he departs presently with Charlemagne and his other
companions, leaving the princess pregnant of a son, who afterwards meets him at Roncesvalles.[1] In 'Girbert de Metz,' an old
Lorrain 'chanson de geste,' the 'empress' urges her knights on to
deeds of valour, and to encourage them promises the favours of the
daughters of her counts and princes as their reward.[2] Similarly,
in the 'Chanson de Doon de Nanteuil,' warriors are promised that,
if they "hit the enemy in the bowels, they will be free to take
their choice of the most beautiful ladies in the court."[3] The
usages are, it will be seen, identical with those of the ancient Britons,[4]
and are the same as those which obtained among the North American Indians and the Araucanians of Chili. As with the Redskins,
it was accounted an honour for a girl or woman to be distinguished
by the embraces of a warrior of repute, and to offer herself to him
was deemed an act worthy of praise. Gawain praises the good taste
of his own lady-love, Orgueilleuse, for having offered her favours to so
valiant a warrior as the Red Knight.[5] In a Provençal romance, a
husband reproaches his wife with her infidelity. She replies : " My
Lord, you have no dishonour on that account, for the man I love is
a noble baron, expert in arms, namely, Roland, the nephew of
King Charles." The husband is reduced to silence by the explanation, and is filled with confusion at his unseemly interference.[6]

As among the American aborigines, one of the fundamental
ideas underlying those customs was the primitive desirability for
a woman and her family of acquiring the noble blood of a

[1] *Pélerinage de Charlemagne*, summarised in C. Nyrop, *Storia dell' epopea
francese nel medio evo*, pp. 116 sq., 120.

[2] E. Stengel, *Romanische Studien*, i, pp. 521 sq. :—

> " Pucelles ai en mes chambres gentis,
> Filles a princes et a contes marchis,
> Je vos otroi le baiser a delis,
> Et l'acoleir, et l'autre chouse ausi."

[3] P. Meyer, " La chanson de Doon de Nanteuil, Fragments inédits,"
Romania, xiii, p. 22 :—

> " Qui mielz pourre feri les Frans jusqu'os boelles
> Cil choisiront des dames et prandront des plus belles."

In the Irish sagas Princess Findabair is offered in turn to every warrior
who will fight Cuchulainn (R. Thurneysen, *Die irische Helden- und Königsage*,
pp. 159, 166, 168 sq., 195 sq., 219, 221).

[4] See above, p. 379.

[5] A. Nutt, *Studies on the Legend of the Holy Grail*, p. 241. Cf. *Raoul de
Cambrai*, ed. P. Meyer and A. Longnon, p. 197 :—

> " Se je vos aim n'en doi estri blasmée,
> Car de vos ert si grans la renoumée."

[6] *Gesta Karoli Magni ad Carcassonam et Narbonam*, ed. by F. E. Schneegans, p. 139.

distinguished warrior. A girl who has bestowed her favours
on a knight laments, when she hears that he has been killed,
that he did not leave her pregnant.[1] The women vied for the
attentions of a famed and victorious warrior. They commonly fall
in love with a famous knight in consequence of his reputation, and
without having set eyes on him.[2] A celebrated hero, like Gawain, is
pestered with the women's solicitations. Throughout the romances
of chivalry, as in the more archaic tales from which they derived,
the first advances come, as a general rule, from the women,[3] and
they are as direct and crude as is possible.[4] "For those primitive
women who obeyed, perhaps too readily, the voice of nature, there
is little interval between words and deeds. They do not repress
their feelings, but give them free play. They express loudly their
admiration, and have no hesitation in openly confessing their love.
They go straight to the goal, and if the coveted hero is diffident
or reserved, they offer him their love in words which are anything

---

[1] *Aiol, chanson de geste*, ed. J. Normand and G. Raymond, vv. 5195 sq. :

> "Pleust or a dieu le fieu sante Marie,
> Que j'en fuisse remese toute grosse et enciente."

[2] *Histoire littéraire de la France*, vol. xxx, p. 56 ; T. Krabbes, *Die
Frau im altfranzoesischen Karls-Epos*, p. 26 n. The same thing occurs
in ancient Irish sagas (see, for instance, the " Togail braidne Ui Dergae," in
R. Thurneysen, *Die irische Helden- und Königsage*, p. 628).

[3] T. Krabbes, *op. cit.*, p. 20. Cf. A. Luchaire, *La société française au
temps de Phillipe-Auguste*, p. 376.

[4] E.g., *Amis et Amile*, ed. C. Hofmann, vv. 669 sqq. :—

> "Sire, dist-elle, je n'aime se voz non.
> En vostre lit une nuit me semoing,
> Trestout mon cors voz mettrai a bandon."

Ibid., vv. 612 sqq. :—

> "Biaus sire Amile, dist la franche meschine,
> Je voz offri l'autre jour mon service,
> De dens ma chambre en pure ma chemise."

Raoul de Cambrai, chanson de geste, ed. P. Meyer and A. Longnon, p. 195:—

> "Veés mon cors, com est amanervis :
> Mamele dure, blanc le col, cler le vis ;
> Et car me baise, frans chevalier gentis,
> Si fai de moi trestot a ton devis."

Aiol, chanson de geste, ed. J. Normand and G. Raynaud, vv. 2172 sqq. :—

> "Car vous tornes vers moi, jovente bele,
> Se vous voles baiser, n'autre ju faire,
> J'ai tres bien talent que je vous serve.
> Si m' ait Dieu del ciel, je suis pucele,
> Si n'euc onques ami en nule terre.
> Mais moi vint a penser, vostre voil estre,
> S'il vos vient a plaisir que je vos serve."

but metaphorical." [1] Not infrequently the men repulse them in the curtest manner ; [2] when rejected the women persevere, by insistence or guile, in achieving their object. [3]

The qualifications which are demanded of an intended husband are also required of a lover. Even the most enamoured young woman does not think of yielding her favours unless she is assured of the man's fighting qualities. " I will give you all my love," says a young girl to a knight, " as soon as I have seen you fight your first joust." [4] If a warrior's reputation was not established, he had to prove his valour ; ' service ' was demanded of a lover before he could claim a ' guerdon,' as of a suitor seeking the woman in marriage. There was, in fact, in pagan society no such definite distinction as we make between ' marriage ' and a more or less temporary liaison. The same terms were used for both relations, and when the latter is spoken of as ' marriage,' modern editors have to explain in a gloss that " only a temporary love-relation is intended." [5] Since, however, the modern editor's distinction did not exist for pre-Christian European barbarians, the usages in such cases are identical. When a lover requests a lady's love, she replies : " I care only that your sword be sharp. It is

---

[1] C. Nyrop, *Storia dell' epopea francese nel medio evo*, p. 351. Cf. T. Krabbes, *Die Frau im altfranzoesischen Karls-Epos*, p. 26.

[2] *Histoire littéraire de la France*, vol. xxx, pp. 34, 55 ; C. Nyrop, *op. cit.*, p. 352. Aiol replies to the above-cited offer which his host's daughter makes to him : " Car vos couchies huimais, bien est terme." Cf. *Raoul de Cambrai*, ed. P. Meyer and A. Longnon, pp. 221 sq. :—

> " Elle parla con ja porres oïr :
> ' Baisiés moi, sire, por Dieu qui ne menti ;
> ' Plus le desir que riens que Diex fesist.'
> Est dist Bernier : ' J'an ai molt grant desir
> Mais de basier n'est il mie or loisir.' "

[3] *Amis et Amile*, vv. 696 sqq. :—

> " Sire, dist elle, un petit m'entendez.
> Vos aviiez le mien cors refuse,
> Par bel engieng voz ai prins et mate,
> D'or en avant, s'il voz plaist si m'aimez
> Et si, soiez mes drus et mes privez."

[4] Adenés li Rois, *Bueves de Commarchis*, ed. A. Scheler, vv. 2398 sq. Cf. D. M. Méon, *Nouveau recueil de fabliaux et de contes inédits*, vol. i, p. 175 :—

> " Si li dist, en riant, sanzire,
> que de s'amor n'ert-il ja sire,
> de si que sache, sans dotance,
> comment il porte escu et lance
> et s'il en set venie à chief."

[5] R. Thurneysen, *Die irische Helden- und Königsage*, p. 286.

necessary that for love of me you should do deeds of chivalry." [1]
When Kahelin somewhat bluntly asks the favours of Kamille, she
replies that she is not a peasant girl; he would have to perform
'services' for some time before he could lay claim to favours. [2]
Even Iseult expects that Tristan shall perform any services
which she may require, and flies in a temper if he appears
negligent in that respect. [3] The 'guerdon' which a knight
expects as payment for the performance of 'services' is referred
to in the most direct terms. "Jesus!" exclaims a love-sick
knight, "that I might hold her naked in my arms!" [4] The ladies
use the same expressions in referring to the promised guerdon. [5]

The usages and principles of 'chivalry' thus appear to have
been continuous with those which had obtained from immemorial
time among the barbaric pagan populations of Europe, and were
similar to those found in every primitive society of warriors
or hunters. The standard of sexual morals which went with
those usages differed likewise but slightly from those current
in barbaric Europe before the introduction of Christianity.
"With such 'Naturmenschen,'" remarks Schultz, "platonic
love is out of the question." [6] In the 'chansons de geste'
and earlier romances, says Professor Nyrop, "the morals of the
heroes and heroines are scanty; we scarcely ever find that they
have a single modest or chaste thought. The conception of morality
does not seem to have been very developed, and great licentiousness and immodesty appear to have been general in every class
of society." [7] It would not be safe to judge of the actual state of
the relations between the sexes in the society which modelled itself
upon the romances of chivalry, by the picture of unbridled licentiousness presented in the literature of 'fabliaux' and 'contes'
of the twelfth and thirteenth centuries. Such testimony must be
discounted as highly seasoned by the satirical wit and salacious

---

[1] *Elie de Saint Gille*, ed. G. Reynaud (*Société des Anciens Textes Français*),
vv. 1732 sqq.
[2] Eilhart von Oberge, *Tristan und Isolde*, ed. F. Lichtenstein, vv. 6672 sqq.
[3] G. Schoepperle, *Tristan and Isolt*, vol. i, p. 134.
[4] *Le Chastelain de Couci*, ed. G. A. Crafelet, v. 6631.
[5] *Gui de Nanteuil*, vv. 2188 sqq. :—

> "Amis Gui de Nanteuil, proesce vous salue,
> Encor me tendrez en vos bras toute nue,
> S'en ferez vo talent com de la vostre drue."

Raoul de Cambrai, ed. P. Meyer and A. Longnon, p. 219 :—

> "Qui le tenrait tot nu soz sa cortine,
> Miex li valroit que nule rien qui vive."

[6] A. Schultz, *Das höfische Leben zur Zeit der Minnesinger*, vol. i, p. 452.
[7] C. Nyrop, *Storia dell' epopea francese nel medio evo*, p. 353.

humour of the writers ; and the world of the satirist and scandal-monger is much the same whether in imperial Rome or present-day Europe. But between those civilised societies and that of the Middle Ages there is one profound difference, that, namely, resulting from the survival in mediaeval Europe of the traditional usages and customs of pagan barbarism, which the influence of Christianity had not yet succeeded in abolishing or transforming. " Feudal society," says so competent and sympathetic an authority as Mr. Thomas Wright, " was, in comparison to what had gone before it, polished and brilliant, and presented many great qualities, but under the surface it was not pure." [1] Of the bearing of the women in that period, Professor Luchaire says : " Modesty and decorum were entirely unknown." [2] This was the result of the persistence of social customs belonging to an order of things entirely different from the official Christian law and principles. It was the duty of young women of noble family to receive all guests that presented themselves at the paternal manor, and to attend personally upon their bath and their bed.[3] The old conceptions of sexual hospitality survived, though

---

[1] T. Wright, *Womankind in Western Europe*, p. 166.

[2] A. Luchaire, in E. Lavisse, *Histoire de France*, vol. ii, Part ii, p. 21.

[3] *Ibid.* ; A. Schultz, *Das höfische Leben zur Zeit der Minnesinger*, vol. i, p. 170 ; P. Paris, *Romans de la Table Ronde*, vol. iii, p. 166 ; C. Nyrop, *op. cit.* pp. 351 sq. ; T. Krabbes, *Die Frau im Altfranzoesischen Karls-Epos*, p. 10 ; K. Weinhold, *Die deutschen Frauen in dem Mittelalter*, pp. 174, 393 ; P. Meyer, *Romania*, iv, pp. 394 sq. ; L. Constans, *Légende d'Oedipe*, p. 268. The prescriptive attendance of the young ladies of the house on the guest while he has a bath is described in some detail in " Enfances Viviens " :—

> " Viviens entre el baing molt doucement,
> Li autre apres : chascuns sa cuve prent ;
> N' i a si povre, tant ait poi tenement,
> N'ait sa pucelle devent lui en present,
> Fille de conte ou de prince ausiment,
> Qui bien les servent et font a lor talent "

(*Enfances Viviens*, ed. Wahlund and H. von Failitzen, p. 265). The custom obtained in the same way among the ancient Irish (R. Thurneysen, *Die irische Helden- und Königsage*, p. 393). It furnishes one of the leading episodes in the romance of Tristan and Iseult, and in the first dramatic scene between the future lovers, the hero is stark naked (J. Bédier, *Le roman de Tristan, par Thomas*, vol. i, p. 133). It was the duty of the attendant lady to massage the guest—" le tastonner doucement "—in order to remove any feelings of lassitude (cf. P. Meyer, " Mélanges de poésie Anglo-Normande," *Romania*, iv, pp. 394 sq.).

The same custom, it may be noted, obtained in ancient Greece. Thus when Telemachus visits Nestor, the King of Pylos, his youngest daughter washes him, rubs him all over, and dresses him again (Homer, *Odyssey*, iii. 464 sqq.). Similarly, Helen pays the same attentions to Ulysses (*ibid.*, iv. 250 sqq. Cf. *ibid.*, iii. 48 sq., 464 sqq. ; xviii. 85 sqq.). A terra cotta from

they gradually became attenuated. In some of the older ' chansons ' it is the host's daughter who is offered to the guest to keep him company during the night ; in the ' Chevalier à l'épée ' the host instructs his daughter " not to deny anything to his guest." [1] Where the chatelaine was unmarried or a widow it was almost obligatory for her to offer herself to her guest ; and the time-honoured custom has survived in the most expurgated redactions of the romances.[2] Elsewhere the hostess provides a substitute, a sister or other relative,[3] or a waiting-maid.[4]

Similar customs were usual in ordinary intercourse. There was " extreme intimacy between the two sexes, who commonly visited each other in their bedrooms." In ' Blonde of Oxford,' for instance, the young Oxford lady visits a young man in his bedroom and stays all night with him, " in perfect innocence, as we are told in the romance ; we must remember that it was the custom in those times

Cyprus in the Louvre Museum represents the hostess assisting her guest at his bath (R. Dussaud, *Les civilisations préhelléniques*, p. 402, fig. 296).

Traces of those ancient usages lingered until quite lately in some parts of the Continent in the customary use of female attendants at baths (J. Casanova, *Mémoires*, vol. iv, pp. 393 sq.). I have observed survivals of the same notion in remote and unsophisticated country districts of Germany ; a bath is a ceremonious affair, and the assistance of a female not from any licentious or mercenary motives, but from some traditional notion of the fitness of things, is looked upon as prescriptive. The custom is still usual in Sweden (A. Harrison, *Pandora's Hope*, p. 164).

[1] *Le chevalier à l'épée*, ed. E. C. Armstrong, pp. 18 sq. Cf. *Aiol*, ed. J. Normand and G. Raynaud, v. 2170 sqq.

[2] *La Livre du chevalier de La Tour Landry*, p. 268. Cf. below, pp. 457 sqq.

[3] E. Méray, *La vie au temps des trouvères*, pp. 76 sqq. In a poem of Garin's, the chatelaine says to her fair cousin :—

> " Tu t'en uras au chevalier
> Que monseigneur heberja hier ;
> Ne cri ne noise ne feras,
> Et avec li te coucheras,
> Et feras du tout son plaisir.
> Et bien li dis que j'y alasse
> Se le conte ne redoutasse."

[4] For numerous examples of the usage, see T. Krabbes, *Die Frau im altfranzoesischen Karls-Epos*, p. 24 ; A. Schultz, *Das höfische Leben zur Zeit der Minnesinger*, vol. i, pp. 464 sq. ; A. Preime, *Die Frau in den altfranzösischen Fabliaux*, pp. 63 sqq. ; G. Schoepperle, *Tristan and Isolt*, vol. i, pp. 254 sqq. In the Tristan romance the hero's companion, Kahelin, is supplied by Iseult with her chief lady-in-waiting (Eilhart von Oberge, *Tristan*, v. 6655 sqq., 9050). The ambassador of King Charles reports, in *Gérard de Rossillon*, the courteous manner in which he has been entertained by the Duke :—

> " Colget-me en un lieh d'aur e d'argen,
> E donet-me donzela tan convien,
> Anc non vistes tan bela "
> 	(*Gérard de Rossillon*, ed. Fr. Michel, p. 124).

for both sexes to go to bed perfectly naked."[1]   Those usages were manifestly survivals of the pre-nuptial freedom of the ancient barbarians and of the manner in which noble damsels were wont amongst them to honour estimable warriors.   The practice known as 'bundling,' has lingered to our time among the populations of districts unaffected by the stream of cultural evolution.   It was, and may still be, prevalent in Wales.   "The lower order of people," says an eighteenth-century visitor, "do actually carry on their love affairs in bed."   He notes the "perfect ease and freedom with which it is done, no awkwardness or confusion appearing on either side."[2]   Another traveller remarks : "Much has been said of the innocence with which their meetings are conducted, but it is a very common thing for the consequences of the interview to make its appearance in the world within two or three months after the marriage ceremony has taken place."[3]   The same usage obtained in Scotland and in some English counties, and was carried over to the American Colonies, where "the ridiculous and pernicious custom which prevailed among the young to a degree which we can scarcely credit sapped the foundations of modesty."[4]   In Holland it was known as 'queesting.'[5]   In Switzerland "these nightly visits, recognised, however, as entirely respectable and conventional, were habitual in every canton."[6]   Stendhal quotes from the works of a Swiss colonel a description of the usage, in this instance in the form of hospitality. The host was the chief magistrate of the town, and his daughter, aged sixteen, offered to keep the guest company during the night. She, however, first requested her mother's permission, who, in turn, consulted her husband.   "With pleasure," replied the latter, "to such a guest I would even lend my wife."[7]   Mediaeval society, in which those usages were habitual amongst all classes, thus differed considerably from our own in its conceptions of sexual morality. How greatly the standards of propriety in speech in the England of Shakespeare differed from those of the present day is known to everyone.   But the naturalism of the Elizabethan age was as nothing compared with that of earlier periods.   The women possessed a matchless gift of direct expression.   "The conversation and

---

[1] T. Wright, *Womankind in Western Europe*, p. 167.

[2] S. J. Pratt, *Gleanings through Wales, Holland and Westphalia*, vol. i, pp. 105 sqq.

[3] W. W. Bingley, *North Wales, including its Scenery, Antiquities, Customs*, vol. ii, p. 282.   Cf. J. T. Barber, *A Tour through South Wales and Monmouthshire*, pp. 103 sqq.

[4] H. R. Stiles, *Bundling*, p. 6.

[5] *Ibid.*, pp. 36 sq.

[6] A. C. Johnson, *The Cottages of the Alps, or Life and Manners in Switzerland*, pp. 77, 91, 132.

[7] Stendhal, *De l'amour*, pp. 207 sq.

repartee of a mediaeval circle would disgrace a modern tavern,"
observes an admirer of the Middle Ages.[1]

Marriage retained for centuries after Europe had become
Christian the loose character, as a matter of pure economic
convenience, that it had in pagan Europe. The matrimonial
history of Henry VIII would not have attracted attention in
the eleventh or twelfth century. Wives were put aside whenever, for any reason, their husbands desired a change ; the women
used the same freedom, and the majority of those whose names
appear in the chronicles have changed husbands three or four
times. Women, together with their domains, were " in circula-
tion." [2] " In the Middle Ages," say Sir Frederic Pollock and
Mr. Maitland, " marriages, or what looked like marriages, were
exceedingly insecure." The Church was compelled to temporise.
The principle of the indissolubility of marriage was, indeed, entirely
neutralised by the amazing extent of the recognised impediments
to valid marriage. Not only were the prohibited degrees of
relationship interpreted in the most comprehensive manner, but
the same sweeping restrictions applied to relatives by marriage,
and even to the blood-relations of any person with whom
illicit intercourse had taken place. To those prohibited degrees
were added such as depended upon ' spiritual affinity,' namely,
relationship through god-parents. Those multiplied impediments
" made the formation of a valid marriage a matter of chance,"

---

[1] C. H. Pearson, *The Early and Middle Ages of England*, p. 434. The
expressions used in the games which were fashionable in polite circles were
such that even the old Norman-French will not bear being reproduced (see
T. Wright, *Anecdota Literaria*, p. 81). The mediaeval standard in this
respect is strikingly instanced by the extraordinary book of the chevalier
de La Tour Landry, published as late as the fourteenth century. It enjoyed
a wide vogue and was translated into English by Chaucer, being one
of the first books to be printed in England. It was expressly composed as a manual of moral instruction for the author's young daughters,
and is written with the most devout and earnest moral intentions.
Yet such are the anecdotes by which the pious knight exhibits the evils
of moral laxity to his beloved children, that no publisher could at
the present day print the work in modern English without rendering himself liable to prosecution. For example, the desirability of observing
proper decorum in church is brought home by the story of a couple who
committed fornication on the high altar : " Si advint un miracle qu'ilz
s'entreprindrent et s'entrebessonnèrent comme chiens, tellement qu'ilz furent
anssy pris de toute le jour à journée, si que ceulx de l'esglise et ceulx du
païx eurent assez loisir de lez venir veoir ; car ils ne se pouvoient departir,
et convint que l'on venist à procession à prier Dieu pour eulx, et au fort sur
le soir ilz se departirent " (*Le livre du chevalier de La Tour Landry pour
l'enseignement de ses filles*, p. 80).

[2] A. Luchaire, *La société française au temps de Philippe-Auguste*, pp. 386
sq. ; Id., in E. Lavisse, *Histoire de France*, vol. ii, Part ii, p. 22.

and whenever annulment was desired it was not difficult to show that the marriage had been invalid from the first.[1]   We hear, for example, of a Duke Albany who entered into negotiations with a view to marrying Edward's daughter Cecilia, although he had only just married Anne de La Tour shortly after divorcing another wife.[2]

It was prescriptive for every married woman to have one or more knightly lovers, and the lack of such a mark of honour entailed disgrace and shame.   The chivalric ' love-service ' had, like ' bundling,' come to be conventionally regarded as ostensibly innocent and ' platonic.'   But that was not the view which ecclesiastical authorities took of it.   The knights who fight in tournaments, says Bishop Jacques of Vitry, " hope to obtain through their success in arms the favours of the shameless women whose tokens they wear." [3] The ideal of the relation was, as usual, a retrospective mirage. " The platonic gallantry of the paladins of old," says a modern historian, sharing that delusion, " had gradually become replaced by a thinly disguised sensuality." [4]   The chevalier de La Tour Landry gives, as a warning to his daughters, a curious account of a discussion on the subject between himself and his wife, a plain practical woman.   The husband declares that he can see no wrong in a woman having a lover, and that, on the contrary, the merit of a good woman is enhanced by her inspiring a man to deeds of prowess.   But his matter-of-fact lady is not to be taken in by such specious sentiments.   She declares her conviction that such relations are invariably dangerous, and that high-flown sentiments and chaste kisses are but sparks applied to a dry haystack, which must needs result in conflagration.[5]   It cannot for a moment be doubted that there were at that period many chaste and faithful wives, and many men and women who were imbued with the principles of Christian morality.   William of Malmesbury assures us that he was personally acquainted with several men, both lay and clerical, who led sober and chaste lives ; but he represents them as exceptions.   The Norman nobility in general were, he says, " given over to gluttony and lechery."   It was usual with them, " when their concubines became pregnant or they tired of them, to establish them as public prostitutes or to traffic their favours amongst their acquaintances." [6]   Shortly after the battle of

---

[1] F. Pollock and F. W. Maitland, *The History of English Law before the Time of Edward I*, vol. ii, pp. 369, 386 sqq., 393.

[2] A. Abrams, *English Life and Manners in the Later Middle Ages*, p. 121.

[3] Jacques de Vitry, *Sermones Vulgares*, in J. B. Pitra, *Analecta Novissima Spicilegii Solesmensis*, vol. ii, p. 431.

[4] A. Lecoy de la Marche, *La chaire française au moyen-âge*, p. 392.

[5] *Le livre du chevalier de La Tour Landry*, pp. 246 sqq.

[6] William of Malmesbury, *De gesta regum Anglorum* (*Chronicles and Memorials of Great Britain and Ireland*), vol. ii, p. 305.

Hastings, a large number of William's knights asked leave of absence and hurried back to their Norman castles on receiving news that their wives were entertaining lovers.[1]   When Richard I arrived at Marseilles to embark for the Holy Land, he found his barons, who had preceded him at the port of embarkation by a few weeks, penniless, having spent on women the money which they had collected from their vassals to redeem the sepulchre of Christ.[2]   "Marital vows are never observed," says Abbot Guibert of Nogent.[3]   A lady of his acquaintance, Sibyll of Château-Porcien, although her husband was young and handsome, had countless lovers, "because her husband could not fulfil his conjugal duties to the extent that she desired."   At the time that she became the mistress of Equerrend de Bores, an elderly man "who was so addicted to the sex that he had always about him some women bought or borrowed," she was pregnant by another lover.[4]   John of Salisbury gives an even more lurid account of the manners of his time.   "After a young woman has come out of the bridal chamber," he says, "her husband is regarded more as a procurer than as a spouse.   He brings her out and exhibits her to his friends, and wherever a hope of profit is held out, he hypocritically offers her love.   When the pretty daughter, or any other female member of the family, pleases a rich man, she is a ware in the market which is offered wherever a purchaser is forthcoming."[5]   In England it is complained that adultery is universal.

> Thys ys now a common synne
> For almost hyt ys every-whore.
> A gentyl man hath a wyfe and a hore ;
> And wyves have now comunly
> Here husbandys and a ludby.[6]

Those manners are set down by ancient and modern writers to 'the corruption of the times.'   But if we go back to an earlier epoch, when Christianity had not long become established in England, instead of pristine purity the accounts we have of sex relations show, on the contrary, a worse 'corruption.'   The

---

[1] Ordericus Vitalis, *Historia ecclesiastica*, v. 4.

[2] Benedict of Peterborough, *Vita et Gesta regis Henrici Secundi*, ann. 1190, in Bouquet, *Recueil des historiens des Gaules et de la France*, vol. vii, p. 500 ; M. Capefigue, *Histoire de Philippe-Auguste*, vol. i, p. 359.

[3] Guibert of Nogent, *Monodiae*, iii. 3, in Migne, *Patrologiae Cursus Completus, Series Latina*, vol. clvi, col. 943.

[4] *Ibid.*, coll. 909 sqq.

[5] John of Salisbury, *Polycraticus*, ed. J. A. Giles, iii. 13.

[6] Robert of Brunne, *Handlyng Synne*, ed. F. J. Furnivall (*Roxburgh Club Publications*), p. 93.

condition of things which they suggest differs little from that represented by Caesar's statement that " the Britons possessed their wives in common." St. Boniface laments again and again the lack of comprehension of the proper relations between the sexes shown by the English. The English, he says, " utterly despise legitimate matrimony." " It fills us with shame for our race," he writes to an English priest, " to be told by both Christians and pagans that the English people, scorning the usages of other nations and the apostolic precepts given under God's law, refuse to have legitimate wives, and continue to live in lechery and adultery after the manner of neighing horses and braying asses, confounding all things in their wickedness and corruption." [1] These are not the exaggerations of a fanatic, for Boniface was not of that type, and his complaints are addressed to English friends who knew as well as he did how matters stood. He addressed a long letter, more in sorrow than in anger, to Ethelbald, the powerful King of Mercia, expressing his grief that he had no legitimate wife, but continued to use—in the traditional pagan manner—the monasteries of Holy Women as his harems. [2] At a still earlier date, Gildas, it will be remembered, speaks of the sexual morals of the Britons in similar terms. " Although they keep a large number of wives, they are fornicators and adulterers "; and elsewhere he says : " There is among you everywhere such fornication as is scarcely to be met with among pagans in any country." [3] About a century after Boniface, Alcuin of York found little improvement in this respect. For a wonder he does not set down the prevalent looseness of sexual morals entirely to the ' corruption of the times.' " I do not say that the sin of fornication did not previously exist among the people," he writes, " but since the time of King Aelfwald, at any rate, the land has been absolutely submerged under a flood of fornication, adultery, and incest, so that the very semblance of modesty is entirely absent." [4]

In spite of the references of Gildas and of Boniface to " the

---

[1] St. Boniface, *Epistola*, lxi, in Migne, *Patrologiae Cursus Completus*, vol. lxxxix, col. 756. Cf. *Epistola*, lii, *ibid.*, col. 750.

[2] Id., *Epistola*, lxii, coll. 758 sqq.

[3] Gildas, *De excidio Britanniae*, ed. J. Stevenson, pp.27, 36.

[4] Alcuin, *Epistolae*, in Pertz, *Monumenta Germaniae Historica, Epistolae Karolini Aevi*, vol. ii, p. 43. Aelfwald was king of Northumbria from 779 to 788. The licentiousness of the Anglo-Saxons is reflected in the penitentiaries of Saint Egbert, Archbishop of York (*S. Egberti Poenitantiale*, in Migne, *Patrologiae Cursus Completus*, vol. lxxxix, coll. 401 sqq.). Among the venial sins which confessors are instructed to deal with are mentioned, for instance, " Si maritus cum uxore more canino coeat. . . . Si cum extis ejus coeat. . . . Si quis cum bestia coeat. . . . Quicumque in os semen effuderit. . . . Qui viri semen biberit."

customs of other nations," these did not, on Boniface's own showing, differ fundamentally from those of the English. He elsewhere warns the latter that if they do not mend their ways they will suffer in consequence, " as has happened to the people of Spain, of Provence, of Burgundy, who, neglecting God, lived in fornication." [1] Salvianus, in fact, draws an even more lurid picture of the morals of Gaul at the close of the fifth century than does Boniface of those of the English. Every estate is a scene of prostitution, all Aquitaine is one vast ' lupanar,' conjugal fidelity is unknown. The state of things is no better in Spain.[2] The fact is that the character of marriage and of sex relations had remained to a large extent unchanged since the days of paganism. A modern ecclesiastical apologist appears to be justified when he claims that " the ideas and customs in regard to marriage were established by the Church ; it was the Church that created marriage." [3]

The apostle of Germany laments in particular the state of the English monasteries : the nunneries were no better than brothels.[4] There can here be no question of ' corruption ' ; most of the monasteries had but recently been established. Boniface's remarks, which represent the nuns as exceeding other women in immorality, refer to the institutions at their origin, and not to what it is customary to regard as abuses and corruptions in the monasteries of the thirteenth and fourteenth centuries in France and Italy. It must be borne in mind that not one person out of a hundred, male or female, who entered the monasteries did so from motives of religion. Throughout the Middle Ages the monasteries were a godsend ; they offered homes, which were comfort and luxury compared with those of the majority of the population, a life free from

---

[1] Boniface, *Epistola*, lxii, *op. cit.*, col. 761. Military reverses have invariably been ascribed by the Church to sexual incontinence. Alcuin sets down the defeat of the Britons by the Saxons in the same manner to ' fornication ' (Alcuin, *op. cit.*, p. 47) ; though it is difficult to see that the Saxon or Norman victors were in this respect superior to the vanquished. The reverses of the Crusaders were likewise accounted for by their fornications (Henry of Huntingdon, *Historia Anglorum*, vii, A.D. 1097, *Chronicles and Memorials of Great Britain and Ireland*, vol. lxxiv, p. 280). The French peasants were told by their ' curés ' during the late war that it was due to the same cause, and also to the expulsion of the monastic orders from France.

[2] Salvianus, *De gubernatione Dei*, vi. 72, vii. 16. 27, in Migne, *op. cit.*, vol. liii, coll. 120 sqq., 132, 135.

[3] L. Gautier, *La chevalerie*, p. 358. For a long while after the introduction of Christianity the Church appears, however, to have paid little attention to the marriages of the common people and serfs. The latter were encouraged to cohabit, but those unions were not spoken of as marriages (nuptiae, matrimonia), but as ' contubernia,' and were contracted without any ceremony or priestly benediction (J. Potgiesserus, *De statu servorum*, ii. 2. 1).

[4] Boniface, *Epistolae*, lii, lxi. lxii. *ut supra*.

care, and the enjoyment of numerous privileges and prerogatives. Men and women of all sorts and conditions flocked to the monasteries. Religious views had nothing to do with their ' vocation '; throughout the Middle Ages the boldest thinkers, the most determined heretics, artists, students of science, have been monks. The men and women who filled the monasteries of barbaric lands soon after their establishment were, most of them, simply incapable of understanding what was expected of them ; they knew scarcely anything of Christianity ; their notions and ideas were purely pagan. Many of the Irish saints who transferred their devotion from old to new idols, as did the priestesses of Brigit, had no more smattering of Christian doctrine than those wild Mexican Indians who, at the present day, mix the myths and rituals of pagan and Christian religions in inextricable confusion. Most of those men and women, when told that they were vowed to chastity, probably did not understand what the word meant. In the earlier Irish monastic foundations the monks had women to wait on them.[1] As Professor Zimmer remarks, and illustrates by a number of examples, the lives of early Irish saints are characterised by conceptions of sexual morality which differ little, if at all, from those of pagan times. St. Brigit is described as solemnly blessing the womb of a pregnant nun.[2] The morals, or absence of morals, of the nunneries were the customary standards which, according to pagan ideas, were understood to apply to unattached women, and to ' sacred women ' in particular. King Ethelbald and other potentates, in regarding the nunneries as their harems, continued the immemorial usage by which priestesses are looked upon as the wives of the king.

Unions were temporary, marriages were trial-marriages. In times of misery and anarchy, when agriculture on a large scale was impossible, and any permanent occupation difficult, thousands of women attached themselves to wandering bands, to ' knights ' seeking adventures. St. Boniface again strongly urges the English synods to discourage pilgrimages, especially in the case of women, whether lay or veiled. They are pretexts for wandering over the continent and leading a licentious life, and most of the women do not return. " There is scarcely a town in Italy, or in France, or in Gaul," he says, " where English prostitutes are not to be found ; which is a scandal and a disgrace to your Church." [3]

It might seem at first sight as if the stern and obsessing

[1] A. W. Haddan and W. Stubbs, *Councils and ecclesiastical documents relating to Great Britain and Ireland*, vol. ii, Part i, p. 292.
[2] H. Zimmer, " Keltische Beiträge," *Zeitschrift für deutsches Alterthum und deutsche Litteratur*, xxxiii, p. 284.
[3] Boniface, *Epistola*, lxiii, *op. cit.*, col. 768.

sentiments of the Christian Church concerning sexual purity, which permitted marriage as the lesser evil, had been without effect upon the established usages and ideas of the peoples who came to constitute the bulk of Christendom. That, however, was not by any means the case. Christianity ultimately effected a profound and momentous, if somewhat indirect, transformation in their conceptions of the relations between the sexes.

In the first place definite legislation restricted the legal conception of marriage. The laws, codified by Christian priests, abolished polygamy, although for a considerable time the prohibition was not taken very seriously. As among the Celts, so also among the Normans, "polygamy would seem to have been the rule, at least among the leaders."[1] It was the custom "with all the Germans, and the victory of Christianity in this matter was only slowly achieved."[2] Polygamy was common among the kings and chieftains in the Merovingian and Carolingian era, and Charlemagne himself, the hero and defender of the Faith, was said to have at least two 'legal' wives at the same time, and was attended by a seraglio of concubines.[3] A beginning was made by insisting that priests should not have more than one legal wife.[4] A distinction which did not previously exist tended to become established between legitimacy and illegitimacy in regard to sex relations and offspring. In the later Middle Ages and thereafter the word 'bastard' is one of the most offensive which it is possible to use, and is accordingly a favourite term of abuse. It is significant, however, that throughout the earlier heroic sagas, not only was no dishonour attached to bastardy, but it appears to have been almost obligatory for every heroic and exalted personage to be a bastard. All the heroes of Irish epical myth—King Conchobar,[5] Cuchulainn,[6] Mongan,[7] Fionn,[8] Conaire [9]—were bastards. King Arthur was a bastard,[10] and so was Gawain.[11] Roland, the hero of Carolingian epics, was a bastard.[12] Historical personages of any distinction were, like

[1] A. Mawer, *The Vikings*, p. 85.

[2] K. Weinhold, *Altnordisches Leben*, p. 249.

[3] M. Capefigue, *Charlemagne*, vol. ii, pp. 227 sq.

[4] *Karoli Magni Capitularia*, in Pertz, *Monumenta Germaniae Historica, Leges*, "Capitularia Regum Francorum," vol. i, p. 45.

[5] "Compert Concobuir," *Revue Celtique*, vi, pp. 179 sq.

[6] L. Duvau, "La légende de la conception de Cuchulainn," *Revue Celtique*, ix, p. 12.

[7] K. Meyer and A. Nutt, *The Voyage of Bran*, vol. i, pp. 44 sq.

[8] J. G. Campbell, *The Fians*, pp. 16 sqq.

[9] R. Thurneysen, *Die irische Helden- und Königsage*, p. 629.

[10] *Perceval le Gallois*, ed. C. Potvin, vol. i, pp. 229 sq.

[11] *Ibid.*, p. 253 ; *Histoire littéraire de la France*, vol. xxx, p. 31 n.

[12] C. Nyrop, *Storia dell' epopea francese nel medio evo*, p. 87 ; G. Paris, *Histoire poétique de Charlemagne*, p. 378.

mythical heroes, under the obligation of being bastards.   Theodoric was a bastard.[1]   Clothwig, the founder of the Frankish
kingdom, the ' eldest son of the Church,' was a bastard ; [2] and
when his kingdom was divided after his death, his bastard
son obtained, according to barbarian usage, by far the largest
share, to the detriment of his three legitimate half-brothers.[3]
Charles Martel was a bastard.[4]   Charlemagne himself was persistently declared to be a bastard.[5]   When, as in the latter instances,
the truth of the allegations is doubtful, they were not scandalous defamations, but were regarded as befitting the character
of the glorified heroes.   Among the barbaric ancestors of modern
Europeans, as among the ancient Hindus or the Guanches, it
added dignity to have been begotten by a ' stranger.' [6]   William
the conqueror nowise resented the appellation of ' William the
Bastard,' by which he was commonly known.   In fact, " bastardy was in credit." [7]   The dishonour that came to be attached to
the term ' bastard ' and its employment as an epithet of abuse were
thus the expression of a complete inversion of ideas, brought about
by the influence of the Christian religion.   The Anglo-Saxon synod
of 786 decreed " that the son of a meretricious union shall be
debarred from legally inheriting, for, in accordance with the
apostolic authority of holy decrees, we regard adulterine children
as spurious. . . . We command then, in order to avoid fornication,
that every layman shall have one legitimate wife, and every woman
one legitimate husband, in order that they may have and beget
legitimate heirs according to God's law." [8]

---

[1] J. Grimm, *Deutsche Rechtsalterthüme*, pp. 407, 472.

[2] *Gesta regum Francorum*, in M. Bouquet, *Recueil des historiens des Gaules
et de la France*, vol. ii, p. 546.

[3] Gregory of Tours, *Historia ecclesiastica Francorum*, ibid., pp. 176,
187 n.

[4] G. Paris, *Histoire poétique de Charlemagne*, pp. 440 sq. ;   G. Huet,
" La légende de Charlemagne bâtard et le témoignage de Jean Baendale,"
Le Moyen Âge, 2ᵉ Série, xv, p. 163.

[5] G. Huet, pp. 161 sqq. ;   G. Paris, *Histoire poétique de Charlemagne*,
pp. 227, 439 sqq.   Cf. C. Nyrop, *Storia dell' epopea francese nel medio
evo*, p. 85.   Professor Nyrop regards Charlemagne as having, in fact,
been the son of Pepin's concubine, Alpaid.   It is significant that Einhard
states that he knows nothing concerning the birth of Charlemagne.   A
legend was current representing Charles as the offspring of an incestuous
union (A. Graf, *Roma nella memoria e nell' immaginazione del medio evo*,
p. 308).

[6] Cf. J. G. Hahn, *Sagwissensschaftlichen Studien*, pp. 341 sqq. ;   A. Nutt,
" The Aryan Expulsion- and Return Formula in the Folk- and Hero Tales
of the Celts," *Folk-lore Record*, iv, pp. 1 sqq.

[7] G. Huet, *op. cit.*, p. 101.   Cf. T. Wright, *Womankind in Western Europe*,
p. 173.

[8] *Monumenta Germaniae Historica, Epistolae*, vol. iv, p. 25.

The Literature of Pagan Europe.

The changes which were gradually effected in sentiments concerning sex relations are, however, far more clearly exhibited in the literature of early Christian Europe than in the manners of its peoples. The facts which we are about to examine show that those changes of sentiment first manifested themselves in theoretical and abstract form in literary productions, and only subsequently extended their influence to actual life. It is as a literary rather than as a social phenomenon that the transition from pagan to Christian sentiment first presents itself.

The manners of the barbarians and their ignorance of the principles of Christian morality were reflected in the unwritten literature which played a prominent part in their lives, and which directly gave rise to the romantic literature of mediaeval Europe. Lays reciting the adventures and loves of heroes and goddesses, the rewards of deeds of valour, the abduction of princesses and queens and the conquests of their realms, had formed a part of every entertainment and gathering among the barbaric nations of Europe. The Germans had no other literature than those ancient songs;[1] among the Celts no ' Round Table ' was complete without the recital of some thrilling tale.[2] The bard was a privileged person, a magical individual to whom nothing could be denied ; knowledge of the sagas and skill in poetical composition were accounted a merit equal to valour in the field. The Germans, says Saxo Grammaticus, " considered that to sing deeds of valour is as meritorious as to perform them." [3] The bard incited the combatants, and as late as the battle of Hastings Taillefer is represented as encouraging the Norman barons, in the ancient manner, by singing ' chansons de geste.' [4] Tristan is pictured as a gifted singer and composer of lays, and is even, as was also Cuchulainn, proficient in entertaining tricks of sleight-of-hand such as were associated in mediaeval Europe with the

---

[1] Tacitus, *Germania*, iii.

[2] Posidonius, in Athenaeus, iv. 12 ; Amminanus Marcellinus, xv. 9. 8 ; Diodorus Siculus, v. 31 ; Lucan, *Pharsalia*, i. 447 sqq. Cf. L. Diefenbach, *Origines Europeae*, p. 245 ; A. T. Holder, *Altceltischer Sprachschatz*, vol. i, col. 347 sq.

[3] Saxo Grammaticus, *Historia Danica*, Praefatio, p. 3.

[4] W. Wace, *Roman de Rou*, ed. Andressen, vol. ii, p. 348 ; Henry of Huntingdon, *Historiae Anglorum*, vi. 30 ; Gui d'Amiens, *Carmen de Hastingae proelio*, ed. Fr. Michel, *Chroniques anglo-normandes*, vol. iii, p. 18 ; Geffrei Gaimar, *Lestorie des Englies*, ed. by Sir T. D. Hardy and C. T. Martin (*Chronicles and Memorials of Great Britain and Ireland*), vol. ii, p. 167. Cf. *Nibelungen Lied*, ed. K. Bartsch, stanza 196 ; Saxo Grammaticus, *op. cit.*, xiv ; *Miracula S. Benedicti*, in M. Bouquet, *Recueil des historiens des Gaules et de la France*, vol. xi, p. 489.

art of the 'jongleur.'[1] The pagan minstrelsy continued during
the Middle Ages to constitute the literature of the illiterate populations ; they heard with the same tense interest the recital, with but
formal modifications, of the themes to which for centuries their
forefathers had listened. The inmates of every castle, court, and
hostel were entertained with lays from the traditional repertoire
of wandering minstrels, 'trouvères,' 'jongleurs.' The social status
of the singers changed with altered conditions. In pagan society
the bard had been 'ex officio' a semi-priestly personage, and
often a distinguished warrior ; none but a freeman could exercise
the calling.[2] In Christian society the singer of pagan lays was
banned by the ecclesiastical authorities.[3] The art of the poet
continued, however, to grace the character of kings, and to be
exercised by noblemen.[4] Every guest of distinction was expected
to provide some entertainment of the kind in return for his host's
hospitality. "It is the custom in Normandy," says a twelfth-
century trouvère—

> Usage est en Normandie,
> Que qui est hebergie, faut qu'l die
> Fable ou chanson a son hoste.[5]

The sharp distinctions of feudal society inevitably reduced,
however, the status of literary entertainers ; the itinerant minstrel,
the 'jongleur,' the gleeman often fell to the lowest depths of

---

[1] G. Schoepperle, *Tristan and Isolt*, pp. 287, 290 sqq. ; *Táin bó Cúalnge*,
tr. H. d'Arbois de Jubainville, pp. 63 sqq. ; S. H. O'Grady, *Silva Gadelica*,
vol. i, pp. 92 sq., vol. ii, pp. 99 sq.

[2] T. Stephens, *The Literature of the Kymry*, p. 95.

[3] See below, pp. 444, sqq.

[4] The Merovingian king Chilperic composed poems (Gregory of Tours,
Historia ecclesiastica Francorum, v. 45, in M. Bouquet, *Recueil des historiens des
Gaules et de la France*, vol. ii, p. 260). The instances of Richard I, of Duke
William of Aquitaine (see below, p. 477), are familiar. Baldwin II, Count
of Guines, was said to be equal to any 'jongleurs' in his knowledge of sagas
and skill in song (Lambert of Ardres, *Historia comitum Ghisnensium*, in Pertz,
Monumenta Germaniae Historica, Scriptores, vol. xxiv, p. 598). The following
passage shows how the art of the 'conteur' was exercised by knights and
nobles : "Then a certain knight, a veteran called Robert of Constantine,
graced his ears by singing, accompanying himself on an instrument, of the
'Roman Emperors,' of 'Charlemagne,' Roland and Oliver, and Arthur
King of Britain . . . and a relative of his, Walter of Clusa, sang concerning
the Deeds of the Angles, and their fables, of Gormund, Sambard, Tristan and
Iseult, Merlin and Merchulf, and the Deeds of the Ardennes " (*ibid.*, p. 607).

[5] Jehan le Chapelain, *Le sacristain de Cluny*, in P. J. B. Legrand d'Aussy,
Fabliaux ou contes du xiie et xiiie siècles, vol. iv, p. 266 ; A. Méray, *La vie
au temps des trouvères*, p. 172. For the custom among the ancient Celts,
see H. d'Arbois de Jubainville, *La civilisation des Celtes*, p. 142.

beggarly parasitism and vagrancy.[1] The delight in the entertainment which he supplied and the influence it exercised were, however, scarcely less than in pagan times. That oral literature was the mental pabulum upon which the imagination of the people, high and low, prince and serf, baron and villein, from York to Palermo, eagerly fed during the Middle Ages, the world of fancy by which their ideals and sentiments were moulded. "The fables of Arthur of Britain and the songs of Charlemagne," sings a minstrel, "are more dearly cherished and more esteemed than the Gospels. The minstrel is listened to more keenly than Saint Paul or Saint Peter." [2]

[1] In his important book on mediaeval 'jongleurs,' Professor Faral puts forward, against the general view, the theory that the minstrels of the Middle Ages derived not from the barbarian bards, but from the Roman 'mimes' (E. Faral, *Les jongleurs en France au moyen âge*, pp. 9 sqq. and *passim*). But although mediaeval minstrels may have inherited some of the characteristics of Roman entertainers, the theory will not bear examination. Early mediaeval minstrelsy flourished more particularly in the north of France, in Flanders and Germany, among the Normans, in Britain, countries where Roman civilisation and its luxuries had not taken deep root. In the south of France, the Roman 'Provincia,' where, if anywhere, the successors of Roman 'mimes' might, on M. Faral's view, be expected to be in evidence, the poets and singers belonged, more especially in the earlier period, prescriptively to the aristocratic class, and only subsequently descended to the level of popular entertainers. We repeatedly hear of the accomplishments of the singers from Britain, who are specially sent for; it is scarcely to Britain that one would send for Roman 'mimes.' The themes of mediaeval narrative poetry are northern and pagan, not classical and Latin. The favourite instrument which was used for accompaniments in early times was the Celtic 'rote.' Literary entertainers among the barbarian nations became to a large extent degraded in mediaeval times to a status and character similar to that of 'mimes' and buffoons among the Romans; ecclesiastical writers who waged an incessant war against them (see below, pp. 444 sqq.) identified them with the 'mimes,' the 'histriones' of classical civilisation, and speak of them—even of a knightly bard like Taillefer—by those terms. The degradation of the noble bard into the 'ribald jongleur' is easily intelligible in the conditions of the times; but it would be difficult, on M. Faral's view, to account for the genesis of the aristocratic bard out of the Roman 'mimes.' M. Faral has not attempted to face the question; he merely refers to some 'mimes' becoming enriched. William of Poitou, Jaufré Rudel, Richard I, the Lord of Couci, the knights mentioned by Lambert, were not "enriched mimes." Cf. G. Paris, *Histoire poétique de Charlemagne*, p. 48: "A cette époque les chanteurs (jongleurs, ménestrels, etc.) ne semblent pas avoir encore formé une classe distincte; en tout cas la plupart des guerriers savaient eux-mêmes répéter des rudes poésies." Cf. Id., in *Romania*, xiii, p. 603.

[2] *Romania*, xviii, p. 509:—

"Les fables d'Artur de Bretagne
E les chansons de Charlemagne
Plus sont cheries e meins viles
Que ne soient les evangiles.
Plus est escoutes li jugliere
Que ne soit saint Pol ou saint Pierre."

The subject of sex relations naturally occupied a large place in that earliest European literature ; but it was not treated from the point of view of morality, still less from that of the principles of Christian morality. The whole literary heritage was of pagan origin, and the contrast between it and the ascetic zeal of the established religion was as great as that between the ideals of the Christian Fathers and the usages of the heathen barbarians ; while the spirit of the former continued to dominate theological and religious writings, an utterly different view of sex relations inspired the popular or ' romantic ' literature. The term ' romance ' was applied to compositions in the current speech of the people of France, who ever since the days of Roman domination had been proud to call themselves Roman citizens, or Romans. The word was originally an adverb, ' romanice,' ' in the Roman tongue,' as opposed to ' latinice,' ' in Latin,' or ' theudisce,' ' in German.' Romantic literature means, therefore, the popular French literature of the early Middle Ages, as opposed to the learned literature of clerks, which was written in Latin. When we speak of ' romance,' of ' romantic sentiments,' of ' romantic love,' the expressions signify, strictly speaking, sentiments and conceptions of love similar to those pictured in the popular literature of mediaeval France, the ' romances.' Those expressions are nowadays generally understood to refer to a form of amatory sentiment which is distinctive of European feeling, and to which nothing, either in the ancient classical world or in any other culture, exactly corresponds. The identification of the two meanings is, in fact, perfectly justified ; it is out of the ' romantic ' literature of the Middle Ages that the type of European ' romantic ' amatory sentiment developed. In the literature of the twelfth and thirteenth centuries the distinctive characteristics of the European conception of romantic love are indeed manifested in full-blown perfection. Not only did they receive poetical expression in the narratives of the sagas re-modelled by the court-poets of the period, but the subject was theoretically analysed, dissected, discussed, and defined with a pedantic minuteness from which later taste would have shrunk.

In the curious book of Andreas, the chaplain, the views and sentiments on the subject of romantic love which obtained in the society of baronial castles and troubadour circles in France during the twelfth and the early part of the thirteenth century are prosaically set forth in detail. Among other documents, thirty-one propositions or principles are laid down which, after mature consideration and discussion by the most eminent authorities on amatory matters, were accepted as canons to which the tender passion was expected to conform. It is appointed, for example, that " Every lover is wont to grow pale at the sight of his lady-love ; that at the sudden and unexpected sight of her the heart of the true lover palpitates ; that a real lover is always a prey to anxiety ; that a person who is under the influence of love eats little and sleeps little ; that a true lover is perpetually enthralled by the image of his lady-love, which never for one moment departs from his mind." We certainly have here, if the Hibernicism may be allowed, the classical picture of romantic love. But side by side, or rather intermingled, with the presentment of the perfect lover and of what until very lately was termed the modern conception of sexual love, as distinguished from all pre-Christian or non-European forms of the sentiment, those same canons of early European romanticism present the definite traces of the social conditions amid which those ideals developed. It is laid down that " It is not becoming to love those ladies who only love with a view to marriage ; that love can deny nothing to love ; that marriage cannot be pleaded by a lady as an excuse for refusing love ; that favours which are yielded unwillingly are insipid ; that a new love banishes the old one completely ; that nothing can prevent one lady being loved by two gentlemen, or one gentleman by two ladies." [1] Even more explicitly it is stated on the authority of the Countess of Narbonne that " conjugal affection and the true love between lovers are two absolutely different things which have nothing in common, and have their source in wholly different sentiments. . . . We say definitely and considerately that love cannot exist between married people." [2] The opinion is endorsed by Eleanor of Aquitaine, afterwards the queen of Henry II, one of the leading patronesses of poetry. The same lady, who was regarded as one of the highest authorities in such matters, was called upon, after the fashion of the times, to give her judgment in a disputed case. A knight had offered his service to a lady, who, her affections being elsewhere engaged, did not accept him, but, not wishing to dismiss him without hope, engaged herself to be his lady should she happen to lose her present lover. She eventually married the latter. The

[1] Andreas, capellanus, *De Amore*, ed. E. Trojel, pp. 310 sqq. The date of the book of Andreas was placed in the fourteenth century by Diez (F. Diez, *Beiträge zur Kenntniss der romanischen Poesie*, p. 76), a writer whose exhaustive industry in the field of Provençal philology imparted the highest authority to his views. He was not, however, aware that the whole of Andreas's book had been translated in the thirteenth century (C. Joret, " Une traduction d'André le Chapelain au XIIIᵉ siècle," *Romania*, xiii, pp. 403 sq.), and that he is several times quoted in the early part of that century (E. Trojel, *op. cit.*, Introduction, p. v ; T. Sundby, *Della vita e delle opere di Brunetto Latini*, pp. 173 sq., 490 ; P. Rajna, in *Studi di filologia romanza*, v, pp. 193 sqq. ; E. G. Parodi, " Le Storie di Cesare nella letteratura dei primi secoli," *ibid.*, iv, pp. 259 sq.).

[2] Andreas, capellanus, *op. cit.*, pp. 280 sq., 290, 153.

other knight, however, having performed his 'service' in her name, claimed his guerdon. The lady stoutly denied any obligation, since, far from losing her lover, she had become married to him. On appeal being made to the Duchess of Aquitaine, she directed that the lady was in honour bound to yield herself to the claimant, since she had in fact lost her lover, he having become her husband.[1]

But such explicit statements are scarcely necessary ; the poetry of romantic love in courtly French literature dealt exclusively with extra-conjugal relations. " Married women alone were idealised by chivalry, and it is to them that are addressed the homage of poets and of knights." [2] The right to manifest jealousy was denied to husbands. Since true jealousy cannot exist without love, and love cannot exist in marriage, argued the Countess of Champagne, daughter of Queen Eleanor, husbands cannot manifest true jealousy.[3] The condemnation of jealous husbands by public opinion was more than a frivolously perverse delight in their discomfiture. In one version of the story of Tristan, the hero, when his guilt is discovered, is killed by the injured husband. The knights of King Arthur's Round Table, however, put King Marc to death in indignation at his conduct.[4] When an aggrieved husband, Count Raimond of Roussillon, killed the troubadour Guilhem de Cabestang, and his wife committed suicide in consequence, the whole country rose. Knights moved a punitive expedition against the vindictive husband ; his castle was seized ; King Alfonso of Aragon publicly degraded him, and deprived him of his fief, distributing his lands among the relatives of the lovers, who were given a sumptuous burial in the church of Perpignan. The count was cast into prison, where he remained

---

[1] Andreas, capellanus, op. cit., p. 290.

[2] J. Anglade, Les troubadours, p. 79. Cf. C. Fauriel, Histoire de la poésie provençale, vol. i, pp. 505 sqq. ; F. Diez, Die Poesie der Troubadours, pp. 132 sq. Andreas quotes the opinion that " virgins are, properly speaking, not capable of love " (Andreas, capellanus, op. cit., p. 175). In the earlier romances of chivalry the heroines are usually unmarried women (see the somewhat panegyrical remarks of M. Gaston Paris in Histoire littéraire de la France, vol. xxx, p. 15) ; in the still earlier sagas, such as those of Ireland, they are indifferently either married or unmarried. Those differences correspond to the changes in custom ; pre-nuptial chastity was, in pagan times, of no account, while in feudal times, when marriage alliances came to be of great economic importance, the freedom of unmarried girls was correspondingly limited, whereas the conduct of married women was relatively of small account.

[3] Andreas, capellanus, op. cit., p. 153.

[4] Jehan des Preis, Ly Myreur des Histors, ed. A. Borguess and S. Bormons, vol. iii, pp. 241 sq.

for the rest of his life.[1]   Such an attitude was not peculiar to the
sophisticated amatory conventions of troubadour Provence.   In
the North as in the South, throughout the romantic literature of
the Middle Ages, the passion of love is understood to refer exclusively to extra-conjugal and illicit relations.   The love-stories
which for ages thrilled the imagination and stirred the emotions
of European populations, in Saxon and Norman England as in
Italy and Spain, are, without an exception, from Tristan and
Iseult, Lancelot and Guinevere, Eric and Enid, to Paolo and
Francesca, presentments of illicit relations.   In Chestien de Troyes'
' Cligès,' unlawful love is put before the duty of a wife to her
husband ; in Tristan it is put before the duty of a husband to a
wife ; in ' Le Conte de la Charette ' it is even put before the duty
of chivalric honour.[2]   The learned M. Gaston Paris, referring more
particularly to the most popular of those love-stories, that of
Tristan, admits to being utterly perplexed.   " How comes it about,"
he asks, without being able to suggest a satisfactory answer—
" how comes it about that this legend, which arose among a semi-
barbarous people, is devoted to the glorification of a love which so
absolutely contravenes the laws which stand for the family, and
which are often more sacred in primitive cultures than in more
advanced societies ? "[3]   I don't know whence M. Paris, than
whose work there is none more admirable in the province of
literary archaeology, derived his impressions of primitive cultures ;
very possibly from Dr. Westermarck.   It is, in any case, precisely
because they originated in the social conditions of primitive pagan
populations as yet untransformed by Christianity, that the conceptions of the relations between the sexes in the romantic literature
of nascent Europe were such as we find them.   As an historian
remarks in reference to the rules of chivalry, so here also, " the
theory followed upon the practice." [4]

The fact is notable.   Romantic love, when at last we come
upon its unmistakable presentment, in the ideal form which
answers to European conceptions and has no exact parallel in any
other stage of culture, that sentiment which has been represented
as the primitive motive of " human marriage," is deliberately and
emphatically regarded as incompatible with, and opposed to,
marriage.

The process of evolution, which ultimately led to the idealisa-

---

[1] F. Hüffer, *Der Trobador Guillem de Cabestanh, sein Leben und seine Werke*,
pp. 12 sq.

[2] G. Schoepperle, *Tristan and Isolt, a Study of the Sources of the Romance*,
vol. ii, pp. 453 sq.

[3] G. Paris, *Poèmes et légendes du moyen-âge*, pp. 173 sq.

[4] E. Lavisse, *Histoire de France*, vol. ii, p. 22.

tion and refinement of conceptions connected with sex relations, began with the re-editing of the mythical and epic material of pagan tradition by Christian redactors. No specimen of that literature has reached us which has not been thus edited and more or less translated in terms of Christian belief and ideas. The gods, demi-gods, and heroes of Celtic Ireland, for instance, became connected with Noah and Biblical History.[1] The Irish mythical king Conchobar was assimilated to Jesus Christ ; his birth and death were made to coincide with the Nativity and Crucifixion of the Saviour, and he fell endeavouring to avenge the death of Christ, which had been predicted to him by a druid.[2] Oberon, that is, the Nibelung king Albericht, performed his feats of magic in the name of Christ and professed to derive his powers from him.[3] The great druid magician Myrdhinn, or Merlin, was baptised and delivered discourses on theology.[4] The Celtic goddess Morgan the Fay attended mass and built a chapel to Our Lady.[5]

Strangely distorted scraps of classical annals and literature were commingled in like manner with Biblical and pagan myth in the mediaeval scheme of history, producing the most amazing medley. The wars between David and the kings of Rome were referred to, and the tunnel at Posilippo had been excavated to afford Romulus and his barons shelter against the assaults of the dreaded armies of the king of Judah.[6] Brutus, " a certain Roman consul," the grandson of Aeneas, became after the siege of Troy the first king of Britain.[7] Turnus, whose father Nerva had re-built the city of Tournay after its destruction by Artaxerxes, had expelled the Romans from Paris, and, after inflicting many defeats upon Caesar and his knights, had liberated France from the foreign yoke.[8] Julius Caesar, king of Hungary and of Austria,

---

[1] H. d'Arbois de Jubainville, *L'épopée celtique en Irlande*, pp. 64 sqq.

[2] E. Hull, *The Cuchullin Saga in Irish Literature*, pp. 3 sqq., 267 sqq.

[3] *Huon de Bordeaux*, ed. F. Guessnard and C. Grandmaison, v. 3711. For the identity of Oberon with the Nibelung Albericht, see P. Rajna, *Le origini dell' epopea francese*, pp. 425, 436 sqq. ; G. Osterhage, " Anklänge an die germanische Mythologie in der altfranzösiche Karlssage," *Zeitschrift für romanische Philologie*, xi, p. 2 ; C. Nyrop, *Storia dell' epopea francese nel medio evo*, pp. 113 sq. ; J. Grimm, *Irische Elfenmärchen*, p. lix.

[4] H. de la Villemarqué, *Myrdhin, ou l'enchanteur Merlin*, pp. 150, 163 sqq.

[5] " Le vallon des faulx amants," in P. J. B. Legrand d'Aussy, *Fabliaux ou contes du xiie et du xiiie siècle*, vol. i, p. 92.

[6] Benjamin of Tudela, cited in A. Graf, *Roma nella memoria e nell' immaginazione del medio evo*, p. 171.

[7] Godfrey of Monmouth, *Historia Britonum*, ed. J. A. Giles, pp. 3 sqq.; Nennius, *Historia Britonum*, ed. J. Stevenson, p. 6.

[8] *Croniques de Tournay* (Turin MS.), in E. G. Parodi, " Le storie di Cesare nellal etteratura italiana dei primi secoli," *Studi di filologia romanza*, iv, pp. 277 sqq.

and prince of Constantinople, was the son of Brinhylde, the daughter of Judas Maccabaeus, and married Morgana, the fairy, by whom he became the father of Oberon and of Saint George.[1] Hanygos, king of Little Britain, wages war against Theodogus, the king of Spain and uncle of Julius Caesar, and cuts off his head. Caesar, full of anger and grief, vows destruction on the Britons, sets their realm on fire, and, having captured Hanygos, causes him to perish amid exquisite tortures. Julius Caesar was, nevertheless, " the flower of chivalry " ; his bodily strength was remarkable ; he had unhorsed countless knights, and was in the habit of lifting up his opponents bodily in the midst of a fray and carrying them away at arm's length.[2] The most accomplished and courteous among the knights of olden time and the pattern of chivalry was, however, Alexander of Macedon. One of his last expeditions was to the Garden of Eden. We learn besides of his voyages in search of wisdom, together with Tholomeus, king of Egypt, who introduced clocks to regulate the Holy Offices in monasteries, Vergil, the great magician, Saint Baudran, and " Monsignor St. Paul." [3]

The startling chaos of anachronisms, heterogeneous names and incidents, and miscellaneous myths which characterises the mediaeval conceptions of history attended the transmission of the ethnic legends which constituted the literature of pre-Christian Europe. The traditional stories of the warlike and amatory adventures of Celtic gods and goddesses, tribal demi-gods and heroes, became ultimately transformed into those romantic narratives which centred round ' King Arthur ' and the knights of his ' Round Table,' and it is in that form that they have for centuries furnished the peoples of Europe with the world of fiction and romance in which their imagination loved to dwell. ' Arthur,' that is to say, ' the Black One ' (arðu = ' black '), is almost certainly the same as ' Bran,' ' the Raven,' and has no historical foundation.[4] The essential feature of the myth of Bran and of

[1] *Huon de Bordeaux*, ed. F. Guessnard and C. Grandmaison, pp. 1, 104 ; *Auberon*, vv., 1211 sqq., 1319 sqq., 1451 sqq., in A. Graf, *I complementi della chanson d'Huon de Bordeaux*.

[2] Jean de Preis, dit d'Outremeuse, *Ly Myreur des histors*, ed. A. Borgnet and S. Bormans, vol. ii, pp. 212 sqq. ; E. G. Parodi, " Le storie di Cesare nella letteratura italiana dei primi secoli," *Studi di filologia romanza*, iv ; A. Birch-Hirschfeld, *Ueber die den provenzalischen Troubadours des XII und XIII Jahrhunderts bekannten epischen Stoffe aus den Alterthum*, pp. 24 sqq ; A. Graf, *Roma nella memoria e nell' immaginazione del medio evo*, pp. 195 sqq.

[3] *L'Ymagene del monde*, summarised in *Histoire littéraire de la France*, vol. xxxiii, p. 318.

[4] The view that a nucleus of historical fact underlies the legend of Arthur—a British leader who, in the words of William of Malmesbury, " sustained the declining fortunes of his native land and maintained the

Arthur was their visit to the Otherworld where they dwelt for a

courage of his people," at the time of the Saxon invasions (William of Malmesbury, *Gesta regum Anglorum*, iii, vol. i, pp. 11 sq.)—is untenable. The passage of Nennius (*Historia Britonum*, ed. J. Stevenson, pp. 47 sqq.), which constitutes practically the only ground in support of such an hypothesis, is in reality strong evidence against it. The sole particular which it mentions, with a quite unintelligible emphasis, is that Arthur fought twelve battles, neither more nor less, one for each month in the year. Tradition places these 'battles' sometimes in England, sometimes in Scotland, at other times in Scandinavia, Ireland, Gaul, Italy, and even Egypt! We are also told that Arthur, 'the Black One,' fasted or disappeared from the world for exactly "three nights and three days" (Nennius, *op. cit.*, Cambridge MS., in Pertz, *Monumenta Germaniae Historica, Auctores antiquissimi*, vol. xiii, p. 200; *Annales Cambriae*, in Petrie, *Monumenta Historica Britanniae*, p. 831). Arthur is described as dwelling, during his period of invisibility, "at the antipodes" (Etienne of Rouen, *Draco Normannicus*, in *Chronicles and Memorials of Great Britain and Ireland, Chronicles of Stephen*, etc., vol. ii, p. 946; *Gesta regum Britanniae*, ed. F. Michel [*Cambrian Archaeological Association Publications*], v. 4155). At his death, according to Heinrich von dem Türlîn, the chief mourner was the moon (Lûne). (*Diu Crône*, v. 300). Arthur has none but mythological relatives. His father is the dragon Uther, his sister the goddess Anu, his wife the "White Lady," who is naturally associated with the "Black Man," his mistress or sister is Morgana, the fairy (see R. H. Fletcher, *The Arthurian Material in the Chronicles*, p. 29). The chief feature of popular belief concerning Arthur was his expected resurrection, a belief "which was a more sacred thing to the men of Cornwall and Devon than church, monks, or miracles" (R. H. Fletcher, *op. cit.*, p. 101). There is nothing in the disasters and sufferings which the Britons sustained in an age when success alone counted to justify the idealisation of any person connected with that period of defeat into the hero of the British race. The complete silence of the contemporary Gildas cannot be disposed of. The only 'graphic touch' in Nennius is the statement that Arthur fought "together with the kings of the Britons, but he himself was leader in the battles." What does this mean? British kings, or chieftains, in those days certainly had no 'generals' or deputy commanders; and in any case a historical "leader in the battles" ('dux bellorum'), commanding the armies of all the British kings, who were always quarrelling amongst themselves, is unintelligible. The facts seem to point to the conclusion that 'the Black One,' 'leader of battles,' is identical with 'Bran,' 'the Raven,' the leader in battles of the Celts in every war which they have fought throughout the ages (cf. below, pp. 452 sq.). A tradition preserved by Cervantes represents Arthur as a raven (M. de Cervantes, *El ingenioso hidalgo Don Quichote de la Mancha*, xiii, 49. Cf. L. A. Paton, *Studies in the Fairy Mythology of Arthurian Romances*, p. 34 n.). Arthur is described as "the eternal ruler of fate," his army is "invincible" (Etienne de Rouen, *Draco Normannicus*, in *Chronicles of the reigns of Stephen, Henry II, and Richard I*, ed. R. Howlett, vol. ii, pp. 945 sqq.). Much could be added, but the reader may perhaps judge whether the above traits apply to an unsuccessful leader in a disastrous struggle or to an ancient Celtic cosmic deity and war-god. As William of Newburgh long since remarked, Geoffrey of Monmouth "disguised under the honourable name of history the fables about Arthur which he took from the fictions of the Britons, and increased out of his own head" (William of Newburgh, *Historia rerum Anglicarum*, ed. R. Howlett, vol. i, p. 12).

time with the Queen of the Dead.[1] The fundamental lunar
myth was applied to all Celtic and Teutonic heroes, and to historical personages. The father of Charlemagne had, like
Tannhäuser, a love adventure with the goddess Bertha 'of the
goose-foot'; Charlemagne himself had a fairy mistress.[2] Julius
Caesar had been the lover of the fairy Morgana.[3] Cuchulainn,
while exhausted with much fighting, received repeated messages
from Morrigan, or Fand, the daughter of 'The Eternal' (Búan),
wife of the god of the Otherworld, Manannan the son of Lir, to
join her in the Blessed Otherworld, the 'Isle of Women,' and be
her lover. He pleads that he is too weak, but she heals his wounds
and he is led to the Blessed World, where he spends some time
with the goddess, until her husband takes her away from him.
Cuchulainn then returns to Ireland, where Morrigan has arranged
to meet him, but the hero's wife, Emer, attends the tryst at
the head of fifty armed women and chases Morrigan away. The
goddess thenceforth becomes the enemy of Cuchulainn and his
wife Emer, and only returns to him when, in his last battle,
she appears by the side of his body in the form of a bird.[4]
Arthur is, like Cuchulainn, Bran, and other heroes, the lover
of Morgana the Fairy,[5] with whom he lives in Avalon, the Walhalla
where all good warriors feast in the arms of immortal mistresses.[6]

[1] For the myth of Bran, see K. Meyer and A. Nutt, *The Voyage of Bran*,
vol. i, pp. 2 sqq.

[2] G. Paris, *Histoire poétique de Charlemagne*, pp. 384 sq.

[3] *Huon de Bordeaux*, ed. F. Guessnard and C. Grandmaison, pp. 1, 104.

[4] H. d'Arbois de Jubainville, *L'épopée celtique en Irlande*, pp. 174 sqq.
Cf. *Táin bó Cúalnge*, ed. Id., pp. 128 sq. ; W. Stokes, " Cuchulainn's Death,"
Revue Celtique, iii, pp. 175 sqq.

[5] *Gesta Regum Britanniae*, ed. F. Michel (*Cambrian Archaeological
Association Publications*, 1862), vv. 4213 sqq. ; Rauf de Boun, *Petit Brut*
(MS. Harleian, 902 fols., 1–11b), cited in R. H. Fletcher, *The Arthurian Matter
in the Chronicles*, p. 211. Arthur has three sons by Morgana : Morgan the
Black, Patrick the Red, and Adeluf II. A reminiscence of the loves of
Arthur and Morgana is found in Spenser, *Faerie Queene*, ix, 13 sqq. Rauf
de Boun says that Arthur owed all his successes to his fairy love ;
and he apologises for not recounting those exploits at greater length
with the significant remark that it is not " amiable de mettre fayerie en
escripture."

[6] ' Avalon,' ' Aualon,' ' Avallon,' ' Avallonia,' was derived by Geoffrey
of Monmouth from ' aval,' which means ' apple ' in Celtic, and was interpreted by him as ' insula pomorum ' (*Vita Merlini*, ed. Fr. Michel and T.
Wright, v. 908) ; and the etymology has until lately been generally accepted.
But, although apples are frequently regarded as love-charms and associated
with love-goddesses (H. Gaidoz, " La requisition d'amour et le symbolisme
de la pomme," *Annuaire de l'école pratique des Hautes Études*, x, 1902 ; B. O.
Foster, " Apples as Love-charms," *Harvard Studies in Classical Philology*, x,
pp. 39 sqq. ; A. Graf, *Miti, leggende e superstizioni del medio evo*, vol. i, p. 141),

She it was who bore him away from his last battle at Camlan and healed his wounds ;[1] and the Britons await the return of the ' leader of armies.'[2] In later redactions of the sagas Arthur's amours with the goddess were thought unbecoming, and Morgana was made a relative of Arthur and finally his sister,[3] thus completely securing the ' platonic ' character of the relation.

Morgana, the Irish Morrigan, or Muirgan, is ' the Lady of the Sea,' or ' of the Lake '[4]—a form, of course, of the Celtic Moon

there is a good deal of uncertainty about the interpretation, and many scholars regard it as unsatisfactory (see J. Rhys, *Studies in the Arthurian Legends*, pp. 336 sq. ; F. Lot, " Études sur la provenance du cycle Arthurien," *Romania*, xxiv, pp. 329 sq. ; San-Marte, *Die Sagen von Merlin*, pp. 89 sqq. ; H. Zimmer, " Bretonische Elemente in der Arthursage des Gottfried von Monmouth," *Zeitschrift für französische Sprache und Literatur*, xii, pp. 238 sqq.). It may perhaps be suggested that ' Avalon ' is not a Celtic word, but that the legend having been transmitted through the intermediary of Saxon versions, the corresponding Teutonic term ' Walhalla ' was used, and that ' Avalon ' is merely a Latinised form of it. Several examples of an analogous translation of Celtic names by Teutonic equivalents are known, as, for instance, Wieland, the Smith, for Gofan, Goswhit, Arthur's helmet (see A. C. L. Brown, " Welsh Traditions in Layamon's Brut," *Modern Philology*, i, pp. 99 sqq.). The addition of an initial *A* is common enough ; Loth, for instance, is called Aloth in ' Brut ' (R. H. Fletcher, *The Arthurian Material in the Chronicles*, p. 218). It may be further pointed out that Aualon was commonly spoken of as a ' vale,' the noun thus appearing as Val-Auallon. There is no Celtic precedent for the Otherworld being represented as a ' valley ' ; it is always an ' isle.' The description of Avalon as a ' vale ' may thus have arisen from some older rendering of ' Walhalla.'

[1] *Le Saint Graal, ou le Joseph d'Arimathée*, ed. E. Hucher, vol. i, p. 502 ; Jean de Preis, *Ly Myreur des Histors*, ed. A. Borgnet and S. Bormans, vol. ii, p. 243 ; Etienne de Rouen, *Draco Normannicus*, p. 703.

[2] See references in R. H. Fletcher, *The Arthurian Material in the Chronicles*, pp. 101, 188.

[3] In Geoffrey of Monmouth Arthur has only one sister, Anne, who marries King Lear (*Historia Britonum*, ed. J. A. Giles, p. 153 ; Etienne de Rouen, *Draco Normannicus*, ed. Howlett, p. 708). Wace likewise knows only Arthur's sister, Anne (*Brut*, vv. 9053, 9872, 1005). With Giraldus Cambrensis Morgana becomes a ' kinswoman ' (cognata) of Arthur, and he scouts the popular notion that she is ' some fantastic goddess,' " dea quaedam fantastica " (*Opera*, ed. J. S. Brewer, *Chronicles and Memorials of Great Britain and Ireland*, vol. iv, pp. 48 sq.). In Chrestien (*Erec*, v. 4218 ; *Sir Gawain and the Green Knight*, vv. 2464 sqq.) Morgana becomes Arthur's sister (see L. A. Paton, *Studies in the Fairy Mythology of Arthurian Romances*, pp. 136 sqq.). On Anne in mythical tradition, see J. Rhys, *Studies in the Arthurian Legends*, pp. 19, 336 sq. ; J. Loth, *Les Mabinogion*, vol. ii, p. 305. She is doubtless no other than the goddess Anu.

[4] The first element of the name, ' mor,' means ' sea,' or ' lake.' The other component has been variously interpreted. Sir John Rhys translates the name ' sea-born ' (*Studies in the Arthurian Legends*, p. 23 ; Id., *Hibbert Lectures on . . . Celtic Heathendom*, pp. 236 sqq. Cf. F. Lot, " Celtica," *Romania*, xxiv, p. 337). J. Grimm interprets it ' mor ' = ' mare,' ' gwenn ' = ' splendens femina ' (*Deutsche Mythologie*, vol. i, p. 342 n.). The

goddess who rules over the sea and dwells by lakes and springs. By a process of which examples have been met with, she became duplicated in Christian times, her more wayward and maleficent aspects being ascribed to Morgana, while her more amiable and beneficent characteristics were associated with ' the Lady of the Lake ' ; and the two names, which are probably identical, thus became opposed.[1] In the myth of Arthur, as in that of Cuchulainn, Morgana becomes hostile to him and to his wife Gwenn-wyfar.[2] The latter, ' the White Lady,' ' la Dame Blanche,' of French popular tradition, was another appellation of the Celtic goddess.[3] As in the typical form of the Celtic hero-myth, Arthur, at the head of his host of warriors, abducts Gwenn-wyfar from her husband, Melwas, the king of " the Land whence none returns," that is, the ' Pluto ' of Caesar's account of Celtic gods.[4] Similarly, in an Irish tale, Eochaid, the king of Ireland, obtains Etain, the wife of Midir, the king of the fairies ; Midir wins her back by playing a game of chess with the king, the lady being the stake. The Irish king, after laying siege for nine years to the castle of the fairy king, once more abducts his queen.[5] The ' fairy-wife theme ' in Celtic literature has, it will be noted, three

Irish Morrigan is usually interpreted as ' woman of the sea.' It is generally out of a lake, not out of the sea, that she rises. ' Mor ' and ' mere ' apply equally to both.

[1] The contrast between the characteristics of the two is dwelt on at length in *Les prophecies de Merlin* (Paris, 1526, p. lxxi). Cf. L. A. Paton, *Studies in the Fairy Mythology of Arthurian Romances*, p. 195.

[2] L. A. Paton, *op. cit.*, pp. 13 sqq., 60 sqq.

[3] A. Maury, *Croyances et légendes du moyen-âge*, p. 23. Cf. above, p. 158. Here, as with Morgana, while the first part of the name is plain, the second has given rise to various interpretations. Sir Edward Anwyl and Mr. Nutt read ' Gwenhwyfar ' and interpret "White Phantom" (E. Anwyl, *Celtic Religion in pre-Christian Times*, p. 63 ; *The Mabinogion*, ed. A. Nutt, p. 374). There are about twenty-two different spellings of the name (R. H. Fletcher, *The Arthurian Matter in the Chronicles*, p. 298). Professor A. C. L. Brown reads Gwenn-wyfar and interprets ' the White Enchantress ' (A. C. L. Brown, ' Welsh Traditions in Layamon's ' Brut,' " *Modern Philology*, i, p. 102). The name is universally spread among Celtic peoples as the name of the goddess. She was the patroness of the Parisians, and her name probably survives in those of Geneva and Genoa. It has been pointed out that most of the acquisitions of Arthur, ' the Black,' contain the attribute of ' whiteness ' (A. C. L. Brown, *loc. cit.*). The facts suggest that in Celtic mythology the god, ' Raven,' ' Black One,' was associated with the ' dark ' aspect of the moon, while the goddess was associated with the ' white ' aspect of the full moon. A curious tradition, which recalls many savage lunar myths, relates that Gwenn-wyfar was *eaten* by Modred, whom we shall identify with her husband Melwas (Jean de Preis, *Ly Myreur des Histors*, ed. A. Borgnet and S. Bormans, vol. ii, p. 244).

[4] Cf. F. Lot, " Celtica," *Romania*, xxiv, p. 327.

[5] A. Leahy, *Heroic Romances of Ireland*, vol. ii, pp. 145 sqq.

aspects : (1) The abduction from her divine husband by the hero, (2) her recovery by the former from the latter, (3) her second recovery by the hero. The emphasis may be laid on one or other of those phases ; all three occur in the myth of Arthur and Gwenn-wyfar. While in the more archaic forms of the story Gwenn-wyfar is originally the wife of Melwas and is abducted by Arthur,[1] Geoffrey of Monmouth substitutes the faithless nephew Modred for the Underworld god Melwas, and it is Modred and not Arthur who is the original abductor.[2] In a German version of some lost redaction, a knight appears at Arthur's Court and requires the king to grant him an unspecified boon ; when Arthur has promised, he demands the queen, and carries her off. Later she is rescued by Gawain.[3] The latter was, in fact, one of the original heroes of the cycle. Gawain, Walwein, Galvanus, the lord of Gallaway,[4] is the British name for the Ultonian hero Cuchulainn,[5] and appears to be in his myths and attributes interchangeable with Arthur. He is usually represented as Arthur's nephew, the son of his sister by the god Lot, Ludg, or Lir, who was likewise the father of Cuchulainn and of Lancelot of the Lake.

In the older versions Arthur's nephew is called Modred, and abducts Gwenn-wyfar on his own account ; for being Arthur's heir, according to matriarchal law, he gains possession of Arthur's wife, as is the custom in African monarchies, in his impatience to secure his heritage. Geoffrey of Monmouth informs us that Arthur gave up the conquest of Rome, and hurried back to Britain, because he learnt that " Modred, his nephew, to whom he had committed the charge of Britain, had seized his crown by tyranny and usurpation, and that the queen, Ganhumara, violating her nuptial vow, had become joined to him." [6] In later

---

[1] Heinrich von dem Türlîn, *Diu Crône*, ed. G. H. F. Scholl, p. 60 ; *Vita Gildae*, in Gildas, *De excidio Britanniae*, ed. J. Stevenson, p. xxxix. Gwenn-wyfar had been possessed by Melwas " for a long time " before she was abducted by Arthur.

[2] Geoffrey of Monmouth, *Historia Britonum*, ed. J. A. Giles, p. 200.

[3] Hartmann von Aue, *Der Löwenritter*, bk. viii, vv. 4530 sqq., 5668 sqq.

[4] William of Malmesbury, *Gesta regum Britanniae*, ed. W. Stubbs, iii, 287, vol. ii, p. 342 ; Sir F. Madden, *Sir Gawayne*, p. xxiv. Cf. F. Lot, " Études sur la provenance du cycle Arthurien," *Romania*, xxv, p. 2 ; *Perceval le Gallois*, ed. C. Potvin, vv. 7964 sqq.

[5] Cf. J. L. Weston, *The Legend of Sir Gawain*, p. 17 ; Id., *The Legend of Sir Perceval*, vol. i, pp. 301 sqq.

[6] Geoffrey of Monmouth, *Historia Britonum*, ed. J. A. Giles, p. 200. In the ' Mabinogion ' Arthur is represented as anxious to settle the dispute with his nephew Medrawd in an amicable manner ; it is only through the mischief-making interference of his ambassador that they come to blows over so trifling a matter (*The Mabinogion*, p. 150). If Medrawd had consented to restore his wife and his kingdom to Arthur, all trouble would have been avoided.

romances Arthur's false nephew became generally known as
Lancelot of the Lake, that is, the son of the Lady of the Lake.
The name is not Celtic, but is a Norman-French rendering of that
of the original personage.[1] In an Irish version of the theme of
the usurping nephew, Grainne, the wife of the King of Ireland,
induces his nephew, Diarmaid, to abduct her.[2] A similar story
was also told of a tribal hero called Drest, Drestan, or Tristan,[3]
the "inventor of engines," and master of minstrelsy.[4] Like all

---

[1] Lancelot, spelt in the earlier MSS. 'L'Ancelot,' is a diminutive of
'ancel,' 'ancillus,' a 'servant,' 'vassal prince,' 'knecht,' 'knight.' The
Celtic term having the corresponding meaning is 'mael,' an element which
is exceedingly common in Celtic names, both Irish and British. 'Mael-
was' has thus exactly the same meaning as 'L'Ancelot,' that is, 'the lesser
or younger prince' (see E. de Villemarqué, Les romans de la Table Ronde,
pp. 58, 61; J. Rhys, Studies on the Arthurian Legend, p. 51). Modred,
who first appears in the character of the false nephew in Geoffrey of Monmouth, seems to be the same as the 'Maglocunus' whom Gildas mentions
as the most powerful king of Britain and as oppressing his uncle with
sword, spear, and fire (Gildas, De excidio Britanniae, ed. J. Stevenson,
p. 42). The name is an attempted Latinisation of Mael-gwinn, that is,
'the Great Prince.' The abductors of Gwenn-wyfar are thus all etymo-
logically related, Lancelot, or Mael the Lesser, being the euhemerised representative of Mael-was, the Otherworld King. The relation of Modred-
Lancelot to Arthur is exceedingly confused and variable. In one tradition
Modred is the brother of Gwenn-wyfar (Wace, Brut, ed. Le Roux de Lincy,
v. 11458), a notion probably reminiscent of the relationship of the King of
the Otherworld to his wife. In another version he is the son of Arthur
by a concubine (R. H. Fletcher, The Arthurian Matter in the Chronicles,
p. 188); in yet another he is the offspring of an incestuous union of Arthur
with his sister (ibid., p. 141). The abduction of Gwenn-wyfar by Lancelot
is represented in Celtic tradition in much coarser terms than in the
romantic version which so deeply moved Paolo and Francesca. The hero,
having learnt that the queen was about to take a walk in a certain
wood, stripped himself naked and hid in a bush; when the queen and her
ladies passed by, he sprang upon her, seized her in his arms and made off
with her, while the frightened attendants ran away (E. de Villemarqué,
op. cit., p. 59). A common version represents, according to true Celtic precedent, Gwenn-wyfar as herself inducing Modred to abduct her (Robert of
Gloucester, Chronicle, v. 4503).
[2] J. G. Campbell, The Fians (Waifs and Strays of Celtic Tradition,
vol. iv), pp. 53 sqq.
[3] J. Loth, Contributions à l'étude des romans de la Table Ronde, pp. 16 sqq.;
J. Bédier, Le Roman de Tristan, par Thomas, vol. ii, pp. 105 sqq.;
G. Schoepperle, Tristan and Isolt, vol. ii. p. 268; H. Zimmer, "Beiträge
zur Namenforschung in den altfranzösischen Arthurepen," Zeitschrift für
franzoesische Sprache und Literatur, xiii, p. 73.
[4] He is called 'gallofyd,' that is, 'master of engines,' in a Mabinogion
(J. Loth, Les Mabinogion, p. 238). Eilhart von Oberge tells us that he was
the first to use fish-hooks (Eilhart von Oberge, Tristan, v. 4339 sqq.); and
from Beroul we learn that he invented a particular form of trap to catch
game (Le roman de Tristan par Beroul, ed. E. Muret, v. 1437). His skill as

Celtic tribal heroes he wins by his exploits several princesses, and like Diarmaid and Lancelot abducts his uncle's wife. In the much-edited version which became popular in the Middle Ages his uncle's wife, Iseult, is the same as a princess whom he has won as a prize for his prowess from a king of Ireland, but whom he is bound by oath to deliver to his uncle, Marc, that is, 'the Horse,' a king of Cornwall with horse's ears.

Such stories of the abduction of women and of contests for their possession abound in ancient Celtic literature ; they constitute a whole class of Irish stories known as 'atheida,' of which the 'Book of Leinster,' in mentioning the tales which every bard should know, names a dozen.[1] Those barbaric love-stories present what, to our taste, are strange contrasts. Many of them breathe a spirit of deep passion ; the love of the women—for it is chiefly in them that it is manifested—is often obsessing, haunting, persistent. They sacrifice everything to it ; love alone counts. They are fiercely devoted and loyal where the interests and honour of their lovers or husbands are concerned—a trait which is characteristic of the love of primitive women ; they will face dangers and death in their defence, they will share every hardship and misfortune with them, they will assist them with their utmost power and at the sacrifice of their own lives. Their pride in them is unbounded, they proclaim their chosen man to be superior to all others.[2] At the loss of the man they love they will not be comforted. Deidre, when Naisi is killed, and she is re-captured by her husband, will neither eat nor sleep ; " she raised not her head from her knee." At last she dashes her brains out against a stone.[3] There is in such stories a passionate emotion ; as a matter of fact, from the point of view of that truth and depth of feeling which constitute genuine pathos and are an element of the highest art, they are a thousand times superior to the euphuistic affectations and artificial delicacies of sentiments of ' courtly love ' in the chivalric romances. They are tales, as an Irish bard himself aptly puts it, " that make women sorrowful." [4] It is that element of primitive

a harpist and a poet was universally famous (see G. Schoepperle, *op. cit.*, p. 287).

[1] E. O'Curry, *Lectures on the Manuscript Materials of ancient Irish History*, p. 590 ; H. Zimmer, " Keltische Beiträge," *Zeitschrift für deutsches Alterthums und deutsche Litteratur*, xxxiii, p. 281.

[2] See, for instance, *Fled Bricrend. The Feast of Bricriu*, ed. G. Henderson (*Irish Texts Society*, No. 2), pp. 27 sqq., where Emer loftily claims precedence of all women in Ireland on account of the superior valour of her husband.

[3] A. H. Leahy, *Heroic Romances of Ireland*, vol. ii, pp. 145 sqq.

[4] " The Death of Diarmaid," ed. by J. H. Lloyd, O. J. Bergin, G. Schoepperle, *Revue Celtique*, xxxiii, p. 163.

passion, and not any later ' refinements,' which has supplied whatever true art there is in ' romantic ' literature.   Little was needed
to make the story of Tristan and Iseult into one of the most
poignant expressions of the pathos and tragedy of love in the
world's literature.

And yet, conjoined with that passion and that emotion, we
come upon features which appear to us incompatible with them,
and which run counter to every sentiment and conception of
romantic love ; we are not for a moment allowed to forget
that we are in the midst of a society to which those sentiments
and those conceptions are foreign.   There does not appear to be
the slightest suspicion, either on the part of the men or on that
of the women, that even the deepest and most passionate attachment implies or calls for sexual fidelity.   The ' Wooing of Emer '
by Cuchulainn has been cited for the tender sentiment and the
constancy of attachment which pervades it, and for its ' modern '
tone.   Yet the hero's love, even during the first period of his
' wooing,' is interspersed with half a dozen other love adventures.[1]
The character of Emer and her attachment to the hero have been
gushed over by sentimental editors, and have been adduced as a
solitary instance contrasting with the glaring dissoluteness and
careless infidelity of the heroines of other love-idylls.[2]   But there
is not the slightest ground for such comments.   Emer offers herself
to any man she pleases with an effrontery and obscenity which
defy description.[3]   She takes a fancy to a Scandinavian visitor ;
she induces him to elope with her ; they spend a long ' villegiatura '
together at the Isle of Man, in the Hebrides, in Scotland.
Cuchulainn pursues them all over the country ; he finally discovers
the pair, defeats his rival, brings his wife back with him to his
home, and their relations continue as affectionate and happy as
if nothing had happened.[4]   When Iseult herself, who has all the

[1] See above, p. 379.
[2] " She is a type of woman altogether Irish.   The Arthurian women are
as gentle (!), but lack the charming sprightliness, the spirit, and self-respect
. . ." etc.   " Once won, she is the faithfullest of wives " (E. Hull, *The Cuchullin Saga in Irish Literature*, pp. xlviii sq.).
[3] H. Zimmer, *Keltische Studien*, vol. i, pp. 79 sq.   She addresses Ailill
in terms which I leave in Dr. Zimmer's language : " Erhebe dich, o wunder-
barer Ailill ! jegliche Ruhe wird Dir, Tapferster !   Schling die Hand um
meinen Nacken : der Anfang der Liebeslust—wonning ist ihre Gabe—ist
Weib und Mann in gegenseitigem Küssen.   Wenn Dir dies nicht genügt, tref-
flicher Mann, o Sohn des Königs, königlicher Herrscher, dann gebe ich
Dir zur Heilung vom Liebesschmerz, o Geliebter, von meinem Knie bis zu
meinem Nabel."
[4] " Aithed Emere le Tuir n-Glesta mac rig Lochainne," ed. K. Meyer,
Revue Celtique, vi, pp. 184 sqq.   In the Arthurian romances ' L'Orguleuse,'
Gawain's special mistress, in some versions his wife, is the double of Emer, as

fierceness of a barbaric virago, is forced by circumstances to betray her love and to give herself to King Marc before her lover's very eyes—for the sleeping arrangements are most primitive, and the wedding night is spent in the common room—there is not the slightest hint of the horror and tragedy of such a situation. On the contrary, we are actually told in the most unconcerned and natural manner that she took pleasure in the caresses of Marc, for he was young, and agreeable company.[1] When Diarmaid elopes with Queen Grainne, one of the first things he does is to play for her as the stake in a game of dice with a stranger, and to lose her temporarily. After he has regained possession of her, the idyll continues on a tone of deep passion without any reference to the trifling incident.[2] Masculine jealousy is in the early romantic literature of Europe, both in its primitive and more sophisticated forms, what it is in savage societies; husbands are jealous of lovers lest they run away with their wives, but there is no hint of lovers ever being jealous of husbands. Of any delicacy, of any reticence, whether in words, deeds, or sentiments, there is not a trace. The women almost invariably do the wooing, and they do it with a directness and determination that ignore rebuffs. Deidre springs at Naisi like a wild beast, seizes him by his ears, refusing to release him till he has promised to elope with her.[3] The terms in which they make their advances will scarcely bear repeating. Deidre tells Naisi that she is a young cow and wants him as her bull.[4] Grainne urges on the hesitating Diarmaid by an obscene jest, which is reproduced in Tristan and Iseult.[5]

It is, indeed, a trait of primitive Celtic tales that the men

Gawain himself is the double of Cuchulainn (see A. Nutt, in J. L. Weston's translation of *Parzival*, vol. ii, p. 205. Cf. Id., *Studies on the Legend of the Holy Grail*, pp. 232 sq). " She has already had several favoured lovers, as indeed she frankly tells Gawain. He proffers his service, which she hardly accepts, but heaps upon him all manner of indignity and insult. . . . He winds up, at midday in the open forest, with a proposition which the repentant scornful lady can only parry by the naïve remark : " Seldom she had found it warm in the embrace of a mail-clad arm." Orgueilleuse, overcome with admiration at the Red Knight's prowess, offers him her love (A. Nutt, *Studies on the Legend of the Holy Grail*, pp. 240 sq.).

[1] Thomas, *Le roman de Tristan*, ed. by J. Bédier, vol. i, p. 157.

[2] J. G. Campbell, *The Fians (Waifs and Strays of Celtic Tradition*, vol. iv), pp 53 sqq.

[3] A. H. Leahy, *Heroic Romances of Ireland*, vol. i, p. 95.

[4] *Ibid.*

[5] " The Pursuit of Diarmaid and Grainne," *Revue Celtique*, xxxiii, p. 48. As she walks by her lover's side through some water, it splashes up to her thighs ; she remarks : " A plague on thee, streaky splash, thou art bolder than Diarmaid." Iseult ' of the white hands ' makes a similar remark (Eilhart von Oberge, *Tristan*, v. 6134 sqq.).

are represented as reluctant lovers. Cuchulainn makes all sorts of excuses before he accepts the invitation of Fand to join her in the Island of the Blessed;[1] Diarmaid, Naisi are literally compelled by force or stratagem to abduct their lady-loves. That trait is doubtless a part of the marked matriarchal character of the sex relations represented; it is the woman who chooses her lover, it is she who insists upon obtaining the man upon whom her choice has fallen. Where the wooing woman is, as was originally the rule, a goddess who seeks to draw her mortal lover to her abode in the Otherworld, the hesitation and reluctance of the man are readily intelligible; to join his immortal mistress in the Realms of the Blessed means, in fact, to die. The mortal lover, after spending a long period of time, of which he does not know the duration, in the arms of his immortal mistress, is usually represented as anxious to leave her and to return to the world of the living. That reluctant character of the lover in Celtic myth and his repulse of the advances of divine women were transmitted to the mediaeval romances which derived from those stories, and were used with effect in the later re-editing of the myths, when the attitude was easily interpreted as arising from regard for chastity. Even the amatory Gawain not uncommonly disdains a lady's proffered love.[2]

In all those stories of women passing backwards and forwards from one associate to another, being exchanged, won as the stake in a game of chance, or demanded as the companion of a night, there is no inkling of any appreciation of chastity as a virtue, still less of virginity.[3] Mr. Nutt assures us that " no Celtic tale

---

[1] H. d'Arbois de Jubainville, *L'épopée celtique en Irlande*, pp. 174 sqq.

[2] *Histoire littéraire de la France*, vol. xxx, pp. 34, 55; C. Nyrop, *Storia dell' epopea francese nel medio evo*, pp. 352 sq.

[3] In the mediaeval versions of the story of Tristan and Iseult, the Irish princess resorts to a stratagem common in later tales to conceal from King Marc on their wedding-night the fact that she is not a virgin. One of her waiting-maids, Brangien, takes her place beside the king. The incident, which is common in mediaeval and Renaissance stories (see for examples G. Schoepperle, *Tristan and Isolt*, vol. i, p. 206), is unknown in Celtic literature. It is beyond doubt an emendation introduced by Christian redactors of the old saga to meet a difficulty which did not arise for Celtic bards and their audiences. Indeed Brangien, or Brangwen, who is represented as offering her virginity in the place of Iseult, is in well-known Celtic tradition an old married woman, the wife of Morhoult (or Matholwch), Iseult's uncle, who is killed by Tristan. In the 'Mabinogion,' Branwen, the daughter of King Llyr, " one of the three chief ladies of the island," is degraded to the position of a waiting-maid in retaliation for an insult offered to Matholwch (*The Mabinogion*, pp. 26 sqq.). The incident in which Iseult plots to have Brangien murdered, from fear of her revealing the queen's amours with Tristan, is connected in the romance with Brangien's supposed sacrifice of her virginity. Doubtless in the original form of the tale it was

I have examined insists upon this idea." [1] Professor Zimmer, referring to the Irish literature, puts it more strongly : " Nowhere in the course of my studies," he says, " have I come upon any literature more pervaded with sensuality or picturing women more devoid of shame." [2] The heroes of the most romantic among those tales are renowned for their countless love-adventures ; Diarmaid, whose loves with Queen Grainne present a close parallel to the story of Tristan and Iseult, is known as ' Diarmaid na mban,' ' Diarmaid of the women.' [3] The numerous achievements of Cuchulainn would entitle him to a similar appellation ; he enjoys the love of " fifty queens." [4]

Those characteristics are not peculiar to the sagas in their primitive form. In spite of the adaptation, remodelling, expurgation to which they have been subjected by Christian and ' chivalric ' romance-makers, the most courtly redactions retain the traces of the same manners. Gawain, the pattern of Arthurian knighthood, is, like Diarmaid, known as " the knight of the ladies." [5] Here also the wooing is done mostly by the women, and is often equally crude ; [6] here also there is no thought of permanent union, except where a valuable dowry is at stake ; deep attachment is not thought of as a bar to other loves. Perceval hurries from one love to another. When the ladies of King Arthur's Court are subjected to a proof of chastity and fidelity, by trying on a magic mantle that will fit a virtuous woman only, not one is found to answer the test.[7] When a similar test is

part of the enmity between Brangwen and Tristan on account of the latter having killed her husband, and the magic potion which she administers to Tristan and Iseult, and which is the cause of their troubles, was, there can be no doubt, prepared by herself, and not by Iseult's mother, who has no motive for doing so. Brangwen was a magic woman who, like Morgana, had the power of sending her lovers to sleep, and is but a form of the threefold goddess, " the three Ladies of Britain."

In another adventure of Tristan, a lady about to be married invites him, in much the same manner as Iseult, to enjoy her favours before the marriage is consummated. But there is no reference to the proceeding being thought of as involving difficulties or complications (F. L. Polidori, *Tavola ritonda*, vol. i, p. 93. Cf. G. Schoepperle, *op. cit.*, pp. 297 sq.).

[1] A. Nutt, *Studies on the Legend of the Holy Grail*, p. 247.

[2] H. Zimmer, " Keltische Beiträge," *Zeitschrift für deutsches Alterthums und deutsche Litteratur*, xxxiii, p. 281 ; cf. p. 284.

[3] G. Schoepperle, *op. cit.*, p. 297.

[4] " Cuchulainn's Death," translated by Whitley Stokes, *Revue Celtique*, iii, p. 185.

[5] Raoul de Houdenc, *Méraugis de Portlesguez*, ed. H. Michelant, p. 58. For some of his amours, see *Histoire littéraire de la France*, vol. xxx, p. 34.

[6] T. Krabbes, *Die Frau in altfranzösichen Karls-Epos* (*Ausgaben und Abhandlungen aus der Gebiet der romanischen Philologie*, No. 8), p. 20.

[7] Ulrich von Zatzihoven, *Lanzelet* (ed. K. A. Hahn), vv. 5746 sqq. ; ' Le Conte du Mantel," ed. Fr.-A. Wulff, *Romania*, xiv, pp. 358 sqq.

applied to the men, King Arthur is the only one that can pass it successfully.[1]

The Christianisation of Pagan Literature.

It would, nevertheless, be difficult to imagine a transmutation more complete than that which was ultimately effected in the pagan material of romantic literature. Its translation into terms of Christian morality was in the end achieved with a thoroughness that cannot but excite admiration for the persistent zeal which, by its incessant pressure through three centuries, brought the apparently hopeless task to a successful issue. The earlier recorders of the pagan sagas contented themselves with a rough and super-ficial Christianisation of the stories, euhemerising their mythology, linking them up somewhat clumsily with Biblical history, and occasionally interpolating professions of Christian doctrine. They were not prepared to undertake the elaborate editorial task of recasting the whole material in order to adapt it to Christian standards of morality. Some adaptation in that respect was carried out from the first where it could be done without too much trouble by a slight modification of the wording or an explanatory gloss putting the matter in a more beseeming light. Such was the perfunctory manner in which the Saxon lay of Beowulf, the large collection of Irish tradition set down at the desire of Finn MacGorman, Bishop of Kildare, and known as the ' Book of Leinster,' and the ' Leabhar na' h Uidhre,' or ' Book of the Dun Cow,' were redacted. It was in those instances the traditional literature of their own people which was set down by clerical redactors, under whose superficial Christianity there lingered a good deal of sympathy with pagan conceptions.

But it was far otherwise on the Continent. The religious authorities there were for the most part Italian, or thoroughly Romanised priests, who saw only in the popular pagan literature heathen abominations. The bards were from the first pursued by the fierce denunciations of the Christian clergy, who regarded their total suppression as almost as essential to the triumph of Christianity as the suppression of idols. At the Court of Charlemagne, Alcuin, that dark obscurantist whom the modern ' poetical history ' of the Middle Ages still represents as a promoter of culture, was untiring in his activity. " It behoves us at banquets," he wrote, " to hear the reading of Scripture, not the twang of harpists; the discourses of the Fathers, not the poems of the pagans. One house is too narrow to harbour both Hinield (a hero

---

[1] Heinrich von dem Türlln, *Diu Crône*, ed. G. H. F. Scholl, vv. 1072 sqq.

of pagan sagas) and Christ; we cannot have both. The King of Heaven will not have anything to do with pagan kings, who are damned; for the Eternal King reigns in heaven, those pagan kings groan in hell. Let the voice of Scripture-readers be heard in thy palace, not a crowd laughing among the dishes."[1] Charlemagne himself, like all the barbarians, cherished the pagan sagas, and, if we are to believe Einhard, even had them collected and set down in writing.[2] He was supported in his taste by many in his entourage, as, for instance, by Angilbert. But the persistent zeal of Alcuin at last wrung from him a decree abolishing the poets. Writing to the Abbot of Corbie, Alcuin thus chuckles over his triumph : " No doubt our Homer (that is, Angilbert) will be much annoyed at this decree abolishing spectacles and diabolical fictions. They are, however, prohibited by all Holy Scriptures, for, as we read in the blessed Augustin : ' The man who introduces histrionic persons, mimes, and dancers in his house does not know what a swarm of foul devils are admitted in their train.' Heaven forbid that the devil should gain power in a Christian household ! "[3] The clergy thundered against the singers. " Let no one presume to allow those inane fables to be sung," orders Hincmar, archbishop of Reims.[4] Leidrad, archbishop of Lyons, denounces " the songs of poets, the elegancies and verses of comedians, which render the mind effeminate."[5] Charles's son, Louis the Pious, who in his youth knew the popular poems by heart, was induced to renounce them, and neither to read nor listen to them, and even to forbid their being taught.[6] Councils reiterated the proscriptions.[7] The duties of kings were defined by the Sixth Council of Paris as being " to prevent thefts, to punish adultery, and to

[1] Alcuin, *Epistola*, cxxiv, in Pertz, *Monumenta Germaniae Historica Epistolae Karolini Aevi*, vol. ii, p. 183.

[2] Einhard, *Vita Karoli Magni*, 29, in *Monumenta Germaniae Historica, Scriptores*, vol. ii, p. 458. If this be correct it is significant that, while all written documents issued by Charlemagne have been so carefully preserved, not a scrap of those redactions of pagan poems made by his order has reached us. Like those poems about ' Hinield,' to which Alcuin refers as so dangerously popular, they have apparently been completely annihilated.

[3] Alcuin, *Epistola*, clxxv, *op. cit.*, p. 290.

[4] Hincmar, *Capitula ad presbyteros*, xiv, in Migne, *Patrologiae Cursus Completus*, vol. cxxv, col. 1067.

[5] Leidrad, *Epistola*, in Pertz, *Monumenta Germaniae Historica, Epistolae Karolini Aevi*, vol. ii, p. 541.

[6] Theganus, *Vita Hludowici imperatoris*, chap. xix, in Pertz, *op. cit., Scriptores*, vol. ii, p. 594. Cf. Benedictus Levita, *Capitularia, ibid., Leges*, vol. ii, part ii, p. 83 ; Rodulfus Glaber, *Historiae sui temporis*, in M. Bouquet, *Recueil des Historiens des Gaules et de la France*, vol. x, p. 42 ; F. Lorenz, *The Life of Alcuin*, p. 149.

[7] E. Faral, *Les jongleurs en France au moyen-âge*, pp. 272 sq.

abstain from feeding ' jongleurs.' " [1] Minstrels were denied communion ; [2] it was declared that they had no hope of salvation, " for they are ministers of Satan." [3]

So essential a part was that oral literature, the only one which they possessed, of the life of the mediaeval populations, that, as we know, all those efforts proved vain. It is admitted after the most drastic prohibitions and acts of repression that " the abominable usage still continues." [4] As in regard to other obstinate survivals of paganism, when suppression proved impossible, compromise and adaptation were resorted to. In the general condemnation of pagan poetry exceptions were allowed in favour of poems of a purely historical character, ' chansons de geste ' celebrating the deeds of heroes, especially of Christian heroes that had merited well of the Church.[5] It is probably owing to those conditions that early continental poetical literature is almost exclusively represented by ' chansons de geste,' and is relatively poor in mythological matter. To the difference in the circumstances which attended the transmission of pagan literature in Ireland and Britain is due doubtless in great part the importance of the ' matter from Britain,' which, when it became available at the comparatively late date of the Norman Conquest, well-nigh superseded other secular literature on the Continent.[6]

---

[1] *Collectio canonum*, in Migne, *Patrologiae Cursus Completus*, vol. cxxxix, col. 477.

[2] W. Hertz, *Spielmans-Buch*, p. 317 ; E. Gautier, *Épopées françaises*, vol. ii, p. 11.

[3] Honorius of Autun, *Elucidarium*, in Migne, *Patrologiae Cursus Completus*, vol. clxxii, col. 1148. For further examples of the Church's war against the minstrels, see E. Gautier, *op. cit.*, vol. ii, pp. 6 sqq. ; H. Reich, *Der Mimus*, pp. 744 sqq. ; E. Faral, *op. cit.*, pp. 24 sqq.

[4] Rodulfus Glaber, *Historiae sui temporis*, in M. Bouquet, *Recueil des historiens de la Gaule et de la France*, vol. x, p. 42.

[5] E. Gautier, *Épopées françaises*, vol. ii, p. 11 ; Thomas Cabham, cited by F. Guessnard and C. Grandmaison, in Introduction to *Huon de Bordeaux*, pp. vi sq. Cf. E. Faral, *Les jongleurs en France au moyen-âge*, p. 67 ; C. Nyrop, *Storia dell' epopea francese*, pp. 279 sq.

[6] Much discussion has taken place on the question whether the ' matière de Bretagne,' as the romances of the Arthurian cycle were called, was derived by the twelfth-century romance-makers who made it popular from British or from continental Celtic sources ; and scholars specialising in the study of that literature have been divided into a ' continental ' and an ' insular ' school of opinion. It may now be regarded as demonstrated that the material reached the authors of the romances mainly through Anglo-Norman redactions of the sagas as preserved by British bards, probably through the medium of Anglo-Saxon interpretations. It appears to me, however, that the opposition between the ' insular ' and the ' continental ' theories is not so sharp and complete as is generally assumed. My opinion on the subject is of no authority ; but I have constantly been impressed

Some specimens of that Celtic literature which have reached us in a form least affected by the doctoring of ecclesiastical redaction have been preserved by a French (or Flemish) lady, known as Marie de France, who resided in England and was familiar with the English, and possibly with the Celtic language. Referring to the treatment of the subject of sex relations in those tales, a critic remarks: " The manners which they depict are rudely and naïvely indecent. . . . The women are not without grace and tender sentiments, but the virtue of which they are most conspicuously devoid is chastity. They sacrifice it very readily and willingly, deeming it as ' a thing of small account,' and the authors, in relating the most outrageous infidelities committed in cold blood, appear to be neither surprised nor indignant. In order to perceive how sentiments of delicacy have developed through the sole progress of the times (par le seul progrès des temps), one has but to compare Marie de France with Froissart. . . . How much more highly developed are those sentiments in the chronicler,

with the essential cultural unity of all Celtic-speaking peoples. Usages, myths, religious conceptions, deities, names are found to be identical from western Scotland and Ireland to the valley of the Po, wherever populations of Celtic speech are found. The themes of Irish and British myths were equally familiar in southern Gaul. Posidonius heard there in the first century B.C. the well-known story of Gawain and the Green Knight, which is the same as the Irish ' Fled Bricrend ' (Athenaeus, iv. 40. Cf. H. d'Arbois de Jubainville, *La civilisation des Celtes et celle de l'épopée Homérique*, pp. 52 sq.). If definite prototypes of the ' Arthurian ' romances are found in Ireland and in Wales, they are also found in Brittany. There can be no doubt as to the derivation of the original materials used by Chrestien de Troyes and his fellow-writers from Anglo-Norman sources and from Britain. But it should not be forgotten that a good deal of Celtic romance had at that time already become embodied in the current themes and materials of trouvères and romance-makers. Merlin, the Lady of the Lake, Morgana, were familiar characters to those romance-makers before the ' matière de Bretagne ' reached them. That older material which derived from continental Celtic sources overlapped in many points the new matter from Norman England, and it is impossible to say to what extent that English material was modified by that overlapping of already established romantic tradition. Professor Rajna has shown that ' Arthurian ' names, such as Galvanus, were used in Italy at the beginning of the twelfth century (P. Rajna, " Gli eroi brettoni nell' onomastica italiana," *Romania*, xvii, p. 355). There was a St. Goulven, bishop of Léon (A. Maury, *Croyances et légendes du moyen-âge*, p. 118), just as there was a St. Leger. There is no more need to trace the former than the latter to romances of chivalry. The fact has generally been assumed to indicate the astonishingly quick spread of the popularity of the romances. But names of Celtic deities and heroes are found in Italy since the days of primitive Rome ; if Bu Anu, the Celtic Mothers, and Bryan were immemorially familiar to Celtic populations in Italy, why not the names of Gawain and other heroes of Celtic mythology ?

how much more delicate is his taste ; how one feels the proximity
of modern times and modern feeling ! " [1]

'The sole progress of the times' can scarcely be accepted
as affording an adequate scientific explanation of psychological
and social phenomena. The process which brought about those
changes is traceable through the countless successive redactions of
the romantic literature. By the thirteenth century, when, enriched
by the 'matter from Britain,' the romances of chivalry attained
the height of their development and popularity, the process of
adaptation of the popular oral literature which it had not been
found possible to suppress to the needs and principles of the
Church had proceeded far. Not only were the Carolingian romances
that celebrated the triumphs of Christian knights over the infidel
tolerated, but the poets had secured for themselves the indulgence,
and even the protection, of the Church by freely lending their
talents to the work of edification. From the general condemna-
tions of the profession had to be excepted not only the singers
of epic romances, but also those of lives of Saints.[2] An enormous
number of such compositions, of poems on the Passion, of 'Histories
of Mary and Jesus,' helped to redeem the profanity of the entertainers.[3] The repertoires of itinerant troupes of 'jongleurs'
abounded in matter of such merit that even the wrath of the
ecclesiastical authorities was disarmed. Thus one of those troupes
presents the following programme : " Adam and Eve in Paradise,
the Three Kings, the Murder of the Innocents, Our Lord and His
Mother eating apples, the apostles telling their beads, the decapita-
tion of John the Baptist, Herod and Caiaphas in their mitres,
Pilate washing his hands, a Paradise with many angels, and a
Hell black and stinking in which the damned fall and are immediately seized by devils." [4] The valuable assistance which 'jongleurs' rendered in organising and lending attraction to Church
festivals and pageants rendered them almost indispensable ;
mystery-plays were probably their creation, in any case they took
a prominent part in their production.[5] At Abbeville we find
troupes of 'jongleurs' giving representations in the church on
the occasion of the Feast of Our Lady.[6] Confraternities of poets
and minstrels came to be attached to churches and monasteries.

[1] M. A. Joly, *Marie de France et les fables du moyen-âge*, pp. 42 sq.
[2] F. Guessnard and C. Grandmaison, *Huon de Bordeaux*, pp. vi sq.
[3] E. Faral, *Les jongleurs en France au moyen-âge*, pp. 45 sqq.
[4] P. J. B. Legrand d'Aussy, *Fabliaux, ou contes du xiie et xiiie siècles*,
vol. ii, p. 177.
[5] L. J. N. Monmerqué and Fr. Michel, *Théâtre français au moyen-âge*,
pp. 396, 501.
[6] F. C. Louandre, *Histoire ancienne et moderne d'Abbeville*, pp. 383 sqq.

One such guild was in the twelfth century connected with the Cathedral of Arras. It was under the patronage of the Virgin Mary, who had herself directed the founder, a repentant minstrel, to offer his services to the bishop in order to establish a school of poets who should devote their talents to the glorification of the Holy Mother.[1] A similar poetical fraternity was under the protection of the ecclesiastical authorities of Amiens, and held a yearly concourse of poetry, in which the prize was allotted to the poem which was judged to be most " pleasing in the ears of God." [2] The ancient Abbey of Fécamp, in Normandy, celebrated for the possession of most holy relics, which included the Blood of Our Lord collected on the cross by Joseph of Arimathea, had also an old-established and noted troupe of poets attached to its service, who were subsidised by William the Conqueror and other Norman nobles.[3]

In the thirteenth-century versions of Celtic legends and sagas, the rude heroes of that age which excited the fierce denunciations of Gildas on account of its barbarity and vices, were transformed, like Alexander and Caesar, into feudal knights distinguished for their ' courtesy,' although their actual behaviour is frequently marked by extreme rudeness.[4] The most startling supernatural characteristics of pagan gods were attenuated and euhemerised.[5] Goddesses, magic women, and matriarchal queens became ' ladies '

---

[1] E. Faral, *Les jongleurs en France au moyen-âge*, pp. 133 sqq.

[2] Id., *ibid.*, pp. 139 sqq.

[3] Leroux de Lincy, *Essai historique et littéraire sur l'abbaye de Fécamp*, p. 378.

[4] " We are very apt to forget," remarks Miss Weston, " that the knights of Arthur's Court are not knights *ab origine*, but bear about them signs and tokens of an earlier state : Perceval's uncouthness, Tristan's shameless mendacity, Gawain's facile morality, are apparent blots upon their perfect knighthood ; but it is not as knights, or even as Arthurian heroes, that such qualities belong to them ; they are legacies from an earlier mythic stage " (J. L. Weston, *The Legend of Sir Perceval*, vol. i, pp. 306 sqq.).

[5] Kay, Arthur's seneschal, " had this peculiarity, that his breath lasted nine nights and nine days under water, and he could exist nine nights and nine days without sleep. . . . When it pleased him he could render himself as tall as the highest tree in the forest.   And he had another peculiarity— so great was the heat of his nature, that, when it rained hardest, whatever he carried remained dry for a handbreadth above and a handbreadth below his hand ; and, when his companions were coldest, it was to them as fuel with which to light their fire " (*The Mabinogion*, ed. A. Nutt, p. 115).   Gawain waxed and waned : " Fro it passed 9 of the clock waxed ever stronger and stronger, for thenne hit cam to the hour of noone and thryes his myghte was encreased.   And thenne whan it was past noone, and whan it drewe toward evensong Syre Gawayne's strengthe febled and waxed passynge faint that unnethe he myght dure ony longer " (Sir T. Malory, *Le Morte d'Arthur*, iv. 18.   Cf. *Perceval le Gallois*, ed. C. Potvin, vol. iii. p. 334 ; *Le Roman de Merlin*, ed. Sommer, p. 137 ; P. Paris, *Les romans de la Table ronde*, vol. iii,

and ' damsels.' The Walhallas, the Isles of the Blessed, the Otherworld abodes of Celtic mythology, became enchanted castles.
Merlin, Bran became Christian magicians. The magic cauldrons
prominent in pagan myth and ritual were transformed into the
sacramental vessel of the Last Supper, in which the blood of Christ
was collected by angels as He lay on the Cross. The San Graal,
containing the true blood of the redemption (' Sanguis realis ') was
said to have been brought to England by Joseph of Arimathea.

This last identification had the most felicitous and important
results ; it imparted to the whole cycle of Celtic myths the
character of a Christian epic, and those features of the pagan
conceptions connected with the magic talisman which were no
longer understood, far from proving difficulties in the way of
the adaptation, helped, on the contrary, to surround it with
that atmosphere of obscure symbolism and mystery which constitutes the essence and suggestiveness of mysticism. The important
part played by the magic cauldrons, fashioned of precious materials,
in the rites of the barbarians, which survived in the rituals of
witchcraft, has already been noted. Into the sacred vessel was
received the blood of the human sacrifices which were understood to redeem the lives which warriors had risked in battle.
With that blood, as Strabo vaguely informs us, the Cymric
priestesses "made a prophecy." [1] In an old Arthurian romance
the wounds of King Arthur are healed by a sorceress, who anoints
them with the blood of a slain enemy.[2] Elsewhere wounded
knights request to be taken to the magic vessel to be healed of
their wounds.[3] Those incidents doubtless contain a reminiscence
of the magic procedures, or ' prophecies,' carried out by the
barbaric priestesses by means of the sacrificial blood. The
magic cauldron was credited with the power of resuscitating dead
warriors. Thus Bran ' the Blessed ' (Bendigeid Vran) gave to
the Irish chieftain Matholwch as a peace offering " a cauldron,
the property of which is that if one of thy men be slain to-day,
and be cast therein, to-morrow he will be as well as ever he
was at the best, except that he will not regain his speech." [4]

---

p. 309 ; Sir F. Madden, *Syr Gawayne*, p. xvi ; *Histoire littéraire de la France*,
vol. xxx, pp. 35 sq.). The strength of Gawain, instead of waxing during the
day, is represented in some MSS. as increasing at midnight. A Celtic legend,
of which no trace appears in the romances, represents him as dwelling at
times, like Arianrhod, in a palace at the bottom of the sea (Peter Bercheure,
Opera omnia ; sive Reductorium, Repertorium et Dictionarium morale, xiv,
Prologum).

[1] See above, vol. ii, p. 542.

[2] ' Didot ' Perceval, in *Perceval le Gallois*, ed. C. Potvin, vol. i, p. 19 ;
Perlesvaus, Hatton Manuscript 82, Branch 1, ed. by J. T. Lister, p. 50.

[3] *La Queste del Saint Graal*, ed. F. S. Furnivall, p. 51.

[4] *The Mabinogion*, ed. A. Nutt, p. 31.

That property of the 'cauldron of regeneration'[1] is commonly mentioned in Irish myths of the cycle of Fionn.[2]   It appears probable that some rite of initiation, similar to those prevalent among primitive peoples, and in which the initiated is supposed to die and be born again with renewed life like the lunar divinity, was connected with the magic uses of the Celtic ritual of the sacred cauldron.[3]   The hero Gawain was called the son of 'Blood.'[4] Magic cauldrons were also the source of prophetic inspiration. Thus the mother of the bard Taliesin endowed her son by means of such a cauldron with prophetic gifts.   "She resolved, according to the arts of the books of Fferyllt, to boil a Cauldron of Inspiration and Science for her son . . . which from the beginning of its boiling might not cease to boil for a year and a day, until three blessed drops were obtained of the Grace of Inspiration"[5]   Like all instruments of primitive magic and religion the magic cauldron was not only the giver, but also the sustainer of life, the giver of food; but it nourished the initiated only: "it will not boil the food of a coward that has not been sworn."[6]   The magic cauldron of the Irish King of Alba supplied the food for the banquet of any company that was assembled, "and no party ever

---

[1] *The Mabinogion*, p. 39.

[2] "Fionn's Enchantment," translated by J. F. Campbell, *Revue Celtique*, i, p. 194.

[3] Such 'cauldrons of regeneration' were familiar in archaic Greece. Medea regenerated people by boiling them in a magic cauldron (Euripides, *Medea*, 9 sq.; Scholiast on Aristophanes, *Equites*, 1321, Apollodorus, i. 9. 27).   Pelops, after he had been boiled in a 'sacred cauldron,' was regenerated by the Moira Klotho, or, according to another version, by Rhea (Pindar, *Olymp.*, i, 40 sqq.; Scholiast, *ad loc.*).   Dionysos was made "whole and entire" after being boiled in a cauldron (Macrobius, *Somnium Scipionis*, i. 12).   Cf. F. M. Cornford, "The Origin of the Olympic Games," in J. E. Harrison, *Themis*, pp. 244 sqq.

[4] *The Mabinogion*, p. 281.   It may be conjectured that when Cuchulainn, Arthur, Tristan, and other Celtic heroes were 'made whole' by the magic women or goddesses to whom they resorted for that purpose, they were in reality resurrected, and that the "cauldrons of regeneration" which were in the possession of those magic females may have played a part in the process.

[5] *Ibid.*, p. 295.

[6] F. Skene, *The Four Ancient Books of Wales*, vol. i, p. 265: "The Book of Taliesin," xxx.   The Welsh 'Bardic' books, as also the Mabinogi of Taliesin, are of late redaction, but they contain materials which belong to the primitive strata of pagan tradition.   Any reference to magic cauldrons, in particular, may without hesitation be accepted as belonging to those strata, for it is manifest that the authors of those compositions, who were familiar with the fully developed legend of the Holy Grail, would not deliberately revert to so primitive a form of the conception.   Of any connection between such magic cauldrons and the holy vessel they were quite unconscious, and the suggestion of such a connection would undoubtedly have been repudiated by them as impious.

went away unsatisfied, for whatever quantity was put into it there was never boiled of it but what was sufficient for the company according to their grade and rank." [1] The Irish poet enumerates several magic cauldrons which were famous in Celtic lands. Some appear to have been fashioned of gold, or, like the cauldron of Jutland, of silver. The rim of the cauldron of Dagda was adorned with pearls. The property of supplying unlimited food is mentioned with reference to most magic cauldrons in Irish legends.[2] The vessel of the Holy Grail had in like manner fed Joseph of Arimathea during his imprisonment,[3] and in the Grail Castle " it proceeded to every place in the hall, and as it came before the tables it filled them with every kind of meat that a man could desire." [4]

The magic cauldrons prominent in Celtic ritual had their counterpart among the talismans of the gods. The Tuatha da Danan guarded four precious talismans. One was the Stone of Virtue, or of Fate, which is no other than the ' Stone of Scone,' upon which English sovereigns since Edward I have been crowned. " It used to roar under each king of Ireland on his being chosen." [5] The second was the sword of the god Lug ; the third was his spear. The fourth was " the Cauldron of Lofty Deeds of Dagda," the Good God. Its property was that " a company used not ever go away from it unsatisfied." [6] The talismans were in Celtic tradition regarded as being in the special keeping of Bran, or Bryan, that is, ' the Raven.' When in 387 B.C. the Gauls crossed the Apennines, captured and sacked primitive Rome, they were understood to be under the leadership of Bran, whom Roman writers called Brennus.[7] When in 280 B.C. Celtic hosts penetrated into Greece and into the very sanctuary of Delphi, they were again understood to be led by Bran, or ' Brennos.' [8] The Asiatic Gauls in Galatia like-

[1] J. O'Donovan, The Banquet of Dun Na N-Gedh and the Battle of Mag Rath (Irish Archaeological Society), pp. 51 sqq.

[2] A. Nutt, Studies on the Legend of the Holy Grail, pp. 74 sqq.

[3] Perceval Le Gallois, ed. C. Potvin, vol. v, p. 154 ; Le Saint Graal, vol. ii, pp. 71 sq.

[4] Perceval le Gallois, vv. 20142 sqq., 20114 sqq., 12 sqq., 171 sqq. ; Seint Graal, ed. R. Williams, pp. 442 sq.

[5] When Perceval seats himself on the Siege Perillous, it gives forth a loud roar (Perceval le Gallois, vol. iv, p. 172 ; Le Saint Graal, vol. i, pp. 426 sq.).

[6] G. Keating, History of Ireland, ed. D. Comyr (Irish Texts Society), vol. i, pp. 205 sqq.

[7] Livy, v. 38. It is noteworthy that neither Diodorus nor Polybius knows the name of the leader of the Gauls. Livy's ' Brennus ' thus appears to be a later ascription, probably derived from information gathered from Cisalpine Gauls to the effect that the leader of the victorious Gauls must needs have been Bran.

[8] Pausanias, x. 19. 7 ; Strabo, iv. 187 ; Justin, xxiv, 6 ; Suidas, s.v.

wise fought under the auspices of Brennos.[1]   The 'Brennos' who thus constantly appears as the leader of the Gauls is clearly the god Bran, ' the Raven ' under whose guidance they were led to victory.[2] The god Bran, Lord of the Otherworld and keeper of the magic cauldron and sacred lance and sword, is in the Christianised myth of the romances, where his name is spelt Brons, the keeper of the Holy Grail ; he is the brother-in-law of Joseph of Arimathea, and brought the Grail to England.[3]

The acquisition of the magic cauldron and of magic weapons is ascribed in Celtic myth to many divine heroes.   It is more particularly associated in the Ultonian cycle with Cuchulainn, who, in the course of his conquest of the land of Scathach, the sorceress who instructs him in deeds of valour, is given " by the daughter of the king "—probably Scathach herself—a magic cauldron.   " They used to frequent that cauldron ; delightful was the contest ; they would not go from it on any side until they left it full.   There was much gold and silver in it—wonderful was the find ; that cauldron was given to us by the daughter of the king." [4]   In British myth the adventure of the Holy Grail was originally associated with Cuchulainn's British counterpart, Gawain.   In the version preserved in Heinrich von dem Türlîn's ' Diu Crône,' which is a very early one and based on several Norman redactions, Gawain is the sole hero of the legend of the Quest which he achieves completely.   The mystic vessel, the quest being accomplished, is translated to Heaven, and Gawain returns triumphant to Arthur's Court, where his achievement is celebrated with " the most magnificent feasts that were ever seen." [5]

In its original pagan form the adventure of the magic cauldron and other talismans was in nowise a ' mystic ' quest, but a conquest like any other.   As was natural among warlike tribes, the conquest of the magic sword and lance was even more important than that of the magic cauldron.   The weapons occupy a more prominent place than the vessel in the earlier versions of the legend, and even Chrestien de Troyes' unfinished version, so far as he was permitted to write it, deals chiefly with the

---

[1] Plutarch, *Parallela minora*, 15.

[2] Cf. C. I. Elton, *Origins of English History*, pp. 291 sq. ;   H. d'Arbois de Jubainville, *Le Cycle mythologique Irlandais*, pp. 148 sq.

[3] According to the ' Didot ' Perceval, however, Bran and the Grail Castle are in Ireland, where they properly belong.

[4] E. Hull, *The Cuchullin Saga*, p. 284.   The obscurity of the wording, which renders it difficult to make out the exact meaning, is not wholly due to the failure of the translators ; it is a common feature of Celtic poetry which frequently adopts such puzzling ' stil clus.'   It is mentioned concerning a poem which was sung before Arthur that no one was able to understand what it meant, except that it was in praise of the king.

[5] Heinrich von dem Türlîn, *Diu Crône*, ed. G. H. F. Scholl, vv. 28252 sqq.

expedition of Gawain, whose main object is to gain possession of the lance and not of the Grail. In the fully developed Grail legend the bloody lance and sword become accessories, the former being explained as the lance with which Longinus pierced the side of Christ, the latter, somewhat clumsily, as the sword with which John the Baptist was beheaded, or as that of Judas Maccabaeus.

A far more serious difficulty than these interpretations and adaptations was presented, in the Christianisation of the myth, by the character of the heroes. It behoved the protagonist of so high a theme, the chosen guardian of the Eucharistic Vessel, to be ritually pure. It was, indeed, scarcely sufficient that he should be reputably chaste ; his quasi-saintly function seemed to require that he should be a celibate and a virgin. How could the office be filled by Gawain who, of all the heroes of the Arthurian cycle, had the most firmly established reputation for amatory adventures, a reputation which had become too proverbial to be obliterated or glossed over ? In later stages of the romance period Lancelot had almost supplanted the more primitive Gawain in popularity as the most famous knight of Arthur's Court, and there was a disposition to transfer to him as Gawain's understudy the high adventure. But even with the help of his supposed repentance, the lover of Guinevere was scarcely better qualified from the moral point of view than the original Gawain. It was indeed a perplexing problem to find among those transformed pagan warriors, half of whose stories consisted of amatory adventures, a hero even potentially chaste. As the best solution that could in those difficult circumstances be devised the part became generally assigned to Perceval.

The attribution of the high office to Perceval, his transformation into the sainted hero of the Holy Grail, presents one of the most curious incidents in literary history, and affords a striking illustration of the changes which traditional myths may undergo in the process of being re-edited with a special aim in view. The character of Perceval in Celtic folklore is a typical and well-defined one. He was not a mythological hero—unlike the other non-historical characters in the cycle he has no mythological attributes—but a pure product of folklore humour. He was, in fact, the clown, or comic personage, of the traditional cycle, a type common in the popular literature of most peoples, and of the Celts in particular.[1] He was spoken of as ' Perceval

---

[1] For illustrations, see A. Nutt, *Studies on the Legend of the Holy Grail*, pp. 152 sqq. Simrock says : "It cannot be doubted that we have in the story of Perceval's youth a variant of the Tale of the Fool found amongst all peoples " (K. Simrock, *Parzival und Titurel*, p. 781).

the Fool.' [1] In Wolfram von Eschenbach's version Perceval makes
his first appearance at the Court of King Arthur attired in the
motley of a Court fool.[2] He leaves his rustic home on " a bony
piebald horse," which was used for carrying firewood, having
" pressed a pack into the form of a saddle, and with the twisted
twigs imitated the trappings which he had seen upon the horses "
of knights. He is armed with pitchforks. In this guise he rides
into the hall of Arthur's Court amid the jeers and laughter of the
company, who throw sticks at him,[3] and a damsel who has not
smiled for ten years bursts into laughter at the sight of him, and
mockingly salutes him as the flower of knighthood.[4] While
clumsily manoeuvring his farm-horse he knocks off King Arthur's
cap.[5] The part of this comic knight in Celtic folklore was to
attempt all the exploits and adventures of the heroic prototypes,
and to accomplish them, with the proverbial fool's luck, even
more easily and more brilliantly than the most renowned heroes,
failing, however, owing to his phenomenal stupidity, to reap the
fruits of his successses. When with his pitchfork he overthrows
his first knight in order to obtain a suit of armour, he is unable
to remove it, and is discovered dragging the corpse about, and
proposing to burn it out of the harness.[6] The favourite manner
in which Perceval's feeble-mindedness was exhibited was by his
scrupulous observance, in the most unintelligent and inopportune
manner, of any advice or instruction given to him. His reason for
proposing to burn the knight is, he says, that

> " My moder bad me
> Whenne the darte should broken be
> Owte of the yren brenne the tree." [7]

He carries out conscientiously his mother's advice to possess
himself of any precious jewel, by stealing the ring of the first lady

---

[1] Wolfram von Eschenbach, *Parzival*, ed. K. Bartsch, vol. i, p. 166:
" Parzivâl der Tumbe." The ' Mons ' MS. speaks of him as " qui moult
avoit de sens petit " (*Perceval le Gallois*, ed. C. Potvin, vol. ii, p. 42).

[2] Wolfram von Eschenbach, *op. cit.*, vol. i, p. 137. In the other versions
he is clad in goat-skins. " The illuminated texts show him dressed in a single
tight-fitting garment, with a pointed hood, drawn over his head. The effect
is really that of a fool's dress, especially when the costume, as in the frescoes
of the great hall at Neu-Schwanstein, is coloured red " (J. L. Weston, *The
Legend of Sir Perceval*, vol. i, p. 78 n.).

[3] *The Mabinogion*, ed. A. Nutt, pp. 246, 248 ; *Perceval le Gallois*, ed.
C. Potvin, vol. i, p. 72.

[4] *The Mabinogion*, p. 249 ; *Perceval le Gallois*, vol. i, p. 76.

[5] *Perceval le Gallois*, loc. cit. ; *The Thornton Romances*, ed. J. C. Halliwell, p. 20.

[6] *Perceval le Gallois*, ed. cit., vol. i, pp. 78 sq. ; Wolfram von Eschenbach,
Parzival, ed. cit., vol. i, pp. 166 sqq. ; *The Mabinogion*, p. 250 ; *The Thornton
Romances*, pp. 29 sq.

[7] *The Thornton Romances*, loc. cit.

he meets,[1] and similarly accompanies all his blunders with the refrain that he had been advised to act thus.

It was inevitable that the conquest of the magic talismans should, like other famous adventures, be undertaken by the comic hero, although in two at least of the most archaic versions of his story that have reached us he has no connection with the enterprise. The point in Perceval the Fool's achievement of that exploit is, however, that, having come upon the talismans, he fails to gain possession or to make use of them, owing to his strict observance of the Polonius-like advice just given him by the sage Gonemans not to show too much curiosity and not to ask the meaning of all he sees. He thus remains ignorant of the talismans' properties, and, having found them and had them within his grasp, returns empty-handed, and is jeered at and cursed for his stupidity. The very servants laugh at him; a valet calls out to him: " You are a goose! you have lost the opportunity of winning the greatest prize." [2]

With the translation of the adventure of the magic talismans

---

[1] *Perceval le Gallois*, vol. i, pp. 62 sqq.; Wolfram von Eschenbach *Parzival*, vol. i, pp. 140 sqq.; *The Mabinogion*, p. 247.

[2] Wolfram von Eschenbach, *Parzival*, ed. cit., vol. i, p. 262 :—

> "Sprach der knappe : 'ir sît ein gans.
> Möht ir gerüeret hân den flans,
> Und het den wirt gevrâget!
> Vil prîss iuch hât betrâget.' "

Cf. *Perceval le Gallois*, ed. C. Potvin, vol. ii, pp. 201 sq.; *Le Saint-Graal ou le Joseph d'Arimathie*, ed. E. Hucher, vol. i, p. 404.

The French romance-makers, taking Perceval the Fool quite seriously, supposed that the questions concerning the meaning of the talismans had in themselves a magic virtue, causing the spell under which the inhabitants of the Grail Castle suffered to be removed. Modern criticism appears to have been to a large extent stultified by the same serious view of the clownish hero. An instance of that misapprehension is afforded by the manifestly inadequate attempts of so acute and competent a critic as Mr. A. Nutt to 'explain' Perceval's silence. He suggests that "the silence of Perceval may, perhaps, be referred to the same myth-root as Fionn's concealment of his name. . . . This prohibition might extend not only to the disclosing of his name . . . but to the utterance of any words at all. . . . An alternative hypothesis is that . . . in the language of Irish mythic tradition Perceval would be under 'geasa' (see above, p. 402) to ask no questions, and Gonemans' advice would be the last faint echo of such an incident" (A. Nutt, *Studies on the Legend of the Holy Grail*, pp. 211 sq.). "That the romance writers did not understand this incident," remarks Mr. Nutt, "is evident from the explanation they give." I venture to think that the same remark applies to Mr. Nutt's explanations. The explanation which the romance-writers give is that Perceval was bent on scrupulously observing the advice he had just received from Gonemans, namely, not to show too much curiosity. And the explanation which Perceval in every known version of his story gives of any of his blunders is that he is carrying out somebody's advice. He continues to bear in mind the same advice

into the holy quest of the San Graal, the mystic and sacred symbol of the miracle of the Mass, any sense of humour with which the Christian redactors might have regarded the story of Perceval the Fool was abolished by the sanctity of the theme, and any levity in relation to it became inadmissible. The clownish knight who had been paradoxically saluted on his arrival at Arthur's Court as " the chief of warriors and flower of knighthood " was taken in all seriousness. An incident which belonged probably to his original story commended him particularly in the eyes of the Christian editors, and marked him out as a more suitable hero than Gawain or Lancelot for the sacred quest. Perceval had been instructed by his mother to make love to every fair woman he met whether she was willing or no, and he had endeavoured to carry out the instruction with the same punctiliousness as her other counsels; but, in harmony with his character and his simplicity, he bungled his first amatory successes in the same manner as his other enterprises. The first woman whom he comes upon he finds asleep in a tent, which he takes to be a church; he roughly kisses her " more than twenty times," steals her jewellery, and eats up all her provisions—his appetite is Gargantuan, his table manners are likened to the operation of filling a manger.[1] Having thus faithfully carried out his mother's instructions, he departs taking no notice of the lady's hints and advances.[2] When the distressed queen, Blancheflor, whose realm is ravaged and her castle besieged by an inacceptable suitor, implores Perceval to assist her, he stipulates in the crudest manner he will do so only on condition that she becomes his mistress, and that he will accept no other guerdon.[3] When she comes in approved fashion

---

when he is sent for by Blancheflor and is first introduced to her presence : he sits stock-dumb :—

> " Sîn manlîch zuht was im sô ganz,
> Sît in der werde Gurnamanz."

(Wolfram von Eschenbach, *op. cit.*, vol. i, p. 200). The only hypothesis which the critic has not considered is that the hero did not ask the question because he was a fool. The original purpose of the quest—as in every primitive version of the theme—is, of course, not the asking of questions, but the acquisition of talismans. Perceval did not acquire them because, not having made any enquiries, he did not know they were talismans.

[1] Wolfram von Eschenbach, *Parzival*, ed. cit., vol. i, p. 176 :—

> " in den bárn er sich sô habete,
> daz er der spîse swande vil."

[2] *Perceval le Gallois*, vol. i, pp. 62 sqq. ; Wolfram von Eschenbach *Parzival*, vol. i, pp. 140 sqq. ; *The Mabinogion*, p. 247.

[3] *Perceval le Gallois*, ed. C. Potvin, vol. i, p. 111 :—

> " . . . se je l'oci et conquier
> Votre druerie requier
> En guerdon, k'ele soit moie ;
> Autres saudées n' en prendroie."

to her guest's bed, coquettishly excusing herself " por ce que je
sui presque nue," he receives her literally with open arms ; but,
in entire accordance with his character, the ' Great Fool ' who
does not know a tent from a church or a hind from a goat, after
covering her with kisses, falls sound asleep in her arms, and—

> " Ensi giurent tote la nuit
> Li un vers l'autre, boce a boce." [1]

The incident became one of the most prominent in the
Christian version of the Perceval legend. It was assimilated
to the ' trials of chastity ' of early Christian saints ; chastity came
to be one of the special virtues of the hero ; and ultimately, in the
later redactions of his myth, he came to be represented as a maiden
knight, and thus worthiest protagonist of the mystic quest of the
Holy Grail.

An exceptional opportunity of following in detail the various
steps of that adaptation is afforded in the numerous redactions
of the theme. The original Perceval was in no way more austere,
though far less courteous in his amours, than his heroic prototypes.
At his second meeting with Blancheflor he is represented by the
continuators of Chrestien de Troyes as having quite lost the simplicity
which distinguished him in his first adventure with her ; and when
she again comes to his bed he is eager to make the most of the
' bonne fortune.' [2]   There is certainly nothing austere about his
behaviour with the " Lady of the Chessboard." [3] The moment

---

[1] *Perceval le Gallois*, ed. C. Potvin, vol. i, pp. 107 sq., 110.

[2] The Montpellier MS. has :—

> " Percevaus le prent dans ses bras
> Qui moult desire le soulas
> Avoir, car moult l'a enamee ;
> C. fois en une randonee
> L'a baisie sans ariester.
> Je ne vous voel mie conter
> Del sorplus comment il ala,
> Mais se dans Percevaus pecha
> En Blanchefleur ne resmet mie ;
> Qui si plaine est de courtoisie,
> Que cose que faire vonst
> Por nule rien ne desdesist.
> Ensi menerent lor deduit
> Petit dormirent cele nuit."

The Mons MS. amends the 7th and 8th lines thus :—

> " Le sorplus, se plus en i a
> Mais, se Percevaus l'en pria."

> > (*Perceval le Gallois*, ed. C. Potvin, vol. iv, p. 163.)

[3] The lady appears to be no other than Morgana. She enters on the
scene by rising out of the waters that surround the castle, and the magic

he beholds her " there came upon Perceval a great love and desire of her body and her beauty " ; he draws her to his arms, kisses her, " and would have done more if he could and she had consented." The lady, however, threatens him if, as he appears disposed to do, he attempts to ravish her, but promises her love if he first duly performs certain required exploits.[1] These he easily achieves, but, in accordance with his traditional character, allows the trophies to be stolen from him, and his endeavours to recover them occupy in the poem of Chrestien's continuators a much more important place than the quest of the Grail, and take up fully a third of the narrative. Having at last regained possession of the proofs of his exploits, he has no other thought but to claim his promised guerdon, and, neglecting all else, hurries to the lady, who, to his joy, duly redeems her promise.[2] In the pursuit of this amour Perceval neglects Blancheflor in a manner so boorish that he is brought to task by her uncle concerning his conduct, and plainly requested to make amends and marry her.[3] In the older versions Blancheflor becomes his wife. In the English lay

chessboard is represented as a gift of Morgana. She is at the time over a hundred years old.

[1] *Perceval le Gallois*, ed. C. Potvin, vol. iv, p. 81 :—

> " Por son cors et por ses biautes
> Vint une si grande volentes
> A Perceval de li amer
> Qu'il commence a souspirer . . .
> A soi le trait, si le baisa,
> De tant com puet se conforta,
> Et plus fesist se il peuist
> Et se cile li consentist."

She, however, tells him :—

> " Mais de tant soies-vos certains
> Que, se vous force me faisie,
> Je seriez tous detrencies.
> Mais se m'amor volis avoir
> M'amor ares sans contreditz."

[2] *Ibid.*, vol. iv, p. 339 :—

> " Percevaus pas ne s'endormi
> Si tost come faire soloit ;
> A la damoiselle pensait
> Qui de biaute resemblait fee.
> Que qu'il estait en la pensee,
> Vint celle a lui, si se couca,
> Envers lui sa foi aquitta
> Tout si com il ot devise
> Et com elle ot acreante,
> S'en lui ne remest par folie ;
> Trestoute la nuit amutie,
> Ont conduie ensemble geu."

[3] *Ibid.*, vol. iv, pp. 182 sq.

of ' Sir Perceval ' his relation to Blancheflor (called here Lufamour) is the old straightforward one of the conquest of a wealthy wife and her dowry. After ridding her of rival claimants to the prize,

> Now has Percevelle the wight,
> Wedden Lufamour the bright,
> And is a kyng fulle righte
>   Of alle that lande brade.[1]

In Wolfram von Eschenbach's ' Parzeval,' Blancheflor, called Condwiramur, instead of making him king of her ' lande brade,' joins him, much to his surprise, after five years of complete desertion on his part, and becomes queen of the Kingdom of the Holy Grail.[2]

Not only is Perceval a married man but his matrimonial arrangements appear to be multiple. One of his traditional amours is with a certain heathenish princess, a wielder of magic arts. He meets her at a tournament given by King Arthur, and sends all the knights he overthrows to pay her homage, retaining, however, the proceeds of their armour and horses, as well as some trifles he obtains from the lady, in order to pay his rent to the miller with whom he is lodging. At the conclusion of the tournament the lady is, according to one manuscript, expressly said to be given in marriage to Perceval by King Arthur. In two other versions, which give the incident in the same way, the writers show a remarkable embarrassment and reticence when it comes to disposing of the lady to the winner of the tournament. They state that she was given by King Arthur to a most distinguished knight, but positively decline to mention his name.[3] We are thus admitted to the perplexities and mental conflicts of the editors. From the Mabinogion version we learn that the lady was " the Empress of Cristinobyl the Great," and that she hailed from the lands " towards India." She entertains Perceval " for fourteen years." [4] By this Indian princess he has a son, Morien, who,

---

[1] " The Romance of Sir Perceval," in *The Thornton Romances*, ed. J. C. Halliwell (*Camden Society*), p. 67.

[2] Wolfram von Eschenbach, *Parzival*, ed. K. Bartsch, vol. iii, p. 180.

[3] J. L. Weston, *The Legend of Sir Perceval*, vol. i, pp. 123 sqq. MS. 12577, Bibliothèque Nationale, has :—

> " La pucele du paveillon
> De celi fist le roi don
> Au bon Perceval le Galois."

MS. 12576 says :—
> " Nel weil nomer a ceste fois."

The Alsatian version of Perceval says :—

> " Einne hoch-gebornen ritter fin
> dez namen sol vergorgan sin."

[4] *The Mabinogion*, pp. 274, 278 sqq.

when he grows up, seeks everywhere his father on behalf of his deserted mother.[1] In the Dutch 'Lancelot' the perplexed editor states that some books declare that Morien was the son of Perceval, " but that cannot be true, because, as is well known, both Perceval and Galahad remained virgins on account of the quest of the Grail." [2]

In the German 'Parzival' the moral difficulties of the adaptation were met by marriages " per onestar la cosa," according to Ariosto's expression ; even Gawain is there a marrying man. But the hero's chastity is nevertheless emphasised at the cost of innumerable incongruities. The classical episode of Blancheflor's visit to her guest's bed—the germ of the whole evolution —had of necessity, as an essential feature of the legend, to be included, in spite of the attribution to the heroine of the most delicate modesty ; but the account of the prescriptive incident, if adorned with rhyme, is certainly destitute of reason. Condwiramur, although she has had an afternoon and evening to confide her troubles to her guest, feels herself " compelled by the necessities of her situation " to do so in the middle of the night, attired in shift and mantle—" What garb could be more gallant and befitting ? "—and enters his bed, " but their limbs never touched." [3] After Perceval has successfully

---

[1] F. Lot, " Celtica," *Romania*, xxiv, p. 336. An epitaph is cited to " Mor, the son of Peredur." In Wolfram von Eschenbach the incident is transferred to Perceval's father, whose son by the heathen queen Belakane goes in search of him, but finds Perceval himself, accompanies him to the Grail Castle, and ultimately becomes the father of Prester John (Wolfram von Eschenbach, *Parzival*, vol. i, pp. 65 sq. ; vol. iii, pp. 124 sqq.).

[2] *Roman van Lancelot*, ed. W. J. A. Jonckbloet, vol. i, pp. 284 sq.

[3] Wolfram von Eschenbach, *Parzival*, ed. K. Bartsch, vol. i, pp. 204 sq :—

> " Das kom als ich íu sagen wil.
> Ez prach niht wîplîchiu zil :
> mit staete kiusche truoc diu maget,
> von der ein teil hie wirt gesaget.
> Die twanc úrlíuges nôt,
> und lieber hélfaére tôt
> ir herze an solhez krachen,
> daz ir óugen muosen wachen.
> Dô gienc diu küneginne,
> niht nâch sölher minne
> diu solhen namen reizet
> der megde wip heizet :
> sie suochte helfe unt friwendes rât.
> An ir was werlîchiu wât,
> ein hemede wîz sîdîn :
> waz möhte kampflîcher sin,
> dan gein dem man sus kómende ein wîp ?
> Ouch swanc diu frouwe umbe ir lîp
> von samît einen mantel lanc. . . ."

[Continued on next page.

overcome Condwiramur's enemies, the marriage of the two is
solemnised; but, as a compromise, their strict observance of the
traditional three nights' delay before consummation is described
with great prolixity, and we are assured that the behaviour of the
hero was such as "would not have pleased most ladies at the
present day." As a result of that comparative chastity, the lady
presents him with twins.[1]

A further phase in the evolution of Perceval the Fool is entered

(Observe that her mantle is 'white' and 'long' in extenuation of her
behaviour.)

> " Gein sînem bette gieng ir pfat;
> ûffen téppech kniete sie für in.
> sie heten beidiu kranken sin,
> er und diu küneginne,
> an bî ligender minne.
> Hie wart alsus geworben:
> an fröudén verdorben
> was diu maget: des twanc sie scheme:
> ob er sie hin an iht neme?
> leider des enkan er niht.
> Âne kunst ez doch geschiht,
> mit eime alsô bewanden vride,
> daz sie diu süenebaeren lide
> niht z'ein ander brâhten.
> wênc sie des gedâhten."

[1] Wolfram von Eschenbach, *op. cit.*, vol. i, pp. 213 sq.; vol. iii, p. 180.
Wolfram, it is now generally recognised, had besides Chrestien another model,
to whom he refers as Kiot. Kiot's work, though embodying some archaic
features, appears to be a comparatively late one. It is clear that it
presented the Perceval story in its connection with the Grail legend, and
was probably highly moralised. Possibly it emanated from Fécamp or
from some of the ecclesiastical trouvères; it had a French (Armorican),
not a British setting—Arthur's Court in Wolfram is situated at Nantes.
Wolfram himself, whose version is one of the most highly elaborated,
freely manipulated his material and introduced a good deal of his own.
To him, or to his immediate entourage, is undoubtedly due the linking
of the Perceval-Grail legend with the Flemish tradition of the Knight
of the Swan. Wolfram was under the patronage of the Count of Brabant,
and part of his task was to adapt his theme to the glorification of his patron
by making his ancestor, Lohengrin, a knight of the Grail and the son of
Perceval. Consequently also the hero's relation with Blancheflor—whose
name is changed, probably in order to connect her with a Brabant princess—
had to be represented in as beseeming a light as possible; her marriage
with the hero is dwelt upon, although it is immediately followed by a
complete separation which lasts at least five years, and she is somewhat
artificially brought in at the end to take her place as queen of the Grail
kingdom. It follows that Gerbert, who knows Lohengrin as the son of
Perceval, must have been posterior to Wolfram, and must have either
known his poem or some version of Flemish source derived from it
(Wolfram's language is almost identical with Flemish), and that the German
poem therefore represents a stage in the direct line of the transformation
of Perceval into a 'maiden knight.'

upon in Gerbert's 'addition' to Chrestien's poem. Here again
the obligatory incident of Blancheflor's nightly visit to Perceval's
bed is necessarily given ; but it is even more devoid of any con-
ceivable 'raison d'être' than in Wolfram. It takes place on the
very eve of their marriage, after Perceval, on the insistent
representations of her uncle, has been compelled to declare
publicly his intention of being joined to Blancheflor " in holy
matrimony." Needless to say, that purposeless escapade is carried
out with scrupulous regard for chastity, if not for common
sense. The betrothed couple, whose indecent haste is quite
unaccountable, sleep with the bed-cover between them, though
we are not told which of the two runs the risk of catching a death
of cold by sleeping outside it.[1] Their wedding is celebrated the
next day with great pomp and solemnity, but, in spite of their
impatient anticipation of it, no change takes place in their
relations, and they resolve to live a life of chastity. No sooner
are they alone, than Blancheflor addresses her husband in a dis-
course paraphrased from Origen : " Let us beware, my beloved
friend," she says, " lest the Enemy of mankind should obtain
power over us. It is easy to perceive that chastity is a holy
thing, but by as much as the rose surpasses all other flowers
in beauty, so doth virginity surpass chastity ; and he who has
both the one and the other, all honour encompasses him, and he
thus gains a double crown before God and in blessed Paradise."
Perceval replies by an antistrophe to that epithalamium : " For
the love of God, dear friend, let us not make an ill use of our lives,
for if, as I believe and know, virginity surpasses all other virtues,
as topaze doth crystal, and gold the baser metals, he who hath
both chastity and virginity must, I trow, obtain the joys and delights
of Paradise." After spending some hours in prayer, they retire
to their chaste couch, " taking care that their bodies do not come
in contact with one another." Their virtuous resolution is commended by a voice from Heaven which, after a further lengthy
disquisition on the merits of virginity, urges them to persevere
in their purpose of preserving theirs, and enters into details as to
the proper use of marriage. As a reward for their saintliness, the
heavenly voice gratifies the pair by the astounding announcement
of the glory which awaits their descendants, from whose seed shall
spring the Knight of the Swan and the deliverer of the Holy
Sepulchre. Since Perceval's only living relatives are a holy
hermit and a nun, it is difficult to imagine how the prophecy can
be realised.[2]

[1] *Perceval le Gallois*, ed. Potvin, vol. vi, pp. 207 sqq.
[2] *Ibid.*, vol. vi, pp. 207 sqq. :—

> " Percheviax, biaux amis,
> Or gaitons ce que l'anemis
> N'ait sor nous force et pooir ;

[*Continued on next page.*

Gerbert's re-interpretation is not, however, the last word in the translation of Perceval; the author of ' La Queste del Saint Graal' goes even farther. Here there is neither marrying nor giving in marriage. What of the classical episode of Blancheflor? To have omitted it altogether would have been tantamount to obliterating the identity of the hero. The author of ' La Queste' merits admiration for the ingenuity with which he solved so difficult a problem. Perceval meets Blancheflor in a desert place and she seduces him by her blandishments; she leads him into a luxurious tent in which is a magnificent bed, and, disrobing, invites him to her arms. Perceval yields to her seductions and, casting off his clothes, is about to step into the bed, when his eyes fall upon the cross-shaped hilt of the sword which he has just removed. At that sight he is reminded of his vows, and draws back. Instantly tent and damsel vanish, and he finds himself once more in the desert, where presently he meets a holy hermit, to whom he relates what has just befallen him. The saintly man has no difficulty in explaining to him the adventure: " Know, my son," he tells him, " that the damsel to whom you spoke just now is no other than the Enemy, the master of Hell." [1]

It is not surprising that under the saintly figure of the chosen knight of the Holy Grail the features of Perceval the Fool became, even to modern critics, barely discernible. Yet, in spite of the bold and resourceful editorship which translated him, it was felt that his ritual purity and virginity were far from being established beyond suspicion, and that his qualifications, which had been secured at the cost of contradicting current and familiar versions, did not render him a wholly satisfactory protagonist for the part. Those misgivings led to a further device. A brand-new hero was created who, unhampered by any rumours of a disputable past, could be made to fulfil the requirements of the most exacting ideals. Galahad, who is entirely unknown, save for a casual mention of the name, in Celtic tradition, " surpassed in goodness and in chivalry all those that went before." [2] The author of ' Le

> Legiere chose est a savoir
> Que chaastez est sainte chose ;
> Mais eusement comme la rose
> Sormonte autre flore de biautez
> Ansi passe virginitez
> Chaastee, ce sachiez de voir ;
> Et qui puet l'une et l'autre avoir
> Sachiez toute honors l'avironne
> Et si en a double coronne
> Devant Dieu, en saint paradis," etc., etc.

[1] *La Queste del Saint Graal*, ed. F. J. Furnivall, pp. 95 sq., 98.
[2] *Le Saint-Graal, ou le Joseph d'Arimathie*, ed. E. Hucher, vol. iii, p. 117.

Saint-Graal' made him the sole hero of the quest of the mystic talismans, obliterating from his account the name of Perceval. " Thus," Sir Thomas Malory concludes his picturesque version— " Thus endeth thistory of the Sancgreal that was breuely drawen oute of Frensshe in to Englysshe, the which is a story cronycled for one of the truest and the holyest that is in this world." [1]

Thus, indeed, was reached the term of a remarkable evolution. The secular literature of romantic adventure which afforded popular imagination its only relief from theological obsessions was not only purged of the grossness of its pagan morals, but was transmuted into an echo of Patristic teaching. In the retrospective mirage which created an ' age of chivalry ' chronologically located among the contemporaries of Gildas and the ' Sioux ' of Carolingian Europe, ideals of chastity came to be included as a part and parcel of perfect knighthood. Chastity, and indeed celibacy and virginity, it came to be understood, appertained to the very essence of chivalry : " there is no chivalry so high as to be virgin and to avoid luxuriousness." [2] The belief became current that the relations between knights and their ' amies ' had always been ' platonic.' That conception of the historical imagination of the later Middle Ages is set forth with his usual lucidity by the ingenious hidalgo, Don Quixote of La Mancha. " Know," he says, instructing his faithful squire, " that in this our style of chivalry it is most honourable for a lady to have a large number of knights in her service, who are devoted to her without venturing farther in their inmost thoughts than a desire to serve her for her own sake, and without expecting other guerdon in return for their many and honourable exploits save that she should deign to acknowledge them for her knights." Sancho's dull mind has some difficulty in grasping the idea. " I have indeed heard our preacher say," he remarks, " that we should love the Lord our God with a love somewhat after that manner, for His own sake, and without reference to any hope of glory or fear of punishment. But, for my part, I prefer to serve Him for the sake of what He can do for me." This masterly definition of primitive religion excites the disgust of the knight, who is moved to exclaim : " To the devil with thee ! Thou art little better than a boor, though at times thou seemest to show signs of sense. One would think that thou hast never studied." And indeed Sancho Panza admits that he cannot read, which accounts for his

---

[1] Sir Thomas Malory, *Le Morte d'Arthur*, iii. 104.

[2] *La Queste del Saint Graal*, ed. F. J. Furnivall, p. 109. The opposite definition was given by Marie de France : " Chivalry is valued for the sake of love and druerie " (Marie de France, *Poésies*, vol. i, p. 114). Elsewhere she casts doubts on the chivalry of a knight who is chaste (*ibid.*, p. 52).

inability to appreciate duly the sentiments brought into existence by European literature.[1]

The popular literature which enshrined the doctrines of Ambrose and of Origen became an instrument of edification, not only to the mediaeval but to the modern world. The Victorian age recognised in the Arthurian knighthood of thirteenth-century romances its own ideals of literary sentiment, " finding there unconsciously some image of " itself. In his well-known studies on that literature Mr. Nutt cites " as a sample of the feelings with which many Englishmen have regarded it," the inevitable ' purple patch ' in which the editor of ' La Queste ' delivers himself with some emotion : " What is the lesson of it all ? Is the example of Galahad and the unswerving pursuit of the highest spiritual object set before him nothing to us ? Is that of Perceval, pure and tempted, on the point of yielding, yet saved by the sight of the symbol of his Faith, to be of no avail to us ? . . . Monkish, to some extent, the exaltation of bodily chastity above almost every other earthly virtue is ; but the feeling is a true one ; it is founded on a deep reverence for woman, which is the most refining and one of the noblest sentiments of man's nature, one which no man can break through without suffering harm in his spiritual life." [2] Mr. Nutt, however, cannot bring that enthusiasm into harmony with a critical view of the facts. " It would be hard," he says, " to find a more striking instance of how the editorial idol may over-ride perception and judgment. He who draws such lofty and noble teachings from ' La Queste del Saint Graal ' must first bring them himself. He must read modern religion, modern morality, into the mediaeval allegory, and on one point he must entirely falsify the mediaeval conception." The work of the author of ' La Queste ' " is a glorification of physical chastity. His conception, says Mr. Furnivall, is founded upon a deep reverence for woman. This is, indeed, such a precious thing that, had the mediaeval ascetic really felt it, we could have forgiven the stupidity which ignores all that constitutes the special dignity and pathos of womanhood. But he felt nothing of the kind. Woman is for him the means whereby sin came into the world, the arch stumbling-block, the tool the devil finds readiest to his hands when he would overcome man. Only in favour of the Virgin Mother, and of those who like her are vowed to mystical maidenhood, does the author pardon woman at all. . . . Wife or leman, it was all one for the author of ' La Queste '; woman could not but be an occasion for deadly sin, and the sin, though in the one case less in degree (and

---

[1] Miguel de Cervantes, *El ingenioso Hidalgo Don Quijote de la Mancha*, Part i, ch. xxxi.

[2] F. J. Furnivall, Introduction to *La Queste del Saint Graal*, pp. ix sq.

even this is uncertain), was the same in kind. Fully one-half of the romance is one long exemplification of the essential vileness of the sex-relation, worked out with the minute and ingenious nastiness of a Jesuit moral theologian."[1]

To charge the Christian Church with supineness or inefficiency, and to suppose that its influence was without effect upon the conceptions and sentiments of modern Europe in regard to sex relations, would be grossly unjust. No more amazing transformation could be imagined than that which its persevering zeal succeeded in bringing about. The only secular literature that could compare in influence on the minds of the people with religious literature, a literature which had sprung out of the traditions of the pagan society which the Church had supplanted, and faithfully reflected its sexual standards and its ignorance of the value of chastity, was remoulded by ecclesiastical influence. Not only was it purged of its grossness and adapted to Christian standards of morality, but it was transmuted into an instrument of edification, and into a transcendent glorification of the most uncompromising doctrines of the Fathers of the Church concerning the supreme worth of chastity and the vileness of sex.

[1] A. Nutt, *Studies on the Legend of the Holy Grail*, pp. 242 sq.

CHAPTER XXIX

ROMANCE (*Continued*)

THE interpretations which transformed, in the romances of the thirteenth century, the pagan sagas' naturalistic presentation of sex relations came to be so intimately associated with the notion of chivalry that it is chiefly in that connotation that the term has survived. But it was not in the romances of chivalry that the conception of chivalric, or 'courtly,' love, in its late thirteenth-century form, was for the most part elaborated. The development of the conception is connected with a branch of literature which developed side by side with that of the romantic narratives, namely, lyrical poetry. While the chief home of chivalric romance was northern France, it was in Provence that lyrical amatory poetry attained in the hands of the troubadours a degree of development so important that its style and standards were imposed upon the northern trouvères.[1] Not only did troubadour poetry stamp its pattern upon northern French literature, but it is the source whence all the lyrical poetry of Europe, in Italy, in Spain, in Germany, in England, has derived.[2] Its influence and effects have been even

---

[1] See P. Meyer, " Des rapports de la poésie des trouvères avec celle des troubadours," *Romania*, xix, pp. 3 sqq.

[2] The derivation of Italian poetry, and hence of all European poetry, which in turn developed under Italian influence, will be referred to presently. It may seem more strange, but is equally true, that early German lyrical poetry, that of the Minnesinger, is the direct product of the poetry of Provence. German emperors held claims over the kingdom of Arles, and the relations between the two countries were constant and close. Frederic I paid a long visit to the south of France, bringing many minstrels in his train (see A. Luduitz, *Die Liebestheorien der Provenzalen bei den Minnesingern der Stauferzeit*, Berlin, 1904). Provençal influence on English literature has been for the most part exercised through the medium of Italian and French ; but much of it also operated directly. Some of the most noted centres of the troubadour movement lay in the Angevin dominions of the Plantagenets, and the most famous patroness of the poets, Eleanor of Aquitaine, grand-daughter of ' the first troubadour ' and mother of a troubadour king, was the queen of Henry II. See on the subject,

more momentous and more profound than those of the romances of chivalry. While the taste for the latter passed more or less completely, the manner in which amatory sentiments and relations were viewed in the romantic love-poetry of the Provençal poets was handed down to the literary tradition of every country in nascent Europe, and has grown into the blood and bone, as it were, of every subsequent European literature. Whereas the theme of sexual love was dealt with in the chivalric romances in the form of cursive narrative and without any subtlety, it constituted the substance of most troubadour poetry, and was treated as an elaborate description of sentiments.

Love-poetry did not occupy an important place in the literature of pagan Europe. Love-songs were originally regarded in the light of magic spells by which the lover endeavoured to bewitch the object of his desire. Among the northern peoples to address a love-song to a girl or woman was an indictable offence, and was often severely punished like any other form of witchcraft, which was regarded as constituting an assault on the person. Cases are cited of poets who were thus brought to justice and convicted of having composed a poem about the daughter of a family that had declined to enter into alliance with theirs, and who were punished for the literary offence by a heavy fine and expulsion from the district. The Scandinavian poet, Ottar the Black, was thus convicted of having dedicated a poem to the daughter of King Olaf of Sweden. He was arrested, tried, and condemned to death. The sentence was only commuted as he was being led to execution, on account of his having had the inspiration to sing an ode in praise of the king.[1] In one version of the story of Tristan, the hero-poet is killed by King Marc for singing a song to Iseult.[2] Those primitive love-poems of the pagan barbarians were extremely crude, and bore scarcely any likeness to what we understand by lyrical love-poetry. The singular development of amatory lyricism in Provence, and the highly elaborate literary and metrical technique which imposed it as a pattern upon all Europe, were due to local conditions, and in particular to close contact with Moorish Spain, whose literature was characterised by the same predominance of love-lyrics and where the same importance was attached to skilful and elaborate technique.[3]

W. H. Schofield, *English Literature from the Norman Conquest to Chaucer*, pp. 69 sq. ; H. Chaytor, *The Troubadours and England* ; J. F. Rowbotham, *The Troubadours and the Courts of Love*, pp. 39 sqq., 114 sqq. ; M. J. Adian, " Les troubadours en Angleterre," *Bulletin de la Société des Lettres, Sciences et Arts de la Corrèze* (Tulle, 1920).

[1] K. Weinhold, *Die deutschen Frauen in dem Mittelalter*, p. 188.

[2] G. Schoepperle, *Tristan and Isolt*, vol. ii, p. 439.

[3] The influence of the poetry of Moorish Spain upon the development of Provençal poetry, which was insisted on by the older literary historians

Troubadour poetry inherited in addition the traditions of chivalry. The two essential avocations and interests of the knight

such as Fauriel, is by modern Romance scholars, chiefly after the example of Diez, dismissed with the contempt of silence. Lyrical poetry, it is pointed out, had always existed among European populations, and Provençal poetry developed out of it. That is not disputable, but it does not appear that either Diez or anyone else has adduced satisfactory reasons, or any reasons at all, to explain why European poetry should, in Provence alone, have assumed a degree of development and technical elaboration which made it the model of all subsequent poetry in Europe. The question cannot be regarded as settled by the attitude of Romance specialists, however competent, for it could only be satisfactorily discussed by a scholar equally competent in Arabic studies. Unfortunately the poetry of Moorish Spain has never been critically edited and collected (cf. R. Briffault, *The Making of Humanity*, pp. 210 sq.). The facts to be taken into account are briefly: (1) The closeness of the intercourse between Provence, the Christian Spanish States, and the Moorish States; southern France itself was for two centuries never entirely free from Moorish domination. (2) European romantic literature is saturated with Arabic importations; "Aucassin (Al-Kasim) and Nicolette," "Floire et Blanchefleur," for example, have passed bodily from Moorish Spain to current Provençal literature (G. Paris, *Poèmes et légendes du moyen-âge*, p. 104); Boccaccio and even Shakespeare teem with plots and themes of Arabic origin, and the romances of chivalry are replete with them. Is it reasonable to suppose that lyrical poetry presented a singular exception? (3) The latter consisted of songs, which were inseparable from the music to which they were sung; the musical instruments employed were, without an exception, derived from the Moors, and the habitual term by which they are referred to in the Middle Ages was 'mauresques.' Is it reasonable to suppose that, while the instruments were imported, the music and the songs were excluded? (4) The characters and forms by which the Arabic poetry of Spain is distinguished from older Arabic poetry, and from the Arabo-Persian poetry of other parts of the Arab dominions, are of the same kind as the characters and forms by which Provençal poetry is distinguished from the antecedent lyrical poetry of Europe. Speaking of the former, Mr. R. A. Nicholson says: "The most interesting features of Spanish-Arabian poetry are the tenderly romantic feeling which not infrequently appears in the love-songs, a feeling that sometimes anticipates the attitude of mediaeval chivalry; and in the second place an almost modern sensibility to the beauties of nature. On account of these characteristics the poems in question appeal to many European readers who do not easily enter into the spirit of the Mu'allaqat. . . . The 'zajal' and 'muwashshah' were favourite types. Both forms were invented in Spain, and their structure is very similar, consisting of several stanzas in which the rhymes are so arranged that the master-rhyme ending each stanza and running through the whole poem like a refrain is continually interrupted by a various succession of subordinate rhymes. Many of these songs and ballads were composed in the vulgar dialect and without regard to the rules of classical prosody. The troubadour Ibn Quzman (+ 1160) first raised the 'zajal' to literary rank. . . . True to the traditions of their family, the Spanish Umayyads loved poetry, music, and polite literature a great deal better than the Koran" (R. A. Nicholson, *A Literary History of the Arabs*, pp. 416 sq. Cf. A. F. von Schack, *Poesie und Kunst der Araber in Spanien und Sicilien*). Everyone acquainted with Troubadour poetry

were arms and love. In a society such as that of Provence in the twelfth century, which enjoyed exceptional prosperity and peace and was for the most part immune from the perpetual violence and private wars which infested the rest of the continent, warlike occupations sank to secondary importance. The aspect of chivalry which, in the absence of urgent call for warlike valour, assumed the chief importance was that which had reference to amatory adventures. "All the people of that society," remarks a critic of troubadour poetry, "live manifestly for the chief purpose of enjoying themselves ; that is the ideal which they openly pursue, and to which they sacrifice everything with an ' insouciance ' which is not without grace, if it somewhat lacks dignity. It is a pleasure-seeking society. . . . The nobles, some of them among the most powerful of their time, are the friends of poets, but they are above all engaged in their attentions to the ladies and always in quest of some new amorous adventure." [1] Of the attributes of the traditional hero of the sagas, that of warlike prowess was over-shadowed by distinction in minstrelsy and the gift of song ; both were equally recognised attributes of the knightly character. Like the bards of pagan times, the early troubadours belonged to the ruling class ; it was obligatory that the poet should be a belted knight.[2] Troubadour poets make constant reference to the cycles of northern romance, and compare themselves to Tristan, to Lancelot, to Perceval.[3] The love-service which the minstrel-knight offered to his lady in the form of poetical homage and adulation was identified with the service by which he might win her with

will recognise some of its technical characteristics in the above description of Moorish poetry ; many more details could be adduced, and those technical characters have not been traced by any of the scholars who ignore the suggestion of Arabic influence, to another source.

[1] P. Andraud, *La vie et l'oeuvre du troubadour Raimon de Miraval, étude sur la littérature et la société méridionales à la veille de la guerre des Albigeois*, p. 162.

[2] See in particular, A. Stimming, "Provenzalische Literatur," in G. Gröber, *Grundriss der romanische Philologie*, vol. ii, part ii, pp. 19 sq. Cf. J. Anglade, *Les troubadours*, pp. 27 sq.

[3] Bertram de Born, in C. A. F. Mahn, *Die Werke der Troubadours*, vol. i, p. 274 ; *Bernart von Ventadorn, seine Lieder*, ed. C. Appel, p. 262 ; Arnaut de Maroill, in K. Bartsch, *Chrestomachie provençale*, p. 97 ; Raimbaut de Vaquieras, in C. A. F. Mahn, *op. cit.*, vol. i, p. 366 ; Hugues de la Blancherie, in C. Raynouard, *Choix des poésies originales des troubadours*, vol. iii, p. 342 ; Riagaut de Barbezieux, in J. Anglade, *Les troubadours*, p. 82 ; Augier Novella, in *Le Parnasse occitanien*, p. 397 ; Bartolomeo Zorzi, in C. A. F. Mahn, *Gedichte der Troubadours*, vol. ii, No. 5 ; F. Diez, *Geschichte der Trouba-dours*, pp. 117 sq. ; A. Birch-Hirschfeld, *Ueber den Troubadours des XII und XIII Jahrhunderts bekannten epische Stoffe*, p. 40 ; L. Sudre, "Les allusions à la légende de Tristan dans la littérature du moyen-âge," *Romania*, xv, pp. 534 sqq.

lance and sword.[1] The poetical serving-knight was the vassal of his mistress, and owed allegiance to her, as she also to him, when she had formally accepted him as her bard.[2] The poetical relation was thus exactly modelled upon the ordinary knightly relation, and the terms of the one applied equally to the other. Like combatant chivalry, that amatory and literary chivalry was regarded as essentially a knightly privilege, which conferred upon men and women of ' gentle ' birth a freedom of extra-connubial amatory relations which belonged to the usages and attributes of the nobility. ' Gallantry,' in the sense which the term has preserved in the French language, ' courtesy,' or ' courtly love,' were part of the character of a gentleman and lady of noble birth. Prudery on the part of a woman, or jealousy on the part of a husband, were ' ungallant,' and ' uncourtly,' and the signs of a vulgar disposition and of ignorance of polite usage. Hence the elaborate insistence on defining the rules of that usage, and on the distinction between courtliness and ill-breeding.

The literary ' service,' which aped the original knightly service much as a tourney aped the realities of war, was regulated by an artificial conventionalism. Poetical inspiration was confined within the frame of fixed literary canons, any breach of which was an offence against artistic taste ; and the merit of a poetical composition was appraised by the degree of its conformity to established precedent. Hence originality in troubadour poetry is confined almost entirely to the skill displayed in variations upon set forms and themes. Subject, sentiments, ' conceits,' even words and phrases, were prescribed by the artistic standards. It was a rule, for example, that an amatory song should begin with some reference to the season of the year, and make some elegant allusion to the flowers that bloom in the spring or to the song of the nightingale—the prescriptive ' bulbul ' of Arabo-Persian poetry.

The like rigorous conventionalism regulated the relation between the ' courtly ' lover and his mistress and the appropriate sentiments which were to furnish the theme of polite effusions. The canons of romantic love-making were worked out with an amazing pedantic exactitude ; every sigh, every blush, the ' cruelty ' of the lady and the ' despair ' of the lover, the graduated scale of ' favours,' were measured and timed according to established rules, from which it would have been a breach of polite taste to depart. The situations to which a love-relation may give rise, the metaphysics of amatory psychology, were formally debated

---

[1] F. Diez, *Die Poesie der Troubadours*, pp. 128 sqq.
[2] M. E. Wechsler, " Frauendienst und Vassalitat," *Zeitschrift für französische Sprache und Literatur*, xxiv, pp. 159 sqq.

in dialectical discussions modelled on scholastic disputations;[1] judgment was pronounced at conferences of expert authorities on erotic problems, which served for the codification of precedents in that amatory jurisprudence.[2] The dialecticians of 'courtly

[1] C. de Lollis, " Dolce stil nuovo e ' noel dig de nova maestria,' " *Studi medievali*, i, p. 21 : " The subtleties, obscurities, contortions, and involved abstractions of the poetry of Arnaud Daniel and Giraut de Borneill arise essentially from a desire to simulate profundity and abstruseness of thought."

[2] A vast amount has been written for and against the existence of ' Courts of Love.' Almost all the older writers implicitly accepted the account of Nostradamus (Jehan de Nostredame, *Les vies des plus celèbres et anciens poètes provençaux*, ed. C. Chabaneau and J. Anglade, pp. 83 sq.) and gave full descriptions of those amatory tribunals (e.g. C. Raynouard, *Choix des Poésies des Troubadours*, vol. ii, pp. 79 sqq. ; V. Balaguer, *Historia politica y literaria de los Trobadores*, vol. i, pp. 277 sqq. ; B. G. Rolland, *Recherches sur les prérogatives des dames chez les Gaulois, sur Cours d'Amour*, etc., pp. 30 sqq. ; J. F. Rowbotham, *The Troubadores and the Courts of Love*, pp. 222 sqq). Diez, and Professor Anglade following him, treated the matter as ' a fable ' (F. Diez, *Ueber die Minnehöfer* ; J. Anglade, *Les Troubadours*, p. 98 ; Id., *Histoire sommaire de la littérature méridionale au moyen-âge*, p. 25. Cf. G. Paris, *Mélanges de littérature française au moyen âge*, pp. 473 sqq. ; P. Rajna, *Le corti d'amore* ; V. Crescini, *Per la questione delle corti d'amore*). The truth appears to lie between those extremes. It is not a question of affirming or denying, but of explaining. Poetical contests, which are represented by the ' tensons ' that form a large proportion of troubadour literature, were habitual ; a ' question of love,' on the correct estimate of a particular quality, or the correct behaviour in a particular amatory situation, was proposed for debate. The affirmative and the negative were maintained by the contestants before an assembly of connoisseurs, mostly ladies. The question debated was then further discussed by the assembled company under the chairmanship of a presiding lady or gentleman, who summed up the result of the discussion and gave the verdict. Such assemblies are referred to as ' Courts ' in a tenson between Peyronnet and Guiraut de Salignac. In most tensons a single individual is appealed to by the competitors, but as each competitor appeals to a different individual, and the verdict could not consist of opposite opinions expressed by two judges, it is clear that the appeal was addressed to individual members of the assembly. Many such discussions, apart from any poetical tenson, undoubtedly took place in the erotico-literary circles of the castles that were the centres of poetical patronage, such as that of Eleanor of Aquitaine, of the Countess of Champagne, of the Countess of Flanders, of Pierrefeu, Signe, Avignon, Romanin. That such questions should at times have arisen out of actual cases, concrete disputes being referred for consideration and judgment to such gatherings, follows almost inevitably from the conventions of those social circles, and is intrinsically as probable as it is improbable that such appeals should have ever assumed a formal and personal character. The possibility of the latter procedure is excluded by the rules of secrecy governing the relation between lovers. What took place, as appears from the book of Andreas Capellanus, was that appeal was made to a well-known authority for a pronouncement on the disputed point. The question at issue was discussed at a gathering of the social circle without mentioning names, and the conclusion arrived at was communicated by letter by the presiding lady to the applicant for an opinion. Such was the character of

love,' remarks a critic, " gave out their views on points of amatory casuistry, according to the spirit of the times, with a gravity and seriousness which make us smile, but which prove to what extent that erotic poetry, so artificial in many respects, was mixed up with actual life." [1]

That strange theoretical interest in the discussion of amatory sentiments which made these the theme of quasi-psychological and philosophical debates, and elaborated with pedantic deliberation a standard of ' courtly love,' is a singular and significant phenomenon. Such a pedantic dealing with erotics is without parallel. There is no precedent for it either in pagan barbarism or in classical literature ; to our own taste it cannot but appear grotesque. ' Love' is about the last subject which we should bethink ourselves of treating as a theme for abstract dialectics. Modern philosophers and even professional psychologists have, as a very general rule, fought shy of discussing it at all.[2] The singular refinement of analysis which made its appearance in a society that had scarcely emerged from the rudest barbarism was a process of adaptation, in a period of transition, between old and new conceptions and social conditions in regard to the relations between the sexes. The theoretical conventions of ' courtly love ' were unconsciously the expression of the clash between opposed standards, and of a desire to give to those sex relations which had never ceased to be customary the sanction of cultivated taste and aristocratic privilege. It was a form of apologetics ; a defence of the old usages and conceptions amid the new order and the new morality of Christianity. By representing it as subject to subtle

the ' Courts of Love,' as described to us by Andreas, whose style is that of an unimaginative chronicler of what he heard and saw. Little more is implied in the account of Nostradamus. As is his way, he embroiders on the facts ; he is a notorious romancer, and his uncorroborated testimony is not valid evidence. In following him too literally those who described the ' Courts of Love ' as regularly instituted mock-courts of amatory justice are misleading. In dismissing them as a pure ' fable ' Diez was led to commit a bad blunder as regards the value of the book of Andreas (see above, p. 428 n.[1]). That ' questions of love ' were constantly debated is certain, that concrete cases not infrequently supplied the subject for such discussions is probable, that such gatherings and debates may have called themselves ' Courts of Love ' is possible (see further, E. Trojel, " Sur les cours d'amour," *Revue des langues romanes*, xxxiv, pp. 179 sqq. ; G. Zonto, " Rileggendo Andrea Capellano," *Studi Medievali*, iii, pp. 49 sqq.).

[1] P. Andraud, *La vie et l'oeuvre du troubadour Raimon de Miraval*, p. 146.

[2] " Most psychologists have been very sparing of details on the subject, and many voluminous treatises might be cited which make no mention of it whatsoever. Is this from some inordinate sentiment of pudicity ? " (T. Ribot, *La psychologie des sentiments*, p. 244).

and esoteric codes unintelligible to the common crowd, as bound up with lofty and heroic principles, and as inspiring elevated sentiments, the customary freedom of sexual relations was dissociated from vulgar licentiousness, the application of Christian standards was eluded, and the charge of immorality parried.

Those elaborate conventions of romantic sentiment and the poetical idealisation of sex relations and of women that went with it had reference, as has been seen, to extra-conjugal relations exclusively. The homage of the troubadour poets was, without an exception, addressed to married women.[1] That circumstance was emphasised as an essential principle of those very conventions which laboured to establish a distinction between 'refined,' 'idealised,' 'courtly,' 'honourable' love and gross, vulgar relations, or 'villeiny,' as the poets called it. A woman who should plead her duty of fidelity to her husband was stigmatised as behaving 'like a bourgeoise.' The husband who was jealous was 'uncourtly,' 'dishonourable.' The poet-knight Mataplana, one of the most powerful nobles of the old school, who were not only patrons of poets but poets themselves, addresses a 'sirvente' to Raimon de Miraval on his unworthy, indelicate, and ungallant conduct. "He has committed," he says, "a grave breach against the rules of that courtly love on the honourable observance of which he has hitherto prided himself : if ever he formerly followed the straight path of a courteous lover, his sentiments have now fallen far below that ideal. . . . He has behaved in such a manner that it will be difficult for him to clear himself from the charge of villeiny. . . . He has renounced, it would seem, his ideal, which was to act as a perfect lover ; for, if he still set any value upon courtliness and the pleasure of love, he would not have committed a fault for which every gentleman will wish his ruin. A husband who loves gallantry must be accommodating, in order that his neighbours may in turn prove accommodating towards him. . . . Conscious of his guilt, he now seeks to become reconciled with his wife. If he sincerely wishes that reconciliation and desires to have her back, he must show himself sufficiently generous to allow her to have a lover after her own heart. When he shall have made his peace with her, joy will return to his home ; . . . let him not complain that his house is graced with courtesy. If he fulfils those conditions he will once more be pleasant to us courtly men."[2] That fundamental

---

[1] J. Anglade, *Les troubadours*, p. 79.
[2] Ugo de Mataplana, in P. Andraud, *La vie et l'oeuvre du troubadour Raimon de Miraval*, pp. 138 sq. :—

"D'un sirventes m'es pres talens,

. . . . . .

[Continued on next page.

tradition of romantic love persisted, indeed, until a late date. As in the barbaric sagas of pagan times, the representative poet of the tender passion in Renaissance Europe, Petrarca, a canon of the Church, a personage of the highest gravity and respectability, celebrated in a lengthy series of songs and sonnets his love, real or fictitious, for a married woman.

Romantic love was thus, in the very essence of the literary tradition which elaborated it, 'immoral.' Yet, as in the transformation of the romances of chivalry, a moralising evolution took place in the ideals and sentiments of lyrical erotics. If Canon Petrarca could, without any unbeseemingness, give poetic expression to a love which, in Tristan, makes M. Gaston Paris marvel at the barbarism of the heathen bard who could thus glorify adultery, it is because the literary treatment of the sentiment had in the course of the intervening centuries undergone a profound change. Although from an artistic point of view the pathos of the love of Tristan and Iseult may be preferred to the flowery elegance of Messer Petrarca, the latter's long-drawn literary passion is, from the moral point of view, well-nigh unobjectionable. For, while it is equally adulterous, it is so highly etherealised, sublimated, and so completely dissociated from any gross sex relation, that not only can little objection be taken to it on moral grounds, but doubt

a N'Raimon, don ai pensanssa,
car fetz tant gran malestanssa
contra dompnei, don totztems s'es vanatz ;
e s'anc tenc dreig viatge
de drut cortes, ar camia son coratge.

. . . . . .

Q'el sol aver s'esperanssa
en ioi et en alegranssa ;
mas aras n'es malamens cambiatz,
que mes a tal usatge,
don nois pot ges esdir de vilanatge.

. . . . . .

Car s'il plagues mais domneis ni solatz,
non feira tal outratge
don tuich cortes volguesson son dampnatge.

Car maritz a cui platz iovens
deu sofrir, per so c'atressi
sofran lui siei autre vezi.
Mas aissi l'es camiatz sos sens ;
e car fetz tal malestanssa,
poing c'ab lieis ai' acordanssa ;
e si la vol ni sos cobrars li platz,
fass'il tant d'avantatge,
q'ill sofr' un drut que trob' a son coratge."

may arise as to whether it is not purely fictitious. The conception of romantic love has in the interval become transformed, purified, spiritualised. That notable transformation took place in the development of troubadour poetry, and it is therefore of particular interest to trace the causes which brought about the change in Provence.

There is in the earlier poetry of the Provençal troubadours no vestige of any such delicacy or etherealisation. The impression of the manners and ideas it pictures which Dr. Weinhold derives from a perusal of it is that " there is no refinement and no shame ; every ideal of womanhood is cast into the dust and trodden under foot." [1] The judgment is too severe, but it would have met with the approval of later taste, when the evolution which that poetry underwent had been accomplished. The first troubadour whose name and works have come down to us—though it is clear from the perfection and fully developed conventions of his art, and also from the fact that he wrote in what was to him a foreign language, that he had behind him a long line of unknown predecessors—is Count William of Poitou, Duke of Aquitaine. His apotheosis of love as the supreme factor in life, the omnipotent inspirer, the source of joy and of sorrow, is not to be distinguished from similar productions in later poetry, save perhaps by a truer ring of sincerity.[2] Yet there is not in that romantic glorification of amatory emotions a thought of sublimating sex relations. His grossness is such that it would be more difficult to render it into printable English than any of the anthropological facts which we have had to note, and he furnished Boccaccio with the prototype of one of his most salacious stories.[3] Other early troubadours,

[1] K. Weinhold, *Die deutschen Frauen in dem Mittelalter*, p. 181.

[2] *Les chansons de Guillaume IX, duc d'Aquitaine* (1071–1172), ed. A. Jeanroy, pp. 21 sqq., " Mout jauzens me prenc en amar " :—

> " Per son joy pot molautz sanar
> e par sa ira sas morir
> e savis hom enfolezir," etc.

Like every other sentiment found in troubadour poetry the ' praise of love ' is a stereotyped formula repeated with variations by more than four hundred poets. One of the forms of the formula is that ' love justifies everything,' a manifestly important principle of the apologetics of ' courtly love.' Miraval, for example, says : ' Tot quant hom fai per amor es gen "— " all that is done for love's sake is ' gentle,' " that is, ' good form ' (Raimon de Miraval, in C. A. F. Mahn, *Die Werke der Troubadours*, vol. ii, p. 118). The whole theory of the ' refinement ' of courtly love turns upon the principle that all must be done for love's sake, and not from mercenary or other motives. Cf. below, pp. 482 sq.

[3] *Ibid.*, pp. 8 sqq., " Farai un vers, pos mi somelh." Cf. G. Boccaccio,

such as Marcabru [1] and Cercamon,[2] are equally direct and unsophisticated. Bernard de Ventador, one of the most graceful exponents of the poetical art of the period, is if anything more ingeniously sensual than William of Poitou.[3] Guillem Ademar

Il Decamerone, iii. 1 ; cf. *ibid.*, pp. 29 sqq., " Farai chansoneta nueva " ; pp. 24 sqq., " Ab la dolchor del temps novel " :—

> " Enquer me lais Dieus viure tan
> c'aja mas manz soz so mantel ! "

> " Que tal se van d'amor gaban,
> nos n'avem la pessa e.l coutel."

[1] *Poésies complètes du troubadour Marcabru* (ed. J.-M. L. Dejeanne), p. 26 :—

> " Ma bon'amia m'acuoill
> ab un baiser, quant me despuoill."

Cf. pp. 14 sqq., 15 sqq., 20, 34, 63, etc.

[2] *Les poésies de Cercamon*, ed. A. Jeanroy, pp. 28, 29 :—

> " Dieus ! si poirai l'ora veder
> qu'eu posca pres de lei jazer ! "

> " E si'm fezes tant de plazer
> que'm laisses pres de si jazer,
> ja d'aquest mal non morira."

[3] He thus expresses the guerdon which he looks to for his poetic service :—

> " Qu' eu la manei e bai
> et estrenha vas me
> so cors blanc, gras e le "

(C. Appell, *Bernart von Ventadorn*, p. 207). Cf. pp. 141, 206 sqq., 152 :—

> " Mal o fara si no.m manda
> venir lai on se despolha,
> qu'eu sia per sa comanda
> pres del leih, josta l'esponda
> e.lh traga.ls sotlars be chaussans,
> a genolhs et umilians,
> si.lh platz que sos pes me tenda ; "

159, 195 ("can eu remir so cors gai"), 70 ("no sai domna, volgues o no volgues,—si.m volia, c'amar no la pogues "). The only passage in Bernard de Ventador that can be, and has been, cited as suggesting the acceptance of platonic love, is—

> " Bona domna, re no.us deman
> mas qu'em prendatz per servidor,
> qu'eus servirai com bo senhor,
> cossi que del gazardo m'an "

(*op. cit.*, p. 191). But the piece in which the passage occurs is in a deliberately jocular tone. M. Lucka says that Bernard de Ventador " was the first to praise chaste love. If any champion of civilisation deserves a monument it is this poet " (E. Lucka, *The Evolution of Love*, p. 121). One may doubt whether M. Lucka has read him ; for there is not a line in his poems which has reference to " chaste love."

holds the same language ;[1] Raimon Jordan prefers a night in
the arms of his beloved to his chance of Paradise ;[2] and Gaucelm
Faidit is even more lascivious.[3] They are, however, surpassed
by other troubadour exponents of courtly love, whose obscenity
is probably unexcelled in any poetical literature.[4] The renowned
Bertran de Born knows no other conception of love.[5] Arnaut
de Maroill defines the motives of his passion in express terms ;
it is " the desire which I have of your sweet body."[6] Raimon
de Miraval, a dialectical theorist of ' courtly love,' and a noted

---

[1] Guillem Ademar, in C. Raynouard, *Choix des poésies originales des
troubadours*, vol. iii, p. 197 :—

> " E non envei el mon nulh home nat,
> sim vol mi dons tener vestit o nut,
> baizan lonc se, en luec de mollerat :
> anc no fon fag al mieu par tals honors
> cm er a mi, s'en aissi s'esdeve ;
> qu'el sieu cors blanc, gras e chauzit e le
> remir baizan, ni m tenc entre mos bratz."

[2] Raimon Jordan, in *Le Parnasse Occitanien*, p. 200.

[3] Gaucelm Faidit, in C. A. F. Mahn, *Gedichte der Troubadours*, vol. i,
p. 36.

[4] Raimon de Durfort, in *Parnasse Occitanien*, p. 75 ; Peire de Bussinhac,
ibid.; p. 292 ; Trucs Molecs, ' Servente,' in " Ueber die in Italien befindlichen
provençalsiche Liederhanschriften," *Archiv für das Studium der neueren
Sprachen und Literatur*, xxxiv, p. 200.

[5] Bertran de Born, in C. A. F. Mahn, *Die Werke der Troubadours*, vol. i,
p. 274 :—

> " A mon ' Miels de Ben' deman
> son adreit nou cors prezan
> de que par a la verguda
> la fassa bon tener nuda."

Cf. *ibid.*, p. 290.

[6] Arnaut de Maroill, in C. Raynouard, *Choix des poésies originales des
troubadours*, vol. iii, p. 218 : " voluntatz qu'ai del vostre cors gen." Cf.
ibid., pp. 203 sq. :—

> " Ai ! bona dona benestans,
> si veira ja est fis amans
> a son viven lo jorn ni'l ser
> que, a selat o per lezer,
> vostre gen cors cuend e prezan
> entre mos bras remir baizan.

> " Tot en aisi con ieu dezir
> la nueg e'l jorn quan m'o cossir,
> a son talan ab vos domreya,
> embrass' e baiza e maneya . . ." etc.

And C. A. F. Mahn, *op. cit.*, vol. i, p. 162 :—

> " E s'ieu auzes dir quar mi fos
> un ser lai on se devestis."

stickler for the observance of its tenets, is equally explicit.[1]
He indeed expressly declares in so many words that it is
" bodily and not spiritual possession which he desires." [2] Not
a whit more veiled are the terms in which Arnaud Daniel, the
' master of love,' the truest artist of them all, refers to his looked-
for guerdon : " May it be the merciful God's pleasure to grant
that my lady and I shall lie in that chamber where our precious
assignation convenes us, holding out the promise of so much joy, and
that I may, amid smiles and kisses, uncover her fair body and feed
my eyes upon it by the light of the lamp." [3]   Dante's estimate of
Daniel is fully merited,[4] for alone perhaps of all the troubadour
poets he dared to make light of the conventional rules of sentiment,
and his verses are the only ones that show unaffected inspiration.
He sets aside the consecrated rule that every lover must be
anxious, melancholy, and despairing, and every lady pitiless.   He
sings in a far other strain : " Beautiful is life, when orbed in joy ;
let those to whom the Fates are harsh decry it ; no cause of plaint
my lot affords.   She is not cruel whose friend I am ; nor is a
fairer this side the Alps.   Fondly I love her, nor ever greater joy
did Paris have of Helen of Troy." [5]   Nowhere in the poetry of the

---

[1] P. Andraud, *La vie et l'oeuvre du troubadour Raimon de Miraval*, p. 43 :—

> " De la belha cui sui cochos
>   dezir lo jazer el baizar
>   el tener el plus conquistar."

[2] C. Raynouard, *Choix de poésies originales des troubadours*, vol. ii,
p. 223 :—

> " Del cors li fos non de l'arma
>   que m consentis a celat dins sa cambra,
>   tos temps serai ab lieys cum cara et ongla."

[3] U. A. Canello, *La vita e le opere del trovatore Arnaldo Daniello*, p. 111 :—

> " Dieus lo chauzitz,
>
>   .   .   .   .   .   .
>
> voilla, sil platz, qu'ieu e midonz jassam
> en la chambra on amdui nos mandem
> uns rics convens don tan gran joi atendi,
> quel seu bel cors baisan rizen descobra
> e quel remir contral lum de la lampa."

[4] Dante Alighieri, *Purgatorio*, xxvi. 119.

[5] U. A. Canello, *op. cit.*, pp. 97 sq. :—

> " Bona as vida
>   pos joia la mante,
>   que tal n'escrida
>   cui ges no vai tan be ;
>   no sai de re
>   coreillar m'escarida,
>   que per ma fe
>   del mieills ai ma partida."

> " Ges non es croia
>   cella cui soi amis ;
>   de sai Savoia
>   plus bella nos noiris ;
>   tals m'abelis
>   don ieu plus ai de joia
>   non ac Paris
>   d'Elena, cel de Troia."

troubadours until the period of its decadence is there any ambiguity as to the nature of their conception of love or a suggestion of ' platonic ' sentiments.[1]

To insist upon the subtle and fanciful barriers which were supposed to mark the exclusiveness of refined sentiments as a privilege of ' gentle ' persons was the essence of the conventions upon which ' courtly ' love was founded. The distinction was the very motive of the theory ; no vulgar burgher, no tradesman, no villein, no person who was not ' learned ' in polite sentiments was capable of appreciating the delicate subtleties which stamped aristocratic gallantry. The constant boast of the poets is that their love is ' courtly ' and ' honourable ' ; their constant taunt against rivals, jealous persons, and detractors is that these are ' discourteous ' and vulgar. Uncourtly love is mere grossness, fit for boors and persons of no refinement and ignorant of the ' rules of love.' ' Courtly ' love, ' drudaria ' as they call it, is the love of a well-bred, ' gentle ' heart, of an ' entendedor,' that is, of a ' connoisseur ' ; and its power of inspiration, of imparting ' joy,' depends upon knowledge and observance of those standards of ' connoisseurship.' The distinction, difficult as it may be to define, is constantly insisted on ; the whole theme of troubadour poetry may, in truth, be said to consist of that insistence. Arnaud

---

[1] Cf. Peire Rogier, in C. A. F. Mahn, *Die Werke der Troubadours*, vol. i, p. 120 :—

> " Molt mi fera gen secors
> s'una vetz ab nueg escura
> mi mezes lai o s'despuelha."

Giraud de Salignac, in C. Raynouard, *Choix de poésies originales des troubadours*, vol. iii, p. 395 :—

> " En vos podon complir tug mey voler."

Bernard Arnaud de Montcuc, *ibid.*, vol. ii, p. 217 :—

> " Dona, que m'esglai
> lo desir qu'ieu n'ay
> Del vostre bel cors cortes,
> Complit de totz bes."

It would be superfluous to dwell on such commonplaces of Provençal poetry but that some writers, trading upon the general public's unacquaintance with an unfamiliar literature, have represented it as picturing a ' platonic ' conception of love. An impression to that effect appears to exist, as in regard to ' chivalric ' love in general.

The same expressions are current among the northern trouvères as among the southern troubadours. Thus the most elegant and distinguished amongst the former, the Lord of Couci, sings :—

> " Que cele où j'ai mon coeur et mon penser
> tiegne une foiz entre mes bras nuete "

(Châtelain de Coucy, *Chansons*, ed. Fr. Michel, p. 33 ; cf. p. 31).

Daniel, frankly sensual as he is, expresses his contempt for " those lovers whose relations are such that they bring shame to the woman and degradation to the man." " I myself," he says, " have more than once renounced the love of some wealthy chatelaine in order to have nought to do with shameful pleasures unredeemed by honour and refinement. . . . From such love as moves me are debarred those disloyal seekers of women who destroy courtliness, however smart and elegant they may be." [1] In Andreas, the chaplain, the most detailed exponent of ' courtly ' ideas, the same distinction is dwelt upon. There is no ambiguity as to the sense in which the term ' love ' is used, or any suggestion of ' platonic ' relations ; the subject is discussed in physiological terms [2] Nevertheless, there is the same repudiation of ' mere ' sensuality, and of lovers who " confound everything by their behaviour, which is no better than that of dogs." [3] Marcabru, who is generally described as a misogynist, has much to say on the subject. He is, in truth, by no means a woman-hater ; on the contrary, he is at one with the most gallant troubadours in the exaltation of women and of the inspiring power of love. [4] The women against whom he inveighs are those who set aside the rules of ' drudaria,' who are grossly mercenary, who keep no faith. What women he means, he does not leave us to guess ; he calls them in plain Provençal ' putanas,' ' harlots.' [5] Mercenary motives were, in fact, regarded as the chief sin against ' courtly love.'

---

[1] Arnaud Daniel, in A. Canello, *op. cit.*, pp. 99, 101 :—

> " D' aquest amor son lunh forsdug
> dompneiador fenhen, fradel,
> pero sis n'an maint pretz destrug
> tal ques fan cueinte et isnel.
>
> Qu'ieu sait drut que si assembla
> don blasm'a leis, el col groma ;
> qu' ieu n'ai ja perdut ric cortil
> car non vuoill gabs ab vergoigna
> ni blasme ab honor loigna,
> per que ieu loing son seignoril."

[2] Andreas capellanus, *De amore*, pp. 292 sq., 175 sq.
[3] *Ibid.*, p. 13. Cf. Marie de France, *Poésies*, vol. i, p. 84 :—

> " Plusur le tienent a gabois,
> Si cumme cil vilain curtois,
> Kil' gulousent par tut le munt,
> Puis se vantent de çou qu' il funt.
> N'est pas amurs, ainz est folie,
> Et mauveiste et lecerie."

[4] *Poésies complètes du troubadour Marcabru*, ed. J. M. L. Dejeanne, pp. 148, 155, 180. 198,
[5] *Ibid.*, pp. 140, 210.

" A woman must yield her favours to her lover, as to a friend, not as to a master," a poetess declares.[1] Hence one of the rules of amatory gallantry was that no woman should have a lover of a more exalted social station than herself. " A woman who accepted a powerful lord as her lover was regarded as being as good as dead." [2] This was the sort of grossness which was regarded as an offence against refinement, and called forth the denunciation of the exponents of courtly love. Raimon de Miraval fulminates against a lady who has been guilty of such misconduct. " He has the first right to enter who pays most," he declares with scorn ; " but that is an evil salary which the lady has received, by her greed she has lost her good name." [3] Marcabru is equally moved to wrath against the men who do not observe, or are incapable of understanding, romantic love, and think that by simply giving themselves up to sensual adventures they are being ' romantic.' " If they call that drudaria," he says, " they lie ; for perfect love is ' joy,' suffering, and moderation." [4] But it must not be supposed that the distinction has any reference to ' platonic ' as against ' sensual ' love, still less that our poet has any thought of associating chastity with ' drudaria.' When he has done denouncing in the fiercest terms those women and those men who debase love, who neglect the good traditional rules of drudaria, who scorn sentiment and high emotions, he betakes himself, in a more gentle mood, to his ' bon amia.' She at least does not fall into those errors, and is worthy of the refined love and cultivated devotion of a true ' entendedor ' ; and he begs her to kiss him—" while he removes his clothes." [5]

With the later troubadours of the thirteenth century those distinctions became even more pronounced and their character was modified. The grossness of the earlier bards becomes more rare ; the blunt and direct terms in which they referred to the object of their desire and the ' guerdon ' of their ' services ' are

---

[1] Maria de Ventadorn, in *Parnasse Occitanien*, p. 267 :—

> " Domna deu a son drut far honor
> Com ad amic e non com a senhor."

[2] " Razo," or commentary, to one of Miraval's poems, cited in P. A. Andraud, *La vie et l'oeuvre du troubadour Raimon de Miraval*, p. 102.

[3] *Ibid.*, p. 124.

[4] Marcabru, *op. cit.*, p. 179 :—

> " . . . benananssa
> as jois, sofrirs e mezura."

[5] *Ibid.*, p. 26 :—

> " Ma bon'amia m'acuoill
> ab un baisar, quant me despuoill."

seldom used. Those rewards are even explicitly disclaimed;[1] the humble lover declares himself sufficiently recompensed by a kiss, or a smile,[2] or even by a gracious glance,[3] or the gift of a hair from his lady's fur-cloak, or a thread from her glove.[4] Nay, it is enough that his services should be accepted, and that the fair one should acknowledge him as her servant.[5] If it be her pleasure to let him perish, he will die happy, and esteem it a favour to end his martyrdom by so sweet a death.[6] The affectation and artificiality of the conventions becomes increasingly pronounced; the 'conceits' are spun out to finest cobwebs; the poets become more prolix, elaborating through several long stanzas the sentiments which the earlier troubadours indicated in a line. The humility and resignation of the lover is unendingly dwelt upon and becomes abject; his tears flow in a perpetual stream; we hear a great deal more of the 'cruelty' and 'heartlessness' of his fair enemy. An evolution is thus manifest in the treatment of the theme of romantic and poetic love as we pass from the earlier troubadours to those of a later period, and becomes more pronounced as we near the last days of Provençal culture. The terms of the conventions of courtly love are unchanged; the stereotyped forms and sentiments are reproduced; but the emphasis is shifted, the stress is laid upon the submission, the disinterestedness and resignation of the patient lover. "It was said at first that love, besides being what it is by nature, ought to be the source of all good things and of every virtue; the decadents, exaggerating this sentiment, said that, in order to be the source of all good things and of every virtue, love ought to retain nothing of what it is by nature."[7]

What were the causes that brought about that evolution? The transformation in the 'conception of love' during the Middle Ages has often been described, down to one of the latest writers

---

[1] Gaucelm Faidit, in C. Raynouard, *Choix des poésies originales des troubadours*, vol. iii, p. 293.

[2] Id., in C. A. F. Mahn, *Gedichte der Troubadours*, vol. i, p. 36; Pons de Capdoill, in Id., *Die Werke der Troubadours*, vol. i, p. 353.

[3] Guiraut Riquier, in C. A. F. Mahn, *Die Werke der Troubadours*, vol. iv, p. 37.

[4] Guillaume de Saint-Didier, in C. Raynouard, *Choix des poésies originales des troubadours*, vol. iii, p. 300.

[5] Guiraut Riquier, *op. cit.*, vol. iv, p. 22.

[6] Augier, in C. Raynouard, *op. cit.*, vol. iii, p. 105. The same formula is used in a very libertine piece, and in connection with an obscene jest, by one of the oldest troubadours, Raimbaud d'Orange, *ibid.*, vol. ii, p. 251.

[7] C. de Lollis, *Vita e poesie di Sordello di Goito*, p. 77. Cf. A. Thomas, *Francesco da Barberino et la littérature provençale en Italie au moyen-âge*, pp. 54 sq.

on the subject,[1] in terms of metaphysical and psychological subtleties scarcely less abstract than the hair-splitting quibbles of the poetical scholasticists themselves. But, without having recourse to speculations on the ' development of the ego,' plain and direct causes for those transformations may be found in the social conditions amid which they took place. The poetic and romantic treatment of sex-relations was older far than any ' platonic ' sublimation ; it was fully developed in the twelfth century in the same literary form which we find in the thirteenth. In the earlier periods of romantic literature it went with manners and customs which had not yet emerged, or which had but incompletely emerged, from the conditions of a heathen society. Sexual freedom was limited by marital rights only, and but incompletely restricted by those rights ; romantic passion had reference to extra-conjugal relations which were a part of recognised and universal usages. The literary tradition continued, while social conditions changed. Extra-conjugal relations became illicit and illegal, though they continued to be lightly looked upon ; their illicit character grew as Christian legislation became more fully established and feudal society more firmly organised. Love became ' platonic ' because the changed social conditions required that it should. The conduct of courtly society in France, in Italy, in Norman England never became austere or puritanical ; it remained to the last what we should call decidedly ' loose.' But the opposition between things permissible and things illicit became, in theory at least, more definite and pronounced. Romantic and chivalrous love was from the first associated, nay, closely identified, with the conception of ' honour.' In the early days of ' chivalry,' a lady was ' bound in honour ' to pay his due meed to the knight who served her, and she would have been ' dishonoured ' by failing to do so. In a later age the dictates of the code of honour became in effect reversed ; Sordello implores his lady-love not to be moved by pity to grant him favours that should compromise her honour ;[2] and Guilhem Montanhagol lays it down that a lover ought to desire nought that could dishonour the object of his sublimated passion—

> c'amans non deu voler per nulh talen
> ren q'a si donz tornes a desonranssa.[3]

---

[1] E. Lucka, *The Evolution of Love*, pp. 115 sqq. and *passim*.
[2] C. de Lollis, *Vita e poesie di Sordello di Goito*, p. 200.
[3] J. Coulet, *Le troubadour Guilhem Montanhagol*, p. 140. Cf. F. da Barberino : " Di lei l'onore e sue forme servare " (A. Thomas, *Francesco da Barberino et la littérature provençale en Italie au moyen-âge*, p. 56). We have seen that one of the primary meanings of ' honour ' was the obligation ' to keep one's pledged word,' a necessary substitute for law in an anarchical society (see above, p. 402). It was thus as much a matter of ' honour '

The early trouvères and troubadours had belonged to the ruling classes ; knighthood was one of their necessary qualifications. Literary talent came later to be independent of class distinctions ; the jongleurs and gleemen who attended a noble bard often became his successors. Bernard de Ventador was the son of a scullion and a kitchen wench.[1] Folquet de Marseille was a burgher in business. His editor comments upon the absurdity of supposing that he would create a scandal by making love to the Viscountess of the Manor, who, with her husband, was good enough to patronise him.[2] The poetical homage which had been offered by knights like William of Poitou to their mistresses came to be offered by poets to ladies with whose character and position it was not always consistent to grant openly the last favours to their poetical admirers. There was a period of transition during which the talented protégé was assimilated to the minstrel knight, and the amatory activities of the former were taken seriously. Bernard de Ventador himself is stated to have been the lover of his protectress, the chatelaine of Ventador. The jealousy of husbands cost Guilhem de Cabestaing his life, and Peire Vidal his tongue.[3] There are indications of the resentment felt by barons of the old school at the gradual elevation of poets of low birth to the same status as the knightly bards. Peire de Mula has a ' sirvente ' against these beggarly parasites.[4] Sometimes the love-poetry of the professional troubadour was composed to order for the purpose of forwarding the intrigues of his noble patron or patroness, and the poet played the part of a go-between.[5] In the same manner as the jongleurs and troupes of itinerant entertainers had gradually supplanted the bard of pagan times, who was a chieftain or the equal of chieftains and kings, so the poet-knight in search of amatory adventures became transformed into the professional provider of poetry, the literary protégé, who depended upon courtly patronage. The ' drue ' whom the noble bard had celebrated became the

for a lady to keep her word to her chosen knight as to keep her pledged word of fidelity to her husband. In either case she would be ' dishonoured ' by breaking her word.

[1] C. Appel, *Bernart von Ventadorn*, pp. xix sqq.

[2] S. Stronski, *Le trouvadour Folquet de Marseille*, pp. 66 sq. It was, of course, expected of every court poet, down to the times of Tasso and Ariosto, and much later, that he should be desperately in love with the lady of the palace. Occasionally, as with Tasso, the poet had the misfortune of being betrayed by the conscientious performance of his duty into taking it seriously.

[3] F. Diez, *Die Gedichte der Troubadours*, p. 131.

[4] *Ibid.*, pp. 47 sq.

[5] P. Andraud, *La vie et l'oeuvre du troubadour Raimon de Miraval*, p. 123 ; M. Pelaez, *Vita e poesie di Bonifazio Calvo*, p. 55. Cf. E. Faral, *Les jongleurs en France au moyen-âge*, p. 216.

gracious patroness of literature upon whose favour an esurient poet, whose status had come to be little more than that of a superior lackey, was dependent for his bread and butter.

Those altered social circumstances were not, however, the only cause of the change that took place in the poetical treatment of romantic love. The Provençal poets of the latter part of the thirteenth century were being pressed by even more urgent and terrible necessities. The elegant semi-Oriental culture of Provence, flourishing in comparative security, had been in a position to make light of, and even to defy and treat with irreverent satire, the Christian clergy's denunciations of its dalliance and profanity. But the time had come when the voice of the Church was to make itself heard. From the early years of the century, when at the repeated summonses of Pope Innocent III the hosts of Simon de Montfort had pounced down upon the doomed abodes of profane culture and heresy, reducing whole districts to deserts, and leaving God to know his own, the times had been scarcely favourable to gaiety and courtly elegance. The struggle had been a long one ; the heroism of the free burghers inspired by the impassioned 'sirventes' of the poets who, like Peire Cardinal, were fired to heights of more ringing eloquence by the stern realities of the strife than they had ever reached while repeating the mawkish conventions of courtly love, had been indomitable. And when De Montfort, in 1218, was, by a sort of poetic justice, killed by the hands of a woman, the southerners had almost reconquered their devastated country, and the invaders were for the most part glad to abandon the fruits of their rapine and to return to their northern domains. What the swords of the Crusaders had failed to achieve was done, and done thoroughly, by the officers of the Holy Inquisition. "In the twelfth century," says the historian, "the south of France had been the most civilised land in (Christian) Europe. There commerce, industry, art, science, had been far in advance of the age. The cities had won virtual self-government, were proud of their wealth and strength, jealous of their liberties, and self-sacrificing in their patriotism. The nobles, for the most part, were cultivated men, poets themselves or patrons of poetry, who had learned that their prosperity depended upon the prosperity of their subjects, and that municipal liberties were a safeguard rather than a menace to the wise ruler. The Crusaders came, and their unfinished work was taken up and executed to the bitter end by the Inquisition. It left a ruined and impoverished country, with shattered industries and failing commerce. The native nobles were broken by confiscation and replaced by strangers. . . . A people of rare gifts had been tortured, decimated, humiliated, despoiled. . . . The precocious civilisation which had promised to lead Europe in the path of culture was gone, and to

Italy was transmitted the honour of the Renaissance." [1]   " The world is changed so much that I can scarcely tell it," sighs Bertran d'Alamanon ; " I was wont to make songs and to enjoy myself, and to devote myself to all those occupations that beseem a courtly knight, and to visit ladies of renown with great delight.   But now I should fear to incur blame if I did such things." [2]   And Guiraut de Bornheil recalls how " formerly I saw singers in brave apparel wandering from court to court solely to praise the ladies.   Now none dares any longer speak ; so that true honour has disappeared." [3] And small wonder ! Bishops and Dominicans were illustrating their own view of ' reverence for women.'   Women, even though sick, were dragged out of their beds, tied to the stake, and burnt.[4] In the middle of the century the last refugees who had taken shelter in some mountain castle that had formerly resounded with the music and songs of the poets, were hunted out and besieged by troops led by the Archbishop of Narbonne.   When famine compelled them to surrender, an enclosure of stakes was formed at the foot of the hill, wood was piled up and set on fire, and over two hundred men and women as they came out of the castle were tossed into the flames.[5]   The idle vanities of the poets, their shameless glorification of sinful passions, were denounced in loud terms by the ministers of religion.[6]   These even warned the bards in their own language.   The Dominican prior of Villemier addressed a theological poem, expounding the doctrines of true Christianity, to the most distinguished of the recalcitrant poets ; the exposition of the creed was clinched with the refrain : " If you will not believe this, look at that raging fire which is consuming your comrades. Reply in one word or two, for you will either roast in that fire or join us." [7]

Such forcible arguments did not fail in their appeal ; they hastened with wonderful effect in the minds of the poets, now inspired by holy terror, the transformation in ' the conception of love.' " Provençal poetry became penetrated with the theory of the sinfulness of love, invented by the Church." [8]   The leading spirit

---

[1] H. C. Lea, *A History of the Inquisition of the Middle Ages*, vol. ii, pp. 109 sq.

[2] J. J. Salverda de Grave, *Le troubadour Bertran d'Alamanon*, pp. 39 sq.

[3] F. Diez, *Die Poesie der Troubadours*, p. 55.

[4] H. C. Lea, *op. cit.*, vol. ii, p. 11.

[5] *Ibid.*, vol. ii, pp. 42 sq.

[6] J. Anglade, *Le troubadour Guiraut Riquier*, p. 336.

[7] C. Raynouard, *Choix de poésies originales des troubadours*, vol. v, p. 230 :—

" E' s'aquest no vols creyre vec te 'l foc aizinat que art tos companhos.
Aras vuelh que m' respondas en un mot o en dos,
Si cauziras en foc o remanras ab nos."

[8] J. Anglade, *Les Troubadours*, p. 297.

in bringing about that moral reform in literature and in raising the ideals of romantic love, was Guilhem Montanhagol. He devoted himself to the rehabilitation and defence of the literary tradition by adapting it to the pressing needs of the time, and the change brought about in public taste by the sight of burning faggots. " The poet strove to reassure those who, terrified by the prohibitions of the clergy, turned away from the cult of romantic love." [1] " Lovers," sang the apologist of that cult, " must continue to serve Love, for love is not a sin, but a virtue which makes the wicked good, and the good better, and puts men in the way of doing good every day. Chastity itself comes from love, for whosoever truly understands love cannot be evil-minded." [2] That is the first mention of the word ' chastity ' in Provençal literature. Montanhagol developed his defence at considerable length. " I do not like," he says, " to hear the manners of our time denounced by wicked people. . . . He who seeks to induce his lady to commit a sin, does not truly love her ; for a lover should on no account desire what would dishonour his lady-love. Love is before all things that which raises the beloved object of pure desire. He who seeks anything else betrays the name of love. Desire never had any power over me to make me wish her to whom I have given myself ought that should not be. I should not reckon that a pleasure which might debase her. . . . A true lover must seek the interest of his beloved a hundred times more than his own . . . Bad lovers do not deserve to be loved by God ; to those, on the other hand, who desire nothing but what is good, He will grant all happiness, sooner or later—in any case when they die." The apologist employs the method which has been freely resorted to down to the present day ; like an apologetical anthropologist, he represents the moral notions which he preconises as having always obtained, and as having been the rule in the old times ; if they are not observed as they should be at the present time, that is due to ' corruption.' " The noble knights of old," he affirms, " sought nothing in love except honour, and those ladies in whom beauty

---

[1] J. Coulet, *Le troubadour Guilhem Montanhagol*, p. 73.
[2] *Ibid.*, p. 70 :—

> " Ben devon li amador
> de bon cor servir amor
> quar amor non es peccatz
> anz es vertutz que.ls malvatz
> fai bos, e.lh bon son melhor,
> e met om'en via
> de ben far tot dia ;
> et d'amor mou castitaz,
> quar qui.n amor ben s'enten
> no pot far que pueis mal renh."

resided did nothing that they should not have done. But nowa-days honour is held in contempt ; lovers have adopted other maxims, which bring about shame. I shall probably be attacked by those evil lovers on account of what I say, for their hearts are full of the faults which I condemn. But who tolerates evil is an accomplice of it ; the duty of a wise man is to protect fools against their errors." [1]

That reform in the poetical ' conception of love, ' that ' new style,' [2] was eagerly adopted " for the sole purpose of disarming the severity of the clergy." To do so was indeed " above all a matter of necessity ; in order that the love-song might survive at all it had to conform to the exigencies of the religious authorities. The troubadours could henceforth sing only a love in accordance with Christian morality, setting aside all evil desires in order to be virtuous and chaste." [3] The principles of the poetical reformation were set forth by Malfre Ermengaud in a prodigious versified treatise of 27,445 lines, the ' Breviari d'Amor,' where the argument is prosily set forth in true scholastic fashion, supported by citations from the old troubadours. The excellence of platonic love is demonstrated ; but the most prominent place is given to long chapters, or cantos, bearing the headings ' On remembering the vileness of sin,' ' On bearing in mind the vileness of the flesh.' [4] In imperfect harmony with the traditional exaltation of poetical love and the praises of women, the apologist, in order to leave no doubt as to his orthodoxy, concludes with the expression of the most unimpeachable canonical views on the subject. " Satan," he says, " in order to make men suffer bitterly, makes them adore women ; for instead of loving, as they should, the Creator, with fervent love, with all their heart, with all their mind and under-standing, they sinfully love women, whom they make into deities. Know ye that whosoever adores them, doth most certainly adore Satan, and make a god of the most disloyal Devil, Belial." [5]

---

[1] *Op. cit.*, pp. 148, 141 sq.

[2] In spite of his assurances concerning the chastity of the noble knights of old, Montanhagol is perfectly conscious of the changed treatment which he is introducing. " The ancient troubadours, in the gay old time," he says, " have not so exhausted the theme of love that we may not after them produce beautiful songs, at once new, pleasant and sincere."

> " Non an tan dig li primier trobador
> del fag d'amor, lai el temps qu'era guays,
> qu'enquera nos no fassam apres lor
> chanson de valor," etc.
>
> (Guilhem Montanhagol, *op. cit.*, pp. 110 sq.).

[3] J. Coulet, *Le troubadour Guilhem Montahangol*, pp. 51 sq.

[4] Matfre Ermengaud, *Le Breviari d'Amor*, ed. G. Azaïs, vol. ii, pp. 2 sqq., 5 sqq.

[5] *Ibid.*, pp. 418 sq.

The new interpretation of amatory sentiment is voiced by the last bards of Provence, as they scatter to foreign lands. Chief among those terror-stricken poets was Guiraut Riquier, ' the last of the Troubadours.' For twenty years he dedicated his poetical homage to Filippa d'Anduza, the wife of the Viscount of Narbonne, whom he celebrated under the name of Belh Deport. The delicacy of his sentiments leaves nothing to be desired. " I account myself well repaid," he sings, " by the inspiration which has been derived from the love I have bestowed upon my Lady, without being requitted by any love on her part. My honoured Lady, adorned with every quality, is loved by me the more deeply and the more respectfully for never having been compromised or blamed by even an evil thought. Had I derived from her the least favour, both she and I would have been degraded thereby." [1]

The literary culture established and perfected by the troubadours, though extinguished in Provence in blood and fire, had before expiring sown in other lands the seeds that were to perpetuate its traditions throughout Europe. In Italy the very language of the creators of lyric love had been adopted, and Dante, in his earlier days, fulminated against " the perverse men of Italy who commend the vulgar tongue of other countries and despise their own, account the Italian speech vile and praise the Provençal." [2] The Italian troubadours, such as Lanfranc Cigala, Zorzi, Sordello, reproduced, with the technique and the stereotyped conventions of Provençal poetry, the latest refinements of its surviving expositors in the days of its decadence, and, like all pupils, outdid their masters in the exaggeration of their tendencies. Sordello, the friend of Guilhem Montanhagol, begged of his ' sweet enemy ' the favour not to grant him any favours ; [3] and protested that " as my love is in its sense of honour unequalled, I prefer to serve her in vain rather than serve another who should condescend to invite me to

---

[1] C. A. F. Mahn, *Die Werke der Troubadours*, vol. iv, p. 30 :—

" Mout me tenc ben per pagatz
Del saber, que m'es uengutz
per ben amar non amatz
ma Dona ; quar mentaugutz
ne suy e n'ai benuolensa
dels pros ; doncx bem ual sabers
Cent aitans d'autres ualers,
Qu'ieu ai d'amar lieys ualensa
Tal, on no s'enten fallensa."

" E quar sos gens cors presatz
en totz bes aperceubutz
No fon repres ni blasmatz
Ni de nulh non degut cutz,
Am lan pus fis ab temensa ;
Quar si m'agues faitz plazers
Tals, que li fos non devers,
A lieys fora dechazensa
Et a mi a ma parvensa."

Cf. J. Anglade, *Le troubadour Guiraut Riquier, étude sur la décadence de l'ancienne poésie provençale*, pp. 243 sqq.

[2] Dante Alighieri, *Il Convito*, i. 11.

[3] See above, p. 485.

her bed."[1] The extravagance of his refinement was startling even to some of his contemporary fellow-bards, who had the bad taste to make merry over it.[2] In a tenson with the Italian poet, Peir Guilham of Toulouse declares his inability to understand him: "Never surely," he says, "was such a 'connoisseur' known as you, Sordello, for what other lovers desire you pretend to account of no value."[3] Bertran d'Alaman expresses regret that Sordello should have taken leave of his senses.[4]

The Italian poets, who at first adopted the language of their Provençal models, presently began to use their native tongue as the medium for their compositions. Thus arose the first Italian poetry, which immediately preceded Dante, and which, after an expression used by him, is generally known as the 'dolce stil nuovo,' the 'sweet new style.' Earliest of thirteenth-century Italian poetry in the vernacular was that produced at the Sicilian court of the emperor Frederic II, the cradle of much European culture. Inspired and stimulated by Provençal poets who took refuge with the great patron of arts and literature, it reproduced the stereotyped themes, conventions, 'conceits,' and even the words and phrases of troubadour poetry as faithfully as the latter had from generation to generation repeated the consecrated formulas of the literary tradition.[5] But, on the authority of an ambiguous ex-

---

[1] C. de Lollis, *Vita e poesie di Sordello di Goito*, p. 182 :—

> "E quar am de bon pretz ses par,
> Am mais servir lieys en perdo
> qu'autra qu' ab sim degnes colgar."

[2] Granet, in C. A. F. Mahn, *Gedichte der Troubadours*, vol. iii, p. 203 :—

> "E d'en Sordel sabem tot son usage
> qe ben ama ses jausimen s'amia,
> e non vol pas qel veinha d'agradage
> qel colc ab si, qe vergoinha i penria."

[3] C. de Lollis, *op. cit.*, pp. 172 sq. :—

> "En Sordell, anc entendedor
> non sai vi mais d'aital color
> com vos iest ; qe lh' autr'amador
> volon lo baizar el jacer,
> e vos metes a no caler
> so q'autre drut volon aver."

[4] J. J. Salveda de Grave, *Le troubadour Bertran d'Alamanon*, p. 95 :—

> "Mout m'es greu d'En Sordel, car l'es faillitz sos senz,
> Qu'eu cuidava qu'el fos savis e connoissenz ;
> Era en mon cug faillitz, don sui dolenz."

[5] See A. Gaspary, *La scuola poetica siciliana del secolo xiii* (A. d'Ancona's transl.), pp. 34 sqq. and *passim* ; G. A. Cesareo, *La poesia siciliana sotto gli Svevi*, pp. 24 sqq.

pression of Dante's, the rise of pre-Dantesque Italian poetry has been erroneously associated too exclusively with the Sicilian court. Independently of the group of poets who flourished there, save possibly for the suggestion of using the Italian vernacular, an equal literary activity, in even closer contact with Provence and the Provençal exiles, prevailed in the north, and it was thence that the 'stil nuovo,' which led up to Dante and established the traditions of Italian literature, directly derived.[1] Pre-Dantesque Italian poetry differs merely in the change of idiom from that of the Italian troubadours who had written in Provençal, but the fixed literary form acquired in the hands of the poets of the 'stil nuovo' a flexibility and variety of expression which surpassed in charm the products of Provençal art. The artistic conventions as regards the treatment of amatory themes were, however, unaltered; in letter and in spirit, in essence and in detail, they remained, not only throughout the poetry of the 'stil nuovo,' but with Dante and Petrarca themselves, those which decandent Provençal poetry and the Italian troubadours had handed down.[2]

The Italian imitations of troubadour poetry which were produced in Sicily show no trace of the later doctrines of its Provençal models; the Provençal poets who took refuge at the semi-pagan court of Frederic II were not likely to belong to the set of Montanhagol and his friends. The most distinguished amongst them was Guilhem Figueira, whose scathing denunciation of the priestly persecutors of his countrymen earned for him their special detestation.[3] In the poems of Guido delle Colonne, Jacopo Lentini, Pier delle Vigne, and the other poets of the Sicilian school, not an inkling is to be found of the ecclesiastical transformation in the 'conception of love,' nor a word about the merit of chastity.[4] In northern Italy, on the other hand, vernacular poetry developed directly out of the Provençal poetry of the Italian minstrels who,

---

[1] See C. de Lollis, " Dolce stil nuovo e 'noel dig de nova maestria,' " *Studi Medievali*, i, pp. 5 sqq.; E. Monaci, " Da Bologna a Palermo," in L. Morandi, *Antologia della nostra critica letteraria moderna*, pp. 237 sqq.

[2] N. Scarano, " Fonti provenzali della lirica Petrarchesca," *Studi di Filologia Romanza*, No. 8; A. C. Gidel, *Les troubadours et Pétrarque*. Petrarca was thoroughly familiar with the poetry of the Provençal troubadours, from which almost every formula and idea in his sonnets and 'trionfi' can be exactly paralleled. There is, however, no occasion to suppose that he deliberately imitated the work of the troubadours, for those formulas had never varied throughout Italian tradition up to his time.

[3] One of the questions asked of a heretic by the inquisitors was whether he had read the poems of Figueiria (*Histoire générale du Languedoc*, vol. vi, p. 653).

[4] K. Vossler, *Die philosophischen Grundlagen zum 'sussen neuen Stil' des Guido Guinicelli, Guido Cavalcanti, und Dante Alighieri*, pp. 47 sq.

with Sordello, Cigala, Zorzi at their head, had been followers of
Montanhagol and Guiraut Riquier.

The first products of the northern Italian muse manifest conspicuously the principles of the school. Some of the earliest, the
poems of Chiaro Davanzati, bear every appearance of being translations of Malfre d'Ermengau's edifying 'Breviari d'Amor.'
"Love, in the true and proper sense," says the first predecessor
of Dante, "is not a sin, and it does not befit a poet to
desire a woman who is not his wife. Every carnal desire is a
temptation of the devil ; woe unto him who yields himself to such
desires ! " [1] The most noted among the early poets of the new
school, Guittone d'Arezzo, goes even farther back for his inspiration. His prolific poems are not so much an echo of the ' Breviari
d'Amor ' as a versified paraphrase of the tractates of the Church
Fathers on chastity and virginity. He has, like them, long hymns
to " Chastity, thou light, thou beauty of the world ! " " To live in
the flesh without the desires of the flesh is more than angelic ; for
the angels have chastity without flesh, but he who has it with the
flesh is even greater than the angels in heaven. . . . Oh ! true
virtue, true love, thou alone art the virtue of virtues." The
expositor of the new ' conception of love ' shows that love " caused
the damnation of humanity, which was on its account put out of
Paradise, and for its sake was Christ killed." He demonstrates
through two volumes " the vile condition of lovers who, forgetting
God, make a divinity of the woman they love." [2]

The ' sweet new style ' assumes the full development of its
characteristics and elegance with Guido Guinicelli of Bologna, the
friend of Guittone, to whom, as to his revered master, he addresses

---

[1] *Le antiche Rime volgari* (ed. A. d'Ancona e Comparetti), vol. iii, pp. 89 sqq.
The connection of Davanzati with the Provençals on the one hand has
been shown by C. de Lollis (" Sul canzoniere di Chiaro Davanzati," *Giornale
Storico della Letteratura Italiana*, Supp. i, pp. 82 sqq., 111 sqq.), and with
Guinicelli and the ' stil nuovo ' by N. Zingarelli (" Dante," *Storia Letteraria
d'Italia*, vol. v, pp. 57 sq. ; C. J. G. W. Koken, *Guittone's von Arezzo Dichtung
und sein Verhältniss zu Guinicelli von Bologna* (Leipzig, 1886).

[2] Guittone d'Arezzo, *Rime*, vol. i, pp. 16 sqq., 184, 185 sq. ; vol. ii, p. 137.

"Castitate, tu luce e tu bellore ! . . .
Ah ! quanto amo e commendo
Donna che tene casto e corpo e core.
vivere in carne fuor voler carnale
è vita angelicale.
Angeli castità hanno fuor carne,
ma chi l'have con carne
in tant'e via maggior d'angel di celo.

Umanitate dannoe
e mise ad onta fuor di paradiso
per lei fù Cristo ucciso," etc.

a sonnet.[1] The crudeness of Patristic dissertations tends to be abandoned, denunciations of sin and sensuality, long-drawn praises of chastity are dispensed with ; they have become superfluous, for those principles are taken for granted. Guinicelli contents himself with referring to the sublimated purity of his love, to his lady's "refined love that is pure, which she bears towards me who am pure."[2] "It is not a sin to bestow his love upon her."[3] It is, however, superfluous to insist upon such apologies, for the object of his love is so ethereal that no suspicion of sensuality could attach to it. His lady "is crowned in heaven and is his hope of Paradise ; and the thought of her is all holiness."[4] Indeed, if she is not expressly identified with the Holy Virgin, she is assimilated to the moon : "The lady who in my heart awakened love seems like unto the orb that measures time and sheds her splendour in the sky of love."[5] Dante's Beatrice, leading him through the seven spheres while she lectures him on theology, is here clearly prefigured. Dante's friend, and the most eminent of his immediate forerunners, Guido Cavalcanti, gave out, in imitation of the ' Roman de la Rose ' of Guillaume de Lorris, a new version of Andreas' laws of love from which all objectionable principles are eliminated, and in their stead the following are substituted : "One must not love another man's lady," "the lover must be mindful to observe religion."[6] He prefaces his first verses with the advertisement that, should anything be found in them that is contrary to honour, it should be set down to some fault of expression ;[7] but the caution appears unnecessary. Sublimated amatory sentiments are now

---

[1] *Poeti del primo secolo della lingua italiana*, vol. i, p. 101.

[2] *Ibid.*, p. 70 :—

> "La sua beltà piacente
> e il fino amor ch'è puro
> in ver me che son puro."

[3] *Ibid.*, p. 93 :—

> "Non mi fù fallo se in lei posi amanza."

[4] *Ibid.*, p. 90 :—

> "La vostra Donna ch'e'n ciel coronata,
> ond'è la vostra speme in paradiso,
> è tutta santa ormai vostra memoria
> contemplando."

[5] *Ibid.*, p. 96 :—

> "La bella stella, che il tempo misura
> sembra la Donna, che m'ha innamorato,
> posta nel ciel d'amore."

[6] G. Salvadori, *La poesia giovanile e la canzon d'amore di Guido Cavalcanti*, p. 95. The sonnets in the Vatican codex, from which this and the following references are taken, are generally ascribed to Guido Cavalcanti, although it is possible, as some think, that they are the work of some other poet.

[7] *Ibid.*, p. 89.

" far removed from every vanity." [1] Scarcely is it possible to detect through the mellifluous flow of musical words any substantial body of meaning. An old troubadour ' conceit ' about love reaching the heart through the eyes suffices to furnish the theme for a mile of sonnets, and a reference to the loadstone will supply the substance of half a dozen ' canzoni.'

" The process of refinement which erotic lyricism underwent at the hands of Montanhagol and his contemporaries arose by an inevitable, but at the same time deliberate, exaggeration of principles which had been present from the first in love-poetry." [2] The same law applies to the development of all sentimental conceptions ; nothing, in the process of psychological evolution, ever arises, except through the modification, often very slight and gradual, though momentous in its cumulative effect, of that which went before. Hence is it always easy to read the conceptions of a later age into the crude germs out of which they have arisen, to read the gods of theology and metaphysics into the fierce deities of the savage, modern sentiments of modesty and propriety into the sexual tabus and superstitious fears of primitive woman, the sanctity of modern institutions into the rude regulations of primitive society, cultured sentiments of romantic love into the crude passions of the barbarian. The development of sentimental conceptions that took place at the very birth of European literature, during the twelfth and thirteenth centuries, illustrates the same phenomenon. The conventions of ' amour courtois,' which had themselves arisen out of the rude usages of warlike matriarchal societies, had, in their original form, no reference whatever to ideals of chastity ; no sentiments could have been more radically opposed to the ascetic conceptions of Christianity. Yet the process by which the former were at last harmonised with the latter needed only to use materials which lay at hand in the conventions of chivalric and poetical love. The process of adaptation which was effected by the troubadour poets of the Albigenses period merely modified the traditional sentiments, and had but to put a slightly altered interpretation upon words and ideas to bring them into harmony with the new requirements. The distinction between ' courtly ' and ' dishonest ' love which ran through the gamut of the poetical erotics was reinterpreted as the opposition between ' pure ' and ' sensual ' love. " Little by little public sentiment was transmuted ; profane poetry, even in its most elevated form, became a ' sin '; poetry of a religious character was alone tolerated or comprehended. Such is

---

[1] G. Salvadori, *La poesia giovanile e la canzon d'amore di Guido Cavalcanti*, p. 97 :—

" d'ogni vanità fatta lontana."

[2] J. Coulet, *Le troubadour Guilhem Montanhagol*, p. 17.

the term of the evolution which the poetry of the troubadours reached by the end of the thirteenth century with Riquier and his contemporaries. In that form it is scarcely recognisable. Yet very little has sufficed to bring about the transformation." [1]

The tenets of poetic love, modelled upon those of chivalric love, centred upon the 'service' required of the poet before he could claim from his lady the 'guerdon' to which he referred in terms no less crude than the barbarian. In that convention, as in the 'service,' or tests of endurance, of the savage, the desires of the impatient lover had to be moderated. That 'moderation,' 'mezura,' was one of the consecrated terms in the scholastic disputations on court love, and was opposed to 'leujairia,' or 'sensuality.' One of the troubadours of the earlier period, Garin le Brun, has a piece in which, after the fashion of the time, the opposing promptings of 'Mezura' and 'Leujairia' are contrasted. "Mezura," he says, "Moderation, tells me not to be over-eager nor desire too much. 'Nor give all at once all thou hast,' she says, 'for if thou give all, what will be left to thee to offer in further service?' Moderation whispers sweet and low, telling me to proceed with my affairs step by step. 'Leujairia' says: 'Wherefore wait? If thou dost not hasten, the opportunity of reaching the goal may pass.' Moderation says to me: 'Be cautious, and thou wilt hold thy guerdon of love.' Leujairia pulls me by the nose and says: 'When once thou hast the cup in thy hand, what more dost thou need?' And thus am I equally divided between 'Mezura' and 'Leujairia.'" [2] It is

[1] J. Anglade, *Les troubadours*, p. 298.
[2] C. Appel, " L'enseignement de Garin le Brun," *Revue des Langues Romanes*, xxiii, pp. 406 sqq. :—

" Mezura.m ditz no si 'escas
ni ja trop d'aver non amas,
ni non dar ges tot so que as ;
quar si dava tot quan mi plas
   pueys de que serviria ?

Mezura.m ditz suave e bas
que fassa mon afar de pas ;
e Leujayria.m ditz : 'que fas ?
si no.i.t cochas, no.i conseguas
   que.l terminis s'embria.

Mezura ditz que sia escas
e gazauh terras et amas
e Leujayria.m pren ple nas
e.m ditz que pueis serai el vas
   pueys avers que.m faria ?

Aissi m'an partit equalme
   Mezura e Leujayria."

The changes which we have been noting are illustrated in the altered

easy to perceive how, by a very slight pressure of exegetic interpretation, the contrast could be turned to account and converted
into the opposition between pure and impure love, between chastity
and lechery. Indeed, in pre-Dantesque Italy Fra Guittone d'Arezzo
actually translates thus the old refrain in one of his most unctuous
and edifying poems : " seguo ragion, non lecceria," ' ragion ' being
in the phraseology of the period the equivalent of chastity.[1] Thus,
while the ' new conception of love ' developed by almost imperceptible modifications from pre-existing conceptions, it came in fact
to reverse completely those conceptions. In the twelfth century
poets had declared that love was incompatible with legal marriage ;
Francesco da Barberino, the philosopher of the ' stil nuovo,' using
the same phraseology as those poets, affirmed, on the contrary, that
" illicit love cannot properly be called by the name of love at all,
but is designated by the common consent of all honest persons as
insanity." [2]

The process of adapting the amatory lyrical poetry of twelfth-
and thirteenth-century Europe to the requirements of Church
morality went, however, as has been seen, a great deal farther
than such a re-interpretation of terms and modification of their
connotation. Nothing short of the conversion of that profane
and sinful poetry into purely religious poetry could satisfy the
requirements of the times and justify its survival. ' Love,' ab-

connotation of words. Romantic courtly love in its most refined form
was denoted by the term ' druerie ' ; a knight standing to his lady-love in
the relation of ' love-service ' was her ' dru ' (Provençal, ' drutz '; Italian,
' drudo '; Celtic, ' druth '). The word is closely related to ' truth,' ' troth ' ;
a king's ' faithful subjects,' or feudal vassals, are spoken of as his ' drutz '
(e.g. *Roman de Renard*, iii. 303). ' Druerie ' was opposed, as courtly,
refined love, to vulgar love, harlotry. The term is applied to divine love :
" Hit is as derworthe a drurie as deore god him-seluen " (William Langland,
Piers the Plowman, Passus i, 85, ed. W. W. Skeat, p. 27). In Thomas's
Tristan the refrain of the hero's lament for Iseult is :—

> " Isôt ma drue, Isôt m'amie
> En vous ma mort, en vous ma vie "

(J. Bédier, *Le roman de Tristan, par Thomas*, vol. i, p. 259). In Dante's
time the connotation of the term had become completely changed. He uses
it in the masculine form as the correlative of the coarsest term for ' harlot.

> " Taide è la puttana che rispose
> Al drudo suo," etc.

(*Inferno*, xviii. 133). In the translation of *Cormac's Glossary*, ' druth '
is rendered ' harlot.' From being applied to the most idealised form of
romantic love the word thus came to mean ' whoredom.' A similar transformation has taken place in the term ' mistress,' which, of course, had
originally reference to the ' vassalage ' of love-service.

[1] Fra Guittone d'Arezzo, *Rime*, vol. i, p. 16.
[2] A. Thomas, *Francesco da Barberino et la littérature provençale en Italie*,
p. 56.

stracted and personified, after the manner that had been habitual with the troubadours, was freely identified with God, with Christ, with the Holy Ghost. The 'Lady' towards whom poetical sentiment was directed was in like manner identified with the Holy Virgin.

A recent Catholic writer states that "respect for women rises and falls with the veneration of the Virgin Mother of God,"[1] and there is some truth in the claim. The independent and influential position of women in pagan barbaric Europe, in which those themes arose that were transformed in the romantic literature of the Middle Ages, was associated with the fervent worship of the Virgin Mother. But she was not as yet Christian, and her freedom and proud independence of bearing corresponded with that of her barbaric votaries. She figures in early romances as the fairy and enchantress who draws wandering knights to her celestial love, and in whose toils they, for a long season, remain imprisoned. Her worship was, as has been seen, at first put down by the Church. By the time of the revival of culture in the twelfth and thirteenth centuries it had, however, together with much that belonged to old pagan sentiment and conceptions, become completely re-established. The Holy Virgin, called by Albertus Magnus the Great Goddess, had, in southern Europe at least, well-nigh displaced the male Trinity in the current devotion of the people. God the Father was regarded as terrible and unapproachable ; Christ, in spite of His compassion, held the office of a judge ; the Queen of Heaven alone could show untrammelled mercy to sinners. She wrought more miracles than all male divine and saintly beings put together, and had, in fact, entirely regained her position as divine prototype of magic-wielding women. She intervened at all times in the order of nature, and there was not a circumstance or situation of daily life too trivial to call for her intervention, or a task too humble for her to undertake. She was the chief source of healing. A poor monk, it is related, was on the point of death, and quite given up by his brethren, on account of an ulcerous disease of a very suspicious nature. His nose was eaten away, and his mouth was one ghastly sore, which stank horribly. He appealed to the Holy Virgin, and recalled the fervent devotion with which he had always served her. Touched by his appeal the Blessed Lady came down in person and treated the case by applying the milk from her own breast to the sores.

> La douce Dame, la piteuse,
> trait sa mamelle savoureuse,
> se li boute dedenz la bouche,
> et puis moult doucement li touche
> par sa dolor et par ses plaies.

[1] A. Rössler, art. "Woman," *The Catholic Encyclopaedia*, vol. xv, p. 690.

The divine application was, of course, instantly effective, and when his brother-monks came with spades to bury him they found the patient uncommonly lively.[1] In a certain convent the reverend abbess was in sore trouble ; the signs of the good understanding between her and her chaplain had become evident, and she knew not what arrangements to make in view of the event. But the Blessed Virgin came to her assistance and acted as midwife, delivering her safely and without any pain of a lusty boy, whom she handed over to the care of a holy hermit in the neighbourhood.[2] In another monastery a nun, who acted as stewardess, having become weary of the monotony of convent life, deposited her keys upon the altar and went into the town, where she led a life of gaiety as a prostitute. In time, however, this mode of life also began to pall upon her, and she longed for the peace and quietness of the convent. Returning there, she knocked at the gate, and, when the porteress opened it, asked if she remembered Sister Agatha, mentioning the name by which she had been known in religion. The porteress answered that indeed she knew her, and that she was a most worthy and holy nun. Surprised at this answer, the repentant sinner looked more closely at the porteress, and found that she was no other than the Blessed Virgin, who had taken her place during her absence from the convent, so that nobody there knew of her escapade.[3] The Holy Virgin also came to the assistance of women who had forsaken the marital couch for the night, and prevented their absence being noticed by their husbands by taking their place.[4] "We must not suppose," the Blessed Alphonso de Liguori tells us, "that such prodigies are extraordinary events ; they are everyday occurrences."[5] On the other hand, the Blessed Virgin was by no means so ready to shelter unfaithful husbands, which, of course, she could hardly do in the same way. A married woman being jealous of her husband's mistress, appealed to the Holy Virgin to avenge her rights and to enforce justice. "But our Blessed Lady replied : ' Justice ! Chastisement ! Dost thou seek them from me ? No, go to others, for I will not grant what thou askest ; for know,' she added, ' that this sinner recites every day a salutation in my honour, and that by whomsoever it is recited, it deprives me of the power of allowing him to suffer or to be chastised for his sins.' "[6]

---

[1] Gautier de Coincy, *Miracles de la Sainte Vierge*, col. 349. Cf. *Sermones Discipuli*, Exemplum xxxii.

[2] *Les Miracles de Nostre Dame par personnages*, vol. i, p. 96. Cf. *Sermones Discipuli*, Exemplum xxiv.

[3] *Sermones Discipuli*, Exemplum xxv.

[4] St. Alphonso Maria de Liguori, *The Glories of Mary*, pp. 547 sq.

[5] *Ibid.*, p. 179.   [6] *Ibid.*, p. 231.

"Let anyone glance through the legends of the Holy Virgin Mary," remarks Dr. Weinhold, " the most pronounced manifestations of mediaeval piety, and he will be compelled, on a fair and impartial judgment, to refuse to allow to them any moral value whatsoever." [1]

Although even in the best period of Provençal poetry some of the troubadours, as for instance Folquet de Marseille and Peire d'Alvergne, had composed religious pieces, the Holy Virgin is not referred to in those compositions. Peire Cardinal was the first to compose a hymn to the Virgin.[2] Concomitantly with the decadence of Provençal literature, and the evolution in the conception of love which took place on the establishment of the Inquisition, poetical devotion to the Holy Virgin assumed enormous proportions.[3] Peire Guilhem of Luzerna, Albert of Sisteron, Peire Espanhol vied with one another in the composition of lyrics in praise of the Holy Virgin. Of the poetry of Guiraut Riquier, the protagonist in the elaboration of the new conception of love, fully three-fourths consists of songs in honour of the Virgin.[4] The earliest troubadour poems to the Holy Virgin are merely poetical paraphrases of Church hymns and have no relation in form to amatory poetry.[5] The troubadours of the decadence transferred the formulas and traditions of Provençal love-poetry to the celebration of the Virgin. They merely substituted the name of the latter for that of the ideal object of their effusions. Guiraut Riquier went so far as to reverse the procedure ; he called the Holy Virgin by the name he had used in celebrating his Countess of Narbonne.[6] " In times past," sang the elderly love-poet, " oft did I sing of love ; but in truth I knew not what love was, for what I took to be such was but folly. But now does Love bid me to love a Lady whom I cannot fear and honour sufficiently, nor love as she deserves to be loved. May the love of her wholly fill me, so that I may obtain from her the guerdon which I seek. I am not jealous of any who desires the love of her I love ; and pray my Lady to protect all her lovers, so that each may see his desires fulfilled." [7]

The fashion was taken up by the Italian troubadours ; Lanfranc Cigala and Bartolomeo Zorzi are no less prolific than Riquier in

---

[1] K. Weinhold, *Die deutschen Frauen in dem Mittelalter*, p. 179.

[2] V. Lowinski, *Zum geistliche Kunstlied*, pp. 10 sq., 17 ; J. Anglade, *Le troubadour Guiraut Riquier*, p. 285.

[3] J. Anglade, *op. cit.*, p. 284 : " Religious poetry developed in the exact measure that profane poetry tended to disappear."

[4] Id., *ibid.*, p. 286.

[5] V. Lowinski, *loc. cit.*

[6] J. Anglade, *op. cit.*, p. 297 ; C. A. F. Mahn, *Die Werke der Troubadours*, vol. iv, p. 75.

[7] C. A. F. Mahn, *op. cit.*, vol. iv, pp. 75 sqq.

songs to the Virgin. Like other formulas of early European
lyricism, it became an established tradition ; it was expected of
every amatory poet that he should furnish some hymns to the
Holy Virgin. The tradition was scrupulously observed as late as
the time of Pulci, in whose ' Morgante Maggiore ' somewhat coarse
blasphemies about the Holy Trinity alternate with invocations to
the Virgin ; and the ' divine ' Aretino supplemented his pornographic sonnets, and his directory to the prostitutes of Venice,
with hymns to the Madonna.

There was nothing very revolutionary in that poetical worship.
By the time it came into vogue amatory poetry had become dissociated from actual life ; it was literature pure and simple. It
cost the troubadours of the Albigenses period nothing to transfer
their poetical homage from some patroness or fictitious object to
the Holy Virgin. The artifice had probably, on one occasion
at least, been adopted long since by an early troubadour who,
like many others, turned in his last days to religion.[1]   In the opinion
of several critics the ' unseen lady ' and ' distant princess ' of Jaufré
Rudel was no other than the Heavenly Virgin, and the fable of the
' Lady of Tripoli ' and the poet's pilgrimage to the Holy Land were,
like much in the ' biographies ' of the troubadours, but aetiological
commentaries in explanation of what was at that time a somewhat
startling eccentricity.[2]   The poets of the Albigenses period were
glad to seize upon the simple device which enabled them to reproduce the traditional literary forms banned by the Church, while
giving at the same time proof of unimpeachable orthodoxy. It is
difficult to see that the poetical Lady-love was elevated by her
identification with the Virgin ; the latter was celebrated in terms
which could not be more exalted than those which in earlier days
had already been applied to the former. The poetical device, at
the time of its introduction at least, can scarcely be said to have
had any elevating effect upon the sentimental feeling toward
women, or upon the conception of sex relations.

The changes in the attitude towards sex-relations and in the
treatment of amatory themes which are illustrated in the early
development of European literature, were not so much psychological changes in sentiment, or even, as has been commonly
said, in the ' conception of love,' as changes in literary treatment
and conventions. With the early princely troubadours poetical
accomplishments had been, as with the warrior bards of an even

---

[1] Lowinsky counts some forty troubadours who became monks
(V. Lowinsky, *Zum geistliche Kunstlied*, p. 10).

[2] A. Jeanroy, *Les poésies de Jaufré Rudel*, pp. 16 sq. Cf. Introduction,
and C. Appel, " Wiederum zu Jaufré Rudel," *Archiv für das Studium der
neueren Sprachen und Literaturen*, cvii, p. 343.

more barbaric age, a means of enhancing their attractions in the
eyes of women, or an elegant pastime. They bore a direct relation
to life. But it was otherwise with the court poets of a later time.
The fixed conventions, the 'rules of the game,' precluded in any
case those feats of technical skill from ever being spontaneous
effusions of feeling. "Love appears to be in their songs rather a
fantasy of the mind than a passion of the heart." [1] Even with
Bernard de Ventador, one of the least artificial of the troubadour
poets, it is the considered verdict of critics that "his poetry lies
outside the world of reality." [2] "He neither wishes to, nor can,
remain bound to the reality of things," says another writer, "and
for him poetry and the real world are two different things"; the
business of the former is "the invention of poetical situations,
invested with technical forms apt to awaken admiration for
virtuosity." [3] In the later period of that literature, when the
refinements and transformations in the 'conception of love' took
place, the divorce between the artistic product and psychological
reality was even more complete. "Instead of presenting themselves to us as very personal revelations, these love-songs are but
laboured reflections on the subject of love, inventions of the various
situations to which love may give rise, a tissue of literary motives
and commonplaces which have no relation to reality. . . . In
general there is no relation between the poets and the ladies.
Everything points to the conclusion that, as a general rule, the
ladies of the songs are imaginary inventions." [4] To this day,
although a whole literature has been written concerning Dante
and Petrarca, opinions are divided as to whether the Beatrices
and Lauras of their poetical idealisation were real or fictitious
personages. No one can suppose that the sentiments of Master
Guiraut Riquier for the good Countess of Narbonne, to whom for
over twenty years he addressed his poetical sighs, went deeper
than the tip of his goose-quill. It is easy enough, in those circumstances, to spiritualise and sublimate 'the conception of love.'
Troubadours, such as Blacatz and Foulquet de Roman, continued
to produce poetic laments over the cruelties of the ladies after they
were well over fifty.[5]

As a rule our poets kept one 'conception of love' for their

[1] J. Anglade, *Le Troubadour Guiraut Riquier*, p. 241. Cf. F. Diez, *Die Poesie der Troubadours*, p. 122.

[2] C. Appel, *Bernart von Ventadorn*, pp. xxiv sq.

[3] N. Zingarelli, "Su Bernart di Ventador," *Studi Medievali*, i, p. 392.

[4] S. Stronski, *Le trouvadour Folquet de Marseille*, pp. 66, 68. It is noteworthy that of the four hundred troubadours who spent their lives in depicting
the mortal anguish which they suffered through the cruelties of their lady-
loves, not one is reported to have committed suicide.

[5] R. Zenker, *Die Gedichte des Folquet von Romans*, p. 13.

literary activities and another for their relations with women. Messer Sordello himself, whose extravagance in the idealisation of the 'conception of love' surprised his contemporaries, was no less distinguished for his exploits as a libertine. He eloped with at least two married women, and was in constant danger from the ire of injured husbands. His name was a by-word for inconstancy, and Bertran d'Alamanon cites him as having changed mistresses a hundred times.[1] He is himself, when the occasion suits, the first to cast aside the convention of his 'conception of love,' and to indite a verse or two in another vein, as when, far from protesting the modesty of his desires, he declares to a lady that he will die " if he does not taste her sweet body." [2] The following is perhaps the most surprising production of a champion of chastity and refinement : " I do not wonder," he boasts, " that husbands are jealous of one so learned as I am in the arts of love, for there is not a woman, however prudish, that can withstand the sweet persuasiveness of my appeals. Therefore do I not blame him who complains of me, and is aggrieved that his wife receives me. But so long as I have my pleasure of her body, little do I reck of his grievance and still less of his complaints." [3]

[1] Bertran d'Alamanon, ed. J. J. Salveda de Grave, p. 119 :—

> " Pas en Sordel n'a ben camiadas cen,
> Ben puese camiar una."

[2] C. de Lollis, *Vita e poesie di Sordello di Goito*, p. 189 :—

> " S'en breu noill pren merces, tan soi cochatz
> dels mals dun sui per s'amor tormentatz,
> q'eu tem morir desiran son cors gai."

[3] Id., *ibid.*, p. 199 :—

> " Nom meraveill sil marit son gilos
> de mi, tan sui en dreig d'amor sabenz,
> qu'el mon non es dompna, tan sia pros,
> ques defendes de mos dolz precs plaisenz ;
> Donc non blasm'on negun que de mes plaingna,
> q'usqecs a dol qant sa moillers m'acoill ;
> mas sol qez eu ab son cors me despueill,
> pauc pretz son dol e meinz blan sa mesclaingna."

Sordello's learned editor is disposed to suggest doubts as to his relations with Cunizza (p. 13 n.), but has some difficulty in disposing of the testimony of all the witnesses, and the poet's relations with Otta di Strasso are too interwoven with numerous particulars of his life for any doubts to be raised. Signor de Lollis passes lightly over the " quizzi carnali " in Sordello's poems, and suggests that they are perhaps reminiscences of ancient poets (pp. 78, 85, " sporconata marziale ") ; but it is remarkable that neither in his summary allusion to the matter, nor in his notes does he make any reference to the contents of the above piece. There is no question of explaining it away by interpreting the poet's ' arts of love ' as a reference to platonic sentiments. The words of the seventh line are unambiguous.

The evolution which has been considered belongs, in fact, to the history of literature rather than to the history of life. Yet ultimately it is not possible to separate literature from life. The literature of a people is part of their traditional heredity, and the sentiments and principles which determine their conduct and conceptions are inseparable from that heredity. The culture of every civilised people is built around its Bibles. The conformity of poets and romance-writers was in its origin a literary conformity, an orthodoxy which did not extend beyond the written page. But the written page is the germ of the living mind of succeeding generations. The standards which were at first imposed by literature upon public taste came later to be imposed by public taste upon literature. The changes that took place in the forms of European literature were not the result of a change in current standards and tastes. The transformation in the conceptions of romantic love, the idealisation of the relations between the sexes which is presented in the course of literary evolution from the primitive sagas of European peoples, from the first outburst of lyrical poetry in southern Europe to the dawn of the Renaissance, were not dictated by changes in public sentiment, but by the influence and by the pressure of the Christian Church. It was imposed upon popular literature by those Patristic conceptions which pronounced the extinction of the human race to be preferable to its reproduction by sexual intercourse. Those conceptions are regarded as the extravagances of a disordered asceticism. The strange pronouncements, culled from the dusty volumes of moral theology, are apt to be perused with a smile as archaeological curiosities. From an ethical point of view, few would have any hesitation in accounting them morbid and even nauseating aberrations. Sexual morality, as currently conceived, has nothing to do with the insane vilification of sex, with the visionary exaltation of virginity, with the condemnation of marriage as a necessary evil. The standards by which the sexual morality of a given society, savage or civilised, is judged, are quite other : they are what is deemed a moderate and healthy view of the matter dictated by considerate judgment and wholesome sentiments. Yet it is to the ascetic ideal that current European standards owe their existence. It was not by moderate and considered views that the agelong traditional usages and conceptions of the people of barbaric Europe were transformed, but by the persistent and strenuous influence of Patristic ideals in their fiercest, crudest, and most uncompromising form. For over ten centuries those ideals did not cease to exercise their unremitting pressure upon the conceptions of European peoples in regard to sex relations ; they imposed themselves upon the nascent literatures of the new cultures and completely transformed them, and have thus determined the course of all subsequent development of European sentiment. The moral standards applied to sex relations are the residual product of that exaltation of ritual purity which pronounced a curse upon sex, stigmatised woman as the instrument of Satan, and poured scorn upon motherhood. It is in the doctrines of Ambrose and of Origen, of Augustine and of Jerome that European sexual morality has its roots.

Those influences have had an even deeper bearing. Their effect has not been confined to promoting new conceptions of sexual morality. Nothing could appear more remote from present-day realities than the fabric of chivalric heroics and conventions, the love-service and the curious codes that grew round that institution. Those seemingly exotic fictions have nevertheless left their indelible imprint. They were, as has been seen, originally associated with extra-connubial relations. As the freedom of pagan barbarism became gradually abolished, the idealisation by which it had been sought to justify and excuse it was transferred to legitimate relations, and came to be regarded as leading to, and as the foundation of, monogamic marriage, with which they had formerly been pronounced to be incompatible. That idealisation of a relation which had remained essentially economic has continued in the tradition of European sentiment. The sexual instincts, confined by ever more rigorous restrictions within one prescribed channel, have become directed, as in no other phase of human culture, towards a single personal object, and have availed themselves of the emotional sublimation of which the romantic and lyrical literature of the Middle Ages supplied the elements. Monogamic relations have created monogamic love. The sentimental idealisation of the sex relation has thus assumed a character which is without equivalent in any other culture, and was unknown in the cradle of European civilisation in the Hellenic world. In the light of it, under the rubrics of love, courtship, and marriage, the modern anthropologist elucidates the psychological and sociological phenomena presented by primitive man and woman, by the savage and the barbarian.

CHAPTER XXX

THE MOTHERS

CIVILISATION, as it presents itself in humanity's powers of control over nature and over its own social conditions, in the higher forms of knowledge and of culture, in the gradual elimination of error and abuses, has developed within a relatively short period of time. Those achievements have been brought about chiefly, if not exclusively, through the operation of man's rational faculty. The creative and controlling powers of intellect, growing by the accumulation of acquired experience and knowledge, by the concomitant elimination through perpetual criticism of invalid conceptions and claims, have transmuted not the intellectual outlook only and the activities that are governed by the powers of the intellect, but, by a necessary extension of their effects, the sentiments, the motives, the moral conceptions that react upon conduct and social relations, and the values and emotions that colour life. That process which has raised civilised humanity above savagery is fundamentally an intellectual process. It has been rendered possible by conditions that have bestowed security and leisure upon favoured classes and emancipated them from the hand-to-mouth organic struggle. Those achievements which constitute what, in the best sense, we term civilisation, have taken place in societies organised on patriarchal principles; they are for the most part the work of men. Women have had very little direct share in them.

Women are constitutionally deficient in the qualities that mark the masculine intellect. Where all values are relative, it is as irrelevant as it is invidious to speak of superiority and inferiority. Feminine differs from masculine intelligence in kind; it is concrete, not abstract; particularising, not generalising. The critical, analytical, and detached creative powers of the intellect are less developed in women than in men. That character arises in all probability from the subordination and sacrifice to maternal functions which limits the physical growth of the mammalian female. Women are more precocious than men, their maturity is reached earlier. There is in their growth the arrest of development, physical and mental, which goes with relative precocity. It has been said that a man learns nothing after forty ; it may be said in the same broad sense that a woman learns nothing after twenty-five. At that age, when a man is often setting out on his career of intellectual adventure and discovery, most women's intellectual outlook has become formed. Hence the innate conservatism of the feminine mind. The prolonged adaptability which constitutes the intellectual advantage of men in progressive societies is opposed to the natural constitution of women. The social conditions of settled material culture have not only enabled men to take over the productive work formerly carried out by female labour, and afforded to leisured ruling classes the opportunity of detaching themselves from the material struggle ; they have opened the way for the exercise by men of their real advantage over women. The intellectual structure of the higher forms of culture and organisation which constitute civilisation are masculine products and are marked by the qualities and characteristics of the masculine intellect.

But that world of civilisation is issued from another which was in many respects very different. The rich superstructure, of which, for all its faults, and for all our divine discontent, we have just cause to be proud and thankful, is the outgrowth of more ancient types of society ; from these it has necessarily drawn its traditional inheritance. In the development of uncultured societies the intellectual powers of the human mind have played a much smaller part, the reactions of instinct to pressing needs a much larger one, than in the development of advanced culture. Thought was less critical ; it was to an even greater extent than in any subsequent stage bound down by the fetters of a tradition that had continued unchallenged since the dawn of the human world, and harked back to the emergence of the race out of animality. The conceptions which have presided over the growth of uncultured societies have been what appear to us the grossest superstitions. The place which critical, analytical, creative thought, which organising intelligence, which science, or in more archaic phases systematised philosophical and theological interpretations, occupy in higher culture, was filled almost exclusively in the uncultured world by the notion of magic. The practical operations and enterprises of life, social relations and organisation, the relation of man to his natural and social environment, were looked upon as immediately dependent upon magical powers and influences. The inheritance which primitive society has handed down is profoundly irrational. There was, in those conditions, none of the predominance of masculine intellectual qualities which marks the products of civilisation. The division and distribution of labour afforded no room for the detached and leisured thinker or for the differentiated specialist ; abstract conceptions and generalisations could have no place where every relation of life was concrete.   On a common level, the respective contributions of men and of women to the growth of the social and traditional inheritance were not distinguished by any superior quality in the former.   It was, on the contrary, from the women's sphere of interest and activity that the group-mind derived its chief stimulus ; it was by these that its features and contents were moulded.   With women were chiefly connected those mysterious magical powers that were accounted paramount in the control of human life and destiny.   The place of women in the social structure was marked by none of the subordination which the powers and achievements of masculine enterprise and activity assign to them. The material conditions of culture were not the outcome of that masculine activity, but were mainly the achievements of women ; they were not the products of organised industry and of male labour, but of the home-building and household avocations of woman.   Social organisation itself—the associated group to which humanity owes its mere existence—was the expression of feminine functions.   Those social sentiments, without which no aggregate of individuals can constitute a society, were the immediate derivatives of the feelings which bind the mother and her offspring, and consisted originally of these, and of these alone.   Upon them the superstructure of humanity, and the powers and possibilities of its development, ultimately rest.

" The family is the foundation of society " ; so ran the postulate of pre-scientific social science.   In the sense in which it was intended the axiom is belied by all the facts, anthropological and biological, which have engaged our attention.   The patriarchal 'family' of academic social science is but a euphemism for the individualistic male with his subordinate dependents.   As a social unit the family means the individual, actuated by his most aggressively individualistic instincts ; it is not the foundation, but the negation of society. Out of an aggregate of conflicting individualistic interests, human society emphatically has not, and could never have, arisen.   It owed its rise to instincts that obliterated individualistic instincts, that moulded by binding sentiments of interdependence, loyalty, solidary devotion a group larger than the patriarchal family, and from its nature capable of indefinite expansion.

Yet the old erroneous aphorism contains, like most fallacies, its core of essential truth.   Whatever the constitution of the 'family,' it is the ties of sentiment which bind its members —sentiments that are not merely self-defensive and aggressive, sentiments which transcend mere principles of organisation and combinations of interests—it is those bonds of sentiment that are the ultimate foundation of any society, its sole living foundation. They are the antithesis of individualism ; and it is on that account that the patriarchal family can never by mere aggregation give rise to, or constitute, a social structure. The primordial family was not the unit, but was the whole of society. The expansion of primitive social groups into larger aggregates, the growth, ultimately, of the historical societies comprising millions of individuals, has been rendered possible only by the character of the bonds which made the primitive group a social entity, and by the evolution out of them of other forms of loyalty. These, multiform though they are, derive from the primordial instinct out of which they have developed, their social character.

The mere principle of ' altruism ' is a discursive philosophical abstraction which never had any existence as a sentiment, nor ever determined human conduct. No people, no individual probably, has ever been actuated by love of the human race. ' Altruism ' is but a misty evaporation distilled by abstract thought from the derivative sentiments of the social instincts prototype in nature. The maternal instinct alone is primitively ' altruistic ' ; every sentiment that has made social aggregation possible by checking self-regard owes its existence to that primal love.

The maternal instinct and the extra-rational sentiments that united the members of the primitive maternal group have germinated, and given rise to, more generalised bonds of union and to a varied growth of loyalties. The natural and biological dominance of the primitive mother over the group which she created, the awe attaching to her magical nature and powers, were the rudiments of the characters of the priestess and the queen. The source of those magical powers was the celestial counterpart of her nature. The supernatural food-giver, the divine progenitor or mother, perpetuated the relationship of the expanded tribe to its earthly mother and extended to larger aggregates the bonds which united the primitive maternal family. The deity was the undying spirit of the tribe ; generations were bound together by their communion with the divine source and controller of their life. That faith has undergone many and profound transformations : but the communion which it established has imparted to the most diverse forms of its products and to the most varied types of societies the solidarity which the primitive mystery of generation and the primitive sacrament of common blood and common food, bestowed upon the ideal tribe of its followers.

The leader of men who established the domination of his people over other groups, who founded kingdoms, who expanded the primitive matriarchal clan or tribe into a society scattered over vast territories, who ultimately led to the evolution of empires and states extending over multitudes, inherited from the primitive mother and priestess her sacred and magical character. The sentiments with which she was regarded became the sentiments which attached to the sacred and divine king, the representative of God on earth. His power, and the power of all rulers, has never rested upon force alone. The multitudes that formed the empires organised under the sway of the divine ruler were controlled less by the swords and spears of his soldiers than by the awe with which his sacred function and character were invested. The labours of those organised workers have created material civilisation and have afforded the conditions of culture. But those achievements have not depended upon the power of the rulers so much as upon the willing loyalty of the ruled. The earliest civilisations have been founded upon that devotion. The superstitious magical character of the divine king may pass away, but in its stead a transformed loyalty inspires and upholds the nation. The glamour of the primitive magic-wielder transmits its glow to the patriotic ideal. The Greek warrior lays down his life with the name of his beloved City on his lips ; the Roman citizen bows with the deepest emotions of his soul before his supreme goddess, ' Dea Roma ' ; the English adventurer seeks the farthest corners of the earth and takes possession of them, murmuring, " England, dear England ! "

Those ideal loyalties, which derived in their emotional aspect from the social instincts of the primitive maternal group, in their conceptual aspect from the magical ideas of the savage, are in our intellectualised age inevitably losing much of their force ; their significance has grown feeble. They have been reformulated as abstract principles, a process which generally constitutes the last mortuary rites of a sentiment that was once living. The condition of Western societies appears to many parlous and precarious ; meditation concerning their constitution is concerned at the present time with remedies and prescriptions for their restoration rather than with enquiries into their nature and origin. Schemes of social reform and readjustment of economic foundations are rife. While conservative statesmen are devising props that may consolidate the structure, there are not a few who are in favour of pulling the whole thing down ; the ingenuity of both schools is alike directed towards the restoration or reconstruction of the social edifice. The conditions which call forth those schemes and that anxiety are due in part to the enfeeblement of the sentimental bonds that held the social structure together, and without which none has hitherto contrived to exist. Human society did not arise as an organisation of adjusted interests. It arose out of an extra-rational sentiment ; it has never existed in any form except through the binding force of such sentiments. The aggregate in which they have lost their force and reality is but a skeleton out of which life has departed ; and, though it may endure a while by virtue of the momentum acquired from organic and vital forces, it must before long crumble down into its constituent dust of individual units.

Not the ' family ' necessarily, but the sentiment that constitutes the warp and woof of social structure, is the foundation of society. The adjustment of interests, the organisation of industry and trade, the fine regulation of economic efficiency, of competition, of cooperation, the devices of government, the schemes of economists, the resources of policy, the guarantees of power, of wealth, of enterprise, of talent—these do not make a society. Its foundations lie in what intellect cannot create, nor science devise, or enterprise achieve, and no wealth can purchase. They lie beyond the sphere of intellect and device, in sentiments and emotions without which the most skilfully contrived Utopia can be no more than a wooden automaton. The animating soul of the organised society lies outside the ' ordinary activities ' of life. Some think of that extra-rational foundation of the social structure as religious faith ; others regard it as the eternal hope of the ideal, the inspiration of art and of thought ; others again see it in charity and love. Upon such faith, upon such hope, upon such charity, every human society has ultimately rested. But the greatest of these is charity.

As the human mind rests upon other foundations than those which are consciously formulated and perceived, so human society is in the last resort founded upon relations other than those which constitute the scheme of political and economic organisation. The theorist conceives it as an association of individuals, of corporations, of classes, of rulers and ruled, of rich and poor, of workers and of holders of capital. But in its primary biological character— and to biological facts appeal must in the last resort be made— human society is none of those things ; it is an association of men and women. Like every biological aggregate it has primarily developed as a group having reproductive functions. From those functions the bonds of sentiment which constitute its psychological basis are derived ; it is as a reproductive group that it has acquired its human characters. If in the foregoing studies the relations between the sexes, the social and psychological phenomena included under the terms ' marriage ' and ' sexual morality ' have chiefly called for attention, it is from no morbid bias for that aspect. Biologically human society is a group of males and females ; all else is superstructure. When the ideal transformations of the primary social sentiments have lost in a large measure their efficacy and validity as bonds of the social aggregate, scientific thought is thrown back upon the primal forms of which those ideal sentiments are but pale reflections. The elements of its constitution which the society, the civilised State, whose ideal loyalties are on the wane, can least afford to ignore, are those upon which its structure was primarily built, the relations between men and women. It must hark back to fundamentals.

The facts of social evolution are the indispensable guide to any valid estimate of social problems. Society is not made up of economic units, but of human souls ; and the human soul is in turn the product of social history, more especially in its primitive and uncultured phases. In that evolution the mind of man has been moulded ; it is the traditional heredity of the race that has transformed its biological impulses into human characters, thoughts, sentiments. Unless the factors and elements of social life are known in their origin and development, unless the motives and purposes which they have served in the past are discerned, speculative thought gropes in darkness. Social life, like the human mind, consists of two sets of facts ; biological facts antecedent to tradition and culture, which are common to humanity and to all life, and products brought into being by social evolution and traditional heredity. The latter have modified the biological elements of human life, the inherited instincts, the primary relations, to such a degree that they are often scarcely discernible under the rich superstructure. But they are the ultimate foundations. Social products and social tradition may transform them out of all recognition ; it has adapted them to new purposes and to new achievements ; but it cannot abolish them. The social inheritance is as real and indestructible as the biological ; it is well-nigh omnipotent ; but it cannot ignore or defy biological facts. As often as it attempts to do so its efforts are fraught with failure and disaster. It is the function of social evolution to utilise and adapt biological forces ; it cannot set them at nought. To distinguish clearly between the two orders of elements, which are constantly liable to be misapprehended and confounded, is the supreme contribution of scientific thought on the subject. We shall have learnt the most valuable lesson which the study of social anthropology has to teach if we are able to distinguish what is primal and founded upon vital laws and functions from the mutable products of traditional inheritance.

But that is not to say that the history of social sentiments can supply ready-made diagnoses and prescriptions. Many appear to think that everything which is ' natural ' must therefore be good, that everything which is ' artificial ' must on that account be worthless. No delusion could be more fantastic. The most precious things in our human heritage are products of social evolution, and what is ' natural ' is for the most part bestial. Because a given sentiment has its roots in what appear to us puerile and absurd superstitions or barbaric claims, it by no means follows that it is destitute of value. In the foregoing pages it has frequently been contended that a given institution or sentiment owed not its origin

to the exalted conceptions and high motives which are associated
with it, but to much more trivial and, in our eyes, baser and less
worthy causes.　But if it be supposed that to trace it to a humbler
origin is to detract from the intrinsic worth of the social or psychological product, the relation of human values is profoundly mis-
understood.　From the point of view of the uses and benefits which
we may hope to derive from the scientific study of human phenomena, one principle should, as regards the intrinsic values of those
phenomena, be ever in view—" Judge not."　There is no element in
our social heritage which, in its effects and products, is wholly good
or wholly bad ; most of the conceptions and sentiments, the foundations of which have been laid down in primitive society, have been
at once the sources of great good and of great evil.　We cannot
have the one without the other.　Many, in inveighing against the
folly and injustice that offend them, are unwittingly denouncing
that which they most highly prize.　The restrictions imposed upon
the sexual instincts by primitive tabus, by superstition, by barbaric
selfishness, by the delusions of fanaticism, have so transformed the
manifestations of those instincts that it is impossible for them to
operate in civilised man in the same manner as in primitive
humanity.　Those restrictions have created sentiments that are
unknown to the savage.　He knows not love as the banking up
of primitive passions into one channel, and the synthesis of
cultural aspirations that derive their moving force from the racial
instincts have created it.　And even though the confined and
concentrated flood may beat about the banks and its course be
full of storm and pain, few would readily forgo the baptism of its
living waters.　But the causes that have exalted and sublimated
primal instincts have also given rise to the mephitic products which
result from their simultaneous stimulation and thwarting.　Restric-
tive sexual morality which has aimed at purity and chastity has
been the source of vice and morbid lubricity.　European morality
places a tabu on the sexual instincts at the time when these are first
developing and when their operation is most potent ; it is a psychological law that whatever form the first manifestations of those
instincts may assume will be indelibly impressed upon the whole
sexual life of the individual.　It is poisoned at its source.　Thus it
is that civilised man imparts to uncultured races morals and vice at
one and the same time, reforms and corrupts them with the same
breath.

　Those features of social evolution, whether in uncultured or
in civilised societies that seem best or worst, are equally fraught
with good and evil.　When we contemplate the social condition of a
primitive society, we perceive features that seem better, more
desirable than the corresponding traits in the society in which we
live.　We are prone to jump to the conclusion that uncultured man

managed these things better, and that the panacea for the evils that beset civilisation is a return to simpler conditions. Hence the cry of ' Back to nature ! ' But to men and women whose soul is the product of an evolution that has transcended the conditions of primal instincts and primitive irrationality, these would for the most part be intolerable and revolting.

And even were it desirable to return to simpler phases, to do so is impossible. Traditional heredity is as indestructible as is natural heredity ; what it has once created can no more be annihilated than the bodily form of man can be altered into that of his marine progenitors. The products of traditional heredity can be modified, adapted ; their original meaning and force may be lost ; but their imprint persists and can never be effaced. We are the heirs of all the ages ; we are ruled by the dead—" los muertos mandan ! " [1] Our material and social culture may conceivably be simplified, but the complexity of our minds cannot be changed. If we were to go into the woods and hunt game with bows and arrows, and our women should make the pots and tend the cabbages, we should carry with us into the wilderness the infinite complexity of the modern mind, which would only be increased by our attempts at adaptation.

The present time offers, as regards the relations between the sexes, an exceptional and perhaps unprecedented situation. The process of intellectual criticism, which has destroyed the validity of many time-honoured elements in our traditional heredity, and swept away ancient claims, has extended to women. In our advanced patriarchal society the fundamental patriarchal principles have, in the eyes of many women as well as of many men, lost their ancient axiomatic authority. The modern woman is ' emancipated ' from the traditional fiction, and looks upon it with the scorn of the neophyte of free-thought who has just ' found out ' his old creed   We live in a patriarchal society in which patriarchal principles have ceased to be valid. The situation is far too complex to be immediately grasped in all its bearings by emancipated woman herself, far less by man. She has heard of primitive matriarchal societies. But any return to the conditions of those societies is as impossible as a return to the Stone Age. Women can never be the chief economic producers and controllers as they were in the housekeeping stage of material culture. Many aim, as a compromise, at economic independence ; the avocations of men can be taken up by women, thus abolishing to some extent the economic lever upon which patriarchal dominance is founded. But that ' equality ' of productive economy is a very different thing from the primitive economic monopoly of women. It is not even a com-

---

[1] The title of one of Señor V. Blasco Ibañez's novels.

promise between it and patriarchal feminine dependence ; for the economic advantage of women in primitive society was part of a strict division of labour, and was, as such, part of the structure of the reproductive group. Productive economic independence as the modern feminist woman conceives it cannot be a part of sex relations as at present established ; it is even flatly opposed to them. Either the woman worker eventually marries, thus return- ing to patriarchal conditions ; or she adopts other forms of sex relations than patriarchal marriage. The situation is more funda- mental than appears on the surface. It is manifest that if the tendencies which have led to the emancipation of women from patriarchal tradition and principles continue to operate, patriarchal marriage itself must undergo modifications.

Patriarchal marriage in its Christian form has combined the economic with the sexual aspect of the association between man and woman. But both those aspects have undergone transforma- tion ; they no longer bear the same values as when they were distinct. The economic relation, instead of consisting in productive contribution from both the man and the woman, and association between them in the primitive division of labour, consists in the maintenance of the woman by the man. The sexual aspect of the relation has been even more profoundly transmuted by the develop- ment of new sentiments. Such has been that development that the recognised and just moral grounds of the marriage association have become shifted from the economic to the sentimental aspect. The former constituted primitively the overt motive for the association ; in modern humanity the woman who sells herself for her maintenance acts immorally. And that estimate is justified ; it is even the basic fact of the problem. However much the senti- ment of sexual love may owe to social and cultural evolution, it is the derivative of the forces that have originated human develop- ment. As such it takes precedence in social as in individual life ; it is the biological price which woman herself offered for the man's permanent association and cooperation in her functions. The woman who deliberately sets aside the basic ground of that associa- tion contributes to the undoing of the fabric of which women have been the founders ; and the association is not in the sense of tabu-values, but of the deepest realism, immoral.

The future of the relation between the sexes and of marriage institutions lies with women. Some suppose that it is a matter of legislative action. But all legislative regulation of sexual associa- tions derives from the same principle as the barbaric claims which regarded them as subject to the authority of the tribe, of rulers, or of parents, and which produced infant-betrothal and marriage by purchase. Such institutions and the conclusion of marriages by external parties are unobjectionable in primitive societies where personal sentiments are undeveloped and economic considerations alone count. But in our societies a sexual association deriving no sanction from the sentiments of the parties to the association is immoral. Legislative action which prescribes a form of marriage and overrides the personal agreement of the parties involved, stands upon the same footing as the Australian tribal council that allots sexual partners or the negro who sells his daughter. Modern legal thought recognises the principle that it is not concerned with sexual morals, but only with safeguarding economic rights and relations, and protecting individuals against prejudicial action. But the law of civilised countries has not yet adapted itself consistently to that principle; marriage is still an 'institution,' and is thought of as resting upon legal sanctions, whereas it rests solely upon the mutual agreement and sentiments of the parties, and the State has no other function in the matter than to register that agreement. It is not the concern of the State to institute any form of marriage, or to put down any form of sex relations so long as the parties involved are responsible and consenting, and the transactions cause no manifest prejudice to others. That is the fundamental objection against established marriage systems which perpetuate the traditional character of marriage as an institution. It was such under other conditions; but it cannot be so when the only validity and moral foundation of the union lie in the sentiments and feelings of the men and women who enter into it. People are either united by love and agreement, or they are united by an 'institution,' and if the latter is the only bond of union, it comes near to being synonymous with prostitution. Legislative action cannot hence institute new forms of marriage. When the State oversteps its function and prescribes a standard for all, it is forcing the most complex manifestations of human nature into a rigid mould. It is not towards a new form, but towards new forms of marriage that existing conditions point. Individual men and women differ profoundly in their fitness for one form or other of sexual association; what is in a given instance desirable is quite unsuitable in others. Some women are by nature and temperament patriarchal wives, others are 'hetairai.' Moral judgments and intellectual scorn are here irrelevant; they will not make the 'hetaira' an ideal housewife, or the perfect housewife an ideal sexual companion.

The lifelong union of one man with one woman constitutes the ideal sex relation, the highest and most precious that life can offer. But, like all ideals, its adequate realisation is beset with all manner of difficulties, and demands both special qualifications and provident effort on the part of those who would achieve it. The ordinary cause of its failure is the ignorant assumption, perpetuated by traditional dogma and fostered by sentimentalising pseudo-science, that it is a ' natural ' relation founded on biological functions, and that marriage, once concluded, can be left to the spontaneous operation of those functions. Marriage is, on the contrary, not a biological, but a social product. It is a compromise and an adaptation of biological facts. And great as is the power of traditional heredity, it cannot alter ultimate biological facts. Transient unions conflict, on the other hand, as deeply with the most valued sentiments that human evolution has created. No ' new form of marriage ' is devisable that shall be of universal applicability to all men and women, bestowing perfect harmony on their relations, proof against all inadaptations. For human mating is not a biological function, but the complex product of many streams of social and cultural evolution, and the disharmony between it and the contrasted primal instincts of men and women cannot be completely obliterated. Tragedy and suffering will continue, love will be attended with pain.

Social evolution, which has its origin in the association and cooperation of the sexes, has accentuated the fundamental opposition between their respective aims and interests. That antagonism is rooted in the profound biological differences between the functions of the reproductive instincts in each—periodic rearing of offspring in the one sex, maximum dissemination of the breed in the other ; and it extends to the entire mentality of each sex, which is coloured by the reproductive functions. Complete identity of interests is never spontaneously possible ; the self-protective individualistic instincts of each sex cannot be laid aside, the male and the female are compelled to remain on their guard against the incompatible instincts of the opposite sex. That primal opposition is enormously increased in human society, that is, in the association of the opposed sexes. Among animals there is little association, and still less cooperation ; both sexes are self-supporting and independent. One of the first results of human association was to create a sharp division of economic labour between the sexes, which rendered them for the first time economically interdependent. The patriarchal order of society in turn abolished that primitive division of labour, and thus brought about the economic dependence of women. In the primitive division of labour spontaneous adjustment resulted in a mutual collective loyalty that was well-nigh unbounded. In existing society there is scarcely a collective social interest common to both sexes. The spheres of masculine activity cannot in general be regarded by women as much more than means to the ends of their primal interests— means to independence, means to the male's subservience to their functions. The world of man's activity is the product of quite other forces than those which actuate woman. It is not of her making ; the enterprise and ambition of the combative male

are alien to her. Her primal instincts do not readily translate
themselves into intellectualised surrogates, or, if they do, never
depart widely from their direct and primary objects. Women
are said to have no ideals. The racial instincts that sublimate
themselves into ideals are, indeed, too real and engrossing in
woman to suffer transformation ; she views ideals concretely
and realistically. Man's intellectualised outlook and activity is
as much his peculiar sphere and outside that of the women of a
patriarchal society as the hunter's and the warrior's pursuits were
outside the sphere of primitive woman. But the woman of patriarchal society has none of the complementary share in the economic
social fabric that primitive woman had. She has but her sex.
The relation, collective and individual, between the sexes thus
acquires an intensified individualism. Whether she aims at freedom
and independence or a home and children, woman is thrown back
on the defence of her own interests ; she must defend herself against
man's attempt to bind her, or sell herself to advantage. Woman is
to man a sexual prey ; man is to woman an economic prey. The
free woman's interests do not lie in the ambitions or in the racial
ideals of men, but in the guarding of her freedom and in the individualistic use of it on her behalf. The marrying woman's interests
are still less concerned with the goals of the masculine world except
in so far as they may be the means of the male's efficient performance of his function towards her. Loyalty and devotion she can
readily give to him, but not to racial aims and ideals. So long as
women were altogether subordinate, so long as society retained its
thoroughgoing patriarchal character, and masculine aims and
activities alone counted, the dissociation of women from those
aims and activities was of no great moment. With the weakening
of patriarchal principles the rift of sex antagonism is added to the
disintegrating individualistic forces which, in the decay of other
bonds of loyalty, make for dissolution.

In a clearer view of facts lies the hope of meliorism. Men have
much of the 'patriarchal theory' to unlearn. Women have to
learn that all racial ideals that are worth while are ultimately
identical with their own elemental instincts, and are the outcome
of them.

The path towards a solution of the problems arising out of the
relations of the sexes lies in the understanding of their causes and
in mutual cooperation. Whether in the social aspect of the relation between the two sex-classes that constitute human society
or in the personal aspect of the association between man and
woman, no advantage can accrue to either sex from the accentuation of sex antagonism, from the self-defensive attitude of
individualistic interests, from the endeavour to impose the aims of
its own instincts upon the opposite sex. All such association is a

compromise, as all the sentiments that have gone to establishing it have been compromises and surrenders of individualism. Maternal love is sacrifice. Love is the expression of that subordination of individualism which has created human society.

Men and women must view with sympathy, not with antagonism, one another's standpoint and the causes that have produced them. Thus may they cooperate in the eternal effort to follow ideals and face realities. The compromises that govern the relations between the sexes are those that condition all true human values. The masculine intellect has battled for its freedom from the dead hand of the irrational heritage bequeathed by a distant past. What is vital and redeeming in that heritage is the outcome of the primal love that created humanity, and upon its first foundation human life and human relations still ultimately stand. It is, as of old, the part of the Vestal Mothers to tend the Sacred Fires. Upon women falls the task not only of throwing off their own economic dependence, but of rescuing from the like thraldom the deepest realities of which they were the first mothers. Women are the repositories of those values. Upon the rude foundations which they laid the restless energy of man has reared a mighty structure ; but the loftier and more complex that structure, the greater the danger in which it stands of crushing the realities of existence. As with the social, so with the structure of the individual life. Power, energy, ambition, intellect, the interests of the combative male, no more achieve the fulfilment of his being than they can of themselves build up a human society. The life that has centred upon those aims finds some day that its achievements have been barren, its idols hollow. " Grey is all theory, green life's golden tree." In the love of the mother, in the mutual devotion of man and woman, the achievements of the organising and constructive intellect fade into mist. These be the primal loyalties. They are, as they have ever been, in the keeping of the women, and in theirs alone. Woe to the woman who makes light of them and tramples upon them ; she merits every anathema that has been pronounced upon womanhood. Honour to the women who can exercise their functions as befits the richer and more complex, if more strenuous and difficult, conditions, which distinguish present human culture from its beginnings ; honour to those who can be mothers, not in the flesh alone, but in the spirit, who can choose, praise, and encourage aright, not only in that function of sexual selection which has always been theirs, but in the selection also of what is truest and best in the complex aims, ideals, and efforts of humanity.

In the Second Part of ' Faust ', Goethe, recalling those threefold, nameless, or many-named divinities who appear in the most ancient beliefs of European peoples, ruling human destinies, dispensing life and death, bringing forth and nursing the gods, referred in mystic terms to The Mothers that dwell beyond space and time, and from whom the manifestations of life proceed as a timeless phantasmagoria of phenomena generated from the abiding reality of their spirit.   The conception applies equally to the racial spirit of Motherhood, of which the higher avatars of human life are derivative manifestations.   And with the symbolic thought of the great poet our long journey may fittingly conclude—

> In your name, ye MOTHERS! who upon the throne
> Of the Illimitable dwell eternally alone—
> Yet not uncompanied. Life's Idols swarm
> About you, lifeless, yet in lifelike form ;
> What has been is, and shall be ; for with you
> Abide what things are ageless, unfading, ever new.

BIBLIOGRAPHY

Aa, Pieter van der, *Naaukeurige versameling der gedenk-waardigste zee- en land-reysen na Oost- en West-Indien*. 28 vols. Leyden, 1707–8.
  Recueil de divers voyages curieux faits en Tartarie, en Perse et ailleurs. 2 vols. Leiden, 1729.
Aa, Pieter J. B. C. Robidé van der, *Reizen naar Nederlandsch Nieuw-Guinea ondernomen in de jaren 1871, 1872, 1875–76, door P. van der Crab en J. E. Teysmann*, etc. 's Gravenhage, 1879.
Abadie, Maurice, " Les Mân du Haut Tonkin," *Revue d'Ethnographie et des Traditions populaires*. Vol. iii. Paris, 1922.
Abbad y Lasiera, Fray Inigo, *Historia geografica, civil y natural de la isla de San Juan Bautista de Puerto Rico*. Porto Rico, 1866.
Abbes, H., " Die Eskimos des Cumberland-Sundes," *Globus*. Vol. xlvi. Braunschweig, 1884.
Abbott, Charles C., *A Naturalist's Rambles about Home*. New York, 1884.
Abbott, G. F., *Macedonian Folklore*. Cambridge, 1905.
'Abd Allah ibn Abd al Kadir, munshi. *Voyage de Abd-Allah ben Abd-el Kader de Singapore à Kalantan*. Traduit par Ed. Dulaurier. Paris, 1850.
Abd-er-Razzak, " Narrative of the Journey of Abd-er-Razzak," in R. H. Major, *India in the Fifteenth Century*. London, 1857.
Abeghian, Manuk, *Der armenische Volksglaube*. Leipzig, 1899.
Abel, C. W., *Savage Life in New Guinea*. London, 1901.
Abelsdorff, G., and others, *Krankheiten und Ehe*. Munich, 1904.
Abercromby, Hon. John, *The Pre- and Proto-Historic Finns*. 2 vols. London, 1898.
  " Marriage Customs of the Mordvins," *Folk-lore*. Vol. i. London, 1890.
  A Study of the Bronze Age Pottery of Great Britain and Ireland and its associated Grave-goods. 2 vols. Oxford, 1902.
  "The Prehistoric Pottery of the Canary Islands and its Makers," *Journal of the Royal Anthropological Institute*. Vol. xliv. London, 1914.
Abès, M., " Les Izayan d'Oulmes," *Archives Berbères*. Vol. i. Paris, 1916.
  " Les Ait Ndhir (Beni Mtir)," *ibid*. Vol. ii. Paris, 1917.
Abhandlungen der historischen Classe der Königlichen Bayerischen Akademie der Wissenschaften. München, 1832–
Abhandlungen der Königlichen Akademie der Wissenschaften. Berlin, 1815–
Abhandlungen der Königlichen Gesellschaft der Wissenschaften. Göttingen, 1843–
Abhandlungen der Königlichen Sächsischen Gesellschaft der Wissenschaften. Leipzig, 1850–
Abhandlungen des Kolonialinstituts. Hamburg, 1910–

Abhandlungen und Berichte des Königliches zoologisches und anthropologisch-ethnologisches Museum zu Dresden. Berlin, 1887–

Abrahams, Israel, *Jewish Life in the Middle Ages.* London, 1896.

Abrams, A., *English Life and Manners in the Later Middle Ages.* London, 1913.

Abreu de Galindo, Juan de, *Historia de la conquista de las sietes islas de Gran Canaria (Biblioteca Isleña,* entregas, 10, 11). Santa Cruz de Tenerife, 1848.

The History of the Discovery and Conquest of the Canary Islands. Transl. by G. Glas. London, 1764.

Abt, Adam, *Die Apologie des Apuleius von Madaura und die antike Zauberei.* (A. Dieterich und R. Wensch, *Religionsgeschichtlich Vesuche und Vorarbeiten.* Vol. iv, Hft. 2.) 1903.

Abu'l Fadah, Ismail ibn Ali, *Historia Anteislamica.* Ed. H. O. Fleischer. Leipzig, 1831.

La Géographie d'Aboulféda traduite de l'Arabe en Français, par M. Reinaud. 2 vols. Paris, 1848–83.

Abu'l Ghazi, Bedadur Khan, *Histoire des Mongols et des Tartares.* Ed. Baron Des Maisons. 2 vols. St. Petersburgh, 1871–74.

Histoire généalogique des Tartars. Leyden, 1726.

A General History of the Turks, Moguls and Tartars. 2 vols. London, 1729–30.

Abu'l Hasan, 'Ali ibn 'Abd Allah ibn Abi Zar, *Annales Regum Mauritaniae.* Ed. C. J. Tornberg, 1843.

An Account of the Present State of Northern Asia (vol. ii of Abu'l Ghazi, *General History of the Turks,* etc.). London, 1830.

Achery, Luc d', *Veterum aliquot scriptorum, maxime Benedictinorum, latuerant Spicilegium* . . . 13 vols. Parisiis, 1655–77.

Achilles Tatius, *Isagoge ad arati phenomena,* in D. Petau, *Uranologion.* Lutetia Parisiorum, 1630.

Acosta, Joseph d', *The Naturall and Morall Historie of the East and West Indies.* London, 1604.

Acta Joannis. Ed. Th. Zahn. Erlangen, 1880.

Acta Sanctorum Bollandiana. Brussels, 1643–

Acta Societatis Scientiarum Fenicae. Helsingfors, 1842–

Actes de la Société d'Ethnographie américaine et orientale. Paris, 1860–

Actes de la Société scientifique de Chili. Santiago, 1892–

Adair, James, *The History of the American Indians.* London, 1775.

Adam, Lucien, *Le parler des hommes et des femmes dans la langue Caraïbe.* Paris, 1890.

Adams, J., *A Treatise on the supposed Hereditary Properties of Diseases.* London, 1814.

Adanson, Michel, *Histoire naturelle du Sénégal. Coquillages. Avec la relation abrégée d'un voyage fait en ce pays.* Paris, 1757.

Adenés li Rois, *Bueves de Commarchis.* Ed. Aug. Scheler. Bruxelles, 1874.

Adian, M. J., "Les troubadours et l'Angleterre," *Bulletin de la Société des Lettres, Sciences et Arts de la Corrèze.* Tulle, 1920.

Adjà îb al-Hind, *Les Merveilles de l'Inde. Ouvrage arabe inédit du Xe siècle.* Transl. by L. M. Devic. Paris, 1878.

Adler, H., "Über den Generationswechsel der Eichen-Gallwespen," *Zeitschrift für wissenschaftlichen Zoologie.* Vol. xxxv. Leipzig, 1881.

Adriani, N., "Mededeelingen omtrent de Toradjas van Midden-Celebes," *Tijdschrift voor Indische taal-, land- en volkenkunde.* Vol. xliv. Batavia, 1901.

and Kruijt, A. C., *De Bare's-sprekende Toradja's van Midden-Celebes.* 3 vols. 's-Gravenhage, 1912–14.

Aduarte, Fray Diego, *The History of the Province of the Holy Rosary, of the Order of Preachers, in Philippines, Japon, and China.* Translated in E. H. Blair and J. A. Robertson, *The Philippine Islands, 1493–1803.* Vols. xxx, xxxi. Cleveland, 1905.

Aelfric, *Lives of Saints.* Ed. by W. W. Skeat. (*Early English Texts Society.*) London, 1881.

Aelianus, *De natura animalium; Varia historia; Epistolae; Fragmenta.* Rec. R. Hucker. Paris, 1858.

Aeschines, *Orationes,* in *Oratores Attici.* Ed. J. G. Baiterus and H. Sauppe. Vol. iii. Turici, 1850.

Aeschylus, *Tragoediae.* Ed. E. A. I. Ahrens. Parisiis, 1842.

Afrika-Bote. Loewenberg, 1895–

L'Afrique Française. Paris, 1909–

Agassiz, Alexander, "Notes of Beaver Dams," *Proceedings of the Boston Society of Natural History.* Vol. xiii. Boston, 1871.

Agathias, *Historiarum libri v.* Bonnae, 1828.

Agrippa, Henricus Cornelius, *De occulta philosophia.* Coloniae, 1533.

Aguilar, Pedro Sanchez de, "Informe contra idolorum cultores del obispado de Yucatan," *Anales del Museo Nacional.* Vol. vi. Mexico, 1900.

Ahlqvist, A., *Die Kulturwörter der westfinnischen Sprachen.* Helsingfors, 1875. "Unter Wogulen und Ostjaken," *Acta Societatis Scientiarum Fennicae.* Vol. xiv. Helsingfors, 1885.

Ahmad Shah, *Four Years in Tibet.* Benares, 1906.

Aiol, chanson de geste. Ed. Jacques Normand et Gaston Raynaud. Paris, 1877.

Aita Reya-Āranyaka. See *Upanishads.*

Aiyar, N. S., "The Nayars," in "Ethnographical Appendices," *Census of India, 1901.* Vol. i. Calcutta, 1903.

Akeley, C. E., *In Brightest Africa.* London, 1924.

Alarcon, Hernando Ruiz, "Tratado de las supersticiones y costumbres gentilicas que oy viven entre los Indios naturales desta Nueva España" (1629), *Anales del Museo Nacional.* Vol. vi. Mexico, 1892.

Alberti, L., *De Kaffers aan de Zuidkust van Afrika.* Amsterdam, 1810. *Die Kaffern auf der Südküste von Afrika.* Gotha, 1815.

Albertis, Luigi M. d', *New Guinea.* Transl. 2 vols. London, 1880.

Albiruni, *India.* Transl. by C. E. Sachau. 2 vols. London, 1888.

Al-Bukhari, *Les traditions islamiques.* Tr. O. Houdas and W. Marçais. 4 vols. Paris, 1903–14.

Alciphron, *Epistolae.* Ed. J. A. Wagner. 2 vols. Lipsiae, 1798.

Alcuin, *Epistolae,* in Pertz, *Monumenta Germaniae Historica, Epistolae.* Vol. iv. *Karoli Aevi.* Vol. ii. Berlin, 1895.
Opera, in Migne, *Patrologiae Cursus Completus.* Vols. c, ci. Parisiis, 1851.

Alecsandri, V., *Ballades et chants populaires de la Roumanie (Principautés danubiennes).* Intr. by M. A. Ubicini. Paris, 1855.

Alexander of Aphrodisias, *Problemata,* in *Physici et Medici Graeci minores.* Ed. Ideler. Vol. i. Berlin, 1841.

Alexander, Sir James Edward, *An Expedition of Discovery into the Interior of Africa.* 2 vols. London, 1838.

Alexander, W. D., *A Brief History of the Hawaiian People.* New York, 1899.

Al-Kindi, *The Apology of Al-Kindy.* Tr. by Sir William Muir. London, 1887.

Alldridge, T. J., *The Sherbro and its Hinterland.* London, 1901.
A Transformed Colony, Sierra Leone as it was and as it is. London, 1910.

Allègre, F., *Étude sur la déesse grecque Tyché.* (*Bibliothèque de la Faculté de Lettres de Lyon.* Vol. xiv.) Paris, 1889.

Allen, Joel Asaph, *History of the North American Pinnipeds.* (*United States Geological and Geographical Survey of Territories.*) Washington, 1880.

Allen, John, *Modern Judaism.* London, 1830.

Allen's Naturalist's Library. London, 1894–

Allen, Capt. W. D., and Thomson, Dr. R. H., *A Narrative of the Expedition sent by Her Majesty's Government to the Niger River in 1841.* 3 vols. London, 1876.

Allgemeine Medizinische Central-Zeitung. Altenburg, 1831–

Allgemeine Missions-Zeitschrift. Gütersloh, 1874–

Allison, S. S., "Account of the Similkamean Indians," *Journal of the Anthropological Institute.* Vol. xxi. London, 1892.

Almeida, Manoel de, *Histoire de ce que c'est passé ès Royaume d'Ethiopie en l'année 1626.* Paris, 1629.

Almeida, W. B. d', *Life in Java.* 2 vols. London, 1804.

Almeida Serra, R. F. de, "Sobre os Indios Uiacuru's, Guana's, etc.," *Revista Trimensal do Instituto de Historia e Geographia do Brasil.* Vol. xiii. Rio de Janeiro, 1872.

Alphonso Maria de Liguori, *The Glories of Mary.* Transl. R. A. Coffin. London, 1868.

  The Glories of Mary, Mother of God. Translated from the Italian of Blessed Alphonso Liguori, and carefully revised by a Catholic Priest. Dublin, 1833.

Al-Tabari, Muhammad Abu Jafar ibn Jarir, *Chronique.* Transl. H. Zotemberg. 4 vols. Paris, 1867–74.

Der Alte Orient. Leipzig, 1900–

Al-Tunisi, Muhammad ibn'Umar, *Voyage au Darfour par le Cheykh Mohammed Ebn-Omar El-Tounsy.* Translated by Dr. Perron. Paris, 1845.

Alvarez, Pedro, "Navigation," in G. B. Ramusio, *Navigationi et Viaggi.* Vol. i. Venetia, 1554.

Al-Wakidi, Muhammad ibn'Umar, *Muhammed in Medina ; d.i., Vakidi's Kitab al-Maghazi in verkürzter deutscher Wiedergabe,* von J. Wellhausen. Berlin, 1882.

Aly, W., "Ursprung und Entwicklung der kretischen Zeusreligion." *Philologus.* Vol. lxxi. Leipzig, 1912.

Ambassades mémorables de la Compagnie des Indes Orientales des Provinces Unies vers les Empereurs du Japon. 2 vols. Amsterdam, 1680.

Ambrose, St., *Opera omnia,* in Migne, *Patrologiae Cursus Completus.* Vols. xiv–xvii. Paris, 1845.

Ambrosetti, Juan B., "Die Kaïngang in Argentinien," *Globus.* Vol. lxxiv. Braunschwieg, 1898.

Ameer Ali, Syed, *A Short History of the Saracens.* London, 1900.

  Personal Law of the Mahommedans. Mahommedan Law compiled from Authorities in the original Arabic. Vol. ii, containing the Law relating to Succession and Status. Calcutta, 1908.

  Woman in Islam. Lahore, 1893.

Amélineau, E., *Prolégomènes à l'étude de la religion égyptienne.* Paris, 1889.

The American Anthropologist. Vols. i–xi. Washington, 1888–1898 ; New Series, New York and Lancaster, 1899–

The American Antiquarian and Oriental Journal. Cleveland, 1878–

The American Journal of Psychology. Worcester, 1888–

The American Journal of Semitic Languages and Literatures. Chicago, London, Leipzig, 1895–

The American Journal of Theology. Chicago, 1897–

The American Naturalist. Salem, Philadelphia and Boston, 1868–

Amicis, Edmondo de, *Constantinople*. Transl. London, 1878.

Amira, Karl von, *Erbenfolge und Verwandschafts-Gliederung nach den alt-niederdeutschen Rechten*. München, 1874.

" *Amis et Amile,*" und " *Jourdains de Balivies.*" Ed. C. Gofman. Erlangen, 1882.

Amman, Jan Coenraad, *Surdus Loquens ; seu, Methodus, qua qui surdus natus est loqui discere possit*. Amstelodami, 1692.

Ammianus Marcellinus, *Rerum gestarum libri qui supersunt*. Rec. V. Gardthausen. 2 vols. Lipsiae, 1874–75.

Ampelius, Lucius, *Liber memorialis*. Rec. E. Woelfflied. Lipsiae, 1854.

Analecta Bollandiana. Bruxelles, 1882–

Anales de la Biblioteca Nacional. Buenos Aires, 1900–

Anales de la Real Sociedad de Historia Natural. Madrid, 1872–

Anales de la Sociedad Científica Argentina. Buenos Aires, 1876–

Anales de la Universidad de Chile. Santiago ; Valparaiso, 1846–

Anales del Museo Nacional de Arqueologia, Historia y Etnologia. Mexico, 1877–

Anantha Krishna Iyer, L. K., *The Cochin Tribes and Castes*. 2 vols. Madras, 1909–12.

Anchieta, Padre José d', "Informaçao dos casamentos dos Indios do Brasil," *Revista Trimensal de Historia e Geographia*. Vol. vii. Rio de Janeiro, 1846.

Ancient Egypt. London, 1914–

Ancient Laws and Institutes of England. London, 1840.

Ancient Laws and Institutes of Ireland. Dublin and London, 1865–79.

Ancient Laws and Institutes of Wales. London, 1841.

Ancona, A. di, and Comparetti, D., *Le antiche rime volgari*. 5 vols. Bologna, 1875–88.

Andagoya, Pascual de, *Relacion de los sucesos de Pedrarias Dávila en las provincias de Tierra firme ó Castilla del oro*, etc., in M. Fernandez de Navarrete, *Coleccion de los viages*, etc. Vol. iii. Madrid, 1829.

    Narrative of the Proceedings of Pedrarias Davila in the Province of Tierra Firme, etc. Trans. by Sir C. R. Markham (*Hakluyt Soc.*). London, 1865.

Anderson, John, *A Report of the Expedition to Western Yunan via Bhamô*. Calcutta, 1871.

    Mandalay to Momien. London, 1876.

Anderson, G. W., *A New Collection of Voyages round the World, containing an authentic history of Captain Cook's First, Second, Third and Last Voyages*. London, 1784.

Anderson, R. G., "Some Tribal Customs in Relation to Medicine and Morals of the Nyam-Nyam and Gour People inhabiting the Eastern Bar-El-Gazhal," *First Report of the Wellcome Tropical Research Laboratory*. Khartum, 1911.

    " Medical Practices and Superstitions amongst the People of Kordofan," *Third Report of the Wellcome Tropical Research Laboratories*. Khartum, 1908.

Andersson, C. J., *Lake Ngami*. London, 1856.

Andocides, in *Oratores Attici*. Ed. I. Bekker. Vol. i. Oxford, 1822.

Andraud, Paul, *La vie et l'oeuvre du troubadour Raimon de Miraval, étude sur la littérature et la société méridionales à la veille de la guerre des Albigeois*. Paris, 1902.

Andreas, *Andreae capellani regii Francorum De Amore libri tres*. Rec. E. Trojel. Habniae, 1892.

Andree, Richard, *Ethnographische Parallele und Vergleiche*. 2 vols. Stutt-
    gart, 1878–89.
  Zur Volkskunde der Juden. Bielefeld, Leipzig, 1881.
Andrews, J. B., in *Revue des Traditions Populaires*. Vol. ix. Paris, 1894.
Andrian, F. von, "Ueber Wortaberglauben," *Correspondenz-Blatt der
    deutsche Gesellschaft für Anthropologie, Ethnologie und Urgeschichte*.
    Jahrg. xxvii. München, Braunschweig, 1896.
Andriezen, W. Lloyd, "The Problem of Heredity with special Reference to
    Pre-Embryonic Life," *The Journal of Mental Science*. Vol. li.
    London, 1905.
Angas, George French, *South Australia Illustrated*. London, 1847.
  Savage Life and Scenes in Australia and New Zealand. 2 vols. London,
    1847.
Anglade, Joseph, *Les Troubadours*. Paris, 1908.
  *Le troubadour Guiraut Riquier, étude sur la décandence de l'ancienne
    poésie provençale*. Paris, 1905.
  Histoire sommaire de la littérature méridionale au moyen-âge. Paris, 1921.
Angus, H. C., "'Chensamwali,' or Initiation Ceremony of Girls as performed
    in Azimba Land, Central Africa," *Verhandlungen der Berliner Gesell-
    schaft für Anthropologie*. Berlin, 1898.
Ankermann, Bernhard, "L'ethnographie actuelle de l'Afrique méridionale,"
    Anthropos. Vol. i. Salzburg, 1906.
Annales Cambriae, in H. Petrie, *Monumenta historica Britannica*. London,
    1848.
Annales de la Propagation de la Foi. Lyon, 1834–
Annales de l'Extrême Orient. Paris, 1879–
Annales de Philosophie Chrétienne. Paris, 1830–
Annales des Missions d'Océanie. Lyon, 1833–
Annales des Sciences Naturelles. Paris, 1824–
Annales du Musée du Congo Belge. Bruxelles, 1898–
Annales du Musée Guimet. Paris, 1880–
Annales Médico-psychologiques. Paris, 1843–
*Annales Regni Francorum inde ab a. 741 ad a. 829, qui dicuntur Annales
    Laurissenses Maiores et Einhardi*. Ed. F. Kurze, in G. H. Pertz,
    Scriptores rerum Germanicarum in usum scholarum. Hanover, 1894.
Annali del Instituto di Corrispondenza Archeologica. Roma, 1829–
Annali del Museo Civico di Storia Naturale di Genoa. Genoa, 1870–
Annals of Archaeology and Anthropology, University of Liverpool. London
    and Liverpool, 1908–
Annandale, N., and Robinson, H. C., *Fasciculi Malayenses*. 2 parts.
    London, 1903–4.
L'Année Sociologique. Paris, 1898–
Annuaire de l'École Pratique des Hautes Études. Paris, 1893–
*Annuaire des établissements français de l'Océanie et du protectorat des îles de
    la Société*. Papeete, 1863–
Annual Archaeological Reports. (*Canadian Institute*.) Toronto, 1888–
The Annual of the British School at Athens. London, 1895–
Annual Report(s) of the Bureau of [American] Ethnology. Washington, 1881–
Annual Report(s) of the Geographical and Natural History Survey of Canada.
    N.S. Ottawa, 1885–
*Annual Report(s) of the Peabody Museum of American Archaeology and
    Ethnology*. Cambridge, Mass., 1868–
[*Annual*] *Report(s) on British New Guinea*. Brisbane, 1889–
Annunzio, Gabriele d', *La Figlia di Iorio*. *Tragedia pastorale*. Milano, 1904.
Anquetil Du Perron, A. H., *Zend-Avesta*. 2 vols. Paris, 1771.

The Antananarivo Annual and Madagascar Magazine. Antananarivo, 1875–

Anthologia Graeca, Res. Brunck and F. Jacobs. 13 vols. Lipsiae, 1794–1814.

Anthropological Essays presented to E. B. Tylor. Oxford, 1907.

Anthropological Papers of the American Museum of Natural History. New York, 1907–

The Anthropological Review. London, 1863.

Anthropos, revue internationale d'ethnologie et de linguistique. Salzburg, etc., 1906–

The Anugîtâ. Trans. by K. T. Telang, *The Sacred Books of the East.* Vol. viii. Oxford, 1898.

Anwyl, Sir Edward, *Celtic Religion in pre-Christian Times.* London, 1906.

" Ancient Celtic Deities," *Transactions of the Gaelic Society of Inverness.* Vol. xxvi. Inverness, 1910.

" Ancient Celtic Goddesses," *The Celtic Review.* Vol. iii. Edinburgh, 1906.

Anz, Wilhelm, " Zur Frage nach dem Ursprung des Gnostizismus," *Texte und Untersuchungen zur Geschichte der altchristlichen Literatur.* Vol. xv. Leipzig, 1897.

Âpastamba. See *Sacred Laws of the Âryas.*

The Apocrypha and Pseudepigrapha of the Old Testament. Edited by R. H. Charles. 2 vols. Oxford, 1913.

Apollodorus, *Bibliotheca.* Ed. R. Wagner, etc. (*Mythographi Graeci.* Vol. i.) Lipsiae, 1894.

" Apollodori Bibliothecae Fragmenta Sabbaitica," *Rheinisches Museum.* Vol. xlvi. Frakfurt a M., 1891.

Apollonius Rhodius, *Argonautica.* Emend. R. Merkel. Lipsiae, 1854.

Appel, C., *Bernart von Ventadorn, seine Lieder mit Einleitung und Glossar.* Halle, 1915.

" L'enseignement de Garin le Brun," *Revue des Langues Romanes.* Vol. xxxiii. Montpellier, 1889.

Poésies prevençales inédites tirées des manuscrits de l'Italie. Paris, Leipzig, 1898.

" Wiederum zu Jaufre Rudel," *Archiv für das Studium der neueren Sprachen und Litteraturen.* Vol. cvii. Braunschweig, 1901.

Appun, K. F., " Die Getränke der Indianer Guayanas," *Globus.* Vol. xviii. Braunschweig, 1870.

" Die Indianer von Britisch-Guayana," *Das Ausland.* Augsburg, 1871.

Apuleius, *Opera omnia.* Rec. G. F. Hildebrand. 2 vols. Lipsiae, 1842.

Arago, J., *Narrative of a Voyage Round the World.* Trans. 2 vols. London, 1823.

Arbois de Jubainville, M. H. d', *Cours de littérature Celtique.* 12 vols. Paris, 1883–1902.

Le Cycle mythologique irlandais et la mythologie celtique (vol. ii. of above). Paris, 1884.

L'Épopée celtique (vol. v of above). Paris, 1892.

Études sur le droit celtique (vol. vii and viii of above). Paris, 1895.

Les Druides et les dieux celtiques à formes d'animaux. Paris, Macon, 1906.

La civilisation des Celtes et celle de l'épopée homérique. Paris, 1899.

La famille celtique. Paris, Macon, 1905.

" Le droit du roi dans l' épopée irlandaise," *Revue archéologique.* Vol. xlii. Paris, 1905.

Arbousset, T., and Daumas, F., *Relation d'un voyage d'exploration au nord-est de la colonie du Cap de Bonne Espérance.* Paris, 1842.

Archäologische Zeitung. Berlin, 1843–

'Αρχαιολογικη 'Εφημερις. Athens, 1862–

Archiv für Anatomie und Physiologie. Berlin, 1884–

Archiv für Anthropologie. Braunschweig, 1866–

Archiv für das Studium der neueren Sprachen und Litteraturen. Braunschweig, 1846–

Archiv für die gesamte Psychologie. Leipzig, 1903–

Archiv für Entwickelungsmechanik der Organismen. Leipzig, 1894–

Archiv für Gynaekologie. Berlin, Leipzig, 1870–

Archiv für Naturgeschichte. Berlin, 1834–

Archiv für Ohrenheilkunde. Würzburg, Leipzig, 1864–

Archiv für Psychiatrie und Nervenkrankheiten. Berlin, 1868–

Archiv für Rassen- und Gesellschaftbiologie. Leipzig, 1904–

Archiv für Religionswissenschaft. Freiburg i. B., 1898–

Archiv für wissenschaftliche Kunde von Russland. Berlin, 1841–

Archives Berbères. Paris, 1916–

Archives de l'Anthropologie criminelle, de criminologie, et de psychologie normale. Paris-Lyon, 1886–

Archives de Médecine Navale. Paris, 1864–

Archives de Zoologie expérimentale et générale. Paris, 1872–

Archives du Muséum d'Histoire Naturelle de Lyon. Lyon, 1872–

Archives Marocaines. Paris, 1904–

Archives of Neurology from the Pathological Laboratory of the London County Asylums. Claybury and London, 1899–

Archives of Ophthalmology and Otology. New York, 1869–

Archives of Pedriatrics. Philadelphia and New York, 1884–

Archives of Philosophy, Psychology, and Scientific Methods. New York, 1905–6.

Archivio italiano di anatomia e di embriologia. Firenze, 1902–

Archivio per l'Antropologia e la Etnologia. Firenze, 1871–

Archivio storico Lombardo. Milano, 1874–

Archivos do Museu Nacional do Rio de Janeiro. Rio de Janeiro, 1876–

Arcin, André, *La Guinée française.* Paris, 1907.

Aristides, Aelius, *Opera.* Rec. G. Dindorf. 3 vols. Leipzig, 1829.

Aristophanes, *Comaediae.* Ed. F. H. M. Blaydes. 12 parts. Halle, 1880–92. *The Comedies.* Edited, translated, and explained by B. B. Rogers. 11 parts. London, 1902–15.

Aristoteles, *Opera omnia.* 5 vols. Parisiis, 1848–74.

Arjan Singh, Sirdar, of Kapurthala, " Early Marriage in India," *The Imperial and Asiatic Quarterly Review.* Third Series, vol. xx. Woking, 1905.

Arkiv för Nordisk Filologi. Christiania, 1883–

Armit, W. E., " Customs of the Australian Aborigines," *Journal of the Anthropological Institute.* Vol. ix. London, 1880.

Árnason, Jóhn, *Íslenzkar þjóðsögur og aefintyri.* 2 vols. Leipzig, 1862–64. *Icelandic Legends.* Trans. 2 vols. London, 1864–66.

Arnaud, R., " Notes sur les montagnards Habe des cercles de Bandiagoro et de Homlori," *Revue d'Ethnographie et des Traditions Populaires.* Vol. iii. Paris, 1922.

Arnaud Daniel. See U. A. Canello.

Arner, G. B. L., *Consanguineous Marriages in the American Population.* (*Columbia University; Studies in History,* etc. Vol. xxxi, No. 3.) New York, 1908.

Arnobius, *Disputationum adversus gentes libri septem,* Migne, *Patrologiae Cursus Completus.* Vol. v. Paris, 1844.

Arnold, Thomas, *Education of Deaf-Mutes*. London, 1888.

Arnould, Louis, *Âmes en prison. L'école française des sourdes-muettes-aveugles et leurs soeurs des deux mondes*. Paris, 1910.

Arpe, Petrus Fridericus, *De prodigiosis naturae et arte operibus, talismanes et amuleta dictis*. Hamburgi, 1717.

Arrhenius, Svante, " Die Einwirkung kosmischer Einflüsse auf physiologischen Verhältnisse," *Skandinavisches Archiv für Physiologie*. Vol. viii. Leipzig, 1896.

" Über den Ursprung des Gestirnkultus," *Scientia*. Vol. ix. Milan, 1911.

Arriaga, Pablo Joseph, *La extirpacion de la idolatria del Piru*. (1621.) (Reprint in *Coleccion de libros y documentos referentes a la historia del Peru*.) Lima, 1920.

Arrian, Flavius, *Expeditionis Alexandri libri septem*. Rec. G. Raphelii. Amsterlaedami, 1757.

Artemidorus, *Oneirocritica*. Ed. J. G. Reiff. 2 vols. Leipzig, 1805.

Arvieux, M. C. Chevalier d', *Mémoires*. 6 vols. Paris, 1735.

Asboth, O., " Ein Hochzeitsbrauch in Südrussland," *Archiv für Anthropologie*. Vol. xiii. Braunschweig, 1881.

Ascherson, " Die Bewohner der kleine Oase in den libyschen Wüste," *Zeitschrift für Ethnologie*. Vol. viii. Berlin, 1876.

Ashe, T., *Travels in America performed in 1806*. London, 1808.

Asiatic Annual Register. London, 1799–

Asiatick Researches. Calcutta, etc., 1788–

Asterius Amasenus, *Encomium in sanctos martyres*, in Migne, *Patrologiae Cursus Completus, Series Graeca*. Vol. xl. Parisiis, 1858.

Astley, T., *A New General Collection of Voyages and Travels*, etc. 4 vols. London, 1745–47.

Athanasius, *Opera omnia quae extant*. Opera monachorum Ord. S. Benedicti. 2 vols. Paris, 1698.

Atharva-Veda.—Atharva-Veda Samhita, translated, with a critical and exegetical commentary, by William Dwight Whitney (*Harvard Oriental Series*. Vols. vii, viii). 2 vols. Cambridge, Mass., 1905.

Hymns of the Atharva-Veda . . . with Commentaries. Transl. by M. Bloomfield. (*The Sacred Books of the East*. Vol. xlvii.) Oxford, 1897.

Ruckert, Fr., *Atharwaweda*. Darmstadt, 1923.

The Hymns of the Atharvaveda. Transl. by R. T. H. Griffith. Benares, 1893.

Athenaeus, *Deipnosophistarum libri quindecim*. J. Casaubon recens. 2 vols. Lugduni, 1657–64.

Athenagoras, *Legatio pro Christianis*, in Migne, *Patrologia Graeca*. Vol. vi. Parisiis, 1857.

Atkinson, Edwin T., *The Himalaya Districts of the North-Western Provinces of India*. (*North-Western Provinces Gazetteers*. Vols. x–xii.) 3 vols. Allahabad, 1882–86.

Atkinson, J. C., " Reason and Instinct," *The Zoologist*. London, 1857.

Atkinson, J. J., " Primal Law," in A Lang and J. J. Atkinson, *Social Origins and Primal Law*. London, 1903.

" Notes on Pointed Forms of Pottery among Primitive Peoples," *Journal of the Anthropological Institute*. Vol. xxiii. London, 1903.

Atkinson, James, *Customs and Manners of the Women of Persia*. London, 1832.

Atkinson, John Christopher, *Forty Years in a Moorland Parish*. London, 1891.

Atkinson, T. W., *Travels in the Regions of the Upper and Lower Amoor*. London, 1860.

Atkinson, Mrs. T. W., *Recollections of Tartar Steppes and their Inhabitants*. London, 1863.

Atti della Reale Accademia archeologica di Napoli. Napoli, 1892.

"Les Attié (Côte d'Ivoire)," par un Missionaire, *Revue d'Ethnographie et des Traditions Populaires*. Vol. iii. Paris, 1922.

Aubrey, John, *Remains of Gentilisme and Judaisme*. Ed. by J. Britten. London, 1881.

Audoenus. See Owen.

Audubon, J. J., and Bachman, J., *The Quadrupeds of North America*. 3 vols. New York, 1856.

Augusti, J. C. W., *Denkwürdigkeiten aus der christliche Archaeologie.* 12 vols. Leipsic, 1817-30.

Augustine, St., *Opera omnia*, Migne, *Patrologiae Cursus Completus*. Vols. xxxii–xlvii. Paris, 1845–49.

Aurelius Victor, Sextus, *Origo gentis Romanae ; De viris illustribus urbis Romae*, etc. ; in B. C. Haurisius, *Scriptores Historiae Romanae Latini Veteres*. Vol. ii. Heidelberg, 1743.

Aus der Anomia. Archäologische Beiträge Carl Robert zur Erinnerung an Berlin dargebracht. Berlin, 1890.

Ausgaben und Abhandlungen aus dem Gebiete der romanischen Philologie. Marburg, 1882.

Das Ausland. München, etc., 1828–

Avebury, Lord (Sir John Lubbock), *The Origin of Civilisation and the Primitive Customs of Man*. 4th edition. London, 1882.

   The Origin of Civilisation. London, 1912.

Avé-Lallemant, Robert, *Reise durch Nord-Brasilien in Jahre, 1859.* 2 vols. Leipzig, 1860.

Avienus, Rufus Festus, *Descriptio Orbis Terrae, Ora maritima, et Carmina minora*, in N. E. Lemaire, *Bibliotheca Classica Latina, Poetae Latini Minores*. Vol. v. Parisiis, 1825.

Avila, Fr. de, *A Narrative of the Errors, False Gods, and other Superstitions and diabolical Rites in which the Indians of the Province of Muazochiri lived in Ancient Times*. Trans. by Sir Clements R. Markham, in *Narratives of the Rites and Laws of the Yncas*. London, 1873.

Authorised Daily Prayer Book of the United Hebrew Congregations of the British Empire, with transl. by R. Simeon Singer. London, 1891.

Aymard, Capt., *Les Touaregs*. Paris, 1911.

Aymonier, Etienne François, *Le Cambodge*. 3 vols. Paris, 1900–4.

   Voyage dans le Laos (Annales du Musée Guimet ; Bibliothèque d'études). 2 vols. Paris, 1895–97.

   "Notes sur les coutumes et croyances superstitieuses des Cambodgiens," *Cochinchine française. Excursions et reconnaissances.* No. xvi. Saigon, 1883.

Azara, Felix de, *Voyage dans l'Amérique méridionale*. 4 vols. Paris, 1809.

Azémar, Père, "Les Stiengs de Brolam," *Cochinchine française. Excursions et reconnaissances.* Vol. xii. Saigon, 1886.

Azzolina, L., *Il dolce stil nuovo*. Palermo, 1903.

B . . . n, "Korte aanstippigen nopens de afdeeling Benkoelen," *Tijdschrift voor Neërlands Indië.* Vol. i. Batavia, 1838.

Baader, B., *Neugesammelte Volksagen aus dem Lande Baden und den angrenzenden Gegenden*. Karlsruhe, 1859.

Baarda, M. J. van, " Fabelen, verhalen en overleveringen der Galelareezen,"
    Bijdragen tot taal-, land- en volkenkunde van Nederlandsch Indië.
    Vol. xlv. 's-Gravenhage, 1895.
Baber (E. Colborne), *Travels and Researches in the Interior of China.* (*Royal
    Geographical Society : Supplementary Papers.*) London, 1886.
Babyloniaca. Paris, 1906–
Babylonian Expedition of the University of Pennsylvania. Ed. H. V.
    Hilprecht. Series A., 30 vols. Philadelphia, 1893–1913.
The Babylonian Talmud. Tractate Berakot. Ed. by A. Cohen. Oxford,
    1921.
Bachofen, Johann Jacob, *Das Mutterrecht.* Basel, 1897.
    *Antiquarische Briefe, vornehmlich zur Kenntniss der ältesten Verwands-
    chaftsbegriffe.* Strassburg, Naumberg, 1880.
    Die Sage von Tanaquil. Heidelberg, Naumberg, 1870.
Back, G., *Narrative of the Arctic Land Expedition to the Mouth of the
    Great Fish River and the Shores of the Arctic Ocean.* London,
    1836.
Backhouse, James, *A Narrative of a Visit to the Australian Colonies.* London,
    1843.
Bader, Clarisse, *La femme dans l'Inde antique.* Paris, 1864.
    La femme Romaine. Paris, 1877.
Badger, George Percy, *The Nestorians and their Ritual.* 2 vols. London,
    1852.
Baedeker, Karl (ed.), *Egypt.* Fifth ed. Leipsic, 1902.
Baegert, Jacob, " An Account of the Aboriginal Inhabitants of the Cali-
    fornian Peninsula," *Smithsonian Report for 1863-64.* Washington,
    1864.
Baessler, A., *Südsee Bilder.* Berlin, 1895.
    Neue Südsee Bilder. Berlin, 1900.
Baessler-Archiv. Berlin, Leipzig, 1911–
Baeyertz, C., " Extracts from an Essay on the Aborigines of Australia,"
    Science of Man, Sydney, 1898.
Bagge, S., " The Circumcision Ceremony among the Naivasha Masai,"
    Journal of the Anthropological Institute. Vol. xxxvi. London,
    1896.
Bailey, John, " An Account of the Wild Tribes of the Veddahs of Ceylon ;
    their Habits, Customs, and Superstitions," *Transactions of the Ethno-
    logical Society of London. New Series.* Vol. ii. London, 1863.
Bainbridge, R. B., "Saorias of the Rajmahal Hills," *Memoirs of the Asiatic
    Society of Bengal.* Vol. ii. Calcutta, 1911.
Baines, J. A., *Census of India, 1891, General Report.* Calcutta, 1893.
Baker, Sir Samuel White, *The Albert N'yanza, and Explorations of the Nile
    Sources.* 2 vols. London, 1867.
    *The Nile Tributaries of Abyssinia, and the Sword Hunters of the Hanran
    Arabs.* London, 1867.
    *Wild Beasts and their Ways, Reminiscences of Europe, Asia, Africa, and
    America.* 2 vols. London, 1890.
Balaguer, Victor, *Historia politica y literaria de los Trovadores.* 6 vols.
    Madrid, 1878–79.
Balbi, Gasparo, *Viaggio dell'Indie Orientali.* Venetia, 1590.
Baldaeus, Philippus, *Naauwkeurige beschrijvinge van Malabar en Choro-
    mandel, der zelver aangrenzende Ryken en Ceijlon.* 3 vols. Amsterdam,
    1672.
Baldwin, J. Mark, *Mental Development in the Child and in the Race.* New
    York, 1895.

Balfour, E., " On a Migratory Tribe of Natives in Central India," *Journal of the Asiatic Society of Bengal.* Vol. xiii. Calcutta, 1844.

Balfour, Edward, *Cyclopaedia of India and of Eastern and South Asia.* 3 vols. London, Edinburgh, 1885.

Balfour, Marie Clothilde, *Examples of printed Folk-lore concerning Northumberland.* (*County Folk-lore.* Vol. iv.) London, 1904.

Ball, J. Dyer, *Things Chinese.* London, 1904.

The Chinese at Home. London, 1911.

Ball, William Platt, *Are the Effects of Use and Disuse Inherited ?* London, 1890.

Banbury, G. A. Lethbridge, *Sierra Leone, or The White Man's Grave.* London, 1888.

Bancroft, H. H., *The Native Races of the Pacific States of North America.* 5 vols. New York, 1875–76.

Bancroft, T. L., " Notes on Mutilations practised by Australian Aborigines," *Journal and Proceedings of the Royal Society of New South Wales.* Vol. xxxi. Sydney, 1897.

Bandelier, Adolf F., *Historical Introduction to Studies among the sedentary Indians of New Mexico* (*Papers of the Archaeological Institute of America, American Series.* Vol. i.) Boston, 1881.

Report of an Archaeological Tour in Mexico (*Ibid.* Vol. ii). Boston, 1881.

Final Report of Investigations among the Indians of the South-western United States. (*Ibid.* Vols. iii and iv.) Cambridge, 1890 and 1892.

Contributions to the History of the South-western Portion of the United States. (*Ibid.* Vol. v.) Cambridge, 1890.

The Delight Makers. New York, 1890.

The Islands of Titicaca and Koati. New York, 1910.

Baraze, Père Cyprien, in *Lettres édifiantes et curieuses.* Vol. viii. Paris, 1781.

Barbas, Josafa, " Viaggio alla Tana," in G. B. Ramusio, *Navigationi et Viaggi.* Vol. ii. Venetia, 1556.

Barbazan, Et., *Fabliaux et Contes des poètes français des xi, xii, xiii, xiv et xv siècles.* 4 vols. Paris, 1808.

Barber, J. T., *A Tour throughout South Wales and Monmouthshire.* London, 1803.

Barbera, Madame de, *Gems and Jewels.* London, 1860.

Barbeyrac, J., *Traité de la morale des Pères de l'Église.* Amsterdam, 1728.

Barbosa, Duarte, " Viaggi," in G. B. Ramusio, *Navigationi et Viaggi.* Vol. i. Venetia, 1564.

Barclay, Edgar, *Mountain Life in Algeria.* London, 1882.

Barclay, W. S., " The Land of Magellanes, with some Account of the Ona and other Indians," *The Geographical Journal.* Vol. xxiii. London, 1904.

Bardesanes, in Eusebius, *Praeparatio Evangelica, q.v.*

Barham, C. N., " Child Marriage in India," *Westminster Review.* Vol. cxxxv. London, 1891.

Baring-Gould, S., *Curious Myths of the Middle Ages.* London, 1897.

Barnart de Ventadorn. See Appel, C.

Barns, T. A., *The Wonderland of the Congo.* London, 1922.

Barret, P., *L'Afrique occidentale.* 2 vols. Paris, 1888.

Barrett, S. M. See Geronimo.

Barrett, W. E. H., "Notes on the Customs and Beliefs of the Wa-Giriama, etc., British East Africa," *Journal of the Royal Anthropological Institute.* Vol. xli. London, 1911.

Barrington Daines, " Experiments and Observations on the Singing of Birds,"
  Philosophical Transactions. Vol. lxiii, part 1. London, 1773.

Barros, Joan de, *Asia : dos fectos que os Portuguezes fizeram no descobrimento
  e conquista dos mares e terras do Oriente*. Lisboa, 1552–53.

  L'Asia, tradotta novamente di lingua Portoghese dal S. A. Ulloa. 2 vols.
  Venice, 1562.

Barrow, Sir John. *Travels in China*. London, 1804.

Barrow, John, " Recent Accounts of the Pitcairn Islanders," *The Journal of
  the Royal Geographical Soicety*. Vol. iii. London, 1834.

Barry, Martin, "Spermatozoa observed within the Mammiferous Ovum,"
  Philosophical Transactions of the Royal Society. London, 1843.

Barsanti, Ottavio, *I Selvaggi dell'Australia*. Roma, 1868.

Bartels, M., " Die spät Lactation," *Verhandlungen der Berliner Gesellschaft
  für Anthropologie*. Berlin, 1896.

Bartels, Olga, " Aus den Leben der weissrussischen Landbevölkerung im
  Gouvernement Smolensk," *Zeitschrift für Ethnologie*. Vol. xxxv.
  Berlin, 1903.

Bartema, Ludovico, *Itinerario*, in G. B. Ramusio, *Navigationi et Viaggi*.
  Vol. i. Venetia, 1554.

  Travels of L. Varthema. Transl. by J. W. Jones. London, 1863.

Barter, Major C., " Notes on Ashanti," *The Scottish Geographical Magazine*.
  Vol. xii. Edinburgh, 1896.

Barth, B., *Liebe und Ehe im altfranzösischen Fabeln und mittelhochdeutschen
  Novelle*. Berlin, 1910.

Barth, Henrich, *Reisen und Entdeckungen in Nord- und Central-Afrika*.
  5 vols. Gotha, 1857–58.

  Travels and Discoveries in North and Central Africa. Transl. 5 vols.
  London, 1857.

Bartholomaeus Anglicus, *De proprietatibus rerum*. Edited by Batman.
  London, 1582.

Barto, Philip Staphan, *Tannhäuser and the Mountain of Venus*. New York,
  1916.

Barton, George Aaron, " Yaweh before Moses," in *Studies in the History of
  Religion presented to Crawford Howell Toy*. New York, 1912.

  A Sketch of Semitic Origins, Social and Religious. New York, 1902.

Barton, Juxon, "Notes on the Suk Tribe of the Kenia Colony,"
  Journal of the Royal Anthropological Institute. Vol. li. London,
  1921.

Bartram, W., " Observations on the Creek and Cherokee Indians," *Transactions of the American Ethnological Society*. Vol. iii. New York,
  1853.

Bartram, William, *Travels through North and South Carolina, Georgia, East
  and West Florida*, etc. Philadelphia, 1791.

Bartsch, K., *Grundriss zur Geschichte der provenzalischen Literatur*. Elberfeld, 1872.

  Chrestomathie provençale. Elberfeld, 1868.

Barua, H. C., *Notes on the Marriage Systems of the Peoples of Assam*.
  Sidsagar, 1909.

Basden, G. T., *Among the Ibos of Nigeria*. London, 1921.

Basedow, Herbert, " Anthropological Notes on the Western Central
  Tribes of the Northern Territory of South Australia," *Transactions
  of the Royal Society of South Australia*. Vol. xxxi. Adelaide, 1907.

  " Anthropological Notes made on the South Australian Government
  North-West Prospecting Expedition, 1903," *Transactions of the Royal
  Society of South Australia*. Vol. xxviii. Adelaide, 1903.

Basil, St., of Caesarea, *Opera omnia*, in Migne, *Patrologiae Cursus Completus, Series Graeca*. Vols. xxix–xxxii. Parisiis, 1857.

Basile, Giambattista, *Der Pentamerone*. Übertragen von Felix Liebrecht. 2 vols. Breslau, 1846.

Bassett, Benjamin, "Fabulous Traditions and Customs of the Indians of Martha's Vineyard," *Collections of the Massachusetts Historical Society*. Vol. i. Boston, 1792.

Li Bastars de Buillon. Ed. Aug. Scheler. Bruxelles, 1877.

Bastian, A., *Der Mensch in der Geschichte*. 3 vols. Leipzig, 1860.

Die Rechtsverhältnisse bei verschiedenen Völkern der Erde. Berlin, 1872.

Geographische und ethnographische Bilder. Jena, 1873.

Die Völker der östlichen Asien. 6 vols. Leipzig, 1866–71.

Inselgruppen in Oceanien. Berlin, 1883.

Allerlei aus Volks- und Menschenkunde. 2 vols. Berlin, 1888.

Die deutsche Expedition an der Loango-Küste. 2 vols. Jena, 1874–75.

Ein Besuch in San Salvador. Bremen, 1859.

Batchelor, John, *The Ainu and their Folk-lore*. London, 1901.

The Ainu of Japan. London, 1892.

Bateman, C. S. L., *The First Ascent of the Kasaï*. London, 1889.

Bates, Daisy M., "The Marriage Laws and some Customs of the West Australian Aborigines," *Victorian Geographical Journal*. Vols. xxiii–xxiv. Melbourne, 1906.

"Social Organisation of some Western Australian Tribes," *Report of the Fourteenth Meeting of the Australasian Association for the Advancement of Science, Melbourne, 1913*. Melbourne, 1914.

Bates, Henry Walter, *The Naturalist on the River Amazons*. 2 vols. London, 1863.

Bateson, W., *The Methods and Scope of Genetics*. Cambridge, 1908.

Mendel's Principles of Heredity. Cambridge, 1909.

Battell, "The Strange Adventures of Andrew Battell of Leigh in Essex, sent by the Portugals Prisoner to Angola," etc., *Hakluytus Posthumus, or Purchas His Pilgrimes*. Vol. vi. Glasgow, 1905.

Batty, John, *The Spirit and Influence of Chivalry*. London, 1890.

Baudesson, Henri, *Indo-China and its Primitive Peoples*. Transl. London, 1919.

Baudhâyana Dharmasastra, in *The Sacred Books of the East*. Vol. xiv. Oxford, 1882.

Baudin, R. P., "Féticheurs ou ministres religieux des Nègres de la Guinée," *Les Missions Catholiques*. Vol. xvi. Lyon, 1884.

Baudissin, W. W. von, *Studien zur semitischen Religionsgeschichte*. 2 vols. Leipzig, 1876–78.

Baumann, Oscar, *Durch Massailand zur Nilquelle*. Berlin, 1894.

Usambara. Berlin, 1891.

Baumstark, "Die Warangi," *Mittheilungen aus den Deutschen Schutzgebieten*. Vol. xiii. Berlin, 1900.

Bavaria. Landes- und Volkskunde des Königreichs Bayern, bearbeitet von einem Kreise bayerischen Gelehrter. 5 vols. Munich, 1861–68.

Bazin, Antoinne P. L., *Théâtre chinois, ou choix de pièces de théâtre composées sous les empereurs Mogols*. Paris, 1838.

Beardmore, E., "The Natives of Mowat, Daudai, New Guinea," *Journal of the Anthropological Institute*. Vol. xix. London, 1890.

Beare, J. I., *Greek Theories of Elementary Cognition, from Alcmaeon to Aristotle*. Oxford, 1906.

Beauchamp, W. M., *The Iroquois Trail or Foot-prints of the Six Nations in Custom, Tradition, and History.* New York, 1892.
" Indian Corn Stories and Customs," *Journal of American Folk-Lore.* Vol. xi. Boston and New York, 1898.
" Iroquois Women," *Journal of American Folk-Lore.* Vol. xiii. Boston and New York, 1901.
Beaudouin, J., " Faits pour servir à l'histoire des effets de la consanguinité chez les animaux domestiques," *Comptes Rendus de l'Académie des Sciences.* Vol. lv. Paris, 1862.
Beauvais, J., " Notes sur les coutumes des indigènes de la région de Long-Tcheou," *Bulletin de l'École Française d'Extrême-Orient.* Vol. vii. Hanoi, 1907.
[Beauvoir, J. M.], *Los Shelknam ; indigenos de la Tierra del Fuego, sus tradiciones, costumbres y lengua, por los missionarios Salesianos.* Buenos Aires, 1915.
Beauvois, M. E., " Deux sources de l'histoire des Quetzalcoatl," *Le Muséon.* Vol. v. Louvain, 1886.
Beaver, Wilfred N., *Unexplored New Guinea.* London, 1920.
" A Description of the Girara District, Western Papua," *The Geographical Journal.* Vol. xliii. London, 1914.
Beccanus, Joannes Goropius, *Origines Antwerpianae, sive Cimmeriorum Beccesciana novem libros complexa.* Antwerp, 1569.
Bechara Chemali, " Naissance et premier âge au Liban," *Anthropos.* Vol. v. Wien, 1910.
Beckwith, H. W., *History of Iroquois County.* Chicago, 1880.
Bede, *Historia Ecclesiastica gentis Anglorum.* Rec. J. Stevenson. London, 1838.
Bédier, J. See Thomas.
Beecham, John, *Ashantee and the Gold Coast.* London, 1841.
Beechey, F. W., *Narrative of a Voyage to the Pacific and Behring's Strait.* 2 vols. London, 1831.
Begbie, P. J., *The Malayan Peninsula.* Madras, 1834.
Béguin, Eugène, *Les Ma-rotsé, étude géographique et ethnologique.* Lausanne, Fontaines, 1903.
Behr, H. F. von, " Die Völker zwischen Rufiyi und Rovuma," *Mittheilungen aus den deutschen Schutzgebieten.* Vol. iv. Berlin, 1893.
Beiträge zur Biologie der Pflanzen. Breslau, 1894–
Beiträge zur Kunde der indogermanischen Sprachen. Göttingen, 1877–
Bekker, Im., *Anecdota Graeca.* 3 vols. Berolini, 1814–21.
Belcher, Sir E., " The Andaman Islands," *Transactions of the Ethnological Society.* N.S., vol. v. London, 1867.
Bell, Alexander Graham, *Memoir upon the Formation of a Deaf Variety of the Human Race.* Washington, 1884.
Bell, Blair, " The Internal Secretions and Female Characteristics," *Proceedings of the Royal Society of Medicine.* Vol. vi. London, 1913.
Bell, C. Napier, *Tangweera.* London, 1899.
" Remarks on the Mosquito Territory, its Climate, People, Productions, etc," *Journal of the Royal Geographical Society.* Vol. xxxii. London, 1862.
Bell, Sanford, " A Preliminary Study of the Emotion of Love between the Sexes," *The American Journal of Psychology.* Vol. xiii. 1902.
Bellamy, " Notes ethnographiques sur le Haut-Sénégal," *Revue d'Ethnographie.* Vol. v. Paris, 1886.
Bellew, H. W., *Journal of a Political Mission to Afghanistan in 1857.* London, 1862.

Bellucci, Giuseppe, *Il feticismo primitivo in Italia e le sue forme di adattamento.* Perugia, 1907.
    Un capitolo di psicologia popolare. Gli Amuleti. Perugia, 1908.
    Amuletti italiani. Perugia, 1898.
Below, E., " Die Ganglienzellen des Gehirnes bei verschiedenen neugeborenen Thieren," *Archiv für Anatomie und Physiologie (Physiologische Abtheilung).* Leipzig, 1888.
Belt, Thomas, *The Naturalist in Nicaragua.* London, 1874.
Benavides, Alonso de, *Memorial que . . J. de Santandes de la Orden de San Francisco presenta a la Magestad Catolica del Rey Felipe Quarto.* Madrid, 1630.
Bender, W., *Mythologie und Metaphysik.* Stuttgart, 1899.
Benedict of Peterborough, *De gestis Heinrici secundi et Riccardi.* Ed. W. Stubbs. (*Chronicles and Memorials of Great Britain and Ireland.*) 2 vols. London, 1867.
Benfey, Theodor, *Die Hymnen des Sâma-Veda.* 2 vols. Leipzig, 1848.
    Pantschatantra. 2 vols. Leipzig, 1859.
Benhazera, Maurice, *Six Mois chez les Touareg du Ahaggar.* Alger, 1908.
Benjamin, Archimandrite, in " Über den religiösen Glauben und Ceremonien der haidnischen Samojeden im Kreise Mesen," *Zeitschrift für allgemeine Erdkunde,* Neue Folge. Vol. viii. Berlin, 1860.
Benjamin, S. G. W., *Persia and the Persians.* London, 1891.
Bennett, A. L., " Ethnological Notes on the Fang," *Journal of the Anthropological Institute.* Vol. xxix. London, 1899.
Bennett, George, *Wanderings in New South Wales, Batavia,* etc. 2 vols. London, 1834.
Benrath, Karl, " Zur Geschichte der Marienverehrung," *Theologische Studien und Kritiken.* Gotha, 1886.
Bent, J. T., *The People of Southern Arabia.* London, 1895.
    The Sacred City of the Ethiopians : Travel in Abyssinia. London, 1868.
Bentham, Jeremy, *Theory of Legislation.* Transl. from the French. London, 1864.
Bentley, Richard, *Dissertation on the Epistles of Phalaris.* London, 1816.
Bentley, W. H., *Pioneering in the Congo.* London, 1900.
    Dictionary and Grammar of the Kongo Languages. London, 1887.
Beowulf. Ed. Thomas Arnold. London, 1876.
    German translation by K. Simrock. Stuttgart, 1859.
Bérard, Victor, *De l'origine des cultes Arcadiens.* Paris, 1894.
Bercheure, Pierre, *Opera omnia ; sive Reductorium, Repertorium et Dictionarium morale utriusque Testamenti quadripartitum.* 3 vols. Coloniae Agrippinae, 1730–31.
Berchon, " Documents sur le Sénégal," *Bulletin de la Société d'Anthropologie.* Série i, vol. i. Paris, 1860.
Berdau, Emil, " Der Mond in Volkzmedizin, Sitte, Gebraüche der mexicanische Grenzbewohnschaft des südliches Texas," *Globus.* Vol. lxxxviii. Braunschweig, 1905.
Bérenger-Feraud, L. J.-B., *Les peuplades de la Sénégambie.* Paris, 1879.
    Les Provençaux à travers les âges. Paris, 1900.
    Superstitions et survivances étudiées au point de vue de leur origine et de leurs transformations. Paris, 1896.
Berger, Hans, " Experimentell-anatomische Studien über die durch den Mangel optischer Reize veranlassten Entwicklungshemmungen in Occipitallappen der Hundes und Katzen," *Archiv für Psychiatrie und Nervenkranheiten.* xxxiii. Berlin, 1900.

Berger, H., " Beiträge zur feineren Anatomie der Gehirnrinde," *Monat-schrift für Psychiatrie und Neurologie.* Vol. xviii. Berlin, 1899.

Bergeron, P., " Traité de la navigation et des voiages de découverte et conquête modernes," in P. van der Aa, *Recueil de divers voyages curieux.* 2 vols. Leiden, 1729.

Bergh van Eysinga, G. A. van den, " Altchristlisches und Orientalisches," *Zeitschrift der deutschen morgenländischen Gesellschaft.* Vol. lx. Leipzig, 1906.

Bergmann, B., *Nomadische Streifereien unter der Kalmüken.* 4 vols. Riga, 1804–5.

Bergmann, Frederic-Guillaume, *Les Gètes.* Strasbourg, Paris, 1859.

Bergström, L., " Semitisk mändyrka," *Nordisk Tidskrift.* Stockholm, 1909.

Berlepsch, H. A., *Die Alpen in Natur- und Lebensbildern.* Jena, 1871.

Bernáldez, Andrés, *Historia de los Reyes Catolicos D. Fernando y Doña Isabel.* 2 vols. Sevilla, 1870–75.

Berichte der Naturforschende Gesellschaft. Freiburg, 1822–

Berichte über die Verhandlungen der königliche Sächsische Gesellschaft der Wissenschaften. Leipzig, 1848–

Bernard, St., Abbot of Clairvaux, *Opera omnia,* in Migne, *Patrologiae Cursus Completus.* Vols. clxxxii–clxxxv. Parisiis, 1854.

Bernard, Augustin, *L'Archipel de la Nouvelle Calédonie.* Paris, 1895.

Les Confins algéro-marocains. Paris, 1911.

Le Maroc. Paris, 1913.

[Bernard, J.-F. and B. Picard], *Cérémonies et Coutumes religieuses de tous les peuples du monde.* 11 vols. Amsterdam, 1723–37.

Bernau, J. H., *Missionary Labours in British Guiana.* London, 1847.

Bernfeld, Siegfried, " Zur Psychologie der Unmusikalischen," *Archiv für die gesamte Psychologie.* Vol. xxxiv. Leipzig, 1915.

Béroul, *Le Roman de Tristan.* Ed. E. Muret. Paris, 1913.

Berthelon, L., " Note on the Modern Pottery Fabrics in Tunisia," comm. by J. L. Myres. *Man,* vol. iii. London, 1903.

" Les formes de la famille chez les premiers habitants de l'Afrique du nord d'après les écrivains de l'antiquité et les coutumes modernes," *Archives d'Anthropologie Criminelle et de Psychologie normale et pathologique.* 8ᵉ année. Paris, 1893.

Berthelot, Sabin, *Ethnographia y anales de la conquista de las Islas Canarias (Biblioteca Isleña).* Santa Cruz de Tenerife, 1849.

Bertran d'Alamanon. See Salverda de Grave, J. J.

Bertran de Born, *Poésies.* Ed. A. Stimming. (*Romainsche Bibliothek,* vol. viii.) Halle a. S. 1892.

Bertrand, A., *La Religion des Gaulois.* Paris, 1897.

Besant, Walter, and E. A. Palmer, *Jerusalem.* London, 1899.

Besnard, H., " Les populations Moï de Darlac," *Bulletin de l'École Française d'Extrême-Orient.* Vol. vii. Hanoi, 1907.

Bessels, Emil, " Einige Worte über die Innuit (Eskimo) des Smiths-Sundes," *Archiv für Anthropologie.* Vol. viii. Braunschweig, 1875.

" The Northernmost Inhabitants of the Earth," *The American Naturalist.* Vol. xviii. Philadelphia, 1884.

Best, Elsdon, " Maori Marriage Customs," *Transactions and Proceedings of the New Zealand Institute.* Vol. xxxvi. Wellington, 1904.

" Notes on Maori Mythology," *Journal of the Polynesian Society.* Vol. viii. Wellington, 1899.

" Omens and Superstitious Beliefs of the Maoris," *Journal of the Polynesian Society.* Vol. vii. Wellington, 1898.

Best, Elsdon, " The Races of the Philippines," *Journal of the Polynesian Society*. Vol. i. Wellington, 1892.

" The Lore of the Whare-Kohanga," *Journal of the Polynesian Society*. Vol. xiv. Wellington, 1905.

" Ceremonial Performances pertaining to Birth as performed by the Maoris of New Zealand," *Journal of the Anthropological Institute*. Vol. xliii. London, 1913.

Beverley, J. E., " Die Wagogo," in S. R. Steinmetz, *Rechtsverhältnisse von eingeborenen Völkern in Afrika und Ozeanien*. Berlin, 1903.

Beveridge, Peter, *The Aborigines of Victoria and Riverina*. Melbourne, 1889.

Beyer, H. Otley, *Population of the Philippine Islands in 1916*. Manila, 1917.

Bezold, Carl, *Orientalische Studien Theodor Nöldeke zum siebzigsten Geburtstag gewidmet*. 2 vols. Gieszen, 1906.

Bezzemberger, A., and Prellwitz, ed., *Beiträge zur Kunde der indogermanischen Sprachen*. 25 vols. Göttingen, 1877–99.

The Bhagavadgîtâ, with the Sânatsugâtîya, and the Anugîtâ. Trans. by Kâshinâth Trimbak Telach. (*The Sacred Books of the East*, vol. viii.) Oxford, 1898.

Bhandarkar, Ramkrishna Gopal, *see* Ramkrishna.

Bhimbhái Kirpárám, " Gujarat Population," in *Gazetteer of the Bombay Presidency*. Vol. ix. Part i. Bombay, 1901.

Bible.—The Holy Bible, Authorised Version. Cambridge, s.d.

Revised Version. Cambridge, s.d.

Biblia Sacra, Vulgaris editio. Parisiis, 1859.

Vetus Testamentum ex versione septuaginta interpretum. 6 vols. Oxford, 1817.

Biblia Hebraica. Cur. C. G. G. Theile. Leipzig, 1849.

Novum Testamentum Graece. Rec. C. Tischendorf. Leipzig, 1850.

Biblioteca de autores españoles, desde la formación del lenguaje hasta nuestros dias. Manuel Rivadeneyra, pub., 71 vols. Madrid, 1846–80.

Biblioteca de las tradiciones popolares Españolas. Sevilla, 1883–

Biblioteca Isleña. 21 parts. Santa Cruz de Tenerife, 1847–49.

Bibliothèque égyptologique. Paris, 1893–

Bickmore, A. S., " Some Notes on the Ainos," *Transactions of the Ethnological Society*. Vol. vii. London, 1869.

Biddulph, J., *Tribes of the Hindoo Koosh*. Calcutta, 1880.

Big Game Shooting (Badminton Library), by C. Phillips-Wolley and others. 2 vols. London, 1894.

Bijdragen tot de taal-, land- en volkenkunde van Neerlandsch Indië. 's Gravehage, Amsterdam, 1853–

Bilharz, Alfons, " Beschreibung der Genitalorgane einiger schwarzen Eunuchen, nebst Bemerkungen über die Beschneidung der Clitoris und kleine Schamlippe," *Zeitschrift für wissenschaftliche Zoologie*. Vol. x. Leipzig, 1859.

Billardière, J. J. H. de la, *Account of a Voyage in Search of La Pérouse*. Transl. 2 vols. London, 1800.

Billson, J. Charles, " The Easter Hare," *Folk-lore*. Vol. iii. London, 1892.

Binger, Louis G., *Du Niger au golfe de Guinée par le pays de Kong et le Mossi*. 2 vols. Paris, 1892.

Bingham, Hiram, *A Residence of Twenty-one Years in the Sandwich Islands*. Hartford, 1849.

Bingley, W. W., *North Wales, including its Scenery, Antiquities, Customs*. 2 vols. London, 1804.

Bink, G.-L., " Réponses faites au Questionnaire de Sociologie et d'Ethnographie de la Société par M. G.-L. Bink, qui, de 1871 à 1883, a séjourné à la Nouvelle-Guinée, spécialement au golfe de Geelwink," *Bulletin de la Société d'Anthropologie.* 3e Série, vol. xi. Paris, 1888.

Biological Bulletin, Marine Biological Laboratory, Wood's Hole. Boston, 1889–

Biologisches Centralblatt. Leipzig, 1881–

Biometrika. Cambridge, 1901–

Biot, E., " Researches into the Manners of the Ancient Chinese, according to the She-King," in J. Legge, *The Chinese Classics.* Vol. iv, Part i. Hong-Kong, 1871.

Birch, Samuel, *Gallery of Antiquities selected from the British Museum by F. Arundale and J. Bononi.* 2 Parts. London, 1842–43.

Birch-Hirschfeld, A., *Ueber die den provenzalischen Troubadours des XII und XIII Jahrhunderts bekannten epische Stoffe.* Halle a. S., 1878.

Bird, I. S. (Mrs. Bishop), *Unbeaten Tracks in Japan.* 2 vols. London, Edinburgh, 1885.

  Korea and its Neighbours. 2 vols. London, 1898.

  Journeys in Persia and Kurdistan. 2 vols. London, 1891.

Bird, Mary Rebecca, *Persian Women and their Creed.* London, 1899.

Birlinger, A., *Volksthümiches aus Schwaben.* 2 vols. Freiberg im Breisgau, 1861.

Bischoff, T. von, " Bemerkungen über die Geschlechtsverhältnisse der Feuerlander," *Sitzungsberichte der königliche bayerische Akademie der Wissenschaften zu München. Mathematisch-physikalischen Classe.* München, 1882.

  Das Hirngewicht des Menschen. Bonn, 1880.

Bischofs, Jos., " Die Niol-Niol, ein Eingeborenenstamm in Nordwest-Australien," *Anthropos.* Vol. iii. Wien, 1908.

Biscoe, C. E. Tyndale, *Kashmir in Sunlight and Shade.* London, 1922.

Bissuel, H., *Les Touaregs de l'ouest.* Alger, 1888.

Black, W. G., " The Hare in Folk-lore," *The Folk-lore Journal.* Vol. i. London, 1883.

Blackbird, A. J., *History of the Ottawa and Chippeway Indians.* Philadelphia, 1860.

Blackman, A. M., " The Pharaoh's Placenta and the Moon-god Khons." *Journal of Egyptian Archaeology.* Vol. iii.

  " Some Remarks on an Emblem upon the Head of an Ancient Egyptian Birth-Goddess." *Ibid.* London, 1916.

Blair, Emma Helen, *The Indian Tribes of the Upper Mississippi Valley and the Region of the Great Lakes.* 2 vols. Cleveland, Ohio, 1911–12.

  and Robertson, J. A., *The Philippine Islands, 1493-1803.* 55 vols. Cleveland, 1903–9.

Blanchard, R., " La prostitution en Palestine," *Bulletin de la Société Française d'Histoire de la Médecine.* Vol. xi. Paris, 1912.

Blau, O., " Nachrichten über kurdische Stämme," *Zeitschrift der Deutschen Morgenländischen Gesellschaft.* Vol. xvi. Leipzig, 1862.

Bleek, W. H. I., *Reynard the Fox in South Africa.* London, 1864.

  A Brief Account of Bushman Folk-lore and other Texts. Cape Town, 1875.

  Report of Dr. Bleek concerning his Researches into the Bushman Language and Customs. Cape Town, 1873.

  and Lloyd, L. C., *Specimens of Bushman Folklore.* London, 1911.

  The Mantis and his Friends ; Bushman Folklore. Ed. by D. F. Bleek. Cape Town, 1924.

Bley, " Sagen der Baininger auf Neupommern," *Anthropos.* Vol. ix. Münster, 1914.

Blind, K., in *Folk-lore*. Vol. iii. London, 1892.

Bliss, Arthur, " A Contribution to the Study of Deaf Mutism," *The Medical News*. Vol. lxvii. Philadelphia, 1895.

Bloch, Iwan, *The Sexual Life of Our Time*. Trans. London, 1908.

Blocqueville, H. Goulibeuf de, " Quatorze mois de captivité chez les Turcomans," *Le Tour de Monde*. Vol. i. Paris, 1860.

Bloomfield, Maurice, " Contributions to the Interpretation of the Veda," *Journal of the American Oriental Society*. Vol. xv. New Haven, 1893.

" On the Frog-hymn of the Rig Veda." *Ibid.*, vol. xvii. New Haven, 1895.

Cerberus, the Dog of Hades. Chicago, 1905.

Blöte, J. F. D., " Das aufkommen des clevischen Schwanritters," *Zeitschrift für deutsches Altertum*. Vol. xiii. Leipzig and Berlin, 1885.

Blumenbach, J. F., *Lives and Anthropological Treatises*. Transl. London, 1865.

Blumentritt, Ferdinand, " Der Ahnencultus und die religiosen Anschaungen der Malaien des Philippinen-Archipels," *Mittheilungen der Kaiserlich und Königlich Geographischen Gesellschaft*. Vol. xxv. Wien, 1882.

Versuch einer Ethnographie der Philippinen. (*Petermann's Mittheilungen, Erganzungsheft*, No. 67.) Gotha, 1882.

Blunt, Lady Anne. *The Seven Golden Odes of Pagan Arabia*. London, 1903.

Blunt, E. A.," United Provinces of Agra and Oudh," *Census of India*, 1911. Vol. xv. Allahabad, 1912.

Blyth, D., " Notes on the Traditions and Customs of the Natives of Fiji relative to Conception, Pregnancy, and Parturition," *Glasgow Medical Journal*. Vol. xxviii. Glasgow, 1887.

Boas, Franz, " The Human Faculty as determined by Race," reprint from *Proceedings of the American Association for the Advancement of Science, 1894*. Salem, 1895.

" First General Report on the Indians of British Columbia," *Report of the Fifty-ninth Meeting of the British Association for the Advancement of Science* (Newcastle-upon-Tyne, 1889). London, 1890.

" Second General Report on the Indians of British Columbia," *Report of the Sixtieth Meeting of the British Association for the Advancement of Science* (Leeds, 1890). London, 1891.

" Third Report on the Indians of British Columbia," *Report of the Sixty-first Meeting of the British Association for the Advancement of Science* (Cardiff, 1891). London, 1892.

" The Indian Tribes of the Lower Fraser River," *Report of the Sixty-fourth Meeting of the British Association for the Advancement of Science* (Oxford, 1894). London, 1894.

" Fifth Report on the Indians of British Columbia," *Report of the Sixty-fifth Meeting of the British Association for the Advancement of Science* (Ipswich, 1895). London, 1895.

" Kathlamet Texts," *Bureau of Ethnology, Bulletin No. 26*. Washington, 1901.

" The Central Eskimo," *Sixth Annual Report of the Bureau of Ethnology*. Washington, 1888.

" The Social Organisation and the Secret Societies of the Kwakiutl Indians," *Smithsonian Report for 1895*. Washington, 1897.

" The Eskimo of Baffin Land and Hudson Bay," *Bulletin of the American Museum of Natural History*. Vol. xv. New York, 1901.

" Sagen aus Britisch-Columbia," *Verhandlungen der Berliner Gesellschaft für Anthropologie*. Berlin, 1892–93.

" Sagen der Indianer an der Nordwest-Küste America's," *Verhandlungen der Berliner Gesellschaft für Anthropologie*. Berlin, 1894–95.

Boas Anniversary Volume. Anthropological Papers presented to Franz Boas.
  New York, 1906.

Boccaccio, Giovanni, *Il Decamerone.* 2 vols. Milano, 1893.

Bock, Carl, *The Head-Hunters of Borneo.* London, 1881.
  Temples and Elephants. London, 1881.
  Een reis in Oost en Zuid-Borneo, van Koetoi naar Banjermassin. 's Hage, 1881.

Bodin, Jean, *De la démonomanie des sorciers.* Rouen, 1604.

Boece, Hector, *The Buik of the Chroniclis of Scotland.* Ed. W. B. Turnbull.
  (*Chronicles and Memorials of Great Britain and Ireland*). 3 vols.
  London, 1858.

Boecler, J. W., *Der Ehsten abergläubische Gebräuche, Weisen und Gewohnheiten.*
  Ed. Fr. K. Kreutzwal. St. Petersburg, 1854.

Boetticher, C. G. W., *Der Baumkultus der Hellener.* Berlin, 1856.

Boggiani, Guido, *Viaggi d'un artista nell' America meridionale. I Caduvei*
  (*Mbayá o Guaycurú*). Roma, 1895.

Bogle, G. See Markham, C. R.

Bogoras, Waldemar, *The Chukchee* (*Publications of the Jesup North Pacific
  Expedition*, vol. vii). Leiden and New York, 1904.

Boguet, Henry, *Discours des Sorciers avec six advis en faict de sorcelerie.*
  Lyon, 1608.

Bohner, H., *Im Lande des Fetisch.* Basel, 1890.

Boismoreau, Dr., *Coutumes médicales et superstitions populaires du Bocage
  vendéen.* Paris, 1911.

Boldetti, Marco Antonio, *Osservazioni sopra i cimiteri de' santi martiri ed
  antichi Cristiani di Roma.* 2 vols. Roma, 1720.

Boll, Franz, " Die Histologie und Histogenese der nervösen Centralorgane,"
  Archiv für Psychiatrie und Nervenkrankheiten. Vol. iv. Berlin, 1874.

Bollani, Mons. Domenico, *De gli errori popolari d'Italia.* Venetia, 1603.

Boller, H. A., *Among the Indians.* Philadelphia, 1868.

Bolletin del Institudo géografico Argentino. Buenos Aires, 1880–

Bolletino della Societá Geografica Italiana. Florence and Rome, 1868–

Bolton, J. Shaw, " The Histological Basis of Amentia and Dementia,"
  Archives of Neurology of the London County Asylums. Vol. ii. Clay-
  bury and London, 1903.
  " Amentia and Dementia," *The Journal of Mental Science.* Vol. li.
  London, 1905.

Boman, E., *Antiquités de la région Andine de la République Argentine et du
  désert d'Atacama.* Paris, 1908.

Bonald, Vicomte L. G. A. de, *Oeuvres complètes.* 3 vols. Paris, 1859.

Boniface, *Opera quae extant*, in Migne, *Patrologiae Cursus Completus.* Vol.
  lxxxix. Paris, 1863.

Bonifacy, " Étude sur les coutumes et la langue des La-Ti," *Bulletin de
  l'École Française d'Extrême-Orient.* Vol. vi. Hanoi, 1906.

Bonneau, A., *Les cadenas et ceintures de chasteté, notice historique, suivie du
  plaidoyer de Freydier, avocat de Nîmes.* Paris, 1883.

Bonnetty, A., " Découverte d'une statuette gauloise d'une Vierge Mère,"
  Annales de Philosophie Chrétienne. 6e Série, vol. ix. Paris, 1875.

Bonney, F., " On some Customs of the Aborigines of the River Darling,"
  Journal of the Anthropological Institute. Vol. xiii. London, 1884.

Bonvalot, G., *En Asie Centrale. Du Kohistan à la Caspienne.* Paris,
  1885.
  Across Thibet. Transl. 2 vols. London, 1891.

Bonwick, James, *The Last of the Tasmanians ; or, the Black War of Van
  Diemen's Land.* London, 1870.
  Daily Life and Origin of the Tasmanians. London, 1870.

Bonwick, James, *Egyptian Belief and Modern Thought.* London, 1878.

Borghéro, Abbé, " Relation sur l'établissement des missions dans le vicariat apostolique de Dahomey," *Annales de la Propagation de la Foi.* Vol. xxxvii. Lyons, 1865.

Borheck, A. C., *Erdbeschreibung von Asien.* 3 vols. Düsseldorf, 1792–94.

The Book of Lays of Fionn. Ed. Eoin MacNeill (*Irish Text Society*). 2 vols. London, 1908.

The Book of the Dead, edited and translated by Sir E. A. Wallis Budge. 3 vols. 1901.

   The Book of the Dead. The Papyrus of Ani in the British Museum. Ed. by Sir E. A. Wallis Budge. London, 1895.

   Das Todtenbuch der Aegypter nach den hieroglyphischen Papyrus in Turin. Ed. by R. Lepsius. Leipzig, 1881.

Boot, W. G., " Korte Schets der Noord-kust van Ceram," *Tijdschrift van het Kon. Nederlandsch Aardrijkskundig Genootschap.* Tweede Serie, vol. x. Leiden, 1893.

Bos, Ritzema, " Untersuchungen über die Folgen der Zucht in engster Blutverwandtschaft," *Biologisches Centralblatt.* Vol. xiv. Leipzig, 1894.

Bosanquet, R. C., " Excavations at Palaikastro," *Annual of the British School at Athens.* Vol. ix. London, 1902.

   " The Sanctuary of Artemis Orthia," *Annual of the British School at Athens.* Vol. xii. London, 1906.

   " Laconia. Excavations at Sparta. The Cult of Orthia as illustrated by the Finds." *Ibid.*, London, 1906.

   " Notes from the Cyclades," *Annual of the British School at Athens.* Vol. iii. London, 1897.

   and Dawkins, R. M., *The Unpublished Objects from the Palaikastro Excavations, 1902-6.* (*The British School at Athens, Supplementary Papers.* No. i.) London, 1923.

Boscana, G. See Robinson, A.

Bosman, W., " A New Description of the Coast of Guinea," in Pinkerton, *Collection of Voyages and Travels.* Vol. xvi. London, 1814.

Bosscher, C., and Mattijssen, P. A., " Schetsen van de rijken van Tomboekoe en Banggaai op de oostkust van Celebes," *Tijdschrift voor Indische taal-, land- en volkenkunde.* Vol. ii. Batavia, 1854.

Bossu, Capt., *Travels through that Part of North America formerly called Louisiana.* Transl. 2 vols. London, 1771.

Boston Journal of Natural History. Boston, 1834–

Boucaut, Sir James Penn, *The Arab Horse, the Thoroughbred and the Turf.* London, 1912.

Bouche, Pierre, *Sept ans en Afrique occidentale. La Côte des Esclaves et le Dahomey.* Paris, 1885.

Bouché-Leclercq, A., *Histoire des Lagides.* 4 vols. Paris, 1903–7.

   Histoire de la divination dans l'antiquité. 4 vols. Paris, 1879–82

   L'astrologie grecque. Paris, 1899.

Boudard, P. A., *Études sur l'aphabet Ibérien et sur quelques monnaies autonomes d'Espagne.* Paris, 1852.

Boudin, J. Ch. M., *Danger des unions consanguines et nécessité des croisements dans l'espèce humaine.* Paris, 1862.

Bougainville, L. A. de, *Voyage autour du Monde par la frégate du Roi, La Boudeuse.* 2 vols. Paris, 1772.

Bouillane de La Coste, E. A. H. de, *Au pays sacré des anciens Turcs et Mongols.* Paris, 1911.

Boulenger, G. A., art. " Teleostei," in *The Cambridge Natural History*. Vol. vii. London, 1904.

Bouquet, M., and others (ed.), *Rerum Gallicarum et Franciscarum Scriptores* (*Recueil des historiens des Gaules et de la France*). 23 vols. Paris, 1738–1876.

Bourien, Le Père, " On the Wild Tribes of the Interior of the Malay Peninsula," *Transactions of the Ethnological Society*. New Series, vol. iii. London, 1865.

Bourke, John Gregory, *The Snake-Dance of the Moquis of Arizona*. London, 1884.

On the Border with Crook. New York, 1891.

" Notes upon the Gentile organisation of the Apaches of Arizona," *Journal of American Folk-Lore*. Vol. iii. Boston and New York, 1890.

" Notes upon the Religion of the Apache Indians," *Folk-lore*. Vol. ii. London, 1891.

Scatological Rites of All Nations. Washington, 1891.

" Superstitions of Rio Grande," *Journal of American Folklore*. Vol. vii. Boston, New York, 1894.

Bourne, B. F., *The Captive in Patagonia*. London, 1853.

Bove, Giacomo, *Patagonia. Terra del Fuoco. Mari Australi*. Genoa, 1883.

Bovis, E. de, " État de la société Taïtienne à l'arrivée des Européens," *Annuaire des établissements français de l'Océanie et du Protectorat des Îles de la Société*. Papeete, 1863.

Bowdich, T. E., *Mission from Cape Coast Castle to Ashantee*. London, 1873.

Bowler, A. C. R., " Aboriginal Customs," *Science of Man*. Sydney, 1902.

Bowman, Isaiah, *The Andes of Southern Peru*. New York, 1916.

Bowring, Sir John, *The Kingdom and People of Siam*. 2 vols. London, 1857.

Boyd, Robert, " Tables of the Weights of the Human Body and Internal Organs in the Sane and Insane of Both Sexes at Various Ages, arranged from 2614 post-mortem examinations," *Philosophical Transactions of the Royal Society*. London, 1861.

Boylan, Patrick, *Thoth, the Hermes of Egypt*. London, Vienna, 1922.

Boyle, D., "On the Paganism of the civilised Iroquois of Ontario," *Journal of the Anthropological Institute*. Vol. xxx. London, 1900.

Brackelmann, *Les plus anciens chansonniers français*. Paris, 1870.

Bradbury, J., *Travels in the Interior of America* (in R. G. Thwaites, *Early Western Travels*. Vol. v). Cleveland, 1904.

Braga, Theophilo, *O povo portuguez, nos seus costumes, crenças e tradições*. 2 vols. Lisboa, 1885.

Brain. London, 1878–

Brainne, C., *La Nouvelle-Calédonie*. Paris, 1854.

Brand's Popular Antiquities of Great Britain. Ed. by W. Carew Hazlitt. 2 vols. London, 1905.

Brandeis, Antonie, " Ethnographische Beobachtungen über die Nauru-Insularen," *Globus*. Vol. xci. Braunschweig, 1907.

Brandt, A. J. W., *Die mandäische Religion ihre Entwickelung und geschichtliche Bedeutung*. Leipzig, 1889.

Brandt, Alexander, " Anatomisches und allgemeines über die sogenannte Hahnenfedrigkeit und über anderweitige Geschlechtsanomalien bei Vögeln," *Zeitschrift für wissenschaftliche Zoologie*. Vol. xlviii. Leipzig, 1889.

Brandt, Mat. von, *Sittenbilden aus China. Mädchen und Frauen*. Stuttgart, 1895.

Brantôme, Pierre de Bourdeilles, seigneur de, *Oeuvres complètes*. 11 vols. Paris, 1864–82.

Brasseur de Bourbourg, E. C., *Histoire des nations civilisées de l'Amérique centrale durant les siècles antérieurs à Christophe Colomb*. 4 vols. Paris, 1857–59.
Popol Vuh. Le livre sacré et les mythes de l'antiquité américaine. Paris, 1861.
Voyage sur l'isthme de Tehuantepec, dans l'État de Thiapas et la République de Guatemala. Paris, 1861.

Brau des Saint-Pol Lias, X., *Île de Sumatra ; chez les Atchés*. Paris, 1884.
Pérak, et les Orang-Sakeys. Paris, 1883.

Braun, Julius, *Naturgeschichte der Sage*. 2 vols. München, 1864–65.

Bray, Denys, "Baluchistan. Report," *Census of India, 1911*. Vol. iv. Calcutta, 1913.

Bréal, Michel, *Pour mieux connaître Homère*. Paris, s.d.

Breasted, J. H., *Ancient Records of Egypt*. Chicago, 1906–
The Development of Religious Thought in Ancient Egypt. New York, 1912.

Breeks, James Wilkinson, *An Account of the Primitive Tribes and Monuments of the Nīlagiris*. London, 1873.

Brehm, A. E., *Thierleben*. 10 vols. Leipzig, 1876–78.
Tierleben. Remodelled edition ed. by Otto zur Strassen. 13 vols. Leipzig, 1912–20.
Reiseskizzen aus Nord-Ost-Afrika. 3 Parts. Jena, 1885.

Brenchley, J. L., *Jottings during the Cruise of H.M.S. Curaçoa among the South Sea Islands in 1865*. London, 1873.

Brenner, J. F. von, *Besuch bei den Kannibalen Sumatras*. Würzburg, 1893.

Brentano, Lujo, " Die Volkswirthschaft und ihre konkrete Grundbedingungen," *Zeitschrift für social- und Wirtschaftgeschichte*. Vol. i. Freiburg i. B. and Leipzig, 1893.

Brereton, John, in *Hackluytus Posthumus, or Purchas His Pilgrimes*. Vol. xviii. Glasgow, 1906.

Bretschneider, E., *Mediaeval Researches from Eastern Asiatic Sources*. 2 vols. London, 1888.

Brett, W. H., *The Indian Tribes of Guiana*. London, 1868.
Legends and Myths of the Aboriginal Indians of British Guiana. London, 1880.

Brewer, W. M., " The Instinctive Interest of Children in Bear and Wolf Stories," *Proceedings of the American Association for the Advancement of Science*. 41st Meeting. Salem, 1893.

Brewster, A. B., *The Hill Tribes of Fiji*. London, 1922.
" Circumcision in Noikoro, Noemolu and Mboumbudho," *Journal of the Royal Anthropological Institute*. Vol. xlix. London, 1919.

Bridges, T. W., " Fishes," *The Cambridge Natural History*. Vol. vii. London, 1904.

Bridges, Thomas, " Das Feuerland und seine Bewohner," *Globus*. Vol. xlvii. Braunschweig, 1885.
In *The South American Missionary Magazine*. Vol. xxv. London, 1875.

Brierly, O. W., " Brief Geographical Sketch of the Friendly Islands," *Journal of the Royal Geographical Society*. Vol. xxii. London, 1852.

Briffault, Robert, *Psyche's Lamp*. London, 1921.
The Making of Humanity. London, 1919.

Brigham, W. T., " Hawaiian Feather Work," *Memoirs of the Berenice Panshı Bishop Museum*. Honolulu, 1903.

Brigham, W. T., *Brihadâranyaka-Upanishad.* See *Upanishads.*

Brincker, P. H., *Wörterbuch und kurzgefasste Grammatik des Otji-Herero.* Leipzig, 1886.

" Charakter, Sitten und Gebräuche speciell der Bantu Deutsch-Südwestafrikas," *Mittheilungen des Seminars für orientalische Sprachen zu Berlin.* Vol. iii, Part iii. Berlin, Stuttgart, 1900.

Brinton, D. G., *American Hero-Myths.* Philadelphia, 1882.

Religions of Primitive Peoples. New York and London, 1897.

Nagualism. A Study in Native American Folk-Lore and History. Philadelphia, 1894.

Races and Peoples. New York, 1890.

The American Race. New York, 1891.

The Lenâpe and their Legends. Philadelphia, 1882.

Essays of an Americanist. Philadelphia, 1890.

Brisley, T., " Some Notes on the Baoule Tribe," *Journal of the African Society.* Vol. viii. London, 1909.

The British and Foreign Medico-Chirurgical Review. London, 1848–

The British Central Africa Gazette. Zomba, 1894–

The British Journal of Psychology. Cambridge, 1905–

The British Medical Journal. London, 1857–

Broca, Paul, " Sur le poids relatif des deux Hemisphères cérébraux et de leurs lobes frontaux," *Bulletins de la Société d'Anthropologie,* 2ᵉ Série, vol. x. Paris, 1875.

" Sur la capacité des crânes parisiens des diverses époques," *ibid.,* vol. iii. Paris, 1862.

Brock, R. G. C., " Some Notes on the Zande Tribe as found in the Meridi District (Bar el Ghazal province)," *Sudan Notes and Records.* Vol. ii. Khartoum, 1918.

Brockhaus, F. A., *Konversations-Lexikon.* 17 vols. Leipzig, 1901–4.

Brockman, Ralph Evelyn Drake, *The Mammals of Somaliland.* London, 1910.

Brogniart, Jules, *Traité des Arts Céramiques ou de Poterie.* 2 vols. Paris, 1854.

Brooke, Charles, *Ten Years in Sarawak.* 2 vols. London, 1848.

Brooke, James, *Narrative of Events in Borneo and Celebes.* Ed. by R. Munday. 2 vols. London, 1848.

Brosses, C. de, *Du culte des dieux fétiches.* Paris, 1760.

Histoire des Navigations aux Terres Australes. 2 vols. Paris, 1756.

Brown, A. C. L., " Welsh Traditions in Layamon's ' Brut,' " *Modern Philology.* Vol. i. Chicago, 1904.

Brown, A. R., *The Andaman Islanders.* Cambridge, 1922.

" Three Tribes of Western Australia," *Journal of the Royal Anthropological Institute.* Vol. xliii. London, 1913.

" Notes on the Social Organisation of Australian Tribes," *Journal of the Royal Anthropological Institute.* Vol. liii. London, 1923.

Brown, George, *Melanesians and Polynesians, Their Life-Histories described and compared.* London, 1910.

" Life History of a Savage," *Report of the Seventh Meeting of the Australasian Association for the Advancement of Science.* Sydney, 1898.

Brown, G. St. J. Orde, " Circumcision Ceremonies among the Amwimbe," *Man.* Vol. xiii. London, 1913.

" Circumcision Ceremonies of the Chuka," *Man.* Vol. xv. London, 1915.

Brown, Rev. J. Tom, *The Bantu of Central South Africa.* (MS.)

Brown, Robert, *The Races of Mankind.* 4 vols. London, 1873–76.

Brown, William, *New Zealand and its Aborigines*. London, 1845.

Browne, James, " The Aborigines of Australia," *The Nautical Magazine and Naval Chronicle*. London, 1856.

Browne, J. Ross, *Adventures in the Apache Country*. New York, 1869.

Browne, Sir Thomas, *Works*. Ed. S. Wilkin. 3 vols. London, 1852.

Brownell, C. de Wolf, *The Indian Races of North and South America*. Boston, 1853.

Broyde, I., art., " Circumcision among the Arabs," in *The Jewish Encyclopaedia*. Vol. iv. Chicago, s.d.

Bruce, C. D., " A Journey across Asia from Leh to Peking," *The Geographical Journal*. Vol. xxix. London, 1907.

Bruce of Kinnaird, James, *Travels to discover the Source of the Nile*. 5 vols. Edinburgh, 1790.

Bruel, G., " Les populations de la Moyenne Sanga. Les Pomo et les Boumali." *Revue d'Ethnographie et de Sociologie*. Vol. i. Paris, 1910.

L'Afrique équatoriale française. Paris, 1918.

Brugsch, H., *Religion und Mythologie der alten Ägypter*. Leipzig, 1885.

Dictionnaire géographique de l'ancienne Égypte. Leipzig, 1879–80.

" Das Osiris-Mysterium von Tentyra," *Zeitschrift für Aegyptische Sprache und Alterthumskunde*. Vol. xix. Leipzig, 1881.

" Der Traum Königs Thutmes IV bei der Sphinx," *Zeitschrift für Aegyptische Sprache und Alterthumskunde*. Vol. xiv. Leipzig, 1876.

Egypt under the Pharaohs. Transl. 2 vols. London, 1879.

Thesaurus inscriptionum Aegyptiacarum. Leipzig, 1883–91.

Bruisaud, E., *Histoire des expressions populaires*. Paris, 1892.

Brumund, J. F. G., *Indiana*. 2 vols. Amsterdam, 1853–54.

Brunache, P., *Au Centre de l'Afrique autour du Tchad*. Paris, 1894.

Brunet, L., and Giethlen L., *Dahomey et dépendances*. Paris, 1900.

Brunner, H., *Deutsche Rechtsgeschichte*. 2 vols. Leipzig, 1887–92.

Bruyerin, J. B., *De re cibaria*. Périgeux, 1560.

Bryant, A. T., *Zulu-English Dictionary*. Pinetown, Natal, 1905.

Buch, Max, " Die Wotjäken." *Acta Societatis Scientiarum Fennicae*. Vol. xii. Helsingfors, 1883.

Buchanan, Angus, *Exploration of Aïr, out of the World North of Nigeria*. London, 1921.

Buchanan, Francis, *A Journey from Madras through the Countries of Mysore, Canara, and Malabar*. 3 vols. London, 1807.

The same, in Pinkerton, *Voyages and Travels*. Vol. viii. London, 1811.

Buchanan, James, *Sketches of the History, Manners and Customs of the North American Indians*. London, 1824.

Buchanan, John, *The Shiré Highlands (East Central Africa)*. Edinburgh, 1885.

Bücheler, Franz, and Zitelmann, Ernst, " Das Recht von Gortyn," *Rheinisches Museum für Philologie*. Vol. xl, Erganzungsheft. Frankfurt a. M., 1885.

Büchner, F. C. C. L., *Liebe und Liebes-Leben in der Thierwelt*. Leipzig, 1885.

Buchner, Max, *Kamerun. Skizzen und Betrachtungen*. Leipzig, 1887.

" Beiträge zur Ethnographie der Bantu," *Das Ausland*. Stuttgart, Augsburg, München, 1883.

Buckingham, J. S., *Travels among the Arab Tribes inhabiting the Countries East of Syria and Palestine*. London, 1825.

Travels in Assyria, Media, and Persia. 2 vols. London, 1830.

Buckland, F., *Natural History of British Fishes*. London, 1881.

Buckle, Henry Thomas, *History of Civilisation in England.* 3 vols. London, 1889.

Budge, Sir E. A. T. Wallis, *On the Hieratic Papyrus of Nesi-Amsu.* London, 1902.
 A History of Egypt. 8 vols. London, 1902.
 The Gods of the Egyptians. 2 vols. London, 1904.
 Osiris and the Egyptian Resurrection. 2 vols. New York, 1911.
 A Short History of the Egyptian People. London, 1923.
 An Egyptian Hieroglyphic Dictionary. London, 1920.
 See *Book of the Dead.*

Buehler, G., *Grundriss der indo-arischen Philologie und Altertumskunde.* Strassbourg, 1896.

Bufe, "Die Bakundu," *Archiv für Anthropologie.* N.V., vol. xii. Braunschweig, 1913.

Buffon, G. L. LcClerc de, *Histoire Naturelle.* Red. par. C. S. Sonnini, 127 vols. Paris, 1798–1808.

Bugge, Sophus, *Der Ursprung der Etrusker durch zwei lemnischen Inschriften erläutert.* Christiania, 1886.

Bulletin de Correspondance Africaine. Alger, 1882–

Bulletin de Correspondance Hellénique. Athènes, Paris, 1877–

Bulletins de l'Académie d'Hippone. Bône, 1865–

Bulletin de l'Académie Royale de Belgique. Bruxelles, 1832–

Bulletins de la Société d'Anthropologie. Paris, 1860–

Bulletin de la Société de Géographie. Paris, 1822–

Bulletin de la Société des Lettres, Sciences et Arts de la Corréze. Tulle, 1920.

Bulletin de la Société d'Études Coloniales. Bruxelles, 1894–

Bulletin de la Société Entomologique de France. Paris, 1896-

Bulletin de la Société Française d'Histoire de la Médecine. Paris, 1902–

Bulletin de la Société Zoologique de France. Paris, 1876–

Bulletin de l'École Française d'Extrème-Orient. Hanoi, 1901–

Bulletin de l'Institut général psychologique. Paris, 1900–

Bulletin des Amis des Sciences Naturelles de Rouen. Rouen, 1875–

Bulletin du Comité de l'Afrique Française. Paris, 1891–

Bulletin of the American Museum of Natural History. New York, 1881–

Bulletin of the United States Fish Commission (Bureau of Fisheries). Washington, 1882–

Bulletin of the United States National Museum. Washington, 1875–

Bulletin Scientifique de la France et de la Belgique. Paris, 1888–

Bullettino di Paletnologia Italiana. Parma, 1875–

Bulmer, John, "Some Account of the Aborigines of the Lower Murray, Wimmera, Gippsland, and Maneroo," *Transactions and Proceedings of the Royal Geographical Society of Australasia (Victoria Branch).* Vol. v. Melbourne, 1888.

Bülow, W. von, "Das ungeschriebenes Gesetz der Samoaner," *Globus.* Vol. lxix. Braunschweig, 1896.
 "Die Eidechsen im Volksglauben der Samoaner," *Globus.* Vol. lxxiv. Braunschweig, 1902.

The Bundahis. See *Pahlavi Texts.*

Bunsen, C. C. J. von, *De jure hereditario Atheniensium.* Gottingae, 1813.

Burchell, W. J., *Travels in the Interior of Southern Africa.* 2 vols. London, 1822–24.

Burckhardt, Jacob, *Die Kultur der Renaissance in Italien.* 2 vols. Leipzig, 1913.

Burckhardt, John Lewis, *Notes on the Bedouins and Wahábys.* London, 1830.
 Arabic Proverbs. London, 1875.

Burckhardt, John Lewis, *Travels in Arabia.* 2 vols. London, 1829.
Travels in Nubia. London, 1822.

Bureau of American Ethnology. (Smithsonian Institution.) Annual Reports. Washington, 1881–
Bulletins. Washington, 1887–

Burg, C. L. van der, *De Geneesheer in Nederlandsch-Indië.* 3 vols. Batavia, 1882–87.

Burger, Friederich, *Die Küsten- und Bergvölker der Gazellehalbinsel.* Stuttgart, 1913.

Burges, Arn., *American Kennel and Sporting Field.* New York, 1876.

Burk, F., "Teasing and Bullying," *Pedagogical Seminary.* Vol. iv. Worcester, 1897.

Burke, R. O'Hara, "Exploring Expedition from Victoria to the Gulf of Carpentaria, under the Command of Mr. Robert O'Hara Burke," *Journal of the Royal Geographical Society.* Vol. xxxii. London, 1862.

Burn, R., "N.-W. Provinces and Oudh," *Census of India, 1901.* Vol. xvi. Allahabad, 1902.

Burne, Miss Charlotte S., "Presidential Address," *Folk-lore.* Vol. xxii. London, 1911.
Shropshire Folk-lore from the collection of Georgina F. Jackson. London, 1882.

Burnes, A., *Travels into Bokhara.* 3 vols. London, 1839.

Burnet, John, *Early Greek Philosophy.* 3rd Edition. London, 1920.
See Plato.

Burrows, Guy, "On the Natives of the Upper Welle District of the Belgian Congo," *Journal of the Anthropological Institute.* Vol. xxviii. London, 1899.
The Land of the Pigmies. London, 1898.

Burrows, R. M., *The Discoveries in Crete.* London, 1907.

Burt, Cyril, "The Inheritance of Mental Characters," *The Eugenics Review.* Vol. iv. London, 1913.
"The Experimental Investigation of General Intelligence," *British Journal of Psychology.* Vol. iii. Cambridge, 1907.

Burton, Sir Richard F., *Two Trips to Gorilla Land and the Cataracts of the Congo.* 2 vols. London, 1876.
Personal Narrative of a Pilgrimage to El-Medinah and Meccah. 3 vols. London, 1855–56.
The same. 2 vols. London, 1906.
Zanzibar : City, Island and Coast. 2 vols. London, 1872.
First Footsteps in East Africa. London, 1856.
The Lake Regions of Central Africa. 2 vols. London, 1864.
A Mission to Gelele, King of Dahome. 2 vols. London, 1864.
Supplemental Nights to the Book of the Thousand Nights and a Night. 6 vols. Benares, 1886–88.
"Notes on Certain Matters connected with the Dahomans," *Memoirs read before the Anthropological Society.* Vol. i. London, 1865.

Burton, Robert, *The Anatomy of Melancholy.* London, 1845.

Buschmann, J. C. E., "Ueber den Naturlaut," *Abhandlungen der Königlich Preussische Akademie der Wissenschaften zu Berlin, Philosophische und historische Classe.* Berlin, 1852.

Bush-Brown, H. K., "Heredity in Horses," *The Journal of Heredity.* Vol. xi. Washington, 1920.

Butcher, E. L., *Things seen in Egypt.* London, 1914.

Butel-Dumont, George M., *Mémoires historiques sur la Louisiane.* 2 vols. Paris, 1753.

Butler, Major John, *Travels and Adventures in the Province of Assam.* London, 1855.

Butler, N. M., " Anaximander on the Prolongation of Infancy in Man," in *Classical Studies in Honour of H. Drisler.* New York, 1894.

Butler, Samuel, *The Authoress of the Odyssey.* London, (1897).

Buttles, Janet R., *The Queens of Egypt.* London, 1908.

Büttner, C. G., " Sozialpolitisches aus dem Leben der Herero in Damaraland," *Das Ausland.* Vol. lv. Stuttgart, 1882.

Byington, Cyrus, *Dictionary of the Choctaw Language.* (*Bureau of Ethnology, Bulletin, No. 46.*) Washington, 1915.

Byng-Hall, F. F. W., " Notes on the Bassa Komo Tribe," *Journal of the African Society.* Vol. viii. London, 1908.

Byron, John, *The Narrative of the Honourable John Byron . . . containing an account of the great distress suffered by himself and his companions on the coasts of Patagonia,* etc. Morpeth, 1812.

Cabaton, A., *Java, Sumatra and Other Islands of the Dutch East Indies.* Transl. London, Leipzig, 1911.

Nouvelles recherches sur les Chams. Paris, 1901.

Cabeza de Vaca, Alvar Nuñez, *Comentarios,* in *Biblioteca de autores españoles.* Vol. xxii.

Naufragios, y relación de la jornada que hizo a la Florida. Ibid. Madrid, 1852.

Ca da Mosto, Alvise, " Navigationi," in G. B. Ramusio, *Navigationi et Viaggi.* Vol. i. Venetia, 1564.

Cadière, R. P., " Coutumes populaires de la vallée de Nguôn-so'n," *Bulletin de l'École Française d'Extrème-Orient.* Vol. ii. Hanoi, 1902.

Caesar, C. Julius, *Commentarii de bello Gallico.* Ed. G. Long. London, 1853.

Caetani, Leone, Principe di Teano, *Studi di Storia Orientale.* 3 vols. Milano, 1911–14.

Caillé, René, *Travels through Central Africa to Timbuctoo.* 2 vols. London, 1830.

Caillemer, E., *Études sur les antiquités juridiques d'Athènes. Le droit de succession légitime à Athènes.* Paris, Caen, 1879.

Cailliaud, Fréderic, *Voyage a Méroë, au Fleuve Blanc, au delà de Fazoql, à Syouah,* etc. 4 vols. Paris, 1826–27.

Caillot, A. C. Eugène, *Mythes, légendes et traditions des Polynésiens.* Paris, 1914.

" Calabar Stories," *Journal of the African Society.* Vol. v. London, 1906.

Caland, W., *Altindisches Zauberritual ; Probe einer Übersetzung der wichtigste Theile des Kauscka Sutra.* Amsterdam, 1900.

The Calcutta Review. Calcutta, 1846–

Calkins, Gary N., " Studies on the Life-History of Protozoa. The Life-cycle of *Paramoecium caudatum,*" *Archiv für Entwickelungsmechanik der Organismen.* Vol. xv. Leipzig, 1902.

Callaway, H., *The Religious System of the Amazulu. Izinyanga Zokubula.* Springvale, Natal ; London, 1870.

Nursery Tales, Traditions, and Histories of the Zulus. Springvale, Natal ; London, 1868.

" On Divination and Analogous Phenomena among the Natives of Natal," *Journal of the Anthropological Institute.* Vol. i. London, 1872.

Callimachus, *Hymni, epigrammata et fragmenta*. Ex rec. Graevi. 2 vols. Ultrajecti, 1697.

Calvert, J., *Vazeeri Rupi, the Silver Country of the Vazeers in Kulu*. London, 1873.

Camboué, P., "Notes sur quelques moeurs et coutumes malgaches," *Anthropos*. Vol. ii. Salzburg, 1907.

"Les dix premiers ans de l'enfant chez les Malgaches," *Anthropos*. Vol. iv. Wien, 1909.

The Cambridge Ancient History. Vol. i. Cambridge, 1923.

The Cambridge History of India. Vol. i. *Ancient India*. Ed. by E. J. Rapson. Cambridge, 1922.

The Cambridge Natural History. 10 vols. London, 1895–1906.

Camden, William, *Britannia*. Transl. and enlarged by Rich. Gough. 3 vols. London, 1789.

Camerarius, P., *Operae horarum subcisivarum, sive meditationes historicae*. 3 vols. Francofurti, 1625–42.

Cameron, A. L. P., "Notes on some Tribes of New South Wales." *Journal of the Anthropological Institute*. Vol. xiv. London, 1885.

"Notes on a Tribe speaking the 'Boontha-Murra' Language," *Science of Man*. Vol. vii. Sydney, 1904.

Cameron, C. V., "Examination of the Southern Half of Lake Tanganyika," *Journal of the Royal Geographical Society*. Vol. xlv. London, 1875.

Cameron, D., "A Sketch of the Customs, Manners, Way of Living of the Natives in the Barren Country about Nipigon," in L. R. Masson, *Les Bourgeois de la Compagnie du Nord-ouest*. Vol. ii. Quebec, 1889.

Cameron, J., *Our Tropical Possessions in Malayan India*. London, 1865.

Cameron, P., *A Monograph of the British Phytophagous Hymenoptera*. (*Ray Society's Annual*.) London, 1882–85.

Cameron, Verney Lovett, *Across Africa*. London, 1885.

Camoens, Luis de, *Os Lusiadas*, with English translation by J. J. Aubertin. 2 vols. London, 1878.

Campbell, Major, "Geographical Memoir of Melville Islane, or the Cobourg Peninsula, North Australia," *The Geographical Journal*. Vol. iv. London, 1834.

Campbell, Lord Archibald (ed.), *Waifs and Strays of Celtic Tradition. Argyllshire Series*. 5 vols. London, 1889–95.

Campbell, Archibald, *A Voyage round the World from 1806 to 1812*. Edinburgh, 1816.

Campbell, Dugald, *In the Heart of Bantuland*. London, 1922.

"A Few Notes on Butwa: an African Secret Society," *Man*. Vol. xiv. London, 1914.

Campbell, J. F., "Fionn's Enchantment," *Revue Celtique*. Vol. i. Paris, 1872.

Campbell, James, "Polygamy: its Influence on Sex and Population," *Journal of Anthropology*. London, 1870–71.

Campbell, John, *Travels in South Africa*. London, 1815.

A Personal Narrative of Thirteen Years' Service amongst the Wild Tribes of Khondistan. London, 1864.

Campbell, John Gregorson, *The Fians* (*Waifs and Strays of Celtic Tradition*. Vol. iv). London, 1891.

Superstitions of the Highlands and Islands of Scotland. Glasgow, 1900.

Campbell, W. D., "An Account of the Aboriginals of Sunday Island, King Sound, Kimberley, Western Australia," *Journal and Proceedings of the Royal Society of Western Australia*. Vol. i. Perth, 1916.

Campen, C. F. H., " De Alfoeren van Halmahera," *Tijdschrift voor Neërlands Indië*. Vol. i. Batavia, 1883.

Canaan, T., *Aberglaube und Volksmedizin im Lande der Bibel (Abhandlungen des Kolonialinstituts*. Vol. xx). Hamburg, 1914.

Cañamaque, Francisco, *Las islas Filipinas, de todo un poco*. Madrid, 1880. *Recuerdos de Filipinas*. 2 vols. Madrid, 1877.

Candelier, H., *Rio-Hacha et les Indiens Goajires*. Paris, 1893.

Candish, Thomas, " Eerste scheeps-togt van T. C." in P. van den Aa, *Naaukeurige versameling der gedenk-waardigste zee- en land- reysen*. Vol. xx. Leyden, 1708.

Canello, U. A. *La vita e le opere del trovatore Arnaldo Daniello*. Halle, 1883.

Canivey, Jules, " Notice sur les moeurs et coutumes des Moï de la région de Dalat," *Revue d'Ethnologie et de Sociologie*. Vol. iv. Paris, 1913.

Canones et Decreta SS. oecumenici Concilii Tridentini. Romae, 1845. *The Canons and Decrees of the Sacred and Oecumenical Council of Trent*. Translated by the Rev. J. Waterworth. London, 1848.

Cantova, J. A., in *Lettres édifiantes et curieuses*. Vol. xv. Paris, 1781.

Capefigue, J. B. H. R., *Historie de Philippe Auguste*. 4 vols. Paris, 1829. *Charlemagne*. 2 vols. Paris, 1842.

Capitularia Regum Francorum. Ed. Alfred Boretius, in Pertz, *Monumenta Historica Germaniae*. *Leges*. Sect. I. 2 vols. Hanover, 1881–97.

Capus, G., " Les Kafirs Siahpouches," *Bulletin de la Société d'Anthropologie*. Série 4, vol. i. Paris, 1890.

Carancha, Antonio de la, *Coronica moralizada del Orden de San Augustin en el Peru*. 2 vols. Barcelona, 1638.

Cardanus Mediolanensis, Hieronymus, *Opera omnia*. Ed. Carolus Sponius. 10 vols. Lugduni, 1663.

Cardinall, A. W., *The Natives of the Northern Territories of the Gold Coast*. London, 1920.
" Customs at the Death of King of Dagomba," *Man*. Vol. xxi. London, 1921.

Carlgreen, O., " Die Brutflege der Actinarien," *Biologisches Centralblatt*. Vol. xxi. Leipzig, 1901.

Carnoy, E. H., and Nicolaïdes, J., *Traditions populaires de l'Asie Mineure*. Paris, 1889.

Carr, Lucien, " The Social and Political Position of Women among the Huron-Iroquois Tribes," *Sixteenth Annual Report of the Peabody Museum of American Archaeology and Ethnology*. Cambridge, Mass., 1883.
" Dress and Ornaments of certain American Indians," *Proceedings of the American Antiquarian Society*. N.S., vol. xi. Worcester, 1898.
Mounds of the Mississippi Valley historically considered. (*Memoirs of the Geological Survey of Kentucky*. Vol. ii.) Frankfort, 1883.

Carr, William, *The History of the Rise and Progress of the Killerby, Studley, and Warlaby Herds of Shorthorns*. London, 1867.

Carruthers, D., *Unknown Mongolia*. 2 vols. London, 1913.

Cartailhac, Émile, *La France préhistorique*. Paris, 1889.

Cartelli, Francesco, *Viaggi da lui racontati in dodici ragionamenti*. (Reprint.) Firenze, 1878.

Carteret, Philip, *An Account of a Voyage round the World*, in Hawkesworth's *Voyages*, etc. Vol. i. London, 1773.

Cartier, Jacques, *Bref récit et succinct narration de la navigation faict en MDXXXV et MDXXVI*. Paris, 1654. Facsimile reprint. 1863.

Cartright, M., " Folk-lore of the Basutos," *Folk-lore*. Vol. xv. London, 1904.

Carver, J., *Travels through the Interior Parts of North America.* London, 1781.

Casalis, E., *Les Bassoutos.* Paris, 1859.

The Basutos. Transl. London, 1861.

Casanova de Seingalt, Jacques Girolamo, *Mémoires.* 8 vols. Paris, 1880.

Casati, C. C. M., *Fortis Etruria. Origines étrusques de droit Romain.* Paris, 1883.

Casati, G., *Ten Years in Equatoria.* Transl. 2 vols. London, 1891.

Caspari, C. P., *Kirchenhistorische Anecdota.* Christiania, 1883.

Casson, S., " Hera of Kanathos and the Ludovisi Throne," *The Journal of Hellenic Studies.* Vol. xl. London, 1920.

Castañeda de Naçera, Pedro de, " Relacion de la jornada de Cibola," in G. P. Winship, " The Coronado Expedition," *Fourteenth Annual Report of the Bureau of Ethnology.* Part i. Washington, 1897.

Castanheda, Ferñao Lopes de, *Historia do descobrimento e conquista da India pelos Portuguezes.* Coimbra, 1551.

Transl. in R. Kerr, *General History and Collection of Voyages and Travels.* Vol. ii. Edinburgh, 1811.

Castellani, C., *Les femmes au Congo.* Paris, 1898.

Castelli, R., *Credenze ed usi siciliani.* Palermo, 1878.

Castelnau, Francis de, *Expédition dans les parties centrales de l'Amérique du Sud, de Rio de Janeiro à Lima et de Lima au Para. Histoire du Voyage.* 6 vols. Paris, 1850–59.

Castrén, Alexander, *Vorlesungen über die Finnische Mythologie.* St. Petersburg, 1853.

Ethnologische Vorlesungen über die Altaischer Völker. St. Petersburg, 1857.

Castro, A. de, " Résumé historique de l'établissement portugais à Timor, des us et coutumes de ses habitants," *Tijdschrift voor Indische taal-, land- en volkenkunde.* Vol. xi. Batavia, 1862.

Castro y Rossi, A., *Discurso acerca las costumbres publicas y privadas de los Españoles en el siglo xvii, fundado en el estudio de las comedias de Calderon.* Madrid, 1881.

Cat, R. P., in *Lettres édifiantes et curieuses.* Vol. ix. Paris, 1781.

The Catholic Encyclopaedia. 17 vols. New York, 1907–18.

Catlin, George, *Illustrations of the Manners, Customs, and Condition of the North American Indians.* 2 vols. London, 1866.

Letters and Notes on the Manners, Customs and Condition of the North American Indians. 2 vols. New York and London, 1844.

O-Kee-pa, a Religious Ceremony, and other Customs of the Mandans. London, 1867.

Cato, Marcus Porcius, *De re rustica.* Ed. Jo. Matt. Gesner. Mannhemii, 1781.

Cator, D., *Everyday Life among Head-hunters.* London, 1905.

Cauer, Paul, *Grundfrager der Homerkritik.* Leipzig, 1923.

Caufeynon (i.e. Dr. Jean Fauconney), *La ceinture de chasteté, son histoire, son emploi, autrefois et aujourd' hui.* Paris, 1905.

Caulin, Antonio, *Historia coro-graphica, natural y evangelica de la Nueva Andalucia, Provincia de Cumana, Guayana y vertientes del Rio Orinoco.* Madrid, 1779.

Caussin de Perceval, *Essai sur l'histoire des Arabes avant l'Islamisme et jusqu'à la réduction de toutes les tribus sous la loi musulmane.* 3 vols. Paris, 1847–48.

Cavazzi da Montecuccoli, G. A., *Istorica descrizione de' tre regni, Congo, Matamba et Angola,* etc. Bologna, 1687.

Relation historique de l'Ethiopie occidentale, contenant la description des royaumes de Congo, Angolle et Matamba, traduit de l'Italien, etc. 5 vols. Paris, 1732.

Cayzac, R. P., " La religion des Kikuyu," *Anthropos.* Vol. v. Wien, 1910.

Cedrenus, Georgius, *Synopsis Historiarum.* Ed. Emm. Bekker. 2 vols. Bonn, 1838.

La Cellule, Recueil de cytologie et d'histologie générale. Lierre, Gand, Louvain, 1885–

The Celtic Review. Edinburgh, 1904–

Census of India, 1881. See *Report on the Census of British India.*

    1891. Calcutta, etc., 1892–

    1901. Calcutta, etc., 1902–

    1911. Calcutta, etc., 1912–

    1921. Calcutta, etc., 1923–

    See under the names of authors of the various reports.

Census of Ireland, 1881. Part ii. *General Report.* Dublin, 1882.

Central Provinces, Ethnological Survey. 7 vols. Allahabad, 1907–11.

The Century Illustrated Magazine. New York, 1881–

Cercamon, *Les poésies de Cercamon.* Ed. by A. Jeanroy. Paris, 1922.

Céresole, Alfred, *Légendes des Alpes Vaudoises.* Lausanne, 1885.

Cerruti, G. B., *Nel Paese dei Veleni. Fra i Sakai.* Verona, 1906.

Certeux, A. et Carnoy, E. H., *L'Algérie traditionelle.* Paris et Alger, 1884.

Cervantes Saavedra, Miguel de, *Obras.* Madrid, 1864.

Cesareo, G. A., *La poesia siciliana sotto gli Svevi.* Catania, 1894.

Chabas, F., " Les maximes du scribe Ani," *L'Égyptologie.* Vols. i. and ii. Chalon-sur-Saône, 1876–77.

    Le papyrus magique Harris. Chalon-sur-Saône, 1868.

    Le calendrier des jours fastes et néfastes de l'année égyptienne. (IVth Sallier Papyrus.) Chalon-sur-Saône and Paris, 1870.

    " Un hymne à Osiris," *Revue archéologique.* Vol. lxii. Paris, 1857.

    " Notice sommaire des papyrus hiératiques," in C. Leeman, *Monuments égyptiens du Musée d'antiquités des Pays-Bas à Leide.* Vol. ii. Leiden, 1839.

Chadwick, H. Munro, *The Origins of the English Nation.* Cambridge, 1907.

    The Heroic Age. Cambridge, 1912.

Chaffanjon, J., *L'Orénoque et le Caura.* Paris, 1889.

Chalmers, James, " On the Manners and Customs of some Tribes of New Guinea," *Proceedings of the Philosophical Society of Glasgow.* Vol. xviii. Glasgow, 1887.

    " Notes on the Natives of Kiwai Island, Fly River, British New Guinea," *Journal of the Anthropological Institute.* Vol. xxxiii. London, 1903.

    Pioneering in New Guinea. London, 1887.

    and Gill, W. W., *Work and Adventure in New Guinea.* London, 1885.

Chamberlain, Alexander Francis, *The Child.* London, 1900.

    " Nanibozhu amongst the Otchipwe, Mississagas, and other Algonkian Tribes," *Journal of American Folk-Lore.* Vol. iv. Boston and New York, 1891.

    " Primitive Woman as Poet " (abstract), *Proceedings of the American Association for the Advancement of Science.* 42nd Meeting. Salem, 1894.

    " Entwicklungshemmung des Kindes bei den Naturvölkern und bei den Völkern von Halbkultur," *Zeitschrift für pädagogische Psychologie.* Vol. ii. Leipzig, 1900.

Chamberlain, Basil Hall, *Aino Folk-Tales.* London, 1888.

    " Ko-Ji-Ki, or Records of Ancient Manners." Transl. by B. H. C., with Introduction. *Transactions of the Asiatic Society of Japan.* Vol. x. Supplement. Yokohama, 1883.

    " The Luchu Islands and their Inhabitants," *The Geographical Journal.* Vol. v. London, 1895.

Chambers's Journal. London, 1832–

Chamisso, Adelbert von, *Reise um die Welt mit der Romanoffischen Entdec kungs-Expedition in den Jahren, 1815–18.* 2 vols. (*Werke*, vols. i, ii.) Leipzig, 1842.

Champion, Arthur M., " The Atharaka," *Journal of the Royal Anthropological Institute.* Vol. xlii. London, 1912.

Champlain, Samuel de, *Œuvres.* 4 vols. Quebec, 1870.

Champollion-Fijeac, J. J., *Égypte ancienne.* (*L'Univers.*) Paris, 1839.

Chance, E., *The Cuckoo's Secret.* London, 1922.

Chandless, W., " Ascent of the River Purus," *The Journal of the Royal Geographical Society.* Vol. xxxvi. London, 1866.

La Chanson de Roland. Ed. L. Gautier. Paris, 1894.

Chantepie de la Saussaye, P. D., *The Religion of the Teutons.* Boston, 1902.

Chantre y Herrera, José, *Historia de las misiones de la Compañia de Jesús en el Marañon español.* Madrid, 1901.

Chapeaurouge, A. de, *Einiges über Inzucht und ihre Leistung auf verschiedenen Zuchtgebieten.* Hamburg, 1909.

Chapman, F. W., " Athapascan Traditions from the Lower Yukon," *Journal of American Folk-Lore.* Vol. xvi. Boston and New York, 1903.

Chapman, J., *Travels in the Interior of South Africa.* 2 vols. London, 1808.

Chardin, Jean, *Voyages en Perse et autres lieux de l'Orient.* 10 vols. Amsterdam, 1711.

Charencey, H. de, *Le fils de la Vierge.* Havre, 1879.

Le Folklore des deux mondes. Paris, 1894.

Charlemagne, an Anglo-Norman Poem of the Twelfth Century. Ed. by Francisque Michel. London, 1836.

Charlevoix, Pierre François Xavier de, *Histoire et description de la Nouvelle France ; avec journal d'un voyage dans l'Amérique Septentrionale.* 6 vols. Paris, 1744.

Histoire du Paraguay. Paris, 1756.

The History of Paraguay. Transl. 2 vols. London, 1769.

Chateaubriand, François René de, *Voyages en Amérique.* 2 vols. (*Oeuvres Complètes*, vols. vi & vii.) Paris, 1828.

Chatelain, H., *Folk-Tales of Angola.* Boston, 1894.

Chatelin, L. N. H. A., " Godsdienst en bijgeloof der Niassers," *Tijdschrift voor Indische taal-, land- en volkenkunde.* Vol. xxvi. Batavia, 1881.

Chaumette-des-Fossés, A., *Voyage en Bosnie dans les années 1807 et 1808.* Berlin, 1812.

Chavanne, J., *Die Sahara.* Wien, Pest, Leipzig, 1879.

Chavero, Alf., " Los dioses astronómicos de los antiguos Mexicanos. Apendice á la interpretación del Codice Borgia," *Anales del Museo Naciónal.* Vol. v. Messico, 1899.

See Riva Palacio.

Chaytor, H., *The Troubadours and England.* Cambridge, 1923.

Cheever, Henry T., *Life in the Sandwich Islands ; or, The Heart of the Pacific, as it was and is.* London, 1851.

The Island World of the Pacific. New York, 1851.

Cheon, A., " Note sur les Muong de la province de Son-Tay," *Bulletin de l'École Française d'Extrême-Orient.* Vol. v. Hanoi, 1905.

Chervin, Arthur, " Aymaras and Quichas ; A Study of Bolivian Anthropology," *International Congress of Americanists. Proceedings of the XVIII Session, London, 1912.* Vol. i. London, 1912.

Chester, H. N., " Native Habits and Customs of the Louisiades District," *Annual Report on British New Guinea, 1892–93.* Brisbane, 1894.

Le chevalier à l'épée, an old French poem. Ed. by E. C. Armstrong. Baltimore, 1900.

Li chevaliers as deus espees. Ed. W. Foerster. Halle a. S., 1877.

Cheyne, Andrew, *A Description of the Islands of the Western Pacific Ocean.* London, 1852.

Cheyne, T. K., *Traditions and Beliefs in Ancient Israel.* London, 1907.

Chil y Naranjo, G., *Estudios historicos, climatologicos y patologicos de las Islas Canarias.* 2 vols. Las Palmas, 1876–80.

Childers, Robert Caesar, *A Dictionary of the Pali Language.* London, 1875.

The China Review : or Notes and Queries on the Far East. Hong-Kong, 1872–1901.

" Chinese Family Life," *The China Review.* Vol. xi. Hong-Kong, 1882.

The Chinese Recorder and Missionary Journal. Shang-Hai, Foo-Chow, 1865–

The Chinese Repository. 20 vols. Canton, 1833–51.

Chinnery, E. W. P., and Beaver, W. N., " Notes on the Initiation Ceremonies of the Koko, Papua," *Journal of the Royal Anthropological Institute.* Vol. xlv. London, 1915.

Chirino, Pedro, S. J., *Relación de las Islas Filipinas i de lo que en ellas an trabaiado los padres de la Compañia de Iesus.* Roma, 1604. Transl. in E. H. Blair and J. A. Robertson, *The Philippine Islands, 1493–1803.* Vols. xii and xiii. Cleveland, 1904.

Chomé, Père Ignace, in *Lettres édifiantes et curieuses.* Vol. viii. Paris, 1781.

Chou-King. Ed. S. Couvreur. Ho Kien Fou, 1897.

Chou-Li.—Le Tcheou-Li. Transl. by Édouard Biot. 2 vols. Paris, 1851.

Chrestien de Troyes, *Perceval le Gallois, publié d'après le manuscrit de Mons,* par Ch. Potvin (*Société des Bibliophiles Belges, No. 21*). 6 vols. Mons, 1866–71.

    Cligès, ed. W. Foerster (*Romanische Bibliothek.* Vol. i). Halle a/S., 1889.

    Yvain, ed. W. Foerster (*Ibid.* Vol. v.). Halle a/S., 1891.

    Erec et Enide. Ed. W. Foerster. Halle, 1896.

    and Godefroy de Laigny, *Le roman du chevalier de la charette.* Ed. P. Tarbe. Reims, 1860.

Christaller, J. G., " Negersagen von der Goldküste," *Zeitschrift für Afrikanischen Sprachen.* Vol. i. Berlin, 1888.

Christian, F. W., *The Caroline Islands.* London, 1899.

    Eastern Pacific Islands. London, 1910.

    " Notes on the Marquesans," *Journal of the Polynesian Society.* Vol. iv. Wellington, 1895.

Chronicles and Memorials of Great Britain and Ireland (Rolls Series). London, 1858–

Chronicles of the Reigns of Stephen, Henry II, and Richard I. Ed. R. Howlett. (*Chronicles of Great Britain and Ireland.*) 4 vols. London, 1884–89.

La Chronique Médicale. Paris, 1894–

The Church Missionary Intelligencer. London, 1850–

Church, George Earl, *Aborigines of South America.* London, 1912.

Churchill, Awnsham and John, *A Collection of Voyages and Travels.* 6 vols. London, 1704–32.

Churchill, William, " The Duk-Duk Ceremonies," *The Popular Science Monthly.* Vol. xxxviii. New York, 1890.

Chwolson, D. A., *Die Ssabier und der Ssabismus.* 2 vols. St. Petersburg, 1856.

    Über Tammuz und die Menschenverehrung bei den alten Babyloniern. St. Petersburg, 1860.

Cicero, Marcus Tullius, *Opera quae supersunt omnia*. Ed. I. C. Orellius. 8 vols. Turici, 1826–38.

Cieza de Leon, Pedro de, *La crónica del Peru* (*Biblioteca de Autores Españoles*. Vol. xxiii.). Madrid, 1853.

  The Second Part of the Chronicle of Peru. Transl. by Sir C. R. Markham. (*Hakluyt Society*, No. 68.) London, 1883.

Claridge, G. Cyril, *Wild Bush Tribes of Tropical Africa*. London, 1922.

Clarke, Robert, " Sketches of the Colony of Sierra Leone and its Inhabitants," *Transactions of the Ethnological Society*. Vol. ii. London, 1863.

The Classical Review. London, 1887–

Classical Studies in Honour of Henry Drisler. New York, 1894.

Claus, Heinrich, *Die Wagogo*. Leipzig, Berlin, 1911.

Clavel, Charles, *Les Marquisiens. Études physiologiques, anthropologiques, et ethnologiques*. Paris, 1885.

Clavigero, F. S., *Storia antica del Messico*. 4 vols. Cesena, 1780–81.

  Storia della California. 2 vols. Venice, 1789.

Clay, A. T., *Light on the Old Testament from Babel*. Philadelphia, 1907.

  " Ellil, the God of Nippur," *The American Journal of Semitic Languages and Literatures*. Vol. xxiii. Chicago, New York, 1907.

Clement of Alexandria, *Opera*, in Migne, *Patrologiae Cursus Completus, Series Graeca*. Vols. viii–ix. Paris, 1857.

Clement of Rome, *Opera*, in Migne, *Patrologiae Cursus Completus, Series Graeca*. Vols. i–ii. Parisiis, 1857.

  Homiliae. Ed. A. Schwegler. Stuttgart, 1847.

Clements, E., " Ethnological Notes on the Western-Australian Aborigines," *Internationales Archiv für Ethnographie*. Vol. xvi. Leiden, 1903.

Clercq, F. S. A. de, " Allerlei over de residentie Manado," *Tijdschrift voor Nederlands Indië*. Vol. ii. Batavia, 1871.

  Bijdragen tot de kennis de Residentie Ternate. Leiden, 1890.

Clerke, E. M., " On the Aborigines of Western Australia," *Report of the Sixty-first Meeting of the British Association for the Advancement of Science. Cardiff, 1891*. London, 1892.

Clifford, Hugh, *Studies in Brown Humanity*. London, 1898.

Clot, A. B., *Aperçu général sur l'Égypte*. 2 vols. Bruxelles, 1840.

Clozel, F. J., " Land Tenure on the Ivory Coast," *Journal of the African Society*. Vol. i. London, 1901.

  and Villamur, R., *Les coutumes indigènes de la Côte d'Ivoire*. Paris, 1902.

Coan, Titus, *Life in Hawaii*. New York, 1882.

Cobb, I. Geikie, *The Organs of Internal Secretion*. London, 1918.

Cochinchine Française. Excursions et reconnaissances. Saigon, 1879–

Codrington, R. H., *The Melanesians*. Oxford, 1891.

  " Religious Beliefs and Practices in Melanesia," *Journal of the Anthropological Institute*. Vol. x. London, 1881.

  and Palmer, J., *A Dictionary of the Language of Mota*. London, 1896.

Cohn, F., " Die Entwicklungsgeschichte der Gattung Volvox," *Beiträge zu Biologie der Pflanzen*. Breslau, 1875.

Coincy, Gautier de, *Les miracles de la Sainte-Vierge*. Paris, 1857.

Cojazzi, A., *Los Indios del Archipélago Fueguino* (Reprint from *Revista Chilena de Historia y Geografia*). Santiago de Chile, 1914.

Cole, Fay-Cooper, *Traditions of the Tinguian, a Study in Philippine Folk-Lore* (*Field Museum of Natural History, Anthropological Series*. Vol. xiv, No. 1). Chicago, 1915.

  The Wild Tribes of Davao District, Mindanao (*Ibid*. Vol. xii, No. 2). Chicago, 1913.

Cole, H., " Notes on the Wagogo of German East Africa," *Journal of the Anthropological Institute*. Vol. xxxii. London, 1902.

Cole, Sir H. W. G., " The Lushais," in *Census of India, 1911*. Vol. iii, Part i. " Assam," Report. Shillong, 1912.

Cole, R. H., *Mental Diseases*. London, 1924.

Colebrooke, Henry Thomas, *Miscellaneous Essays*. 2 vols. London, 1837.

" On the Religious Ceremonies of the Hindus, and of the Brahmens especially," *Asiatic Researches*. Vol. vii. Calcutta, 1801.

Colebrooke, T. E., " On the Proper Names of the Mohammedans," *Journal of the Royal Asiatic Society*. N.S., vol. xi. London, 1879.

Colección de Documentos ineditos relativos al descubrimiento conquista y colonización de las possessiones Españolas en America y Oceania, sacados, en su mayor parte del Reale Archivio de Indias. Madrid, 1865.

Coleman, Charles, *Mythology of the Hindus*. London, 1832.

Colenso, J. W., *Zulu-English Dictionary*. Natal, 1905.

Colenso, William, *On the Maori Races of New Zealand*. Wanganui, 1865.

Ancient Tide-Lore and the Tales of the Sea. Napier, 1889.

Colgan, John, *Acta Sanctorum veteris et majoris Scotiae seu Hiberniae Sanctorum insulae*. 2 vols. Louvain, 1645–47.

Colin, Francisco, S.J., *Labor Evangelica, ministerios apostolicos de los obreros de la Compañia de Iesus, fundación y progressos de su provincia en las Islas Filipinas*. Madrid, 1663.

Extr. transl. in E. H. Blair and J. A. Robertson, *The Philippine Islands, 1493-1803*. Vol. xl. Cleveland, 1906.

Colini, G. A. See Boggiani, G.

Coll, C. van, " Matrimonia indigenarum Surinamensium," *Anthropos*. Vol. ii. Salzburg, 1907.

Colle, R. P., *Les Baluba*. 2 vols. Bruxelles, 1913.

Collecção de noticias para a historia e geografia das nações ultramarinas, que vivem nos dominios portuguezes. Lisboa, 1812–

Collectio canonum, in Migne, *Patrologiae Cursus Completus*. Vol. cxxxix. Parisiis, 1853.

Collections of the Massachusetts Historical Society. Boston, 1792–

Collections of the Minnesota Historical Society. St. Paul, Minn., 1860–

Collections of the New York Historical Society. New York, 1809–

Collens, H. J., *A Guide to Trinidad*. London, 1888.

Collins, David, *An Account of the English Colony of New South Wales*. 2 vols. London, 1798–1802.

Collocot, E. E. V., " Notes on Tongan Religion," *Journal of the Polynesian Society*. Vol. xxx. New Plymouth, 1921.

Colman, Charles, *The Mythology of the Hindus, with notices of various mountain and island tribes*. London, 1832.

Columella, *De re rustica*, in *Scriptores Rei Rusticae Veteres Latini*. Leipzig, 1794–97.

Combe, E., *Histoire du culte de Sin en Babylonie et en Assyrie*. Paris, 1908.

Combes, E., and Tamisier, M., *Voyage en Abyssinie, dans le pays des Galla, de Choa, et d'Ifet*. 4 vols. Paris, 1835–37.

Combés, Francisco, *Historia de las islas de Mindanao, Iolo, y sus adjacentes*. Madrid, 1667.

Extracts translated in E. H. Blair and J. A. Robertson, *The Philippine Islands, 1493–1803*. Vol. xl. Cleveland, 1906.

Comes, Natalis, *Mythologiae, sive explicationum fabularum libri decem*. Lugduni, 1602.

Comparetti, Domenico, *Virgilio nel Medio Evo.* 2 vols. Firenze, 1896.
  The Traditional Poetry of the Finns, transl. with preface by A. Lang. London, 1898.

Compayré, G., *L'évolution intellectuelle et morale de l'enfant.* Paris, 1893.

"Compert Concobuir," *Revue Celtique.* Vol. iv. Paris, 1859.

Comptes-Rendus de l'Académie des Inscriptions et Belles Lettres. Paris, 1858–

Comptes-rendus, etc., *de la Société de Biologie.* Paris, 1850–

Comptes Rendus hebdomadaire des Séances de l'Académie des Sciences. Paris, 1835–

Comrie, P., "Anthropological Notes on New Guinea," *Journal of the Anthropological Institute.* Vol. vi. London, 1877.

Concepcion, Juan de la, *Historia general de Philipinas.* 14 vols. Manila, 1788–92.

Conder, C. R., "The Present Condition of the Native Tribes in Bechuanaland," *Journal of the Anthropological Institute.* Vol. xvi. London, 1887.

Condon, M. A., "Contribution to the Ethnography of the Basoga-Batamba, Uganda Protectorate," *Anthropos.* Vols. v, vi. Wien, 1910–11.

Congrès International des Américanistes. Comptes-rendus. Nancy, etc., 1875–

Le Congo Illustré. Bruxelles, 1892–

Conklin, Edwin Grant, *Heredity and Environment in the Development of Man.* Princeton, 1915.

Connelley, W. E., "Notes on the Folk-Lore of the Wyandots," *Journal of American Folk-Lore.* Vol. xii. Boston, New York, 1899.
  "The Wyandots," *Archaeological Report.* Toronto, 1899.

Connolly, R. M., "Social Life in Fanti-Land," *Journal of the Anthropological Institute.* Vol. xxvi. London, 1897.

Connor, Bernard, *The History of Poland, in letters to persons of quality.* 2 vols. London, 1698.

Conradi, Edward, "Song and Call-Notes of English Sparrows when reared with Canaries," *American Journal of Psychology.* Vol. xvi. Worcester, 1905.

Consiglieri Pedroso, "Sur quelques formes du mariage populaire en Portugal," *Congrès international d'Anthropologie et d'Archéologie préhistorique,* IXᵉ Session. Lisbon, 1884.

"Conte du Mantel." Ed. Wulff. *Romania.* Vol. xiv. Paris, 1885.

The Contemporary Review. London, 1866–

Conti, Nicoló, "The Travels of Nicoló Conti in the Early Part of the Fifteenth Century," Transl. in R. H. Major, *India in the Fifteenth Century.* London, 1857.

Contributions to North American Ethnology (Department of the Interior. United States Geographical and Geological Survey of the Rocky Mountains Region). Washington, 1877–

Conway, W. M., "The Pre-Hellenic Inscriptions of Praesos," *Annual of the British School at Athens.* Vol. viii. London, 1902.

Conybeare, Fred. Cornwallis, *Myth, Magic, and Morals : a Study of Christian Origins.* London, 1910.

Cook, Alice Carter, "The Aborigines of the Canary Islands," *American Anthropologist.* N.S., vol. ii. New York, 1900.

Cook, Arthur Bernard, "The European Sky God : The Celts." *Folk-lore.* Vol. xviii. London, 1907.
  "The Bee in Greek Mythology," *Journal of Hellenic Studies.* Vol. xv. London, 1895.

Cook, James, *An Account of a Voyage round the World,* in J. Hawkesworth's *Voyages,* etc. Vols. ii. and iii. London, 1773.
  Journal of Captain Cook's Last Voyage to the Pacific Ocean. London, 1785.

Cook, James, *The Voyages of Captain Cook.* 7 vols. London, 1813.
    See Anderson, G. W.
Cook, S. A., in *The Cambridge Ancient History.* Vol. i. Cambridge, 1923.
Cooke, E., *A Voyage to the South Sea and round the World.* 2 vols. London, 1712.
Cooper, H. S., *The Coral Islands of the Pacific.* London, 1882.
Cooper, John M., *Analytical and Critical Bibliography of the Tribes of Tierra del Fuego and Adjacent Territory (Smithsonian Institution. Bureau of American Ethnology, Bulletin, 63).* Washington, 1917.
Cooper, Thomas, " Fabulous Traditions and Customs of the Indians of Martha's Vineyard," *Collection of the Massachussetts Historical Society.* Vol. i. Boston, 1792.
Cooper, T. T., *The Mishmee Hills.* London, 1873.
Cooper, W., *Mystery of Witchcraft.* London, 1617.
Copies of, or Extracts from, Dispatches of the Governors of the Australian Colonies, with Reports of the Protector of the Aborigines. House of Commons Accounts and Papers, 1844. Vol. xxxiv. London, 1844.
Copp, Evelyn Fletcher, " Musical Ability," *The Journal of Heredity.* Vol. vii. Washington, 1916.
Cordier, E., " Le droit de famille aux Pyrénées," *Revue du droit français et értanger.* Vol. v. Paris, 1859.
    Croyances des anciens Basques. Bagnère-de-Bigorre, s.d.
    Superstitions et légendes des Pyrénées. Bagnère-de-Bigorre, 1867.
Cordier, Henri, *Histoire générale de la Chine.* 4 vols. Paris, 1920–21.
Cornaby, W. A., art. " God, Chinese," in Hastings's *Encyclopaedia of Religion and Ethics.* Vol. vi. Edinburgh, 1913.
Cornford, F. M., *From Religion to Philosophy. A Study in the Origins of Western Speculation.* London, 1912.
    " The Origin of the Olympic Games," in J. E. Harrison, *Themis.* Cambridge, 1912.
The Cornhill Magazine. London, 1860–
Cornutus, Lucius Annaeus, *Theologiae Graecae Compendium.* Rec. C. Lang. Leipzig, 1881.
Corpus Inscriptionum Atticarum. (Now incorporated in the following.) Berlin, 1873–
Corpus Inscriptionum Graecarum. Berlin, 1828–
Corpus Inscriptionum Latinarum. Berlin, 1863–
Corpus Inscriptionum Rhenanarum. Ed. W. Brambach. Elberfeldae, 1867.
Corpus Inscriptionum Semiticarum. Parisiis, 1881–
Corpus Juris Canonici. Rec. Aem. Friedberg. 2 vols. Lipsiae, 1879–81.
Corpus Juris Civilis. 3 vols. : Vol. i, *Institutiones,* rec. P. Krueger ; *Digesta,* rec. Th. Mommsen. Vol. ii, *Codex Justinianus,* rec. P. Krueger ; Vol. iii, *Novellae,* rec. R. Schoell. Berolini, 1889–95.
Corpus Juris Sueo-Gotorum antiqui. Samling of Sveriges Gamla Lagar. Ed. H. S. Collin and C. J. Schlyter. 13 vols. Stockholm, Lund, 1827–77.
Corpus Scriptorum Ecclesiasticorum Latinorum. 65 vols. Vindobonae, 1866–1916.
Correspondenz-Blatt der deutsche Gesellschaft für Anthropologie, Ethnologie und Urgeschichte. München, Braunschweig, 1869–
Cortes, F., " History of the Province of Mindanao." Transl. in E. H. Blair and J. A. Robertson, *The Philippine Islands, 1493–1803.* Vol. xl. Cleveland, 1906.
Cortet, Eugène, *Essai sur les fêtes religieuses.* Paris, 1867.

Cortez, José. *History of the Apache Nations and other Tribes near the parallel of 35° north latitude (Pacific Railroad Reports.* Vol. iii, Part iii.). Washington, 1856.

The Cosmopolitan. New York, 1886–

Cosmos. Ed. Guido Cora. Torino, 1873–

Costermans, Lieut., " Le district de Stanley-Pool," *Bulletin de la Société d'Études Coloniales.* Vol. ii. Bruxelles, 1895.

Coucy, Le châtelain de, *Chansons.* Ed. Francisque Michel. Paris, 1830.

Coudreau, Henri, *La France équinoxiale.* 2 vols. Paris, 1887.
  Chez nos Indiens. Paris, 1893.

Coulet, Jules, *Le troubadour Guilhem Montanhagol.* Toulouse, 1898.

Couling, Samuel, *The Encyclopaedia Sinica.* London, 1917.

County Folklore. London, 1895–

Couperus, C. Th., " De instelligen der Maleiers in de Padangsche Boven-landen," *Tijdschrift voor Indische taal-, land- en volkenkunde.* Vol. iv. Batavia, 1856.

Couppé, Mgr., " En Nouvelle-Poméranie," *Les Missions Catholiques.* Vol. xxiii. Lyon, 1881.

Courbon, " Observations topographiques et médicales recueillies dans un voyage en Abyssinie," *Bulletin de la Société de Géographie.* Vol. iii. Paris, 1824.

Court de Gebelin, A., *Monde primitif analysé et comparé avec le monde moderne.* 9 vols. Paris, 1773–82.

Couto de Magalhães, J. V., *O Selvagem.* Rio de Janiero, 1876.
  " Reise an der Araguaya," *Petermann's Mittheilungen.* Vol. xxii. Gotha, 1876.

Coutouly, F. de, " Le mariage et ses coutumes chez les Foula du Koïu," *Revue d'Ethnographie et de Sociologie.* Vol. i. Paris, 1910.

Couve, L., art. " Kernos," in C. V. Daremberg and E. Saglio, *Dictionnaire des antiquités grecques et romaines.* Vol. iii. Paris, 1899.

Cowan, J., *The Maoris of New Zealand.* Christchurch, 1910.

Cox, A. F., *Madras District Manuals. North Arcot.* 2 vols. Madras, 1894–95.

Cox, Sir George William, *The Mythology of the Aryan Nations.* 2 vols. London, 1882.

Cox, Hiram, *Journal of a Residence in the Burman Empire.* London, 1821.

Cox, R., *Adventures on the Columbia River.* 2 vols. London, 1831.

Cox, Samuel S., *Diversions of a Diplomatist in Turkey.* New York, 1887.

Coxe, William, *Account of the Russian Discoveries between Asia and America.* London, 1804.

Craig, James A., *Assyrian and Babylonian Religious Texts (Assyriologische Bibliothek).* 2 vols. Leipzig, 1895, 1897.

Craigie, W. A., *Scandinavian Folklore.* London, 1896.

Craik, G. L., *The New Zealanders.* London, 1830.

Cranz, David, *The History of Greenland, containing a description of the Country and its Inhabitants.* Transl. 2 vols. London, 1767.

Craufurd, in *Journal of the Anthropological Institute.* Vol. xxiv. London, 1894.

Craven, C. H., " Traces of Fraternal Polyandry among the Santals," *Journal of the Asiatic Society of Bengal.* Vol. lxxii, Part iii. Calcutta, 1904.

Craven, Lady Elizabeth, *A Journey through the Crimea to Constantinople . . . in a series of Letters written in the year 1786.* London, 1789.

Crawford, Alexander, Earl of, *Etruscan Inscriptions Analysed and Trans-lated.* London, 1872.

Crawford, D., *Thinking Black.* London, 1912.

Crawford, M. D. C., " Peruvian Textiles," *Anthropological Papers of the American Museum of Natural History*. Vol. xii. Washington, 1915.

Crawfurd, John, *Journal of an Embassy from the Governor-general of India to the Court of Ava*. 2 vols. London, 1830.

History of the Indian Archipelago. 3 vols. Edinburgh, 1820.

Crawley, A. E., *The Mystic Rose*. London, 1902.

Creagh, James, *Armenians, Koords, and Turks*. 2 vols. London, 1880.

Creagh, S. M., " Notes on the Loyalty Islands," *Report of the Fourth Meeting of the Australasian Association for the Advancement of Science*. Sydney 1894.

Cremony, John C., *Life among the Apaches*. San Francisco, 1868.

Crescini, V., *Per la questione delle Corti d'Amore*. Padova, 1891.

Creuzer, G. F., *Symbolik und Mythologie der alten Völker*. 6 vols. Leipzig, Darmstadt, 1819–23.

The same, transl. and remodelled by G. F. Guigniart under the title *Religions de l'antiquité*, etc. 4 vols. Paris, 1825–51.

Crèvecoeur, M. G. J. de, *Voyage dans la haute Pensylvanie et dans l'état de New York*. 3 vols. Paris, 1801.

Crisp, John, " An Account of the Inhabitants of the Poggy, or Nassau Islands, lying off Sumatra," *Asiatick Researches*. Vol. vi. Calcutta, 1799.

Cromer, Lord, *Modern Egypt*. London, 1911.

Cronise, Titus Fey, *The Natural Wealth of California*. San Francisco, 1868.

Crooke, W., *The Popular Religion and Folk-lore of Northern India*. 2 vols. Westminster, 1896.

Tribes and Castes of the North-Western Provinces and Oudh. 4 vols. Calcutta, 1896.

" The Lifting of the Bride," *Folk-lore*. Vol. xiii. London, 1902.

" Nudity in India in Custom and Ritual," *Journal of the Royal Anthropological Institute*. Vol. xlix. London, 1919.

" The Cults of the Mother Goddesses in India," *Folk-lore*. Vol. xxx. London, 1919.

" The Holi : a Vernal Festival of the Hindus," *Folk-lore*. Vol. xxv. London, 1914.

Art. " Charms and Amulets (Indian)," in Hastings's, *Encyclopaedia of Religion and Ethics*, vol. iii. Edinburgh, 1910.

Crosby, Oscar Terry, *Tibet and Turkestan*. London, 1905.

Cross, D. Kerr, " Notes on the Country lying between Lakes Nyassa and Tanganyika," *Proceedings of the Royal Geographical Society*, N.S., vol. xiii. London, 1891.

Crowfoot, J. W., " Customs of the Rubatab," *Sudan Notes and Records*. Vol. i. Khartoum, 1918.

" Wedding Customs in the Northern Sudan," *ibid*. Vol. v. Khartoum, 1922.

Cruikshank, Brodie, *Eighteen Years on the Gold Coast of Africa*. 2 vols. London, 1853.

Cruise, R. A., *Journal of a Ten Months' Residence in New Zealand*. London, 1824.

Cujacus, Jacobus. *Opera Omnia in decem tomos distributa jam a C. A. Fabroto disposita*. 11 vols. Neapolis, 1758.

Cumming, Constance F. Gordon, *In the Himalayas and on the Indian Plains*. London, 1884.

From the Hebrides to the Himalayas. 2 vols. London, 1876.

Cummins, S. L., " Sub-tribes of the Bahr-el-Ghazal Dinkas," *Journal of the Anthropological Institute*. Vol. xxxiv. London, 1904.

Cunningham, Sir Alexander, *Ladak*. London, 1854.
  in *Reports of the Archaeological Survey of India*, q.v.
Cunningham, J. D., *A History of the Sikhs*. London, 1849.
Cunningham, J. F., *Uganda and its Peoples*. London, 1905.
Cunningham, J. T., *Sexual Dimorphism in the Animal Kingdom*. London, 1900.
  The Natural History of the Marketable Marine Fishes of the British Islands. London, 1896.
Cuoq, Jean A., *Lexique de la langue algonquine*. Montreal, 1886.
  Lexique de la langue iroquoise. Montreal, 1882.
Cureau, A. L., *Savage Man in Central Africa*. Transl. London, 1915.
Curr, E. M., *The Australian Race*. 4 vols. Melbourne, London, 1886–87.
  Recollections of Squatting in Victoria. Melbourne, 1883.
Currier, Andrew F., " A Study relative to the Functions of the Reproductive Apparatus in American Indian Women," *Transactions of the American Gynecological Society*. Vol. xvi. Philadelphia, 1891.
Curtin, J., *A Journey in Southern Siberia*. London, 1910.
  The Mongols, their religion and their myths. Boston, 1909.
  The Mongols : A history. Boston, 1908.
Curtiss, Samuel Ives, *Primitive Semitic Religion To-day*. London, 1902.
Cushing, Frank H., " My Adventures in Zuñi," *The Century Magazine*. Vol. xxvi. New York, 1883.
  " Zuñi Fetishes," *Second Annual Report of the Bureau of Ethnology*. Washington, 1883.
  " A Study of Pueblo Pottery illustrating of Zuñi cultural growth." *Fourth Annual Report of the Bureau of Ethnology*. Washington, 1886.
  " Outlines of Zuñi Creation Myths," *Thirteenth Annual Report of the Bureau of Ethnology*. Washington, 1896.
  " Primitive Motherhood," *Proceedings of the National Congress of Mothers*. Washington, 1897.
Cusick, David, *Sketches of the Ancient History of the Six Nations*. See Beauchamp, W. M., *The Iroquois Trail*.
Cypria, in *Epicorum Graecorum Fragmenta*. Ed. G. Kinkel. Leipzig, 1878.
Cyprian, *Opera omnia*, in Migne, *Patrologiae Cursus Completus*. Vols. iii–iv. Parisiis, 1844.
Cyril of Jerusalem, *Opera*, in Migne, *Patrologiae Cursus Completus, Series Graeca*. Vol. xxxiii. Parisiis, 1857.
Czaplicka, M. A., *My Siberian Year*. London [1916].
  Aboriginal Siberia. Oxford, 1914.

The Dâdistân-î Dînîk and the Epistles of Mânûskîhar. Transl. by E. W. West. *The Sacred Books of the East*. Vol. xviii. Oxford, 1882.
Dahlgrün, H., " Heiratsgebräuche der Schambaa," *Mitteilungen aus den Deutschen Schutzgebieten*. Vol. xvi. Berlin, 1903.
Dale, G., " An Account of the Principal Customs and Habits of the Natives inhabiting the Bondei Country," *Journal of the Anthropological Institute*. Vol. xxv. London, 1896.
Danhnhardt, O, *Natursagen*. 4 vols. Leipzig, 1907–12.
Dahmen, F., " The Paliyans, a Hill-tribe of the Palni Hills (South India)," *Anthropos*. Vol. iii. Wien, 1908.
  " The Kunnuvans or Mannalis, a Hill-tribe of the Palnis, South India," *Anthropos*. Vol. v. Wien, 1910.

Dalager, Lars, *Grønlandske Relationer*. Kiøbenhaven, s.d.

Dall, W. H., " Social Life among our Aborigines," *The American Naturalist*. Vol. xii. Philadelphia, 1878.

Alaska and its Resources. London, 1870.

" On Masks, Labrets, and certain Aboriginal Customs," *Third Annual Report of the Bureau of Ethnology*. Washington, 1884.

Tribes of the Extreme Northwest (*Contributions to North American Ethnology*. Vol. i). Washington, 1877.

Dalla Torre, K. W. von, " Die Erforschungsgeschichte der Parthenogenesis bei den Schmetterlinge," *Entomologische Jahrbücher*. Vol. xxv. Leipzig, 1916.

" Die Parthenogenesis bei den Hönigbiene," *Zoologisches Zentralblatt*. Vol. xvi. Leipzig, 1910.

Dally, E., *Recherches sur les mariages consanguins et sur les races pures*, reprint from the *Bulletin de la Société d'Anthropologie*. Paris, 1864.

Dalton, E. T., *Descriptive Ethnology of Bengal*. Calcutta, 1872.

" The Kols of Chota-Nagpore," *Transactions of the Ethnological Society*. N.S., vol. vi. London, 1868.

" The Bhuiyas," *Calcutta Review*. Vol. ciii. Calcutta, 1871.

Dalton, Henry G., *History of British Guiana*. 2 vols. London, 1855.

Dalyell, J. G., *The Darker Superstitions of Scotland*. Edinburgh, 1834.

Damartin, Herbert le duc de, *Le roman de Foulque de Candie*. Ed. P. Tarbé. (*Collection des poètes de Champagne antérieurs au xvie siècle*.) Reims, 1860.

Danks, B., " Marriage Customs of the New Britain Group," *Journal of the Anthropological Institute*. Vol. xviii.

Dannert, E., " Soziale Verhältnisse der Ovaherero," *Mitteilungen der Geographischen Gesellschaft (für Thuringen) zu Jena*. Vol. vi. Jena, 1888.

Zum Rechte der Herero. Berlin, 1906.

" Customs of the Ovaherero," *Folk-lore Journal*. Vol. ii. Cape Town, 1880.

Dante Alighieri, *La Divina Commedia*. Firenze, 1840–42.

Opere minori. 3 vols. Firenze, 1856–57.

Danz, H. A. A., *Lehrbuch der Geschichte des römischen Rechts*. 2 Parts. Leipzig, 1840–46.

Dapper, Olfert, *Description de l'Afrique*. Amsterdam, 1686.

Die unbekante Neue Welt, oder Beschreibung des Weltteils Amerika. Amsterdam, 1673.

Daremberg, Ch., and Saglio, Edm., *Dictionnaire des antiquités grecques et romaines*. 5 vols (in 8). Paris, 1873–1919.

Dareste, Rodolphe, *Nouvelles études d'histoire du droit*. Paris, 1902.

Dargun, L., *Mutterrecht und Raubehe und ihre Reste im germanischen Recht und Leben*. Breslau, 1883.

Darwin, Charles, *The Descent of Man and Selection in Relation to Sex*. 2 vols. London, 1888.

The Variation of Animals and Plants under Domestication. 2 vols. London, 1890.

A Naturalist's Voyage round the World. London, 1890.

" A Biographical Sketch of an Infant," *Mind*. Vol. ii. London, 1877.

Darwin, George H., " Marriages between First-Cousins in England and their Effects," *Journal of the Statistical Society*. Vol. xxxviii. London, 1875.

Daumas, M. J. E., *Moeurs et coutumes de l'Algérie*. Paris, 1855.

La Femme Arabe. Alger, 1913.

Le Sahara Algérien. Paris, 1845.

Daumer, G. F., *Enthüllung über Kaspar Hauser*. Frankfurt a. M., 1859.

Davay, Francis, *Du danger des mariages consanguins sous le rapport sanitaire*. Paris, 1862.

Davenport, C. B., *Heredity in relation to Eugenics*. London, 1912.
  The Feebly Inhibited. Nomadism, or the Wandering Impulse, with Special Reference to Heredity. Washington, 1915.
  and Scudder, M. T., *Naval Officers, their Heredity and Development*. Washington, 1919.

David, J., "Notizen über die Pygmäen des Ituriwaldes," *Globus*. Vol. lxxxvi. Braunschweig, 1904.

David, Mrs. T. W. Edgeworth, *Funafuti ; or Three Months on a Coral Island*. London, 1899.

Davids, T. W. Rhys, *Buddhist Birth-Stories*. London, 1877.

Davidson, J. W., *The Island of Formosa, Past and Present*. London and Yokohama, 1903.

Davies, R. H., "On the Aborigines of Van Diemen's Land," *The Tasmanian Journal of Natural Science*. Vol. ii. Hobart, 1846.

Davis, Arthur William, *Gazetteer of the North Lushai Hills*. Shillong, 1894.

Davis, C. O. B., *Maori Mementos ; being a series of Addresses presented by the Native People to His Excellency Sir George Grey*. Auckland, 1855.

Davis, Gladys M. N., *The Asiatic Dionysos*. London, 1914.

Davis, J. B., "Some Cherokee Stories," *Annals of Archaeology and Anthropology, University of Liverpool*. Vol. iii. London and Liverpool, 1910.

Davis, Sir John Francis, *China : a general Description of the Empire and its Inhabitants*. 2 vols. London, 1857.

Davis, Theodore M., *Excavations : Bibàn el Molûk. The Tomb of Queen Tîyi*. London, 1910.
  The Tomb of Hâtshopsîtû. London, 1906.

Davis, W. W. H., *El Gringo ; or New Mexico and her People*. New York, 1857.

Davy, John, *An Account of the Interior of Ceylon*. London, 1821.

Dawkins, R. M., "Excavations at Palaikastro," *Annual of the British School at Athens*. Vol. x. Athens, 1904.

Dawson, George M., *On the Haida Indians of the Queen Charlotte Islands* (*Geological Survey of Canada. Reports of Explorations and Surveys, 1878–79*). Montreal, 1880.
  "Report on an Exploration in the Yukon District, North Western Territory, and adjacent northern portion of British Columbia," *Annual Report of the Geological and Natural History Survey of Canada*, N.S. Vol. iii, part i. Montreal, 1889.

Dawson, J., *The Australian Aborigines*. Melbourne, 1881.

Day, Francis, *British and Irish Salmonidae*. London, 1887.

De Amicis, see Amicis.

Dean, B., *Fishes, Living and Fossil*. London, 1895.

Deane, Wallace, *Fijian Society*. London, 1921.

"The Death of Diarmaid." Ed. and tr. by J. H. Lloyd, O. J. Bergin, and G. Schoepperle, *Revue Celtique*. Vol. xxxiii. Paris, 1912.

Debret, J. B., *Voyage pittoresque et historique au Brésil*. 3 vols. Paris, 1834–39.

Déchelette, J., "Croissants lacustres et cornes sacrées," *Revue préhistorique et de paléontologie*. Vol. iii. Paris, 1908.

Decle, Lionel, *Three Years in Savage Africa*. London, 1898.

De C[lercq], "Over eenige maatschappelijke instelligen der inlandsche Christenen in de Minahassa," *Tijdschrift voor Nederlands Indië*. Vol. i. Batavia, 1838.

Deecke, W., in *Jahrbuch für Geschichte, Sprache und Litteratur Elsass-Löth-ringen.* Strassburg, 1881.

Deevall, H. van, "Aanteekeningen omtrent de Nordoostkuste van Borneo," *Tijdschrift voor Indische taal-, land- en volkenkunde.* Vol. iv. Batavia, 1855.

Defrémery, Ch., Review of Makrizi's *De valle Hadramaut libellus*, ed. P. B. Noskowyi, Bonn, 1866, in *Journal Asiatique.* VIe Série. Vol. ix. Paris, 1867.

De Grandpré, L. M., *Voyage à la côte occidentale d'Afrique, fait dans les années 1786 et 1787.* 2 vols. Paris, 1801.

Deguignes, Joseph, *Histoire générale des Huns, des Turcs, des Mogols et des autres Tartares occidentaux.* 5 vols. Paris, 1756–58.

Delacour, A., "Les Tenda (Koniagui, Bassari, Badyaranke) de la Guinée Française," *Revue d'Ethnographie et de Sociologie.* Vol. iv. Paris, 1913.

De la Flotte, *Essais historiques sur l'Inde, précédes d'un journal de voyages et d'une description de la Côte de Coromandel.* Paris, 1769.

Delafosse, Maurice, "Le peuple Siéna ou Sénoufo," *Revue des études ethno-graphiques et sociologiques.* Vol. i. Paris, 1908.

Delage, Yves, and Hérouard, Edgard, *Traité de Zoologie concrète.* 9 vols. Paris, 1896–

De la Mare, Walter, *Down-adown-derry.* London, 1922.

De Lancre, Pierre, *Tableau de l'inconstance des mauvais anges et des démons.* Paris, 1612.

Delbrück, Berthold, "Die Enstehung des Mythos bei den indogermanische Völker," *Zeitschrift für Völkerpsychologie und Sprachwissenschaft.* Vol. iii. Berlin, 1863.

"Die indogermanischen Verwandschaftsnamen," *Abhandlungen der König-lichen Sächsischen Gesellschaft der Wissenschaften.* Vol. xxv. Leipzig, 1890.

Délégation en Perse. Mémoires publiés sous la direction de M. J. de Morgan. 13 vols. Paris, 1900–12.

Delegorgue, A., *Voyage dans l'Afrique Australe.* 2 vols. Paris, 1847.

Delhaise, C., *Les Warega.* Bruxelles, 1909.

Notes ethnographiques sur quelques peuplades du Tanganika. Bruxelles, 1905.

De l'Isle, A., "Mémoire sur les moeurs et l'accouchement de l'Alytes obste-tricans," *Annales des Sciences naturelles, 6e Série, Zoologie.* Vol. iii. Paris, 1 76.

Delisle, F., review of J. Truffert, "Le Massif des M'Brés," *Revue générale des Sciences, 1902*, in *L'Anthropologie.* Vol. xiv. Paris, 1903.

Delitzsch, Fr., *Assyrisches Handwörterbuch.* Leipzig, 1894.

Babel und Bibel. Stuttgart, 1904.

Babel and Bible. Transl. Chicago, 1906.

Dellon, Dr., *Nouvelle Relation d'un Voyage fait aux Indes orientales.* Amster-dam, 1699.

Del Mar, A., *History of Money in Ancient Countries.* London, 1885.

Deloche, M., "La procession dite de la Lunade et les feux de la Saint-Jean à Tulle (Bas Limousin). La Fête du solstice d'été." *Revue Celtique.* Vol. ix. Paris, 1888.

De Lollis, C., *Vita e poesie di Sordello di Goito.* Halle, 1896.

"Sul canzoniere di Chiaro Davanzati," *Giornale storico della Letteratura Italiana*, Suppl. i. Torino, 1898.

"Dolce stil nuovo e 'noel dig de nova maestria.'" *Studi Medievali.* Vol. i. Torino, 1904.

Demelič, F., *Le droit coutumier des Slaves Méridionaux*. Paris, 1877.

Demeunier, Jean-Nicholas, *L'esprit des usages et des coutumes des différents peuples*. Londres et Paris, 1786.

Demosthenes, *Opera*. Ed. J. T. Voemel. Paris, 1843.

Denham, Major Dixon, Capt. Clapperton and Dr. Oudney, *Travels and Discoveries in North and Central Africa*. 4 vols. London, 1826.

Deniker, J., *Les races et peuples de la terre*. Paris, 1900.

Denis, Ferd., *Brésil*. (*L'Univers.*) Paris, 1837.

Denis, Jacques, *Histoire des théories et des idées morales dans l'antiquité*. 2 vols. Paris, 1856.

Denkschriften der philosophisch-historische Classe der Kön.-Kais. Akademie der Wissenschaften. Wien, 1850–

Dennett, R. E., " Laws and Customs of the Fjort or Bavili Family, Kingdom of Loango," *Journal of the African Society*. Vol i. London, 1901.

   Nigerian Studies, or the Religious and Political System of the Yoruba. London, 1910.

   At the Back of the Black Man's Mind. London, 1904.

   Notes on the Folklore of the Fjort (French Congo). London, 1898.

Dennis, George, *The Cities and Cemeteries of Etruria*. 2 vols. London, 1878.

Dennys, Nicholas Belfield, *The Folklore of China and its affinities with that of the Aryan and Semitic Races*. London, Hong-Kong, 1876.

   A Descriptive Dictionary of British Malaya. London, 1894.

Denys, Nicholas, *Description géographique et historique des costes de l'Amérique septentrionale, avec l'histoire naturelle du païs*. 2 vols (the second volume bears a different title-page). Paris, 1672.

Depelchin, H., and Croonenberghs, Ch., *Trois ans dans l'Afrique Australe. Le Pays des Matabèles*. Bruxelles, 1882.

Derembourg, H., " Le Culte de la déesse Al'Ouzza dans l'ancienne Arabie vers l'an 300 de notre ère," *Verhandlungen der Zweiten Kongress für allgemeine Religionsgeschichte*. Basel, 1904.

Deschamps, E., *Au Pays des Veddas : Ceylon*. Paris, 1892.

   " Les Veddas de Ceylan," *L'Anthropologie*. Vol. ii. Paris, 1891.

Deschamps, Paul, " Les différences sociologiques entre les sauvages et les anthropoïdes," *L'Anthropologie*. Vol. xxx. Paris, 1920.

" Descripção geographica da America Portugueza (sem nome de autor)," *Revista Trimensal do Instituto Historico e Geographico do Brazil*. Vol. i. Rio de Janeiro, 1839.

" A Description and Historicall Declaration of the Gold Kingdom of Guinea," etc. Translated out of Dutch. *Hakluytus Posthumus, or Purchas His Pilgrimes*. Vol. vi. Glasgow, 1905.

" A Description of China," in Astley, *A New General Collection of Voyages and Travels*. Vol. iv. London, 1847.

Desgodins, C. H., *Le Thibet d'après la correspondance des Missionaires*. Paris, 1885.

De Smedt, C., and De Backer, J., *Acta Sanctorum Hiberniae ex codice Salmatico*. Edinburgh, 1888.

Desoignies, " Die Msalala," in S. R. Steinmetz, *Rechtsverhältnisse von eingeborenen Völker in Afrika und Ozeanien*. Berlin, 1903.

Desor, E., *Die Pfahlbauten des Neuenburger Sees*. Frankfurt a. M., 1867.

Desplagnes, Aug. M. L., *Le plateau central nigérien. Une mission archéologique et ethnologique au Soudan Français*. Paris, 1907.

Des Preis, Jehan, *Ly Myreur des histors*. Ed. A. Borgnet and S. Bormans. 6 vols. Bruxelles, 1864–87.

Des Vergers, A. N., *L'Étrurie et les Étrusques*. 2 vols. Paris, 1862–64.

Detzner, H., *Vier Jahre unter Kannibalen*. Berlin, 1920.

Deubner, Lugwig, *De Incubatione capita quattuor.* Leipzig, 1900.

Devay, F., *Du danger des mariages consanguins sous le rapport sanitaire.* Paris, Lyon, 1857.

Devéria, T., *Catalogue des manuscrits égyptiens qui sont conservés au musée du Louvre.* Paris, 1877.

Dewall, H. von, " Aanterkenigen omtrent de nordoostkust van Borneo," *Tijdschrift voor Indische taal-, land- en volkenkunde.* Vol. iv. Batavia, 1855.

Dewey, John and A. C., *Letters from China and Japan.* New York, 1920.

D'Hancarville, *Recherches sur l'origine, l'esprit et le progrés des arts de la Grèce.* 2 vols. Londres, 1785.

Diaz, Casimiro, " Conquests of the Filipinas Islands and chronicle of the religious of our Father St. Augustine," in E. H. Blair and J. A. Robertson, *The Philippine Islands, 1493–1803.* Vols. xxxvii., xlii. Cleveland, 1906.

Dibble, S., *History of the Sandwich Islands.* Lahainaluna, 1843.

Dickinson, F. A., *Big Game Shooting on the Equator.* London, 1908.

Dickinson, G. Lowes, *The Greek View of Life.* London, 1896.

Diderot, Denis, *Oeuvres complètes.* Ed. J. Assezat. 20 vols. Paris, 1875–77.

Didron, A. N. D., *Iconographie chrétienne.* Paris, 1843.

" Die Eingeborenen von Neuholland," *Evangelisches Missions-Magazin,* N.F. Vol. iv. Basel, 1860.

Diefenbach, Lorenz, *Origines Europaeae.* Frankfurt a. M., 1861.

Dieffenbach, Ernst, *Travels in New Zealand.* 2 vols. 1843.

Diels, Hermann, *Die Fragmente der Vorsokratiker.* 2 vols. Berlin, 1906–10. *Heracleitos von Ephesos.* Berlin, 1909.

Diéreville, *Relation du voyage du Port Royal de l'Acadie, ou de la Nouvelle France.* Amsterdam, 1710.

Dieterich, Albrecht, *Mutter Erde, ein Versuch über Volksreligion.* Berlin, 1913.

Diez, F., *Beiträge zur Kenntniss der romantische Poesie.* Berlin, 1825. *Über die Minnehöfe.* Berlin, 1825. *Leben und Werke der Troubadours.* Leipzig, 1883. *Die Poesie der Troubadours.* Leipzig, 1882.

Digesta. See *Corpus Juris Civilis.*

Dilich, Wilhelm, *Hessische Chronika.* Cassel, 1608.

Dill, Samuel, *Roman Society from Nero to Marcus Aurelius.* London, 1911.

Din Dayal, Munshi, " Note on various Birth Customs," in E. H. Kealy, " Rajputana and Ajmer-Merwara," Report, *Census of India, 1911.* Vol. xxii. Ajmer, 1913.

Dio Cassius, *Historiarum Romanarum quae supersunt.* Ed. L. Dindorf. 5 vols. Leipzig, 1863–65.

Diodorus Siculus, *Bibliotheca historica.* 11 vols. Biponti, 1793–1807.

Diogenes Laertius, *De vitis philosophorum.* Ed. H. G. Huebner. 2 vols. Leipzig, 1828–31.

Diomedes, *Ars Grammatica,* in *Grammatici Latini,* Ed. H. Keil. Vol. i. Leipzig, 1857.

Dion Chrysostom, *Orationes.* Ed. I. Casaubon and Morelli. Lutetia, 1704.

Dionysius of Halicarnassus, *Opera omnia.* 6 vols. Leipsic, 1774–77.

Dionysius Periegetes, *Orbis descriptio* in G. Bernhardy, *Geographi Graeci Minores.* Vol. ii. Leipzig, 1828.

Distant, W. L. " The Inhabitants of Car Nicobar," *Journal of the Anthropological Institute.* Vol. iii. London, 1874.

Dixie, Lady Florence, *Across Patagonia.* London, 1880.

Dixon, J. M., " The Tsuishikari Ainos," *Transactions of the Asiatic Society of Japan*. Vol. xi, Part i. Yokohama, 1883.

Dixon, Roland B., " The Northern Maidu," *Bulletin of the American Museum of Natural History*. Vol. xvii, Part iii. New York, 1905.

" The Shasta," *Ibid.* Part v. New York, 1907.

" Notes on the Achomawi and Astsugewi Indians of Northern California," *The American Anthropologist*. N.S., vol. x. Lancaster, 1908.

The Chimariko Indians and Language (University of California Publications in American Archaeology and Ethnology. Vol. v, No. 5). Berkeley, 1910.

" Basketry Designs of the Maidu Indians," *The American Anthropologist*. Vol. ii. Lancaster, 1900.

" Maidu Myths," *Bulletin of the American Museum of Natural History*. Vol. xvii. New York, 1902.

Dobell, Peter, *Travels in Kamtchatka and Siberia*. 2 vols. London, 1830.

Dobers, E., " Über die Biologie der Bdelloidea," *Internationale Revue der gesamten Hydrobiologie und Hydrographie*. Vol. vii, Supplement. 1916.

Dobrizhoffer, M., *Historia de Abiponibus*. Vienna, 1784.

An Account of the Abipones. Trans. 3 vols. London, 1822.

Dobrowsky, Josef, *Geschichte der böhmischen Sprache und ältern Litteratur*. Prague, 1818.

Dodge, R. Irving, *Our Wild Indians*. Hartford, 1882.

Dodwell, Edward, *A Classical and Topographical Tour through Greece*. 2 vols. London, 1819.

Döhne, J. L., *Zulu-Kafir Dictionary*. Cape Town, 1857.

Dölger, Franz Jos., " IXΘYC," *Römische Quartalschrift für christliche Altertumskunde und Kirchengeschichte*. Vol. xxiii. Rome, 1909.

Domenech, Emmanuel, *Journal d'une mission au Texas et au Mexique*. Paris, 1857.

Dominguez, Luis de, *The Conquest of the River Plate (Hakluyt Society)*. London, 1891.

Donaldson, Henry Herbert, *The Growth of the Brain*. London, 1895.

" Anatomical observations on the brain and several sense-organs of the blind deaf-mute Laura Dewey Bridgman," *American Journal of Psychology*. Vol. iii. and iv. Baltimore, 1891-92.

" The extent of the visual area of the cortex in man deduced from the study of Laura Bridgman's brain," *American Journal of Psychology*. Vol. iv. Baltimore, 1893.

Donaldson, Thomas, " The Moqui Indians of Arizona and Pueblo Indians of New Mexico," *Eleventh Census, United States, Extra Bulletin*. Washington, 1893.

Donath, J., *Die Anfänge des menschlichen Geistes*. Stuttgart, 1898.

Doolittle, J., *Social Life of the Chinese*. 2 vols. New York, 1867.

Doon de Mayence, chanson de geste. Ed. by A. Peÿ. Paris, 1859.

Dopsch, A., *Die Wirtschaftsentwicklung des Karolingerzeit*. 2 vols. Weimar, 1912–13.

Doré, H. (S. J.), *Recherches sur les Superstitions en Chine*. Chang-Hai, 1915–

Dornan, S. S., " The Tati Bushmen and their Language," *Journal of the Royal Anthropological Institute*. Vol. xlvii. London, 1917.

Döropfeld, Wilhelm, " Verbrennung und Bestattung der Toten im alten Griechenland," *Mélanges Nicole. Recueil de Mémoires offert a Jules Nicole*. Genève, 1905.

Döropfeld, Wilhelm, " Die kretischen Paläste," *Mitteilungen des kaiserlich deutschen archäologischen Instituts, Athenische Abteilung.* Vol. xxxii. Athens, 1907.

Dorsey, George A, *Mythology of the Wichita (Carnegie Institute Publications, No. 21).* Washington, 1904.

Traditions of the Caddo. Washington, 1905.

The Pawnee Mythology. Washington, 1906.

" Social Organization of the Skidi Pawnee," *Congrès international des Américanistes XVᵉ Session tenue à Québec en 1906.* Vol. 2. Quebec, 1907.

" A Pawnee Ritual of Instruction," *Boas Anniversary Volume.* New York, 1906.

The Arapaho Sun Dance (Field-Columbian Museum, Publication 75, Anthropological Series. Vol. iv). Chicago, 1903.

The Cheyenne (Ibid., Publication 99, Anthropological Series. Vol. ix). Chicago, 1905.

Traditions of the Skidi Pawnees (Memoirs of the American Folklore Society. Vol. viii.). Boston, 1894.

Dorsey, J. Owen, " Omaha Sociology," *Third Annual Report of the Bureau of Ethnology.* Washington, 1884.

" Siouan Sociology," *Fifteenth Annual Report of the Bureau of Ethnology.* Washington, 1897.

" Osage Traditions," *Sixth Annual Report of the Bureau of Ethnology.* Washington, 1888.

" A Study of Siouan Cult," *Eleventh Annual Report of the Bureau of Ethnology.* Washington, 1894.

" Omaha Dwellings, Furniture and Implements," *Thirteenth Annual Report of the Bureau of Ethnology.* Washington, 1896.

" Nanibozhu in Siouan Mythology," *Journal of American Folk-lore.* Vol. v. Boston and New York, 1892.

and Swanton, J. R., *A Dictionary of the Biloxi and Ofo Languages (Bureau of Ethnology, Bulletin No. 47).* Washington, 1912.

Douce, Francis, *Illustrations of Shakespeare and of Ancient Manners.* 2 vols. London, 1807.

Douceré, Mgr. V., " Notes sur les populations indigènes des Nouvelles Hébrides," *Revue d'Ethnographie et des Traditions Populaires.* Vol. iii. Paris, 1922.

Doughty, C. M., *Travels in Arabia Deserta.* 2 vols. Cambridge, 1888.

Douglas, R. S., " An Expedition to the Back Country of Central Borneo," *The Sarawak Museum Journal.* Vol. i. Singapore, 1912.

Doutté, E., *La Société musulmane du Maghreb. Magie et religion de l'Afrique du Nord.* Algier, 1909.

Douville, Jean Baptiste, *Voyage au Congo et dans l'intérieur de l'Afrique équinoxiale.* 3 vols. Paris, 1832.

Dove, T., " Moral and Social Characteristics of the Aborigines of Tasmania," *The Tasmanian Journal of Natural Science.* Vol i. Hobart, 1842.

Down, J. Langdon, *On the Education and Training of the Feeble in Mind.* London, 1876.

Dowson, J., *A Classical Dictionary of Hindu Mythology, Religion, History and Literature.* London, 1879.

Dozon, Auguste, *Poésies populaires Serbes.* Paris, 1859.

Dozy, R., *Spanish Islam.* Transl. London, 1913.

Dictionnaire détaillé des noms de vêtements chez les Arabes. Amsterdam, 1845.

Drabbe, P., "Het heidensch huwelijk op Tanimbar," *Bijdragen tot de taal-, land- en volkenkunde van Nederlandsch-Indië*. Vol. lxxix. 's Gravenhage, 1923.

Drach, "Croyances des peuples de l'antiquité sur une Vierge-mère," *Annales de Philosophie Chrétienne*. Vol. vii. Paris, 1833.

Drake Brockman, R. E., *The Mammals of Somaliland*. London, 1910.

Drever, James, *Instinct in Man*. Cambridge, 1917.

Drew, Frederic, *The Jummoo and Kashmir Territories*. London, 1875.

Driberg, J. H., *The Lango, a Native Tribe of Uganda*. London, 1923.

"A Preliminary Account of the Didinga." *Sudan Notes and Records*. Vol. v. Khartoum, 1922.

Dribers, J. H., "Rain-making in Loango," *Journal of the Royal Anthropological Institute*. Vol. xlix. London, 1919.

Driver, S. R., *The Book of Genesis*. London, 1906.

Drummond, James, *Philo Judaeus, or the Jewish-Alexandrian Philosophy*. 2 vols. London, 1888.

Drury, Robert, *Madagascar, or R.D.'s Journal*. Ed. by P. Oliver. London, 1890.

Dubeux et Valmont, V., *Tartarie, Belouchistan, Boutan et Nepal*. (*L'Univers*.) Paris, 1848.

Du Bois, Constance Goddard, "Mythology of the Mission Indians," *The Journal of American Folk-Lore*. Vol. xvii. Boston and New York, 1904.

"The Mythology of the Diegueños," *ibid*. Vol. xiv. Boston and New York, 1901.

Dubois, Eugène, "The Proto-Australian Fossil Man of Wadjak, Java," *Koninklijke Akademie van Wetenschappen te Amsterdam*. 2d Section, Proceedings (English edition). Vol. xxiii. Amsterdam, 1922.

Dubois, Jean Antoine, *Moeurs, institutions et cérémonies des peuples de l'Inde*. 2 vols. Paris, 1825.

Hindu Manners, Customs and Ceremonies. Transl. by Henry K. Beauchamp. 2 vols. Oxford, 1897.

Du Boys, Albert, *Histoire du droit civile des peuples anciens*. Paris, 1845.

Du Camp, Maxime, "L'enseignement exceptionel. L'institut des sourds-muets," *La Revue des Deux Mondes*. Vol. civ. Paris, 1873.

Du Cange, C. du Fresne, Sieur, *Glossarium mediae et infimae latinitatis*. 6 vols. Niort, 1883–87.

Du Chaillu, Paul B., *A Journey to Ashango Land*. London, 1867.

In African Forest and Jungle. London, 1903.

"Second Journey into Equatorial Western Africa," *The Journal of the Royal Geographical Society*. Vol. xxxvi. London, 1866.

Du Chesne, André, *Historiae Normannorum Scriptores antiqui*. Lutetiae, Paris, 1619.

Duemmler, F., and Studniczka, F., "Zur Herkunft der mykenischen Cultur," *Mitteilungen des kaiserlich deutschen archäologischen Instituts. Athenische Abteilung*. Vol. xii. Athens, 1887.

Duff, H. L., *Nyasaland under the Foreign Office*. London, 1906.

Duffield, A. J., "On the Natives of New Ireland," *Journal of the Anthropological Institute*. Vol. xv. London, 1886.

Dugmore, A. A. Radclyffe, *The Romance of the Newfoundland Caribou*. London, 1913.

Du Halde, J. B., *The General History of China*. Transl. 4 vols. London, 1741.

Description de la Chine et de la Tartarie chinoise. La Haye, 1736.

Dümichen, J., *Geographische Inschriften* (in H. Brugsch, *Recueil de monuments égyptiens*). 2 vols. Leipzig, 1867–66.

"Geographie des alten Aegyptens. Schrift und Sprache seiner Bewohner," in E. Meyer, *Geschichte des alten Aegypten*. Berlin, 1887.

Dumont d'Urville, J. S. C., *Voyage de la Corvette l'Astrolabe. Histoire du Voyage*. 5 vols. Paris, 1830–34.

Voyage pittoresque autour du monde. 2 vols. Paris, 1834–35.

Duncan, John, *Travels in Western Africa in 1845–1846*. 2 vols. London, 1847.

Duncan, J. Matthew, *Fecundity, Fertility, Sterility, and Allied Topics*. Edinburgh, 1871.

Duncan, Jonathan, "Historical Remarks on the Coast of Malabar with some description of the Manners of its Inhabitants," *Asiatic Researches*. Vol. v. London, 1799.

Duncan, W., in *The Church Missionary Intelligencer*. London, 1856.

Duncker, Maximilian W., *The History of Antiquity*. Transl. 6 vols. London, 1877–82.

Dundas, Hon. Charles, "History of Kitui," *Journal of the Royal Anthropological Institute*. Vol. xliii. London, 1913.

"The Organisation of some Bantu Tribes of East Africa," *Journal of the Royal Anthropological Institute*. Vol. xl. London, 1910.

"Native Laws of some Bantu Tribes of East Africa," *Journal of the Royal Anthropological Institute*. Vol. li. London, 1921.

Dundas, Hon. Kenneth R., "Notes on the Tribes inhabiting the Baringo District, East African Protectorate," *Journal of the Royal Anthropological Institute*. Vol. xl. London, 1910.

"The Wawanga and other Tribes of the Elgon District, British East Africa," *Journal of the Royal Anthropological Institute*. Vol. xliii. London, 1913.

Dunham, S. Astley, *History of the Germanic Empire*. 3 vols. London, 1834–35.

Dunlop, R. H. W., *Hunting in the Himalaya*. London, 1860.

Dunn, John, *The Oregon Territory and the British North American Fur Trade*. Philadelphia, 1845.

Du Pin, L. Ellies, *Nouvelle Bibliothèque des Auteurs Ecclésiastiques*. 33 vols. Paris, 1690.

Du Pratz, Le Page, *Histoire de la Louisiane*. 2 vols. Paris, 1758.

Dupuis, Joseph, *Journal of a Residence in Ashantee*. London, 1824.

Du Quesne, *Journal d'un voyage aux Indes Orientales*. 3 vols. Paris, 1721.

Durand, J. B. L., *Voyage au Sénégal*. Paris, 1802.

Durand-Fardel, Max, "Étude sur le suicide chez les enfants," *Annales Médico-psychologiques*. Paris, 1855.

Durham, M. Edith, "High Albania and its Customs in 1908," *Journal of the Royal Anthropological Institute*. Vol. xl. London, 1910.

Düringsfeld, Ida von, and Reinsberg-Düringsfeld, Otto von, *Hochzeitsbuch*. Leipzig, 1871.

Durkheim, Émile, "La prohibition de l'inceste et ses origines," *L'Année Sociologique*. Vol. i. Paris, 1898.

Düsing, C., *Die Regulierung des Geschlechtsverhältnisses bei der Vermehrung der Menschen, Tiere und Pflanzen*. Iena, 1884.

Dussaud, René, *Les civilisations préhelléniques dans le bassin de la Mer Egée*. Paris, 1914.

"Questions Mycénéennes," *Revue de l'Histoire des Religions*, Vol. li. Paris, 1905.

Du Tertre, J.-B., *Histoire générale des Isles de S. Christophe, de la Guadaloupe, de la Martinique, et autres dans l'Amérique.* Paris, 1654.
  Histoire générale des Antilles habitées par les Français. 4 vols. Paris, 1667.
Dutreuil de Rhins, J.-L., *Mission scientifique de la Haute Asie.* Paris, 1890–95.
Duvan, L., " Légende de la conception de Cuchulainn," *Revue Celtique.* Vol. ix. Paris, 1888.
Duveyrier, Henri, *Les Touaregs du Nord.* Paris, 1864.
Dwight, T., *Travels in New England and New York.* 4 vols. London, 1823.
Dybowski, B., *Okwestyi Kobiacej.* Leopol, 1896.
Dyer, T. F. Thiselton, *English Folk-Lore.* London, 1889.
Dyke, H. H., in *Man.* Vol. xvii. London, 1917.

Ealand, C. A., *Insect Life.* London, 1921.
Earl, G. W., *Papuans.* London, 1853.
Early Voyages to Terra Australis. Ed. by R. H. Major. *(Hakluyt Society.)* London, 1859.
" East Greenland Eskimo," *Science.* Vol. vii. New York, 1886.
Eastman, Mrs. Mary, *Dahcotah, or Life and Legends of the Siou around Fort Snelling.* New York, 1849.
Ecker, A., " Ueber die Excision der Clitoris bei afrikanische Völkerschaften," *Archiv für Anthropologie.* Vol. vii. Braunschweig, 1872.
Eckermann, Johann Peter, *Gespräche mit Goethe in den letzten Jahren seines Lebens.* Leipzig, 1909.
Eckstein, Baron F. von, " La gynécocratie des Cariens," *Revue Archéologique.* Paris, 1858.
Edelfelt, E. G., " Notes on New Guinea," *Proceedings and Transactions of the Queensland Branch of the Geographical Society of Australasia.* Vol. ii, Part i. Brisbane, 1886.
Edersheim, Alfred, *Sketches of Jewish Social Life in the Days of Christ.* London, [1876].
Edge, J. G., " The Mika Ceremony," *Science of Man.* Sydney, 1899.
Edinburgh Medical and Surgical Journal. Edinburgh, 1855–
Edkins, J., " The Yue-ti or Massagetae," *Journal of the (north) China Branch of the Royal Asiatic Society.* Vol. xxi. Shanghai, 1886.
  " The Ephthalites," *Ibid.*
  Chinese Buddhism. London, 1880.
Edwardes, Tickner, *The Lore of the Honey-Bee.* London, s.d.
Edwards, Amelia B., " Relics from the Tombs of the Priest-kings at Dayr-el-Baharee," *Recueil de Travaux relatifs à la philologie et à l'archéologie Égyptiennes et Assyriennes.* Vol. iv. Paris, 1883.
Eerde, J. C. van (ed.), *De Volken van Nederlandsch Indië in monograpieen,* 2 vols. Amsterdam, 1920.
  " Een huwelijk bij de Minangkabausche Maleiers," *Tijdschrift voor Indische taal-, land- en volkenkunde.* Vol. xliv. Batavia, 1901.
Egbert, Archbishop of York, *Poenitentiale,* in Migne, *Patrologiae Cursus Completus.* Vol. lxxxix. Parisiis, 1850.
Egede, Hans, *A Description of Greenland.* Transl. London, 1818.
  Nachrichten von Grönland aus einen Tagebuch vom Bischof Paul Egede. Kopenhagen, 1790.
Eggleston, E., " The Aborigines and the Colonists," *The Century Magazine.* Vol. xxvi. New York, 1883.
Egidi, M., " La tribú di Tanata," *Anthropos.* Vol. ii. Salzburg, 1907.
Eginhard, *Vita Karoli Magni Imperatoris.* Ed. Louis Halphen. Paris, 1923.

Ehmann, P., " Japanische Sprichwörter und sprichwörtliche Redensarten,"
    *Mittheilungen der deutschen Gesellschaft für Natur- und Völkerkunde
    Ostasiens.* Vol. vi. Tokyo, 1897.

" Volksthümliche Vorstellungen in Japan," *Mitteilungen der deutschen
    Gesellschaft für Natur- und Völkerkunde Ostasiens.* Vol. vi. Tokyo, 1897.

Ehrenreich, Paul, *Beiträge zur Völkerkunde Brasiliens (Veröffentlichungen aus
    dem königlichen Museum für Völkerkunde.* Vol. ii). Berlin, 1891.

" Ueber die Botocudos der brasilianischen Provinzen Espiritu Santo und
    Minas Geraes," *Zeitschrift für Ethnologie.* Vol. xix. Berlin, 1887.

" Die Mythen und Legenden der südamerikanische Urvölker," *Zeitschrift
    für Ethnologie.* Vol. xxxvii. Supplement. Berlin, 1905.

Eigenmann, C. H., " The Development of *Micrometrus aggregatus,* one of the
    viviparous surf-perches." *American Naturalist.* Vol. xxiii. Salem,
    Philadelphia, Boston, 1889.

Eilhart von Oberge, *Tristan.* Ed. F. Lichtenstein (*Quellen und Forschungen.*
    Vol. xix). Strassburg, 1877.

" Die Eingeborenen von Neuholland," *Evangelisches Missions-Magazin,*
    Neue Folge. Vol. iv. Basel, 1860.

Eisenmenger, Johann Andrea, *Entdecktes Judenthum.* 2 vols. Frankfurt,
    1700.

Eisler, Robert, *Weltenmantel und Himmelszelt,* 2 vols. München, 1910.

Ekris, A. van, " Iets over Ceram en de Alfoeren," *Bijdragen tot de taal-, land-
    en volkenkunde van Nederlandsch-Indië.* N.V., vol. i. 's Gravenhage,
    1857.

" Het Ceramsche Kakianverbond," *Mededeelingen van wege het Neder-
    landsche Zendelinggenootschap.* Vol. ix. Rotterdam, 1865.

Elias, Ney, " Narrative of a Journey through Mongolia," *The Geographical
    Journal.* Vol. xliii. London, 1873.

Élie de Saint Gille, *Oeuvres.* Ed. Gaston Raynaud (*Société des Anciens Textes
    Français*). Paris, 1879.

Eliot, Sir C., *The East African Protectorate.* London, 1905.

Ella, Samuel, " Polynesian Native Clothing," *Journal of the Polynesian
    Society.* Vol. viii. Wellington, 1899.

" Samoa," *Report of the Fourth Meeting of the Australasian Association
    for the Advancement of Science, Tasmania, 1893.* Sydney, 1894.

Elliot, H. M., *The History of India as told by its own Historians.* Ed. and
    continued by J. Dowson. 8 vols. London, 1867–77.

Elliot, Henry W., " Report on the Seal Islands of Alaska," *Tenth Census of
    the United States.* Vol. viii. Washington, 1884.

Ellis, Alfred Burdon, *The Ewé-speaking Peoples of the Slave Coast of West
    Africa.* London, 1890.

The Tshi-speaking Peoples of the Gold Coast of West Africa. London, 1887,

The Yoruba-speaking Peoples of the Slave Coast of West Africa. London,
    1894.

Ellis, F. W. See Tiruvalluvar.

Ellis, Henry Havelock, *Man and Woman.* London, 1914.

Studies in the Psychology of Sex. 6 vols. Philadelphia, 1906–12.

The Criminal. London, 1901.

Ellis, W., *Polynesian Researches.* 4 vols. London, 1859.

History of Madagascar. 2 vols. London, 1838.

Narrative of a Tour through Hawaii. London, 1826.

Ellis, W., " The Moon and the Weather," *The Observatory.* Vol. xvii.
    London, 1894.

" Supposed dispersion of Clouds under the Full Moon. *Ibid.* London,
    1894.

Elmslie, W. A., *Among the Wild Ngoni*. Edinburgh, London, 1899.

Elphinstone, Montstuart, *An Account of the Kingdom of Caubul*. 2 vols. London, 1815.

History of India. 2 vols. London, 1841.

Elton, Charles Isaac, *Origins of English History*. London, 1890.

Elton, F., " Notes on Natives of the Solomon Islands," *Journal of the Anthropological Institute*. Vol. xvii. London, 1888.

Elworthy, F. T., *The Evil Eye*. London, 1895.

" On Perforated Stone Amulets," *Man*. Vol. iii. London, 1903.

Emerson, Ellen Russell, *Indian Myths, or Legends and Symbols of the Aborigines of America compared with those of other Countries*. Boston, Cambridge, 1884.

Emin Pasha in Central Africa. London, 1888.

Emory, W. H., *Notes of a military Reconnaissance from Port Leavermouth in Missouri to San Diego in California*. New York, 1848.

Encyclopaedia Biblica. 4 vols. London, 1899–1903.

Encyclopaedia Britannica, 11th ed. 29 vols. Cambridge, 1910–11.

Encyclopaedie van Nederlandsch Indië. Ed. P. A. van der Lith, A. J. Spaan, F. Folkes, and J. F. Snellman. 4 vols. 's Gravenhage, Leiden, 1895–1905.

Second edition. Ed. S. de Graaf and D. G. Stibbe. 1917–22.

Endemann, K., " Mittheilungen über die Sotho-Neger," *Zeitschrift für Ethnologie*. Vol. vi. Berlin, 1874.

Endle, Sidney, *The Kacháris*. London, 1911.

Les Enfances Viviens. Ed. by C. Wahlund and H. von Feititzen. Upsala, Paris, 1895.

English, A. C., " Native Habits of the Rigo District," *Annual Report on British New Guinea*, 1892–93. Brisbane, 1893.

" Native Habits and Customs of the Rigo District," *Annual Report on British New Guinea*, 1893–94. Brisbane, 1894.

" Report of the Government Agent for the Rigo District," *Annual Report on British New Guinea*, 1891–92. Brisbane, 1893.

Enjoy, Paul d', " Le baiser en Europe et en Chine," *Bulletins de la Société d'Anthropologie de Paris*. IVe Série. Vol. viii. Paris, 1897.

Entomologische Jahrbücher. Leipzig, 1892–

Entomologische Zeitung. Stettin, Leipzig, 1840–

Epicorum Graecorum Fragmenta. Ed. G. Kinkel. Leipzig, 1878.

Epiphanius, Bishop of Constantia, *Opera*, in Migne, *Patrologiae Cursus Completus, Series Graeca*. Vols. xli–xliii. Parisiis, 1858.

Epp, F., reviewed in *Allgemeine Medicinische Central-Zeitung*. Altenburg, 1853.

Erasthothenes, *Catasterismi*. Ed. J. C. Schubach. Gottingae, 1795.

Erdland, P. August, *Die Marshall-Insulaner*. Wien, 1914.

" Die Stellung der Frauen in den Häuptlingsfamilien der Marshallinseln (Südsee)," *Anthropos*. Vol. iv. Wien, 1909.

Erdweg, M. J., " Die Bewohner der Insel Tumleo, Berlinhafen, Deutsch Neu-Guinea," *Mittheilungen der Anthropologischen Gesellschaft in Wien*. Vol. xxxii. Wien, 1902.

Erman, Adolf, " Ein Denkmal memphitischer Theologie," *Sitzungsberichte der königlich preussische Akademie der Wissenschaften, Philosophisch-historische Classe*. Vol. xliii. Berlin, 1911.

Life in Ancient Egypt. Transl. London, 1894.

Handbook of Egyptian Religion. Transl. London, 1907.

and Krebs, Fritz, *Aus der Papyrus der königlichen Museen*. Berlin, 1899.

Erman, Georg Adolph, " Ethnographische Wahrnehmungen und Erfah-
    rungen an den Küsten des Berings-Meeres," *Zeitschrift für Eth-
    nologie*. Vol. iii. Berlin, 1871.
    Travels through Siberia. Transl. 2 vols. London, 1848.
Ermengaud, Matfre, *Le Breviari d'Amor*. Ed. G. Azaïs. 2 vols. Béziers,
    Paris, 1862–81.
Errington de La Croix, J., " Étude sur les Sakaies de Pérak," *Revue d'Ethno-
    graphie*. Vol. i. Paris, 1882.
Erro, J. B., *El Mundo primitivo filosofico de la antequedad y cultura de la nacion
    Bascongoda*. Madrid, 1815.
Erskine, J. Elphinstone, *Journal of a Cruise among the Islands of the Western
    Pacific*. London, 1853.
Es, Anton H. G. P. van der, *De jure familiarum apud Athenienses*. Lugduni
    Batavorum, 1864.
Eschelmann, P. Henri, " L'enfant chez les Kuni (Nouvelle Guinée Anglaise),"
    Anthropos. Vol. vi. Salzburg, 1911.
Eschwege, W. C. von, *Journal von Brasilien, oder vermischte Nachrichten aus
    Brasilien, aus wissenschaftlichen Reisen gesammelt*. 2 vols. Weimar,
    1818.
Espinas, A., *Les sociétés animales*. Paris, 1878.
Espinosa, Alonso de, *Del origen y milagros de N.S. de Candelaria que aparecio
    en la isla de Teneriffe, con la descripcion de esta isla*. Sevilla, 1594.
    Reprinted in *Biblioteca Isleña*. Santa Cruz de Tenerife, 1848.
    The Guanches of Tenerife. Transl. by Sir Clements Markham. London, 1907.
Esquirol, E., *Des maladies mentales considérées sous les rapports médical,
    hygiénique et médico-légal*. 2 vols. Paris, 1838.
*Essays on some Biblical Questions of the Day by Members of the University of
    Cambridge*. Ed. by H. R. Swete. London, 1909.
Estrée, P. d', " La ceinture de chasteté," *Journal de Médecine de Paris*,
    3ᵉ Série. Vol. xiv. Paris, 1902.
L'État Présent de la Boucharie, etc. Cologne, 1723.
Die ethnographisch-anthropologischen Abtheilung des Museum Godeffroy.
    Ed. J. D. E. Schmeltz and R. Krause. Hamburg, 1881.
Ethnologisches Notizblatt. Berlin, 1894–
Étienne de Rouen, *Draco Normannicus*, in *Chronicles of the Reigns of Stephen,
    Henry II, and Richard I* (*Chronicles and Memorials of Great Britain
    and Ireland*. Vol. lxxxii). Vol. ii. London, 1886.
Etré, P. Guillaume, in *Lettres édifiantes et curieuses*. Vol. viii. Paris, 1783.
Etymologicum Magnum. Ed. F. Sylburg. Leipzig, 1816.
The Eugenics Review. London, 1909–
Eugénien, Fr., " Les Chiites d'aujourd'hui," *Anthropos*. Vol. ii. Salzburg,
    1907.
Euripides, *Fabulae*. Res. T. Fix. Parisiis, 1843.
    The Bacchae, with critical and explanatory notes by John Edwin Sandys.
    Cambridge, 1885.
    The Plays of Euripides, translated into English rhyming verse by Gilbert
    Murray. 2 vols. London, s.d.
Eusebius Pamphilus, *Evangelicae Praeparationis libri xv*. Ed. E. G. Gifford.
    6 vols. Oxonii, 1903.
    Historia ecclesiastica. 2 vols. Cambridge, 1720.
    Opera omnia, in Migne, *Patrologiae Cursus Completus, Series Graeca*.
    Vols. xix–xxiv. Parisiis, 1857.
Eustathius, " Commentarius in Dionysium Periegetem," in *Geographi Graeci
    Minores*, ed. C. Müller. Vol. ii. Parisiis, 1882.
    Commentarius ad Iliadem. 4 vols. Leipzig, 1827–30.

Eutropius, Flavius, *Breviarium Historiae Romanae*. Rec. F. Ruehl. Leipzig, 1887.

Eutychius, *Annales*, in Migne, *Patrologiae Cursus Completus, Patrologia Graeca*. Vol. iii. Parisiis, 1856.

Evangeliorum secundum Hebraeos, Petrum, Aegyptios, Matthiae traditionum, etc., *quae supersunt*. Ed. A. Hilgenfeld. Berlin, 1884.

Evangelisch-Lutheranisches Missionsblatt. Dresden, Leipzig, 1846–

Evangelisches Missions-Magazin, Neue Folge. Basel, 1857–

Evans, Arthur J., " The Minoan and Mycenean Element in Hellenic Life," *The Journal of Hellenic Studies*. Vol. xxxii. London, 1912.

" Knossos, The Palace," *The Annual of the British School at Athens*. Vol. vi. Athens, 1899–1900.

" Further Discoveries of Cretan and Aegean Script, with Libyan and Proto-Egyptian Comparisons," *The Journal of Hellenic Studies*. Vol. xvii. London, 1897.

" Mycenean Tree and Pillar Cult and its Mediterranean Relations," *Journal of Hellenic Studies*. Vol. xxi. London, 1901.

" Temple Repositories," *Annual of the British School at Athens*. Vol. ix. London, 1902.

" The Palace of Knossos," *Annual of the British School at Athens*. Vol. ix. Athens, 1903.

Scripta Minoa. Oxford, 1909–

Prehistoric Tombs in Knossos. London, 1906.

Evans, Ivor H. N., *Among Primitive Peoples in Borneo*. London, 1921.

Studies in Religion, Folk-lore and Custom in British North Borneo and the Malay Peninsula. Cambridge, 1923.

" Notes on the Religion, Beliefs, Superstitions, Ceremonies, and Tabus of the Dusuns of the Tuaran and Tempassuk Districts of British North Borneo," *Journal of the Royal Anthropological Institute*. Vol. xlii. London, 1912.

" Folk Stories of the Tempassuk and Tuaran Districts, British North Borneo," *Journal of the Royal Anthropological Institute*. Vol. xliii. London, 1913.

" Some Sakai Beliefs and Customs," *Journal of the Royal Anthropological Institute*. Vol. xlviii. London, 1921.

" Notes on some Beliefs and Customs of the Orang Dusun, of British North Borneo," *Journal of the Royal Anthropological Institute*. Vol. xlvii. London, 1917.

Ewald, H., *The Antiquities of Israel*. London, 1876.

Ewers, J. Ph. G., *Das älteste Recht der Russen in seiner geschichtlichen Entwickelung*. Dorpat, Hamburg, 1826.

" Examen filosofico de un peregrino suceso do estos tiempos," *Semanario erudito*. Vol. viii. Madrid, 1788.

The Expository Times. Edinburgh, 1889–

Eycleshymer, Albert C., " Observations on the Breeding Habits of *Ameiurus Nebulosus*," *The American Naturalist*. Vol. xxxv. Boston, 1901.

Eylmann, Erhard, *Die Eingeborenen der Kolonie Südaustralien*. Berlin, 1908.

Eyre, E. J., *Journals of Expeditions of Discovery into Central Australia*. 2 vols. London, 1845.

Faa di Bruno, the Very Rev. J., *Catholic Belief, a short and simple exposition of Catholic Doctrine*. London, 1913.

Faber, Felix, *Evagatorium in Terrae Sanctae, Arabiae et Egypti peregrinationes*. Ed. C. D. Hassler. 3 vols. Stuttgart, 1843.

Fabretti, A., *Corpus inscriptionum Italicarum antiquioris aevi, et glossarium Italicum.* Aug. Taurin., 1867.

Fabricius, J. A., *Codex apocryphus Novi Testamenti.* 3 vols. Hamburghi, 1703–19.

Fabry, Hermann, "Aus dem Leben der Wapogoro," *Globus.* Vol. xci. Braunschweig, 1907.

Faidherbe, L. L. C., "Recherches sur les tombeaux mégalithiques de Roknia," *Bulletin de l'Académie d'Hippone.* Bone, 1868.

Fairbridge, D., *A History of South Africa.* London, 1918.

Falk, F., "Zur Statistik der Taubstummen," *Archiv für Psychiatrie und Nervenkrankheiten.* Vol. iii. Berlin, 1872.

Falkner, T., *A Description of Patagonia and the adjoining parts of South America.* Hereford, 1774.

Fallow, T. M., art. "Cross," *Encyclopaedia Britannica.* Vol. vii. Cambridge, 1910.

Farabee. W. Curtis, *The Central Arawaks* (*University of Pennsylvania Anthropological Publications*, No. ix). Philadelphia, 1819.

Indian Tribes of Eastern Peru (*Papers of the Peabody Museum of American Archaeology and Ethnology, Harvard University.* Vol. x.). Cambridge, Mass., 1922.

Faral, Edmond, *Les jongleurs en France au moyen âge.* Paris, 1910.

Fardel, M. Durand, "Études sur le suicide chez les enfants," *Annales médico-psychologiques.* Paris, 1855.

Farini, G. A., *Huit Mois au Kalahari.* Paris, 1887.

Farley, J. Lewis, *Modern Turkey.* London, 1872.

Farnell, L. R., *The Cults of the Greek States.* 5 vols. London, 1896–1909.

"Sociological Hypotheses concerning the Position of Women in Ancient Religion," *Archiv für Religionswissenschaft.* Vol. vii. Leipzig, 1904.

Farrand, L., "Basketry Designs of the Salish Indians," *Publications of the Jesup North Pacific Expedition.* Vol. i. Leiden, New York, 1900.

"Traditions of the Chilcotin Indians," *ibid.* Vol. ii. Leiden, New York, 1900.

"Traditions of the Quinault Indians," *ibid.* Vol. ii. Leiden, New York, 1902.

Faulkner, R. O., "The God Setekh in the Pyramid Texts," *Ancient Egypt.* London, 1925.

Favre, P., *An Account of the Wild Tribes inhabiting the Malayan Peninsula, Sumatra . . . with a Journey to Johore.* Paris, 1865.

Fawcett, F., "On the Soaras (or Savaras)," *Journal of the Anthropological Society of Bombay.* Vol. i. Bombay, 1888.

"The Kondayamkottai Marvars, a Dravidian Tribe of Tinnevelly, Southern India," *Journal of the Anthropological Institute.* Vol. xxxiii. London, 1906.

Fawcett, J. W., "Customs of the Wanuah-Ruah Tribe," *Science of Man.* Sydney, 1898.

Fay, Edward Allen, *Marriages of the Deaf in America.* Washington, 1898.

Featherman, A., *Social History of the Races of Mankind.* 7 vols. London, 1881–91.

Fehling, H., "Beiträge zur Physiologie des placentaren Stoffverkehr," *Archiv für Gynaekologie.* Vol. xi. Berlin, Leipzig, 1877.

Fehlinger, Hans, "Beiträge zur Kentniss der Lebens- und Entwicklungsbedingungen der Inder," *Archiv für Rassen- und Gesellschaftsbiologie.* Vol. iv. Leipzig, 1907.

Fehrle, Eugen, *Die kultische Keuscheit im Altertum.* Giesen, 1910.

Feldner, W. C. G., *Reisen durch mehrere Provinzen Brasiliens.* 2 vols. Liegnitz, 1828.

Felkin, R. W., " Notes on the Madi or Moru Tribe of Central Africa," *Proceedings of the Royal Society of Edinburgh.* Vol. xii. Edinburgh, 1884.
" Notes on the Waganda Tribe of Central Africa," *Proceedings of the Royal Society of Edinburgh.* Vol. xiii. Edinburgh, 1886.

Fellows, C., *Travels and Researches in Asia Minor, particularly in Lycia.* London, 1852.

Féré, Ch., " Les perversions sexuelles chez les animaux," *Revue Philosophique de la France et de l'Étranger.* Vol. xxii. Paris, 1897.
" Sur la psychologie de l'infanticide chez les animaux," *Comptes Rendus de la Société de Biologie.* Paris, 1897.

Ferguson, James, *Tree and Serpent Worship.* London, 1868.

Ferishta, Muhammad Kasim, *History of the Rise of the Mahometan Power in India.* Transl. by John Briggs. 4 vols. London, 1829.

Fernandez, F. Andre, in G. M. McCall Theal, *Records of South-East Africa.* Vol. ii. London, 1898.

Fernandez, J. P., *Relacion historial de las missiones de los Indios que llaman Chiquitos.* Madrid, 1726.

Ferraro, Giuseppe, *Superstizioni usi e proverbi Monferrini (Curiosità popolari tradizionali.* Ed. G. Pitré. Vol. iii). Palermo, 1886.

Ferraz de Macedo, F., *Ethnogenia brazilica.* Lisboa, 1886.

Ferrero, G., *Grandezza e decadenza di Roma.* 5 vols. Milano, 1912–14.

Ferriani, L., *Minderjährige Verbrecher.* Berlin, 1896.

Ferrier, J. P., *Caravan Journeys and Wanderings in Persia, Afghanistan, Turkistan and Beloochistan.* London, 1857.

Festgruss an Rudolf von Roth zum Doktor-Jubiläum. Stuttgart, 1893.

Festschrift zum 70 Geburtstage Rudolph Leuckart's. Leipzig, 1892.

Festschrift zur Juberlfeier des 25 jährigen Bestehens des Vereins für Erdkunde zu Dresden. Dresden, 1888.

Festus, Sextus Pompeius, *De verborum significatione.* Ed. C. O. Mueller. Lipsiae, 1839.

Fewkes, J. Walter, " The Winter Solstice Altars at Hano Pueblo," *The American Anthropologist,* N.S. Vol. i. New York, 1899.
" Tusayan Snake Ceremonies," *Sixteenth Annual Report of the Bureau of Ethnology.* Washington, 1897.
" Hopi Katcinas," *Twenty-first Annual Report of the Bureau of American Ethnology.* Washington, 1903.
" Tusayan Migration Traditions," *Nineteenth Annual Report of the Bureau of American Ethnology.* Part ii. Washington, 1900.
" An Interpretation of Katcina Worship," *Journal of American Folk-Lore.* Vol. xiv. Boston and New York, 1901.
" A few Summer Ceremonies at Zuñi Pueblo," *Journal of American Ethnology and Archaeology.* Vol. i. Boston and New York, 1891.
" The Growth of Hopi Ritual," *Journal of American Folk-Lore.* Vol. xi. Boston and New York, 1898.
" The Snake Ceremonial at Walpi," *Journal of American Ethnology and Archaeology.* Vol. iv. Boston and New York, 1894.
" The Aborigines of Porto Rico and the Neighbouring Islands," *Twenty-fifth Annual Report of the Bureau of American Ethnology.* Washington, 1907.
" The Group of Tusayan Ceremonial called Katcina," *Fifteenth Annual Report of the Bureau of Ethnology.* Washington, 1897.
and Owens, J. G., " The La-la-kon-ta : a Tusayan Dance," *The American Anthropologist.* Vol. v. Washington, 1892.

ffoulkes, Arthur, " The Fanti Family System," *Journal of the African Society*.
    Vol. vii. London, 1908.
    " Fanti Marriage Customs," *Journal of the African Society*. Vol. viii.
    London, 1909.
Fiala, F., Hoernes, M., and others, *Die neolitische Station von Butmir bei
    Sarajevo in Bosnien*. 2 vols. Wien, 1895–98.
Fiamingo, G., " The Conflict of Races, Classes, and Societies," *The Monist*.
    Vol. vii. Chicago, 1896.
Fick, August, *Vorgriechische Ortsnamen, als Quelle für die Vorgeschichte
    Griechenlands*. Göttingen, 1905.
    Die Enstehung der Odyssee. Göttingen, 1901.
    Die homerische Odyssee in der ursprunglichen Sprachform. Göttingen,
    1905.
Fies, K., " Der Hostamm in Deutsch-Togo," *Globus*. Vol. xxxvii. Braun-
    schweig, 1905.
Finamore, Gennaro, *Tradizioni popolari abruzzesi (Curiosità popolari tradi-
    zionali*. Ed. G. Pitré. Vol. xiii). Torino, Palermo, 1894.
    Credenze, usi e costumi abruzzesi (Curiosità popolari tradizionali. Ed.
    G. Pitré. Vol. vii). Palermo, 1890.
Finck, H. T., *Primitive Love and Love-Stories*. New York, 1899.
Finlay, George, *History of the Byzantine Empire*. London, 1906.
Finley, John Park, and Churchill, William, *The Subanu. Studies of a Sub-
    Visayan Mountain Folk of Mindanao (Carnegie Institute Publications)*.
    Washington, 1913.
Finsch, Otto, *Neu-Guinea und seine Bewohner*. Bremen, 1865.
    " Töpferei in Neu Guinea," *Verhandlungen der Berliner Gesellschaft für
    Anthropologie*. Berlin, 1882.
    " Ueber die Bewohner von Ponapé (östl. Carolinen)," *Zeitschrift für
    Ethnologie*. Vol. xii. Berlin, 1880.
    Samoafahrten. Leipzig, 1888.
" Fionn's Enchantment," transl. by J. F. Campbell, *Revue Celtique*. Vol. i.
    Paris, 1872.
Fischer, E., " Paparuda und Scaloian," *Globus*. Vol. xciii. Braunschweig,
    1908.
Fischer, G. A., " Das Wapokomo-Land und seine Bewohner," *Mittheilungen
    der geographische Gesellschaft in Hamburg, 1876-77*. Hamburg,
    1878.
Fischer, J. E., *Sibirische Geschichte*. St. Petersburg, 1773.
Fishberg, Maurice, *The Jews : a Study of Race and Environment*. London
    1911.
Fisher, Captain, " Memoir of Sylhet, Kachar, and the adjacent Districts,"
    Journal of the Asiatic Society of Bengal. Vol. ix, Part ii. Calcutta,
    1840.
Fisher, Ruth B., *On the Borders of Pigmy Land*. London, 1905.
Fiske, John, *Excursions of an Evolutionist*. London, 1884.
    Outlines of Cosmic Philosophy. 2 vols. London, 1874.
Fison, Lorimer, " The Nanga, or Sacred Stone Enclosure of Wainimala, Fiji,"
    Journal of the Anthropological Institute. Vol. xiv. London, 1885.
    " The Classificatory System of Relationship," *Journal of the Anthropological
    Institute*. Vol. xxi. London, 1892.
    and Howitt, A. W., *Kamilaroi and Kurnai*. Melbourne and Sydney, 1880.
Fitzgerald, David, " Popular Tales of Ireland," *Revue Celtique*. Vol. iv.
    Paris, 1879–89.
Fitzsimons, F. W., *The Natural History of South Africa*. London, 1919.
    The Monkeyfolk of South Africa. London, 1911.

Flad, M., *Kurze Schilderung der abissinischen Juden.* Kornthal, 1869.

Flaubert, Gustave, " Mémoires d'un fou," in *Oeuvres de jeunesse inédites.* Paris, 1910.

Flechsig, Paul, *Gehirn und Seele*, 2nd Edition. Leipzig, 1896.

Fled Bricrend : The Feast of Bricriu. Ed. G. Henderson (*Irish Texts Society*). Dublin, 1899.

Fletcher, A. C., " Indian Songs and Music," *The Journal of American Folk-Lore.* Vol. xi. Boston, New York, 1898.

" Laieikawai, a Legend of the Hawaiian Islands," *Journal of American Folk-Lore.* Vol. xiii. Boston, New York, 1900.

and La Flesche, Francis, " The Omaha Tribe," *Twenty-seventh Annual Report of the Bureau of American Ethnology.* Washington, 1911.

Fletcher, Banister and B. F., *A History of Architecture on the Comparative Method.* London, 1901.

Fletcher, Giles, " A Treatise of Russia and adjoining Regions," in *Hakluytus Posthumus or Purchas His Pilgrimes.* Vol. xii. Glasgow, 1906.

Fletcher, Robert Huntington, *The Arthurian Material in the Chronicles (Harvard Studies in Literature).* Cambridge, Mass, 1906.

Flint, L. A., " Muguru at Torobina, Bamu River, New Guinea," *Man.* Vol. xix. London, 1919.

Foa, Ed., *Le Dahomey.* Paris, 1895.

Fol, H, " Recherches sur la fécondation et le commencement de l'hénogénie chez divers animaux, " *Mémoires de la Société de Physique et d'Histoire Naturelle de Genève.* Vol. xxvi. Genève, 1879.

Folk-Lore. London, 1883–

Folk-Lore Journal. London, 1883–89.

Folk-Lore Journal. Cape Town, 1879–80.

Folk-Lore Record. London, 1878–1882.

Fontana, Nicholas, " On the Nicobar Isles and the Fruit Mellori," *Asiatick Researches.* Vol. iii. London, 1799.

Forbes, Alexander, *California : a History of Upper and Lower California.* London, 1839.

Forbes, Anna, *Insulinde.* Edinburgh, London, 1887.

Forbes, A. K., *Râs Mâla, or Hindoo Annals of the Province of Goozerat.* 2 vols. London, 1856.

Forbes, C. J. F. S., *British Burma and its People.* London, 1878.

Forbes, C. S., " The Western Shores of Volcano Bay, Yesso," *Journal of the Royal Geographical Society.* Vol. xxxvi. London, 1866.

Forbes, D., " On the Aymara Indians of Bolivia and Peru," *Journal of the Ethnological Society.* Vol. ii. London, 1870.

Forbes, James, *Oriental Memoirs, a Narrative of Seventeen Years' Residence in India.* 4 vols. London, 1813.

Forbes, Jonathan, *Eleven Years in Ceylon.* 2 vols. London, 1840.

Forbes, H. O., *A Handbook to the Primates (Allen's Naturalist's Library).* 2 vols. London, 1894.

A Naturalist's Wanderings in the Eastern Archipelago. London, 1885.

" On Some Tribes of the Island of Timor," *Journal of the Anthropological Institute.* Vol. xiii. London, 1884.

" On the Ethnology of the Timor-Laut," *Ibid.* Vol. xiii. London, 1884.

" On the Kubus of Sumatra," *Ibid.* Vol. xiv. London, 1885.

Ford R., in *Murray's Handbook to Spain.* 3rd Edition. London, 1855.

Foreman, John, *The Philippine Islands.* London, 1899.

Fornander Abraham, *An Account of the Polynesian Race.* 3 vols. London, 1878–85.

Forster, George, *Voyage round the World in H.M.S. " Resolution," commanded by Capt. Cook, 1772-75.* 2 vols. London, 1777.

Forster, John Reinold, *Observations made during a Voyage round the World.* London, 1778.

Forsyth, James, *The Highlands of Central India.* London, 1919.

Forsyth, T., "An Account of the Manners and Customs of the Sauk and Fox Nations," in E. H. Blair, *The Indian Tribes of the Upper Mississippi Valley and the Region of the Great Lakes.* Cleveland, Ohio, 1912.

The Fortnightly Review. London, 1865–

The Forum. New York, 1886–

Fossey, M. de, *Le Mexique.* Paris, 1857.

Foster, B. O., *Apples as Lovecharms (Harvard Studies in Classical Philology.* Vol. xx.). Boston, 1899.

Foucart, Paul, *Recherches sur l'origine et la nature des mystères d'Éleusis.* Paris, 1895.

" Le culte de Pluton dans la religion Éleusinienne," *Bulletin de Correspondance Hellénique.* Vol. vii. Athens, Paris, 1883.

Fouillée, Alfred, *Nietzsche et l'immoralisme.* Paris, 1902.

Foureau, F., *Documents scientifiques de la la mission saharienne.* 2 vols. Paris, 1905.

Fowler, W. Warde, *Roman Essays and Interpretations.* Oxford, 1920.

The Roman Festivals of the Period of the Republic. London, 1899.

Fox, C. E., "Social Organisation in San Cristoval, Solomon Islands," *Journal of the Royal Anthropological Institute.* Vol. xlix. London, 1919.

and Drew, F. H., " Beliefs and Tales of San Cristobal (Solomon Islands)," *Journal of the Royal Anthropological Institute.* Vol. xlv. London, 1915.

Fox, H. Munro, " Lunar Periodicity in Living Organisms," *Science Progress in the Twentieth Century.* Vol. xvii. London, 1923.

Fracastoro, Hieronymus, *Opera.* 2 vols. Genevae, 1637.

Fragmenta historicorum Graecorum. Ed. C. Müller. 5 vols. Parisiis, 1841–84.

Francis, E. A., " Benkoelen in 1833," *Tijdschrift voor Neërlands-Indië.* Jahrg. iv. Deel i. Batavia, 1842.

Herinneringe uit den levensloop van een Indisch' Ambtenaar van 1815 to 1851. 3 vols. Batavia, 1856–60.

" Westkust van Borneo," *Tijdschrift voor Neërlands-Indië.* Vol. iv, Part ii. Batavia, 1842.

Francis, W.," Agricultural Superstitions in Bellany," *Folk-lore.* Vol. xviii. London, 1907.

The Nilgiris (Madras District Gazetteers). 2 vols. Madras, 1908–15.

" Madras," *Census of India, 1901.* Vol. xv. Madras, 1902.

François, H. von, *Nama und Damara, Deutsch-Süd-West-Afrika.* Magdeburg, 1896.

Frank, Ludwig, *Handbuch der Anatomie der Hausthiere.* Stuttgart, 1870.

Franke, Erich, *Die geistige Entwicklung der Negerkinde.* Leipzig, 1915.

Franke, O., " Beiträge aus chinesischen Quelle zur Kenntniss der Türkvölker und Skythe Zentral Asiens," *Abhandlungen der Königlich Preussische Akademie der Wissenschaften.* Berlin, 1914.

Frankenberger, Ottokar, " Adenoide Vegetationen bei Taubstummen nebst einigen Bemerkungen über die Aetiologie der Taubstummheit," *Monatschrift für Ohrenheilkunde, sovie für Kehlkopf-, Nasen-, Rache-Krankheiten.* Vol. xxx. Berlin, 1896.

Franklin, Sir John, *Narrative of a Journey to the Shores of the Polar Sea.* London, 1823.

Narrative of a Second Expedition to the Shores of the Polar Sea. London, 1828.

Fraser, A., " The Moon Myth," *Science of Man.* Sydney, 1899.

Fraser, Donald, *Winning a Primitive People.* London, 1914.

Fraser, J., and G. Platt, " Some Folksongs and Myths from Samoa," *Journal and Proceedings of the Royal Society of New South Wales.* Vol. xxvi. Sydney, 1892.

Fraser, James Baillie, *A Winter's Journey (Tátar) from Constantinople to Tehran.* 2 vols. 1838.

Journal of a Tour through Part of the Snowy Range of the Himālā Mountains. London, 1820.

Fraser, John, *The Aborigines of New South Wales.* Sydney, 1892.

" The Aborigines of New South Wales," *Journal and Proceedings of the Royal Society of New South Wales.* Vol. xvi. Sydney, 1883.

Frazer, Sir James George, *The Golden Bough,* 3rd Edition. 12 vols. London, 1907–15.

Totemism and Exogamy. 4 vols. London, 1910.

Folk-Lore in the Old Testament. 3 vols. London, 1918.

Psyche's Task. London, 1909.

The Magical Origin of Kings. London, 1920.

Fredericke (Federici), Caesar, " The Voyage of M. Caesar Fredericke, Merchant of Venice, into the East India and beyond the Indies," in R. Hakluyt, *Collection of the Early Voyages, Travels and Discoveries of the English Nation.* Vol. v. London, 1812.

Extracts from the above in *Hakluytus Posthumus, or Purchas His Pilgrimes.* Vol. x. Glasgow, 1905.

Freeman, Edward Augustus, *History of the Norman Conquest of England.* 4 vols. Oxford, 1870–76.

Freimark, Hans, *Das Sexualleben der Afrikaner.* Leipzig [1919].

Freman, R. A., *Travels in Ashanti and Japan.* Westminster, 1898.

French, B. F., *Historical Collections of Louisiana.* 5 vols. New York, 1846–53.

French-Sheldon, Mrs., " Customs among the Natives of East Africa, from Teita to Kilimegalia," *Journal of the Anthropological Institute.* Vol. xxi. London, 1892.

Fréret, " Recherches sur le culte de Bacchus parmi les Grecs," *Mémoires de Littérature tirés des Registres de l'Académie Royale des Inscriptions et Belles-Lettres.* Vol. xxiii. Paris, 1756.

Fresnel, F., " Note sur quelques tribus de l'Arabie," *Bulletin de la Société de Géographie.* 2e Série, vol. xi. Paris, 1839.

Freud, Siegmund, *Vorlesungen zur Einführung in die Psycho-analyse.* Leipzig, Wien, 1916.

Die Traumdeutung. Leipzig, Wien, 1919.

Three Contributions to the Theory of Sex. Transl. New York, Washington, 1918.

Freycinet, Louis Desaulses de, *Voyage autour du monde par ordre du roi. Historique.* 2 vols. Paris, 1825–39.

Freytag, G. W., *Arabum Proverbia.* 2 vols. Bonn, 1838–43.

Einleitung in das Studium der Arabischen Sprache. Bonn, 1861.

Frič, Vojtěck, and Radin, Paul, " Contribution to the Study of the Bororo Indians." *Journal of the Anthropological Institute.* Vol. xxxvi. London, 1906.

Fricz, J., and Leger, L., *La Bohème historique, pittoresque et littéraire*. Paris, 1867.

Friederichs, C., *Matronaeum monumenta*. Bonn, 1886.

Friedländer, B., " Ueber den sogenanten Palolowurm," *Biologisches Central-blatt*. Vol. xviii. Leipzig, 1896.

" Nochmals der Palolowurm und die Frage nach unbekannte kosmische Einflüsse auf physiologischen Vorgänge," *ibid*. Vol. xix. Leipzig, 1897.

Friedmann, M., " The Sabbath Light," *Jewish Quarterly Review*. Vol. iii. London, 1891.

Friend, Hilderic, " Euphemism and Tabu in China," *The Folk-lore Record*. Vol. iv. London, 1881.

Friend-Pereira, J. E., " The Rabhas," in *Census of India, 1911*. Vol. iii, " Assam." Shillong, 1912.

Fries, C., *Die griechische Götter und Heroen vom astral mythologischen Standpunkt betrachtet*. Berlin, 1911.

" Babylonische und griechische Mythologie," *Neue Jahrbücher für das klassische Altertum*. Vol. ix. 1902.

Fritsch, Gustav, *Die Eingeborenen Süd-Afrika's*. Breslau, 1872.

Drei Jahre in Südafrika. Breslau, 1868.

Fritz, G., " Die Chamorro, eine Geschichte und Ethnographie der Marianen," *Ethnologisches Notizblatt*. Vol. iii, Part iii. Berlin, 1904.

Frobenius, H., *Die Heiden-Neger des ägyptischen Sudan*. Berlin, 1893.

Frobenius, Leo, *Das Zeitalter des Sonnengottes*. Berlin, 1904.

Die Weltanschaung der Naturvölker. Berlin, 1898.

Volksmärchen der Kabylen. 3 vols. Jena, 1921.

Froude, James Anthony, *A History of England from the Fall of Wolsey to the death of Elizabeth*. 12 vols. London, 1856–70.

Fryer, John, *A New Account of East India and Persia*. London, 1698.

Fuchs, Paul, " Ethnologische Beschreibung der Osseten," *Das Ausland*. Stuttgart, 1876.

Fujioka and Hizade, *Nipon Fuzoku-Shi* (History of Japanese Civilisation). 3 vols. Tokyo, 1895.

Fülleborn, Friedrich, *Das deutsche Njassa- und Ruwuna-Gebiet, Land und Leute, nebst Bemerkungen über die Schire-Länder*. Berlin, 1906.

Fuller, Sir Francis, *A Vanished Dynasty : Ashanti*. London, 1921.

Funnell, William, *A Voyage round the World*. London, 1707.

Furlong, Charles Wellington, " The Southernmost People of the World," *Harper's Monthly Magazine*. Vol. cxix. New York, 1909.

" The Vanishing People of the Land of Fire," *ibid*. Vol. cxx. New York, 1910.

Furness, W. H., *The Home Life of the Borneo Head-Hunters*. Philadelphia, 1902.

Furtwängler, Adolf, *Die antike Gemmen*. 3 vols. Leipzig, 1900.

Fustel de Coulanges, N. D., *La cité antique*. Paris, 1870.

Fynn, A. J., *The American Indian as a Product of Environment*. Boston, 1907.

Fytche, A., *Burma, Past and Present*. London, 1878.

Gaarstang, J., *The Land of the Hittites*. London, 1910.

Gadeau de Kerville, H., " Faune de la Normandie," *Bulletin des Amis des Sciences Naturelles de Rouen*. Année xxiii. Rouén, 1887.

Gafe, T., *A New Survey of the West Indies*. London, 1655.

Gaffarel, Paul, *L'Algérie conquise*. Paris, 1888.

Gaguière, " Les Béni-bou Zeggou," *Bulletin de la Société de Géographie*. Paris, 1910.

Gaidoz, Henri, " Superstitions de la Basse Bretagne au xviie Siècle," *Revue Celtique*. Vol. ii. Paris, 1875.

" La requisition d'amour et le symbolisme de la pomme," *Annuaire de l'École Pratique des Hautes Études*. Vol. x. Paris, 1902.

Gaillard, Le P. Louis, *Croix et swastika en Chine*. Chang-Hai, 1893.

Gaimard, Geffrei, *Lestorie des Englies*, ed. by Sir Thomas Duffus Hardy and C. T. Martin (*Chronicles and Memorials of Great Britain and Ireland*). 2 vols. London, 1888–89.

The Gaina Sûtras, trans. by H. Jacobi (*The Sacred Books of the East*. Vols. xxii, xlv). Oxford, 1884, 1895.

Gait, E. A., " India," Report, *Census of India, 1911*. Vol. i. Calcutta, 1913.

" Assam," Report, *Census of India, 1891*. Shillong, 1892.

Gaius, *Institutionum commentarii*, Rec. Goeschen. Berolini, 1842.

Galitzin, Prince Ern, " Manners and Customs of the Yakoutes," transl. by Norton Shaw, *Journal of the Ethnological Society*. Vol. iv. London, 1856.

Gallardo, Carlos R., *Los Onas*. Buenos Aires, 1910.

Gallaud, R. P., " A la Côte d'Or," *Les Missions Catholiques*. Vol. xxv. Lyon, 1893.

Gallieni, J. S., *Voyage dans le Soudan Français et Pays de Ségour*. Paris, 1885.

Galton, Francis, *Hereditary Genius*. London, 1869.

The Narrative of an Explorer in Tropical South Africa. London, 1853.

Galvano, Antonio, " Booke of the Discoveries of the World," extracts in *Hakluytus Posthumus, or Purchas His Pilgrimes*. Vol. x. Glasgow, 1905.

Garbutt, H. W., " Native Witchcraft and Superstition in South Africa," *Journal of the Royal Anthropological Institute*. Vol. xxxix. London, 1909.

Garcia, Fra Gregorio, *Origen de los Indios de el Nuevo Mundo*. Madrid, 1729.

G[arcia], Mathias, *Lettres sur les Îles Marquises, ou mémoires pour servir à l'étude religieuse, morale, politique et statistique des Îles Marquises et de l'Océanie Orientale*. Paris, 1843.

Garcilasso de la Vega, *First Part of the Royal Commentaries of the Yncas*. Transl. by C. R. Markham. 2 vols. London, 1869–71.

Garcin de Tassy, J. H., *Science des religions. L'Islamisme selon le Coran*. Paris, 1874.

Gardiner, A. F., *A Journey to the Zoolu Country*. London, 1836.

Gardiner, J. Stanley, " The Natives of Rotuma," *Journal of the Anthropological Institute*. Vol. xxvii. London, 1898.

Gardiner, Samuel Rawson, and Mullinger, J. B., *Introduction to the Study of English History*. London, 1894.

Garner, R. L., *Gorillas and Chimpanzees*. London, 1896.

" Native Institutions of the Ogowe Tribe of West Central Africa," *Journal of the African Society*. Vol. i. London, 1901.

Garnett, Lucy M. J., *The Women of Turkey and their Folk-lore*. 2 vols. London, 1892.

Turkish Life in Town and Country. London, 1904.

Garnier, Jules, *Océanie. Les Îles des Pins, Loyalty et Tahiti*. Paris, 1871.

Garrett, T. R. H., " The Natives of the Eastern Part of Borneo and Java," *Journal of the Royal Anthropological Institute*. Vol. xlii. London, 1912.

Die Gartenlaube. Leipzig, 1853–

Gason, Samuel, *The Dieyerie Tribe of Australian Aborigines*. Adelaide, 1874.
" Notes on the Australian Aborigines," *Journal of the Anthropological Institute*. Vol. xxiv. London, 1894.
in Woods, J. D., *The Native Tribes of South Australia*. q.v.

Gaspary, Adolf., *La scuola poetica siciliana del secolo xiii*. Transl. Livorno, 1882.

Gates, R. Ruggles, " Heredity and Eugenics," *The Eugenics Review*. Vol. xii. London, 1920.

Gatschet, Albert Samuel, *The Klamath Indians of Southwestern Oregon (Contributions to North American Ethnology*. Vol. ii). 2 Parts. Washington, 1890.
" Der Yuma-Sprachstamm nach den neuesten handschriftlichen Quellen," *Zeitschrift für Ethnologie*. Vol. ix. Berlin, 1877.
" Human Bones," *Journal of American Folk-Lore*. Vol. i. Boston, New York, 1880.

Gaubil, Antoine, *Traité de la chronologie chinoise*, in *Mémoires concernant l'histoire*, etc., *des Chinois*. Vol. xvii. Paris, 1814.

Gaupp, E. Th., *Das alte Gesetz der Thüringer*. Breslau, 1834.

Gautier, A., " Voyage au pays des Moïs," *Cochinchine française*. *Excursions et reconnaissances*. Vol. v. Saigon, 1882.

Gautier, Léon, *La Chevalerie*. Paris, s.d.
Les épopées françaises. 3 vols. Paris, 1865–69.

Gaydon, chanson de geste, ed. F. Guessard and S. Luce (*Anciens Poètes de la France*). Paris, 1862.

Gazette archéologique. Paris, 1875–

Gazette Médicale de Paris. Paris, 1830–

Gazetteer of the Bombay Presidency. Ed. by Sir J. M. Campbell. 27 vols. Bombay, 1877–1904.

Gazetteer of the Kangra District. In four parts, ed. by A. H. Diack. Lahore, 1899.

Gazetteer of the Karnal District, 1883-84. Lahore, 1884.

Gazetteer of the Karnal District. Ed. by J. M. Douie. Lahore, 1892.

Gazetteer of the Province of Oudh. Ed. by J. C. Nesfield. 3 vols. Lucknow, Allahabad, 1877–78.

Gazetteer of the Simla District. Calcutta, 1888–89.

Geddes, Patrick, and Thomson, J. Arthur, *The Evolution of Sex*. London, 1889.

Gehrts, M., *A Camera Actress in the Wilds of Togoland*. London, 1915.

Geiger, Wilhelm, *Civilization of the Eastern Iranians in ancient times*. Transl. 2 vols. London, 1885–86.
Ostiranische Kultur im Altertum. Erlangen, 1882.
and Kuhn, E., *Grundriss der iranischen Philologie*. 2 vols. Strassburg, 1895–1904.

Geiseler, *Die Oster-Insel*. Berlin, 1883.

Geldart, E. M., *Folklore of Modern Greece*. London, 1884.

Geldner, K. F., " Awestalitteratur," in W. Geiger and E. Kuhn, *Grundriss der iranischen Philologie*. Vol. ii. Strassburg, 1904.
See Pischel, R.

Gellius, Aulus, *Noctes Atticae*. Rec. A. Lion. 2 vols. Gottingae, 1824.

Gemelli Careri, Giovan Francesco, *Giro del Mondo*. 9 vols. Venezia, 1728.

Gennep, A. van, *Les rites de passage*. Paris, 1911.
Tabou et totémisme à Madagascar. Paris, 1904.
Études d'ethnographie algérienne (reprinted from *Revue d'Ethnographie et de Sociologie*, 1911). Paris, 1911.

The Gentleman's Magazine. London, 1731–

Geoffrey of Monmouth, *Historia Britonum*. Ed. J. A. Giles. London, 1844.

Geoffroy, Auguste, *Les arabes pasteurs et nomades de la tribu Larbaa, Sahara Algérien*. Paris, 1887.

Geografisk Tidskrift. Kjøbenhavn, 1877–

Geographi Graeci minores. Ed. C. Müller. 3 vols. Parisiis, 1855–61.

Georgeakis, G., and Pineau, L., *Le folk-lore de Lesbos*. Paris, 1894.

Georgevitch, T. R., " Parthenogenesis in Serbian Popular Tradition," *Folk-lore*. Vol. xxix. London, 1918.

Georgi, A. A., *Alphabetum Tibetanum*. Rome, 1762.

Georgi, Johann Gottlieb, *Description de toutes les nations de l'Empire de Russie*. 3 vols. St. Petersburg, 1776.

Gérard de Rossillon, chanson de geste ancienne. Ed. by Francisque-Michel, Paris, 1856.

Gerard, Alexander, *Account of Koonawur in the Himalaya*. London, 1841.

Gerard, Emily, *The Land beyond the Forest : Transylvania*. 2 vols. Edinburgh, 1888.

Gerebtzoff, Nicolaï de, *Essai sur l'histoire de la civilisation en Russie*. 2 vols. Paris, 1858.

Gerhard, Eduard, *Gesammelte akademische Abhandlungen*. 3 vols. Berlin, 1866–68.

    Griechische Mythologie. 2 vols. Berlin, 1854–55.

Gerland, Georg, " Bannu und die Afghanen," *Globus*. Vol. xxxi. Braunschweig, 1877.

Geronimo, Apache chief. *Geronimo's Story of his Life, taken down and edited by S. M. Barett*. New York, 1906.

Gersen, G. J. " Oedang-oedang, of verzameling van voorschriften in de Lemantang-Oeloe en Ilir en de Pasemah-landen," *Tijdschrift voor Indische taal-, land- en volkenkunde*. Vol. xx. Batavia, 's Hage, 1873.

Gervinus, Georg Gottfried, *Geschichte der deutsche Dichtung*. 5 vols. Leipzig, 1871–74.

Gesenius, F. H. W., *Scripturae linguaeque Phoeniciae monumenta quotquot supersunt*. Leipzig, 1837.

Gesta Karoli Magni ad Carcassonam et Narbonam. Ed. F. E. Schneegans. Halle a. S., 1898.

Gesta Regum Britanniae. Ed. F. Michel (*Cambrian Archaeological Association Publications*). London, 1862.

Gesta Regum Francorum, in Dom Martin Bouquet, *Rerum Gallicarum et Francicarum Scriptores*. Vol. ii. Paris, 1739.

Gesta Romanorum. Ed. A. Keller. Tübingen, 1842.

Geyer, R., " Die arabische Frauen in der Schlacht," *Mitteilungen der anthropologischen Gesellschaft*. Vol. xxxix. Wien, 1909.

Gfrörer, A. F., *Kritische Geschichte des Urchristenthums : Philo und die Alexandrinische Theosophie*. Stuttgart, 1835.

Ghali, Wacyf Boutros, *La tradition chevaleresque des Arabes*. Paris, 1919.

Ghinzoni, P., " Usi e costumi principeschi," *Archivio Storico Lombardo*. Vol. xv. Milan, 1888.

Giard, Alfred, " À propos de la parthénogénèse artificielle des oeufs d'Echinodermes," *Comptes Rendus Hebdomadaires de la Société de Biologie*. Paris, 1900.

    Oeuvres diverses. 2 vols. Paris, 1911–13.

Gibbon, Edward, *The History of the Decline and Fall of the Roman Empire*. Ed. J. B. Bury. 7 vols. London, 1896–1900.

Gibbons, A. St. Hill, *Africa from South to North through Marotseland*. 2 vols. London, 1904.

Gibbs, George, *Tribes of western Washington and northwestern Oregon (Contributions to North American Ethnology*. Vol. i). Washington, 1877.
" Notes on the Tinneh or Chepewyan Indians of British and Russian America," *Smithsonian Reports for 1866*. Washington, 1867.

Gidel, C. A., *Les troubadours et Pétrarque*. Angers, 1857.

De Gids. Amsterdam, 1837–

Gierke, O. von, *Der Humor in deutschen Recht*. Berlin, 1871.

Gildas, *De excidio Britanniae*. Ed. J. Stephenson. London, 1838.

Gilder, W. H., *Schwatka's Search*. London, 1882.

Giles, Herbert Allen, *Chinese Sketches*. London, 1876.
China and the Chinese. New York, 1902.

Gilhodes, Ch., " Mythologie et Religion des Katchins (Birmanie)," *Anthropos*. Vol. iii. Salzburg, 1908.

Gilii, Filippo Salvador, *Saggio di Storia Americana*. 4 vols. Roma, 1780–84.

Gill, Thomas, " Parental Care among Fresh Water Fishes," *Annual Report of the Smithsonian Institution*. Washington, 1906.

Gill, W., *The River of the Golden Sand*. London, 1880.

Gill, William, *Gems from the Coral Islands*. London, 1871.

Gill, William Wyatt, *Life in the Southern Isles*. London, 1876.
" Childbirth Customs in the Loyalty Islands," *Journal of the Anthropological Institute*. Vol. xix. London, 1890.
The South Pacific and New Guinea, Past and Present. Sydney, 1893.
Myths and Songs of the South Pacific. London, 1876.
" Extracts from the Papers of the late Rev. W. Wyatt Gill, LL.D.," *Journal of the Polynesian Society*. Vol. xx. Wellington, 1911.

Gillen, F. J., " Notes on some Manners and Customs of the Aborigines of the McDonnell Ranges belonging to the Arunta Tribe," *Report on the Work of the Horn Scientific Expedition to Central Australia*. Part iv. London, Melbourne, 1896.
" The Natives of Central Australia," *Proceedings of the Royal Geographical Society of Australasia ; South Australian Branch*. Vol. iv. Adelaide, 1901.

Gillier, " Les Banda," *L'Afrique Française*, Supplément. Paris, 1913.

Gillings, J., " On the Veddahs of Bitenne," *Journal of the Ceylon Branch of the Royal Asiatic Society*. Colombo, 1853.

Gilmour, James, *Among the Mongols*. London, 1888.

Ginsburg, C. D., art. " Essenes," in W. Smith and H. Wace, *Dictionary of Christian Biography, Literature, Sects, and Doctrines*. Vol. i. London, 1877.

Giornale Storico della Letteratura Italiana. Roma, Torino, Firenze, 1883–

Giraldus Cambrensis, *Opera*. Ed. S. Brewer (*Chronicles and Memorials of Great Britain and Ireland*). 4 vols. London, 1861–91.

Giran, Paul, *Magie et religion Annamites*. Paris, 1912.

Girard de Raille, J., *Mémoire sur l'Asie Centrale, son histoire, ses populations*. Paris, 1875.

Giraud, Gaston, in *Revue Coloniale*. Paris, 1909.

Giraud-Teulon, Alexis, *Origines du mariage et de la famille*. Genève, 1884.

Girschner, M., " Die Karolinen und Namöluk und ihre Bewohner," *Baessler-Archiv*. Vol. ii. Leipszig, 1912.

Giuseppe di Santa Maria, *Prima speditione all' Indie orientali*. Roma, 1666.

Gjerset, Knut, *History of the Norwegian Peoples*. 2 vols. New York, 1915.

Glaber, Rodulfus, *Historiae sui temporis.*, in M. Bouquet, *Recueil des historiens des Gaules et de la France*. Vol. x. Parisiis, 1760.

Glaser, Eduard, *Die Abessinier in Arabien und Afrika*. München, 1895.

" Polyandrie oder Gesellschaftehe bei den alten Sabaern," *Beilage zur Münchener Allgemeine Zeitung*. München, 1897.

The Glasgow Medical Journal. Glasgow, 1828–

Glassberg, A., *Die Beschneidung in ihre geschichtliche, ethnographiche, religiöse und medicinische Bedeutung*. Berlin, 1896.

Glaumont, " Usages, moeurs et coutumes des Néo-Calédoniens," *Revue d'Ethnographie*. Vol. vii. Paris, 1889.

Glave, E. J., *Six Years of Adventure in Congo Land*. London, 1893.

Gleichen, Count (ed.), *The Anglo-Egyptian Sudan*. 2 vols. London, 1905.

Globus. Braunschweig, 1862–

Glotz, G., *Études sociales et juridiques sur l'antiquité grecque*. Paris, 1906.

Godard, Ernest, *Égypte et Palestine, observations médicales et scientifiques*. Paris, 1867.

Goddard, Pliny Earle, *Life and Culture of the Hupa* (*University of California Publications in American Archaeology and Ethnology*. Vol. i). Berkeley, 1903.

Hupa Texts (*University of California Publications in American Archaeology and Ethnology*. Vol. i). Berkeley, 1903.

Godden, Gertrude M., " Nágá and other Frontier Tribes of North-Eastern India," *Journal of the Anthropological Institute*. Vol. xxvii. London, 1898.

Godwin-Austen, H. H., " On the Stone Monuments of the Khasi Hill Tribe and on some of the Peculiar Rites and Customs of the People," *Journal of the Anthropological Institute*. Vol. i. London, 1871.

Goeje, M. J. de, " De Berbers," *De Gids*. Amsterdam, 1867.

Goethe, Johann Wolfgang von, *Sämtliche Werke*. 36 vols. Cotta, 1882–85.

Goetsch, Wilhelm, " Neue Beobachtungen und Versuchen an Hydra," *Biologisches Centralblatt*. Vol. xxxix. Leipzig, 1919.

Gogerly, G., " Essay on Buddhism," *Journal of the Ceylon Branch of the Royal Asiatic Society*. Vol. i. Colombo, 1845.

Golder, F. A., " Tales from Kadiak Island," *Journal of American Folk-Lore*. Vol. xvi. Boston and New York, 1903.

" The Songs and Stories of the Aleuts, with Translations from Veniaminov," *Journal of American Folk-Lore*. Vol. xx. Boston, New York, 1907.

Goldschmidt, L., *Die Doktrine der Liebe bei den iteliänischen Lyrikern des XIII Jahrhundert*. Breslau, 1889.

Goldstein, Ferdinand, " Die Frauen in Haussafulbien und Adamana," *Globus*. Vol. xciv. Braunschweig, 1908.

Goldziher, Ignacz, *Abhandlungen zur arabischen Philologie*. 2 vols. Leiden, 1896.

Mythology among the Hebrews. Transl. London, 1877.

Review of *Kinship and Marriage in Early Arabia*, by W. Robertson Smith, in *Literatur-Blatt für orientalische Philologie*. Vol. iii. Leipzig, 1887.

" Eisen als Schutz gegen Dämonen," *Archiv für Religionswissenschaft*. Vol. x. Freiburg i. B., 1907.

Golther, Wolfgang, *Handbuch der germanischen Mythologie*. Leipzig, 1895.

Goltz, Freiherr von der, " Zauberei und Hexenkünste, Spiritismus und Chamanismus in China," *Mittheilungen der deutschen Gesellschaft für Natur- und Volkenkunde Ostasiens*. Vol. vi. Tokyo, 1897.

Goltzius, H., *Sicilia et Magna Graecia*. Antuerpiae, 1617.

Gomara, Francisco Lopez de, *Historia general de las Indias* (*Biblioteca de Autores Españoles*. Vol. xxii.) Madrid, 1852.

Italian translation in G. B. Ramusio, *Navigationi et Viaggi*. Vol. iii. Venetia, 1559.

Gomes, E. H., *Seventeen Years among the Sea Dyaks of Borneo*. London, 1911.

Gomme, George Laurence, *Handbook of Folklore*. London, 1890.

Goncourt, E. L. A. and J. A. de, *La Femme au dix-huitième siècle*. Paris, 1862.

Gondavo, Pero de Magalhães, " Historia da Provincia Sãta Cruz," *Revista Trimensal do Instituto Historico e Geographico Brasileiro*. Vol. xxi. Rio de Janeiro, 1858.

" The Gonds and Bygas of the Eastern Sathpuras," *The Cornhill Magazine*. Vol. xxvi. London, 1872.

Goodwin, C. W., " On the Word Kamen," *Zeitschrift für Aegyptische Sprache und Alterthumskunde*. Vol. xi. Leipzig, 1873.

Gookin, Daniel, " Historical Collections of the Indians in New England," *Collections of the Massachusetts Historical Society*. Vol. i. Boston, 1806.

Gordon, Mary Margaret, *The Home Life of Sir David Brewster*. Edinburgh, 1869.

Görres, J. J. von, *Das Heldenbuch von Iran aus dem Schah Nameh des Firdussi*. 2 vols. Berlin, 1820.

Gosselin, A., " Les Sauvages du Mississipi d'après la correspondance des Missions étrangères à Québec," *Congrès international des Américanistes. XVe Session tenue à Québec en 1906*. Vol. i. Québec, 1907.

Gottschling, E., " The Bawenda, a Sketch of their History and Customs," *Journal of the Anthropological Institute*. Vol. xxxv. London, 1905.

Goudswaard, A., *De Papoewa's van de Geelvinksbaai*. Schiedam, 1863.

Gougard, L., " Les saints irlandais dans la tradition populaire des pays continentaux," *Revue Celtique*. Vol. xxxix. Paris, 1922.

Gough, Archibald Edward, *The Philosophy of the Upanishads and Ancient Indian Metaphysics*. London, 1882.

Gouldsbury, Cullen, and Sheane, Hubert, *The Great Plateau of Northern Rhodesia*. London, 1911.

Gourmont, Remy de, *Physique de l'amour ; essai sir l'instinct sexuel*. Paris, 1912.

Gowan, W. B., " Mongolia," *Imperial and Asiatic Quarterly Review*. Vol. v. London, 1898.

Graafland, A. F. P., " De verbreiding van het matriarchaat in het landschap Indragiri," *Bijdragen tot de taal-, land- en volkenkunde van Nederlandsch-Indië*. Vol. xxxix. 's Gravenhage, 1890.

Graafland, N., *De Minahassa : haar verleden en haar tegenwoordige toestand*. 2 vols. Rotterdam, 1867–69.

Grabowsky, F., " Der Distrikt Dusson Timor in Südost-Borneo, und seine Bewohner," *Das Ausland*. Vol. lvii. Stuttgart and Munich, 1884.

Graevell, Paul, *Die Charakteristik der Personen im Rolandsliede*. Heilbronn, 1880.

Graf, A., *I complementi della Chanson d'Huon de Bordeaux*. Halle, 1878.
Miti, leggende e superstizioni del medio evo. 2 vols. Torino, 1892–93.
Roma nella memoria e nelle immaginazioni del medio evo. Torino, 1915.

Graham, " Report on the Manners, Customs and Superstitions of the People of Shoa," *Journal of the Asiatic Society of Bengal*. Vol. xii. Calcutta, 1843.

Gramberg, J. S. G., " Eene maand in de binnenlanden van Timor," *Verhandelingen van het Bataviaasch Genootschap van Kunsten en Wetenschappen*. Vol. xxxvi. Batavia, 1872.

Grammatici Latini. Ed. H. Keil. 8 vols. Leipzig, 1857–70.

Grandidier, Alfred, " Funeral Ceremonies of the Malagasy," *Antananarivo Annual and Madagascar Magazine*. No. xv. Antananarivo, 1891.
and Guillaume, *Histoire physique et politique de Madagascar*. 39 vols. (in progress). Paris, 1875–

Grandidier, E., *Voyage dans l'Amérique du Sud. Pérou et Bolivie.* Paris, 1861.

Granger, Fr. S., *The Worship of the Romans viewed in relation to the Roman Temperament.* London, 1895.

Grant, P., "The Sauteux Indians," in L. R. Masson, *Les Bourgeois de la Compagnie du Nord-Ouest.* Vol. ii. Vol. ii. Quebec, 1890.

Grant, W., "Magato and his Tribe," *Journal of the Anthropological Institute.* Vol. xxxv. Bondon, 1905.

Granville, R. K., and Roth, F. N., "Notes on the Jekris, Sobos and Ijas of the Ware District of the Niger Colony Protectorate," *Journal of the Anthropological Society.* Vol. xxviii. London, 1899.

Gratarolus, Guglielmus, *A Direction for the Health of Magistrates and Studentes . . . Englished by T. N.* London, 1574.

Graul, Karl, *Die Reise nach Ostindien in den Jahre 1849 bis 1853.* 4 vols. Leipzig, 1854.

Gray, Florence L., art. "Easter Island," Hastings's *Encyclopaedia of Religion and Ethics.* Vol. v. Edinburgh, 1912.

Gray, J. E., in *Proceedings of the Zoological Society.* Vol. xxix. London, 1861.

Gray, J. H., *China ; a History of the Laws, Manners, and Customs of the People.* 2 vols. London, 1878.

Gray, L. H., art. "Iroquois," in Hastings's *Encyclopaedia of Religion and Ethics.* Vol. xii. Edinburgh, 1914.

Gray, W., "Some Notes on the Tannese," *Internationales Archiv für Ethnographie.* Vol. vii. Leiden, 1894.

Grébaut, E., "Hymne à Ammon-Ra," *Revue archéologique.* Vol. i. Paris, 1873.

"Des deux yeux du disque solaire," *Recueil de travaux relatifs à la philologie et à l'archéologie égyptiennes et assyriennes.* Vol. i. Paris, 1870.

Green, J. R., *A Short History of the English People.* London, 1917.

Gregg, Josiah, *Commerce of the Prairies, or the Journal of a Santa Fé Trader,* etc. 2 vols. New York, 1844.

Gregor, Walter, *Notes on the Folk-Lore of the North-East of Scotland.* London, 1881.

An Echo of the Olden Time from the North of Scotland. Edinburgh, Glasgow, 1874.

Gregorio e Russo, Giuseppe, *Dissertazioni critico-fisiche delle varie osservazioni della luna intorno ai salassi, ed alle purghe, in cui trattasi della epilessia, crisi e purghe mestruali, inoltre di alcuni animali, pesci, piante, pietre ed altre cose diverse per nulla dipendenti dei movimenti di luna.* Palermo, 1742.

Gregory of Nazianzus, *Opera,* 4 vols., in Migne, *Patrologiae Cursus, Series Graeca.* Vols. xxxv–xxxviii. Paris, 1857–58.

Gregory of Nyssa, *Opera,* 3 vols., in Migne, *Patrologiae Cursus, Series Graeca.* Vols. xliv–xlvi. Paris, 1858.

Gregory of Tours, *Historia ecclesiastica Francorum,* in Dom Martin Bouquet, *Rerum Gallicarum et Francicarum Scriptores.* Vol. ii. Paris, 1739.

Liber de Gloria Confessorum, in J. P. Migne, *Patrologiae Cursus.* Vol. lxxi. Parisiis, 1849.

Gregory, J. W., *The Great Rift Valley.* London, 1896.

Grenard, F., *Le Turkestan et le Tibet,* in J.-L. Dutreuil de Rhins, *Mission scientifique de la Haute Asie.* Part ii. Paris, 1898.

Tibet, the Country and its Inhabitants. Transl. London, 1904.

Grey, Sir George, *Journals of two Expeditions of Discovery in North-West and Western Australia.* 2 vols. London, 1841.

Vocabulary of the Dialects of South-Western Australia. London, 1840.

Grey, Sir George, *Polynesian Mythology*. London, 1855.
    in *House of Commons Accounts and Papers, 1844*. Vol. xxxiv. London, 1844.
Gribble, J. B., *Black but Comely, or Glimpses of Aboriginal Life in Australia*. London, 1884.
Grierson, G. H., "The Battle between the Pandavas and Kauravas," *Journal of the Royal Asiatic Society*. London, 1908.
    Review of T. Graham Bailey's "The Languages of the Northern Himalayas, being Studies in the Grammar of Twenty-six Himalayan Dialects," *Journal of the Royal Asiatic Society*. London, 1909.
Griffis, W. E., *Japanese Fairy World*. Schenectady, 1880.
Griffith, F. L., *A Collection of Hieroglyphs (Egypt Exploration Fund)*. London, 1898.
    "Notes on some Royal Names and Families," *Proceedings of the Society of Biblical Archaeology*. Vol. xiv. London, 1892.
Grigg, H. B., *A Manual of the Nilagiri District in the Madras Presidency*. Madras, 1880.
Grimble, Arthur, "From Birth to Death in the Gilbert Islands," *Journal of the Royal Anthropological Institute*. Vol. li. London, 1921.
Grimm, Jacob L. C., *Deutsche Mythologie*. 3 vols. Göttingen, 1843–44.
    Teutonic Mythology. Transl. 4 vols. (pagination consecutive). London, Aberdeen, 1880–88.
    Deutsche Rechts-Alterthümer. Göttingen, 1828.
    Kleinere Schriften. 5 vols. Berlin, 1864–90.
    Geschichte der deutschen Sprache. Leipzig, 1853.
    and W., *Irische Elfenmärchen*. Transl. Leipzig, 1826.
Grimme, Hubert, "Der Logos in Südarabien," in C. Bezold, *Orientalische Studien Theodor Nöldeke zum siebzigsten Geburtstag gewidmet*. Vol. i. Gierzen, 1906.
Grinnell, George Bird, *The Cheyenne Indians*. 2 vols. New Haven, 1923.
    "Marriage among the Pawnees," *The American Anthropologist*. Vol. iv. Washington, 1891.
    The Story of the Indian. London, 1896.
    Pawnee Hero Stories and Folk-Tales. New York, 1889.
    "Pawnee Mythology," *Journal of American Folk-Lore*. Vol. vi. Boston and New York, 1893.
    Blackfoot Lodge Tales. London, 1893.
    "Cheyenne Woman Customs," *The American Anthropologist*. N.S., vol. iv. New York, 1902.
    "The Lodges of the Blackfeet," *The American Anthropologist*, N.S., vol. iii. New York, 1901.
The Griya Sūtras. Transl. by H. Oldenberg (*The Sacred Books of the East*. Vols. xxix, xxx). Oxford, 1886, 1892.
Gröber, Gustav, *Grundriss der romanische Philologie*. 2 vols (in 4 parts). Strassburg, 1888–1902.
Groeneveldt, W. P., "Notes on the Malay Archipelago and Malacca, compiled from Chinese Sources," *Verhandelingen van het Bataviaasch Genootschap van Kunsten en Wetenschappen*. Vol. xxxix. Batavia, 's Hagen, 1880.
Grohmann, Adolf, "Göttersymbole und Symboltiere in südarabische Denkmäler," *Kais. Akademie der Wissenschaften in Wien; Denkschriften Philologisch-historische Klasse*. Vol. lix. Wien, 1917.
Groot, J. J. M. de, *Les fêtes annuellement célébrées à Émoui (Amoy)*. 2 vols. (*Annales du Musée Guimet*. Vols. xi and xii.) Paris, 1886.
    The Religious System of China. Leyden, 1892–

Grose, John Henry, *A Voyage to the East Indies.* 2 vols. London, 1766.

Grosier, J. B. G. A., *A General Description of China.* Transl. 2 vols. London, 1795.

Groskurd, C. G., *Strabons Erdbeschreibung.* 4 vols. Berlin, Stettin, 1831–34.

Grote, George, *A History of Greece.* 10 vols. London, 1872.

Grout, Lewis, *Zulu-land, or Life among the Zulu Kafirs.* Philadelphia, n.d.

Grove, E. T. N., "Customs of the Acholi," *Sudan Notes and Records.* Vol. ii. Khartoum, 1919.

Grubb, W. Barbrooke, *An Unknown People in an Unknown Land.* London, 1911.

   Among the Indians of the Paraguayan Chaco. London, 1904.

Gruber, A., "Beiträge zur Kentniss der Physiologie und Biologie der Protozoen," *Berichte der Naturforschende Gesellschaft zu Freiburg.* Freiburg, 1886.

Grübner, H., "Ueber die Gebräuche der Basutos," *Verhandlungen der Berliner Gesellschaft für Anthropologie.* Berlin, 1877.

Gruppe, O., *Griechische Mythologie und Religionsgeschichte.* 2 vols. Munich, 1906.

Gruterus, Janus, *Inscriptiones Antiquae totius Orbis Romani.* 2 vols. Amsteraedami, 1707.

Grützner, H., "Über die Gebräuche der Basuto," *Verhandlungen der Berliner Gesellschaft für Anthropologie.* Berlin, 1877.

Gubernatis, Angelo de, *Storia dei viaggiatori Italiani nelle Indie Orientali.* Livorno, 1875.

   Storia comparata degli usi nuziali in Italia e presso gli altri popoli Indo-Europei. Milano, 1878.

   Zoological Mythology. Transl. 2 vols. London, 1872.

   La mythologie des plantes. 2 vols. Paris, 1878–82.

Gudgeon, W. E., "On Matakite," *Journal of the Polynesian Society.* Vol. xx. Wellington, 1910.

Gudmundsson, Valtȳn and Kålund, Kristian, "Sitte, Skandinavische Verhältnisse," in H. Paul, *Grundriss der Germanischen Philologie.* Vol. iii. Strassburg, 1900.

Guer, M., *Moeurs et usages des Turcs.* 2 vols. Paris, 1747.

Guerville, A. B. de, *New Egypt.* Transl. London, 1905.

Guevara, José, *Historia del Paraguay, Rio de la Plata y Tucuman.* 2 vols. (*Anales de la Biblioteca Nacional.* Vols. v and vi.) Buenos Ayres, 1908–10.

Guevara, Tomas, "Folklore Araucano," *Anales de la Universidad de Chile.* Vol. cxxvii. Santiago de Chile, 1911.

   Historia de la civilisación de Araucania. 3 vols. Santiago de Chile, 1898–1902.

Guibert of Nogent, *Opera,* in Migne, *Patrologiae Cursus Completus, Series Latina.* Vol. clvi. Paris, 1853.

Guichot y Sierra, A., "Superstitiones populares andaluzas," *Biblioteca de las tradiciones populares españolas.* Vol. i. Sevilla, 1883.

Gui d'Amiens, *Carmen Hastingae,* in F. Michel, *Chroniques anglo-normandes.* Vol. iii. Rouen, 1840.

Gui de Nanteuil, ed. P. Meyer (*Anciens Poètes de la France*). Paris, 1861.

Guignes, Joseph de. See Deguignes, Joseph.

Guigniart, G. F. See Creuzer, G. F.

Guillaume de Tudèle, *La chanson de la croisade contre les Albigeois.* Ed. by P. Meyer. 2 vols. Paris, 1875–79.

Guillelmus Brito-Armoricus, *Phillipides, sive gesta Philippi Augusti, Francorum regis*, in M. Bouquet, *Recueil des historiens des Gaules et de la France*. Vol. xvii. Paris, 1718.

Guillem de Cabestanh. See Hüffer.

Guillemard, F. H. H., *The Cruise of the " Marchesa " to Kamschatka and New Guinea*. London, 1889.

Guillemé, Père, " Au Bengouéolo," *Les Missions Catholiques*. Vol. xxxiv. Lyon, 1902.

Guimarães, José da Silva, " Memoria sobre os usos, costumes, e linguagem dos Appiacas," *Revista Trimensal de Historia e Geographia*. Vol. vi Rio de Janeiro, 1844.

Guinnard, A., *Trois ans d'esclavage chez les Patagons*. Paris, 1864.
Three Years' Slavery among the Patagonians. Transl. London, 1871.

Guiraut Riquier. See Anglade, J.

Guis, R. P., " Les Canaques, ce qu'ils font, ce qu'ils disent," *Les Missions Catholiques*. Vol. xxx. Lyon, 1898.

Guise, R. E., " On the Tribes inhabiting the Mouth of the Wanigela River, New Guinea," *Journal of the Anthropological Institute*. Vol. xxviii. London, 1899.

Guittone d'Arezzo, *Rime*. 2 vols. Firenze, 1828.

Gulgowski, " Sonne, Mond und Sterne in Volksglaube der Kaschuben am Weitsee " (Abstract). *Globus*. Vol. xliii. Braunschweig, 1908.

Gumilla, J., *El Orinoco ilustrado*. 2 vols. Madrid, 1745.

Günther, A. C. L. G., *Introduction to the Study of Fishes*. Edinburgh, 1880.

Guppy, H. B., *The Solomon Islands*. London, 1887.

Gurdon, P. R. T., *The Khasis*, with introduction by Sir G. Lyall. London, 1907.
" Note on the Khasis, Syntegs, and allied Tribes, inhabiting the Khasi and Jaintia Hills District in Assam," *Journal of the Asiatic Society of Bengal*. Vol. lxxiii, Part iii. Calcutta, 1905.

Güssfeldt, Paul, Falkenstein, Julius, Pechuël-Loesche, E., *Die Loango-Expedition*. 3 vols. Leipzig, 1879.

Gutch, Mrs., and M. Peacock, *Folklore concerning Lincolnshire (County Folklore*. Vol. v). London, 1908.

Guthrie, Douglas, " Notes on 13 cases of Aural Tuberculosis in Infants," *The Journal of Laryngology, Rhinology, and Otology*. Vol. xxxv. London, 1920.

Gutierez de Santa Clara, Pedro, *Historia de la guerras civiles del Peru (1544-1548) y de otros sucesos de las Indias*. 2 vols. Madrid, 1904.

Gutmann, " Die Frau bei den Wadschagga," *Globus*. Vol. xcii. Braunschweig, 1907.

Guyau, M., *Éducation et hérédité*. Paris, 1890.

Guyon, C. M., *A New History of the East Indies, Ancient and Modern*. Transl. 2 vols. London, 1757.

H. L. D., " A Strange Marriage Custom," *The China Review*. Vol. i. Hong-Kong, 1872.

Haas, E., " Die Heiratsgebräuche der alten Inder," *Indische Studien*. Vol. v. Berlin, 1862.

Haddan, A. W., and Stubbs, W., *Councils and Ecclesiastical Documents relating to Great Britain and Ireland*. 3 vols. Oxford, 1869–78.

Haddon, A. C., *Evolution in Art as illustrated by the life-history of design*. London, 1895.

Haddon, A. C., " The Ethnography of the Western Tribe of Torres Straits," *Journal of the Anthropological Institute*. Vol. xix. London, 1890.

Head-Hunters, Black, White, and Brown. London, 1901.

The Decorative Art of British New Guinea. Dublin, 1894.

" Migrations of Culture in New Guinea," *Journal of the Royal Anthropological Institute*. Vol. i. London, 1920.

" Legends of Torres Straits," *Folk-lore*. Vol. i. London, 1890.

" The Kopiravi Cult of the Namau Papua," *Man*. Vol. xix. London, 1919.

in *Reports of the Cambridge Anthropological Expedition to Torres Straits*. *Magic and Fetichism*. London, 1906.

and Meyers, C. S., " The Cult of Bomai and Malu," in *Reports of the Cambridge Anthropological Expedition to Torres Straits*. Vol. vi. Cambridge, 1908.

Hadfield, E., *Among the Natives of the Loyalty Group*. London, 1920.

Haeckel, Ernst, *Indische Reisebriefe*. Berlin, 1884.

Hagen, A., and Pineau, A., " Les Nouvelles Hébrides," *Revue d'Ethnographie*. Vol. vii. Paris, 1889.

Hagen, B., " Beiträge zur Kenntniss der Battareligion," *Tijdschrift voor Indische taal-, land- en volkenkunde*. Vol. xlv. Batavia, 1902.

Die Orang Kubu auf Sumatra (Veröffentlichungen aus dem städtischen Völker-Museum, Frankfurt am Main. Vol. ii). Frankfurt a. M., 1908.

Unter den Papua's. Wiesbaden, 1899.

Hagen, Gunther von, " Die Bana," *Baessler-Archiv*. Vol. ii. Berlin-Leipzig, 1912.

Hagenbeck, Carl, *Beast and Man*. Abridged transl. London, 1909.

Haggenmacher, G. A., " Reise in Somali-lande," *Petermann's Mittheilungen*. Vol. x. Erganzungsheft No. 47. Gotha, 1876.

Hahl, Alb., " Das mittlere Neumecklenburg," *Globus*. Vol. xci. Braunschweig, 1906.

" Über die Rechtsanschauungen der Eingeborenen eines Theiles der Blanchebucht und des Innern der Gazelle-halbinsel," *Nachrichten über Kaiser Wilhelms-Land und den Bismarck-Archipel*. Berlin, 1897.

Hahn, C. von, " Die Täler der ' Grossen Ljachwa,' und Ksanka (Ksan) und das südliche Ossetien," *Globus*. Vol. lxxxviii. Braunschweig, 1905.

Hahn, Eduard, *Demeter und Baubo*. Lübeck, 1897.

Die Enstehung der Pflugkultur. Heidelberg, 1909.

Hahn, Rev. F., " Some Notes on the Religion and Superstitions of the Oraos," *Journal of the Asiatic Society of Bengal*. Vol. lxxii, Part 3. Calcutta, 1904.

Hahn, Josaphat, " Die Ovaherero," *Zeitschrift der Gesellschaft für Erdkunde zu Berlin*. Vol. iv. Berlin, 1869.

" Das Land der Herero," *Zeitschrift der Gesellschaft für Erdkunde zu Berlin*. Vol. iii. Berlin, 1868.

Hahn, J. G., *Albanische Studien*. Jena, 1854.

Sagenwissenschaftliche Studien. Jena, 1876.

Hahn, Ph. " La Mère et l'enfant chez les Fuégiens du Sud (Yaghan)," *Bulletin de la Société d'Anthropologie*. 3e Série. Vol. iii. Paris, 1883.

Hahn, Theophilus, *Tsuni-Goam, the Supreme Being of the Khoi-Khoi*. London, 1881.

" Die Nama-Hottentoten, ein Beitrag zur süd-afrikanische Ethnographie," *Globus*. Vol. xii. Braunschweig, 1867.

Haile, John H., " Some Betsileo Ideas," *Antananarivo Annual and Madagascar Magazine*, No. xxiv. Antananarivo, 1900.

Hailes, David Dalrymple, Lord, *Annals of Scotland from the Accession of Malcolm III to the Accession of the House of Stewart*. 3 vols. Edinburgh, 1819.

Hakluyt, Richard, *The Principal Navigations, Voyages, Traffiques and Discoveries of the English Nation*. 16 vols. Edinburgh, 1884–90.

Hakluytus Posthumus, or Purchas His Pilgrimes. 20 vols. Glasgow, 1905–7.

Hale, Horatio, *Ethnography and Philology in the United States Exploring Expedition*. Philadelphia, 1846.

Halévy, Joseph, *Mélanges de critique et d'histoire relatifs aux peuples sémitiques*. Paris, 1883.

Haliburton, R. G., *New Materials for the History of Man*. Halifax, 1863.

Halkin, J., and Viaenne, E., *Les Ababua*. Bruxelles, 1911.

Hall, C. F., *Life with the Esquimaux*. 2 vols. London, 1864.
   Arctic Researches and Life among the Esquimaux. New York, 1865.

Hall, G. Stanley, *Adolescence and its Psychology*. 2 vols. New York, 1904.
   " A Study of Fears," *The American Journal of Psychology*. Vol. viii. Worcester, 1897.
   " A Study of Anger," *The American Journal of Psychology*. Vol. x. Worcester, 1899.
   " Some Aspects of the Early Sense of Self," *The American Journal of Psychology*. Vol. ix. Worcester, 1898.

Hall, H. R., *The Ancient History of the Near East*. London, 1916.
   " Keftiu and the Peoples of the Sea," *Annual of the British School at Athens*. Vol. viii (1901–2). London, 1902.
   Art. " Family (Egyptian)," in Hastings's *Encyclopaedia of Religion and Ethics*. Vol. v. Edinburgh, 1912.
   Review of " The Excavations at Phylakopi," *The Classical Review*. Vol. xix. London, 1905.
   " A Note on the Phaistos Disk," *The Journal of Hellenic Studies*. London, 1911.
   The Oldest Civilisation of Greece. London, 1901.
   " The Two Labyrinths," *The Journal of Hellenic Studies*. Vol. xxv. London, 1905.

Hallam, H., *View of the State of Europe during the Middle Ages*. 3 vols. London, 1853.

Halphen, L., *Étude critique sur l'histoire de Charlemagne*. Paris, 1921.
   See Eginhard.

Hamilton, Alex., *A New Account of the East Indies*, in Pinkerton, *Collection of Voyages and Travels*. Vol. viii. London, 1811.

Hamilton, Augustus, *The Art Workmanship of the Maori Race in New Zealand*. Dunedin, 1896–1901.

Hamilton, Francis, *An Account of the Kingdom of Nepal*. Edinburgh, 1819.

Hamilton, Gavin, " Customs of the New Caledonian Women," *Journal of the Anthropological Institute*. Vol. vii. London, 1878.

Hamilton, James, *Sinai, the Hedjaz, and Soudan*. London, 1857.

Hamilton, James Stevenson, *Animals in Africa*. 3 vols. London, 1917.

Hamlyn-Harris, R., " Some Anthropological Considerations of Queensland and the History of its Ethnology," *Proceedings of the Royal Society of Queensland*. Vol. xxix. Brisbane, 1917.

Hammer-Purgstall, Joseph, Baron von, *Histoire de l'Empire Ottoman*. Transl. 3 vols. Paris, 1840–42.

Hammerschlag, Victor, " Ein neues Eintheilungsprincip für die verschiedenen Formen der Taubstummheit," *Archiv für Ohrenheilkunde*. Vol. lvi. Leipzig, 1902.

Hammurabi. See H. Winckler.

Hanauer, E., *Les paysans de l'Alsace au moyen-âge*. Paris, Strasbourg, 1865.

Hanauer, J. E., in *Quarterly Statement of the Palestine Exploration Fund*. London, 1910.

Hancock, A., " Observations on the Nidification of *Gastrosteus aculatus* and *Gastrosteus spinachia*," *Transactions of the Tyneside Naturalists' Field Club*. Vol. ii. Newcastle-upon-Tyne, 1851.

Handbook of American Indians North of Mexico. Edited by Frederick Webb Hodge (*Smithsonian Institution. Bureau of American Ethnology, Bulletin* 30). 2 vols. Washington, 1907.

Handelingen en Mededeelingen van de Maatschapij der Nederlandsche Letterkunde. Leyden, 1846–

Hanoteau, L. A., and Letourneux, A., *La Kabylie et les coutumes Kabyles*. 3 vols. Paris, 1872.

Hansen, J. F. K., " De groep Noord- en Zuid-Pageh van de Mentaweieilanden," *Bijdragen tot de taal-, land- en volkenkunde van Nederlandsch-Indië*. Vol. lxx. 's Gravenhage, 1915.

Hanusch, Ignaz Jhann, *Die Wissenschaft des slavischen Mythus*. Lemberg, Stanislawow, and Tarnow, 1842.

Harcourt, A. F. B., *The Himalayan Districts of Kooloo, Lahoul, and Spiti*. London, 1871.

Hardeland, August, *Dajacksch-Deutsches Wörterbuch*. Amsterdam, 1859.

Hardenburg, W. E., " The Indians of the Putumayo, Upper Amazon," *Man*. Vol. x. London, 1910.

   The Putumayo. London, 1912.

Hardisty, W. L., " The Loucheux Indians," *Smithsonian Report for 1866*. Washington, 1867.

Hardman, E. T., " Notes on some Habits and Customs of the Natives of the Kimberley District, Western Australia," *Proceedings of the Royal Irish Academy*. Ser. iii, vol. i. Dublin, 1889–91.

Hardwick, C., *Traditions, Superstitions and Folk-Lore, chiefly Lancashire and North of England*. Manchester, 1872.

Hardy, R. Spence, *Eastern Monachism*. London, 1850.

Hardy, Thomas, *The Return of the Native*. London, 1895.

Harger, R. L., " The Desiccation of Africa," *The Journal of the East African and Uganda Natural History Society*. Vol. vi. London, 1917.

Harkness, H., *Description of a Singular Aboriginal Race inhabiting the Summit of the Neilgherry Hills*. London, 1832.

Harley, Timothy, *Moon-lore*. London, 1885.

Harmon, Daniel Williams, *A Journal of Voyages and Travels in the Interiour of North America*. Andover, 1820.

Harnack, C. G. A., *History of Dogma*. Transl. 7 vols. London, 1894–99.

Harper's New Monthly Magazine. New York, 1850–

Harper, C. H., " Notes on the Totemism of the Gold Coast," *Journal of the Anthropological Institute*. Vol. xxxvi. London, 1906.

Harper, R. F., *Assyrian and Babylonian Literature*. New York, 1901.

Harpocration, Valerius, *Lexicon*. Rec. I. Bekker. Berolini, 1833.

Harris, J. M., " Some Remarks on the Origin, Manners, Customs, and Superstitions of the Gallinas People of Sierra Leone." *Memoirs read before the Anthropological Society of London*. Vol. ii. London, 1866.

Harris, John, *Navigantium atque Itinerantium Bibliotheca. Voyages and Travels above six Hundred*. 2 vols. London, 1744–48.

Harris, W. B., *Tafilet ; the Narrative of a Journey of Exploration to the Atlas Mountain and the Oases of the North West Sahara.* Edinburgh and London, 1895.

"The Nomadic Berbers of Central Morocco," *The Geographical Journal.* Vol. i. London, 1897.

Harrison, Austin, *Pandora's Hope.* London, 1925.

Harrison, Charles, *Ancient Warriors of the North Pacific, the Haidas.* London, 1925.

Harrison, Jane Ellen, *Prolegomena to the Study of Greek Religion.* Cambridge, 1908.

Themis. Cambridge, 1912.

Harry, Gerard, *Man's Miracle, the Story of Helen Keller and her European sisters.* From the French. London, 1914.

Hart, C. F., "Notes on the Manufacture of Pottery among Savage Races," *The American Naturalist.* Vol. xiii. Boston, 1880.

"Contribuições para a ethnologia do valle do Amazonas," *Archivos do Museu Nacional do Rio de Janeiro.* Vol. vi. Rio de Janeiro, 1885.

Hartland, Edwin Sydney, *The Science of Fairy Tales.* London, 1891.

Primitive Paternity. 2 vols. London, 1909.

The Legend of Perseus. 3 vols. London, 1894–96.

"Notes on some South African Tribes," *Man.* Vol. vii. London, 1907.

Hartmann, A., *Deafmutism and the Education of Deaf-mutes.* Transl. London, 1881.

Hartmann, Robert, *Anthropoid Apes.* Transl. London, 1904.

Die Völker Afrikas. Leipzig, 1879.

Naturgeschichtlichemedizinische Skisse der Nillande. Berlin, 1866.

Hartmann von Aue, *Iwein, der Ritter mit dem Lewen.* Ed. Benecke and Lachman. Berlin, 1827.

Hartnock, C., *De Republica Polonica.* Frankfurt, Leipzig, 1687.

Hartog, Marcus, "Rotifera," in *The Cambridge Natural History.* Vol. ii. London, 1896.

Hartshorne, Bertram, F. "The Weddas," *The Fortnightly Review.* Vol. xix. London, 1876.

"The Weddas," *The Indian Antiquary.* Vol. viii. Bombay, 1879.

Hartung, G., and Dulk, A. F. B., *Fahrten durch Norwegen und die Lappmark.* Stuttgart, 1877.

Hartzer, Le Père Fernand, *Les Îles Blanches du Sud.* Paris, 1900.

Harvard African Studies. Cambridge, Mass, 1917–

Harvard Studies and Notes in Philology. Cambridge, Mass., 1892–

Harvard Studies in Classical Philology. Cambridge, Mass., 1890–98.

Harvey, Alexander, "Some Types of Egyptian Women," *The Cosmopolitan,* Vol. xxviii. New York, 1900.

Hass, E., "Die Heiratsgebräuche der alten Inder nach der Griyasutra," *Indische Studien.* Vol. v. Berlin, 1861.

Hasselt, A. L. van, "Aanteekenigen omtrent de Pottenbakkerij in de Residentie Tapanoeli," *Internationales Archiv für Ethnographie.* Vol. vi. Leiden, 1893.

Volksbeschrijving van Midden-Sumatra. Leiden, 1882.

Hasselt, J. B. van, "Die Noeforezen," *Zeitschrift für Ethnologie.* Vol. viii. Berlin, 1876.

Hasselt, Th. J. F. van, "Gebruik van vermonde taal door de Nufooren," *Tijdschrift voor Indische taal-, land- en volkenkunde.* Vol. xlv. Batavia, 's Hage, 1902.

Hastings, James (ed.) *Encyclopaedia of Religion and Ethics.* 12 vols. Edinburgh, 1908–21.

Hastings, James, *A Dictionary of the Bible.* 5 vols. Edinburgh, 1899–1904.

Hastings, Warren, " On the Gods of Greece, Italy, and India," *Asiatick Researches.* Vol. i. Calcutta, 1788.

Haug, Martin, *Essays on the Sacred Language, Writings, and Religion of the Parsees.* Bombay, 1878.

Haupt, Paul, *Akkadische und Sumerische Keilschrifttexte.* Leipzig, 1881.

Hausen, J. F. K., " De groep Noord- en Zuid-Pageh van de Mentawei-eilanden," *Bijdragen tot de taal-, land- en volkenkunde van Nederlandsch-Indië.* Vol. lxx, 's Gravenhage, 1915.

Hautecoeur, H., *Le Folklore de l'île de Kythnos.* Bruxelles, 1898.

Hauvette-Besnault, Am., " Fouilles de Délos," *Bulletin de Correspondance Hellénique.* Vol. vi. Athènes, Paris, 1882.

Havard, Henry, *La Hollande pittoresque. Le Coeur du pays.* Paris, 1878.

Hawes, Charles Henry, *In the Uttermost East.* London, New York, 1903.

and Harriet Boyd, *Crete the Forerunner of Greece.* London, New York, 1916.

Hawes, Harriet Boyd, *Gournia.* Philadelphia, 1908.

Hawkes, E. W., *The Labrador Eskimo.* Ottawa, 1916.

Hawkesworth, John, *An Account of the Voyages undertaken by the order of His present Majesty for making discoveries in the Southern Hemisphere.* 3 vols. London, 1773.

Hawkins, Col. Benjamin, *Sketch of the Creek Country and Customs of the Creek Indians.* Savannah, 1848.

Haxthausen, A. von, *Transcaucasia.* Transl. London, 1854.

Hayavadana Rao, C., " The Kasubas, a Forest Tribe of the Nilgiris," *Anthropos.* Vol iv. Wirn, 1909.

" The Irulans of the Gingee Hills," *Anthropos.* Vol. vi. Wien, 1911.

Haywood, A. H. W., *Through Timbuctoo and across the Great Sahara.* London, 1912.

Hazard, Ebenezer, *Historical Collections ; consisting of State Papers and other authentic documents, intended for an history of the United States of America.* 2 vols. Philadelphia, 1792–1794.

Hazeu, G. A. J., " Kleine bijdragen tot de ethnografie en folklore van Java," *Tijdschrift voor Indische taal-, and- en volkenkunde.* Vol. xlvi. Batavia, 's Hage, 1903.

Head, V. Barclay, *Historia Numorum.* Oxford, 1911.

Head, W. B., " Notes on the Yezidis," *Journal of the Royal Anthropological Institute.* Vol. xli. London, 1911.

Headland, I. T., " Chinese Women from a Chinese Standpoint," *The Chinese Recorder.* Shang-Hai, Foo-Chow, 1897.

Heape, Walter, *Sex Antagonism.* London, 1913.

Hearn, Lafcadio, *Glimpses of Unfamiliar Japan.* 2 vols. London, 1905.

" Out of the East," *Reveries and Studies in New Japan.* Boston and New York, 1895.

Hearne, Samuel, *Journey from the Prince of Wales's Fort in Hudson's Bay to the Northern Ocean.* London, 1795.

Heckewelder, J. G. E., *History, Manners, and Customs of the Indian Nations who once inhabited Pennsylvania and the surrounding States* (Reprint in *Memoirs of the Historical Society in Pennsylvania.* Vol. xii). Philadelphia, 1876.

Hecquard, Hyacynthe, *Voyage sur la côte et dans l'intérieur de l'Afrique occidentale.* Paris, 1855.

Hector, Sir James, reported in *Nature.* Vol. xii. London, 1875.

Hedley, Charles, " The Atoll of Funafuti, Ellice Group," *Memoirs of the Australian Museum.* Vol. iii, Part iii. Sydney, 1897.

Heese, " Sitte und Brauch der Sango," *Archiv für Anthropologie.* N.F., vol. xii. Braunschweig, 1913.

Heffter, August Wilhelm, *Die athenäische Gerichtsverfassung.* Cöln, 1822.

Hehn, J., *Siebenzahl und Sabbat bei den Babyloniern und im Alten Testament.* Leipzig, 1907.

Heim, Ricardus, *Incantamenta magica graeca latina (Jahrbücher für Philologie.* N.F. der Supplement, Bd. 19, Heft 12). Leipzig, 1855.

Heinrich von dem Türlin, *Diu Crône.* Ed. G. H. F. Scholl. Stuttgart, 1852.

Helbig, W., *Das homerische Epos aus den Denkmälern erläutert.* Leipzig, 1887.

Hellwald, Friederich von *Die Menschliche Familie nach ihrer Enstehung und natürlichen Entwickelung.* Leipzig, 1889.

Helmont, J. B. van, *Workes.* London, 1644.

Hely, B. A., " Native Habits and Customs in the Western Division," *Annual Report on British New Guinea, 1893-94.* Brisbane, 1894.

Hempelmann Friederich, " Zur Naturgeschichte von *Nereis dumerlii*, Aud. et Edw." *Zoologica.* Vol. xxv. Stuttgart, 1911.

Henderson, George, *Survivals in Belief among the Celts.* Glasgow, 1911.

Henderson, J., *Observations on the Colonies of New South Wales and van Diemen's Land.* Calcutta, 1832.

Henderson, William, *Notes on the Folk-Lore of the Northern Counties of England and the Borders.* London, 1879.

Henne-Am Rhyn, O. *Kulturgeschichte des Judenthums von den ältesten Zeiten bis zur Gegenwart.* Jena, 1880.

Die deutsche Volkssage im Verhältniss zu den Mythen aller Zeiten und Völker. Wien, 1879.

Hennepin, R. P. Louis, *Voyage ou nouvelle découverte à un très-grand pays dans l'Amérique entre le nouveau Mexique et la Mer Glaciale.* Amsterdam, 1704.

Hennessy, J. M., " Native Habits and Customs of the Eastern Division," *Annual Report on British New Guinea, 1893-94.* Brisbane, 1894.

Henny, W. A., " Reis naar Si Gompoelon en Si Lindong in Maart en April 1858. Bijdrage tot de kennis der Bataklande," *Tijdschrift voor taal-, land- en volkenkunde van Nederlandsch Indië.* Vol. xvii. Batavia, 's Hage, 1869.

Henry of Huntingdon, *Historia Anglorum.* Ed. by Thomas Arnold (*Chronicles and Memorials of Great Britain and Ireland*). London, 1879.

Henry, A., " The Lolos and other Tribes of Western China," *Journal of the Anthropological Institute.* Vol. xxxiii. London, 1903.

Henry, Alexander, *Travels and Adventures in the Years 1760-1776.* Chicago, 1921.

Henry, Jos., *L'Âme d'un peuple Africain. Les Bambara.* Münster i. W., 1910.

Henry, Miss Teuria, " Tahitian Folk-Lore," *Journal of the Polynesian Society.* Vol. x. Wellington, 1901.

" The Tahitian Version of the Names Ra'iatea and Taputapu-alea," *Journal of the Polynesian Society.* Vol. xxi. Wellington, 1912.

Henry, Victor, *La Magie dans l'Inde antique.* Paris, 1909.

Heraklides Ponticus, *Fragmenta*, in C. Müller, *Fragmenta Historicorum Graecorum.* Vol. ii. Parisiis, 1848.

Herbelot, B. D. d', *Bibliothèque Orientale.* Paris, 1697.

Herber, J., " Tatouage du pubis au Maroc," *Revue d'Ethnographie et des Traditions Populaires.* Vol. iii. Paris, 1922.

Herbert, Thomas, *Some Yeares Travels into Divers Parts of Africa and Asia the Great.* London, 1677.

Herbert de Damartin, *Le roman de Foulque de Candie.* Ed. P. Tarbe. Reims, 1860.

Herdings, A., " Report on the East African Protectorate," *House of Commons Accounts and Papers*, 1897, No. 7. London, 1897.

Herennius, Caius, *Rhetoricorum ad C. H. libri iv.* Venetiis, 1564.

Hering, O., " Die Frauen Japans im Spiegel der für sie bestimmten Litteratur," *Mitteilungen der deutschen Gesellschaft für Natur- und Völkerkunde Ostasiens.* Vol. v. Yokohama, 1892.

Heriot, George, *Travels through the Canadas.* London, 1807.

Hermann, Lt., " Ugogo, das Land und seine Bewohner," *Mitteilungen aus den Deutschen Schutzgebieten.* Vol. v. Berlin, 1892.

Hermann, Wilhelm, " Die ethnographischen Ergebnisse der Deutschen Pilcomayo-Expedition," *Zeitschrift für Ethnologie.* Vol. xl. Berlin, 1908.

Hermathena ; Papers by Members of Trinity College, Dublin. Dublin, 1874–

Hermes, Berlin, 1866–

Hernandez, Pablo, *Missiones del Paraguay. Organización social del las doctrinas Guaranies de la Compañia de Jesús.* 2 vols. Barcelona, 1913.

Herndon, W. L., *Exploration of the Valley of the Amazon.* 2 Parts (Part ii, by L. Gibbon). Washington, 1854.

Hernsheim F., " Die Marshall-Inseln," *Mittheilungen der geographischen Gesellschaft in Hamburg, 1878-79.* Hamburg, 1879.

Herodian, *Historiarum libri octo.* Ed. T. G. Irmisch. 5 vols. Lipsiae, 1789–1805.

Herodotus, *Historiae.* Rec. C. Hude. Oxonii, s.d.

Heron, David, *The Influence of Defective Physique and unfavourable Home Environment on the Intelligence of School Children (Eugenics Laboratory Memoirs, No. 8).* London, 1910.

Heron de Villefosse, A., *Notice des Monuments provenant de la Palestine et conservés ay Musée du Louvre.* Paris, 1876.

Herport, Albrecht, *Eine kurtze Ost-Indianische Reiss-Beschreibung.* Bern, 1669.

Herrera, A. de, *Historia general de los hechos de los Castellanos en las islas i tierra firme del mar oceano.* 4 vols. Madrid, 1726–30.
    General History of America, commonly called the West Indies. Transl. 6 vols. London, 1740.

Hershon, Paul Isaac, *A Talmudic Miscellany.* London, 1880.

Hertwig, C. W. T. R., " Über die Conjugation der Infusorien," *Sitzungsberichte der Gesellschaft für Morphologie und Physiologie.* Vol. v. München, 1890.
    " Über befruchtung und Conjugation," *Verhandlungen der deutschen Zoologischen Gesellschaft.* Leipzig, 1892.
    " Was veranlasst die Befruchtung der Protozoen ? " *Sitzungsberichte der Gesellschaft für Morphologie und Physiologie.* Vol. xv. München, 1900.

Hertz, W., *Spielmanns-Buch.* Stuttgart, 1886.

Hervey D. F. A., " The Mentra Traditions," *Journal of the Straits Branch of the Royal Asiatic Society.* No. 10. Singapore, 1882.

Hervey, E. A., " The Endau and its Tributaries," *Journal of the Straits Branch of the Royal Asiatic Society.* Vol. iv. Singapore, 1881.

Hesiod, *Carmina.* Rec. C. Goettling. Gothae, 1843.

Hesse-Wartegg, Ernst von, *Samoa, Bismark Archipel und Neuguinea.* Leipzig, 1902.

Hesychius, *Lexicon.* Rec. M. Schmidt. 4 vols. Ienae, 1858–62.

Hewan, Archibald, " On some Customs of the People of Old Malabar relative to Pregnancy and Parturition," *Edinburgh Medical and Surgical Journal.* Vol. x. Edinburgh, 1865.

Hewett, Edgar L., " Archaeology of Pajarito Park, New Mexico," *The American Anthropologist*, N.S., Vol vi. Lancaster, 1904.

Hewitt, J. N. B., " The Cosmogonic Gods of the Iroquois," *Proceedings of the American Association for the Advancement of Science for the 44th Meeting*. Salem, 1896.

"Iroquois Cosmology," *Twenty-first Annual Report of the Bureau of American Ethnology*. Washington, 1903.

Hewitt, W. M. G., *The Diagnosis and Treatment of Diseases of Women*. London, 1868.

Heymans, G., and Wiersma, E., " Beiträge zur speziellen Psychologie auf Grund einer Massenuntersuchung," *Zeitschrift für Psychologie*. Vol. xlii. Leipzig, 1906.

Heywood, Thomas (T. H. Gent.), *The Generall History of Women*. London, 1657.

The Hibbert Journal. London, Oxford, 1892–

Hickson, S. J., *A Naturalist in North Celebes*. London, 1889.

" Notes on the Sengirese," *Journal of the Anthropological Institute*. Vol. xvi. London, 1887.

Hieronimo di Santo Stefano, " Account of the Journey of Hieronimo di Santo Stefano," transl. in R. H. Major, *India in the Fifteenth Century*. London, 1857.

Hild, J. A., art. " Vestalis," in C. Daremberg and E. Saglio, *Dictionnaire des antiquités grecques et romaines*. Vol. v. Paris, 1919.

Hildburgh, W. L., " Some Japanese Charms connected with the Making of Clothes," *Man*. Vol. xvii. London, 1917.

" Notes on some Tibetan and Bhutia Amulets and Folk Medicines, and a few Nepalese Amulets," *Journal of the Royal Anthropological Institute*. Vol. xxxix. London, 1909.

Hildebrandt, J. M., " Ethnographische Notizen über Wakamba und ihre Nachbaren," *Zeitschrift für Ethnologie*. Vol. x. Berlin, 1878.

Hilgenfeld, Adolf, *Ketzergeschichte des Urchristenthums*. Leipzig, 1884.

Hermae Pastor ; Elxai libri Fragmenta. Berlin, 1881.

See *Evangeliorum secundum Hebraeos*, etc.

Hill, Richard, and Thornton, George, *Notes on the Aborigines of New South Wales*. Sydney, 1892.

Hill, S. S., *Travels in the Sandwich and Society Islands*. London, 1856.

Hill, Sid, " Ceremonies, Customs, and Foods of the Myoli Tribe," *Science of Man*. Sydney, 1901.

Hillebrandt, Alfred, *Vedische Mythologie*. 3 vols. Breslau, 1891–1902.

" Ritualliteratur. Vedische Opfer und Zauber," in G. Buehler, *Grundriss der indo-arischem Philogie*. Strassburg, 1897.

" Eine Miscelle aus dem Vedaritual," *Zeitschrift der deutschen morgenländische Gesellschaft*. Vol. xl. Leipzig, 1886.

Hillelson, S., " Arabic Proverbs, Sayings, Riddles, and Popular Beliefs," *Sudan Notes and Records*. Vol. iv. Khartoum, 1921.

Hilprecht Anniversary Volume. Studies in Assyriology and Archaeology. Leipzig, 1909.

Hincmar, *Capitula ad presbyteros*, in Migne, *Patrologiae Cursus Completus*. Vol. cxxv. Parisiis, 1852.

Hinde, S. L., and Hildegarde, *The Last of the Masai*. London, 1901.

Hinlopen, Wijlen, P. A. M. Sen Severijn, P., " Verslag van een onderzoek der Poggi-Eilanden." *Tijdschrift voor Indische taal-, land- en volkenkunde*. Vol. iii. Batavia, 1855.

Hippolytus, *Refutatio omnium Haeresium*. Ed. L. Duncker and F. G. Schneidewin. Gottingae, 1859.

Hirsch, E. G., art., " Sabbath," *The Jewish Encyclopaedia*. Vol. x. Chicago, s.d.

Hirschfeld, H., " Remarks on the Etymology of Sabbath," *Journal of the Royal Asiatic Society*. Vol. xxviii. London, 1896.

Hirst, C. C., " Mendelian Heredity in Man," *The Eugenics Review*. Vol. iv. London, 1913.

Histoire générale de Languedoc. 15 vols. Toulouse, 1872–92.

Histoire littéraire de la France par des religieux bénédictins de la Congréga-tion de Saint-Maur continuée par des membres de l'Institut. Paris, 1733–

Historiae Augustae Scriptores. 2 vols. Lugd. Batav., 1671.

The History of Fulk Fitz Warine. Ed. T. Wright. London, 1855.

Hitchcock, R., " The Ainos of Yezo, Japan," *Smithsonian Report for 1891*. Washington, 1892.

Hoang, P. Pierre, *Le mariage Chinois au point de vue légal (Variétés sino-logiques*. Vol. xiv.). Chang-Hai, 1898.

Hobhouse, L. T., *Morals in Evolution*. London, 1915.

Wheeler, G. C., and Ginsberg, M., *The Material Culture and Social Insti-tutions of the Simpler Peoples. An Essay in Correlation*. London, 1915.

Hobley, C. W., *Eastern Uganda*. London, 1902.

" Kikuyu Customs and Beliefs," *Journal of the Royal Anthropological Institute*. Vol. xl. London, 1910.

Ethnology of A-Kamba and other East African Tribes. Cambridge, 1910.

" British East Africa. Anthropological Studies in Kavirondo and Nandi," *Journal of the Royal Anthropological Institute*. Vol. xxxv. London, 1903.

" Further Researches into Kikuyu and Karba Religious Beliefs," *Journal of the Royal Anthropological Institute*. Vol. xli. London, 1911.

Bantu Beliefs and Magic. London, 1922.

Hocart, A. M., " Notes on the Dual Organisation in Fiji," *Man*. Vol. xiv. London, 1914.

" Pierres magiques au Lau, Fiji," *Anthropos*. Vol. vi. Wien, 1911.

Hodgkinson, Clement, *Australia from Port Macquarie to Moreton Bay ; with a Description of the Natives*. London, 1845.

Hodgson, B. H., *Miscellaneous Essays relating to Indian Subjects*. 2 vols. London, 1880.

" On the Origin, Location, Numbers, Creed, Customs, Character, and Condition of the Kocch, Bodo and Dhimal People, with a General Description of the Climate they dwell in," *Journal of the Asiatic Society of Bengal*. Vol. xviii. Part ii. Calcutta, 1850.

Hodgson, Christopher Pemberton, *Reminiscences of Australia*. London, 1846.

Hodson, T. C., *The Metheis*. London, 1908.

The Nāga Tribes of Manipur. London, 1911.

" The ' Genna ' amongst the Tribes of Assam," *Journal of the Anthropo-logical Institute*. Vol. xxxvi. London, 1906.

" Head-hunting among the Hill Tribes of Assam," *Folk-lore*. Vol. xx. London, 1909.

" The Native Tribes of Manipur," *Journal of the Anthropological Institute*. Vol. xxxi. London, 1901.

Hoeck, Karl, *Kreta*. 3 vols. Göttingen, 1823.

Hoernes, M., *Urgeschichte der Bildende Kunst in Europa*. Wien, 1915.

Hoernle, A. F. R., " Some Problems in Ancient Indian History," *Journal of the Royal Asiatic Society*. London, 1909.

Hoëvell, G. W. W. C. Baron van, *Ambon en meer bepaaldelijk de Oeliasers*. Dordrecht, 1875.

Hoëvell, G. W. W. C. Baron van, " Einige weitere Notizen über die Forme der Gotterverehrung auf den süd-wester und süd-oster Inseln," *Internationales Archiv für Ethnographie*. Vol. viii. Leiden, 1895.

Höffding, Harald, *Outlines of Psychology*. Transl. London, 1891.

Hoffman, W. J., " The Menomini Indians," *Fourteenth Annual Report of the Bureau of Ethnology*. Washington, 1896.

" The Midē'wivin or ' Grand Medicine Society ' of the Ojibwa," *Seventh Annual Report of the Bureau of Ethnology*. Washington, 1892.

Höfler, M., *Deutsches Krankheitsnamen-Buch*. München, 1899.

" Kröte und Gebärmutter," *Globus*. Vol. lxxxviii. Braunschweig, 1905.

Hofman, O., " Beiträge zur Kenntniss der Parthenogenesis," *Entomologische Zeitung*. Stettin, 1869.

Hogarth, D. G., art., " Aegean Religion," in Hastings's *Encyclopaedia of Religion and Ethics*. Vol. i. Edinburgh, 1908.

Höhnel, Ludwig von, *Discovery of Lakes Rudolf and Stefanie*. Transl. 2 vols. London, 1894.

Holden, W. C., *The Past and Future of the Kaffir Races*. London, 1866.

Holder, Alfred T., *Altceltischer Sprachschatz*. 3 vols. Leipzig, 1896.

Holder, C. F., " The nest-builders of the sea," *Harper's New Monthly Magazine*. Vol. lxviii. New York, 1884.

Holland, S. C., " On the Ainos," *Journal of the Anthropological Institute*. Vol. iii. London, 1874.

Hollander, J. J. de, *Handleiding bij de beoefening der land- en volkenkunde van Nederlandsch Oost-Indië*. 2 vols. Breda, 1861–62.

Hollhausen, F., " Zu der altschwedische Ratten- und Mäusezauber," *Arkiv för Nordisk Filologi*. Vol. xiv. Lund, 1898.

Hollis, A. C., *The Masai, Their Language and Folk-lore*. Oxford, 1905.

The Nandi, Their Language and Folk-lore. Oxford, 1909.

" Notes on the History and Customs of the People of Taveta, East Africa," *Journal of the African Society*. Vol. i. London, 1901.

" A Note on the Masai System of Relationship and other Matters connected therewith," *Journal of the Anthropological Institute*. Vol. xl. London, 1910.

Holm, G. F., " Sagn og Fortaellinger fra Angmagsalik, samt 4 Trommensange, 2 Tryllesange og 1 Trylleformular," *Meddelelser om Grønland*. Vol. x. Kjøbenhaver, 1885.

" Konebaads-Expeditionen til Grønlands Østkyst, 1883–85," *Geografisk Tidskrift*. Vol. viii. Kjøbenhavn, 1886.

Holmberg, Eduardo A., *Viaje al interior de Tierra del Fuego*. Buenos Aires, 1906.

Holmberg, H. J., " Ethnographische Skizzen über die Völker des russischen Amerika," *Acta Societatis Scientiarum Fennicae*. Vol. iv. Helsingfors, 1856. ..

Holmes, W. H., " Pottery of the American Pueblos," *Fourth Annual Report of the Bureau of Ethnology*. Washington, 1886.

" Origin and Development of Form and Ornament in Ceramic Art," *Ibid*.

" Aboriginal Pottery of the Eastern United States," *Twentieth Annual Report of the Bureau of American Ethnology*. Washington, 1903.

" Prehistoric Textile Fabrics of the United States derived from Impressions on Pottery." *Third Annual Report of the Bureau of Ethnology*. Washington, 1884.

" The Use of Textile Fabrics in Pottery Making," *The American Anthropologist*, N.S. Vol. iii. Lancaster. 1901.

" Art in Shell of the Ancient Americans," *Second Annual Report of the Bureau of Ethnology*. Washington, 1883.

Holtzmann, A., *Deutsche Mythologie*. Leipzig, 1874.

    Indische Sagen. 3 vols. Karlsruhe, 1845–47.

Holub, Emil, *Von der Capstadt ins Land der Maschukulumbe*. 2 vols. Wien, 1890.

    Sieben Jahre in Süd-Afrika. 2 vols. Wien, 1881.

    Seven Years in South Africa. 2 vols. Transl. London, 1881.

Homer, *Carmina*. Ed. J. F. Dübner. Parisiis, 1837.

    Scholia in Iliadem. Rec. Bekkeri. 2 vols. Berolini, 1821.

Hommel, Fritz, " Neue Werke über die älteste Bevölkerung Kleinasiens," *Archiv für Anthropologie*. Vol. xix. Braunschweig, 1890.

    The Ancient Hebrew Tradition and the Monuments. Transl. London, 1897.

    Der Gestirndienst der alten Araber und die israelitische Überlieferung. München, 1901.

    Aufsätze und Abhandlungen arabisch-semitologische Inhalts. München, 1892–1901.

Honorius of Autun, *Elucidarium*, in Migne, *Patrologiae Cursus Completus*. Vol. clxxii. Parisiis, 1854.

Hood, T. H., *Notes of a Cruise in H.M.S. " Fawn " in the Western Pacific, 1862*. Edinburgh, 1863.

Hooper, W. H., *Ten Months among the Tents of the Tuski*. London, 1853.

Hoorn, G. van, " De origine cistophorum," *Mnemosyne*. Vol. xliii. 1914.

Hope, R. C., *The Legendary Lore of Holy Wells in England*. London, 1893.

Hopf, L., *The Human Species*. New York, 1909.

Hopkins, E. Washburn, in *The Cambridge History of India*. Vol. i. Cambridge, 1922.

    The Religions of India. London, 1896.

    " The Social and Military Position of the Ruling Caste in Ancient India, as represented by the Sansckrit Epic," *Journal of the American Oriental Society*. Vol. xiii. New Haven, 1889.

Hopkins, Manley, *Hawaii. The Past, Present, and Future of the Island-Kingdom*. London, 1866.

Horapollo Nilous, *The Hieroglyphics*. Ed. by Alex. Turner Cory. London, 1840.

Horatius Flaccus, Quintus, *Poemata*. Ed. C. Anthon et J. Boyd. Londini, 1847.

Hornaday, W. T., " On the Species of the Bornean Orangs, with Notes on their Habits," *Proceedings of the American Association for the Advancement of Science, 20th Meeting*. Salem, 1880.

    The Mind and Manners of Wild Animals. New York and London, 1922.

Horne, C., " Notes on Villages in the Himalayas, in Kumaon, Gahrwal, and on the Satlek," *The Indian Antiquary*. Vol. v. Bombay, 1876.

Hornell, J., " The Indian Conch (*Turbinella pyrum*, Linn.) and its relation to Hindu Life and Religion," *Report to the Government of Baroda on the Marine Zoology of Okhamandal in Kattiawar*. Part ii. London, 1910.

Horrack, J. de, *Les lamentations d'Isis et de Nephthys*. Paris, 1866.

Horst, D. W., " Uit de Lampongs," *De Indische Gids*. Jahrg. i. Vol. ii. Amsterdam, 1879.

Horst, R., " Over Wavo (*Lysidice oele*, n. sp.)," *Rumphius Gedenkboek*. Haarlem, 1905.

Hort, Dora, *Tahiti, the Garden of the Pacific*. London, 1891.

Hose, C. and McDougall, W., *The Pagan Tribes of Borneo*. 2 vols. London, 1912.

Houghton, E. P., " On the Land Dayaks of Upper Sarawak," *Memoirs of the Anthropological Society of London*. Vol. iii. London, 1870.

Hovelacque, Abel, *Les nègres de l'Afrique sus-équatoriale*. Paris, 1889.
   L'Avesta, Zoroastre et le Mazdéisme. Paris, 1880.
    Picot, E., and Vinson, J., *Mélanges de linguistique et d'anthropologie*.
    Paris, 1880.
Howard, H. E., *Territory in Bird Life*. London, 1920.
Howe, Maud, and Hall, Florence Howe, *Laura Bridgman, Dr. Howe's famous
   pupil, and what he taught her*. London, 1904.
Howe, Samuel Grindley. *On the Causes of Idiocy*. Edinburgh, 1858.
Howell, John, *The Life and Adventures of Alexander Selkirk*. Edinburgh, 1829.
Howitt, A. W., " Australian Group Relations," *Smithsonian Report, 1883*.
   Washington, 1885.
   " On the Organization of Australian Tribes," *Transactions of the Royal
   Society of Victoria*. Vol. i., Part i. Melbourne, 1889.
   The Native Tribes of South-East Australia. London, 1904.
   " On Australian Medicine Men ; or Doctors and Wizards of some Aus-
   tralian Tribes," *Journal of the Anthropological Institute*. Vol. xvi.
   London, 1887.
   " Notes on Songs and Song-makers of some Australian Tribes," *Journal
   of the Anthropological Institute*. Vol. xvi. London, 1887.
   " The Jeraeil, or Initiation Ceremonies of the Kurnai Tribe," *Journal of
   the Anthropological Institute*. Vol. xiv. London, 1885.
   " Native Tribes of South-East Australia," *Journal of the Royal Anthro-
   pological Institute*. Vol. xxxvii. London, 1907.
   " Further Notes on the Australian Class System," *Journal of the Anthro-
   pological Institute*. Vol. xviii. London, 1890.
   " The Diery and other kindred Tribes of Central Australia," *Journal of
   the Anthropological Institute*. Vol. xx. London, 1891.
   " On some Australian Ceremonies of Initiation," *Journal of the Anthro-
   pological Institute*. Vol. xiii. London, 1884.
Hozumi, Nobushige, *Lectures on the New Japanese Civil Code*. Tokyo, 1912.
   Ancestor-Worship and Japanese Law. Tokyo, 1913.
Hrdlička, Aleš, " The Region of the Ancient Chchimecs, with Notes on the
   Tepecanos and the Ruins of La Quemada, Mexico," *The American
   Anthropologist*. N.S., vol. v. Washington, 1903.
Hruza, Ernst, *Beiträge zur Geschichte des griechischen und römischen Familien-
   rechtes*. 2 vols. Erlangen and Leipzig, 1892–94.
Hübner, " Die Duk-Duk-Ceremonie," *Die ethnologisch-anthropologische Abthei-
   lung des Museum Godeffroy*. Hamburg, 1881.
Huc, Evariste Regis, *Travels in Tartary, Thibet, and China during the years
   1844–5–6*. Transl. by W. Hazlitt. 2 vols. London, 1852.
   The Chinese Empire. Transl. 2 vols. London, 1855.
Hudson, W. H., *The Naturalist in La Plata*. London, 1895.
Huet, G., " La légende de Charlemagne bâtard et le témoignage de Jean
   Boendale," *Le Moyen Âge*. 2ᵉ Série, vol. xv. Paris, 1911.
Hüffer, *Der Trobador Guillem de Cabestanh, sein Leben und seine Werke*.
   Berlin, 1869.
Huish, Robert, *A Narrative of the Voyages of Captain Beechey and Captain
   Back*. London, 1836.
Hull, Eleanor, *The Cuchullin Saga in Irish Literature*. London, 1898.
Humbert de Romans, in A. Lecoy de la Marche, *La chaire française au moyen-
   âge*. Paris, 1886.
Humboldt, F. H. Alex. von, *Gesammelte Werke*. 12 vols. Stuttgart [1889]
   *Personal Narrative of Travels in the Equinoctial Regions of the New Conti-
   nent*. Transl. 7 vols. London, 1814–29.
   The same. 3 vols. London, 1852–53.

Humboldt, F. H. Alex von, *Cosmos*. Transl. 5 vols. London, 1848–59.
   Vues des Cordillères et monumens des peuples indigènes de l'Amérique.
   2 vols. Paris, 1816.
Humboldt, Wilhelm von, *Gesammelte Werke.* 7 vols. Berlin, 1841–52.
Hunt, A. E., "Ethnographical Notes on the Murray Islands, Torres Straits,"
   Journal of the Anthropological Institute. Vol. xxviii. London, 1899.
Hunt, Robert, *Popular Romances of the West of England ; or Drolls, Tradi-*
   tions, and Superstitions of old Cornwall. London, 1881.
Hunter, W. A., *Exposition of Roman Law.* London, 1876.
Hunter, William Wilson, *A Statistical Account of Assam.* 2 vols. London,
   1879.
   A Statistical Account of Bengal. London, 1875–77.
   The Annals of Rural Bengal. 3 vols. London, 1868–72.
Huntington, Ellsworth, *The Pulse of Asia.* Boston and New York, 1907.
   "The Mountains of Turkestan," *The Geographical Journal.* Vol. xxv.
   London, 1905.
Huon de Bordeaux. Ed. F. Guessard and C. Grandmaison (*Anciens Poètes*
   de la France). Paris, 1860.
Hurd, R., *Letters on Chivalry and Romance.* Ed. E. J. Morley. London, 1911.
Hurel, E., "Religion et vie domestique des Bakerewe," *Anthropos.* Vol. vi.
   Wien, 1911.
Hurgronje, C. Snouck, *De Atjéhers.* 2 vols. Batavia, Leiden, 1893–94.
   Mekka, 2 vols. Haag, 1888–89.
Hurley, F., *Pearls and Savages.* New York and London, 1924.
Hurst, C. C., "Mendelian Heredity in Man," *The Eugenics Review.* Vol. iv.
   London, 1913.
Huschke, P. E., *Der Verfassung des Königs Servius Tullius.* Leipzig,
   1840.
Hussey, Mary Inda, "Some Sumerian-Babylonian Hymns of the Berlin
   Collection," *American Journal of Semitic Languages and Literatures.*
   Vol. xxiii. Chicago, 1907.
Hutchinson, R. H. Sneyd, *An Account of the Chittagong Hill Tracts.* Cal-
   cutta, 1906.
Hutchinson, Thomas H., *Ten Years' Wandering among the Ethiopians.*
   London, 1861.
Hutchinson, Th. J., "The Tehuelche Indians of Patagonia," *Transactions of*
   the Ethnological Society. Vol. vii. London, 1869.
Hutchinson, Woods, "Animal Marriage," *The Contemporary Review.*
   London, 1904.
Hutereau, A., *Notes sur la vie familiale et juridique de quelques populations du*
   Congo belge (Annales du Musée du Congo). Bruxelles, 1909.
Huth, Alfred Henry, *The Marriage of Near Kin.* London, 1887.
Hutton, J. H., *The Sema Nagas.* London, 1921.
   The Angami Nagas. London, 1921.
Hutton, J., *Central Asia from the Aryan to the Cossack.* London, 1875.
Hutton, William, *A Voyage to Africa.* London, 1821.
Hyades, P., "Ethnographie des Fuégiens," *Bulletin de la Société d'Anthro-*
   pologie. 3e Série, vol. x. Paris, 1887.
   and Deniker, J., in *Mission scientifique du cap Horn.* Vol. vii. "Anthro-
   pologie ethnographie." Paris, 1891.
Hyde, Douglas, *A Literary History of Ireland.* London, 1899.
Hyde, Thomas, *Historia religionis veterum Persarum.* Oxonii, 1760.
Hyginus, C. Julius, *Fabulae,* in *Mythographi Latini,* ed. T. Munckerus. Am-
   sterlodami, 1681.
Hylten-Cavallius, G. O., *Wärend och Wirdarne.* 2 vols. Stockholm, 1868.

Iamblichus Chalcidensis, *De mysteriis.* Ed. T. Gale. Oxford, 1678.

Ibbetson, Sir Denzil Charles Jelf, *Report on the Census of the Panjáb, taken on the 17th of February, 1881.* 3 vols. Calcutta, 1883.

Ibn Batutah, Muhammad ibn 'Abd Allah, *Voyages.* Ed. and transl. by C. Défrémery and B. R. Sanguinetti. Paris, 1853–58.
The same. Transl. by S. Lee. London, 1829.

Ibn Khaldun, 'Abd al-Rahman ibn Muhammad, *Histoire des Berbères et des Dynasties Musulmanes de l'Afrique Septentrionale* par Ibn Khaldoun, traduite de l'Arabe par M. le Baron de Slane. 4 vols. Alger, 1852–56.

Icard, S., *La femme pendant la période menstruelle.* Paris, 1890.

Icazbalceta, Joaquin Garcia (ed.), *Coleccion de documentos para la Historia de Mexico.* 2 vols. Mexico, 1855–66.

Iden-Zeller, Oscar, " Ethnographische Beobachtungen bei den Tschuktschen," *Zeitschrift für Ethnologie.* Vol. xliii. Berlin, 1911.

Ignace, Abbé, " Les Capiekrans," *Anthropos.* Vol. v. Wien, 1910.

Ihering, H. von, " Die künstliche Deformierung der Zähne," *Zeitschrift für Ethnologie.* Vol. xiv. Berlin, 1882.

Ihering, Rudolph von, *Geist des römischen Rechts auf den verschiedenen Stufen seines Entwickelung.* 3 vols. Leipzig, 1888–98.

Ihne, Wilhelm, *Römische Geschichte.* 8 vols. Leipzig, 1868–90.

Imhaus, E. N., *Les Nouvelles-Hébrides.* Paris, 1890.

Imhoof-Blumer, F., *Kleinasiatische Münzen.* Vienna, 1901–

Immerwahr, W., *Die Kulte und Mythen Arkadiens.* Leipzig, 1891.

Imperial and Asiatic Quarterly Review. London, 1891–

Imperial Gazetteer of India. 26 vols. Oxford, 1907–09.

Im Thurn, E. F., *Among the Indians of Guiana.* London, 1883.

The Indian Antiquary. Bombay, 1872–

Indische Gids. Amsterdam, 1879–

Indische Studien, Zeitschrift für die Kunde der indischen Alterthums. Berlin, Leipzig, 1850–98.

Inglis, John, *In the New Hebrides.* London, 1887.

Inman, Thomas, *Ancient Faiths embodied in Ancient Names.* 2 vols. London, 1872.

Inscriptiones Graecae Insularum Maris Aegei. Berlin, 1895–

The Institutes of Vishnu. Transl. by J. Jolly ; *The Sacred Books of the East.* Vol. vii. Oxford, 1880.

Interiano, Giorgio, " Della vita de Zychi, chiamati : Circassi," in G. B. Ramusio, *Secondo volume delle Navigationi et Viaggi.* Venetia, 1559.

Internationale Revue der gesamten Hydrobiologie und Hydrographie. Leipzig, 1908–

Internationales Archiv für Ethnographie. Leiden, 1888–

Inwards, Richard, *Weather Lore.* London, 1893.

Ireland, William W., *The Blot upon the Brain : Studies in History and Psychology.* Edinburgh, 1893.
The Mental Affections of Children ; Idiocy, Imbecility, and Insanity. London, 1900.

Irenaeus, *Contra Haereses,* in Migne, *Patrologiae Cursus Completus, Series Graeca.* Vol. vii. Parisiis, 1857.

Irle, J., *Die Herero.* Gütersloh, 1906.

Isaeus, *Orationes,* in *Oratores Attici,* ed. I. Bekker. Oxford, 1822–23.

Isidorus Characenus, in C. Müller, *Geographi Graeci Minores.* Vol. i. Parisiis, 1855.

Isidore of Seville, *Opera omnia.* Ed. F. Arevalo. 7 vols. Romae, 1787–1803.

Isle, A. de l', " Mémoire sur les moeurs et l'accouchement de l'Alyte obstetri-
cans," *Annales des Sciences Naturelles*, 5ᵉ Série, Zoologie. Vol. iii.
Paris, 1876.

Itard, J. E. M. G., *De l'éducation d'un homme sauvage et des premiers développe-
ments physiques et moraux du jeune sauvage de l'Aveyron.* Paris, 1801.

Itinerarium Peregrinorum et Gesta Regis Ricardi, in *Chronicles and Memorials
of the Reign of Richard I* (*Chronicles and Memorials of Great Britain
and Ireland*). Ed. by W. Stubbs. Vol. i. London, 1864.

Iti-vuttaka, or Sayings of Buddha. Transl. by J. H. More. New York,
1908.

Iu-Kiao-Li, ou Les deux cousines. Transl. by J. P. Abel Rémusat. 2 vols.
Paris, 1826.

Izuka, Akira, " Observations on the Japanese Palolo, *Ceratocephale osawai,*
n. sp.," *Journal of the College of Science, Imperial University of Tokyo.*
Vol. xvii. Tokyo, 1903.

Jackson, A. V. Williams, " Die Iranische Religion," in W. Geiger and E. Kuhn,
Grundriss der Iranischen Philologie. Vol. ii. Strassburg, 1904.

Jackson, F. G., " Notes on the Samoyads of the Great Tundra ; with prefatory
remarks by Arthur Montefiore," *Journal of the Anthropological Institute.* Vol. xxiv. London, 1895.

Jackson, F. J., in *Big Game Shooting.* Vol. i. (*Badminton Library.*) London, 1894.

Jackson, H. C., " The Nuer of the Upper Nile Province, " *Sudan Notes and
Records.* Vol. vi. Khartum, 1923.

Jackson, J. Wilfrid, *Shells as Evidence of the Migrations of Early Culture.*
Manchester, 1915.

Jacobi, Hermann, G., " Über das Alter des Rig-Veda," in *Festgruss an Rudolf
von Roth.* Stuttgart, 1893.
" On the Date of the Rig-Veda," *The Indian Antiquary.* Vol. xxiii.
Bombay, 1894.
" On the Antiquity of Vedic Culture," *Journal of the Royal Asiatic Society.*
London, 1909.

Jacobowski, Ludwig, " Das Weib in der Poesie der Hottentotten," *Globus.*
Vol. lxx. Braunschweig, 1896.

Jacobs, Joseph, *An Inquiry into the Sources of the History of the Jews in Spain.*
London, 1894.
" Studies in Jewish Statistics," *The Jewish Chronicle.* N.S., No. 720.
London, 1883.
" On the Racial Characteristics of Modern Jews," *Journal of the Anthro-
pological Institute.* Vol. xv. London, 1885.

Jacobsen, J. A., *Captain Jacobsen's Reise an der Nordwestküste Amerikas.*
Herausg. A. Woldt. Leipzig, 1884.

Jacottet, E., *The Treasury of Ba-suto Lore.* Vol. i. Morijo, London, 1908.
Textes Soubiya (Bulletin de Correspondance Africaine, xvi). Paris, 1899.

Jacquemont, Victor, *Voyages dans l'Inde.* 4 vols. Paris, 1835–44.
*Correspondance de V . . . J . . . avec sa famille et ses amis pendant son
voyage dans l'Inde.* 2 vols. Paris, 1869.

Jacques de Vitry, *Sermones Vulgares*, in J. B. Pitra, *Analecta novissima ;
Specilegii Solesmensis altera continuatio.* Vol. ii. Paris, 1888.

Jadrinzew, N. H., " Ueber die Bewohner des Altai und die Tschernschen
Tartaren," *Russische Revue.* Vol. xxi. St. Petersburg, 1882.

Jafar Sharif, *Qanoon-e-Islam, or The Customs of the Moosulmans of India.*
Transl. by G. A. Herklots. London, 1832.

Jagor F., " Einige Sklaven-Kasten in Malabar," *Zeitschrift für Ethnologie.* Vol. x. Berlin, 1878.

Jagor, A. F., *Reisen in den Philippinen.* Berlin, 1873.

Jahn, Otto, " Die Cista Mystica," *Hermes,* Vol. iii. Berlin, 1868.

" Über den Aberglauben des bösen Blicks bei den Alten," *Berichte über die Verhandlungen der Königlich Sächsischen Gesellschaft der Wissenschaften zu Leipzig.* Philologisch-historische Classe. Vol. vii. Leipzig, 1885.

Jahrbuch der kaiserlich deutsches archäologisches Instituts. Berlin, 1886–

Jahrbuch für Geschichte, Sprache und Litteratur Elsass-Löthringen. Strassburg, 1872–

Jahrbücher für classiche Philologie. Leipzig, 1826–

Jahrbücher für wissenschaftliche Botanik. Berlin, Leipzig, 1858–

Jahresbericht der Verein für Erdkunde in Dresden. Dresden, 1865–

Jahresberichten des königliches-kaiserliches Franx-Josef Gymnasium. Wien, 1875–

Jaime, G., *De Koulikoro à Timbouctou.* Paris, 1892.

James, Edwin, *Account of an Expedition from Pittsburgh to the Rocky Mountains, performed in the years 1819 and '20 under the command of S. H. Long.* 2 vols. Philadelphia, 1823.

James, George Wharton, *Indians of the Painted Desert Region.* Boston, 1903.

James, H. E. M., *The Long White Mountain; a Journey in Manchuria.* London, 1888.

James, William, *The Principles of Psychology.* 2 vols. London, 1900.

Jamieson, G., " Cases in Chinese Criminal Law," *The China Review.* Vol. x. Hong-Kong, 1881–82.

Jannet, Claudio, *Les institutions sociales et le droit civil à Sparte.* Paris, 1880.

Jardin, Gomes, " Sobre os Indios Uiacurús e Guanás," *Revista Trimensal de historia e geographia.* Vols. vii, xiii. Rio de Janeiro, 1845.

Jardine, John, *Notes on Buddhist Law.* III, *Marriage.* Rangoon, 1883.

Jardine, John, " Description of the Neighbourhood of Somerset, Cape York. Australia," *The Journal of the Royal Geographical Society.* Vol. xxxvi. London, 1866.

Jarves, J. J., *History of the Hawaiian Islands.* Honolulu, 1872.

Jastrow, Morris, *Die Religion Babyloniens und Assyriens.* 2 vols. Giessen, 1905–12.

Religion of the Babylonians and Assyrians. Boston, 1898.

Hebrew and Babylonian Traditions. New York, 1914.

" The Original Character of the Hebrew Sabbath," *The American Journal of Theology.* Vol. ii. Chicago, 1898.

Art. " Asusa, " in *The Jewish Encyclopaedia.* Vol. ii. New York, London, s.d.

The Jātaka, or Stories of the Buddha's former Births. Transl. from the Päli and ed. by E. B. Cowell. 6 vols. Cambridge, 1895–97.

Jaussen, A., *Coutumes Arabes au pays de Moab.* Paris, 1908.

Jean, C., *Les Touaregs du Sud-Est; L'Aïr.* Paris, 1909.

Une Jeanne d'Arc africaine, épisode de l'invasion des Arabes en Afrique. Paris, 1891.

Jeanroy, A., *Les poésies de Jaufré Rudel.* Paris, 1914.

Jebb, R. C., *Bentley (English Men of Letters).* London, 1882.

Jehan de Waurin, *Recueil des croniques et anchiennes istories de la Grant Bretaigne, à présent nommé Engleterre (Chronicles and Memorials of Great Britain and Ireland).* 5 vols. London, 1864–91.

Jellinghaus, Th., " Sagen und Gebräuche der Munda-Kohls in Chota Nagpore,"
  Zeitschrift für Ethnologie. Vol. iii. Berlin, 1871.
Jenks, Albert Ernest, *The Bontoc Igorot (Ethnological Survey Publications.*
  Vol. i). Manila, 1905.
" Bulu knowledge of the Gorilla and Chimpanzee," *American Anthro-*
  pologist. N.S., vol. xiii. Lancaster, 1911.
Jerdon, T. C., *The Mammals of India.* London, 1874.
Jeremias, Alfred, *Handbuch der altorientalischen Geisteskultur.* Leipzig, 1913.
  Arts. " Ea-Oannes," " Marduk," in W. H. Roscher, *Ausführliches Lexikon*
  der griechischen und römischen Mythologie.
  Das Alte Testament im Lichte des alten Orients. Leipzig, 1906.
Jesuit Relations and Allied Documents. Edited by Reuben Gold Thwaites.
  73 vols. Cleveland, 1896–1901.
  Relations des Jésuites contenant ce qui s'est passé de plus remarquable
  dans les missions des Pères de la Compagnie de Jésus dans la Nouvelle
  France. 3 vols. (Each relation is paged separately.) Quebec, 1858.
The Jesup North Pacific Expedition. Edited by Franz Boas (*Memoir of the*
  American Natural History Museum). 12 vols. Leiden, New York,
  1898–1909.
Jetté, Julius, " On the Superstitions of the Ten'a Indians (Middle Part of the
  Yukon Valley, Alaska)," *Anthropos.* Vol. vi. Wien, 1911.
  " L'organisation sociale des Ten'as," *Quinzième Congrès International*
  des Américanistes, Québec, 1906. 2 vols. Quebec, 1907.
Jevons, F. B., " Graeco-Italian Magic," in R. B. Marret, *Anthropology and the*
  Classics. Oxford, 1908.
Jevons, J. B. See Plutarch.
The Jewish Chronicle. London, 1845–
The Jewish Encyclopaedia. 12 vols. New York, 1901–25.
The Jewish Quarterly Review. London, 1888–
Jewitt, John R., *Narrative of the Adventures and Sufferings of John R. Jewitt*
  among the Savages of Nootka Sound. New York, 1816.
Jiriczek, Otto, *Northern Hero Legends.* Transl. London, 1902.
Jivanji Jamshedji Modi, *Marriage Customs of the Parsees.* Bombay, 1900.
João dos Santos, Fra, in G. MacCall Theal, *Records of South Africa.* Vol.
  vii. London, 1899.
Job Ben Solomon, " The Remarkable Captivity and Deliverance of Job Ben
  Solomon," in Astley, *New General Collection of Voyages and Travels.*
  Vol. ii. London, 1745.
Jochelson, Waldemar, *The Koryak (Publications of the Jesup North Pacific*
  Expedition. Vol. vi). Leiden and New York, 1908.
  The Yukaghir and the Yukaghirized Tungus (Publications of the Jesup
  North Pacific Expedition. Vol. ix, Part i). Leiden, New York,
  1910.
" Scientific Results of the Ethnological Section of the Riabouschinsky
  Expedition of the Imperial Russian Geographical Society to the Aleu-
  tian Islands and Kamtchatka," *International Congress of Americanists.*
  Proceedings of the XVIII Session, London, 1912. Vol. ii. London,
  1912.
Joelson, F. S., *The Tanganyika Territory.* London, 1921.
Joest, W., " Beiträge zur Kenntniss der Eingebornen der Inseln Formosa
  und Ceram," *Verhandlungen der Berliner Gesellschaft für Anthropologie.*
  Berlin, 1882.
  " Bei den Barolong," *Das Ausland.* Vol. lvii. München, 1884.
Johannes Damascenus, *Opera omnia.* 3 vols, in Migne, *Patrologiae Cursus,*
  Series Graeca. Vols. xciv–xcvi. Paris, 1860.

John of Oxenede, *Chronica*. Ed. by Sir H. Ellis (*Chronicles and Memorials of Great Britain and Ireland*). London, 1859.

John of Salisbury, *Opera omnia*. Ed. by J. A. Giles. 5 vols. Oxford, 1848.

[Johnson, A. C.], *The Cottages of the Alps, or Life and Manners in Switzerland*. New York, 1860.

Johnson, J., "The Savagery of Boyhood," *The Popular Science Monthly*. Vol. xxxi. New York, 1887.

Johnson, S. and O., *The History of the Yoruba*. London, 1921.

Johnston, Sir Harry Hamilton, *The Uganda Protectorate*. London, 1902.
British Central Africa. London, 1807.
The River Congo. London, 1884.
The Kilima-njaro Expedition. London, 1886.
George Grenfell and the Congo. London, 1908.
"The People of Eastern Equatorial Africa," *Journal of the Anthropological Institute*. Vol. xv. London, 1886.
Liberia. 2 vols. London, 1906.

Johnstone, J. C., *Maoria*. London, 1874.

Joinville, "On the Religion and Manners of the People of Ceylon," *Asiatick Researches*. Vol. vii. Calcutta, 1801.

Joly, M. A., *Marie de France et les fables au moyen-âge*. Paris, 1863.

Jomard, M., "Noticia sobre os Botocudos," *Revista Trimensal do Instituto Historico e Geographico Brasileiro*. Vol. ix. Rio de Janeiro, 1847.

Jones, David, *Journal of Two Visits made to some Nations of Indians on the South Side of the River Ohio*. New York, 1865.

Jones, Peter, *History of the Ojebway Indians*. London, 1861.

Jordanes of Ravenna, *De Getarum sive Gothorum origine et rebus gestis*. Ed. C. A. Closs. Stuttgart, 1861.

Joret, Ch., "Une traduction d'André le Chapelain au xiiie siècle," *Romania*. Vol. xiii. Paris, 1884.

Josephus, Flavius, *Opera omnia*. Rec. S. A. Naber. 6 vols. Lipsiae, 1888–95.

Joske, A. B., "The Nanga of Viti-Levu," *Internationales Archiv für Ethnographie*. Vol. ii. Leiden, 1889.

Journal and Proceedings of the Royal Society of Western Australia. Perth, 1916–

Journal and Transactions of the Royal Society of New South Wales. Sydney, 1868–

Journal Asiatique. Paris, 1822–

Journal de Médecine de Paris. Paris–

Journal des Missions Évangeliques. Paris, 1826–

Journal des Museum Godeffroy. Hamburg, 1873–

Journal des savants. Paris, 1816–

Journal of American Ethnology and Archaeology. Boston, New York, 1891–

Journal of American Folk-Lore. Boston, New York, 1888–

Journal of Anthropology. London, 1871–

Journal of Biblical Literature. Boston, 1882–

Journal of Comparative Neurology and Psychology. Baltimore, 1921–

Journal of Egyptian Archaeology. London, 1914–

Journal of Experimental Zoology. Baltimore, 1904–

Journal of Hellenic Studies. London, 1880–

The Journal of Heredity. Washington, 1909–

The Journal of Laryngology, Rhinology, and Otology. London, 1887–

The Journal of Mental Science. London, 1855–

Journal of Philology. London, Cambridge, 1868–

Journal of the African Society. London, 1901–

Journal of the American Oriental Society. Boston, 1849–
Journal of the Anthropological Society of Bombay. Bombay, London, 1886–
Journal of the Asiatic Society of Bengal. Calcutta, 1832–
Journal of the Ceylon Branch of the Royal Asiatic Society. Colombo, 1845–
Journal of the College of Science, Imperial University of Tokio. Tokio, 1886–
Journal of the East African and Uganda Natural History Society. London,
    1902–
Journal of the Indian Archipelago and Eastern Asia. Singapore, 1847–1862.
Journal of the Madras Literary Society. Madras, 1859–
Journal of the (North) China Branch to the Royal Asiatic Society. Shanghai,
    1858–
Journal of the Polynesian Society. Wellington, 1892–
Journal of the (Royal) Anthropological Institute of Great Britain and Ireland.
    London, 1872.
Journal of the Royal Asiatic Society. London, 1834–
Journal of the Royal Geographical Society. London, 1832–
Journal of the (Royal) Statistical Society. London, 1839–
Journal of the Straits Branch of the Royal Asiatic Society. Singapore, 1878–
Jousseaume, " Observations anthropologiques faites par le comte Teleki sur
    quelques peuplades du centre de l'Afrique," *Bulletin de la Société
    d'Anthropologie de Paris.* 4ᵉ Série, vol. i. Paris, 1890.
Joustra, M., " Het leven, de zeden en gewoonten der Bataks," *Mededeelingen
    van wege het Nederlandsche Zendelinggenootschap.* Vol. xlvi. Rotter-
    dam, 1902.
Joyce, P. W., *A Social History of Ancient Ireland.* 2 vols. London, 1903.
Jukes, J. Beete, *Narrative of the Surveying Voyage of H.M.S. " Fly," in
    Torres Strait, New Guinea, and other Islands of the Eastern Archipelago.*
    2 vols. London, 1847.
Julin, C., " Recherches sur la phylogenèse des Tuniciers," *Mittheilungen aus
    der zooligischen Station zu Neapel.* Vol. xvi. Berlin, 1904.
Jullian, C., *Recherches sur la religion des Gaulois.* Paris, 1903.
    Art. " Flamen," in C. Daremberg and E. Saglio, *Dictionnaire des antiquités
    grecques et romaines.* Vol. ii, Part ii. Paris, 1896.
Jung, " Aufzeichnungen über die Rechtsanschauungen der Eingeborenen von
    Nauru," *Mitteilungen aus den Deutschen Schutzgebieten.* Vol. x.
    Berlin, 1897.
Jung, Emil, " Japanischer Aberglaube," *Zeitschrift für Ethnologie.* Vol. ix.
    Berlin, 1877.
Junghuhn, Franz, *Die Battaländer auf Sumatra.* 3 vols. Berlin, 1847.
Junke, Hermann, " Die Onuris Legende," *Kais. Akademie der Wissenschaften
    in Wien. Denkschriften, philologisch-historische Klasse.* Vol. xlix.
    Wien, 1917.
Junker, W., *Reisen in Afrika, 1875–1886.* 3 vols. Wien, Olmutz, 1889–91.
    Travels in Africa. Transl. 3 vols. London, 1890–92.
Junod, H. A., *The Life of a South African Tribe.* 2 vols. London, Neu-
    châtel, 1912.
    Les Ba-Ronga. Neuchâtel, 1898.
    Les chants et contes des Ba-Ronga de la baie de Delagoa. Lausanne, 1897.
    " Some Remarks on the Folk-lore of the Ba-Thonga," *Folk-lore.* Vol.
    xiv. London, 1903.
    " The Fate of Widows amongst the Ba-Ronga," *Report of the South African
    Association for the Advancement of Science. Sixth Meeting, Grahams-
    town, 1908.* Cape Town, Johannesburg, 1909.
Jurisprudentiae antejustinianae quae supersunt. Ed. P. E. Huschke. Leipzig,
    1861.

Juse, E. F., " Breeding Habits of *Heteronereis* form of *Platynereis megalops*,"
    Biological Bulletin of the Marine Biological Laboratory, Woods Hole.
    Vol. xxxvii.   Woods Hole, Mass., 1914.
Justi, F., " Geschichte Irans," in W. Geiger and E. Kuhn, *Grundriss der
    iranischen Philologie*.   Vol. ii.   Strassburg, 1904.
Justin, *Historiae Philippicae*.   Lugd. Batav., 1719.
Justin Martyr, *Opera quae extant omnia*, in Migne *Patrologiae Cursus Completus,
    Series Graeca*.   Vol. vi.   Parisiis, 1857.
Justinian.   See *Corpus Juris Civilis*.
Juynboll, T. G. J., *Chronicon Samaritanum, arabice conscriptum cui Titulus
    est Liber Josuae*.   Leyden, 1848.

Kaindl, R. F. von, " Zauberglaube bei den Huzulen," *Globus*.   Vol. lxxvi.
    Braunschweig, 1899.
Kalevala, the epic poem of Finland.   Tr. by J. M. Crawford.   2 vols.   New York,
    1888.
    Le Kalévala.   Transl. by Ch. de Ujfalvy.   Paris, 1876.
Kalyanakrishna, Aiyar T. A., in *Malabar Quarterly Review*.   Vol. ii.   Trivan-
    drum, 1908.
Kames, Henry Home, Lord, *Sketches of the History of Man*.   3 vols.   Edin-
    burgh, 1813.
Kannan Nayar, K., " The Matrimonial Customs of the Nayars," *The Malabar
    Quarterly Review*.   Vol. vii.   Trivandrum, 1908.
Kanshîtaki-Upanishad.   See *Upanishads*.
Karlowa, Otto, *Römische Rechtsgeschichte*.   2 vols.   Leipzig, 1885–1901.
Karo, G., " Altkretische Kultstätten," *Archiv für Religionswissenschaft*.
    Vols. vii., viii.   Freiburg i. B., 1904–05.
    " Die ' tyrsenische ' Stele von Lemnos," *Mitteilungen des kaiserlich
    deutschen archäologischen Instituts. Athenische Abteilung*.   Vol. xxxiii.
    Athens, 1908.
Karoli Magni Capitularia.   See *Capitularia Regum Francorum*.
Karusio, A., " Pregiudizzi popolari Putignatesi," *Archivio per l'Antropologia
    e l'Etnologia*.   Vol. xvii.   Firenze, 1887.
Karsten, Rafael, *Indian Dances in the Gran Chaco* (*S. America*) (*Ofversigt af
    Finska Vetenskaps-Societetens Förhandlingar*.   Vol. lvii).   Helsing-
    fors, 1915.
    Contributions to the Sociology of the Indian Tribes of Ecuador.   Abo, 1920.
    " Die ethnographischen Ergebnisse der deutschen Pilcomayo-Expedition,"
    Zeitschrift für Ethnologie.   Vol. xl.   Berlin, 1908.
    Studies in South American Anthropology, I.   Helsingfors, 1920.
Kater, C., " De Dajaks van Sidin " *Tijd schrift voor Indische taal-, land- en
    volkenkunde*.   Vol. xvi.   Batavia, 's Hage, 1867.
Kâthaka Upanishad (Samhita).   Ed. Apte.   Poona, 1889.
Die Katholischen Missionen.   Freiburg, 1873–
Katscher, Leopold, *Bilder aus dem Chinesischen Leben*.   Leipzig and Heidel-
    berg, 1881.
Kaufmann, Hans, " Die Auin, Ein Beitrag zur Buschmannforschung,"
    Mittheilungen aus den Deutscher Schutzgebieten.   Vol. xxiii.   Berlin,
    1910.
Kaufman Kohler, art. " Huppah " in *The Jewish Encyclopaedia*.   Vol. vi.
    New York, s.d.
Kaul, Pandit Harikishan, " Punjab," Part i.   *Census of India, 1911*.   Vol.
    xiv.   Lahore, 1912.

Kausch, H., and Hahn, Ferd., *Fünfzig Bilder aus der gossnerscher Kols-Mission.* Friedenau-Berlin, 1895.

Kaushîtaki Brâhmana (Upanishad). Ed. G. B. Lindner. Jena, 1887.

Kay S., *Travels and Researches in Caffraria.* London, 1833.

Kealy, E. H., " Rajputana and Ajmer-Merwara," Report, in *Census of India, 1911.* Vol. xxii. Ajmer, 1913.

Keane, Augustus Henry, *Ethnology.* Cambridge, 1896.

 " On the Botocudos," *Journal of the Anthropological Institute.* Vol. xiii. London, 1884.

Keane, Marcus, *The Towers and Temples of Ancient Ireland.* Dublin, 1867.

Keate, George, *An Account of the Pelew Islands.* London, 1803.

Keating, George, *History of Ireland.* 3 vols. Dublin, 1902–08.

Keating, William H., *Narrative of an Expedition to the Source of St. Peter's River, Lake Winnipeek, etc. Compiled from the Notes of Major Long, Messrs. Say, Keating, and Colhoun.* 2 vols. London, 1825.

Keith, A. Berriedale, in *The Cambridge History of India.* Vol. i., Cambridge, 1922.

 " On the Antiquity of Vedic Culture," *Journal of the Royal Asiatic Society.* London, 1909.

Keith, Sir Arthur, *The Antiquity of Man.* London, 1915.

Keith, George, " Letters to the Hon. Roderic McKenzie," in L. R. Masson, *Les Bourgeois de la Compagnie du Nord-ouest.* Vol. ii. Quebec, 1890.

 " The Filthy Lake and Ground River Indians," in L. R. Masson, *Les Bourgeois de la Compagnie du Nord-ouest.* Vol. ii. Quebec, 1890.

Keleti Szemle. Kozlemenyek ar Ural-altaje nep-es nyelvtudomany kokebol (Revue orientale pour les études ouralo-altaïques). Budapest, Leipzig, 1906.

Keller, Ferdinand, *The Lake Dwellings of Switzerland and other Parts of Europe.* Trans. 2 vols. London, 1878.

Keller, Helen, *The World I Live in.* London, 1908.

 The Story of My Life. London, 1903.

Keller, I., " Knowledge and Theories of Astronomy on the part of the Isubu Natives of the Western Slopes of the Cameron Mountains in German West Africa (Kamerun)," *Journal of the African Society.* Vol. ii. London, 1902.

Keller, Victor, " *Le siège de Barbastre,*" *und die Bearbeitung von Adenet le roi.* Marburg, 1875.

Kelly, Walter K., *Curiosities of Indo-European Tradition and Folk-lore.* London, 1863.

Kennan, G., *Tent Life in Siberia and Adventures among the Koraks and other Tribes of Kamtchatka and Northern Asia.* London, Edinburgh, 1871.

Kennedy, James, " The Aryan Invasion of Northern India," *Journal of the Royal Asiatic Society.* London, 1919–20.

Keppel, The Hon. Henry, *A Visit to the Indian Archipelago.* London, 1853.

Kern, J. H., *Der Buddhismus und seine Geschichte in Indien.* Transl. from the Dutch. 2 vols. Leipzig, 1882–84.

Kerr, Robert, *A General History and Collection of Voyages and Travels.* 18 vols. Edinburgh, 1811–24.

Kerr, W. M., " Journey from Cape Town Inland to Lake Nyassa," *Proceedings of the Royal Geographical Society,* New Series. Vol. viii. London, 1886.

Kerry-Nichols, J. H., " The Origin, Physical Characteristics, and Manners and Customs of the Maori Race," *Journal of the Anthropological Institute.* Vol. xv. London, 1886.

Kessel, J., " Ueber das Mobilisiren des Steigbügels durch Ausschneiden des Trommelfelles, Hammers und Ambosses bei Undurchgängigheit der Tuba," *Archiv für Ohrenheilkunde*. Vol. xiii. Leipzig, 1878.

Ketjen, E., " De Kalangers," *Tijdschrift voor Indische taal-, land- en volkenkunde*. Batavia, 's Hage, 1877.

Keysser, C., " Aus dem Leben der Kaileute," in R. Neuhauss, *Deutsch Neu-Guinea*. Vol. iii. Berlin, 1911.

Kicherer, J. J., *An Extract from the Rev. Mr. Kicherer's Narrative of his Mission in South Africa*. Wiscasset, 1805.

Kidd, Benjamin, *Social Evolution*. London, 1894.

Kidd, Dudley, *The Essential Kafir*. London, 1904.

    Savage Childhood. London, 1906.

Kielhorn, F., " Epigraphic Notes," *Nachrichten von der königlich Gesellschaft der Wissenschaften zu Göttingen. Philol.-histor. Klasse*. Gottingen, 1904.

King, L. W., *A History of Sumer and Akkad*. London, 1910.

    Babylonian Religion and Mythology. London, 1900.

    The Seven Tablets of Creation. London, 1902.

King, P. Parker, and Fitzroy, R., *Narrative of the surveying Voyages of the " Adventure " and " Beagle,"* 3 vols. London, 1839.

King, W. Ross, " The Aboriginal Tribes of the Nilgiri Hills," *Journal of Anthropology*. London, 1871.

Kingdom, E. C., and Russell, J. S. R., " Infantile Cerebral Degeneration with Symmetrical Changes at the Macula," *Proceedings of the Royal Medical and Chirurgical Society of London*. London, 1896–97.

Kingsley, Mary H., *Travels in West Africa*. London, 1897.

    West African Studies. London, 1901.

Kipling, Rudyard, *The Second Jungle Book*. London, 1895.

Kirby, Frederick Vaughan, *In Haunts of Wild Game*. London, 1896.

Kircher, A., *China monumentis illustrata*. Amsterdam, 1667.

Kirchhoff, A., *Die homerische Odyssee*. 2nd Edition. Berlin, 1879.

Kirke, Henry, *Twenty-Five Years in British Guiana*. London, 1908.

Kirkpatrick, C. S., " Polyandry in the Panjab," *The Indian Antiquary*. Vol. vii. Bombay, 1878.

Kirkpatrick, W., *An Account of the Kingdom of Nepaul*. London, 1811.

Kishen, Kant Bose, " Some Account of the Country of Bhútan," *Asiatick Researches*. Vol. xv. Serangore, 1825.

Kissenberth, W., " Bei den Canella-Indianern in Zentral Maranhao (Brazil)," *Baessler-Archiv*. Vol. ii. Berlin-Leipzig, 1912.

Kitching, A. L., *On the Backwaters of the Nile*. London, Leipzig, 1912.

Klaatsch, H., " Some Notes in Scientific Travels amongst the Black Population of Tropical Australia in 1904, 1905, 1906," *Proceedings of the Australasian Association for the Advancement of Science, Adelaide, 1907*. Adelaide, 1908.

Klaproth, Heinrich Julius von, *Tableaux historiques de l'Asie depuis la monarchie de Cyrus jusqu'à nos jours*. Paris, 1826.

    Reise in dem Kaukasus und nach Georgien. 2 vols. Halle, Berlin, 1812–14.

Kleintitschen, P. A., *Die Küstenbewohner der Gazellehalbinsel*. Hiltrup bei Münster, 1906.

Klemm, G., *Allgemeine Cultur-Geschichte der Menscheit*. 10 vols. Leipzig, 1843–52.

Klose, Heinrich, *Togo unter deutscher Flagge*. Berlin, 1899.

Kloss, C. Boden, *In the Andamans and Nicobars*. London, 1903.

Kluge, F., *Mitelenglisches Lesebuch*, Halle a. S., 1912.

Klunzinger, C. B., *Upper Egypt*. Transl. London, 1878.

Klutschak, H. W., *Als Eskimo unter den Eskimos*. Wien, Pest, Leipzig, 1881.

Knaft, " Die Wapokomo," in S. R. Steinmetz, *Rechtsverhältnisse von einge-borenen Völkern in Afrika und Ozeanien.* Berlin, 1903.

Knight, E. F., *Where Three Empires meet.* London, 1893.

Knight, Richard Payne, *Le culte de Priape.* Transl. Luxembourg, 1866.

Knox, Robert, *An Historical Relation of the Island of Ceylon.* London, 1817.

Kobelt, W., " Das Volk der Omaha," *Globus.* Vol. l. Braunschweig, 1886.

Kock-Grünberg, Theodor, *Zwei Jahre unter den Indianern.* 2 vols. Stuttgart, 1909–10.

" Frauenarbeit bei den Indianern Nord-West Brasiliens," *Mitteilungen der anthropologischen Gesellschaft.* Vol. xxxviii. Wien, 1908.

Ködding, W., " Die batakschen Götter und ihr Verhältniss zum Brahmanismus," *Allgemeine Missions Zeitschrift.* Vol. xii. Gütersloh, 1885.

" Die Batakken auf Sumatra," *Globus.* Vol. liii. Braunschweig, 1885.

Koeler, Hermann, " Einige Notizen über die Eingebornen an die Ostküste des St.-Vincent Golfs, Süd Australien," *Monatsberichte über die Verhandlungen der Gesellschaft für Erdkunde zu Berlin,* Neue Folge. Vol. i. Berlin, 1844.

Koenig, H. C., *De Hominum inter feras educatorum statu naturali solitario.* Hanover, 1730.

Koenigswald, G. von, " Die Coroados in südlichen Brasilien," *Globus.* Vol. xciv. Braunschweig, 1908.

" Die Caraja-Indianer," *Globus.* Vol. xciv. Braunschweig, 1908.

" Die Botokudo in Südbrasilien," *Globus.* Vol. xciii. Braunschweig, 1907.

" Die Cayuás," *Globus.* Vol. xciii. Braunschweig, 1907.

Koeppen, C. F., *Die Religion des Buddha und ihre Enstehung.* 2 vols. Berlin, 1857–59.

Kögel, J., " Notizen über Sitten und Gebräuche der Javanen und Maduresen," *Das Ausland.* München, 1863.

Kohlbrugge, J. H. F., " Naamgeving in Insulinde," *Bijdragen tot de taal-, land- en volkenkunde van Nederlandsch-Indië.* Vol. lii. Leiden, 1901.

Kohler, Josef, " Studien über Frauengemeinschaft, Frauenraub und Frauenkauf," *Zeitschrift für vergleichende Rechtswissenschaft.* Vol. v. Stuttgart, 1884.

" Das Banturecht in Ostafrika," *Zeitschrift für vergleichende Rechtswissenschaft.* Vol. xv. Stuttgart, 1901.

" Das Recht der Herero," *Zeitschrift für vergleichende Rechtswissenschaft.* Vol. xiv. Stuttgart, 1900.

" Das Recht der Papuas," *Zeitschrift für vergleichende Rechtswissenschaft.* Vol. xiv. Stuttgart, 1900.

" Das Recht der Marschallinsulaner," in *Zeitschrift für vergleichende Rechtswissenschaft.* Vol. vii. Stuttgart, 1900.

" Das Recht der Hottentotten," *Zeitschrift für vergleichende Rechtswissenschaft.* Vol. xv. Stuttgart, 1901.

" Kleinere Skizzen aus der ethnologischen Jurisprudenz," *Zeitschrift für vergleichende Rechtswissenschaft.* Vol. vi. Stuttgart, 1886.

Rechtsvergleichende Studien. Berlin, 1889.

Kohler, Kaufman, art. " Huppah," in *The Jewish Encyclopaedia.* Vol. vi. Chicago, s.d.

Köhler, R., *Über die Dionysiaca des Nonnus von Panopolis.* Halle, 1853.

Köhler, Wolfgang, *The Mentality of Apes.* Transl. London, 1925.

Kohls, S. C., " New Light on Eugenics," *The Journal of Heredity.* Vol. vi. Menasha, Wisc., 1915.

Ko-Ji-Ki. See Camberlain, B. H.

Koken, C. J. G. W., *Guittone's von Arezzo Dichtung und sein Verhältniss zu Guinicelli von Bologna.* Leipzig, 1886.

Kolbe, Peter, *The Present State of the Cape of Good Hope*. Transl. 2 vols. London, 1731.

Kolbing, *Die nordische und die englische Version der Tristansage*. Heilbronn, 1878–82.

Kookel Keloo Nair, " Memorandum on the Syrian and Jewish Copper Plate of Malabar," *Madras Journal of Literature and Science*, N.S. Vol. v. Madras, 1859.

Kopec, *Dziennik podrozy po Syberyi*. Leopol, s.d.

Koppenfels, Hugo von, "Meine Jagden auf Gorillas," *Die Gartenlaube*. Leipzig, 1877.

The Koran. Transl. by G. Sale. London, 1844.

Koslow, L., " Das Gewohnheitsrechts der Kirghisen," *Russische Revue*. Vol. xxi. St. Petersburg, 1882.

Kossmann, Robbi, " Menstruation, Schwangershaft, Wochenbett, Lactation und ihre Beziehungen zur Ehe," in G. Abelslorff and others, *Krankheiten und Ehe*. Munich, 1904.

Kostromitonow, in F. P. Wrangell, *Statistische und ethnographische Nachrichten über die russischen Besitzungen an der Nordküste von Amerika*. St. Petersburg, 1839.

Kostyleff, N., " Contribution à l'étude du sentiment amoureux," *Revue Philosophique de la France et de l'Étranger*. Paris, 1914.

" Sur la formation du complexus érotique dans le sentiment amoureux," *ibid*. Paris, 1915.

Kotzebue, Otto von, *A New Voyage round the World*. Transl. 2 vols. London, 1830.

A Voyage of Discovery into the South Sea and Behring's Straits. Transl. 3 vols. London, 1821.

Kowald, C., " Report of the Government Agent for the Mekeo District," *Annual Report on British New Guinea, 1891–92*. Brisbane, 1893.

" Native Habits and Customs of the Mekeo District (Central Division)," *Annual Report on British New Guinea, 1892-93*. Brisbane, 1893.

Kowalewski, Maxime, *Modern Customs and Ancient Laws of Russia*. London, 1891.

" La famille matriarcale au Caucase," *L'Anthropologie*. Vol. iv. Paris, 1893.

Coutume contemporaine et loi ancienne. Droit coutumier ossétien. Paris, 1893.

" Marriage among the early Slavs," *Folk-lore*. Vol. i. London, 1890.

Krabbes, Theodor. *Die Frau in altfranzösischen Karls-Epos*. Marburg, 1884.

Krall, J., *Demotische und assyrische Contracte*. Wien, 1881.

Krämer, Augustin, *Hawaii, Ostmikronesien und Samoa*. Stuttgart, 1906.

Die Samoa-Inseln. 2 vols. Stuttgart, 1901–02.

Ueber den Bau der Korallenriffe und die Planktonverteilung an dem Samoanischen Küsten. Kiel and Leipzig, 1897.

Kramer, F., " Der Götzendienst der Niasser," *Tijdschrift voor Indische taal-, land- en volkenkunde*. Vol. xxviii. Batavia, 1890.

Kramer, Wilhelm, *Die Erkenntniss und Heilung der Ohrenkrankheiten*. Berlin, 1836.

Kranz, A., *Natur- und Kulturleben der Zulus*. Wiesbaden, 1880.

Krapf, J. Lewis, *Travels, Researches, and Missionary Labours during an Eighteen Years' Residence in Eastern Africa*. 2 vols. London, 1860.

Reisen in Ost-Afrika. Stuttgart, 1858.

Krasheninnikoff, S. P., *The History of Kamtschatka and the Kurilski Islands*. Transl. Glocester, 1764.

Krause, Aurel, *Die Tlinkit Indianer, Ergebnisse einer Reise nach der Nord-westküste von America und der Beringstrasse (Auftrage der Bremer geographischen Gesellschaft).* Jena, 1885.

Krause, Fritz, *In den Wildnissen Brasiliens.* Leipzig, 1911.

" Bericht über seine ethnographische Forschungsreise in Zentralbrasilien," *Zeitschrift für Ethnologie.* Vol. xli. Berlin, 1909.

Krauss, Friederich S., *Sitte und Brauch der Südslaven.* Wien, 1885.

Sagen und Märchen der Südslaven. Leipzig, 1883.

Volksglaube und religiöser Brauch der Südslaven. Münster i. W., 1890.

Krauss, S., *Das Leben Jesu nach jüdischen Quellen.* Berlin, 1902.

Kreemer, J., " De Loeboes in Mandailing," *Bijdragen tot de taal-, land- en volkenkunde van Nederlandsch-Indië.* Vol. lxvi. 's Gravenhage, 1912.

Krefft, Gerard, *On the Manners and Customs of the Aborigines of the Lower Murray and Darling.* Sydney, 1865.

Krehl, C. L. E., *Ueber die Religion der vorislamischen Araber.* Leipzig, 1863.

Kremer, A. von, *Culturgeschichte des Orients unter den Chalifen.* 2 vols. Vienna, 1875-77.

Kretschmer, P. W., *Einleitung in die Geschichte der griechischen Sprache.* Göttingen, 1896.

in *Aus der Anomia.* Berlin, 1890.

Krichauff, F. E. H. W., " Further Notes on the ' Aldolinga ' or ' Mbender-inga ' Tribe of Aborigines," *Proceedings of the Royal Geographical Society of Australasia : South Australia Branch.* Vol. ii. Adelaide, 1890.

Krick, R. P., in *Annales de la Propagation de la Foi.* Vol. xxvi. Lyon, 1854.

Krieger, Maximilian, *Neu-Guinea.* Berlin, 1899.

Kroeber, A. L., " Wishosk Myths," *Journal of Aerican Folk-Lore.* Vol. xviii. Boston, New York, 1905.

" Zuñi Kin and Clan," *Anthropological Papers of the American Museum of Natural History.* Vol. xviii, Part ii. New York, 1917.

" The Arapaho," *Bulletin of the American Museum of Natural History.* Vol. xviii, Part i. New York, 1902.

" Indian Myths of South Central California," *University of California Publications in American Archaeology and Ethnology.* Vol. iv. No. 4. Berkeley, 1906-7.

" The Myths of the Mission Indians of California," *Journal of American Folk-Lore.* Vol. xix. Boston and New York, 1906.

The Peoples of the Philippines (American Museum of Natural History, A Handbook, No. 8). New York, 1919.

" The Eskimo of Smith Sound," *Bulletin of the American Museum of Natural History.* Vol. x. New York, 1899.

" Tales of the Smith Sound Eskimo," *Journal of American Folk-Lore.* Vol. xii. Boston, New York, 1899.

" Cheyenne Tales," *Journal of American Folk-Lore.* Vol. xiii. Boston and New York, 1900.

" Preliminary Sketch of the Mohave Indians," *The American Anthropologist*, N.S. Vol. iv. New York, 1902.

" Ethnology of the Gros Ventres," *Anthropological Papers of the American Museum of Natural History.* Vol. i. New York, 1907.

Kronheim, W., " Die Tschuwachen," *Archiv für wissenschaftliche kunde von Russland.* Vol. iii. Berlin, 1843.

Kropf, A., *Das Volk der Xosa-Kaffern im östlichen Südafrika.* Berlin, 1889.

Kropotkin, P., " The Desiccation of Eur-Asia," *The Geographical Journal.* Vol. xxiii. London, 1904.

Kruijt, A. C., *Het Animisme in dem Indische Archipel.* 's Gravenhage, 1906.

" Eēnige ethnografische aanterkeningen omtrent de Toboengkoe en de Tomori," *Mededeelingen van wege het Nederlandsche Zendelinggenoot-schap.* Vol. xliv. Rotterdam, 1900.

" De legenden der Poso-Alfoeren aangaande de ersten menschen," *Mede-deelingen van wege het Nederlandsche Zendelinggenootschap.* Vol. xxxviii. Rotterdam, 1894.

" De Timoreezen," *Bijdragen tot de taal-, land- en volkenkunde van Neder-landsch-Indië.* Vol. lxxix. 's Gravenhage, 1923.

Kruseman, " Enkele dagen onder de Buduwis," *De Indische Gids.* Amster-dam, 1879.

Krusenstern, A. J. von, *Voyage round the World in the Years 1803–1806.* Transl. London, 1813.

Kubary, J., " Die Bewohner der Mortlock Inseln," *Mittheilungen der Geo-graphischen Gesellschaft in Hamburg, 1878-79.* Hamburg, 1879.

" Die Palau-Inseln in der Südsee," *Journal des Museum Godeffroy.* Vol. iv. Hamburg, 1873.

Ethnographische Beiträge zur Kentniss der Karolinschen Insel-gruppe und Nachbarschaft. Heft. I, *Die Socialen Einrichtungen der Pelauer.* Berlin, 1885.

" Die Religion der Pelauer," in A. Bastian, *Allerlei aus Volks- und Mensch-enkunde.* Vol. i. Berlin, 1888.

Küchler, L. W., " Marriage in Japan," *Transactions of the Asiatic Society of Japan.* Vol. xiii. Yokohama, 1885.

Kuhn, A., " Raranyu-'Εριννύς," *Zeitschrift für Sprachforschung.* Vol. i. Berlin, 1851.

Kuhn, F. F. A., and Schwartz, F. L. M., *Norddeutsche Sagen, Märchen, und Gebräuche aus Meklemburg, Pommern,* etc. Leipzig, 1848.

Kulischer, M., " Intercommunale Ehe durch Raub und Kauf," *Zeitschrift für Ethnologie.* Vol. x. Berlin, 1878.

Kumlien, Ludwig, *Contributions to the Natural History of Arctic America (Bulletin of the United States Museum of Natural History,* No. 15). Washington, 1879.

Kurth, G., *Histoire poétique des Mérovingiens.* Paris, 1893.

Kurze, G., " Sitten und Gebräuche der Lengua-Indianer," *Mitteilungen der geographischen Gesellschaft (für Thuringen) zu Iena.* Vol. xxiii. Iena, 1905.

" Die Samoaner in den heidnischen Zeit," *Mitteilungen der geographischen Gesellschaft (für Thuringen) zu Jena.* Vol. xix. Jena, 1901.

Kussmaul, A., *Die Störungen der Sprache.* Leipzig, 1877.

Kwang-Zze, transl. by J. Legge (*The Sacred Books of the East.* Vol. xxxix). Oxford, 1891.

Kyriaka, Mansour, " Fiançailles et mariage à Mossoul," *Anthropos.* Vol. vi. Wienn, 1911.

Laband, P., " Die rechtliche Stellung der Frauen im altrömischen und germanischen Recht," *Zeitschrift für Völkerpsychologie und Sprach-wissenschaft.* Vol. iii. Berlin, 1865.

Labat, J. B., *Relation historique de l'Éthiopie occidentale.* 5 vols. Paris, 1732.

Nouveau voyage aux isles de l'Amérique. 6 vols. Paris, 1722.

Voyage du chevalier Des Marchais en Guinée, isles voisines et Cayenne. Amsterdam, 1731.

Labbé, Paul, *Un bagne russe, L'île de Sakhaline*. Paris, 1903.
  Chez les lamas de Sibérie. Paris, 1909.

Labbé, Ph., *Sacrorum Conciliorum Collectio*. 31 vols. Florentiae, Venetiis, 1759–98.

La Billardière, J. J. Houton de, *An Account of a Voyage in Search of La Pérouse in the Years 1791, 1792, 1793*. Transl. 2 vols. London, 1800.

La Borde, Le Sieur de, *Voyage qui contient une relation exacte de l'origine, moeurs, coutumes, religions, guerres et voyages des Caraïbes*. Amsterdam, 1704.

Laboulaye, E. S. L., *Recherches sur la condition civile et politique des femmes depuis les Romains jusqu'à nos jours*. Paris, 1843.

Labouret, H., " Mariage et polyandrie parmi les Dagari et les Oule (Volta moyenne, Afrique occidentale) " *Revue d'Ethnographie et des Traditions populaires*. Vol. l. Paris, 1920.

La Condamine, C. M. de, *Historie d'une jeune fille sauvage trouvée dans les bois à l'âge de dix ans*. Paris, 1755.

Lacroix, F., *Patagonie Terre-de-Feu et îles Malouines (L'Univers)*. Paris, 1841.

La Croix, J. Errington de, " Études sur les Sakaies de Pérak," *Revue d'Ethnologie*. Vol. i. Paris, 1882.

Lactantius, *Opera omnia*, in Migne, *Patrologiae Cursus Completus*. Vols. vi, vii. Parisiis, 1844.

Laet, Joannes de, *Novus Orbis ; seu descriptionis Indiae occidentalis libri xviii*. Ludg. Batav., 1633.

Laffitte, K., *Le Dahomé, Souvenirs de voyage et de Mission*. Tours, 1873.

Lafitau, Joseph François, *Moeurs des sauvages amériquains comparées aux moeurs des premiers temps*. 2 vols. Paris, 1724.

La Flesche, Francis, " Osage Marriage Customs," *The American Anthropologist*, N.S. Vol. xiv. Lancaster, 1912.

Lafone Quevedo, Samuel A., *La raza pampeana y la raza Guarani, o los indios del Rio de la Plata en el siglo XVI*. Buenos Aires, 1900.

Lagae, C. R., " Les Arande sont-ils animistes ? " *Sudan Notes and Records*. Vol. iii. Khartoum, 1920.

Lageniensis (i.e. John O'Hanlon), *Irish Local Legends*. S.d.

Lagrange, M., *Études sur les religions sémitiques*. Paris, 1905.

La Hontan, Armand L. de D., *Nouveaux voyages dans l'Amérique Septentrionale*. La Haye, 1703.
  New Voyages to North America. Transl. 2 vols. London, 1735.

Laing, A. Gordon, *Travels in the Timannee, Kooranko, and Soolima Countries in Western Africa*. London, 1825.

Laisnel de la Salle, *Croyances et Légendes du Centre de la France*. 2 vols. Paris, 1875.

Lajard, J. B. F., *Recherches sur le culte les symboles, les attributs, et les monuments figurés de Vénus en Orient et en Occident*. Paris, 1837–49.

La Marmora, G. A. F. de, *Voyage en Sardaigne*. Paris, 1839.

La Martinière, H. M. P., et Lacroix, N., *Documents pour servir à l'étude du Nord-Ouest africain*. 4 vols. Alger, 1894–97.

Lambert of Ardres, *Historia comitum Ghisnensium*. Ed. Ioh. Heller, in Pertz, *Monumenta Germaniae Historica : Scriptores*. Vol. xxiv. Hannoveriae, 1879.

Lambert, R. P., *Moeurs et superstitions des Néo-Caledoniens*. Nouméa, 1900.

Lammert, Gottfried, *Volksmedizin und medizinischer Aberglaube in Bayern und den angrenzenden Bezirken*. Würzburg, 1869.

Lamont, E. H., *Wild Life among the Pacific Islanders*. London, 1867.

Lamouroux, R., " La région du Toubouri. Notes sur les populations de la subdivision de Fianga," *L'Anthropologie*. Vol. xxiv. Paris, 1913.

Lamprecht, Karl, *Deutsche Geschichte*. 6 vols. Leipzig, 1894–96.

Lamprey, J., " Note by the Secretary," *Journal of the Royal Asiatic Society, Ceylon Branch*. Vol. ii. Colombo, 1853.

" On the Veddahs of Ceylon," *The Natural History Review*. Dublin, 1856.

Lamson, Mary Swift, *Life and Education of Laura Dewey Bridgman, the Deaf, Dumb, and Blind Girl*. Boston, 1878.

Landes, A., " Contes et légendes annamites," *Cochinchine Française. Excursions et Reconnaissances*. Vol. xi. Saigon, 1886.

Landis, E. B. L., " Mourning and Burial Rites of Corea," *Journal of the Anthropological Institute*. Vol. xxv. London, 1896.

Landolphe, J. F., *Mémoires du Capitaine Landolphe contenant l'histoire de ses voyages pendant trente-six ans aux côtes d'Afrique et aux deux Amériques*. 2 vols. Paris, 1823.

Landor, A. Henry Savage, *Alone with the Hairy Ainu*. London, 1893.

In the Forbidden Land. 2 vols. London, 1898.

Landtman, Gunnar, " The Folk-tales of the Kiwai Papuans," *Acta Societatis Scientiarum Fennicae*. Vol. xlvii. Helsingfors, 1917.

Nya Guinea färden. Helsingfors, 1913.

" The Magic of the Kiwai Papuans in Warfare," *Journal of the Royal Anthropological Institute*. Vol. xlvi. London, 1916.

Lane, Edward W., *An Account of the Manners and Customs of the Modern Egyptians*. 2 vols. London, 1871.

The same (1 vol.). London, 1890.

Arabic-English Lexicon. 8 vols. London, 1863–93.

Lane-Poole, Stanley, *Cairo*. London, 1892.

The Mohammadan Dynasties. London, 1894.

Lang, Andrew, *The Making of Religion*. London, 1898.

The Secret of the Totem. London, 1905.

and Atkinson, J. J., *Social Origins and Primal Law*. London, 1903.

Lang, F. H., " Die Waschambala," in S. R. Steinmetz, *Rechtverhältnisse von eingeborenen Völkern in Afrika und Oceanien*. Berlin, 1903.

Lang, G. S., *The Aborigines of Australia*. Melbourne, 1865.

Lang, J. D., *Cooksland in North-Eastern Australia*. London, 1847.

Queensland. London, 1861.

Lang, R. Hamilton, " On Archaic Survivals in Cyprus," *Journal of the Anthropological Institute*. Vol. xvi. London, 1887.

Langdon, S., " The Babylonian Conception of the Logos," *Journal of the Royal Asiatic Society*. London, 1918.

" The Derivation of ' Sabattu ' and Other Notes," *Zeitschrift der deutschen morgenländischen Gesellschaft*. Leipzig, 1908.

Tammuz and Ishtar. Oxford, 1914.

Babylonian Liturgies. Paris, 1913.

Sumerian and Babylonian Psalms. Paris, 1909.

Langdon-Down, J., *On the Education and Training of the Feeble in Mind*. London, 1876.

Lange, A., " Unsere gegenwärtige Kenntnis von den Fortpflanzungsver-hältnisse der Radiolarien," *Internationale Revue der gesamten Hydrobiologie und Hydrographie*. Vol. vi. Leipzig, 1913–14.

Langland, William, *The Vision of Piers Plowman*. Ed. W. W. Skeat. Oxford, 1886.

Langsdorf, G. H. von, *Voyages and Travels in Various Parts of the World during the Years 1785–88*. Transl. 3 vols. London, 1799.

Lankester, E. Ray, art. " Marsupials," in *Encyclopaedia Britannica*. Vol. xvii. Cambridge, 1911.

Lansdell, Henry, *Chinese Central Asia*. London, 1893.
  Through Siberia. 2 vols. London, 1882.

Lanzi, L. A., *Saggio di Lingua Etrusca e di altre antiche d'Italia*. 2 vols. Firenze, 1824-25.

Lanzone, R. V., *Dizionario di mitologia egizia*. 5 vols. Torino, 1881-86.

La Pérouse, J. F. Galaup, *Voyage de La. P. autour du monde*. 4 vols. Paris, 1797.

La Potherie, C. Le Roy Bacqueville de, *Histoire de l'Amérique septentrionale*. 4 vols. Paris, 1722.

Large, J. T., " Some Notes on Atiu Island, Cook Group, South Pacific," *Journal of the Polynesian Society*. Vol. xxii. Wellington, 1913.

Largeau, Victor, *Le Sahara algérien. Les déserts de l'Erg*. Paris, 1902.

Lartet, Edouard, and Christy, H., *Reliquiae Aquitanicae*. London, 1875.

Lasaulx, E. von, *Studien des classischen Alterthums*. Regensburg, 1854.

Las Casas, Bartolomé de, *De las antiguas gentes del Peru*. Madrid, 1892.

Lasch, R., " Der Selbsmord aus erotischen Motiven bei den primitiven Völkern," *Zeitschrift für Socialwissenscaft*. Vol. ii. Berlin, 1899.
  " Rache als Selbsmordmotive," *Globus*. Vol. lxxiv. Braunschweig, 1898.
  " Über Sondersprachen und ihre Enstehung," *Mitteilungen der anthropologischen Gesellschaft*. Vol. xxxvii. Wien, 1907.

Laski, H. J., " A Mendelian View of Racial Heredity," *Biometrika*. Vol. viii. Cambridge, 1912.

Lassen, Christian, *Indische Alterthumskunde*. 4 vols. Bonn and Leipzig, 1847-61.

Latcham, R. E., " Ethnology of the Araucanos," *Journal of the Royal Anthropological Institute*. Vol. xxxix. London, 1909.

Latorre, G., *Relaciones geográficas de Indias, contenidas en el Archivio General de Indias de Sevilla*. Sevilla, 1919.

La Tour Landry, Geoffrey de, *Le livre du chevalier de La Tour Landry pour l'enseignement de ses filles*. Paris, 1854.

Laufer, Berthold, " Preliminary Notes on Explorations among the Amoor Tribes," *The American Anthropologist*: N.S., vol. ii. New York, 1900.
  " The Decorative Art of the Amur Tribes," *Publications of the Jesup North Pacific Expedition*. Vol. iv. Leiden and New York, 1902.

Laval, R. P., in *Annales de la Propagation de la Foi*. Vol. xiv. Lyon, 1847.

Lavallie, A., " Notes ethnographiques sur diverses tribus de sud-est de l'Indo-Chine," *Bulletin de l'École Française d'Extrême-Orient*. Vol. i. Hanoi, 1900.

Laverack, Edward, *The Setter, with notices of the most eminent Breeds now extant*. London, 1872.

La Vaulx, Henri de, *Voyage en Patagonie*. Paris, 1901.

Lavisse, E., and others, *Histoire de France*. 9 vols. Paris, 1901-11.
  and Rambaud, A., *Histoire générale du IVᵉ siècle à nos jours*. 12 vols. Paris, 1893-1901.

The Laws of Manu. Translated by G. Buhler (*The Sacred Books of the East*. Vol. xxv). Oxford, 1886.

Lawson, John, *History of Carolina*. London, 1714.

Lawson, J. C., *Modern Greek Folklore and Ancient Greek Religion*. Cambridge, 1910.

Lawson, M. S., *Life and Education of Laura Dewey Bridgman, the Deaf, Dumb and Blind Girl*. Boston, 1878.

Layamon, *Le roman de Brut*. Ed. Le Roux de Lincy. 2 vols. Rouen, 1836-38.

Laycock, Thomas, " A Chapter on some Organic Laws of Personal and Ancestral Memory," *Journal of Mental Science*. Vol. xxi. London, 1876.

Lea, Henry Charles, *History of the Inquisition of the Middle Ages*. 3 vols. London, 1888.

Leabhar na g-Ceart, or the Book of Rights. Ed. with notes by J. O'Donovan. Dublin, 1847.

Leahy, A. H , *Heroic Romances of Ireland (Irish Saga Library No. 2)*. 2 vols. London, 1905.

Leared, Arthur, *Morocco and the Moors*. London, 1876.

Le Bas, P., et Waddington, W. H., *Voyage archéologique en Grèce et en Asie Mineure*. Paris, 1847.

Lebeau, Charles, *Histoire du Bas-Empire*. 21 vols. Paris, 1824–36.

Lebedew, " Die simbirskischen Tschuwaschen," *Archiv für wissenschaftliche Kunde von Russland*. Vol. ix. Berlin, 1851.

" Leben in den Faktoreien bei Sherbro," *Globus*. Vol. xlvii. Braunschweig, 1885.

Le Bon, Gustave, *Les civilisations des Indes*. Paris, 1887.

Lechaptois, Mgr., *Aux rives du Tanganika*. Algiers, 1913.

Lecky, W. E. Hartpole, *A History of England in the Eighteenth Century*. 7 vols. London, 1892.

Le Clercq, *Nouvelle Relation de la Gaspesie*. Paris, 1691.

Leclère, A., " Moeurs et coutumes des Cambodgiens," *Revue Scientifique*. Vol. li. Paris, 1893.

Lacoy de La Marche, A., *La chaire française au moyen-âge*. Paris, 1886.

Leeder, S. H., *Veiled Mysteries of Egypt*. London, 1912.

Leems, Knud, " An Account of the Laplanders of Finmark, their Language, Manners, and Religion." Transl. Pinkerton's *Voyages and Travels*. Vol. i. London, 1908.

Lefébure, E., " La Vertu du nom. Égypte," *Mélusine*. Vol. viii. Paris, 1896–97.

"Le Mythe Osirien," *Études Égyptologiques*. Livraisons iii and iv. Paris, 1874–75.

" Le lièvre dans la mythologie," *Bibliothèque égyptologique*. Vol. xxxv. Paris, 1912.

" Sur différents mots et noms égyptiens," *ibid*. Paris, 1912.

Lefèvre et Nehil, " La région de Tafrata et les tribus qui l'habitent," *L'Afrique française*. Supplément. Paris, 1910.

Legazpi, Miguel Lopez de, " Relation of the Filipinas Islands and of the Character and Conditions of their Inhabitants " (1569). Transl. in E. H. Blair and J. A. Robertson, *The Philippine Islands, 1493–1903*. Vol. iii. Cleveland, 1903.

La légende d'Oedipe, en particulier dans le Roman de Thèbes. Ed. L. Constans. Paris, 1881.

Leggatt, T. Watt, " Malekula, New Hebrides," *Report of the Fourth Meeting of the Australasian Association for the Advancement of Science, Tasmania, 1893*. Sydney, 1894.

Legge, J., *The Chinese Classics*. 5 vols. Hongkong, 1861–72.

Le Gobien, C., *Histoire des Isles Marianes*. Paris, 1700.

Legrand, Dr. M. A., *Au pays des Canaques. La Nouvelle Calédonie et ses habitants en 1890*. Paris, 1893.

Legrand d'Aussy, P. J. B., *Fabliaux ou contes du XIIᵉ et du XIIIᵉ siècle*. 5 vols. Paris, 1829.

Lehndorff, G., *Horse Breeding Recollections*. London, 1883.

Leidrad, *Epistolae*, in Pertz, *Monumenta Historica Germaniae, Epistolae Karolini Aevi*. Vol. ii. Berolini, 1895.

Leitner, G. W., *Results of a Tour in Dardistan, Kashmir, Little Tibet, etc.* Lahore, London, 1873.

Lekkerkerker, C., " Enkele opmerkingen over sporen van shamanisme biji Modoereezen an Javanen," *Tijdschrift von taal-, land- en volkenkunde.* Vol. xlv. Batavia, 1902.

Leland, C. G., *The Algonquin Legends of New England.* London, 1884.
Etruscan Roman Remains in Popular Tradition. London, 1892.
and Prince, John D., *Kuloskap the Master, and other Algonquin Poems.* New York and London, 1902.

Lemcke, Chr., " Die Taubstummenschüler in Ludwiglust," *Zeitschrift für Ohrenkrankheiten.* Vol. xvi. Leipzig, 1886.
Die Taubstummheit in Mecklenburg-Schwerin, ihre Ursache und ihre Verhütung. Leipzig, 1892.

Le Mesurier, C. J. R., " The Veddas of Ceylon," *Journal of the Royal Asiatic Society, Ceylon Branch.* Vol. ix. Colombo, 1887.

Le Moyen Âge. Paris, 1888–

Lenormant, F., " Quelques observations sur les symboles religieux des stèles puniques," *Gazette archéologique.* Vol. ii. Paris, 1876.

Lent, D., *Statistik der Taunstummen des Regirungsbezirkes Köln.* Köln, 1870.

Lenz, Oscar, *Skizzen aus Westafrika.* Berlin, 1878.

Leo Africanus (Hasan ibn Muhammad al Wazzan), *Descrittione dell' Africa e delle cose notabili che ivi sono,* in G. B. Ramusio, *Navigationi et Viaggi.* Vol. i. Venetia, 1564.

Le Page du Pratz, Antoine S., *Histoire de la Louisiane.* 3 vols. Paris, 1758.

Lepechin, I. I., *Tagebuch der Reise durch verschiedenen Provinzen des Russiches Reiches.* 3 vols. Altenburg, 1774–83.

Lepsius, R. A. M., *Denkmäler aus Ägypyten und Äthiopien.* 6 Abhand., 12 vols. Berlin, 1849–59.
Die Chornologie der Aegypter. Berlin, 1849.
See *Book of the Dead.*

Le Roux de Lincy, A. J. V., *Le livre des proverbes français.* 2 vols. Paris, 1859.
Essai historique et littéraire sur l'abbaye de Fécamp. Rouen, 1840.

Le Roy, A., " Au Zanguebar Anglais," *Les Missions Catholiques.* Vol. xxii. Lyon, 1890.

Le Roy, J. D., *Mémoire sur les travaux qui ont rapport à l'exploitation de la mâture dans les Pyrennées.* Londres, 1776.

Le Roy, Mgr., " Les Pygmées," *Les Missions Catholiques.* Vol. xxix. Lyon, 1897.
La religion des primitifs. Paris, 1909.

Lery, Jean de, *Histoire d'un voyage faict en terre de Brésil, autrement dite Amérique.* Paris, 1585.

Lescarbot, Marc, *Histoire de la Nouvelle France.* 3 vols. (Reprint.) Paris, 1866.

Leslie, R. M., art. " Pygmies," in *Encyclopaedia Britannica.* Vol. xxii. Cambridge, 1911.

Le Muséon. Louvain, 1882–

Lesseps, J. B. B. de, *Voyage de M. de Lesseps du Kamtschatka en France.* Paris, Lagny, 1800.

Lesson, P. Adolphe, *Les Polynésiens.* 4 vols. Paris, 1880–84.

Lesson, R. P., *Voyage autour du monde sur La Coquille.* 2 vols. Paris, 1838–39.

Le Strange, G., *The Lands of the Eastern Caliphate.* Cambridge, 1905.

Lethbridge, A., *West Africa the Elusive.* London, 1921.

Letherman, J., "Sketch of the Navajo Tribe of Indians, Territory of New Mexico," *Smithsonian Report for 1855.* Washington, 1856.

Letourneau, C. J. M., *La condition de la femme dans les diverses races et civilisations.* Paris, 1903.

Lettres édifiantes et curieuses, écrites des missions étrangères de la Compagnie de Jésus. 26 vols. Paris, 1780–83.

Leuschner, "Die Bakwiri," in S. R. Steinmetz, *Rechtsverhältnisse von eingeborenen Völkern in Afrika und Ozeanien.* Berlin, 1903.

Le Vaillant, François, *Voyage dans l'intérieur de l'Afrique par le Cap de Bonne Espérance.* 2 vols. Paris, 1798.

Levchin, A. de, *Description des hordes et des steppes des Kirghiz-Karak, ou Kirghiz-Kaïssaks.* Transl. Paris, 1840.

Levi, G., "Studi sulla grandezza delle cellule," *Archivio italiano di Anatomia e Embriologia.* Vol. v. Firenze, 1906.

Lévi, Sylvain, "Notes sur les Indo-Scythes," *Journal Asiatique,* 9e Série. Vol. ix. Paris, 1897.

Levrault, "Rapport sur les provinces de Canélos et du Napo," *Bulletin de la Société de Géographie.* 2e Série, vol. xi. Paris, 1839.

Levy, E., *Guilhem Figueira, ein provenzalischer Troubadour.* Berlin, 1880.

Levy-Bruhl, L., *Les fonctions mentales dans les sociétés inférieures.* Paris, 1910.

Lewin, T. H., *The Hill Tracts of Chittagong and the Dwellers therein.* Calcutta, 1869.

Wild Races of South-Eastern India. London, 1870.

Lewis, W. Bevan, *A Text-book of Mental Diseases, with special reference to the pathological aspects of insanity.* London, 1899.

in *Brain.* London, 1879.

Lex Gundobada, in *Monumenta Germaniae Historica; Legum.* Sect. i, Vol. ii, Part i. Hanover, 1892.

Liber Josuae. See Juynboll, T. G. J.

Lichtenstein, M. H., *Travels in Southern Africa.* Trans. 2 vols. London, 1812–15.

Liddell, H. C., and Scott, R., *Greek-English Lexicon.* Oxford, 1901.

Liebrecht, F., *Zur Volkskunde.* Heilbronn, 1879.

Des Gervasii von Tilbüry Otia Imperialia, in einen Auswahl neu herausgegaben und mit Anmerkungen begleitet. Hanover, 1856.

Liétard, Alfred, *Au Yun-nan. Les Lo-Lo P'o. Une tribu des aborigènes de la Chine méridionale.* Munster i-W., 1913.

Life of Lucilio (alias Julius Caesar) Vanini, burnt for Atheism at Thoulouse; with an Abstract of his Writings. Transl. from the French. London, 1730.

Lî Kî, tr. by J. Legge (*The Sacred Books of the East.* Vols. xxvii, xxviii). Oxford, 1885.

The same, edited and translated by S. Couvreur. 2 vols. Ho Kien Fou, 1913.

Lillie, Frank R., and Just, E. E., "Breeding Habits of the *Heteronereis* forms of *Nereis limbata,*" *Biological Bulletin of the Marine Biological Laboratory, Woods Hole.* Vol. xxiv. Woods Hole, Mass., 1913.

Lillo de Garcia, Maximino, *Filippinas. Distritto de Lepanto.* Manila, 1877.

Liltmann, Enno, "Sternensagen und Astrologisches aus Nordabessinien," *Archiv für Religionswisseschaft.* Vol. xi. Leipzig. 1908.

Lindblom, Gerhard, *The Akamba in British East Africa.* Upsala, 1920.

Lindeman, M., *Les Upotos.* Bruxelles, 1906.

Lindsay of Piscottie, Robert, *The Chronicles of Scotland.* 2 vols. Edinburgh, 1814.

Lindt, J. W., *Picturesque New Guinea.* London, 1887.

Linke, Franz, " Samoanische Bezeichnung für Wind und Wetter," *Globus*. Vol. xciv. Braunschweig, 1908.

Linschotten, J. H. van, *The Voyage of J. H. van L. to the East Indies*. Transl. by A. C. Burnell and P. A. Tiele. 2 vols. London, 1885.

Lipinska, Mélanie, *Histoire des femmes médecins*. Paris, 1900.

Lipsius, Justus, *De cruce*. Antverpiae, 1629.

Lipsius, R. A., *Die apokryphen Apostelgeschichten und Apostellegenden*. 3 vols. Braunschweig, 1883–90.

    art. " Gospels, Apocryphal," in W. Smith and H. Wace, *Dictionary of Christian Biography, Literature, Sects, and Doctrines*. Vol. ii. London, 1880.

Li Rois, Adenés, *Beuves de Commarchis*. Ed. Aug. Scheler. Bruxelles, 1874.

Lisiansky, Urey, *A Voyage round the World in the Years 1803–6*. London, 1814.

Lista, Ramon, *Los Indios Tehuelches*. Buenos Aires, 1894.

Lister, J. J., " Notes on the Natives of Fakaofu (Bowditch Island), Union Group," *Journal of the Anthropological Institute*. Vol. xxi. London, 1892.

Liston-Blyth, A., " Notes on the Native Customs of the Baniera District (N.E.D.), Papua," *Journal of the Royal Anthropological Institute*. Vol. liii. London, 1923.

Literatur-Blatt für orientalische Philologie. Leipzig, 1883–

Lith, Pieter Antonie van der, *Nederlandsch Oost-Indië, beschreven en afgebeeld*. Doesborgh, Arnhem, 1875.

Livingstone, David, *Missionary Travels and Researches in South Africa*. London, 1857.

    The Last Journals of David Livingstone in Central Africa. Ed. by H. Waller. 2 vols. London, 1874.

    and Livingstone, Charles, *Narrative of an Expedition to the Zambesi and its Tributaries*. London, 1865.

Livius Patavanus, Titus, *Historiarum Romanorum libri qui supersunt*. Ex. rec. Io. Nic. Madvigii. 4 vols. Hanniae, 1873.

Lloyd, George Thomas, *Thirty-three Years in Tasmania and Victoria*. London, 1862.

Lloyd, L. C., *A Short Account of further Bushman Material*, London, 1889.

    Specimens of Bushman Folklore, collected by the late W. H. I. Bleek and L. C. Lloyd. London, 1911.

Die Loango Expedition, 1873–76, by P. Grussfeldt, J. Falkenstein, E. Pechuël-Loesche. 3 vols. Leipzig, 1879–82.

Loarca, Miguel de, " Tratado de las yslas Philipinas " (1582), in E. H. Blair and J. A. Robertson, *The Philippine Islands, 1493–1802*. Vol. v. Cleveland, 1903.

Lobeck, Ch. Aug., *Aglaophamus, sive de theologiae mysticae Graecorum causis*. 2 vols. Königsberg, 1829.

Löbel, T., *Hochzeigebräuche in der Türkei*. Amsterdam, 1897.

Logan, J. R., " Five Days in Naning," *Journal of the Indian Archipelago*. Vol. iii. Singapore, 1849.

    " The Orang Binua of Johore," " The Orang Muka Kuning," " The Orang Sabimba of the Extremity of the Malay Peninsula," " The Biduanda Kallang of the River Pulai in Johore," *Journal of the Indian Archipelago*. Vol. i. Singapore, 1847.

    " The Manners and Customs of the Malays," *Journal of the Indian Archipelago*. Vol. iii. Singapore, 1849.

Logan, James, *The Scottish Gaël ; or Celtic Manners*. 2 vols. London, 1831.

Logan, M. H., " The Beirs," *Sudan Notes and Records*. Vol. i. Khartoum, 1918.

Loisel, G. Stave, " Relations entre les phénomènes du rut, de la lactation, de la mue et de l'amour maternel chez une chienne hybride, " *Comptes rendus hebdomadaires de la Société de Biologie*. Vol. i. Paris, 1906.

Lollis, Cesare de, *Vita e poesie di Sordello di Goito*. Halle a. S., 1896.

" Dolce stil nuovo e 'noel dig de nova maestria,'" *Studi Medievali*. Vol. i. Torino, 1904–5.

Lombroso, Gina, *L'Anima della Donna*. Bologna, 1920.

Lombroso, Paola, *Saggi di psicologia del bambino*. Torino-Roma, 1894.

Long, C. Chaillé, *Central Africa ; Naked Truths of Naked People*. London, 1876.

Long, J., *Voyages and Travels of an Indian interpreter and trader, describing the manners and customs of the North American Indians*. London, 1791.

Lopes, Manoel Monteiro, " Usages and Customs of the Natives of Sena," *Journal of the African Society*. Vol. vi. London, 1907.

Lörcher, E., *Die Basler Mission in China*. Basel, 1882.

Lorenz, Frederick, *The Life of Alcuin*. Transl. London, 1837.

Lortet, V., " Les fêtes d'Osiris au mois de Khoiak," *Recueil de travaux relatifs à la philologie et à l'archéologie égyptiennes et assyriennes*. Vol. iii. Paris, 1872.

— and Gaillard, C., " La Faune momifiée de l'ancienne Égypte," *Archives du Muséum d'Histoire Naturelle de Lyon*. Vols. ix, x. Lyon, 1907–9.

Loskiel, George Henry, *History of the Mission of the United Brethren among the Indians in North America*. London, 1794.

Lot, F., " Celtica," *Romania*. Vol. xxiv. Paris, 1875.

" Études sur la provenance du cycle arthurien," *Romania*. Vols. xxiv, xxv. Paris, 1895–96.

Loth, J., " L'année celtique," *Revue Celtique*. Vol. xxv. Paris, 1904.

Contributions à l'étude des romans de la Table ronde. Paris, 1912.

Les Mabinogion. Paris, 1889.

Loti, Pierre, *Le mariage de Loti*. Paris, 1888.

Les désenchantées. Paris, 1906.

Lott, Emmeline, *The English Governess in Egypt. Harem Life in Egypt and Constantinople*. London, 1867.

Louandre, F. C., *Histoire ancienne et moderne d'Abbeville et de son arrondissement*. Abbeville, 1834.

Love, James Kerr, *Deaf Mutism*. Glasgow, 1896.

" Deafness and Mendelism : an Essay in Eugenics " (abstract), *Maternity and Child Welfare*. Vol. v. London, 1921.

" The Origin of Sporadic Congenital Deafness," *The Journal of Laryngology*. Vol. xxxv. London, 1920.

Lovisato, Domenico, " Appunti etnografici con accenni geologici sulla Terra del Fuoco," *Cosmos di Guido Cora*. Vol. viii. Torino, 1884–85.

Low, David, *On the Domesticated Animals of the British Islands*. London, 1845.

Low, Hugh, *Sarawak*. London, 1848.

Low, James, " The Karean Tribes or Aborigines of Martalan and Tavai, with Notices of the Aborigenes in Keddah and Perak," *Journal of the Indian Archipelago*. Vol. iv. Singapore, 1850.

Löwe, F., *Schulchan Aruch, oder die vier jüdischen Gesetzbücher*. Transl. 4 vols. Hamburg, 1837–40.

Löwe, F., " Wenjaminow über die Aleutischen Inseln und deren Bewohners," *Archiv für wissenschaftliche Kunde von Russland*. Vol. ii. Berlin, 1842.

Lowie, R. H., " The Assiniboines," *Anthropological Papers of the American Museum of Natural History*. Vol. iv. New York, 1910.
" The Northern Shoshone," *Anthropological Papers of the American Museum of Natural History*. Vol. ii, Part ii. New York, 1908.

Lowinsky, V., *Zum geistlichen Kunstlied*. Berlin, 1898.

Lowis, R. F., " The Andaman and Nicobar Islands," *Census of India*, 1911. Vol ii. Calcutta, 1912.

Loyer, Godefroy, *Relation du voyage du royaume d'Issyny, Côte d'Or, Paris de Guinée*. Paris, 1714.

Lozano, Pedro, *Descripcion Chorographica del terreno, rios, arboles, y animales de las dilatadissimas Provincias del Gran Chaco, Gualamba*, etc. Cordoba, 1733.

Lucas, A. H. S., and Le Souëf, W. H. D., *The Animals of Australia*. Vol. i. Melbourne, 1909.

Lucas, Prosper, *Traité philosophique et physiologique de l'hérédité naturelle*. 2 vols. Paris, 1847, 1850.

Lucian of Samosata. *Opera*. Ex res. G. Dindorfii. Parisiis, 1867.

Luchaire, Achille, *La société française au temps de Philippe-Auguste*. Paris, 1909.

Lucka, Emil, *The Evolution of Love*. Transl. London, 1922.

Ludeking, E. W. A., " Schets van de Residentie Amboina," *Bijdragen tot de taal-, land- en volkenkunde van Nederlandsch-Indië*. 3e Serie, vol. iii. 's Gravenhage, 1868.

Ludolfus, Iobus, alias Leutholf dictus, *Ad suam Historiam Aethiopicam ante hoc editam Commentarius*. Francofurti ad Maenum, 1691.

Luduitz, A., *Die Liebestheorie der Provenzalen bei den Minnesingern der Stauferzeit*. Berlin, 1904.

Luis de Jesús, " General History of the Discalced Religious of St. Augustine " (1681), in E. H. Blair and J. A. Robertson, *The Philippine Islands, 1493–1803*. Vol. xxi. Cleveland, 1905.

Lujan, Pedro de, *Colloquios matrimoniales*. Seville, 1552.

Lumbroso, J., *Recherches sur l'économie politique de l'Égypte sous les Lagides*. Turin, 1870.

Lumholtz, Carl, *Through Central Borneo*. 2 vols. London, 1920.
Among Cannibals. London, 1889.
Unknown Mexico. 2 vols. London, 1903.

Lummis, C. F., *The Man who Married the Moon, and other Pueblo Folk Stories*. New York, 1884.

Lundborg, H., " Über die Erblichkeitsverhältnisse der konstitutionellen (hereditären) Taubstummheit und einige Worte über die Bedeutung der Erblichkeitsforschung für Krankheitslehre," *Archiv für Rassen- und Gesellschafts-Biologie*. Vol. ix. München, Berlin, 1912.

Lunet de Lajonquière, E., *Ethnographie du Tonquin septentrional*. Paris, 1906.

Luschan, Felix, von, " Beiträge zur Anthropologie von Kreta," *Zeitschrift für Ethnologie*. Vol. xlv. Berlin, 1913.

Lutfullah, *The Autobiography of Lutfullah, a Mahommedan Gentleman*, etc. Ed. by E. B. Eastwick. London, 1857.

Lutteroth, Henri, *O-Taïti*. Paris, 1845.

Lüttke, Theodor, Путешествіе вокругъ свѣта (Voyage round the World). 3 vols. St. Petersburg, 1834–36.

Lutz, F. E., " The Inheritance of the Manner of Clasping Hands," *The American Naturalist*. Vol. xlii. Boston, 1908.

Lux, A. E., *Von Loanda nach Kimbuda*. Wien, 1880.

Luzel, F. M., " La lune," *Revue Celtique*. Vol. iii. Paris, 1878.

Lyall, Sir Alfred C., *Asiatic Studies, religious and social. First Series.* London, 1899.

Lyall, J. B., *Report of the Land Revenue Settlement of the Kangra District*, Panjab. Lahore, 1874.

Lyddeker, R., *A Hand-book to the Carnivora*, Part I, *Cats, Civets, and Mongooses. (Allen's Naturalist's Library.)* London, s.d.

 and Sclater, P. L., *The Royal Natural History.* 6 vols. London, 1893–96.

Lydgate, John, *The Siege of Thebes, (Chaucer Society).* London, 1911.

Lynde, James William, "Religion of the Dakotas," *Collections of the Minnesota Historical Society.* No. ii. St. Paul, 1867.

Lyon, D. G., " The Consecrated Women of the Hammurabi Code," in *Studies presented to C. N. Toy.* New York, 1912.

Maas, A., " Ta-kä-käi-käi tabu," *Zeitschrift für Ethnologie.* Vol. xxxvii. Berlin, 1905.

 " Durch Zentral-Sumatra," *Zeitschrift für Ethnologie.* Vol. xli. Berlin, 1909.

Mabille, A., " The Basuto of Basutoland," *Journal of the African Society.* Vol. v. London, 1905–6.

The Mabinogion. Transl. by Lady Charlotte Guest, ed. A. Nutt. London, 1904.

 See Loth, J.

Macalister College Contributions : Department of History, Literature and Political Science. Saint Paul, Minnesota, 1889–

Macalister, R. A. Stewart, " Tremair Breg : A Study of the Remains and Traditions of Tara," *Proceedings of the Irish Academy.* Vol. xxxiv, Section C. Dublin, 1917–19.

Bible Side-lights from the Mount of Gezer. London, 1906.

McCandish, A. C., " Environment and Breeding as Factors influencing Milk Production," *The Journal of Heredity.* Vol. xi. Washington, 1920.

MacCauley, Clay, " The Seminole Indians of Florida," *Fifth Annual Report of the Bureau of Ethnology.* Washington, 1887.

Macchioro, Vittorio, *Zagreus, studi sull' Orfismo.* Bari, 1920.

 " Dionysiaka," *Atti della Reale Accademia archeologica di Napoli.* Vol. v. Napoli, 1897.

MacCulloch, J. A., *The Religion of the Ancient Celts.* Edinburgh, 1911.

 Art. " Celts," in Hastings's *Encyclopaedia of Religion and Ethics.* Vol. iii. Edinburgh, 1910.

McCulloch, J. H., *Researches Philosophical and Antiquarian concerning the Aboriginal History of America.* Baltimore, 1829.

McDonald, A., " Mode of Preparing the Dead among the Natives of Upper Mary River, Queensland," *Journal of the Anthropological Institute.* Vol. i. London, 1872.

Macdonald, C. R., " St. Kilda, the Inhabitants and the Diseases peculiar to them," *The British Medical Journal.* London, 1886.

Macdonald, Duff, *Africana ; or the Heart of Heathen Africa.* 2 vols. London, 1882.

Oceania, Linguistic and Anthropological. London, 1889.

Macdonald, D. G. F., *Cattle, Sheep, and Deer.* London, 1871.

Macdonald, James, " East Central African Customs," *Journal of the Anthropological Institute.* Vol. xxii. London, 1893.

 " Manners, Customs, Superstitions, and Religions of South African Tribes," *Journal of the Anthropological Institute.* Vol. xx. London, 1891.

Macdonald, James, "Bantu Customs and Legends," *Folk-lore*. Vol. iii. London, 1892.

Macdonald, K., *Social and Religious Life in the Highlands from the earliest time to the Reign of King Edward VII*. Edinburgh, 1902.

Macdonell, A. A., "Vedic Mythology," in G. Bühler, *Grundriss der indoarischen Philologie und Altertumskunde*. Vol. iii, Heft 1. Strassburg, 1897.

    and Keith, A. B., *Vedic Index of Names and Subjects*. 2 vols. London, 1912.

Macdonell, J., "Some Account of the Red River," in L. R. Masson, *Les Bourgeois de la Compagnie du Nord-Ouest*. Vol. i. Quebec, 1889.

McDougall, A. C., "Manners, Customs and Legends of the Coombangree Tribe," *Science of Man*. Sydney, 1901.

McDougall, William, *An Introduction to Social Psychology*. London, 1915.

Macedo, Joaquin Manoel de, "Noticia sobre os selvajens du Mucury," *Revista Trimensal de Historia e Geographia*. Vol. x. Rio de Janeiro, 1870.

Macfarlane, W., *Geographical Collection relating to Scotland*. Edinburgh, 1906.

McGee, W. J., "The Seri Indians," *Seventeenth Annual Report of the Bureau of Ethnology*. Part i. Washington, 1898.

    "The Siouan Indians," *Fifteenth Annual Report of the Bureau of Ethnology*. Washington, 1897.

Macgillivray, John, *Narrative of the Voyage of H.M.S. "Rattlesnake."* 2 vols. London, 1852.

Macgregor, William, "Lagos, Abeokuta, and the Alake," *Journal of the African Society*. Vol. iii. London, 1904.

Machado y Alvarez, A. (ed.), *Folk-lore Español. Biblioteca de las traditiones españoles*. Sevilla, 1883–86.

Machal, J., *Slavic Mythology*. Boston, 1918.

Macieiowski, W. A., *Slavische Rechtsgeschichte*. 4 vols. Stuttgart, Leipzig, 1835–39.

MacInnes, D., *Folk and Hero Tales (Waifs and Strays of Celtic Tradition : Argyllshire Series*, ed. J. Campbell, No. ii). London, 1890.

Mackay, G. L., "Unter den Aboriginalstämmen Formosas," *Mittheilungen der geographischen Gesellschaft (für Thüringen) zu Jena*. Vol. xv. Jena, 1897.

McKenney, T. L., *Sketches of a Tour to the Lakes, of the Character and Customs of the Chippeway Indians*, etc. Baltimore, 1827.

Mackenzie, Sir Alexander, *Voyages from Montreal on the River St. Laurence through the Continent of North America to the Frozen and Pacific Oceans, in the years 1789 and 1793*. London, 1801.

Mackenzie, A., "Australian Languages and Traditions," *Journal of the Anthropological Institute*. Vol. vii. London, 1878.

Mackenzie, C., "The Mississouri Indians," in L. R. Masson, *Les Bourgeois de la Compagnie du Nord-Ouest*. Vol. i. Quebec, 1889.

Mc'Kenzie, Dan, "Children and Wells," *Folk-lore*. Vol. xviii. London, 1907.

Mackenzie, Duncan, "Cretan Palaces and the Aegean Civilisation," *Annual of the British School at Athens*. Vol. xii. London, 1906.

McKenzie, J., "The King's Posts," in L. R. Masson, *Les Bourgeois de la Compagnie du Nord-Ouest*. Vol. ii. Quebec, 1889.

McKiernan, Bernard, "Some Notes on the Aborigines of the Lower Hunter River, New South Wales," *Anthropos*. Vol. vi. Wien, 1911.

Maclagan, E. D., "The Punjab and its Feudatories," *Census of India, 1891*. Vol. xix. Calcutta, 1892.

Maclagan, Robert Craig, *Our Ancestors, Scots, Picts, and Cymry*. London, Edinburgh, 1913.

Maclean, J., *Canadian Savage Folk*. Toronto, 1896.

McLean, John, *Notes of Twenty-five Years' Service in the Hudson's Bay Territory*. 2 vols. London, 1849.

Maclean, John, *A Compendium of Kafir Law and Custom*. Mount Coke, 1858.

McLennan, J. F., *Studies in Ancient History*. London, 1886.

Studies in Ancient History. The Second Series. London, 1896.

Macmichael, H. A., " Pottery Making on the Blue Nile," *Sudan Notes and Records*. Vol. v. Khartoum, 1922.

Macmillan's Magazine. London, 1860–

Macmillan, D. A., " The Bhuiyas," *Calcutta Review*. Vol. ciii. Calcutta, 1896.

McMillan, D. P., and Bruner, F. H., " The Children attending the Public Day Schools for the Deaf in Chicago," *Special Report of the Department of Child Study and Pedagogic Investigation. Chicago Public Schools*. Chicago, 1906.

Macpherson, S. Ch., *An Account of the Religion of the Khonds in Orissa*. London, 1852.

MacRitchie, David, " The Aïnos," *Internationales Archiv für Ethnographie*. Supplement to vol. iv. Leiden, 1892.

Macrizi, *Abhandlung über die in Aegypten eingewanderten Stämme*. Ed. F. Wuestenfeld. Göttingen, 1847.

Macrobius, Ambrosius Theodorius, *Opera*. Recog. Franciscus Eyssenhardt. Leipzig, 1893.

McSwiney, J., " Assam," Report, *Census of India, 1911*. Vol. iii. Shillong, 1912.

Madden, Sir Frederick, *Syr Gawayne ; a collection of ancient romantic poems*. Edinburgh, 1839.

Mademba, Fama, " Die Sansanding-Staaten," in S. R. Steinmetz, *Rechtsverhältnisse von eingeborenen Völkern in Afrika und Ozeanien*. Berlin, 1903.

Madras District Gazetteers. Madras, 1904–

Madras District Gazetteers. Madura. Madras, 1906–

Madras Journal of Literature and Science. Madras, 1835–

Madrolle, Claude, *En Guinée*. Paris, 1895.

Maes, J., " Notes sur quelques objets des pygmés-Wambuti," *Anthropos*. Vol. vi. Wien, 1911.

Maffei, F. S., *Museum Veronense ; hoc est antiquarum inscriptionum atque anaglyphorum collectio*. Verona, 1749.

Magalhães Gandavo, Pedro de," Historia da Provincia Sãta Cruz, a que vulgarmête chamamos Brasil," *Revista Trimensal do instituto historico e geographico Brasileiro*. Vol. xxi. Rio de Janeiro, 1858.

Magyar, L., *Reisen in Süd-Afrika*. Pest and Leipzig, 1859.

The Mahabharata of Krishna-Dwaipayana-Vyasa. Transl. into English. 2 vols. Calcutta, 1884.

Mahānāma, *The Mahāwanso*. With translation by the Hon. G. Turnour. Ceylon, 1837.

The Mahâvagga. Transl. from the Pâli by T. W. Rhys Davids and H. Oldemberg. (*The Sacred Books of the East*, vol. xiii.) Oxford, 1881.

Mahn, C. A. F., *Gedichte der Troubadours in provenzalischer Sprache*. 4 vols. Berlin, 1856–73.

Die Werke der Troubadours. 4 vols. Berlin, 1846-

Mailla, J. A. M. de Moyria de, *Histoire générale de la Chine, ou annales de cet empire traduites de Tong-Kien-Kang-Mou.* 13 vols. Paris, 1777–85. in *Lettres édifiantes et curieuses.* Vol. xviii. Paris, 1781.

Maine, Sir Henry J. S., *Ancient Law.* London, 1885.
Lectures on the early history of Institutions. London, 1875.
Village Communities in the East and West. London, 1876.
Dissertations on Early Law and Custom. London, 1883.

Majerus, "Brautwerbung und Hochzeit bei den Wabende (Deutsch-Ostafrika)," *Anthropos.* Vol. vi. Wien, 1911.

Major, R. H., *India in the Fifteenth Century.* London, 1857.

Malala, Ioannes, *Chronographia.* Ex. rec. Lud. Dindorfii. (*Corpus Scriptorum Historiae Byzantinae.*) Bonn, 1831.

Malcolm, L. W. G., "Notes on Birth, Marriage, and Death Ceremonies of the Etap Tribe, Central Cameroons," *Journal of the Royal Anthropological Institute.* Vol. liii. London, 1923.
"Note on the Seclusion of Girls among the Efik of Old Calabar," *Man.* Vol. xxv. London, 1925.

Malinowski, Bronislaw, *The Family among the Australian Aborigines.* London, 1913.
"Baloma; the Spirits of the Dead in the Trobriand Islands," *Journal of the Royal Anthropological Institute.* Vol. xlvi. London, 1916.
"The Natives of Mailu," *Transactions of the Royal Society of South Australia.* Vol. xxxix. Adelaide, 1915.
Argonauts of the Western Pacific. London, 1922.

Mallat, J., *Les Philippines.* 2 vols. Paris, 1846.

Malleolus, Felix (F. Haemmerlein), *De nobilitate et rusticitate dialogus.* Strasburgh, 1490.

Mallet, D., *Le culte de Neit à Saïs.* Paris, 1888.

Malo, David, *Hawaiian Antiquities.* Translated from the Hawaiian by Dr. N. B. Emerson. Honolulu, 1903.

Malory, Sir Thomas, *Le Morte d'Arthur.* London, 1898.

Mama Rinso, "To-tato Ki Ko, d.i., Reise nach der östlichen Tatarei," *Nippon, Archief voor de beschrijving van Japan.* Vol. vii. Leyden, 1854.

Man, A Monthly Record of Anthropological Science. London, 1901–

Man, E. H., "On the Aboriginal Inhabitants of the Andaman Islands," *Journal of the Anthropological Institute.* Vol. xii. London, 1883.
"Nicobar Pottery," *Journal of the Anthropological Institute.* Vol. xxiii. London, 1894.

Man, John F., "Notes on the Aborigines of Australia," *Proceedings of the Geographical Society of Australasia; New South Wales and Victoria Branch.* Vol. i. Sydney, 1885.

Mandelsloe, J. H. de, in J. Harris, *Navigantium et Itinerantium Bibliotheca.* Vol. i. London, 1744.

Manella, Filippo, *La razza negra nel suo stato selvaggio in Africa.* Torino, 1864.

Mangin, E., "Essai sur les us et coutumes du peuple Mossi au Soudan Occidental," *Anthropos.* Vol. ix. Wien, 1914.

Il Manicomio (moderno). Giornale di psichiatria. Nocera, 1885–

Maning, F. E. (ps. Pakeha Maori), *Old New Zealand.* London, 1863.

Mannert, Conrad, *Geographie der Griechen und Römer aus ihren schriften dargestellt.* 10 vols. Leipzig, Nuremberg, Landshut, 1829–35.

Mannhardt, W., *Wald und Feldkulte.* 2 vols. Berlin, 1904.
Mythologische Forschungen. Berlin, 1884.

Manning, James, "Notes on the Aborigines of New Holland," *Journal and Proceedings of the Royal Society of New South Wales, 1882.* Sydney, 1883.

Manouvrier, " Un rapt de progéniture entre femelles de rat blanc," *Bulletin international de Psychologie*. Paris, 1905. Cited by E. Rabaud in *Bulletin de la Société Zoologique*, vol. xlvi.

Mansfeld, " Einiges uber Taubstummheit und die Taubstummen," *Wochenschrift für die gesammte Heilkunde.* 1834.

Mansfeld, Alfred, *Urwald Dokumente, vier Jahre unter den Crossflutnegern Kameruns.* Berlin, 1908.

Mantegazza, Paolo, *Fisiologia del Amore.* Milano, 1875.

  Quadri della natura umana. 2 vols. Milano, 1871.

  Gli amori degli uomini. 2 vols. Milan, 1886.

  " Studi sui matrimonii consanguinei," *Rendiconti dell' Instituto Lombardo di Scienze e Lettere.* Vol. i. Milano, 1868.

A Manual of Belgian Congo, compiled by the Naval Intelligence Division, Admiralty. London, 1920.

Mapes, Walter, *De Nugis Curalium.* Ed. T. Wright. London, 1850.

Marcabru, *Poésies completes.* Ed. by J.-M. L. Dejearre. (*Biblothèque Méridionale*, vol. xii.) Toulouse, 1909.

Marcel, M. G., " Les Fuégiens à la fin du XVIIe siècle d'après des documents français inédits," *Congrès International des Américanistes. Compte-rendu de la Huitième Session.* Paris, 1892.

Marchal, P., " La reproduction et l'évolution des guêpes sociales," *Archives de Zoologie expérimentale et générale.* 3e Série, vol. iv. Paris, 1896.

  " Les ouvières pondeuses chez les abeilles," *Bulletin de la Société Entomologique de France.* Paris, 1894.

Marcoy, Paul, *Voyage à travers l'Amérique du Sud de l'océan Pacifique à l'océan Atlantique.* 2 vols. Paris, 1861.

Marett, R. B. (ed.) *Anthropology and the Classics.* Oxford, 1908.

Margolis, M. L., art. " Celibacy," in *The Jewish Encyclopaedia.* Vol. iii. Chicago, s.d.

Marguin, G., " La Terre de Feu," *Bulletin de la Société de Géographie.* 6e Série, vol. x. Paris, 1875.

Mariana, Juan de, *Historia general de España.* 20 vols. Madrid, 1817–22.

Marie de France, *Poésies.* Ed. B. de Roquefort. 2 vols. Paris, 1820.

Mariette, A., " Lettre sur les fouilles de Tanis," *Revue archéologique.* Paris, 1862.

  Denderah. Paris, Alexandrie, 1875.

  Le Sérapéon de Memphis. Paris, 1857.

  Notice des principaux monuments exposés dans les galéries provisoires du Musée d'Antiquités Égyptiennes . . . à Boulaq. Paris, Poitiers, 1869.

  Abydos. 3 vols. Paris, 1869–80.

Mariner, William, *An Account of the Natives of the Tonga Islands compiled by John Martin.* 2 vols. London, 1817.

Marino de Lovera, Pedro, *Cronica del reino de Chile.* (*Colleción de historiadores de Chile.* Vol. vi.) 1801.

Markham, Sir C. R., " A List of the Tribes in the Valley of the Amazon," *Journal of the Anthropological Institute.* Vol. xxiv. London, 1895.

  The same, 3rd ed., *Journal of the Royal Anthropological Institute.* Vol. xv. London, 1910.

  Narratives of the Mission of George Bogle to Tibet and of the Journey of Thomas Manning to Lhasa. London, 1876.

  Narrative of the Rites and Laws of the Yncas. (*Hakluyt Society.*) London, 1873.

Marno, Ernst, *Reise in der Egyptischen Aequatorial-Provinz und in Kordofan.* Wien, 1878.

  Reisen im Gebiete des blauen und weissen Nil. Wien, 1874.

Marquardt, Joachim, and Mommsen, T., *Handbuch der römischen Alterthümer*. 7 vols. Leipzig, 1874–88.

Marquette, Jacques, " Récit des voyages et des découvertes du Père J. Marquette," in B. F. French, *Historical Collections of Louisiana*. Part iv. New York, 1851.

Marquordt, F., " Bericht über die Kavirondo," *Zeitschrift für Ethnologie*. Vol. xli. Berlin, 1909.

Marracius, Hippolytus, *Polyanthea Mariana*. Coloniae Agrippinae, 1700.

Marriott, H. P. Fitzgerald, " The Secret Societies of West Africa," *Journal of the Anthropological Institute*. Vol. xxix. London, 1899.

Marro, A., " The Influence of the Age of Parents upon the Psycho-physical Characters of the Children," *Problems in Eugenics*. London, 1912.

Marsden, S., in *The Missionary Register*. London, 1816.

Marsden, W., *The Histroy of Sumatra*. London, 1811.

Marshall, A. E. M. A., *History of the Universities Mission to Central Africa, 1859–96*. London, 1897.

Marshall, F. H. A., *The Physiology of Reproduction*. London, 1910.

Marshall, Henry Rutgers, *Instinct and Reason*. London, 1898.

Marshall, W. E., *A Phrenologist among the Todas*. London, 1873.

Marston, M., " Letter to the Rev. Dr. Jedidah Morse," in E. H. Blair, *The Indian Tribes of the Upper Mississippi Valley and the Region of the Great Lakes*. Vol. ii. Cleveland, 1912.

Marten, J. T., " India," *Census of India, 1921*. Vol. i. Calcutta, 1924.

Martène, Edmond, *De antiquis Ecclesiae ritibus*. 4 vols. Venetiis, 1783.

Martial, L. F., *Mission scientifique du Cap Horn, 1882–83*. Vol. i. " Histoire du Voyage." Paris, 1888.

Martin, K., *Reisen in den Molukken, in Ambon, den Uliassern, Seran (Ceram) und Buru*. Leiden, 1894.

Martin, M., *Basutoland ; its Legends and Customs*. London, 1903.

Martin, R., *Les Mammifères de la France*. Paris, 1910.

Martin, Rudolf, *Die Inlandstämme der malayischen Halbinsel*. Jena, 1905.

Martini, Martinus, *Sinicae Historiae*. Monachii, 1658.

  Novus Atlas Sinensis. Amsterdam, 1655.

Martial, *Epigrammaton libri*. Ed. L. Friedlaender. 2 vols. Leipzig, 1886.

Martial de Salviac, R. P., *Un peuple antique, ou une colonie gauloise au pays de Ménélik. Les Galla*. Cahors, 1900.

Martianus Capella, *Opera*. Ed. F. Eyssenhardt. Leipzig, 1866.

Martius, C. F. Ph. von, *Beiträge zur Ethnographie und Sprachenkunde Amerika's zumal Brasiliens*. 2 vols. Leipzig, 1867.

  " On the State of Civil and Natural Rights among the Aboriginal Inhabitants of Brazil," *Journal of the Royal Geographical Society*. Vol. ii. London, 1834.

  Von den Rechtszustande unter den Ureinwohnern Brasiliens. 2 vols. München, 1832.

Martrou, Louis, " Les ' Eki ' des Fang," *Anthropos*. Vol. i. Salzburg, 1906.

Marvin, Charles, *Merv, the Queen of the World, and the Scourge of the Man-stealing Turcomans*. London, 1881.

Marx, L., " Die Amahlubi," in S. R. Steinmetz, *Rechtsverhältnisse von eingeborenen Völkern in Afrika und Ozeanien*. Berlin, 1903.

Mas, Sinibaldo de, *Informe sobre el estado de las Yslas Filipinas en 1842*. 2 vols. Madrid, 1843.

Mason, J. Alden, *The Ethnology of the Salinan Indians (University of California Publications in American Archaeology and Ethnology*. Vol. x, No. 4.) Berkeley, 1912.

Mason, Otis T., *Woman's Share in Primitive Culture*. New York, 1894.

" Aboriginal Skin-Dressing," *Report of the United States National Museum for 1888-89*. Washington, 1891.

Maspéro, G., " Les chants d'amour du papyrus de Turin et du papyrus Harris," *Journal Asiatique*. 8e Série, vol. i. Paris, 1883.

" Sur la toute-puissance de la parole," *Recueil de travaux relatifs à la philologie et à l'archéologie Égyptiennes et Assyriennes*. Vol. xxiv. Paris, 1902.

" Les forgerons d'Horus et la légende d'Horus d'Edfou," *Bibliothèque Égyptologique*. Vol. ii. Paris, 1894.

" Sur l'Ennéade," *Revue de l'Histoire des Religions*. Vol. xxv. Paris, 1892.

Life in Ancient Egypt and Assyria. London, 1901.

Guide du visiteur au Musée de Boulaq. Boulaq, Vienne, 1883.

Histoire ancienne des peuples de l'orient classique. Paris, 1886.

Les momies royales de Déir el-Baharî (Mémoires publiés par les membres de la Mission Archéologique Française au Caire. Vol. i). Paris, 1889.

Les Contes populaires de l'Égypte ancienne, Paris. 1911.

The Dawn of Civilisation. London, 1910.

The Struggle of the Nations. London, 1910.

The Passing of the Empires. London, 1900.

Massenat, E., Lalande, Ph., and Cartailhac, E., " Description d'un squelette humain de l'âge du renne à Lugerie Basse (Dordogne)," *Comptes Rendus hebdomadaires de l'Académie des Sciences*. Vol. lxxiv. Paris, 1872.

Masson, Charles, *Narrative of various Journeys in Balochistan, Afghanistan, the Panjab*. 4 vols. London, 1842–43.

Masson, L. R., *Les Bourgeois de la Compagnie du Nord-Ouest*. 2 vols. Québec, 1889–90.

Masúdi, *Muruju'l-Dhahab* (Maçoudi, *Les Prairies d'Or*). Text and transl. by C. Barbier de Meynard and Pavet de Courteille. 9 vols. Paris, 1861–77.

Mateer, S., " Nepotism in Travancore," *Journal of the Anthropological Institute*. Vol. xii. London, 1884.

Native Life in Travancore. London, 1883.

Maternity and Child Welfare. London, 1817–

Mathew, John, " The Australian Aborigines," *Journal and Proceedings of New South Wales*. Vol. xxiii. Sydney, 1889.

Eaglehawk and Crow. Melbourne, 1899.

Two Representative Tribes of Queensland. London, 1910.

Mathews, R. H., " The Bora, or Initiation Ceremonies of the Kamilaroi Tribe," *Journal and Proceedings of the Royal Society of New South Wales*. Vol. xxiv. Sydney, 1890.

" The Group Divisions and Initiations Ceremonies of the Barkunjee Tribe," *Journal and Proceedings of the Royal Society of New South Wales*. Vol. xxxii. Sydney, 1898.

" Aboriginal Bora held at Gundabloni in 1894," *Journal and Proceedings of the Royal Society of New South Wales*. Vol. xxxviii. Sydney, 1904.

" Initiation in Australian Tribes," *Proceedings of the American Philosophical Society*. Vol. xxxvii. Philadelphia, 1898.

" The Origin, Organization and Ceremonies of the Australian Aborigines," *Proceedings of the American Philosophical Society*. Vol. xxxix. Philadelphia, 1900.

" Phallic Rites and Initiation Ceremonies of the South Australian Aborigines," *Proceedings of the American Philosophical Society*. Vol. xxxix. Philadelphia, 1900.

Mathews, R. H., " Australian Ground and Tree Drawings," *The American Anthropologist*. Vol. ix. Washington, 1896.

" Ethnological Notes on the Aboriginal Tribes of N.S. Wales and Victoria," *Journal of the Royal Society of New South Wales*. Vol. xxxviii. Sydney, 1905.

" Notes on the Arranda Tribe," *Journal and Proceedings of the Royal Society of New South Wales*. Vol. xli. Sydney, 1908.

" The Bunan Ceremony of New South Wales," *The American Anthropologist*. Vol. ix. Washington, 1896.

" Australian Tribes : their Formation and Government," *Zeitschrift für Ethnologie*. Vol. xxxviii. Berlin, 1906.

" Ethnological Notes on the Aboriginal Tribes of Queensland," *Queensland Geographical Journal*. New Series. Vol. xx. Brisbane, 1905.

" Initiation Ceremonies of the Murawarri and other Aboriginal Tribes of Queensland," *ibid*. Vol. xxii. Brisbane, 1907.

" Notes on some Native Tribes of Australia," *Journal and Proceedings of the Royal Society of New South Wales*. Vol. xl. Sydney, 1907.

and Everitt, M. N., " The Organisation, Language and Initiation Ceremonies of the South-East Coast of New South Wales," *Journal and Proceedings of the Royal Society of New South Wales*. Vol. xxxiv. Sydney, 1900.

Mathieu, Père, in *Annales de la Propagation de la Foi*. Vol. xxviii. Lyons, 1856.

Matthes, B. F., *Bijdragen tot de Ethnologie van Zuid-Celebes*. 's Hage, 1875.

" Over de adas of Gewoonten der Makassaren en Boegineezen," *Verslagen en Mededeelingen van het Koninklijke Akademie van Wetenschappen*. Derde Serie, vol. ii. Amsterdam, 1885.

" Over de bisoes, of heidensche priester en priesteressen der Boeginezen," *Verslagen en Mededeelingen van het Koninglijke Akademie van Wetenschappen*. Vol. vii. Amsterdam, 1872.

Matthew Paris, *Chronica Majora*. Ed. by S. Henry Richards Luard (*Chronicles and Memorials of Great Britain and Ireland*). 7 vols. London, 1872–83.

Matthews, John, *A Voyage to the River Sierra Leone on the Coast of Africa*. London, 1791.

Matthews, Washington, *Ethnography and Philology of the Hidatsa Indians*. (*United States Geological and Geographical Survey, Miscellaneous Publications*. No. 7.) Washington, 1877.

" Navajo Weavers," *Third Report, American Bureau of Ethnology*. Washington, 1884.

" The Mountain Chant : a Navajo Ceremony," *Fifth Annual Report of the Bureau of Ethnology*. Washington, 1887.

" Some Deities and Demons of the Navajos," *The American Naturalist*. Vol. xx. Boston, 1886.

Navaho Legends (*Memoirs of the American Folk-Lore Society*). Vol. v. Boston and New York, 1897.

Maudsley, Henry, *The Pathology of Mind*. London, 1895.

Maundeville, Sir John, *The Voiage and Travaile of Sir J. M.* Reprint, by J. O. Halliwell. London, 1839.

Maupas, E., " Sur la conjugaison des infusoires ciliés," *Comptes Rendus de l'Académie des Sciences*. Vol. ciii. Paris, 1886.

" Sur la puissance de multiplication des infusoires ciliés." *Ibid.*, vol. civ. Paris, 1887.

Maupas, E., " Recherches expérimentales sur la multiplication des infusoires ciliés," *Archives de Zoologie expérimentale et générale.* 2e Série, vol. vi. Paris, 1888.

" Modes et formes de reproduction des Nématodes," *Archives de Zoologie Expérimentale.* 3e Série, vol. viii. Paris, 1900.

Maurer, Conrad von, *Isländische Volksagen der Gegenwart.* Leipzig; Munich, 1860.

Maurer, G. L. von, *Geschichte der Dorfverfassung in Deutschland.* 2 vols. Erlangen, 1865–66.

Maury, L. F. Alfred, *Croyances et légendes du moyen-âge.* Paris, 1896.

Mawer, A., *The Vikings.* Cambridge, 1913.

Maxwell, W. E., " The Folk-lore of the Malays," *Journal of the Straits Branch of the Royal Asiatic Society.* No. 7. Singapore, 1881.

May, F., " The Zulu Kafirs of Natal," *Anthropos.* Vol. ii. Salzburg, 1907.

May, J.-B., *Saint-Petersbourg et La Russie en 1829.* 2 vols. Paris, 1830.

Maya Das, " Some Marriage Customs among the Khatris of the Panjab," *The Indian Antiquary.* Vol. xxix. Bombay, 1900.

Mayer, Alfred Goldsborough, " The Annual Breeding-swarm of the Atlantic Palolo," *Papers from the Tortugas Laboratory of the Carnegie Institute of Washington.* Vol. i. Washington, 1908.

Mayer, Paulin, " La Chanson de Doon de Nanteuil ; Fragments inédits," *Romania.* Vol. xiii. Paris, 1884.

Mayers, W. F., *The Chinese Reader's Manual.* Shanghai, 1874.

Mayeux, F. J., *Les Bédouins, ou Arabes du désert.* 3 vols. Paris, 1816.

Mayhew, Henry, and Binny, John, *The Criminal Prisons of London, and Scenes from Prison Life.* London, 1862.

Mayne, J. D, *A Treatise on Hindu Law and Usage.* Madras, 1914.

Mayne, R. C., *Four Years in British Columbia and Vancouver Island.* London, 1862.

Mayr, A., *Die vorgeschichtlichen Denkmäler von Malta.* München, 1901.

Die Insel Malta in Altertum. München, 1909.

Mead, G. R. S., *Fragments of a Faith Forgotten.* London and Benares, 1906.

Mecklenburg-Strelitz, Duke Adolph Frederick of, *In the Heart of Africa.* Transl. London, 1910.

From the Congo to the Niger and the Nile. Transl. 2 vols. London, 1913.

Meddelelser om Grönland, udgivine af Commissionen for Ledelsen af de geologiske og geographiske Undersögelse i Grönland. Kjøbenhaven, 1879–

Mededeelingen van wege het Nederlandsche Zendelinggenootschap. Rotterdam, 1857–

Medhurst, W. H., " Marriage Affinity, and Inheritance in China," *Transactions of the Royal Asiatic Society, China Branch.* Vol. iv. Hongkong, 1855.

China, its State and Prospect, with special reference to the Spread of the Gospel. London, 1840.

The Medical News. Philadelphia, 1882–

Meeker, L. L., " Siouan Mythological Tales," *Journal of American Folk-Lore.* Vol. xiii. Boston and New York, 1901.

Megapolensis, John, " A Short Account of the Maquaas Indians in New Netherland . . . written in the year 1644." Transl. from the Dutch, in E. Hazard, *Historical Collections.* Vol. i. Philadelphia, 1792.

Megasthenes, *Fragmenta*, in *Fragmenta Historicorum Graecorum*. Ed. C. Müller. Vol. ii. Paris, 1848.

Mehlis, C., "Die Ligurerfrage," *Archiv für Anthropologie*. Vol. xxvi. Braunschweig, 1899.

Meier, E., *Deutsche Sagen, Sitten und Gebräuche aus Schwaben*. Stuttgart, 1852.

Meier, J., *Mythen und Erzählungen der Küstenbewohner der Gazelle-halbinsel*. Münster, 1909.

" Primitive Völker und ' Paradies-' Zustand. Mit besonderer Beruchsichtigung der früheren Verhältnisse bei Oststamm der Gazellehalbinsel in Bismarck-Archipel," *Anthropos*. Vol. ii. Salzburg, 1907.

" Mythen und Sagen der Admiralitäts-Insulaner," *Anthropos*. Vol. iii. Wien, 1908.

" Der Glaube an der ' inal ' und den ' tutana vurakit ' bei den Eingeborenen im Küstegebiet der Blanchebucht," *Anthropos*. Vol. v. Wien, 1910.

Meiners, C., *Vermischte philosophische Schriften*. 3 vols. Leipzig, 1775–76.

Meinhof, Carl, " Die Geheimsprachen Afrikas," *Globus*. Vol. lxvi. Braunschweig, 1894.

Meinicke, C. E., *Die Inseln des Stillen Oceans*. 2 vols. Leipzig, 1875–76.

Meissner, Bruno, *Beiträge zum altbabylonischen Privatrecht*. Leipzig, 1893.

Meissner, F. L., *Taubstummheit und Taubstummbildung*. Leipzig and Heidelberg, 1856.

Mela, Pomponius, *De situ orbis*. Rec. C. H. Tzchuckio. 3 vols. Leipzig, 1806–07.

Mélanges Nicole. Recueil de mémoires de philologie classique et d'archéologie offert à Jules Nicole. Genève, 1905.

Melland, F. H., " Some Ethnological Notes on the Awemba Tribe of North-East Rhodesia," *Journal of the African Society*. Vol. iii. London, 1904.

Melnikow, N., " Die Burjäten des irkutschkischen Governments," *Verhandlungen der Berliner Gesellschaft für Anthropologie*. Berlin, 1889.

Mélusine, Revue de Mythologie, etc. Paris, 1878–

Melville, H., *Typee*. London, 1892.

Mémoire sur la Lousiane ou le Mississipi. Luxembourg, 1752.

Mémoires concernant l'histoire, les sciences, les arts, les moeurs, les usages, etc., *des Chinois*, per les Missionaires de Pékin. 17 vols. Paris, 1776–1814.

Mémoires de l'Academie Celtique. Paris, 1807–12.

Mémoires de la Société d'Anthropologie de Paris. Paris, 1860–

Mémoires de la Société de Physique et d'Histoire Naturelle de Genève. Genève, 1821–

Mémoires de la Société d'Ethnographie. Paris, 1871–

Mémoires de l'Institut de France. Académie des Inscriptions. Paris, 1831–

Mémoires de Littérature tirés des régistres de l'Académie des Inscriptions et Belles Lettres. La Haye, 1719–

Mémoires et Documents publiés par la Société d'Histoire de la Suisse Romande. Lausanne, 1838–

Memorie della Reale Accademia delle Scienze di Torino. Torino, 1818–

Memoirs of the American Anthropological Association. Lancaster, Pa., 1907–

Memoirs of the American Folk-Lore Society. Boston, 1894–

Memoirs of the American Museum of Natural History. New York, 1898–

Memoirs of the Asiatic Society of Bengal. Calcutta, 1907–

" Memoirs of the Malay," *Journal of the Indian Archipelago*. Vol. ii. Singapore, 1848.

Memoirs of the Peabody Museum. Cambridge, U.S., 1896–

Memoirs read before the Anthropological Society of London. London, 1865–

Menander, *Reliquiae.* Ed. Meinecke. Berolini, 1823.

Menant, Joachin, *Les Yezidiz.* Paris, 1892.

    Pierres gravées de la Haute-Asie. 2 vols. Paris, 1883–86.

    Catalogue de cylindres orientaux du Cabinet Royal des Médailles de La Haye. La Haye, 1878.

Ménare, L., *Hermès Trismégiste.* Paris, 1867.

Mendieta, Fray Geromimo de, *Historia eclesiastica Indiana.* Mexico, 1880.

Menière, M. P., " Recherches sur l'origine de la surdi-mutité," *Gazette Médicale de Paris.* Paris, 1846.

Méon, Dominique Martin, *Nouveau recueil de fabliaux et de contes inédits des xiie–xve siècles.* 2 vols. Paris, 1823.

Méray, Antony, *La vie au temps des trouvères ; croyances, usages et moeurs intimes du xie, xiie, et xiiie siècles.* Paris, 1873.

    La Vie au temps des cours d'amours. Paris, 1876.

Mercier, Charles, *Sanity and Insanity.* London, 1890.

Le Mercure de France. Paris, 1724–

Mercurii, S., *Degli errori popolari d'Italia.* Venezia, 1603.

Meredith, C., in *Proceedings of the Royal Society of Tasmania.* Hobart, 1873.

Merensky, A., " Die Hottentotten," *Verhandlungen der Berliner Gesellschaft für Anthropologie.* Berlin, 1878.

    Beiträge zur Kenntniss Süd-Afrikas. Berlin, 1875.

Merker, M., *Rechtsverhältnisse und Sitten der Wadschagga,* in *Petermann's Mitteilungen,* Erganzungsheft. No. 138. Gotha, 1902.

    Die Masai. Berlin, 1904.

Merlet, J. F. L., *Nitokris, légende de l'ancienne Egypte, poème.* Paris, 1912.

Merolla da Sorrento, J., " A Voyage to Congo and several other Countries." Transl. in Pinkerton, *Voyages and Travels.* Vol. xvi. London, 1814.

Merriam, Clinton Hart, " The Vertebrates of the Adirondack Region, Northeastern New York," *Transactions of the Linnaean Society of New York.* Vols. i. and ii. New York, 1882–84.

Metcalfe, R. B., " Report to the Commisioner of Indian Affairs," in *Executive Documents printed by Order of the House of Representatives, First Session of the 35th Congress, 1857–58.* Washington, 1858.

Metz, J. F., *Die Volkstämme der Nilagiri's.* Basel, 1858.

    The Tribes inhabiting the Neilgherry Hills. Mangalore, 1864.

Metzger, Emil, " Die Bewohner der Karolinen," *Globus.* Vol. xlix. Braunschweig, 1886.

    " Herrscher und Beherrschte auf Java," *Globus.* Vol. lvi. Braunschweig, 1883.

    " Mittheilung über Glauben und Aberglaugen bei Sundanesen und Javanen," *Globus.* Vol. xliv. Braunschweig, 1883.

Meursius, Joannis, *Creta, Cyprus, Rhodus.* Amsterlodami, 1675.

Meuse, F. de, " De la condition de la femme, " *Le Congo Illustré.* Vol. iii. Bruxelles, 1894.

Meyer, A. B., " Über der Perforation des Penis bei der Malayen," *Mittheilungen der anthropologische Gesellschaft.* Vol. vii. Wien, 1877.

Meyer, E. H., *Badisches Volksleben im neunzehnten Jahrhundert.* Strasburg, 1900.

Meyer, Eduard, *Geschichte des Altertums.* (3rd. ed.) Stuttgart and Berlin, 1913.

    Geschichte des Alten Aegypten (W. Oncken, *Allgemeine Geschichte in Einzeldarstellungen).* Berlin, 1887.

    Der Papyrusfund von Elephantine. Leipzig, 1912.

Meyer, Elard Hugo, *Mythologie der Germanen.* Strasburg, 1903.
  Germanische Mythologie. Berlin, 1891.
  Art. " Astarte," in W. H. Roscher, *Ausfürliches Lexikon der griechischen
    und römischen Mythologie.* Vol. i. Leipzig, 1886.
Meyer, G., " Die Karier ; ein ethnographisch-linguistische Untersuchung,"
    Beiträge zur Kunde der indogermanischen Sprachen. Vol. x. Göt-
    tingen, 1886.
Meyer, Hans, " Die Igorrotes von Luzon (Philippinen)," *Verhandlungen
    der Berliner Gesellschaft für Anthropologie.* Berlin, 1883.
Meyer, Kuno, " The Edinburgh Gaelic Manuscript xl," *The Celtic Review.*
    Vol. xii. Inverness, 1887.
  The Death-Tales of the Ulster Heroes. (*Royal Irish Academy : Todd
    Lectures Series.*) Vol. xiv. Dublin, 1906.
  " Aithed Emere le Tuir n-Glesta mac rig Lochaine," *Revue Celtique.*
    Vol. vi. Paris, 1877.
  " Irish Miscellanies," *Revue Celtique.* Vol. vi. Paris, 1885.
  and A. Nutt, *The Voyage of Bran.* 2 vols. London, 1895–97.
Meyer, Otto, " Mythen und Erzählungen von der Insel Vuatom (Bismark-
    Archipel, Südsee)," *Anthropos.* Vol. v. Wien, 1910.
Meyer, Paul, " Notice sur deux anciens manuscrits français ayant appartenu
    au marquis de la Clayette (Bibliothèque Nationale, Moreau, 1715,
    1719)," *Notices et Extraits des Manuscrits de la Bibliothèque Nationale
    et autres Bibliothèques.* Paris, 1890.
  " Des rapports de la poésie des trouvères avec celle des troubadours,"
    Romania. Vol. xix. Paris, 1890.
  " Mélanges de poésie anglo-normande," *Romania.* Vol. iv. Paris, 1875.
Meyers Konversations-Lexikon. 19 vols. Leipzig, 1893–99.
Meyners d'Estrey, C., *La Papouaisie ou Nouvelle-Guinée occidentale.* Rotter-
    dam, 1881.
  " Les Nouvelles Hébrides," *Annales de l'Extrème Orient.* Vol. i. Paris,
    1879.
  " Moeurs des Arfda," *Annales de l'Extrème Orient.* Vol. i. Paris,
    1879.
Mian Durga Singh, " A Report on the Panjab Hill Tribes," *The Indian
    Antiquary.* Vol. xxxvi. Bombay, 1907.
Michel, Charles, *Recueil d'inscriptions grecques.* Bruxelles, 1900.
Michel, Francisque, *Chroniques Anglo-Normandes.* 3 vols. Rouen, 1836–40.
Michel, George Babington, " The Berbers," *Journal of the African Society.*
    Vol. ii. London, 1903.
Michelet, Jules, *Origines du droit français.* Paris, 1898.
Middendorff, A.Th. von, *Reise in den äussersten Norden und Osten Sibiriens.*
    4 vols. St. Petersburg, 1856–75.
Midrash (*Leviticus*).—*Der Midrasch Wajikra Rabba.* Transl. by A.
    Wünsche. Leipzig, 1884.
Mielberg, K., " Eine Exkursion nach Chiwa und Audienz beim Chan,"
    Russische Revue. Vol. xvi. St. Petersburg, 1880.
Mielziner, M., *The Jewish Law of Marriage and Divorce in Ancient and
    Modern Times.* Cincinnati, 1884.
Miesen, W. van der, " Eeen en ander over Boeroe," *Mededeelingen van wege
    het Nederlandsche Zendelinggenootschap.* Vol. xlvi. Rotterdam, 1902.
Migeod, F. W. H., " A Talk with some Gaboon Pygmies," *Man.* Vol. xxii.
    London, 1922.
Migne, J. P., *Encyclopédie théologique.* 168 vols. Paris, 1844–66.
  Patrologiae Cursus completus ; Series Latina. 221 vols. Parisiis, 1844–55.
  Series Greaeca. 162 vols. Parisiis, 1856–66.

Mikhailovskii, V. M., "Shamanism in Siberia and European Russia."
  Trans., *Journal of the Anthropological Institute*. Vol. xxiv. London,
  1895.
Miklucho-Maclay, N. von, "Ethnological Excursions in the Malay Peninsula,"
  Journal of the Straits Branch of the Royal Asiatic Society. Vol. i.
  Singapore, 1878.
"Anthropologische Bemerkungen ueber die Papuas der Maclay-Küste
  in Neu-Guinea," *Natuurkundig Tijdschrift voor Nederlandsch Indië*.
  Vol. xxxiii. Batavia, 's Gravenhage, 1873.
"Über die künstliche Perforatio Penis bei den Dajaks auf Borneo,"
  Verhandlungen der Berliner Gesellschaft für Anthropologie. Berlin, 1876.
"Über die Mika-Operation in Central Australien, "*ibid*. Berlin, 1880.
Millais, J. G., *Mammals of Great Britain and Ireland*. 3 vols. London,
  1904–6.
Miller, Edward Y., *The Bataks of Palawan*. Manila, 1905.
Milligan, Joseph, *Vocabulary of the dialects of some Aboriginal Tribes of
  Tasmania*. Hobart Town, 1866.
Millin de Grandmaison, A., *Voyage dans les départements du midi de la France*.
  4 vols. Paris, 1807–11.
Millington, W. H., and Maxfield, B. L., "Philippine (Tagalog) Superstitions,"
  Journal of American Folk-Lore. Vol. xix. New York, 1906.
Millot Jacques, "Signification biologique de l'argenture des poissons,"
  Bulletin de la Société de Zoologie. Vol. xlvii. Paris, 1922.
Milloué L. de, *Catalogue du Musée Guimet. Première partie. Inde, Chine
  et Japon*. Lyon, 1883.
Milne, Mrs. Leslie, *Shans at Home*. London, 1910.
Milne, William C., *Life in China*. London, 1858.
Milton, John, *Poetical Works*. Oxford, 1900.
Mind. London, 1876–
Mindeleff, Cosmos, "Aboriginal Remains in Verde Valley, Arizona,"
  Thirteenth Annual Report of the Bureau of Ethnology. Washington, 1896.
Minns, Ellis H., *Scythians and Greeks*. Cambridge, 1913.
Minot, Charles S., *The Problem of Age, Growth, and Death*. London, 1908.
*Minutes of Evidence taken before the Royal Commission on the Blind, the Deaf
  and Dumb*, etc. 3 vols. London, 1889.
Les Miracles de Notre Dame par personnages. 8 vols. Paris, 1876–93.
Miracula S. Benedicti, in M. Bouquet, *Recueil des historiens des Gaules et
  de la France*. Vol. xi. Paris, 1767.
Mishna.—Eighteen Treatises from the Mishna. Transl. by D. A. De Sola
  and M. J. Raphall. London, 1843.
Mismer, Ch., *Souvenirs de la Martinique et du Mexique pendant l'intervention
  française*. Paris, 1890.
Mission, Maximilien, *Nouveau voyage en Italie*. 2 vols. La Haye, 1702.
The Missionary Register. London, 1813–
Les Missions Catholiques, Bulletins hebdomadaires. Lyon, 1868–
Mitchell, Arthur, "Blood-Relationship in Marriage considered in its Influence
  upon the Offspring," *Memoirs read before the Anthropological Society
  of London*. Vol. ii. London, 1866.
  in *Edinburgh Medical Journal*. Edinburgh, 1865.
Mitchell, P. Chalmers, *The Childhood of Animals*. London, 1912.
Mitchell, Sir Thomas L., *Three Expeditions into the Interior of Eastern
  Australia*. 2 vols. London, 1839.
Mitteis, Ludwig, *Reichsrecht und Volksrecht in den östlichen Provinzen des
  römischen Kaiserreichs*. Leipzig, 1891.
Mitteilungen aus dem Deutschen Schutzgebieten. Berlin, 1907–

Mitteilungen der Vorderasiatische Gesellschaft. Berlin, 1896–

Mittheilungen aus der zoologischen Station zu Neapel. Berlin, Naples, Leipzig, 1879–

Mittheilungen der anthropologischen Gesellschaft in Wien. Wien, 1871–

Mittheilungen der Deutschen Archaeologischen Institut, Athenische Abtheilung. Athens, 1876–

Mittheilungen der kaiserlich-königliche geographische Gesellschaft. Wien, 1857–

Mittheilungen der deutschen Gesellschaft für Natur- und Völkerkunde Ostasiens. Yokohama, 1873–

Mittheilungen der geographischen Gesellschaft (für Thuringen) zu Jena. Jena, 1882–

Mittheilungen der geographischen Gesellschaft zu Hamburg. Hamburg, 1878–

Mittheilungen des Seminars für orientalische Sprachen. Berlin, Stuttgart, 1898–

Mivart, St George, *Dogs, Jackals, Wolves, Foxes ; a Monograph of the Canidae.* London, 1890.

Mnemosyne. Tijdschrift voor classieke Litteratuur. Leyden, 1852–

Mockler-Ferryman, A. F., *British Nigeria.* London, 1902.

Modera, J., *Verhaal van eene reize naar en langs de zuidwest-kust van Nieuw Guinea in 1828.* Haarlem, 1830.

Modern Philology. Chicago, 1904–

Modi, Jivanji Jamshedji, *Marriage Customs of the Parsees.* Bombay, 1900.

Modigliani, Elio, *Un Viaggio a Nias.* Milano, 1890.

   L'Isola delle Donne, Viaggio ad Engano. Milano, 1894.

Modio, Gian Battista, *Il Convito.* Rome, 1554.

Moerenhout, J. A., *Voyages aux îles du Grand Océan.* 2 vols. Paris, 1837.

Moffat, Robert, *Missionary Labours and Scenes in South Africa.* London, 1846.

Moggridge, L. T., " The Nyassaland Tribes, their Customs and Poison Ordeal," *Journal of the Anthropological Institute.* Vol. xxxii. London, 1902.

Mogk, E., Review of Finnur Jónsson, " Den oldnorske og oldislandscke litteraturs historie " (Kóbenhavn, 1893–94), *Arkiv för Nordisk Filologi.* Vol. xii. Lund, 1896.

   " Mythologie," in H. Paul, *Grundriss der germanischen Philologie.* Vol. iii. Strasburg, 1893.

Mohl, Jules, " Extraits du Modjmel al-Tawarikh relatifs a l'histoire de la Perse," *Journal Asiatique.* 3ᵉ Série, vol. xii. Paris, 1841.

Mohnike, O., " Die Affen auf die indischen Inseln," *Das Ausland.* Vol. xlv. Augsburg, 1872.

Mökern, Ph. van, *Ostindien.* 2 vols. Leipzig, 1857.

Molina, Christobal de, *An Account of the Fables and Rites of the Yncas.* Trans. in Sir Clements R. Markham, *Narratives of the Rites and Laws of the Yncas.* London, 1873.

Molina, J. J., *The Geographical, Natural, and Civil History of Chili.* Transl. 2 vols. London, 1809.

Moll, A., *The Sexual Life of the Child.* London, 1912.

Mollendorff, P. G. von, " The Family Law of the Chinese in its comparative Relation with that of other Nations," *Journal of the North-China Branch of the Royal Asiatic Society.* N.S., No. 13. Shanghai, 1879.

Moloni, J. Chartres, " Madras," *Census of India, 1911.* Vol. xii, Part i. Madras, 1912.

De Moluccis Insulis. Transl. in E. H. Blair and J. A. Robertson, *The Philippine Islands, 1493–1803.* Vol. i. Cleveland, 1903.

Mommsen, Th., *Die unteritalischen Dialekte.* Leipzig, 1850.

   Römische Forschungen. 2 vols. Berlin, 1864–79.

Mommsen, Th., *Abriss des römische Staatsrecht.* Leipzig, 1893.

Monaci, E., " Da Bologna a Palermo," in L. Morandi, *Antologia della nostra critica letteraria moderna.* Città di Castello, 1893.

Monakow, C. von, *Die Lokalisation in Grosshirn und Abbau der Functionen durch korticale Herde.* Wiesbaden, 1914.

Monatsbericht über die Verhandlungen der Gesellschaft für Erdkunde zu Berlin. Neue Folge. Berlin, 1840–

Monatschrift für Ohrenheilkunde, sovie für Kehlkopf-, Nasen-, Rache-Krankheiten. Berlin, 1867–

Monatschrift für Psychiatrie und Neurologie. Berlin, 1897–

Monboddo, James Burnet, Lord, *On the History and Progress of Languages.* 6 vols. Edinburgh, 1773–92.

Antient Metaphysics. 6 vols. London, 1784–

Moncelon, Léon, " Réponse alinéa par alinéa, pour les Néo-Calédoniens, au Questionnaire de Sociologie et d'Ethnographie de la Société," *Bulletin de la Société d'Anthropologie de Paris.* Ser. iii, vol. ix. Paris, 1886.

Monckton, Whitmore, " Some Recollections of New Guinea Customs," *Journal of the Polynesian Society.* Vol. v. Wellington, 1896.

Monfat, A., *Les Tonga, ou Archipel des Amis.* Lyon, 1893.

Le missionnaire des Samoa, Mgr. L. Elloy. Lyon, 1890.

Dix années en Mélanésie. Lyon, 1891.

Monier-Williams, Sir M., *Sanskrit-English Dictionary.* Oxford, 1899.

Indian Epic Poetry. London, 1873.

Brahmanism and Hinduism. London, 1887.

The Monist. Chicago, 1890–

Monk of St. Gall, *De gestis Karoli imperatoris,* in *Monumenta Germaniae Historica, Scriptores.* Vol. ii. Hannoverii, 1828.

Monmerqué, L. J. N., and Michel, Francisque, *Théatre français au moyen-âge.* Paris, 1842.

Monnier, D., *Traditions populaires comparées,* etc. Paris, 1854.

and Vigtriner, *Croyances et traditions populaires recueillies dans la Franche-Comté, le Lyonnais, la Bresse, et le Bugey.* Lyon, 1874.

Monrad, H. E., *Gemälde der Küste von Guinea und der Einwöhner derselber.* Weimar, 1824.

Montagu, Lady Mary Wortley, *Letters and Works.* 2 vols. London, 1887.

Montaigne, Michael, Lord of, *Essays,* Florio's translation. 3 vols. London, 1908.

Montanhagol. See Coulet, J.

Montanus (W. von Waldbruehl), *Die deutschen Volksfeste, Volksbräuche und deutscher Volksglaube.* Iserlohn and Elberfeld [1854].

Monteil, C., *Les Khassonké. Monographie d'une peuplade du Soudan français.* Paris, 1915.

Monteiro, J. J., *Angola and the River Congo.* 2 vols. London, 1875.

Monteiro, Rose, *Delagoa Bay, its Natives and Natural History.* London, 1891.

Montelius, Osc., *Les temps préhistoriques en Suède.* Transl. Paris, 1895.

Montfaucon, Bernard de, *L'Antiquité expliquée.* 5 vols. Paris, 1722.

Montgomery, J., *Journal of Voyages and Travels by the Rev. Daniel Tyerman and George Bennet, Esq. . . . in the South Sea Islands.* 2 vols. London, 1831.

Monthly Journal of Medical Science. London, Edinburgh, 1845–

Montiton, R. P. Albert, " Les Paumotou," *Les Missions Catholiques.* Vol. vi. Lyon, 1874.

Montoto, Luis, " Costumbres populares Andaluzas," *Biblioteca de las Tradiciones populares Españolas.* Vol. i. Sevilla, 1883.

Monumenta Germaniae Historica. Ed. by G. H. Pertz, Th. Mommsen, and others. Hanover, Berlin, 1826–

Monumenta Hebraica. Wien, Leipzig, 1913–

Monumenti Antichi Inediti. Roma, 1784–

Monumenti Antichi pubblicati per cura della Reale Accademia dei Lincei. Milano, 1890–

Mooney, Jas., "The Calendar History of the Kiowa," *Seventeenth Annual Report of the Bureau of Ethnology.* Part i. Washington, 1898.

"The Sacred Formulas of the Cherokees," *Seventh Annual Report of the Bureau of Ethnology.* Washington, 1891.

"The Ghost-Dance Religion and the Sioux Outbreak of 1890," *Fourteenth Annual Report of the Bureau of Ethnology.* Washington. 1896.

"Myths of the Cherokees," *Nineteenth Annual Report of the Bureau of American Ethnology.* Washington, 1900.

"The Cheyenne Indians," *Memoirs of the American Anthropological Association.* Vol. i, Part vi. Lancaster, 1907.

"The Jicarilla Genesis," *The American Anthropologist.* Vol. xi. Washington, 1898.

Moorcroft, William, and Trebeck, George, *Travels in the Himalayan Provinces of Hindustan and the Panjab.* 2 vols. London, 1841.

Moore, A. W., *The Folk-lore of the Isle of Man.* London, 1891.

Moore, George Fletcher, *A Descriptive Vocabulary of the Language in common use amongst the Aborigines of Western Australia.* London, 1842.

Moore, Lewis, *Malabar Law and Custom.* Madras, 1905.

Moore, T., *Marriage Customs, Modes of Courtship, and Singular Propensities of the Various Nations of the Universe.* London, 1814.

Moraes, A. I. de Mello, *Corographia historica, etc. . . . . do Imperio do Brasil.* 4 vols. Rio de Janeiro, 1858.

Morandi, Luigi, *Antologia della nostra critica letteraria moderna.* Città di Castello, 1893.

Mordtmann, J. H., *Beiträge zur Minaischen Epigraphik.* Leipzig, 1897.

Morelet, Arthur, *Voyage dans l'Amérique centrale, l'isle de Cuba et le Yucatan.* 2 vols. Paris, 1857.

Moreno, F. P., *Viaje á la Patagonia austral.* Buenos Aires, 1879.

Moret, A., *Mystères égyptiens.* Paris, 1913.

Morga, Antonio de, *The Philippine Islands, Moluccas, Siam, Cambodia, Japan, and China at the close of the Sixteenth Century.* Transl. by H. E. Stanley. London, 1868.

Sucesos de las Islas Filipinas, in E. H. Blair and J. A. Robertson, *The Philippine Islands, 1493–1898.* Vol. xvi. Cleveland, 1904.

Morgan, C. Lloyd, *Habit and Instinct.* London, 1896.

Introduction to Comparative Psychology. London, 1894.

Morgan, John, *The Life and Adventures of William Buckley, thirty-two years a wanderer amongst the Aborigines of the unexplored country round Port Phillip.* Hobart, 1852.

Morgan, Lewis Henry, *Ancient Society.* London, 1877.

The American Beaver and his Works. Philadelphia, 1868.

League of the Ho-de-no-sau-nee, or Iroquois. Rochester, 1851.

Houses and House-life of the American Aborigines (Contributions to North American Ethnology). Vol. iv. Washington, 1881.

Systems of Consanguinity and Affinity of the Human Family (Smithsonian Contributions to Knowledge. Vol. xvii). Washington, 1871.

Morice, A. G., "The Western Dénés, their Manners and Customs," *Proceedings of the Canadian Institute.* Series iii, vol. vii. Toronto, 1890.

Morice, A. G., " The Great Déné Race," *Anthropos*. Vols. i-v. Salzburg, 1906–10.

" La Femme chez les Dénés," *Congrès international des Américanistes. XVe Session*. Vol. i. Quebec, 1907.

Art. "Déné," in Hastings's, *Encyclopaedia of Religion and Ethics*. Vol. iv. Edinburgh, 1911.

The History of the Northern Interior of British Columbia, formerly New Caledonia. Toronto, 1904.

Morill, James, *Sketch of a Residence among the Aborigines of Northern Queensland, for seventeen years*. Boston, 1864.

Morris, Margaretta (Mrs. Samuel Bryan Scott), " The Influence of War and of Agriculture upon the Religion of the Karyan and Sea-Dyaks of Borneo," *Journal of the American Oriental Society*. Vol. xxv. New Haven, Conn., 1904.

" Harvest Festivals of the Land Dyaks," *ibid*. Vol. xxix. New Haven, Conn., 1909.

Morse, Jedidah, *A Report to the Secretary of War of the United States on Indian Affairs*. New Haven, 1822.

Morshead, A. E. M. A., *History of the Universities Mission to Central Africa, 1859–96*. London, 1897.

La mort de Garin le Loherain. Ed. Edelstand Du Meril. Paris, 1846.

Mortillet, G. de, *Le signe de la croix avant le Christianisme*. Paris, 1866.

Mortimer, Geoffrey, *Chapters on Human Love*. London, 1898.

Moryson, Fynes, *Travels*. London, 1617.

Moscatelli, A., *La Condizione della donna nelle società primitive e nell' antico diritto romano*. Bologna, 1886.

Moseley, H. N., " On the Inhabitants of the Admiralty Islands, etc.," *Journal of the Anthropological Institute*. Vol. vi. London, 1877.

Moses of Choren, *Historiae Armenicae Libri III*. Ed. Gugl and Georg Whiston. London, 1736.

Moss, F. J., " The Maori Polity in the Island of Raratonga," *Journal of the Polynesian Society*. Vol. iii. Wellington, 1894.

Mosso, Angelo, *La paura*. Milano, 1901.

Le Origini della Civiltà Mediterranea. Milano, 1912.

Escursioni nel Mediterraneo e gli scavi di Creta. Milano, 1910.

Moszkowski, M., " Bei den letzten Weddas," *Globus*. Vol. xciv. Braunschweig, 1908.

" The Pagan Races of East Sumatra," *Journal of the Royal Asiatic Society*. London, 1909.

Auf neuen Wegen durch Sumatra. Berlin, 1909.

" Die Volkerstämme am Mamberamo in Holländisch-Neuguinea und auf den vorgelagerten Inseln," *Zeitschrift für Ethnologie*. Vol. xliii. Berlin, 1911.

" Über zwei nicht-malayische Stämme von Ost-Sumatra," *Zeitschrift für Ethnologie*. Vol. xl. Berlin, 1908.

Mott, Sir Frederick W., *Nature and Nurture*. London, 1914.

" The Progressive Evolution of the Structure and Functions of the Visual Cortex in Mammalia," *Archives of Neurology from the Pathological Laboratory of the London County Asylums*. Vol. iii. Claybury, London, 1901.

Motte, T., " Narrative of a Journey to the Diamond Mines at Sumbhulpoor," *The Asiatic Annual Register*. London, 1799.

Mouat, F. J., " Narrative of an Expedition to the Andaman Islands in 1857," *Journal of the Royal Geographical Society*. Vol. xxxii. London, 1862.

Moudgah d'Ohsson, *Tableau général de l'Empire Othoman.* 3 vols. Paris, 1788.

Mouhot, Henry, "Voyage dans les royaumes de Siam, de Cambodge, de Laos," etc., *Le Tour du Monde.* Paris, 1863.

Mouliéras, A., *Le Maroc inconnu.* 2 vols. Paris, 1899.
Une tribu Zénète anti-musulmane au Maroc. Les Zkara. Paris, 1905.

Moulton, J. H., *Early Religious Poetry of Persia.* Cambridge, 1911.
Early Zoroastrianism. London, 1913.

Moura, J., *Le Royaume du Cambodge.* 2 vols. Paris, 1883.

Moura-Para, Ignacio Baptista de, "Sur le progrès de l'Amazonie et sur les Indiens," *Verhandlungen des XVI Internationales Amerikanisten Kongress, Wien, 1908.* Vol. ii. Wien, Leipzig, 1910.

Movers, F. C., *Die Phönizier.* 3 vols. Bonn, 1841.

Mowry, Sylvester, "Report to the Commissioner on Indian Affairs," *Executive Documents printed by Order of the House of Representatives, First Session of the 35th Congress, 1857–58.* Washington, 1858.

Much, M., *Die Trubspielung orientalische Kultur in den vorgeschichtliche Zeitalterns Nord- und Mittel-Europas.* Jena, 1907.

Muir, John, "On the Question whether Polyandry ever existed in Northern Hindustan," *The Indian Antiquary.* Vol. vi. Bombay, 1877.
Original Sanskrit Texts. 5 vols. London, 1868–84.

Muir, Sir William, *The Life of Mahomet.* London, 1894.

Müllenhoff, K. von, *Beovulf. Untersuchungen über das angelsächsische Epos.* Berlin, 1889.
Deutsche Altertumskunde. 5 vols. Berlin, 1883–1900.

Müller, Dr., "Essai sur la langue pehlvie," *Journal Asiatique.* 3e Série, vol. vii. Paris, 1839.

Müller, Carl Otfried, *The History and Antiquities of the Doric Race.* Transl. 2 vols. London, 1839.
Die Etrusker, neu bearbeitet von W. Deecke. 2 vols. Stuttgart, 1877.
Denkmäler der alten Kunst. Göttingen, 1854.

Müller, F., "Die Religionen Togos in Einzeldarstellungen," *Anthropos.* Vol. ii. Salzburg, 1907.

Müller, F. A., *Der Islam im Morgen und Abendland* (in W. Oncken, *Allgemeine Geschichte in Einzeldarstellungen*). 2 vols. Berlin, 1885–87.

Müller, Friederich, in *Reise der österreichischen Fregatte Novara um die Welt. Anthropologischer Theil.* Vol. iii. Ethnologie. Wien, 1869.

Müller, Friederich Max, *Lectures on the Science of Language.* London, 1871.
Biographies of Words and the Home of the Aryas. London, 1888.
Introduction to the Science of Religion. London, 1882.

Müller, H. D., *Mythologie der griechischen Stämme.* 2 vols. Göttingen, 1857–61.

Müller, J. G., *Geschichte der Amerikanischen Urreligionen.* Basel, 1855.

Müller, P. Fr., "Fetischistisches aus Atakpane (Deutsch-Togo)," *Globus.* Vol. lxxxi. Braunschweig, 1902.

Müller, Robert, *Sexualbiologie.* Berlin, 1907.

Müller, Salomon, *Reizen en onderzoekingen in den Indischen Archipel.* Amsterdam, 1857.

Müller, Sophus, "Det store solukar fra Gundestrup i Jylland," *Nordiske Fortidsminder.* Heft ii. Kjøbenhaven, 1892.

Müller, W. Max, *Die Liebespoesie der alten Ägypter.* Leipzig, 1899.
Asien und Europa nach altaegyptischen Denkmälern. Leipzig, 1893.

Mundy, R., *Narrative of Events in Borneo and Celebes down to the occupation of Labuan ; from the Journals of James Brooke.* 2 vols. London, 1848.

Munkácsi, Bernhard, " Die Weltgottheiten der wogulischen Mythologie,"
    Keleti Szemle. Vols. viii, ix, x. Budapest, 1907-9.
Munro, J. Arthur R., " Inscriptions from Mysia," *The Journal of Hellenic
    Studies*. Vol. xvii. London, 1897.
Munro, Robert, *The Lake-Dwellings of Europe*. London, 1890.
Munzinger, W., *Ostafrikanische Studien*. Schaffhausen, 1864.
    Ueber die Sitten und das Recht der Bogos. Winterthur, 1859.
Murad Efendi (Franz von Werner), *Turkische Skizzen*. 2 vols. Leipzig,
    1878.
Muratori, L. A., *Rerum Italicarum Scriptores*. 25 vols. Mediolani, 1723-51.
    Antiquitates Italicae medii aevi. 6 vols. Mediolani, 1738-42.
Murdoch, John, " Ethnological Results of the Point Barrow Expedition,"
    Ninth Annual Report of the Bureau of Ethnology. Washington, 1892.
Murray, C. A., *Travels in North America during the years 1834, 1835 and
    1836*. 2 vols. London, 1839.
Murray, Gilbert, *The Rise of the Greek Epic*. Oxford, 1911.
Murray, G. W., " Marriage Ceremonial of the Barabra," *Man*. Vol. xvii.
    London, 1917.
    " The Ababda," *Journal of the Royal Anthropological Institute*. Vol. liii.
    London, 1923.
Murray, James A. H., *A New English Dictionary on Historical Principles*.
    10 vols. Oxford, 1888-1920.
Murray, J. H. P., in *Annual Report for New Guinea, 1921-22*. Brisbane,
    1922.
Murray, Margaret, " Priesthoods of Women in Egypt," *Transactions of the
    Third International Congress for the History of Religions*. Vol. i.
    Oxford, 1908.
    The Osiirion at Abydos (*Egypt Research Account, Ninth Year, 1903*).
    London, 1904.
    " Child-sacrifice among European Witches," *Man*. Vol. xviii. London,
    1918.
    " Witches and Fertility," *Man*. Vol. xix. London, 1919.
    The Witch-Cult in Western Europe. A Study in Anthropology. Oxford,
    1921.
Murtadha Ibn Al-Khafil, *L'Égypte de Murtadi, fils du Gaphile*. Transl. by
    P. Wattier. Paris, 1666.
Musters, G. C., *At Home with the Patagonians*. London, 1873.
    " On the Races of Patagonia," *Journal of the Anthropological Institute*.
    Vol. i. London, 1872.
Mygge, Johannes, *Om Ægteskaber mellem Blodbeslaegtede, met specielt Hensyn
    til deres Betydning foe Dovstumhedens Ætiologi*. Kjøbenhavn, 1879.
Mygind, Holger, *Deaf-Mutism*. London, 1894.
Myres, J. L., " Notes on the History of the Kabyle Pottery," *Journal of the
    Anthropological Institute*. Vol. xxxii. London, 1902.
    " A History of the Pelasgian Theory," *The Journal of Hellenic Studies*.
    Vol. xxvii. London, 1907.
Mythographi Latini. Ed. Thomas Munckerus. Amsterlodami, 1681.

N. . . ., M. A. M., " Lettre écrite de Chalons en Champagne, le 9 décembre
    1731, par M. A. M. N. . . ., au sujet de la fille sauvage trouvée aux
    environs de cette ville," *Le Mercure de France*. Paris, 1731.
Nachrichten über Kaiser Wilhelms-Land und den Bismarck-Archipel. Berlin,
    1886-

Nachrichten von der Königlichen Gesellschaft der Wissenschaften und der Georg-Augusts-Universität zu Göttingen. Göttingen, 1845–

Nachtigal, G., *Sahara und Sudan.* 3 vols. Berlin, 1879–89.

" Die Tibbu," *Zeitschrift für Erdkunde zu Berlin.* Vol. v. Berlin, 1870.

Nafzawi, *Le Jardin parfumé du Cheikh Nefzaoui.* Paris, 1912.

Nagam Aiya, V., *The Travancore State Manual.* 3 vols. Trivandrum, 1906.

Nanjundayya, H. V., *The Ethnographical Survey of Mysore.* Bangalore, 1906.

Nansen, F., *Eskimo Life.* London, 1894.

Eskimoleben. Berlin, 1903.

The First Crossing of Greenland. 2 vols. London, 1890.

Napier, James, *Folk-lore : Beliefs in the West of Scotland.* Paisley, 1879.

Nassau, R. H., *Fetichism in West Africa.* London, 1904.

Natesa Sastri, S. M., *Hindu Feasts, Fasts, and Ceremonies.* Madras, 1903.

The Natives of South Africa, their Economic and Social Condition. Ed. by the South African Native Races Committee. London, 1901.

The Natural History Review. Dublin, London, 1854–

Nature. London, 1870–

Natuurkundig Tijdschrift voor Nederlandsch Indië. Batavia, 's Gravenhage, 1850–

Nauhaus, C. T., " Familienleben, Heiratsgebräuche und Erbrecht der Kaffern," *Verhandlungen der Berliner Gesellschaft für Anthropologie.* Berlin, 1882.

Navagero, A., *Il viaggio fatto in Spagna et in Francia dal Magnifico M. Andrea Navagiero.* Venetia, 1563.

Navarrete, D. Fernandes, " An Account of the Empire of China," in A. J. Churchill, *A Collection of Voyages and Travels.* Vol. i. London, 1704.

Navarrete, Martin Fernandez de, *Coleccion de los viages y descubrimientos que hiciero por mar los Españoles.* 5 vols. Madrid, 1825–37.

Naville, Edouard, *Textes relatifs au mythe d'Horus recueillis dans le temple d'Edfou.* Geneva, Bale, 1870.

The XIth Dynasty Temple at Deir El-Bahari (Memoirs of the Egypt Exploration Fund, No. 28). London, 1907.

Nayer, K. Kannan, " The Matrimonial Customs of the Nayars," *The Malabar Quarterly Review.* Vol. vii. Trivandrum, 1908.

Neill, Edward D., " Dakota Land and Dakota Life," *Collections of the Minnesota Historical Society.* Vol. i. St. Paul, 1872.

" Memoir of the Sioux : a Manuscript in the French Archives, now for the first time published," *Macalister College Contributions : Department of History, Literature and Political Science,* No. 5. St. Paul, Minnesota, 1890.

Nelson, E. W., " The Eskimo about Bering Strait," *Eighteenth Annual Report of the Bureau of Ethnology.* Washington, 1899.

Nennius, *Historia Britonum.* Ed. J. Stevenson. London, 1838.

The same, in Pertz, *Monumenta Germaniae Historica, Chronica minora.* Vol. iii. Berlin, 1898.

Nepos, Cornelius, *Vitae excellentium imperatorum.* Amsterlodami, 1707.

Netto, C., and Wagner, G., *Japanischer Humor.* Leipzig, 1901.

Netto, Ladislau, " Invetigaçoes sobre a archeologia Brazileira," *Archivos do Museu Nacional de Rio de Janeiro.* Vol. vi. Rio de Janeiro, 1885.

Neue Jahrbücher für das klassische Altertum. Leipzig, 1898–

Neuhauss, R., *Deutsch Neu-Guinea.* 3 vols. Berlin, 1911.

Neumann, J. B., " Het Pane– en Bila-stromgebied op het eiland Sumatra," *Tijdschrift van het Nederlandsch Aardrijkskundig Genootschap.* 2ᵉ Serie, vol. iii. Amsterdam, 1886.

Neustadt, E., *De Iove Cretico.* Berlin, 1906.

Nevill, Hugh, "The Vaeddas," *The Taprobanian*. Vol. i. Bombay, 1887.

Newberry, Percy E., *Beni Hasan*. (*Memoirs of the Archaeological Survey of Egypt ; Egypt Exploration Fund.*) London, 1890.

— and Garstang, John, *A Short History of Ancient Egypt*. London, 1907.

Newbold, T. J., *Political and Statistical Account of the British Settlements in the Straits of Malacca*. 2 vols. London, 1839.

Newland, S., "The Parkengees, or Aboriginal Tribes on the Darling River," *Proceedings of the Royal Geographical Society of Australasia, South Australian Branch*. Vol. ii. Adelaide, 1890.

Newton, A., *A Dictionary of Birds*. London, 1893–96.

Der Nibelungenlied. Ed. K. Bartsch. Leipzig, 1875.

Nibelunge Not. Ed. K. Bartsch. 3 vols. Leipzig, 1870–80.

Nicander, in *Poetae bucolici et didactici*. Ed. F. S. Lehrs. Parisiis, 1846.

Nicholas of Damascus, *Fragmenta*, in *Fragmenta Historicorum Graecorum*. Ed. C. Müller. Vol. iii. Parisiis, 1849.

Nicholas, F. C., "The Aborigines of the Province of Santa Marta, Colombia," *The American Anthropologist*. N.S., vol. iii. New York, 1901.

Nicholas, John Liddiard, *Narrative of a Voyage to New Zealand, performed in the Years 1814 and 1815*. 2 vols. London, 1817.

Nicholson, Reynold A., *A Literary History of the Arabs*. London, 1914.

Nicole, "Die Diakite-sarakolesen im Kreise Kita, westlicher Sudan," in S. R. Steinmetz, *Rechtsverhältnisse von eingeborenen Völkern in Afrika und Ozeanien*. Berlin, 1903.

Nicolls, James A., and Eglington, W., *The Sportsman in South Africa*. London, 1892.

Niebhur, C., 'Travels in Arabia," in Pinkerton, *Voyages and Travels*. Vol. x. London, 1811.

Nieboer, H. J., *Slavery as an Industrial System*. The Hague, 1900.

Nielsen, D., *Die altarabische Mondreligion*. Strassburg, 1904.

Nietzold, Gabriel, *Die Ehe in Ägypten zur ptolemäisch-römischen zeit nach den griechischen Heiratskontrakten und verwandten Urkunden*. Leipzig, 1903.

Nietzsche, Friedrich, *Menschliches, allzumenschliches*. (Taschen-Ausgabe.) 2 vols. Leipzig, 1906.

— *Die Geburt der Tragödie*. Leipzig, 1906.

Nieuport, G. H., *Rituum qui olim apud Romanos obtinuerunt succinta explicatio*. Ludg. Batav., 1802.

Nieuw Guinea, ethnographisch en natuurkundig onderzocht en beschreven in 1858 door een Nederlandsch Indische Commissie, uitgegeven door het Koninklijk Institut voor Taal-, Land-, en Volkenkunde van Nederlandsch Indië. Amsterdam, 1862.

Nieuwenhuis, A. W., *In Central Borneo ; Reis van Pontinak naar Samarinda*. 2 vols. Leiden, 1900.

— *Quer durch Borneo*. 2 vols. Leyden, 1904–7.

Nieuwenhuisen, J. T., and Rosenberg, H. C. B. von, "Verslag omtrent het eiland Nias en deszelf bewoners," *Verhandelingen van het Bataviaasch genootschap van Kunsten en Wetenschappen*. Vol. xxx. Batavia, 1863.

Nigmann, E., *Die Wahehe*. Berlin, 1908.

Nigrinum, M. Georgius, *Von Zaübereri, Hexen und Unholden*. Frankfurt a. M., 1592.

Nikander of Colophon, *Alexipharmaca*. Parisiis, 1557.

Nikolski, D., "Ueber die Tschutschen des kolymsker Bezirk," *Moscauer Arbeiten*, i. (in Russian), Moscow, 1900, reviewed by L. Stieda, in *Archiv für Anthropologie*. Vol. xxvii. Braunschweig, 1901.

Nillson, Martin P., *Griechische Feste von religiöser Bedeutung*. Leipzig, 1906.

Nind, Scott, " Description of the Natives of King George's Sound (Swan River Colony) and adjoining Country," *Journal of the Royal Geographical Society*. Vol. i. London, 1832.

Nippon, Archief voor de beschrijving van Japan. Ed. by P. Fr. von Siebold. 7 vols. Leyden, 1832–54.

Nixon, Francis Russell, Bishop of Tasmania, *The Cruise of the " Beacon" : a Narrative of a visit to the Islands in Bass's Straits*. London, 1857.

Nobrega, Manoel da, " Informação das terras de Brasil," *Revista Trimensal de historia e geographia*. Vol. vi. Rio de Janeiro, 1844.

Noel, V., " Île de Madagascar, Recherches sur les Sakkalava," *Bulletin de la Société de Géographie*. Série ii, vol. xx. Paris, 1843.

Nöldeke, Th., *Beiträge zur Kenntniss der Poesie der alten Araber*. Hanover, 1864.

    " Vorstellungen der Araber vom Schicksal," *Zeitschrift für Völkerpsychologie und Sprachwissenschaft*. Vol. iii. Berlin, 1863.

    "Die Schlange nach arabischen Volksglauben," *Zeitschrift für Völkerspsychologie und Sprachenwissenschaft*. Vol. i. Berlin, 1860.

Nordenskiöld, A. E., *Den andra Dicksonska expeditionen till Grönland*. Stockholm, 1910.

    The Voyage of the Vega round Asia and Europe. Transl. 2 vols. London, 1881.

Nordenskiöld, Erland, *Indianerleben*. *El Gran Chaco*. Leipzig, 1912.

Nordenskjöld, Nils O. G., " Algunos datos sobre la parte austral del continente sud-americano segun estudios hechos por la comision cientifica sueca," *Actes de la Société Scientifique du Chili*. Vol. vii. Santiago, 1897.

Nordisk Tidskrift. Stockholm, 1854–

Nordiske Fortidsminder. Kjøbenhavn, 1890–

Nore, Alfred de, *Coutumes, mythes et traditions des provinces de France*. Paris, Lyon, 1846.

Norris, E., " Memoir on the Scythic Version of the Behistun Inscription," *Journal of the Royal Asiatic Society*. Vol. xv. London, 1840.

Norsworthy, Naomi, and Whitley, Mary Theodora, *The Psychology of Childhood*. New York, 1920.

North Indian Notes and Queries. Allahabad, 1891–93.

North, " Puberty Rites of the Basuto," *Report of the Seventh Annual Meeting of the South African Association for the Advancement of Science, Bloemfontein*. Cape Town, 1909.

Northbrook, John, *A Treatise against Dicing, Dancing, Plays and Interludes, with other idle Pastimes* (1577). Reprint. London, 1843.

Northcote, G. A. S., " The Nilotic Kavirondo," *Journal of the Royal Anthropological Institute*. Vol. xxxvii. London, 1907.

Norwood, G., *The Riddle of the " Bacchae."* Manchester, 1908.

Nostredame, Jehan de, *Les vies des plus célèbres et anciens poètes provençaux*. Ed. C. Chabaneau and J. Anglade. Paris, 1913.

Notes and Queries on China and Japan. Hong-Kong, 1867–69.

Notices et extraits des manuscrits de la Bibliothèque Nationale (*du Roi Impériale*). Paris, 1787–

Noticia do Brasil, in *Colleção de Noticias para a historia e Geografia das naçoes ultramarinas que vivem nos dominios Portuguezes*. Vol. iii. Lisboã. 1825.

" Noticia sobre os Indios Tupinambas, sens costumos," etc. (sem nome de autor), *Revista Trimensal do Instituto Historico e Geographico do Brasil*. Vol. i. Rio de Janeiro, 1839.

" Noticias geographicas da Capitania do Rio Negro no Grande Rio Amazonas," *Revista Trimensal de Historia e Geographia.* Vol. x. Rio de
Janeiro, 1870.

Nott, J. F., *Wild Animals Photographed and Described.* London, 1886.

Noury, P., " Les entraves mécaniques à la fonction de reproduction," *La
Chronique médicale.* Vol. xiii. Paris, 1906.

Nouveau dictionnaire d'histoire naturalle, appliquée aux arts. 36 vols. Paris,
1816–19.

Nouvel, Suzanne, *Nomades et sédentaires au Maroc.* Paris, 1919.

Nouvelles Archives d'Obstétrique et de Gynécologie. Paris, 1886–

Nuñez, Alvaro, " Relation," in G. B. Ramusio, *Navigationi et Viaggi.*
Vol. iii. Venetia, 1574.

Nutt, Alfred, " The Aryan Expulsion- and Return Formula in the Folk-
and Hero Tales of the Celts," *The Folk-lore Record.* Vol. iv. London,
1822.

    Studies on the Legends of the Holy Grail. London, 1888.

    " The Lai of Eriduc and the Märchen of Little Snow-White,"
Folk-lore. Vol. iii. London, 1892.

Nynak, L., " Religious Rites and Customs of the Iban, or Dayak of Sarawak," *Anthropos.* Vol i. Salzburg. 1906.

Nyrop, Cristoforo, *Storia dell' epopea francese nel medio evo.* Transl. by
Egidio Gorra. Torino. 1888.

Obersteiner, H., *Anleitung beim Studium des Baues des nervösen Centralorgane
in gesunden und kranken Zustande.* Leipzig, Vienna, 1888.

The Observatory. A Monthly Journal of Astronomy. London, 1877–

Ochenius, Carl, *Chile, Land und Leute.* Leipzig, 1884.

O'Curry, E., *On the Manners and Customs of the Ancient Irish.* 3 vols.
London, Dublin, 1873.

O'Donovan, *The Banquet of Dun Na N-Gedh and the Battle of Mag Rath*
(*Irish Archaeological Society*). Dublin, 1842.

    See *Leabhar na g-Caert.*

Oertzen, von, " Die Banaka und Bapuki," in S. R. Steinmetz, *Rechtsverhältnisse von eingeborenen Völkern in Afrika und Ozeanien.* Berlin,
1903.

O'Ferrall, W., " Native Stories from Santa Cruz," *Journal of the Anthropological Institute.* Vol. xxxiv. London, 1907.

Offord, Joseph, " Ashteroth-Karnaim," *Proceedings of the Society of
Biblical Archaeology.* Vol. xxi. London, 1899.

Ofversigt af Finska Vetenskaps-Societetens Förhandlingar. Helingfors, 1838–

O'Grady, S. H., *Silva Gadelica, a Collection of Tales in Irish.* London and
Edinburgh, 1892.

O'Hallaran, S., *A General History of Ireland from the Earliest Accounts
to the close of the Twelfth Century.* 2 vols. London, 1778.

O'Kearney, Nicholas, " Folk-Lore," *Transactions of the Kilkenny Archaeological Society.* Vol. ii. Dublin, 1855.

Olaus Magnus, *Historia de Gentibus septentrionalibus.* Rome, 1555.

Old and New. Boston, 1870–

Oldenberg, Hermann, *Die Religion des Veda.* Berin, 1894.

    " Der vedische Kalender und das Alter des Veda," *Zeitschrift der deutschen
morgenländischen Gesellschaft.* Vols. xlviii and xlix. Leipzig, 1894–95.

    " On the Antiquity of Vedic Culture," *Journal of the Royal Asiatic
Society.* London, 1909.

Oldendorp, S. G. A., *Geschichte der Mission der evangelischen Brüder auf den caraibischen Inseln S. Thomas, S. Croix und S. Jan.* Brandeburgh. 1777.

Oldfield, A., "On the Aborigines of Australia," *Transactions of the Ethnological Society.* N.S., vol. iii. London, 1865.

Oliveira, J. F. de, "The Cherentes of Brazil," *International Congress of Americanists. Proceedings of the XVIII Session.* London, 1912. Vol. ii. London, 1913.

Oliveira, Jose Joaquim Machado, "Se todos os indigenas do Brasil conhecidos até hoje tinham idéa de una unica divinidade," etc., *Revista Trimensal de historia e geographia.* Vol. vi. Rio de Janeiro, 1865.

O'Malley, L. S. S., "Bengal, Bihar and Orissa and Sikkim." Report. *Census of India, 1911.* Vol. v. Calcutta, 1913.

Oman, John Campbell, *The Brahmans, Theists, and Muslims of India.* London, 1907.
    Cults, Customs, and Superstitions of India. London, 1908.

"On the Weddos," by a Tamil native of Ceylon, *Transactions of the Ethnological Society.* N.S., vol. iii. London, 1864.

Oncken, Wilhelm, ed., *Allgemeine Geschichte in Einzeldarstellungen.* 37 vols. Berlin, 1870–93.

Ondegardo, Polo do, "Report." Transl. by Sir Clements R. Markham in *Narratives of the Rites and Laws of the Yncas.* London, 1873.

Opet, O., *Die erbrechtliche Stellung der Weiber in der Zeit der Volksrechte.* Breslau, 1888.

Oppé, A. P., "The Chasm at Delphi," *Journal of Hellenic Studies.* Vol. xxiv. London, 1904.

Oppenheimer Heinrich, *The Rationale of Punishment.* London, 1913.

Oppert, G., *On the Original Inhabitants of Bharatavarsa or India.* London, 1893.

Oratores Attici. Ed. I. Bekker. 4 vols. Oxford, 1822–23.

Orbigny, A. Dessalines d', *Voyage dans l'Amérique méridionale.* 9 vols. Paris, Strassbourg, 1835–47.
    L'homme américain (de l'Amérique méridionale). 2 vols. Paris, 1839.

Ordericus Vitalis, *Historia ecclesiastica,* in A. Du Chesne, *Historiae Normannorum Scriptores antiqui.* Lutetiae, Paris, 1619.

Ordinaire, Olivier, "Les sauvages du Pérou," *Revue d'Ethnographie.* Vol. vi. Paris, 1887.

Orelli, J. C. von, *Inscriptionum Latinarum selectarum amplissima collectio.* 3 vols. Turici, 1828–56.

Orientalische Studien Theodor Nöldeke zum siebzigsten Geburtstag gewidmet. 2 vols. Gieszen, 1906.

Origen, *Opera omnia.* Ed. C. Delarue. 4 vols. Parisiis, 1733–59.

Origo Gentis Langobardorum, in *Monumenta Germaniae Historica, Scriptores rerum Langobardicarum et Italicarum saec. vi–ix.* Hanover, 1878.

Orioli, Francesco, *Dei sette re di Roma, e del comminciamento del consolato ; Nuove ricerche storiche.* Fiesole, 1839.

Orozco y Berra, Manuel, *Historia antigua y de la conquista de Mexico.* 4 vols. Mexico, 1880.

Orpen, J. M., "A Glimpse into the Mythology of the Maluti Bushmen," *Folk-lore.* Vol. xxx. London, 1919.

Orphica. Ed. by E. Abel. Prague, Leipzig, 1885.

Orsi, Paolo, "Pantellaria," *Monumenti Antichi, Accademia dei Lincei.* Vol. ix. Milano, 1890.

Orton, James, *The Andes and the Amazon.* New York, 1876.

Osiander, E., "Studien über die vorislamische Religion der Araber," *Zeitschrift der deutschen Morgenländische Gesellschaft.* Vol. vii. Leipzig, 1856.

Oslhoff, H., *Etymologische Parerga.* Leipzig, 1901.

Osorius Lusitanus, Hieronymus, Episcopus, *De Rebus Emmanuelis Regis Lusitaniae.* Coloniae, 1576.

Osterhage, G., "Anklänge an die germanische Mythologie in der altfranzösiche Karlssage," *Zeitschrift für Romanische Philologie.* Vol. xi. Halle, 1887.

Ostermann, Leop, "The Navajo Indians of New Mexico and Arizona," *Anthropos.* Vol. iii. Wien, 1908.

O'Sullivan, Hugh, "Dinka Laws and Customs," *Journal of the Royal Anthropological Institute.* Vol. xl. London, 1910.

Ott, O., "Des lois de la périodicité de la fonction physiologique de l'organisme féminin," *Nouvelles Archives d'Obstétrique et de Gynécologie.* Paris, 1890.

Ottoni, Fr. João, "Breve noticia sobre os selvagens Mucury," *Revista Trimensal do Instituto Historico e Geographico Brasilero.* Vol. xxi. Rio de Janeiro, 1858.

Ouffroy de Thoron, E. vicomte de, *La langue primitive depuis Adam jusqu'à Babel ; son passage en Amérique.* Paris, 1886.

Ouseley, Sir William, *Travels in various Countries of the East, more particularly Persia.* 3 vols. London, 1819–23.

Overbeck, J., *Griechische Kunstmythologie.* 4 vols. 1871–89.

Overbergh, Cyr. van, *Les Basonge.* Bruxelles, 1908.

  Les Bangala. Bruxelles, 1908.

  Les Mangbetu. Bruxelles, 1909.

  Les Mayombe. Bruxelles, 1907.

The Overland Monthly. San Francisco. 1865–

Oviedo y Valdes, Gonzalo Hernandez de, *Sumario de la Natural Historia de las Indias (Biblioteca de Autores Españoles.* Vol. xxii). Madrid, 1852.

  The same, trans., in G. B. Ramusio, *Navigationi et Viaggi.* Vol. iii. Venice, 1559.

Owen, Saint, *Vita S. Eligii* (in Luc d'Achery, *Spicilegium.* Vol. v). Parisiis, 1657.

Owen, Mary A., *Folklore of the Musquakie Indians.* London, 1904.

Owen, Sir Richard, "On the Osteology and Dentition of the Aborigines of the Andaman Islands, and the Relations thereby indicated to other Races of Mankind," *Transactions of the Ethnological Society.* Vol. ii. London, 1850.

Owen, W. F. W., *Narrative of Voyages to explore the shores of Africa, Arabia and Madagascar.* 2 vols. London, 1833.

Oyler, D. S., "The Shilluk's Belief in the Evil Eye," *Sudan Notes and Records.* Vol. ii. Khartoum, 1919.

Padfield, J. E., *The Hindu at Home.* Madras, 1896.

Palafox y Mendoza, José, *The History of the Tartars, being an account of their religion, manners and customs, etc.* Transl. London, 1679.

Palgrave, F. T., *History of the Anglo-Saxons.* London, 1887.

Palladius, *De re rustica,* in *Scriptores rei rusticae veteres Latini.* Ed. J. G. Schreiber. Leipzig, 1794–97.

Pallas, P. S., *Reise durch verschiedene Provinzen des russischen Reichs.* 3 vols. Frankfurt, Leipzig, 1776–78.

Pallas, P. S., *Voyages en différentes provinces de l'Empire de Russie et dans l'Asie septentrionale.* 5 vols. Paris, 1788–93.

Travels through the Southern Provinces of the Russian Empire in 1793 and 1794. 2 vols. London, 1812.

Travels into Siberia and Tartary. London, 1788.

Merkwürdigkeiten der obischen Ostjaken, Samojeden, etc. Frankfurt, Leipzig, 1777.

Pallegroix, J. B. *Description du royaume Thaï ou Siam.* 2 vols. Paris, 1854.

Palmer, Edward, " Notes on some Australian Tribes," *Journal of the Anthropological Institute.* Vol. xiii. London, 1884.

Pañcaviṃça Brâhmana. Ed. A. Vedântavâgîça. Calcutta, 1869–74.

Panceri, Paolo. " Lettera a Mantegazza," *Archivio per l'Antropologia e la Etnologia.* Vol. iii. Firenze, 1874.

Panikkar, K. M. " Some Aspects of Nayar Life," *Journal of the Royal Anthropological Institute.* Vol. xlviii. London, 1918.

Panikkar, T. K. Gopal, *Malabar and its Folk.* Madras, 1901.

Papers of the Archaeological Institute of America. American Series. New York, 1881–

Papers from the Tortugas Laboratory of the Carnegie Institute of Washington. Washington, 1908–

Papers on Malay Subjects. Published by the Committee for Malay Studies, Federated Malay States. Kuala Lumpur, 1907–

Papon, J. P., *Histoire générale de Provence.* 4 vols. Paris, 1877–86.

Pargiter, F. E., " Ancient Indian Genealogies and Chronology," *Journal of the Royal Asiatic Society.* London, 1910.

" Sagara and the Haihayas, Vasisthra and Aurva," *Journal of the Royal Asiatic Society.* London, 1919.

Paribeni, R., " Il sarcofago dipinto di Haghia Triada," *Monumenti antichi pubblicati per cura della Reale Accademia dei Lincei.* Vol. xix. Milano, 1908.

" Corni di consecrazione nella prima età del ferro europea," *Bullettino di paletnologia italiana.* Ann. xxx. Parma, 1904.

Paris, Gaston, *Poèmes et légendes du moyen-âge.* Paris, 1900.

" Lancelot du Lac," *Romania.* Vol. xii. Paris, 1883.

Histoire poétique de Charlemagne. Paris, 1865.

" Le conte de la Charette," *Romania.* Vol. xii. 1883.

" Les cours d'amour," *Journal des Savants.* Paris, 1888.

De Pseudo-Turpino. Parisiis, 1865.

Mélanges de littérature française du moyen-âge. Paris, 1912.

Paris, Paulin, *Les romans de la Table Ronde mis en nouveau langage.* 5 vols. Paris, 1868–77.

Park, Mungo, *Travels in the Interior of Africa.* Edinburgh, 1860.

The same, in Pinkerton, *Voyages and Travels.* Vol. xvi. London, 1814.

Parke, T. H., *My Experiences in Equatorial Africa.* London, 1891.

Parker, E. H., " The History of the Wei-Wan, or Wei-Whan Tunguses of the First Century," *The China Review.* Vol. xx. Hong-Kong, 1893.

" Comparative Chinese Family Law," *The China Review.* Vol. viii. Hong-Kong, 1879–80.

Parker, Edward Stone, *The Aborigines of Australia.* Melbourne, 1854.

Parker, Mrs. K. Langloh, *The Euahlayi Tribe.* London, 1905.

Australian Legendary Tales. London, 1896.

Parker, T. Jeffery, and Haswell, William A., *A Text-book of Zoology.* 2 vols. London, 1897.

Parkinson, J., " Note on the Asaba People (Ibos) of the Niger," *Journal of the Anthropological Institute.* Vol. xxxvi. London, 1906.

Parkinson, R., *Dreissig Jahre in der Südsee*. Stuttgart, 1907.

  Im Bismarck-Archipel. Leipzig, 1887.

  " Beiträge zur Ethnologie der Gilbert Insulaner," *Internationales Archiv für Ethnographie*. Vol. ii. Leiden, 1889.

  " Beiträge zur Ethnographie der Matty- und Durour-Inseln (Bismark Archipelago)," *Internationales Archiv für Ethnographie*. Vol. ix. Leiden, 1896.

  " Beiträge zur Kenntniss des deutschen Schutzgebiete der Südsee," *Mittheilungen der geographischen Gesellschaft in Hamburg, 1887–88*. Hamburg, 1888.

  Zur Ethnographie der nordwestlichen Salomo Inseln. (*Abhandlungen und Berichte des königlichen zoologischen und anthropologisch-ethnographischen Museums zu Dresden.* Vol. vii, No. 6.) Berlin, 1899.

Parkman, Francis. *The Jesuits in North America in the Seventeenth Century.* Toronto, 1901.

Parkyns, M., *Life in Abyssinia.* 2 vols. London, 1853.

Le Parnasse occitanien, ou choix de poésies originales des troubadours. Ed. by De Rochegude. Toulouse, 1817.

Παρνασσος, συγγραμμα περιοδικον. ἐν Αθηναις, 1877–

Parodi, E. G., " Le storie di Cesare nella letteratura italiana dei primi secoli," *Studi di Filologia Romanza*. Vol. iv. Roma, 1889.

Parrot, J., " Sur l'origine de l'une des formes du dieu Ptah," *Recueil de travaux relatifs à la philologie et à l'archéologie égyptiennes et assyriennes*. Vol. ii. Paris, 1880.

Parry, H. Oswald, *Six Months in a Syrian Monastery.* London, 1895.

Parry, W. E., *Journal of a Second Voyage for the Discovery of a North-West Passage from the Atlantic to the Pacific.* London, 1824.

Parsons, E. C., " The Reluctant Bridegroom," *Anthropos*. Vol. x–xi. Wien, 1915–16.

Parthey, G. F. C., " Das Orakel und die Oase Ammon," *Abhandlungen der königliche Akademie der Wissenschaften*. Berlin, 1862.

Partington, J. E., " Extracts from the Diary of Dr. Samwell, Surgeon to the ' Discovery,' " *Journal of the Polynesian Society*. Vol. viii. Wellington, 1899.

Partridge, C., *Cross River Natives.* London, 1905.

Pascal, J.-B.-E., *Origines et raison de la liturgie Catholique*, in Migne, *Encyclopédie Théologique*. Vol. viii. Paris, 1844.

Passarge, L., " Die Weltanschaung der Lappen," *Das Ausland*. Stuttgart, 1881.

Passarge, S. *Die Buschimänner der Kalahari.* Berlin, 1907.

Pater, Walter, *Plato and Platonism.* London, 1901.

Patherick, John, *Egypt, the Soudan and Central Africa.* Edinburgh and London, 1861.

Paton, D. N., *The Nervous and Chemical Regulators of Metabolism.* London, 1913.

Paton, Lewis Bayles, art " Ishtar," in Hastings's *Encyclopaedia of Religion and Ethics*. Vol. vii. Edinburgh, 1914.

Paton, Lucy Allen, *Studies in the Fairy Mythology of Arthurian Romances.* (*Radcliffe College Monographs*, No. 13). Boston, 1903.

Paton, W. R., " The φαρμακοι and the Story of the Fall," *Revue Archéologique.* 4ᵉ Série. Vol. ix. Paris, 1907.

  and J. L. Myres, " Karian Sites and Inscriptions," *Journal of Hellenic Studies*. Vol. xvi. London, 1896.

Paturet, G., *La condition juridique de la femme dans l'ancienne Égypte.* Paris, 1886.

Pauli Carl, *Altitalische Forschungen.* 3 vols. Leipzig, 1885–91.

Paulinus a Sancto Bartholomeo, *Systema Brahminicum, liturgicum, mythologicum, civile.* Roma, 1791.
Alphabetum tibetanum. Roma, 1793.

Paulitschke, Ph., *Ethnographie Nordost-Afrikas.* 2 vols. Berlin, 1893–96.

Paulus diaconus, *Historia Langobardorum,* in G. H. Pertz, *Monumenta Historica Germaniae ; Scriptores rerum Langobardicarum et Italicarum, saec. vi–ix.* Hannoverae, 1878.

Pauly, August F. von, and Wissowa, G., *Real-Encyclopédie der classischen Alterthumswissenschaft.* In progress. Stuttgart, 1894–

Pauw, Cornelius, *Recherches philosophiques sur les Américains.* 3 vols. Paris, 1770.

Pavitt, W. T. and K., *The Book of Talismans, Amulets, and Zodiacal Gems.* London, 1914.

Payne, Arnold Hill, art. "Deaf and Dumb," *Encyclopaedia Britannica.* Vol. vii. Cambridge, 1910.

Payne, E. J., *History of the New World called America.* 2 vols. Oxford, 1892–99.

Peacock, T. B., "Tables of the Weight of the Brains and some other Organs of the Human Body," *Monthly Journal of Medical Science.* London, Edinburgh, 1847.

Peal, S. E., "On the Morong as possible relic of pre-marriage communism," *Journal of the Anthropological Institute.* Vol. xx. London, 1880.

Pearce, Nathaniel, *Life and Adventure of N. Pearce during his Residence in Abyssinia, 1810–19.* 2 vols. London, 1831.

Pearl, Raymond, "A Biometrical Study of Conjugation in Paramoecium," *Biometrika.* Vol. v. Cambridge, 1907.

Pearse, J., "Women in Madagascar, their Social Position, Employment, etc." *Antananarivo Annual and Madagascar Magazine.* No. XXIII. Antananarivo, 1899.

Pearson, Charles H., *The Early and Middle Ages of England.* London, 1861.

Pearson, Karl, "On the Inheritance of Mental and Moral Characters in Man," *Biometrika.* Vol. iii. Cambridge, 1904.
Treasury of Human Inheritance (University of London Eugenics Laboratory Memoirs. Vol. i). London, 1912.
"Inheritance of Psychical Characters," *Biometrika.* Vol. xii. Cambridge, 1919.
Nature and Nurture. London, 1910.

Pease, A. E., *The Book of the Lion.* London, 1913.

Pechuël-Loesche, Edward, "Indiscretes aus Loango," *Zeitschrift für Ethnologie.* Vol. x. Berlin, 1878.

Peckel, P. G., *Religion und Zauberei auf dem mittleren Neu-Mecklenburg, Bismarck-Archipel, Südsee.* Munster i. W., 1910.

The Pedagogical Seminary. Worcester, Mass., 1891–

Peet, S. O., "Mythology of the Menominees," *The American Antiquarian and Oriental Journal.* Vol. xxxi. Cleveland, 1909.

Peet, T. Eric, in *The Cambridge Ancient History.* Vol. i. Cambridge, 1923.

Pelaez, M., *Vita e poesie di Bonifazio Calvo, trovatore genovese.* Torino, 1897.

Pellegrin, Jacques, "Contributions à l'étude anatomique, etc., des Cichlides," *Mémoires de la Société Zoologique.* Vol. xvi. Paris, 1904.

Peggs, Ada Janet, "Notes on the Aborigines of Roebuck Bay, Western Australia," *Folk-lore.* Vol. xiv. London, 1903.

Pelleschi, Juan. *Los Indios Matacos y su Lengua.* Buenos Aires, 1897.

Pelleschi, Juan, *Eight Months on the Gran Chaco of the Argentine Republic.* Transl. London, 1886.

Pellizzari, *La vita e le opere di Guittone d'Arezzo.* (*Annali della R. Scuola Normale Superiore di Pisa : Filosofia e filologia.* Vol. xx.) Pisa, 1907.

Peggs, J., " Notes on the Aborigines of Roebuck Bay, Western Australia," *Folk-lore.* Vol. xiv. London, 1903.

Peney, " Études sur l'ethnographie, la physiologie, l'anatomie et les maladies des races du Soudan," *Bulletin de la Société de Géographie.* Série iv, vol. xviii. Paris, 1859.

Penha, Geo. d', " Superstitions and Customs in Salsette," *The Indian Antiquary.* Vol. xxviii. Bombay, 1899.

Penick, C. C., " The Devil Bush of West Africa," *Journal of American Folk-Lore.* Vol. ix. Boston, New York, 1896.

Penna, Orazio, *Breve Notizia del regno di Tibet,* published by H. J. von Klaproth, *Journal Asiatique.* 2e Série, vol. xiv. Paris, 1835.

Pennant, Thomas, *Tour in Scotland,* London, 1798.

Pennell, T. L., *Among the Wild Tribes of the Afghan Frontier.* London, 1909.

Penny, Alfred, *Ten Years in Melanesia.* London, s.d.

Penrose, C. A., " Sanitary Conditions of the Bahama Islands," *Geographical Society of Baltimore,* 1905, cited by P. Popenoe, *The Journal of Heredity.* Vol. iv. Washington, 1916.

Perdrizet, P., " Mên," *Bulletin de Correspondance Hellénique.* Vol. xx. Athènes, Paris, 1896.

 " Le fragment de Satyros sur les dèmes d'Alexandrie," *Revue des Études Anciennes.* Vol. xii. Bordeaux, 1910.

 " La miraculeuse histoire de Pandare et d'Echedore suivie de recherches sur la marque dans l'Antiquité," *Archiv für Religionswissenschaft.* Vol. xiv. Leipzig, 1911.

Perelaer, Michael, Th. H., *Ethnographische beschrijving des Dajaks.* Zalt-Bommel, 1870.

Perera, A. A., *Glimpses of Singhalese Social Life.* Bombay, 1904.

Perez, Bernard. *La Psychologie de l'Enfant. Les trois premières années de l'enfant.* Paris, 1886.

 The First Three Years of Childhood. Trans., intr. by J. Sully. London, 1885.

 L'art et la poésie chez l'enfant. Paris, 1888.

Perham, J., " Petara, or Sea Dyak Gods," *Journal of the Straits Branch of the Royal Asiatic Society.* No. 8. Singapore, 1881.

 " Sea Dyak Gods," *ibid.* No. 10. Singapore, 1882. No. 14. Singapore, 1884.

 " Manangism in Borneo," *Journal of the Straits Branch of the Royal Asiatic Society.* No. 19. Singapore, 1887.

Perlesvaus, Hatton Manuscript 82, Branch 1. Ed. with intr. and notes by John Thomas Lister. Menaska, 1921.

Pérot, F., *Folklore Bourbonnais.* Paris, 1908.

Perregaux, E., *Chez les Achantis.* Neufchâtel, 1906.

Perron, N., *Les Femmes Arabes avant et depuis l'Islamisme.* Alger, 1858.

Perrot, Georges, and Chipiez, C., *Histoire de l'art dans l'antiquité.* 7 vols. Paris, 1882–99.

Perrot, Nicolas, *Mémoire sur les moeurs, coutumes et religion des sauvages de l'Amérique Septentrionale,* publié pour la première fois par le R. P. J. Tailhan. Leipzig, Paris, 1864.

Perry, W. C., *The Women of Homer.* London, 1898.

Pertz, G. H., *Monumenta Germaniae Historica.* Hanover, 1826–

Petau, D., *Uranologion*. Lutetia Parisiorum, 1630.

Peter of Blois, *Opera Omnia*, in Migne, *Patrologiae Cursus Completus*. Vol. ccvii. Parisiis, 1855.

Petermann's Mittheilungen aus Justes Perthes' geographischer Anstalt. Gotha, 1855–

Erganzungsband. Gotha, 1874–

Petersen, E., *Kritische Bemerkungen zur älteste Geschichte der griechischen Kunst*. Berlin, 1871.

and Luschan, F. von, *Reisen in Lykien, Milyas, und Kibyratis*. Wien, 1889.

Petit, André, " Un suicide chez les Noirs," *Revue d'Ethnographie et des Traditions populaires*. Vol. i. Paris, 1920.

Petitot, E., " Les Déné-Dindjiés," *Congrès international des Américanistes*. Iᵉ Session. Vol. ii. Nancy, Paris, 1875.

Dictionnaire de la langue Déné-Dindjié. Paris, 1908.

Autour du Grand Lac des Esclaves. Paris, 1891.

Les grands Esquimaux. Paris, 1887.

in *Annales de la Propagation de la Foi*. Vol. xliii. Lyon, 1871.

" Étude sur la nation montagnaise ou Tchippewayne," *Missions Catholiques*. Lyon, 1868.

Petrie, Miss, *Tom Petrie's Reminiscences of Early Queensland*. Brisbane, 1904.

Petrie, G., " On the History and Antiquities of Tara Hill," *Transactions of the Royal Irish Academy, Department of Antiquities*. Vol. xviii. Dublin, 1838.

Petrie, H., *Monumenta Historica Britannica*. Vol. i. London, 1848.

Petrie, W. H. Flinders, *Social Life in Ancient Egypt*. London, 1923.

History of Egypt. 6 vols. London, 1894–1901.

Amulets. London, 1914.

The Royal Tombs of the First Dynasty. (*Egypt Exploration Fund*.) London, 1900–

Petroff, Ivan, " Report on the Population, Industries, and Resources of Alaska," *United States Department of the Interior, Tenth Census*. Vol. viii. Washington, 1881.

Petronius Arbiter, *Satyricon*. Ed. P. Burmannus. 2 vols. Amsterlaedami, 1743.

Peyron, Bernardino, " Papiri greci del Museo Britannico di Londra e delle Biblioteche Vaticane," *Memorie della Reale Accademia delle Scienze di Torino*. Serie ii. Vol. iii, Part ii. Torino, 1841.

Pfefferkorn, *Beschreibung der Landschaft Sonora*. 2 vols. Köln, 1794.

Pfeil, Joachim Graf von, *Studien und Beobachtungen aus der Südsee*. Brunswick, 1899.

" Duk Duk and other Customs as forms of Experience of Melanesian Intellectual Life," *Journal of the Anthropological Institute*. Vol. xxvii. London, 1898.

Pflugk-Harttung, J. von, " Les cycles épiques d'Irlande, leur date et leur charactère," *Revue Celtique*. Vol. xiii. Paris, 1892.

Philaster, bishop of Brescia, *De haeresibus liber*, in Migne, *Patrologiae Cursus Completus*. Vol. xii. Parisiis, 1845.

The Philippine Journal of Science. Manila, 1906–

Phillips, C., *Samoa, Past and Present*. London, 1890.

Phillips, R. C., " The Lower Congo, a Sociological Study," *Journal of the Anthropological Institute*. Vol. xvii. London, 1888.

Philo Judaeus, *Opera*, ed. T. Mangey. 2 vols. London, 1742.

About the Contemplative Life, or the Fourth Book of the Treatise concerning Virtues. Ed. F. C. Conybeare. Oxford, 1895.

Philologus. Stolberg, Leipzig, 1846–

Philosophical Transactions of the Royal Society. London, 1665–

Philostratos, *Heroica.* Ed. J. Fr. Boissonade. Parisiis, 1806.
  Quae supersunt. Rec. G. Olearius. Lipsiae, 1709.

Philpot, Mrs. J. H., *The Sacred Tree, or The Tree in Religion and Myth.* London, 1897.

Photius, *Lexicon.* Ed. G. Hermann. Lipsiae, 1808.

Physici et medici graeci minores. Ed. Ideler. 2 vols. Berlin, 1841.

Picard, F., " Note préliminaire sur l'atrophie de l'oeil chez le mâle d'un hyménoptère chalcidien (*Melittobia acasta,* Walk.)," *Bulletin de la Société Zoologique de France.* Vol. xlvii. Paris, 1922.

Picarda, R. P., " Autour du Mandera, Notes sur l'Ouzigoua, l'Oukwere et l'Oudoe (Zanguebar)," *Les Missions Catholiques.* Vol. xviii. Lyon, 1886.

Piedrahita, Lucas Fernandez de, *Historia general de las conquistas del nuevo Reyno de Granada.* Amberes, 1688.

Pierre de Vaux-de-Cernay, *Historia Albigensum et sacri belli in eos suscepti,* in M. Bouquet, *Recueil des historiens des Gaules et de la France.* Vol. xix. Paris, 1733.

Pierret, Paul, *Dictionnaire d'archéologie égyptienne.* Paris, 1875.

Piers, Sir Henry, *Description of the County of Westmeath,* in C. Vallancey, *Collectanea de rebus Hibernicis.* Vol. i. Dublin, 1786.

Pietro della Valle, *The Travels of Pietro della Valle in India.* Transl. by G. Havers (1664), ed. by Edward Grey. 2 vols. London, 1892.

Pietro Martire (Pedro Martir), " Segundo viage de Cristoforo Colon," in M. Fernandez de Navarrete, *Colección de los viages y descubrimientos.* Vol. i. Madrid, 1825.
  in G. B. Ramusio, *Navigationi et Viaggi.* Vol. iii. Venetia, 1559.

Piette, E., " La station de Brassempouy et les statuettes humaines de la période glyptique," *L'Anthropologie.* Vol. vi. Paris, 1895.

Pigafetta, Antonio, *Primo viaggio intorno al mondo,* in E. H. Blair and J. A. Robertson, *The Philippine Islands, 1493–1803.* Vol. xxxiii. Cleveland, 1906.

Pilins, C., in *The American Anthropologist.* Vol. vi. Washington, 1893.

Pilsudski, Bronislaw, *Materials for the study of the Ainu Language and Folklore.* Cracow, 1912.
  " Schwangerschaft, Entbindung und Fehlgeburt bei den Bewohnern der Insel Sachalen," *Anthropos.* Vol. v. Salzburg, 1910.

Pimental, J., " Relación de esta provincia de Caracas," in G. Latorre, *Relaciones geográficas de Indias, contenidas en el Archivio General de Indias de Sevilla.* Sevilla, 1919.

Pinart, Alphonse, " Les Aléoutes, leurs origines et leurs légendes," *Actes de la Société d'Ethnographie.* Vol. viii. Paris, 1873.
  " Notes sur les Koloches," *Bulletin de la Société d'Anthropologie.* 2e Série, vol. vii. Paris, 1872.

Pinches, T. G., art. " Sabbath (Babylonian)," in J. Hastings's *Encyclopaedia of Religion and Ethics.* Vol. x. Edinburgh, 1910.
  " ' Sapattu,' the Babylonian Sabbath," *Proceedings of the Society of Biblical Archaeology.* Vol. xxvi. London, 1904.
  " The Goddess Ištar in Assyrian-Babylonian Literature," *Proceedings of the Society for Biblical Archaeology.* Vol. xxxi. London, 1909.
  " Assyro-Babylonian Astrologers and their Lore," *The Expository Times,* Vol. xxx. Edinburgh, 1919.
  " The Babylonian Paradise and its Rivers," *ibid.* Vol. xxix. Edinburgh, 1918.

Pinches, T. G., "Early Babylonian Chronology and the Book of Genesis," *ibid.* Vol. xxvii. Edinburgh, 1916.

The *Old Testament in the Light of the Historical Records of Babylonia and Assyria.* London, 1902.

Pindar, *Carmina.* Rec. O. Schröder. Leipzig, 1900.

Pineda, Vicente, *Historia de las sublevationes indigenas habidas en el Estado de Chiapas.* Chiapas, 1888.

Pinto, Fernando Mendez, *Voyages advantureux de F. M. P. fidèlement traduicts de Portugais en François.* Paris, 1626.

"Observations of China, Tartaria and other Easterne parts of the World," in *Hakluytus Posthumus, or Purchas His Pilgrimes.* Vol. xii. Glasgow, 1906.

Piprek, Johannes, *Slawische Brautwerbungs und Hochzeitsgebräuche.* Stuttgart, 1914.

Pirie, George, "North-East Rhodesia," *Journal of the African Society.* Vol. vi. London, 1907.

Pischel, R., and Geldner, K. F., *Vedische Studien.* 3 vols. Stuttgart, 1888–91.

Pischon, C. N., *Der Einfluss des Islam auf das häusliche, sociale und politische Leben seiner Bekenner.* Leipzig, 1881.

Pistorius Nidanus, J., *Rerum Germanicarum Scriptores aliquot insignes* 3 vols. Ratisbonae, 1731.

Pistorius, A. W. P. Verkerk, *Studien over de inlandische huishouding in de Padangsche Bovenlanden.* Zalt-Bommel, 1871.

Pitra, Cardinal J. B., *Analecta novissima ; Spicilegii Solesmensis altera continuatio.* 2 vols. Paris, 1885–88.

Pitré, Giuseppe, *Usi e costumi, credenze e pregiudizi del popolo Siciliano.* 4 vols. Palermo, 1889.

Usi *natalizi, nuziali e funebri del popolo siciliano.* Palermo, 1879.

Medicina popolare siciliana. Palermo, Torino, 1896.

Pitt, Frances, *Wild Creatures of Garden and Hedgerows.* London, 1920.

Pittier de Fabrega, H., "Die Sprache der Bribri-Indianer in Costa Rica," *Sitzungsberichte der philosophischen-historischen Classe der kaiserliche Akademie der Wissenschaften, Wien.* Vol. cxxxviii. Wien, 1898.

Placucci, M., *Usi e pregiudizi dei contadini di Romagna.* Palermo, 1885.

Plancy, J. Collin de, *Dictionnaire infernal.* Paris, 1863.

Plas, Joseph Vanden, *Les Kuku.* Bruxelles, 1910.

Plassard, Louis, "Les Guaranos et le delta de l'Orinoque," *Bulletin de la Société de Geographie.* 5ᵉ Série, vol. xv. Paris, 1868.

Plath, H. S., "Die hausliche Verhältnisse der alten Chinesen," *Sitzungberichten der Münchener Akademie.* Part ii. Munich, 1862.

"Gesetz und Recht in Alten China nach Chinesischen Quellen," *Abhandlungen der philosophisch-philologischen Classe der Königlich Bayerischen Akademie der Wissenschaften.* Munich, 1864.

Plato, *Scripta Graeca omnia.* Rec. I. Bekker. 11 vols. Londini, 1826.

Phaedo. Ed. with introd. and notes by John Burnet. Oxford, 1911.

Platt, Arthur, "Homer's Similes," *The Journal of Philology.* Vol. xxiv. London, Cambridge, 1896.

Plautus, Titus Marcius, *Comaediae et deperditarum fragmenta.* Rec. B. F. Schmieder. Gottingae, 1804.

Playfair, A., *The Garos.* London, 1909.

Plehn, A., "Beobachtungen in Kamerun," *Zeitschrift für Ethnologie.* Vol. xxxvi. Berlin, 1904.

Pleyte, C. M., " De geographische verbreiding van het koppensnellen in den Oost Indischen Archipel," *Tijdschrift van het Kon. Nederlandsch Aardrijkskundig Genootschap*. Tweede Serie, vol. viii. Leiden, 1891.

" Ethnographische beschrijving der Kei-eilanden," *Tijdschrift van het Kon. Nederlandsch Aardrijkskundig Genootschap*. Tweede Serie, vol. x. Leiden, 1893.

Bataksche Vertellingen. Utrecht, 1894.

" Die Schlange im Volksgläuben der Indonesier," *Globus*. Vol. lxxxv. Braunschweig, 1894.

Pleyte, W., *Chapîtres supplémentaires du Livre des Morts*. Leiden, 1881.

La religion des Pré-Israélites : recherches sur le dieu Seth. Utrecht, 1862.

and F. Rossi, *Papyrus de Turin*. Leiden, 1901.

Pliny, the elder, *Naturalis Historia*. 5 vols. Leipzig, 1830.

The Historie of the World, commonly called, The Naturall Historie of Pliny. Translated by Philemon Holland. London, 1601.

Ploix, M., " Les Hottentots, ou Khoi-Khoi et leur religion," *Revue d'Anthropologie*. Vol. xvi. Paris, 1887.

Ploss, H. H., *Das Kind im Brauch und Sitte der Völker*. 2 vols. Leipzig 1884.

" Die operative Behandlung der weiblichen Geschlechtstheile bei verschiedenen Völkern," *Zeitschrift für Ethnologie*. Vol. iii. Berlin, 1871.

and Bartels, M., *Das Weib in der Natur und Völkerkunde*. 2 vols. Leipzig, 1905.

Plotinus, *Enneades*. Ed. F. Dübner. Parisiis, 1855.

Plutarch, *Quae supersunt omnia*. Ed. I. I. Reiske. 12 vols. Leipzig, 1774–82.

De Iside et Osiride. Ed. Parthey. Berlin, 1850.

Romane Questions. Transl. by F. B. Jevons. London, 1892.

Pocock, Edward, *Specimen historiae Arabum*. London, 1649.

Poeta Saxo, *Annales de gestis Caroli Magni imperatoris*, in Pertz, *Monumenta Germaniae Historica, Poetae Latini*. Vol. iv, Part i. Hanover, 1890.

Poetae Bucolici et Didactici. Recog. F. S. Lehrs. Parisiis, 1846.

Poeti del primo secolo della lingua italiana. 2 vols. Firenze, 1816.

Pöch, R., " Eine Reise an der Nordküste von Britisch-Neuguinea," *Globus*. Vol. xcii. Braunschweig, 1908.

Pogge, Paul, *Im Reiche des Muata Jamwo*. Berlin, 1880.

and Wissmann, *Unter deutscher Flagge quer durch Afrika*. Berlin, 1889.

Pohl, J. E., *Reise im Innern von Brasilien*. 2 vols. Wien, 1832–37.

Polack, J. E., *Persien : das Land und seine Bewohner*. 2 vols. Leipzig, 1865.

Polack, J. S., *Manners and Customs of the New Zealanders*. 2 vols. London, 1840.

Polek, J., " Regenzauber in Ost-Europa," *Zeitschrift des Vereins für Volkskunde*. Vol. iii. Berlin, 1893.

Polidori, F. L., *Tavola ritonda*. 2 vols. Bologna, 1864–65.

Politis, N. G., " Der Mond in Sage und Glaube der heutigen Hellenen," in W. H. Roscher, *Über Selene und Verwandtes*. Leipzig, 1890.

Politzer, Adam, *A Text-Book of the Diseases of the Ear*. Trans. London, 1909.

Pollard, S. *In Unknown China*. London, 1921.

Pollock, Sir Frederick, and Maitland, R. W., *The History of English Law before the Time of Edward I*. 2 vols. Cambridge, 1898.

Pollux, *Onomasticum*. Ed. J. H. Lederlin and T. Hemsterhuis. 2 Parts. Amsterlaedami, 1706.

Polo, Marco. *The Book of Ser Marco Polo.* Ed. H. Yule. 2 vols. London, 1903.

Polyaenus, *Strategematum libri viii.* Rec. P. Maasvicius. Lugd. Batav., 1690.

Polybius, *Historiarum quae supersunt.* Ex recog. I. Bekkeri. Berolini, 1844.

Pommerol, Mme. Jean. *Among the Women of the Sahara.* Translated by Mrs. Arthur Bell. London, 1900.

Ponce, Don Pedro, " Breve relación de los dioses y ritos de la gentilidad," *Anales del Museo Nacional.* Vol. vi. Mexico, 1892.

Pond, G. H., " Dakota Superstitions," *Collections of the Minnesota Historical Society.* No. vii. Saint Paul, 1867.

Pontow, H., " Die Kultstätte der ' anderen Götter ' von Delphi," *Philologus.* Vol. lxxi. Leipzig, 1912.

Popenoe, Paul, " Heredity and the Mind," " Experimental Inbreeding," *The Journal of Heredity.* Vol. vii. Washington, 1916.
" Consanguineous Marriage," *ibid.* Vol. iv. Washington, 1913.

Pöppig, Eduard, *Reise in Chili, Peru und auf dem Amazonenstrome.* 2 vols. Leipzig, 1835–36.

The Popular Science Monthly, New York, 1872–

Porphyrius, *De Abstinentia et De Antro Nympharum.* Ed. R. Hersche. Paris, 1858.

Porter, David, *Journal of a Cruise into the Pacific Ocean.* New York, 1822.

Porthan, Heinricus Gabriel, *Opera Selecta.* 5 vols. Helsingfors, 1859–73.

Portman, M. V., *A History of our Relations with the Andamanese.* 2 vols. Calcutta, 1899.

Post, A. H., *Studien zur Entwicklungsgeschichte des Familiensrecht.* Oldenburg, Leipzig, 1890.
Bausteine für eine allgemeine Rechtswissenschaft auf vergleichend-ethnologischer Basis. 2 vols. Oldenburg, 1880–81.
Afrikanische Jurisprudenz. 2 vols. Oldenburg, Leipzig, 1887.
Die Anfange des Staats-und Rechtslebens. Oldenburg, 1878.
Die Geschlechtsgenossenschaft der Urzeit und die Entstehung der Ehe. Oldenburg, 1875.

Potanin, G. N., " Survey of G. N. Potanin's Journey in North-west Mongolia," *Petermann's Mittheilungen.* Vol. xxvii. Gotha, 1881.

Potgiesserus, Joachimus, *De conditione et statu servorum apud Germanos tam veteri quam novo.* Coloniae Agrippinae, 1707.

Pottinger, Sir Henry, *Travels in Beloochistan and Sinde.* London, 1816.

Potts, F. A., " Notes on the Free-living Nematodes," *Quarterly Journal of Microscopical Science.* Vol. x. London, 1914.

Pouchot, *Memoir upon the Late War in North America between the French and the English.* Transl. 2 vols. Roxbury, 1866.

Poulsen, F., *Der Orient und die frühgriechische Kunst.* Leipzig, Berlin, 1912.

Poupon, A., " Étude ethnographique des Baya de la circonscription du M'Bimou," *L'Anthropologie.* Vol. xxvi. Paris, 1915.

Pouqueville, F. C. H. L., *Voyage en Morée, à Constantinople, en Albanie et dans plusieurs autres parties de l'Empire Ottoman.* 3 vols. Paris, 1805.

Powell, B., *Erichthonus and the Three Daughters of Cecrops.* New York, 1906.

Powell, J. W., " Wyandot Government"; " Sketch of the Mythology of the North American Indians," *First Annual Report of the Bureau of Ethnology.* Washington, 1881.

Powell, T., " Some Folk-Songs and Myths from Samoa," *Journal and Proceedings of the Royal Society of New South Wales.* Vol. xxiv. Sydney, 1890.

Powell, Wilfrid, *Wanderings in a Wild Country ; or Three Years amongst the Cannibals of New Britain.* London, 1883.

Powell-Cotton, Major P. H. G., *In Unknown Africa, a Narrative of Twenty Months' Travels and Sport in Unknown Lands and Among New Tribes.* London, 1904.

Powers, Stephen, *Tribes of California (United States Geographical and Geological Survey of the Rocky Mountain Region. Contributions to North American Ethnology.* Vol. iii). Washington, 1877.

" The Northern Californian Indians," *The Overland Monthly.* Vol. viii. San Francisco, 1872.

Prado, Francisco Rodriguez, " Historia dos Indios Cavalleiros ou de nação Guaycuru," *Revista Trimensal do Instituto historico geographico e ethnographico do Brasil.* Vol. i. Rio de Janeiro, 1839.

Prain, David, " The Angami Nagas," *Revue coloniale internationale.* Vol. v. Amsterdam, 1887.

Pratt, G., " Some Folk-songs and Myths from Samoa," *Journal and Proceedings of the Royal Society of New South Wales.* Vol. xxv. Sydney, 1891.

Pratt, S. J., *Gleanings through Wales, Holland, and Westphalia.* 4 vols. London, 1797–99.

Preime, A., *Die Frau in altfranzösischen Fabliaux.* Cassel, 1901.

Prejevalsky, N. *From Kulja across the Tian Shan to Lob-nor.* London, 1879. *Mongolia, the Tangut Country and the Solitudes of Northern Tibet.* 2 vols. London, 1876.

Preller, L., *Griechische Mythologie.* Bearbetit von C. Robert. 2 vols. Berlin, 1904.

Römische Mythologie. Berlin, 1858.

Demeter und Persephone. Hamburg, 1837.

Prémare, J. H. de, " Vestiges choises des principaux dogmes de la religion chrétienne, extraits des anciens livres chinois," *Annales de Philosophie Chrétienne.* 6e Série. Vols. vii, viii, ix, x. Paris, 1874–75.

Preuner, August, *Hestia-Vesta.* Tübingen, 1864.

Preuss, Konrad Theodor, *Religion und Mythologie der Uitoto.* 2 vols. Göttingen, Leipzig, 1921–23.

" Die Astralreligion in Mexiko in vorspanischer Zeit und in der Gegenwart," *Transactions of the Third International Congress for the History of Religions.* Vol. i. Oxford, 1908.

" Der Ursprung der Religion und Kunst," *Globus.* Vol. lxxxvi. Braunschweig, 1904.

Preyer, W., *Die Seele des Kindes.* Leipzig, 1882.

Price, F. G. H., " A Description of the Quissaura Tribe," *Journal of the Anthropological Institute.* Vol. i. London, 1872.

Prichard, H. H., *Through the Heart of Patagonia.* London, 1902.

Pridham, Charles, *An Historical, Political and Statistical Account of Ceylon.* 2 vols. London, 1849.

Prilonski, W. L., " Ueber der Schamanisten bei den Jakuti," in A. Bastian, *Allerlei aus Volk- und Menschenkunde.* Vol. i. Berlin, 1888.

Priminius, " Dicta abbatis Priminii de singulis libris canonicis scarapsus," in C. P. Caspari, *Kirchenhistorische Anecdota.* Christiania, 1883.

Prince, J. Dyneley, " The Hymn to Bêlit, K. 257 (HT. 126–131)," *Journal of the American Oriental Society.* Vol. xxiv. New Haven, 1903.

Prinz, Hugo, "Bemerkungen zur altkretische Religion, I.," *Mitteilungen der Kaiserlich deutschen archäologischen Institut. Athenische Abteilung.* Vol. xxxv. Athens, 1910.

Priscian, *Opera.* Ed. A. Krehl. 2 vols. Leipzig, 1819–20.

Pritchard, W. T., *Polynesian Reminiscences, or Life in the South Pacific Islands.* London, 1866.

Pritchard, W. T., "Notes on Certain Anthropological Matters respecting the South Sea Islanders," *Memoirs read before the Anthropological Society of London.* Vol. i. London, 1865.

Problems in Eugenics. London, 1912.

Proceedings of the American Antiquarian Society. Worcester, 1843–

Proceedings of the American Association for the Advancement of Science. Salem, etc., 1849–

Proceedings of the American Oriental Society. New Haven, 1860–

Proceedings of the Boston Society of Natural History. Boston, 1844–

Proceedings of the Canadian Institute. Third Series. Toronto, 1879–

Proceedings of the Royal Geographical Society. London, 1855–

Proceedings of the Royal Geographical Society of Australasia: N.S.W. and Victoria Branch. Sydney, 1885–

Proceedings of the Royal Geographical Society of Australasia: South Australian Branch. Adelaide, 1889–

Proceedings of the Royal Irish Academy. Dublin, 1837–

Proceedings of the Royal Medical and Chirurgical Society of London. London, 1856–

Proceedings of the Royal Physical Society of Edinburgh. Edinburgh, 1858–

Proceedings of the Royal Society of Medicine. London, 1908–

Proceedings of the Royal Society of Queensland. Brisbane, 1885–

Proceedings of the Society of Biblical Archaeology. London, 1879–

Proceedings of the United States National Museum. Washington, 1879–

Proclus, *Commentarius in Platonis Timaeum.* Rec. C. E. S. Schreider. Vratislaviae, 1847.

Procopius, *Opera.* Ex recensione Guilielmi Dindorfii. 3 vols. Bonn, 1833.

Les Prophécies de Merlin. Paris, 1526.

Proyart, L. B., *Histoire de Loango, Kakongo, et autres royaumes d'Afrique.* Paris, 1776.

Prudentius, Bishop of Troyes, *Annales Bertinianorum,* in *Monumenta Germaniae Historica, Scriptores.* Vol. i. Hanover, 1826.

Pruyssenaere, E. de, "Reisen und Forschungen in Gebiete des Weissen und Blauen Nil," *Petermann's Mittheilungen, Erganzungsband.* Vol. xi. Heften, 50, 51. Gotha, 1877.

Psellus, *Quaenam sunt Graecorum opiniones de daemonibus.* Ed. J. F. Boissonade. Nuremberg, 1838.

Psichari, Jean, "La Ballade de Lénore en Grèce," *Revue de l'Histoire des Religions.* Vol. ix. Paris, 1884.

Ptolemaeus, *Geographia.* Ed. C. F. A. Nobbe. 3 vols. Lipsiae, 1843–45.

Publications of the Field Columbian Museum: Anthropological Series. Chicago, 1895–

Puini, C., *Il Tibet secondo la relazione del viaggio del P. Ippolito Desideri* (*Memorie della Società Geografica Italiana.* Vol. x.) Roma, 1904.

Pumpelly, Raphael, *Exploration in Turkestan. Expedition of 1904. Prehistoric Civilisation of Anau.* 2 vols. Washington, 1908.

Punjab Notes and Queries. Allahabad, 1886–

Punnett, R. C., *Mendelism.* Cambridge, 1905.

Purcell, Brabazon Harry, "The Aborigines of Australia (Queensland and North Territory)," *Transactions of the Royal Geographical Society of Australasia* (*Victoria Branch*). Vol. xi. Melbourne, 1894.

"Rites and Customs of Australian Aborigines," *Verhandlungen der Berliner Gesellschaft für Anthropologie, 1893.* Berlin, 1893.

Purchas, Samuel, *Purchas, His Pilgrimage.* London, 1613. *See* Hakluytus.

"The Pursuit of Diarmaide and Grainne," *Revue Celtique.* Vol. xxxiii. Paris, 1912.

Putnam, F. W., " Symbolism in Ancient American Art," *Proceedings of the American Association for the Advancement of Science for the 44th Meeting.* Salem, 1896.

Puybonnieux, I. B., *Mutisme et surdité, ou influence de la surdité naturelle sur les facultés physiques, intellectuelles et morales.* Paris, 1846.

Puymaigre, T. J. de Boudet de, *Les Vieux Auteurs Castillans.* 2 vols. Paris, 1861.

Pycraft, W. P., *The Infancy of Animals.* London, 1912.

The Courtship of Animals. London, 1913.

Pyrard de Laval, *Voyage de contenant sa navigation aux Indes Orientales.* Paris, 1619.

Quandt, C., *Nachricht von Suriname und seine Einwohnern, sonderlich den Arawaken, Warauen,* etc. Leipzig, 1808.

Quantz, J. O., " Dendro-Psychoses," *American Journal of Psychology.* Vol. ix. Worcester, 1898.

Quarterly Journal of the Microscopical Society. London, 1853–

Quarterly Statement of the Palestine Exploration Fund. London, 1870–

Quatremère, Étienne M., *Mémoires géographiques et historiques sur l'Égypte et sur quelques contrées voisines, recueillis des manuscrits coptes, arabes,* etc., *de la Bibliothéque Impériale.* 2 vols. Paris, 1841.

Mélanges d'histoire et de philologie orientale. Paris, 1861.

Queensland Geographical Journal. N.S. Bisbane, 1900–

La Queste del Saint Graal, in the French Prose of Maistres Gautiers Map. Ed. F. S. Furnivall (*Roxburghe Club*). London, 1862.

Quibell, J. E., *Hierakonpolis.* (*Egyptian Research Account.*) London, 1900.

The Ramesseum. (*Egyptian Research Account.*) London, 1898.

Quiller-Couch, Sir Arthur, *On the Art of Writing.* Cambridge, 1916.

Quintillian, *Instituti oratoris libri xii.* Rec. C. Halm. 2 vols. Leipzig, 1868–69.

Quiroga, Adan, *La Cruz en America.* Buenos Aires, 1901.

Quiroga, P. José, " Breve noticia del viaje que hizo por el rio Paraguay, 1753–54," *Coleccion de Documentos Ineditos para la Historia de España.* Vol. civ. Madrid, 1892.

Rabaud, Étienne, " L'instinct maternel chez les mammifères," *Bulletin de la Société Zoologique.* Vol. xlvi. Paris, 1921.

Rabelais, François, *Oeuvres.* 2 vols. Paris, 1887–93.

Rabot, Paul, *La Terre de Feu, d'après Otto Nordenskjöld.* Paris, 1902.

Radau, Hugo, " Miscellaneous Sumerian Texts from the Temple Library of Nippur," in *Hilprecht Anniversary Volume.* Leipzig, 1909.

Sumerian Hymns and Prayers to God Nin-ib, from the Temple Library of Nippur. (*Babylonian Expedition of the University of Pennsylvania.* Vol. xxix, Part i.) Philadelphia, 1911.

Early Babylonian History. New York, 1900.

Radde, G., *Die Chewsúren und ihr Land.* Cassel, 1878.

Radiguet, Max, " La reine blanche. Aux Îles Marquises, Souvenirs et paysages d'Océanie," *Revue des Deux Mondes.* Vol. xxiii. Paris, 1859.

" Les derniers sauvages," *Revue des Deux Mondes.* Paris, 1859.

Radloff, W., " Observations sur les Kirghis," *Journal Asiatique.* VIᵉ Série. Vol. ii. Paris, 1863.

Radloff, W., *Aus Sibirien*. 2 vols. Leipzig, 1884.

Raeder, H., *Platons philosophische Entwickelung*. Leipzig, 1905.

Raffenel, Anne, *Voyage dans l'Afrique occidentale*. Paris, 1846.
Nouveau voyage dans le pays des nègres. Paris, 1856.

Raffles, Sir Th. Stamford, *The History of Java*. 2 vols. London, 1830.

Raggi, A., " Osservazioni e considerazioni cliniche sul soliloquio dei pazzi," *Il Manicomio moderno*. Vol. xiv. Nocera, 1898.

Raimbert de Paris, *La chevalerie Ogier de Danemarche*. Ed. J. Barrois. 2 vols. Paris, 1842.

Rainsford, W. S., *The Land of the Lion*. London, 1909.

Rajacsich, *Das Leben, die Sitten und Gebräuche der im Kaiserthume Oesterreich lebenden Südslaven*. Wien, 1873.

The *Rájávaliya : or a Historical Narrative of the Sinhalese Kings*. Ed. by B. Gunasékara. Colombo, 1900.

Rajna, Pio, *Le origini dell' epopea francese*. Firenze, 1884.
Le corti d'amore. Milano, 1890.
" Un frammento di un codice perduto di poesie provenzali," *Studi di filologia romanza*. Vol. v. 1889.
" Gli eroi brettoni nell' onomastica italiana," *Romania*. Vol. xvii. Paris, 1887.

Ralston, W. R. S., *Russian Folk-tales*. London, 1873.
The Songs of the Russian People. London, 1872.

Ramayana.—*The Ramayan of Valmiki translated into English Verse*, by R. T. H. Griffith. 5 vols. London, 1870–74.

Rambaud, Alfred N., *La Russie épique ; étude sur les chansons héroiques*. Paris, 1876.

Ramkrishna Gopal Bhandarkar, " The Nasik Cave Inscriptions," *Transactions of the Second Session of the International Congress of Orientalists, held in London in September 1874*. London, 1874.
" Vaisnavism, Saivism and Minor Religions," in G. Buehler, *Grundriss der Indoarische Philologie und Altertumskunde*. Vol. iii. Strassburg, 1913.

Ramon y Cajal, S., " Estructura de la corteza occipital de los pequenos mammiferos," *Anales de la Real Sociedad de Historia Natural*. Madrid, 1893.
Textura del sistema nervioso del hombre y de los vertebrados. 3 vols. Madrid, 1897–1904.
" Sur la structure de l'écorce cérébrale de quelques mammifères," *La Cellule*. Vol. vii. Lierre, 1891.

Ramsay, Sir Wm., *The Cities and Bishoprics of Phrygia*. 2 vols. Oxford, 1895–97.

Ramusio, Giovan Battista, *Primo (Secondo, Terzo) volume delle Navigationi et Viaggi in molti luoghi*. Venetia, 1554.

Rand, Silas Tertius, *Legends of the Micmacs*. New York and London, 1894.

Randall-Maciver, David, and Wilk, Anthony, *Libyan Notes*. London, 1901.

Rannie, Douglas, " New Ireland," *Proceedings and Transactions of the Queensland Branch of the Geographical Society of Australasia*. Vol. ii, Part i. Brisbane, 1886.

Raoul de Cambrai, chanson de geste. Ed. Paul Meyer and A. Lognon (*Société des Anciens Textes*). Paris, 1882.

Raoul de Houdenc, *Méraugis de Portlesguez, roman de la Table Ronde*. Ed. H. Michelant. Paris, 1869.

Raoul-Rochette, Desiré, " Sur les Antiquités chrétiennes," *Mémoires de l'Institut Royal de France. Académie des Inscriptions*. Vol. xiii. Paris, 1838.

Rapp, Adolf, " Die Religion und Sitte der Perser und übrigen Iranier, nach den griechischen und römischen Quellen," *Zeitschrift der deutschen morgenländischen Gesellschaft.* Vol. xx. Leipzig, 1866.

Rascher, P., " Die Sulka, ein Beitrag zur Ethnographie Neu-Pommern," *Archiv für Anthropologie.* Vol. xxix. Braunschweig, 1904.

Rasmussen, Knud, *The People of the Polar North.* Transl. London, 1908.

Rat, J. N., " The Carib Language as now spoken in Dominica, West Indies," *Journal of the Anthropological Institute.* Vol. xxvii. London, 1898.

Rattray, R. S., *Some Folk-lore Stories and Songs in Chinyanja.* London, 1907.

Ratzel, Friederich, *History of Mankind.* Transl. 3 vols. London, 1896–98. *Völkerkunde.* 3 vols. Leipzig, 1885–88.

Rau, C., " Indian Pottery," *Smithsonian Reports.* Washington, 1866.

Rauber, A., *Homo sapiens ferus, oder die zustände der verwildeten,* etc. Leipzig, 1885.

Raum, J., " Die Religion der Landschaft Moschi am Kilimandjaro," *Archiv für Religionswissenschaft.* Vol. xiv. Leipzig, 1911.

in *Evangelisch-Lutheranisches Missionsblatt.* Leipzig, 1909.

Rautenen, M., ' Die Ondonga," in S. R. Steinmetz, *Rechtsverhältnisse von eingeborenen Völker in Afrika und Ozeanien.* Berlin, 1903.

Ravenstein, E. G., *The Russians on the Amur.* London, 1861.

Rawlinson, George, *The Five Great Monarchies of the Ancient Eastern World.* 3 vols. London, 1871.

History of Phoenicia. London, 1889.

Rawlinson, Sir Henry Creswicke, *The Cuneiform Inscriptions of Western Asia.* London, 1861.

" The Persian Cuneiform Inscriptions at Behistun," *Journal of the Royal Asiatic Society.* Vol. xi, Part i. London, 1849.

" Notes on the Early History of Babylonia," *Journal of the Royal Asiatic Society.* Vol. xv. London, 1840.

Ray, P. Henry, *Report on an International Expedition to Point Barrow, 1881–1884.* Washington, 1885.

Raymond, Xavier, *Afghanistan.* (*L'Univers.*) Paris, 1848.

Raynouard, F. J. M., *Choix des poésies des troubadours.* 6 vols. Paris, 1816–21.

Read, Carveth, " On the Differentiation of Man from the Anthropoids." *Man.* Vol. xiv. London, 1914.

" No Paternity," *Journal of the Royal Anthropological Institute.* Vol. xlviii. London, 1918.

Reade, W. Winwood, " The Habits of the Gorilla," *The American Naturalist.* Vol. i. Salem, Mass., 1861.

Savage Africa. London, 1863.

" Notes on the Derbyan Eland, the African Elephant, and the Gorilla," *Proceedings of the Zoological Society.* Vol. xxxi. London, 1863.

Reamer, Jeanette Chase, " Mental and Educational Measurements of the Deaf," *Psychological Review Publications : Psychological Monographs.* Vol. xxix. No. 3. Princeton and Lancaster, 1921.

Reclus, Élie, *Les Primitifs.* Paris, 1885.

Primitive Folk. Transl. London, 1891.

Records of the Past ; being English Translations of the Assyrian and Egyptian Monuments. 12 vols. London, 1873–81.

Recueil de travaux relatifs à la philologie et à l'archéologie égyptiennes et assyriennes. Paris 1870–

The Red Deer (Fur, Feather, and Fin Series), by H. A. Macpherson and others London, 1912.

Reed, William Allan, *Negritos of Zambales.* Manila, 1904.

Rees, W. A. van, *De annexatie der Redjang*. Rotterdam, 1860.

Regino Prumiensis abbas, *Chronica*, in Migne, *Patrologiae Cursus Completus*. Vol. cxxxii. Parisiis, 1853.

Rehse, Hermann, *Kiziba, Land und Leute*. Stuttgart, 1910.

Reich, Alfred, " Die Kampa und die Kunibo des Urubamba," *Globus*. Vol. lxxxiii. Braunschweig, 1903.

Reich, Hermann, *Der Mimus*. Berlin, 1903.

Reichard, " Die Wanjamuesi," *Zeitschrift der Gesellschaft für Erdkunde zu Berlin*. Vol. xxiv. Berlin, 1889.

Reid, G. Archdall, " The Biological Foundation of Sociology," *Sociological Papers*. Vol. iii. London, 1907.

Reid, William Jameson, " Among the Farthest People," *The Cosmopolitan*. Vol. xxviii. New York, 1900.

Reiffenberg, Baron Frederic de, *Le Chevalier au cygne et Godefroy de Bouillon*. 2 vols. Bruxelles, 1846–48.

Rein, G. K., *Abessinien*. 3 vols. Berlin, 1918–20.

Rein, W., *Das Criminalrecht der Römer von Romulus bis auf Justinianus*. Leipzig, 1844.

Reina, Paul, " Über die Bewohner der Insel Rook, ostlich von Neu-Guinea," *Zeitschrift für allgemeine Erdkunde*. N.F, vol. iv. Berlin, 1858.

Reinach, Salomon, " Statuette de femme nue découverte dans la grotte de Menton," *L'Anthropologie*. Vol. ix. Paris, 1898.

Reinach, Salomon, *Répertoire de l'art quaternaire*. Paris, 1913.
 Cultes, mythes et religions. 4 vols. Paris, 1905–12.

Reinaud, J. T., *Mémoire géographique, historique et scientifique sur l'Inde . . . d'après les écrivains arabes, persans et chinois*. Paris, 1849.

Reinecke, " Die Samoaner und die Kokospalme," *Globus*. Vol. lxxv. Braunschweig, 1903.

Reinwardt, C. G. S., *Reis naar het oosterlijk gedeelte van den Indischen Archipel*. 's Gravenhagen, 1857.

Reise der oesterreichischen Fregatte Novara um die Erde in den Jahren 1857–59. Ed. by C. von Scherzer. 3 vols. Wien, 1861–62.

Reisner, G., Sumerisch-babylonische Hymnen (*Mitteilungen an dem orientalischen Sammlungen der Königlichen Museen*. Vol. x). Berlin, 1896.
 The Early Dynastic Cemeteries of Naga ed-Der. Berkeley, 1908–

Reiter, P. F., " Traditions tonguiennes," *Anthropos*. Vol. ii. Salzburg, 1907.

Reitzenstein, F. von, " Der Kausalzusammenhang zwischen Geschlechtsverkehr und Empfängniss in Glaube und Brauch der Natur- und Kulturvölker," *Zeitschrift für Ethnologie*. Vol. xli. Berlin, 1909.

" Relación de algunas cosas de la Nueva España y de la gran ciudad de Temestitan Mexico, escrita por un companero de Cortes," in J. G. Icaszbalceta, *Coleción de Documentos para la Historia de Mexico*. Vol. i. Mexico, 1858.

Relation des missions du Paraguai, traduite de l'Italien. Paris, 1754.

Relations des Jésuites. See *Jesuit Relations*.

Rémusat, J. P. A. *Nouveaux mélanges asiatiques*. 2 vols. Paris, 1830.
 Ju-kiao-li ; or The Two Fair Cousins (*Chinese Romance*). London, 1827.

Remy, Jules, *Ka Moolelo Hawai. Histoire de l'archipel. Hawaien*. Paris, Leipzig, 1862.

Remy, N., *Die Judische Weibe*. Leipzig, 1892.

Renan, Ernest, " La société Berbère," *Revue des Deux Mondes*. Vol. cvii. Paris, 1873.

Renaud de Beaujeu, *Le Bel Inconnu*. Ed. C. Hippeau. Paris, 1860.

Renaus de Montauban. Ed. by H. Michelant. Stuttgart, 1862.

Rendiconti della Reale Accademia dei Lincei. Classe di Scienze morali, storiche e filologiche. Roma, 1892–

Rendiconti dell'Instituto Lombardo di Scienze e Lettere. Milano, 1868–

Rengger, Johan Rudolph, *Naturgeschichte der Säugethiere von Paraguay.* Basel, 1830.

Report of the First (etc.) *Meeting of the Australian Association for the Advancement of Science.* Sydney, 1889–

Report of the First (etc.) *Meeting of the British Association for the Advancement of Science.* London, 1833–

Report of the Malabar Marriage Commission, with Enclosures and Appendices. Madras, 1891.

(*First*, etc.) *Report of the Wellcome Tropical Research Laboratory, Gordon College.* Khartum, 1904–

Report on the Census of British India taken on the 17th February, 1881. 3 vols. London, 1883.

Report on the Work of the Horn Scientific Expedition to Central Australia. Part iv. London, Melbourne, 1896.

Reports of the Archaeological Survey of India. 23 vols. Simla, Calcutta, 1871–87.

Reports of the Cambridge Anthropological Expedition to Torres Straits. 6 vols. Cambridge, 1901–8.

Reports of the United States National Museum. Washington, 1883–

Reports to the Commissioner on Indian Affairs. Department of the Interior. Executive Documents printed by Order of the House of Representatives. Washington, 1849–

Résumé statistique de l'Empire du Japon. Tokyo, 1888.

Réville, Albert, *Les religions du Mexique, de l'Amérique Centrale et du Pérou.* Paris, 1885.

Revillout, E., "La question du divorce chez les Égyptiens"; "Les régimes matrimoniaux dans le droit égyptien"; "Union légitimée après seduction"; "Hypothèque légale de la femme et donations entre époux"; "L'omnipotence des femmes"; *Revue Égyptologique.* Vol. i. Paris, 1880.

"Un quasi-mariage après concubinat," *Revue Égyptologique.* Vol. ii. Paris, 1881.

L'ancienne Égypte d'après les papyrus et les monuments. Vol. ii. *La Femme dans l'antiquité égyptienne.* Paris, 1909.

Cours de droit égyptien. Paris, Anger, 1884.

Revista Brazileira. Rio de Janeiro, 1879–

Revista trimensal de Historia-Geographia ou Jornal do Instituto historico geographico Brasileiro. (Title varies.) Rio de Janeiro, 1839–

Revue Celtique. Paris, 1854–

Revue Coloniale. Paris, 1901–

Revue Coloniale Internationale. Amsterdam, 1885–

Revue d'Anthropologie. Paris, 1872–

Revue de l'Histoire des Religions. Paris, 1879–

La Revue des Deux Mondes. Paris, 1831–

Revue des Études Anciennes. Bordeaux, 1899–

Revue des Études Ethnographiques et Sociologiques. Paris, 1908–

Revue des Langues Romanes. Montpellier, 1870–

Revue des Traditions Populaires. Paris, 1886–

Revue d'Ethnographie. Paris, 1882–

Revue d'Ethnographie et de Sociologie. Paris, 1910–

Revue d'Ethnographie et des Traditions Populaires. Paris, 1920–

Revue du Droit Français et Étranger. Paris, 1855–

Revue Égyptologique. Paris, 1880–

Revue Numismatique. Blois, Paris, 1838–

Revue Orientale et Américaine. Paris, 1859–

Revue Philosophique de la France et de l'Étranger. Paris, 1876–

Revue Préhistorique et de Paléontologie. Paris, 1906–

Revue Scientifique. Paris, 1884–

Reyes Lala, Ramon, *The Philippine Islands.* New York, 1899.

Reynolds, H., " Notes on the Azandé Tribe of the Congo," *Journal of the African Society.* Vol. iii. London, 1904.

Rheinisches Museum für Philologie. Bonn, 1827–

Rheinwald, G. F. H., *Die kirkliche Archäologie.* Berlin, 1830.

Rhode, R., in *Mittheilungen des Kaiselich-Königliches österreichisches Museum.* Wien, 1885.

Rhys, John, *Celtic Folklore, Welsh and Manx.* 2 vols. Oxford, 1901.
  Hibbert Lectures on the Origin and Growth of Religion as illustrated by Celtic Heathendom. London, 1898.
  President's Address in *Transactions of the Third International Congress for the History of Religions.* Section VII. Oxford, 1908.
  Studies in the Arthurian Legend. Oxford, 1891.

Ribbe, Carl, *Zwei Jahre unter den Kannibalen der Salomo-Inseln.* Dresden-Blasewitz, 1903.

Ribbe, Carl, " Die Aru-Inseln," in *Festschrift zur Jubelfeier des 25 jährigen Bestehens des Vereins für Erdkunde zu Dresden.* Dresden, 1888.

Ribbeck, Otto, *Anfänge und Entwickelung des Dionysoscultus in Attika.* Kiel, 1869.

Ribeiro, F. de Paulo, " Memoria sobre as nações gentias que presentemente habitam o continente do Maranhão," *Revista Trimensal de Historia e Geographia.* Vol. iii. Rio de Janeiro, 1841.

Ribiero, *History of Celao.* Transl. by P. E. Pieris. Colombo, 1909.

Ribot, T., *La psychologie des sentiments.* Paris, 1896.

Riccardi, P., *Pregiudizii e superstizioni del popolo modenese.* Firenze, 1891.

Richard, J., *Histoire naturelle, civile et politique du Tonquin.* Paris, 1778.

Richards, F. J., " Cross-Cousin Marriage in India," *Man.* Vol. xiv. London, 1914.

Richardson, J., *Travels in the Great Sahara.* 2 vols. London, 1848.

Richardson, J., Tanala Customs, Superstitions and Beliefs, *Antananarivo Annual and Madagascar Magazine.* No. ii. Antananarivo, 1876.
  " Remarkable Burial Customs of the Betsileo," *ibid.* No. i. Antananarivo, 1875.

Richardson, John, *Arctic Searching Expedition.* 2 vols. London, 1851.

Richardtz, J. M. Firmenich, Τραγουδια 'Ρωμαικα. *Neugriechische Volkgesänge.* Berlin, 1840.

Richter, " Das Bezirk Bukoba," *Mittheilungen aus den Deutschen Schutzgebieten.* Vol. xii. Berlin, 1899.

Richthofen, Ferdinand von, *China : Ergebnisse eigener Reisen und darauf gegründeten Studien.* 3 vols. Berlin, 1877–83.

Rickard, R. H., " The Dukduk Association of New Britain," *Proceedings of the Royal Society of Victoria.* Vol. iii. Melbourne, 1891.

Ridley, W., *The Aborigines of Australia.* Sydney, 1864.

Ridgeway, W., *The Early Age of Greece.* Cambridge, 1901.
  The Origin of Tragedy. Cambridge, 1910.

Ridley, William, " Report on Australian Languages and Traditions," *Journal of the Anthropological Institute.* Vol. ii. London, 1873.
  Kamilaroi and other Australian Languages. New South Wales, 1875.

Riedel, J. G. F., " De Minahasa in 1825 ; Bijdrage tot de kennis van Noord-Selebes," *Tijdschrift voor Indische Taal-Land en Volkenkunde.* Vol. xviii. Batavia, 1872.

De sluik- en kroesharige rassen tusschen Selebes en Papua. 's Gravenhage, 1886.

" De vroegere regten en verpliggtigen der Alifoeroes van Noord-Selebes," *Tijdschrift voor Indische Taal-, Land- en Volkenkunde.* Vol. xviii. Batavia, 1872.

" The Sawu Group," *Revue Coloniale Internationale.* Amsterdam, 1885.

" The Island of Flores," *Revue Coloniale Internationale.* Amsterdam, 1886.

" Die Lanschafte Holontalo, Limveto, Bone, Boalemo, und Kattingola oder Andagile," etc., *Zeitschrift für Ethnologie.* Vol. iii. Berlin, 1871.

Riemann, G., " Taubstumm und blind zugleich," *Zeitschrift für Pädagogische Psychologie und Pathologie.* Vol. ii. Berlin, 1900.

Riemer, J. A., *Missionsreise nach Surinam und Barbia, zu einer an Surinamfluss in dritten Grade der Linie wohnenden Freineger-Nation.* Zittau, Leipzig, 1801.

Rienzi, G. L. Domeny de, *Océanie, ou cinquième partie du monde (L'Univers).* 3 vols. Paris, 1836–37.

Riess, E., art. " Aberglaube," in Pauly-Wissowa, *Real-Encyclopädie der classischen Altertumswissenschaft.* Vol. i. Stuttgart, 1894.

Riggs, Stephen Return, *Dakota Grammar, Texts, and Ethnography (Contributions to North American Ethnology.* Vol. ix). Washington, 1893.

Dakota-English Dictionary (Contributions to North American Ethnology. Vol. vii). Washington, 1890.

Rig-Veda.—Aufrecht, Th., " Die Hymnen des Rigveda," *Indische Studien.* Vols. vi and vii. Berlin, 1861–62.

Transl. by A. Ludwig. 6 vols. Prague, 1876–88.

Rig-Veda-Sanhita : the Sacred Hymns of the Brahmans. Ed. F. Max Müller. 6 vols. London, 1849–74.

Rigveda lib. i, Sanskrit and Latin. Ed. F. Rosen (*Oriental Translation Fund*). London, 1838.

Rig-Veda. Transl. by H. Grassmann. 3 vols. Leipzig, 1876–77.

Langlois, A., *Rig-Véda.* Paris, 1870.

Rijn van Alkemale, J. A. van, " Verslag eener reis van Siak naar Pija Kombo," *Tijdschrift van het Koninklijk Nederlandsch Aardrijkskundig Genootschap.* 2e Serie, vol. ii. Amsterdam, 1885.

" Beschrijving eener reis van Bengkalis langs de Rokan-rivier naar Rantau-Binoewang," *Bijdragen tot de taal-, land- en volkenkunde van Nederlandsch-Indië.* 4e Serie, vol. viii. 's Gravenhage, 1884.

Ripley, W. Z., *The Races of Europe.* London, 1900.

Rink, Heinrich Johannes, *Tales and Traditions of the Eskimo, with a Sketch of their habits, religion, language, and other peculiarities.* Transl. Edinburgh, London, 1875.

Ris, H., " De onderafdeeling Klein Mandailing, Oeloe en Pahantan en hare bevolking met uitzondering van de Oeloes," *Bijdragen tot de taal-, land- en volkenkunde van Nederlandsch-Indië.* Vol. xlvi. 's Gravenhage, 1896.

Risley, H. H., *Tribes and Castes of Bengal.* 4 vols. Calcutta, 1891.

The People of India. London, 1915.

" Ethnographical Appendices," *Census of India, 1901.* Vol. i. Calcutta, 1903.

Ritter, Carl, *Allgemeine Erdkunde.* Berlin, 1862.

Ritter, H., " Land und Leute im russischen Amerika, nach den russischen Marine-Archiv (Morskoi Sbornik, 1862, No. i)," *Zeitschrift für allgemeine Erdkunde*, N.F. Vol. xiii. Berlin, 1862.

Riva Palacio, D. V. *Mexico a travès de los siglos*. First volume by D. Alf. Chavero. Mexico, s.d.

Rivero, M. E., and J. J. von Tschudi, *Peruvian Antiquities*. Transl. London, 1854.

Rivers, W. H. R., " The Marriage of Cousins in India," *Journal of the Royal Asiatic Society*. London, 1907.
> *The Todas*. London, 1906.
> *The History of Melanesian Society*. 2 vols. Cambridge, 1914.
> " Totemism in Polynesia and Melanesia," *Journal of the Royal Anthropological Institute*. Vol. xxxix. London, 1909.
> *Kinship and Social Organisation*. London, 1914.
> Art. "New Hebrides," in Hastings's *Encyclopaedia of Religion and Ethics*. Vol. ix. Edinburgh, 1917.

Rivet, P., " Les Indiens in Jivaros," *L'Anthropologie*. Vol. xviii. Paris, 1907.
> " La race Lagoa-Santa chez les populations précolombiennes de l'équateur," *Bulletin de la Société d'Anthropologie*. 5e Série, vol. ix. Paris, 1908.

Rivier, Alphonse, *Introduction historique au droit Romain*. Bruxelles, 1872.

Rivista marittima. Firenze, Roma, 1868–

Robelo, Cecilio A., *Diccionario de Mitologia Nahoa*. Mexico, 1905.

Robert of Brunne, *Handlyng Synne*. Ed. F. J. Furnivall (*Roxburghe Club Publications*). London, 1862.

Robert, C., " Sosipolis in Olympia," *Mittheilungen des kaiserlich deutschen archaeologischen Gesellschaft. Athenische Abtheilung*. Vol. xviii. Athens, 1893.

Roberts, Emma, *Scenes and Characteristics of Hindostan*. 3 vols. London, 1835.

Robertson, Sir George Scott, *The Kafirs of the Hindu-Kush*. London, 1896.

Robin, C. C., *Voyages dans l'intérieur de la Louisanne, de la Floride occidentale, et dans les isles de la Martinique et de Saint-Domingue, pendant les années 1802, 1803, 1804, 1805, et 1806*. 3 vols. Paris, 1807.

[Robinson, A.], *Life in California, by an American*. New York, 1846.

Robinson, F. N., " Satirists and Enchanters in Early Irish Literature," *Studies in the History of Religions presented to Crawford Howell Toy*. New York, 1912.

Robiou, Félix, *Mémoire sur l'économie politique, l'administration et la législation de l'Égypte au temps des Lagides*. Paris, 1875.

Rocha, Andres Diego, *Origen de los Indios*. 2 vols. Madrid, 1891.

Rochas, Victor de, *La Nouvelle Calédonie et ses habitants*. Paris, 1862.
> *Essai sur la topographie hygiénique et médicale de la Nouvelle Calédonie*. Paris, 1860.
> " Îles Loyalty," *Bulletin de la Société de Géographie*. 4e Série, vol. xx. Paris, 1860.

Rochebrune, A. T. de, " Étude morphologique sur la femme et l'enfant dans la race Ouolove," *Revue d'Anthropologie*. Vol. iv. Paris, 1875.

Rochefort, H. de, *Histoire naturelle et morale des îles Antilles de l'Amérique*. Rotterdam, 1658.

Rocher, Émile, *La province chinoise du Yün-Nan*. 2 vols. Paris, 1879–80.

Rochet d'Héricourt, C. E. X., *Voyage sur la côte orientale de la Mer Rouge, dans le pays d'Adel, et le royaume de Choa*. Paris, 1841.

Rochholz, E. L., *Deutscher Glaube und Brauch im Spiegel den heidnische Vorzeit*. 2 vols. Berlin, 1867.

Rochholz, E. L., *Drei Gaugöttinen, Walburg, Verena und Gertrud als deutsche Kirchenheilige.* Leipzig, 1870.

Rochon, Abbé, "Description of Madagascar," in *Madagascar, or Robert Drury's Journal.* Ed. by P. Oliver. London, 1890.

Rockhill, W. W., *The Land of the Lamas.* London, 1891.

Life of Buddha, and early History of his Order, from Tibetan works. London, 1884.

Rodenwaldt, G., in *Tyrins. Die Ergebnisse der Ausgrabungen.* q.v.

Rodin, Paul and Gray, Louis H., art. "Eskimos," in Hastings, *Encyclopaedia of Religion and Ethics.* Vol. ii. Edinburgh, 1909.

Rodocanachi, *La femme italienne à l'époque de la Renaissance.* Paris, 1907.

Rodulfus, *Gesta Abbatium Trudoniensium,* in Pertz, *Monumenta Germaniae Historica : Scriptores.* Vol. x. Hannoveriae, 1852.

Rodulfus Glaber, *Historiae sui temporis* in M. Bouquet, *Recueil des historiens de la Gaule et de la France.* Vol. x. Paris, 1740.

Roero, O., dei Marchesi di Cortanze, *Ricordi dei Viaggi al Cashemir, Piccolo e Medio Thibet, e Turkestan.* 3 vols. Torino, 1881.

Rogers, C., *Scotland, Social and Domestic.* London, 1869.

Rogers, R. W., *A History of Babylonia and Assyria.* 2 vols. New York, 1915.

The Religion of Babylonia and Assyria. London, 1908.

Cuneiform Parallels to the Old Testament. London, 1912.

Rogers, Woodes, *A Cruising Voyage round the World.* London, 1718.

Roggewein, Jacob, "An Account of Commodore Roggewein's Expedition," in J. Harris's *Navigantium atque Itinerantium Bibliotheca.* Vol. i. London, 1744.

Rohde, Erwin, *Psyche : Seelencult und Unsterblichkeitsglaube der Griechen.* 2 vols. Freiburg i. B., 1898.

Róheim, G., *Australian Totemism.* London, 1926.

Rohlfs, Gerhard. *Reise durch Marokko.* Bremen, 1868.

Rolland, B. G., *Recherches sur les prérogatives des dames chez les Gaulois, sur les Cours d'Amour,* etc. Paris, 1787.

Rolland, Eugène, *Faune populaire de la France.* 6 vols. Paris, 1877–83.

Rolle, P. N., *Recherches sur le culte de Bacchus.* 3 vols. Paris, 1824.

Le Roman de Merlin, or the Early History of King Arthur. Ed. H. O. Sommer. London, 1894.

Roman de Renart. Ed. D. M. Méon. Paris, 1826.

Le Roman de Thèbes. Ed. L. Constans. 2 vols. Paris, 1890.

Roman y Zamora, *Republicas de Indias, idolatrias y gobierno en Mexico y Peru ante de la conquista.* 2 vols. Madrid, 1897.

"The Romance of Sir Perceval of Galles," in *The Thornton Romances (Camden Society).* London, 1844.

Romanes, George John, *Animal Intelligence.* London, 1883.

Romania. Paris, 1872–

Romanische Studien veröffentlich von Emil Ebering. Berlin, 1897–

Li romans de Parise la Duchesse. Ed. G.-F. de Martonne. (*Anciens Poètes de la France.*) Paris, 1838.

Römer, L. F., *Nachrichten von der Küste Guinea.* Kopenhagen, Leipzig, 1769.

Romilly, Hugh Hastings, *The Western Pacific and New Guinea.* London, 1887.

"The Islands of the New Britain Group," *Proceedings of the Royal Geographical Society,* N.S. Vol. ix. London, 1887.

Letters from the Western Pacific and Mashonaland. London, 1893.

Römische Quartalschrift für christliche Altertumskunde und für Kirchengeschichte. Roma, 1887–

Roos, S., " Iets over Endeh," *Tijdschrift voor Indische taal-, land- en volken-kunde*. Vol. xxiv. Batavia, 's Hage, 1877.

Roosevelt, Théodore, and Heller, Edmund, *Life Histories of African Game Animals*. 2 vols. London, New York, 1915.

Rosales, Diego de, *Historia general de el Reyno de Chile*. 3 vols. Valparaiso, 1877–78.

Roscher, W. H., *Ausführliches Lexicon der griechischen und römischen Mythologie*. Leipzig, 1884–

Über Selene und Verwandtes. Leipzig, 1890.

Nachtrage, Leipzig, 1895.

Nektar und Ambrosia. Leipzig, 1883.

Roscio, Fr. João, " Breve noticia dos sete povos das missoes Guaranis, chamados commummente Tapes," *Revista Trimensal do Instituto Historico e Geographico Brasileiro*. Vol. xxi. Rio de Janeiro, 1858.

Roscoe, John, *The Baganda*. London, 1911.

The Northern Bantu. Cambridge, 1915.

The Soul of Central Africa, London, 1922.

" Notes on the Manners and Customs of the Baganda," *Journal of the Anthropological Institute*. Vol. xxxi. London, 1901.

" Further Notes on the Manners and Customs of the Baganda," *Journal of the Anthropological Institute*. Vol. xxxi. London, 1901.

" The Bahima," *Journal of the Royal Anthropological Institute*. Vol. xxxvii. London, 1907.

" Notes on the Bageshu," *Journal of the Royal Anthropological Institute*. Vol. xxxix. London, 1909.

The Bakitara or Banyoro. (*The First Part of the Report of the Mackie Ethnological Expedition to Central Africa*.) Cambridge, 1923.

The Banyankole. (*The Second Part of the Report of the Mackie Ethnological Expedition to Central Africa*.) Cambridge, 1923.

The Bagesu and other Tribes of the Uganda Protectorate. (*The Third Part of the Report of the Mackie Ethnological Expedition to Central Africa*.) Cambridge, 1924.

" Worship of the Dead as practised by some African Tribes," *Harvard African Studies*. Vol. i. Cambridge, 1917.

Rose, Archibald, and Brown, J. Coggin, " Lisu (Yawyin) Tribes of the Burma-China Frontier," *Memoirs of the Asiatic Society of Bengal*. Vol. iii. Calcutta, 1910.

Rose, H. A., *A Glossary of the Tribes and Castles of the Punjab and North-West Frontier Province*. 3 vols. Lahore, 1911–19.

" Hindu Pregnancy Observances in the Punjab," *Journal of the Anthropological Institute*. Vol. xxxv. London, 1905.

" The Khokhars and the Gakkhars in Panjab History," *The Indian Antiquary*. Vol. xxxvi. Bombay, 1907.

Rose, H. J., " On the Alleged Evidence for Mother-right in Early Greece," *Folk-lore*. Vol. xxii. London, 1911.

" Mother-right in Ancient Italy," *ibid.*, vol. xxxi. London, 1920.

Rosegarten, J. G. W., " Ueber der Vornamen oder ' Kunje ' der Araber," *Zeitschrift für die Kunde des Morgenlandes*. Vol. i. Göttingen, 1837.

Rosen, F. A., see *Rig-Veda*.

Rosenberg, C. A., *Die Erinyen*. Berlin, 1874.

Rosenberg, H. von, *Der malayische Archipel*. Leipzig, 1878.

" Bescchrijving van Engano en van deszelfs bewoners," *Tijdschrift voor Indische taal-, land- en volkenkunde*. Vol. iii. Batavia, 1854.

Ross, Alexander, *Adventures of the First Settlers on the Oregon or Columbia River*. London, 1849.

Ross, B. R., " The Eastern Tinneh," *Smithsonian Report for 1866.* Washington, 1867.

Ross, Sir John, *Narrative of a Second Voyage in Search of a North-West Passage.* London, 1835.

Rossbach, A., *Untersuchungen über die römische Ehe.* Stuttgart, 1853.

Rosset, C. W., " On the Maldive Islands more especially treating of Málé Atol," *Journal of the Anthropological Institute.* Vol. xvi. London, 1887.

Rössler, A., art. " Woman," in *The Catholic Encyclopaedia.* Vol. xv. New York, s.d.

Roth, H. Ling, *The Natives of Sarawak and British North Borneo.* 2 vols. London, 1896.

" The Natives of Borneo, edited from Papers of the late Brooke Low," *Journal of the Anthropological Institute.* Vol. xxi. London, 1898.

The Aborigines of Tasmania. London, 1890.

Great Benin. Halifax, 1903.

"American Quill Work; a possible clue to its origin," *Man.* Vol. xxiii. London, 1923.

"Studies in Primitive Looms," *Journal of the Royal Anthropological Institute.* Vols. xlvii, xlviii. London, 1917–18.

Roth, Walter, E., *Ethnological Studies among the North-West-Central Queensland Aborigines.* Brisbane, 1897.

North Queensland Ethnography. Bulletins Nos. 1–8. Brisbane, 1901–6.

Bulletins Nos. 10–11, *Records of the Australian Museum.* Vol. vii. Sydney, 1910.

" An Inquiry into the Animism and Folk-Lore of the Guiana Indians." *Thirtieth Annual Report of the Bureau of American Ethnology.* Washington, 1915.

Rougé, E. de, *Notices sommaires des monuments exposés dans la galerie d'antiquités égyptiennes au Musée du Louvre.* Paris, 1872.

" Note sur l'usage de régler certaines fêtes en Égypte par la nouvelle lune," *Bibliothèque Égyptologique.* Vol. xxiv. Paris, 1911.

Rougier, Emmanuel, " Maladies et médecines à Fiji, autrefois et aujourd'hui," *Anthropos.* Vol. ii. Salzburg, 1907.

Rouquette, H. E., " A Few Notes on the Farming, etc., of the Kafirs and Basutos," *Journal of the Anthropological Institute.* Vol. xvi. London, 1887.

Rouse, W. H. D., " Folklore from the Southern Sporades," *Folk-lore.* Vol. x. London, 1899.

Rousseau, Jean-Jacques, *Oeuvres complètes.* 4 vols. Paris, 1837.

Rousselet, Louis, *India and its Native Princes.* Transl. London, 1876.

Routledge, W. S. and K., *With a Prehistoric People, The Akikuyu of British East Africa.* London, 1910.

Roux, Wilhelm, *Der Kampf der Theile im Organismus.* Leipzig, 1881.

Rovings in the Pacific from 1837 to 1849. By a Merchant long resident at Tahiti. 2 vols. London, 1851.

Rowe, G. S., *A Pioneer. A Memoir of the Rev. John Thomas, Missionary to the Friendly Islands.* London, 1885.

Rowley, Henry, *Africa Unveiled.* London, 1876.

The Story of the Universities' Mission to Central Africa. London, 1867.

Rowney, H. B., *The Wild Tribes of India.* London, 1882.

Roy, Sarat Chandra, *The Orāons of Chōtā Nāgpur.* Ranchi, 1915.

The Mundas and Their Country. Calcutta, 1912.

Roy, S. H., " Melanesia and New Guinea," *Journal of the Anthropological Institute.* Vol. xxxi. London, 1901.

Royce, C. C., " The Cherokee Nation of Indians," *Fifth Annual Report of the Bureau of Ethnology.* Washington, 1887.

Rubbens, Clement, " Préjugés en Louisiane," *Revue des Traditions Populaires.* Vol. v. Paris, 1890.

Rudbeck, Olf, *Atlantica seu Manheim.* Pars altera. Upsalae, 1689. Pars quarta. Upsalae, 1702.

Rudel, Jaufré. See Jeanroy, A.

Ruiz de Montoya, Antonio, *Conquista espiritual hecha por les religiosos de la Compañia de Jesús en las Provincias del Paraguay, Parana, Vruguay y Tape.* Madrid, 1639.

Rumphius, Georgius Everhardus, *D'Amboinsche rareteikamer, behelzende eene beschrijvinge van . . . schaalvisschen . . . die men in d'Amboische zee vierdt,* etc. Amsterdam, 1741.

Rumphius-gedenkboek, 1702–1902. Amsterdam, 1902.

Rupp, H., " Ueber die Prüfung musikalischen Fähigkeiten," *Zeitschrift für angewandte Psychologie.* Vol. ix. Leipzig, 1915.

Rüppell, Ed., *Reisen in Abyssinien.* 2 vols. Frankfurt, 1838–40.

Russeger, Jos., *Reise in Europa, Asien und Africa.* 5 vols. Stuttgart, 1847–49.

Russell, Frank, " Myths of the Jicarille Apaches," *Journal of American Folk-Lore.* Vol. xi. Boston, New York, 1898.

" The Pima Indians," *Twenty-sixth Annual Report of the American Bureau of Ethnology.* Washington, 1908.

Russell, R. V., *The Tribes and Castes of the Central Provinces of India.* 4 vols. London, 1916.

Russische Revue. St. Petersburg, 1873–91.

Rutter, Owen, *British North Borneo.* London, 1922.

Rzaczynski, P. Gabriel, *Historia naturalis curiosa regni Poloniae, Magni Ducatis Lituaniae . . .* Sandomiriae, 1721.

S——, I. F., *Algemeine Geschichte der Lander und Völker von America, nebst eine Vorrede von S. J. Baumgarten.* Halle, 1752.

Saabye, Hans Egede, *Bruckstücke eines Tagebuches gehalten in Grönland.* Transl. Hamburg, 1817.

Sachse, F. J. P., *Het Eiland Seran en zijne bewoners.* Leiden, 1907.

The Sacred Books of China. Transl. by J. Legge (*The Sacred Books of the East.* Vols. iii, xvi.) Oxford, 1897, 1882.

The Sacred Books of the East, transl. by various scholars. Edited by F. Max Müller. 50 vols. Oxford, 1879–1910.

The Sacred Laws of the Âryas as taught in the Schools of Âpastamba, Gautama, Vâsishta, and Bhadhâyana. Transl. by G. Bühler. (*The Sacred Books of the East.* Vols. ii, xiv.) Oxford, 1882, 1897.

Sacy, A. I. Silvestre de, *Mémoires sur diverses antiquités de la Perse et sur les médailles des Sassanides, suivis de l'histoire de Mirkhond.* Paris, 1793.

Sad-Dar. Transl. by E. W. West. (*The Sacred Books of the East*). Vol. xxiv. Oxford, 1885.

Saegert, C. W., *Das Taubstummen-Bildungswesen in Preusen.* Berlin, 1850.

Saegher, M. de, " Les coutumes des indigènes de l'état indépendant du Congo," *Bulletin de la Société d'Études Coloniales.* Bruxelles, 1894.

Safford, W. E., " Guam and its People," *The American Anthropologist.* N.S., vol. iv. New York, 1902.

agard Théodat, F. Gabriel, *Le Grand Voyage du Pays des Hurons.* Paris, 1632. Reprint, Paris, 1865.

Sager, J. W., " Notes on the History, Religion and Customs of the Nuba,"
Sudan Notes and Records. Vol. v. Khartoum, 1922.

Sahagún Bernardino de, *Historia de las cosas de la Nueva España*. 3 vols.
Mexico, 1829.

St. Élie, A. M., " La femme du désert autrefois et aujourd'hui," *Anthropos*.
Vol. iii. Wien, 1908.

Le Saint-Graal, ou le Joseph d'Arimathée. Ed. E. Hucher. 3 vols. Le
Mans, Paris, 1875–78.

Saint-Hilaire, Auguste de, *Voyages dans l'intérieur du Bresil*. 4 Parts
(bearing different titles). Paris, 1830–51.

St. John, H. C., *Notes and Sketches from the Wild Country of Nipon*. Edinburgh,
1880.

" The Aino : Aborigines of Yeso," *Journal of the Anthropological Institute*,
Vol. ii. London, 1873.

St. John, Spencer, *Life in the Forests of the Far East*. 2 vols. London,
1862.

" Wild Tribes of the North-West Coast of Borneo," *Transactions of the
Ethnological Society*. N.S., vol. ii. London, 1863.

St. Johnston, T. R., *The Islanders of the Pacific*. London, 1921.

The Lau Islands, Fiji, and their Fairy Tales and Folklore. London, 1918.

St. Reymond, Lasislas, *The Peasants. Autumn*. Transl. London, 1925.

Saintyves, P., *Les vierges mères et les naissances miraculeuses*. Paris, 1908.

Les saints successeurs des dieux. Paris, 1907.

Sajous, Charles de M., *The Internal Secretions and the Principles of Medicine*.
2 vols. Philadelphia, London, 1903–7.

Sakamoto, *Das Ehescheidungsrecht Japans*. Berlin, 1903.

Salcamayhua, Juan de Santa Cruz Pachacuti-Yamqui, " An Account of the
Antiquities of Peru." Transl. by Sir Clements R. Markham. *Narratives
of the Rites and Laws of the Yncas*. London, 1873.

Salimbene Parmigiano, Fra, *Cronaca, volgarizzata da Carlo Cantarelli*.
2 vols. Parma, 1882.

Salle, Laisnel de la, *Croyances et légendes du centre de la France*. Paris, 1875.

Sallustius Crispus, C., *Catilinae Conjuratio ; Bellum Jugurthinum*. Recog.
Axel. W. Ahlberg. Lipsiae, 1919.

Salmon, G., " Les institutions berbères au Maroc," *Archives Marocaines*.
Vol. i. Paris, 1904.

" Une tribu marocaine," *ibid*.

" Les Bd'ad'oua," *ibid*. Vol. ii. Paris, 1905.

Salmon, George, *A Historical Introduction to the Study of the Books of the New
Testament*. London, 1897.

Art. " Saturninus," in W. Smith and H. Wace, *Dictionary of Christian
Biography, Literature, Sects and Doctrines*. Vol. iv. London, 1887.

" The Cross-References in the ' Philosophumena,' " *Hermathena*. Vol. v.
Dublin, 1885.

Salt, H., *A Voyage to Abyssinia*. London, 1814.

Salvado, Rudesindo, *Memorie storiche dell' Australia, particolarmente della
missione Benedettina di Nuova Norcia, e degli usi e costumi degli
Australiani*. Roma, 1851.

Mémoires historiques sur l'Australie. Paris, 1854.

Salvadori, Giulio, *La poesia giovanile e la canzone d'amore di Guido Cavalcanti*.
Roma, 1895.

Salverda de Grave, J. J., *Le troubadour Bertran d'Alamanon*. Toulouse,
1902.

Salvianus, *Opera*, in Migne, *Patrologiae Cursus Completus*. Vol. liii. Parisiis,
1847.

Sammlungen von Natur- und Medicin wie auch hierzu gehörigen Kunst- und Literatur- Geschichte so sich in Schlesien und andern Landern begeben von einigen Breslauischen Medicis. Winter-Quartal, 1718.

Samter, Ernst, *Geburt, Hochzeit und Tod.* Leipzig, Berlin, 1911.

Sanas Chormaic. Cormac's Glossary. Transl. by J. O'Donovan. Ed. by Whitley Stokes. Calcutta, 1868.

Sanchez, Jesús, " Estatua colosal de la diosa del agua," *Anales del Museo Nacional.* Vol. iii. Mexico, 1886.

Sánchez Labrador, José, *El Paraguay Católico.* 2 vols. Buenos Aires, 1910.

Sand, George, *La Mare au Diable.* Paris, 1884.

Sanderson, George P., *Thirteen Years among the Wild Beasts of India.* London, 1878.

" Die Sandwich Inseln, einst und jeis," *Evangelisches Missions-Magazine.* Neue Folge. Basel, 1865.

Sangermano, A., *Description of the Burmese Empire.* Transl. Rome, 1833.

Sankara Menon, M., " Cochin," Report, *Census of India, 1901.* Vol. xx. Ernakulam, 1903.

Sankarâkârya. See *Vedânta-Sûtras.*

San-Marte (A. Schulz), *Die Sagen von Merlin.* Halle, 1853.

Sanson, André, *L'hérédité normale et pathologique.* Paris, 1893.

Sanson, André, " Sur les unions consanguine chez les animaux domestiques." *Bulletin de la Société d'Anthropologie.* 1e Série, vol. iii. Paris, 1862.

Santa-Anna Nery, F.-J., *Folk-lore Brésilien.* Paris, 1889.

Santa Clara, Pedro Gutierrez de, *Historia de las guerras civiles del Peru (1544–1548) y de otros sucesos de las Indias.* 3 vols. Madrid, 1904–5.

Santa Ines, " Cronica de la Provincia San Gregorio Magno," in E. H. Blair and J. A. Robertson, *The Philippine Islands, 1493–1808.* Vol. vii. Cleveland, 1903.

Sapir, Edward, " Notes on the Takelma Indians of the South-western Oregon," *The American Anthropologist.* N.S., vol. ix. Lancaster, 1907.

" Religious Ideas of the Takelma Indians," *Journal of American Folk-Lore.* Vol. xix. New York, 1906.

Sapper, Carl, " The Old Settlements and Architectural Structures in North America," *Smithsonian Report for 1895.* Washington, 1896.

" Die Gebräuche und religiosen Anschaungen der Kekchi-Indianer," *Internationales Archiv für Ethnographie.* Vol. viii. Leiden, 1895.

Sarasin, Fritz, *La Nouvelle-Calédonie et les îles Loyalty.* Bâle, 1917.

Sarasin, Paul, " Ueber die Entwicklung des griechischen Tempel aus der Pfahlhaus," *Zeitschrift für Ethnologie.* Vol. xxxix. Berlin, 1907.

and Sarasin, F., *Reisen in Celebes.* 2 vols. Wiesbaden, 1905.

Ergebnisse naturwissenschaftlicher Forschungen auf Ceylon. 4 vols. Wiesbaden, 1887–93.

Sarat Chandra Das, " The Marriage Customs of Tibet," *Journal of the Asiatic Society of Bengal.* Vol. lxii, Part iii. Calcutta, 1893.

Sarat Chandra Mitra, " On the Har Parauri, or the Behari Women's Ceremony for producing rain," *Journal of the Royal Asiatic Society.* N.S., vol. xxix. London, 1897.

" On some Ceremonies for producing Rain," *Journal of the Anthropological Society of Bombay.* Vol. iii. Bombay, 1893.

The Sarawak Museum Journal. Singapore, 1912–

Sarbah, J. M., *Fanti Customary Law.* London, 1904.

Sarmiento de Gamboa, P., *History of the Incas.* Transl. by Sir C. Markham. (*Hakluyt Society.*) London, 1907.

Sarrazin, H., *Les races humaines du Soudan français.* Paris, 1901.

Sars, M., "Mémoire sur le développement des astéries," *Annales des Sciences Naturelles.* 3e Série, Zoologie. Vol. ii. Paris, 1844.

Sarzec, E. de, *Découvertes en Chaldée.* Ed. by Leon Henzey. Paris, 1912.

Sassetti, Filippo, "Lettere," in A. de Gubernatis, *Storia dei Viaggiatori Italiani nelle Indie Orientali.* Livorno, 1875.

The Satapatha-Brâhmana. Transl. by Julius Eggeling. (*The Sacred Books of the East.*) Vols. xii, xli, xliii. Oxford, 1882–1900.

Saunderson, H. S., "Notes on Corea and its People," *Journal of the Anthropological Institute.* Vol. xxiv. London, 1895.

Sauson, A., *L'hérédité normale et pathologique.* Paris, 1893.

Sauvé, L. F., *Le Folk-lore des Hautes-Vosges.* Paris, 1889.

Savage, George H., *Insanity and Allied Neuroses.* London, 1891.

Savage, Dr. John, *Some Account of New Zealand, particularly of the Bay of Islands, and surrounding country.* London, 1807.

Savage, T. S., and Wyman, J., "Observations on the External Characters and Habits of Troglodytes Niger," *Boston Journal of Natural History.* Vol. iv. Boston, 1844.

Sawyer, Frederic H., *The Inhabitants of the Philippines.* London, 1900.

Saxo Grammaticus, *Gesta Danorum.* Ed. A. Holder. Strassburg, 1886.

The First Nine Books of the Danish History of Saxo Grammaticus. Transl. by F. York Powell. London, 1894.

Sayce, A. H., "A Babylonian Saints' Calendar," *Records of the Past.* Vol. vii. London, 1876.

The Hibbert Lectures, 1887. London, 1887.

The Religions of Ancient Egypt and Babylonia. Edinburgh, 1902.

Sayous, Edouard, *Les origines et l'époque païenne de l'histoire des Hongrois.* Paris, 1874.

Scarano, N., "Fonti provenzali della lirica Petrarchesca," *Studi di Filologia Romanza.* Vol. ii. Roma, 1886.

Schaafhausen, Hermann, *Anthropologischen Studien.* Bonn, 1885.

"Darwinism and Anthropology, "*The Anthropological Review.* Vol. vi. London, 1868.

Schack, Adolf F., Graf von, *Poesie und Kunst der Araber in Spanien und Sicilien.* 2 vols. Stuttgart, 1877.

Schadee, M. C., "Heirats- und andere Gebräuche bei den Mansela und Nusawele Alfuren in der Unterscheilung Wahaai der Insel Seram," *Internationales Archiv für Ethnologie.* Vol. xxii. Leiden, 1913.

Schandein, L., in *Bavaria, Landes- und Volkskunde des Königsreichs Bayern.* Vol. iv. München, 1866.

Schandenberg, Alex., "Die Bewohner von Süd-Mindanao und der Insel Samal," *Zeitschrift für Ethnologie.* Vol. xii. Berlin, 1880.

Schaudinn, F., "Ueber den Zeugungskreis von *Paramoeba Eilhardi,*" *Sitzungsberichte der Königliche Preussiche Akademie der Wissenschaften.* Berlin, 1896.

Schayer, "Abhandlung über die Verhältnisse der Eingeborenen von Australia und die Ursachen der Abnahmung der Bevölkerung," *Monatsberichte über die Verhandlungen der Gesellschaft für Erdkunde zu Berlin, Neue Folge.* Vol. iv. Berlin, 1847.

Schedius, Elias, *De diis germanis.* Halae, 1728.

Scheffer, John, *The History of Lapland wherein are shewed the original manners, habits, marriages, conjurations,* etc., *of that people.* Oxford, 1674.

Scheftelowitz, I., "Das Fischsymbol im Judentum und Christentum," *Archiv für Religionswissenschaft.* Vol. xiv. Leipzig, 1911.

Schellong, O., "Beiträge zur Anthropologie der Papua," *Zeitschrift für Ethnologie.* Vol. xxiii. Berlin, 1891.

Schellong, O., " Das Barlum-Fest der Gegend Fischhafens," *Internationales Archiv für Ethnographie.* Vol. ii. Leiden, 1889.

Scheube, B., " Die Ainos," *Mittheilungen der deutsche Gesellschaft für Natur- und Volkerkunde Ostasiens.* Vol. iii. Yokohama, 1880–84.

Schillings, C. B., *Mit Blitzlicht und Büchse.* Leipzig, 1907.

Schinz, Hans, *Deutsch-Süd-West-Afrika.* Oldenburg, Leipzig, 1891.

Schirmer, H., *Le Sahara.* Paris, 1893.

Schlagintweit-Sakünlünski, Hermann von, *Reisen in Indien und Hochasien,* 1854–58. 4 vols. Jena, 1871–80.

Schlegel, C. W. Friederich von, *The Philosophy of History.* Transl. London, 1846.

Schlegel, Gustav, *La Femme Chinoise.* Leide, 1896.

" The Secret of the Chinese Method of transcribing Foreign Sounds," *T'oung Pao.* Series ii, vol. i. Leiden, 1900.

Sing chin khao youen, Uranographie Chinoise. Leiden, 1875.

Mai Yu Lang Tou Tchen Hoa Kouei. Le vendeur-d'huile qui seul possède la reine-de-beauté. Roman chinois traduit pour la première fois par. G. S. Leiden, 1877.

Schlegel, H., en Müller, S., " Bijdragen tot de natuurlijke historie van den Orang-oetan (*Simia Satyrus*)," *Verhandelingen over de natuurlijke geschiedenis der Nederlandsche overzeesche bezittingen : Zoologie.* Leiden, 1839–44.

Schleinitz, — von, " Die Markesas Inseln und ihre Bevölkerung," *Verhandlungen der Gesellschaft für Erdkunde zu Berlin.* Vol. vi. Berlin, 1879.

Schliemann, Heinrich, *Troja.* Leipzig, 1884.

Schmaltz, Heinrich, *Die Taubstummen im Königreich Sachsen.* Leipzig, 1884.

Ueber die Taubstumme und ihren Bildung. Dresden, Leipzig, 1838.

Schmeller, J. A., *Bayerisches Wörterbuch.* Ed. by G. K. Fromman. 2 vols. München, 1872–78.

Schmeltz, J. D. E., " Ethnographical Notes on the West Australian Aborigines," *Internationales Archiv für Ethnographie.* Vol. xvi. Leiden, 1903.

" Über einige religiöse Gebräuche der Melanesier," *Globus.* Vol. xli. Braunschweig, 1882.

Schmid, Von, " Het Kakihansch verbond op het eiland Ceram," *Tijdschrift voor Neerlands Indië.* Vol. ii. Batavia, 1843.

Schmidt, Karl, " Das Streit über das jus primae noctis," *Zeitschrift für Ethnologie.* Vol. xvi. Berlin, 1884.

Schmidt, Max, *Indianerstudien in Zentralbrasiliern.* Berlin, 1905.

" Die Guato," *Verhandlungen der Berliner Gesellschaft für Anthropologie.* Berlin, 1902.

" Ueber das Recht der tropische Naturvölker Sudamerikas," *Zeitschrift für vergleichende Rechtswissenschaft.* Vol. xiii. Stuttgart, 1899.

Schmidt, P. W., " Ethnographisches von Berlinhafen, Deutsch-Neu-Guinea," *Mittheilungen der Anthropologischen Gesellschaft in Wien.* Vol. xxx. Wien, 1899.

" Grundlinien einer Vergleichung der Religionen und Mythologien der Austronesischen Völkern," *Denkschriften der Kaiserlichen Akademie der Wissenschaften in Wien. Philosophisch-historische Klasse.* Vol. liii. Vienna, 1910.

Schmidt, Richard, *Cukasaptati.* Kiel, 1894.

Liebe und Ehe im alten und modernen Indien. Berlin, 1904.

Schmidt, W., *Das Jahr und seine Tage in Meinung und Brauch der Romänen Siebenbürgens.* Hermannstadt, 1866.

Schmidt, W. A., *Forschungen auf dem Gebiet des Alterthums*. Part i (no more published). *Die griechischen Papyruskunden der königliche Bibliothek zu Berlin*. Berlin, 1842.

Schmitz, J. H., *Sitten und Sagen, Lieder, Spruchwörter und Räthsel des Eifler Volkes*. 2 vols. Trier, 1856.

Schmitz, Robert, *Les Baholoholo*. Bruxelles, 1912.

Schneider, G. H., *Der Menschliche Wille vom Standpunkt der neueren Entwicke-lungstheorien*. Berlin, 1882.

Schneider, J. G., see *Scriptores Rei Rusticae*.

Schneider, Oscar, *Muschelgeldt-Studien*. Dresden, 1905.

Schneider, W., *Die Religion der afrikanischen Naturvölker*. Munster i. W. 1891.

Schoepperle, Gertrude, *Tristan and Isolt, a Study of the Sources of Romance*. 2 vols. Frankfurt a. M., London, 1913.

Schofield, A. T., *The Springs of Character*. London, s.d.

Schofield, W. H., *English Literature from the Norman Conquest to Chaucer*. London, 1906.

Schömann, G. F., *Opuscula academica*. 3 vols. Berlin, 1856–58.

Schomburgk, R., "Ueber einige Sitten und Gebräuche der tief im Innern Süd-Australiens, am Peake-Flusse und dessen Umgebung hausenden Stämme," *Verhandlungen der Berliner Gesellschaft für Anthropologie*. Berlin, 1879.

Schomburgk, Richard, *Reisen in Britisch-Guiana in den Jahren 1840–44*. 3 vols. Leipzig, 1847–48.

Schöne, G., and Mannhardt, W., "Die Eisfrau von Ichstedt," *Zeitschrift für deutsche Mythologie und Sittenkunde*. Vol. iii. Göttingen, 1853.

Schoolcraft, H. R., *Algic Researches*. New York, 1839.
    The Indian in his Wigwam. New York, 1848.
    Historical and Statistical Information respecting the History, Condition, and Prospects of the Indian Tribes of the United States. 6 vols. Philadelphia, 1851–60.
    The Myth of Hiawatha, and other oral legends and allegories of the North American Indians. Philadelphia, London, 1856.

Schopenhauer, Arthur, *Parerga und Paralipomena*. 2 vols. Berlin, 1862.

Schott, "Ueber die Sage von Geser-Chan," *Abhandlungen der königlichen Akademie der Wissenschaften zu Berlin*. Berlin, 1851.

Schott, Gaspar, *Magia universalis naturae et artis*. Herbipolis, 1657–59.

Schotter, Aloys, "Notes ethnographiques sur les tribus de Kouy-tcheou (Chine)," *Anthropos*. Vol. vi. Wien, 1911.

Schouten, Wouter, *Ost-Indische Reyse*. Amsterdam, 1676.

Schrader, E., *Die Keilinschriften und das Alte Testament*. Berlin, 1903.
    Keilinschriftliche Bibliothek. Berlin, 1889–
    Die Höllenfahrt der Istar. Giessen, 1874.

Schrader, Otto, *Sprachvergleichung und Urgeschichte*. Jena, 1890.
    Art. "Charms and Amulets (Slavic)" in Hastings's *Encyclopaedia of Religion and Ethics*. Vol. iii. Edinburgh, 1910.

Schreiber, A., *Die Battas in ihren Verhältnisse zu den Malaien von Sumatra*. Barmen, 1874.

Schreiber, Emmanuel, *Die Principien des Judenthums verglichen mit denen des Christenthums*. Leipzig, 1877.

Schreiner, Olive, *Woman and Labour*. London, 1911.

Schrenk, Alex. Gustav, *Reise nach dem Nordoste der europäischen Russlands durch die Tundren der Samoyeden*. 2 vols. Dorpat, 1848.

Schren(c)k, L. von, *Reisen und Forschungen im Amur-Lande*. 4 vols. St. Petersburg, 1858–1900.

Schröder, Edward, " Ueber das Spell," *Zeitschrift für deutches Alterthum und deutche Litteratur.* Vol. xxxvii. Berlin, 1893.

Schroeder, Leopold von, *Die Hochzeitsgebräuche der Esten und einiger anderer finnisch-ugrischer Völkerschaften in Vergleichung mit denen der indogermanischen Völker.* Berlin, 1888.

Schultz, Alwin, *Das höfische Leben zur Zeit der Minnesinger.* 2 vols. Leipzig, 1879–80.

Schültz, H. G., in *Annali del Instituto di corrispondenza archeologica.* Roma, 1839.

Schultz-Sellack, C., " Die amerikanischen Götter der vier Weltrichtungen und ihre Temple in Palanque," *Zeitschrift für Ethnologie.* Vol. xi. Berlin, 1879.

Schultze, E., *Die Prostitution bei gelben Völker.* Bonn, 1918.

Schultze, F., *Der Fetichismus.* Leipzig, 1871.

Schultze, L., *Aus Namaland und Kalahari.* Jena, 1907.

Schulze, Rev. Louis, " The Aborigines of the Upper and Middle Finke River : their Habits and Customs." Translated from the German by J. G. Tepper, *Transactions and Proceedings of the Royal Society of South Australia.* Vol. xiv. Adelaide, 1891.

Schulze, Wilhelm, " Zur Geschichte lateinischer Eigennamen," *Abhandlungen der Königlichen Gesellschaft der Wissenschaften, Philologisch-historisch klasse.* N.F. v., No. 5. Göttingen, 1847.

Schumacher, P., " Das Eherecht in Ruanda," *Anthropos.* Vol. vii. Wien, 1912.

Schure, E., " Le Miracle Hellénique. L'Apollon de Delphes et la Pythonisse," *Revue des Deux Mondes.* Paris, 1912.

Schürer, Emil, *History of the Jewish People in the Time of Jesus Christ.* Transl. 5 vols. Edinburgh, 1885–90.

Schurtz, H., *Urgeschichte der Kultur.* Leipzig, Wien, 1900.

" Zur Ornamentik der Ainos," *Internationales Archiv für Ethnographie.* Vol. ix. Leiden, 1896.

Schuster, E., and Elderton, E. M., " Inheritance of Psychical Characters," *Biometrika.* Vol. v. Cambridge, 1907.

Schuster, F., " Die sozialen Verhältnisse des Banjange-Stammes (Kamerun)," *Anthropos.* Vol. ix. Wien, 1914.

Schütt, O., *Reise in Südwestlichen Becken des Congo.* Berlin, 1881.

Schuyler, Eugene, *Turkistan.* 2 vols. London, 1876.

Schwaner, C. A. L. M., *Borneo. Beschrijving van het stroomgebied van den Barito,* etc. Amsterdam, 1853–54.

" Aanteekenigen betreffende eenige maatschappelijke instelligen en gebruiken der Dajaks van Doesson, Moeroeng en Siang " (nader bewerkt door Dr. J. H. Croockewit), *Tijdschrift voor Indische taal-, land- en volkenkunde.* Vol. i. Batavia, 1853.

Schwanhäuser, Hans, *Das Seelenleben der Dschagga-Neger.* Erlangen, 1910.

Schwartz, F. L. W., *Sonne, Mond und Sterne.* Berlin, 1864.

Der Ursprung der Mythologie. Berlin, 1860.

Schwartz, J. Alb. T., " Ethnographica uit Minahassa," *Internationales Archiv für Ethnographie.* Vol. xviii. Leiden, 1906.

Schwarz, B., *Algerien.* Leipzig, 1881.

Schweinfurth, Georg, *Im Herzen von Afrika.* 2 vols. Leipzig, 1874.

The Heart of Africa. Transl. 2 vols. London, 1874.

" Das Volk der Monbuttu in Central-Africa," *Zeitschrift für Ethnologie.* Vol. v. Berlin, 1873.

Artes Africanae. Leipzig, 1875.

Schwela-Schorbus, " Die ' grosse ' wendische Hochzeit," *Zeitschrift für Volkskunde.* Vol. iii. Leipzig, 1891.

Scialoia, Vittorio, " Il testamento di Acca Larentia," *Rendiconti della Reale Accademia dei Lincei. Classe di Scienze morali, storiche e filologiche.* Ser. 5, vol. xiv. Roma, 1905.

Science. Cambridge (Mass.), 1883–

Science Progress in the Twentieth Century. London, 1906–

Scientia. Bologna, Milano, 1910–

Sclater, Philip Lutley, and Thomas, Oldfield, *The Book of Antelopes.* 4 vols. London, 1894–1900.

Scory, Sir Edmund, " Extracts taken out of the observations of the Right Worshipfull Sir Edmund Scory, Knight of the Pike of Tenariffe," in *Purchas His Pilgrimage.* London, 1626.

Scott, A. W., *Seal, Dugongs, Whales.* Sydney, 1873.

Scott, Sir James George, and Hardiman, J. P., *Gazetteer of Upper Burma and the Shan States.* 5 vols. Rangoon, 1900–1.

See Shway Yoe.

Scott, John W., " Some Egg-laying Habits of *Amphitrite ornata*," *Biological Bulletin of the Marine Biological Laboratory, Woods Hole.* Vol. xvii. Woods Hole, Mass., 1909.

Scott, Reginald, *The Discoverie of Witchcraft.* London, 1654.

Scott, Mrs., Samuel Bryan. See Morris, Margaretta.

Scott, Sir Walter, *Demonology and Witchcraft.* London, 1876.

Scott, W. E. D., " Data on Song in Birds," *Science.* Vol. xiv, vol. xv, New York, 1901. Vol. xix, vol. xx, New York, 1904.

The Scottish Geographical Magazine. Edinburgh, 1885–

Scriptores rei rusticae veteres Latini. Ed. J. G. Schneider. 4 vols. Leipzig, 1794–97.

Scriptores rerum Germanicarum in usum scholarum. Ed. G. H. Pertz. 63 vols. Hanover, 1839–1921.

Scröder, Leopold von, *Die Hochzeitsbräuche der Este und einige andre finnish-ugrischen Völkerschaften.* Berlin, 1888.

Sébillot, Paul, *Le Folk-Lore de France.* 4 vols. Paris, 1904–7.

Légendes, croyances, et superstitions de la mer. Paris, 1886.

Traditions et superstitions de la Haute-Bretagne. Paris, 1882.

" Secret Societies of the South Sudan," *Sudan Notes and Records.* Vol. iv. Khartoum, 1921.

Sedgwick, William, " On Sexual Limitations in Hereditary Disease," *The British and Foreign Medico-Chirurgical Review.* Vol. xxviii. London, 1861.

Seeland, N., " Die Ghiliaken (auf der Insel Sachalin). Eine ethnographische Skizze." *Russische Revue.* Vol. xxi. St. Petersburg, 1882.

Seemann, B., *Viti.* Cambridge, 1862.

Segers, P. A., " Habitos y costumbres de los Indios Aonas," *Bolletin del Institudo geografico Argentino.* Vol. xii. Buenos Aires, 1891.

Segonzac, Marquis René de, *Voyages au Maroc, 1899–1903.* Paris, 1903.

Séguin, E., *Idiocy, and its treatment by the Physiological Method.* New York, 1870.

Seidlitz, N. von, " Gemeinde- und Familienleben der Chewsuren," *Das Ausland.* Stuttgart, 1891.

Selden, Johannis, *Uxor Ebraica.* 2 vols. Francofurti ad Oberden, 1695.

Selections from the Records of the Government of India. Calcutta, 1853–75.

Seler, Eduard, *Codex Fejervary-Mayer.* Berlin, London, 1901–2.

Codex Borgia. 2 vols. Berlin, 1904–6.

" Einiges über die natürliche Grundlagen mexicanischer Mythen," *Zeitschrift für Ethnologie.* Vol. xxxix. Berlin, 1907.

Seler, Eduard, " Die Sage von Quetzalcouatl," *Verhandlungen des XVI internationales Amerikanisten-Kongressen.* Vol. i. Wien, 1910.

Seler, Eduard, art. " Mexicans (ancient)," in Hastings's *Encyclopaedia of Religion and Ethics.* Vol. viii. Edinburgh, 1916.

Seligman, C. G., *The Melanesians of British New Guinea.* Cambridge, 1910.
Report on Totemism and Religion of the Dinka of the White Nile. Khartoum, s.d.
" The Medicine, Surgery, and Midwifery of the Sinaugolo," *Journal of the Anthropological Institute.* Vol. xxxii. London, 1902.
" The Cult of Nyakang and the Divine Kings of the Shilluk," *Fourth Report of the Wellcome Tropical Research Laboratory at the Gordon Memorial College, Khartoum.* Khartoum, 1911.
" Some Aspects of the Hamitic Problem in the Anglo-Egyptian Sudan," *Journal of the Royal Anthropological Institute.* Vol. xliii. London, 1913.
and Seligman, Brenda Z., *The Veddas.* Cambridge, 1911.

Seligman, B. Z., " Marital Gerontocracy in Africa," *Journal of the Royal Anthropological Institute.* Vol. liv. London, 1924.

Seligmann, S., *Der Böse Blick und Verwandtes.* 2 vols. Berlin, 1910.

Seligsohn, M., art. " Moon," in *The Jewish Encyclopaedia.* Vol. viii. Chicago, s.d.

Seljan, Mirko and Stevo, " Tupi and Guarani, eine theo-kosmogonische Indianer Legend," *Globus,* xcvii. Braunschweig, 1910.

Selous, F. Courtney, *African Nature Notes and Reminiscences.* London, 1908.
A Hunter's Wanderings in Africa. London, 1881.

Semanario Erudito. Madrid, 1788–

Se-Ma-Ts'ien, *Les Mémoires Historiques, traduits par E. Chavannes.* Paris, 1895.

Semper, Karl, *Die Philippinen und ihre Bewohner.* Würzburg, 1869.
Die Palou-Insel im Stillen Ocean. Leipzig, 1873.

Seneca, Lucius Annaeus, *Opera.* Rec. F. Haase. 3 vols. Leipsic, 1884–92.

Senfft, Arno, " Die Rechtssitten der Jap Eingeborenen," *Globus.* Vol. xci. Braunschweig, 1907.
" Die Marshall-Insulaner," in S. R. Steinmetz, *Rechtsverhältnisse von eingeborenen Völkern in Afrika und Ozeanien.* Berlin, 1903.
" Die Insel Nauru," *Mitteilungen aus den Deutschen Schutzgebieten.* Vol. ix. Berlin, 1896.

Sepp, Anthony, and Behme, Anthony, " An Account of a Voyage from Spain to Paraquaria," in Churchill's *New Collection of Voyages and Travels.* Vol. iv. London, 1704.

Sera, Leo G., *Sulle Tracce della Vita.* Roma, 1907.

Serbelov, Gerda, " The Social Position of Men and Women among the Natives of East Malekula, New Hebrides," *The American Anthropologist.* N.S., vol. xv. Lancaster, 1913.

Sergi, Giuseppe, *The Mediterranean Race.* London, 1901.
Europa, l'origine dei popoli europei, e loro relazioni coi popoli d'Africa, d'Asia e d'Oceania. Torino, 1908.

Sermones Discipuli. Reutlingen, 1480.

Serpa Pinto, A. de, *Comment j'ai traversé l'Afrique.* 2 vols. Paris, 1882.

Servius Maurus Honoratus, *Servii grammatici qui feruntur in Vergilii carmina commentarii.* Rec. G. Thilo and H. Hagen. 3 vols. Lipsiae, 1878–1902.

Seton, Ernest Thompson, *Life Histories of Northern Animals.* 2 vols. London, New York, 1910.

Settegast, F., " Der Ehrbegriff in altfranzösische Rolandsliede," *Zeitschrift für romanische Philologie.* Vol. ix. Halle, 1886.

Settegast, Hermann Gustav, *Die Thierzucht.* Breslau, 1868.

Sextus Empiricus, *Opera*. Ed. Io. Albertus Fabricius. 2 vols. Leipzig, 1842.

Seynt Graal, or the Sank Ryal ; The History of the Holy Graal by H. Lonelick and R. de Borron. Ed. F. J. Furnivall. London, 1874.

Shakespear, J., *The Lushei Kuki Clans.* London, 1912.

" The Kuki-Lushai clans," *Journal of the Royal Anthropological Institute.* Vol. xxxix. London, 1909.

Shakespeare, William, *The Complete Works.* Oxford, s.d.

Shams-ul-Ulma Jivangi Jamshedij Modi, " Haoma in the Avesta," *Journal of the Anthropological Society of Bombay.* Vol. v. Bombay, 1890.

Shand, Alexander, " The Moriori People of the Chatham Islands ; their Traditions and History," *Journal of the Polynesian Society.* Vols. iii, iv, v, vi. Wellington, 1894–97.

Shand, A. F., *The Foundations of Character.* London, 1914.

Sharp, David, " Insects," in *The Cambridge Natural History.* Vols. v and vi. Cambridge, 1895, 1899.

Sharpe, Samuel, *Egyptian Antiquities in the British Museum.* London, 1862.

Egyptian Inscriptions from the British Museum and other Sources. 2 Parts. London, 1837–55.

Shaw, G. A., " The Betiseleo Country and People," *Antananarivo Annual and Madagascar Magazine.* No. III. Antananarivo, 1877.

" The Betsileo : Religious and Social Customs," *ibid.* No. IV. Antananarivo, 1878.

Shaw, Thomas, " On the Inhabitants of the Hills near Rájamahall," *Asiatick Researches.* Vol. iv. Calcutta, 1795.

Shâyast Lâ-Shâyast, in Pahlavi Texts translated by E. W. West, *The Sacred Books of the East.* Vol. v. Oxford, 1880.

She-King, in J. Legge, *The Chinese Classics.* Vol. iv. Hong-Kong, 1871.

Shea, J. Gilmary, *Early Voyages up and down the Mississippi.* Albany, 1861.

History of the Catholic Missions among the Indians of the United States, 1529–1854. New York, 1855.

" Discovery and Exploration of the Mississippi Valley," in B. F. French, *Historical Collections of Louisiana.* Vol. iv. q.v.

Sheane, J. H. West, " Some Aspects of the Awemba Religion and Superstitious Observances," *Journal of the Anthropological Institute.* Vol. xxxvi. London, 1906.

Sherring, C. A., *Western Tibet and the British Borderland.* London, 1906.

" Notes on the Bhotias of Almora and British Garwhal," *Memoirs of the Asiatic Society of Bengal.* Vol. i. Calcutta, 1907.

Shinn, Milicent Washburn, *Notes on the Development of a Child.* 2 vols. (*University of California Publications in Education.* Vols. i and iv.) Berkeley, 1893, 1907.

The Biography of a Baby. Boston, New York, 1900.

Shooter, Joseph, *The Kafirs of Natal and the Zulu Country.* London, 1857.

Shortland, E., *Southern Districts of New Zealand.* London, 1851.

Traditions and Superstitions of the New Zealanders. London, 1856.

Shortt, J., ed. *The Hill Ranges of Southern India.* 5 vols. Madras, 1868–76.

" An Account of the Hill Tribes of the Neilgherries " *Transactions of the Ethnological Society of London.* N.S., vol. vii. London, 1869.

" A Contribution to the Ethnology of Jeypore," *Transactions of the Ethnological Society.* N.S., vol. vi. London, 1868.

" The Bayadere, or Dancing Girls of Southern India," *Memoirs read before the Anthropological Society.* Vol. iii. London, 1870.

Shu-Ching (Chou-King). Ed. and transl. by S. Couvreur. Ho Kien Fou. 1897.

Shufeldt, R. W., "Notes on Certain Traits of Infant Navajos," *Nature.* Vol. xxxv. London, 1887.

"The Navajo Tanner," *Proceedings of the United States National Museum.* Vol. xi. Washington, 1889.

Shu-Li (Chou-Li, Le Tcheou-Li). Transl. by Édouard Biot. 2 vols. Paris, 1851.

Shway Yoe (i.e. Sir James George Scott), *The Burman, his Life and Notions.* 2 vols. London, 1882.

Sibree, James, *The Great African Island : Madagascar.* London, 1880.

"Remarkable Ceremonial at the Decease and Burial of a Betsileo Prince," *Antananarivo Annual and Madagascar Magazine.* No. XXII. Antananarivo, 1898.

"The Manners and Customs, Superstitions and Dialect of the Betsimisaraka," *ibid.* No. XXI. Antananarivo, 1897.

"Relationships and Names used for them among the Peoples of Madagascar," *Journal of the Anthropological Institute.* Vol. ix. London, 1880.

Siebert, Otto, "Sagen und Sitten der Dieri und Nachbarstämme Zentral-Australiens," *Globus,* Vol. xcvii. Braunschweig, 1910.

Siebold, C. Th. von, *Beiträge zur Parthenogenesis der Arthropoden.* Leipzig, 1871.

Wahre Parthenogenesis bei Schmetterlingen und Bienen. Leipzig, 1856.

Sieg, E., and Siegling, W., "Tocharisch, die Sprache der Indoskythen, vorläufige Bemerkungen über ein bisher unbekannte indogermanische Litteratur," *Sitzungsberichte der königlich preussische Akademie der Wissenschaften.* Berlin, 1908.

Sierozewski, Wenceslas, "The Yakut," abridged from the Russian of S. by W. G. Sumner, *Journal of the Anthropological Instititute.* Vol. xxxi. London, 1901.

"Du Chamanisme d'après les croyances des Yakoutes," *Revue de l'Histoire des Religions.* Vol. xlvi. Paris, 1902.

12 lat w kraju Jakutow (Twelve Years in the Land of the Yakut). Warsaw, 1900.

Sievers, W., *Reise in der Sierra Nevada de Santa Maria.* Leipzig, 1887.

Silvestre, Capt., "Les Thaï blancs de Phong-Tho," *Bulletin de l'École Française d'Extrème-Orient.* Vol. xviii. Hanoi, 1918.

Simeon Ben Asai, *Jalkut Schimoni.* Frankfurt a. Mayn, 1687.

Simms, S. C., "A Crow Monument to Shame," *The American Anthropologist.* N.S., vol. v. New York, 1903.

Simons, F. A. A., "An Exploration of the Goajira Peninsula," *Proceedings of the Royal Geographical Society.* N.S., vol. vii. London, 1885.

Simpson, J., "Observations on the Western Eskimo and the Country they Inhabit," in *Further Papers relative to the Recent Arctic Expeditions.* London, 1855.

Simrock, K., *Handbuch der deutschen Mythologie.* Bonn, 1878.

Parzival und Titurel. Stuttgart, Tübingen, 1842.

See *Beowulf.*

Siret, Henri and Louis, *Les premiers âges du métal dans le sud-est de l'Espagne.* Anvers, 1887.

Sirr, H. Charles, *Ceylon and the Cingalese.* 2 vols. London, 1909.

Sismondi, J. C. L. de, *History of the Fall of the Roman Empire.* 2 vols. London, 1834.

Histoire des Français. 22 vols. Bruxelles, 1836–46.

Sitzungsberichte der Gesellschaft für Morphologie und Physiologie. München, 1886–

Sitzungsberichte der königlich baierischen Akademie der Wissenschaften : philosophisch-philologischen und historischen Classe. München, 1871–

Sitzungsberichte der königliche preussichen Akademie der Wissenschaften. Berlin, 1882–

Sitzungsberichte der philosophisch-historischen Classe der kaiserlich Akademie der Wissenschaften. Wien, 1849–

Skandinavisches Archiv für Physiologie. Leipzig, 1889–

Skeat, W. W., *Malay Magic.* London, 1900.

—— and Blagden, C. O., *Pagan Races of the Malay Peninsula.* 2 vols. London, 1906.

Skene, William Forbes, *The Four Ancient Books of Wales.* 2 vols. Edinburgh, 1868.

Skertchly, J. A., *Dahomey as it is.* London, 1874.

Skinner, A., *Notes on the Bribri of Costa Rica. (Indian Notes and Monographs.* Vol. vi, No. 3.) New York, 1921.

—— *Notes on Iroquois Archaeology.* New York, 1921.

—— " Notes on the Plains Crees," *The American Anthropologist.* Vol. xvi. Washington, 1914.

—— " Social Life and Ceremonial Bundles of the Menomini Indians," *Anthropological Papers of the American Museum of Natural History.* Vol. xiii. Washington, 1916.

Skottsberg, Carl, " Observations on the Natives of the Patagonian Channel Region," *The American Anthropologist.* N.S., vol. xv. Lancaster, 1913.

—— *The Wilds of Patagonia.* London, 1911.

Skrefsrud, L. O., " Traces of Fraternal Polyandry amongst the Santals," *Journal of the Asiatic Society of Bengal.* Vol. lxxii, Part iii. Calcutta, 1904.

Sladen, Douglas, *Queer Things about Japan.* London, 1904.

—— *In Sicily.* 2 vols. London, 1901.

Sladen, E. B., " Official Narrative of the Expedition to explore the Trade Route to China via Bhamo," *Selections from the Records of the Government of India. Foreign Department, 1870.* No. lxxix. Calcutta, 1870.

Sleeman, W. H., *Journey through the Kingdom of Oude.* 2 vols. London, 1855.

—— *Rambles and Recollections of an Indian Official.* 2 vols. London, 1893.

Slosse, Eugène, " Le chemin de fer du Congo. En avant avec la brigade d'études," *Le Congo illustré.* Vol. iii. Bruxelles, 1894.

Small, John Frederick, " Customs and Traditions of the Clarence River Aboriginals," *Science of Man.* Sydney, 1898.

Smet, P. J. de, *Oregon Missions, and Travels over the Rocky Mountains.* New York, 1847.

Smith, A. D., *Through Unknown African Countries. The First Expedition from Somaliland to Lake Lau.* Cambridge, Mass., 1897.

Smith, E. A., " Myths of the Iroquois," *Second Annual Report of the Bureau of Ethnology.* Washington, 1883.

Smith, E. R., *The Araucanians.* New York, 1855.

Smith, E. W., and Dale, A. M., *The Ila-speaking Peoples of Northern Rhodesia.* 2 vols. London, 1921.

Smith, George, *Assyrian Discoveries.* London, 1883.

Smith, G., " Crustacea," in *The Cambridge Natural History.* Vol. iv. Cambridge, 1909.

Smith, G. Elliott, *The Evolution of the Dragon.* London, 1919.

Smith, H. H., *Brazil, the Amazons and the Coast*. London, 1879.

Smith, N. H., *Observations on Breeding for the Turf*. London, 1825.

Smith, V. A., " The Kushan, or Indo-Scythian, Period of Indian History," *Journal of the Royal Asiatic Society*. London, 1903.

" The Gurjaras of Rajputana and Kanauj," *Journal of the Royal Asiatic Society*. London, 1909.

Smith, T., *Narrative of a Five Years' Residence in Nepaul*. 2 vols. London, 1852.

Smith, Sir William, Wayte, W., and Maridin, G. E., *A Dictionary of Greek and Roman Antiquities*. 2 vols. London, 1890-91.

and Wace, H., *Dictionary of Christian Biography, Literature, Sects, and Doctrines*. 4 vols. London, 1877-87.

Smith, W., *A New Voyage to Guinea*. London, 1744.

Smith, William, *History of the Province of New York*. London, 1776.

Smith, W. Robertson, *Kinship and Marriage in early Arabia*. Edited by S. A. Cook. London, 1903.

Lectures on the Religion of the Semites. London, 1894.

Smyth, Robert Brough, *The Aborigines of Victoria*. 2 vols. Melbourne, 1870.

Smyth, W., and Lowe, F., *Narrative of a Journey from Lima to Para*. London, 1836.

Snellman, J. F., " Die Töpferei auf den Kei-Inseln," *Globus*. Vol. xcii. Braunschweig, 1907.

Snessareff, A., " Religion und Gebräuche der Bergvölker des westlichen Pamir," *Keleti Szemle*. Vol. ix. Budapest, Leipzig, 1908.

Sociological Papers. 3 vols. London, 1905-7.

Söderblom, N., *Les Fravashis. Étude sur les traces dans le Mazdéisme d'un ancien concept sur la survivance des morts*. Paris, 1899.

Solberg, O., " Gebräuche der Mittelmesa-Hopi (Moqui) bei Namengebung, Heirat, und Tod," *Zeitschrift für Ethnologie*. Vol. xxxvii. Berlin, 1905.

Sollas, W. J., *Ancient Hunters and their Modern Representatives*. London, 1911.

Sollier, Paul, art. " Idiocy," in *Twentieth Century Practice*. Vol. xii. London, 1897.

Somerset, Hon. Fitz. R. R., " The Lotuko," *Sudan Notes and Records*. Vol. i. Khartoum, 1918.

" Sommario di tutti i regni, città, e popoli orientali," in G. B. Ramusio, *Navigationi et Viaggi*. Vol. i. Venetia, 1554.

Sommer, L., *Das Haar in Religion und Aberglauben der Griechen*. Munster, 1912.

Sommerville, B. T., " Ethnological Notes on the New Hebrides," *Journal of the Anthropological Institute*. Vol. xxiii. London, 1894.

Song Yun, *Voyage de Song Yun dans l'Udyana et le Gaudhara (518-522 p. C.)*. Transl. by E. Chavannes. Hanoi, 1903.

Sonnerat, Pierre, *Voyage aux Indes orientales et à la Chine*. 2 vols. Paris, 1782.

Sophokles, *Tragoediae et Fragmenta*. Ed. E. A. J. Ahrens. Parisiis, 1842.

Soppitt, C. A., *A Short Account of the Kachcha Naga Tribe of the North Cachar Hills*. Shillong, 1885.

A Short Account of the Kuki-Lushai Tribes of the North-East Frontier. Shillong, 1887.

Sordello. See De Lollis, C.

Sorge, F., " Nissan-Inseln im Bismarck-Archipel," in S. R. Steinmetz, *Rechtsverhältnisse von eingeborenen Völkern in Afrika und Ozeanien*. Berlin, 1903.

Soripatrus Charisius, Flavius, *Ars Grammatica*, in *Grammatici Latini*. Ed. H. Keil. Vol. i. Leipzig, 1857.

Sousa, Andre Fernandes de, "Noticias geographicas da Capitania do Rio Negro no grande Rio Amazonas," *Revista Trimensal de Historia e Geographia*. Vol. x. Rio de Janeiro, 1848.

The South American Missionary Magazine. London, 1867.

The Voice of Pity for South America. London, 1854– (published as— *A Voice for South America*. London, 1863–)

South Canara Manual (Madras District Manuals). Ed. by J. Sturroch and H. A. Sturt. 2 vols. Madras, 1894–95.

Southey, Robert, *History of Brazil*. 3 vols. London, 1810–19.

Soyaux, Hermann, *Aus West-Afrika*. Leipzig, 1879.

Sozomenus, *Historia ecclesiastica*, in Migne, *Patrologiae Cursus Completus, Series Graeca*. Vol. lxvii. Parisiis, 1859.

Spalding, Douglas A., "Instinct; with Original Observations on Young Animals," *Macmillan's Magazine*. Vol. xxvii. Cambridge, 1873.

Spallanzani, Lazaro, *Expériences pour servir à l'histoire naturelle de la génération des animaux et des plantes*. Genève, 1785.

Sparkman, Ph. Stedman, *The Culture of the Luiseño Indians (University of California Publications in American Archaeology and Ethnology*. Vol. viii.) Berkeley, 1908.

Spearman, C., "'General Intelligence,' objectively determined and measured," *American Journal of Psychology*. Vol. xv. Worcester, 1904.

"The Proof and Measurement of Association between Two Things," *American Journal of Psychology*. Vol. xv. Worcester, 1904.

Specht, Edouard, "Les Indo-Scythes et l'époque du règne de Kanichka d'après les sources chinoises," *Journal Asiatique*. 9e Série, vol. x. Paris, 1897.

"Étude sur l'Asie centrale d'après les historiens chinois," *Journal Asiatique*. 8e Série. Paris, 1883.

Speck, Frank G., *Ethnology of the Yuchi Indians (University of Pennsylvania Anthropological Publications*. Vol. i, No. 1). Philadelphia, 1909.

Speckmann, F., *Die Hermannsburger Mission in Afrika*. Hermannsburg, 1876.

Spegazzini, Carlos, "Costumbres de los habitantes de la Tierra de Fuego," *Anales de la Sociedad científica Argentina*. Vol. xiv. Buenos Aires, 1882.

"Costumbres de los Patagones," *Anales de la Sociedad científica Argentina*. Vol. xvii. Buenos Aires, 1884.

Speiser, Felix, *Two Years with the Natives in the Western Pacific*. 2 vols. London, 1883.

Speke, J. H., *Journal of the Discovery of the Source of the Nile*. Edinburgh, 1863.

Spelman, Henry, *Concilia, Decreta, Leges, Constitutiones in re Ecclesiarum Orbis Britannici*. 2 vols. Londini, 1727.

Spence, L., art., "Brazil," in J. Hastings's *Encyclopaedia of Religion and Ethics*. Vol. ii. Edinburgh, 1909.

Spencer, H., *Descriptive Sociology*. 8 vols. London, 1872–96.

The Principles of Psychology. 2 vols. London, 1870–72.

Spencer, Sir Walter Baldwin, *Native Tribes of the Northern Territory of Australia*. London, 1914.

and Gillen, F. J., *The Native Tribes of Central Australia*. London, 1899.

The Northern Tribes of Central Australia. London, 1904.

Spengel, J. W., "Die Fortpflanzung des *Rhinoderma Darwinii*," translated from Jimenez de la Espada, *Zeitschrift für wissenschaftliche Zoologie*. Vol. xxix. Leipzig, 1877.

Speyer, J. S., " Eene Indische verwandte van de Germansche godi Nerthus," *Mededeelingen van de Maatschapij der Nederlandsche Letterkunde te Leiden, 1901-2.* Leiden, 1902.

Spiegel, Friederich, *Die altpersische Keilinschriften.* Leipzig, 1862.

" Zur vergleichenden Religionsgeschichte," *Das Ausland.* München, 1872.

Spielberg, W., *Der Papyrus Libbey, ein ägyptischer Heiratsvertrag (Schriften der wissenschaftlichen Gesellschaft in Strassburg.* No. 1). Strassburg, 1907.

Spieth, Jakob, *Die Ewe-Stämme. Material zur Kunde des Ewe-Volkes in Deutsch-Togo.* Berlin, 1906.

Die Religion der Eweer in Süd-Togo. Berlin, 1911.

Spix, Joh. Bapt. von, and Martius, Carl Fried. Phil. von, *Reise in Brasilien.* 3 vols. Munich, 1824-31.

Sproat, Gilbert M., *Scenes and Studies of Savage Life.* London, 1868.

Squier, E. G., *Adventure on the Mosquito Shore.* New York, 1891.

The Serpent Symbol and the Worship of Reciprocal Symbols of Nature in America. New York, 1851.

Stack, Edward, *The Mikirs.* London, 1908.

Stade, H., *The Captivity of Hans Stade of Hesse, in A.D. 1547-1555, among the Wild Tribes of Eastern Brazil.* London, 1874.

Stadling, J., *Through Siberia.* London, 1901.

" Shamanism," *The Contemporary Review.* London, 1901.

Stair, John B., *Old Samoa.* London, 1897.

Stanbridge, W. E., " Some Particulars of the General Characteristics, Astronomy, and Mythology of the Tribes in the Central Parts of Victoria, Southern Australia," *Transactions of the Ethnological Society.* N.S., vol. i. London, 1861.

Standing, H. F., " Malagasy ' Fady,' " *Antananarivo Annual and Madagascar Magazine.* No. VII. Antananarivo, 1884.

Stanley, H. M., *Through the Dark Continent.* 2 vols. London, 1878.

Stannus, H. S., " Notes on some Tribes of British Central Africa," *Journal of the Royal Anthropological Institute.* Vol. xl. London, 1910.

Starch, Daniel, *Educational Psychology.* New York, 1920.

Starcke, C. N., *The Primitive Family in its Origin and Development.* London, 1889.

Stark, C. B., *Gaza und die philistäische Küste.* Jena, 1852.

Statius, Publius Papinius, *Opera quae extant.* Ed. F. Dubner. 2 vols. Leipzig, 1837.

Staunton, Sir G., *An Authentic Account of an Embassy from the King of Great Britain to the Emperor of China.* 2 vols. London, 1797.

Stefanson, V., *My Life with the Eskimo.* New York, 1913.

Steinen, Karl von den, *Durch Central-Brasilien.* Leipzig, 1886.

Unter den Naturvölkern Zentral-Brasiliens. Berlin, 1894.

Steiner, J. W. C., *Codex Inscriptionum Romanarum Rheni.* 2 vols. Darmstadt, 1837.

Steinmetz, S. R., *Ethnologischen Studien zur ersten Entwickelung der Strafe.* 2 vols. Leiden, 1894.

Rechtsverhältnisse von eingeborenen Völkern in Afrika und Ozeanien. Berlin, 1903.

" Suicide among Primitive Peoples," *The American Anthropologist.* Vol. vii. Washington, 1894.

Steinthal, H., " The Legend of Samson," in I. Goldziher, *Mythology among the Hebrews.* London, 1877.

Steller, G. W., *Beschreibung von dem Lande Kamtschatka.* Frankfurt, Leipzig, 1774.

Stendhal (Henry Beyle), *De l'amour.* Paris, 1887.

Stengel, E., *Ausgaben und Abhandlungen aus dem Gebiete der romanischen Philologie.* Marburg, 1882–
  in *Romanische Studien.* Berlin, 1897.

Stephan, E., and Graebner, F., *Neu-Mecklenburg (Bismarck-Archipel).* Berlin, 1907.

Stephen, A. M., " The Navajo," *The American Anthropologist.* Vol. vi. Washington, 1893.

Stephens, H., *The Book of the Farm.* 2 vols. London, 1852.

Stephens, T., *The Literature of the Kymry.* London, 1876.

Stern, B., *Medizin, Aberglaube und Geschlechtsleben in der Türkei.* 2 vols. Berlin, 1903.

Stern, Bolko, *Ägyptische Kulturgeschichte.* Magdeburg, 1896.

Stern, L.-C., " Le manuscrit irlandais de Leide," *Revue Celtique.* Vol. xiii. Paris, 1892.

Stern, Ludw., " Die Nilstele von Gebel Silsilek," *Zeitschrift für Ägyptische Sprache und Alterthumskunde.* Vol. xi. Leipzig, 1873.

Sternberg, Leo, " Die Giljaken," *Verhandlungen der Berliner Gesellschaft für Anthropologie, Ethnologie and Urgeschichte.* Berlin, 1901.

" The Turano-Ganowanian System and the Nations of North-East Asia," *International Congress of Americanists. Proceedings of the XVIII Session, London, 1912.* Vol. ii. London, 1912.

" The Inau cult of the Ainu," *Boas Anniversary Volume.* New York, 1906.

Sterndale, R. A., *Natural History of the Mammalia of India and Ceylon.* Calcutta, 1884.

Stevens, Hrolf Vaughan, " Mittheilungen aus dem Frauenleben der Ôrang Belendas, der Ôrang Djâkun und der Ôrang Lâut," *Zeitschrift für Ethnologie.* Vol. xxvii. Berlin, 1896.

Stevenson, James, " Ceremonial of Hasjelti Dailjis and Mythical Sand Painting of the Navaho Indians," *Eighth Annual Report of the Bureau of Ethnology.* Washington, 1892.

Stevenson, Matilda Cox, " The Sia," *Eleventh Annual Report of the Bureau of Ethnology.* Washington, 1894.

" The Zuñi Indians," *Twenty-third Annual Report of the Bureau of American Ethnology.* Washington, 1904.

" The Religious Life of the Zuñi Child," *Fifth Annual Report of the Bureau of Ethnology.* Washington, 1883.

Stevenson, Robert Louis, *In the South Seas.* London, 1900.

Stevenson-Hamilton, James, *Animal Life in Africa.* London, 1912.

Stevenson-Moore, C. J., " Harvest Festivals in Muzuffarpur," *Journal of the Asiatic Society of Bengal.* Vol. lxxii, Part iii. Calcutta, 1904.

Stewart, C. S., *A Visit to the South Seas.* 2 vols. London, 1832.

Stewart, Dugald, *Elements of the Philosophy of the Human Mind.* 3 vols. Edinburgh, 1854–55.

Stieda, L. review of D. Nikolski, " Über die Tschuktschen des kolymschen Bezirk," in *Moskauer Arbeiten,* 1900, *Archiv für Anthropologie.* Vol. xxvii. Braunschweig, 1901.

Stigand, C. H., *Equatoria. The Lado Enclave.* London, 1923.

" Notes on the Natives of Nyasaland, North-East Rhodesia and Portuguese Zambesia," *Journal of the Anthropological Institute.* Vol. xxxvii. London, 1907.

Stiles, Henry Reed, *Bundling ; its Origin, Progress and Decline in America.* Albany, 1869.

Stimming, A., " Provenzalische Litteratur," in G. Gröber, *Grundriss der romanische Philologie.* Vol. ii, Part iii. Strassburg, 1897.

Stirling, E. C., " Answers to Questions by Sir James Frazer," in *Journal of the Anthropological Institute*. Vol. xxiv. London, 1895.

in *Report of the Work of the Horn Scientific Expedition to Central Australia*. Part iv, " Anthropology." London, Melbourne, 1896.

Stirling, W. H., " A Residence in Tierra del Fuego," *The South American Missionary Magazine*. Vol. iv. London, 1870.

Stobaeus, Ioannis, *Florilegium*. Ed. A. Meineke. 3 vols. Leipzig, 1856.

Stokes, Whitley, " The Second Battle of Moytura," *Revue Celtique*. Vol. xii. Paris, 1891.

" Annals of Tigernach," *Revue Celtique*. Vol. xvii. Paris, 1896.

" The Bodleian Amra Choluimb Chille," *Revue Celtique*. Vol. xx. Paris, 1899.

" Cuchullainn's Death," abridged from the *Book of Leinster*, fol. 77 a 1, 78 b 2," *Revue Celtique*. Vol. iii. Paris, 1878.

" On the Death of some Irish Heroes," *Revue Celtique*. Vol. xxiii. Paris, 1902.

" The Destruction of Da Derga's Hostel," *Revue Celtique*. Vol. xxii. Paris, 1901.

" Rennes Dindsenchas," *Revue Celtique*. Vol. xvi. Paris, 1895.

Stoll, Otto, " Die Ethnologie der Indianerstämme von Gautemala," *Internationales Archiv für Ethnographie*. Vol. i, Supplement. Leyden, 1889.

Stone, S., " Facts connected with the History of a Wasps' Nest," *Transactions of the Entomological Society of London*. 2nd Series, vol. v. London, 1860.

Stordy, R. J., in *The Veterinarian*. London, 1900.

Stout, G. F., " Instinct and Intelligence," *The British Journal of Psychology*. Vol. iii. London, 1910.

Stow, G. W., *The Native Races of South Africa*. London, 1905.

" Account of an Interview with a Tribe of Bushmans in South Africa," *Journal of the Anthropological Institute*. Vol. iii. London, 1874.

Straaten, J. van der, and Severijn, P., " Verslag van een in 1854 bewerkstelligd onderzoek op het eiland Engano," *Tijdschrift voor Indische taal-, land- en volkenkunde*. Vol. iii. Batavia, 1855.

Strackerjan, L., *Aberglauben und Sagen aus den Herzogthum Oldenburg*. 2 vols. Oldenburg, 1867.

Stradelli, Ermanno, " L'Uaupes e gli Uaupes "; " Leggenda di Jurupary," *Bolletino della Societá Geografica Italiana*. Vol. iii. Roma, 1890.

Strahan, S. A. K., *Marriage and Disease*. London, 1892.

Stratz, C. H., *Die Frauen auf Java. Eine gynäcologische Studie*. Stuttgart, 1897.

Strauch, H., " Allgemeine Bemerkungen ethnologischen Inhalts über Neu-Guinea, die Anachoreten-Inseln, Neu-Hannover, Neu-Irland, Neu-Britannien und Bougainville." *Zeitschrift für Ethnologie*. Vol. ix. Berlin, 1877.

Strehlow, Carl, *Die Aranda- und Loritja-Stämme in Zentral-Australien*. Ed. Moritz von Leonhardi. 4 vols. Frankfurt a. M., 1907–13.

Stricker, W., " Der Fuss der Chinesinnen," *Archiv fur Anthropologie*. Vol. iv. Braunschweig, 1870.

Stritter, Johann Gotthilf, *Memoriae populorum, olim ad Danubium, P. Euxinum, Paludem Maeotidem, Caucasum, Mare Caspium et inde ad septentriones incolentium, e Scriptoribus Historiae Byzantinae erutae*. 4 vols. Petropoli, 1771–79.

Stronski, S., *Le troubadour Folquet de Marseille*. Cracovie, 1910.

Struck, Bernhard, " Die Erdmutter in Afrika," *Archiv für Religionswissenschaft.* Vols. x, xi. Freiburg, 1908–9.

" African Ideas on the Subject of Earthquakes," *Journal of the African Society.* Vols. viii. London, 1909.

" Niederlegen und Aufheben der Kinder von der Erde," *Archiv für Religionswissenschaft.* Vol. x. Freiburg, 1907.

Struve, B. von, " Einiges über die Samojeden im Norden von Sibirien," *Das Ausland.* München, 1880.

Strzoda, Walter, " Die Li auf Hainan und ihre Beziehungen zum asiatischen Kontinent," *Zeitschrift für Ethnologie.* Vol. xliii. Berlin, 1911.

Stuart, H. A., " Madras," *Census of India, 1891.* Vol. xiii. Madras, 1893.

Stuart, H. B., *A History of Infantry from the Earliest Times to the Present.* London, 1862.

Stuart, T. P. A., " The ' Mika ' or ' Kulpi ' Operation of the Australian Aborigines," *Journal and Proceedings of the Royal Society of New South Wales.* Vol. xxx. Sydney, 1896.

Stubbes, Phillip, *The Anatomie of Abuses.* Reprint by F. J. Furnivall. London, 1882.

Studi di Filologia Romanza. Roma, 1885–

Studi Medievali. Torino, 1904–

Studies in the History of Religions presented to Crawford Howell Toy. New York, 1912.

Stuebel, O., *Samoanische Texte.* Berlin, 1896.

Stuhlamnn, Franz, *Mit Emin Pasha ins Herz von Afrika.* Berlin, 1894.

Stulpnagel, C. R., " Polyandry in the Himalayas,"*The Indian Antiquary.* Vol. vii. Bombay, 1878.

Sturler, W. L. de, *Proeve eener beschrijving van het gebied van Palembang.* Gronigen, 1843.

Sturt, Charles, *Narrative of an Expedition into Central Australia.* 2 vols. London, 1849.

Suarez de Cepeda, J., " Relación de la ciudad de la Trinidad y desta de la Palma," in G. Latorre, *Relaciones geograficas de Indias.* Sevilla, 1919.

Suas, J. Bapt., " Mythes et légendes des indigènes des Nouvelles-Hébrides, (Océanie)," *Anthropos.* Vol. vi. Wien, 1911.

Subbaraya Aiyar, N., " The Nambudiri," *The Malabar Quarterly Review.* Vol. vii. Trivandrum, 1908.

" Substance of the Speech of Good Peter to Governor Clinton and the Commissioners of Indian Affairs at Albany," *Collections of the New York Historical Society.* Vol. ii. New York, 1814.

Sudan Notes and Records. Khartoum, 1918–

Sudre, L., " Les allusions à la légende de Tristan dans la littérature du moyen-âge," *Romania.* Vol. xv. Paris, 1886.

Suidas, *Lexicon.* Ed. G. Bernherdy. 2 vols. Halis, Brunsvigae, 1853.

Sully, James, *Studies of Childhood.* London, 1903.

The Human Mind. 2 vols. London, 1892.

Introduction to Bernard Perez' *The First Three Years of Childhood.* London, 1885.

Sulpicius Severus, *Vita S. Martini,* in *Corpus Scriptorum Ecclesiasticorum Latinorum.* Vol. i. Vindobonae, 1866.

Sumner, W. G. See Sierosewski.

Sundby, Thor B., *Della vita e delle opere di Brunetto Latini.* Transl. Firenze, 1884.

Sundermann, H., *Die Insel Nias und die Mission daselbst.* Barmen, 1905.

" Die Insel Nias und die Mission daselbst," *Allgemeine Missions-Zeitschrift.* Vol. xi. Freiburg, 1884.

Sundermann, H., " Die Olon Maanjan und die Missionsarbeit unter denselben," *Allgemeine Missions-Zeitschrift*. Gütersloh, 1899.

" Die Insel Nias," *ibid.* Gütersloh, 1884.

Sundstral, F., *Aus dem Reiche der Inkas*. Berlin, 1902.

Sunkuni Wariyar, " A Variant of the Bloody Cloth," *The Indian Antiquary*. Vol. xviii. Bombay, 1889.

Supplementary Papers of the Royal Geographical Society. London, 1886–

Süssmilch, Johann Peter, *Versuch eines Beweises dass die erste Sprache ihres Ursprung nicht vom Menschen, sondern allein vom Schöpfer erhalten habe*. Berlin, 1766.

Sutherland, A., *The Origin and Growth of the Moral Instinct*. 2 vols. London, 1898.

Sûtrakritânga Sûtra. See *Gaina Sûtras*.

The Sutta-Nipâta. Transl. from Pâli by V. Fausböll. (*The Sacred Books of the East.* Vol. x, Part ii.) Oxford, 1898.

Sutton, T. M., " The Adjahdurah Tribe of Aborigines on Yorke's Peninsula : some of their Early Customs and Traditions," *Proceedings of the Royal Geographical Society of Australasia : South Australian Branch*. Vol. ii. Adelaide, 1890.

Swammerdam, Jan, *Miraculum naturae sive uteri muliebris fabrica, notis in J. van Horne prodromum illustratum*. Lugduni Batavorum, 1672.

Swan, James G., *The Northwest Coast, or Three Years' Residence in Washington Territory*. New York. 1857.

Haidah Indians of Queen Charlotte's Islands, British Columbia (Smithsonian Contributions to Knowledge. Vol. xvi). Washington, 1874.

Swanton, J. R., " Social Condition, Beliefs, and Linguistic Relationship of the Tlingit Indians," *Twenty-sixth Annual Report of the Bureau of American Ethnology*. Washington, 1908.

Indian Tribes of the Lower Mississippi Valley (Bureau of American Ethnology, Bulletin No. 43). Washington, 1911.

Early History of the Creek Indians and their Neighbors (Bureau of American Ethnology, Bulletin 73). Washington, 1922.

Swettenham, F. A., " Comparative Vocabulary of the Dialects of some of the Wild Tribes inhabiting the Malayan Peninsula, Borneo, etc., " *Journal of the Straits Branch of the Royal Asiatic Society*. No. 5. Singapore, 1880.

Swift, Jonathan, *Works*. 16 vols. London, 1755–65.

Sykes, E. and P., *Through Deserts and Oases of Central Asia*. London, 1920.

Symes, Michael, *An Account of an Embassy to the Kingdom of Ava*. London, 1800.

Synge, M. B., *A Short History of Social Life in England*. London, 1908.

Szanto, Emil, " Zum lykischen Mutterrecht," in *Festschrift für Otto Benndorf*. Wien, 1898.

Tabari, *Chronique d'Abou-Djafar Mohammed Tabari, fils de Djarir, fils d'Yezid.* Transl. by Louis Dubeux. Paris, 1836.

Taberer, W. S., " Mashonaland Natives," *Journal of the African Society*. Vol. iv. London, 1905.

Tacitus, *Opera*. Ed. F. Ritter. 2 vols. Cambridge, 1848.

Táin bó Cúalnge. Enlèvement (du taureau divin et) des vaches de Cooley. Trad. par H. d'Arbois de Jubainville. Paris, 1907.

Taittirîya Samhita, with Sâyana's commentary. Ed. by Subrahmanya. Madras, 1883.

Talbot, D. Amaury, *Woman's Mysteries of a Primitive People. The Ibibios of Southern Nigeria.* London, 1915.

Talbot, Eugène, *Essai sur la légende d'Alexandre-le-grand dans les romans français du XIIᵉ siècle.* Paris, 1850.

Talbot, P. Amaury, *In the Shadow of the Bush.* London, 1912.

" The Buduma of Lake Chad," *Journal of the Royal Anthropological Institute.* Vol. xli. London, 1911.

Talmud, Original text, edited, etc., and transl. into English by M. L. Rodkinson. 17 vols. New York, 1896–1903.

Talton, J., " Voyage of Captain G. Castleton to Priaman in 1612," in Astley's *New Collection of Voyages and Travels.* Vol. i. London, 1745.

Tamil, " On the Weddas," by a Tamil, *Transactions of the Ethnological Society.* Vol. iii. London, 1863.

Tanner, John, *Narrative of the Captivity and Adventures of John Tanner during Thirty Years' Residence among the Indians.* Ed. by Edwin James. London, 1830.

Taplin, George, *The Folklore, Manners, Customs, and Languages of the South Australian Aborigines.* Adelaide, 1879.

" The Narrinyeri," in Woods, *Native Tribes of South Australia.* Adelaide, 1879.

Tappenbeck, Ernst, *Deutsch-Neuguinea.* Berlin, 1901.

The Taprobanian, a Dravidian Journal of Oriental Studies in and around Ceylon. Bombay, 1887–

Tarde, Gabriel, *Les lois de l'imitation.* Paris, 1895.

La logique sociale. Paris, 1898.

Tarikhi-i Mamalik-i Hind, in H. M. Elliot, *The History of India as told by its own Historians.* Vol. viii. London, 1877.

The Tasmanian Journal of Natural Science, Agriculture, Statistics, etc. Hobart, 1842–47.

Tassoni, Alessandro, *La secchia rapita.* Venezia, 1747.

Tassy, J. H. Garcin de, *Science des religions ; l'Islamisme d'après le Coran.* Paris, 1874.

Tata, H. R., " Further Notes on the Kikuyu Tribe of British East Africa," *Journal of the Anthropological Institute.* Vol. xxxiv. London, 1904.

Ta Tsing Leu Lee, being the fundamental laws . . . of China. Transl. by Sir G. T. Staunton. London, 1810.

Tauern, O. D., " Ceram," *Zeitschrift für Ethnologie.* Vol. xlv. Berlin, 1913.

Tautain, L., " Études critiques sur l'ethnologie et l'ethnographie des peuples du bassin du Sénégal," *Revue d'Ethnographie.* Paris, 1885.

" Étude sur le mariage chez les Polynésiens des îles Marquises," *L'Anthropologie.* Vol. vi. Paris, 1895.

Tauxier, L., *Le Noir du Soudan.* Paris, 1912.

Études soudanaises. Le Noir de Bondoukou. Paris, 1921.

Études soudanaises. Le Noir du Yatenga. Paris, 1917.

Tavernier, Jean-Baptiste, *Les six voyages de Tavernier en Turquie, en Perse et aux Indes.* 3 vols. Paris, 1692.

Taylor, A. E., *Varia Socratica, First Series (University of St. Andrew's Publications. No. IX).* Oxford, 1911.

Taylor, G., " Folklore of Aboriginal Formosa," *Folk-Lore Journal.* Vol. v. London, 1887.

Taylor, Isaac, *Etruscan Researches.* London, 1874.

Taylor, R., *Te Ika a Maui, or New Zealand and its Inhabitants.* London, 1870.

Tcheng-ki-t'ong, *China und die Chinesen.* Transl. Leipzig, 1885.

Tcheou Ta-Kouan, " Mémoire sur les coutumes du Cambodge," traduit et annoté par M. P. Pelliot, *Bulletin de l'École Française d'Extrême-Orient*. Vol. ii. Hanoi, 1902.

Tchihatcheff, Paul de, *Espagne, Algérie et Tunisie*. Paris, 1880.

Voyage scientifique dans l'Altaï oriental et des parties adjacentes de la frontière de Chine. Paris, 1845.

Techo, Nicholas del, " The History of the Provinces of Paraguay, Tucuman, Rio de la Plata, Parana, Guaira and Urvaica," in Churchill, *A Collection of Voyages and Travels*. Vol. iv. Transl. London, 1704.

Teit, James A., " The Thompson Indians of British Columbia," *Jesup North Pacific Expedition Publications*. Vol. i. Leiden, New York, 1900.

" The Lillooet Indians," *ibid*. Vol. ii. Leiden, New York, 1905.

" The Shuswap," *ibid*. Vol. ii. Leiden, New York, 1905.

Traditions of the Thompson River Indians of British Columbia (*Memoirs of the American Folk-Lore Society*. Vol. vi). Boston, 1894.

Tei-ziro, Kouri-Moto, " Sur la condition de la femme au Japon," *Revue Orientale et Américaine*. Vol. xi. Paris, 1872.

Tellier, " Maluihe Fulbe, Bambaras in Kreise Kita, westlicher Sudan," in S. R. Steinmetz, *Rechtsverhältnisse von eingeborenen Völkern in Afrika und Ozeanien*. Berlin, 1903.

Temme, J. D. H., *Die Volkssagen der Altmark*. Berlin, 1839.

Volksagen aus Pommern und Rügen. Berlin, 1840.

Temminck, C. J., *Coup d'oeil sur les possessions néerlandaises dans l'Inde archipélagique*. 3 vols. Leiden, 1847–49.

Temple, Sir Richard C., " The Andaman and Nicobar Islands," *Census of India, 1901*. Vol. iii. Calcutta, 1903.

Art. " Burma," in Hastings's *Encyclopaedia of Religion and Ethics*. Vol. iii. Edinburgh, 1910.

Temple, O., *Notes on the Tribes, Provinces, Emirates and States of the Northern Provinces of Nigeria. Compiled from official Reports*. Lagos, 1922.

Tench, Watkin, *A Complete Account of the Settlement of Port Jackson in New South Wales*. London, 1793.

Tendeloe, " De toestand der vrouw in de Minahassa," *Mededeelingen van wege het Nederlandsche Zendelinggenootschap*. Vol. xvii. Rotterdam, 1873.

Ten Kate, H. F. C., " Notes ethnographiques sur les Comanches," *Revue d'Ethnographie*. Vol. iv. Paris, 1885.

" Verslag eener reis in de Timorgroep en Polynesie," *Tijdschrift van het kon. Nederlandsch Aardrijkskundig Genootschap*. 2ᵉ Serie, vol. xi. Leiden, 1894.

Tennent, Sir James Emerson, *Ceylon*. 2 vols. London, 1860.

Ternaux-Compans, Henri, *Voyages, relations et mémoires originaux pour servir à l'histoire de la découverte de l'Amérique*. 20 vols. Paris, 1837–41.

" La Terre de Feu et ses habitants," *Journal des Missions Evangéliques*, 51ᵉ année. Paris, 1876.

Tertre, Jean Baptiste, *Histoire générale des isles de S. Christophe, de la Guadeloupe, de la Martinique et autres dans l'Amérique*. Paris, 1654.

Histoire générale des Antilles habitées par les Français. 4 vols. Paris, 1667.

Tertullian, *Opera*, in Migne, *Patrologiae Cursus Completus*. Vols. i, ii. Parisiis, 1842.

Teschauer, C., " Die Caingang oder Coroados-Indianer im brasilianischen Staate Rio Grande do Sul," *Anthropos*. Vol. ix. Wien, 1914.

Tessmann, Günter, *Die Pangwe. Völkerkundliche Monographie eines westafrikanischen Negerstammes*. 2 vols. Berlin, 1913.

The Testaments of the Twelve Patriarchs. Ed. R. H. Charles. London, 1908.

Texte und Untersuchungen zur Geschichte der altchristlichen Literatur. Leipzig, 1882.

Tezner, F., " Feste und Spiele der Litauer," *Globus.* Vol. lxxii. Braunschweig, 1898.

Thalbitzer, W., " The Heathen Priests of East Greenland (Angakut)," *Verhandlungen des XVI Internationales Amerikanisten-Kongress, Wien, 1908.* Vol. ii. Wien, Leipzig, 1910.

Thaumas de la Thaumasière, G., *Histoire de Berry.* 4 vols. Bourges, 1865–71.

Theal, George McCall, *The Portuguese in South Africa.* London, 1896.
  The Yellow and Dark-skinned People of Africa South of the Zambesi. London, 1910.
  Records of South-East Africa collected in Libraries and Archive Departments in Europe. 8 vols. London, 1898–1902.
  Ethnography and Condition of South Africa. London, 1919.
  The Beginning of South African History. London, 1902.

Theganus, *Vita Hludowici imperatoris,* in *Monumenta Germaniae Historica, Scriptores.* Vol. ii. Hanover, 1828.

Theodoret, *Opera omnia.* Ed. J. Sirmond. 3 vols. Parisiis, 1642–84.

Theodori, Archiepiscopi Cantuariensis, *Poenitentiale. Capitula.* In Migne, *Patrologiae Cursus Completus.* Vol. xcix. Paris, 1851.

Theodoric " Epistolae," in M. Bouquet, *Recueil des historiens des Gaules et de la France.* Vol. iv. Paris, 1741.

Theophanes monachus, *Chronographia.* 2 vols. Bonnae, 1839–41.

Theophylactus Simocatta, *Historiarum libri viii.* Rec. I. Bekker. Bonnae, 1834.

Thévenin, M., *Textes relatifs aux institutions privées et publiques aux époques mérovingienne et carolingienne.* Paris, 1887.

Thévet, André, *Les Singularitez de la France antartique autrement nommée Amérique.* Paris, 1878.

Thibault, " Mariages consanguins dans la race noire," *Archives de Médecine Navale.* Vol. i. Paris, 1864.

Thibaut, G., " On some recent Attempts to determine the Date of Vedic Civilisation," *The Indian Antiquary.* Vol. xxiv. Bombay, 1895.

Thiers, Jean-Baptiste, *Traité des superstitions qui regardent les sacremens.* 4 vols. Avignon, 1767.

Thiersch, H., " Gjölbaschi und Lykischen Mutterrecht," *Jahrbuch des kaiserliches deutsches archäologischen Instituts.* Vol. xxii. Berlin, 1908.

Thilenius, G., " Kröte und Gebärmutter," *Globus.* Vol. lxxxvii. Braunschweig, 1905.

Thomas, *Le roman de Tristan (Soc. des anciens textes français).* Ed. J. Bédier. Paris, 1902–5.

Thomas, Antoine, *Francesco da Barberino et la littérature provençale en Italie au Moyen Âge.* Paris, 1883.

Thomas, Cyrus, " Burial Mounds of the Northern Sections of the United States," *Fifth Annual Report of the Bureau of Ethnology.* Washington, 1887.

Thomas, Edward, " On the Position of Women in the East in Olden Time," *Journal of the Royal Asiatic Society.* N.S., vol. xi. London, 1879.

Thomas, N. W., " Totemism in Southern Nigeria," *Anthropos.* Vol. x–xi. Wien, 1916.
  " Notes on Edo Burial Customs," *Journal of the Royal Anthropological Institute.* Vol. i. London, 1920.

Thomas, N. W., *Anthropological Report on the Ibo-speaking Peoples of Nigeria.* 6 Parts. London, 1913–14.

Kinship Organisations and Group Marriage in Australia. Cambridge, 1906.

Anthropological Report on the Edo-speaking Peoples of Nigeria. 2 vols. London, 1910.

Anthropological Report on Sierra Leone. 3 Parts. London, 1916.

Thomas, P. E., " Report to the Commissioner of Indian Affairs, " *Executive Documents printed by Order of the House of Representatives, First Session of the 35th Congress, 1857–58.* Washington, 1858.

Thomassin, Louis, *Dictionnaire de discipline ecclésiastique,* in Migne, *Encyclopédie Théologique.* Série III, vol. xxv–xxvi. Paris, 1856.

Thompson, Augustus C., *Moravian Missions.* New York, 1882.

Thomsen, Anthon, " Orthia," *Archiv für Religionswissenschaft.* Vol. ix. Leipzig, 1906.

Thomson, A. S., *The Story of New Zealand.* 2 vols. London, 1859.

Thomson, Sir Basil Hugh, *The Diversions of a Prime Minister.* London, 1894.

" The Kalou-Vu (Ancestor-Gods) of the Fijians," *Journal of the Anthropological Institute.* Vol. xxiv. London, 1895.

" Note upon the Natives of Savage Island, or Niue," *Journal of the Anthropological Institute.* Vol. xxxi. London, 1901.

The Fijians. A Study of the Decay of Custom. London, 1908.

Savage Island. London, 1902.

Thomson, George M., *The Naturalisation of Animals and Plants in New Zealand.* Cambridge, 1922.

Thomson, H. C., *Rhodesia and its Government.* London, 1898.

Thomson, J., " On Certain so-called ' Bad Habits ' in Children," *Archives of Pedriatics.* Vol. xxiv. Philadelphia, New York, 1907.

Thomson, J. A., *Heredity.* London, 1908.

Thomson, J. A. K., *Studies in the " Odyssey."* Oxford, 1914.

Thomson, Joseph, *Through Masai Land.* London, 1887.

Thornber, William, *An historical and descriptive Account of Blackpool and its Neighbourhood.* Blackpool, 1844.

Thorndike, Edward L., *Educational Psychology.* 3 vols. New York, 1912–14.

Educational Psychology. Briefer Course. New York, 1915.

" Measurements of Twins," *Archives of Philosophy, Psychology, and Scientific Methods.* Vol. i. New York, 1906.

Thorne, E., *The Queen of the Colonies : Queensland.* London, 1876.

The Thornton Romances. Ed. by James Orchard Halliwell (*Camden Society*). London, 1844.

Thorpe, Benjamin, *Northern Mythology.* 3 vols. London, 1851–52.

Thouar, A., *Explorations dans l'Amérique du Sud.* Paris, 1891.

Thrämer, E., *Pergamos.* Leipzig, 1888.

Thunberg, C. P., " An Account of the Cape of Good Hope and some parts of the interior of southern Africa," in Pinkerton, *Voyages and Travels.* Vol. xvi. London, 1814.

Thureau-Dangin, François, *Les inscriptions de Sumer et d'Akkade.* Paris, 1905.

Thurneysen, Rudolf, *Die irische Helden und Königsage biss zum siebzichten Jahrhundert.* Halle, 1921.

Thurnwald, Richard, *Forschungen auf den Salomo-Inseln und dem Bismarck-Archipel.* 2 vols. Berlin, 1912–

" Im Bismarckarchipel und auf den Salomoinseln," *Zeitschrift für Ethnologie.* Vol. xlii. Berlin, 1910.

Thurnwald, Richard, "Ermittlungen über Eingeborenenrechte der Südsee," *Zeitschrift für vergleichende Rechtswissenschaft*. Vol. xxiii. Stuttgart, 1910.

—— *Bánaro Society ; Social Organisation and Kinship System of a Tribe in the Interior of New Guinea*. (*Memoirs of the American Anthropological Association*. Vol. iii, No. 4.) Lancaster, 1916.

Thurston, E., *Omens and Superstitions of Southern India*. London, 1912.

—— *Castes and Tribes of Southern India*. 7 vols. Madras, 1909.

—— *Ethnographic Notes in Southern India*. Madras, 1906.

Thwaites, R. G., ed., *Early Western Travels, 1748–1846*. 32 vols. Cleveland, Ohio, 1904–7.

Tickell, S. R., " Notes on the Gibbon of Tenasserim, *Hylobates lar*," *Journal of the Asiatic Society of Bengal*. Vol. xxxiii. Calcutta, 1865.

Tijdschrift van het Aardrijkskundig Genootschap. Amsterdam, 1876–

Tijdschrift voor Indische Taal-, Land- en Volkenkunde. Batavia, 1853–

Tijdschrift voor Neêrlands Indië. Batavia, 1838–

Tikhomirov, L., *La Russie politique et sociale*. Paris, 1886.

Tillier, L., *L'instinct sexuel chez l'homme et chez les animaux*. Paris, 1889.

Timberlake, Lt. Henry, *The Memoirs of Lt. H . . . T . . .* London, 1765.

Tiruvalluvar, Nayanar, *The Kural ; with translation and commentary in English* by F. W. Ellis. Madras, 1816.

Tiryns. Die Ergebnisse der Ausgrabungen des Instituts (*Kaiserlich deutsches archaeologischen Institut in Athen*). 2 vols. Athen, 1912.

Tissandier, Gaston, *L'océan aérien*. Paris, s.d.

Tisseire, Léon T., *Études sur la vipère cornue bicorne du sud de l'Algérie*. Alger, 1858.

Tissot, Charles Joseph, *Géographie comparée de la Province Romaine d'Afrique* (*Exploration scientifique de la Tunisie*). 2 vols. Paris, 1884–88.

Tobler, Adolf, " Ueber das volksthumliche Epos der Franzosen," *Zeitschrift für Völkerpsychologie und Sprachwissenschaft*. Vol. iv. Leipzig, 1866.

—— " Plus a paroles an plain pot De vin qu'an un mui de cervoise," *Zeitschrift für romanische Philologie*. Vol. iv. Halle, 1878.

Tocantins, Antonio, Manoel Gonçalves, " Estudios sobre a tribu ' Mundurucu,' " *Revista Trimensal do Instituto Historico Geographico e Ethnographico do Brasil*. Vol. xl, Part ii. Rio de Janeiro, 1877.

Tod, A. J., *The Primitive Family as an Educational Agency*. New York, London, 1913.

Tod, Hunter, *Diseases of the Ear*. London, 1907.

Tod, James, *Annals and Antiquities of Rajast'han, or the Central and Western Rajpoot States of India*. 2 vols. London, 1829.

Tollius, Jacobus, *Fortuita, in quibus praeter critica nonulla, tota fabularis historia Graeca, Phaenicia, Aegyptiaca ad chemiam pertinere asseritur*. Amsterlaedamii, 1687.

Toorn, J. L. van der, " Het animisme bij den Minangkabauer der Palangsche Bovenlande," *Bijdragen tot de taal-, land- en volkenkunde van Neerlandsch Indië*. Vol. xxxix. 's Gravenhage, 1890.

Toorn, J. L. van der, " Aanteekenigen uit het familieleven bij de Maleier in de Padangsche Bovenlanden," *Tijdschrift voor Indische taal-, land-en volkenkunde*. Vol. xxvi. Batavia, 1881.

Topinard, Paul, *L'Anthropologie et la Science Sociale*. Paris, 1900.

Torday, E., and Joyce, T. A., *Notes ethnographiques sur les peuples communément appelés Bakuba, ainsi que sur les peuplades apparentés—Les Bushongo* (*Annales du Musée du Congo*). Bruxelles, 1911.

Torday, E., and Joyce, T.A., "Notes on the Ethnography of the Ba-Huana," *Journal of the Anthropological Institute*. Vol. xxxvi. London, 1906.

" Notes on the Ethnography of the Ba-Mbala," *Journal of the Anthropological Institute*. Vol. xxxv. London, 1905.

" Notes on the Ethnography of the Ba-Yaka," *Journal of the Anthropological Institute*. Vol. xxxvi. London, 1906.

Torquemada, E. Juan de, *Veinte i un libros rituales i monarchia Indiana*. 3 vols. Madrid, 1723.

Torres, Lúis María, *Los primitivos habitantes del delta dell Paraná*. Buenos Aires, 1911.

Le Tour du Monde. Paris, 1863–

Tout, C. Hill, "Report on the Ethnology of the Stlatlumh of British Columbia," *Journal of the Anthropological Institute*. Vol. xxxv. London, 1905.

" Report on the Ethnology of the South-Eastern Tribes of Vancouver Island, British Columbia," *Journal of the Anthropological Institute*. Vol. xxxvii. London, 1907.

" Ethnological Report on the Stseelis and Skaulits Tribes of the Halokmelem Division of the Salish of British Columbia," *Journal of the Anthropological Institute*. Vol. xxxiv. London, 1904.

The Far West, the Home of the Salish and Déné. London, 1907.

Toutée, G., *De Dahomé au Sahara*. Paris, 1899.

Townsend, C. O., "Der Einfluss des Zellkerns auf die Bildung der Zellhaut," *Jahrbücher für wissenschaftliche Botanik*. Vol. xxx. Berlin, 1897.

Toy, C. H., "The Earliest Form of the Hebrew Sabbath," *Journal of Biblical Literature*. Vol. xviii. Boston, 1899.

Introduction to the History of Religions. Boston, 1913.

Traill, H. D., and Mann, J. S., (ed.) *Social England*. 6 vols. London, 1893–97.

Tran-Nuong Hanh, "Moeurs et coutumes annamites," *Annales de l'Extrème Orient*. Vol. xiv. Paris, 1882.

Transactions and Proceedings of the New Zealand Institute. Wellington, 1869–

Transactions and Proceedings of the Royal Geographical Society of Australasia (New South Wales Branch). Sydney, 1888–

Transactions and Proceedings of the Royal Society of South Australia. Adelaide, 1877–

Transactions of the American Ethnological Society. New York, 1845–

Transactions of the American Gynecological Society. Boston, 1876–

Transactions of the Anthropological Society of Washington. Washington, 1881–

Transactions of the Asiatic Society of Japan. Yokohama, 1874–

Transactions of the China Branch of the Royal Asiatic Society. Hong-Kong, 1848–

Transactions of the Entomological Society. London, 1807–

Transactions of the Ethnological Society of London. London, 1861–

Transactions of the Gaelic Society of Inverness. Inverness, 1872–

Transactions of the Kilkenny Archaeological Society. Dublin, 1850–

Transactions of the Linnaean Society of New York. New York, 1882–

Transactions of the Second Session of the International Congress of Orientalists held in London in September 1874. London, 1876.

Transactions of the Royal Society of New South Wales (published as *Journal and Proceedings* after 1877). Sydney, 1868–

Transactions of the Royal Society of Victoria. Melbourne, 1855–

Transactions of the Third International Congress for the History of Religions. 2 vols. Oxford, 1908.

Transactions of the Tyneside Naturalists' Field Club. Newcastle-upon-Tyne, 1850–

Transilvano, Massimiliano, " Epistola della ammirabile e stupenda navigatione fatta per li Spagnoli lo anno MDXIX attorno il mondo," in G. B. Ramusio, *Navigationi et Viaggi.* Vol. ii. Venetia, 1554.

" A Treatise of Brasil, written by a Portugall, which had long lived there." *Hakluytus Posthumus, or Purchas His Pilgrimes.* Vol. xvi. Glasgow, 1906.

Tredgold, A. F., *Mental Deficiency (Amentia).* London, 1922.

" Amentia (Idiocy and Imbecility)," *Archives of Neurology of the London County Asylums.* Vol. ii. Claybury, London, 1903.

Treffers, F., " Het landcshap Laiwoei in Z-O. Celebes en zijne bevolking," *Tijdschrift van het Koninklijk Nederlandsch Aardrijkskundig Genootschap.* 2e Serie, vol. xxx. Leiden, 1914.

Tregear, E., *The Maori-Polynesian Comparative Dictionary.* Wellington, 1891.

" The Maoris of New Zealand," *Journal of the Anthropological Institute.* Vol. xix. London, 1890.

The Maori Race. Wanganui, 1904.

Tellier, G., " Kreis Kita, Französischer Sudan," in S. R. Steinmetz, *Rechtsverhältnisse von eingeborenen Völkern in Afrika und Ozeanien.* Berlin, 1903.

Tremearne, Major A. J. N., " Bori Beliefs and Ceremonies," *Journal of the Royal Anthropological Institute.* Vol. xliv. London, 1915.

The Ban of the Bori. London, 1914.

Hausa Superstitions and Customs. London, 1913.

" Notes on Some Nigerian Head-Hunters," *Journal of the Royal Anthropological Institute.* Vol. xlii. London, 1912.

Trenk, " Die Buschleute der Namib, ihre Rechts- und Familienverhältnisse," *Mittheilungen aus den deutschen Schutzgebieten.* Vol. xxiii. Berlin, 1910.

Trent, William, *Journal of Captain William Trent from Logstown to Pickawillany, A.D. 1752.* Ed. by Alfred T. Goodman. Cincinnati, 1871.

Treuber, O., *Geschichte der Lykier.* Stuttgart, 1887.

Trevelyan, Marie, *Folk-lore and Folk-stories of Wales.* London, 1909.

Trilles, H., *Le totémisme chez les Fân (Bibliothèque Anthropos).* Münster i. W., 1912.

Trinchese, S., " Descrizione di un feto di orang-utan," *Annali del Museo Civico di Storia Naturale di Genoa.* Vol. i. Genoa, 1870.

Trojel, E., " Sur les cours d'amour," *Revue des langues romanes.* Vol. xxxiv. Montpellier, 1890.

See Andreas capellanus.

Tromp, S. W., " Eeen reis naar de bovenlanden van Koetei," *Tijdschrift voor Indische taal-, land- en volkenkunde.* Vol. xxiii. Batavia, 's Hage, 1876.

Trousseau, Armand, *Clinique médicale de l'Hôtel Dieu de Paris.* 3 vols. Paris, 1865.

Troyon, F., *Habitations lacustres des temps anciens et modernes.* (*Mémoires de la Société d'Histoire de la Suisse Romande.* Vol. xxv.) Lausanne, 1860.

Trucs Malecs, *Sirventes,* in *Archiv für das Studium der neueren Sprachen und Litteraturen.* Vol. xxxiv. Braunschweig, 1863.

Truffert, J. See Delisle, F.

Trumbull, Henry, *History of the Indian Wars.* Philadelphia, 1851.

Trumbull, J. H., " On the Algonkin name ' manit ' (or ' manitou '), sometimes translated ' great spirit,' and ' god,' " *Old and New.* Vol. i. Boston, 1870.

Tschudi, Friederich von, *Das Thierleben der Alpenwelt.* Leipzig, 1854.

Tschudi, J. J. von, " Culturhistorische und sprachliche Beiträge zur Kentniss des alten Peru," *Denkschriften der Kaiserliche Akademie der Wissenschaften ; Philosophisch-historische Classe*. Vol. xxxix. Vienna, 1850. *Travels in Peru during the years 1838–1842*. Transl. London, 1847.

Tsountas, Chrestos, and Massatt, J. Irving, *The Mycenaean Age*. Boston, New York, 1897.

Tsugaru, Fusamaro, *Die Lehre der Japonischen Adoption*. Berlin, 1903.

Tuch, F., " Sinaitischen Inschriften," *Zeitschrift der deutschen morgenländische Gesellschaft*. Vol. iii. Leipzig, 1850.

Tuke, John Batty, " Medical Notes on New Zealand," *Edinburgh Medical and Surgical Journal*. Vol. ix. Edinburgh, 1864.

Tupper, C. L., *Punjab Customary Law*. 3 vols. Calcutta, 1881.

Tur, J., " Observations sur les perversions de l'amour maternel," *Bulletin scientifique de la France et de la Belgique*. Vol. xliii. Paris, 1909.

Türlim, Heinrich von dem, *Diu Crône*. Ed. by G. H. F. Scholl. Stuttgart, 1852.

Turner, George, *Samoa, a Hundred Years ago and long before*. London, 1884. *Nineteen Years in Polynesia*. London, 1861.

Turner, L. M., " Ethnology of the Ungava District, Hudson Bay Territory," *Eleventh Annual Report of the Bureau of Ethnology*. Washington, 1894.

Turner, Samuel, *An Account of an Embassy to the Court of the Teshoo Lama, in Tibet*. London, 1800.

Turner, W. Y., " On the Ethnology of Motu," *Journal of the Anthropological Institute*. Vol. vii. London, 1878.

Turnour, George, *An Epitome of the History of Ceylon, compiled from native annals*. Ceylon, 1836.

See Mahānāma.

Turpin, F. H., *Histoire civile et naturelle du royaume de Siam*. 2 vols. Paris, 1771.

Twasaki, Kojiro, *Das Japanische Eherecht*. Leipzig, 1904.

Twentieth Century Practice. 20 vols. London, 1895–1900.

Tyler, Josiah, *Forty Years among the Zulus*. Boston, Chicago, 1891.

Tylor, Edward Burnett, " Wild Men and Beast-Children," *Anthropological Review*. Vol. i. London, 1863.

" The Matriarchal Family System," *The Nineteenth Century*. Vol. xl. London, 1896.

Primitive Culture. 2 vols. London, 1903.

Researches into the Early History of Mankind. London, 1878.

" Notes on the Modern Survival of Ancient Amulets against the Evil Eye," *Journal of the Anthropological Institute*. Vol. xix. London, 1890.

" On a Method of investigating the Development of Institutions, applied to Laws of Marriage and Descent," *Journal of the Anthropological Institute*. Vol. xviii. London, 1889.

Tzetzes, I. and J., *Scholia ad Lycophorn*. Ed. C. R. Müller. Leipsic, 1811. *Chiliades*. Ed. T. Kiesseling. Leipsic, 1826.

" Ueber den religiösen Glauben und die Ceremonien der heidnischen Samojeden im Kreise Mesen, nach dem Russischen," *Zeitschrift für allgemeine Erdkunde*. N.F., vol. viii. 1860.

" Ueber die in Italien befindlichen provençalische Liederhandschrifte," *Archiv für das Studium der neueren Sprachen und Literatur*. Vol. xxxiv. Braunschweig, 1863.

Uhlhorn, J. G. W., *Die Homilien und Recognitionen des Clemens Romanus.*
  Göttingen, 1852.
Ujfalvy, Karl Eugen von, *Aus den westlichen Himalaya.* Leipzig, 1884.
  Les Aryens au Nord et au Sud de l'Hindou-Kouch. Paris, 1896.
  Expédition scientifique française en Russie, en Sibérie et dans le Turkestan.
  6 vols. Paris, Le Puy, 1878–80.
  " Die Ptolemäer. Ein Beitrag zur historischen Anthropologie," *Archiv
  für Anthropologie.* N.F., vol. ii. Braunschweig, 1904.
  " Voyage dans l'Himalaya occidental (le Koulou, le Cachemire et le Petit
  Thibet)," *Bulletin de la Société d'Anthropologie.* Série iii, vol. v.
  Paris, 1882.
Ulloa, A. de, *Relación historica del viage á la America meridional.* 2 vols.
  Madrid, 1748.
Ulloa, G. J. and A. de, " A Voyage to South America," in Pinkerton, *Voyages
  and Travels.* Transl. Vol. xiv. London, 1813.
Ulrich von Zatzihoven, *Lanzelet.* Ed. K. A. Hahn. Frankfurt a. M., 1845.
Ungnad, A., and Gressmann, H., *Das Gilgamesh-Epos.* Göttingen, 1911.
University of California Publications in American Archaeology and Ethnology.
  Berkeley, 1903–
University of California Publications in Education. Berkeley, 1893–
University of London. Eugenics Laboratory Memoirs. London, 1912–
L'Univers: histoire et description de tous les peuples. 70 vols. Paris,
  1835–63.
The Upanishads. Transl. by F. Max Müller. (*The Sacred Books of the East.*
  Vols. i. and xv.) Oxford, 1879, 1884.
Up de Graff, F. W., *Head-Hunters of the Amazon.* London, 1922.
Upham, Edward, *The Mahávansi, the Rája-Ratnácari, and the Rája-Vali,
  forming the Sacred and Historical Books of Ceylon.* 3 vols. London,
  1833.
Usener, Hermann, *Götternamen.* Bonn, 1896.
  " Dreiheit," *Rheinisches Museum für Philologie.* Neue folge, vol. lviii.
  Frankfurt a. M., 1903.
Uticšenovič, Og., M., *Die Hauskommunionen der Südsclaven.* Wien, 1859.
Uzel, H., *Monographie der Ordnung Thysanoptera.* Könnigrätz, 1895.

Vaërting, Mathilde and Mathias, *Neubegrundung der Psychologie von Mann
  und Weib.* Karlsruhe, 1921.
  English transl., *The Dominant Sex.* London, 1923.
Valenta, Joseph, " Volkskrankheiten und ärtzliche Zustände in Serbien,"
  Mittheilungen der kais. und königl. geographische Gesellschaft in Wien.
  Vol. xv. Vienna, 1873.
Valentijn, F., *Oud en nieuw Oost-Indië.* 3 vols. Dordrecht, Amsterdam,
  1724–26.
Valentini, Ph. J. J., " Trique Theogony," *Journal of American Folk-Lore.*
  Vol. xii. Boston, New York, 1899.
Valerius Flaccua, Caius, *Argonauticon,* lib. viii. Rec. Aem. Baehrens. Lip-
  siae, 1875.
Valerius Maximus, *Opera.* Ex. ed. J. Kappii. Londini, 1819.
Vallancey, Charles, *Collectanea de rebus Hibernicis.* Dublin, 1786.
Vámbéry, H., *Reise in Mittelasien.* Leipzig, 1873.
  Sketches of Central Asia. London, 1868.
  Travels in Central Asia. London, 1864.
Vanden Bergh, L. J., *On the Trail of the Pygmies.* London, 1922.

Van der Burght, J. M. M., *Un grand peuple de l'Afrique équatoriale. Éléments d'une monographie sur l'Urunde et les Warundi.* Bois-le-Duc, 1904.

Van Schmid, " Aanteekeningen nopens de zeden, gewoonten en gebruiken, benevens de vooroordeelen en bijgeloovigheden der bevolking van der eilanden Saparoea, Haroekoe, Noessa Laut, en van een gedeelte van de zuidkust van Ceram, in vroegeren en lateren tijd," *Tijdschrift voor Neerlands Indië.* Vol. v, Part ii. Batavia, 1843.

Varnhagen, F. A. de, *Historia geral do Brasil.* 10 vols. Rio de Janeiro, 1854-57.

Varro, Marcus Terentius, *Rerum rusticarum libri iii.* Rec. H. Keil. Leipzig, 1889.

Vasconcellos, Simão de, *Noticias curiosas e necessarias dos cousas do Brasil.* Lisboa, 1668.

Vaublanc, V. H. de, *La France au temps des croisades.* 4 vols. Paris, 1844-47.

Vaugeois, Mme, " Rimes et jeux du pays Nantois," *Revue des Traditions Populaires.* Vol. xiii. Paris, 1898.

Vaux, Carra de, art. " Family (Muslim)," in Hastings's, *Encyclopaedia of Religion and Ethics.* Vol. v. Edinburgh, 1912.

Vaux, L. de, " Les Canaques de la Nouvelle Calédonie," *Revue d'Ethnographie.* Vol. ii. Paris, 1883.

Vaz d'Almada, Francisco, " An Account of the Misfortunes that befell the Ship São Joãn Baptista," in G. MacCall Theal, *Records of South-East Africa.* Vol. viii. London, 1902.

The Vedânta-Sûtras, with the commentary by Sankârakarya. Transl. by George Thibaut. (*The Sacred Books of the East.* Vol. xxxiv.) Oxford, 1890.

Vega, Chritophorus, Soc. Jesu., *Theologia Mariana.* 2 Parts. Lugduni, 1655.

Veigl, Fr. Xavier, *Gründliche Nachrichten über die Verfassung der Landschaft von Maynas in Süd-America.* Nürenberg, 1798.

Velarde, Pedro Murillo, *Historia de la Provincia de Philipinas.* Manila, 1749. Extracts transl. in E. H. Blair and J. A. Robertson, *The Philippine Islands, 1493-1803.* Vol. xliv. Cleveland, 1906.

Velleius Paterculus, Caius, *Ex historiae Romanae lib. ii quae supersunt.* Ed. C. Halm. Leipzig, 1876.

Venegas, M. A., *Natural and Civil History of California.* Transl. 2 vols. London, 1759.

Veniukof, M., " The Belors and their Country," *The Journal of the Royal Geographical Society.* Vol. xxxvi. London, 1866.

Venkata Subra Rau, R., *Kamala's Letters to her Husband.* Madras, 1904.

Vergil Maro, *Opera.* Ed. C. G. Heyne. 4 vols. London, 1818.

Verhandelingen van het Bataviaasch Genootschap van Kunsten en Wetenschappen. Batavia, 1779–

Verhandlungen der Kaiserliche Akademie der Wissenschaften. Wien, 1858–

Verhandlungen der Berliner Gesellschaft für Anthropologie, Ethnologie und Urgeschichte. Berlin, 1869–

Verhandlungen der Gesellschaft für Erdkunde zu Berlin. Berlin, 1873–

Verhandlungen der deutschen Zoologische Gesellschaft. Leipzig, 1877–

Verhandlungen der zweiten Kongress für Allgemeine Religionswissenschaft. Basel, 1904.

Verhoeven, P. W., *Kurtze Beschreibung einer Reyse, so von den Holländern und Seeländern, in die Ost Indien.* Frankfurt a. M., 1613.

Verneau, René, *Les anciens Patagons.* Monaco, 1903.

— *Les races humaines.* Paris, 1890.

Verneau, René, *Le Bassin suivant les sexes et les races*. Paris, 1875.

Verrall, A. W., *The " Bacchants " of Euripides and other Essays*. Cambridge, 1910.

    Euripides, the Rationalist. Cambridge, 1895.

Verslagen en Mededeelingen van het Koninklijke Akademie van Wetenschappen. Amsterdam, 1853.

Vespucci, Amerigo, *Quatuor Americi Vesputii Navigationes*, in F. de Navarrete, *Colección de los viages y descubrimientos*, etc. Vol. iii. Madrid, 1829.

The Veterinarian. London, 1828–

Veth, P. J., *Borneo's Wester-Afdeeling*. 2 vols. Zaltbommel, 1854–56.

    Het eiland Timor. Amsterdam, 1855.

    Java, geographisch, ethnologisch, historisch. 4 vols. Haarlem, 1896–1907.

    " Het landschap Aboeng en de Aboengers," *Tijdschrift van het Kon. Nederlandsch Aardrijkskundig Genootaschap*. Vol. ii. Leiden, 1877.

Vetter, Konrad, " Bericht des Missionars Herrn Konrad Vetter in Simbang über papuanische Rechtsverhältnisse, wie solche namentlich bei den Jabin beobachtet wurden," *Nachrichten über Kaiser Wilhelms-Land und den Bismarck-Archipel*. Berlin, 1897.

Veuillot, Louis, *Le droit du seigneur au moyen-âge*. Paris, 1854.

Veytia, M. F. de Echeverria y, *Historia antigua de Méjico*. 3 vols. Mexico, 1836.

Viehe, G., " Die Ovaherero," in S. R. Steinmetz, *Rechtsverhältnisse von eingeborenen Völkern in Afrika und Ozeanien*. Berlin, 1903.

    " Some Customs of the Ovaherero," communicated by W. Coates Palgrave, *Folk-lore Journal*. Vol. i. Cape Town, 1879.

Vigne, G. T., *Travels in Kashmir, Ladak, Iskardo*. 2 vols. London, 1842.

Villemarqué, T. C. H. de la, *Les romans de la Table Ronde et les contes des anciens Bretons*. Paris, 1860.

    Myrdhin, ou l'enchanteur Merlin. Paris, 1862.

Villeneuve, Hureau de, *De l'accouchement dans la race jaune*. Paris, 1863.

Vincendon-Dumoulin and Desgraz, C., *Îles Marquises ou Nouka-Hiva*. Paris, 1843.

Vincent de Beauvais, *Speculum historiale*. Douai, 1624.

Vincenti, C. von, *Die Ehe in Islam*. Wien, 1876.

Vinson, Julien, *Le Folk-lore du Pays Basque*. Paris, 1883.

Virchow, Rudolf L. C., *Menschen- und Affenschadel*. (*Sammlung gemeinverständlicher wissenschaftlichen Vorträge*. Heft 96.) Leipzig, 1866.

    " Die Weddas von Ceylon in ihre Beziehungen zu der Nachbarstammen," *Abhandlungen der Konigliche Akademie der Wissenschaften*. Berlin, 1881.

    The same. Trans. in *Journal of the Ceylon Branch of the Royal Asiatic Society*. Vol. ix. Colombo, 1888.

Viré, Armand, *La faune souterraine de France*. Paris, 1900.

Virey, J. J., *Histoire naturelle du genre humain*. 3 vols. Paris, 1924.

Virey, Philippe, *Études sur le papyrus Prisse, le livre de Kaquimna et les leçons de Ptah-Hotep*. Paris, 1887.

Virolleaud, Ch., *L'astrologie chaldéenne : Le livre intitulé, Enuma Anu il Lil*. Paris, 1908.

Vishnu Purana, transl. by H. H. Wilson, ed. by F. Hall. 5 vols. London, 1864–70.

Vishwanath, Pandit, " Ancient Royal Hindu Marriage Customs," with notes by H. A. Rose, *Journal of the Royal Anthropological Institute*. Vol. xlvii. London, 1917.

Vita Merlini (attributed to Geoffrey of Monmouth). Ed. Fr. Michel and T. Wright. Paris, 1837.

Vitruvius Pollio, Marcus, *De architectura*. Rec. J. G. Schneider. 3 vols. Lipsiae, 1807–8.

Vivien de Saint Martin, Louis, *Les Huns blancs, ou Ephthalites*. Paris, 1849.

Vogel, Hans, *Eine Forschungsreise im Bismarck-Archipel*. Hamburg, 1911.

Vogel, Johan Wilhelm, *Zehen-Jährig Ost-Indianische Reise-Beschreibung*. Altenburg, 1704.

Vogt, Carl, *Vorlesungen über den Menschen, seine Stellung in der Schöpfung und in der Geschichte der Erde*. 2 vols. Giessen, 1863.

Vogüé, E. M., de, *Syrie centrale*. 3 vols. Paris, 1865–77.

Voigt, M., *Geschichte und System des Civil-und-Criminal-Rechtes wie Processes der XII Tafeln ueber deren Fragmenten*. Leipzig, 1883.

Voison, A., "Contribution à l'histoire des mariages entre consanguins," *Mémoires de la Société d'Anthropologie de Paris*. Vol. ii. Paris, 1865.

Volkens, Georg, *Der Kilimandscharo*. Berlin, 1897.

Volmann, F., "Zur Psychologie, Religion, Sociologie und Geschichte der Monumbo-Papua, Deutsch Neu-Guinea," *Anthropos*. Vol. v. Wien, 1910.

Volz, W., "Beiträge zur Anthropologie und Ethnographie von Indonesien," *Archiv für Anthropologie*. Vol. xxxii. Braunschweig, 1906.

Nord Sumatra. 2 vols. Berlin, 1912.

Vopiscus, Flavius, in *Historiae Augustus Scriptores*. Vol. ii. Lugd. Batav. 1671.

Vormann, F., "Zur Psychologie, Religion, Soziologie und Geschichte der Monumbo-Papua, in Deutsch Neu-Guinea," *Anthropos*. Vol. v. Salzburg, 1910.

Vortisch, H., "Die Neger der Goldkuste," *Globus*. Vol. lxxxix. Braunschweig, 1906.

Vossler, Karl, *Die philosophischen Grundlagen zum "süssen neuen Stil" des Guido Ginicelli, Guido Cavalcanti, und Dante Alighieri*. Heidelberg, 1904.

Voth, H. R., *The Traditions of the Hopi*. (*Field-Columbian Museum, Publication 96 ; Anthropological Series*. Vol. viii.) Chicago, 1905.

Vuk, Karadzić Stephanović, *Montenegro und die Montenegriner*. Stuttgart, 1837.

Wace, Robert, *Le roman de Rou*. Ed. F. Pluquet. 2 vols. Rouen, 1827.

Wachsmuth, C., *Das alte Griechenland im neuen*. Bonn, 1864.

Wachsmuth, E. W. Gottlieb, *Hellenische Alterthumskunde*. 2 vols. Halle, 1846.

Wade, William, *The Blind-Deaf*. Indianopolis, 1904.

Waddell, L. A., *The Buddhism of Tibet, or Lamaism*. London, 1895.

"The Tribes of the Brahmaputra Valley," *Journal of the Asiatic Society of Bengal*. Vol. lxix, Part iii. Calcutta, 1901.

"Frog-worship amongst the Newars, with a note on the Etymology of the word ' Nepal,' " *The Indian Antiquary*. Vol. xxii. Bombay, 1893.

Wagner, Nicholas, "Ueber die viviparen Gallmuckenlarva," *Zeitschrift für wissenschaftliche Zoologie*. Vol. xv. Leipzig, 1865.

Meinert, Pagenstecher, and Ganine, "Observations sur la reproduction parthénogénésique chez quelques larves d'insectes diptères," *Annales des Sciences Naturelles*. 5e Série, Zoologie. Vol. iv. Paris, 1865.

Wahlen, A. (J. F. N. Coumyer), *Moeurs, usages et costumes de tous les peuples du monde*. 4 vols. Bruxelles, 1843–44.

Waitz, Georg, *Das alte Recht der Salischen Franken*. Kiel, 1846.

Waitz, Th., *Anthropologie der Naturvölker*. 6 vols. Part ii of vol. v and vol. vi by G. Gerland. Leipzig, 1859–72.

Wake, C. S., " The Origin of Serpent Worship." *Journal of the Anthropological Institute*. Vol. ii. London, 1873.

Wakefield, E. J., *Adventure in New Zealand, 1839–44*. 2 vols. London, 1845.

Waldegrave, Hon. W., " Extracts from a private Journal kept on board H.M.S. 'Seringapatam,' in the Pacific, 1830," *The Journal of the Royal Geographical Society*. Vol. iii. London, 1834.

Walen, A., " The Sakalava," *Antananarivo Annual and Madagascar Magazine*, Nos. v–viii. Antananarivo, 1881–84,

Walhouse, M. J., " Devil and Ghost Worship in Western India," *Journal of the Anthropological Institute*. Vol. v. London, 1883.

Walker, R. B. N., " Letter to Dr. J. E. Gray," *Proceedings of the Zoological Society*. Vol. xli. London, 1873.

Wallace, A. R., *The Malay Archipelago*. 2 vols. London, 1869.
Darwinism. London, 1889.
Travels on the Amazon and Rio Negro. London, 1853.

Walpole, Hon. Fred., *Four Years in the Pacific*. 2 vols. London, 1849.

Walshe, W. G., art. " Chastity (Chinese)," in Hastings's *Encyclopaedia of Religion and Ethics*. Vol. iii. Edinburgh, 1910.
Ways that are Dark. Shanghai, 1907.

Walter, Ferdinand, *Corpus Juris Germanici antiqui*. 3 vols. Berlin, 1824.

Walter, P., " Die Inseln Nossi-Be und Mayotte," in S. R. Steinmetz, *Rechtsverhältnisse von eingeborenen Völkern in Afrika und Ozeanien*. Berlin, 1903.

Walters, H. B., in *The Classical Review*. Vol. viii. London, 1894.

Wanderer, C., " Die Khoi-Khoin oder Naman," in S. R. Steinmetz, *Rechtsverhältnisse von eingeborenen Völkern in Afrika und Ozeanien*. Berlin, 1903.

Wangemann, Th., *Die Berliner Mission im Bassuto-Lande (Transvaal-Republik)*. (*Geschichte der Berliner Missionsgesellschaft und ihrer Arbeiten in Süd-Afrika*. Vol. iv.) Berlin, 1877.

Ward, B. C., " Geographical and Statistical Memoir of a Survey of the Neelgherry Mountains in the Province of Coimbatore," in H. B. Grigg, *A Manual of the Nilagiri District in the Madras Presidency*. Madras, 1880.

Ward, F. Kingdom, *In Farthest Burma*. London, 1921.

Ward, Herbert, *Five Years among Congo Cannibals*. London, 1890.

Ward, Lester F., " Our Better Halves," *The Forum*. Vol. vi. New York, 1888.
Dynamic Sociology. 2 vols. New York, 1907.

Ward, W., *A View of the History, Literature, and Religion of the Hindoos*. 4 vols. London, 1817–20.

Ward, William Hayes, *The Seal Cylinders of Western Asia*. Washington, 1910.
" The Greek and the Hittite Gods," in *Essays presented to C. A. Briggs*. New York, 1911.

Wardle, H. Newell, " The Sedna Cycle : A Study in Myth Evolution," *The American Anthropologist*. N.S., vol. ii. Boston, New York, 1900.

Warneck, F., " Das Eherecht bei den Toba-Batak," *Bijdragen tot de taalland-, en volkenkunde van Nederlandsch-Indië*. Vol. liii. Leiden, 1901,

Warneck, J., " Studien über die Literatur der Tobabatak," *Mitteilungen des Seminars für orientalische Sprachen*. Vol. ii. Berlin, 1898.
Die Religion der Batak. Leipzig, 1909.

Warren, Willar W., " History of the Ojibways based upon Traditions and Oral Statements," *Collections of the Minnesota Historical Society*. Vol. v. Saint Paul, 1885.

Waterhouse, Joseph, *The King and People of Fiji*. London, 1876.

Waterson, D., " Report upon the Physical Characters of some Nilotic Negroid Tribes," *Third Report of the Wellcome Research Laboratories at the Gordon Memorial College, Khartum*. Khartum, 1908.

Watson, J. B., " The effect of the bearing of Young upon the Body-weight and the weight of the Central Nervous System of the Female White Rat," *Journal of Comparative Neurology and Psychology*. Vol. xv. Baltimore, 1905.

Watt, Agnes C. P., *Twenty-five years Mission Life on Tanna, New Hebrides*. London, 1896.

Watt, George, " The Aboriginal Tribes of Manipur," *Journal of the Anthropological Institute*. Vol. xvi. London, 1887.

Watt, Mrs. Stuart, *In the Heart of Savagedom*. London, 1923.

Wauters, A.-J., *L'état indépendant du Congo*. Bruxelles, 1890.

Webb, C. Morgan, " Burma " Report, *Census of India, 1911*. Vol. ix. Rangoon, 1912.

Weber, Albrecht, " Vac und λόγος," *Indische Studien*. Vol. ix. Leipzig, 1865.
" Zur Kenntniss des vedische Opferrituals," *Indische Studien*. Vol. x. Leipzig, 1868.
" Indische Hochzeitssprüche," *Indische Studien*. Vol. v. Berlin, 1861.
The History of Indian Literature. Transl. London, 1878.
" Collectanea über die Kastenverhältnisse in der Brahmana und Sutra," *Indische Studien*. Vol. x. Leipzig, 1868.

Weber, E. von, *Vier Jahre in Afrika*. 2 vols. Leipzig, 1878.

Weber, Otto, *Arabien vor dem Islam (Der Alte Orient)*. Leipzig, 1901.
" Studien zur südarabischen Alterthumskunde," *Mitteilungen der Vorderasiatische Gesellschaft*. Vol. vi. Berlin, 1901.
Altorientalische Siegebilder (Der Alte Orient). Leipzig, 1920.

Webster, Hutton, *Primitive Secret Societies*. New York, 1908.
Rest Days. New York, 1916.

Wechsler, M. E., " Frauendienst und Vasalitat," *Zeitschrift für französische Sprache und Literatur*. Vol. xxiv.

Weeks, John, *Among the Primitive Bakongo*. London, 1914.
Among Congo Cannibals. London, 1913.
" Anthropological Notes on the Bangala of the Upper Congo River," *Journal of the Royal Anthropological Institute*. Vols. xxxix, xl. London, 1909–10.
" Notes on some Customs of the Lower Congo People," *Folk-lore*. Vol. xix. London, 1908.

Wehrli, H. J., " Beitrag zur Ethnologie der Chingpaw (Kachin) von Ober-Burma," *Internationales Archiv für Ethnographie*. Vol. xvi, Supplement. Leiden, 1903.

Weidener, E., " Zur babylonischen Astronomie," *Babyloniaca*. Vol. vi. 1911.

Weinhold, Karl, *Altnordisches Leben*. Berlin, 1856.
Die deutschen Frauen in dem Mittelalter. 2 vols. Wien, 1882.

Weipert, H., " Japanisches Familien und Erbrecht," *Mitteilungen der deutschen Gesellschaft für Natur- und Völkerkunde Ostasiens*. Vol. v. Yokohama, 1892.

Weismann, August, *The Germ-Plasm*. Transl. London, 1893.
Amphimixis, oder Vermischung der Individuen. Jena, 1891.
" Parthenogenesis bei Ostracoden," *Zoologischer Anzeiger*. Vol. iii. Leipzig, 1880.

Weiss, M., " Land und Leute von Mpororo (Nord-west von Deutschen Öst-
afrika)," *Globus*, Vol. xci. Braunschweig, 1907.

Weiss, Max, *Die Völkerstämme im Norden Deutsch-Ostafrikas.* Berlin, 1910.

Weissenberg, S., " Die Falaschas," *Globus*. Vol. xcvi. Braunschweig, 1909.

Weissmann, A., " Beitrage zur Naturgeschichte der Daphnoiden," *Zeitschrift für wissenschaftliche Zoologie.* Vol. xxxiii. Leipzig, 1880.

Welcker, F. G., *Griechische Gotterlehre.* 3 vols. Gottingen, 1857-63.

Wellhausen, J., *Prolegomena to the History of Israel.* Transl. Edinburgh,
1885.

Reste arabischen Heidentums. Berlin, 1897.

" Die Ehe bei den Arabern," *Nachrichten von der königlichen Gesellschaft
der Wissenschaften und der Georg-August-Universität zu Göttingen.*
Göttingen, 1893.

Wells, Francis H., " The Habits, Customs, and Ceremonies of the Aboriginals
of the Diamentina, Herbert, and Eleanor Rivers in East Central
Australia," *Report of the Fifth Meeting of the Australasian Association
for the Advancement of Science.* Adelaide, 1893.

Wenckstern, A. von, " Orang-Utan's von der Ostkuste von Sumatra," *Correspondenz-Blatt der deutsche Gesellschaft für Anthropologie, Ethnologie
und Urgeschichte.* Vol. xxii. Munich, 1892.

Wendland, P., and Kern, O., *Beiträge zur Geschichte der griechischen Philosophie
und Religion.* Berlin, 1895.

Weniaminof, Ivan, " Chrakter-Züge der Aleuten von den Fuchs-Inseln," in
F. Wrangell, *Statistische und ethnographische Nachrichten über die
russischen Besitzungen an der Nordwestküste von Amerika. (Beiträge
zur Kenntniss des Russischen Reiches und der angränzenden Länder
Asiens.* Vol. i.) St. Petersburg, 1839.

Wentzel, W. F., " Letters to the Hon. Roderic McKenzie," in L. R. Masson,
Les Bourgeois de la Compagnie du Nord-Ouest. Vol. i. Quebec, 1889.

Werenfels, Samuel, *A Dissertation upon Superstition in Natural Things.*
London, 1748.

Werner, Alice, *The Natives of British Central Africa.* London, 1906.

" Two Galla Legends," *Man.* Vol. xii. London, 1912.

" The Evolution of Agriculture," *Journal of the African Society.* Vol. ix.
London, 1910.

Wessely, Carl, " Studien über das Verhältniss des griechischen zum ägyptischen Recht im Lagidenreich," *Sitzungsberichte der philosophisch-
historischen Classe der kaiserlichen Akademie der Wissenschaften.*
Vol. cxxiv. Wien, 1891.

" Die griechischen Papyri der kaiserlichen Sammlungen Wiens," *XI
Jahresbericht des königliches-kaiserliches Franz-Josef-Gymnasium.* Wien,
1885.

" Griechische Zauberpapyrus von Paris und London," *Denkschriften der
Kaiserlichen Akademie der Wissenschaften ; Philologisch-historische
Classe.* Vol. xxxvi, Part ii. Wien, 1888.

Wessman, R., in *Verhandlungen der Berliner Gesellschaft für Anthropologie.*
Berlin, 1877.

West, John, *The Substance of a Journal during a Residence at the Red River
Colony, British North America.* London, 1634.

West, Rev. John, *The History of Tasmania.* 2 vols. Launceston, 1852.

West, Thomas, *Ten Years in South-Central Polynesia.* London, 1865.

Westervelt, W. D., *Legends of Ma-ui, a Demi-God of Polynesia and of his
Mother Hina.* Honolulu, 1910.

Legends of Gods and Ghosts. Hawaiian Mythology. Boston, 1915.

Westermanns illustrierte deutsche Monats-Hefte. Braunschweig, 1882–

Westermarck, Edward, *The History of Human Marriage*. Fifth edition, rewritten. 3 vols. London, 1921.
    The same, 3rd edition, 1901 ; 4th edition, 1911.
    The Origin and Development of Moral Ideas. 2 vols. London, 1908.
Westgarth, William, *Australia Felix*. Edinburgh, 1848.
    A Report on the Condition, Capabilities, and Prospects of the Australian Aborigines. Melbourne, 1846.
Westminster Review, New Series. London, 1887–
Weston, Jessie L., *The Legend of Sir Gawain*. London, 1897.
    The Legend of Sir Launcelot du Lac. London, 1901.
    The Legend of Sir Perceval. 2 vols. London, 1906.
    Parzival. Transl. London, 1904.
Weule, Karl, " Aus den afrikanischen Kinderleben," *Westermanns illustrierte deutsche Monats-Hefte*. Vol. lxxxv. Braunschweig, 1899.
    Wissenschaftliche Ergebnisse meiner ethnologische Forschungen in der Südkoste Deutschostafrikas. Berlin, 1908.
    Native Life in East Africa. Transl. London, 1909.
Wheeler, Sir George, *Voyage de Dalmatie, de Grèce et du Levant*. 2 vols. Amsterdam, 1689.
Wheelright, C. A., " Native Circumcision Lodges in the Zoutpansberg District," *Journal of the Anthropological Institute*. Vol. xxxv. London, 1905.
Whiffen, Thomas, *The North-West Amazons*. London, 1915.
White, Gilbert, *The Natural History of Selborne*. Ed. R. Kearton. London, 1902.
White, J. Claude, *Sikkim and Bhutan*. London, 1909.
White, Gilbert, *The Natural History of Selborne*. London, 1900.
White, John, *Maori Superstitions*. Auckland, 1856.
    The Ancient History of the Maori, his Mythology and Traditions. 4 vols. Wellington, 1886–89.
Whitehead, H., *The Village Gods of South India*. Calcutta, 1916.
Whitney, W. D., " On Jacobi and Tilaka on the Age of the Veda," *Proceedings of the American Oriental Society*. New Haven, 1894.
    Oriental and Linguistic Studies. 2 vols. New York, 1873–75.
Whymper, F., " Russian America, or ' Alaska,' the Natives of the Youkon River and Adjacent Country," *Transactions of the Ethnological Society*. Vol. vii. London, 1869.
Wide, S., *De sacris Troezeniorum, Hermionensium, Epidauriorum*. Upsala, 1898.
    Lakonische Kulte. Leipzig, 1893.
Widenmann, " Beschneidung bei den Massai," *Verhandlungen der Berliner Gesellschaft für Anthropologie*. Berlin, 1895.
Wied-Neuwied, Prince Maximilian zu, *Reise in das Innere Nord Amerika's*. Coblenz, 1839–41.
    Voyages in the Interior of North America. 3 vols. (in R. G. Thwaites, *Early Western Travels, 1748-1846*). Cleveland, 1906.
Wiedemann, A., *Religion of the Ancient Egyptians*. London, 1897.
    " Le roi dans l'ancienne Égypte," *Le Muséon*. Vol. xiii. Louvain, 1894.
    Ägyptische Geschichte. 2 Parts. Gotha, 1884.
    Hieratische Texte aus den Museen zu Berlin und Paris. Berlin, 1879.
Wiedemann, F. J., *Aus dem inneren und äusseren Leben der Ehsten*. St. Petersburg, 1876.
Wiese, Carl, " Beiträge zur Geschichte der Zulu im Norden des Zambesi, namentlich der Angoni," *Zeitschrift für Ethnologie*. Vol. xxxii. Berlin, 1900.

Wieseler, F., *Der Hildesheimer Silberfund.* Bonn, 1868.

Wigan, A. L., *A New View of Insanity. The Duality of the Mind.* London, 1844.

Wilamowitz-Moellendorff, Ulrich von, *Homerische Untersuchungen.* (*Philologische Untersuchungen.* Heft 7.) Berlin, 1884.

Aristoteles und Athen. 2 vols. Berlin, 1893.

Wilcken, Ulrich, *Griechische Ostraka aus Ägypten und Nubian.* Leipzig, Berlin, 1899.

" Arsinotische Steuerprofesionen aus dem Jahre 189 n. Chr. und verwandte Urkunde," *Sitzungsberichte der königlich Preussische Akademie der Wissenschaften zu Berlin, 1883.* Vol. ii. Berlin, 1883.

Wilde, Lady Jane, *Ancient Legends, Mystic Charms, and Superstitions of Ireland.* 2 vols. London, 1887.

Wilde, William R., *Practical Observations on Aural Surgery and the Nature and Treatment of Diseases of the Ear.* London, 1853.

Wilhelmi, Barnum Felix, *Statistik der Taubstummen des Regierungsbezirkes Magdeburg nach der Volkzählung von 1871. Beilage zur Deutschen Klinik.* Berlin, 1873.

Wilhelmi, Charles, " Manners and Customs of the Australian Natives," *Transactions of the Royal Society of Victoria.* Vol. v. Melbourne, 1860.

Wilken, G. A., *De Verspreide Geschriften,* verzameld door Mr. F. D. E. van Ossenbruggen, Semarang, Soerabaja. 4 vols. 's Gravenhage, 1912. *Handleiding voor de vergelijkende volkenkunde van Nederlandsch-Indië.* Ed. by C. M. Pleyte. Leiden, 1893.

" Die Ehe zwischen Blutsverwandten," *Globus.* Vol. lix. Braunschweig, 1891.

Wilken, P. N., " Bijjdragen tot de kennis van de zeden en gewoonten der Alfoeren in de Minahassa," *Mededeelingen van wege het Nederlandsche Zendelinggenootschap.* Vol. vii. Rotterdam, 1863.

Wilkes, C., *Narrative of the United States Exploring Expedition during the years 1838, 1839, 1840, 1841, 1842.* 5 vols and atlas. London, 1845.

Wilkinson, R. J., *Papers on Malay Subjects, Supplement : The Aboriginal Tribes.* Kuala Lumpur, 1910.

Papers on Malay Subjects. Life and Customs, Part i : The Incidents of Malay Life. Kuala Lumpur, 1908.

Willer, T. J., *Het eiland Boeroe, zijne exploratie en Halfoerische instellinge.* Amsterdam, 1858.

" Verzameling der Battasche wetten en instellingen in Mandheling en Pertibie," *Tijdschrift voor Neërlands Indië.* Vol. viii, deel ii. Batavia, 1846.

William of Malmesbury, *De gestis regum Anglorum.* Ed. W. Stubbs (*Chronicles and Memorials of Great Britain and Ireland*). 2 vols. London, 1887–89.

William of Newburgh, *Historia rerum Anglicarum,* in *Chronicles of the Reigns of Stephen, Henry II and Richard I.* Ed. R. Howlett. 2 vols. London, 1884–89.

William of Poitou, *Les chansons de Guillaume IX, duc d'Acquitaine* (1071–1127). Ed. by Alfred Jeanfroy, Paris, 1913.

William, Prince of Sweden, *Among Pygmies and Gorillas.* London, 1923.

Williams, Blanche E., " Religion of the Minaons," in B. H. Hawes, *Gournia.* Philadelphia, 1908.

Williams, Clement, *Through Burmah to Western China.* London, 1868.

Williams, G. R. C., *Historical and Statistical Memoir of Dehra Doon.* Roorkee, 1874.

Williams, John, *A Narrative of Missionary Enterprises in the South Sea Islands*. London, 1837.

Williams, Thomas, and Calvert, James, *Fiji and the Fijians*. London, 1870.

Williams, Jackson, A.V., " Die Iranische Religion," in W. Geiger and E. Kuhn, *Grundriss der Iranischen Philologie*. Vol. ii. Strassburg, 1896–1904.

Williams, S. W., *The Middle Kingdom*. 2 vols. London, 1883.

Williamson, R. W., *The Social and Political System of Central Polynesia*. 3 vols. Cambridge, 1924.

The Mafulu Mountain People of British New Guinea. London, 1912.

"Some Unrecorded Customs of the Mekeo People of British New Guinea," *Journal of the Royal Anthropological Institute*. Vol. xliii. London, 1913.

The Ways of the South Sea Savage. London, 1914.

Willinck, G. D., *Het rechtsleven bij Minangkabausche Maleiers*. Leyden, 1900.

Willoughby, W. C., " Notes on the Totemism of the Becwana," *Journal of the Anthropological Institute*. Vol. xxxv. London, 1905.

Wills, Charles James, M.D., *Persia as it is. Being sketches of modern Persian Life and Character*. London, 1886.

Willshire, W. H., *The Aborigines of Central Australia*. Adelaide, 1891.

Wilson, Capt., " Report on the Indian Tribes inhabiting the Vicinity of the 49th Parallel of North Latitude, North America," *Transactions of the Ethnological Society*. N.S., vol. iv. London, 1866.

Wilson, Andrew, *The Abode of Snow*. Edinburgh, London, 1876.

Wilson, C. T., *Peasant Life in the Holy Land*. London, 1906.

and Felkin, R. W., *Uganda and the Egyptian Soudan*. 2 vols. London, 1882.

Wilson, Capt. James, *A Missionary Voyage to the South Pacific Ocean, performed in the years 1796, 1797, 1798, in the Ship " Duff."* London, 1799.

Wilson, H. D., *The Province of South Australia*. Adelaide, 1894.

Wilson, Horace Hayman, *Ariana Antiqua ; an Account of the Antiquities and Coins of Afghanistan*. London, 1841.

Select Specimens of the Theatre of the Hindus. 2 vols. London, 1871.

" An Essay on the Hindu History of Cashmir," *Asiatick Researches*. Vol. xv. Serampore, 1825.

Wilson, J. L., *Western Africa*. London, 1856.

Wilson, T. B., *Narrative of a Voyage round the World*. London, 1835.

Winckler, Hugo, *The Tell-el-Amarna Letters*. London, 1896.

Altorientalische Forschungen. 3 Series. Leipzig, 1893–96.

Völker und Staate des alten Orients. 3 vols. Leipzig, 1892–1900.

Musri, Meluhla, Ma'in. Berlin, 1898.

Geschichte Israels in Einzeldarstellungen (Völker und Staaten des alten Orients). 2 vols. Leipzig, 1895, 1900.

Die Gesetze Hammurabis im Umschrift und Ubersetzung. Leipzig, 1904.

" North Arabia and the Bible," *The Hibbert Journal*. London, 1904.

" Polyandrie bei den Semiten," *Zeitschrift für Ethnologie*. Berlin, 1898.

Winckler, J., " Bericht über die zweite Untersuchungsreise nach der Insel Engano," *Tijdschrift voor Indische taal- land- en volkenkunde*. Vol. i. Batavia, s' Hage, 1908.

Windisch, W. O. E., *Irische Texte mit Wörterbuch*. 4 Series. Leipzig, 1880–1909.

Windishmann, F. H., " Ueber den Somacultus der Arier," *Abhandlungen der I klasse der Münchener Akademie*. Vol. iv. München, 1846.

Wines, Frederick Howard, " Report on the Defective, Dependent, and Delinquent Classes of the Population of the United States as returned at the Tenth Census," *Tenth Census of the United States; Statistical Reports.* Vol. xiii, part 21. Washington, 1883.

Wing, J. van, *Études Bakongo. Histoire et Sociologie.* Bruxelles, 1921.

De geheime sekte van't Kimpasi. Brussels, 1921.

Winkler, Hans, *Verbreitung und Ursache der Parthenogenesis in Pflanzen- und Tierreiche.* Jena, 1920.

Winship, George Parker, " The Coronado Expedition," *Fourteenth Annual Report of the Bureau of Ethnology.* Part i. Washington, 1897.

Winstedt, R. O., *Malaya, the Straits Settlements and the Federated and Unfederated Malay States.* London, 1923.

Winter, C. F., " Instelligen, gewoonten en gebruiken der Javanen te Soerakarta," *Tijdschrift voor Neêrlands Indië.* Vol. v, Part i. Batavia, 1843.

Winterbottom, Thomas, *An Account of the Native Africans in the Neighbourhood of Sierra Leone.* 2 vols. London, 1803.

Winternitz, M., *Geschichte der indischen Litteratur.* Leipzig, 1905.

" Das altindische Hochzeitsrituell nach dem Apastambiya-Grihyasutra und einigen anderen verwandten Werken," *Denkschriften der kaiserlichen Akademie der Wissenschaften. Philosophisch-historische Classe.* Vol. xl. Wien, 1892.

" Notes on the ' Mahābhārata,' with special reference to Dahlmann's ' Mahābhārata,' " *Journal of the Royal Asiatic Society.* London, 1897.

Wirnt von Gravenberg, *Wigalois.* Ed. Pfeffer. Leipzig, 1847.

Wise, James, *Notes on the Races, Castes and Tribes of Eastern Bengal.* London, 1883.

Wissendorff, Henri Zincien, " Légendes mythologiques lataviennes," *Revue des Traditions populaires.* Vol. vii. Paris, 1892.

Wissendorff de Wissukuok, Henri, " Légendes Lataviennes," *Revue des Traditions populaires.* Vol. viii. Paris, 1893.

Wissmann, H. von, *Unter deutscher Flagge quer durch Afrika.* Berlin, 1889.

Witchell, C. A., *The Evolution of Bird Song with Observations on the Influence of Heredity and Imitation.* London, 1896.

Cries and Call-notes of Wild Birds. London, 1899.

Wissowa, Georg, *Religion und Kultus der Römer.* Munich, 1902.

Withnell, J. G., *The Customs and Traditions of the Aboriginal Natives of North-Western Australia.* Roeburn, 1901.

Wlislocki, H. von, *Volksglaube und Volksbrauch der Siebenbürger Sachsen.* Berlin, 1893.

Wochenschrift für die gesammte Heilkunde. Berlin, 1833–

Wohlers, J. F. H., " The Mythology and Traditions of the Maori in New Zealand," *Transactions and Proceedings of the New Zealand Institute.* Vols. vii and viii. Wellington, 1875–76.

Wolf, J. W., *Hessische Sagen.* Leipzig, 1853.

Beiträge zur deutschen Mythologie. 2 vols. Göttingen, 1852–57.

Wolf, L., " Reisen in Central Afrika," *Verhandlungen der Gesellschaft für Erdkunde zu Berlin.* Vol. xiv. Berlin, 1807.

" Volkstämme Central-Afrika's," *Verhandlungen der Berliner Gesellschaft für Anthropologie.* Berlin, 1886.

Wolfram von Eschenbach, ' *Parzival' und ' Titurel.*' Ed. Karl Bartsch. 3 vols. Leipzig, 1875–77.

Wollaston, A. F. R., *Pygmies and Papuans. The Stone Age To-day in Dutch New Guinea.* London, 1912.

Wonderful History of Virgilius the Sorcerer of Rome. London, 1893.

Wood, A., *Survey of the Antiquities of the City of Oxford.* (*Oxford Historical Society.* Vol. i.) Oxford, 1889.

Wood, W. H., " The Hairy Men of Yesso," *Transactions of the Ethnological Society.* N.S., vol. iv. London, 1866.

Woods J. D., *The Native Tribes of South Australia.* Adelaide, 1879.

The Province of South Australia. Adelaide, 1894.

Woods Hutchinson, " Animal Marriage," *The Contemporary Review.* London, October 1904.

Woodworth, R. S., " Racial Differences in Mental Traits," *Science.* N. S., vol. xxxi. Cambridge, Mass., 1910.

" Address of the Vice-President and Chairman of the Section of Anthropology and Psychology," *American Association for the Advancement of Science.* Boston, 1909.

Worcester, Dean C., " The non-Christian Tribes of North Luzon," *The Philippine Journal of Science.* Vol. i. Manila, 1906.

The Philippine Islands and their People. New York, 1898.

Wrag, R., " A Description of a Voiage to Constantinople and Syria," in R. Hakluyt, *The Principal Navigations, Voyages, Traffiques and Discoveries of the English Nation.* Vol. vi. Edinburgh, 1885.

Wrangell, F. P., *Statistische und ethnographische Nachrichten über die russischen Besitzungen an der Nordwestküste von Amerika.* (*Beiträge zur Kenntniss des Russischen Reiches und angränzenden Länder Asiens.* Vol. i.) St. Petersburg, 1839.

" Observations recueillies par l'Amiral Wrangell sur les habitants des côtes nord-ouest de l'Amérique ; extraites du Russe par M. le prince Emanuel Galitzin." (*Nouvelles Annales des Voyages.* Vol. i.) Paris, 1853.

Wray, L., " The Malay Pottery of Perak," *Journal of the Anthropological Institute.* Vol. xxiii. London, 1903.

Wrede, Adolph von, *Reise in Hadhramaut, Beled Benr'Yssa und Beled el Hadsh.* Braunschweig, 1870.

Wriedt, C., in an interview reported in *The Journal of Heredity.* Vol. vii. Washington, 1916.

Wright, E. Blackwood, " Native Races in South Africa," *Journal of the African Society.* Vol. ii. London, 1902.

Wright, Thomas, *Womankind in Western Europe to the Seventeenth Century.* London, 1862.

Anecdota Literaria ; Short Poems in English, Latin, French, illustrative of England in the Thirteenth Century. London, 1844.

Wright, W. H., *The Grizzly Bear.* London, s.d.

Wuttke, C. F. Adolf, *Der deutsche Volksaberglaube der Gegenwart.* Dritte Bearbeitung von E. M. Meyer. Berlin, 1900.

Wyndham, W. T., " The Aborigines of Australia," *Journal and Proceedings of the Royal Society of New South Wales.* Vol. xxiii. Sydney, 1889.

Xanthoudides, " Cretan Kernoi," *Annual of the British School at Athens.* Vol. xii. London, 1906.

Xenophon, *Quae extant.* Ed. I. G. Schneider. 6 vols. Leipzig, 1821–38.

Ximenes Francisco, *Las historias del origen de los Indios de esta provincia de Guatemala.* Vienna, 1857.

Xiphilinus, Johannis, *Epitome Dionis Cassii.* Ed. Reimari. Hamburgi, 1752.

Yarrell, William, " On the Change in the Plumage of some Hen-pheasants,"
Philosophical Transactions. London, 1827.
A Dictionary of British Birds. 4th ed. rev. by A. Newton. 4 vols.
London, 1871.
Yarrow, H. C., " A further Contribution to the Study of the Mortuary Cus-
toms of the North American Indians, " *First Annual Report of the
Bureau of Ethnology."* Washington, 1881.
Yate, William, *An Account of New Zealand.* London, 1835.
Yî King, translated by James Legge. (*The Sacred Books of the East.*
Vol. xvi). Oxford, 1882.
Youatt, William, *The Pig.* London, 1847.
The Dog. London, 1845.
The Horse. London, 1859.
Young, Arthur, *A Tour in Ireland.* 2 vols. London, 1892.
Young, E., *The Kingdom of the Yellow Robe.* Westminster, 1900.
Yule, H., " Notes on the Kasia Hills and People," *Journal of the Asiatic
Society of Bengal.* Vol. xiii, Part ii. Calcutta, 1844.
Yuzbaski, " Tribes of the Upper Nile, The Bari," *Journal of the African
Society.* Vol. iv. London, 1905.
Yves d'Evreux, *Voyage dans le Nord du Brésil fait durant les années 1613 et
1614.* Ed. Ferdinand Denis. Leipzig, Paris, 1864.

Zaborowski, M., " La circomcision, ses origines et sa repartition en Afrique
et à Madagascar," *L'Anthropologie.* Vol. vii. Paris, 1896.
" De la circoncision des garçons et de l'excision des filles comme pratiques
d'initiation," *Bulletins de la Société d'Anthropologie.* 4e Série, vol. v.
Paris, 1894.
Zache, H., " Sitten und Gebräuche der Suaheli," *Zeitschrift für Ethnologie.*
Vol. xxxi. Berlin, 1899.
Zahn, H., " Die Jabim," in R. Neuhauss, *Deutsch Neu-Guinea.* Vol. iii.
Berlin, 1911.
Zanetti, A., " La Società fra gli animali," *Nuova Antologia.* Firenze, 1875–76.
Zangronitz, J. Zobel, " Spanische Münzen und bisher unerklärte Aufschriften,"
Zeitschrift der deutschen Morgenländische Gesellschaft. Vol. xvii.
Leipzig, 1863.
Zárate, Augustin de, *Historia del decubrimento y conquista de la provincia del
Peru.* (*Biblioteca de Autores Españoles.* Vol. xxiii.) Madrid,
1853.
Zeirreddin Mukhdom, transl. in J. Duncan, " Historical Remarks on the Coast
of Malabar," *Asiatick Researches.* Vol. v. Calcutta, 1799.
Zeitschrift der deutschen morgenländischen Gesellschaft. Leipzig, 1847–
Zeitschrift der Gesellschaft für Erdkunde. Berlin, 1866–
Zeitschrift des Vereins für Volkskunde. Berlin, 1891–
Zeitschrift für ägyptische Sprache und Alterthumskunde. Leipzig, Berlin,
1863–
Zeitschrift für afrikanischen Sprachen. Berlin, 1888–
Zeitschrift für allgemeine Erdkunde. Berlin, 1853–
Zeitschrift für angewandte Psychologie. Leipzig, 1907–
Zeitschrift für Assyriologie und verwandte Gebiete. Leipzig, etc., 1886–
Zeitschrift für die Kunde des Morgenlandes. Göttingen, 1837–
Zeitschrift für deutsches Althertum und deutsche Litteratur. Leipzig and
Berlin, 1872–
Zeitschrift für deutsche Mythologie und Sittenkunde. Göttingen, 1853–
Zeitschrift für Ethnologie. Berlin, 1869–

Zeitschrift für französische Sprache und Litteratur. Oppel, Leipzig, Berlin, 1889–

Zeitschrift für Ohrenheilkunde. Wiesbaden, 1879–

Zeitschrift für pädagogische Psychologie und Pathologie. Berlin, 1899–

Zeitschrift für Psychologie. Leipzig, 1906–

Zeitschrift für romanische Philologie. Halle, 1875–

Zeitschrift für Social- und Wirthschaftsgeschichte. Freiburg i. B., Leipzig, Weimar, 1893–

Zeitschrift für Socialwissenschaft. Berlin, 1898–

Zeitschrift für Sprachforschung auf dem Gebiete des Deutschen, Griechischen und Lateinischen. Berlin, 1851–

Zeitschrift fur Völkerpsychologie und Sprachwissenschaft. Berlin, Leipzig, 1860–

Zeitschrift für Volkskunde. Leipzig, 1889–

Zeitschrift für wissenschaftliche Zoologie. Leipzig, 1848–

Zell, Th., "Das Einfangen ausgewachsener Gorillas," *Die Gartenlaube.* Leipzig, 1907,

Zeller, Eduard, *Philosophie der Griechen.* 3 vols. Tübingen, 1856–68.

Zeltner, Fr. de, "Les Touaregs du Sud," *Journal of the Royal Anthropological Institute.* Vol. xliv. London, 1914.

Zend-Avesta. Transl. by James Darmesteter and L. H. Mills. *Sacred Books of the East.* Vols. iv, xxiii, xxxi. Oxford, 1880–87.

See Anquatil Du Perron.

Zenker, G., "Die Mobea," *Ethnologisches Notizblatt.* Vol. iii, Heft. 3. Berlin, 1904.

Zenker, R., *Die Gedichte des Folquet von Romans.* Halle, 1896.

Zernitz, A., *La Luna nelle credenze popolari e nella poesia.* Trieste, 1889.

Zhishman, J., *Das Eherecht der orientalischen Kirche.* Wien, 1863.

Zielinski, Th., "Hermes und die Hermetik," *Archiv für Religionswissenschaft.* Vols. viii, ix. Leipzig, 1905–6.

Zimmer, Heinrich, *Altindisches Leben.* Berlin, 1879.

"Keltische Beiträge," *Zeitschrift für deutsches Alterthum und deutsche Litteratur.* Vol. xxxiii. Berlin, 1889.

"Der Kulturgeschichtliche Hintergrund in den Erzählungen der alten irische Heldensagen," *Sitzungsberichte der Königliche Preussische Akademie der Wissenschaften.* Berlin, 1911.

Keltische Studien. 2 vols. Berlin, 1881–84.

"Bretonische Elemente in der Arthursage des Gottfried von Monmouth," *Zeitschrift für französische Sprache und Litteratur.* Vol. xii. Leipzig, 1890.

"Beiträge zur Namenforschung in den altfranzösischen Arthurepen," *ibid.* Vol. xiii. Leipzig, 1891.

Zimmern, H., "Zur Vollständingung von K 2001," *Zeitschrift für Assyriologie.* Vol. xxv. Strassburg, 1911.

Babylonische Hymnen und Gebete in Auswahl. (*Das alte Orient.*) 2 vols. Berlin, 1905–11.

Zingarelli, N., "Su Bernart de Ventadorn," *Studi Medievali.* Vol. i. Torino, 1904–5.

Dante (in *Storia letteraria d'Italia*). Milano, 1903.

Zoeckler, O., *The Cross of Christ.* Transl. London, 1877.

Zoeller, Max, *Latium und Rom.* Leipzig, 1878.

Zöller, Hugo, *Forschungsreisen in der deutschen Colonie Kamerun.* 3 vols. Berlin and Stuttgart, 1885.

Deutsch-Neuguinea. Stuttgart, Berlin, Leipzig, 1891.

Zonara, Johannis, *Lexicon.* Ed. I. A. H. Tittman. 2 vols. Lipsiae, 1808.

Zonto, Giuseppe, " Rileggendo Andrea Capellano," *Studi Medievali*.   Vol. iii.
    Torino, 1908–11.

Zoologischer Anzeiger.   Leipzig, 1877–

Zoologisches Zentralblatt.   Leipzig, 1894–

Zoologist.   London, 1843–

Zuazo, Alonso, " Carta del licenciato A. Z., al Padre Fray Luis de Figueroa,
    Prior de la Mejorada," in J. G. Icazbalceta, *Coleccion de Documentos
    para la Historia de Mexico*.   Vol. i.   Mexico, 1858.

Zucchelli, Antonio, *Relazione del viaggio e missione di Congo*.   Venezia, 1712.

Zündel, G., " Land und Volk der Eweer auf der Sclavenküste in Westafrika,"
    Zeitschrift der Gesellschaft für Erdkunde zu Berlin.   Vol. xii.   Berlin,
    1877.

Zündel, J., " Ein griechischer Bücherkatalog, aus Aegypten," *Rheinisches
    Museum für Philologie*.   Neue Folge.   Vol. xxi.   Frankfurt am Main,
    1866.

Zurita, Alonso de, " Breve i sumaria relacion de los señores de la Nueva
    España," *Coleccion de documentos ineditos para la historia de España*.
    Vol. iii.   Madrid, 1891.

INDEX

ah, name of the moon and of the moon-god among the ancient Egyptians, ii, 772 ; cross worn by, 752 ; possibly an element in the name of Osiris, 773n ; identified with Thoth, 786.

ah-Tehuti (Aah-Thoth), ii, 786.

ataensic, moon-goddess and supreme deity of the Iroquois, Hurons, and Algonkin tribes, ii, 572, 728 ; iii, 53 ; plants poisonous trees to destroy mankind, ii, 572 sq. ; requires the dead to dance to her, 748 ; called ' The Eternal One,' 601 ; represented as a serpent, 661 ; mother, or grandmother of the Great Manitu, 730 and n[1].

babua of the Belgian Congo, old wives procure new wives for their husbands, ii, 262.

bandia, Belgian Congo, maternal uncle disposes of nieces in marriage, i, 542 sq.

bbeville, guild of ' jongleurs ' perform in the church, iii, 448.

bduction, prevalence of, in uncultured societies, ii, 105, 110, 235 sq. ; with consent of the woman's family, 237 sq. ; of married women, 104 sq., 109 ; confounded in ethnological reports with adultery, 101 sqq., 109–111 ; men's fear of losing their wives by, 107 sq. ; primitive jealousy has reference to, 101–112 ; establishes the right of the abductor to the woman after a given period, 107 sq.

beokuta (West Africa), disastrous expedition of King Gueso against, i, 455.

Ability, tests of, i, 55 sq. ; specific, not inherited, 56 sq.

Abipones of the Paraguayan Chaco, infanticide, ii, 28 ; alleged regard for chastity, 36 ; weaving, i, 464 ; priestesses, ii, 523 sq. ; ritual rules about drawing water, 638 ; moon-cult, 744 ; reported lack of interest in cosmology and metaphysics, 503.

Abors of Assam, polyandry, i, 669.

Abortion, employed in order to preserve sexual freedom, ii, 29 ; among the North American Indians, 71.

Abraham, his name and cult, iii, 108 n[4] ; worshipped in the Ka'-aba, 80 ; his sacrifice and resurrection, 104 ; circumcises himself, 323 ; his sister-wife, i, 372 ; his two wives, iii, 82.

Abrons of the Ivory Coast, adoption among, i, 602 sq. ; adultery of king's wives a source of royal revenue, ii, 125 sq.

Abu-Simbel, temples of, iii, 42.

Abyssinia, position of women, i, 326 ; adultery punished with a fine of fivepence, ii, 134 ; official monogamy with extensive polygyny, 269 sq. ; domination of younger favourites among wives, 309 sq. ; life regarded as dependent upon the moon, 654 ; infibulation, iii, 344 ; circumcision of girls among the Jews, 324.

Acca Larentia gives land to the Roman people, i, 423.

Acclimatisation of animals from small numbers, i, 206 sq.

Achaeans, i, 394 sq., 398 n[3].

for inefficient housekeeping, ii,
136 ; adultery not a ground for
divorce, *ibid.* ; widower must
cohabit with deceased wife's sister
before he can marry again, i, 623.

Bahuana of the Congo, position of
maternal uncle, i, 499 sq.

Baiame, an Australian god, ii, 696–
701 ; said to have gone away
long ago, 512 ; fights his brother
to obtain his wives, 205 ; as a
turtle, 479.

Baila of northern Rhodesia, traces
of matrilocal customs, i, 303 ;
pre-nuptial sexual intercourse encouraged, ii, 40 ; compensation
demanded for pre-nuptial motherhood, iii, 339 ; female cross-
cousins termed ' wives,' i, 571 ;
wife selected by bridegroom's
mother, 544 ; marriage ceremony not completed till after
birth of child, ii, 85 ; instability
of marriage, 81 ; menstrual tabu,
379 ; cessation of marital relations, during pregnancy and
nursing, 394 ; importance attached to amulets, iii, 271.

Baiswar, Rajput tribe of Mirzapur,
ceremonial purification after adultery, ii, 136.

Bakairi of Brazil, matrilocal marriage, i, 279 ; wives accompany
husband on visits to other wives,
ii, 258 ; maternal uncle, 498 sq. ;
moon-cult, 744 ; reluctance to
be seen eating, iii, 291 ; modesty
as regards the exposure of their
feet, 300.

' Bakchai ' of Euripides, iii, 122 sq.

Bakers' Feast in Ancient Rome,
iii, 18 sq. ; chastity recommended
in, 356.

Bakitara. See Banyoro.

Bakoki of Central Africa, pre-
nuptial motherhood regarded as
unlucky, ii, 26.

Bakongo (Ba-Congo), maternal descent in clans, paternal succession
in families, i, 582 sq. ; cross-
cousin marriage, 570 ; sororal
polygyny, 618 ; levirate, 768 n ;
menstrual tabu, ii, 379.

Bakumbi of British East Africa,
matrilocal marriage, i, 281.

Bakunta of central East Africa,
collective sexual relations, i,
717.

Bakyiga of the Uganda Protectorate, constant state of war between
intermarrying clans, i, 561 ; punishment of unmarried mothers,
ii, 26.

Balante of Senegal, women choose
their husbands, ii, 172.

Balasore, Bengal, polyandry, i, 673.

Balearic Islands, ancient inhabitants of, Nasamonian custom, iii,
224, 318.

Bali, island of (Indonesia), capture
of women, real and conventional,
ii, 243.

Ball, games of, as a means of
assisting the moon, ii, 749.

Baluba of the Congo, levirate
observance, i, 776 sq. ; barbarous
punishment of adultery, ii, 126 ;
secret societies, 551 ; ritual eating
of the totem by women, 465 ;
myth of the origin of death, 646,
757 sq. ; morning and evening
stars regarded as wives of the
moon, iii, 82.

Baluchistan, intermarriage groups
in, i, 576 sq. ; artificial defloration,
iii, 319 ; licentious customs at
weddings, 225.
    See Brahin.

Bambala of the Congo, fishing an
occupation of women, i, 448 ; first
wife must be of Bushongo blood,
ii, 312 ; pre-nuptial motherhood
forbidden, iii, 339 ; sexual communism, i, 719.

Bambara of West Africa, marriage
negotiated by ' go-betweens,'
i, 530 ; pre-nuptial licence and
licentiousness, ii, 41 ; women's
moon-cult, 754 sq. ; sacred tree,
ibid.

Bana of Cameroons, pre-nuptial
motherhood resented, but virginity not claimed, ii, 26.

Banaka of West Africa, frequent
changes of partners, ii, 82.

Banana in myths of the origin of
death, ii, 655 sq. ; said to contain
an image of Christ, 656 n[4].

Banaro of New Guinea, bride must
have a child by a ' goblin ' before

Boucaut, Sir James Penn, on English race-horse, i, 211.

Boudicca, queen of the Iceni, i, 420, 458 ; ii, 541, 614 ; iii, 70.

Boudin, Major, his statistics on the association of deaf-mutism with consanguine marriages, i, 227 sq.

Bovidae, collective parental instincts among, i, 596.

Bowditch Island, matrilocal marriage, i, 295 ; observance of tabu days, ii, 427 sq. ; myths, 680.

Boys brought up as girls, ii, 532 sq.

Brahmans, their contest with the Kshatriya, or warrior caste, i, 688 sq. ; regarded as gods, 15 ; fraternal polyandry opposed to their theocratic interests, 679, 689 ; traces of matriarchal usage among, 361 sq. ; union with them desired, 689 ; sometimes play the part of stallions, iii, 229 ; have intercourse with sacred hierodules, 227 ; indifference to adultery unless publicly known, ii, 128 ; eat only sacrificial meat, 470 ; rites of sexual licence, iii, 203.

Brahmans, Nambutiri, of Travancore, impartite fraternal polyandrous family among, i, 653, 689 sq.

Brahui of Baluchistan, maternal uncle conducts marriage ceremony, i, 541 ; examination of the proofs of virginity by a jury of matrons, iii, 342 ; circumcision of women as a cure for sterility, 324.

Brain, growth of, i, 100–103 ; of idiots, 30 sq. ; brain-cells, larger in larger animals, 96.

Brames of West Africa, prefer a wife who has had many lovers, iii, 316.

Bran, the Raven, Celtic deity, iii, 452 sq. ; probably the same as Brennus, *ibid.* ; i, 418 ; and as Arthur, iii, 432 sq. ; keeper of the sacred cauldron of the Irish gods, 452 ; called Brons, keeper of the Holy Grail, 453 ; dies by drinking up a well, 387 n[1].

Brangien, in the story of Tristan and Iseult, iii, 442.

Brazil, Indian tribes of, power of chiefs, i, 449 sq. ; pottery manufacture, 472 ; clothing, iii, 297, 288 sq. ; maternal love, i, 127 ; children not chastised, 131 ; pre-nuptial sexual freedom, ii, 4 n ; women offer themselves to warriors, 182 ; matrilocal marriage, i, 277 sq. ; position of the maternal uncle, 499 ; polygamy and alleged monogamy, ii, 279–286 ; absence of jealousy between wives, 258 ; indifference to adultery, 114 ; trial-marriage, 73 sq. ; instability of marriage, 82 sq. ; polyandry, i, 646 ; levirate, 768 n ;

religious myths and cults, ii, 741–745 ; menstrual tabu, 371 sq. ; separation during pregnancy and nursing, 393 ; medicine-men, i, 17 ; priestesses and shamanesses, 523–525 ; theory of paradigms, or ' mothers,' 7 ; modesty, iii, 298 sq.

Breasts, thought to be endangered by exposure during pregnancy and suckling, iii, 301 sq. ; effects of exposure on Flaubert, 311 ; pendulous, admired, ii, 163 ; pottery in the shape of woman's, i, 473 ; development in men, 446.

Breeches, adopted by Celts, iii, 380 n[3] ; elder sister represented by, at wedding of younger sister in China, ii, 655 ; intermarrying groups called, in Baluchistan, i, 577.

Breeding-seasons, i, 180–182, ii, 401–403 ; lunar influence on, 429 sq.

Brennus, Brennos, war-leader of the Celts, iii, 452 sq. See Bran.

' Breviari d'Amor,' iii, 490.

Brewster, Sir David, his intuitive fear, i, 46 sq.

Bribri Indians of Costa Rica, matrilocal marriage, i, 276.

Bride and bridegroom exchange clothes, ii, 534 n[5] ; not present at wedding, i, 556 sq.

Bride, not present at wedding, i, 556 sq. ; non-virgin preferred, iii, 313–317 ; claim to virginity of, 334-346 ; marked with blood,

Manta of Peru, Nasamonian custom, iii, 225.

Mantenerys of the Purus River, Brazil, position of women, i, 319.

Mantegazza, Professor P., on love, 145 n[1]; his attempt to show the evil effects of consanguineous unions, i, 224.

Mantinea, priestesses at, iii, 128.

Mantram, or magic words of the Hindus, i, 15.

Mantras of the Malay Peninsula, successive polygyny, ii, 295; myth of the origin of death, 656; their life dependent on the moon, 652.

Man Tseu, tribe of southern China, ruled by a queen, iii, 23.

Manu, Laws of, incongruities and self-contradictions in, i, 689; on position of wife, 345.

Manuscripts, Oriental, defaced by intentional blots, iii, 358.

Manyema of the Congo, strength of the women, i, 444.

Maori of New Zealand, plaiting of baskets, i, 465; mats, 466; horn blown on approaching a village, 159; cannibalism repudiated, 713; suicide, 330, ii, 145 sq.; intermarriage, i, 219; position of women, 322; women attend the men in battle, 452; women's labour, 328; pre-nuptial sexual freedom, ii, 11 n., 18; girl with child preferred as bride, iii, 315; refusal of sexual hospitality resented, 636; betrothal, 325 sq.; advances generally come from the women, ii, 169; athletic contests of suitors, 205; simulated capture, 244 sq.; permission of all members required for intertribal marriages, i, 552; husband and wife not regarded as related, 509; lack of conjugal affection, 126; abduction, ii, 235 sq.; fidelity of married women, 18; adultery generally compounded for, 117; husband punished for wife's misconduct, 129; husband and lover agree to share wife, 120 sq.; instability of marriage, 83; sororal polygyny, 629 sq.; harmony between wives,

259; chief wife the first who bears an heir, 313; levirate, i, 771 n.; modest bearing of women, ii, 24; indifference to the presence of witnesses during sexual intercourse, iii, 261; menstrual and puerperal tabus, ii, 384; tabu days, 427; tabu objects marked with red paint, 412 sq.; objection to women stepping over their legs, 419; to leaning against a house, 419; ideas concerning menstruation, 432; the moon the real husband of women, *ibid.*; triune, 603 sq.; cross amulet, 751; hei-tiki amulet, 584; moon associated with immortality, 657; formerly ruled over both day and night, 580; earthquakes not dreaded, 582; mythology, 712–716; priestesses, 529.

Mappellas of Malabar, survival of matrilocal marriage, i, 303.

Marae, Polynesian sacred places, ii, 529, 719.

Maratha, military caste of southern India, their amazonian leaders, i, 456.

Marathon, absence of the Spartans at the battle of, iii, 140.

Marc, King of Cornwall, iii, 429, 439, 469.

Marcabru, troubadour, iii, 478, 482.

Marcomanni, women warriors among the, i, 458.

Mares develop canine teeth, i, 135; thought to be fecundated by the wind, ii, 451.

Maria Candelaria, ii, 523.

Marianne Islands, see Ladrones Islands.

Marie de France, iii, 404, 407 sq.

Maries, the Three, ii, 608.

Markets in Africa, i, 484; in Nicaragua, 485 sq.

Marotse, matrilocal marriage, i, 281; bride-racing, ii, 208; instability of, 81.

Marquesas Islands, high civic morality, ii, 356; pre-nuptial licence, 11 n.; women doctors, i, 487; matrilocal marriage, 295; sororal polygyny and polyandry, 621, 723 sq.; modesty of women, iii, 309; cultivation of 'Hot-

Semiramis, her love for a horse, iii, 188.

Semites, their aversion to agriculture, ii, 315 ; matriarchal order among, i, 370–377 ; polyandry, 714 sq. ; capture of women, ii, 233.

Semitic religion, moon in, iii, 77 sq.

Sena, the priestesses of, ii, 538 sq.

Senecas, the chief tribe of the Iroquois, marriage customs, i, 270 ; separation after birth of children, ii, 87 ; polyandry, i, 645 sq.

Senegambia, husband and wife live separate, i, 513 ; chief wife as forewoman, ii, 310 ; menstruating women marked by scarlet scarf, 397 ; privileges of poets, i, 18 sq.

Seniority, rule of, in fraternal group-marriage, i, 651–654 ; in levirate, 773.

Sentiments, social, iii, 511 sq.

Sepulchre, Holy, iii, 120, 138, 144, 157.

Serbia, impurity of women at childbirth, ii, 374 sq. ; poetry, i, 505.

Seresmundo, Himalaya, polyandry, i, 658.

Sergi, Professor G., on Mediterranean race, i, 395 n[7].

Seri Indians of Tiburon and New Mexico, material culture and social organisation, i, 274–276 ; arrows, 461 ; hostility towards strangers, 158 ; maternal love, i, 129 ; marriages discussed by tribal council, 553 ; test of endurance, ii, 200 ; fraternal-sororal polygamy, 303, 645 ; objections of women respected, i, 548 ; tribal marks painted on visitor, 635 ; dread of being photographed, iii, 300 ; witchcraft, ii, 559 sq. ; religious rites, 471 ; Great Pelican, ibid. ; chief chosen for his wife's magic power, iii, 15 sq.

Serpent deities, ii, 515, 540, 661 sq., 664, 666, 670, 683, 699 sq., 733, 737, 739, 742, 766 ; iii, 21, 62, 78, 108, 112, 118, 154, 642, 661.

Serpents, thought to be immortal owing to power of changing their skin, ii, 641–651 ; associated with the moon, 660–662, 659 ; thought to have thirty ribs, 661 ; defraud men of the gift of immortality, 645–647 ; immortality obtained through, 642 ; the source of magic powers, 662 sq., 663 sq. ; and witches, 662 ; and women, 662–671 ; ravish women, 664–670 ; steal women's milk, 668 ; and water, 667, 668 sq., 670–673 ; guardians of treasure, i, 482 ; charming of, by magic women, ii, 663 sq. ; assist women in weaving, 625 ; women's hair turns to, 662 ; in women's cults, 548–664 ; as souls of the departed, 651 ; equivalent to lizards, 671 ; to dragon, 670 ; to eels, 671 ; to fish, 643, 671 sq.

Serpent-stones, ii, 702–704.

Service, see Marriage by service, Love-service.

Set, Egyptian god, ii, 768, 784 sq.

Sethosis, Manetho's account of, iii, 43 sq.

Settegast, Professor H. G., disastrous effects of his doctrines on the art of breeding, i, 214.

Seventh son or daughter, endowed with magic powers, ii, 533.

Sewing, i, 462.

Sex antagonism, iii, 518 sq.

Sex, not a principle of nature, i, 91.

Sexes, respective size in animals, i, 442 sq. ; physical differences between, 442–447 ; proportion supposed to have bearing on polygamy, ii, 274, i, 169 ; division of labour between the, 435 sq. ;
    separation of, among mammals, 122–124, 177, 255.

Sexual characters, present in opposite sex, i, 133–141 ; masculine developed in females, 135 sq. ; feminine developed in males, 136 sq. ; transference to opposite sex, 133–141.

Sexual hospitality, see Hospitality, sexual.

Sexual instincts, transformation of, i, 51, 163 ; originally associated with cruelty, 118–120 ; and mating

Travancore, menstruating goddess at, ii, 435 sq.

Tree, World, or Tree of Life, ii, 630, iii, 68.

Trees, sacred, ii, 629–631, iii, 78, 90, 137, 218; women united to, iii, 218; deities as, 118, ii, 742; in the moon, ii, 628 sq.

Trengganu, see Trangganore.

Trent, Council of, Decrees, iii, 241 n[3], 249, 375.

Trial marriage, ii, 72–74, 86, iii, 368.

Tribe and family, i, 421.

Trichinopoly, pot-goddesses in, i, 474.

Trieterica, iii, 124.

Trinidad, natives of, name kept secret, i, 13.

Trinity, of lunar deities, ii, 603–606, iii, 84 sq., 682 sq.; solar and others, ii, 607; Gnostic, i, 6 n.

Trinity, Holy, compared by Canadian Indians to a piece of pork, ii, 503; monstrous representations of condemned by the Church, 608.

Tripod, prophetic, ii, 605.

Tristan and Iseult, iii, 405, 412, 424, 438, 440, 442 n[3], 469, 476.

Triune, deities, ii, 603–608, iii, 69 sq.

Trobriand Islands, New Guinea, pre-nuptial licence, ii, 71; polygamy, 334 sq.

Troglodyte dwellings, i, 470.

Troubadours, chap. xxix; influence of poetry on European literatures, iii, 468 n[2]; conventions, 472–474; transformations of conception of love, 476 sq.; Italian, 491 sq.

Trousers, misuse of, in the Congo, iii, 298; in Chinese wedding ceremonies, i, 655.

Tsalisans of Formosa, courtship discontinued if prospective bride does not become pregnant, ii, 86; visiting husbands, ibid.

Tsetse fly, driven away by women, ii, 411.

Tshi-speaking peoples of the Gold Coast, infanticide, ii, 27; abduction resented if bride-price is not refunded, 102.
See Ashanti.

'Tsi' and Tsie,' great and little wives, ii, 325.

Tsimshian of British Columbia, skin-changing hero, ii, 641; religious dances, 723.

Tsoroti of central Brazil, matrilocal marriage, i, 279.

Tsuni-goam, the supreme being of the Hottentots, ii, 745 sq.

Tuareg, relation to Mediterranean and Aegean populations, i, 284 sq., 395 sq.; alphabet, 286, 396 n[1]; formerly Christians, ii, 287 n[10]; maternal descent, i, 285 sq.; matrilocal marriage, 285; loose sexual relations, iii, 256; position of women, i, 326; late marriage and avoidance of marriage, ii, 156 sq.; accumulation of property in the hands of women, 219; marriages negotiated by 'marabuts,' i, 530; widows and divorcées preferred, iii, 314; concubines not resented by wives, 259; absence of jealousy, ii, 113; rhetorical punishment of adultery by death, 133; women give preference to effeminate men, 182 sq.; monogamy of some tribes, 287; displays of horsemanship at weddings, ii, 207.

Tuberculosis, as a cause of deaf-mutism, i, 226 sq.; acquisition of comparative immunity, 235 n[1].

Tubori of Senegambia, equality of wives, ii, 309.

Tucunas of the Amazon, menstrual tabu, ii, 371.

Tui-tonga, or sacred king of Tonga, ii, 718; descended from the moon, ibid., pays homage to wife and daughter, iii, 27; not circumcised, 336.

Tully River tribes of Queensland, fraternal-sororal sexual communism, i, 735.

Tum (Atum, Temu), the god of Heliopolis, ii, 766.

Tumbuka of East Africa, i, 281.

Tungus, women hunters, i, 448; maternal descent, 297, 364; partial matrilocal marriage, 297; avoidance of marriage, ii, 155;